D1321393

EDWARD III

Also in the Yale English Monarchs Series

* Available in the U.S. from University of California Press

EDWARD III

W. Mark Ormrod

YALE UNIVERSITY PRESS
NEW HAVEN AND LONDON

For information about this and other Yale University Press publications, please contact:
U.S. Office: sales.press@yale.edu   www.yalebooks.com
Europe Office: sales@yaleup.co.uk   www.yalebooks.co.uk

Set in Baskerville by IDSUK (DataConnection) Ltd
Printed in Great Britain by TJ International Ltd, Padstow, Cornwall.

Library of Congress Cataloging-in-Publication Data

Ormrod, W. M., 1957–
   Edward III/W. Mark Ormrod.
      p. cm.
   Includes bibliographical references and index.
   ISBN 978-0-300-11910-7 (cl:alk. paper)
      1. Edward III, King of England, 1312–1377. 2. Great Britain—History—Edward III, 1327–1377. 3. Great Britain—Kings and rulers—Biography. 4. Great Britain—Politics and government—1327–1377. I. Title.
   DA233.O737 2012
   942.03'7092—dc22
   [B]
                                                                                    2011013536

A catalogue record for this book is available from the British Library.

10 9 8 7 6 5 4 3 2 1

For Richard

CONTENTS

ILLUSTRATIONS

Maps

Genealogical Tables

PREFACE & ACKNOWLEDGEMENTS

The book has an eventful prehistory. In the early days of the English Monarchs series, the commission for *Edward III* went to John Le Patourel, Professor of Medieval History at the University of Leeds. In the 1950s and early 1960s Le Patourel had written a series of penetrating and influential articles on Edward III's relations with France. Thereafter, however, his attention was directed mainly to his project on *The Norman Empire* (published in 1976) and its planned successor, *The Plantagenet Realm* (which remained incomplete at the time of his death in 1981). Early in the 1970s, therefore, Le Patourel gave up the *Edward III* contract to A. R. (Alec) Myers, Professor of Medieval History at the University of Liverpool. Myers prepared a chronological account of the reign, in ten chapters, drawn almost entirely from the published chronicles and Rymer's *Foedera* and dominated by the history of war with Scotland and France. This was, I believe, his first attempt to organize the book on the model of a number of the early contributions to the English Monarchs series, with a first half providing a narrative of the reign and a second half taking up the major themes of politics and governance and providing an assessment of the king's character and achievements. When Myers died in 1980, the second part remained unplanned and unwritten.

I was first approached to take up the contract for *Edward III* in the late 1980s by the then general editor of the English Monarchs series, Professor J. J. Scarisbrick. At the time I had already embarked on an analytical study of the domestic politics of the period, published in 1990 as *The Reign of Edward III: Crown and Political Society in England, 1327–1377*. In the early 1990s, after the death of Alec Myers's widow, I was contacted by his colleague at Liverpool, Alan Harding, and offered the rediscovered fragment of Myers's biography. It seemed most appropriate to set the typescript aside unread and to return to it only when I was at an advanced stage in my own work. I then embarked on a series of studies on the fiscal, judicial and parliamentary records and institutions of later medieval England, and only came back to Edward III with serious purpose in the mid-2000s. When I eventually read Myers's typescript in 2010, after finishing the first draft of the present work, I found myself incorporating into my text a handful of his observations on the set pieces of the reign and a few of the well-turned translations that he had already employed in his 1969 edition of *English Historical Documents, 1327–1485*. But I detected few clues as to how my predecessor had imagined the king, other than to sense his frustration with the immensity of the project and his strong desire to bring Edward to rather a brisker end than the monarch himself ever managed. In good conscience, I can therefore say that, for better or worse, the work that follows is not Myers's but my own.

Much of the final programme of research and most of the writing of this book was undertaken during my tenure of a Leverhulme Trust Senior Research Fellowship in 2007–10. I am profoundly grateful to the Trust for the precious gift of time that made all things possible. I also record my thanks to Professor Brian Cantor, Vice-Chancellor of the University of York, and to my successive Heads of Department, Professor Miles Taylor and Professor Bill Sheils, for the release from other responsibilities that allowed me to take up the fellowship. My colleagues in the Department of History and the Centre for Medieval Studies have enormously enriched my understanding of the past, as well as taking up the burden in my absence, and I am grateful to Timothy Ayers, Peter Biller, James Binns, Gabriella Corona, Dee Dyas, Jeremy Goldberg, Guy Halsall, Nicholas Havely, Philippa Hoskin, Nicola McDonald, Richard Marks, Linne Mooney, Christopher Norton, Sarah Rees Jones, Felicity Riddy, Craig Taylor, Sethina Watson and Jocelyn Wogan-Browne for much advice and support. To have had the opportunity to write this book among such a stimulating community of scholars working together in one of the great medieval cities of Europe has been a source of constant personal satisfaction and intellectual inspiration.

I have also been exceptionally favoured in having the opportunity to work with a group of outstanding PhD students at the University of York, and I acknowledge with great sincerity and warmth my indebtedness to Alison Basil, Lisa Benz, Phillip Bradford, Alex Brayson, Joel Burden, Catherine Casson, Antonio Castro Henriques, Lesley Coote, Gwilym Dodd, Keith Fieldes, Barbara Gribling, Mark Honeywell, Ralph Kaner, Esther Ketskemety, Helen Killick, Robert Kinsey, Helen Lacey, Martyn Lawrence, Joanna Laynesmith, Christian Liddy, Jonathan Mackman, Mark Punshon, Thom Richardson, Monika Simon and Danielle Westerhof. To James Bothwell and Gwilym Dodd, whom I mentored during their postdoctoral research fellowships, I owe special thanks for their long-running advice and assistance. It has also been my distinct good fortune to work with cohorts of wonderful undergraduate and Master's students; to these, and especially to the survivors of my Special Subject, 'England at War, 1290–1360' and innumerable dissertation projects, I offer my warmest thanks. My research assistants, Simon Harris, Lisa Liddy, Jonathan Mackman and Shelagh Sneddon, have helped me in so many ways to understand the complexities of medieval documents.

The fourteenth century, once a rather lonely patch, has become much more intensively cultivated by historians in the generation since I plucked my own first seedlings, and to list all those who have influenced my work would only run the risk of omission. I am especially grateful to the late James Gillespie and to Mark Arvanigian, Douglas Biggs, Jeffrey Hamilton and Sharon Michalove for their organization of the justly famous Society of the White Hart sessions at the International Congress on Medieval Studies, University of Western Michigan, Kalamazoo. Chris Give-Wilson, Jeffrey Hamilton and Nigel Saul, my fellow convenors of the Society for Fourteenth-Century Studies sessions at the International Medieval Congress, University of Leeds, and co-editors of the biennial *Fourteenth Century England*, have also given generously of their advice and expertise. I thank my hosts at a sequence of conferences and seminars at the National Archives, Kew (funded by the Arts and Humanities Research Council), the Universities of Exeter and Nottingham, the Institute of Historical Research and the Institute of Advanced Legal Studies, University of London, the Ohio State University, the University of Toronto (hosted by the Medieval Academy of America), the University of California, Los Angeles (funded by the Andrew W. Mellon Foundation), the University of Rochester and the Datini Institute, Prato, for the opportunities offered to develop some of the ideas that have gone into the making of this book. The British Academy and the University of York made generous travel grants that facilitated some of these and other international visits.

A number of colleagues have generously given me access to their notes on primary sources and allowed me to make use of their findings and interpretations in advance of publication: here I especially record my appreciation to Adrian Ailes, Martin Allen, Roger Axworthy, Richard Barber, Michael Bennett, Maurizio Campanelli, Paul Dryburgh, Christopher Fletcher, Phillip Lindley, Marilyn Livingstone, Jessica Lutkin, John Maddicott, Alison Marshall, Ralph Moffat, Ian Mortimer, David A. L. Morgan, Clementine Oliver, Robert Palmer, John Carmi Parsons, Guilhem Pépin, Clifford Rogers, Graham St John, Caroline Shenton and Anthony Verduyn. Anthony Musson has been a great support throughout. The readers of my manuscript, subsequently revealed as Michael Prestwich and Anthony Goodman, have helped enormously to improve the detail, shape and sense of my text; Richard Barber also generously read the entire work and offered many valuable insights.

I record my appreciation of the services provided by the University of York Library & Archives, the National Archives, the Library of the Institute of Historical Research, University of London, and the British Library. I also owe considerable thanks to Robert Baldock, Heather McCallum, Rachael Lonsdale, Candida Brazil and Beth Humphries at Yale University Press for their patience and expertise in bringing this long and large project home, and to Robert Kinsey for his work with proofs and index. For any errors of fact or interpretation that remain within this book, I naturally take full responsibility.

The families Ormrod, Dobson and Wilson have borne the intrusion of Edward III into their lives for many years; public expressions of appreciation seem an inadequate return, to say the least, for their enormous investment of love and support. If there are limits to Richard's tolerance of this book, then he has rarely shown it; certainly, it is to his patience and indulgence that I owe my ability to finish it.

W. Mark Ormrod
November 2010

ABBREVIATED REFERENCES

Unless otherwise stated, all unpublished documents are in Kew, The National Archives.

AC	*The Anonimalle Chronicle, 1333–1381*, ed. V. H. Galbraith (Manchester, 1927)
Age of Chivalry	*Age of Chivalry: Art in Plantagenet England, 1200–1400*, ed. J. Alexander and P. Binski (London, 1987)
Ann. Paulini	'Annales Paulini', *Chronicles of the Reigns of Edward I and Edward II*, ed. W. Stubbs, 2 vols (RS, 1882–3), i
Anon. Cant.	*Chronicon Anonymi Cantuariensis: The Chronicle of Anonymous of Canterbury, 1346–1365*, ed. C. Scott-Stokes and C. Given-Wilson (Oxford, 2008)
Anon. Chron. 1307–34	*The Anonimalle Chronicle, 1307–1334*, ed. W. R. Childs and J. Taylor (Yorkshire Archaeological Society record series, cxlvii, 1987)
Antient Kalendars	*The Antient Kalendars and Inventories of the Treasury of His Majesty's Exchequer*, ed. F. Palgrave, 3 vols (London, 1836)
ASR	*Anglo-Scottish Relations, 1174–1328*, ed. E. L. G. Stones, revised edn (Oxford, 1970)
Avesbury	Robert of Avesbury, *De gestis mirabilibus regis Edwardi Tertii*, ed. E. M. Thompson (RS, 1889)
Baker	Geoffrey le Baker, *Chronicon Galfridi le Baker de Swynebroke*, ed. E. M. Thompson (Oxford, 1889)
Battle of Crécy	A. Ayton and P. Preston, with F. Autrand, C. Piel, M. Prestwich and B. Schnerb, *The Battle of Crécy, 1346* (Woodbridge, 2005)
BIA	York, Borthwick Institute for Archives
BIHR	*Bulletin of the Institute of Historical Research*
BJRL	*Bulletin of the John Rylands Library*

BL   London, British Library
Bower   W. Bower, *Scotichronicon*, ed. D. E. R. Watt,
                            9 vols (Aberdeen, 1993–8)
BPR   *Register of Edward the Black Prince*, 4 vols.
                            (London, 1930–3)
Bridlington   'Gesta Edwardi de Carnarvan auctore
                            canonico Bridlingtoniensi, cum continua-
                            tione', *Chronicles of the Reigns of Edward I and
                            Edward II*, ed. W. Stubbs, 2 vols. (RS,
                            London, 1882–3), ii
BRUO   A. B. Emden, *Biographical Register of the
                            University of Oxford to 1500*, 3 vols (Oxford,
                            1957–9)
Brut   *The Brut, or, The Chronicles of England*, ed. F. W.
                            D. Brie, 2 vols (Early English Texts Society,
                            original series, cxxxi, cxxxvi, 1906–8)
Cal. Mem. Rolls 1326–7   *Calendar of Memoranda Rolls (Exchequer),
                            Michaelmas 1326–Michaelmas 1327* (London,
                            1968)
CCCC   Corpus Christi College, Cambridge
CChR   *Calendar of Charter Rolls, Henry III–Henry VIII*,
                            6 vols (London, 1903–27)
CCR   *Calendar of Close Rolls, Edward II–Richard II*,
                            24 vols (London, 1892–1927)
CCW 1244–1326   *Calendar of Chancery Warrants 1244–1326*
                            (London, 1927)
CDS   *Calendar of Documents Relating to Scotland*, ed.
                            J. Bain, G. G. Simpson and J. D. Galbraith,
                            5 vols (Edinburgh, 1881–1987)
CFR   *Calendar of Fine Rolls, Edward II–Richard II*, 10
                            vols (London, 1912–29)
Chron. J&C   *Chroniques des règnes de Jean II et Charles V*, ed.
                            R. Delachenal, 4 vols (Société de l'Histoire de
                            France, 1910–20)
Chron. Lanercost   *Chronicon de Lanercost*, ed. J. Stevenson
                            (Edinburgh, 1839)
Chron. Meaux   *Chronica Monasterii de Melsa*, ed. E. A. Bond,
                            3 vols (RS, 1866–8)
Chron. QPV   *Chronique des quatre premiers Valois (1327–1393)*,
                            ed. S. Luce (Société de l'Histoire de France,
                            1862)
CIM   *Calendar of Inquisitions Miscellaneous, Henry
                            III–Henry V*, 7 vols (London, 1916–69)
CIPM   *Calendar of Inquisitions Post Mortem, Edward
                            I–Richard II*, 17 vols (London, 1904–88)

CLBL	*Calendar of Letter Books of the City of London*, ed. R. R. Sharpe, 11 vols (London, 1899–1912)
CPL	*Calendar of Entries in the Papal Registers Relating to Great Britain and Ireland: Papal Letters*, ii–iv (London, 1895–1902)
CPMR	*Calendar of Plea and Memoranda Rolls of the City of London*, ed. A. H. Thomas and P. E. Jones, 6 vols (Cambridge, 1926–61)
CPP	*Calendar of Entries in the Papal Registers Relating to Great Britain and Ireland: Petitions to the Pope, 1342–1419* (London, 1896)
CPR	*Calendar of Patent Rolls, Edward II–Richard II*, 27 vols (London, 1894–1916)
CUL	Cambridge University Library
CYS	Canterbury and York Society
Delachenal	R. Delachenal, *Histoire de Charles V*, 5 vols (Paris, 1909–31)
EcHR	*Economic History Review*
EETS	Early English Texts Society
EHD	*English Historical Documents*
EHR	*English Historical Review*
EMDP	*English Medieval Diplomatic Practice*, ed. P. Chaplais, 2 vols in 3 parts (London, 1975–82)
Eng. Govt at Work	*The English Government at Work, 1327–1336*, ed. J. F. Willard, W. A. Morris and W. H. Dunham, 3 vols (Cambridge, Mass., 1940–50)
Eulogium	*Eulogium Historiarum*, ed. F. S. Haydon, 3 vols (London, 1858–63)
Fasti 1300–1541	J. Le Neve, *Fasti Ecclesiae Anglicanae, 1300–1541*, comp. H. P. F. King, J. M. Horn and B Jones, 12 vols (London, 1962–7)
Foedera	*Foedera, Conventions, Literae et Cujuscunque Generic Acta Publica*, ed. T. Rymer, 3 vols in 6 parts (London, 1816–30)
French Chronicle	*Croniques de London*, ed. G. J. Aungier (Camden Society, original series, xxviii, 1844)
Froissart	J. Froissart, *Chroniques*, ed. S. Luce et al., 15 vols (Société de l'Histoire de France, 1869–1975)
Froissart, *Oeuvres*	J. Froissart, *Oeuvres complètes: Chroniques*, ed. J. M. B. C. Kervyn de Lettenhove, 25 vols (Brussels, 1867–77)
Froissart, trans. Brereton	J. Froissart, *Chronicles*, trans. G. Brereton (Harmondsworth, 1978)

GEC	G. E. Cokayne, *The Complete Peerage of England, Scotland, Ireland, Great Britain and the United Kingdom*, rev. V. Gibbs et al., 13 vols (London, 1910–59)
HBC	*Handbook of British Chronology*, ed. E. B. Fryde, D. E. Greenway, S. Porter and I Roy, 3rd edn (Cambridge, 1986)
Hist. Angl.	T. Walsingham, *Historia Anglicana*, ed. H. T. Riley, 2 vols (RS, 1863–4)
HR	*Historical Research*
Issues	*Issues of the Exchequer, Henry III–Henry VI*, ed. F. Devon (London, 1847)
JBS	*Journal of British Studies*
JMH	*Journal of Medieval History*
JRUL	Manchester, John Rylands University Library
King's Works	R. A. Brown, H. M. Colvin and A. J. Taylor, *The History of the King's Works: The Middle Ages*, 2 vols (London, 1963)
Knighton	*Knighton's Chronicle, 1337–1396*, ed. G. H. Martin (Oxford, 1995)
le Bel	*Chronique de Jean le Bel*, ed. J. Viard and E. Déprez, 2 vols (Société de l'Historie de France, 1904–5)
Melsa	*Chronica Monasterii de Melsa*, ed. E. A. Bond, 3 vols (RS, 1866–8)
Murimuth	A. Murimuth, *Continuatio chronicarum*, ed. E. M. Thompson (RS, 1889)
Norwell	*The Wardrobe Book of William de Norwell*, ed. M. Lyon, B. Lyon, H. S. Lucas and J. de Sturler (Brussels, 1983)
'Observations'	'Observations on the Institution of the Most Noble Order of the Garter', ed. N. H. Nicolas, *Archaeologia*, xxxi (1846)
ODNB	*Oxford Dictionary of National Biography*, ed. H. C. G. Matthew and B. H. Harrison, 60 vols (Oxford, 2004)
Parl. Writs	*Parliamentary Writs and Writs of Personal Summons*, ed. F. Palgrave, 2 vols in 4 parts (London, 1827–34)
Political Poems	*Political Poems and Songs Relating to English History*, ed. T. Wright, 2 vols (RS, 1859–61)
Polychronicon	R. Higden, *Polychronicon*, ed. C. Babington and J. R. Lumby, 9 vols (RS, 1865–82)
PROME	*The Parliament Rolls of Medieval England*, ed. and trans. P. Brand, A. Curry, C. Given-Wilson,

	R. E. Horrox, G. Martin, W. M. Ormrod and J. R. S. Phillips, 16 vols (Woodbridge, 2005)
RDP	*Report from the Lords Committee for All Matters Touching the Dignity of a Peer*, 5 vols (London, 1820–9)
Reading	J. Reading, 'Chronicon', *Chronica Johannis de Reading et Anonymi Cantuariensis*, ed. J. Tait (Manchester, 1914)
Rot. Scot.	*Rotuli Scotiae*, 2 vols (London, 1814–19)
RP	*Rotuli Parliamentorum*, 6 vols (London, 1787)
RPHI	*Rotuli Parliamentorum Anglie hactenus inediti*, ed. H. G. Richardson and G. O. Sayles (Camden Society, 3rd series, li, 1935)
RS	Rolls series
SAL	Society of Antiquaries of London
Scalacronica	T. Gray, *Scalacronica*, ed. and trans. A. King (Surtees Society, ccix, 2005)
SCCKB	*Select Cases in the Court of King's Bench*, ed. G. O. Sayles, 7 vols (Selden Society, lv, lvii, lviii, lxxiv, lxxvi, lxxxii, lxxxviii, 1936–71)
SR	*Statutes of the Realm*, 11 vols (London, 1810–28)
St Albans	T. Walsingham, *The St Albans Chronicle: The 'Chronica Maiora' of Thomas Walsingham*, ed. J. Taylor, W. R. Childs and L. Watkiss, in progress (Oxford, 2003–)
Sumption	J. Sumption, *The Hundred Years War*, in progress (London, 1990–)
Tout, *Chapters*	T. F. Tout, *Chapters in the Administrative History of Medieval England*, 6 vols (Manchester, 1920–33)
TRHS	*Transactions of the Royal Historical Society*
VCH	*Victoria County History*
Vie du Prince Noir	Chandos Herald, *La vie du Prince Noir*, ed. D. B. Tyson (Tübingen, 1975)
Vita	*Vita Edwardi Secundi*, ed. and trans. W. R. Childs (Oxford, 2005)
WAM	London, Westminster Abbey Muniments
'Wigmore Chronicle'	'A Wigmore Chronicle, 1355–1377', ed. J. Taylor, in J. Taylor, *English Historical Literature in the Fourteenth Century* (Oxford, 1987)
Wyntoun	*The Original Chronicle of Andrew of Wyntoun*, vi, ed. F. J. Amours (Edinburgh, 1908)

NOTE ON MONEY

The monetary system of medieval England was usually expressed in the three units of pounds (£), shillings (s) and pence (d), with 12 pence in a shilling and 20 shillings in a pound. Another unit of account was the mark, which was worth 13s 4d, or two-thirds of a pound. In France there were two principal moneys of account based in silver currency, the *livre parisis* and the *livre tournois*. Exchange rates fluctuated significantly over time, but in the fourteenth century one English pound usually converted to 4 *livres parisis* and 5 *livres tournois*. The everyday currencies of England and France comprised low-denomination silver coins, but France experimented with gold coins from the mid-thirteenth century and securely established them by the opening of the Hundred Years War; in England, a gold coinage was first introduced in the 1340s. Gold coins were usually high-denomination and were used chiefly for large-scale trade and international exchange.

Map 1 Edward III's Europe.

The English royal family

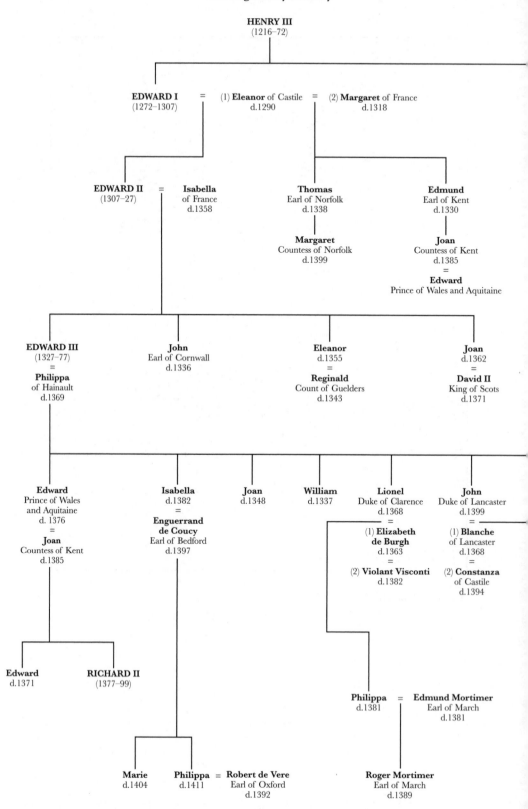

HENRY III
(1216–72)

EDWARD I = (1) **Eleanor** of Castile = (2) **Margaret** of France
(1272–1307)   d.1290   d.1318

EDWARD II = Isabella   Thomas   Edmund
(1307–27)   of France   Earl of Norfolk Earl of Kent
            d.1358   d.1338   d.1330

Margaret   Joan
Countess of Norfolk   Countess of Kent
d.1399   d.1385
                  =
                  Edward
                  Prince of Wales and Aquitaine

EDWARD III   John   Eleanor   Joan
(1327–77)   Earl of Cornwall d.1355   d.1362
=   d.1336   =   =
Philippa   Reginald   David II
of Hainault   Count of Guelders King of Scots
d.1369   d.1343   d.1371

Edward   Isabella   Joan   William   Lionel   John
Prince of Wales d.1382   d.1348   d.1337   Duke of Clarence Duke of Lancaster
and Aquitaine   =   d.1368   d.1399
d. 1376   Enguerrand   =   =
=   de Coucy   (1) **Elizabeth** (1) **Blanche**
Joan   Earl of Bedford   **de Burgh**   of Lancaster
Countess of Kent d.1397   d.1363   d.1368
d.1385   =   =
                                                 (2) **Violant Visconti** (2) **Constanza**
                                                 d.1382   of Castile
                                                                 d.1394

Edward   RICHARD II
d.1371   (1377–99)

Philippa = **Edmund Mortimer**
d.1381   Earl of March
           d.1381

Marie   Philippa = **Robert de Vere**   Roger Mortimer
d.1404   d.1411   Earl of Oxford   Earl of March
                     d.1392   d.1389

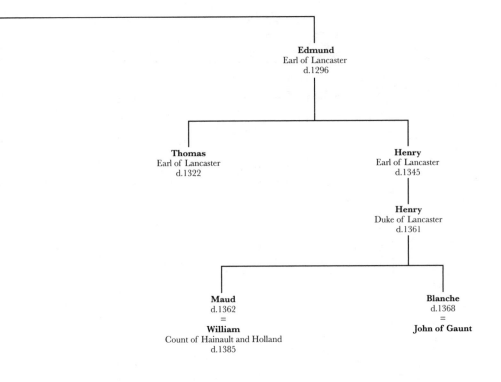

Edmund
Earl of Lancaster
d.1296

Thomas
Earl of Lancaster
d.1322

Henry
Earl of Lancaster
d.1345

Henry
Duke of Lancaster
d.1361

Maud
d.1362
=
William
Count of Hainault and Holland
d.1385

Blanche
d.1368
=
John of Gaunt

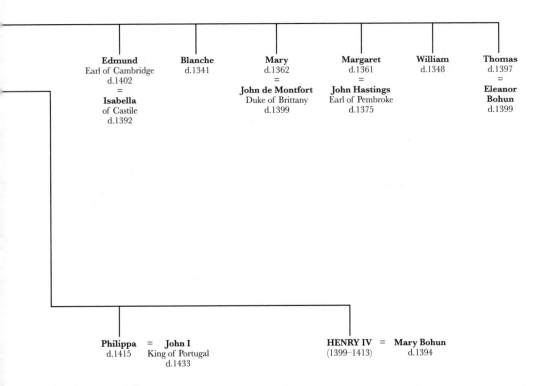

Edmund
Earl of Cambridge
d.1402
=
Isabella
of Castile
d.1392

Blanche
d.1341

Mary
d.1362
=
John de Montfort
Duke of Brittany
d.1399

Margaret
d.1361
=
John Hastings
Earl of Pembroke
d.1375

William
d.1348

Thomas
d.1397
=
**Eleanor
Bohun**
d.1399

Philippa   =   **John I**
d.1415   King of Portugal
              d.1433

HENRY IV   =   **Mary Bohun**
(1399–1413)   d.1394

Rulers of France, Navarre, Flanders and Hainault

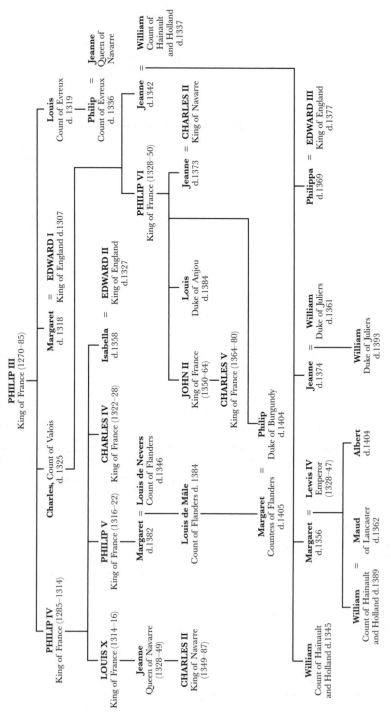

Rulers of Scotland

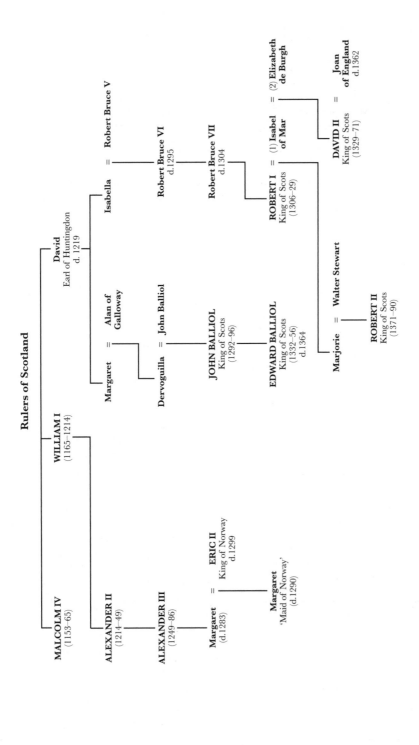

Chapter 1

EDWARD OF WINDSOR, 1312–1322

Edward III was king of England for over fifty years. Among his predecessors, only Henry III reigned longer, and it was only much later that these records of longevity came to be exceeded by George III, Queen Victoria and Elizabeth II.[1] Edward lived out virtually all of his life in the public eye. An adolescent of just fourteen when he was placed prematurely on the throne in 1327, he spent his twenties and thirties in active military leadership. Moving into a more sedentary role in government during his forties and fifties, he then declined into infirmity and died in 1377 at the age of sixty-four. Edward's sheer capacity for survival is remarkable in a period when both the medical and the political odds seemed so much stacked against long life. He outlived his three siblings, his wife and eight of their twelve children. At a time when military commanders took it for granted that they might die in battle, in tournaments, or from debilitating diseases contracted on campaign, and in an age when significant numbers of Edward's close associates succumbed to the ravages of the Black Death, the survival of the king came, not surprisingly, to look like something of a mark of divine favour. The collective sense of loss experienced by his subjects in the months and years after the old king's death was, indeed, palpable. In 1377 there were very few people in England who could remember – and fewer still who would wish to compare – what life had been like before the triumphant Edward had come to the throne.

The events, environments and personalities of Edward III's life and reign come down to us as a series of snatched moments and impressionistic vignettes. Only tiny fragments remain today of the buildings, artefacts, fabrics and furnishings that provided the spatial contexts, ceremonial trappings and domestic comforts of the Edwardian court.[2] What survives is, for the most part, in the form of the written word: the chronicles, treatises and poetry composed by contemporary monks, clerks and occasional high-status laymen; the archives of the Church and of the principal cities and towns; and above all the extraordinarily voluminous records generated by royal government, especially those of the royal secretariat (the chancery, privy seal and signet) and the financial offices (the exchequer, the wardrobe or treasury

---

[1] James VI was ruler of Scotland for 57 years, but (as James I) was king of England only from 1603 to 1625.

[2] *Age of Chivalry*, 489–504.

of the king's household, and the chamber).[3] These texts and documents almost always represent the king at some remove. Since England lacked any real tradition of official history or polemic, most writers had little or no personal knowledge of the events they described: only rarely, as in the cases of Adam Murimuth and Thomas Gray for the first half of Edward III's reign or of Jean Froissart and Thomas Walsingham for its later stages, did chroniclers have sufficiently privileged access to information to give their accounts a real ring of authenticity.[4] Most of the records maintained by the great offices of central government, moreover, were highly formulaic, their self-conscious artificiality further emphasized by the fact that the majority were written in academic Latin. Only where letters, petitions and poems survive in the Anglo-Norman French still then used as a regular language of speech at court and in polite circles do we begin to approach something of an authentic register.[5] And until the latter part of Edward III's reign Middle English, the everyday language of most of the king's ordinary subjects, was virtually never employed as a means of written expression and communication beyond the literary genre of poetry.[6]

All of this, then, makes for major challenges of comprehension. We can know reasonably surely what Edward III looked like, what he wore, where he travelled, how he conducted himself in war and what he said in ceremonial acts of state. We may even fleetingly discern something of the quality of his personal relationships in his fondness for his family, his occasional impatience with his administrators, his fun and games with friends, and the affectionate nicknames he gave to his intimate domestic servants. But to address the greater task of establishing the king's character and motivations is constantly to remark just how much remains unknown and unknowable. This book aims, as much as is possible, to recover Edward III's experiences, deeds, words, behaviour and demeanour, and thus to evaluate the degree to which the king's own character and ambitions defined, shaped and transcended the institutional structures and political conventions of his day. Only in this way, it is argued, can we reach an overall assessment of Edward both as king and as man.[7] It is for the

[3] For a useful summary of the structure of government and its archives in this period, see A. L. Brown, *The Governance of Late Medieval England, 1272–1461* (London, 1989).

[4] P. S. Lewis, 'War, Propaganda and Historiography in Fifteenth-Century France and England', *TRHS*, 5th series, xv (1965), 1–21; A. Gransden, 'Propaganda in English Medieval Historiography', *JMH*, i (1975), 363–81.

[5] H. Suggett, 'The Use of French in England in the Later Middle Ages', *TRHS*, 4th series, xxviii (1946), 61–83. Note particularly the complex relationship between *spoken* English and *written* Latin and French in the activities of the royal law courts: J. H. Baker, *The Common Law Tradition: Lawyers, Books and the Law* (London, 2000), 225–46; P. Brand, 'The Languages of the Law in Later Medieval England', *Multilingualism in Later Medieval Britain*, ed. D. A. Trotter (Cambridge, 2000), 63–76.

[6] See pp. 455–61.

[7] For the use of such techniques in other modern biographies of medieval rulers, see M. Vale, 'The Return of the Event', *Times Literary Supplement*, 16 Aug. 1996, 3–4.

reader to decide whether the darkness of the intervening centuries ultimately allows such a meaningful relationship to be established between the
medieval monarch and his modern biographer.

The future Edward III was born at Windsor castle on 13 November 1312.
Later in his life he was to make much of his association with Windsor
and would transform the castle into a great memorial to his monarchy.
In the early fourteenth century, however, the royal residence had relatively
few palatial pretensions. Henry III had carried out improvements in the
mid-thirteenth century, but Edward I had preferred to use the royal manor
house in the Great Park, a much-favoured venue for hunting parties.
Edward II was a more frequent visitor to the castle and, recalling that both
his mother and his grandmother had borne and raised children there,
consciously selected the castle as the appropriate venue for the birth of his
own first child in 1312. The court had been at Windsor more or less contin-
uously since mid-September, though the king initially spent much of his
time away from the queen, hunting in the park. His brief foray to the castle
between 15 and 18 October could have been provoked by fears that his wife,
Isabella of France, was about to undergo a premature delivery, but things
became sufficiently stable again for him to make a visit to Westminster at
the end of the month. He was back at Windsor on 12 November, just in
time for the birth, early on Monday 13 November, of his new baby son.[8]
The prince's birthday was the Feast of St Brice; when he became king, the
day was celebrated with distributions of special alms and was sometimes
annotated in the household accounts for its royal significance.[9]
    The queen's uncle, Louis of Evreux, was in attendance at the English
court at the time of the birth, and a rumour developed that he and
Isabella had demanded that the prince be given one of the names used
by the recent kings of France. Considering the general influence that
Philip IV had expected to enjoy over the English royal family as a result of
the marriage of his daughter to Edward II in 1308, the story seems reasonably plausible.[10] It is likely, though, that Evreux expected to exercise the
prerogative of the godparent and have the boy christened Louis rather
than Philip. To modern nationalist sensibilities this may seem unrealistic;
however, contemporaries may have been more persuaded. The proposal
harked back to the great thirteenth-century French model of kingly

---

[8] E 101/375/2, m. 2–3; E. M. Hallam, *The Itinerary of Edward II and his Household* (List &
Index Society, ccxi, 1984), 92; *Foedera*, II.i, 18.
    [9] E.g., E 101/387/9, m. 3.
    [10] *Johannis de Trokelowe et Henrici de Blandeforde Chronica et Annales*, ed. H. T. Riley (RS, 1866),
79; *Hist. Angl.*, i, 13; E. A. R. Brown, 'The Political Repercussions of Family Ties in the
Early Fourteenth Century: The Marriage of Edward II of England and Isabelle of
France', *Speculum*, lxiii (1988), 573–95; E. A. R. Brown, 'The Marriage of Edward II of
England and Isabelle of France: A Postscript', *Speculum*, lxiv (1989), 373–9; S. Phillips,
Edward II (London, 2010), 201–2.

sanctity, Louis IX: later, when Edward III explicitly claimed the throne of France as heir of St Louis, he was dubbed by one continental satirist with the double style 'Edward Louis'.[11] In the end, however, the accident that had delivered two successive kings with the distinctly English name of Edward proved more powerful. The selection of this name placed the new heir to the throne in a line running back through his own father and grandfather to England's own most powerful king-saint, Edward the Confessor. In due course, the prince was therefore destined to become 'King Edward the Third after the Conquest' – the first ruler of England, in fact, to have a number formally included in his official title.[12]

King and people had more than usual cause for celebration at the birth. Since Edward II's accession in 1307 the throne had lacked an heir apparent, and there was some concern that the king's sudden death might create a succession crisis.[13] This was no idle speculation. Edward II's older brothers, John, Henry and Alfonso, had all died young.[14] The line had been strengthened after Edward I's second marriage to Margaret of France and the birth of two more sons, Thomas of Brotherton and Edmund of Woodstock, but they were still only boys at the birth of their nephew in 1312. Of the other cadet branches of the royal family, the line of King John's younger son, Richard of Cornwall, had become extinct on the death of Edmund of Almaine, earl of Cornwall, in 1300, leaving only the house of Lancaster, descended through Henry III's younger son, Edmund Crouchback (d. 1296), and represented in the opening decades of the fourteenth century by the latter's son, Thomas of Lancaster. Thomas never cast himself in the role of pretender,[15] but his extraordinary wealth and high political profile may have led some to conclude that he was a viable heir presumptive. Disputed successions, as the situations in Scotland in 1290 and subsequently in France in 1328 made clear, fundamentally threatened the political and moral order of the realm. Accordingly it was much to England's relief, as well as her pride, that King Edward II was provided with an heir apparent in 1312.

The new royal child was, by all accounts, gratifyingly robust. While we have a considerable body of information on the medical treatments of

---

[11] *The Vows of the Heron (Les Voeux du héron): A Middle French Vowing Poem*, ed. J. L. Grigsby and N. J. Lacy (New York, 1992), 32–7.

[12] *CCR 1327–30*, 100; Baker, 6; Murimuth, 55. Initially the style used for his father was extended, and for a short while Edward III was called 'King Edward, son of King Edward, son of King Edward' (sometimes with 'son of King Henry' for good measure): *Cal. Mem. Rolls 1326–7*, viii; *RPHI*, 110.

[13] *Vita*, 63.

[14] J. C. Parsons, 'The Year of Eleanor of Castile's Birth and her Children by Edward I', *Mediaeval Studies*, xlvi (1984), 257–65; J. C. Parsons, *Eleanor of Castile: Queenship and Society in Thirteenth-Century England* (Basingstoke, 1995), 38.

[15] J. R. Maddicott, *Thomas of Lancaster, 1307–1322: A Study in the Reign of Edward II* (Oxford, 1970), 318–34.

Edward II and Queen Isabella, it is striking that there are no extant references to Prince Edward being administered medicines or tended by doctors in his infancy.[16] The famous Oxford physician John Gaddesden, who later treated Edward's own children, referred in his treatise, the *Rosa Anglica*, to having saved 'the son of the illustrious king of England' from smallpox by the dubious but time-honoured practice of wrapping the child in a red blanket. But although it is often assumed that the boy in question was the future Edward III, it seems much more likely from other dating evidence that the reference is to one of Edward I's younger sons, Thomas or Edmund.[17]

For Edward II, the birth of an heir was a cause of obvious celebration in a year otherwise dominated by difficulty and tragedy. The flamboyant and unpredictable Edward had flouted political and social convention by blatantly promoting the interests of his closest friend, Piers Gaveston. The nature of the relationship between these two men has been much discussed. Edward II's decision in 1307 to override his father's plans and grant the earldom of Cornwall not to one of his half-brothers but to the newcomer Piers suggests that he bestowed on his favourite the special status of adopted brother. In liberal twenty-first-century cultures it can be much more openly speculated as to whether this was indeed a same-sex love affair. But even supposing the friendship to have been platonic, there were many ready explanations for the extraordinary hatred shown towards Gaveston by other members of the elite. Piers was an alien (his family came from Gascony) and an upstart. He may have been more interested in the trappings than the substance of power. But his overbearing influence on Edward threatened to shut off channels of communication between the crown and its 'natural' (native-born) advisers, the high nobility, and thus fundamentally to disrupt the sense of balance and cohesion within the ruling elite.[18]

In 1310 an unusually united nobility led first by the earl of Lincoln and then by Thomas of Lancaster had forced the king to accept a reformist agenda, the 'New Ordinances', whose central clause required that Piers Gaveston 'be forever exiled from the realm, never to return'. Although the king initially complied with this demand, he quickly sought opportunities to confound the Ordinances and called the unrepentant Piers back to his side, pronouncing him pardoned and restored to his estates in January 1312.[19] This flagrant breach of faith galvanized the opposition, and

[16] J. S. Hamilton, 'Some Notes on "Royal" Medicine in the Reign of Edward II', *Fourteenth Century England II*, ed. C. Given-Wilson (Woodbridge, 2002), 34–43.

[17] G. Dock, 'Printed Editions of the *Rosa Anglica* of John of Gaddesden', *Janus*, viii (1907), 3; *BRUO*, ii, 739; C. H. Talbot and E. A. Hammond, *The Medical Practitioners in Medieval England: A Biographical Register* (London, 1965), 148–50.

[18] J. S. Hamilton, *Piers Gaveston, Earl of Cornwall 1307–1312* (London, 1988), 16–17, 109–10; P. Chaplais, *Piers Gaveston: Edward II's Adoptive Brother* (Oxford, 1994), 30–1.

[19] *SR*, i, 162; *CCR 1307–13*, 448–9.

Gaveston, who was placed in the custody of the earl of Pembroke, was seized by Warwick and put to death at Blacklow Hill, on the road between Warwick and Kenilworth, in June. A number of contemporary chroniclers commented that Edward II's resulting grief lifted, if only briefly, at his son's birth in November.[20] Something of the quality of that joy is certainly revealed by the grant subsequently made to John Launge, the queen's yeoman, and his wife Joan, one of Isabella's damsels, of a handsome annuity of £80 for bringing the king news of the queen's safe delivery.[21]

It was in the new spirit of optimism engendered by the birth of the prince that Edward II also sought a rapprochement with the queen. Isabella of France had been only twelve years old at the time of her marriage in 1308, and had been placed in an extremely difficult situation as a result of the king's favouring Gaveston. It is doubtful how much credence we can give to the story that Piers had dressed in the royal purple and usurped the queen's role at the banquet following the royal couple's coronation.[22] But it is clear that Isabella's father, Philip the Fair, had strong concerns over her treatment at the English court. It is possible that her family forbade the consummation of the marriage for some years, even perhaps until the conception of Prince Edward at York in the spring of 1312.[23] The queen's loneliness during the intervening period is touchingly revealed by her adoption of a Scottish orphan boy named Thomalin in 1311. It is hardly surprising that by early 1312 Isabella was already engaged in secret correspondence with the earl of Lancaster, deriving a personal assurance from him that Gaveston would be separated, once and for all, from the king. As the time for the birth of the queen's first child approached, her father also grew increasingly solicitous for her welfare. Although Isabella had her own physician, Master Theobald, Philip IV dispatched his surgeon, Henri de Mondeville, to supervise the confinement.[24]

The death of Gaveston and the arrival of the prince therefore did much to improve the young Queen Isabella's political and personal standing. A public holiday was proclaimed in London on 14 November and a great service of thanksgiving was held at St Paul's Cathedral.

---

[20] *Vita*, 36; *Trokelowe*, 79; Baker, 6.

[21] *CPR 1307–13*, 519. For the Launges' subsequent problems in securing this annuity, see *CCR 1313–18*, 54; *CCR 1318–23*, 611; *CPR 1321–4*, 128.

[22] *Ann. Paulini*, 262; H. G. Richardson, 'The *Annales Paulini*', *Speculum*, xxiii (1948), 630–40.

[23] P. C. Doherty, 'The Date of the Birth of Isabella, Queen of England (1308–58)', *BIHR*, xlviii (1975), 246–8; Brown, 'Political Repercussions of Family Ties', 583 n. 25; J. C. Parsons, 'Mothers, Daughters, Marriage, Power: Some Plantagenet Evidence, 1150–1500', *Medieval Queenship*, ed. J. C. Parsons (Stroud, 1994), 67–8. If the pregnancy ran its full course, then Edward of Windsor must have been conceived at York shortly after Gaveston's own daughter was born there: Hamilton, *Gaveston*, 93–4; Chaplais, *Gaveston*, 78–9. Isabella had arrived in York by 24 Feb. 1312: *The Household Book of Queen Isabella of England, 8th July 1311 to 7 July 1312*, ed. F. D. Blackley and G. Hermansen (Edmonton, 1971), xxiv.

[24] *Household Book of Queen Isabella*, xix, xxiii, xxv–vi; *Trokelowe*, 75–6; Hamilton, 'Notes on "Royal" Medicine', 35 n. 16.

A week later, following a similar ceremony at Westminster Abbey, Londoners enjoyed further celebrations, during which the conduit in Cheapside ran with wine.[25] The *Vita Edwardi Secundi* summed up Edward II's achievements by 1313 in strikingly domestic terms: 'Our King Edward has now reigned six full years and up until now he has achieved nothing praiseworthy or memorable, except that he has made a splendid marriage and has produced a handsome son and heir to the kingdom.'[26]

Meanwhile, the new prince had been christened in St Edward's Chapel, Windsor, on 16 November 1312, the Feast of St Edmund Rich. A precious fragment of the font in which he 'was washed in the water of holy baptism' still survives. Taking advantage of the current round of talks with the papacy and the French, Edward II secured the services of Arnold, cardinal priest of St Prisca, to perform the ceremony and elected as the child's godfathers Richard, cardinal bishop of Poitiers, John Droxford, bishop of Bath and Wells, Walter Reynolds, bishop of Worcester, Louis, count of Evreux, the earls of Richmond and Pembroke and Hugh Despenser the Elder.[27] The event had a distinctly political air about it, and a number of people were notable by their absence. The omission of the archbishop of Canterbury, Robert Winchelsey, for example, may have been a deliberate snub, for he had been a conspicuous supporter of the Ordainers. It is certainly significant that on his death the following May, Winchelsey was to be succeeded at Canterbury by one of the prince's new godfathers, the loyal Walter Reynolds.[28] Nor, inevitably, were any of those implicated in Gaveston's murder present at the event. Indeed, the fractious Lancaster and his confederates were still in arms against the king.

The celebrations following the christening were inevitably somewhat forced. The costs of the king's hall, which normally stood at about £30, rose only to a relatively modest £57 on the day of the prince's baptism.[29] Little over a month later, however, a tribunal presided over by the cardinals, where Edward II was represented by Pembroke and Despenser the Elder, produced proposals for a political reconciliation between the king and his errant barons. Thus, while the chroniclers were generally agreed that Gaveston's death created a personal blood feud between the king and Lancaster, it was not at all certain that there was any general commitment

---

[25] *Memorials of London and London Life in the XIIIth, XIVth, and XVth Centuries*, ed. H. T. Riley (RS, 1868), 105–7; 'Annales Londoniensis', *Chronicles of the Reigns of Edward I and Edward II*, ed. W. Stubbs, 2 vols (RS, 1882–3), i, 22–1; *CLBL, D,* 310

[26] *Vita,* 69.

[27] *Foedera,* II.i, 187; *CPR 1348–50,* 144; P. Tudor-Craig, 'The Fonts of St George's Chapel', *St George's Chapel Windsor in the Fourteenth Century,* ed. N. Saul (Woodbridge, 2005), 156–7. The anniversary of the king's baptism was later marked by special gifts of alms: e.g., E 101/387/9, m. 3; E 101/393/11, fol. 61v.

[28] J. R. Wright, *The Church and the English Crown, 1305–1334* (Toronto, 1980), 263–4.

[29] E 101/375/2, m. 3.

among the political elite to the perpetuation of hostilities.[30] The royal family itself passed much of the winter of 1312–13 together at Windsor, where Christmas was celebrated with considerable magnificence. It was in such moments of relative calm that Edward II and Queen Isabella expressed for public benefit whatever elements of natural affection might have emerged in their newly established nuclear unit.[31] For some time after the birth of Edward of Windsor, the general mood of the court was therefore both celebratory and conciliatory.

It was incumbent on Edward II to provide resources fitting to the prince's great estate. On 24 November 1312, the king accordingly granted his son the palatinate county of Chester. The earldom had been particularly associated with the heir to the throne since the time of Henry III, and Edward III himself would later entail it upon the monarch and his eldest son in perpetuity. However, Prince Edward was not to enjoy possession of all the other lands and titles associated with the heir to the throne since Henry III's endowment of the Lord Edward in 1254.[32] The lordship of Ireland, which had provided income for the future Edward I, was too important a source of money and manpower to be ceded by Edward II, and the duchy of Aquitaine was not transferred to the prince's control until 1325. The Channel Islands, another of the Plantagenets' offshore interests included in the endowment of 1254, had been granted for life to Otto de Grandisson, scion of a Savoyard dynasty who had made a successful military and political career in the service of Edward I. Otto had since departed England, and in 1318 the king, believing him dead, granted the islands to Prince Edward. In point of fact, Grandisson lived until 1328, and there is no evidence that Edward III came into possession of the Channel Islands until after he became king.[33] Finally, the earldom of Cornwall, though linked with the royal family, was not yet associated specifically with the heir to the throne: after Gaveston's demise it remained vacant until Edward III revived it for his brother, John of Eltham, in 1328, and it was only after the latter's death that it was entailed upon the king and his eldest son and raised to the status of a duchy in 1337.

It was soon evident that the earldom of Chester was inadequate to provide the material needs of the prince and his entourage. The transfer of the earldom was treated rather casually by Edward II, who continued

---

[30] Maddicott, *Thomas of Lancaster*, 130, 134–54; J. R. S. Phillips, *Aymer de Valence, Earl of Pembroke 1307–1324* (Oxford, 1972), 46–69.

[31] *CFR 1307–19*, 158.

[32] *CChR 1300–26*, 202; Tout, *Chapters*, iv, 69 and n. 2; M. Prestwich, *Edward I* (London, 1988), 11–14.

[33] *ODNB*, xxiii, 269–70; *CChR 1300–26*, 407–8. In 1319 the islanders petitioned Queen Isabella concerning their request for the resumption of the islands into the hands of the king or his eldest son: SC 1/37/39.

to draw on its resources whenever he needed.[34] The earlier separation of the honour of Macclesfield from the county and its grant to Queen Isabella created inevitable frictions between the ministers of the prince and his mother.[35] And the political disruptions of the 1310s took their toll; in 1318 there was a serious riot in the city of Chester, and the financial administration of the county fell into some disarray.[36] Consequently, it was necessary from an early stage to supplement the prince's landed income. One of the earliest such arrangements came in December 1312, when the king granted his son Carisbrooke castle and all other royal lands and rights on the Isle of Wight. As with Cheshire, so with Wight: the youth of the lord prince made his administration susceptible to corruption, and two successive constables of Carisbrooke, Henry Tyeys and Richard Byfleet, were later to be fined for abusing their place as the young prince's agents.[37] But in spite of such difficulties, Edward's material wealth accrued quickly. By 1318 he enjoyed the issues of the honour of Wallingford and the manor of Petworth and 1,000 marks per annum from the Cornish tin mines.[38] In the mid-1320s, Edward's annual income was running at about £4,000. This was well in excess of any other contemporary household in England, barring those of the prince's own parents, the earl of Lancaster and Hugh Despenser the Younger.[39] By the time he was ten years old, Edward of Windsor was truly one of the greatest lords of the realm.

As was customary, the heir to the throne was also provided from birth with his own independent household staffed by loyal servants of his father and mother.[40] Edward's first steward was Sir John Sapy, who gave way to the more prominent courtier Sir Robert Mauley in 1314; Hugh Leominster, the original treasurer, was replaced in or before 1319 by the distinguished Yorkshire-born clerk Nicholas Huggate.[41] From the start, the prince's household moved around more or less independently of those of

[34] *CCR 1323–7*, 455–6; P. H. W. Booth, *The Financial Administration of the Lordship and County of Chester, 1272–1377* (Chetham Society, 3rd series, xxviii, 1981), 58, 64.

[35] *CChrR 1300–26*, 202; *CCR 1313–18*, 373; *CCW 1244–1326*, 403.

[36] *CCR 1318–23*, 12, 23–4; *CPR 1317–21*, 200; SC 8/6/267, printed in *RP*, i, 401–2; Booth, *Financial Administration*, 60–1.

[37] *CChR 1300–26*, 202, 377; *CPR 1317–21*, 546, 598; *CPR 1324–7*, 23, 86; *CCW 1244–1326*, 560; SC 8/154/7685. Tyeys was put to death after Boroughbridge: N. M. Fryde, *The Tyranny and Fall of Edward II, 1321–1326* (Cambridge, 1977), 61.

[38] *CCR 1313–18*, 64; *CPR 1317–21*, 5; *CCR 1318–23*, 193; *CCR 1323–7*, 7, 102–3; *CPR 1317–21*, 141, 162.

[39] N. Denholm-Young, *Collected Papers* (Cardiff, 1969), 166; Maddicott, *Thomas of Lancaster*, 27; C. M. Woolgar, *The Great Household in Late Medieval England* (London, 1999), 15–17.

[40] E 101/375/3; Tout, *Chapters*, iv, 70–1; *Household Book of Queen Isabella*, xiii.

[41] Tout, *Chapters*, iv, 71; Leominster's term of office is datable by E 101/376/7, fol. 20. Sapy went on to be justiciar of Chester but fell from favour and was victimized by the Despensers after 1322: J. C. Davies, *The Baronial Opposition to Edward II* (Cambridge, 1918), 455; T. F. Tout, *The Place of the Reign of Edward II in English History*, 2nd edn (Manchester, 1936), 337; Fryde, *Tyranny*, 230.

the king and queen. During the first six months of 1313, for instance, the baby prince spent only about four weeks at court. For most of the time he was lodged at the recently confiscated preceptory of the Knights Templar at Bisham in Berkshire, where his parents made fleeting visits in February, May and August. From late May to mid-July, both the king and the queen were out of the country on a visit to Paris, and the only family visitor to the child recorded during this period was his step-grandmother, the kindly dowager Queen Margaret.[42] Similarly, the prince's mother was again absent from the realm on a diplomatic mission to France in the spring of 1314. When the king marched north that summer en route to the disaster of Bannockburn, the baby Edward's household went into residence at the royal manor of Ludgershall in Wiltshire.[43]

This is not to say that the royal couple were not solicitous of their son's welfare. Both Edward II and Queen Isabella wrote regularly to the child (or rather, to his keepers) when they were separated from him. Nothing of this correspondence survives, but we know that in early 1316 the king sent to the three-year-old toddler his 'blessing'.[44] The indulgent Edward II was also careful, for the first few years, to make discretionary grants to the young prince's household from the sheriffs' revenues, the profits of taxation and the receipts of North Wales.[45] From 8 July to 25 October 1315 Prince Edward was recorded as living at least partially at the king's direct cost, at a rate of about £3 a day; over the same period the king also covered special purchases such as the £35 that his son's entourage managed to spend on sugar and spices.[46] In material terms at least, the precious prince lacked for nothing.

Nor was Edward of Windsor's early life entirely devoid of emotional stability. Queen Isabella went on to bear her husband three further surviving children: John of Eltham (b. August 1316), Eleanor of Woodstock (b. June 1318) and Joan of the Tower (b. July 1321). In 1319 John and Eleanor were moved from Isabella's household and placed with their brother, an arrangement that prompted the transfer to the prince of several of the queen's estates, including the honours of Macclesfield and the High Peak. The experiment proved short-lived, and was abandoned in 1320.[47] It is possible, however, that the prince and his siblings continued to spend a certain amount of time together. In common

---

[42] Tout, *Chapters*, iv, 70–1; Hallam, *Itinerary of Edward II*, 95, 98; *VCH Berks*, iii, 139, 146.

[43] E 179/377/7; *CCR 1313–18*, 53, 57.

[44] E 101/375/9, fols 33v, 34; E 101/376/7, fol. 75v, 99v; E 101/376/25; SAL, MS 121, fol. 33v.

[45] *CCR 1307–13*, 530; *CCR 1313–18*, 3, 11, 45, 47, 106; E 179/377/7.

[46] E 101/376/7, fol. 20. Compare the £20 a day received from the Bardi for the upkeep of Edward's household after he became king: *CPR 1330–4*, 52; *CCR 1330–3*, 15. In 1317–18 the king also made a discretionary gift to the prince in recompense of expenses: SAL, MS 121, fol. 33v.

[47] *CFR 1307–19*, 389; Tout, *Chapters*, iv, 72 n. 9, 74–5.

with generations of royals and aristocrats, they developed powerful emotional bonds with wet-nurses and other female attendants. Edward of Windsor's first nurse was named Margaret Chaundeler. But it was Margaret Daventry who was really to dominate his early life. She certainly reaped the rewards of that affection. Margaret's daughter, Hawise, received a notably generous gift of 100 marks from Edward III on the occasion of her marriage in 1337. And as late as the 1350s, the forty-something Edward was still intervening in the courts to protect the elderly Margaret's property and financial interests.[48] Edward of Windsor's bonding with his nurse was probably the only truly natural and spontaneous relationship of his life.

Until the early 1320s the young prince's horizons continued to be fixed, and his attitudes formed, largely by those set around him in his own household and administration. The physical separation of the prince from his parents necessitated the appointment of an official tutor or 'keeper of the body' to be directly responsible for his physical safety, his education and military training, and the general overseeing of his household and estates. By April 1318 this post was held by Sir Richard Damory, who retained it at least until 1320.[49] Though initially overshadowed by his younger brother, Roger, Sir Richard went on to a distinguished career and, like the prince's former steward, Robert Mauley, survived the revolution of 1327 to be retained in Edward III's household.[50] It was presumably under Damory that Edward began the training in manners and etiquette, in the accomplishments of dancing, singing and playing musical instruments, and in riding, hunting and jousting, that formed the core of a royal education in this period.[51] It was later claimed that Richard Bury, who went on to become one of Edward's most trusted advisers and ended his days as bishop of Durham, was the prince's tutor. Bury was very well connected in the world of scholarship and became an avid book collector; it is easy to see why his own panegyrists should have wished to cast him in the role of royal instructor. The claim that the pair actually engaged in formal lessons is generally refuted in modern scholarship, but it remains entirely possible that Bury, who was in the prince's service from at least 1319, acted more generally as a mentor and father-figure. If so, then Edward was indeed a lucky boy, for he found in Richard precisely those qualities

[48] *CFR 1307–19*, 189; E 101/383/10; *Cal. Mem. Rolls 1326–7*, nos. 986, 2270, 2271; *CIM*, ii, no. 1317; *CFR 1337–47*, 180; E 403/297, 23 Feb 1337; E 159/136, *Brev. bar.*, Trin., rot. 15d.

[49] *CCW 1244–1326*, 485. Compare *CPR 1317–21*, 134, 453–4; *CFR 1307–19*, 389, where Damory is associated with other members of Edward's household, though his own post is not specified.

[50] Maddicott, *Thomas of Lancaster*, 192–6; Phillips, *Aymer de Valence*, 131–3; Tout, *Chapters*, vi, 42, 59–60; *Cal. Mem. Rolls 1326–7*, no. 2270.

[51] N. Orme, *From Childhood to Chivalry: The Education of the English Kings and Aristocracy, 1066–1530* (London, 1984), 20.

of reliability and fortitude that he would value in his successful adult relationships.[52]

The cultural environment in which Edward of Windsor spent his early years was of the cosmopolitan sophistication that properly befitted a major European prince. Before her death in 1318, Margaret of France may have assisted her niece, Queen Isabella, in introducing the infant prince to the illustrious legacy of his maternal ancestors of the house of Capet. Edward II's mother, Eleanor of Castile, had also brought significant Spanish influences to the court, and the Iberian cultural connection was still strong in the 1310s.[53] Edward of Windsor's godfathers, John of Brittany, earl of Richmond, and Aymer de Valence, earl of Pembroke, were connected by family ties to the royal dynasties on both sides of the Channel and felt quite as much at home at the court of Paris as at that of Westminster. Pembroke's second wife, Marie de Saint-Pol, stood at the centre of a vast network of French princely and aristocratic houses and became an important conduit of cross-Channel cultural exchange throughout the reign of Edward III.[54] Edward's nurses would have taught him his first words in English, but after being handed over into the care of the male members of his household he would have tended to speak the Anglo-Norman French that was the mainstay of courtly communication in the early fourteenth century.

We know that the future Edward III received formal instruction in his letters from John Paynel, another administrator in the earldom of Chester; this would have given him reading fluency in insular and continental French as well as in administrative Latin.[55] Literacy in a ruler did not necessarily run to writing: to wield a pen was the job of a clerk, not of a king. Nevertheless, Edward III is the earliest English ruler to leave us examples of his own handwriting inscribed on official documents.[56] With these basic skills Edward would have progressed to lessons and conversations with the scholars and bibliophiles in his entourage: men such Bury and the prince's confessor, Roger Stanegrave.[57] These and other clerics would also have

---

[52] *Historia Dunelmensis Scritores Tres*, ed J. Raine (Surtees Society, ix, 1839), 127; Tout, *Chapters*, iii, 25–7; Denholm-Young, *Collected Papers*, 3–4; *BRUO*, i, 324.

[53] T. Tolley, 'Eleanor of Castile and the "Spanish" Style in England', *England in the Thirteenth Century: Proceedings of the 1989 Harlaxton Symposium*, ed. W. M. Ormrod (Stamford, 1991), 167–92; C. L. Chamberlin, 'A Castilian in King Edward's Court: The Career of Giles Despaigne, 1313–27', *England and Iberia in the Middle Ages, 12th–15th Century: Cultural, Literary and Political Exchanges*, ed. M. Bullón-Fernández (Basingstoke, 2007), 89–117.

[54] C. H. Jenkinson, 'Mary de Sancto Paulo, Foundress of Pembroke College, Cambridge', *Archaeologia*, lxvi (1915), 401–46; M. Vale, *The Angevin Legacy and the Hundred Years War, 1250–1340* (Oxford, 1990), 26–7.

[55] Tout, *Chapters*, iii. 25 n. 2; Orme, *Childhood to Chivalry*, 20–1, 88.

[56] V. H. Galbraith, *Kings and Chroniclers: Essays in English Medieval History* (London, 1982), chap. i, 103.

[57] Denholm-Young, *Collected Papers*, 166; E. Déprez, *Les Préliminaires de la Guerre de Cent Ans* (Paris, 1902), 85 and n. 2; C. Tyerman, *England and the Crusades, 1095–1588* (Chicago, 1988), 251–2.

been charged with responsibility for instructing the prince in the articles of faith and preparing him to take up the role of Christian king.

Formal learning was not a prescribed part of a royal education in fourteenth-century England, and the future Edward III's academic education would later seem woefully inadequate to fit him for the more cerebral challenges of monarchy. This is not to say that parents of the future Edward III were neglectful. Edward II, who had received little academic instruction of his own in youth, must have felt keenly the barbs that compared him, so unfavourably, both with his learned grandfather of Castile, Alfonso X, and his father, the great law-giver Edward I.[58] And Queen Isabella, who had a keen sense of the need to impose some rigour on the rather relaxed traditions of the English court, seems at least from 1325 to have prescribed a book-based curriculum for her son's personal development and political training.[59] By English standards of the day at least, Edward of Windsor's education provided all the intellectual and moral guidance appropriate to the destiny that awaited him.

The texts on which this educational programme was based were various. Vegetius' *Epitoma rei militaris*, the classical treatise on military strategy, had already been translated into Anglo-Norman French for Edward I or Edward II and was probably available to Edward of Windsor in the 1320s.[60] It is likely that Edward II also possessed a French translation of *De regimine principum*, written in the thirteenth century by Giles of Rome as a handbook on government for the future Philip IV of France. As king, Edward III acquired another French version of this text, in a manuscript given to him by Queen Philippa at the time of their nuptials in 1328.[61] This latter collection also included a French translation of the *Secreta secretorum*, a treatise on statecraft purportedly written by Aristotle for Alexander the Great. Walter Milemete dedicated to the young Edward III a Latin commentary on the *Secreta* that made quite pointed reference to the political failures of his father.[62] When William of Pagula addressed his

---

[58] *Vita*, 62–3, in calling down the positive attributes of his ancestors on the future Edward III, chose the wisdom of Edward I but could muster only the good looks of Edward II.

[59] A. R. Stanton, *The Queen Mary Psalter: A Study of Affect and Audience* (Philadelphia, 2001), 9–10, 237.

[60] Orme, *Childhood to Chivalry*, 185–6.

[61] C. F. Briggs, *Giles of Rome's* De regimine principum: *Reading and Writing Politics at Court and University, c.1275–c.1525* (Cambridge, 1999), 53–6.

[62] Oxford, Christ Church, MS 92, reproduced in facsimile in Walter Milemete, *De nobilitatibus, sapientiis et prudentiis regum*, ed. M. R. James (Oxford, 1913). The original of the accompanying copy of the *Secreta* is BL, Add. MS 47680. Since neither manuscript was in fact completed, there remains some doubt as to whether they were presented to their royal addressee. See L. F. Sandler, *Gothic Manuscripts, 1285–1385*, 2 vols (London, 1985), ii, nos 84–5; M. Michael, 'The Iconography of Kingship in the Walter of Milemete Treatise', *Journal of the Warburg and Courtauld Institutes*, lvii (1994), 35–47; F. Lachaud, 'Un "Miroir au prince" méconnu: Le *De nobilitatibus, sapienciis et prudenciis regum* de Walter de Milemete (vers 1326–1327)', *Guerre, pouvoir et noblesse au Moyen Âge: Mélanges en l'honneur de Philippe Contamine*, ed. J. Paviot and J. Verger (Paris, 2000), 401–10.

Speculum regis Edwardi tercii to the young king in the early 1330s, he also drew on another French text of the 'mirrors for princes' tradition, the *Enseignements* of St Louis.[63]

The other books readily available at court during Edward of Windsor's upbringing fell into three broad categories.[64] The largest group comprised liturgical texts for use in the king's chapel and in private prayer. The dominance of religion is no surprise: the majority of extant illuminated manuscripts that can be associated directly with Edward III and his queen were psalters.[65] A second group comprised 'books of romances', stories (usually in Anglo-Norman French verse) from the classics, the Bible, the Arthurian legends and other stock medieval tales such as the *Roman de Renard*. Finally, chronicles provided an especially significant source of information and instruction. Edward III almost certainly owned at least one copy of the great set text of England's island story, the Anglo-Norman prose *Brut*.[66] In later life, at least, he also borrowed books: the abbot of Nutley (Buckinghamshire) was ordered in the early 1340s to send to court a copy of the twelfth-century chronicle of William of Newburgh, and in 1352 the Chester monk Ranulph Higden was instructed to bring his own *Polychronicon* before the king.[67]

It is from a combination of such varied texts that Edward of Windsor's instructors would have guided his earliest introductions to the formal art of kingship. It is less easy to determine how biddable Edward might have been, and how much he actually internalized the education thus provided. Much as one would like to find it, there is absolutely no evidence to suggest either that Edward carried Vegetius in his mind on the military campaigns of his adult career or, indeed, that his contemporaries saw his successes of war as the result of adherence to this text.[68] Most of the extant books known to have been presented to Edward were de luxe illuminated manuscripts intended as much for display as for didactic

[63] *De Speculo Regis Edwardi Tertii*, ed. J. Moisant (Paris, 1891); *Medieval Political Theory – A Reader: The Quest for the Body Politic, 1100–1400*, ed. C. J. Nederman and K. L. Forhan (London, 1993), 200–6; L. E. Boyle, 'William of Pagula and the *Speculum Regis Edwardi III*'. *Mediaeval Studies*, xxxii (1970), 329–36.

[64] J. Vale, *Edward III and Chivalry: Chivalric Society and its Contexts, 1270–1350* (Woodbridge, 1982), 42–56.

[65] J. J. G. Alexander, 'Painting and Manuscript Illumination for Royal Patrons in the Later Middle Ages', *English Court Culture in the Later Middle Ages*, ed. V. J. Scattergood and J. W. Sherborne (London, 1983), 141–3; Sandler, *Gothic Manuscripts*, ii, nos 74, 106, 110.

[66] R. F. Green, *Poets and Princepleasers: Literature and the English Court in the Later Middle Ages* (Toronto, 1980), 92, 135; L. M. Matheson, *The Prose Brut: The Development of a Middle English Chronicle* (Tempe, 1998), 10. In 1358 new ligatures were purchased for a 'book called *cronicles*': E 403/392, 31 Apr. 1358.

[67] SC 1/39/161, printed in W. M. Ormrod, 'Edward III and his Family', *JBS*, xxvi (1987), 421–2; *CCR 1349–54*, 499; J. G. Edwards, 'Ranulph, Monk of Chester', *EHR*, xlvii (1932), 94.

[68] C. D. Taylor, 'English Writings on Warfare and Chivalry during the Hundred Years War', *Soldiers, Nobles and Gentlemen: Essays in Honour of Maurice Keen*, ed. P. Coss and C. Tyerman (Woodbridge, 2009), 82.

purposes. In one respect at least, however, Edward showed himself open to direction, for his adult sense of royal dignity was powerfully informed by mythological and historical models of knighthood and kingship. The set of great classical, biblical and Christian heroes known as the Nine Worthies became a popular convention in literature and art during the fourteenth century, and found early patronage at the court of the young Edward III. In 1332 Edward's young wife would present him with a spectacular silver cup and ewer decorated with images of the Worthies, including Charlemagne, Arthur, Roland, Oliver, Gawain and Lancelot.[69] A little later in the reign, the king also commissioned a bed-set that included six pillows decorated with scenes from the life of another of the Worthies, Alexander the Great.[70]

Most vividly of all, Edward was surrounded by physical mementos and reminders of the ready legacy of his heroes and ancestors. The prince owned a relic of St George, his active interest in the cult of George no doubt further reinforced by a striking illumination in Milemete's treatise that depicted a royal youth receiving the trappings of knighthood directly from the great patron of chivalry.[71] Still more arrestingly, the royal cabinet of curiosities included both the steel helmet thought to have been taken by Richard I from Saladin and the knife with which the Ismailian assassins had attempted to murder Edward I at Acre in 1272.[72] In later life Edward of Windsor made something of a fetish of the tomb at Westminster Abbey of his esteemed grandfather, the mighty Edward I.[73] For the youthful prince to have sought to model himself on the most recent epitome of great kingship was an obvious enough reaction to the blatant inadequacies of Edward II. But the degree of interest that he was to show in the records both of his grandfather and of his other great empire-building ancestor, Henry II, went sufficiently far as to suggest that, of all the arts, it was History that had most obviously engaged the attention and imagination of the young Edward of Windsor.

The first ten years of Prince Edward's life witnessed one of the most dismal periods in a century renowned for its natural and man-made

---

[69] E 101/385/19, fol. 11; BL, Add. MS 35181, fols 5–8; Vale, *Edward III and Chivalry*, 44.

[70] E 101/392/4, m. 4.

[71] E 101/385/19, fol. 10; Oxford, Christ Church, MS 92, fol. 3. Queen Isabella had a statue of St George decorated with pearls: E 101/393/4, fol. 9v. For other examples of Edward's early interest in the cult of St George, see D. A. L. Morgan, 'The Banner-Bearer of Christ and Our Lady's Knight: How God Became an Englishman Revisited', *St George's Chapel Windsor*, ed. Saul, 58–9.

[72] J. Vale, 'Image and Identity in the Prehistory of the Order of the Garter', *St George's Chapel Windsor*, ed. Saul, 36; Vale, *Edward III and Chivalry*, 45, 93; *Antient Kalendars*, iii, 174, 202. A 1356 inventory of the king's treasury records a golden rose given by the pope to Edward I: *Antient Kalendars*, iii, 227.

[73] See pp. 101–2.

disasters. Since 1296 the English crown had committed itself to the eradication of the independent kingdom of the Scots and the subjection of the
lands beyond the Tweed and Solway Firth to the sovereign control of an
expansionist Plantagenet state. Under this dispensation, formalized in
1305 and observed throughout Edward II's reign, Scotland was defined as
a 'land' or dependent dominion of the English crown. The hopelessness
of this claim had become apparent even before the death of Edward I
when, in 1306, the charismatic Robert Bruce had been inaugurated at
Scone as king of an independent Scotland. The first years of Edward II's
reign witnessed a slow but alarming erosion of effective English control in
the Lowlands, and by the time of Edward of Windsor's first birthday in
1313 many strategically important positions, including Linlithgow, Perth,
Roxburgh and Edinburgh, had already been lost. When Edward II's
representative at Stirling, Sir Philip Mowbray, made a private agreement
to hand over the castle to Robert Bruce's brother, Edward, unless an
English army appeared to defend it, Edward II was finally forced to
announce a major northern campaign early in 1314. Despite the refusal of
Lancaster and Warwick to join the muster, the majority of the nobility
recognized the threat and assisted in mounting a large army.[74] This,
however, simply increased the sense of shame that resulted from the
ensuing debacle at the battle of Bannockburn on 24 June. The earl of
Gloucester was killed, the earl of Hereford and a host of English knights
were taken prisoner and held to ransom, and the Scots embarked on a
series of cross-border raids that, over the following years, inflicted significant damage on the economic infrastructure of large parts of the north of
England and raised serious questions over the ability of the English crown
to guarantee the security of its own borders.

Bannockburn provided the otherwise lacklustre earl of Lancaster with
just the excuse he needed to revive interest in the reform programme of
1311. Meeting with the king in parliament at York in September 1314, Earl
Thomas made his offer of assistance against the Scots conditional on
Edward's acceptance of the Ordinances. For several years, control of
government passed to the king's cousin. But Lancaster's single-minded
adherence to the principles of the Ordinances had increasingly less relevance in a period dominated by Scottish raids and intense economic
hardship. The harvests of 1315–17 were disastrous, and the government's
attempts to control food prices resulted in the withdrawal of already
acutely short supplies from the market.[75] Famine was rife across much of
Europe, and between 10 and 15 per cent of the English population may
have died from starvation and malnutrition in these desperate years.

---

[74] For the size of the two armies at Bannockburn, see G. W. S. Barrow, *Robert Bruce and
the Community of the Realm of Scotland*, 3rd edn (Edinburgh, 1988), 204–9.

[75] W. C. Jordan, *The Great Famine: Northern Europe in the Early Fourteenth Century* (Princeton,
1996), 171–2.

Prince Edward and his household were obviously shielded from such shortages by their ability to pay high prices in the market and by their exercise of the prerogative of purveyance, which allowed royal agents to requisition foodstuffs by compulsory purchase. Abuses of the latter system had been roundly condemned in the Ordinances, and their continuation clearly did little to endear the royal family to hard-pressed peasant farmers in areas visited by the king, the queen and their children. In 1320, indeed, a specific complaint was to be made in parliament about the purveyances conducted by officers of the prince's household, and after his accession Edward III had to deal with an embarrassing number of demands for the repayment of outstanding debts run up by his entourage when he was heir to throne.[76]

Edward II's reluctance to be constrained by the Ordinances also produced continued political tension. The emergence of a new group of royal favourites – Hugh Audley, Roger Damory and William Montagu – created a threat to the role of chief councillor accorded to the earl of Lancaster at the Lincoln parliament of 1316. Despite the arrangements made to guarantee Lancaster's influence in a new form of conciliar government set up under the so-called treaty of Leake in 1318, the king's developing affections for Hugh Despenser the Elder's son, another Hugh, provoked widespread mistrust. That the earliest explicit accusations of homosexual acts committed by Edward II with a named partner were in reference to this relationship, rather than that with Piers Gaveston, tells us something about the degree of political anxiety created by the emergence of the new favourite.[77] For whereas Gaveston had lacked any sense of focused ambition, Despenser the Younger was obviously intent on establishing himself as nothing less than the greatest magnate of the land. The threat helped briefly to galvanize political opinion, and Lancaster managed to win sufficient support to have the two Despensers banished from the realm in July 1321. But with the king's revocation of the exile in December, full-scale military activity became more or less inevitable. Before his tenth year was out, Edward of Windsor would witness that ultimate aberration, civil war.

The raising of arms during the winter of 1321–2 created real disruption in many parts of England, as national rivalries were played out in a great wave of local disputes and personal vendettas. The collapse of public order was to leave a powerful imprint on the collective memory; on becoming king in 1327, Edward III would face a barrage of complaints from men and women who claimed to have been the innocent victims of indiscriminate violence and intimidation during the Despenser war. Edward II marched from Coventry to meet his cousin at Burton upon Trent in early March 1322. Lancaster had burned the town bridge and,

---

[76] *PROME*, iii, 395–6; SC 8/66/3300.

[77] R. E. Zeikowitz, *Homoeroticism and Chivalry: Discourses of Male Same-Sex Desire in the Fourteenth Century* (New York, 2003), 113–18.

fearing the force of the royalist army, decided to retreat. When he and his forces attempted to make their way from Tutbury to his Northumberland stronghold of Dunstanburgh, they were intercepted at Boroughbridge in Yorkshire by a royal army under Sir Andrew Harcla and were roundly defeated on 17 March. The earl of Hereford was killed in the battle. Lancaster himself was made a prisoner in his own castle of Pontefract and, after summary trial, was put to death on 22 March. The king's forces ran riot, and much of the town of Boroughbridge was looted and burned.[78]

There followed one of the most bitter and unrestrained acts of political vengeance ever witnessed in medieval England, as the triumphant king and the Despensers applied the full rigours of martial law and the penalties of treason against their opponents. A number of prominent Lancastrians were put to death with Earl Thomas at Pontefract, and Lords Mowbray and Clifford were executed at York. Other contrariants, as the Lancastrian lords became known, were sent for public execution to London, Gloucester, Windsor, Canterbury and Winchelsea.[79] Nor was it only the rebels of Boroughbridge who fell to the king's campaign of revenge. Harcla, awarded the earldom of Carlisle for his services in the civil war, now fell foul of the regime as a result of a rumoured private deal with Bruce and was executed as a traitor at Knaresborough in February 1323. Those who had capitulated before Boroughbridge were also subject to ruthless punishment. Sir Roger Mortimer of Wigmore, who had surrendered at Shrewsbury in January 1322 and been imprisoned in the Tower of London, was condemned to death. It was to avoid this fate that Mortimer subsequently made his dramatic escape from the Tower in 1323, fleeing to the continent where he became the self-appointed spokesperson of a group of political exiles gathering together in France during the years of the Despenser ascendancy.[80] Of Mortimer and his tribe the realm of England was destined to know much more.

Meanwhile, the Ordinances were formally revoked under the terms of the Statute of York of 1322 and the king was theoretically restored to the plenitude of power. Hugh Despenser the Elder was created earl of Winchester, and the spoils of the civil war were used to endow his son with an enormous landed estate concentrated on South Wales and the marches, worth over £7,000 a year.[81] Modern historians stress that the Despensers had little coherent programme beyond their own aggrandizement, and the idea that they engaged in a systematic attempt to usurp the structures of local and central government has been too often exaggerated in

---

[78] W. M. Ormrod, 'The Road to Boroughbridge: The Civil War of 1321–2 in the Ancient Petitions', *Foundations of Medieval Scholarship: Records Edited in Honour of David Crook*, ed. P. Brand and S. Cunningham (York, 2008), 77–88.

[79] BL, MS Cotton Faustina B. V, fols 39–39v.

[80] Baker, 12, 15–16.

[81] Fryde, *Tyranny*, 106–18.

the past.[82] On the other hand, their influence over the king and the uncompromising brutality they showed to former Lancastrian supporters broke all the conventions of responsible monarchy, and rendered Edward liable to the charge of tyranny. As the author of the *Vita Edwardi Secundi* put it in 1325, 'The king's harshness has indeed increased so much today that no one, however great or wise, dares to cross the king's will . . . Thus, today will conquers reason. For whatever pleases the king, though lacking in reason, has the force of law.'[83]

The tender age of the prince and the very real dangers attaching at times to the security of the heir to the throne meant that the future Edward III played no active part in the politics of the 1310s and early 1320s. Indeed, it would later be to his distinct advantage that Edward of Windsor could so readily claim the innocence of youth and dissociate himself from the troubled events of his father's reign. Prior to 1325, the king gave his eldest son no recognizably public function. On his missions to France, for example, Edward II did not appoint the infant prince as titular custodian of the realm but preferred to select proven officials or close friends – men such as John Droxford, bishop of Bath and Wells, in 1313 and the loyal earl of Pembroke in 1320 – as keepers. Nor was the earl of Chester even included in the witness lists to royal charters during these years.[84]

It seems reasonable to suggest that the prince made appearances at domestic and courtly events from an early age. In 1315, when he was nearly three, and perhaps in preparation for some special ceremony, he was given a silver and gold clasp for his robes and a pair of silver buckles for his shoes.[85] We can suppose that Edward was also present at the churchings of his mother and the baptisms of his siblings.[86] The only moment in the court calendar when the prince was explicitly recorded in the royal household accounts, however, was at the Feast of the Circumcision, 1 January, when it was usual for the king to distribute gifts to members of the royal family and especially distinguished courtiers. Prince Edward was on the list of recipients of gold plate given by Edward II at the New Year celebrations at Windsor in 1318 and at York in 1320.[87] But even in these instances, there is some doubt that the young boy was always present. At New Year 1316, Edward II sent a messenger to deliver

[82] N. Saul, 'The Despensers and the Downfall of Edward II', *EHR*, xcix (1984), 1–33.

[83] *Vita*, 230–1.

[84] *HBC*, 39; *The Royal Charter Witness Lists of Edward II (1307–1326)*, ed. J. S. Hamilton (List and Index Soc., cclxxxviii, 2010).

[85] E 101/376/7, fol. 20.

[86] The expenses of Edward II and Queen Isabella for the baptism of John of Eltham on 22 Aug. 1316 are recorded in SAL, MS 120, fol. 97v, though there is no specific mention of the presence of Edward of Windsor.

[87] SAL, MS 121, fol. 67; BL, Add. MS 17362, fol. 49.

to the prince a gold clasp encrusted with six emeralds.[88] Similarly in 1321, when the court spent the New Year at Marlborough, the king's presents were carried to all three of his children by the messenger Llewelyn ap Madoc.[89] Such as they are, the fragmentary records of the early years of Edward of Windsor suggest that he remained distinctly detached from life at court.

Around the time of his seventh birthday in 1319, however, there was a modest but significant change in the young prince's responsibilities to his father and to the realm at large. The scale and frequency of written communication between Edward II and his son now increased appreciably. Much of this correspondence was inevitably in the form of public instruments addressed to the earl of Chester and dealt with by the prince's administrators. But some of it was personal.[90] By January 1324 at the latest, Edward of Windsor was also instigating written exchanges with his father.[91] It is very tempting to assume that Edward II took such opportunities not only to enquire into the growing boy's welfare but also to introduce his heir to the adult world that he was even now joining.

In August 1320, at the age of seven, Edward received his first personal summons to attend parliament as a peer of the realm.[92] Omitted from the parliament of 1321, he was again summoned to the parliament and great council held at York in May and June 1322, and thereafter to all such assemblies held before his departure to France in 1325.[93] Despite his tender years, it is quite possible that Edward attended these gatherings of the political elite. One petition submitted in parliament early in 1320 addressed itself not, as was usual, to the king and council, but directly to Prince Edward in his capacity as earl of Chester.[94] Such a premature entry on to the political stage was perhaps deliberately organized by Edward II in the hope that the boy's appearance would provide a sense of optimism for an otherwise increasingly disaffected and demanding polity.

These first, faltering steps into the world of high politics can scarcely have failed to impress themselves on the boy's emotional and psychological development. If Prince Edward was indeed at York in the spring of 1322, then he was also on hand to witness the full and terrifying

---

[88] E 101/376/7, fol. 99v.

[89] BL, Add. MS 9951, fol. 41v.

[90] For evidence of letters under the king's secret seal sent to the prince see BL, Add. MS 17362, fol. 39v; E 101/379/19, fol. 6r; 'The First Journal of Edward II's Chamber', ed. J. C. Davies, *EHR*, xxx (1915), 669.

[91] E 101/379/19, fol. 7.

[92] *Parl. Writs*, II.ii, 219; *PROME*, iii, 365.

[93] *PROME*, iii, 422, 434, 437, 440, 443, 447; E 101/379/19, fol. 5r. An older tradition that Edward of Windsor was made prince of Wales at the York parliament of May 1322 was disproved by J. Barnes, *The History of that Most Victorious Monarch Edward III* (Cambridge, 1688), 2.

[94] SC 8/99/4920, printed in *RP*, i, 413–14.

application of royal wrath in the executions of the contrariants carried out in the royal castle within the city. He would also soon share in the shock and humiliation of further military failure. Along with the other tenants-in-chief of the crown, Edward received a personal summons to meet with the feudal host at Newcastle in August 1322 and proceed in the king's impending campaign against Robert Bruce.[95] The order was not to be taken literally, but as the mechanism by which the prince's own military tenants from the county of Chester – itself an important recruiting ground for royal armies – could be mustered for service.[96] It is not impossible that Edward II intended the nine-year-old to progress at least as far as the border, as Queen Isabella did; the sense of a family outing is enhanced by the presence in the royal party of the king's twelve-year-old illegitimate son, Adam.[97] On balance, though, it seems likely that Prince Edward was left at York. The principal offices of royal administration had moved to the northern capital earlier in the year to provide effective management for the upcoming war, and the prince would have provided a suitable and convenient figurehead for meetings of the king's council in the city.[98] On 21 September, for the first time on record, the earl of Chester effectively deputized for his father as president of a royal feast in York to honour the visit of the French nobleman Henri de Sully.[99] No record survives of the impression that the young boy made upon the multitude. But there is something curiously prescient about the fact that the future Edward III's first official engagement celebrated the entente between the realms of England and France.

Wiser heads than Edward II's might well have thought beyond the ceremonial advantages of the prince's residence at York in 1322 and considered the threat that this posed to his safety. Once before, in 1319, there had been a Scottish plot to capture Queen Isabella while she was at York. The great campaign of 1322 having proved fruitless, the thwarted Edward II returned south in late September and headed for Rievaulx Abbey. English intelligence proved inept, and in mid-October the king was very nearly ambushed by a Scottish raiding party at Byland. He had to flee eastwards to Bridlington, whence he limped his way back to York by boat. Henri de Sully, who had gone to the king's aid, and Prince Edward's godfather, the earl of Richmond, were among those taken prisoner at Byland. The queen also found herself in extreme jeopardy, stranded at Tynemouth Priory, and was forced to make a dramatic escape

[95] *Foedera*, II.i, 485–6.
[96] P. Morgan, *War and Society in Medieval Cheshire, 1277–1403* (Chetham Society, 3rd series, xxxiv, 1987), 38.
[97] F. D. Blackley, 'Adam, the Bastard Son of Edward II', *BIHR*, xxxvii (1964), 76–7.
[98] W. M. Ormrod, 'Competing Capitals? York and London in the Fourteenth Century', *Courts and Regions in Medieval Europe*, ed. S. Rees Jones, R. Marks and A. J. Minnis (York, 2000), 83.
[99] E 101/379/9.

by sea.[100] Bruce's forces bore down upon York and then moved east, first to Beverley and then to Malton; after an orgy of destruction, they eventually withdrew in early November. With the king and queen back in the northern capital, the temporary threat to the prince's security lifted. But all parties were well aware that Edward of Windsor had come uncomfortably close to the reality of military action and the ever-present threat of capture. In the four years that followed, both king and queen would have occasion to want to keep the precious prince altogether closer at hand.

Ironically, then, the ill-judged efforts to define a role for Edward of Windsor in 1322 resulted in the temporary withdrawal of the prince from public life. While the prince may have continued to attend some parliaments and great councils, the conspicuous shortage of references to his activities between late 1322 and early 1325 strongly suggests that he was now subjected to fairly strict constraints imposed for the preservation of his own safety. The boy was in London with his mother in February 1323 at the time when the king issued plans for a further, subsequently aborted, campaign against the Scots.[101] He was definitely not at the great council held at the archbishop of York's palace of Bishopthorpe in May 1323 when the elite assented to the king's controversial plan for an Anglo-Scottish truce.[102] He may perhaps have been at the Northampton tournament of September 1323, at which the jousting teams were headed by his two young uncles, the earls of Norfolk and Kent.[103] Otherwise, there is a resounding silence. The one further campaign of the reign in which Prince Edward might conceivably have served, that planned in Gascony in 1325, was called off at the last moment.[104] For the present, then, the prince remained withdrawn from the polity, his activities carefully circumscribed by the will of his parents.

It was in this environment of enforced domesticity that Edward developed some of the close friendships that would endure through the trials of the coming years. A fragmentary account of Edward's household in 1325 reveals that the prince was having lessons in swordsmanship. It also contains a number of references to his 'playing' with Henry Beaumont, the man who had now evidently taken over the role of royal tutor.[105] Beaumont was the son of Louis de Brienne, vicomte of Beaumont in

---

[100] R. M. Haines, *King Edward II: Edward of Caernarfon, his Life, his Reign, and its Aftermath, 1284–1330* (Montreal, 2003), 266; P. Doherty, *Isabella and the Strange Death of Edward II* (London, 2003), 76–8. This episode was to be remembered later, when Isabella had her moment of retribution against the Despensers: G. A. Holmes, 'Judgement on the Younger Despenser, 1326', *EHR*, lxx (1955), 265.

[101] E 101/379/9; *CCR 1318–23*, 699, 700; Phillips, *Edward II*, 439.

[102] Davies, *Baronial Opposition*, 584–5.

[103] J. R. V. Barker, *The Tournament in England 1100–1400* (Woodbridge, 1986), pp. 61–2.

[104] *Parl. Writs*, II.ii, 663, 683, 696, 714, 723.

[105] Denholm-Young, *Collected Papers*, 165.

Maine, and was distantly related to Edward II through their common Castilian connections. Henry and his sister Isabella, Lady Vescy, had been prominent courtiers since Edward I's time, and their brother, Louis, had been made bishop of Durham in 1317. Henry was a controversial personality who had been specifically criticized in the Ordinances of 1311 and was taken prisoner by the Lancastrian supporter Sir Gilbert Middleton in 1317. By 1325 he had ample cause for grievance against the crown. Edward II had reluctantly agreed to a truce with the Scots in 1323, which effectively forced Beaumont to abandon his claims, via his wife Alice, to the earldom of Buchan.[106] Nevertheless, his appointment as one of Prince Edward's guardians for the latter's journey to France in 1325 suggests that the king continued to hold Henry in high trust. Beaumont was also destined to have a huge impact on Edward III's later policies on Scotland.

A number of other members of the prince's circle began to emerge as fixed points of security during these same years. In 1323 the treasurership of Edward's household was taken by William Cusance, a Burgundian clerk who had served as secretary to the younger Despenser and keeper of the king's great wardrobe, and who, like Richard Bury, went on to a prominent career in royal administration. About the same time, John Claroun, another foreigner and very possibly a relative of Cusance, became the prince's steward.[107] The internationalism of Edward's household goes a long way to explaining the confidence with which he subsequently entered into his first engagements with the kings and princes of western Europe.

There was also a widening circle of aristocratic companions. Among those who may have been members of the prince's household and circle from his earliest years were Robert Ufford, William Montagu, son of Edward II's steward, and William Bohun, the prince's cousin. Bohun's three older brothers, John, Humphrey and Edward, were all placed in the custody of the crown after the death of their father, the earl of Hereford, at the battle of Boroughbridge and were held as prisoners at the Tower of London. But their deceased mother's distinguished status as a daughter of Edward I ensured them a relatively privileged lifestyle, and the young prince is likely to have encountered them regularly; the youngest, Edward Bohun, was later to rise high in Edward III's favour.[108] The knights Edward Chandos, Gilbert Talbot and John Melton, the esquires John Molyns and John Seckford, and the serjeant Henry Ditton were among a longer list of household stalwarts who went on to serve Edward after his

[106] *ODNB*, iv, 659. Both Isabella Vescy and Alice Beaumont were ladies of the queen: *Household Book of Queen Isabella*, xiii–xiv.

[107] Tout, *Chapters*, ii, 272; iv, 71, 72 and n. 4; *ODNB*, xiv, 811. For the Cusance family see C. L. Kingsford, 'Sir Otho de Grandison, 1238?–1328', *TRHS*, 3rd series, iii (1909), 181–2.

[108] E 101/378/16; E 101/379/10; E 101/380/5; E 101/382/23; E 403/225, 7 Mar. 1327.

accession to the throne in 1327. The equally long service provided by comparatively lowly figures such as the falconer Thomas Corbet and the groom John Gloucester suggests that, as in later life, Edward of Windsor tended to develop a strong affection for the menials and domestics of his personal staff.

Whatever the individual political attitudes of these and other members of Edward's circle, it remains highly doubtful that the prince's household was perceived before 1325 as some form of alternative power base that might act in competition with, or provide a refuge from, the court and administration of the king. The fact that Gilbert Talbot and a number of other members of the young Edward's retinue had supported the Ordainers and fought against the king at Boroughbridge led an older generation of historians to suppose that the prince's household was increasingly 'Lancastrian' in its political sympathies in the 1320s.[109] But it is hardly likely that the king, who exercised such strong control over the prince's affairs and the appointment of his officers, would have allowed his son's domestic establishment to turn into a hotbed of anti-Despenser conspiracy. Rather, the men who survived and thrived in the prince's service were precisely those who had the wit and judgement to adjust to the dramatic shifts in political fortunes that marked the period 1321–7. In this respect, their instincts and actions may well have influenced Edward's own later and much-advertised preference for the politics of reconciliation. It was also surely from this circle of friends and allies that the prince acquired an understanding of the political attribute he would come to prize above all others: loyalty.

Contemporary chroniclers and later legend have bequeathed much vivid, not to say prurient, detail about the characters of Edward II and Isabella, and history has built on this material to create the very model of the medieval dysfunctional family. Edward of Caernarfon was seen as a degenerate who spent his time 'idling, and applying himself to making ditches and digging', indulging in the sports of rowing and swimming and engaging in heavy drinking sessions with disreputable company. His easy susceptibility to sin may well account for the still more damaging speculation, beginning around the time of his deposition, that Edward was a heretic and a sodomite.[110] It is hardly surprising that in 1318, when an impostor claiming to be the true heir of Edward I challenged the throne, at least some people were readily inclined to believe

[109] CPR 1324–7, 170–1; Cal. Mem. Rolls 1326–7, nos 2270, 2271; Denholm-Young, Collected Papers, 166; C. Shenton, 'The English Court and the Restoration of Royal Prestige, 1327–1345' (University of Oxford DPhil. thesis, 1995), 114–15; J. S. Bothwell, Edward III and the English Peerage (Woodbridge, 2004), 17–18.

[110] Polychronicon, vii, 298; H. Johnstone, 'The Eccentricities of Edward II', EHR, xlviii (1933), 264–7; Haines, Edward II, 42.

him.[111] Meanwhile, Queen Isabella's later role in the downfall of her husband, though justified by some contemporaries as an act of deliverance, earned her the unenviable label of Jezebel, the vindictive wife who committed treason against her own husband in order to pursue her adulterous relationship with the equally infamous Roger Mortimer.[112] These later representations cast a long shadow and can easily create the impression of a deep incompatibility that doomed the royal marriage from the very start.

It is therefore highly tempting to apply the principles of psychohistory to Edward of Windsor and suggest – as has been done for his grandfather, Philip IV of France – that some of his later ambitions for the English monarchy reflected a need constantly to overcome the insecurity experienced during an unhappy childhood.[113] Clearly, it would be a mistake to apply modern bourgeois values to the domestic and emotional life of the young prince. The period of Edward's boyhood, between the fall of Gaveston in 1312 and the ascendancy of the Despensers in 1321, was one of relative calm within the royal family, and there is little evidence that Edward II and Isabella were particularly at odds with each other while the prince remained a boy.[114] As the events of 1321–2 demonstrated, a medieval king could not allow his eldest son a long, carefree and indulgent childhood. The collapse of the royal marriage – and with it the descent into civil strife, open war and, eventually, deposition – was therefore played out against the prince's emergence into adolescence and maturity, stages of life when he would be deemed capable of rationalizing his personal circumstances and developing an independent political profile. For all these qualifications, however, it remains true that Edward III's approach to his own kingship was conditioned to a quite extraordinary degree by the humiliation of his parents' very public quarrel and the trauma of the political crisis that it provoked. By the time he assumed control of his own regime in 1330, when still just seventeen, Edward III understood only too well that the future of the monarchy would depend on his ability to liberate himself, constitutionally and emotionally, from the thrall of his parents.

---

[111] W. R. Childs, 'Edward II, John of Powderham and the Chronicles, 1318', *Church and Chronicle in the Middle Ages: Essays Presented to John Taylor*, ed. I. Wood and G. A. Loud (London, 1991), 149–63.

[112] H. Johnstone, 'Isabella, the She-Wolf of France', *History*, xxi (1936–7), 208–18; S. Menache, 'Isabella of France, Queen of England: A Reconsideration', *JMH*, x (1984), 107–24.

[113] E. A. R. Brown, 'The Prince is Father of the King: The Character and Childhood of Philip the Fair of France', *Mediaeval Studies*, xlix (1987), 282–334.

[114] M. McKisack, *The Fourteenth Century* (Oxford, 1959), 79–80. It should be remarked that no one ever challenged the paternity of Edward III or any of his siblings: C. T. Wood, *Joan of Arc and Richard III: Sex, Saints, and Government in the Middle Ages* (Oxford, 1988), 12–28.

Chapter 2

EXILE AND SUCCESSION, 1322–1327

The events that were to lead to Prince Edward's first real emergence on to the public stage in 1325 find their context in a tangled history of Anglo-French relations stretching back to the time of the treaty of Paris in 1259. Under the terms of this settlement, Henry III of England had agreed to renounce for ever his dynastic claims to lands already lost to the French crown during the previous half-century in Normandy, Anjou, Maine, Touraine and Poitou, and to render liege homage to Louis IX for his remaining continental possession, the duchy of Aquitaine. In return, Louis had agreed greatly to expand the boundaries of Aquitaine by ceding to Henry III extensive territories in Saintonge, the Agenais and the dioceses of Limoges, Cahors and Périgueux.

As all parties had very soon realized, it was a good deal easier to pronounce such major redistributions of lands and loyalties than it was to enforce them. Although Henry III performed the required homage in 1259, the process of transferring territories proved cumbersome and slow. When Edward I's wife, Eleanor of Castile, came into possession of the northern French counties of Ponthieu and Montreuil through her mother in 1279, the English king was once again prepared to allow that he and his successors would in future pay homage for these lordships within the spirit of the treaty of Paris. In 1294, however, as a result of a series of disputes at sea, the ambitious and resolute Philip IV declared Edward I a contumacious vassal and confiscated his lands in France. Edward was forced to undertake a massively expensive war in defence of his rights in Aquitaine and Ponthieu. The dispute was eventually patched up in 1303, and the marriage of Edward II to Philip IV's daughter Isabella in 1308 was specifically intended to heal the rift that had recently opened up between the two ruling families. Edward of Windsor was therefore the direct genetic result of a new commitment by the Capetians and Plantagenets to the terms of peace agreed by their ancestors fifty years before.

In reality, though, the war of 1294–8 had created a significant and permanent shift in the attitudes of the two ruling houses. The issues were threefold. First was the problem of establishing English control over the territories promised to Henry III in 1259. The privileged nobles of the area formally defined as greater Aquitaine were not keen to acknowledge any overlordship, either Plantagenet or Capetian, and in 1311 the two sides agreed to set up a summit conference or 'process' at Périgueux to try to rationalize the myriad legal issues raised by the transfer of jurisdiction.[1] Secondly, the English crown had begun, from the 1290s, to argue that the ancient duchy of Gascony, which formed the ancestral core of their newly enlarged interests in greater Aquitaine, was in fact an allod (a possession held in absolute and unconditional tenure) and that no Capetian king had the right to intervene in its affairs.[2] Edward I and his successor hoped by this means to challenge the right of the French crown, through the *parlement* of Paris, to act as court of appeal for legal cases brought within the jurisdiction of the duke of Aquitaine. Thirdly, there were endless squabbles over the form of feudal homage that the Plantagenets ought to perform for their continental lands. From the 1280s the English had taken the position that homage ought only to be binding once all the agreed territories were in English hands. It was for this reason that Edward I refused to renew his oath of homage to Philip IV after the war of 1294–8. And when Edward II performed the required ceremonies in 1308 and 1320, he was careful to promise only simple homage, omitting the additional oath of fealty. On the latter occasion, indeed, the English king showed some rare mettle, rounding on the courtiers of Philip V who dared to suggest that the wording of the oath should be anything other than in the conditional form used since 1285.[3]

For all this posturing, the English were only too well aware of the vulnerability of their position. Philip IV and Edward I had both developed quite clear visions of sovereignty, claiming that no earthly power could exercise a jurisdiction superior to their own in their lands.[4] Neither, however, had found a way to reconcile this with the English determination to hold on to an ancestral dependency within the realm of France. Ironically, it was Edward I who showed the way forward by his aggressive stance towards Scotland. His attempt at establishing feudal suzerainty over John Balliol in the early 1290s having failed, Edward had simply treated the northern kingdom as a rebellious dominion and placed it directly under the jurisdiction of Westminster. Edward II, who was left with the impossible task of making good that claim, could see perfectly well how the same principles might be readily applied against his own duchy of Aquitaine by his wife's royal relatives in Paris. For twenty years after the treaty of 1303, the English and French crowns continued their interminable bickering over the 1259 settlement. The mutual refusal to admit

---

[1] The earlier process of Montreuil-sur-Mer (1306) had been concerned much more narrowly with the resolution of maritime disputes. G. P. Cuttino, *English Medieval Diplomacy* (Bloomington, 1985), 65–6, 69–72.

[2] P. Chaplais, 'English Arguments concerning the Feudal Status of Aquitaine in the Fourteenth Century', *BIHR*, xxi (1948), 203–13.

[3] A. Curry, *The Hundred Years War*, 2nd edn (Basingstoke, 2003), 34; E. P. Stuart, 'The Interview between Philip V and Edward II at Amiens in 1320', *EHR*, xli (1926), 412–15.

[4] J. R. Strayer, *On the Medieval Origins of the Modern State* (Princeton, 1970), 3–56.

an impasse and agree some new way forward revealed both sides' reluctance to jeopardize their interests in the name of lasting peace. In fact, it was Edward III who would in due course force the issue to a different level and transform the dispute over Aquitaine from an act of feudal rebellion to a full-scale struggle for sovereignty.

Edward II's brother-in-law, the politically adept Philip V, died at the tender age of thirty in January 1322, leaving a clutch of infant daughters but no surviving son. As on the death of his older brother, Louis X, in 1316, the rights of female offspring were ignored and the succession passed to the nearest male, the last surviving son of Philip IV, now duly crowned as Charles IV. In July 1323 the king of England was summoned to the Capetian court and required to submit himself once again to an act of homage for Aquitaine.[5] All sides expected some prevarication: Louis X had died before he could persuade Edward to perform the necessary ceremonies, and it had taken another four years to set up the meeting with Philip V at Amiens in 1320. But there was now an additional complication to Anglo-French relations. Charles IV's first marriage, to Blanche of Burgundy, had been annulled in 1322 and he was currently without surviving offspring from this or his recent second marriage, to Marie of Luxembourg. His closest living male relatives, and potential contenders for the title of heir presumptive, were therefore his uncle, Charles, count of Valois, and his nephew, Edward, earl of Chester. In the spring of 1323 the French attempted to suggest a marriage alliance between Edward of Windsor and one of Count Charles's daughters. Detecting a plot to compromise his son's potential rights, Edward II replied that he could not make such decisions without the consent of parliament. There, for the present, the matter ended.[6] The ten-year-old English prince could no doubt well afford to wait a little longer for a suitable bride. But an unexpected set of events would now prompt an extended diplomatic crisis from which Edward of Windsor would emerge as duke of Aquitaine, king of England and, ultimately, claimant to the throne of France.

In 1323 the abbot of Sarlat decided to found a new *bastide*, or fortified settlement, at Saint-Sardos in the Agenais, one of the territories that went to make up the duchy of Aquitaine as defined under the treaty of Paris. The latter settlement had allowed privileged landholders in this area the right of free consent in the transfer of land and jurisdiction to the Plantagenets, and the abbey of Sarlat, realizing where its interests lay, had insisted on remaining under Capetian rule, claiming that the monastery and its dependencies were inseparably bound to the crown of France. Charles IV agreed to support the new enterprise at Saint-Sardos in 1323,

---

[5] *The War of Saint-Sardos (1323–1325): Gascon Correspondence and Diplomatic Documents*, ed. P. Chaplais (Camden Society, 3rd series, lxxxvii, 1954), ix.

[6] *Foedera*, II.i, 524. In Jan. 1324 an alternative marriage alliance involving Edward II's two daughters was in discussion: *War of Saint-Sardos*, 16; Phillips, *Edward II*, 457.

Map 2 Aquitaine under Edward III.

and the French royal standard was raised over the site in October. It was promptly torn down by a group of armed men assumed to be in the pay of Raymond Bernard of Montpezat, a local lord loyal to Edward II, and Ralph Basset, the English seneschal of Gascony. The aggressive stance of Charles IV and the count of Valois must account for much of the resulting acrimony, but the affair was also badly mishandled by Edward II's representatives in Paris, the earl of Kent and the archbishop of Dublin. When the English forces in the Agenais refused to comply in the surrender of the castle of Montpezat and the envoys rather undiplomatically requested yet another postponement of Edward's homage, the stout-hearted Charles IV was forced to take direct action against his contumacious brother-in-law. Aquitaine and Ponthieu were declared forfeit, and preparations were put in place in the summer of 1324 for a full-scale military occupation of the English territories.[7]

Thirty years earlier, under similar circumstances, Edward I had been forced to divert the resources badly needed for his wars in Wales and Scotland to fight a vastly expensive and extremely unpopular war with Philip IV for the recovery of his French lands. Edward II's otherwise deeply humiliating truce with the upstart Bruce in 1323 had at least offered him the opportunity to withdraw from the northern war that had proved such a liability to his monarchy. Now, and much against his inclination, he was being forced by circumstances beyond his control to organize a war of defiance against the mighty house of Capet. At the very most, Edward could expect only a restoration of the uneasy status quo that had been in place since 1303. At worst, he might suffer serious setbacks and recriminations that could jeopardize all the rights invested in the settlement of 1259.

As things turned out, the ensuing hostilities, known as the war of Saint-Sardos, proved sporadic and short-lived. Much of English Aquitaine remained loyal to Edward II and resisted Capetian occupation, and it was only in Saintonge and the Agenais that Charles of Valois, the French commander, was able to make any real headway. The Plantagenet forces, led by the earl of Kent, were mainly local, though they were later supplemented by infantry and light cavalry sent over from England in 1325 under the earl of Surrey. In the parliament of October 1324 the elite agreed to support the recruitment of an army of Aquitaine so long as the king himself led the expedition.[8] As in 1322 and 1323, Edward of Windsor was issued with a writ of summons for the muster of this army at Portsmouth in March 1325, though it is again to be doubted that the king intended his twelve-year-old son to serve in person. In any case, this muster was successively postponed and, on 10 July 1325, cancelled.[9] The fact that Edward II did not launch a personal expedition either in Aquitaine or (as Edward I had done in 1297) in northern France certainly helped to keep down the costs, which were met from the tax originally granted for the aborted Scottish campaign of 1323 and from the liquid capital recently confiscated from the contrariant lords.[10] All sides seem quickly to have agreed with Edward's view that English interests were best served by a minimal approach to the aggression of Charles IV.

* * *

[7] Vale, *Angevin Legacy*, 232–6.
[8] *PROME*, iii, 443.
[9] *Parl. Writs*, II.ii, 683, 696, 714, 723.
[10] *PROME*, iii, 438, 439; Vale, *Angevin Legacy*, 236–7.

It was against this background of somewhat desultory military action that Edward of Windsor came to be given his first proper role in international diplomacy. Shortly after Christmas 1324, Charles IV suggested in an apparently sincere gesture of peace that if Queen Isabella and Prince Edward were sent to France and the king or his son were to perform homage for the Plantagenet fiefs, he would be prepared to make peace, to revive the agenda of 1259, and to honour English rights in greater Aquitaine.[11] The idea that Prince Edward should have to stand as a kind of hostage for his father's homage did not go down well, and Edward II's council refused to countenance the proposal. It was, however, agreed that the queen should visit her brother and undertake the role of peacemaker. The truce already made by the young earl of Kent the previous September was extended for the upcoming talks in the spring of 1325, and a template was agreed on 31 May. As the English had feared, Charles was determined to extract a heavy price for peace. Edward II was required formally to submit the whole of Aquitaine to French control. The heart-lands of the Plantagenet patrimony in the ancient duchies of Gascony and Guyenne would be restored to him in return for the performance of homage at Beauvais in August. But the areas recently occupied by the French would remain in their hands at least until the resolution of outstanding disputes, and would then only be restored on payment of 60,000 *livres parisis*, or about £15,000. The latter condition was especially serious, for it gave Charles legitimate rights to hold on to the Agenais and other parts of greater Aquitaine until such time as the English fulfilled all their side of the bargain. And by requiring a cash sum for the return of the occupied territories, the French were in effect indicating their intention to impose the feudal inheritance tax known as relief.[12] If Edward agreed to these conditions, it would only be a matter of time before the French insisted on reviving the claim for liege homage and applying the full force of feudal suzerainty over their Plantagenet vassals in Aquitaine and Ponthieu.

Whatever his other deficiencies, Edward of Caernarfon tended to be resolute in the defence of his theoretical rights. It is a marker of the seriousness of the new situation, then, that the draft treaty of May 1325 was not in fact ratified until after his fall from power in 1327. To mollify the French and reduce the liability involved in the new proposals, the English government decided to focus on the performance of the act of homage. On 5 July the highly capable John Stratford, bishop of Winchester, the loyal earl of Richmond and the prominent royal clerk

[11] *War of Saint-Sardos*, 195-6; R. M. Haines, *Archbishop John Stratford: Political Revolutionary and Champion of the Liberties of the Church, ca. 1275/80-1348* (Toronto, 1986), 152-4.

[12] *EMDP*, I.ii, no. 300; Haines, *Stratford*, 158; Sumption, 98. Edward II accepted the obligation of the relief in Oct.: Phillips, *Edward II*, 479 n. 145.

William Airmyn were commissioned to discuss with the French the possibility of transferring the titles of duke of Aquitaine, count of Ponthieu and
count of Montreuil to Prince Edward.[13] Placing the French dependencies
under the titular rule of the heir apparent would not alter the constitutional
position of Aquitaine as a parcel of the English crown. But it would
save the already humiliated king of England from undergoing the additional embarrassment of obeisance before the king of France. It would also
allow the full restoration of the Plantagenet regime in south-western
France without prejudice to the terms of a final peace. The idea was not
wholly new: Edward I had made preparation for just such a transfer of
rights to Edward of Caernarfon in 1306, though he had died before the
ceremony of homage could take place. Edward of Windsor now became
the essential decoy in an English strategy designed to restore control in
Aquitaine while continuing to obfuscate the terms under which the duchy
was held.

If this initiative was clever and bold, it was also extremely risky. Queen
Isabella's recent mission to Paris had been prompted in part by the acrimony now obtaining between her and the Despensers. In September 1324
Isabella had been subjected to the extreme humiliation of being declared
an enemy alien, a pretext for the confiscation of all her English estates and
the disbanding of her independent household. The episode had created
grave public scandal: some even believed that, by imposing such penalties
on the king's wife, Hugh Despenser the Younger was planning to secure a
papal annulment of the royal marriage.[14] Isabella had seized on the
chance of the mission to Paris to get away from the threats and taunts of
her husband's favourite and clearly had no intention of rushing home
again. If Prince Edward were also to be dispatched to France, he could
well become a pawn in the queen's campaign for the removal of the
Despensers, especially if Charles IV were inclined to support his sister in
her act of resistance. The king therefore prevaricated over the prospect of
his son's departure abroad. In the end, the idea that the prince, rather than
the king, should perform the ceremony of homage seems to have been
forced through by the Despensers on the grounds that it was simply too
hazardous to their own interests, and that of the crown, for Edward II to
leave the realm.[15]

In August, the king removed to Kent to prepare either for his own
crossing or, if possible, the sending of his son to the upcoming meeting

---

[13] *Treaty Rolls 1234–1325* (London, 1955), nos 654–6.
[14] *Chron. Lanercost,* 254; M. Buck, *Politics, Finance and the Church in the Reign of Edward II:
Walter Stapeldon, Treasurer of England* (Cambridge, 1983), 151.
[15] Murimuth, 43–4; Baker, 19. The waspish Rochester chronicler, writing with hindsight,
was very clear that the decision to send the prince to France was directly responsible for
the 'desolation and confusion' into which Isabella subsequently drove the kingdom: BL,
MS Cotton Faustina B. V, fol. 45v.

planned at Beauvais. Prince Edward's household reached Dover on the 23rd, taking up residence in the Maison Dieu. The next day the king wrote to Charles IV claiming to be indisposed and requesting a postponement of the ceremony of homage.[16] Still with no news from the French court, on 30 August Edward II appointed his son keeper of the realm for the period of his impending absence.[17] At the last moment, however, on 4 September, Charles IV graciously agreed that he would accept the homage of the prince. The clerks of the English royal chancery immediately began to draw up the documentation detailing the transfer of Aquitaine and Ponthieu to Edward of Windsor, which was completed by 10 September.[18] At the same time, protections were issued to the thirty men who would make up the core of the prince's entourage in the impending visit to France. These included the Despensers' close ally Walter Stapeldon, bishop of Exeter, the royal envoys John Shoreditch and Richard Gloucester, and the prince's own men, Henry Beaumont and William Montagu. Edward of Windsor and his following embarked from Dover on 12 September; two days later, Bishops Stratford and Stapeldon, along with Henry Beaumont, were officially appointed as his guardians.[19] Edward II, with an acute awareness of the possible consequences, dictated that the king of France should have no power to arrange a marriage for the prince or to assign him a protector.[20]

The prince and his entourage probably took the well established sea route from Dover to Wissant, in the Pas de Calais, recently used by both Queen Isabella and Bishop Stratford.[21] On 22 September Edward joined his mother at Paris, and two days later, at Bois de Vincennes, he performed simple homage to Charles IV as duke of Aquitaine, count of Ponthieu and count of Montreuil, in the presence of a large number of the prelates and nobles of France.[22] The show of might and splendour by the court of France no doubt left a powerful impression on the adolescent prince. But all sides freely acknowledged that the ceremony was only really a sideshow to the intense and fractious discussions continuing over Charles's terms for a permanent peace. Edward of Windsor was not yet thirteen years old, and his capacity for independent political action remained subject to severe limitations. In spite of the transfer of titles, therefore, it was Edward II who continued emphatically to dictate policy with regard to

---

[16] *Parl. Writs*, II.ii, App., 275; Murimuth, 43–4.

[17] *CPR 1324–7*, 171. See also *CCR 1323–7*, 399.

[18] Only some of this material is printed in *Foedera*, II.i, 607–8, with the result that it has usually been stated that the grant of Ponthieu and Montreuil was dated 4 Sept. and that of Aquitaine followed on 10 Sept. For the full documentation, which indicates three different versions of both grants, see *CPR 1324–7*, 173–4, 175.

[19] *CPR 1324–7*, 168, 170–1, 174, 175. See also *EMDP*, I.i, no. 49.

[20] Murimuth, 44.

[21] Haines, *Stratford*, 473–4.

[22] SC 1/49/97; *War of Saint-Sardos*, 243–5, 269.

Aquitaine.[23] At the same time, the prince's introduction into the public business of state meant that his interests would soon have to be more amply accommodated in the broad outlines of royal policy. A medieval king's obligations to his office required that he preserve intact the rights of the crown and pass them on, uncompromised, to his successor. From the summer of 1325, Prince Edward inevitably became the primary focus of attention and aspiration for those who felt that Edward II's own performance of kingship was becoming a liability to his realm.

It was essential to the political stability of England that both the queen and the prince should return home as soon as the ceremonies and festivities of homage were complete. Bishop Stapeldon was specifically charged with responsibility for escorting Isabella home.[24] A number of the prince's entourage returned without undue delay: Stratford crossed to Dover on 12 October; John Molyns was in England in the same month; and Adam Southwick, who had been charged with delivering the prince into the queen's custody, wrote to the king that his own return was delayed only by illness.[25] But the queen, newly reinforced in her sense of self-importance through engagement with her French royal relatives, showed no sign either of packing her bags or of relinquishing control of her son. Prince Edward dined with his mother at Poissy on 14 October, in Paris on 15 and 17 and at Le Bourget on 22 October. From the latter date he remained consistently in Isabella's company, and proceeded with her to Reims at the end of October, where he had his first glimpse of the coronation place of the kings of France. Never before in his brief life had Edward of Windsor experienced so powerfully and so long the full force of Isabella's dominant personality and her strident assertion of maternal authority.

It was during this progress that there emerged definite indications of a public rift between Edward II and his queen. The increasingly articulate and confident Isabella was easily persuaded by some of her relatives and friends on the continent that she should not return to England until she was given proper guarantees that both her husband and the two Hugh Despensers would behave appropriately towards her. The queen roundly criticized Bishop Stapeldon for the insult he had shown to herself and her brother of France by returning to England, for his failure to provide her with money for the expenses of her household, and for his

---

[23] C 61/38, m. 6.

[24] Buck, *Stapeldon*, 156. For the form of the oath given on this occasion, see SC 1/37/74, printed in Déprez, *Préliminaires*, 20 n. 5.

[25] SC 1/49/97; Haines, *Stratford*, 474; N. M. Fryde, 'A Medieval Robber Baron: Sir John Molyns of Stoke Poges, Buckinghamshire', *Medieval Legal Records*, ed. R. F. Hunnisett and J. B. Post (London, 1978), 199.

association with the evil Despensers.[26] When John Stratford was sent back to France on 28 October on a secret mission to persuade Isabella and the prince to return without further delay, the queen told the bishop that she dared not venture into England for fear of the younger Hugh.[27] From the end of October at the latest, the queen publicly represented herself and her son as refugees from a hostile family and court in England.

To the scandal of family breakdown was now added the further dimension of adultery. Over the winter of 1325–6 it became known that the queen had entered into a liaison with Roger Mortimer, one of the discontents who had fled from England in the aftermath of Boroughbridge. Edward II had been aware for some months that Mortimer was aiming to stir up trouble abroad and, if possible, at home. One Thomas Newbiggin had tried to get himself released from prison in London in 1324 by claiming that he had valuable information about Mortimer's plots against the crown.[28] And in February 1325 the king's representatives at Charles IV's court, Bishop Salmon of Norwich and John, earl of Richmond, had been instructed to ensure that Roger Mortimer and other English nobles exiled after Boroughbridge should be expelled from France before the coming of the queen.[29] What Edward II did not expect was Isabella's decision to reject her marriage and enter into an openly adulterous relationship with the rebel adventurer.

To some degree this scandalous liaison played to Edward II's hand by offering him the opportunity to take the moral high ground. A decade earlier the French court had been the focus of much salacious gossip as a result of allegations of adultery brought against two of Philip the Fair's daughters-in-law. Charles IV, with a keen sense of his royal and familial dignity, was therefore more than conventionally embarrassed by his own sister's descent into wantonness. In March 1325, when writing to Charles to ask for his assistance in the swift return of the queen and her son to England, Edward II asked that his brother-in-law proceed 'according to reason, good faith and fraternal affection, without having regard to the wilful pleasure of woman'.[30] None of this, however, reckoned with the forcefulness and resourcefulness of Isabella, who now sought publicly to justify her actions on two counts: that she could not be expected to return to her husband's side because of the threat of physical violence; and that her marriage had collapsed not because of Mortimer but because of

---

[26] F. D. Blackley, 'Isabella and the Bishop of Exeter', *Essays in Medieval History Presented to Bertie Wilkinson*, ed. T. A. Sandquist and M. R. Powicke (Toronto, 1969), 230–1.

[27] Haines, *Stratford*, 161–2.

[28] SC 8/128/6395, related to *Parl. Writs*, II, ii, App., 244–9. See also SC 8/90/4482.

[29] *War of Saint-Sardos*, 196.

[30] *CCR 1323–7*, 579.

Hugh Despenser.[31] The sexual insinuation was unmistakable. Edward II's attempt to assert his husbandly authority had simply served to expose the blatant hypocrisy of his own case.

Faced with the public refusal of Isabella to accept her wifely and political responsibilities, the king now tried to appeal directly to their son. It is not known what attitude Edward of Windsor took to the breakdown of his parents' marriage. It is reasonable to suppose that he sympathized with his mother's plight, though it is also true that he later showed neither affection nor mercy to Mortimer, whom he emphatically represented as the true cause of the enmity between Edward II and Isabella.[32] Once Mortimer had ingratiated himself into the queen's company and her bed, then, it may be that the prince became a good deal less than enthusiastic about his enforced exile. On 2 December 1325 the king opened direct correspondence with his son, appealing to the prince's loyalty and begging him to return home with or without Isabella.[33] Any hope of a reunion between father and son was rapidly eroded, however, by Edward II's increasingly threatening behaviour. In January 1326 the prince's English estates were put under royal administration, though their revenues were still made available for the young Edward's needs. More startlingly, in February the sheriffs were instructed that the queen and her son were to be arrested if and when they arrived in England, and that their foreign supporters were to be treated as the king's enemies.[34] In March Edward II assumed the role of 'governor and administrator' of Aquitaine and Ponthieu in an attempt to deprive Prince Edward of an authority that might otherwise be used against the English crown.[35] Ironically, the only effect was to drive Charles IV to reoccupy the parts of greater Aquitaine from which his forces had only recently begun to withdraw.

Edward II's last-ditch efforts to appeal to filial loyalty, in March and June 1326, were entirely lacking in a sense of fatherly affection. Indeed, they were ominously threatening: the king warned that 'he will ordain in such wise that Edward shall feel [his wrath] all the days of his life, and that all other sons shall take example thereby of disobeying their lords and fathers'.[36] The impact of this correspondence on an impressionable young teenager can only be guessed. However, the self-conscious displays of loyalty that Edward III showed to his father's name after the latter's deposition and death almost certainly represented a necessary public

---

[31] *Vita*, 242–7.

[32] *PROME*, iv, 105.

[33] *Foedera*, II.ii, 579–80; Froissart, *Oeuvres*, xviii, 9. For news sent to the king in Jan. 1326 of the proposed return of the queen and prince, see SC 1/49/92.

[34] *CFR 1319–27*, 372; *CCR 1323–7*, 543.

[35] *EMDP*, I.i, no. 49 (where Edward II's policy is explained in more innocent terms).

[36] *Foedera*, II.ii, 543, 576–7, 578; translation from *CCR 1323–7*, 576–7.

act of atonement for the blatant act of defiance in which he had been implicated, either willingly or unwillingly, in 1325–6.

One of the major sources of contention between father and son during 1326 was the rumour of Prince Edward's impending betrothal to the daughter of the count of Hainault. Since 1323 Edward II's dynastic strategy had been dominated by the need to create allies for the war against France, and hopes had centred on an alliance with one of the Iberian kingdoms. After initially exploring the possibility of a match between Prince Edward and the daughter of James II, the cultivated and uxorious king of Aragon, the English monarch had decided to offer his younger daughter, Joan, to James himself, or, 'because it was said that James is old and decrepit and it is not certain that he is not dead', to the latter's son and heir, Alfonso. He had then concentrated his attention on a double union involving Prince Edward and Princess Eleanor on the English side and the young and forceful Alfonso XI of Castile and his sister, also Eleanor, on the other. On 1 January 1326 Edward II found it necessary to issue a denial that his son was about to embark on another marriage in France, and was still pursuing the Castilian alliance when approached by the king and queen of Portugal with offers of an alternative dynastic match in April.[37] Meanwhile, however, an altogether different alliance was being concocted by those who had the custody and control of the prince on the continent.

The union with Hainault was of particular importance since it would subsequently provide Isabella and Mortimer with the military backing they needed to launch their invasion of England in September 1326. There had been close diplomatic and dynastic connections between the Plantagenets and the princes of the Low Countries since the time of Edward I, and the prospect of a royal marriage with the family of the counts of Hainault was not in itself a surprise.[38] But there were significant complications arising from the fact that William of Hainault was married to Jeanne, the daughter of Charles of Valois. As early as 1319 there had been a suggestion that Edward of Windsor might marry William and Jeanne's eldest daughter, Margaret. The court of Philip V had interpreted this as a unilateral attempt by the Plantagenets to insinuate themselves further into the extended royal family of France, and had vigorously resisted the proposal.[39] Although Charles IV had felt confident about the

[37] *Foedera*, II.i, 548–9, 573, 585, 589, 617, 625–6; *CPR 1324–7*, 103–4; *War of Saint-Sardos*, 214–17.

[38] M. G. A. Vale, 'The Anglo-French Wars, 1294–1340: Allies and Alliances', *Guerre et société en France, en Angleterre et en Bourgogne XIVe-XVe siècle*, ed. P. Contamine, C. Giry-Deloison and M. H. Keen (Lille, 1991), 15–31.

[39] A. Wathey, 'The Marriage of Edward III and the Transmission of French Motets to England', *Journal of the American Musicological Society*, xlv (1992), 13–14.

implications of his own proposed alliance between Edward of Windsor and one of Jeanne's much younger half-sisters in 1323, Edward II himself was now suspicious of further involvement with the house of Valois, newly headed by Count Charles's son, Philip. And Edward's instinct was, in this matter at least, sound. Over the winter of 1325–6, the self-confident Philip of Valois sought to make direct capital out of the queen of England's situation by requesting a guarantee that, in the event of a failure of Charles IV's male line, Isabella would not assert her own right, or that of her son, to the throne of France.[40] Edward II had few illusions that such a far-fetched claim could ever be made good, but in a moment of high tension in Anglo-French diplomacy he could ill afford the compromises implied. The new match proposed between Edward of Windsor and a daughter of Count William was therefore very much the product of Isabella's own desperation. Nor were Charles IV, Philip of Valois and William of Hainault much disposed to give public support to the queen in her obvious act of defiance against Edward II. Rather, it was Count William's brother, the adventurer John of Hainault, who now emerged in the guise of chivalric champion to the wronged queen of England, openly offering her refuge and aid against her husband.[41] Alongside these short-term tactical considerations, the wider interests of Edward of Windsor seem to have figured hardly at all.

Isabella's plot with John of Hainault seems first to have been aired in December 1325 when the queen and Prince Edward met the Countess Jeanne in Paris at the funeral of Charles of Valois. The proposal was now for a marriage with one of Jeanne's younger daughters, Philippa.[42] Discreet negotiations opened at Valenciennes early in 1326. After attending the celebrations in Paris following the coronation of Charles IV's queen, Jeanne of Evreux, in May,[43] Isabella and her son crossed into Hainault some time during the summer. Edward II's last, desperate appeal to the king, bishops, peers and magnates of France in June to facilitate the return of the queen and prince went unheeded, and in July the king ordered reprisals against all Frenchmen dwelling in England. Charles, much offended by the insult, quickly retaliated, and in August all Englishmen in France were subjected to imprisonment and seizure of

[40] Fryde, *Tyranny*, 180–2. It was later claimed that before his death in 1325, Charles of Valois had actively promoted the Plantagenet–Hainault alliance, perhaps with the same end in mind: *Autobiography of Emperor Charles IV and his Legend of St Wenceslas*, ed. B. Nagy and F. Schaer (Budapest, 2001), 26–7.

[41] Le Bel, i, 14–16; *Récits d'un Bourgeois de Valenciennes*, ed. Kervyn de Lettenhove (Louvain, 1877), 140–3.

[42] M. Vale, *The Princely Court: Medieval Courts and Culture in North-West Europe* (Oxford, 2001), 159. Messengers reached Edward II with news of Charles of Valois's death while the king was at Bury St Edmunds on 28 Dec.: SAL, MS 122, fol. 26.

[43] C. Lord, 'Queen Isabella at the Court of France', *Fourteenth Century England II*, ed. Given-Wilson, 45–52.

goods.[44] Prince Edward was evidently keenly aware of this further deterioration in diplomacy. On 23 August, apparently with the intention of preparing his own household for war, the young earl of Chester and duke of Aquitaine retained the services of the Hainaulter Simon Hale.[45]

The final terms of the marriage contract between Edward of Windsor and Philippa of Hainault were agreed and sealed at Mons on 27 August.[46] The prince swore on the Gospels to provide Philippa with a suitable dower and to marry her within two years on pain of a fine of £10,000. The guarantors of the contract were Roger Mortimer and the earl of Kent. The latter had fallen out of favour with his half-brother the king since the surrender of La Réole to the French in September 1324; his growing identification with Isabella's party had recently resulted in the confiscation of his English lands.[47] The arrangements had been conducted with no reference to Edward II and in clear opposition to his wishes. This, coupled with the fact that Edward of Windsor was still below the age of consent, made the legality of the process highly questionable. Indeed, the prospects for a future wedding hung entirely on Isabella's ability, by one means or another, to gain control of the government of England. On the day that he stood in the cathedral church of Mons, Prince Edward can have been under few illusions that he was now inextricably implicated in his mother's advertised bid to deliver the kingdom of England from the Despensers' thrall.

It is difficult to determine who else was present in the prince's party at Mons. Roger Mortimer and John of Hainault, the 'most intimate and principal members of the queen's privy household', were certainly there.[48] Many others of Isabella's household, and most of those who had been dispatched on the various diplomatic missions of 1325, had now returned home, and Alexander Bicknor, archbishop of Dublin, was evidently the only English bishop still in attendance on the queen.[49] But the prince's godfather, the earl of Richmond, who had previously been resolutely loyal to Edward II, had remained in France after acting as ambassador there in 1325, and had now openly defected to Isabella's party. Edward of Windsor also had the service, on this occasion, of various of the knights who had originally travelled to the continent in his entourage, including Henry

---

[44] *Foedera*, II.i, 576–8, 581–2; *CFR 1319–27*, 404, 410; Fryde, *Tyranny*, 182.

[45] C 47/2/23/45; Shenton, 'English Court', 256.

[46] Froissart, *Oeuvres*, ii, 502–4; K. Petit, 'Le Mariage de Philippa de Hainault, reine d'Angleterre', *Le Moyen Age*, lxxxvii (1981), 376–7.

[47] Buck, *Stapeldon*, 161.

[48] Baker, 21. In Aug. 1327 the new regime of Edward III considered pawning the crown jewels in order to pay its considerable debts to John of Hainault: SC 1/36/161.

[49] R. M. Haines, *The Church and Politics in Fourteenth-Century England: The Career of Adam Orleton* (Cambridge, 1978), 157, 160.

Beaumont, Gilbert Talbot and William Montagu.[50] It is clear that active support for the queen had been growing significantly over the summer: the sheriff of Essex and Hertfordshire, Richard Perers, joined the prince's retinue on the continent during this time.[51] But the majority of those clustering around Isabella and Prince Edward were still those, like Mortimer, who had been forced into exile by the vindictiveness of the Despenser regime. These included William Trussell and Thomas Roscelyn, who had lost their lands and titles as a result of the persecution of the contrariants in 1322, as well as more recent fugitives from the Despenser tyranny such as John Crombewell and John Roos.[52] Edward II had every right to be contemptuous of his queen for consorting with such company, and particularly with his mortal enemy Mortimer.[53] What the inept and insensitive king had not bargained for was the degree of hostility that his own regime had recently engendered in England, and the widespread support that would rapidly materialize within the kingdom for the invasion of this little band of rebels.

Throughout the summer of 1326 Edward II attempted to mobilize his kingdom against Queen Isabella and their son. The Church was called upon to rouse the people to loyalty. Writing to the Dominican order at the time of their annual general chapter with the accustomed request for prayers, the self-righteous king pointedly excluded the queen and the prince from any resulting spiritual benefits.[54] More practically, magnates were appointed to supervise the defence of the shires; the king's cousin, Henry, earl of Leicester, was to act as lieutenant in the Midlands and his brother the earl of Norfolk in East Anglia. Edward himself planned to make his way to the Welsh marches 'to rouse the good and loyal men of that land'.[55] The king apparently believed that Isabella might land her forces at Bristol, and placed scouts in the Forest of Dean to look out for any signs and news of invasion.[56] He also ordered a number of secret missions to the continent to foil Isabella's plans, though the deficiencies of intelligence reports rendered his efforts futile: one expedition headed for Normandy under the misapprehension that Prince Edward was residing there.[57]

It was only at a comparatively late stage that the king's council was properly informed of Isabella's emerging plan. On 2 September, in a clear

---

[50] Richmond, Talbot and Beaumont were all witnesses to the act of homage for Aquitaine and Ponthieu in Sept. 1325: *War of Saint-Sardos*, 243. Richmond's English estates were seized in Jan. 1326: Buck, *Stapeldon*, 161 n. 237.

[51] *Cal. Mem. Rolls 1326–7*, no. 216. See also Fryde, *Tyranny*, 187.

[52] Fryde, *Tyranny*, 186.

[53] *Foedera*, II.ii, 153.

[54] Haines, *Stratford*, 169–70; *CCR 1324–6*, 556, 643.

[55] C 49/5/17; Fryde, *Tyranny*, 183–4.

[56] SAL, MS 122, fol. 45v.

[57] Haines, *Stratford*, 169; Fryde, *Tyranny*, 184–5.

response to news that the queen intended to land in East Anglia, the crown ordered a general levy of ships from the eastern ports to muster at the Orwell estuary in Suffolk on 21 September. There is little evidence, however, to suggest that a significant force had materialized by the time the queen, the prince and their supporters embarked from Dordrecht on 23 September and landed near the mouth of the Orwell on the following day. Indeed, there are suspicions that Robert Wateville, commander of the royal fleet, actually assisted the queen by allowing safe passage to her little fleet of ten fishing vessels.[58] If so, his was the first of a flood of defections that would rapidly ensure victory for the invading force. As yet, the true intentions of the queen and her lover remained undeclared and uncertain. Whether or not he was privy to their scheming, Edward of Windsor must readily have felt the obvious mixture of foreboding and exhilaration at the apparently imminent confrontation with his frustrated and discredited father the king.

If Isabella and Mortimer already had definite intentions to overthrow Edward II and assume responsibility for the government of England on that day when they and the prince stood upon the Suffolk shore, then their existing force was hardly adequate to the cause. John of Hainault had supplied Isabella with a force of about 700 men-at-arms, and the entire army probably comprised some 1,500 men.[59] Edward II may have been repeatedly humiliated by the Scots but, as the events of 1321–2 had shown, he had resources at his control sufficient to put down even major rebellion. The royal orders for the array of the shires, issued three days after the queen's landing, demanded the service of nearly 50,000 infantry and archers in defence of the king and his crown.[60] At the outset, then, Isabella's miniature army can hardly have been regarded as a serious military threat by either side. For the first few weeks of the ensuing campaign, the majority of people who had any knowledge of the queen's coming assumed that its purpose was solely to apply pressure for the removal of the Despensers and the restoration of her own estates, interests and powers. This essentially loyalist agenda was one to which all could readily subscribe: as Adam Orleton, bishop of Hereford, put it before a meeting of the conspirators early in their campaign, the eradication of the Despensers would allow the restoration of that wise counsel on which notions of good kingship so strongly relied.[61]

---

[58] *CCR 1323–7*, 643–4; *Chron. Lanercost*, 255; BL, MS Cotton Faustina B. V, fol. 47; Fryde, *Tyranny*, 185–6.

[59] H. S. Lucas, *The Low Countries and the Hundred Years' War, 1326–1347* (Ann Arbor, 1929), 56; Fryde, *Tyranny*, 185; Buck, *Stapeldon*, 217.

[60] *Parl. Writs*, II.ii, App., 292–3.

[61] Baker, 21; Haines, *Orleton*, 164.

This was to reckon without the ability of the queen and her party to mobilize the support of key political figures in England. The resourceful Isabella quickly circulated letters to the prelates and magnates, calling upon them to join her for the good of the kingdom. Mindful of the vital role the Londoners played in supporting the government, she entered into correspondence with the authorities in the capital. The increasingly nervous king also suspected her of writing to other cities and towns, and ordered that such letters be intercepted, warning that any favour shown to the queen and her party was tantamount to treason.[62] Given that Mortimer and his adherents were already condemned traitors and that any engagement with the invading force was to be treated as an act of open rebellion, it is all the more striking how many great men were prepared to enter upon such a high-risk venture at so early a stage in its prosecution. In this respect at least the presence of the heir to the throne in the queen's entourage may have proved decisive. The earl of Norfolk quickly abandoned his military command to join the queen and his brother the earl of Kent, as did Bishops Orleton of Hereford, Burghersh of Lincoln, Hothum of Ely and (probably) Airmyn of Norwich. The town of Ipswich loaned the queen and prince £100 soon after their landing. The few sailors who had turned out to resist the rebels' landing were later said to have refused to fight on the grounds of their common contempt for the Despensers.[63]

The queen and prince remained for some time at Walton, and then progressed via Bury St Edmunds to Cambridge, where they lodged at Barnwell Priory.[64] Moving on to Dunstable, they were joined by the earl of Leicester. Isabella now enjoyed the public support of the king's two half-brothers and his cousin. Meanwhile, news from London provided much encouragement. The citizens failed to be duped by the bogus papal excommunication pronounced against the queen and her son by Archbishop Reynolds on 30 September, and with the city in tumult, Edward II fled from the Tower with the Despensers and his chancellor, Robert Baldock, on 2 October. The former treasurer, Bishop Stapeldon, a stalwart of the royalist regime and much hated by the queen, now became the most readily available target of popular wrath. Reynolds's attempts to negotiate a truce with the queen failed and Isabella sent an open letter to the citizens of London on 6 October beseeching their assistance specifically in the arrest of the younger Despenser.[65] On 15 October a gathering at the London Guildhall instructed the mayor, Hamo Chigwell, that

---

[62] *CPMR 1323–64*, 42; Haines, *Stratford*, 170 and n. 41; *CCW 1244–1326*, 582.

[63] Baker, 21; *French Chronicle*, 51; *Cal. Mem. Rolls 1326–7*, no. 2235.

[64] J. H. Round, 'The Landing of Queen Isabella in 1326', *EHR*, xiv (1899), 104–5; Haines, *Stratford*, 170 n. 39.

[65] *CPMR 1323–64*, 41–2; 'Extracts from the *Historia Aurea* and a French "Brut" (1317–1377)', ed. V. H. Galbraith, *EHR*, xliii (1928), 211–12; Buck, *Stapeldon*, 218–19.

Stapeldon was the queen's enemy and that all those hostile to Isabella and her cause should be put to death. Stapeldon was seized as he tried to escape into sanctuary at St Paul's and was pulled through the streets to Cheapside, where he was decapitated with a bread knife. The following day, the keeper of the Tower handed over his keys, and his prisoners, including Mortimer's two sons, were released. The king's authority was effectively nullified by the proclamation of the infant Prince John, then residing at the Tower, as guardian of the city. On 17 October the tablet that Thomas of Lancaster had earlier set up in St Paul's to commemorate the Ordinances, and which had been removed on the king's orders in 1323, was re-erected.[66] The city had provided a decisive lead. It was up to the queen, and the country, to follow.

Edward II's rapid flight from London did not necessarily signify the end of his cause. The panicked king was clearly making for South Wales and thence possibly for Ireland, where he assumed that he would find powerful support; he also had large sums of ready cash in his baggage to pay for extra military aid. The queen and the prince accordingly set off across the country, passing via Wallingford and Oxford to Gloucester and Bristol. Along the way Isabella continued to gather allies: at Gloucester she was joined by Leicester's son-in-law, Sir Thomas Wake, along with Henry Percy and other northern and marcher lords.[67] Edward II, who had moved via Tintern and Chepstow en route for Caerphilly, had left the elder Despenser at Bristol. Although he made some efforts to defend the castle,[68] Despenser was forced to capitulate to the queen on 26 October and, after trial under martial law in a court of chivalry, was hanged, drawn and quartered.[69] With one Despenser down, it was surely a matter of time before the other should succumb and the realm finally be liberated from their intolerable yoke.

Later on the day of the execution, the rebels gathered in the presence of the queen and her eldest son to make formal provision for the governance of England. Bishop John Stratford of Winchester was there, along with Alexander Bicknor and the bishops of Ely, Lincoln, Hereford and Norwich. To the existing list of earls, barons and knights – Norfolk and Kent, Leicester, Thomas Wake, Henry Beaumont, Robert Mauley, Robert Wateville – were now added the names of previously loyal barons such as

[66] C 49/6/7; M. McKisack, 'London and the Succession to the Crown during the Middle Ages', *Studies in Medieval History Presented to Frederick Maurice Powicke*, ed. R. W. Hunt, W. A. Pantin and R. W. Southern (Oxford, 1948), 81–3; Buck, *Stapeldon*, 218–20.

[67] Murimuth, 47. Wake had already been threatened with forfeiture by the king on 10 Oct.: *Parl. Writs*, II.ii, App., 294–5.

[68] In 1327 Sir John Beauchamp of Somerset complained that Richard Brown of Halford had forced a number of his tenants at Shepton Mallet to go with him to defend Bristol against the queen and her son: SC 8/32/1573.

[69] *Ann. Paulini*, 317–18; M. Keen, *Nobles, Knights and Men-at-Arms in the Middle Ages* (London, 1996), 155, 163.

William de la Zouche of Ashby and Robert Morley.[70] The rumour of the
king's attempt to flee to Ireland made it possible to argue that he had made
no proper provision for the government of the realm during his absence.
Assuming power to themselves, the members of the queen's party agreed
that Prince Edward ought to exercise the authority of a keeper of the realm
'in the name and right of the king'.[71] It was at once an act of open defiance
of Edward II and the most explicit statement yet made as to the crucial role
that Edward of Windsor must play in the renegotiation of rule.

The decision to bestow this striking title on the young king was taken,
according to the official record, with the assent of 'the whole community
of the realm there present'. It seems likely that the phrase 'community of
the realm' was used in much the same way as it had been employed against
Henry III in 1258, to denote a sworn league or 'commune' dedicated to a
specific programme of reform.[72] The oaths subsequently taken by
Isabella's supporters at London in January 1327 would refer explicitly to the
queen's quarrel with the Despensers and with Baldock,[73] who by that point
were in fact already condemned and (in the case of the Despensers)
executed. This suggests that the London oaths were a repeat of earlier
oath-swearings in which the rebel leaders formally and publicly committed
themselves to a blood feud against Edward II's favourites. According to an
open letter issued in the names of the queen, the prince and the earl of
Kent on 15 October, the rebels' aim was explicitly and solely to rid the land
of the tyranny of the younger Despenser.[74] It is easy to see why Isabella
promoted this cause as long and as loudly as she did, for it helped avoid the
awkward issue of the act of rebellion being read as treason. Equally,
though, it is almost impossible to resist the conclusion that the key players
in the commune of 26 October were complicit in the revolutionary notion
that, should the king prove resistant to their purpose, they might yet force
him from the throne and have his son crowned in his stead.

The emergence of the prince as an active, if not willing, player in this
conspiracy was a direct corollary of his newly assumed status as keeper of
the realm. Initially and pragmatically, it was decided that Edward of
Windsor's personal privy seal should be used to authorize documents
issued in his new formal capacity.[75] Subsequently, in mid-November, the

[70] GEC, ix, 211–14; xii, 957–60. Zouche (definitely) and Morley (probably) had fought for
the king at Boroughbridge. The fact that Leicester is named as earl of Lancaster and
Leicester in this list may suggest that the record was made after the formal accession of
Edward III and the restoration of Leicester to his brother's title in 1327.

[71] CCR 1324–7, 655; Foedera, II.i, 646; Parl. Writs, II.ii, 349–50.

[72] M. T. Clanchy, England and its Rulers, 1066–1272, 2nd edn (Oxford, 1998), 193–5;
C. Valente, The Theory and Practice of Revolt in Medieval England (Aldershot, 2003), 49–162.

[73] Parl. Writs, II.ii, 354.

[74] Letters of the Queens of England, 1100–1547, ed. A. Crawford (Stroud, 1994), 88–9.

[75] CCR 1324–7, 655. The seal was entrusted to Robert Wyvil, one of the queen's clerks:
Tout, Chapters, ii, 309–10; iii, 2.

great seal of absence that had been created for Edward II's first visit to France in 1308 and been used during his subsequent absences on the continent was sent down to Prince Edward at Hereford. In fact, the need for a substitute seal of state had already almost passed, since the great seal itself was about to be surrendered by the king.[76] These various arrangements suggest that, despite the usurpation of royal authority implicit in the prince's assumption of the keepership of the realm, the queen and her party were attempting to proceed with as much legitimacy as possible.[77] It was in accordance with this contrived punctiliousness that, until 20 November, the central administration was required, rather confusingly, to act on instructions issued both by the prince and by the king.[78]

Under normal circumstances, the powers of a keeper of the realm were carefully circumscribed. There can be little doubt, however, that the new rival government set up at Hereford in early November rapidly assumed a wide range of functions.[79] The earl of Leicester was now recognized as rightful holder of his deceased brother's earldom of Lancaster, and another royal cousin, John Bohun, was given his inheritance as earl of Hereford and Essex.[80] One of the most dramatic indications of the new keeper's authority was the appointment of Bishop Stratford as acting treasurer of the exchequer on 6 November. The doughty Stratford arrived at Westminster on 14 November in the company of the mayor and 'a great crowd' of Londoners; in the absence of the king's treasurer and supporter William Melton, archbishop of York, the staff of the exchequer had no choice but to yield to the new regime.[81] One of Stratford's first duties was to swear to maintain the liberties of the city of London in a public ceremony at the Guildhall on 15 November.[82] Everything suggested that the ground was being laid for the triumphant entry of the queen and her son into the capital city of the realm.

On the day after Stratford's pronouncement at the Guildhall, Edward II and his followers were finally ambushed and captured by a military force dispatched from Hereford under the leadership of Leicester. In early November, Edward II had moved along the coast of South Wales. On 10 November, he sent a final and fruitless deputation to the queen led by the abbot of Neath and Edward Bohun. The king may have

[76] Tout, *Chapters*, iii, 3 n. 1.

[77] L. Benz, 'Queen Consort, Queen Mother: The Power and Authority of Fourteenth-Century Plantagenet Queens' (University of York PhD thesis, 2009), 202–5.

[78] For authorizations under the prince's seal in the exchequer see *Cal. Mem. Rolls 1326–7*, nos. 203, 204, 213, 215, 1100.

[79] A number of grants made by the prince during the period 20 Oct.–30 Nov. had subsequently to be confirmed under the great seal and enrolled: *CPR 1324–7*, 338, 342.

[80] GEC, vi, 470; vii, 398.

[81] *Cal. Mem. Rolls 1326–7*, no. 832; Davies, *Baronial Opposition*, 568.

[82] *Ann. Paulini*, 318.

been planning to escape by sea from Swansea, for some of the records
of the royal chancery were later discovered in the castle there. But for
some reason, he decided to move east again, possibly in the hope of
re-establishing himself behind the prodigious water defences at the
Despenser castle of Caerphilly. He departed from Neath in an evident
state of emergency, and a significant part of the £29,000 that he had
carried in cash into Wales was left behind at the abbey. The journey was
also to prove his last as a free man, for the royal party was betrayed and
ambushed at Llantrisant on 16 November.[83] The eagerly sought younger
Despenser, who had remained with the king to the last, was taken immediately to Hereford where he was subjected to summary trial and execution. The traitor's head was cut off and sent for display on London Bridge,
where it excited a ready audience.[84] The king's other principal supporter
in the marches, the earl of Arundel, was captured on 17 November and
also put to death at Hereford, where the queen and her son took delivery
of all his money and plate. Arundel's estates in the Isle of Axholme were
promptly granted to John de Warenne, the earl of Surrey, who, despite
initially siding with the king, had been allowed to make his peace with
Isabella and was thereafter regarded as one of her allies.[85] The obnoxious
Robert Baldock was also condemned at Hereford, but claimed benefit of
clergy and was placed in the custody of Bishop Orleton, who transferred
him to London and promptly abandoned him to the city authorities;
Baldock subsequently died in torment in Newgate prison in May 1327.[86]
   The captive Edward II was, not surprisingly, treated in a very different
manner. The king was lodged first at Monmouth castle and then, by
5 December, at the earl of Leicester's castle of Kenilworth. Edward was
still the source of his wife's and son's authority, and it was essential that he
be kept safe from his friends and enemies alike. Behind such clear strategy,
however, lay a trail of chaos. Isabella was soon to appropriate the £62,000
left in cash deposits by Edward II at the royal treasuries in Westminster
and the Tower of London. But it would be the best part of a year before
the plate, armour and other goods left at Neath and Swansea were handed
over to the queen, and by that time the locals had helped themselves
to at least £3,000 worth of royal property.[87] Over twenty years later,
Edward III was to receive an anonymous tip-off that Robert Gyene, a
prominent merchant of Bristol, was still holding some 2,000 marks of

[83] *CPR 1324–7*, 336, 337; *CFR 1319–27*, 422; Fryde, *Tyranny*, 105, 189; Hallam, *Itinerary of Edward II*, 291.

[84] Holmes, 'Judgement on the Younger Despenser', 261–7; J. Taylor, 'The Judgement on Hugh Despenser the Younger', *Medievalia et Humanistica*, xii (1958), 70–7.

[85] C 47/3/53, no. 7; *CPR 1324–7*, 338; McKisack, *Fourteenth Century*, 84, 88 n. 2.

[86] *Ann. Paulini*, 320–1; Baker, 25–6; Haines, *Orleton*, 167.

[87] *CFR 1319–27*, 429; *CPR 1324–7*, 339; *List of Welsh Entries in the Memoranda Rolls, 1282–43*, ed. N. Fryde (Cardiff, 1974), 69; 'Inquisition on the Effects of Edward II', ed. C. H. Hartshorne, *Archaeologia Cambrensis*, 3rd series, ix (1863), 163–7.

Baldock's goods;[88] during the inquiry that ensued, the king's commissioners uncovered a huge stash of treasure, valued at an extraordinary £20,000, left over from the personal wealth of Baldock and the younger Despenser.[89] In the wake of Isabella's well-organized plan for the disposal of her foes and the safekeeping of her husband came a veritable flood of indiscriminate violence and bounty-hunting.

Prince Edward had cause to consider carefully the implications of the events at Neath, Hereford and London. His experience at York in 1322 had already provided a powerful glimpse of the hazards that befell those who dared challenge the will of the vengeful Edward II. Now, precisely the same level of brutality was being applied against the enemies of the queen. The younger Despenser was subjected to a particularly agonizing execution; the first phase of the torture, the cutting off of his genitals, may have been chosen deliberately to play on public disgust at Hugh's rumoured sodomy with the king.[90] Though his later actions do not suggest a man who took pleasure in sadistic acts of vengeance, Prince Edward may well have been prepared to condone the human sacrifices of the Despensers and Baldock. Of much greater concern to him as the winter rolled in was the fate that his mother might now have in store for the captive and abject Edward II.

The public knowledge that Edward II lay under arrest on the authority of his son put to swift end the experiment in power-sharing that had obtained since late October. On 20 November 1326 the queen's advisers determined that, since the king had now officially re-entered the realm, it was impossible for Prince Edward to continue to function as keeper. Bishop Orleton and Sir William Blount were accordingly sent to the king and required him to deliver up the great seal to his son. They returned to meet the queen and her son a few miles south-east of Hereford, at Much Marcle, on 26 November.[91] The official record conveniently claimed that Edward II had authorized his wife and son to 'cause to be done under the great seal not only what was necessary for right and peace but also what they may do of grace'.[92] Accordingly, the new regime immediately began to dispose of royal patronage. Among the grants warranted 'by the queen and the king's first-born son' was a reservation of the valuable wardship of Laurence Hastings, heir to the earldom of Pembroke, to the use of Prince

[88] SC 8/153/7650.

[89] *CFR 1347–56*, 324, 388; *CPR 1350–4*, 232, 279; E 368/126, *Brev. retorn.*, Mich., rot. 15d; E 142/47, m. 3; E101/333/23, no. 5; JUST 1/1451, rot. 5. For the further history of this treasure, see p. 374.

[90] C. Sponsler, 'The King's Boyfriend: Froissart's Political Theater of 1326', *Queering the Middle Ages*, ed. G. Burger and S. F. Kruger (Minneapolis, 2001), 143–67; D. Westerhof, 'Deconstructing Identities on the Scaffold: The Execution of Hugh Despenser the Younger, 1326', *JMH*, xxxiii (2007), 87–106.

[91] *CCR 1324–7*, 655–6; Tout, *Chapters*, vi, 10–11.

[92] *Foedera*, II.i, 646; *Parl. Writs*, II.ii, 350.

Edward himself.[93] Ironically the chancery insisted on maintaining the fiction that it worked to the king's instructions and dated the great majority of such grants not at Woodstock, where the queen and prince resided until removing to Wallingford for Christmas, but from the royal prison of Kenilworth.[94] Such fictions helped serve the sensibilities of bureaucrats. But no one actively involved in the regime was now under any illusion as to where the source of royal authority lay.

The most surprising thing about the arrangement of 26 November is not the acknowledgement that it provided of Prince Edward's position as de facto ruler of the realm but the new and very special status it accorded to the queen. Prince Edward had just celebrated his fourteenth birthday, and was thus of an age at which he could be formally assumed to be capable of exercising his own will and taking responsibility for his actions.[95] No official power-sharing was actually necessary. But Isabella clearly had no intention of giving up the influence that went with the custody of the heir to the throne. On two previous occasions she had been given executive custody of her husband's great seal.[96] And her name had already appeared alongside the prince's in formal documents issued since the time that Edward of Windsor was keeper of the realm.[97] Even so, the new scheme implied a kind of female sovereignty that had not been known in England since the twelfth century. Its essential justification was moral rather than legal or constitutional. Isabella was the saviour of the realm from the tyranny of Despenser rule; so long as her husband proved incapable of providing effective leadership, it was fitting that his authority should be devolved in part to her. The fact that petitioners seeking redress from the crown over the winter of 1326–7 addressed the queen and the prince as joint sources of royal grace certainly indicates a public readiness to hail Isabella as active ruler.[98] We can only assume that the likes of Norfolk, Kent and Leicester, who might otherwise have assumed responsibility for the

[93] *CPR 1324–7*, 341. For grants specifically warranted by the queen and prince, see *CPR 1324–7*, 340, 341. It is interesting that the restoration of the estates of John of Brittany on 25 Dec. was, by contrast, warranted 'by the king on the information of the queen': *CPR 1324–7*, 343–4.

[94] Tout, *Chapters*, iii, 3 n. 1.

[95] Orme, *Childhood to Chivalry*, 6.

[96] Benz, 'Queen Consort, Queen Mother', 195–7.

[97] SC 1/37/46; SC 1/49/189; *Cal. Mem. Rolls 1326–7*, no. 616; *The Registers of Roger Martival, Bishop of Salisbury, 1315–1330, III*, ed. S. Reynolds (CYS, lix, 1965), no. 680.

[98] SC 1/37/19; SC 1/37/210; SC 8/46/2256; SC 8/74/3669; SC 8/307/15307; S. A. Sneddon, 'Words and Realities: The Language and Dating of Petitions, 1326–7', *Medieval Petitions: Grace and Grievance*, ed. W. M. Ormrod, G. Dodd and A. Musson (York, 2009), 198–200; F. L. Wiswall III, 'Politics, Procedure and the "Non-Minority" of Edward III: Some Comparisons', *The Age of Richard II*, ed. J. L. Gillespie (Stroud, 1997), 10. For a petition addressed to the prince alone, see SC 8/277/13818. From 1 Nov. 1326 to 11 Mar. 1327 the households of the queen and her son were treated as one: E 101/382/9; Tout, *Chapters*, v, 246–7.

custody of the prince and the presidency of his council, were also prepared to acknowledge the queen's ascendancy and comply, for the present, with her wishes.

On 28 October the new emergency administration took the decision to issue writs for a parliament planned to assemble at Westminster on 14 December. The summonses stated that the king would be absent from the realm at the time of the session and that business would therefore be conducted before the queen and her son. The summonses were very obviously irregular; the bishop of Salisbury's registrar, for example, took strong exception to the use of the great seal of absence to authenticate the writ sent to Bishop Martival.[99] Behind such niceties lay a major anxiety as to whether anyone other the king had the right to call a parliament. But the queen, determined and increasingly assertive in her new role, pressed ahead. After it had taken control of the great seal, and in order to assuage continuing anxieties about the legality of the assembly, the prince's administration issued supplementary writs in the king's own name proroguing the parliament to 7 January.[100]

Whether Isabella and her allies had a clear and agreed plan in place in advance of this meeting remains something of a mystery. The fact that Roger Mortimer's name appeared at the head of the list of barons summoned to parliament, in the place previously occupied by the younger Despenser, certainly hints at a determination to drive through a settlement that guaranteed the interests of the queen. Shortly before parliament met, Bishops Orleton, Stratford and Airmyn, together with the archbishop of Canterbury, Walter Reynolds, met with Leicester, Kent and other nobles at Prince Edward's residence of Woodstock. They agreed that the articulate and impressive Orleton should make a speech in the upcoming assembly explaining that the queen feared the king's vicious anger and that any reconciliation between the royal couple was therefore impossible. Orleton claimed that the king carried a dagger with which he intended to attack his wife, and if necessary would simply crush her with his own teeth. Such images played on common perceptions of Edward's uncontrollable anger and lack of kingly clemency.[101] But they were also intended to provide substantive justification for what was otherwise a blatant breach of wifely responsibilities. Isabella had earlier justified her resistance to patriarchal authority by arguing that the younger Despenser had ruined her marriage.[102] With Hugh now dead, and with many conservative-minded members of the polity uncomfortable about the idea of a wife in open revolt against her husband, further justifications for Isabella's resistance needed to be found. Beyond this point, though, the queen's party

[99] *Registers of Roger Martival III*, no. 681.
[100] *Parl. Writs*, II.ii, 350–66; *HBC*, 556; *PROME*, iv, 5.
[101] Haines, *Orleton*, 167–8; Haines, *Edward II*, 41, 46.
[102] *Vita*, 243.

could not, for the present, go. No solution was offered to the impasse within the royal marriage. Either Isabella's supporters were genuinely at odds on the matter or else, for the present, they simply dared not articulate the revolutionary implications of their schemes.

If the wider political community believed that parliament might provide an occasion for reconciliation between the king and queen and a return to the normal conventions of counsel and consent, it was soon disabused of the idea.[103] Isabella had kept a safe distance from the unsettled city of London since her invasion in September, and Prince Edward's slow progress from Wallingford via Windsor to Westminster in early January marked his first appearance in the capital since he had left for France in 1325. The tumult that had prevailed in the city over the previous two months had hardly abated, and on the opening day of the assembly, 7 January, a crowd of Londoners forced its way into Westminster Hall. Both the city authorities and the mob were to play a significant part in moulding the opinion of the assembly over the following weeks. For Prince Edward, the heady mixture of extreme emotions, from real fright over a possible descent into anarchy to intense nervous excitement at the prospect of political liberation, must have been almost too much to bear.

In spite of the mounting pressure from the Londoners, there remained a deep division of opinion among the queen's party as to whether parliament could legitimately function in the absence of the king, and procedural debates stalled substantive business for several days.[104] Eventually a deputation led by Bishops Burghersh and Stratford was sent to Kenilworth on behalf of the queen, her son and 'all the earls and barons and all the community of the land gathered at London' to request that Edward II come to parliament. His haughty and perverse refusal to comply was announced on the return of the bishops on Monday, 12 January. This was probably a defining moment in the minds of the assembled polity, the

---

[103] The account that follows relies largely on C. Valente, 'The Deposition and Abdication of Edward II', *EHR*, cxiii (1998), 852–81. See also *PROME*, iv, 5–7, from which the present study diverges on certain details. Previous scholarship on the deposition (much of it driven by a desire to determine the degree to which 1327 set a precedent for the forcible removals of later kings in and after 1399), was often wary about ascribing to parliament a very conspicuous role in the transfer of authority from Edward II to Edward III, and focused instead on the possible precedents for the overthrow of monarchs in earlier papal and imperial policy and in the canon-law notion of the personal inadequacy of the ruler. See, *inter alia*, M. V. Clarke, *Medieval Representation and Consent* (London, 1936), 173–95; B. Wilkinson, 'The Deposition of Richard II and the Accession of Henry IV', *Historical Studies of the English Parliament*, ed. E. B. Fryde and E. Miller, 2 vols (Cambridge, 1970), i, 337–44; E. Peters, *The Shadow King: Rex Inutilis in Medieval Law and Literature, 751–1327* (New Haven, 1970), 232–41; and more recent discussions, with references, by Haines, *Edward II*, 186–94, and M. Prestwich, *Plantagenet England, 1225–1360* (Oxford, 2005), 213–20.

[104] *Anglia Sacra*, ed. H. Wharton, 2 vols (London, 1691), i, 367; Haines, *Orleton*, 171; Valente, 'Deposition', 855 n. 4.

point when previously loyal lords, clerics, knights and townsmen began to consider seriously the possibility of a full-scale regime change.

On the day of the dramatic announcement of the king's decision to resist the counsel of his subjects, the mayor and aldermen of London invited some of the magnates to join the city in maintaining the cause of the queen and prince and in seeking the deposition of Edward II and the coronation of his son. On 13 January, a large number of notables attended the Guildhall and swore a common oath to safeguard Queen Isabella and Prince Edward, to maintain their quarrel against the adherents of the Despensers, to support the ordinances made in the current parliament and, significantly, to uphold the freedoms of the city of London.[105] Later that day, Roger Mortimer himself announced in parliament that it had been agreed among the lords that Edward should be deposed and replaced by his son.[106] The queen's episcopal supporters then gave a series of sermon-like speeches on biblical texts and proverbs designed to justify and popularize the rebels' cause. When Bishop Orleton preached on the text, 'A foolish king shall ruin his people' (Ecclesiastes 10: 16), his audience reportedly cried out 'We do not wish him to reign over us any longer!'[107] John Stratford drew on the conventional organic imagery of the state in a sermon on 'My head is sick' (2 Kings 4: 19). Finally, after preaching on the proverb *Vox populi, vox Dei* ('The voice of the people is the voice of God'), Archbishop Reynolds read out a series of articles composed the previous evening at a meeting of the magnates and prelates. These charged the king with weakness and incompetence, taking evil counsel, losing his possessions and rights in Scotland, Ireland and France, and abandoning the realm.[108] Reynolds concluded by declaring that the magnates, clergy and people had given their unanimous consent to the deposition of Edward II and desired that his eldest son, the Lord Edward, should succeed to the crown. Immediately, there was a threefold shout of *fiat* – 'Let it be done!'[109]

On 15 January a deputation was dispatched to Kenilworth to announce this momentous decision to the king. Some attention was given to ensuring that this mission was fully representative of all the estates of the realm. This offered a convenient way out of the difficulties that might arise if the king were to argue – as well he might – that parliament was his creature and had no right on its own to defy his royal authority.[110] In reality, the

---

[105] *CPMR 1323–64*, 11–14; *Litterae Cantuariensis*, ed. J. B. Sheppard, 3 vols (RS, 1887–9), i, 204–7. For the composition of the confederacy, see Clarke, *Medieval Representation and Consent*, 181–2.

[106] Fryde, *Tyranny*, 233; Valente, 'Deposition', 856.

[107] *Chron. Lanercost*, 257; Haines, *Stratford*, 183. Other accounts give different texts for Orleton's sermon: Valente, 'Deposition', 858 n. 4.

[108] *Foedera*, II.i, 650; Valente, 'Deposition', 879–81.

[109] *Chron. Lanercost*, 258; *Anglia Sacra*, i, 367.

[110] *Litterae Cantuariensis*, i, 204–5.

commission was dominated by the will of its leading members, the earls of Leicester and Surrey, the bishops of Winchester and Hereford, and the barons Hugh Courtenay and William Ros. Arriving at Kenilworth on 20 or 21 January, the members of the deputation informed the king that, unless he resigned the crown, the people would repudiate both him and his sons and have some other person, not of the royal blood, as king. Such extremism reveals not only the considerable moral pressure that had to be put on the notably obdurate king but also the considerable unease felt within the polity about the increasingly dominant presence of the queen's lover, Roger Mortimer.

It was this piece of moral blackmail that finally forced the humiliated and hopeless king to admit the futility of his cause. After a due show of histrionics, Edward announced that he would consent to the will of his subjects so long as his eldest son was accepted as king in his place. Faced with the trauma of deposition, both king and lords were quick to revert to a conservative position and present the exchange of power as a simple drawing forward of Edward of Windsor's future accession to the throne. The next day William Trussell, one of the refugees from the Despenser regime who had returned to England with the queen and the prince, acted for the deputation in renouncing all homage and allegiance to Edward II. The king's steward, Sir Thomas Blount, then broke his staff of office to denote the termination of the royal household.[111]

Some members of the Kenilworth deputation were still on the road back to London on 25 January, but the outcome of their visit to the king was probably communicated by fast-moving messengers who reached the capital a couple of days earlier. In the absence of Leicester and his colleagues, parliament had gone into abeyance. But the Londoners had continued their clamour for change, and as early as 20 January some of the bishops had taken an oath in which they recognized Prince Edward as king. Finally, on 24 January, the chancery issued a public statement to the effect that, with the consent of the prelates, earls and barons and the community of the realm, Edward II had, of his own free will, renounced the throne and wished that his eldest son should govern the kingdom and be crowned as king.[112] Following the convention first adopted on the succession of Edward II and observed for the following two hundred years, the new reign was deemed to begin on the day after the old one ended. Edward III therefore began his reign on 25 January 1327.[113]

---

[111] *RPHI*, 101; *Litterae Cantuariensis*, iii, 414; *Ann. Paulini*, 324; Baker, 28.

[112] *Foedera*, II.ii, 683.

[113] B. Guenée, *States and Rulers in Later Medieval Europe*, trans. J. Vale (Oxford, 1985), 68–9. It is to be noted, however, that pardons issued on the eve of the Stanhope Park campaign later in 1327 took the coronation, rather than the accession, as the date when the king's peace was established: *CPR 1327–30*, 161–3.

The proclamations made in the shire towns and markets of England over the following weeks marked the first step in a sustained campaign to present the recent palace coup as a legitimate process palatable to the conservative instincts of the wider realm. In the proclamations, as in a more detailed account of proceedings circulated to some of the monastic houses, the events of 13 and 21 January were conveniently reversed so as to place the abdication of Edward II before his subjects' withdrawal of fealty.[114] By contrast, the articles of deposition read out by Reynolds on 13 January were never publicized and seem to have been rapidly suppressed: we have the substance of them only because they were cited in a later dispute between two of the chief players in the crisis, Bishops Orleton and Stratford.[115] In particular, those with detailed knowledge of civil and canon law seem to have recommended that it was better to avoid the scholastic notion that the people had the right forcibly to remove a tyrant from the throne.[116] It says much for the character of contemporary politics that the elite drew back so quickly from the more radical implications of its actions in 1327. It was indeed a very English kind of revolution that put Edward III prematurely on his father's throne.

Edward of Windsor is a very shadowy figure in the official and unofficial accounts of the deposition proceedings of January 1327. It is not clear whether he attended any of the set pieces in London and Westminster over those momentous days in mid-January. Rather, he seems to have remained holed up with his mother, either in the privy palace of Westminster or perhaps within the sterner defences of the Tower, where the court busied itself with the preliminaries of an impending coronation.[117] The queen and her advisers certainly had good reason to keep the prince away from the main theatres of action. Had he made a formal appearance in parliament, asserted his role as keeper of the realm and taken the presidency of the meeting, Edward would have been immediately implicated in the plot against his father. Much better, then, to plead the innocence of the prince's youth and to keep him at one remove from his kingmakers. This slightly disingenuous position was nicely captured in the coin struck to record Edward III's coronation, which bore the motto 'I did not take; I received'.[118]

Beyond such constitutional niceties there lay the starker reality of Queen Isabella's political supremacy. A number of the chroniclers referred to the assembly of January 1327 not as the king's parliament, nor

[114] Valente, 'Deposition', 871–5. This text, the so-called *Forma depositionis Regis Edwardi*, may reflect the particular anxieties of a number of the bishops at the time of the Guildhall oaths: Haines, *Orleton*, 172.

[115] Haines, *Stratford*, 183–4.

[116] J. Dunbabin, 'Government', *The Cambridge History of Medieval Political Thought, c.350–c.1450*, ed. J. H. Burns (Cambridge, 1988), 495–6.

[117] Valente, 'Deposition', 861.

[118] Barnes, *Edward III*, 4.

as the prince's, but as the queen's.[119] Isabella's successful assertion of equal status with her son in the recent arrangement for the custody of the realm had already revealed the queen's determination to be an active player in the new dispensation. Edward of Windsor may have successfully defied and defeated his father. But it would be another three years before he could shake off the stifling protection of his mother.

[119] Haines, *Stratford*, 181; Valente, 'Deposition', 862.

Chapter 3

TUTELAGE, 1327–1330

The coronation of Edward III took place at Westminster Abbey on 1 February 1327.[1] It was unusual to hold such an event quite so quickly after the succession. In this case, however, no funeral and mourning were necessary for the previous monarch. And with an obvious concern to confirm the legitimacy of the regime, it made every sense to rush the ceremonies through. With most of the political elite already in the capital, it was also comparatively easy to ensure that all the key players were present. The prelates attended in force, as did the king's uncles of Norfolk and Kent and his cousins, the earls of Leicester and Hereford. The ubiquitous John of Hainault and Henry Beaumont were there. Lurking everywhere during the proceedings was the queen's lover and henchman, Roger Mortimer.[2] There was insufficient time to set up a court of claims, but those who asserted the right to fulfil various ritual functions at the coronation banquet were allowed to make their case in advance of the ceremonies; the resulting documentation provides the earliest reference to the office of king's champion, held on this occasion by Henry Hillary.[3]

There were three main parts to the coronation: the knighting of the king, the crowning ceremony, and the subsequent feast. On the days immediately before the main rite, Edward of Windsor, along with his cousins John and Edward Bohun and Mortimer's three sons, received knighthood at the hands of Henry of Lancaster. The king then went on to dub a number of new knights of his own, including two acquaintances from his princely household, Edward Chandos and John Melton, and the Herefordshire man Hugh Frene, who may have come into his service

---

[1] *CCR 1327–30*, 100. Plate from the treasury of the exchequer was transferred to the keeper of the wardrobe on 31 Jan. in preparation for the event: BL, Cotton Ch. IV. 9. There are three manuscript traditions that provide a liturgical record of the 1327 ceremony. 1: C 49/83 (formerly C 49 Roll 11), printed in *Three Coronation Orders*, ed. J. Wickham Legge (London, 1900), 121–4. 2: CCCC, MS 20, printed in *Three Coronation Orders*, pp. 39–4; BL, MS Cotton Vitellus C. XII. 3: CUL, MS Mm.3.21, printed in *Monumenta Ritualia Ecclesiae Anglicanane*, ed. W. Maskell (London, 1847), 3–48; BL, MS Lansdowne 451.

[2] *CCR 1327–30*, 100.

[3] H. G. Richardson and G. O. Sayles, 'Early Coronation Records', *BIHR*, xiv (1936–7), 1–9. For the office of butler at the coronation, see *Cal. Mem. Rolls 1326–7*, 306, 884.

during the winter of 1326–7.[4] On the coronation day itself, the king was conducted in state to Westminster Abbey where he swore the oath, was anointed, and received the sword of state. The so-called crown of St Edward was placed on his head by Archbishop Reynolds, with Bishops Gravesend and Stratford reputedly helping to support its great weight. The king was then given the sceptre and rod of office.[5] According to a later chronicle, the boy-king bore the discomfort of the regalia with a gratifying manliness. In point of fact, it had been necessary to put some padding inside the crown so that it did not wobble at the crucial moment of investiture.[6]

Edward III's coronation may have given special prominence to the process in which the king was 'elected' or acclaimed by the magnates and people assembled in the nave of the abbey church.[7] In light of recent events in parliament, it would perhaps be surprising to find things being done otherwise. But popular acclamation was probably well established in the liturgy by 1327, and there is nothing to suggest that contemporaries believed Edward III's monarchy to be in any sense in the gift of his subjects; it was by right of inheritance and divine approval, not election, that the new king was inaugurated. Much more significant is the fact that Edward was required to take the additional oath included at his father's coronation in 1308. Along with the traditional threefold commitment to uphold the laws and customs of the realm, to maintain God's peace and to act with equity and right judgement, the new king therefore swore that he would 'hold and preserve the laws and righteous customs which the community of [the] realm shall have chosen'.[8] This amounted to a contractual commitment to respect the customs inherited from his ancestors as well as the new laws that would come into being during the course of the forthcoming reign. It was said that the outspoken Hamo Hethe, bishop of Rochester, when asked whether Edward III was to take this supplementary oath, retorted that, unless he did so, he would not be

[4] E 101/383/4; *CPR 1327–30*, 39; Murimuth, 51; GEC, vi, 470; Barnes, *Edward III*, 3–4. A number of chroniclers believed that the king received knighthood at the hands of John of Hainault and or/the earl of Hereford: *Bridlington*, 95; *Récits d'un Bourgeois de Valenciennes*, 143; Phillips, *Edward II*, 539.

[5] Baker, 34–5; BL, MS Cotton Faustina B. V, fol. 50; J. Burden, 'Rituals of Royalty: Prescription, Politics and Practice in English Coronation and Royal Funeral Rituals, *c*.1327–*c*.1485' (University of York DPhil. thesis, 1999), 75–7. The use of the regalia of St Edward in 1327 is discussed by D. Carpenter, *The Reign of Henry III* (London, 1996), 455.

[6] Baker, 34–5; L. Monnas, 'Textiles for the Coronation of Edward III', *Textile History*, xxxii (2001), 19. Cf. Haines, *Stratford*, 187–8.

[7] This argument rests on a date of 1327 for the *ordo* in CUL, MS Mm.3.21. Cf. H. G. Richardson, 'The Coronation in Medieval England: The Evolution of the Office and the Oath', *Traditio*, xvi (1960), 113–202.

[8] *Foedera*, II.i, 36; *CCR 1327–30*, 100; R. S. Hoyt, 'The Coronation Oath of 1308', *EHR*, lxxi (1956), 353–83.

crowned.[9] The story is a powerful reminder of the sensitivities raised by the failure of Edward II's monarchy and of the hopes of a new accommodation in the succeeding regime.

The coronation feast that followed in Westminster Hall was an event of breathtaking scale and grandeur. The royal dais was festooned with violet, red and grey coverings, and the king's throne, adorned with samite cushions, was placed under a canopy of gold-coloured canvas and hung with curtains of gold silk.[10] The surviving financial accounts indicate expenditure of well over £1,000 on other soft furnishings for the abbey and palace.[11] Details of the expenditure on the provision of jewels and plate are lacking, but the cost is likely to have run to several thousand pounds. And the expenses of the royal household on food and other provisions for the occasion ran to over £1,300, by far the largest recorded amount for a single feast in the whole of Edward III's reign.[12] This very deliberate extravagance was intended to create the appropriate impression of political stability and royal magnificence. Few of those in attendance can, however, have been in any doubt that the new regime faced a formidable task in rebuilding the political authority and moral credibility of the crown.

Edward and his advisers were soon at work in earnest on just such a project. The parliament that had sat in January was reconvened in the name of the new king on 3 February, and remained in session for the following month. Its first actions were carefully stage-managed to promote the new theme of reconciliation. The sentences of treason passed against Thomas of Lancaster and some of his major supporters in 1322 were annulled, and the crown agreed to begin negotiations with the papacy for Lancaster's canonization.[13] This removed the final impediment to the restoration of Thomas's brother, Henry, to the earldom of Lancaster. The penalties imposed on Roger Mortimer in 1322 were also now lifted, and the victorious Mortimer set about asserting his right not only to his own former estates but also to those of his recently deceased uncle, Roger Mortimer of Chirk.[14] Those who had been in rebellion with Thomas of

[9] BL, MS Cotton Faustina B. V, fol. 50; H. G. Richardson, 'The English Coronation Oath', *Speculum*, xxiv (1949), 65; B. Wilkinson, 'Notes on the Coronation Records of the Fourteenth Century', *EHR*, lxx (1955), 587–90.

[10] E 101/382/10; E 101/383/6; Monnas, 'Textiles', 2–35; Shenton, 'English Court', 135–45. For robes provided for Queen Isabella on the occasion of the coronation, see E 101/383/3. For other expenses see *Issues*, 139.

[11] Edward subsequently gave a set of cloths, carpets and cushions commissioned for the event as a permanent gift to the abbot and monks of Westminster: E 159/108, rot. 91d.

[12] E 101/382/9.

[13] *PROME*, iv, 2, 9, 11–12, 27–8; *RPHI*, 99; *Foedera*, II.ii, 695, 707, 782, 814. Edward III subsequently sponsored the ecclesiastical career of Thomas's bastard son, John of Lancaster: *CPP*, 193.

[14] C 49/84; *CPR 1327–30*, 141–3; GEC, viii, 438; ix, 253–6.

Lancaster in 1321–2 and lost their rights and estates in the Despensers' redistribution of spoils secured a well-timed guarantee that they would be allowed unimpeded access to justice and restitution.[15]

Understandably, a good deal of attention was given by parliament to the question of establishing effective rule. Since the king was of the age of discretion, it was not necessary to appoint a personal governor responsible for his physical safekeeping. Nor, for the same reason, was it appropriate to put royal authority into commission and have public functions fulfilled by a regent. Instead, the favoured form of administration was a collective. A continual council, made up of 'good, suitable and wise men', would be chosen by the magnates with the assent of the commons and be made subject, in the event of malpractice, to dismissal in parliament. The tribunal would comprise four bishops, four earls and six barons, at least four of whom should always be present about the king. The persistent and loyal Henry of Lancaster was, predictably enough, appointed as president; other members included the archbishops of Canterbury and York, the earls of Norfolk, Kent and Surrey, and the northern lords, Wake, Percy and Ros. They would be joined in their deliberations by the new chancellor, John Hothum, and treasurer, Adam Orleton.[16] The king's ambiguous status, at once of age and yet not fully in command, forced some awkward compromises. Proposals for significant changes to the law, such as a suggested reform of the Charter of the Forest, were simply shelved 'until the king's [full] age'.[17] On the other hand, later attempts to challenge the authority of royal grants made during Edward III's tutelage were confounded by the legal principle that 'the king is always within age'.[18] In 1327 the elite was prepared to countenance a whole series of fictions and compromises as the price for avoiding formal regency. The irony was that just such a situation was rapidly establishing itself through the unilateral actions of the queen and her lover.

It took a month for king, council and parliament to work their way through the large amount of business caused by the forced removal of Edward II. Henry Beaumont and Isabella Vescy successfully petitioned for indemnity against the penalties previously imposed on them in the Ordinances.[19] The belligerent abbot of Bury St Edmunds took advantage of his presence in parliament to declare invalid the charter that the

[15] *CCR 1327–30*, 101–2; C 49/6/2.
[16] *PROME*, iv, 31, 103; Murimuth, 51; *Anon. Chron. 1307–34*, 140–1; *Brut*, i, 254, 258; J. F. Baldwin, 'The King's Council', *Eng. Govt at Work*, i, 132–3; Tout, *Chapters*, iii, 10–11; J. S. Bothwell, 'The More Things Change: Isabella and Mortimer, Edward III, and the Painful Delay of a Royal Majority (1327–1330)', *The Royal Minorities of Medieval and Early Modern England*, ed. C. Beem (New York, 2008), 73. Orleton was replaced in Mar. by Henry Burghersh. Tout, *Chapters*, vi, 11, 21.
[17] *PROME*, iv, 22, 24, 25; *Cal. Mem. Rolls 1326–7*, no. 518.
[18] E. H. Kantorowicz, *The King's Two Bodies* (Princeton, 1957), 378 and n. 216.
[19] *PROME*, iv, 12.

townsmen had recently extracted from him during the violent distur-
bances that had accompanied the queen's invasion.[20] The citizens of
London were also quick to take advantage of their recent support for
the deposition by securing pardon of all offences and debts and a comprehensive new charter of liberties guaranteeing the city's right to self-
government.[21] Meanwhile huge numbers of private petitions flooded in
from the farthest corners of the realm, recounting hair-raising stories of
the unscrupulous activities of the Despenser regime and expressing high
hopes that the new king would redress the wrongs thus sustained.[22]
This public campaign of vindication was an important opportunity to
express commitment to the new regime. Robert Sencler of Stone
(Buckinghamshire) complained that, during the queen's invasion in the
previous winter, some of the Hainaulters in her entourage had attacked
his home and wounded his wife on the pretext, now vigorously denied by
the petitioner, that he was a servant of the Despensers.[23]

Top of the agenda sat the forty-two common petitions promoted by the
lords and commons. These addressed a whole series of hotly topical issues,
including demands for the abolition of recent controversial military and
fiscal demands, confirmation of the earlier judgments against the
Despensers, and the indemnification of those who had joined the queen's
party during the previous winter. The crown responded magnanimously
on these and other matters, though it balked at the request that it reinstate
the Ordinances of 1311.[24] One of the more remarkable demands was that
the text of the common petitions and of the resulting statutes should be
sent into the counties for proclamation, and that the clergy and commons
of the realm be charged to swear oaths, 'as we have sworn, to maintain the
enterprise now begun'.[25] This notion of perpetuating the sworn
communes earlier undertaken at Hereford and at the London Guildhall
reflected a keen awareness that the revolution had still to run its course.
During the ascendancy of the Despensers, when the lords had been
so depleted and cowed, it had been left to the knights and burgesses in

[20] M. D. Lobel, 'A Detailed Account of the 1327 Rising at Bury St Edmunds and the
Subsequent Trial', *Proceedings of the Suffolk Institute of Archaeology*, xxi (1933), 215–31. For other
risings around the time of the invasion, see W. M. Ormrod, *The Reign of Edward III: Crown
and Political Society in England, 1327–1377* (London, 1990), 123, 177.

[21] *PROME*, iv, 44–56; *Ann. Paulini*, 325–32; C. M. Barron, *London in the Later Middle Ages:
Government and People, 1200–1500* (Oxford, 2004), 17, 31–42.

[22] R. W. Kaeuper, 'Law and Order in Fourteenth-Century England: The Evidence of
Special Commissions of Oyer and Terminer', *Speculum*, liv (1979), 741; S. J. Harris, 'Taking
your Chances: Petitioning in the Last Years of Edward II and the First Years of Edward
III', *Medieval Petitions*, ed. Ormrod, Dodd and Musson, 173–92.

[23] SC 8/74/3668; Sneddon, 'Words and Realities', 201–3.

[24] *PROME*, iv, 11–22, 27–35; *SR*, i, 252–7.

[25] *PROME*, iv, 20–1, 35. For the resulting circulation of texts see ibid., iv, 2; *RPHI*, 101;
J. R. Maddicott, 'Parliament and the Constituencies, 1272–1377', *The English Parliament in the
Middle Ages*, ed. R. G. Davies and J. H. Denton (Manchester, 1984), 84.

parliament to take up the baronial tradition of articulating the collective grievances of the realm. The common petitions of 1327, with their self-conscious appeal to the interests of all the estates, marked a defining moment in the evolution of the 'community of the realm' away from a sworn league of barons and towards the representative element in parliament, the commons.[26]

Edward III struck a curiously inconspicuous figure in the parliament of February 1327. He must surely now have assumed his rightful role as formal president of the assembly, and some of the more important business was referred on to him by the council for formal approval.[27] For the most part, however, Edward conformed to his mother's strategy and lay low. Isabella was reported to have stayed away from the coronation, biding her time at Eltham.[28] Edward's continued dependency on the queen was a matter of practical necessity: extraordinarily, the king had yet to be provided with a domestic establishment of his own, and was still being fed and clothed in his mother's household.[29] The later *Brut* chronicle commented ruefully that the young Edward's sustenance depended entirely on the discretion of his mother.[30] The events of January–March helped to distract attention from Queen Isabella and her lover by concentrating on the theme of political reconciliation between the new king and the political community. But those who attended parliament can hardly have been blind to the blunter realities of the new dispensation.

On 10 January 1327, during the interregnum, the queen had seen fit to take back to her use the lands previously granted by her husband in fulfilment of her agreed dower of £4,500.[31] Then, by letters patent dated on coronation day, and as a reward for her good services, Edward III granted his mother a life interest in a long list of additional estates that raised her income to the unprecedented level of 20,000 marks.[32] This was far in excess of any previous endowment for a dowager queen, and significantly more than the landed income even of such mighty magnates as Thomas of Lancaster and Hugh Despenser.[33] Some of the queen's new estates, including the valuable honours of Tickhill, Pontefract and Clitheroe, were

[26] W. M. Ormrod, 'Agenda for Legislation, 1322–c.1340', *EHR*, cv (1990), 1–33; Valente, 'Deposition', 865–8.

[27] Thus the repeated annotation 'It pleases the king': *PROME*, iv, 9, 21–6.

[28] BL, MS Cotton Faustina B. V, fol. 50.

[29] For provisions supplied to this household during the time of parliament, see *Cal. Mem. Rolls 1326–7*, nos 1608, 1717.

[30] *Brut*, i, 248.

[31] *CPR 1317–21*, 115–16; *CPR 1324–7*, 346.

[32] C 49/45/16; *CPR 1327–30*, 66–9.

[33] H. Johnstone, 'The Queen's Household', *Eng. Govt at Work*, i, 253–7. Lancaster's income has been estimated at £11,000 a year, Despenser's at £7,000: Maddicott, *Thomas of Lancaster*, 22; Fryde, *Tyranny*, 107.

drawn from the earldom of Lincoln formerly held by Thomas of Lancaster through his wife, Alice Lacy. Alice's own residual rights, and those of her brother-in-law Henry of Lancaster, were simply ignored. Parliament was understandably chary, and asked that the crown use its patrimony sparingly so as to avoid unnecessary pressure on public resources.[34] A few months later, however, Isabella was to appropriate 10,000 marks from lay and clerical taxes to purchase the lands of Robert de Mohalt for Prince John.[35] The grants to the queen and prince were for life only, and Isabella's enormous dower may well have been designed to protect, rather than to squander, the royal domain.[36] But hostile contemporaries inevitably took her unprecedented wealth as a clear sign of Isabella's unbridled greed and of her unscrupulous manipulation of the crown's assets to serve her own selfish interests.[37]

On 11 March 1327 the domestic establishment that had functioned since the queen's return from France was finally wound up and Edward III took control of his own independent household.[38] Under normal circumstances, this would have marked the end of the transition between the regimes of the two kings and thus of the formal role that had been ascribed to Isabella since the previous November. But the queen was not to be so easily marginalized, and clung resolutely to two principles of rule. First, Edward remained too young to assume control of the full prerogatives of the crown, and ought, like boy-kings in her own French family, to be placed in the custody of his mother.[39] Secondly, if the position of regent were to be denied her, Isabella might at least continue to play the traditional queenly role of royal supporter and intercessor for the king's grace. Many of her actions over the following three years could be readily accommodated within the customary prescriptions of the consort.[40] When it suited her, Isabella could be coy about her sex and status: on at least one occasion she is said to have told the members of her son's council that she, a mere woman, could not be expected to know or do what was best for the realm.[41] All of this makes it easier to understand how the queen mother initially found it so easy to involve herself in the work of the continual council, to receive and answer petitions for royal favour, and to control crown appointments and grants of patronage. In none of this was her rule held at first to be unlawful or overbearing. Rather, her later unpopularity

---

[34] *PROME*, iv, 18, 33.

[35] *CPR 1327–30*, 267.

[36] B. P. Wolffe, *The Royal Demesne in English History* (London, 1971), 54–5, 232–5.

[37] Baker, 28; *Brut*, i, 257, 258; Baldwin, 'King's Council', 134.

[38] E 101/382/9.

[39] For Capetian practice in this regard see A. Poulet, 'Capetian Women and the Regency: The Genesis of a Vocation', *Medieval Queenship*, ed. Parsons, 93–116.

[40] Benz, 'Queen Consort, Queen Mother', 205–18.

[41] BL, MS Cotton Faustina B. V, fol. 55v.

arose from two emergent problems: the disruptive influence in domestic politics of Roger Mortimer, and her controversial diplomatic policies on Scotland and France.[42]

Isabella's greatest misjudgement after 1327 was her loyalty to the lover who had helped depose her husband. The idea that a queen mother should conduct any kind of relationship, clandestine or open, with a member of the English baronage was anathema: a century later, when Katherine of Valois was left a young widow on the death of Henry V, parliament actually passed a statute declaring that she could not remarry without the consent of the council.[43] Isabella and Mortimer were both still bound in wedlock to their respective spouses in 1327, and their double adultery was liable, in theory, to harsh punishment in the Church courts. Only a few years before, during one of Isabella's visits to Paris, the French court had been rocked by the scandalous revelation of acts of adultery committed by two of her royal sisters-in-law, Margaret of Navarre and Blanche of Burgundy.[44] At the Stamford great council of April 1327 the bishops and lords continued their debate as to whether Isabella ought to return to live with her now imprisoned husband. In the end it was decided as before that there was no chance of reconciliation, and that forcing the queen to submit would simply expose her to physical and psychological abuse by the ex-Edward II. Ironically, therefore, Archbishop Reynolds was obliged to issue a public statement threatening sanctions against anyone who spoke out against Queen Isabella's otherwise distinctly irregular domestic arrangements.[45]

It proved a good deal more difficult to silence concerns about Mortimer's political power. Not surprisingly, the former rebel did well from the coup of 1327, securing a full pardon for the offences that had led to his earlier exile and beginning to consolidate and extend his family's traditional interests in Wales and the marches. Until 1328, there was no particular suggestion that these rewards were disproportionate.[46] Mortimer was given no great office of state and was not even a member of the continual council. That he was present with the queen at meetings with members of that council and other advisers is, however, amply attested by his regular appearance in the witness lists to royal charters of

---

[42] Benz, 'Queen Consort, Queen Mother', 205–23.

[43] R. A. Griffiths, *The Reign of King Henry VI* (London, 1981), 60–1.

[44] E. A. R. Brown, 'Diplomacy, Adultery and Domestic Politics at the Court of Philip the Fair: Queen Isabelle's Mission to France in 1314', *Documenting the Past: Essays in Medieval History Presented to G. P. Cuttino*, ed. J. S. Hamilton and P. J. Bradley (Woodbridge, 1989), 53–83.

[45] Murimuth, 52; Baker, 29; P. C. Doherty, 'Isabella, Queen of England, 1296–1330' (University of Oxford DPhil. thesis, 1977), 206–11; R. M. Haines, 'The Stamford Council of April 1327', *EHR*, cxxii (2007), 141–8.

[46] GEC, viii, 437–8; I. Mortimer, *The Greatest Traitor: The Life of Sir Roger Mortimer* (London, 2003), 171–2; Bothwell, 'The More Things Change', 76–7.

this period.[47] It was this anomalous position – at once excluded from the formal structures of politics, yet acting as intimate confidant to the queen – that generated such suspicion and speculation. The Rochester chronicler, a vociferous critic of the adulterous pair, articulated the point nicely: the queen ruled, but Mortimer reigned.[48] Roger Mortimer achieved notoriety because his position at court was at once so influential and so utterly without accountability. The personal frictions thus generated within the elite were to lead, within two years of the deposition, to further threats of civil war.

For a while, such tensions were put aside as the crown went about the accustomed task of confirming the rights and privileges of the great magnates, cities and ecclesiastical institutions of the realm. After Edward III's first parliament was dissolved on 9 March, the new king set off on pilgrimage to Canterbury, returning to Westminster before moving northwards, via Ramsey Abbey, to spend Easter with his mother at Peterborough. Prior to 1327, Edward's knowledge of the geography of power was rather limited. He had been north at least as far as York, west to Hereford and Bristol and, momentously, had made one visit to northern France and Hainault. Over the next few years the need to show himself to his new subjects, coupled with the exigencies of war, would give him a much greater acquaintance with his dominions, taking him on extensive progresses around the Midlands and East Anglia, on other briefer forays into southern counties from Kent to Wiltshire, to the northern extremities of County Durham and, across the Channel, to his mother's county of Ponthieu. On these journeys the king's entourage would take up residence in religious houses, episcopal palaces and aristocratic castles; sometimes, the entire party had to sleep in requisitioned cottages and tents. Until 1330 Edward made little use of any of his own major residences outside the capital; Windsor was not much frequented by the king in this period, though it was the venue for celebrations after Queen Philippa's coronation and for a great council in 1329. Some parts of the kingdom and dominions remained neglected: Edward was never to set foot in Devon and Cornwall, in Cheshire and Lancashire, or in Wales, Ireland and Aquitaine. But it was undoubtedly in the weeks and months that followed his coronation that the new king first acquired an understanding of the traditions of itinerant kingship inherited from his Angevin predecessors and developed the know-how of a constant and often intrepid traveller.[49]

* * *

[47] Baldwin, 'King's Council', 135–6; C. Given-Wilson, 'Royal Charter Witness Lists, 1327–1399', *Medieval Prosopography*, xii² (1991), 61–71.

[48] BL, MS Cotton Faustina B. V, fol. 50v.

[49] Shenton, 'English Court', 123–33; C. Shenton, *The Itinerary of Edward III and his Household, 1327–1345* (List and Index Society, cccxviii, 2007), 15–65, 125–31.

Once the initial excitement of the coronation parliament was over, business of state was dominated for most of 1327 by foreign affairs. The Anglo-French peace proposals in which Queen Isabella and Prince Edward had played such an important part had faltered even as they were apparently being brought to conclusion. In October 1325, the robust English soldier Sir Oliver Ingham had been appointed seneschal of Gascony and had begun a series of incursions into the reoccupied territories in the Agenais and Saintonge. By February 1327, the English government had very real concerns that Charles IV's forces would make a sustained attack on the loyal Plantagenet heartlands in Gascony and Guyenne, and Bishops Stratford and Airmyn, the earl of Richmond and John of Hainault were dispatched to effect an urgent peace. Terms were agreed on 31 March and were probably reported to the king during the great council held at Stamford on 19 April.[50]

The precise status of the 1327 treaty of Paris is somewhat uncertain. It was proclaimed in Gascony in September, but its detailed contents seem not to have been publicized in England. There were good reasons for such caution, for the terms were potentially ruinous. Edward III was to be left in control of the coastal zone in Gascony between Bordeaux and Bayonne. But the remainder of greater Aquitaine, including Ingham's recent reconquests, was to be returned to Capetian control. To the relief of £15,000 demanded in 1325 was now added a bill for reparations running to 50,000 marks.[51] It was subsequently claimed that the intransigent Charles IV had sought to make it impossible for the English to re-establish legal title to any of their lands in south-western France without paying the sums demanded in 1327.[52] It is thus easy to see why the new settlement came to be so roundly criticized during the majority regime of Edward III. There was a particularly bitter irony to the apparent abandonment of English efforts to secure the French territories promised by the settlement of 1259. One of the charges levied against Edward II in the recent articles of deposition was that he had neglected his responsibilities to the duchy of Aquitaine. Now his usurpers were presiding over the effective dismemberment of that same dominion.[53]

The crown was driven to accept the ruinous peace with France by the prospect of yet more urgent military engagement on England's northern border. On the night of 1 February 1327, a Scottish force had crossed the

<hr/>

[50] Déprez, *Préliminaires*, 22–3; Haines, *Stratford*, 189–90; Vale, *Angevin Legacy*, 246–7; E 101/309/37. It is likely that C 47/28/1, no. 37, titled *Cedula missa de partibus Francie* and listing various texts needed by unnamed commissioners (including the forms of homage made for Aquitaine to Philip V and Charles IV), was dispatched to England by this mission, which from internal evidence must date from before the accession of Philip VI.

[51] *Foedera*, II.ii, 700–1; Vale, *Angevin Legacy*, 248.

[52] C 47/28/5, no. 5.

[53] Sumption, i, 102.

Tweed and stormed Norham castle. The timing of the event, within hours of Edward III's coronation, was taken as a direct affront to the new king's dignity and legitimacy.[54] On 15 February Henry Percy, Ralph Neville and others were appointed to enforce the existing Anglo-Scottish truce, which was duly confirmed on 6 March.[55] But serious plans for a campaign were put in place, and a major muster was ordered at Newcastle upon Tyne in mid-April. This was the first and last time that Edward III demanded the traditional feudal service owed by his tenants-in-chief. The crown had just agreed in parliament to abandon some of Edward II's more contentious experiments in conscripting both cavalry and foot for his armies of Scotland and France. The use of the feudal summons, together with a traditional array of infantry promised wages from the time that they left their own counties, was therefore an important means of advertising the new regime's commitment to those promises.[56]

In the event, the muster was much delayed. The king and his mother had held a great council at Stamford on 19 April and had then proceeded to York, arriving in late May and passing the whole of June in the northern capital. The visit to England's second city was one of some political importance: the mayor and citizens, and the dean of the minster, presented ceremonial bowls at the king's triumphal entry.[57] The royal household was now joined by a number of military contingents, including a significant force of 500 Netherlandish knights under the leadership of John of Hainault.[58] The makeshift army was not well disciplined, and the foreigners were accused of running amok in the streets of York.[59] Meanwhile, news that at least three separate Scottish war bands had crossed the border led to a change of plan, and additional contingents were gathered at York in order to allow an advance across the Tees against the army of Sir James Douglas. In early July the king's uncle, the earl of Norfolk, wrote to inform him of a night-time raid launched by the Scots into Cumberland; he had been kept from his bed that night, and would have to stay on guard again the next lest they repeat their tricks.[60] It was

[54] *Chron. Lanercost*, 258–9.

[55] *Foedera*, II.ii, 689; *CPR 1327–30*, pp. 20, 25; R. Nicholson, *Edward III and the Scots: The Formative Years of a Military Career* (Oxford, 1965), 15–16.

[56] *SR*, i, 255; A. R. Prince, 'The Army and Navy', *Eng. Govt at Work*, i, 344–8; M. Powicke, *Military Obligation in Medieval England* (Oxford, 1962), 159–61; N. B. Lewis, 'The Summons of the English Feudal Levy, 5 April 1327', *Essays Presented to Bertie Wilkinson*, ed. Sandquist and Powicke, 236–49.

[57] E 101/383/8, fol. 21v; E 361/2, m. 30d. The bowl presented by the dean was decorated with the arms of the Mauleys, a local aristocratic family: see GEC, viii, 560–8.

[58] Prince, 'Army and Navy', 347. For armour provided for the king for this campaign see E 101/383/19.

[59] Le Bel, i, 39–47; Murimuth, 53; *Anon. Chron. 1307–34*, 136–7; *VCH Yorks: City of York*, 55, 56.

[60] *CDS*, iii, no. 920.

in this highly charged atmosphere that the young king bade farewell to his
mother and siblings, who were to remain at York for the duration, and
embarked on his first official military expedition.[61]

During the second half of July, the English army desperately sought to
cut off the Scottish forces and provoke open battle. Yet everywhere they
moved, the Scots managed to evade them. Arriving in the Wear valley at
the end of the month and taking up a position at Stanhope, Edward
narrowly escaped capture when Douglas raided the encampment; later
tradition spun a dramatic story of the Scottish leader hacking his way
right up to the royal tent and the boy-king fleeing for life. Then, on the
night of 6–7 August, the Scots surreptitiously stole away and headed
home. Edward III had now seen two military campaigns – his mother's
invasion of England, and his own pursuit of the Scots – yet was still
without the blooding of a battle. A number of the chroniclers commented
that the young king wept tears of frustration.[62] There was equally dispiriting news from Ireland, where Robert Bruce had moved earlier in the
spring in order to create a further distraction.[63] A parliament was called to
convene at Lincoln in mid-September and discuss the urgent situation.
Meanwhile, Edward III's own force, hungry and weary, returned south.
After holding a tournament at Clipstone in Sherwood Forest at the end of
August, the king and his mother retired to Nottingham to await events.[64]

In the midst of the Scottish incursion came the equally troubling rumour
that the earl of Mar, who had been brought up at the English court, was
plotting to set Edward II back on his throne.[65] In April 1327 the captive
king had been moved from Kenilworth to Berkeley, there to be held in
secure custody by the lord of the castle, the recently restored Sir Thomas
Berkeley, and the steward of the royal household, Sir John Maltravers. At
least two other plots to release the ex-king were revealed during the
following spring and summer. In the first, led by Thomas Dunheved, the
conspirators managed to breach the defences of Berkeley and actually
allowed the ex-king to escape briefly to Corfe.[66] When news reached the
court in early September of a further restoration conspiracy hatched in
South Wales by Sir Rhys ap Gruffydd, Roger Mortimer decided to take
matters into his own hands. His henchmen William Ogle and Sir Thomas
Gurney were sent to Berkeley where, in conspiracy with Maltravers, they

[61] Le Bel, i, 63–77; Doherty, 'Isabella, Queen of England', 218; E 403/228, 23 Sept. 1327.
[62] *Chron. Lanercost*, 260; *Scalacronica*, 99; *Brut*, i, 251.
[63] C. McNamee, *The Wars of the Bruces: Scotland, England and Ireland, 1306–1328* (East
Linton, 1997), 242–5.
[64] *RDP*, iv, 376–8; E 101/383/3.
[65] T. F. Tout, *Collected Papers*, 3 vols (Manchester, 1932–4), iii, 145–90; Nicholson, *Edward
III and the Scots*, 13–14, 46.
[66] *Ann. Paulini*, 337; F. J. Tanquerey, 'The Conspiracy of Thomas Dunheved, 1327', *EHR*,
xxi (1916), 119–24.

put the hapless Edward of Caernarfon to death on 21 September. Messengers bearing the fateful news of the ex-king's demise – though not the traumatic circumstances of it – arrived in Edward III's presence at Lincoln the following night.[67]

The colourful tale of Edward II's murder has become a great set piece of fourteenth-century political history. The best-remembered element of the story is the gruesome method of murder, in which a red-hot iron rod was reputedly pushed through a 'trumpet' up the king's rectum. This particular detail was not widely reported in Edward III's own time, though it may still have been part of a popular tradition that fitted the punishment to the crime and imagined the ex-king as having been effectively sodomized to death.[68] For the past hundred years and more, some historians have in any case been rather more intrigued by a counter-narrative in which Edward II did not die at all, but lived on for another decade and more in self-imposed exile.[69] If, as has been argued, Edward III was told of his father's survival within weeks of the events at Berkeley, some serious implications arise for his own personal integrity.[70] But in point of fact, there is no direct evidence that such rumours reached the young king before the spring of 1330. It therefore remains entirely plausible that Edward III acted in good faith in organizing a royal funeral for the corpse found at Berkeley in September 1327. Above all, it needs to be emphasized that there were very few people in England who ever doubted after this date that Edward II was indeed dead, and fewer still who had cause to mourn his passing. The rumours of a royal survival, like the earlier speculations about a restoration, are really only significant in what they tell us about a descent into the refuge of fantasy by those so rapidly disillusioned by the negative impact of the revolution of 1327 and the floundering regime of Isabella and Mortimer.

The Lincoln parliament that sat between 15 and 23 September 1327 was persuaded of the continued threat from Scotland and granted Edward III his first direct tax, in the form of a twentieth of moveable property, for the defence of the northern border.[71] Some desultory preparations were made for further hostilities against the Scots.[72] But the government's main concern was to clear existing debts. In her confident espousal of martial

---

[67] Phillips, *Edward II*, 548 and n. 164.

[68] W. M. Ormrod, 'The Sexualities of Edward II', and I. Mortimer, 'Sermons of Sodomy: A Reconsideration of Edward II's Sodomitical Reputation', *The Reign of Edward II: New Perspectives*, ed. G. Dodd and A. Musson (York, 2006), 21–47, 48–60. This form of death, like suffocation, would also have had the advantage of leaving no external marks on the body: M. Evans, *The Death of Kings: Royal Deaths in Medieval England* (London, 2003), 127.

[69] Mortimer, *Greatest Traitor*, 244–64; I. Mortimer, 'The Death of Edward II in Berkeley Castle', *EHR*, cxx (2005), 1175–214.

[70] I. Mortimer, *The Perfect King: The Life of Edward III* (London, 2006), 66.

[71] *PROME*, iv, 82–3.

[72] Nicholson, *Edward III and the Scots*, 46.

values, Isabella had committed war wages of over £8,000 to the invasion of 1326 and at least £9,000 to the Weardale campaign of 1327.[73] But she had already been obliged to draw down over £50,000 from the personal treasure of Edward II to support these and other burdens. With both the lay tax and the accompanying clerical tenth heavily mortgaged to pay off Edward II's creditors, there was no realistic chance of another major engagement in the north.[74] Nor, evidently, was there much pressure to maintain the fight: such was the poverty into which the recent Scottish raids had plunged the border region that the county community of Northumberland claimed it would be unable even to pay the expenses of its parliamentary representatives, let alone offer any taxes.[75] The English government accordingly informed the Scots that it wished to come to terms. A truce was established, ambassadors for peace were appointed, and another parliament was called to meet at York on 7 February.[76]

The Lincoln assembly had been dissolved on the very day that news of Edward II's death reached the king,[77] and elaborate preparations were at once put in place for a funeral fitting to an abdicated monarch. From Nottingham, Edward removed through the West Midlands to Gloucester Abbey, where his father's body was buried with due pomp on 20 December 1327.[78] The site represented a suitable compromise. Edward II was to be denied interment at the emerging royal mausoleum of Westminster Abbey, but would have the dignity of burial in a church with strong royal associations, the burial place of Robert Curthose, son of the Conqueror, and the location of Henry III's coronation.[79] A novelty of the ceremony was the use of a funeral effigy, a wooden, life-sized mannequin

[73] E 101/382/9; E 159/104, rot. 82d; J. F. Willard, *Parliamentary Taxes on Personal Property, 1290 to 1334* (Cambridge, Mass., 1934), 21–2. These were only partly covered by the forced loan on wool exports authorized in the spring of 1327, which raised £7,400: W. M. Ormrod, 'The Crown and the English Economy, 1290–1348', *Before the Black Death: Studies in the 'Crisis' of the Early Fourteenth Century*, ed. B. M. S. Campbell (Manchester, 1991), 168. For the particular problem of Isabella's indebtedness to John of Hainault see E. B. Fryde, *Studies in Medieval Trade and Finance* (London, 1983), chap. iv, 202–3, 206–7, 210.

[74] Fryde, *Tyranny*, 209; J. F. Willard, 'The Crown and its Creditors, 1327–33', *EHR*, xlii (1927), 12–19; W. E. Lunt, 'The Collectors of Clerical Subsidies Granted to the King by the English Clergy', *Eng. Govt at Work*, ii, 262.

[75] C 219/5, part 1, file 1. Northumberland, Cumberland and Westmorland were exempted from the twentieth: J. F. Willard, 'The Taxes upon Moveables of the Reign of Edward III', *EHR*, xxx (1915), 72.

[76] *Rot. Scot.*, i, 223, 224; *Foedera*, II.ii, 724, 728; *RDP*, iv, 378–80; Nicholson, *Edward III and the Scots*, 47–8.

[77] DL 10/253, cited by Mortimer, *Perfect King*, 407. For further dating evidence see Haines, *Stratford*, 191.

[78] 'Documents relating to the Death and Burial of King Edward II', ed. S. A. Moore, *Archaeologia*, l (1887), 215–26. On leaving Nottingham on 11 Nov. the king ordered that swift attention be paid to the deficiencies in the fabric of the castle: E 159/104, rot. 26.

[79] M. Biddle, 'Seasonal Festivals and Residence: Winchester, Westminster and Gloucester in the Tenth to Twelfth Centuries', *Anglo-Norman Studies*, viii (1985), 51–72.

representing the deceased king, which was placed on top of the coffin. It is obviously tempting to suggest that this was done in order that the face of the dead body could remain covered and its true identity undiscovered. On the other hand, the long delay between death and burial that was a normal feature of royal funerals necessitated the full embalming of the body, and the failure to expose the visage of Edward II created no speculation in itself. The mannequin was dressed in the robes that Edward of Caernarfon had worn at his coronation in 1308, and adorned with regalia – crown, sceptre and rod – provided from the royal treasury. Its principal function, therefore, was to represent the legitimacy of Edward II's rule and thus, by extension, that of his son.[80] As a further act of deference, and in recognition of the new ruler's tender years, Edward III probably sat with his mother in a private pew while the bishops and lords performed the obsequies and only took presidency of the occasion at the funeral repast that followed. Once these proper observations were completed, the royal family moved on to spend Christmas at Worcester, where they no doubt remarked the tomb of that other great blot on the record of post-Conquest monarchy, King John. The monks of the cathedral priory, anxious not to pass up the opportunity of the royal visit, eagerly sought out Edward III's support in their attempt to have their prior, Wulfstan Bransford, accepted as the new bishop.[81]

Throughout this period, the young king's attention was much taken up with preparations for his impending marriage. The dynastic alliance sealed at Mons in 1326 had reaped military dividends for Isabella and Mortimer in their invasion of England and in the Weardale campaign, and it was time for the English to carry out their side of the bargain.[82] The necessary papal dispensations were produced during the summer, and the terms were finally confirmed by the bishop of Coventry and Lichfield at Valenciennes at the end of October.[83] Philippa of Hainault arrived in London late in 1327 and, amidst much public celebration, was lodged at the bishop of Ely's town house in Holborn.[84] There is little indication of Philippa's appearance or personality at this defining moment in her life: a surviving description of one of the count of Hainault's daughters, which

[80] For the various interpretations that have been attached to this novelty, see P. Lindley, *Gothic to Renaissance: Essays on Sculpture in England* (Stamford, 1995), 97–112; J. Burden, 'Rewriting a Rite of Passage: The Peculiar Funeral of Edward II', *Rites of Passage: Cultures of Transition in the Fourteenth Century*, ed. N. F. McDonald and W. M. Ormrod (York, 2004), 13–29. For an explicit reference to the delivery to Gloucester of 'the vestments in which Edward, king of England, father of the present king used on the day of his coronation', see E 403/232, 19 Dec. 1327.

[81] *Fasti 1300–1541*, iv, 56.

[82] *CPR 1327–30*, 179.

[83] *CPL*, ii, 260; E 101/309/38; E 403/232, 4 Mar. 1328; Petit, 'Mariage de Philippa de Hainault', 380–1.

[84] *Ann. Paulini*, 338–9; *Bridlington*, 99; *CPR 1327–30*, 190. For gifts from the city of London to the new queen see *CLBL, E*, 216–17.

refers to the girl's dark complexion, brown eyes, good physical form and pronounced overbite, has often been thought to refer to the future queen of England, but is in fact much more likely to be a pen-portrait of Philippa's older sister, Margaret.[85] In any case, looks were now much less important than politics: in the face of a continued stand-off with the court of France, the English alliance with Hainault was the one diplomatic constant to which Isabella, and perforce her son, could now cling.

The royal wedding was celebrated, unusually, at York. Walter Reynolds had died in November and, with a vacancy in the archbishopric of Canterbury, it was decided that the nuptials ought to be performed by England's second archbishop, William Melton, in his own archiepiscopal church.[86] On 27 December Philippa accordingly left London for the north. The wedding ceremony took place in York Minster on 26 January 1328, with the general festivities spreading over a number of days.[87] In spite of the cash crisis of the moment, the event was celebrated in a manner scarcely less ostentatious than at the king's coronation a year before. Gold, silver and jewels were purchased in Paris in preparation for the event; over £2,400 was paid out to the Bardi of Florence for other plate and jewels; Queen Isabella received a new set of robes from the king's household; and lavish cloth of gold was purchased to decorate the dais and throne.[88] In the midst of the liturgy and feasting came the required formal exchange of gifts between the newly married couple. The obliging Philippa presented her husband with an illuminated manuscript containing, among other things, copies of two motets that were probably performed at the wedding.[89]

There remained important questions about the status to be accorded to the new consort. Philippa of Hainault's age remains something of a mystery: she could have been born anywhere between 1310 and 1315, and may thus have been a little older, or a little younger, than her fifteen-

[85] *The Register of Walter de Stapeldon, Bishop of Exeter (A.D. 1307–1326)*, ed. F. C. Hingeston-Randolph (London, 1892), 169; D. Trotter, 'Walter of Stapeldon and the Pre-marital Inspection of Philippa of Hainault', *French Studies Bulletin*, xlix (1993), 1–4. The reference to the complexion of the young woman as *brune*, and certain other of her features as described in this letter, have led to the widely circulated modern notion that Philippa was black, or of black ancestry.

[86] Melton's reluctance to preside in the southern province is explained by the long-standing dispute over whether the archbishop of York had a right to exercise metropolitan jurisdiction there. See R. M. Haines, *Ecclesia Anglicana: Studies in the English Church of the Later Middle Ages* (Toronto, 1989), 69–105.

[87] *Anon. Chron. 1307–34*, 139; Shenton, 'English Court', 148–50. E 101/383/20 records relatively heavy expenditure of £114 and £191 in the king's hall on 25 and 26 Jan. The exchequer was ordered to make account with Nicholas Huggate for special costs in relation to the wedding: E 159/104, rot. 64.

[88] E 101/383/14, m. 1; E 403/240, 27 Jan. 1329; L. Monnas, 'Silk Cloths Purchased for the Great Wardrobe of the Kings of England, 1325–1462', *Textile History*, xx (1989), 284.

[89] Wathey, 'Marriage of Edward III', 1–29.

year-old husband.[90] Under Church law, the couple are likely to have been considered ready to consummate their marriage. But royal practice often delayed the beginning of sexual activity until the female was at least fourteen, and it seems likely that Philippa was kept from her new husband's bed for at least a year after their ceremonial union.[91] The grant of 1,000 marks for the expenses of the young queen's chamber in April 1329 may hint at some change in this regard.[92] But she continued to be denied her own independent household for at least a year after this. Behind these arrangements lay the heavy hand of Queen Isabella, who now had to balance her son's desire for the swift production of an heir against her own equal determination to continue in the role of consort. Philippa would need, at some point, to be provided with a queenly dower and crowned at Westminster Abbey. But preliminary preparations for the latter event were rapidly called off in mid-February 1328, and for two years the new queen remained in a kind of limbo, without a crown or an estate of her own.[93] The infantilizing of Queen Philippa stands as one of the most remarkable elements in Isabella of France's increasingly obsessive efforts to maintain power and influence over the new regime. It takes little imagination to appreciate its likely impact on her future personal relations with both her son and her daughter-in-law.

The early months of 1328 continued to be occupied with the matter of Scotland. The February parliament at York remained in session for a month, but with no immediate sign of a way forward in negotiations with Bruce, the king dismissed the assembly and called another to meet at Northampton on 24 April. The court moved south into Nottinghamshire and Lincolnshire and spent Easter at the Gilbertine priory of Sempringham. Here Edward III made the acquaintance of one of the house's longest-standing inmates, Gwenllian, daughter of the last independent prince of Wales, Llewelyn ap Gruffydd.[94] On 17 March a group of English envoys led by the bishops of Lincoln and Norwich and Lord Percy finally reached an agreement on a lasting peace with the Scots, duly ratified by the Scottish parliament at Edinburgh. The terms were even more damaging to English interests and pride than those recently incurred in the settlement with the French. Edward III would abandon the policy followed by the English crown since 1296 by renouncing his right to treat Scotland as a conquered territory and

---

[90] *ODNB*, xliv, 34; Mortimer, *Perfect King*, 403–4.

[91] Froissart, i, 76, 287, believed that Philippa was quickly removed from Edward's presence and taken back to London after the wedding.

[92] *CPR 1327–30*, 389, E 403/243, 30 May 1329.

[93] Shenton, 'English Court', 145–8. Philippa was promised dower lands to the value of £3,000 at the time of her betrothal, but nothing was done about this until the time of her coronation: *Foedera*, II.ii, 743; *CPR 1327–30*, 270, 501.

[94] J. B. Smith, *Llywelyn ap Gruffudd, Prince of Wales* (Cardiff, 1998), 579–80, 586. For the king's grants and gifts to Gwenllian and to the prior of Sempringham on this occasion, see E 159/105, rot. 36; E 101/384/7.

instead would openly recognize Robert Bruce as legitimate ruler of an independent northern kingdom. The two realms would undertake to support each other against their enemies, but the Scots would be allowed to retain their long-standing alliance with the French recently confirmed at Corbeil in 1326. The new settlement was to be guaranteed by the marriage of Robert's heir, the four-year-old Prince David, to Edward's young sister, Joan. As with Aquitaine, so now with Scotland: Isabella and Mortimer, who had deposed Edward II on the grounds of his inability to maintain his father's foreign dominions, were presiding over the veritable dismemberment of the Plantagenet empire. Not surprisingly, the resulting settlement was soon being dubbed by Edward III's subjects the 'shameful peace'.[95]

Edward's council was in no position to challenge these proposals, and the ensuing parliament of Northampton was induced to accept the treaty in its entirety on 4 May. (This explains why what the Scots called the treaty of Edinburgh was more usually known on the English side as the treaty of Northampton.) Two small concessions made it possible to placate the otherwise restive polity. Edward's government was offered 20,000 marks by way of compensation for the Scots' recent devastation of the northern English counties. And English lords with interests in Scotland were offered some expectation that they would yet be able to retain their lands north of the border.[96] Neither of these sweeteners was, however, to amount to much. Henry Percy managed to secure recognition of his Scottish titles by the newly ascendant Bruce regime, but the subsequent defection of other leading cross-border magnates from Isabella's cause meant that the English crown was disinclined to press their cases any further.[97] It is also doubtful that Bruce paid anything other than a small contribution towards the promised reparations, though this did not prevent Edward III from subsequently accusing the unscrupulous Mortimer of pocketing the entire proceeds.[98] Sharing his subjects' strong sense of humiliation, Edward III now gave tacit support to the successful resistance mounted by the Londoners and the abbot of Westminster to the proposal that the Stone of Scone, confiscated by Edward I and incorporated into the English coronation chair, should be returned to Robert I.[99] One of the young king's

[95] Murimuth, 56; Avesbury, 283; Baker, 40; *Brut*, i, 255–6; Nicholson, *Edward III and the Scots*, 54–5.

[96] *ASR*, 328–41; E. L. G. Stones, 'The Treaty of Northampton, 1328', *History*, xxxviii (1953), 54–61; J. Scammell, 'Robert I and the North of England', *EHR*, lxxiv (1958), 385–403.

[97] S. Cameron and A. Ross, 'The Treaty of Edinburgh and the Disinherited (1328–1332)', *History*, lxxxiv (1999), 237–56.

[98] *PROME*, iv, 105.

[99] *CPMR 1323–64*, 63, 65; WAM, 51112; *English Coronation Records*, ed. L. G. Wickham Legge (London, 1901), 77–8; Baker, 40–1; *Chron. Meaux*, ii, 361; Doherty, 'Isabella, Queen of England', 249–50. The Black Rood of Scotland seems to have been returned, only to be taken again by the English at Neville's Cross: E. L. G. Stones, 'An Addition to the "Rotuli Scotiae" ', *Scottish Historical Review*, xxix (1950), 33; *Scalacronica*, 101; *Antient Kalendars*, i, 160.

first open displays of discontent with his mother's direction of policy was his refusal to grant his infant sister a dowry. His decision not to attend the nuptials held, in his mother's presence, at Berwick in mid-July was as much to do with protocol as with petulance, for Robert Bruce was known to be seriously indisposed and would therefore not attend to represent regal authority on his side. Nevertheless, it is easy to see why Edward's skulking around the West Midlands during the summer of 1328 was readily interpreted in his own lifetime as an emphatic statement of determined opposition to the whole sorry episode.[100]

One reason why the parliament of Northampton was prepared to accept an otherwise obviously ruinous settlement with the Scots was the prospect that this might allow the crown at last to turn its attention properly to the general state of disorder prevailing within England. Already in 1327 the minority administration had revived the practice of appointing standing 'keepers of the peace' in the shires, charged to receive suspected criminals and hold them until the arrival of the justices of gaol delivery in the local area.[101] The 1328 Statute of Northampton, which addressed a range of issues in the administration of criminal justice, subsequently came to be seen as something of a landmark in English legal history.[102] It included an important statement that the king and nobles had sworn in parliament to keep the peace, assist royal justices and desist from the practice of maintenance (that is, interfering in the courts to protect their followers from liability to prosecution). Its main aim, however, was to set up a series of general commissions of oyer and terminer ('to hear and determine'), headed by senior lawyers from the central courts, which would visit the shires, hear the charges against alleged criminals held in the local gaols and make more general investigations into common lawlessness. Such wider-ranging commissions had, since Edward's I's time, been nicknamed 'trailbastons' from the clubs or bastons carried by criminal gangs. Trailbastons were perceived by provincial political society as a distinctly mixed blessing, not least because they were often accompanied by inquiries into the local official corruption that so often condoned the violent crimes perpetrated by influential people. Unfortunately for the

---

[100] *Ann. Paulini*, 341, *Bridlington*, 98–9; *Chron. Lanercost*, 261–2; Nicholson, *Edward III and the Scots*, 51–2; Barrow, *Robert Bruce*, 260. Isabella, en route to Berwick, presided over a council meeting at Pontefract on 3 June and travelled on via Durham: SC 1/36/90; E 403/237, 16 July 1328. The commitment to the marriage of Princess Joan was later thought to comprise one of Mortimer's acts of treason against the crown: P. R. Dryburgh, 'The Career of Roger Mortimer, First Earl of March (*c.*1287–1330)' (University of Bristol PhD thesis, 2002), 126 n. 131.

[101] *PROME*, iv, 21, 25; *SR*, i, 257; A. Verduyn, 'The Politics of Law and Order during the Early Years of Edward III', *EHR*, cviii (1993), 842–67.

[102] *SR*, i, 257–8; E. L. G. Stones, 'Sir Geoffrey le Scrope (*c.*1280 to 1340), Chief Justice of the King's Bench', *EHR*, lxix (1954), 9–11; A. Musson, *Public Order and Law Enforcement: The Local Administration of Criminal Justice, 1294–1350* (Woodbridge, 1996), 55–6, 108–10.

reputation of the minority, the crown's newly advertised determination to re-establish effective public order was all too obviously short-lived, and fewer than half the counties of England were covered before the trailbastons collapsed, under political pressure, at the end of 1328.[103] The failure of this obvious attempt to win back the confidence of the polity simply added, in the short term, to the growing sense of political disillusionment with the work of the new regime.

Edward III was to be subjected to a good deal more humiliation before he was able finally to wrest control from Isabella and Mortimer. The material poverty of his regime began to become painfully evident once the treaties with France and Scotland removed the possibility of further extraordinary taxes. Having exhausted the huge cash resources left by Edward II, the queen now turned to the time-honoured resort of loans; between August 1328 and November 1330 the crown's main bankers, the Bardi of Florence, advanced at least £30,000 to support the king's household, the costs of diplomacy and the continuing burden of gifts and repayment of debts to Mortimer.[104] Throughout 1328–9 Edward was required to attend a series of ostentatious tournaments at Hereford, Ludlow, Bedford and Wigmore at which Mortimer brazenly paraded his supremacy over the crown.[105] The queen's man now set aside all pretence at modesty and began to consolidate a great bloc of territories and titles in the marches, making notably free with some of the great Welsh lordships recently confiscated from the younger Despenser and the earl of Arundel.[106] Only in September 1328 was the young king apparently allowed to absent himself briefly from his mother's side and undertake an independent progress, moving into East Anglia to visit the religious sites at Walsingham, Norwich, Thetford and Bury St Edmunds. But Isabella was her usual solicitous self, and quickly summoned her son to rejoin her at Cambridge for the journey south to a parliament summoned to Salisbury in October.[107] If in 1325 Edward of Windsor had accepted, and even welcomed, the refuge provided by his mother's arms, there is every reason to believe that by 1328 he felt increasingly infantilized and frustrated by maternal suffocation.

Many members of the elite believed that the Salisbury parliament was called for the sole purpose of Mortimer's further aggrandizement. Armed

[103] CPR 1327–30, 297.

[104] Fryde, Studies, chap. iv, 205–6.

[105] McKisack, Fourteenth Century, p. 97; Vale, Edward III and Chivalry, p. 172; Mortimer, Greatest Traitor, 225–6. Around the time of the Wigmore tournament of Sept. 1329, jousts were also held at Hereford, Gloucester and Worcester: E 101/384/6; E 101/384/7.

[106] G. A. Holmes, The Estates of the Higher Nobility in Fourteenth-Century England (Cambridge, 1957), 13.

[107] CPMR 1323–64, 80.

with his vast new endowment, Roger was ready to be elevated to the highest reaches of the nobility. Even so, the details proved a surprise and shock. The young king was now induced to bestow on the queen's lover not the earldom of Shrewsbury, as apparently planned, but the title of earl of March, an unprecedented style that had connotations of regalian authority throughout the marches of Wales. At the same time, Roger's determination to re-establish control over his ancestral lands in Ireland and to take effective political control of the lordship was advertised through the elevation of his protégé, James Butler, to the earldom of Ormond.[108] The third of the creations in the Salisbury parliament, the dubbing of the king's younger brother, John of Eltham, as earl of Cornwall, was something of a sop to those who distrusted Mortimer's motives. But it scarcely distracted from the very obvious comparisons now beginning to be made between Mortimer and the Despensers. For some of the nobility at least, there was now no alternative but openly to challenge the court and its creatures.

The hostile mood of the Salisbury parliament can hardly have taken Isabella and Mortimer by surprise. According to an official account of the resulting rupture sent to the citizens of London at the end of 1328, Henry of Lancaster had already emerged as a leading discontent during a council held at Worcester in mid-June.[109] Lancaster had also refused, very publicly, to attend either the great council at York at the end of July or the Salisbury parliament in October. As the court had made its way south after the York council, Earl Henry had appeared before the king at Barlings in Lincolnshire with an armed force of retainers. Around the same time the earl's associates, Thomas Wake and John Stratford, had informed the Londoners of his grievances: the king was badly advised, had no good counsel about him, and had been deprived of the resources even to support his own household. It was Mortimer's new title bestowed at Salisbury that really forced Lancaster into open opposition. From his subsequent base at Winchester, Earl Henry sent out a series of stinging accusations. Mortimer, he claimed, had made the injurious peace with the Scots with the sole and malicious intention of proceeding to destroy his enemy of Lancaster. The new earl of March swore that he bore Henry no ill will, and Bishops Stratford and Gravesend agreed to mediate for reconciliation. But they returned with yet another set of demands: the king should have resources to live of his own; the queen should support herself from her own dower; there should be a clampdown on the wave of violent crime supposedly flooding the realm; and the continual council ordained in the parliament of 1327 should be confirmed and reinstated. It was Henry of Lancaster's finest hour. But in the face of such powerful

---

[108] *CChR 1327–41, 94*; *CPR 1327–30*, 336; GEC, viii, 439 and n. (h).
[109] For what follows see *CPMR 1323–64*, 77–83; *PROME*, iv, 92–4; Haines, *Stratford*, 196–8.

assertions of political principle, the crown's response was as petulant as it was inflammatory: it was the earl's own withdrawal from parliament and council that was now declared the one and true cause of the crisis.

It was in this uneasy state of impasse that the parliament was called to an end. As the royal party passed Winchester en route back to London, a great force of Lancaster's men, armed in manner of war, came out of the city to jeer and intimidate the queen and her lover.[110] Earl Henry made off quickly to the Midlands to gather his forces from the Lancastrian strongholds of Higham Ferrers, Leicester and Kenilworth. The queen and her lover took the king west to mark the first anniversary of Edward II's funeral at Gloucester and spend Christmas, as in the previous year, at Worcester, which now also provided a convenient location from which, if necessary, to call out Mortimer's marcher retainers. The stage was set for open war.

In the face of this imminent emergency, the king's uncles of Norfolk and Kent took it upon themselves to summon the prelates to London to meet with some of Lancaster's allies, including Thomas Wake and William Trussell, and discuss an accommodation. But the royal earls were forced to acknowledge that the young Edward III, led astray by Mortimer, was acting contrary to Magna Carta and his coronation oath.[111] The statement had real force, for it played to the powerful notion that the baronage was entitled actively to resist an unreasonable regime. The new archbishop of Canterbury, Simon Meopham, addressed a letter on the same theme to the young king on 23 December. Rather than seeking to destroy his critics, Edward III should honour a strategy agreed at Salisbury and suspend all further discussion of the dispute between Lancaster and Mortimer until parliament reconvened. Meopham claimed to speak not just for those present at the London meeting but for 'the community of the people of the kingdom of England'.[112] There is more than a hint here, and in subsequent meetings between Lancaster and other disaffected parties, that the tradition of the sworn commune was being revived as part of a sustained campaign against Roger Mortimer.[113] Such open threats could hardly be countenanced, and on 29 December the king was required to announce his intention to proceed in arms against Lancaster. If this ultimatum was the work of the earl of March, it nonetheless impacted immediately on the person of Edward III. In anticipation of the impending battle, the king was provided with a new set of armour.[114]

[110] G. A. Holmes, 'The Rebellion of the Earl of Lancaster, 1328–9', *BIHR*, xxviii (1955), 88. Compare the account given in *CIM*, ii, no. 1039.

[111] *Anglia Sacra*, i, 368.

[112] *CPMR 1323–64*, 84; *Litterae Cantuariensis*, iii, 414–16; Holmes, 'Rebellion', 87 n. 9.

[113] *Ann. Paulini*, 344; Haines, *Stratford*, 202–3.

[114] *CPMR 1323–64*, 85–6; E 101/383/19. The queen also allegedly rode in arms: Haines, *Stratford*, 203.

Few of those implicated in Lancaster's conspiracy had the stomach for open rebellion, and the threat of royal reprisals had the desired effect. The wary Norfolk and his somewhat pusillanimous brother Kent disowned their cousin of Lancaster around the time that the king's party arrived at Leicester on 6 January. The hostile earls of March and Lancaster eventually confronted each other at Bedford, where Edward III was present on 20 and 21 January. But no lines were drawn, and no blood was spilled. The two sides submitted to the formal arbitration of the queen, and it was agreed once again that differences should be resolved by peaceful process in a future parliament. The avoidance of an affray allowed the crown to treat the rebels with leniency, and Earl Henry and most of his followers escaped the draconian penalties of forfeiture and execution. They were, however, forced to make humiliating oaths binding them to render large sums of money to the crown as surety for future good behaviour.[115] Furthermore, some seventy named men were specifically excluded from pardon. These included such notable figures as Thomas Wake, Thomas Roscelyn and the king's former tutor, Henry Beaumont, who were now forced to flee to exile on the continent. The begrudging magnanimity of the regime therefore appeased no one, and criticism of the earl of March's regime continued to grow steadily. Adam Orleton, who had secured the bishopric of Worcester earlier in 1328, had already fallen out with the court by the end of that year, and the formidable John Stratford, one of the chief architects of the revolution of 1327, now emerged as one of Mortimer's implacable enemies.[116]

For Edward III, the confrontation at Bedford had particularly bitter and ironic repercussions. Having experienced at first hand some of the dramatic consequences of the battle of Boroughbridge six years before, the young king was only too well aware how easily the new altercation with Thomas of Lancaster's brother might have descended into civil war. The episode had revealed the anomaly of his own position, at once accountable for, and yet unable to determine, the direction of policy. It had also exposed his continued dependence on his mother and her lover. Mortimer had saved the king from grave danger, acting at considerable personal risk and financial cost. The elaborate gifts that Edward was forced to bestow on the puffed-up earl of March in the weeks and months after Lancaster's rebellion indicate the extent of his indebtedness and, in some sense, the

---

[115] H. Knighton, *Chronicon Henrici Knighton*, ed. J. R. Lumby, 2 vols (RS, 1889–95), i, 450; *Anon. Chron. 1307–34*, 140–1; V. B. Redstone, 'Some Mercenaries of Henry of Lancaster, 1327–1330', *TRHS*, 3rd series, vii (1913), 163–4. The recognizances must already have been agreed by 21 Jan., but the record made on the close roll dated them on the first day of the reconvened parliament, 9 Feb.: E 159/106, rot. 43d; *CCR 1327–30*, 528–30; KB 27/280, *Rex*, rot. 22; KB 27/281, *Rex*, rot. 17; KB 27/282, *Rex*, rot. 20. Bishop Stratford was subsequently subjected to a charge of contempt and a fine of 1,000 marks: Haines, *Stratford*, 205–6.

[116] *Chron. Lanercost*, 265, 266; *Chron. Meaux*, ii, 359; Haines, *Orleton*, 161–88; Haines, *Stratford*, 191–214.

intensity of his personal humiliation. As late as August 1330 the king was still making arrangements to recompense the earl for expenditure undertaken in raising troops for the late 'riding' against the rebels at Bedford.[117] Others, too, understood this essential truth: private parties now began to write directly to the earl of March to seek his intervention in government.[118] Ironically, therefore, the collapse of the earl of Lancaster's rebellion served only to perpetuate the young Edward's subordination to the will of Roger Mortimer.

The political impasse reached in January 1329 had a permanent effect on the minority regime of Edward III. The parliament that reconvened at Westminster on 9 February failed to resolve the standing differences between the earls of Lancaster and March. The sullen mood of the prelates and lords left the queen and her lover increasingly distrustful of organized political gatherings. Between the dissolution of the parliament of February 1329 and the downfall of Roger Mortimer in late 1330, only one further full parliament was held, at Winchester in March 1330, and two great councils, in July 1329 at Windsor and July 1330 at Osney. The preference for meetings at provincial locations, always a feature of the minority, thus became more pronounced. With the exception of Philippa of Hainault's coronation in February 1330, Edward III seems to have stayed away – or, rather have been kept away – from London and Westminster for the entire period from February 1329 to November 1330.

There is little sense that the regular workings of government were compromised by this distance. The chancellor and chancery often followed in the wake of the court. In January 1329, for example, the king kept the great seal in his possession for a week at Northampton before returning it to Chancellor Burghersh and riding out against Lancaster at Bedford.[119] The moving court seems also to have included in its midst some of the members of the 1327 continual council who had not as yet fallen openly into dispute with Mortimer and the queen; the veteran earl of Surrey continued to draw his fee for remaining at the king's side in times of peace throughout 1329 and early 1330.[120] It was also during this period that Edward's long-standing confidant, Richard Bury, seems to have engineered a rather more active role for Edward in the daily business of state and the distribution of royal patronage. A striking hint of their compact comes in April 1330 when the king broke the convention against the use of the privy seal to interfere in the courts by ordering special bail for Bury's cousin, Thomas d'Augerville, one of the many minor lords

---

[117] E 159/107, rot. 23; Dryburgh, 'Career of Roger Mortimer', 133, 134. See also Fryde, *Studies*, chap. iv, 206.

[118] *Litterae Cantuariensis*, i, 292–5.

[119] *CCR 1327–30*, 425; B. Wilkinson, 'The Chancery', *Eng. Govt. at Work*, i, 195–6.

[120] *CCR 1327–30*, 445, 491; E 43/19.

who had been implicated and imprisoned after the earl of Lancaster's attempted rising.[121]

Nor was this period devoid of major initiatives in domestic administration. In the Windsor great council of 1329 the crown returned to the issue of public order. The king's advisers expressed interest in reviving the eyre, the special itinerant commissions that had been sent periodically into the shires during the thirteenth century. The eyre was preferred over the trailbastons of the previous years for the specific reason that it could be applied selectively and could therefore concentrate on those areas where the greatest problems were perceived to lie. The counties chosen for the first visitations, Northamptonshire and Nottinghamshire, sat in a region that had suffered major disruption during the civil war of 1321–2 and were close to the headquarters of some of the country's most notorious criminal gangs.[122] In practice, however, these good intentions were considerably blunted by the sheer comprehensiveness of the eyre. Far too much time was swallowed up in civil pleas and the investigation of royal rights. New eyres were announced in the spring of 1330 for Bedfordshire and Derbyshire. At this rate it would take a whole generation to visit the entirety of the kingdom, by which time the first targeted areas would simply, of course, have reverted to type. As in 1328, so in 1329, the minority government's eagerness to prove its law and order credentials tended only to expose the inadequacy of its methods.

For all the efficiency of moveable monarchy, then, it is hard to escape the conclusion that the young king's effective exile to the provinces caused his administration to lose touch with the public opinion that ought to help drive it. Nowhere were the results more obvious than in the capital. The Londoners may have given ready support to the coup of 1326–7, but they had also responded enthusiastically to Lancaster's protest movement in the winter of 1328–9. Continuing concerns about hostile conspiracies in the city led the crown to appoint an extraordinary judicial inquiry under two of Mortimer's most prominent supporters, Oliver Ingham and John Maltravers, in February 1329. This, as the Londoners were quick to point out, was in direct contravention of the charter of liberties granted at the time of the king's succession two years earlier.[123] Edward III's physical remoteness from the natural heart of royal power therefore served only to expose the increasing insecurity of his kingship and the

[121] KB 27/280, Rex, rot. 14d; W. M. Ormrod, 'The King's Secrets: Richard de Bury and the Monarchy of Edward III', *War, Government and Aristocracy in the British Isles, c.1150–1500*, ed. A. Kettle, C. Given-Wilson and L. E. Scales (Woodbridge, 2008), 168, 170–1.

[122] H. M. Cam, *Liberties and Communities in Medieval England* (London, 1963), 150–62; D. Crook, 'The Later Eyres', *EHR*, xcvii (1982), 241–68; *The Eyre of Northamptonshire 3–4 Edward III, A.D. 1329–1330*, ed. D. W. Sutherland, 2 vols (Selden Society, xcvii, cxviii, 1983–4).

[123] *CPR 1327–30*, 359, 423; G. A. Williams, *Medieval London: From Commune to Capital* (London, 1963), 301–2.

continued reluctance of his mother to allow him a public and active role within it.

Another no less dramatic indicator of nervousness was Mortimer's attempt to infiltrate his agents into Edward's immediate social circle. Maltravers, who had been deeply implicated in the murder of Edward II, was restored to the stewardship of the king's household in February 1329. His successor in the summer of 1330, Hugh Turplington, was also a conspicuous henchman of the earl of March. A third man, John Wyard, was later publicly named as one of the spies set by Mortimer around the king.[124] It was in these increasingly stifling conditions that Edward III began to put to the test the friendships made over the previous few years. In a secret letter written early in 1330, the king set out a mechanism by which the pope might be able to identify business that genuinely represented his personal wishes: all such correspondence would contain the code-words *Pater sancte* ('Holy Father'), written in the king's own hand. The letter, penned by Richard Bury, stated that the only people who would know about this new scheme were William Montagu and Bury himself, 'both of whom, we are sure, will keep it secret in all cases'. The king then scrawled *Pater sancte* across the bottom as a sample autograph. The letter, which still survives in the papal archives, stands as vivid testimony to the desperate subterfuges that Edward III was driven to undertake during the last months of Mortimer's ascendancy.[125]

As in 1325, so in 1329, it was relations with France that provided Edward with the most obvious opportunity to undertake the public functions of monarchy. In February 1328 the last of his Capetian uncles, Charles IV, had died, leaving no direct male heir. Since Charles's widow, Jeanne of Evreux, was pregnant, an interregnum was announced under the presidency of the deceased king's cousin, Philip of Valois. But when Jeanne was delivered of a daughter on 1 April, the question arose as to whether reason of state required that the succession should override the rights of girls and women in preference for adult males. There were three potential claimants: Philip of Valois, his cousin Philip of Evreux, and Edward III. No time was lost, and the emergency assembly convened by Valois on 2 April delivered the predictable outcome, agreeing that the regent himself should assume the throne as Philip VI. Little is known as to the precise arguments put forward in favour of Philip's candidacy. No attempt was made formally to entail the French throne in the male line, and there is no evidence that the Salic law was explicitly debated between French and English diplomats until the very end of the

---

[124] *PROME*, iv, 103; Tout, *Chapters*, iii, 18–19.

[125] *EMDP*, I.i, no. 18; *CPL*, ii, 497; C. G. Crump, 'The Arrest of Roger Mortimer and Queen Isabel', *EHR*, xxvi (1911), 331–2; Ormrod, 'The King's Secrets', 166–7.

fourteenth century.[126] It is much more likely that the French nobility saw the exigencies of the moment as the primary justification for preferring Philip. As if Edward III's status as king of England was not sufficient reason in itself to reject him, there was also the appalling prospect that Queen Isabella, that usurper of her own husband's divinely ordained kingship, would doubtless intend to take up her destiny and assume the role of regent for her youthful son's administration in Paris.

These insults notwithstanding, the English government knew full well that it could not let the moment pass entirely unnoticed. On 16 May, a fortnight before the date announced for Philip VI's coronation, an embassy was dispatched to the French court under Roger Northburgh and Adam Orleton to register Edward III's rights as the sole surviving grandson of Philip IV.[127] The self-possessed and haughty Philip was in no mood to entertain such presumption, and gave the envoys short shrift. Not surprisingly, many modern historians have dismissed the episode as so much foolishness, a piece of unnecessary tokenism that ran the risk of ridiculing the fragile new regime of Edward III and revealing, yet again, the political liability that was the regency of Queen Isabella.[128] There is no reason to suppose, however, that Edward III considered the protest of 1328 as in any way comparable to the damaging treaty with the Scots, or that he ever felt his mother to have acted in anything other than a proper and responsible manner in relation to his dynastic rights in France. Isabella and her advisers felt bound to preserve the young Edward III's claims in such a way that he might be able to reassert them, according to circumstance, when he came into his majority. It was a similar concern that explains the parallel protest made against the division of the thrones of France and Navarre and the succession to the latter of Louis X's surviving daughter Jeanne and her husband Philip of Evreux.[129] Whereas Edward II had thought it appropriate after Louis's death in 1316 to argue the case for the dividing up of the French kingdom between the latter's surviving siblings, Isabella knew well that the future strength of her son's residual claim would lie in the notion that, in 1328, he had been the sole eligible successor to the Capetian inheritance.[130]

---

[126] P. Viollet, 'Comment les Femmes ont été exclues, en France, de la succession à la couronne', *Mémoires de l'Académie des Inscriptions et Belles-lettres*, xxxiv (1895), 125–78; C. Taylor, 'The Salic Law and the Valois Succession to the French Crown', *French History*, xv (2001), 358–77; C. Taylor, 'The Salic Law, French Queenship, and the Defense of Women in the Late Middle Ages', *French Historical Studies*, xxix (2006), 548.

[127] *Foedera*, II.ii, 743.

[128] E. Perroy, *The Hundred Years War*, trans. W. B. Wells (London, 1951), 81–2; Curry, *Hundred Years War*, 40–1; Sumption, i, 100–12.

[129] *Foedera*, II.ii, 736; E. Meyer, *Charles II, roi de Navarre, comte d'Evreux, et la Normandie au XIVe siècle* (Paris, 1898), 1–7.

[130] P. Chaplais, *Essays in Medieval Diplomacy and Administration* (London, 1981), chap. x.

Finally, Isabella clearly intended to use the bid for her son's rights in France to articulate the notion that the change of dynasty required a readjustment of the feudal relationship between the French crown and its major vassals. Just as Edward III's later formal assumption of the title of king of France in 1340 was precipitated by the need for an Anglo-Flemish alliance, so in 1328 Isabella's administration may have been encouraged to assert such claims by dissident townsmen of Flanders eager to challenge Philip VI's suzerainty over their count, Louis de Nevers.[131] More substantively, the English seem to have thought that Northburgh and Orleton's mission might apply useful pressure for a revision of the 1327 Anglo-French peace. The abbot of Fécamp, the future Pope Clement VI, was sharply rebuffed when he was sent to England to demand Edward III's performance of homage.[132] Early in 1329, the queen delivered two silver cups to her son, one decorated with the quartered arms of England and France and the other with heraldic devices of England, France and Castile.[133] By Isabella's reckoning, Edward's possession of the Capetian bloodline required that the jumped-up Philip treat his cousin of England not as some abject vassal but as his respected equal, a crowned and anointed king.

Such aspirations were not easily reconciled with the exigencies of diplomacy. Unlike Isabella's brothers, Philip VI was determined to have the act of homage completed in timely fashion, not least because it would serve to confirm his occupation of greater Aquitaine under the terms of the 1327 settlement. The threat of a further confiscation of the Plantagenet fiefs was sufficient to bring the English government to its senses, and at the Westminster parliament of February 1329 it was agreed that Edward III should pass beyond the sea to perform homage to King Philip. The meeting was delayed for some weeks, mainly because of the perennial problem of agreeing an appropriate formula for Edward's oath. The court spent March touring the Home Counties before moving on to pass much of Lent and the Easter season at Queen Isabella's castle of Wallingford. At last, in May, the king proceeded to Dover and took ship for the continent, accompanied by Henry Burghersh and a large retinue. Arriving at Wissant on 26 May, he made his way via Montreuil and Crécy (his first glimpse of a place that would witness one of the greatest military achievements of his reign) to Saint-Riquier, and thence on to Amiens, the agreed location for the ceremonies. On 6 June, in the choir of the cathedral, Edward knelt in homage before Philip VI. The formal ceremonies

---

[131] H. Pirenne, 'La Première Tentative Faite pour reconnoitre Edouard III d'Angleterre comme roi de France (1328)', *Annales de la Société de'Histoire et d'Archéologie de Gand*, v (1902), 5–11.

[132] Déprez, *Préliminaires*, 81–2.

[133] E 101/384/1, fol. 16v. The latter was of a set with a silver ewer having images of the kingdoms of Denmark, Germany and Aragon. See also E 101/385/19, fol. 8.

concluded with a great tournament.[134] Edward had taken with him a precious ornament of a fleur-de-lis encrusted with rubies, sapphires, emeralds and pearls and probably made a gift of the spectacular object to his gracious host.[135] Celebrations continued in England where, after his landing on 10 June, Edward hosted jousts at Canterbury, Dartford and Reigate. Much excitement was expressed over Edward's sound decision at Dartford to dismount from an unruly horse whose subsequent flight into the water of the Thames might otherwise surely have killed the king. Such encouraging tales, along with more substantive business from the recent visit to France, were reported with satisfaction to a great council which convened at Windsor in July.[136]

Despite the high mood maintained in these public settings, there were deep misgivings on both sides. The French had tried to push for new conditions that would reserve the recently forfeited territories to Philip VI and thus effectively reclaim the Agenais and the three dioceses of Périgueux, Limoges and Cahors for Valois control. Edward's party had been ready for such slipperiness: the bishop of Lincoln had firmly announced that the king-duke would give up none of his rights in Aquitaine and would perform only simple homage subject to the usual condition of the fulfilment of the 1259 treaty of Paris.[137] But such stubbornness came at a price. Edward's refusal to place his hands inside those of the king of France in the manner that denoted the full bonds of fealty clearly infuriated Philip of Valois. Despite his confident assertion that the matter could be resolved amicably in subsequent negotiations, it soon became evident that Philip intended to press his rights, and through 1329 and 1330 he set a series of deadlines for the performance of the required oath of fealty. Edward's trip to Amiens had been his first solo diplomatic engagement, undertaken without the accompaniment of either his mother or the earl of March. Much more than his previous homage in 1325, however, it had left him with a distinct sense of anticlimax and an uncomfortable awareness of the compromises now imposed not just on the escapist notion of his claim to the throne of France but also on the future integrity of his duchy of Aquitaine.

In the fourteenth century there was no law about the age at which boy-kings could emerge into full enjoyment of their powers. Feudal tenants-in-chief of the crown were eligible to take up their lands and responsibilities when they were twenty-one, but even this strongly held convention was often adjusted in individual cases. The crown was also understood to stand

---

[134] *PROME*, iv, 96; *CPR 1327–30*, 388; E 101/384/6; *Foedera*, II.ii, 765; *EMDP*, I.i, no. 200; Vale, *Edward III and Chivalry*, 172.

[135] E 101/ 384/1, fol. 17v.

[136] E 101/384/6; C 49/66/26; *Ann. Paulini*, 352–3; *RDP*, iv, 390–1.

[137] Murimuth, 58; Déprez, *Préliminaires*, 45–6.

outside such limitations. Henry III had taken control of his own regime in 1227, when he was just over nineteen. To the extent that Henry's example provided a precedent, two general principles seem to have been agreed: that Edward III might assume charge of the realm whenever he (and, by implication, those about him) deemed it appropriate to do so; and that he had to mark such a moment by a public assertion of his personal will and royal prerogative.[138] In November 1329, Edward reached the age of seventeen. This was still quite young to take on full responsibility for his regime, and in other circumstances Queen Isabella and her lover could have reasonably assumed that their informal regency might continue for several years more. In the course of the following year, however, a series of dramatic changes in the king's family were to transform his political status and ultimately propel him, in the most dramatic fashion, into a public declaration of his majority.

By Christmas 1329 it was a matter of common knowledge that the young Philippa of Hainault was expecting the royal couple's first child. The queen's pregnancy proved in the most potent manner the maturity and vigour of her husband. It also impacted directly on her own status. Measures were now put in hand to set up the young queen with her own dower; in February 1330 she was granted the valuable honour of Pontefract and the former Despenser lordship of Glamorgan.[139] Her long-delayed coronation was now to take place at Westminster Abbey on 18 February. On the eve and morrow of the event, the queen made oblations at St Paul's Cathedral and at the high altar and tomb of Edward the Confessor in Westminster Abbey.[140] Whereas she had stayed away from her son's coronation, Queen Isabella played a conspicuous role in that of her daughter-in-law, duly decked out in a new set of robes provided at the king's expense. The coronation of Philippa of Hainault seemed to mark a definitive end to Isabella's artificially extended period as consort. But it remained to be seen whether the dowager would be inclined to accept the resulting constraints. Isabella herself accompanied the young royal pair to Windsor, where Edward lost at the gaming tables to the still ubiquitous Mortimer.[141]

The other piece of family information that Edward received over the winter of 1329–30 was altogether less welcome. Rumours had begun to

[138] Wood, *Joan of Arc and Richard III*, 29–50; D. Carpenter, *The Minority of Henry III* (London, 1990), 389; W. M. Ormrod, 'Coming to Kingship: Boy Kings and the Passage to Power in Fourteenth-Century England', *Rites of Passage*, ed. McDonald and Ormrod, 31–49.

[139] *CPR 1327–30*, 501. For the insufficiency of these estates to cover the agreed dower of £3,000 see SC 8/265/13210; *CPR 1327–30*, 541.

[140] E 101/383/13, m. 3; *Ann. Paulini*, 349. The king's itinerary makes it evident that this was the date of the occasion, but other historians have preferred various dates in Feb. and Mar.: Shenton, *Itinerary of Edward III*, 26, 28.

[141] SC 1/38/191; E 101/399/1; E 101/383/13, m. 3.

circulate that Edward II was still alive.[142] In the fifteenth century, the English monarchy would become inured to such survival tales and treat them as the inevitable and necessary fallout from any act of deposition. But Edward III and his contemporaries were not yet quite so cynical. In late October 1329, after a tournament at Dunstable, the king and his mother moved to the great fortress of Kenilworth – the very place, coincidentally, where Edward II had been held prior to his abdication – and remained there, in distinctly sombre mood, throughout Advent and Christmas. Public statements were issued in an attempt to discredit current rumours and stamp out possible insurrections.[143] In spite of the hazards, some men in extremely high places seem momentarily to have believed in the possibility of Edward II's living existence. In a secret letter written in January 1330 to Simon Swanlond, the mayor of London, Archbishop Melton announced that Edward of Caernarfon was 'alive and in good health'; in preparation for the latter's restoration to freedom, Swanlond was to provide money and clothing for his support and comfort.[144] It is an ironic twist that Swanlond was, at just the same moment, purchasing gifts from the city of London for the upcoming coronation of Queen Philippa.[145]

Edward III's legitimacy rested on three articles of faith: that Edward II had given up the throne willingly; that he had subsequently died of natural causes; and that he now lay buried at Gloucester Abbey. An impostor – especially one properly briefed by men in high places – would threaten to expose the young king as both a usurper and a perjurer. What was needed was a timely strike against those who were seeking to make mischief by giving disingenuous support to the second coming of Edward of Caernarfon. The focus fell on the king's uncle, Edmund, earl of Kent, who had been at odds with the court since the time of the Salisbury parliament of 1328. It remains unclear whether Kent really believed, as Melton apparently did, that the old king was still alive. After their withdrawal from Henry of Lancaster's loyal conspiracy in 1328, both Kent and his brother Norfolk were keen to protest their uncompromising loyalty to the crown, sometimes indeed against their own better interests;[146] and it is not impossible that Kent took refuge in the fantasy of Edward II's survival because it offered a more harmonious interpretation of the transfer of power to Edward of Windsor in the winter of 1326–7. Later, Edward III was himself to accuse Roger Mortimer of encouraging the gullible Edmund into

---

[142] *Ann. Paulini*, 349; *Brut*, i, 262.

[143] *Foedera*, II.ii, 775.

[144] Mortimer, 'Death of Edward II', 1203–4; R. M. Haines, 'Sumptuous Apparel for a Royal Prisoner: Archbishop Melton's Letter, 14 January 1330', *EHR*, cxxiv (2009), 885–94. For Swanlond see Barron, *London*, 238.

[145] *Memorials of London*, 187–8.

[146] *ODNB*, liv, 276.

believing stories that the earl of March himself knew perfectly well to be untrue.[147] This is hardly objective evidence, but it may indeed suggest that the survival rumours were, at least in part, of Mortimer's own invention. When he struck out at Kent in the spring of 1330, the earl of March intended to take pre-emptive action against a personal enemy and to demonstrate the pressing and continued need for his assumed role as the young king's governor and protector.

The Winchester parliament of March 1330 was summoned with the express purpose of discussing measures needed to resist a likely French occupation of the king's remaining continental possessions. The debate did not go well. The assembly agreed only that the king's thirteen-year-old brother, John of Eltham, should be dispatched to Aquitaine to represent a continued commitment to the defence of the duchy.[148] To the urgent issue of Philip VI's continuing demands for the performance of liege homage, the polity could suggest only silence. Mortimer pressed ahead with demands for more active military engagement in Gascony. But he created further controversy by attempting to revive earlier experiments, specifically condemned by parliament in 1327, at taxing local communities to recruit, equip and pay contingents for the planned army. When the polity refused, the queen's lover simply resorted to hounding members of the aristocracy with arbitrary fines and ransoms.[149] The crown's desperate lack of cash provoked the council to launch an investigation into possible peculation by the former receivers of Edward II's personal treasury, the chamber. This was immediately resisted by the current staff of the royal chamber, who insisted that they were not accountable to anyone other than the person of the king. Behind this minor administrative squabble lay a wider campaign to investigate illegal appropriations of crown lands and of the liquid capital that ought to have fallen to the king after the forfeiture of the Despensers, Arundel and Baldock.[150] As Edward I and II had learned to their cost, any attempt to activate the crown's feudal prerogatives for fiscal ends tended to cause controversy. The new campaign of fiscal feudalism therefore simply reinforced the general view, recently articulated by Lancaster, that the proper resources available to support the king were being squandered through Mortimer's own greed and liberality.

It was in this already febrile atmosphere that Mortimer launched his daring attack on Kent. At the end of the parliament, the king's uncle was suddenly and unexpectedly arrested on charges of treason. Edmund, it

---

[147] *PROME*, iv, 104, 106–7.

[148] Ibid., iv, 97; Sumption, i, 111–13.

[149] *PROME*, iv, 104; Powicke, *Military Obligation*, 187–8.

[150] E 159/106, rots 46, 65, 70d, 71; *CCR 1330–3*, 131. In April Edward III was forced to give personal authorization for the chamber inquiry to go ahead: *CCR 1330–3*, 27–9; Tout, *Chapters*, ii, 346.

was alleged, had given credence to the rumours of Edward II's survival and had gone to seek out his royal half-brother at Corfe Castle in Dorset. Mortimer was able to produce a letter supposedly written by Edmund (or his wife, Margaret) to the keeper of Corfe, Sir John Deverel, offering firm support for the restoration of the deposed king to the throne.[151] A kangaroo court was promptly set up under the presidency of the coroner of the royal household, Robert Howel, with Mortimer himself acting as chief prosecutor. Kent, induced to confess, said that the whole story had been a deception of the devil. The outcome was surely never in doubt: the naive young earl was promptly condemned to forfeit both his property and his life.[152] Such was the public outrage at this arbitrary and merciless judgment that nobody could be found to carry out the sentence; Kent's final humiliation was to have to wait around outside the gates of Winchester castle until an obscure member of the royal household eventually came forward to perform the beheading. The dead man's pregnant wife was spared, but she and her children were subjected to strict imprisonment, in notably straitened circumstances, at Salisbury castle.[153] The ruthless disposal of the earl of Kent raised real anxieties as to where Mortimer's vengeance might next fall; the king's other uncle, the earl of Norfolk, perhaps only narrowly missed a similar fate through his recent and fortuitous arrangement of a marriage between his son, Edward, and one of the earl of March's many daughters.[154] Events at Winchester bore comparison with some of the worst excesses of Edward II's campaign against the contrariants in 1322. If Edward III's minority government had to resort to such desperate and ruthless measures, was not it, too, an expendable force?

Those who subsequently wrote up the death of Kent in the chronicles went to some lengths, as well they might, to stress that the young king would have preferred to pardon his uncle, but was persuaded by Isabella and Mortimer that the needs of state came before family sentiment.[155] To give him his credit, the queen's lover did not pursue his vendetta by launching a general campaign against Kent's supporters. Orders went out for the arrest of some forty alleged conspirators, but few were actually apprehended and brought to trial. The most prominent person on this list, Fulk Fitzwarin, shared the fate of his namesake, the fictional hero of the romance *Fulk le Fitz Waryn*, and escaped royal wrath by a well-timed flight

---

[151] *Brut*, i, 263–7; Haines, *Stratford*, 211–12.

[152] Murimuth, 253–7; Baker, 44; *Hist. Angl.*, ii, 251–2. Howel had connections with Queen Isabella, at whose request he had been appointed to his post in the king's household in 1329: *CPR 1327–30*, 380. He was ousted following the Nottingham coup: SC 8/53/2617.

[153] *Chronicon Henrici Knighton*, i, 452; *CPR 1327–30*, 499.

[154] A. F. Marshall, 'Thomas of Brotherton, Earl of Norfolk and Marshal of England: A Study in Early Fourteenth-Century Aristocracy' (University of Bristol PhD thesis, 2006), 111–12.

[155] *Brut*, i, 267; Haines, *Stratford*, 212.

to the continent.[156] Those like Sir William de la Zouche who gave themselves up to the king's mercy were generally accorded at least the guarantee of due process.[157] And no attempts were made to confiscate the estates of Archbishop Melton of York and Bishop Gravesend of London, who were put to answer before the council at Woodstock in late April for their alleged complicity with Kent.[158] Nevertheless, any sense of goodwill was lost by Mortimer's flagrant abuse of the available spoils. A large portion of the executed earl's estates were reserved for the earl of March's own son, Geoffrey, and most of the rest was given to the Mortimer henchmen Maltravers, Turplington and Wyard.[159] It was this extraordinary display of partisanship that finally forced Edward III to confront the necessity of Mortimer's own demise.

Following the prorogation of the Winchester parliament the court left for Woodstock, where it remained for three whole months. This remarkably long sojourn is explained primarily by the impending birth of the king's first child.[160] It was not unusual for a king to keep close to his wife during her first confinement. But Edward's long residence at his mother's manor suggests that Mortimer felt particularly beleaguered after Kent's execution.[161] The hoped-for heir, duly named Edward, was born on 15 June, and both the queen's subsequent churching and the prince's baptism were celebrated with zeal. Philippa's new status as mother of a prince allowed her, at last, the dignity of her own independent household. Immediately after the festivities at Woodstock, and as though finally to put an end to the unfortunate speculations raised by the rebellion of the earl of Kent, the king and his mother made a formal visit to Edward II's burial place at Gloucester.[162]

Behind this show of solidarity, however, lay a potentially very urgent problem. It was later reported by a number of chroniclers that Queen Isabella fell pregnant with Mortimer's child some time during 1330 and that, on this basis, the earl of March began by the end of the summer to

---

[156] *CFR 1327–37*, 169–70; KB 27/280, *Rex*, rots 19d, 20, 20d; KB 27/281, *Rex*, rot. 8; KB 27/282, *Rex*, rot. 20; M. H. Keen, *The Outlaws of Medieval Legend*, rev. edn (London, 1977), 39–52.

[157] *CCR 1330–3*, 17. Zouche's implication is largely explained by his recent abduction of Eleanor, widow of Hugh Despenser the Younger, and his attempts, by violence, to secure her portion of the Clare inheritance: see pp. 139–40.

[158] *SCCKB*, v, no. 17; *CPR 1327–30*, 507; *PROME*, iv, 107.

[159] *CChR 1327–1341*, 176; Mortimer, *Greatest Traitor*, 234; J. S. Bothwell, *Falling from Grace: Reversal of Fortune and the English Nobility, 1075–1455* (Manchester, 2008), 105–6.

[160] BL, MS Cotton Faustina B. V, fol. 56v.

[161] Mortimer, *Greatest Traitor*, 316–17. Isabella was at Woodstock on 30 May: SC 1/38/193.

[162] E 101/383/14, m. 3: E 101/398/22; Tout, *Chapters*, v, 314. Isabella's involvement in the relevant progress is demonstrated by her presence at Tewkesbury on 26 June: SC 1/38/195.

plan his own usurpation of the throne.[163] This may be no more than a piece of salacious gossip, but it reveals the essence of Edward's dilemma. Mortimer's greed was becoming a major liability to the regime. Buoyed up by his brief triumph at Winchester, Roger now took to himself the queen's lordship of Montgomery and the valuable marcher lands of Clifford and Glasbury, as well as securing a special annual fee of 500 marks 'in consideration of his continual stay with the king'.[164] The exchequer's attempts to rebuild some stability in the king's finances were finally doomed when Mortimer took control of all the moveable capital left in the marches of Wales from the confiscated estates of Arundel and the Despensers. The disillusioned keeper of the great wardrobe, William Zouche, was now on the point of resigning for lack of money with which to pay the mounting debts of the household.[165] When the king eventually assumed effective control of his own finances later in the year, there was less than £50 left in cash reserves in the royal treasury.[166] If Edward III intended to retain his throne, it was imperative that he should strike a blow for his independence. The wonder, indeed, is not that this happened, but that it was so long in the coming.

[163] Le Bel, i, 102–3; Baker, 45–6; Froissart, *Oeuvres*, xii, 247; Doherty, 'Isabella, Queen of England', 287; C. Shenton, 'Edward III and the Coup of 1330', *The Age of Edward III*, ed. J. S. Bothwell (York, 2001), 15 and n. 10.

[164] *CPR 1327–30*, 506, 535, 546.

[165] Mortimer, *Greatest Traitor*, 234; Fryde, *Tyranny*, 223–4.

[166] E 101/333/3.

Chapter 4

ENGLAND'S LITTLE LION, 1330–1337

In October 1330 Queen Isabella and the earl of March moved to Nottingham to hold a council on the state of affairs in Gascony. Arriving in advance of the king, they installed themselves in the castle, Isabella taking personal possession of the keys to the fortress.[1] The tensions within the royal family had now reached such a level that Mortimer apparently feared for his personal safety when in the presence of Edward III. Accordingly, when the king arrived on the outskirts of the town he was informed that he would not be allowed into the castle with his entourage, but would have to enter with just three or four of his servants. A stand-off ensued. Mortimer occupied himself in secret discussions with his advisers, Bishop Burghersh, Hugh Turplington, Oliver Ingham and Simon Bereford. The king, meanwhile, discussed his options with the group of trusted friends he had brought to the council. Foremost among this group were William Montagu, Edward Bohun, Robert Ufford, William Clinton and John Neville of Hornby, along with a number of up-and-coming knights and esquires of the household such as Thomas Bradeston, John Molyns and Thomas West. The judicious and forthright Montagu reportedly told the king that 'it is better to eat the dog than to have the dog eat you'.[2] The king's companions were all agreed that Edward should arrest the earl of March. Their decision to act seems to have been taken in the knowledge that the powerful Henry of Lancaster, who had recently arrived in the city, was prepared to give support to their plan and to provide additional manpower for the predicted ambush. When Mortimer caught wind of the plot, he had the temerity to interrogate the king and his followers. This final insult sealed his fate. Montagu secured the assistance of the keeper of the castle, William Eland, who informed the king's party that, whilst the castle gate would remain locked to them, he could guide them through a secret tunnel in the cliff that opened directly into the keep.[3]

On 19 October Edward and his allies took horse and rode out of Nottingham. That night, they quietly made their way back into the town and, with Eland's assistance, stole into the castle. Proceeding straight to

---

[1] For what follows see Shenton, 'Coup of 1330', 21–8.

[2] *Scalacronica*, 105.

[3] For the passages in the cliff face under Nottingham castle, see C. Drage, 'Nottingham Castle', *Transactions of the Thoroton Society*, xciii (1989), 50–1.

the queen's apartments, they took the party by storm, killing two of Mortimer's servants in the fray and putting Turplington instantly to death. While Henry Burghersh tried to escape down a privy, Mortimer hid, Polonius-like, behind a curtain.[4] The queen emerged to plead for the life of her paramour: 'Fair son, fair son, have pity on the noble Mortimer.' Amid the confusion, however, the king kept a proper distance, watching the escape routes, urging his men on to their real target and generally displaying that cool head and steady judgement that would serve him so well in many future military ventures. Such strong direction was all the more necessary since Edward badly needed to take Mortimer alive. His strategy prevailed, and the earl of March and his son Geoffrey, along with Bereford and Ingham, were put in shackles and locked up to await the trial and execution for which they seemed destined.[5] It was in the ensuing bois- terous carousing of the king and his companions that the notably exuberant character of Edward III's majority regime was born.

In the cold light of morning, celebration necessarily gave way to more serious planning as the royal entourage began to prepare a triumphal march to London. The sheriffs of the realm were ordered to proclaim the arrest of Mortimer and the king's renewed commitment to rule 'according to right and reason, as befits his royal dignity'.[6] On 21 October the proces- sion stopped off at Castle Donington, the former residence of the earl of Kent and more recently the centre of Geoffrey Mortimer's regime in the Midlands. Edward made a personal gift of the entire contents of the castle, including Geoffrey's tournament armour, to his young wife.[7] Two days later, at the earl of Lancaster's seat of Leicester, Edward III gave orders for the summons of a full parliament to meet at Westminster on 26 November, at which he would make good the intention declared in the earlier proclamation.[8] The process of formalizing the majority regime had begun.

The events of 19 October 1330 have come down to us in a series of accounts that grew progressively more elaborate with the telling. It is necessary to treat some of the details of the story as fictional embellish- ments, and the words put into the mouths of the principal players as so much dramatic licence. Nevertheless, it is hard to exaggerate the impor- tance of the Nottingham coup in the history of Edward III's life and reign. The king's actions in his mother's apartments provided the first example of something that was to be a recurring theme of Edward's kingship: his

---

[4] *Chron. Meaux*, ii, 360; J. Capgrave, *John Capgrave's Abbreuiacion of Cronicles*, ed. P. J. Lucas (EETS, cclxxxv, 1983), 156.

[5] Baker, 46–7; *Brut*, ii, 271.

[6] *CCR 1330–3*, 158–9.

[7] *CPR 1330–4*, 57; E 199/44/8; JRUL, MS Latin 234, fols 2v, 3r; JRUL, MS Latin 235, fols 31–31v.

[8] *RDP*, iv, 397–9.

ability to seize the moment, to take decisive action and to win the day. The arrest of Mortimer represented a clear statement to the political community that the king had the bravery, determination and judgement to make him a worthy vessel of the royal grace. The proclamations issued on 20 October represented the final and substantive element in the king's assumption of control in his regime, setting aside all fictions of minority and asserting Edward's right to rule. For the time being, the king could evidently count on the great goodwill of the elite and the country at large. He could also play, to a significant degree, on the fact that the misrule imposed during the first three years of his reign was not of his own making. It remained to be seen whether Edward could break the cycles of self-serving government and divisive politics to which the country had now been subject for ten years and more.

The Westminster parliament of 26 November 1330 convened in a mood of high excitement and positive anticipation. The forcible removal of Mortimer allowed the restoration of the accustomed conventions of government. In parliament, these expectations would be represented by the king's active presidency, his eagerness to listen to the advice of his great men, and his willingness to respond to the concerns of the commons. The king obviously intended the assembly to offer discussion of a whole range of issues raised by the previous four years of misrule: an order to compile summaries of all documents relating to the dispute with France for discussion in council during the forthcoming parliament provides a foretaste of Edward's later explicit efforts to withdraw from the diplomatic commitments made by Mortimer and Isabella.[9] More immediately, the assembly was to provide the forum for the trial and condemnation of the disgraced earl of March. A prepared statement of Mortimer's crimes was presented to the lords temporal, who were asked to consider them and deliver judgment as peers of the realm. The crown asserted that Mortimer's offences were 'notorious': that is, that he was self-evidently guilty and did not need the opportunity to defend himself. The lords took little time to reach their judgment: Mortimer was to be drawn and hanged as a traitor and an enemy of the king and realm.[10] The execution took place on 29 November at Tyburn – the 'common gallows of thieves', as the chronicler Geoffrey le Baker acutely remarked. The only concession was that the abject body was not quartered and sent for display in the leading cities of England, but was allowed the dignity of Christian burial, first in London and then in Coventry. A year later Roger's widow, Joan, was given licence to have the remains reinterred at Wigmore Abbey; when she subsequently complained that this had not

[9] C 47/28/1, no. 52.
[10] *PROME*, iv, 105–6; E 159/107, rot. 89.

been allowed, the crown replied tartly that her husband's remains should rest in peace.[11]

The accusations against Mortimer in the parliament of 1330 bore all the hallmarks of careful composition. They amounted to a comprehensive indictment of Roger's baleful influence over the king's family and the public interest throughout the previous four years. He had maliciously bred discord between Edward II and Isabella and had been instrumental in bringing about the murder of the ex-king. He had usurped Edward III's continual council, assuming the right to appoint and dismiss members of the king's household and making free with the resources of the crown. He had broken the peace by raising arms at Salisbury, and he had contravened Magna Carta and the law of the land by his unreasonable treatment of Lancaster's followers. He and his faction had deliberately misled the earl of Kent into believing that Edward II was still alive. He had said openly that the young king's friends wanted to make prejudicial alliances with his enemies on the continent. The charges managed to combine political crimes well understood to be acts of treason with a more general process of demonization that conveniently transferred blame for all the defects of the minority regime on to the slumped shoulders of this one condemned man.[12]

To the modern eye, the summary nature of Mortimer's trial remains somewhat disturbing. For the medieval elite, however, what was most important was who gave the final judgment. Mortimer had conducted Edmund of Kent's trial without the proper involvement of the lords of parliament. Edward III was now presented with a valuable opportunity to redress that wrong and demonstrate his commitment to the consent of the nobility in matters affecting their own number. The lists of those receiving personal summonses to attend parliament as members of the lords became reasonably stable by the 1320s, and the sixty or so earls and barons normally in attendance in the early years of Edward III were developing a keen sense of their status as 'peers of the realm'. The process observed in November 1330 was therefore carefully chosen to meet with their approval and create the air of legitimacy that had been so strikingly lacking in the condemnations of the Despensers and Arundel in 1326 and of Kent in 1330.[13]

Similar considerations explain the treatment of the only other member of the peerage to be put to answer for alleged treason, Sir Thomas Berkeley. Berkeley was quick to wriggle out of the accusation that, as the formal custodian of the ex-king, he was culpable of the murder of Edward II. A jury subsequently confirmed his testimony, agreeing that, at the crucial moment, Thomas had been absent from Berkeley and detained by illness at Bradley. Later investigation of the Berkeleys' household accounts

[11] Dryburgh, 'Career of Roger Mortimer', 206.
[12] *PROME*, iv, 103–5; Doherty, 'Isabella, Queen of England', 319–20.
[13] J. E. Powell and K. Wallis, *The House of Lords in the Middle Ages* (London, 1967), 303–46; Bothwell, *Falling from Grace*, 40–1.

by their steward and historian, John Smyth of Nibley, were to reveal that
the jurors had been put under some pressure and that Thomas might in
fact have been at or near his castle at the time that Edward II was put to
death.[14] But no such qualms were raised in 1330–1, and the case was simply
put into abeyance, not to be revived again for some five years.[15] Berkeley's
rather disingenuous protest and Edward III's reluctance to pursue the
matter have inevitably bred speculation that both men believed, in their
hearts, that Edward II was still alive.[16] On balance, however, it seems much
more likely that the king simply could not afford to have Berkeley
condemned. Both Thomas and his father, Maurice, had fought for Thomas
of Lancaster at Boroughbridge and paid a heavy price, Maurice dying in
1326 while still a prisoner in Wallingford castle. Thomas himself had played
an important part in the coup of 1326–7 and in the subsequent pacification
of the West Country; Thomas's younger brother, Maurice, had entered
Edward III's household earlier in 1330 and been in the king's party at the
ambush of Nottingham in October.[17] Faced with such a record of adherence to the honest causes of the 1320s, the peers were probably eager to
convince themselves that Thomas's only real offence had been to act as the
unwitting accessory of his father-in-law, the earl of March. At a defining
moment in his regime, Edward III wisely drew back from the terrible
consequences that would have befallen the Berkeley family had Thomas
indeed become the first English peer ever to be condemned for regicide.

The parliament of November 1330 was also called on to try others who
(as the lords themselves pointed out) were not themselves peers of the land.
Simon Bereford, imprisoned at the Tower, was declared guilty of treason
and put to death on 24 December. John Maltravers, John Deverel and Bogo
de Bayouse were condemned for their part in the murder of the earl of
Kent, and Thomas Gurney and William Ogle for killing Edward II. These
five all being fugitives, blood money was now put on their heads.[18] In other

[14] *PROME*, iv, 114–15; J. Smyth, *The Lives of the Berkeleys*, 2 vols (Gloucester, 1883), i, 293, 296–7.

[15] See pp. 121–3.

[16] There is considerable debate as to the whether the phrasing used on the parliament roll (*nec unquam scivit de morte sua usque in presenti parliament isto*) implies Berkeley's denial of any previous knowledge of the murder itself (which, as Mortimer emphasizes, allows for the deduction that he actually believed Edward II to be still alive) or (as Phillips argues) merely suggests that he had not previously been aware of any hint of foul play: Mortimer, 'Death of Edward II', 1186; Phillips, *Edward II*, 579–80 and n. 18.

[17] GEC, ii, 128–30; Tout, *Collected Papers*, iii, 159; N. Saul, *Knights and Esquires: The Gloucestershire Gentry in the Fourteenth Century* (Oxford, 1981), 77 and n. 75; Shenton, 'Coup of 1330', 24–5.

[18] *PROME*, iv, 106–7; *CPR 1327–30*, 141–3; C 49/84; E 403/254, 14 Dec. 1330. For the fugitives' subsequent histories see J. S. Bothwell, 'Agnes Maltravers (d. 1375) and her Husband, John (d. 1364)', *Fourteenth Century England IV*, ed. J. S. Hamilton (Woodbridge, 2006), 80–92; J. R. S. Phillips, 'An Englishman in Rome, 1330–1334', *Dublin in the Medieval World: Studies in Honour of Howard B. Clarke*, ed. J. Bradley, A. J. Fletcher and A. Simms (Dublin, 2009), 422–32.

cases, however, the assembly was quick to show the same kind of discretion from which Berkeley benefited. The adept political trimmer Sir Oliver Ingham was pardoned his alliance with Mortimer on 8 December and restored to his family estates, though not, significantly, to those that he had received from the crown during the minority.[19] And a little later, in March 1331, Geoffrey Mortimer was given licence to go abroad; after a suitable interval, he was subsequently allowed to carve out a successful position for himself as heir to some of his mother's inheritances in England and France.[20]

The deliberate efforts of the new regime to moderate its vengeance were intended as a stark contrast to the terrors of 1322 and 1326–7. No less important was that the new regime should show itself properly responsive to the private and public grievances against the recent tyranny of Mortimer. The king provided appropriately generous responses to the large numbers of petitions that flooded in to the November parliament. Among many thus at least partially placated were the townsmen of Bristol, whose expectations of benefit from their involvement in the downfall of the younger Despenser in October 1326 had hitherto been thwarted by the malign intentions of Mortimer's nominee as constable of the town's castle, Thomas Gurney.[21] And in the treatment of the nobility, Edward III demonstrated his inclination to be gracious and liberal to enemies and friends alike. The parliament ended with the posthumous rehabilitation of Mortimer's principal aristocratic victims, the earls of Arundel and Kent, and the promise to their heirs of future restoration of estates. Henry of Lancaster, Hugh Audley and Thomas Wake, along with the knights who had supported them in open opposition at Bedford in January 1329, were formally released from the bail imposed on them by Mortimer. Archbishop Melton and Bishop Gravesend, along with the others impli-cated in the earl of Kent's rebellion, were also pardoned.[22] Edward then sought advice on the rewards that ought to be bestowed on William Montagu, Edward Bohun, Robert Ufford and John Neville for their support in the Nottingham coup. The lords declared that the honourable Montagu had worked selflessly and ceaselessly for the good of the king, and agreed that William be awarded lands to the value of £1,000 a year.

---

[19] *CPR 1330–4*, 22. As was common in such cases, commissioners were appointed to investigate the possessions of all the traitors, including (initially) Ingham: *CPR 1330–4*, 57; E 142/63–74. Ingham quickly returned to Aquitaine to serve a second term as royal seneschal of the duchy: Vale, *Angevin Legacy*, 253.

[20] *CPR 1330–4*, 87; Dryburgh, 'Career of Roger Mortimer', 206–7; C. Given-Wilson, 'Chronicles of the Mortimer Family, c.1250–1450', *Family and Dynasty*, ed. Eales and Tyas, 80 n. 29.

[21] *PROME*, iv, 102, 122–51; C. D. Liddy, 'Bristol and the Crown, 1326–31: Local and National Politics in the Early Years of Edward III's Reign', *Fourteenth Century England III*, ed. W. M. Ormrod (Woodbridge, 2004), 47–65.

[22] *PROME*, iv, 108–12; *CCR 1327–30*, 528–30; SC 8/173/8613.

The first such grant should comprise one of the great prizes that had just resulted from Mortimer's disgrace: the lordship of Denbigh.[23] Edward III's assumption of personal rule had thus served to advertise both the evils of the minority regime and the distinct advantages of loyalty to the person of the young king.

Between the arrest of Mortimer at Nottingham and the opening of the November parliament of 1330, Edward III had passed his eighteenth birthday. Already a husband and a father, and now publicly declared to be in full command of his own monarchy, he could finally be assumed to have moved from adolescence to maturity. Medieval social convention was clear that the essential difference between a boy and a man was a matter of attitude and outlook. Infant rulers were, by their very nature, a liability: contemporaries were only too inclined to quote the biblical text 'Woe to thee, o land, when the king is a child' (Ecclesiastes 10: 16).[24] But an even worse fate was held to befall the country whose king was adult in years and adolescent in behaviour.[25] One of the motets sung at Edward III's wedding in 1328 had turned the usual biblical precept on its head by representing the new monarch's youth as a positive alternative to the ex-king's wilful childishness: 'Woe to the land if [the king] be childish./ Better to be poor and wise/ and a boy, than a foolish king.'[26] For those who were intent on making the very best of the new start, Edward III's youthfulness could be construed as a positive asset to the new regime of 1330.

It is no surprise, then, that contemporaries drew a dramatic distinction between the wintry gloom of Mortimer's regime and the sunny spring of Edward's majority. Sir Thomas Gray of Heton, writing in the 1350s, recounted how the new regime was heralded by a great burst of celebration in which the king and his companions indulged to the full in tournaments, hunting, feasting and ceremony.[27] The Christmas court held at Guildford in 1330 was an especially splendid occasion, filled with the fun of indoor games and outdoor jousts.[28] So, too, was the great cycle of tournaments held at Dartford, Havering, Stepney, Bedford and Cheapside in the summer of 1331, which offered particular opportunities for the king and his courtiers to engage in fanciful chivalric display.[29] It may have been for one of these early tournaments that Edward first adopted the personal

[23] *PROME*, iv, 112–13; *CChR 1327–41*, 210.

[24] For the possibility that this text was employed during the succession crisis of 1326–7 see Valente, 'Deposition', 858 n. 4.

[25] C. Fletcher, *Richard II: Manhood, Youth, and Politics, 1377–99* (Oxford, 2008), 1–24.

[26] Wathey, 'Marriage of Edward III', 20.

[27] *Scalacronica*, 107, 127. See also le Bel, i, 104–5.

[28] E 101/385/4, m. 79; Mortimer, *Perfect King*, 87.

[29] Vale, *Edward III and Chivalry*, 62, 138–9. See also p. 142. The tournaments at Havering (late Apr./early May) and Bedford (20 Aug.) are recorded in E 101/398/22.

badge of the sunburst with which he subsequently became closely associated. The ray of light or breath of wind bursting from clouds to reveal the hidden sun was a rebus for Edward's birthplace and natal style ('winds' and '*or*' [gold] = Windsor).[30] It provided a dramatic and enduring representation of the brave new dawn brought in by the Nottingham coup.

It would be fair to say that Edward III exploited to the full the new celebrity status thus accorded him. Indeed, it is conventional to suggest that the king was distinctly nonchalant about the higher purposes of his office and relied for far too long on the fickleness of public popularity. The huge pressures that he placed on the realm to support the enterprise of war against the Scots and the French exhausted much of the initial goodwill that had buoyed up his regime, and after the major political crisis of 1340–1 he was forced to take a much more considered view of his responsibilities as ruler of England. It is easy, however, to overplay the distinction between the reckless knight of the 1330s and the judicious statesman of the 1340s. The celebrations of monarchy in which the king and his court indulged to the full during the 1330s were more than spontaneous displays of youthful exuberance and princely excess. They were also very deliberately designed to revive the credibility of a damaged institution and to win it new respect at home and abroad. It was in the early years of his reign that Edward turned his personal style into a political art and created the public image that would sustain his monarchy over the following two generations.

At the heart of that public image lay Edward's belief in the providential nature of kingship. The king was brought up to believe that the monarch's task was not merely to respond to events but also actively to shape the destinies of crown and people. He was therefore both fascinated by, and sometimes rightly suspicious of, the various forms of fortune-telling available to fourteenth-century rulers. There is little to indicate that Edward or anyone else made anything of the astrological auspices of his birth and coronation, though his mother or wife kept a crib for the interpretation of horoscopes and the king himself may have felt the need to take astrology rather more seriously after it was held to have foretold the onset of the Black Death in 1348.[31] Much more influential on the young Edward of Windsor, however, was the tradition of political prophecy, which ascribed to past and future kings specific places in the great cycle of Fortune.[32] The well-known *Prophecies of Merlin*, which circulated widely in

[30] Barker, *Tournament*, 183. For literary uses of this pun see L. A. Coote, *Prophecy and Public Affairs in Later Medieval England* (York, 2000), 123–4.

[31] H. M. Carey, *Courting Disaster: Astrology at the English Court and University in the later Middle Ages* (Basingstoke, 1992), 58–116.

[32] For what follows see J. R. S. Phillips, 'Edward II and the Prophets', *England in the Fourteenth Century: Proceedings of the 1985 Harlaxton Symposium*, ed. W. M. Ormrod (Woodbridge, 1986), 189–201; Coote, *Prophecy and Public Affairs*, 83–119.

the later Middle Ages, represented King Arthur as the 'boar of Cornwall' who had saved his people from travail and united Britain and Gaul under one rule. Early in Edward III's reign there emerged a new variant of the Merlin tradition known as *The Last Kings of the English*. This captured a recognizable history of Henry III, Edward I and Edward II, represented by the mythological figures of the lamb, the dragon and the goat, and predicted the fortunes that would befall the land under the next three kings, the boar, the second lamb and the mole. The 'boar of Windsor' would 'whet his teeth upon the gates of Paris' and subdue France; he would go on to reconquer the Holy Land and would be buried at the shrine of the Three Kings in Cologne.[33] Another text that began to circulate at the same time told how the leopard (the king of England) would crush the crab (Scotland) and tear apart the lilies of Gaul (France) before taking Acre and Jerusalem and winning general dominion of Christendom.[34] Although some of the specifics may have been adopted only after the opening of the French war in 1337, most of these ideas were the product of a more enduring fantasy of world domination that had already been deeply embedded in English political culture in Edward I's time. Edward III's uncanny ability to fulfil some of the details and rise to the expectations of this tradition made his subjects eager to hail him as the triumphant boar of public prophecy.

These escapist notions were underpinned, in turn, by the universal and enduring cult of King Arthur. The initial excitement accompanying the Nottingham coup very much encouraged Edward's subjects to hail him as Arthur *redivivus*.[35] The king was only too pleased to respond. In December 1331, he and Queen Philippa affirmed his family's long commitment to the cult by making a tour of the Arthurian sites at Cadbury and Glastonbury. The putative remains of Arthur and Guinevere, discovered in the late twelfth century, had been interred before the high altar of Glastonbury Abbey by Edward I, and in 1345 Edward III attempted to emulate his grandfather by ordering a search for the tomb of the other great cult figure at Glastonbury, Joseph of Arimathea.[36] In the intervening years the young king was also assiduous in performing the role of knight errant and military commander that might associated him with the great worthies of chivalry. Rarely, indeed, had England seen a king quite so ready to align himself with the antiquities and achievements of the fabled Arthur.[37]

---

[33] *Brut*, i, 74–6. See also Froissart, ii, 226.

[34] *Eulogium*, i, 420.

[35] *Bridlington*, 95–6.

[36] J. Taylor, *English Historical Literature in the Fourteenth Century* (Oxford, 1987), 44–5; C. Shenton, 'Royal Interest in Glastonbury and Cadbury: Two Arthurian Itineraries, 1278–1331', *EHR*, cxiv (1999), 1249–55.

[37] See also pp. 300–7.

Yet despite his general enthusiasm for the heroes of chivalry, it is noticeable that the young Edward III was cautious about making too presumptuous an association with the specific figure of Arthur. Roger Mortimer's
flirtations with Arthuriana, which had been the cause of much critical
comment and scorn, taught Edward the real hazards, as well as the
possible benefits, of adherence to the cult.[38] Until the early 1340s, the king
was in fact much more inclined to cast himself as one of the simple knights
of the Round Table, and developed a particularly abiding association with
the figure of Sir Lionel. It is Mortimer who may have had the idea in the
first place, for he gave Edward a cup decorated with the fictitious arms of
Sir Lionel at the Wigmore tournament of 1329.[39] In spite of such an
inauspicious start, the theme persisted. In February 1333, embroidery with
the arms of Lionel was prepared for the king's use. The following year,
Edward appeared at a great tournament at Dunstable in the guise of Sir
Lionel, bearing the arms *argent a quarter gules*. A seal 'with the arms of
Lionel' was made for Edward's personal use in 1337, and in the following
year the king named his third son Lionel. Even after the prince's baptism,
Edward occasionally reverted to the conceit; at another tournament held
in Dunstable, in 1342, he again bore the arms of Lionel.[40] The choice of
Lionel can be explained by the fact that the name, 'little lion', provided a
ready association with the leopard, or heraldic lion *passant guardant*, found
on the royal arms. Lionel therefore became part of a wider repertoire of
cultural associations that linked Edward with the leopard of England.
One of Queen Philippa's gifts to her husband in 1331–2 was a silver cup
decorated with castles, banners, ships, beasts and the figure of a king, with
a stand decorated with enamelled leopards clothed in the royal arms.[41]
The heraldic leopard was also integrated more fully into the public
iconography of Edward's monarchy through its inclusion on a new great
seal in 1338 and the new gold half-florin first issued in 1344.[42] The complex
associations between Edward, Lionel and the leopard therefore served to
communicate both the young knight's aspiration to sit at Arthur's table
and the young king's already powerful sense of his public destiny.

If Arthurian chivalry was an increasingly significant element in Edward
III's articulation of his kingship, then religion was surely its *sine qua non*.[43]
Edward's observation of Christianity was entirely conventional and

[38] *Brut*, i, 262.

[39] E 101/385/19, fol. 8. For the Dunstable tournament held the following month, a
harness of white silk and red velvet was prepared 'for Lionel': E 101/384/6.

[40] E 101/386/9; BL, MS Cotton Nero C. VIII, fol. 210; E 101/389/14.

[41] E 101/385/19, fol. 11.

[42] C. Shenton, 'Edward III and the Symbol of the Leopard', *Heraldry, Pageantry and Social
Display*, ed. P. R. Coss and M. H. Keen (Woodbridge, 2002), 69–81; Vale, 'Image and
Identity', 37–9, 44.

[43] Unless otherwise stated, this and the following two paragraphs are based on W. M.
Ormrod, 'The Personal Religion of Edward III', *Speculum*, lxiv (1989), 849–77.

suggests a hearty, straightforward and rather mechanistic approach to the mysteries of faith. This is not to suggest that the king was a cynic. It is more than likely that he believed in the message of his own propaganda, which cast his accumulating military victories as acts of divine deliverance. To maintain his covenant with the Almighty and continue such success, Edward understood that he needed to undertake regular propitiation for himself and his people. Royal pilgrimages provided one obvious opportunity to combine piety with public display. Edward was a regular visitor to England's main shrine, the tomb of Thomas Becket at Canterbury Cathedral. In the early period of his reign, when he was so often occupied against the Scots, he was also a conscientious pilgrim to the great northern English shrines of St William at York, St John at Beverley, St Wilfrid at Ripon, St Oswin at Tynemouth and St Cuthbert at Durham. In January 1329, while moving around the Home Counties, Edward visited the relic collections at the abbeys of Woburn and St Albans.[44] In keeping with his more general devotion to the cult of the Virgin, he frequented Marian shrines and cults at Walsingham, London, Canterbury, York, Scarborough and Darlington.[45] During these and the more regular progresses of the royal household around the realm, it was conventional for the king's almoner to organize regular distributions of cash doles to the poor. By Edward III's time the indiscriminate generosity of the thirteenth century had given way to a more regulated system confined to the major religious festivals, the king's birthday and the anniversary of his father's death. But Edward III sometimes went much further than this. Between July 1334 and January 1335, for example, 2,500 people received the usual alms associated with the calendar of festivals. But a further 250 were given payment as part of the king's penance for failing to fast on the vigils of saints' days, and no fewer than 7,600 people received discretionary alms 'at the king's particular order'.[46] Such ostentatious acts of charity confirmed Edward's Christian credentials and symbolized his commitment to ruling for the benefit of rich and poor alike.

Religion did more than provide monarchy with an ideology: it gave it miraculous powers. Since at least the thirteenth century the kings of France and England had publicly advertised the perceived special status that went with their anointing at the time of coronation by performing the ceremony known as the royal touch, in which they blessed – and, so it was hoped, healed – persons suffering from scrofula. Edward III was not especially zealous in the pursuit of the royal touch, but he certainly knew how to deploy it to good effect. In bold statements of the legitimacy of his

[44] E 101/383/14, m. 5.

[45] E 101/383/13, m. 5; E 101/383/14, m. 2; BL, MS Cotton Nero C. VIII, fols 204, 205v, 206v; E 101/388/5; E 36/204, fols 72, 72v.

[46] BL, MS Cotton Nero C. VIII, fol. 203v.

foreign causes, Edward exercised his healing powers in the Low Countries in 1338–40 and possibly also in Scotland in 1336 and Brittany in 1342–3. Edward also continued his grandfather's and father's practice of placing money on the altar of the royal chapel on Good Friday and having the coin made up into cramp rings for the cure of persons suffering from muscular spasms and epilepsy. On these occasions the most precious object in the royal relic collection, the Croes Nawdd (or Neith Cross), was deployed to invest the precious metal with the appropriate miraculous powers. This fragment of the True Cross was thought to have been brought to England by St Helena, mother of the Emperor Constantine, and had been confiscated by Edward I during his conquest of Wales. Such a potent combination of the religious, the mythological and the historical appealed particularly to the imagination of Edward III, and it is no accident that the Croes Nawdd became, in due course, the centrepiece of Edward's own personal cult of chivalry at Windsor castle.[47]

The commitment to the practices of his forebears that is revealed by the king's performance of the ritual elements of monarchy was part of a wider sense of obligation to the memory of the former kings of England. Edward III's personal religion sometimes seems to have been largely a matter of ancestor worship. The king regularly patronized the cults of the Anglo-Saxon royal saints, especially Edmund of East Anglia and Edward the Confessor, and possessed his own relics of the latter. Lacking a more recent Plantagenet saint to vie with the French monarchy's St Louis, Edward III made a virtue of necessity and enthusiastically promoted the secular cult that had already grown up around the epitome of martial prowess and statesmanship: his grandfather, Edward I.[48] At the coronation in 1327, Edward I's tomb was distinguished from the other shrines and monuments in Westminster Abbey by being decked in cloth of gold. In the spring of 1330, when the young king was still struggling to assert his voice in politics, he personally ordered that the 'great men and others of these [southern] parts' be summoned to attend the solemn rites at Westminster that would mark the anniversary of his grandfather's death on 7 July.[49] And when the subsequent Scottish and French campaigns prevented the king from attending the solemnities in person, he regularly dispatched cloth of gold to Westminster and had the anniversary observed by his own chaplains in

[47] M. Bloch, *The Royal Touch: Sacred Monarchy and Scrofula in England and France*, trans. J. E. Anderson (London, 1973), 53, 57, 62, 100–3.

[48] For an argument that Edward III's consensual policy towards the nobility was a conscious emulation of his grandfather's true strategy, see A. M. Spencer, 'Royal Patronage and the Earls in the Reign of Edward I', *History*, xciii (2008), 20–46.

[49] E 159/106, rot. 90. Since a great council was summoned to Osney for 9 July (*RDP*, iv, 394–5), it is evident that this personal instruction was somewhat at variance with the plans of Mortimer and Isabella, and in reality the anniversary is likely to have been attended mainly by members of the clergy.

the field.[50] It is hardly surprising that when, in due course, Edward came to make arrangements for his own interment at Westminster, he should have stated explicitly his desire to be buried close to the sepulchre of his esteemed grandfather.[51] The only oddity in all of this is perhaps Edward's failure to commission a permanent effigy to sit upon the plain tomb-chest of his ancestor-hero. In all other respects, he showed profoundly internalized commitment to the bold and expansive vision of kingship that had been espoused by the mighty and revered figure of Edward I.

Edward III's performance of monarchy during the 1330s sought to make clear statements of serious intent about the providential and sacral nature of his office. In attempting to illuminate the inner man, however, we should certainly not be blind to Edward's very obvious indulgence in the pleasures of the over-privileged. If being king was onerous, it could also be a lot of fun. Edward pursued his love of blood sports with a relentlessness bordering on mania. Clipstone, in Sherwood Forest, was a favourite hunting venue in the early years of the reign, but the king also spent significant amounts of time in the royal parks of Clarendon, Woodstock and Windsor. In September 1339, when he was at Anderlecht in the Low Countries and deeply preoccupied with matters military and financial, Edward still found time to order his ministers at home to speed up the current programme of improvements at Clipstone.[52] As in town, so in the forest, Edward was always keen to cut a dash. In the early 1340s he commissioned two suits of green for his own use in the hunt and ordered special robes and liveries for the lords and ladies joining him in the chase.[53] The king's gimlet eye was also alert to the proper maintenance of hunting enclosures: during one trip to Sherwood he ordered the seizure of Lady Furnivall's private hunting park at Worksop on the grounds that he had personally witnessed a stag jumping to freedom over a badly maintained fence.[54] Although the pressures of summer campaigning meant that Edward often missed the open season for stag-hunting between June and September, there were numerous opportunities for blood sports in winter and spring; at these times Edward was wont to pursue wild boar, swans, and even hares and otters.[55]

[50] Ormrod, 'Personal Religion', 871–2. Edward III's avid observation of the anniversary of his grandfather's death is all the more striking given that the equivalent solemnities for Eleanor of Castile, observed with great diligence under Edward II (E 101/379/19, fol. 3v; BL, Add. MS 17362, fol. 3r; BL, MS Cotton Faustina B. V, fol. 46), were not performed in the royal household after 1327.

[51] See pp. 466–7.

[52] E 159/116, rot. 12.

[53] E 101/390/2, m. 1.

[54] SC 8/48/2356; *CCR 1354–60*, 121.

[55] S. A. Mileson, *Parks in Medieval England* (Oxford, 2009), 24; Shenton, 'English Court', 177–84. The eight dogs that Edward lodged at Windsor in 1356 were probably hunters: *Issues*, 163.

Surpassing even the thrill of hunting with horses and dogs was Edward's great and lasting passion for the royal sport of falconry. The king maintained a staff of up to twenty falconers in his household under the formal direction of Sir Thomas Wake of Blisworth, and treated his favourite hawks as prized and pampered pets.[56] On one occasion he made free with his prerogative to order the confiscation of ten top-quality falcons impounded in the port of London.[57] As if to complete his medley of field sports, Edward developed a penchant for fishing. In 1342 he gave a personal gift of 5 shillings to the fishermen who re-stocked the ponds at Woolmer Green against his arrival there, and in 1344 his great wardrobe purchased him a new, and no doubt suitably stylish, fishing rod.[58] In common with a European courtly vogue for the exotic, Edward also kept a menagerie of wild animals, including lions and leopards, a bear and assorted apes and monkeys, and had the animals moved around to his various residences in order to provide entertainment and spectacle.[59]

In the evenings, or when the weather was too bad for outdoor activities, Edward III spent a good deal of his time gambling at dice and board games. His recklessness at the tables was no doubt compounded by the knowledge that the debts he ran up were no part of the obligation of his privy purse but would ultimately have to be covered by the exchequer.[60] Both Edward and his queen possessed sets for chess and chequers.[61] The king was accustomed to keeping a jester at court: Robert 'the fool', who had served both Eleanor of Castile and Edward II, was still a member of the royal household early in the new reign.[62] There was also much indoor merrymaking to match the magnificence of outdoor tournaments. The Christmas festivities were marked by elaborate indoor masques and games.[63] In 1337 the

[56] E 101/386/18; B. Lyon, 'What Were Edward III's Priorities: The Pleasures of Sports or Charity?', *Revue d'histoire ecclesiastique*, xcii (1997), 126–34; R. S. Oggins, *The Kings and their Hawks: Falconry in Medieval England* (London, 2004), 185 n. 141. In 1347 sixteen royal falconers were named: E 403/340, 16 Oct. 1347. For Edward's personal intervention on behalf of one of his falconers, see *CCR 1354–60*, 95.

[57] *CCR 1354–60*, 410; *CIM*, iii, no. 261.

[58] E 36/204, fol. 82; E 101/390/5. For Edward's interest in the creation and refurbishment of fishponds at Clarendon in 1335 and Clipstone in 1355 see *CCR 1333–7*, 425–6; E 159/132, *Brev. bar.*, Mich., rot. 1.

[59] Shenton, 'Symbol of the Leopard', 76–7. For the keeper of the king's *babewyns* (apes and monkeys) in 1336, see BL, MS Cotton Nero C. VIII, fol. 276.

[60] E 101/383/14, m. 1; BL, MS Cotton Nero. C VIII, fols 210, 211, 213, 213v, 214v, 216; Norwell, lxxxiii, 212, 213, 215–16.

[61] E 101/391/6; E 101/392/14, m. 4. For Philippa's gaming debts see JRUL, MS Latin 235, fol. 10v.

[62] E 101/398/13; BL, MS Cotton Galba E. III, fol. 188v; C. Bullock-Davies, *A Register of Royal and Baronial Domestic Minstrels, 1272–1327* (Woodbridge, 1986), 167–8. Robert was still alive in 1355, when he was in receipt of a pension of £2: E 403/377, 11 July.

[63] Murimuth, 65; K. Staniland, 'Clothing and Textiles at the Court of Edward III, 1342–52', *Collectanea Londiniensia*, ed. J. Bird et al. (London and Middlesex Archaeological Society Special Paper, ii, 1978), 228–9.

expenditure on the Christmas court included the provision of woodland scenery, a pillory and a ducking stool. And by the late 1340s, courtiers were being supplied with costumes of birds, lions, elephants and dragons for similar Christmas and New Year entertainments.[64] Christmas was a time for misrule, when authority was turned on its head, fools became lords, ladies courted knights and boys were made bishops.[65] The great wardrobe provided fourteen hobby horses for Christmas and New Year games at Wallingford in 1333–4, and the twenty monks' outfits provided for the king and members of his chamber in 1334–5 may have been intended for similar Christmas fun.[66] It may well be supposed that the king was a leading player in the practical jokes and hearty horseplay that were a feature of the midwinter season.

In this high-spiritedness and bonhomie we can see three special traits that were to become particularly associated with the personal style of Edward III. The first is an emphasis on affective bonds of friendship forged and celebrated within the culture of chivalry. In November 1330 Edward commissioned seven ceremonial jackets of green and purple velvet and silk embroidered with gold and silver thread, apparently as gifts to key individuals who had served in the night raid on Nottingham castle a few weeks before.[67] This marked the beginning of a strong tradition whereby groups of knights especially distinguished in arms or conspicuously close to the king were given the privilege of dressing in team colours. On certain ceremonial occasions such as the processions before the jousts at Stepney and Cheapside in 1331, Edward himself might dress in the colours of the day and ride visored, merging inconspicuously into the tournament teams. At the Dunstable jousts of 1342, for example, the king appeared as a 'simple knight'.[68] These conceits were part of a chivalric tradition that regarded all knights as of equal status and gave distinction on the basis not of birth but of valour and virtue. Edward's inclination to subsume his regal identity into the collective of knighthood provided potent messages about his allegiance to his friends and to the dominant militaristic values of their generation.

A second and connected trait was Edward III's enthusiasm for acts of personal bravery. In battle, the king understood the necessity for good discipline in the ranks of his armies. He managed to resist the individualistic tendencies that drove members of the heavy cavalry to compete

[64] Vale, 'Image and Identity', 45; Shenton, 'English Court', 188. See also pp. 299–300.

[65] For boy bishops at the Christmas celebrations of 1335 and 1338, see BL, MS Cotton Nero C. VIII, fol. 203; Norwell, 250–1. Boy singers appeared before the king's children at Bristol on St Nicholas's eve in 1357: JRUL, MS Latin 236, fol. 3r.

[66] E 101/386/18; E 101/387/14. For other references to games *in aula* at Wallingford and Thame in this season, see E 101/387/9, mm. 1, 4; BL, Add. MS 46350, mm. 1, 2.

[67] Shenton, 'Coup of 1330', 24–6.

[68] Murimuth, 123.

among themselves in life-threatening charges. Away from major set-piece engagements, however, Edward delighted in the sense of adventure to be had from small-scale acts of derring-do. The Nottingham coup of 1330 had given him his first taste for such adventure, and he obviously yearned for more of it. The Scottish and Breton campaigns of 1336 and 1342 were remembered for Edward's acts of knightly heroism in rescuing two belea-guered ladies, the countess of Atholl and the duchess of Brittany, from the hands of their enemies. In different circumstances but with the same spirit of heroic individualism, Edward made a dramatic return home from the Low Countries in November 1340, using deliberate subterfuge to catch his ministers unawares and launch a strike at his enemies within the home administration.[69] Edward III must have relished the adrenalin rush to be had from adventures of this kind, and he persisted in them in spite of the very obvious threats they posed to his own safety.

The other habit that Edward may have developed in these and other early adventures was a certain natural ease and gracious condescension in the presence of his common subjects. By the fifteenth century there was a strong tradition that Edward III had been accustomed to go out among his people incognito – as Thomas Hoccleve put it, 'in simple array, alone' – in order secretly to learn their opinion of him.[70] Edward certainly used disguises in court entertainment and, at least on one occasion, for a diplomatic mission to the continent.[71] Whether he actually conducted secret tours of his realm is hardly provable. But there are certainly lots of hints of ordinary human exchanges with his lesser subjects. In 1334 the king twice made gifts to archers whose bows he had broken, presumably in good-natured encounters at the butts.[72] And in 1336, on a campaign in the north, Edward managed to break a nacker (the shallow kettledrum used by mounted musicians in medieval armies) belonging to one John Pot, presumably in an over-enthusiastic display of his percussion skills.

Above all, rubbing shoulders with his ordinary subjects gave the king invaluable opportunities to demonstrate his beneficence. John Milner was paid the considerable sum of 13s 4d for accommodating the king at Doddington (Northumberland) in November 1334, and Edward made a personal gift of 5 shillings to Matilda Stokenchurch in 1342 in gratitude for the 'ease' that he had taken in her house.[73] Acts of charity and discretion were shown to those who brought their grievances to the visiting king. In

[69] See pp. 173, 231, 249.

[70] J. Fernster, *Fictions of Advice: The Literature of Counsel in Late Medieval England* (Philadelphia, 1996), 149; T. Ohlgren, '*Edwardus redivivus* in *A Gest of Robyn Hode*', *Journal of English and Germanic Philology*, xcix (2000), 1–29; D. Matthews, *Writing to the King: Nation, Kingship and Literature in England, 1250–1350* (Cambridge, 2010), 113–15.

[71] See p. 179.

[72] E 101/387/9, m. 7; Shenton, 'English Court', 190.

[73] BL, MS Cotton Nero C. VIII, fol. 269, 279; E 36/204, fol. 82.

June 1335 Richard Swan, 'late a merchant, now a pauper', managed to catch Edward's attention at York and secured payment of over £25 for military supplies provided over twenty years earlier to Edward II. And in 1344 the king intervened personally to support the Plymouth innkeeper John Baygge in seeking compensation after his premises had been burgled and all his wine stocks lost.[74] Such positive benefits of access to majesty created a powerful and enduring notion of grace. Whereas Edward II's biographers were beginning in the mid-fourteenth century to elaborate their critique of the former king's penchant for low-life, neither his subjects nor his later critics seem ever to have seen Edward III's common touch as anything other than a positive marker of his monarchical style.

Medieval principles of good government were perceived and expressed in strikingly personal terms. The king was more than the symbolic embodiment of the state: he was the personal instrument through which its good intentions were promulgated. There was a huge amount of routine business performed in the king's name with which he had, in reality, nothing directly to do. But the monarch was expected to inform the most important aspects of crown policy by the direct application of his grace and will. Acts of patronage and other dispensations of the royal prerogative were specified by the chancery as having been authorized *per ipsum regem*, 'by the king himself'.[75] The particular responsibility of the king in matters of public policy was twofold: to ensure that his strategies were properly informed by wise counsel; and to protect his subjects against oppression by his ministers and officials in central and local government. Underpinning all of this was the principle, captured in Magna Carta and the coronation oath, that the king guaranteed his free subjects' unrestricted access to justice. To demonstrate his commitment to these notions, Edward III was required at once to deal with the multiplicity of individual cases that constantly clamoured for his attention and to inform and drive the general agenda of policy and reform. Administration, if done well, was a strain on the patience of even the most bureaucratically minded monarch.

The dominant issue in domestic government throughout the early stages of Edward III's reign was undoubtedly that of public order. The harvest failures of 1315–22 and the political disruptions of 1321–2, 1326–7 and 1330 had created serious concern about a general descent into

---

[74] BL, MS Cotton Nero C. VIII, fol. 202; SC 8/239/11918; C 81/1336/46; *CPR 1343–5*, 587.

[75] B. Wilkinson, 'The Authorisation of Chancery Writs under Edward III', *BJRL*, viii (1924), 107–39; W. M. Ormrod, 'Accountability and Collegiality: The English Royal Secretariat in the Mid-Fourteenth Century', *Ecrit et pouvoir dans les chancelleries médiévales: Espace français, espace anglais*, ed. K. Fianu and D. J. Guth (Louvain la Neuve, 1997), 61–76. Written memoranda of Edward III's time resulting in instruments warranted *per ipsum regem* survive in C 81/1394.

criminality.[76] Regime change had also shown how unscrupulously the crown could sometimes manipulate justice for its own ends. The Folvilles, a gentry family in Leicestershire, had taken to a life of crime in the mid-1320s and achieved great notoriety for the murder of Roger Bellers, baron of the exchequer, in January 1326. Calling in their credentials as fervent opponents of the Despensers, however, the Folvilles had taken advantage of the accession of Edward III to secure pardon of this outrageous offence.[77] The condoning of criminal behaviour was to remain a constant anxiety for the political community over the following two decades as a consequence of Edward III's extensive use of pardons as a means of recruiting men to military service.[78] There was always an element of hypocrisy in such debates, for many of those who complained when they were victims of rough justice were just as inclined to improper practice when it suited them. 'Folvilles' law' became a proverb for self-help, and the Robin Hood legends, which may well have their origins in the 1320s and 1330s, repeatedly proclaimed the principle that violence was a valid alternative to justice.[79] Edward III must have understood from an early age just how difficult – perhaps, indeed, impossible – it was to satisfy the many competing voices that called for the better preservation of the king's peace.

For a year after his seizure of power at Nottingham, Edward concentrated on making public displays of his personal commitment to order. The unpopular eyres set up in 1329–30 were promptly withdrawn.[80] The king specifically invited petitions to the November parliament of 1330 from those who wished to complain about oppressions committed by magnates, ministers and others during the minority. New trailbastons, staffed by lords and senior lawyers, were then set up to deal with the resulting flood of business.[81] There were also appropriate signals of Edward's personal commitment to good order. In May 1331 the king was present at Bury St Edmunds for important proceedings designed to bring an end to the endemic violence between the townsmen and the abbey.[82] Later that summer, he broke off from a hunting expedition to Sherwood

[76] B. A. Hanawalt, *Crime and Conflict in English Communities, 1300–1348* (Cambridge, Mass., 1979), 238–60.

[77] *CPR 1327–30*, 10; E. L. G. Stones, 'The Folvilles of Ashby Folville, Leicestershire, and their Associates in Crime, 1326–1347', *TRHS*, 5th series, vii (1957), 117–36.

[78] H. E. Lacey, *The Royal Pardon: Access to Mercy in Fourteenth-Century England* (York, 2009), 100–6.

[79] J. R. Maddicott, 'The Birth and Setting of the Ballads of Robin Hood', *EHR*, xciii (1978), 276–99; O. de Ville, 'The Deyvilles and the Genesis of the Robin Hood Legend', *Nottingham Medieval Studies*, xliii (1999), 90–109; R. F. Green, *A Crisis of Truth: Literature and Law in Ricardian England* (Philadelphia, 2002), 165–205.

[80] *CCR 1330–3*, 164; D. Crook, *Records of the General Eyre* (London, 1982), 183.

[81] *CCR 1330–3*, 161–2; *CPR 1330–4*, 133–4, 138–9.

[82] *CCR 1330–3*, 320–1.

Forest in order to move to Sheffield and preside over a major inquiry into the activities of an outlaw known as 'the king of the Peak' – probably James Coterel, the leader of an infamous criminal gang then operating in Derbyshire.[83] A similar crowd-pleaser was organized in October 1331, when the king had it proclaimed throughout the land that the nobles had promised in parliament to refrain from breaking the law, to eschew maintenance and to assist the king's agents in upholding and enforcing justice.[84]

Much as Edward's initiatives were admired, they offered comparatively little by way of immediate improvement. In January 1331 the Folvilles actually captured and ransomed one of the trailbaston commissioners, Sir Richard Willoughby, on the highway between Melton Mowbray and Grantham. Such open contempt for the king's peace sent a shiver through the senior judiciary, for whom the East Midlands in particular seemed to be turning into a no-go area. In the parliament of March 1332 the chief justice of the king's bench, Sir Geoffrey Scrope, initiated a major debate on law and order. The lords argued that the best guarantee of good order was to appoint keepers of the counties with powers to try and determine criminals. To the obvious question of who might then supervise the keepers, they responded with the naïve but emotive suggestion that 'our lord the king [should] ride around his realm from county to county and learn how the said great men and others are conducting themselves'. Commissions were accordingly issued to earls, barons, knights and senior judges to act as supervisors of the counties, regulating the work of lesser officials, including the keepers of the peace.[85] A special court was set up to tour the Midlands and deal with the particular problems raised by the Folvilles and Coterels. In April Edward went down to Stamford to observe in person the sessions and preside over some of the judgments delivered.[86] As so often, however, bold statement of intent lacked momentum. In October, several of the special judicial commissions were withdrawn.[87] Thereafter, the maintenance of public order relied mainly, once again, on the keepers of the peace and the justices of gaol delivery.

The experiments of 1332 were made partly in the context of Edward III's expected departure for Ireland and the need to stamp out insurgency

[83] BL, MS Cotton Faustina B. V, fols 60, 61. For other evidence of Edward's presence in the High Peak at this time see E 101/398/22, m. 11. This otherwise obscure episode sheds light on other usurpations and parodies of the royal style by outlaw bands in this period: see especially the famous letter of 'Lionel, king of the rout of raveners', printed in *SCCKB*, v, 93. For James Coterel see J. G. Bellamy, 'The Coterel Gang: An Anatomy of a Band of Fourteenth-Century Criminals', *EHR*, lxxix (1964), 698–717.

[84] *PROME*, iv, 158; Ormrod, *Reign of Edward III*, 98.

[85] *PROME*, iv, 166–7; *CPR 1330–4*, 292–5, 296–7, 348–9.

[86] Stones, 'Folvilles', 122–7. The king lodged at the Stamford Blackfriars: E 403/262, 14 May 1332.

[87] *CCR 1330–3*, 610; Verduyn, 'Attitude', 40.

prior to his absence from the realm.[88] Ironically, however, similar strategic issues were subsequently to cause the withdrawal of the keepers of the counties. By the autumn of 1332 the king was keen to free up the magnates and knights of England in order that they could prepare for likely new war in Scotland. In 1334, the parliamentary commons were highly critical of what remained of the 1332 scheme, demanding the dismissal of corrupt keepers of counties and their replacement by men properly accountable to king and council.[89] The mid-1330s saw a number of continuing efforts to satisfy public opinion on law and order. The king's bench was dispatched to eastern and midland England; arrangements were made for those holding pardons to provide guarantors for future good behaviour; and the bishops were asked to issue excommunications against notorious offenders.[90] Before leaving for a campaign in Scotland in 1335, Edward III announced his determination that those who rode armed against the king's peace should be treated not just as felons but as rebels and, potentially, traitors.[91] But even in a state of emergency, such extraordinary measures had a habit of generating controversy. In 1336 an ordinance was granted in parliament allowing the indefinite detention of suspected criminals. This was perceived directly to contravene the explicit statements in Magna Carta against arbitrary imprisonment and access to speedy and fair justice, and the crown was eventually forced to abandon the legislation in 1341.[92] The example is a useful reminder that sensitivities about civil rights could impose very practical constraints on efforts to preserve the peace. In general, however, it cannot be said that Edward III gave a great deal of attention to the maintenance of order in England during the mid-1330s. In June 1337 a new series of oyer and terminer commissions was actually withdrawn in order to provide guarantees against prosecution for those preparing to serve the king in Scotland and France.[93] There could be few clearer signs of the subordination of justice to the dynamics of war.

All that said, the preparations for Edward III's departure to the continent at the start of the French war in 1337–8 involved an extensive and ambitious programme of law enforcement. After consulting with groups of shire knights in councils at York and Westminster, the crown elaborated

[88] See pp. 150–1.

[89] *PROME*, iv, 197–8.

[90] *SCCKB*, iv, xliii n. 1, civ; *CCR 1333–7*, 129; *SR*, i, 275; 33–4; *Registrum Thome de Charlton, episcopi Herefordensis*, ed. W. C. Capes (CYS, ix, 1913), 33–4; *RDP*, iv, 44–6; B. H. Putnam, 'Shire Officials: Keepers of the Peace and Justices of the Peace', *Eng. Govt at Work*, iii, 194.

[91] J. G. Bellamy, *The Law of Treason in England in the Later Middle Ages* (Cambridge, 1970), 74–5.

[92] *SR*, i, 277; *CPR 1334–8*, 367–71; *PROME*, iv, 311, 316.

[93] *CCR 1337–9*, 134. A common petition probably dating to 1339 (but possibly 1337) called for the reinstatement of these commissions: *RPHI*, 268.

on the system first considered in 1332. Groups of magnates were appointed as 'overseers' of the counties, with special responsibility for the defence of the realm.[94] Under them, in each shire, groups of local gentry were empowered to organize the array of troops and deal with breaches of the peace. By authorizing the latter group not just to receive indictments but also to hear and determine cases, the crown promoted the commissioners from 'keepers' to 'justices' of the peace. Similar delegation of responsibilities had been attempted as early as 1329, but it was the experiment of 1338 that really set a template for the future organization of criminal justice, partly because it lasted for six years and partly because it seemed so quickly to satisfy the political elite's priorities pertaining to public order.[95] Both the home administration in 1338 and the parliamentary commons in October 1339 expressed general confidence in the new system for the keeping of the peace.[96] There were some signs of difficulty in the north, where over-enthusiastic pursuit of malefactors forced some people to escape over the border and make common cause with the Scots.[97] And by 1340 the material burden of war was beginning to precipitate acts of civil disobedience that some commentators took for signs of open rebellion.[98] But the quantitative data, such as they are, supply no evidence that the king's long absence on the continent in 1338–40 caused any real crisis of public order.[99] Although a great deal was to happen before the justices of the peace were finally established as a permanent element in the judicial structure, the successful initiative of 1338 would condition much of the subsequent thinking of both crown and polity on the effective preservation of public order.

To the high principles of right and justice was added the rather more prosaic challenge of keeping the crown solvent. Throughout the 1330s the king was almost always short of ready cash. The stripping away, during the minority, of virtually all the liquid capital confiscated from Edward II and his followers meant that the adult Edward III had no personal deposits on which he might draw either to sustain the regular expenditure of his household or subsidize the enterprise of war. The crown's gross ordinary income stood at around £30,000 a year, derived mainly from the farms paid by the sheriffs, the customs collected at the ports and a range

[94] *Foedera*, II.ii, 1013–14; *CPR 1338–40*, 134–40, 141–2; A. Verduyn, 'The Selection and Appointment of Justices of the Peace in 1338', *HR*, lxviii (1995), 1–25.
[95] A. Musson and W. M. Ormrod, *The Evolution of English Justice: Law, Politics and Society in the Fourteenth Century* (Basingstoke, 1999), 50–1.
[96] C 49/7/9, printed (and wrongly dated) in Baldwin, *King's Council*, 478–9; *PROME*, iv, 242.
[97] *CCR 1337–9*, 94; Verduyn, 'Attitude', 70–1.
[98] See pp. 228–9.
[99] Hanawalt, *Crime and Conflict*, 229–38.

of feudal and judicial rights.[100] A large proportion of this revenue was taken up in servicing royal patronage, and much of what was left was committed in advance of collection to cover the costs of the king's household, the central administration and the pursuit of diplomacy. Even in times of peace, then, the crown often had regularly to resort to borrowing cash and issuing credit notes to its suppliers.

During the first decade of his reign Edward III continued the practices of his grandfather and father and borrowed extensively from the Italian banking companies operating in London. By far and away the most conspicuous of these were the Bardi and Peruzzi of Florence, though the Portinari of Florence and the Busdraghi of Lucca were also significant lenders to the crown. A long tradition, beginning in Edward's own time, has it that the bankruptcy of the Bardi and Peruzzi in the 1340s was the direct consequence of the English king's inability or refusal to repay the loans that he raised from them at the start of the Hundred Years War. In point of fact, neither the lending nor the defaulting was of a scale sufficient to cause such chaos. The collapse of the two banks was really the consequence of their general over-commitment and the onset of a serious economic recession in Italy.[101] Either way, however, their withdrawal forced Edward to seek new sources of finance. Already by 1340 the king had significantly diversified his portfolio of lenders to include members of the German Hanse, especially Tidemann Limbergh and Conrad Clipping, and some of the merchant communities of the Low Countries, particularly the towns of Malines and Brussels.[102] Most important of all was the shift towards home-based credit. A number of the largest loans raised by the crown in the period 1337–41 were organized by the Hull-born merchant William de la Pole, whose significant services in this regard were duly rewarded with the honorary status of banneret in the royal household. It was de la Pole who also organized the major syndicate that raised a loan of £200,000 for Edward III in 1337.[103] Between June 1338 and October 1339, when the combined credit made available from the Bardi and Peruzzi was around £126,000, de la Pole alone acted as agent for loans of at least £112,000.[104] Behind these schemes stood some powerful

[100] J. R. Strayer, 'Introduction', *Eng. Govt at Work*, ii, 4–6; N. Barratt, 'English Royal Revenue in the Early Thirteenth Century and its Wider Context, 1130–1330', *Crises, Revolutions and Self-Sustained Growth: Essays in European Fiscal History, 1130–1830*, ed. W. M. Ormrod, M. Bonney and R. Bonney (Stamford, 1999), 77.

[101] E. S. Hunt, 'A New Look at the Dealings of the Bardi and Peruzzi with Edward III', *Journal of Economic History*, l (1990), 149–62; E. S. Hunt, *The Medieval Super-Companies: A Study of the Peruzzi Company of Florence* (Cambridge, 1994).

[102] Fryde, *Studies*, chap. vii; R. L. Axworthy, 'The Financial Relationship of the London Merchant Community with Edward III, 1327 to 1377' (University of London PhD thesis, 2001), 45–67.

[103] See pp. 188–94.

[104] Fryde, *Studies*, chap. xii, 17.

cartels of merchants in London, York and other provincial towns, whose new prominence as major investors gave them a political leverage unimaginable even a generation earlier.

The crown's ability to raise commercial loans relied on three things: the availability of security, the expectation of repayment, and the amount of interest promised. It was not uncommon for kings to pawn their own jewels and plate in the Middle Ages, and Edward III regularly used the 'great crown' and two lesser crowns held in his personal treasury to provide collateral for loans raised at home and abroad.[105] When the great crown was pawned in 1338, it was assayed as having four great and four little foliations encrusted with thirty-four rubies, thirty-four emeralds and eighty-eight pearls.[106] In the same year Edward extracted an enormous stockpile of gold and silver plate from English religious houses and used it as security for his loans and debts on the continent.[107] Such pledging in 1337–8 was of sufficient scale to prompt an unfounded rumour that the crown of St Edward, that most precious element of the coronation regalia, had passed into hands of mere merchants.[108]

Repayment of loans raised during times of war was normally organized in the form of assignments of future revenues from direct and indirect taxation. The higher the level of risk involved in recovering the capital and the shorter the period agreed for repayment, then the higher the rates of interest set by the lenders. To get around the Christian Church's injunctions against usury, Edward III used a variety of techniques. The Jews, on whom earlier generations of English royals had relied heavily as moneylenders, had been expelled from England in 1290 and were only officially tolerated in the land when they submitted as converts to Christianity. But they remained a significant force in parts of continental Europe, and figures such as Vivelin Rufus of Strasbourg acted as middlemen for a number of the loans raised in Germany at the end of the 1330s.[109] In loans raised directly from fellow Christians, there were also plenty of clever book-keeping devices that disguised the extremely high accumulation of interest on the king's debts. The Italians and Flemings usually expected an annualized return of somewhere between 25 and 40 per cent on their capital, and when Edward III's creditworthiness became especially stretched in the later 1330s some smaller lenders were able to negotiate the equivalent of annualized rates as high as 67 per cent.[110] Hardly

---

[105] SC 1/36/161; E 101/391/12.

[106] E 101/624/29.

[107] BL, MS Cotton Faustina B. V, fol. 82; E 101/624/29; C 81/1548B; *CPR 1339–40*, 122; Fryde, *Studies*, chap. vii, 1154.

[108] CCCC, MS 78, fol. 172v.

[109] *CPR 1338–40*, 371.

[110] A. Bell, C. Brooks and T. K. Moore, 'Interest in Medieval Accounts: Examples from England, 1272–1340', *History*, xciv (2009), 418–19.

surprisingly, the king was later to claim that the borrowing at the start of the Hundred Years War forced him into the 'devouring gulf of usury'.[111]

These problems were compounded by three very considerable limitations acting on the crown's finances in the 1330s. The first was a general bullion famine resulting from the recent exhaustion of the silver mines of eastern Europe. Natural wastage and transfers abroad meant that the total amount of silver coin in circulation in England fell from in excess of £2 million in the 1320s to under £1 million by the late 1340s.[112] Secondly, the resulting deflation jeopardized the crown's income from direct taxes on the laity, which were based on the market price of grain, livestock and other merchandise. And finally, the experience of taxation over the previous generation had made Edward III's subjects increasingly adept at tax avoidance. The combined effects can be seen to dramatic effect in the fifteenth and tenth of 1332, which raised less than 30 per cent of what Edward I had taken from a comparable grant in 1290.[113] It was to prevent any further depreciation of the assessable tax base that, when parliament conceded a fifteenth and tenth for the Scottish war in 1334, the crown decided not to carry out a new valuation of goods but simply to impose on each collection district a sum at least equivalent to that paid by its inhabitants in 1332. As a consequence, the maximum possible yield from the regular form of lay taxation was now set at about £38,000. In the parallel system of clerical taxation, the same process of ossification had in fact already set in two generations earlier, in the 1290s. A clerical tenth levied on the two provinces of Canterbury and York could therefore raise no more than £19,000. These ceilings, subject to further downward revision to reflect demographic and economic changes, were to apply for the remainder of Edward III's reign and long beyond.[114]

The quota system adopted for fifteenths and tenths after 1334 had some attractions for the crown. It allowed the government to predict with some certainty the yield of a tax and thus to budget more effectively for its expenditure. It also allowed taxes to be put into commission more speedily. And it reduced overheads by requiring the inhabitants of each tax district to sort out among themselves the way in which they might assess individual contributions. In the latter respect the new system had the

---

[111] *Foedera*, II.ii, 1152–3; G. Seabourne, *Royal Regulation of Loans and Sales in Medieval England* (Woodbridge, 2003), 62.

[112] M. Allen, 'The Volume of the English Currency, 1158–1470', *EcHR*, 2nd series, liv (2001), 607. Allen's figures are significantly larger than most previous estimates, but confirm the speed and magnitude of the reduction during the 1330s.

[113] J. F. Hadwin, 'The Medieval Lay Subsidies and Economic History', *EcHR*, 2nd series, xxxvi (1983), 200–17.

[114] Willard, *Parliamentary Taxes*, 5–6, 54–72; Ormrod, 'Crown and the English Economy', 151–67. The expenses of the royal clerks detained in 1334 to write out the sums previously collected from each vill in 1332 are detailed in E 403/279, 3 Nov., 18 Nov. 1334.

unintended but serious consequence of shifting the tax threshold down the social scale. Prior to 1334 more than half the population had been deemed too poor to pay taxes. After that date a rather larger number of modest householders in town and countryside were brought within the tax net. And since tax quotas were now fixed, this gave the clear impression that the rich were offsetting their economic problems by forcing the burden of taxation on to the poor.[115] There can be little doubt that the new system condoned a higher level of corruption in the local administration of royal subsidies.[116] But we need to be cautious about the notion that Edward III's government was set on the systemic exploitation of the most vulnerable elements of society. Discontented taxpayers were driven rather too readily to make accusations of extortion and embezzlement against local tax collectors because they hoped thereby to be able to recoup some of their own contributions.[117] Nor did the elite necessarily shrug off its obligations. For the most part, the notion that the poorest elements in society ought to be free of direct taxation still prevailed. Even in 1340, under enormous pressure, the parliamentary commons insisted that smallholders and land-less labourers should be exempt from the fifteenth.[118] Pre-plague England was certainly no tax paradise. In the end, though, the increasing resistance that Edward III's fiscal agents were to encounter in the late 1330s was a comment less on the social distribution of taxes than on their sheer number and virtually unprecedented scale.[119]

It was also, in a very real sense, a comment on the considerable inge-nuity that the crown demonstrated in overcoming the limitations of fiscal capacity imposed by the standard lay and clerical subsidies. The 1330s witnessed a very important series of experiments in royal finance. While not all the schemes were successful or enduring, it was out of this process of trial and error that Edward III formed the fiscal system that would sustain his successors for the rest of the Hundred Years War. First, and least successfully, the crown revived Edward I's controversial efforts to appropriate stocks of wool and to sell them, for its own profit, in the markets of the Low Countries.[120] Secondly, and with considerably more success, it secured a series of direct taxes that were assessed and collected not in cash but in kind: a subsidy in wool in 1338; and in 1340, in imitation of the ecclesiastical tithe, a ninth part of all wool, wheat and newborn

[115] C. Dyer, 'Taxation and Communities in Late Medieval England', *Progress and Problems*, ed. Britnell and Hatcher, 168–190.

[116] R. W. Kaeuper, *War, Justice, and Public Order: England and France in the Later Middle Ages* (Oxford, 1988), 132.

[117] W. M. Ormrod, 'Poverty and Privilege: The Fiscal Burden in England (XIIIth–XVth Centuries)', *La fiscalità nell'economia europea secc. XIII–XVIII*, ed. S. Cavaciocchi, 2 vols (Prato, 2008), ii, 641.

[118] *SR*, i, 288–9; *CPR 1338–40*, 499.

[119] See pp. 210–11.

[120] See pp. 188–206.

lambs. Taking subsidies in kind was partly a means of alleviating the continued scarcity of coin. But it also allowed the crown to break free of the restrictions imposed by the standard forms of taxation. The 1338 subsidy in wool raised the equivalent, in domestic market prices, of £73,000, more or less twice what could be expected from one of the fifteenths and tenths that ran alongside it.[121] These extraordinary measures provided a powerful marker of the crown's continued ability, in moments of high emergency, to exploit the real wealth of the realm in the service of its wars.

The third and more enduring of the changes introduced into royal finance during the 1330s was the subsidy on wool exports. Edward I had begun the practice of imposing extraordinary indirect taxes over and above the standard customs rates in 1294. The *maltolt* or 'bad tax', as it had then been dubbed, was deeply unpopular not so much with the merchants who paid it at the ports as with the sheep farmers, who feared that exporters would pass back the additional costs of the subsidy in the form of lower prices on the domestic market. After 1297 there had therefore been only one brief attempt to revive the *maltolt*, in 1322–3.[122] The reintroduction of the tax for one year in 1333–4, at the rate of 10 shillings a sack, was scarcely less controversial.[123] After 1336, however, the crown managed through a series of commercial deals with the merchants to secure a virtually unbroken sequence of grants. It also dramatically increased the rate, which by 1338 stood at £1 3s 4d a sack for English merchants and £2 13s 4d for foreigners. Although the parliament of March 1340 secured a reduction in the charges on aliens and a promise that the tax would soon cease, the crown would continue to negotiate further subsidies with merchant assemblies and parliaments throughout the 1340s at the now more or less standard rate of £2 a sack.[124]

The result was a permanent transformation in the crown's ability to exploit the wealth represented by the English export trade. Before 1336, income from the permanent customs had stood at about £15,000 a year. The various seizures of wool and other short-term interventions in trade disrupted income from the *maltolt* during the early stages of the French war, but within a few years parliament was claiming that the combined revenue from the customs and the wool subsidy was four times that of the period before the war, or around £60,000; and the subsequent history of indirect taxation suggests that even this large figure was a conservative

[121] Ormrod, 'Crown and the English Economy', 177–8.

[122] Ibid., 168–9. This statement excludes forced loans on exports, which were repayable out of future revenue from the customs.

[123] See p. 153.

[124] *PROME*, iv, 264; *SR*, i, 291; *CFR 1337–47*, 196; G. L. Harriss, *King, Parliament and Public Finance in Medieval England to 1369* (Oxford, 1975), 420–49.

estimate.[125] It was the enduring success of the wool subsidy that also allowed the crown, after the initial frenetic activity of the war, to move away from cripplingly heavy direct taxes and concentrate instead on the exploitation of overseas trade. From the mid-1340s the wool subsidy became the single largest regular element in the crown's wartime revenues, and remained so for the rest of the Hundred Years War.[126]

The long-term impact of the various fiscal initiatives undertaken by Edward III's government between 1336 and 1340 ought not to blind us to the equally serious short-term failure of royal finance during these years. The tax experiments that accompanied the opening of the French war were not part of some master plan for the transformation of the medieval fiscal state but desperate measures forced on the country by a king whose spending was out of all proportion to a sustainable income. The high level of taxation in the first years of the Hundred Years War was altogether exceptional, and bears comparison only with a few great peaks of fiscal activity in medieval England, as under Richard I and King John in the 1190s and 1200s, Edward I in the 1290s and Henry V in the 1410s.[127] No less significantly, however, it served to expose the comparative weakness of the contemporary regime in France. Philip VI's peacetime income was three times that of his English counterpart. Between 1337 and 1342, however, his ordinary and extraordinary revenues combined probably still did not amount to as much, in real terms, as those of Edward III.[128] It was the superior capacity of the English crown to transform and maintain itself as a war state that ultimately explains why Edward was able, even after such a disastrously false start, to stave off the bankruptcy that apparently faced him 1340 and to continue to eventual triumph the great adventure that he had begun against the Valois.

To understand how Edward III was able to obtain the consent and acquiescence of his subjects in the great explosion of taxation that accompanied the Scottish and French wars is to appreciate something of the careful groundwork laid in economic policy during the 1330s. Some elements of this policy tended rather obviously to subordinate commercial considerations to short-term fiscal or political gains. This is especially the case with

[125] Ormrod, *Reign of Edward III*, 182, 207; Fryde, *Studies*, chap. x, 6.

[126] W. M. Ormrod, 'England in the Middle Ages', *The Rise of the Fiscal State in Europe, c.1200–1815*, ed. R. Bonney (Oxford, 1999), 41–2.

[127] M. Prestwich, 'War and Taxation in England in the XIIIth and XIVth Centuries', *Genèse de l'état moderne: Prélèvement et redistribution*, ed. J.-P. Genet and M. le Mené (Paris, 1987), 181–3; Ormrod, 'England in the Middle Ages', 30–1.

[128] J. B. Henneman, *Royal Taxation in Fourteenth-Century France: The Development of War Financing, 1320–1356* (Princeton, 1971), 80–114; W. M. Ormrod, 'The West European Monarchies in the Later Middle Ages', *Economic Systems and State Finance*, ed. R. Bonney (Oxford, 1995), 138–44.

the strategy for the wool staple, a system whereby the crown periodically forced all those intending to export wool to the continent to take their goods through one or several entrepôts. Most wool producers in England regarded the staple as a regrettable nuisance and for logistical reasons preferred it to be located in the ports or inland towns of England. This is how two temporary staple operations, in 1326–8 and 1332–4, were implemented. For the crown, however, the fixing of the staple in the Low Countries, the main continental market for English wool, presented a particularly valuable means of winning co-operation for its military endeavours. Accordingly, and much to the chagrin of English producers, the opening of the French war was accompanied by the setting up of a new English staple, first at Antwerp and then, following the Flemish alliance of 1340, at Bruges, where it remained until 1348.[129]

There were many other elements of economic policy that could, however, be more readily and convincingly represented as actively beneficial to English commercial interests. Edward III's interventions in the domestic cloth trade were an especially important case in point. The crown had been under pressure for some time to promote the native cloth industry by encouraging Flemish and other foreign weavers to settle in England.[130] In 1333 parliament returned to this theme, claiming that immigrant clothmakers 'will readily teach the people of this land to work the cloth, to the great profit of our lord the king and of his people'.[131] In 1335 the Statute of York established the crucial principle that all merchants, foreign as well as native, ought to be able to trade freely in England.[132] And in 1337, further legislation provided significant guarantees to manufacturers coming into England and tried to impose mercantilist protectionism by forbidding the wearing of foreign cloth.[133] These initiatives, especially the Statute of York, would become key elements of commercial policy in later years of the reign, and would be read by Edward III's successors as clear examples of his far-sighted economic strategy.[134]

In his management of the currency, too, Edward was careful to be seen to uphold the economic welfare of the realm. The chronic shortage of bullion forced a number of European monarchies, including the Valois, to embark on radical and often disastrous devaluations. Since kings usually

---

[129] T. H. Lloyd, *The English Wool Trade in the Middle Ages* (Cambridge, 1977), 115–18, 121, 193–4, 202–3.

[130] E. Lipson, *The Economic History of England, I: The Middle Ages*, 10th edn (London, 1949), 451–2.

[131] *PROME*, iv, 191.

[132] *SR*, i, 270–1; T. H. Lloyd, *England the German Hanse, 1157–1611* (Cambridge, 1991), 30.

[133] *PROME*, iv, 230; *SR*, i, 280–1; *CLBL, E*, 303; Murimuth, 79; G. Unwin, 'The Estate of Merchants, 1336–1365', *Finance and Trade under Edward III*, ed. G. Unwin (Manchester, 1918), 187.

[134] Ormrod, *Reign of Edward III*, 173–4.

made profits from the outputs of the mints, the re-coinages required by
Philip VI in the later 1330s rapidly came to be seen by his subjects as just
another form of arbitrary taxation.[135] Edward III's government occasionally resorted to desperate measures of its own: in 1329, in a creative effort
to establish new supplies of silver, the government summoned two
rumoured alchemists, John Rous and William Dalby, to come before the
king and demonstrate their miraculous craft.[136] Such escapism apart,
however, the English crown generally preferred to maintain a strong
currency, and for the first five years of his personal rule Edward III
resolutely refused to permit any reduction in the weight or fineness of
sterling. In April 1331 he also issued an important ordinance that
attempted to prevent the outflow of bullion by banning exports of coin
and plate. Such protectionism became a regular feature of monetary
policy in the following years.[137]

Although serious measures were initiated to enforce this embargo,[138]
the very strength of English sterling in the foreign currency markets also
made it virtually impossible, in the longer term, to prevent the further
egress of coin. Accordingly, in 1335, the crown was forced to make a slight
reduction in the fineness of the new halfpennies issued from the mints,
thus at once increasing the amount of coin in circulation and making it
marginally less attractive for export.[139] Mindful of his responsibilities,
however, the king was careful to let it be known that his government
intended to restore sterling standards as soon as circumstances permitted.
In 1338, and again in 1341, English landholders were given an incentive to
contribute additional bullion to the mints by being allowed to take a
proportion of any silver found as mineral deposits or as treasure trove on
their estates.[140] Such desperate measures may seem to the modern eye like
admissions of defeat. But public allegiance to the idea of a strong and
stable currency was important not only for its own sake but also as part of
the social compact that bound the king to promote the material prosperity
of the realm.

Rhetoric, of course, has an uncomfortable tendency sometimes to
deviate from reality. The experience of the first phase of the French war
very rapidly persuaded many of Edward III's ordinary subjects that
economic and monetary policy, far from promoting the common good,
was being ruthlessly subordinated to the king's pursuit of a reckless foreign

---

[135] J. Kaye, *Economy and Nature in the Fourteenth Century* (Cambridge, 1998), 19–28.

[136] *CPR 1327–30*, 386.

[137] *CCR 1330–3*, 303; *SR*, i, 291, 299.

[138] *CFR 1327–37*, 251–2; E 159/107, rot. 122; *The Enrolled Customs Accounts*, ed. S. Jenks, 5
vols (List and Index Society, ccciii, cccvi, cccvii, cccxiii, cccxiv, 2004–6), i, 289 n. 7.

[139] N. J. Mayhew, 'From Regional to Central Minting, 1158–1464', *A New History of the
Royal Mint*, ed. C. E. Challis (Cambridge, 1992), 144–5.

[140] *CFR 1337–47*, 234.

adventure.[141] Yet it was in the policies pursued over the previous decade that Edward now found the moral authority that allowed his regime to survive. When he asserted his right to be considered the legitimate ruler of France in 1340, he wrote a long and carefully worded statement of his adherence to the principles of good kingship, promising his prospective subjects on the other side of the Channel that he would provide justice for all, eliminate arbitrary taxes and restore a sound currency.[142] The parallel initiatives that Edward had already taken in England for the better preservation of public order, the rebuilding of royal finance, the development of manufacture and trade and the stability of the coinage had built up great public confidence which was not completely exhausted even in the darkest moments of the political crisis of 1340–1. The purposefulness and activism of his pre-war regime therefore goes a long way to explaining how Edward III was able in due course to re-emerge in England as the very exemplar of beneficent rule.

[141] See pp. 228–9.
[142] *Foedera*, II.ii, 1108–9.

Chapter 5

FAMILY AND FRIENDS, 1330–1344

If medieval monarchy was a bureaucratic and political institution, it was also very obviously a social performance. Not least of the consequences of the collapse of the minority regime in 1330 was the opportunity thus provided for the young king to exercise much more actively his personal choice over the membership of the royal household, court and council. The Nottingham coup allowed those who had been conspicuous in the young king's service to reap the material rewards of personal loyalty. It also required a rather larger group of ministers, magnates and ecclesiastics to renegotiate their relationship with the crown and prove their worth as reliable counsellors and friends. In his late teens and twenties Edward III had a distinctly conservative, even perhaps old-fashioned, attitude towards political society. Given the new prominence of the commons in the deposition of Edward II and the first parliament of his own reign, it is striking that Edward's early *politique* betrayed comparatively few of the obviously populist strategies that were to become hallmarks of his later regime. On the other hand, the successful prosecution of policy still relied to a considerable degree on the ability of the king to manage the nobles and bishops who comprised his natural social circle and provided the advice and consent that was held necessary to validate so much of the public business of the realm. It was especially important in this regard that the court of the young king should be freed from the political factionalism that had endured through so much of the previous decade. In practice, the only realistic way to achieve this was through a conscious and consistent policy of reconciliation and inclusivity. It was fortunate indeed for the elite that it found in Edward III a king so obviously inclined, both by instinct and by experience, to that strategy.

The greatest test of the king's commitment to clemency lay in his treatment of those responsible for the murder of his father. If all parties had rapidly agreed to the convenient fiction of Edward II's free and open abdication in 1327, there still remained very serious and unresolved issues about the nature of the crime perpetrated at Berkeley later that year. Edward III's deliberate efforts in the parliament of November 1330 to place the blame on Mortimer indicated from the start his disinclination to pursue a more general vengeance. Thomas Gurney, that 'satellite of Satan', was hunted down in Naples and probably escaped trial and execution only because he died at Bayonne while being escorted back to England in 1333.[1] One of Gurney's servants, John Trilly, was still being held at Bordeaux, awaiting the king's pleasure in 1334.[2] In the York parliament of May 1335, however, the lords were readily persuaded to put an end to any remaining uncertainty as to the culpability of Sir Thomas Berkeley, approving the king's pardon and release of Berkeley from all future liability for Edward II's assassination.[3] Around the same time the former steward, John Maltravers, who was under threat of execution for the death of the earl of Kent, made a temporary visit home in the hope of securing a royal pardon.[4] Once his vengeance on Mortimer was complete, Edward III evidently had no intention of pursuing much further the men who had had the misfortune to be implicated in the deaths of his father and uncle.

It was in this atmosphere of reconciliation that the king set about the necessary task of turning the memory of his deceased father to the service of the new regime. In spite of Edward II's blatant inadequacies as monarch and man, a cult had begun to develop around his final resting place at Gloucester. For a short while this had seemed likely to provide a rallying-point for those alienated from the rule of Isabella and Mortimer.[5] It was imperative for the stability of his own regime, then, that Edward III should assume active patronage of the developing cult. In 1331 the king paid £10 to a member of the order of St John of Jerusalem who had gone to the Holy Land for the benefit of the soul of Edward II.[6] After 1330 the anniversary of the ex-king's death continued to be observed every year in the royal chapel, and crown representatives were usually sent to Gloucester to supervise the parallel commemorations held there.[7] Although documentary evidence is lacking, it seems highly likely on stylistic grounds that Edward III commissioned the splendid tomb erected over his father's sepulchre in the abbey church, with its refined and stately alabaster figure of a crowned king. But just as he had resisted the over-zealous pursuit of his father's murderers, so also did Edward III artfully avoid too close an association with the blatant defects of the ex-king's rule. In particular, and unlike his successor Richard II, Edward never provided

---

[1] BL, MS Cotton Faustina B. V, fol. 51; J. Hunter, 'On the Measures taken for the Apprehension of Sir Thomas de Gournay', *Archaeologia*, xxvii (1838), 274–97; 'Extracts from the *Historia Aurea* and a French "Brut" ', 217.

[2] C 47/24/5, fol. 9v.

[3] C 81/1708/34; Ormrod, 'The King's Secrets', 172–4.

[4] Mortimer, 'Death of Edward II', 1205. For Maltravers's eventual rehabilitation in 1351 see p. 364.

[5] S. Walker, *Political Culture in Later Medieval England*, ed. M. J. Braddick (Manchester, 2006), 203.

[6] *CCR 1330–3*, 315; E 403/256, 4 July 1331.

[7] E 101/383/14, m. 2; E 101/398/22; BL, Add. MS 46350, m. 1; BL, MS Cotton Nero C. VIII, fol. 203; Ormrod, 'Personal Religion', 871.

official support for the unlikely campaign of the monks of Gloucester to have Edward of Caernarfon canonized.[8]

Ironically, it was the very low key nature of this official policy that may have contributed to renewed speculation outside England about the survival and potential re-adeption of the ex-king. Some time in or shortly after 1336 Manuel Fieschi, a papal notary and later bishop of Vercelli, wrote a letter to Edward III claiming that the former king had not been assassinated at Berkeley but had escaped, first to Corfe Castle and, after the execution of the earl of Kent, to Ireland. He had then returned to England in the disguise of a pilgrim and later departed the shores of his former realm for the Low Countries, travelling extensively through France and the Rhineland until he had finally taken up residence at Cecima in the diocese of Pavia, where he was now said to be happily settled into the life of a hermit performing prayers and penances for his son and family.[9] That rumours of Edward II's survival persisted on the continent is borne out by a curious incident that took place while the king was at Koblenz in September 1338 en route to seal an alliance with the emperor. One William le Galeys ('the Welshman'), 'who claims that he is the father of the present king', was brought before Edward III and subsequently taken back, in the king's train, to Antwerp.[10] Not surprisingly, these tantalizing snippets have provoked much speculation in modern times about the plausibility of the escape story and raised the intriguing possibility that Edward of Caernarfon did indeed live on in obscure and romantic circumstances on the continent for some years after his supposed burial at Gloucester.[11]

How did Edward III respond to such fantastical tales? If he suspected that there was any truth in them, then there is of course a major issue to confront as to whether Edward was an arch-hypocrite who preferred, for reasons of self-preservation, to support the fiction of Edward II's death at the hands of Mortimer's toadies over the fact of the former king's biding in wait for his return to the throne. We cannot expect to know Edward of Windsor's innermost thoughts on the subject, and always need to keep open the possibility that he did at least momentarily experience the pangs of filial disloyalty and the panic of political threat. Certainly, some of the king's actions around the time of these stories might suggest the need to

[8] *Age of Chivalry*, no. 497; Phillips, *Edward II*, 334–60.

[9] G. P. Cuttino and T. W. Lyman, 'Where is Edward II?', *Speculum*, liii (1978), 526–7, 537–8. For a detailed account of the complex archival history and historiography of this letter see Phillips, *Edward II*, 582–7.

[10] Norwell, 212.

[11] The most detailed case in favour of Edward II's survival is Mortimer, 'Death of Edward II', 1175–1214. For the case against, see R. M. Haines, '*Edwardus redivivus*: The "Afterlife" of Edward of Caernarvon', *Transactions of the Bristol and Gloucestershire Archaeological Society*, cxiv (1996), 65–86; J. R. S. Phillips, ' "Edward II" in Italy: English and Welsh Political Exiles and Fugitives in Continental Europe, 1322–1364', *Thirteenth Century England X*, ed. M. Prestwich, R. H. Britnell and R. Frame (Woodbridge, 2005), 209–26.

pre-empt the admission of dangerous rumours into the realm. In the parliament of March 1337 Edward effectively confirmed his official recognition of his father's death by reissuing Sir Thomas Berkeley's indemnity from liability in the old king's murder.[12] And in September of the same year the king made his first personal visit since the fall of Mortimer to Edward II's tomb at Gloucester.[13] If these are signs of defensiveness and nervousness, then Edward III can indeed be thought to have fallen victim, as did the successors of so many other usurped kings in the late Middle Ages, to the tendency for disaffected parties to focus on the idea of a restoration of the old order.

All that said, we also need to emphasize just how tenuous is the evidence after 1330 for the survival of Edward II. There is nothing to prove that Manuel Fieschi's correspondence ever actually reached its intended recipient, for the only copy of the letter that exists today is in Montpellier. And in any case, the letter carried no imputation that Edward of Caernarfon was ever likely to challenge his son's authority, and was emphatic in its recognition of Edward III as rightful ruler of England. If it carried any warning, it was probably more by way of suggesting that any other impostor stories or re-adeption plots would indeed be inauthentic and invalid.[14] This may well explain why Edward III treated William le Galeys as a deluded simpleton. Whereas his father had been forced in his insecurity to execute the impostor John of Powderham in 1318, Edward III took no recorded action against Galeys in 1338 and presumably set him free from Antwerp to go wandering wherever circumstance and inclination took him. Above all, Edward of Windsor was safe in the knowledge that he had been the undisputed heir to the throne and the natural successor of the former king in the revolution of 1326–7. Later successors to usurped kings lacked such uncontested dynastic authority, and reaped the consequences: one has only to look ahead to the persistent rumours in English high politics and popular culture of Richard II's survival, and the resulting plots that dogged much of the reign of the usurper Henry IV, to make the point.[15]

Whatever his inner thoughts, then, Edward III's calm and firm approach to the rumour mill had the desired effect. There is no direct evidence that the gossip communicated by Fieschi ever again found any currency in England. In 1330 some of the highest in the land had been all too ready to express their hatred of Mortimer by indulging in the escapist

[12] *CPR 1334–8*, 398; *PROME*, iv, 230.

[13] E 101/388/5.

[14] As stressed by Phillips, *Edward II*, 591–2.

[15] Walker, *Political Culture*, 156–73; P. Strohm, *England's Empty Throne: Usurpation and the Language of Legitimation, 1399–1422* (London, 1998), 119–24; J. Burden, 'How do You Bury a Deposed King? The Funeral of Richard II and the Establishment of Lancastrian Royal Authority in 1400', *Henry IV: The Establishment of the Regime, 1399–1406*, ed. G. Dodd and D. Biggs (York, 2003), 35–53.

notion of the return of Edward of Caernarfon. Seven years later, however, no one was likely to want to reject the brilliant young Edward III for
the sake of restoring his dangerously incompetent father. The momentary
flurry of survival stories surrounding the hapless Edward of Caernarfon
had simply dissolved, like the proverbial frost of May, in the warm glow of
Edward of Windsor's charisma.

In many ways it was not the deceased Edward II but the surviving Queen
Isabella who posed the greatest challenge to their son's general policy of
rehabilitation. Pope John XXII believed that Edward III intended
emphatically to punish his mother for her abuse of royal power during the
minority.[16] The king's immediate action after the Nottingham coup in
requiring the queen to surrender all of her dower lands suggests just such
an act of humiliation.[17] Edward even went so far as to set guards on his
mother's jewels and other goods at the Tower and to issue injunctions
against her agents making any further distributions of her confiscated
possessions.[18] Isabella was lodged first at her manor of Berkhamsted and
then at Windsor, where she remained for some two years in close seclusion.[19] For a short while Edward may indeed have thought of his mother
as his prisoner. On the other hand, it may simply be that the queen
suffered a kind of nervous breakdown that required her temporary withdrawal from public life.[20] The idea that Edward III subsequently locked
his mother up at Castle Rising is certainly a fiction. But there is more than
a hint that he sought actively to ensure that the queen showed appropriate
contrition.[21] The French poem known as the *Lament of Edward II* may have
been commissioned by the young king specifically to remind his mother of
her crimes against his father, creatively recast here as the epitome of the
heterosexual courtly lover.[22] And the arduous programme of religious
observance to which the queen became addicted in the later years of her
life bears more than a hint of a penitential regime.[23]
    The eventual re-emergence of Isabella of France on to the public stage
could therefore be regarded as a uniquely sensitive issue for Edward III.
The 1330 parliament agreed that Isabella should be restored to some parts
of her dower, though at the modest and conventional limit of £3,000 a

---

[16] *CPL*, ii, 498, 500, 501.

[17] *CPR 1327–30*, 48; E 159/107, rots 94, 95.

[18] E 159/107, rots 57B, 59.

[19] *CPR 1330–4*, 36; SC 1/63/247; Doherty, 'Isabella, Queen of England', 319. E 403/254,
18 Jan. 1331 records her (temporary) removal from Windsor to Odiham.

[20] Doherty, *Isabella and the Strange Death of Edward II*, 173–4.

[21] Le Bel, i, 103–4; Froissart, i, 89–90; A. Strickland, *Lives of the Queens of England*, 6 vols
(London, 1842), ii, 287–92; Ormrod, 'Sexualities of Edward II', 45–6.

[22] C. Valente, 'The "Lament of Edward II": Religious Lyric, Political Propaganda',
Speculum, lxxvii (2002), 422–39; Matthews, *Writing to the King*, 101–7.

[23] *Chron. Lanercost*, 266; Vale, *Edward III and Chivalry*, 52.

year. Her agents also took several years before they managed to secure effective control of the new estate.[24] With the landed property went the privileged access to justice customarily enjoyed by queens, and in the mid-1330s Isabella's agents were once more aggressively pursuing her rights in an acrimonious dispute with the burgesses and prior of Coventry.[25] The one thing that probably saved the contrite Isabella from political oblivion was her very special status as the sole surviving sibling of the last Capetian king of France and her resulting role as transmitter of the French royal title to her son. In 1331 Edward gave his mother a set of relics that he had recently received as a gift from Philip VI.[26] After the opening of the new Anglo-French war in 1337 and Edward's announcement in 1340 that he intended to exercise his rights as king of France, it was incumbent on him that he show rather more by way of public respect to his imperious mother. From the early 1340s Edward's visits to Isabella became more regular. Very gradually, the dowager queen merged back into the activities of the court so that, by the end of her long life in 1358, she was once more playing a regular and quite conspicuous role in hosting the visits of French nobles engaged in diplomacy with her son.[27] By a mixture of accident and design, Edward III eventually found Queen Isabella an appropriate function within his majority regime. But whatever respect and gratitude the king thus accorded to his mother in public, theirs is hardly likely to have been an affectionate relationship. No matter how hard he tried, Edward III could never quite free himself from the embarrassment of his parents.

That vexed legacy was inevitably shared by Edward's siblings. The departure of the seven-year-old Princess Joan to Scotland in 1328 made her a virtual stranger to her kingly brother. There was some suggestion in 1332 and 1334 that Joan might repudiate her marriage to David Bruce, but the English brought no particular pressure to achieve this point and Edward and his sister were not to be reunited until much later in their lives.[28] With the middle children, John and Eleanor, however, Edward had at least a brief opportunity to build affectionate relationships. From 1330, Eleanor lived in the household of Queen Philippa, where she emerged with the appropriate reputation of a fine beauty.[29] Two years later, just

---

[24] *CPR 1330–4*, 48; SC 1/38/77; Johnstone, 'Queen's Household', 257–9; Wolffe, *Royal Demesne*, 235–6.

[25] *RPHI*, 240–66; *VCH Warks*, viii, 256–9; A. and E. Gooder, 'Coventry before 1355: Unity or Division?', *Midland History*, vi (1981), 19–24; R. Goddard, *Lordship and Medieval Urbanisation: Coventry, 1043–1355* (Woodbridge, 2004), 116–17, 282–3; A. Musson, 'The Prior of Coventry v. Queen Isabella of England: Re-assessing the Archival Evidence', *Archives*, xxxii (2007), 93–103.

[26] *Foedera*, II.ii, 825.

[27] See pp. 254, 388.

[28] Stones, 'Addition to the "Rotuli Scotiae" ', 30–1.

[29] *CPR 1330–4*, 78; E 43/520; JRUL, MS Latin 234, fols. 3r, 5v, 8r, 20r–20v, 33r; JRUL, MS Latin 235, fol. 7r.

short of her sixteenth birthday, she was given in marriage to Reginald II, count of Guelders (Geldern), who marked his gratitude and pleasure by sending Edward III the gift of a wild bear.[30] The king and his sister kept in contact after the wedding,[31] and met again several times during Edward's residence in the Low Countries. In 1342 the count attempted to divorce his wife on the dubious grounds of leprosy (perhaps mental instability), and after his demise in 1343 she took the veil. But she kept up her communications with the English court until her death, at the age of thirty-seven, in 1355.[32]

John of Eltham was just twelve when, at the Salisbury parliament of 1328, he was raised to the peerage as earl of Cornwall. Prince John's personality is not easy to disentangle from the conventional representations of the age. But Edward III and he seem to have been much of a type. In particular, the royal brothers found obvious common ground in martial exploits, and John became an enthusiastic participant in the Scottish campaigns of the 1330s. It was in the midst of one such campaign that he died, tragically and unexpectedly, at Perth in September 1336 when still barely twenty years old. There were predictable rumours in Scotland, perhaps sponsored by the Bruce party, that Edward III had had his brother put to death.[33] Edward was certainly upset by the tragedy: a year later, after having a nightmare about his brother, the king offered special alms for the benefit of his soul.[34] In 1339 he determined to honour John's remains with a major alabaster monument set among the royal tombs in Westminster Abbey, and over thirty years later the king was still making distributions of cloth of gold to the abbey for the requiem masses said every year at the anniversary of John's death.[35] It was Edward III's misfortune that he may only fully have appreciated the special gift of blood brotherhood when it was so cruelly taken from him.

By great and happy contrast, Edward III's home life with his own wife and children seems to have been a matter of genuine affection and unalloyed

---

[30] A. K. McHardy, 'Paying for the Wedding: Edward III as Fundraiser, 1332–3', *Fourteenth Century England IV*, ed. Hamilton, 43–60; Lucas, *Low Countries*, 100–1. For the household established to deliver Eleanor to her husband, see 'An Account of the Expenses of Eleanor, Sister of Edward III, on the Occasion of her Marriage to Reynald, Count of Guelders', ed. E. W. Safford, *Archaeologia*, lxxvii (1927), 111–40; Vale, *Princely Court*, 311–13.

[31] BL, MS Cotton Nero C. VIII, fol. 270.

[32] M. A. E. Green, *Lives of the Princesses of England*, 6 vols (London, 1849–55), iii, 84, 86, 88–91, 96; E. Andre, *Ein Königshof auf Reisen: Der Kontinentaufenthalt Eduards III von England, 1338–40* (Cologne, 1996), 192 n. 6.

[33] T. B. James, 'John of Eltham, History and Story: Abusive International Discourse in Late Medieval England, France and Scotland', *Fourteenth Century England II*, ed. Given-Wilson, 63–78.

[34] E 101/388/5; E 101/396/20.

[35] WAM, 6300*; P. Binski, *Westminster Abbey and the Plantagenets* (London, 1995), 177–9.

joy. Queen Philippa very rapidly emerged as the antithesis of the Jezebel Isabella, a consort entirely devoid of political ambition and content to provide loyal support to an adored husband. The close ties established between England and Hainault since the thirteenth century probably explain why the chroniclers, who so often berated queens for bringing foreign people and suspicious ways into England, had so little to say against Philippa: it was over a century before commentators began to attribute the figure-hugging styles of clothing that were a feature of mid-fourteenth-century fashions to the supposed evil influence of the Hainaulters.[36] Her marriage also amply fulfilled its diplomatic objectives, putting Edward III at the centre of a vast network of Netherlandish and German in-laws and allies. Philippa's older sister, Margaret, who had once been proposed as a possible spouse for Edward, had since wed the emperor, Lewis of Bavaria. Another sister, Jeanne, was married to William, count (later margrave) of Juliers. Edward held William in particularly high trust, named him his personal adviser or 'private and very special sovereign secretary' in 1339, and accorded him the title of earl of Cambridge in 1340.[37] Edward and Philippa maintained close contact with the queen's female relatives and for some years contemplated marrying some of their own children into the same web of imperial ruling families.[38]

The one and only blot on Philippa's historical reputation is that she was a notorious spendthrift. This notion was already in full swing by the sixteenth century, when one of Elizabeth I's keepers of the records in the Tower of London annotated some of Philippa's household accounts to reveal 'the great riches, lavish expenses, and debts of ye queene'.[39] Given the straitened circumstances in which Philippa had lived on her first arrival in England, it would be tempting to suggest that the revolution of 1330 raised her expectations artificially high. Around the time of the Nottingham coup it was reported to the king that her dower was generating barely £150 a year, and that she did not even have the cash with which to pay for food and Christmas robes for her household.[40] As things turned out, the king was certainly not prepared to see the continuation of

---

[36] *Brut*, ii, 296–7.

[37] C 47/30/8, no. 8; *Récits d'un Bourgeois de Valenciennes*, 160–1; *PROME*, iv, 271; *CChR 1327–41*, 471.

[38] For letters passing between Philippa and the Empress Margaret, see E 101/387/23. Philippa's mother was a regular correspondent with both the king and the queen: E 101/388/5; E 403/291, 8 Nov. 1336; E 403/294, 30 July 1337; JRUL, MS Latin 235, fol. 17r. Edward III's letters to Jeanne of Juliers are recorded in BL, MS Cotton Nero C. VIII, fol. 272. For Philippa's role in the abortive negotiations for the marriage of her daughter, Joan, to the son of Otto, duke of Austria, see Lucas, *Low Countries*, 193.

[39] JRUL, MS Latin 235, verso of cover; R. Fawtier, *Hand-List of Additions to the Collection of Latin Manuscripts in the John Rylands Library, 1908–1920* (Manchester, 1921), 2, 11–13.

[40] SC 8/265/13210.

the huge dower allowed to Queen Isabella in 1327, and the landed estate worked out for Philippa between 1330 and 1335 provided the more normal queenly income of about £4,500 a year. It quickly became apparent that this was insufficient, and throughout the 1330s the queen's household was constantly running at a serious deficit.[41]

In the face of this evidence it is as well to remember that a large part of Philippa's expenditure was undertaken to service Edward III's own vision of courtly splendour. In 1330, the year in which she was crowned, produced her first child and effectively supplanted her mother-in-law as the first lady of the English court, Philippa's agents made huge purchases of the finest Flemish and Italian cloth at the great international fairs of Boston and St Ives, including the sumptuous green Italian silk decorated with griffins' heads used to make her robes for the Feast of All Saints.[42] Edward's active endorsement of such extravagance is especially evident in the arrangements for the queen's churchings, the ceremonies that accompanied her re-emergence from confinement following the births of her children. The king's great wardrobe provided the cloth for the baby Edward of Woodstock and his entourage at the queen's first churching in 1330, but it was Philippa herself who sustained the principal cost of the event, including her own set of purple velvet robes embroidered with golden squirrels and lined with ermine and miniver.[43] Perhaps in recognition of the strain this created, the king stepped in more directly for the ceremony that followed the birth of their second child, Princess Isabella, in July 1332, and gave Philippa a flamboyant set of garments decorated with the letters E and P and a set of bed hangings depicting sky and sea, the latter full of mermaids bearing the arms of England and Hainault.[44] Opulence was not, then, simply a matter of the personal whim of the queen; it was indicative of the conscious cultural and political programme of her king.

This sense of complementarity was evident in many other aspects of the personal and public lives of the royal couple. Edward and Philippa were much more often in each other's company than had been the case with the king's parents. They were together, for example, at Clipstone and Stamford in 1337, celebrating the marriage of one of the king's esquires, Roger Beauchamp, with the queen's damsel Sybil Patteshull, and then,

---

[41] Johnstone, 'Queen's Household', 259–62.

[42] JRUL, MS Latin 234, fol. 2r and *passim*.

[43] Ibid., fol. 1v; S. M. Newton, 'Queen Philippa's Squirrel Suit', *Documenta Textila*, ed. M. Flury-Lemberg and K. Stolleis (Munich, 1981), 342–8.

[44] C. Shenton, 'Philippa of Hainault's Churchings: The Politics of Motherhood at the Court of Edward III', *Family and Dynasty in Late Medieval England*, ed. R. Eales and S. Tyas (Donington, 2003), 108–9. The date of this churching, 19 July 1332, can be determined from an annotation in the daily household accounts, E 101/386/1, which records expenses of £292 against the associated feast. See also Vale, *Edward III and Chivalry*, 172. For the churching following the birth of Blanche of the Tower in 1342, see E 403/328, 3 July 1343.

dolefully, attending a requiem mass for Philippa's recently deceased father.[45] Whenever possible, the queen accompanied her husband to the northern marches prior to his departure on campaign. On their first such journey in 1333 it was noted with satisfaction by the monks of Durham that Edward and Philippa agreed, unusually, to sleep apart while at the cathedral priory out of respect for its infamously misogynist patron saint, Cuthbert.[46] On this and other occasions in the 1330s Philippa removed as far north as Bamburgh to await news of her husband's operations in the field, and at least once she travelled north of the border to join Edward at Roxburgh.[47] She also took up long-term residence at Antwerp and Ghent during Edward's sojourn in the Low Countries in 1338–40, where she gave birth to two of her growing brood of children.[48] Edward and Philippa's close partnership was thus advertised to large numbers of people at home and abroad as a veritable model of companionate marriage and familial harmony.

Nor was their relationship one only of utility. Much of the contact between the king and queen is recorded in the formalities of gift-giving, which tend to emphasize the material value rather than the affective significance of their exchanges. At New Year 1332, for example, Edward gave his queen an expensive sapphire set in a gold brooch.[49] But there are also hints of intimacies not governed by the protocol of seasons and ceremonies. The king and queen often sent each other gifts of fresh meat or fish; when they were apart, they would sometimes send hawks or horses that symbolized the means by which they could be reunited.[50] In March 1335 Edward, then on pilgrimage at Walsingham, sent in haste to Philippa at Knaresborough to report the death of a horse.[51] And when necessity and affairs of state kept them apart, the royal couple kept up regular contact by letter.[52] Writing from Brittany in 1342 on the arrangements to be made for the funeral of their common relative, Robert of Artois, Edward repeatedly addressed his wife as *douce cuer* (sweetheart).[53]

[45] BL, MS Cotton Nero C. VIII, fols 207, 207v. For Roger and Sybil's son Philip, see p. 310.

[46] *Historia Dunelmensis*, 117.

[47] SC 1/39/33, 34; BL, MS Cotton Nero C. VIII, fol. 269; E 403/288, 2 Sept. 1336; B. C. Hardy, *Philippa of Hainault and her Times* (London, 1910), 72–88.

[48] SC 1/50/189; SC 1/51/4; Norwell, lxxiv–lxxxv, 226–7. For the membership of Philippa's household on this occasion see *Foedera*, II.ii, 1044.

[49] E 101/385/16. In the previous autumn the king had bought a total of £320 worth of jewels for the queen: E 403/260, 24 Oct. 1331.

[50] E.g., E 101/383/13; E 101/387/9, m. 2; Norwell, 253; E 36/205, fol. 13; E 101/396/2, fol. 31; JRUL, MS Latin 236, fol. 3v.

[51] BL, MS Cotton Nero C. VIII, fol. 270v.

[52] E.g., in 1331 the queen sent her husband a letter during his visit to Philip VI in France: JRUL, MS Latin 235, fol. 17v.

[53] SC 1/56/79, printed in E. Déprez, 'La Mort de Robert d'Artois', *Revue historique*, xciv (1907), 65. For another surviving letter from the king to the queen see SC 1/54/28 (ii).

For contemporaries, the success of the royal marriage was inevitably judged by the abundance of its offspring. After giving birth to a healthy heir in 1330, Philippa went on to have ten further children between 1332 and 1348: Isabella of Woodstock (b. May 1332), Joan of the Tower (b. late 1333), William of Hatfield (b. December 1336), Lionel of Antwerp (b. November 1338), John of Gaunt (b. February 1340), Edmund of Langley (b. June 1341), Blanche of the Tower (b. June 1342), Mary of Waltham (b. October 1344), Margaret of Windsor (b. July 1346) and William of Windsor (b. June 1348). A further late pregnancy, when Philippa was in her early forties, led to the birth of Thomas of Woodstock in January 1355.[54] The couple's oldest child, Edward, was rapidly set up with his own domestic establishment under the direction of the queen's lady, Elizabeth de Saint-Omer.[55] The younger children were cared for partly in the household of their brother, but mainly by the queen.[56] In 1338, Philippa took the unusual step of moving Isabella and Joan with her to the continent. It was only after the births of John and Lionel that the royal couple decided that the security risks were too great and sent the four siblings home in the summer of 1340 to be placed under the custody of another of the queen's ladies, Isabella de la Mote.[57] As soon as the queen returned to England and Prince Edmund was born in the spring of 1341, the royal children were again returned to their mother's care.[58] After Prince Lionel's infant betrothal to the ten-year-old Elizabeth de Burgh, heiress to the earldom of Ulster, in August 1342, the young bride also resided in the safekeeping of the queen.[59] Philippa's very obvious maternal instincts no doubt explain the otherwise fallacious tradition that she eschewed the services of wet-nurses and breastfed her children.[60]

Although the demands of office inevitably kept Edward more frequently from the family fold, he too seems to have been a doting parent. In the summer of 1331, when the countesses of Hainault and Juliers made a long visit to court, the king wrote in great concern to ensure that the baby Prince Edward would have a fitting array of clothing in which to be presented to his grandmother and aunt.[61] As for the birth of their first

[54] *HBC*, 39–40, is inaccurate on a number of dates, and reverses the births of Edmund of Langley and Blanche of the Tower.

[55] SC 8/171/8543; *CPR 1330–4*, 78; JRUL, MS Latin 234, fols 13v, 18v.

[56] Tout, *Chapters*, v, 319–20; BL, MS Cotton Nero C. VIII, fol. 270v. Lady Saint-Omer is found as late as 1358 charged with custody of the young Prince Thomas in the queen's household: JRUL, MS Latin 236, fol. 2.

[57] Knighton, 27; W. M. Ormrod, 'The Royal Nursery: A Household for the Younger Children of Edward III', *EHR*, cxx (2005), 398–415.

[58] It was for this reason that John of Gaunt's resources as earl of Richmond were put at the queen's disposal in 1342: Tout, *Chapters*, v, 282.

[59] E 101/390/8; SAL, MS 208, fol. 3. The date of the betrothal ceremony can be precisely fixed at 15 Aug. 1342: Ormrod, 'Royal Nursery', 411 n. 74; *CPMR 1323–64*, 153.

[60] Barnes, *Edward III*, 44.

[61] E 101/385/20.

child in 1330, so for the second in 1332, the king remained close to his wife at Woodstock throughout her confinement.[62] In 1341 Edward gave orders 'by his own mouth' for the domestic needs of Prince John, and in 1342 he reserved the vacant earldom of Richmond for the special endowment of his third son. And in March 1343, probably at the queen's manor of Havering, the king dined *en famille* with the three infant princes, Lionel, John and Edmund. As they grew older, the royal children also regularly joined their parents for evenings at the gaming tables.[63] It was in such rare moments of domesticity that Edward III forged the bonds that would maintain a remarkable unity within the royal family for the rest of his long life.

If the family was the soul of the king's social body, then the household was surely its heart. The household was part domestic establishment, part council, part war office and part ministry of magnificence. In the early years of Edward III's reign, it numbered between 550 and 650 people. These were divided into two unequal sections. The larger group, comprising roughly two-thirds of the total, was made up of relatively low-status functionaries: kitchen workers, grooms and stable hands, pages, messengers, hunters, falconers and so on. The other, much more prestigious group, which served 'above stairs', was made up of clerks, bannerets, knights, esquires and sergeants-at-arms. The royal household was a great source of sinecures. At the beginning of the reign, for example, John Warblington claimed the office of 'master of the harlots and dismemberer of malefactors' in the young Edward III's household. It also attracted its fair share of hangers-on. Elizabeth of Louth, who followed the household 'as a beggar' in 1328–9, eventually secured a special payment of £1 in royal alms, and a few years later Agnes 'the fruiterer' stayed with the royal entourage all the way from her home base in York to the king's manor of Woodstock.[64]

It is hardly surprising, then, that the king's subjects viewed the arrival of the royal household in their locality as a distinctly mixed blessing. Through the so-called court of the verge, the steward and marshal enjoyed special judicial powers within a twelve-mile radius of the court and used it (so their critics argued) to tyrannize the king's subjects.[65] In

[62] Initially the king had planned that his second child be born at Clarendon: *Foedera*, II.ii, 829; *King's Works*, ii, 917.

[63] E 159/120, rot. 17d; *CChR 1341–1417*, 63; E 43/204, fol. 41v; *BPR*, iv, 74–6.

[64] *Cal. Mem. Rolls 1326–7*, no. 1005; E 101/384/14, m. 5; BL, MS Cotton Nero C. VIII, fol. 205.

[65] W. R. Jones, 'The Court of the Verge: The Jurisdiction of the Steward and Marshal of the Household in Later Medieval England', *Journal of British Studies*, x[1] (1970), 1–29; C. Given-Wilson, *The Royal Household and the King's Affinity: Service, Politics and Finance in England, 1360–1413* (London, 1986), 48–53.

1336 the burgesses of Nottingham accused Peter Greet, the deputy of the steward and marshal, of extracting a ransom of £5 from them to be free of this jurisdiction.[66] A much greater cause of controversy was the prerogative of purveyance, by which the royal households – not just that of the king, but also those of the queen and of the royal children – enjoyed first claim on marketable foodstuffs available both in the areas where they resided and, potentially, across the realm at large. Edward III cannily attempted to offload responsibility for abuses of purveyance during the minority on to the shoulders of Roger Mortimer, but this merely had the effect of throwing up further complaints. In 1331, for example, the people of Leicester complained that they had still not been paid for the many goods taken by Mortimer's men when he and the king had ridden out to hunt down the earl of Lancaster in January 1329.[67] Nor did the majority bring an end to abuse. Public attitudes in the early 1330s were vividly captured by William of Pagula, the parish priest of Winkfield (Berkshire), who depicted himself and his fellow villagers rushing for cover at the dreaded sound of the purveyors' horns.[68] The necessarily makeshift nature of royal logistics was another cause of constant tension. The prior of Blyth, whose house was a regular stopping-off point for Edward III on his travels up and down the Great North Road, complained that the king's men had done £40 worth of damage to the priory. And in 1332 Edward personally authorized payment of £5 to a poor chaplain whose house had been burned to the ground when Queen Isabella's entourage passed through his village.[69]

The major offices and senior ranks of the household were highly politicized. After the Nottingham coup, Edward III took advantage of the claim that Mortimer had packed the household with his henchmen to dismiss over 40 per cent of his staff, replacing them with men who had either served him as prince or who had no previous association with the court.[70] Among the new generation of clerks emerging as the king's conspicuous supporters in the household during the 1330s was William Kilsby, receiver of the chamber (1335–8) and keeper of the privy seal (1338–42). Like many household administrators, Kilsby came of humble origins; his rapid rise to power, and his evident talent for creating offence, were a source of some anxiety and trial for certain members of the political and ecclesiastical elite, who in 1340–1 sought to make him a scapegoat for the king's own manifest errors in the management of the French war.[71] The greatest of the

---

[66] C 49/6/31; SC 8/112/5590; *CPR 1340–3*, 429.
[67] *PROME*, iv, 105; SC 8/123/6129. For other accusations of Mortimer's use of the right of prise see BL, MS Cotton Faustina B. V, fol. 55v.
[68] *De speculo regis Edwardi Tertii*, 99, 134; Matthews, *Writing to the King*, 108–13.
[69] SC 8/34/1691; E 403/262, 4 June 1332.
[70] Shenton, 'English Court', 116–18.
[71] See pp. 231–7.

household clerks of this early period of the reign, however, was the king's old mentor, Richard Bury, who reaped the full rewards of his earlier loyalty to Edward of Windsor by rapid promotion to the keepership of the privy seal (1329–33). Bury was elevated to the bishopric of Durham in 1333 and, as was customary, gave up his position in the household. But his appointments successively as treasurer of the exchequer (1334) and chancellor (1334–5), and his regular involvement in diplomacy until shortly before his death in 1345, ensured that he remained a central figure in the political community and a guiding and benign influence over the king.[72]

Much as he admired and needed the support of churchmen, Edward III was most readily drawn to the comradeship of the principal lay members of the household, the bannerets and knights. In the first decade of his majority rule, Edward III usually retained about fifty men in these roles. Figures such as Gilbert Talbot, who had served in Edward's household before his accession and went on to become chamberlain from 1327 to 1334, or John Darcy, successively chamberlain and steward in 1337–46, were already in high favour when Edward took charge in 1330. Both went on to glittering careers in war, diplomacy and government and amassed the associated prizes in titles and land. Many others were new recruits whose elevation owed much to the king's preference and favour. Reginald Cobham of Sterborough, one of Edward's leading household knights in the 1330s, was another great stalwart of the regime, undertaking a distinguished and entirely unblemished career in civilian government, war and diplomacy. A number of the Hainaulters who entered Edward's service at the beginning of the reign merged without apparent controversy into English political life. The outstanding figure in this respect was Walter Mauny, who worked his way up through the ranks of the household from queen's trencherman to king's esquire (1328), knight (1330) and banneret (1338), and later became a peer of the realm. Mauny's particular achievement, attesting to his remarkable skill in public relations, was his double success in winning public admiration both in his adopted home of England and among her enemies abroad. A less public instance at the time, but still more significant in the long term, was that of the Hainaulter Sir Payn de Roelt, whose daughters Philippa and Katherine later married, respectively, the poet Geoffrey Chaucer and the royal prince John of Gaunt.[73]

It was a commonplace of medieval politics that the lay members of the royal household were sycophants who exploited their intimacy with the king for the pursuit of unscrupulous ambition. Edward III may have eschewed his father's more blatant abuses of legal process to protect

---

[72] Ormrod, 'The King's Secrets', 163–78.
[73] Shenton, 'English Court', 265; Bothwell, *Peerage*, 17–18, 19–20, 21–2; D. Pearsall, *The Life of Geoffrey Chaucer* (Oxford, 1992), 49–51.

friends and followers, but he also seems to have regarded it as a duty of office to intervene personally in the courts on behalf of members of his household.[74] The arrogance of courtiers could generate particular tensions in the regions where they had personal interests. In 1332 the household records marked out three men – Walter Mauny, Thomas Bradeston and Hugh Frene – as knights of the king's chamber, denoting the special favour of access to the king's most private apartments.[75] If Mauny became a model of rectitude in the new regime, then the other two chamber knights were, by all accounts, distinctly insalubrious. Bradeston, who won notable patronage as a result of his presence with the king at Nottingham in 1330, was considered a highly disruptive influence in his native Gloucestershire. The people of King's Barton complained that he was a 'little saint' at court but a 'rampant lion' in their own neighbourhood; were it not for Thomas's intimacy with the king, they alleged, a thousand bills could be brought against him for the crimes he had committed against those less powerful than himself.[76] In 1341 serious charges of murder, terrorism, kidnapping and subversion of justice were also to be laid against John Molyns, who had until recently been a banneret of the household and in high favour with the king.[77] The exposure of such close associates of the king did nothing to revise public perceptions of the court as a hotbed of every imaginable vice.[78]

Chief among the bannerets and knights of the household during the first decade of the reign, and the man who undoubtedly enjoyed closest familiarity with the king, was William Montagu. The two men's habit of exchanging identities and heraldic devices hints that they considered themselves bound by a contract of brotherhood in arms.[79] In 1333, the friends appeared at court in a pair of identical red taffeta surcoats embroidered with birds; five years later, the king had a set of three white tunics made for himself, his cousin Henry of Grosmont and his special friend William Montagu, each embroidered in gold with representations of castles and knights and jauntily finished off with green hems to resemble moats.[80] In 1335 Edward bestowed on Montagu the singular right to bear the royal crest of an eagle, and around the same time the latter seems to have reciprocated by giving the king his own family's emblem of the

[74] E.g., SC 1/55/86.
[75] E 101/385/16. For Frene see p. 145.
[76] Saul, *Knights and Esquires*, 266–7.
[77] Fryde, 'Robber Baron', 201–2.
[78] R. Horrox, 'Caterpillars of the Commonwealth? Courtiers in Late Medieval England', *Rulers and Ruled in Late Medieval England: Essays Presented to Gerald Harriss*, ed. R. E. Archer and S. Walker (London, 1995), 1–15.
[79] For brotherhood in arms see Keen, *Nobles, Knights*, 43–62. For the special assistance that Edward provided to Montagu after the latter's capture by Philip VI in 1340 see pp. 227, 250–1.
[80] Shenton, 'English Court', 195; E 101/388/8, m. 6.

griffin.[81] Conspicuous material benefits soon followed. In return for his loyalty in the 1320s and his unstinting service in the 1330s, Montagu was transformed from a minor West Country landowner to one of the wealthiest and most powerful magnates in the land. By the time of his elevation to the earldom of Salisbury in March 1337, he already had major landed interests in England, Wales and Scotland. Members of his family benefited significantly from their connection at court. One brother, Simon, became bishop of Ely; another, Edward, became a knight of the royal household, married the king's cousin, Alice of Brotherton, and was raised to the baronage.[82] William's wife Catherine (née Grandisson) was the greatest of Queen Philippa's ladies; in 1332 Edward III rewarded her with the extraordinarily generous sum of 500 marks for bringing him the 'happy news' of the birth of his first daughter.[83] And in the winter of 1340–1 the couple's eldest son, another William, was affianced to the king's cousin, the twelve-year-old Joan of Kent. The complex and intimate knot of relationships formed by Edward, Philippa, William and Catherine may be said to have become the very centre-point of the king's social and emotional existence during the first decade of his majority rule.

Given the propensity of courtiers to abuse their position of influence, it might be expected that contemporaries would have poured on William Montagu some of the opprobrium used against the likes of Thomas Bradeston and John Molyns. Yet it was only among hostile continental commentators that the Plantagenet–Montagu friendship came in for criticism. Shortly after William Montagu's death in 1344, the northern French author of the satirical poem the *Vows of the Heron* depicted the king, Queen Philippa and the earl and countess of Salisbury as the chief perpetrators of a series of chivalric fantasies built around Edward's claims in France. On the eve of the war in 1337, he claimed, Salisbury had vowed not to open his right eye until he had vindicated his master's honour by fighting Philip of Valois in battle.[84] The author was clearly well informed: Montagu had actually lost an eye fighting in Scotland in 1333, and thus

---

[81] *CDS*, iii, no. 1116; GEC, xi, 386 n. (i). The king's use of the griffin motif is best evidenced in the new private seal, the 'griffin', adopted c.1335: Tout, *Chapters*, iii, 52. For the Montagu association with the griffin see C. Boutel, *Boutell's Heraldry* (London, 1973), 81, 137, 161; S. Crane, *The Performance of Self: Ritual, Clothing, and Identity during the Hundred Years War* (Philadelphia, 2002), 110.

[82] Holmes, *Estates*, 26–8; R. M. Haines, 'Simon de Montacute, Brother of William, Earl of Salisbury, Bishop of Worcester (1333–7) and of Ely (1337–45)', *Fourteenth Century England I*, ed. N. Saul (Woodbridge, 2000), 37–71; GEC, ix, 84–5. Alice was originally intended as bride of William Montagu's eldest son, John: Marshall, 'Thomas of Brotherton', 141–3.

[83] Ormrod, *Reign of Edward III*, 107; E 101/384/18; E 101/385/16; BL MS Cotton Galba E.III, fols 183, 189v; E 403/282, 30 May 1335. The transcription of the last of these references in *Issues*, 144, mistakes the sex of the child.

[84] *Vows of the Heron*. The poem identifies the countess of Salisbury erroneously as the daughter of the king's cousin, the earl of Derby.

bore upon his body dramatic proof of his absolute and continued allegiance to Edward's cause. In spite of the mocking tones, however, the *Vows of the Heron* regarded Salisbury as doing nothing more than his rightful duty by confirming and supporting his lord in the decision to start the Hundred Years War.

When more specific criticism of the royal friendship was made by England's enemies abroad, furthermore, it was intended not to discredit the earl but deliberately to defame the king. Shortly after Montagu's death a scurrilous story began to circulate on the continent, claiming that Edward III had developed an uncontrollable passion for the countess of Salisbury and had raped her while her husband was away on his service in the early 1340s. This tale, redolent of biblical and classical themes, is very likely to have had its origins in anti-English propaganda put out by Philip VI. It derived its potency from the idea that Edward had committed an act of gross betrayal against a brother in arms and thus broken the very code of chivalry that he claimed so stridently to exemplify. The story was taken up, with some reluctance, by the otherwise pro-English Liège chronicler, Jean le Bel and, through him, by Jean Froissart, though the latter eventually turned the story into a parable of Edward's victory over the temptations of the flesh.[85]

It is, of course, perfectly possible that the king made advances to Catherine Montagu. He may even have had a fully fledged consensual affair with her. Even so, there is no hint of such a scandal becoming public knowledge in England while William and Catherine lived. Any such speculation was effectively scotched, at least in official terms, by the countess's decision to take a widow's vow of chastity after her husband's death.[86] Indeed, what is surely most striking about the rather obvious attempt to defame Edward III is that, so long as the king lived, it had no recorded currency in England.[87] That absence of rumour also hints strongly at the generally positive reaction of the English polity to the friendship between Edward and William. The king's obvious preoccupation with martial virtues did not blind him to the importance of surrounding himself with men of sensibility and sound judgement. Montagu himself bore with fortitude Edward's failure to grant him possession of all his promised estates or to repay the large debts that the earl ran up in his service.[88] Far from

[85] Le Bel, i, 290–4; ii, 30–4; Froissart, ii, 131–5, 293; A. Gransden, 'The Alleged Rape by Edward III of the Countess of Salisbury', *EHR*, lxxxvii (1972), 333–44; P. F. Ainsworth, *Jean Froissart and the Fabric of History* (Oxford, 1990), 254–302.

[86] Haines, 'Simon de Montacute', 40 n. 18.

[87] F. Ingledew, *Sir Gawain and the Green Knight and the Order of the Garter* (Notre Dame, 2006), 31–80, provides the latest attempt to argue the veracity of the story, but the evidence adduced is all circumstantial.

[88] In 1346 Salisbury's executors wrote off £6,733 of outstanding debts owed by the crown to the earl's estate: *CPR 1343–6*, 473.

emerging as a new Piers Gaveston or Hugh Despenser, then, the earl of Salisbury was seen as deserving of his rewards precisely because of the moderating influence he brought to bear on a sometimes impetuous and hot-headed king.[89] And since Edward III's friendship with William Montagu never threatened to destabilize domestic politics or foreign policy, his subjects quite simply never needed to turn it into a scandal, sexual or otherwise.

Although he spent the majority of his time in the company of household men, Edward III necessarily commanded a wider circle of high-ranking clergy and aristocrats who regarded themselves as welcome guests at court and rightful royal counsellors.[90] Chief among the noblemen in the king's circle during the 1330s were the earls of Surrey, Warwick and Arundel,[91] and the cluster of northern barons – Henry Percy, Thomas Wake of Liddell, William Ros of Helmsley and the steward, Ralph Neville – now made newly prominent by their heavy involvement in the war against Scotland. The king's surviving uncle, Thomas of Brotherton, earl of Norfolk, though still active in the wars until his death in 1338, seems to have been rarely at court, and his only son, Edward, never emerged into political life, dying while still a teenager in 1337.[92] Other absences from the king's side could be readily explained: Hugh Courtenay, who was recognized by Edward III as earl of Devon in 1335, was by then nearly sixty; Henry of Lancaster, who seems long to have suffered some physical disability, was now incapacitated by blindness;[93] and the king's young cousins and successive earls of Hereford, John and Humphrey Bohun, suffered from a congenital and debilitating illness that kept them confined to home.[94] The ranks of the nobility had become seriously depleted as a result of the successive executions and forfeitures of the previous decade, and the few earls still active in the business of the realm felt themselves significantly compromised in their ability fully to represent the views of the wider elite.

In the Westminster parliament of March 1337 Edward III explicitly amended this serious defect by elevating six of his closest associates and most distinguished companions-in-arms, William Montagu, William Bohun, William Clinton, Robert Ufford, Henry of Grosmont and Hugh Audley, to the earldoms of Salisbury, Northampton, Huntingdon, Suffolk,

[89] See pp. 176–7, 237–8.

[90] For what follows, see Given-Wilson, 'Royal Charter Witness Lists', 61–71.

[91] See also their appearances among lists of councillors on the dorses of the close rolls: *CCR 1333–7*, 327, 346, 493, 507.

[92] Marshall, 'Thomas of Brotherton', 100–34, 204–5.

[93] Baker, 43; *ONDB*, xxvii, 572.

[94] Holmes, *Estates*, 20–1. In 1327 Edward III paid the expenses of Humphrey while he stayed in London to 'take the cure' at a rate of £1 a week, and continued to maintain him at the rate of 10 shillings a week after his removal back to Pleshey: E 403/225–229, *passim*.

Derby and Gloucester, respectively. While there were a few inevitable rumblings about the strain that the accompanying endowments might put on the royal domain, the king himself explicitly justified his actions in terms readily understandable to, and praised by, the contemporary elite. According to their charters of creation, the new earls would stand as proof of the crown's capacity and duty to bestow patronage on worthy recipients and thus to be 'buttressed by wise counsels and fortified by mighty powers'.[95] Nor did such an unusually large number of new creations significantly threaten the innate conservatism of the established nobility. William Montagu, Robert Ufford and William Clinton all came of solid baronial stock, while William Bohun and Henry of Grosmont were prominent members of the wider royal family, and Hugh Audley was already in effect an earl-in-waiting as husband of one of the co-heiresses of the vacant title to Gloucester. Furthermore, the allusion to the nobility as the armour of monarchy was especially apposite, for the very assembly in which these creations took place witnessed high excitement over the likely opening of major hostilities with France. With the exception of the elderly Audley, all the new earls of 1337 had already amply proved their worth through valiant service in the Scottish campaigns of the mid-decade, and were to go on to give equally conspicuous service as diplomats and commanders in the first stages of the Hundred Year War. As if to emphasize the point about the upcoming great dispute over the king's rights across the Channel, Edward used the same occasion to raise his six-year-old son to the style of duke and endow the heir to the throne with the former earldom, now duchy, of Cornwall. This rank had not been known in England before and its deployment represented a direct and bold assertion of Edward's right, as sovereign ruler, to bestow the same high-flown titles of nobility that were enjoyed by the great peers of France.

There were obviously rather fewer opportunities for Edward III to make a major impact on the personnel of the episcopate during the early years of the reign, though his mentor Bury's promotion to the prestigious bishopric of Durham in 1333 was certainly a sign of the young king's potential for influence in the promotion of senior churchmen. Two of the chief supporters and dominant personalities in the revolution of 1327, Henry Burghersh, bishop of Lincoln, and John Stratford, bishop of Winchester, were now rapidly restored to favour and remained highly influential figures in government throughout the 1330s. Stratford, who became archbishop of Canterbury in 1333, served as chancellor in 1330–4 and 1335–7, and Burghersh returned for a second term as treasurer in 1334–7. Robert Stratford, brother of John, was appointed bishop of Chichester in 1337 and himself served as chancellor in 1337–8 and 1340;

[95] *RDP*, v, 28–32; Bothwell, *Peerage*, 15; C. Given-Wilson, *The English Nobility in the Late Middle Ages* (London, 1987), 35.

yet a third Stratford, Ralph, nephew of John and Robert, became bishop
of London in 1340. Some members of the episcopate had been born into
the aristocracy and shared its values and outlook: Henry Burghersh, for
example, was the brother of Sir Bartholomew Burghersh the elder, a
prominent political figure who successfully survived the collapse of
Mortimer's regime to emerge as one of the major military leaders of the
1330s and completed his career with a long term as chamberlain of the
royal household (1347–55).[96] The Stratfords, who came of bourgeois stock,
were perhaps less convinced of the innate superiority of martial values.
On the other hand, the hostilities in Scotland and France provided the
episcopate with an important opportunity to demonstrate its collective
commitment, and it responded enthusiastically to Edward's expectation
that the country would mobilize in prayer, as well as in arms, for the sake
of the wars.[97] William Melton of York, whose earlier credulity about
Edward II's survival might under different circumstances have cost him his
head, was quick to establish himself as a vociferous supporter of the
majority regime, lending extensively to the cash-strapped exchequer and
exhorting his no doubt rather unimpressed flock to bear the burden of
royal taxation 'kindly and charitably'.[98]

The collective political role of the nobility and the bishops was most
obviously demonstrated in parliaments and great councils. The parliament of November 1330 had been deliberately managed to provide timely
assurances of Edward's regard for the rights, individually and collectively,
of the peerage, and the early stages of the majority regime saw such principles readily applied in practice. In the assembly of September 1331 the
king agreed that the son of Hugh Despenser the Younger, another Hugh,
should be fully pardoned and released from custody, and thus set a
powerful marker of his disinclination to allow the sins of the father to be
visited upon the son.[99] The same parliament heard news of the quarrel
between Sir William de la Zouche of Ashby and Sir John Grey of
Rotherfield over the widow of the younger Despenser, Eleanor, who was

[96] *ODNB*, viii, 798–9.

[97] W. R. Jones, 'The English Church and Royal Propaganda during the Hundred Years
War', *JBS*, xix[1] (1979), 18–30; A. K. McHardy, 'The English Clergy and the Hundred Years
War', *Studies in Church History*, xx (1983), 171–8; A. K. McHardy, 'Religious Ritual and
Political Persuasion: The Case of England in the Hundred Years War', *Journal of Moral and
Social Studies*, iii (1988), 41–57.

[98] *The Register of John Kirkby, Bishop of Carlisle, 1332–1352, and the Register of John Ross, Bishop
of Carlisle, 1325–1332*, ed. R. L. Storey, 2 vols (CYS, lxxix, lxxxi, 1993–5), i, 82–3; R. M. T.
Hill, 'An English Archbishop and the Scottish War of Independence', *Innes Review*, xxii
(1971), 59–71; A. K. McHardy, 'Some Reflections of Edward III's Use of Propaganda', *Age
of Edward III*, ed. Bothwell, 185.

[99] *PROME*, iv, 157. The king also granted permission for the honourable reburial of
Despenser's remains: D. Westerhof, *Death and the Noble Body in Medieval England* (Woodbridge,
2008), 125–6, 131.

one of the co-heiresses to the great Clare estate.[100] Grey, who claimed Eleanor as his lawful wife, alleged that Zouche had abducted and married her against her will. Edward now confirmed the legality of the latter match. But Grey was determined to press his case, and early in 1332 'hot words' and violent blows were exchanged between the two men during a disputation held before the king. The case was therefore put back before the lords in parliament the following September. They followed the king's line and declared in favour of Zouche, but at the same time recommended that Grey be pardoned his offence.[101] The story is a vivid reminder of the importance attached to the king's responsibility to provide effective arbitration between the great men of the realm, and of the highly personalised nature of so much of the business with which he and his parliaments had to deal.[102]

Apart from the set pieces of parliament, there were many other occasions within the cycle of royal ceremonial that attracted significant numbers of nobles and ecclesiastics to court. Edward III regularly held what the household accounts of the 1330s call 'halls' and 'great halls' at the Christian festivals of Easter, Pentecost, All Saints and Christmas.[103] The king's place at the high table was marked out on these occasions by cloth of gold hung in a canopy or as a banner.[104] If a parliament or great council was in session at the time, the lords spiritual and temporal were usually invited to join the feast.[105] On 2 July 1336, while Edward was in Scotland, Queen Philippa presided at a council and hall held at Northampton and attended by eight bishops, eight lords and thirty-eight knights.[106] A few years later, on 15 August 1342, Edward III held a great banquet at the Tower of London to mark the wedding of his four-year-old son, Prince Lionel, to the heiress to the earldom of Ulster. The creation of Edward of Woodstock as prince of Wales on 12 May 1343 was similarly

[100] Eleanor had remained a favoured courtier after the demise of her husband and of Edward II, and had briefly been mistress of John of Eltham's household: CCR 1323–7, 620; CPR 1327–30, 243; E 403/228, 9 May 1327; E 101/382/12; Tout, Chapters, iv, 75 n. 2. But she had been imprisoned in 1329–30 and cajoled by Mortimer into buying back her estates from the crown for a ruinous £50,000, subsequently remitted by Edward III to £5,000: GEC, iv, 270–1; PROME, iv, 116–18; SC 8/157/7801; CPR 1330–4, 51.

[101] CPR 1327–30, 422, 492; PROME, iv, 159, 169; CPL, ii, 394; Ann. Paulini, 355; Powell and Wallace, House of Lords, 319–21.

[102] See also the king's intervention in the disputes between Robert Ufford and Walter Mauny in 1338 and John Ferrers and Giles Beauchamp in 1340: Norwell, lxxxviii, 251; SCCKB, v, cxxxix.

[103] As in 1336: BL, MS Cotton Nero C. VIII, fol. 279v. In 1335, halls were held at York (Pentecost), Doddington (All Saints) and Newcastle upon Tyne (Christmas): BL, MS Cotton Nero C. VIII, fols 271, 272v, 273v.

[104] E.g., E 101/383/14, m. 5; E 101/387/9, mm. 5, 6; E 101/388/5, mm. 3, 6; Norwell, 250; E 101/390/10.

[105] As at York in June 1335: BL, MS Cotton Nero C. VIII, fol. 271.

[106] E 101/387/19.

celebrated with a solemn feast attended by Archbishop Stratford and other bishops and magnates.[107] The most spectacular such event before 1344, however, was undoubtedly the great hall held on 16 March 1337 to mark the new creations of peerage declared in parliament. Where most great banquets might cost between £100 and £200, this came in at a prodigious £439.[108]

In the highly charged atmosphere of militarism that prevailed throughout most of the 1330s and early 1340s it would not be surprising to find that these feasts were sometimes accompanied by elaborate vows of the kind known to have been taken at Edward I's Feast of the Swans in 1306 and later satirized by Edward III's enemies in the *Vows of the Heron*.[109] That Edward commonly feasted at least his inner circle of senior commanders prior to a campaign is suggested by a chance reference from September 1342 when, before departing for Brittany, the king held a banquet at Eastry in Kent for the queen, their eldest son, the earls of Derby, Warwick, Salisbury and Suffolk 'and other magnates'.[110] In a more general sense, seasonal great halls and ad hoc feasts were the natural successors to the great crown-wearing ceremonies that had been undertaken by Edward's Anglo-Saxon and Norman ancestors and the carefully dramatized pieces of political theatre mounted more recently in parliament by Henry III and Edward I.[111] Such constant reaffirmations of the king's sense of camaraderie with the political and chivalric elite provide a powerful explanation of Edward's ability to turn the optimism of 1330 into a tangible and enduring confidence in his rule.

The great set piece of royal entertainment, and the essential accompaniment to many of the early feasts of the reign, was the tournament. By the 1330s tournaments were usually single-handed feats of arms *à plaisance*: that is, fought in the lists with blunted weapons and intended merely for training and pleasure. Contemporaries sometimes called these kinds of staged games hastiludes or jousts to distinguish them from the tournament *à outrance*, a general mêlée fought over open ground as a real battle with attendant risk to life and limb. In reality, though, the distinctions were often less clear. Hastiludes could be extremely dangerous occasions. John

---

[107] E 36/204, fols 26v, 45. Jewels and plate provided for the wedding of Prince Lionel are recorded in E 403/326, 9 Sept. 1342. The 1343 banquet cost £119.

[108] BL, MS Cotton Nero C. VIII, fol. 284v; E 101/388/2; Tout, *Chapters*, iii, 63 and n. 1. A great hall at Northampton at Pentecost 1328 cost £109 (E 101/383/15; E 101/383/20); the feast at the churching following the birth of Princess Isabella in 1332 cost £292 (E 101/386/1); and the feast at the Dunstable tournament of Feb. 1342 cost a mighty £317 (E 36/204, fol. 21v).

[109] P. Coss, *The Knight in Medieval England, 1000–1400* (Stroud, 1993), 84–5.

[110] E 36/204, fol. 26v.

[111] Biddle, 'Seasonal Festivals'; R. C. Stacey, 'Parliamentary Negotiation and the Expulsion of the Jews from England', *Thirteenth Century England VI*, ed. M. Prestwich, R. H. Britnell and R. Frame (Woodbridge, 1997), 86–93.

Beaumont, son of Edward III's old master, Henry Beaumont, and brother-in-law of Henry of Grosmont, was killed in his prime at a particularly bloody tournament held at Northampton in 1342.[112] The traditional season for tournaments was between Easter and Midsummer's Day, and Arthurian tradition associated such sports particularly with the three springtide feasts of the Ascension, Pentecost and Trinity. Edward III held or attended tournaments regularly at these festivals, as, for example, at Hereford in 1328, Burstwick (Yorkshire) in 1334, Kings Langley in 1341 and Eltham in 1342. Weather permitting, however, they might be held at virtually any time outside the penitential seasons of Lent and Advent and so long as the court was not in mourning.[113] When he was on campaign, Edward was especially inclined to take time out over Christmas and the New Year for the appropriate celebration of military values: he hosted midwinter tournaments at Roxburgh in 1334–5, Antwerp in 1338–9 and Melrose in 1341–2.

The king's enthusiasm for the tournament was thus of an order comparable only to his enthusiasm for hunting – with which it was, in some important senses, connected. The venues were usually carefully prepared well in advance of the arrival of the royal party. At Dunstable in 1329, for instance, carpenters and labourers created a wooden stand, a sandpit and a walkway, and the surrounding buildings were freshly plastered in order to set off the banners that would hang from their walls during the festivities. New horses purchased for the king's use in the lists on this occasion cost £160.[114] During the first decade or so of his majority Edward also experimented with some more exotic and fantastical tournament themes. At the Stepney and Cheapside hastiludes in June and September 1331, the king and his fellows wore tunics and mantles embroidered with Cupid's arrows and costumes and masks 'in the likeness of Tartars'; for the second event, each mounted knight was escorted into the arena by a young noblewoman leading her champion at the end of a silver chain.[115] And at the Smithfield hastiludes of June 1343, held to mark the debut of the prince of Wales in the lists, the king and his twelve companions dressed as the pope and cardinals.[116]

---

[112] Murimuth, 124; Vale, *Edward III and Chivalry*, 58. For concern over the custody of the Beaumont estates, see SC 1/39/143.

[113] Mortimer, *Perfect King*, 449 n. 22 interprets entries in E 101/383/3 as references to tournaments held between the announcement of Edward II's death and his burial at Gloucester in Sept.–Dec. 1327. In fact, the Clipstone tournament was held in July 1327 and the tournaments of Worcester and Rothwell were held at Christmas and Epiphany 1327–8.

[114] E 101/384/14; E 403/246, 19 Oct. 1329. The tournament took place on 20 Oct.; the dates given in Vale, *Edward III and Chivalry*, 172, are for the works.

[115] Murimuth, 63; Avesbury, 285–6; *Ann. Paulini*, 353–4.

[116] Vale, *Edward III and Chivalry*, 64–5, 173.

These exercises in self-indulgence, like the feasts that accompanied them, were, of course, crucial elements in Edward III's evolving art of political management. Edward II had feared tournaments because they might provide the political elite with the opportunity to foment rebellion and recruit private armies for civil war. Isabella and Mortimer were at times equally nervous: tournaments should be permitted only on their terms. Edward III, by contrast, was predictably permissive: private tournaments were rarely banned, and the king simply aimed, through vigorous presidency of his own major events, to make himself the undoubted principal patron of these great displays and tests of chivalric commitment. Serious-minded clerics continued to be critical of the licentiousness that they believed accompanied such events, but the Church took no systematic measures to oppose the king in this matter, and the tournament again became a regular beat in the rhythm of court life.[117] Between 1331 and 1343 the young Edward III is known to have hosted at least thirty tournaments. There were probably significantly more: in peak years, they may have run at a rate of one a month. In 1334, for instance, when he was keen to celebrate his achievements in Scotland, Edward held three rounds of tournaments: at Dunstable, Woodstock and Newmarket prior to a meeting of parliament at York in February; at Burstwick and Nottingham on either side of his visit to Newcastle in June; and, in quick succession, at Guildford, Westminster and Smithfield before the parliament that convened at Westminster in late September.[118] The royal jousts held at Dunstable in 1334 and 1342 also yield some rare details on attendance. There were 135 participants at the first, and the second was attended by the earls of Derby, Warwick, Northampton, Pembroke and Suffolk and (so it was claimed) 236 knights.[119] Not all such occasions drew comparably large crowds, and a significant number of the hastiludes of this period were probably rather exclusive gatherings of members of the royal household. But those held in urban centres, particularly in the great outdoor spaces of Smithfield and Cheapside in London, were certainly open to all comers and were specifically organized to provide a spectacle for the onlooking crowds. The tournaments of the 1330s and early 1340s must therefore be regarded as among the key events that bound together the king and the knightly class and publicized more widely Edward III's exuberant and ambitious royal style.

The king's avid pursuit of the jousts offers a timely reminder that his social and political world was inhabited just as much by women as by men. The participation of young ladies of the court in the procession prior to the

---

[117] Knighton, 92–5; Baker, 97; *Chron. Meaux*, iii, 69.
[118] E 101/386/18; E 101/387/9; E 101/387/10.
[119] Vale, *Edward III and Chivalry*, 172–3.

Cheapside tournament of 1331 seems typical; later in the reign, thirty pairs of white shoes were provided for the 'damsels' at the Lichfield tournament of 1348.[120] Before her first pregnancy, Queen Philippa seems to have ridden in the tournament processions.[121] So many ladies tried to cram into the queen's stand at Cheapside in 1331 that the structure collapsed, severely injuring a number of people.[122] By 1342 the Princesses Isabella and Joan were considered old enough to accompany their mother to tournaments.[123] More generally, the cult of courtly love that was in full swing in the fourteenth century set great store by women's sensibility and by the moral purpose they were supposed to inspire in their menfolk. One of the sets of hangings that adorned the royal chambers under Edward III depicted the theme of the *Assault on the Castle of Love*, a popular courtly image that celebrated the relationship between the sexes in terms of the knight's need to prove his valour and the lady's equal need to defend her virtue.[124] Both the moral ethos and the practical functioning of court life therefore required the regular and active presence of royal and aristocratic women.

In a more pragmatic sense, Edward III also quickly realized that women were key to the general process of political reconciliation. When Elizabeth Badlesmere, the widow of Roger Mortimer's deceased heir, married the king's friend William Bohun in 1335, the documentation supplied to the pope specified that their alliance was intended to heal old wounds.[125] Similarly the king's widowed aunt, Margaret, countess of Kent, was quickly released from confinement in October 1330, and Edward maintained her and her children at his own expense for some time thereafter.[126] He later organized the marriage of his cousin John, the new earl of Kent, to one of Philippa of Hainault's German nieces, Elizabeth of Juliers. And John's sister, Joan of Kent, seems to have been brought up from a young age in the queen's household, where she was quickly identified as one of the emergent beauties of her generation.[127] The king was also especially keen to act as chivalric champion to the English wives of Scottish noblemen caught up in the unfortunate dispute

---

[120] E 101/391/14, m. 16. In 1344 seven *cotes pur femmes* were provided 'for the tournay': E 101/390/7.

[121] See the reference to tournament saddles and super-tunics *ad modum domicellarum* provided for the queen in 1329: E 101/384/6; E 101/384/7.

[122] *Ann. Paulini*, 354–5; Baker, 48; *Anon. Chron. 1307–34*, 147.

[123] 'Observations', 27; S. M. Newton, *Fashion in the Age of the Black Prince* (Woodbridge, 1980), 21–2.

[124] E 101/387/11; E 101/387/14.

[125] GEC, 665, n. (a); *ODNB*, vi, 447.

[126] E 403/254, 4 Dec. 1330, 9 Jan. 1331, 26 Jan. 1331, 1 Feb. 1331. The countess was given her own residence inside the bounds of Westminster Palace: E 101/683/56.

[127] GEC, vii, 148–50; *ODNB*, xxx, 137–8. For Joan's position in the queen's household see E 36/205, fol. 11.

between the two realms; for many years he maintained his cousin Mary, countess of Fife, as a refugee at the English court.[128] The general sense of obligation accommodated even those royal ladies who had never fallen victim to politics or war. Mary Brewes, the wife of the earl of Norfolk, took up residence with the queen shortly before her husband's death in 1338 and continued to be maintained at court until her own death in the early 1360s.[129] Along with Catherine Montagu and those hardy perennials, Marie de Saint-Pol and Elizabeth de Saint-Omer, this group of wives and widows represented, in their own right, a mighty phalanx of support for the youthful Edward III.

Not all of the older generation of aristocratic women, it must be said, were so easily persuaded of the king's good intentions towards their sex. Elizabeth de Burgh, dowager countess of Ulster, who had been a regular and prominent member of the court under Edward II, was notably cool in her relations with Edward III, even refusing to attend the wedding of her granddaughter to Prince Lionel in 1342.[130] And Alice Lacy, who had suffered harshly at the hands of successive regimes in the 1320s, certainly had no reason to feel any better treated by the majority rule of Edward III. The king refused to let her reclaim her family's ancestral lordship of Denbigh after its confiscation from Roger Mortimer. Still more controversially, he gave open support to his chamber knight Hugh Frene in an unscrupulous bid to abduct and marry the dowager when she was already well into her fifties and under a vow of chastity.[131] This scandal may, in fact, provide some clue to the myth about the king's rape of the countess of Salisbury: Jean le Bel named his countess figure 'Alice', and Alice Lacy's own family had earlier held the earldom of Salisbury as a courtesy title. Hugh Frene's antics provide a salutary reminder that Edward's strong sense of personal duty to high-status women was always contingent. More generally it is a reminder that even Edward III's characteristically consensual style had its necessary, if small, share of victims and losers.

By the time he was in his mid-twenties, Edward III enjoyed the unconditional support of a group of close followers in the royal household and had begun to promote the most loyal and conspicuous of his friends to the highest noble and episcopal titles in the land. By exploiting his sociability,

---

[128] *Foedera*, II.ii, 936, 946, 1123, 1160; E 101/388/8. Mary was the daughter of Joan of Acre (daughter of Edward I) by Ralph Monthermer.

[129] E 101/388/13; 'Observations', 19; E 101/392/12, fol. 44v. For private correspondence passing between countess and king see E 403/330, 4 Mar. 1344.

[130] F. A. Underhill, *For Her Good Estate: The Life of Elizabeth de Burgh* (Basingstoke, 1999), 112–13; J. Ward, *Women of the English Nobility and Gentry, 1066–1500* (Manchester, 1995), 155.

[131] GEC, v, 572–4; vii, 311; *SCCKB*, v, no. 45; L. E. Mitchell, *Portraits of Medieval Women: Family, Marriage, and Politics in England, 1225–1350* (Basingstoke, 2003), 117–21. That Alice actively opposed her abduction by Frene is proved by her arguments set out in SC 8/64/3163.

his talent for showmanship, and his instinctive resistance to the politics of vengeance, Edward had encouraged the political elite to participate actively in court and council and provide strong and unified support for the wars that now opened up again in Scotland and France. Had the king failed to build such solidarity, the political strains that became evident by the end of the decade would have been a good deal more serious. As it was, Edward managed to retain the active or passive support of the majority of the elite and see off the challenge to his credibility mounted by the obstreperous John Stratford over the winter of 1340–1. His survival of a political crisis that might otherwise have precipitated his deposition provides powerful proof of the veritable transformation of attitudes that Edward had effected among the elite during the 1330s.

Chapter 6

SCOURGE OF THE SCOTS, 1330–1338

Of all the troubled legacies of Isabella and Mortimer's regime, the one that was probably felt most personally and bitterly by Edward III was the treaty of Northampton of 1328. Contemporary and later English chroniclers were at one in seeing this ruinous settlement as having been made against the will and judgement of the young king.[1] It therefore comes as something of a surprise that Edward never formally repudiated the treaty. An argument was made by his representatives in parliament in 1332 that he had been underage at the time and had been counselled (badly) by others. And in 1333 there seem to have been plans afoot to make a formal renunciation to the pope on the similar grounds that the king had been constrained to accept the treaty and had (he alleged) set down his opposition in writing at the time.[2] But such initiatives were never pursued. Treaties lasted only as long as both sides observed them, and by 1333 Edward himself had decided to break the peace in a unilateral act of aggression against the Scots. On the other hand, hindsight demonstrates that Edward's strategy was in many respects framed by the treaty of 1328. The war that broke out in 1333 was not just a continuation of the squabbles of the previous thirty years but also a conscious harking back to a vision of English empire that Edward I had espoused when he first intervened in Scotland after the death of Alexander III in 1286 and of his sole direct heiress Margaret in 1290.

Edward I had originally intended to allow the northern kingdom to retain its own monarchy and integrity and merely submit its new king, John Balliol, to the suzerainty of the throne of England. It was only when this policy failed in 1296 that Edward had taken the more radical and ambitious step of conquering Scotland for himself. For nearly thirty years, from 1296 to 1328, Edward I and Edward II had maintained the position that Scotland was a dominion of the English crown, that the sovereign monarchy claimed by Robert Bruce from 1306 was illegitimate, and (at least in theory) that the Scots who resisted Plantagenet rule were traitors. The agreement of the minority regime of Edward III to acknowledge Robert I as rightful ruler of Scotland had represented a massive climb-down by the

---

[1] Murimuth, 57; Baker, 40; Avesbury, 283; *Chron. Lanercost*, 261.
[2] *PROME*, iv, 182; *Brut*, i, 257–8; Nicholson, *Edward III and the Scots*, 55.

English. But it also created the prospect of a different level of engagement in the future. The death of Robert Bruce just a year after the sealing of the treaty of Northampton and the succession of a five-year-old boy in the feeble frame of David II seemed set to cause a repetition of the succession crisis of 1290. It was this situation that allowed Edward III, in due course, to recognize Edward Balliol, the son of Edward I's former puppet-king, as a legitimate pretender to David's monarchy and to assert over him the same feudal suzerainty that his grandfather had sought to apply between 1292 and 1296. In formal terms, then, the hostilities of the 1330s and 1340s were not simply a continuation of the Scottish war of independence of 1296–1328, but a dynastic dispute between two rival claimants for the throne, David Bruce and Edward Balliol, the one seeking to keep Scotland free and the other equally obviously prepared to reduce it to a feudal dependency of England.[3]

Edward III's highly developed interest in the achievements of his grandfather inevitably meant that he informed himself fully of the historical context of his new strategy.[4] But Edward was certainly no slave to precedent. In particular, he demonstrated far more sensitivity than Edward I to the nature of the suzerainty that he claimed, through Balliol, over Scotland. The treaty of Northampton confirmed the alliance that the Scots had made with the French at the beginning of the war of independence. Edward III understood all too well the anomalous position thus created: if he were to make overly assertive claims as feudal lord of Scotland, it was more than likely that Philip VI would retaliate in like kind over the fiefs that Edward held from him in France. Such practical recognition of current realities also explains why, in spite of the obvious opportunities, Edward chose not to apply the language of sovereignty in Scotland; to abandon Balliol and treat the Scots simply as rebellious subjects liable to the penalties of treason would be to risk having exactly the same harsh penalties applied against the Plantagenets' loyal supporters in Aquitaine.[5] Inevitably, not all of these considerations were fully evident to Edward at the beginning of the Scottish wars in 1332–3. The elation brought on by early and easy victory undoubtedly led the English king to a rather over-ambitious assertion of lordship in the settlement engineered with Balliol in 1333–4. But the idea that Edward III blithely led his forces into an unnecessary and unwinnable war against the Scots simply in order

[3] M. Prestwich, 'England and Scotland during the Wars of Independence', *England and her Neighbours, 1066–1453: Essays in Honour of Pierre Chaplais*, ed. M. Jones and M. Vale (London, 1989), 181–97.

[4] See, e.g., the historical materials collected towards the arguments for English intervention in Scotland presented at the parliament of 1332: *CDS*, v, no. 727.

[5] Nicholson, *Edward III and the Scots*, 105; J. Campbell, 'England, Scotland and the Hundred Years War in the Fourteenth Century', *Europe in the Late Middle Ages*, ed. J. R. Hale, J. R. L. Highfield and B. Smalley (London, 1965), 187–91.

to satisfy his friends' territorial ambitions and his own desire for martial glory does less than credit to the strategic thinking that he and his counsellors clearly applied to the matter of Scotland during the build-up to war in the early 1330s.

On 20 December 1330 Edward III wrote to his brother-in-law David II to ask for fulfilment of a promise undertaken by the latter's father to restore to Thomas Wake, Henry Beaumont and Henry Percy their rightful ancestral lands and titles in the kingdom of Scotland.[6] The Scots' reply was highly evasive, and after some further desultory efforts Edward III seems quickly to have realized the impossibility of a diplomatic solution that might satisfy the concerns of these and other English lords.[7] In the spring of 1331 the young Queen Joan wrote to her sister-in-law Philippa of Hainault, perhaps in a somewhat desperate attempt to launch a joint intercession for peace.[8] Within a year of Edward III's achievement of his majority, Anglo-Scottish relations seemed set on a path to open hostility.

The principal issue in 1330–1 was that of the 'disinherited', the English lords who claimed rights to lands north of the border. Edward was well aware of the personal and political debt that he owed to Henry Beaumont, who had shown his loyalty by going into temporary exile in France rather than reconciling himself with Mortimer after the altercation at Bedford in 1329. Beaumont's fellow claimants were a tight-knit group. His own son, John, like Thomas Wake, Henry Percy and John Mowbray, was married to a daughter of Henry of Lancaster. David of Strathbogie, pretender to the Scottish earldom of Atholl, was Beaumont's son-in-law. And Richard Talbot, co-claimant to the Comyn estate, was Strathbogie's uncle by marriage. To these and other names was added, by late 1331, that of Edward Balliol. After the forced resignation of his father as king of Scots in 1296, Balliol had lived in quiet obscurity first in England and then in Picardy. It seems unlikely that he had as yet any serious designs on the throne of David II, and his alliance with Beaumont was much more obviously focused on the possible restoration of his own ancestral lands. But the presence of such a useful figurehead – and the imminent death of the guardian of Scotland, the earl of Moray – stirred Beaumont's party to action, and at the end of July 1332 the majority of the disinherited sailed from various ports on the Humber, arriving a week later in the Firth of Forth and landing at Kinghorn in Fife.[9]

Edward III must have known about Beaumont's plans for a war of private enterprise, and there can be little doubt that he gave it his

[6] *Foedera*, II.ii, 804, 806–7.
[7] *CDS*, iii, no. 1023; *Foedera*, II.ii, 809–10; Nicholson, *Edward III and the Scots*, 68–70, 77.
[8] JRUL, MS Latin 235, fol. 17.
[9] *Bridlington*, 103–4; *Chron. Meaux*, ii, 362.

unofficial blessing.[10] He sanctioned various mortgages and transfers of property by which the disinherited lords were able to raise money for their campaign; he probably gave instructions to the sheriffs to comply with the military preparations being made in the eastern ports; and he may even have taken Balliol's homage as titular king of Scotland before the lords set sail. All of these initiatives, however, were made under a cloak of secrecy designed to minimize the king's liability. In public, Edward was firm and uncompromising, condemning the invasion as a breach of the peace with the Scots.[11]

This reluctance to implicate himself directly in the campaign was driven less by Edward's commitment to the 1328 settlement and much more by very pressing concern about the state of Ireland. After the battle of Bannockburn, Robert Bruce and his brother Edward had made a number of armed interventions in the lordship. Edward II's deposition had also provoked widespread civil disorder. Roger Mortimer, who himself had important interests in Ireland, had attempted to take matters in hand, dispatching the young William de Burgh, earl of Ulster, to take up leadership of the Anglo-Irish political community in 1328 and organizing the creation of James Butler and Maurice fitz Thomas Fitzgerald as earls of Ormond (1328) and Desmond (1329). But Mortimer's own unscrupulous acquisition of lands and titles in the Irish midlands after the assassination of the earl of Louth in 1329 had exposed the self-serving nature of his regime and encouraged the Anglo-Irish elite back into their accustomed habits of violent self-help.[12]

Thus it was that Ireland, rather than Scotland, moved to the top of Edward III's agenda in the months after the Nottingham coup. In March 1331 ordinances were enacted at Westminster for the better government of the lordship. Sir Anthony Lucy was appointed justiciar and the earl of Ulster created lieutenant of Ireland.[13] A number of the leading trouble-makers, including the earl of Desmond, were rounded up and imprisoned. Such were the mounting problems, however, that the September parliament actually decided that the king himself should cross to the lordship. A search of the royal archives was ordered to find out 'what has been done in the past as regards the correction of the land of Ireland'.[14] The appeal to precedent was stark, for no king of England had set foot in his Irish dominion since King John's expedition there in 1210. The continued

---

[10] *CDS*, iii, no. 1057.

[11] *Brut*, i, 275; *CDS*, iii, nos. 1050–1; *Foedera*, II.ii, 833, 843–4; *Chron. Meaux*, ii, 362–3; Nicholson, *Edward III and the Scots*, 76–9.

[12] R. Frame, *English Lordship in Ireland, 1318–1361* (Oxford, 1982), 174–95.

[13] *Foedera*, II.ii, 811–12, 818. For the additional ordinances issued in Ireland in November, see *Statutes and Ordinances, and Acts of the Parliament of Ireland, King John to Henry V*, ed. H. F. Berry (Dublin, 1907), 332–9.

[14] *PROME*, iv, 156–7.

discussions of Edward III's projected mission in the great council of January 1332 and the parliament of March 1332 indicates a general consensus that Ireland had precedence over all the many urgent calls upon the king's attention.[15] During the summer of 1332 extensive plans were in place to gather military forces for the expedition, now set for the end of September; in the meantime, a parliament was summoned explicitly to discuss 'various arduous affairs touching the king and the state of the realm and the land of Ireland'.[16]

In the midst of these preparations came dramatic news that was to transform the whole military and political landscape. On 11 August at Dupplin Moor, south of Perth, the disinherited had won a crushing victory against the combined forces of the Bruce.[17] The earls of Mar, Moray and Menteith and many other Scottish lords and knights lay slain on the field, while the much smaller English army remained virtually, and miraculously, unscathed. In the panic and disarray that followed, a number of Scottish barons and bishops speedily threw in their lot with Balliol, who on 24 September was proclaimed king of Scots at the abbey of Scone. Immediately, Edward III reordered his priorities. Rather than subduing Ireland, he now launched a plan, with the active support of William de Burgh, to draw an Anglo-Irish army into Scotland. This came to nothing, for de Burgh was assassinated by a group of his own relatives at Carrickfergus in June 1333. In spite of the resulting panic and the continuing and very obvious neglect from Westminster, order did not entirely collapse in the lordship, and by 1335 Edward III was able to raise significant military forces from Ireland for the continuing commitment in Scotland.[18] Nevertheless, the abandonment of the Irish expedition in 1332 resulted in a dramatic and permanent shift in policy. Edward was never to fulfil his personal promise to appear in the lordship, and he delayed for nearly thirty years the decisive intervention to which his early regime had made such a public commitment.

Parliament opened at Westminster on 9 September 1332 in a state of high excitement. It was quickly agreed that the king's Irish expedition be called off and that he make his way instead to the north to prepare for the reprisals that would undoubtedly arise from the recent activities of the disinherited. Such, indeed, was the urgency of news 'coming from the

---

[15] *RDP*, iv, 406–7; *Foedera*, II, ii, 825, 828, 829, 831; *PROME*, iv, 168; BL, MS Cotton Faustina B. V, fols 63v, 64v. For the resulting policy of containment towards the Scots see *Foedera*, II.ii, 833, 837.

[16] *Foedera*, II.ii, 840, 841, 842–3; *RDP*, iv, 411–13; E 403/262, 29 July, 3 Aug., 10 Aug. 1332; C 47/2/25, no. 2; Frame, *English Lordship*, 199–200.

[17] For full accounts of the battle see Nicholson, *Edward III and the Scots*, 83–94; C. J. Rogers, *War Cruel and Sharp: English Strategy under Edward III, 1327–1360* (Woodbridge, 2000), 27–47.

[18] Frame, *English Lordship*, 218–27.

regions of Scotland from day to day' that on 11 September it was agreed
that all other business be set aside and the king be allowed to set forth
without further delay.[19] Edward had probably intended to finance the
Irish expedition out of loans on the security of a tallage, a form of prerogative taxation collected in the towns and on the royal domain; a clerk of
the exchequer had already been set to read through Domesday Book and
extract a list of the king's lands as a basis for the new levy.[20] In recognition
of the fact that the defence of the northern border represented a public
emergency deserving of general taxation, parliament now agreed to
replace the tallage with a general tax of a fifteenth and tenth on moveable
property.[21] The assembly did not, however, sanction any form of direct
military intervention in Scotland, and it seems likely that the king agreed
before his departure to hold further discussions at York before any decisive
intervention was made on behalf of Edward Balliol.

As soon as parliament was over, Edward III and his queen rushed down
to Canterbury to ask for Becket's blessing on the forthcoming expedition.[22]
The king then proceeded north via Leicester and Nottingham to York,
where he arrived on 17 October. The news was mixed. Perth, taken briefly
by the disinherited after Dupplin Moor, had been recaptured by the Scots
on 7 October. Although the new Scottish guardian, Sir Andrew Murray,
was taken prisoner at Roxburgh and sent as a hostage to the English court,
Balliol's forces were surprised as they lay naked in their beds at Annan.
The so-called king of Scots was forced to flee over the border and throw
himself on the mercy of the Franciscan friars of Carlisle.[23] There is no
evidence that Edward III had given permission for Balliol's inauguration
at Scone. But whatever his original ambivalence, he now fully embraced
the opportunities that were presented by the pretender king. In return for
English recognition of his title to the Scottish throne, Edward Balliol
offered to recognize the historical validity of Plantagenet claims to feudal

---

[19] *PROME*, iv, 173–4; *CPR 1330–4*, 323.

[20] *Foedera*, II.ii, 840; E 403/262, 14 July 1332. The grounds for the tallage were not specified, but since its announcement was accompanied by a request for clerical *dona* in support
of the marriage of Princess Eleanor, it seems that Edward had decided to exploit the tradition of the *aide pur fille marier*, the feudal levy made on the occasion of the marriage of his
eldest daughter, in retrospective application to the daughter of Edward II: J. H. Ramsay, *A
History of the Revenues of the Kings of England, 1066–1399*, 2 vols (Oxford, 1925), ii, 162–3. It
should be noted, however, that no attempt was made to levy a customary aid from the
king's feudal tenants, and in 1339 the council was clear that in strict terms no *aide pur fille
marier* had therefore been levied since Edward I's time: C 49/7/10, printed in D. Hughes,
A Study of Social and Constitutional Tendencies in the Early Years of Edward III (London, 1915), 245.
The abbot of Reading attempted to secure exemption from the *donum* requested in 1332 by
claiming that he was not liable to pay an *aide pur fille marier*: C 47/1/18, no. 10.

[21] *Foedera*, II.ii, 845. The raising of troops for the defence of the north was ordered on
7 Oct.: ibid., II.ii, 846.

[22] See p. 614.

[23] *Chron. Lanercost*, 270–1; *Scalacronica*, 113; *Chron. Meaux*, ii, 367; Bower, vii, 83.

lordship over the northern kingdom, to perform homage and fealty to Edward III and to do him military service when summoned, both on the island of Britain and overseas. He would also cede to the English crown, unconditionally and in perpetuity, the town and county of Berwick and a swathe of lands worth a nominal £2,000 a year across the counties adjacent to the English border.[24] The plan would at once shatter the 1328 agreement, restore Edward I's strategy of 1292, and redraw the political map of the border region to the dramatic advantage of the English.

It is likely that Balliol's proposal reached Edward via Beaumont during the session of parliament that convened at York on 4 December. Winter weather and a disinclination to become too involved in hare-brained schemes meant that attendance was unusually poor. On 8 December Sir Geoffrey Scrope, the chief justice of the king's bench, asked the lords and commons to offer their opinion on whether Edward should proceed to claim feudal suzerainty over a Balliol king or simply claim Scotland for himself. Significantly, he seems not to have offered the third option, of withdrawal. Possibly because of this blatant effort to push through such a hazardous enterprise those present refused to give a clear opinion, and after a day of inconclusive discussion it was simply decided to adjourn until the New Year.[25] Edward retired to consider his position over the Christmas festivities at Beverley.

By the time parliament reconvened in York in January 1333, now with a rather fuller turnout, the king was clearly determined to force the issue. Scrope charged the assembly to break into three discussion groups: an inner circle of bishops and lords (including Henry Beaumont) who could be counted on to follow the official line; the rest of the lords spiritual and temporal; and the knights and burgesses of the commons. Five days later Chancellor Stratford announced that, since the assembly had still not made up its collective mind on how to counsel the king, Edward had decided to take matters into his own hands and appoint keepers of the march with whom he could consult on a regular basis about the events unfolding in Scotland.[26] The only tax offered by the assembly, a retrospective subsidy on wool exports, proved highly controversial and had to be withdrawn the following June, though only after the crown had managed to negotiate a similar levy to be collected in 1333–4.[27] In the face of such ambivalence, the king began to exhibit traits that would reveal themselves repeatedly over the following decade: a stubborn belief in the superiority of his own views, a preference for the advice of the like-minded and a

[24] *Foedera*, II.ii, 847–8.
[25] *PROME*, iv, 182–3; J. S. Roskell, 'The Problem of the Attendance of the Lords in Medieval Parliaments', *BIHR*, xxix (1956), 165; Nicholson, *Edward III and the Scots*, 99.
[26] *PROME*, iv, 188–9.
[27] F. R. Barnes, 'The Taxation of Wool, 1327–1348', *Finance and Trade*, ed. Unwin, 140–1. The subsidy raised £15,600: Ormrod, 'Crown and the English Economy', 168.

disinclination to acknowledge ambivalence or opposition.[28] In February the king wrote to the exchequer announcing his firm intention to press ahead with a campaign in Scotland and ordering the swift collection of revenues for its support.[29] No further session of parliament would be held until early 1334, by which time the course of war would have been firmly set, and triumphantly justified.

During the early months of 1333 the formidable logistical machine of English government swung into full power in preparation for a campaign against the Scots. The exchequer and chancery were transferred to York in order to provide effective management of the northern war. Where the exchequer went, the court of common pleas followed, and where common pleas sat, there too sat the court of king's bench and parliament. The city of York thus became the temporary administrative and judicial capital of the kingdom, and remained so until the opening of the French war in 1337.[30] The inhabitants of York were well used to such incursions, which had been a regular occurrence since the 1290s, and while the arrival of the offices of central government could create serious logistical problems, it also opened up welcome opportunities. The abbot of the great York Benedictine house of St Mary's was commissioned to act as the king's temporary treasurer in the spring of 1333, and other York-based clergy became regularly involved in the financial administration of the northern campaigns.[31] A whole range of local tradespeople – carpenters, smiths, ropers, bowyers, fletchers, victuallers and clothiers – benefited from the additional business generated by the crown.[32] The city also provided an important recruitment pool for the army: John the quilt-maker of York had lost an ear fighting for the king at Stanhope Park in 1327.[33]

Fourteenth-century kings raised military forces by a wide variety of methods.[34] The most conservative element in the army was the heavy

---

[28] Rogers, *War Cruel and Sharp*, 58.

[29] E 159/109, rots 46d, 53.

[30] *Chron. Meaux*, ii, 373; Tout, *Collected Papers*, ii, 143–71; D. M. Broome, 'Exchequer Migrations to York in the Thirteenth and Fourteenth Centuries', *Essays in Medieval History Presented to T. F. Tout*, ed. A. G. Little and F. M. Powicke (Manchester, 1925), 291–300; Ormrod, 'Competing Capitals?', 75–98.

[31] E 403/265, 4 Mar. 1333; E 403/267, *passim*; Nicholson, *Edward III and the Scots*, 108; Harriss, *King, Parliament*, 348–54.

[32] *VCH Yorks: City of York*, 87. During the 1327 visit to York, the staff of the king's chapel commissioned a series of vestments from Alice of Blake Street: E 101/383/19. In 1333 Hugh le Seler of York made the seal used for the royal administration of the temporalities of the vacant bishopric of Durham: E 403/270, 20 Oct. 1333.

[33] *CDS*, iii, no. 933.

[34] For what follows see Prince, 'Army and Navy', 332–93; A. E. Prince, 'The Indenture System under Edward III', *Historical Essays in Honour of James Tait*, ed. J. G. Edwards, V. H. Galbraith and E. F. Jacob (Manchester, 1933), 283–97; A. E. Prince, 'The Payment of Army

cavalry (or men-at-arms), commanded by nobles, barons and high-ranking household knights. After 1327, Edward III's government never again attempted to call out the feudal host to perform its traditional forty days' unpaid service. Nor, until the 1340s, did it attempt to revive earlier, controversial experiments designed to impose a public obligation of military service on all free landholders. Rather, the cavalry element in Edward's armies of Scotland during the 1330s was an unstable mix of three elements. First were the bannerets, knights and esquires of the royal household, who were committed to following the king whenever he went personally on campaign. Second were the feudal tenants-in-chief and those holding from them in knight service. In spite of the shift away from the traditional feudal summons, the crown could still mobilize these forces quite effectively by offering them the opportunity to share in the glory of war. Indeed, Edward III occasionally sought to swell the size of this group by inducing landholders to take up knighthood and thus assume the military vocation associated with this status.[35] Finally, and most importantly, there were retinues of men-at-arms who were present not because they had any tenurial or public obligation but because they were contracted to do so. The captains of these latter contingents were sometimes household knights and tenants-in-chief, but might also be free agents in their own right. The Hainaulters and other European knights who brought contract forces to the Scottish wars were therefore essentially mercenaries – though they would have strongly despised the modern connotations that go with that label.

Whether mercenaries or not, all these disparate elements of cavalry usually expected to be paid, from the point of muster, at the rate of 8 shillings a day for an earl, 4 shillings for a banneret, 2 shillings for a knight and 1 shilling for an esquire. By the 1330s the high aristocracy had generally overcome the notion that receipt of payment would somehow demean them and lessen their freedom of action in the theatre of war. Not that pay itself was a major inducement to serve. The impoverished English crown sometimes attempted to economize on the expense of war in the 1330s by offering lump-sum payments fixed well below the real cost of wages. Nor as yet did it generally offer the additional financial incentives that became the norm in the later French wars, such as bonus payments and the right to a share of the ransoms and plunder taken on campaign.

Wages in Edward III's Reign', *Speculum*, xix (1944), 137–60; N. B. Lewis, 'The Organisation of Indentures of Retinue in Fourteenth-Century England', *TRHS*, 4th series, xxvii (1945), 29–39; Powicke, *Military Obligation*, 166–212; N. B. Lewis, 'The Recruitment and Organization of a Contract Army, May to November 1337', *BIHR*, xxxvii (1964), 1–19; M. Prestwich, 'Cavalry Service in Early Fourteenth Century England', *War and Government in the Middle Ages: Essays in Honour of J. O. Prestwich* (Woodbridge, 1984), 147–58.

[35] For these twin tactics see, e.g., the arrangements of 1333: *Foedera*, II.ii, 855–6. Returns to the distraint of knighthood ordered in 1334 (ibid., II.ii, 899) are found in C 47/1/13.

What wages did do was to create some sense of uniformity among the higher ranks and thus, without unduly forcing the issue, to promote a greater sense of collective commitment to a common cause. The English men-at-arms who marched into Scotland in support of Edward III and Edward Balliol had a whole range of motives for doing so. But it remained essential to their status and honour that they were there out of personal loyalty to the king and public obligation to the realm.

The normal method for raising infantry to fight within mainland Britain was the commission of array, by which able-bodied men armed with the basic equipment of war were either freely recruited or more usually press-ganged into service. The principles that underpinned this practice, enshrined in the Statute of Winchester of 1285, had originally been intended primarily for the purposes of local peace-keeping and defence. By 1330, however, it was well established that the crown had the right to move arrayed troops to distant theatres of war so long as it paid them wages from the time they left their own shires. Edward III therefore used commissions of array on a regular basis to recruit infantry for the Scottish campaigns and, despite his promise of 1327, began to push beyond the limits of custom and statute in order to improve both the numbers and the equipment of troops. His determination in this respect is glimpsed in his equally striking determination to secure the appropriate contributions from those parts of the country normally immune from arrays. By the end of the 1330s Edward was regularly calling on the palatinates of Durham and Chester, the principality of Wales and the Welsh marcher lordships to organize their own conscripted forces for the king's wars.[36]

There were three types of soldier raised by array. First were the hobelars, an elite force of light cavalrymen used mainly for reconnaissance and guerrilla warfare, and normally paid at the rate of 6d a day. Second were the contingents of Welsh infantry, who fought with bows, spears and knives; they were normally paid the lowest rate, 2d a day. Third, and most important, were the English archers or longbowmen. Foot archers were paid a daily rate of 2d or 3d. But increasingly significant in the armies of the 1330s were the mounted archers, who received between 4d and 6d a day. All archers fought on foot in set-piece battles, but the mounting of

---

[36] C. D. Liddy, *The Bishopric of Durham in the Late Middle Ages: Lordship, Community and the Cult of St Cuthbert* (Woodbridge, 2008), 165–6. When parliament approved arrays of the shires in Feb. 1339, the king requested the bishop of Durham and the duke of Cornwall to array the laity and clergy of their liberties to provide 230 and 675 men, respectively: *Foedera*, III.ii, 1070–2; C 76/14, m. 14d. For a similar request to Welsh marcher lords for the provision of archers in Mar. 1340 see C 76/15, m. 28d. In 1343–4 Bishop Bury gave jurisdiction within his palatinate to a group of royal commissioners empowered to raise shipping in the north: Durham University Library, Durham Cathedral Muniments, Register of Richard Bury, fol. vii.

such infantry offered commanders the opportunity to move their forces around at much greater speed and thus to respond much more readily as need and emergency arose. Horse archers were not altogether new in the 1330s, but it was in this period that they became an integral part of the English military machine. By 1334, moreover, they were being recruited not by array but by contract. This important shift is indicative of the relatively high status of mounted archers who, while not formally part of the traditional cavalry, were nonetheless often drawn from minor gentry families and espoused much the same value system as the men-at-arms. This binding together of the officer class and the elite infantry into a much more cohesive fighting force was to be one of the essential ingredients of success in the military strategy of Edward III.

The logistics required to move royal armies around, to keep the men well fed and their horses equipped and foddered, was a formidable challenge for the English crown and its local agents.[37] Edward III maintained the position adopted by his immediate predecessors and insisted that the considerable amounts of hardware and consumables needed in the field – horseshoes and nails, hay and oats, replacement longbows, huge stocks of arrows, wheat, pulses, salted meat and cheese, and so on – should be raised by purveyance. The compulsory purchases used to feed the king and his entourage were thus applied on a national scale and enforced through the fiction that the king and his army were simply an extension of the royal household.[38] The system was often inadequate to this greater task. Perishables taken in the shires not infrequently rotted before they reached the theatre of war. And the money required to pay off suppliers was often not forthcoming. While the clerks appointed to receive victuals and other supplies on the frontier were supplied with reasonably ample funds to pay the purveyors, the latter often had far too little cash in hand when they made their initial seizures. In the first large-scale purveyance ordered for the Scottish war in 1333, for example, the sheriffs were forced to give most suppliers IOUs in the form of tallies, wooden sticks on to which the amount owed was inscribed in a series of notches.[39] Few of the little people on whom royal purveyors often preyed had realistic expectations of being able to redeem such credit notes. Partly for these reasons, and partly for its sheer unpredictability and arbitrary application, purveyance

---

[37] M. Prestwich, 'Military Logistics: The Case of 1322', *Armies, Chivalry and Warfare in Medieval Britain and France*, ed. M. Strickland (Stamford, 1998), 276–88; M. Prestwich, 'The Victualling of Castles', *Soldiers, Nobles*, ed. Coss and Tyerman, 169–82.

[38] J. R. Maddicott, 'The English Peasantry and the Demands of the Crown, 1294–1341', *Landlords, Peasants and Politics in Medieval England*, ed. T. H. Aston (Cambridge, 1987), 299–318.

[39] *CCR 1333–7*, 25–6; E 358/2, mm. 1–1d. Compare the accounts of Robert Tonge, receiver of victuals at Newcastle and Berwick, who received over £5,700 in excess of his expenditure between 1334 and 1338: E 138/2, mm. 14–15d.

continued to be a regular source of acrimony between the crown and the political community throughout the first half of Edward III's reign.[40]

English armies of this period did not wear uniforms in the way that the term is understood today. The earls, bannerets and knights bore their own personal heraldry on banners, pennants, shields, over-tunics and horse trappers; any attempt to have them parade only in the king's colours would have been a major affront to the essential individualism of medieval chivalry. In the 1330s, various infantry and support groups – engineers in 1333, the 600 foot levied by Sir Thomas Ughtred in 1335, and the Welsh contingents in 1337 – were required to wear clothing 'of one type'. It remains unclear, however, whether this extended much beyond a basic colour. Edward I had sometimes required English infantry fighting in Wales to wear armbands with the cross of St George.[41] But if badges were worn under Edward III, they are just as likely to have been those of the respective captains as of the king. The one way in which Edward did emphatically stamp the royal style on the army was in his use of flags. In 1331–2 he had built up a stock of armour 'for war and tournament' and personally commissioned thirty banners bearing the arms of St George, forty-four of the arms of England, ten of St Edward and five of St Edmund.[42] Over the course of 1333–5, the royal armourer, William Standewyk, commissioned a large number of painted standards, banners and pennants, including at least twelve standards and twelve banners bearing the king's arms and no fewer than sixty standards and 800 pennants of the arms of St George.[43] If there was indeed a unifying theme and overwhelming 'look' to the armies of the mid-1330s, it was that of England's emergent patron saint.

In the spring of 1333 Edward Balliol again crossed into Scotland in warlike fashion, in the company of the earl of Arundel, Henry of Grosmont, Henry Percy and William Montagu. After rampaging around Roxburghshire, he made for the town of Berwick, to which his army laid siege by mid-March. Berwick had been held by England between 1296 and 1318 but had been lost by Edward II in the aftermath of Bannockburn. Its recapture was essential, both for the development of a viable military strategy in Scotland

---

[40] T. F. T. Plucknett, 'Parliament', *Eng. Govt at Work*, i, 117–19; W. R. Jones, 'Purveyance for War and the Community of the Realm in Late Medieval England', *Albion*, vii (1975), 300–16.

[41] A. J. Taylor, 'Edward I and the Shrine of St Thomas of Canterbury', *Journal of the British Archaeological Association*, cxxxii (1979), 22–8; M. Prestwich, *Armies and Warfare in the Middle Ages: The English Experience* (London, 1996), 141.

[42] E 101/385/20. New armour and two horse trappers had earlier been made for him against the Stanhope Park campaign: E 101/383/3; E 101/383/19.

[43] E 101/386/18; E 101/387/14. See also the order for 1,800 little pennants (*penocellae*) of St George for the Stanhope Park campaign: E 101/383/3.

and for the morale of the English. Edward III's resulting commitment to this enterprise was immediate and enduring. He commissioned two major siege engines in Yorkshire and organized their dispatch by sea to the mouth of the Tweed. John Crabbe, a Flemish adventurer who had masterminded the successful Scottish defence of Berwick in 1318–19 but had recently been taken prisoner by Sir Walter Mauny, was swiftly bought up as a royal prisoner of war and deployed to take charge of the trebuchets and other catapults erected around the bastions of the town. The king ordered prayers to be said by the clergy throughout England for the general defence and salvation of the realm.[44] Having purchased a new steel hauberk in preparation for the impending encounter,[45] Edward then moved off from Yorkshire in April, proceeding via Durham and Newcastle to arrive at Berwick on 17 May, where he remained for the next two months. Despite the daily preoccupations of the siege, the king retained overall mastery of the position in the north. The new guardian of Scotland, Sir Archibald Douglas, aimed to create as many diversionary tactics as possible, launching raids across the border into Northumberland and Cumberland. But Edward refused to accept the Scots' claim that they had managed to retake Berwick on 11 July, and under terms agreed a few days later the people of Berwick were made to concede that, unless they were rescued in the interim, they would give up the town to Edward III on 20 July.[46] Douglas, who was at Morpeth, now had no choice but to confront the English army, and moved swiftly back across the border to take up camp at Duns on 18 July.

The following day, Edward's forces took up a position on Halidon Hill, two miles outside Berwick. The men-at-arms, dismounted, were split into three divisions, headed on the right by the earl of Norfolk and Edward Bohun, on the left by Balliol, and in the centre by the king himself. Each division was flanked by a wing of dismounted archers. The English force probably numbered fewer than 10,000 men, the Scots twice that number.[47] Although Edward's troops were obviously alarmed at the sight of their mighty enemy, those who had been present at Dupplin Moor the year before had reason to think that their chances were good. The decision to replicate the tactics of that battle and take up a defensive position against the Scots represented a radical departure from the traditional English reliance on an offensive cavalry charge. Edward understood the challenges that his grandfather and father had faced in fighting the Scots and the ruination brought on Edward II's forces when he had tried to use the customary methods at Bannockburn. Given the king's very limited experience, it is hardly likely

[44] *Foedera*, II.ii, 856, 858–9; Nicholson, *Edward III and the Scots*, 110, 121–2; H. S. Lucas, 'John Crabbe: Flemish Pirate, Merchant, and Adventurer', *Speculum*, xx (1945), 342–5.

[45] E 101/387/10, m. 1.

[46] *Foedera*, II.ii, 864–5.

[47] Rogers, *War Cruel and Sharp*, 69–70.

that the tactics of Halidon Hill were merely his personal choice or invention. Among those present with Edward before Berwick in July 1333, Henry Beaumont stands out as the obvious mastermind of the project. To say, however, that Edward's contribution was merely symbolic is to neglect the very considerable effect that his personal presence and fixed purpose had on the forces in his company. A number of the chroniclers agreed that this was the moment of sweet revenge for which the king and his friends had been eagerly waiting ever since the ill-fated campaign of 1327.[48]

The Scots advanced in their own characteristic formation, the schiltrons, tightly packed groups of spearmen whose appearance drew analogies with hedgehogs or porcupines. They were a mighty force. But they were already exhausted from several days' hard marching and now had the terrain against them, struggling through waterlogged ground before clambering up the steep slope of the hill. As the Scots approached, the English archers let forth a great hail of arrows. Almost as soon as they reached the third English division, the Scottish pikemen began to melt away, knocked to the ground by the blows of the men-at-arms or, if they were lucky, running for their lives back down the hill. Even so, a number of the Scots successfully broke through the lines, and Edward III's division had to contend with an onslaught by the seventeen-year-old Robert Stewart, steward of Scotland, in which the king himself seems to have fought hand-to-hand. In one of the defining events of his long life, Edward of Windsor passed the supreme test of his leadership, vigour and bravery in that hour when hundreds of the finest Scottish troops were hacked down on the slopes of Halidon.

If the outcome of the battle was scarcely in doubt, there nonetheless remained the need to capitalize to the full on the spectacular collapse of Scottish might. While the earl of Norfolk's forces, including Beaumont, Strathbogie and John of Eltham, continued to battle with the Scottish division led by Douglas, Edward III and Balliol now set off with their re-mounted men-at-arms in ferocious pursuit of the fleeing enemy forces. As the English knights and footmen toured the field and its environs in their search for prisoners and booty, the enormity of the event began to strike home. No fewer than six Scottish lords – Atholl, Carrick, Douglas, Lennox, Ross and Sutherland – had been killed, and hundreds of knights slain. Chroniclers in England, relishing the bloodiness of the victory, proclaimed great losses to the enemy and indulged in their accustomed exaggerations of numbers: one managed somehow to conjure up the figure of 35,712 Scottish dead.[49] On the English side, by contrast, all the earls and bannerets survived unscathed, and the official line at least was

[48] Nicholson, *Edward III and the Scots*, 133; Rogers, *War Cruel and Sharp*, 68.
[49] 'Annales de Bermundeseia', *Annales Monastici*, ed. H. R. Luard, 5 vols (RS, 1863–8), iii, 473.

that no more than one knight and a handful of infantry were lost.[50] The king piously took responsibility for the proper burial of the enemy dead. Edward III had miraculously redeemed himself from the shameful legacy of the Stanhope Park campaign and, in the process, begun to build a reputation as the greatest general of his generation. The victory was formally announced to the English clergy three days later, with the appropriate orders for public celebration throughout the realm.[51]

Under the conventions established on 15–16 July, Berwick was bound to cede peacefully into Edward's hands, and on the day after the battle, 20 July, the keepers of the town duly handed it into English control. Balliol's existing agreement that the town should pass to the sovereign control of the English crown meant that Edward III was within his rights to impose uncharacteristically ruthless punishment on the inhabitants. One of the sons of Alexander Seton, the Scottish keeper of the town, had already been put to death on Edward's orders during the course of the siege.[52] Many of the men who had surrendered and been taken captive at Halidon Hill were reportedly executed on 20 July in a parallel show of Plantagenet domination. The terms of the surrender of Berwick seemed at first to provide guarantees against its formal annexation to the realm and crown of England and to offer the inhabitants their rights under Scottish law. But Edward's subsequent actions indicated very clearly his absolute determination to re-establish the direct rule that had prevailed between Edward I's annexation of Scotland in 1296 and Edward II's loss of Berwick in 1318. The town was not only strategically important; it was also the most important commercial centre in Scotland, the customs duties on wool exported out of its port representing the single largest item in the Bruces' royal revenues.[53] If Edward could now make good the other territorial concessions offered by Balliol, he would have all the benefits of extended control in the Lowlands with none of the liabilities associated with ruling the Highlands. At an emergency Scottish parliament held at Edinburgh in early 1334, Balliol forced through this new vision for his hobbled realm. He would place Scotland once more under the feudal suzerainty of the crown of England, would grant Edward III sovereign control of the town, castle and county of Berwick, and would make additional alienations of territory in the Lowlands up the promised value of £2,000.[54]

[50] Rogers, *War Cruel and Sharp*, 73–4.

[51] E 101/398/22; *CCR 1333–7*, 128; *Foedera*, II.ii, 866; *Bridlington*, 116–18; 'Annales Londoniensis', 358–9.

[52] Nicholson, *Edward III and the Scots*, 126; Prestwich, 'England and Scotland', 196.

[53] A. Tuck, 'A Medieval Tax Haven: Berwick-upon-Tweed and the English Crown, 1333–1461', *Progress and Problems in Medieval England: Essays in Honour of Edward Miller*, ed. R. Britnell and J. Hatcher (Cambridge, 1996), 148–9; Campbell, 'England, Scotland', 185.

[54] *Foedera*, II.ii, 870, 875, 876–8; *CDS*, iii, nos 1107–12.

For Edward III, the opinion of a few remaining Scottish noblemen mattered a good deal less than the fact of his own supremacy. Already in the immediate aftermath of Halidon Hill he had begun unilaterally to dispose of patronage in Scotland, doling out lands forfeited by his recently fallen enemies to the likes of Warenne, Montagu, Beaumont, Percy, Edward Bohun, David of Strathbogie and Thomas Ughtred.[55] In August 1333, on distinctly tenuous grounds, he asserted the right to dispose of the Isle of Man and granted it, as a sovereign territory, to William Montagu.[56] Everything about his approach suggests that Edward regarded the matter of Scotland as briskly and authoritatively settled. After the fall of Berwick he moved south, spending the second half of 1333 and the ensuing winter chiefly in the Home Counties and East Anglia. A great council was held at Waltham Abbey at the end of September, but much of the king's time over the ensuing autumn and winter was spent in the duties of pilgrimage, the pleasures of the chase and the escapism of the tournament.[57]

The English acceptance of Balliol's proposals was formally promulgated at York on 1 March 1334 while Edward III was presiding over parliament.[58] In May the king and the queen moved north again, taking in the enthronement of Richard Bury as bishop of Durham in early June and proceeding on to Newcastle. There, on 19 June, in the Dominican friary, the newly confirmed king of Scots, Edward Balliol, performed liege homage to the king of England. Edward III and Queen Philippa hosted a great feast to mark the conclusion of the terms of peace and honour their new vassal and ally.[59] During the preparations for this great event Edward was informed that David Bruce and his wife had been smuggled out of Scotland to take refuge in Normandy under the protection of Philip VI.[60] Whether the king read this as proof of the disarray into which he had thrown the Bruce regime or as an omen of the common cause that might yet be made between the Scots and the French is uncertain. By force of arms, Edward had effected a change of dynasty, had broken the stranglehold of the 1328 treaty and had re-established his ancestors' long-held claims to suzerainty of Scotland. He had also gained sovereignty over a huge swathe of southern Scotland, stretching from Dumfries in the south and west to Edinburgh and Linlithgow in the north and east. Wiser heads might have warned Edward III to beware. But the extraordinary regime

[55] Nicholson, Edward III and the Scots, 139–62.

[56] Foedera, II.ii, 868; Munimenta de Insula Manniae, ed. J. R. Oliver, 3 vols (Manx Society Publications, iv, vii, ix, 1860–2), ii, 182–4 (incorrectly dated).

[57] E 159/110, rot. 15d; Murimuth, 69; Ann. Paulini, 359.

[58] Rot. Scot., i, 261–3.

[59] Murimuth, 72; Chron. Lanercost, 277; Anon. Chron. 1307–34, 168–71; Foedera, II.ii, 888–90; CDS, iii, no. 1127; E 101/311/7.

[60] Chron. Lanercost, 278; Scalacronica, 117; Froissart, i, 146–8, 429–31, 433–4; Bower, vii, 83; Campbell, 'England, Scotland', 187–8.

change that he had effected through one brilliant and devastating intervention had dramatically confirmed the king's sense of imperial destiny. In
the spring of 1334 it would have been difficult, indeed, to argue that he
was wrong.

During the months following Balliol's homage, Edward III's government
set to work to establish itself in the newly ceded Lowland shires. The
existing administrative structures, in many cases the product of earlier
Norman and Plantagenet influence on the northern kingdom, remained
more or less intact. The area was put under the general jurisdiction of a
separate chamberlain, chancellor and justiciar, and interference from
Westminster – or rather, in this period, from York – was kept to a
minimum.[61] There were good precedents for the creation of an enclave of
this kind. It is clear, though, that Edward was hoping to offload on to this
region the great burden of continuing defence against those Scots who
remained rebellious to Balliol's cause. The York administration invested
very little in the rebuilding, garrisoning or supplying of the newly acquired
castles in the Lowlands, apparently assuming that these could all be
supported locally. This was surely a triumph of hope over experience.
Organized resistance against Balliol, first manifest in Renfrewshire and the
Clyde estuary, quickly spread to the Lowlands. Widespread forfeitures
ordered in 1335, coupled with a continuing campaign of retribution and
destruction, sent a distinctly uncompromising message about the difficult
reality of English sovereignty.[62] Ironically, of course, this vengeful stance
defeated any real hopes of establishing a sustainable English hold on the
Lowlands. The gross profits from Edward III's new territories in Scotland
were no more than £1,000 a year.[63] It soon became starkly obvious that
Edward's regime north of the Solway–Tweed border would only be viable
so long as his subjects in England were prepared to fund it.

In July 1334, John Randolph, the new earl of Moray, whose father had
briefly been guardian of Scotland in 1332 and whose brother had died at
Dupplin Moor, returned from France to make common cause with Robert
Stewart. As the son of Robert Bruce's daughter, Stewart had some claim
to be the heir presumptive to David II, and was in due course to succeed
him as king of Scots in 1371. The allies focused their attention on the
Clyde, taking Dunoon castle and sending guerrilla forces out into Kyle,

---

[61] Nicholson, *Edward III and the Scots*, 163–4.

[62] G. W. S. Barrow, 'The Aftermath of War', *TRHS*, 5th series, xxviiii (1978), 121–5.

[63] The income from the Scottish shrievalties subject to English rule was about £700:
CDS, iii, nos 1214, 1246; R. Nicholson, *Scotland: The Later Middle Ages* (Edinburgh, 1974),
134–5. The customs at Berwick also generated £399 between Sept. 1333 and July 1334:
E 356/6, m. 24. The wardrobe account for 1335 records receipts of £533 levied in fines in
aid of the Scottish war and £66 from the customs at Edinburgh: BL, MS Cotton Nero C.
VIII, fol. 198.

Carrick and Galloway. Balliol, who had been planning to set up the head-quarters of his new administration in Scotland at Perth, found himself plagued by rivalry within the ranks of his own supporters. Edward Bohun and Henry Percy were at loggerheads over their claims to rights in the lordship of Annandale. There was also a serious falling out among the competitors for the rights of the deceased Scottish lord, Philip Mowbray, as a result of which David of Strathbogie and Mowbray's brother, Alexander, both defected to the Bruce party. With effective resistance to Moray and Stewart confined to Henry Beaumont's lordship of Buchan, Edward Balliol was forced once more to retreat to Berwick in September and request a further direct intervention by Edward III.

The English response was quick. Under the terms of the feudal suzerainty he had recently asserted over Balliol, Edward was required to assist his vassal in recovering his position in the kingdom of Scotland. He also had a direct incentive to try to recover some semblance of his own authority in the Lowland shires. Hardly less pressing was the increasingly tenuous condition of the English lords who had started the war. In some cases the king could take instant measures to relieve such problems. In the Westminster parliament of September 1334 he acted as arbitrator in the Percy–Bohun dispute: Edward Bohun was given Annandale, but Percy was handsomely compensated with grants in the Lowland shires to keep him actively committed to the maintenance of the Plantagenet regime there.[64] In other respects, though, military intervention was the only possible way to rescue Edward's comrades. One of the king's main – though unfulfilled – intentions in launching the winter campaign of 1334–5 was to relieve Henry Beaumont, now cut off from allies and supplies in his coastal fortress of Dundarg, north of Aberdeen. Another equally elusive aim was to rescue the English knight Richard Talbot, who just a week before the September parliament had been captured at Linlithgow and was now being held to ransom in Dumbarton.[65]

Such chivalric impulses may have impressed some of the lay magnates in parliament, but a more inclusive sense of benefit had to be communi-cated if the country at large was to be called upon to support a new campaign in the north. Since the start of hostilities Edward had been quick to make the case that the war was fought primarily to keep the Scots at bay. The same rhetoric was now employed to argue the case for general taxation of both laity and clergy and to justify the extensive arrays ordered in December.[66] The well-informed Rochester chronicler says that the taxes

---

[64] Nicholson, *Edward III and the Scots*, 170.

[65] Murimuth, 72; *Chron. Meaux*, ii, 372–3.

[66] *PROME*, iv, 204; *RP*, ii, 447; *Foedera*, II.ii, 887, 888, 900; Willard, *Parliamentary Taxes*, 22; Lunt, 'Collectors of Clerical Subsidies', 229–30; Powicke, *Military Obligation*, 190–1; Harriss, *King, Parliament*, 317 and n. 4.

of 1334 were granted 'to eject the Scots from the limits of England'.[67] A very similar theme is evident in Edward's correspondence with the French around this time, where he argued that his interventions were intended 'to avoid injuries and dangers menacing the English nation'.[68] Having formally allowed the Scots to determine their own fate and taken the homage of their lawful ruler, Edward III could now legitimately represent his continued involvement north of the border as a just war for the protection of his own rights and dominions.

Behind such compelling discourses, however, the strains were already beginning to tell. The magnates who had supported the previous campaign duly turned out again in the army that Edward led from Newcastle in mid-November. Along with the ever-present earls of Arundel and Warwick and the king's brother, John of Eltham, were the earl of Oxford, Lords Neville and Percy, and the massed ranks of the royal household. Henry of Grosmont, who had been at the siege of Berwick but not apparently at Halidon Hill, also now joined the royal party.[69] The talk at York was all blustering confidence: Bruce's supporters, it was said, were retreating beyond the Forth and would not dare to fight.[70] But if Edward was indeed planning a major foray far into the heart of Scotland in relief of Beaumont, he would need a large force to accomplish it. Finding the muster slow, Edward set off for Roxburgh, hoping that further forces would follow. The dim prospects, coupled with exceptionally cold weather, meant that few others responded, and in mid-December the king's accumulated force stood at no more than 5,300 men.[71] Despite their involvement in some action in the forest of Ettrick and the welcome distractions of Christmas games and jousts, Edward found conditions at Roxburgh and Melrose miserable, and by February the army was authorized to disperse. Beaumont had been forced to give up the defence of Dundarg, but had at least been allowed safe passage to return south. The defection of a number of Balliol's Scottish supporters, including Patrick Dunbar, earl of March, had also forced at least a temporary cessation of hostilities. Edward's only compensation was that, unlike the campaign of 1327, his withdrawal was on his own terms: meagre though the army of Roxburgh had been, no Scottish force had dared to approach it.

The English retreat, and Edward's agreement to undertake a truce with the Scots from Easter to midsummer, represented little more than a delaying tactic. A great council meeting at Nottingham in late March 1335

---

[67] BL, MS Cotton Faustina B. V, fol. 76.

[68] C 47/28/3/8–10; Nicholson, *Edward III and the Scots*, 158.

[69] Nicholson, *Edward III and the Scots*, 176–7; K. Fowler, *The King's Lieutenant: Henry of Grosmont, First Duke of Lancaster, 1310–1361* (London, 1969), 30–1.

[70] SC 1/42/202; *CDS*, v, no. 744.

[71] *Bridlington*, 120; Rogers, *War Cruel and Sharp*, 84–6.

authorized a new muster at Newcastle on 11 June.[72] Meanwhile, a full parliament was summoned to meet at York on 26 May. Edward and his ministers no doubt felt somewhat thwarted that, in spite of their expenditure on the Roxburgh campaign, political convention prevented them from asking for any further direct taxes while the grants made in 1334 were still in collection. But where there was room for manoeuvre, they certainly took it. The counties had been ordered to array over 2,500 hobelars and 7,000 archers and, controversially, to support these troops until they reached Newcastle.[73] At the York parliament the commons grumbled about this violation of the Statute of Winchester, but agreed to a compromise whereby their respective county communities would pay fines in lieu of direct service.[74] By this and other expedients, the crown was able to mount one of the largest armies ever put into the field during Edward III's reign. Including the significant contribution of the magnate retinues and a large contingent of Welsh, the force stood at upwards of 13,000 men.[75]

Even taking into account the greater attractions of a summer campaign, it is clear that Edward had worked hard during the early months of 1335 to win back the confidence of the polity for his Scottish policy. In April he had issued proclamations against false rumours of political dissension between king, magnates and people.[76] The bishops and lords of the West Midlands were asked to be vigilant for rumoured insurrections and raids by the Welsh.[77] In particular, the king showed proper sensitivity to anxieties about possible reprisals from the French. Before he set off from Carlisle in late July, Edward arranged a number of meetings of prelates and other notables in York, London and elsewhere. Bishops Gravesend and Orleton were deputed to speak for the king at the London assembly and explain the measures that he was taking to ensure the safekeeping of the kingdom during his absence.[78] In the weeks that followed, Edward would argue that all parts of his dominions had the responsibility to assist him in the increasingly likely event that the Bruce party in France would attempt a seaborne invasion of either Scotland or England.[79]

The campaign of 1335 was one notably devoid of sustained action, successful sieges or major set-piece battles, and its achievement is much

[72] C 47/2/26, no. 15; *PROME*, iv, 206; Nicholson, *Edward III and the Scots*, 194.

[73] *Rot. Scot.*, i, 328–9; Powicke, *Military Obligation*, 202.

[74] *CPR 1334–8*, 131–3. There was to be much subsequent complaint about the fact that the arrayers had held on to the sums of money raised to support the original quotas, rather than paying them back after the commutation: ibid., 289; *CCR 1333–7*, 525, 530; etc.

[75] Nicholson, *Edward III and the Scots*, 200.

[76] *Foedera*, II.ii, 904. See also *AC*, 3; *Chron. Lanercost*, 279.

[77] *Registrum Thome de Charlton*, 59–60.

[78] *RDP*, iv, 452–3; Haines, *Stratford*, 240.

[79] Nicholson, *Edward III and the Scots*, 209–10, 219.

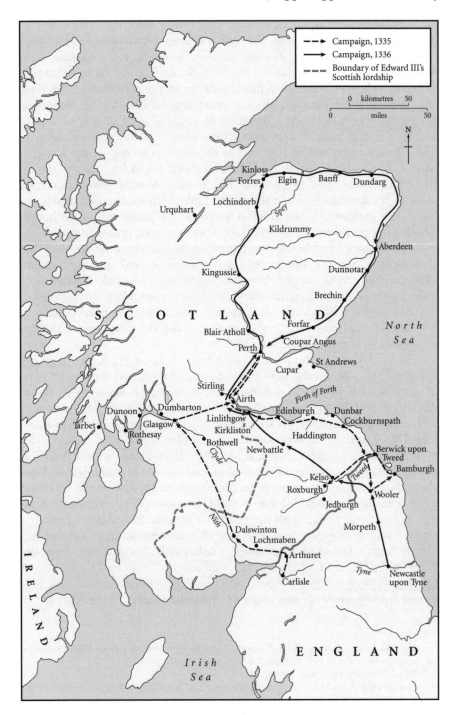

Map 3 The Scottish campaigns of 1335 and 1336.

more difficult to grasp than that of 1333. After their council of war at Newcastle at the end of June, Edward and Balliol had agreed to launch a two-pronged attack, the English king proceeding from Carlisle into Annandale and his vassal advancing from Berwick along the coastal route to Edinburgh. At Carlisle on 9 July the clergy of the cathedral set out their relic collection on the high altar to provide good luck for the departing troops, and the king made a donation of cloth of gold by way of thanks for this spiritual boost.[80] The twin armies met, as planned, at Glasgow in mid-July and marched in triumph to the Forth. Having set up a supply base at Airth, they crossed the Firth and made for Perth, where Edward III remained for most of August. The main action of this period took place in the Lowlands, when the Bruce party's leader, the earl of Moray, was taken prisoner by the English garrisons of Roxburgh or Jedburgh. The legacy of Edward's great march was, however, considerable. A co-ordinated attack launched from Ireland on Arran and Bute ensured that even Robert Stewart was at least temporarily cowed into submission. Wherever they went, English forces indulged in orgies of destruction on a scale rarely seen even in the most vindictive campaigns of Edward I. Berwick alone was spared. It was later said that the only people in Scotland who dared to say they supported 'King Davy' in those dark days of 1335 were, like him, guileless children.[81]

Edward III's main intention in marching as far as Perth was probably to extend this sustained programme of intimidation into the coastal zone of north-east Scotland and make a great riding or *chevauchée* as far as Aberdeen and Elgin. In late August the opportunity arose for similar action in the west, when an Irish force of 1,500 men led by the justiciar, John Darcy, and the earls of Desmond and Ormond landed on the Kyles of Bute and laid siege to Rothesay castle.[82] Balliol, the earl of Warwick, Henry Beaumont, Henry of Grosmont and a force of mounted archers, about 800 men in all, were immediately dispatched to make common cause with the Anglo-Irish lords 'beyond the mountains'.[83] Edward's deci-sion not to press ahead with the northern expedition was not so much a mark of failure, however, as a reflection of improved conditions elsewhere. On 18 August David of Strathbogie made public his defection from the Bruce camp. He and others had been sufficiently impressed by the recent English show of force to be persuaded that their interests were now best served by allegiance to the cause of Edward Balliol.[84] The capture of

---

[80] BL, MS Cotton Nero C. VIII, fol. 202v. Victuals were provided from Richmondshire for the support of the king's forces at Carlisle: E 358/2 m. 38d.

[81] Bower, vii, 103; Wyntoun, 38, 39.

[82] Frame, *English Lordship*, 147–8; A. E. Prince, 'The Strength of English Armies in the Reign of Edward III', *EHR*, xlvi (1931), 357.

[83] Nicholson, *Edward III and the Scots*, 218–23.

[84] *Foedera*, II.ii, 920.

Moray and the re-engagement of Strathbogie simply allowed Edward to return to his bases in the border zone, mainly at Roxburgh, Berwick and Newcastle where he resided until the end of November to oversee a succession of truces. It was during this period that the English king put in place ambitious plans for the rebuilding and garrisoning of Edinburgh castle.

Above all, Edward continued to pursue the inspired policy of allowing his close friends a direct interest in the preservation of the English lordships beyond the Tweed. At the end of the 1335 campaign, Edward gave his closest friend, William Montagu, almost independent jurisdiction over a great arc of estates, including the forest of Selkirk and Ettrick and the town and county of Peebles.[85] The Lowlands were gradually emerging as a set of great marcher lordships of similar scale and importance to those held in Wales and Ireland. If the king could keep the forces of Bruce and Stewart contained in the Highlands, then the English-controlled shires of the border region might yet look after themselves and the security and prosperity of the north of England might finally be assured. The Christmas court at Newcastle in December 1335 had good reason to celebrate. In his later years, Edward III is likely to have looked back on this season as the true high point of his achievement in Scotland.

In spite of these encouraging signs, Edward's knowledge of the history of Anglo-Scottish affairs might have cautioned him against too ready an expectation of long-term success. While diplomatic negotiations were going on further south in 1335, David of Strathbogie, newly installed as Balliol's guardian north of the Forth, laid siege to Kildrummy castle, east of Aberdeen at the foot of the Cairngorms. The castle was an important point of reference for the English: Edward I had taken it on his marches through the north-east of Scotland in 1296 and 1303, and Edward II, in a rare moment of military competence, had successfully besieged it in 1306.[86] It was currently held by Christian, the sister of Robert Bruce and wife of the guardian of David II's monarchy, Andrew Murray. Since Balliol was not formally a party to the truce incepted by the English and the Bruce party, Murray was probably within his rights to proceed to the relief of Kildrummy. He may even have sought permission from Edward III's representative at the current talks, Montagu.[87] If the latter did indeed consent, it must surely have been because he believed Strathbogie capable of victory. The two armies – 3,000 allegedly on Strathbogie's side, and just 800 on Murray's – met at Culblean Hill some miles south of Kildrummy,

[85] *CChR 1327–41*, 348–9; *Foedera*, II.ii, 924.
[86] Prestwich, *Edward I*, 472, 488, 508.
[87] J. Fordun, *Chronica gestis Scotorum*, ed. W. F. Skene (Edinburgh, 1871), 360.

near the River Dee.[88] The engagement – which took place mostly in the ford of a stream called the Burn of the Vat – was brief. But the unthinkable happened. Strathbogie's men were put to flight, and he and his principal followers, including Walter Comyn, were killed. The guardian and his dynamic lieutenant Sir William Douglas then moved on and laid siege to the castles of Lochindorb and Cupar. Their success significantly raised the morale of those Scots still covertly loyal to the Bruce cause; later, indeed, the battle of Culblean became famous as the beginning of the end of Balliol rule.[89] Whether Edward III thought the affray quite so significant is doubtful. What he did know, however, was that the Scottish problem was now becoming irretrievably tangled up in the still bigger question of his relations with the French.

Edward III was brought up to understand the durability of the Auld Alliance between Scotland and France. The changes of regime in France in 1328 and in Scotland in 1329 had not affected the commitment made by the two realms at Corbeil in 1326. From the very beginning of his intervention on behalf of the disinherited in 1333, Edward had therefore been anxious to justify his actions to Philip VI and persuade the latter that he ought to remain neutral.[90] In the aftermath of Halidon Hill, Edward may even have thought that Philip might switch allegiance from David Bruce to Edward Balliol. Such fantasies were destroyed once and for all when Philip offered refuge to the young David II and installed him at the great Norman fortress of Château Gaillard in May 1334.[91] The following month, at what was otherwise an encouraging conference at Senlis on the resolution of disputes over Aquitaine, Philip made the unexpected announcement that any final settlement between England and France would have to take into account the rights and status of the Bruce monarchy in Scotland.[92] Thereafter, the Scottish question became an integral part of the agenda both at Anglo-French diplomatic sessions and in the various arbitrations attempted by two successive popes, John XXII and Benedict XII.

The strength of the English position in 1335 caused Edward III to be somewhat contemptuous of these moves. In August, while he was still at Perth, the English king wrote in high-handed fashion to Philip VI, arguing that his involvement in Scotland was a consequence of his obligation as Balliol's feudal lord. Rather than succouring England's enemies, Philip should recognize his own obligations as Edward's suzerain, relative and friend and come to his aid against the rebellious Scots.[93] There was

---

[88] Bower, vii, 117; Wyntoun, vi, 58–9, 62–3. The estimate for Strathbogie's force is a likely exaggeration: Rogers, *War Cruel and Sharp*, 107 n. 136.

[89] Nicholson, *Edward III and the Scots*, 236.

[90] See, e.g., his letter of May 1333: *Foedera*, II.ii, 860.

[91] *The Exchequer Rolls of Scotland, 1264–1359*, ed. J. Stuart (Edinburgh, 1878), 464.

[92] Déprez, *Préliminaires*, 97.

[93] *Bridlington*, 124–6; Sumption, i, 146; Rogers, *War Cruel and Sharp*, 102.

substance to such an argument, but it was flawed by the fact that Edward and his friends had started the Scottish war in an open act of aggression. During the winter of 1335–6, moderation appeared to prevail. Papal envoys arrived in England and began talks with Murray's supporters; they then moved on to Newcastle and Berwick to take part in discussions with deputations from both David II and Philip VI.[94] Having failed fully to grasp the seriousness of Philip's purpose, Edward was now gambling everything on a belief that the French were never likely to give real military backing to such a blatantly hopeless case as David II.

Under the protection of the truces extended to the spring of 1336, Edward III's negotiators tried to find a way through this tangle of diplomacy that might preserve English honour while accommodating the newly assertive demands of the Scots and the French. The resulting draft treaty of Newcastle proposed that Edward Balliol be accepted as ruler of Scotland north of the Forth, with Edward III retaining sovereignty over the Lowland counties ceded in 1334. However, it also suggested that Balliol, who was in his forties and unmarried, should at his death be succeeded by David Bruce. To this notable concession there were significant conditions. As king-in-waiting, David would be required to give up his exile in France and live under the jurisdiction of the English king. On succeeding to the Scottish throne, moreover, he would be required to perform homage and fealty to Edward III.[95] The idea that Balliol should see out his days as king of Scots ran in the face of reality: with very few effective strongholds in his titular kingdom, Edward the pretender had already moved to the safety of the English zone and taken up residence at Berwick.[96] For David II's supporters, however, the real sticking point was not the question of timing but the issue of the long-term integrity and independence of Scotland. Messengers dispatched to discuss the proposal with the Bruce party reported back to the Westminster parliament in March.[97] The obdurate Scots had refused the terms of peace and rejected the idea of an extended truce. It is hard to believe that Edward III had expected or wanted any other outcome. The English chroniclers made much of David's refusal, attributing it variously to Scottish pride and French interference.[98] The collapse of the talks allowed the English king to turn the *casus belli* on its head and represent the Bruce party as blatant aggressors against his own legitimate overlordship of Scotland.

---

[94] For instructions to the exchequer to provide documents needed for the talks with the French, see C 47/28/8, no. 56.

[95] *Bridlington*, 127; *AC*, 6; *Chron. Lanercost*, 284–5.

[96] Balliol was careful to ingratiate himself with his kingmaker at this point, sending Edward the personal gift of a prize gerfalcon: BL, MS Cotton Nero C. VIII, fol. 268.

[97] *RDP*, iv, 454–6; *PROME*, iv, 208–9; *Foedera*, II.ii, 935; *AC*, 6. Prior to the parliament the king had his clerks prepare a detailed list of the lands owing to him in Scotland under the terms of the proposed peace: E 403/285, 1 Mar. 1336.

[98] *Bridlington*, 128; *AC*, 6.

All was now set for a further major expedition against Scotland. Laity and clergy granted the necessary taxes, extensive arrays were ordered, and Henry of Grosmont was appointed 'captain and commander' of the new army.[99] With new business arising in relation to France, Edward could not afford to commit himself personally to the campaign, but kept himself properly informed of its planning and progress.[100] In the event, many of the resources intended for Scotland had to be redirected. In May Edward learned that Philip VI had finally decided to give material backing to his moral position and either dispatch relief forces to Scotland or launch a diversionary attack on the south coast of England. The northern campaign was therefore radically cut back, and Grosmont left with only about 1,000 men of his own, though the ranks were swollen when he managed to penetrate as far as Perth and link up with Warwick, Montagu, Beaumont and others.[101] English intelligence now suggested that a French fleet was likely to make for the east coast of Scotland. Eager to be part of the action, Edward III set aside his planning role and immediately determined to join his friends. In early June he left Woodstock with no more than a hundred men and proceeded north at lightning speed, taking the inland route through the Lowlands via Kelso to reach Linlithgow on the 17th and Perth two days later. Sir Thomas Lucy reported to the chancellor that preparations were well in hand for the reinforcements to be supplied from the border counties.[102] But moving ahead with such a small force was highly risky. The queen's cousin, Guy of Namur, had attempted a similar feat the previous year, and had been taken prisoner by the earl of Moray.[103] It is hardly surprising that Grosmont's men, holed up in the badly damaged defences at Perth, were said to have wept tears of joy at the miracle of the king's arrival.[104]

Edward's visit was not just a morale-booster; it also had a serious strategic purpose. In mid-July, with a small force of only 400 men-at-arms and about the same number of hobelars and mounted archers, the king set off north from Perth via Blair Atholl, Glen Garry and Glen Truim, and

[99] M. Jurkowski, C. L. Smith and D. Crook, *Lay Taxes in England and Wales, 1188–1688* (London, 1998), 39; Lunt, 'Collectors of Clerical Subsidies', 230; *Foedera*, II.ii, 931; *Rot. Scot.*, i, 422–4; Powicke, *Military Obligation*, 190–1; Lewis, 'Contract Army', 5; Fowler, *King's Lieutenant*, 32. Grosmont had 520 men-at-arms in his service: A. Ayton, *Knights and Warhorses: Military Service and the English Aristocracy under Edward III* (Woodbridge, 1994), 173.

[100] *AC*, 6; E 403/288, 19 June 1336.

[101] *Original Letters Illustrative of English History*, ed. H. Ellis, 3rd series, 3 vols (London, 1866), i, 29–33; Sumption, i, 159; N. A. M. Rodger, *The Safeguard of the Sea: A Naval History of Britain*, 2 vols (London, 1997–2004), i, 93–6; Sumption, i, 158; Rogers, *War Cruel and Sharp*, 116 and n. 181.

[102] SC 1/39/32.

[103] *CDS*, iii, nos 1238–9; *AC*, 4; *Chron. Lanercost*, 282–3; Bower, vii, 111–15; Nicholson, *Edward III and the Scots*, 212–14.

[104] Murimuth, 77; Baker, 57; Rogers, *War Cruel and Sharp*, 116.

thence down the Spey to Lochindorb.[105] This elite, mobile force was capable of moving swiftly over difficult terrain: a detailed account of the expedition written on behalf of the king to Queen Philippa bears witness to its exacting schedule.[106] The first part of the campaign was later remembered for a notable chivalric interlude at Lochindorb castle. In successfully raising the siege there, Edward displayed his credentials as a heroic knight errant by rescuing a group of 'lovely ladies' led by David of Strathbogie's widow, Catherine Beaumont, the titular countess of Atholl.[107] In fact, the taking of Lochindorb was an important marker of renewed English fortunes in the Highlands. The main purpose of the expedition, however, was revealed once Edward's little army moved down to the coastal plain and made its way along the Moray Firth from Forres to Aberdeen. All along the road, the English devastated the countryside, seizing foodstuffs and indiscriminately torching farms and settlements. At Aberdeen their ferocity reached its peak: the town and its hinterland were left in ashes. Returning via Brechin and Forfar to Perth at the end of July, Edward had some justification for believing that he had at once cowed the area beyond the Tay and decisively thwarted French efforts to land a major army there. The king remained in the war zone for over a month, overseeing the reinforcement of defences and garrisons at Perth, Stirling and St Andrews.[108] The *chevauchée* of 1336 marked Edward III's furthest foray into northern Scotland, and proved the dramatic effectiveness of a scorched-earth policy which was to be applied on a hugely ambitious level in his later campaigns in France.

The immediate outcomes of the campaign were, however, somewhat less than encouraging. Rejecting English attempts to sideline the Scottish question, Philip VI declared to the English negotiators at his court, the bishops of Durham and Winchester, that he would make no agreement with Edward unless Scotland was fully returned to the condition of 1328. The ambassadors' messenger reached Archbishop Stratford and other royal councillors at Northampton on 24 August, and they promptly authorized a great council to meet a month later at Nottingham.[109] Edward hurried south and arrived just in time for the opening of the assembly on 23 September. With taxes secured and special defence arrangements put in place against the continued threat of French invasion, he immediately returned north to Newcastle to await news from

---

[105] Prince, 'Strength of English Armies', 358.

[106] *Original Letters*, i, 33–9.

[107] *Scalacronica*, 123; Wyntoun, vi, 74–5; Bower, vii, 119. Catherine later claimed to have spent 400 marks of her own money on the defence of Lochindorb: *CDS*, iii, no. 223. The king intervened personally to ensure the delivery of her dower (SC 1/39/25) and provided for her death in England until her death in 1368.

[108] *Chron. Lanercost*, 286–7; *AC*, 7; Rogers, *War Cruel and Sharp*, 119.

[109] *EMDP*, I.ii, no. 376; *RDP*, iv, 458–64; *AC*, 8; *Chron. Lanercost*, 287.

Scotland. But the majority of the forces that had been maintained under Henry of Grosmont during the king's absence were now being disbanded, and Henry himself was dispatched back to England in early November to undertake responsibilities in the defence of the south coast.[110]

These shifts of priority notwithstanding, the king was clearly determined to press on at least with the ongoing task of the submission of the Lowlands. In mid-October Edward made a dash via Hawick and Peebles to reach the important strategic position of Bothwell castle on the River Clyde outside Glasgow. Plans were put in hand for the rebuilding of the castle under the financial direction of Thomas Hatfield, Edward's future faithful bishop of Durham.[111] An agreement between Balliol and John Og of Islay provided a potentially useful ally in the far west; within a year John was claiming the title of lord of the Isles.[112] But with Andrew Murray actively challenging the remaining outposts of Balliol sympathy in the Highlands and Douglas's guerrilla groups continuing to roam the southern shires, there was in reality little that Edward could do. In early December he left Bothwell, travelling via Berwick to spend Christmas at Hatfield in Yorkshire, where the queen had just given birth to their short-lived second son, William. Over the first weeks of 1337 he moved back and forth between the capital and Hatfield, busy with family responsibilities at the funeral of John of Eltham at Westminster Abbey and the equally solemn churching of the queen held after the demise of their baby boy.[113] In between these doleful duties, the king was also actively involved in preparations for the major business of France that would be discussed in the upcoming parliament summoned to Westminster for March 1337. Edward's intervention in Scotland in 1333 had been a miraculous and glorious moment. The manner of his engagement and withdrawal in 1336–7, by contrast, simply revealed the enormous and intractable problems facing those charged with establishing an enduring Balliol and Plantagenet regime there.

The redirection of English ambition and energy towards the war that broke out with France in 1337 undoubtedly exposed and exacerbated the systemic weaknesses of the English position in the north. Andrew Murray recovered control of his ancestral castle of Bothwell early in 1337. Although he died unexpectedly in April 1338, he was succeeded as guardian by the

---

[110] BL, MS Cotton Faustina B. V, fol. 79; Fowler, *King's Lieutenant*, 33.

[111] Rogers, *War Cruel and Sharp*, 123.

[112] M. Brown, *The Wars of Scotland, 1214–1371* (Edinburgh, 2004), 269–70.

[113] *Bridlington*, 128–9; Murimuth, 78. William was buried in York Minster on 10 Feb., while his father was in the south, but Edward III returned to Hatfield for the solemn ceremonies of the queen's churching on 16th: *The Register of William Melton, Archbishop of York, 1317–1340*, ed. R. M. Hill, D. Robinson, R. Brocklesby and T. C. B. Timmins, 5 vols (CYS, lxx, lxxi, lxxvi, lxxxv, xciii, 1977–2002), i, no. 370: E 101/388/2, m. 1.

able and energetic Robert Stewart. The English garrisons at Edinburgh and Stirling were threatened with sieges, and the remaining forces at Perth were finally required to surrender in 1339. Balliol himself was now a spent force. After 1338 he lived mainly in northern England, though he continued occasionally to take charge of campaigns and had some success in regaining control of ancestral lands in the south-west of Scotland.[114] For the most part, however, his personal monarchy had collapsed into a mere fiction of diplomacy. Edward III's efforts to relocate the border and its associated problems had also failed, and by 1340 the northern English counties of Cumberland, Westmorland and Northumberland had once more fallen prey to the regular depredations of Scottish soldiers and cattle rustlers.[115]

It would be quite wrong, however, to suppose that Edward III gave up on Scotland in 1337.[116] So long as the Scots resisted his settlement with Balliol, he would continue to send forces against them. The parliament of March 1337, which gave its consent to hostilities with the French, also approved a new campaign against the Scots under the earl of Warwick. Warwick and Bishop Bury were ordered to hold a special assembly of northern lords at York to drum up support for the expedition, and the king made a well-timed appearance at this important gathering in early May.[117] According to one chronicle, the March parliament actually insisted that the king should remain in England and persist with the business in the north.[118] The note of caution was well judged. News soon reached Edward that his enemies were laying siege to Stirling castle, and following a council at Stamford on 30 May he set off north again, joining his household in arms at Newcastle by 5 June. By the time he reached Stirling a few days later, the Scots had already withdrawn. Lacking the resources to undertake any other mission, Edward had to content himself with making arrangements for the defence and provisioning of the castle. He returned as quickly as he had gone, reaching Stamford in time for another council meeting on 16 June.[119] Even so, the forces sent into Scotland under the

[114] *ODNB*, iii, 604.

[115] *AC*, 10–14; J. F. Willard, 'The Scotch Raids and the Fourteenth-Century Taxation of Northern England', *University of Colorado Studies*, v (1907–8), 240–2; A. Ayton, 'Sir Thomas Ughtred and the Edwardian Military Revolution', *Age of Edward III*, ed. Bothwell, 107–8, 121–2.

[116] A. Grant, 'Scottish Foundations: Late Medieval Contributions', *Uniting the Kingdom? The Making of British History*, ed. A. Grant and K. J. Stringer (London, 1995), 97–108.

[117] C 47/2/29, nos 1–5, datable to before 25 Mar. 1337 by *Rot. Scot.*, i, 487–8; *Bridlington*, 129; *Chron. Meaux*, ii, 379–80. E 101/388/2, m. 4, records a dinner hosted by the king at York on 11 May attended by the bishop of Durham, the earls of Northampton and Gloucester 'and others'.

[118] *Chron. Lanercost*, 288–9.

[119] Ibid., 290; BL, MS Cotton Faustina B. V, fols 80–80v; Lewis, 'Contract Army', 1 n. 4; *HBC*, 448. Works carried out at Perth and Stirling during this period are listed in E 101/388/5, mm. 17–18.

earls of Warwick, Arundel and Salisbury continued to provide a formidable presence; there were about 4,000 English troops operating in
Scotland in 1337 and 1338.[120]

The great focus of activity for this army, and the major set piece over
the winter of 1337–8, was the siege of Dunbar, where the earl of Moray's
sister, the indefatigable 'Black Agnes' Randolph, held out in legendary
style against the prodigious manpower and equipment of her English
enemies. Edward III was very concerned at this resistance to his authority
and let it be known that it would be punished, under the laws of war, by
the execution of the imprisoned Moray.[121] Still more dramatically, he
made two attempts to visit the siege, in January and March 1338. On the
first occasion he reached Whitekirk, outside Dunbar, and is likely to have
made direct contact with Salisbury and his men. In March he probably
got no further than Alnwick, though a quick dash into the Lowlands is not
impossible.[122] Like his quick ride to Perth in 1336, the visit was in part
designed to lift the flagging spirits of English troops. On his way south in
January the king wrote to the officials of the exchequer to insist on more
adequate supplies for the armies of Scotland and warned them, in tones
that would become all too common over the next few years, that any reversals of fortunes would be put down to their own failure to manage the
financing and logistics of the war properly.[123] At the same time, his observation of the state of play at Dunbar seems to have convinced Edward
that the siege was doomed. In the spring he issued a highly controversial
order for the withdrawal of Salisbury's army and its redeployment as
part of the great force now being put together against the French.
This abnegation of responsibilities seems to have sparked a temporary row
with Montagu, who allegedly used the September parliament of 1337
as an opportunity openly to criticize the king's handling of northern
affairs.[124]

If Edward III ever thought that he could simply drop the Scottish war
in preference for the greater prospects of glory now presenting across the
Channel, the fallout from the siege of Dunbar taught him otherwise.
During his prolonged absence in the Low Countries in 1338–40, and in

[120] Prince, 'Strength of English Armies', 358–9; Lewis, 'Contract Army', 9–11.

[121] *Chron. Lanercost*, 296, 297; Bower, vii, 127–31; Sumption, i, 237.

[122] These expeditions are poorly documented. For the Jan. mission see *Bridlington*, 134–5;
Scalacronica, 124. The king did not take any of his own seals with him on this journey, but
used those of others in his entourage; see instruments sealed at Blyth on 11 Jan. and at
Aberford on 29 Jan.: E 159/114, rots 58, 62d. For the visit in Mar. see E 101/388/5, m. 14;
Chron. Meaux, ii, 385; *Bridlington*, 135–6; *Scalacronica*, 124–5. The privy seal moved only as far
as Newcastle on this second occasion: Shenton, *Itinerary of Edward III*, 175–6.

[123] E 159/114, rot. 62d.

[124] *Scalacronica*, 125; Bower, vii, 130–1. For Salisbury's expenses in connection with the
siege of Dunbar see Norwell, 266.

spite of the now overwhelming pressure for the defence of the southern coast, Edward's council was careful to ensure that the manpower and resources of northern England continued to be reserved, as much as possible, for the defence of the northern border.[125] This commitment no doubt helped persuade Salisbury quickly to make his peace and engage enthusiastically in the continental expedition of 1338. Edward's return home in February 1340 was also seen in some circles as an important marker of his continuing concern about the position in Scotland.[126]

Above all, it was in these years that Edward came to appreciate the ability of his propaganda machine to advertise his sense of obligation to the war in the north. His correspondence with the northern bishops and magnates contained repeated assurance that, wherever his body might be, his heart remained with them in their great enterprise against the Scots.[127] In his proclamations and orders for prayers in support of that war, Edward dug deep into a popular rhetoric that stressed the need for persistent vigilance against a barbarous and fickle enemy.[128] Even those commentators who, like Robert Manning of Bourne (Lincolnshire), took little pleasure in the gruesome messiness of war were nonetheless emphatic in their condemnation of the 'scabbed Scotte'.[129] In the early 1350s when the enthusiastic patriot Laurence Minot put together a sequence of poems on Edward III's achievements in Scotland and France, he was quick to warn his audience against complacency: 'Watch the Scots,' ran his refrain, 'they're full of guile'.[130] The feeling, of course, was mutual: the Scots thought the English as slippery as eels.[131]

The Scottish campaigns of the 1330s had given Edward III a huge sense of entitlement. The papacy, the king of France and other European rulers might look askance at such a blatant act of aggression against a boy-king and a vulnerable realm. But Edward had convinced himself, and most of his English subjects, that his cause was just. By 1338 English war aims had

[125] Powicke, *Military Obligation*, 192.

[126] Le Bel, i, 168; Froissart, i, 481.

[127] *Register of John Kirkby*, nos 413, 419.

[128] A. Ruddick, 'Ethnic Identities and Political Language in the King of England's Dominions: A Fourteenth-Century Perspective', *Identity and Insurgency in the Late Middle Ages*, ed. L. Clark (Woodbridge, 2006), 15–31.

[129] [R. Manning, 'Chronicle', published as] *Peter Langtoft's Chronicle*, ed. T. Hearne, 2 vols (Oxford, 1725), ii, 282; T. Turville-Petre, *England the Nation: Language, Literature, and National Identity, 1290–1340* (Oxford, 1996), 100–3.

[130] L. Minot, *Poems*, ed. T. B. James and J. Simons (Exeter, 1989), 26–30. See also *Anon. Chron. 1307–34*, 156–61. For other traditions of English invective against the Scots see A. G. Rigg, *A History of Anglo-Latin Literature, 1066–1422* (Cambridge, 1992), 53, 96–7, 228–9, 244–5.

[131] Bower, vii, 85–6; *Debating the Hundred Years War: Pour ce que plusieurs (La Loy Salique) and A Declaracion of the Trew and Dewe Title of Henry VIII*, ed. C. Taylor (Camden Society, 5th series, xxix, 2006), 23–4.

settled into an established and acknowledged pattern. Their major imperative was the need to guarantee the security of northern England. If at all
possible, however, Edward also wanted to hold on to Berwick and to the
larger buffer zone in the Lowlands, not least in order to maintain his
commitment to those of his leading men who now had interests there. He
was increasingly concerned to ensure that any lasting peace between
England and Scotland would be without prejudice to his own relations
with France. Above all, he clung resolutely to the argument that any king
of Scots, be he Balliol or Bruce, should perform liege homage to the crown
of England. The emphasis on a feudal relationship between the two
monarchies was typical of Edward's conservative instincts and his strong
adherence to the strategies of his grandfather. Ironically, though, it was at
just this time that Edward also began to experiment with positions that
might finally liberate his family from its own feudal subordination to the
king of France. Those changes, and the necessary adjustments to the
reality of David II's monarchy, would in the longer term transform
Edward's sense of what could and should be achieved from Plantagenet
domination over Scotland.

Chapter 7

THE LEOPARD AND THE LILY, 1331–1339

When Edward III emerged triumphantly from the controlling power of Roger Mortimer in 1330, the most pressing issue in relation to France remained that of the English monarch's responsibilities and liabilities as feudal vassal of the king of France. The compromise that had been struck when Edward performed simple homage to Philip VI at Amiens in 1329 had not really suited either side. But it was Philip who had set the pace over the following eighteen months, insisting that the status of the Agenais and the other provinces confiscated under the terms of the 1327 treaty from English control could only be discussed once Edward had performed full liege homage. He had fixed a series of deadlines for the king-duke to appear before the *parlement* of Paris and take the required oath of fealty. The final deadline ran out on 15 December 1330, and Philip was now technically within his rights to confiscate the whole of Aquitaine. A military force was dispatched under the leadership of Philip's brother Charles, count of Alençon, and Saintes, the northernmost English military position in the duchy, was taken and sacked. In spite of the preparations for war that had been put in place within Aquitaine, Edward was in no position to counter a Valois occupation, and a deputation was dispatched to the French court under Bishops Orleton and Airmyn in January 1331.[1] The only way out of the impasse, it seemed, was for Edward to present himself in person before his cousin of France.

The meeting between Edward and Philip at Pont-Sainte-Maxence in April 1331 was a very different affair from that held at Amiens eighteen months earlier. Edward, now released from the thrall of his mother and Mortimer, was determined to strike an appropriately assertive stance. He ordered that the mission be conducted under terms of strict secrecy. Accordingly, the king crossed the Channel with only a small entourage of close friends, including John Stratford and William Montagu, and assumed the identity of a merchant in order not to excite the attention of his own subjects.[2] The need for confidentiality is explained by the contents

---

[1] *Foedera*, II.ii, 805–6.

[2] Murimuth, 63. On 17 Apr. the crown ordered wheat and bacon to be sent to Portsmouth 'for the sustenance of the magnates', perhaps in reference to the king's return: E 358/2, m. 3; E 358/4, m. 3d. The outward and return crossings were, however, made via Dover.

of a document sent to Philip in preparation for the meeting, in which Edward admitted, presumably much against his better instinct, that he had responsibilities as a liege vassal of the king of France.[3] Philip was prepared to accept this as a statement of honourable intent, and decided not to press his demand that Edward undertake the oath of fealty in person. But Edward understood the wider implications of the partial concession and was determined not to allow others to exploit it as an admission of weakness. He allowed no associated documentation to be put on record at home, and his letters patent setting out his understanding of the issue of homage are known only because the original document was preserved in Paris.[4] The suspicion that had prevailed in relations between Plantagenet and Valois since Philip's succession in 1328 now gave way, on both sides, to a simmering rancour.

The cloak of secrecy surrounding this diplomatic summit left English commentators struggling to come to terms with what had actually happened in this encounter between Philip and Edward. The curmudgeonly Rochester chronicler, unable to define the business of the meeting, could only rail in general terms against the risks involved to the king's welfare by a little adventure undertaken 'without the counsel or consent of the community of the realm'.[5] Even when parliament met at Westminster in September 1331 to consider the making of peace with the French, nothing was said on the matter of homage.[6] And when the king and his advisers subsequently put together a public manifesto of the causes of the war in 1337, the description of the 1331 mission was notable for its vagueness: 'the king of England crossed secretly into France and came to [Philip VI], humbly requesting the delivery of his lands, offering and doing to the king *as much as he ought and more*'.[7] In his domestic politics, the astute Edward III immediately drew back from the truth of 1331 and, without ever actually denying the matter, consistently refused to make a precise statement about what had happened at his last peacetime encounter with Philip VI.

Some of the outcomes from the meeting at Pont-Sainte-Maxence were, however, rather more readily suitable for public advertisement. A new commission, the so-called process of Agen, was set up to address jurisdictional disputes arising in the parts of greater Aquitaine still subject to Valois confiscation. Secondly, a new strand of diplomacy was opened up around the proposal, first mooted in July 1331, for a marriage alliance between the infant Edward of Woodstock and one of the daughters of Philip VI.[8] This might allow Edward to revive the strategies of 1306 and

---

[3] *Foedera*, II.ii, 813.
[4] Ibid., II.ii, 815–18; Déprez, *Préliminaires*, 72–3, 77.
[5] BL, MS Cotton Faustina B. V, fol. 57v.
[6] *PROME*, iv, 155–6.
[7] *EHD*, iv, 62–3 (emphasis added).
[8] *Foedera*, II.ii, 822.

1325 and transfer Aquitaine to his eldest son. After discussion in the parliament of September 1331, the king dispatched John Stratford, Henry Beaumont and William Montagu to organize a treaty of marriage with Philip.[9] In the spring of 1332 Stratford, this time accompanied by Adam Orleton and William Clinton, reiterated this offer and, at the prompting of parliament, suggested a further meeting between the two monarchs.[10] Thereafter, however, the prospect of a settlement for Aquitaine was much reduced. Edward now dropped the offer of a marriage involving his own heir and focused instead on an alliance between his brother and various female members of the extended French royal family, including the daughters of the count of Eu, the count of Blois and the lord of Coucy.[11] When the Valois eventually agreed terms in September 1334, it was for an altogether lesser match between John of Eltham and Marie d'Espagne, the illegitimate daughter of the deceased sire de Lara. It is hard to see this as anything other than a deliberate snub. While a marriage alliance would have done little in itself to resolve the intractable differences between the two realms, it was with some justification that Edward III was able to claim in 1337 that Philip had deliberately obstructed the attempts to find a dynastic solution to their two families' continuing difficulties.

The other significant element in Anglo-French relations after the meeting at Pont-Sainte-Maxence was the public commitment by the two monarchs to join in a crusade. Joint crusading was a well-established part of the rhetoric of Anglo-French peace. Edward II had joined Philip IV and his three sons in taking the Cross at Paris in 1313 and thus committing themselves, when circumstances allowed, to fighting in the Holy Land. Already in 1330 Edward III had offered to assist Philip VI in finding allies for his planned crusade against the Moors in southern Spain, and as part of the settlement of April 1331 he committed himself to participate in person in this expedition. Then, in the autumn of 1331, Philip approached Edward with the suggestion of a much larger and bolder enterprise: a joint crusade to the Holy Land. The notion that the princes of the West should unite in common cause to recover Christian control of the holy places in the Middle East offered a compelling prospect, and for the next few years the crusading venture was to form a regular and often dominant theme in Edward's relations with both the king of France and the pope.

It has become conventional in modern times to draw a deep contrast between Philip VI's sincerity and Edward III's hypocrisy on the issue of crusade. It is rather too easy, though, to cast Edward III as a blatant dissembler who used his supposed commitment to the campaign in the

[9] *PROME*, iv, 155–6; Haines, *Stratford*, 221.
[10] *Foedera*, II.ii, 836, 837–8; *PROME*, iv, 16; Déprez, *Préliminaires*, 84–5.
[11] Déprez, *Préliminaires*, 90 n. 3, 96 n. 3; Haines, *Stratford*, 235.

Holy Land merely to disguise his intention and preparations for full-scale war against France.[12] Crusading motives were almost always mixed. The English crown believed that Philip IV had used his own vow of 1313 simply as a means of distracting attention from his aggressive stance towards Gascony.[13] Edward III was probably just as committed to the romantic ideal of the crusade as his ancestors on both sides of the Channel. His understanding of the tradition was indeed partly informed by family memorabilia: his possession of the helmet of Saladin and the knife used against Edward I at Acre in 1272 gave emotive reminders of earlier kings' commitment to crusading.[14] There must also have been at least a semblance of spiritual obligation: Edward's former confessor, Roger Stanegrave, dedicated a treatise on the Holy Land to him in the early 1330s.[15] Several of the king's closest friends, including William Montagu and Henry of Grosmont, were actively involved in the current crusades against the Moors in southern Spain and against the last outposts of European paganism in Lithuania.[16] At the parliament of March 1332, there was much excitement over 'the good intentions and genuine wish that our lord the king has to go [on crusade]'.[17] If none of this proves Edward's personal commitment to take up the ultimate challenge of Christian knighthood, then neither does it expose him as a jaded cynic.

By 1333 Edward III had established two essential preconditions for his involvement in Philip's crusade: the return of the lands in the Agenais and other parts of greater Aquitaine confiscated in 1324–7, and a guarantee that the French would not make capital out of their alliance with the supporters of David Bruce in Scotland.[18] When Philip retaliated by insisting that David II's rights be included in any further diplomacy, it became evident to almost everyone else concerned that the venture had no

[12] Compare the different approaches of C. Tyerman, 'Philip VI and the Recovery of the Holy Land', *EHR*, C (1985), 25–52, and N. Housley, *The Later Crusades, 1274–1580* (Oxford, 1992), 33–6.

[13] C 47/28/4, no. 24, datable from internal evidence to before 1328.

[14] See above, p. 15. By the mid-1330s Edward III also possessed wall hangings depicting the *pas Saladin*: E 101/387/11. These may have moved into the possession of the Black Prince, who left Richard II hangings of the *pas Saladin* in his will: *A Collection of the Wills . . . of the Kings and Queens of England*, ed. J. Nichols (London, 1780), 72; W. M. Ormrod, 'Richard II's Sense of English History', *The Reign of Richard II*, ed. G. Dodd (Stroud, 2000), 105.

[15] Tyerman, *England and the Crusades*, 251–2. A few years later Edward announced to Alfonso IX his intention to make pilgrimage to Castile, perhaps in order to participate in the war against the Moors: SC 1/37/127.

[16] Housley, *Later Crusades*, 278–81; T. Jones, *Chaucer's Knight: The Portrait of a Medieval Mercenary*, rev. edn (London, 1985), 60–4.

[17] *PROME*, iv, 166, 168; *Litterae Cantuariensis*, i, 438–41.

[18] *Les Grandes Chroniques de France*, ed. J. Viard, 10 vols (Société de l'Histoire de France, 1920–53), ix, 134; *EMDP*, I.ii, no. 325; Baker, 55; Déprez, *Préliminaires*, 96–7; Nicholson, *Edward III and the Scots*, 146.

realistic chance of fulfilment. In the English parliament of September 1334, with the state of affairs in Scotland taking clear precedence, it was agreed that the king would have to postpone his passage to the Holy Land for another five years.[19] It was from this point that Edward sought rather more ruthlessly to manipulate the discourse of crusade for his own good and gain. By apparently complying with Philip VI and Pope Benedict XII's plans, Edward was able to inhabit that place he liked best, the moral high ground. He engaged in new discussions with the envoys of Leo IV, king of Armenia, promising them that he would take the Cross as soon as he had sorted out problems closer to home.[20] He maintained the necessary scruples over the crusading tax that John XXII had imposed on the English clergy in 1333, resisting the temptation to draw down the profits to pay for the Scottish wars until Benedict XII had formally cancelled the passage in March 1336.[21] And right down to the opening of the French war in 1337 he continued to insist that the crusade had collapsed not because of his withdrawal of support but because Philip VI had refused to accept his terms of service. By that stage he is likely to have amply satis-fied his conscience with the not unreasonable conclusion that Philip VI had indeed concocted the whole fantastic scheme as a ruse to distract from his unwarranted assimilation of the Plantagenet fiefs in France.[22]

By the end of 1334, Anglo-French diplomacy had reached an impasse. In most respects, the following three years represented no more than a preliminary cold war to the inevitable hostilities that ensued. To the collapse of the marriage discussions and the mutual recriminations over the failed crusade were now added renewed and serious squabbles about jurisdiction. Philip VI's agents were furious that the English had not surrendered castles deemed to belong to the French side, and the process of Agen had to be wound up completely at the end of 1334 as a result of bitter disputes over the sending of unresolved cases for arbitration before the *parlement* of Paris.[23] Philip's determined and continued insistence on

[19] Murimuth, 72–3; Haines, *Stratford*, 236–7.

[20] E 403/260, 16 Mar. 1332; Nicholson, *Edward III and the Scots*, 106; Haines, *Stratford*, 241 n. 160. For a further mission in 1343 see E 403/328, 8 Aug. 1343.

[21] John XXII ordered a universal crusading tenth on the clergy of Christendom for six years in 1333, but the fact that he had already authorized the levy of four tenths on the English clergy in 1330 to be shared equally with Edward III (for general, rather than crusading, costs) meant that only two further tenths were to be levied. The convocations of Sept. and Oct. 1336 converted these two crusading tenths into two tenths payable to the king for the costs of his wars. Lunt, 'Collectors of Clerical Subsidies', 228–9, 231–2, 260–1; W. E. Lunt, *Financial Relations of the Papacy with England*, 2 vols (Cambridge, Mass., 1939–62), ii, 75–94. Compare Philip VI's appropriation of ecclesiastical wealth in 1337, which brought down the wrath of Benedict XII: Déprez, *Préliminaires*, 142–4.

[22] *EHD*, iv, 62–3.

[23] Cuttino, *English Medieval Diplomacy*, 75–6.

the authority of this high court to hear appeals from the duchy of Aquitaine was causing problems even within those areas theoretically still under English control and loyal to the Plantagenet cause. In 1334 the seneschal of Gascony, Sir Oliver Ingham, complained that the warlike people of the remote Landes region were becoming regular appellants at the *parlement* of Paris, not because they relished the prospect of Valois rule but simply as a means of prolonging the violent vendettas to which they were habituated.[24]

Such open challenges to the Plantagenets' claims to sovereignty within Gascony, however motivated, could not go unpunished. In 1336 Garcie-Arnauld, lord of Sault-de-Navailles, appealed at Paris against Edward III, claiming that he was still owed 31,000 *livres tournois* (just over £6,000) for damages that his father had been forced to pay to Philip IV for his adherence to the English cause in the war of 1294–8. The English were fearful that a judgment in favour of Garcie-Arnauld would open up a spate of similar claims and sought to challenge his right to make the appeal. Had a clear judgment been given by the *parlement* before the start of war in 1337, this dispute might have been sufficient in itself to justify Philip VI's full-scale confiscation of the Plantagenet fiefs. As it was, Edward's subsequent declaration of Garcie-Arnauld as a rebel merely served to demonstrate the way in which appeals to Paris so often drove previously loyal Gascon families into open conflict with the Plantagenet administrations of Bordeaux and Westminster.[25]

The uncertainty and nervousness of the Gascon nobility as to the fate of their duchy was greatly compounded by many rumours and counter-rumours in the mid-1330s. Edward III's supporters retaliated to Philip's aggressive stance on appeals by arguing that the Valois regime was intimidating the Gascon nobility into a compliance that they would never willingly bestow.[26] It may have been around this time that a clerk in the English government made the suggestion that Edward III should assert all his titles, principal and subordinate alike, in the form 'king of England, lord of Ireland, Gascony and the Isles, duke of Aquitaine, count of Ponthieu and Montreuil'.[27] The implied distinction between the ancient duchy of Gascony, a lordship in sovereignty, and the fictional greater

[24] C 47/24/5, fol. 2v.

[25] Vale, *Angevin Legacy*, 259.

[26] G. P. Cuttino, *English Diplomatic Administration, 1259–1339*, 2nd edn (Oxford, 1971), 101–11.

[27] *EMDP*, I.i, no. 95. The reference to Edward as 'lord of the Isles' (*dominus . . . insularum maris*) refers to a claim already asserted by his predecessors to control all the islands in the 'sea of England', specifically the Channel Islands and Oléron: see ibid., I.i, no. 206. It does not carry connotations of the lordship of the Western Isles of Scotland, since this title only emerged in the course of the fourteenth century and in 1327 the entirety of Scotland and the Isles were formally considered an assimilated conquest of the crown of England.

Aquitaine defined in 1259, a fief held in conditional tenure, may have been thought useful to English diplomacy at this difficult moment. But it was also a matter of considerable concern to the pro-English nobles in the Agenais and other confiscated territories, for it implied that the English possession of their regions might be sacrificed to the preservation of the Plantagenets' rule in the coastal strip from Bordeaux to Bayonne. In the summer of 1334 the political community of Gascony complained that the king of England was about to exchange greater Aquitaine for 'other lands' as the price of a settlement with France, and Edward III had to move briskly to counter the resulting ill will.[28] If he was to retain the support of the Gascon nobility for his presence in France Edward had no choice but to remain fully committed to the recovery of the parts of Aquitaine confiscated after the war of Saint-Sardos. Ironically, this uncompromising position also now began to threaten the integrity of his smaller fiefs in northern France. In October 1334, Oliver Ingham felt obliged to report news that Philip VI intended to seize Ponthieu as ransom for the return of disputed castles in the Agenais.[29]

In November 1334 Edward III wrote formally to Philip VI to express his hope that they might yet find a way to lasting peace. He pointed out that he and his Gascon subjects had had no satisfaction from Philip on any of the issues raised by the war of 1324–5, the settlement of 1327 or the initiative of 1331. The long-standing sequence of 'processes' ought to be revived, but should be accompanied by a thorough assessment of the existing terms of peace between the two sides.[30] The letter reveals both the limits and the extent of Edward's vision. The idea of reviving the process of Agen represents the dead weight of tradition that hung upon so much of the diplomacy of the 1330s. Nor was there anything especially novel about the idea of unravelling the complex history of the tenure of Aquitaine. Edward I's advisers had earlier used historical precedents as a means of arguing the allodial status of Gascony, and Edward III had already made a number of surveys of the archives for similar purposes.[31] In the early 1330s, however, the English council tended only to concern itself with issues that could be tracked through the documentation of Anglo-French diplomacy since the treaty of Paris. The proposal of 1334 pushed the agenda back beyond the watershed of 1259 into a time when the Plantagenets' presence in France had been far stronger. A

---

[28] C 47/24/6, fol. 2v.

[29] Cuttino, *English Medieval Diplomacy*, 76.

[30] SC 1/37/135, printed in Déprez, *Préliminaires*, 407; Sumption, i, 138–9.

[31] E 403/253, 15 Nov. 1330, records a survey of 'divers peaces and treaties and truces between the kings of England and France' on the subject of Aquitaine, made for the council on the instruction of the bishops of Norwich and Coventry. See also E 403/262, 14 July 1332; SC 8/114/5666; E. B. Fryde, 'Parliament and the French War, 1336–40', *Historical Studies*, ed. Fryde and Miller, i., 243.

memorandum drawn up during the later 1330s reveals Edward III's growing interest not just in the technical issues of feudal tenure but also in the various intrusions of earlier kings of France into English affairs and the 'damage and dishonour' that the 'nation of England' had suffered at their hands since the time of Richard I.[32] By extending his historical range back to the era before King John's loss of Normandy and Henry III's acceptance of the treaty of Paris, Edward gave the first inklings of a new and more expansive definition of his dominions that would seek to re-establish his Norman and Angevin predecessors' control of the whole of western France from the Channel to the Bay of Biscay.

For the present, however, any such notions remained pure fantasies of the king's romantic imagination. Above all, Edward's existing commit-ments in Scotland continued fundamentally to compromise the more aggressive stance that he might wish to adopt towards France. Throughout 1334 and 1335 Edward III's agents worked consistently to persuade Philip VI of the worthiness of English motives towards the Scots.[33] But this cautious strategy did no more than pander to Philip's already over-inflated ego. Sir Geoffrey Scrope, who had spent over six months in fruitless discus-sion at Paris and Senlis between October 1333 and July 1334, clearly had had more than enough of the whole business, and on his return to England secured an exemption from being required ever again to take part in diplomatic missions.[34] Others must surely have felt the same. In the winter of 1334–5 when John Stratford, William Montagu and William Clinton met with the French negotiators at Paris, the obdurate Philip VI treated his visitors to a lecture on political morality and natural justice. He declared that it was impossible to consider the return of territory in Aquitaine while he remained inadequately compensated for the costs of the war against the English in the 1320s. And he upbraided Edward III for the blatant injustice of his policy against the Scots. In a final and ominous flourish, Philip declared that there would never be peace until there was a single ruler over the three kingdoms of France, England and Scotland. The English ambassadors, deeply indignant, were forced to withdraw.[35] Rarely in the previous eight decades had the two sides so obviously admitted the impossibility of a peace based on the treaty of Paris.

Of all the many elements that went to make up the Anglo-French war of 1337, the most crucial in the short term was the cancellation of the crusade

---

[32] C 47/28/5, no. 17. C 47/28/5, no. 27 is a draft account of quarrels between the English and the French, Scots and Welsh, since the time of King John.

[33] Déprez, *Préliminaires*, 109–18.

[34] *CPR 1330–4*, 565; Stones, 'Sir Geoffrey le Scrope', 8–9, 17.

[35] Baker, 55–6; Haines, *Stratford*, 237–8. Rogers, *War Cruel and Sharp*, 120–1 and n. 203 places this episode later, in 1336.

in March 1336. The keeper of processes with France, John Peres, was ordered to draw up a summary of the most pressing diplomatic issues in time for a parliament ordered to Westminster in March, at which Edward very publicly rejected Philip's latest appeal for a joint meeting to resolve urgent differences.[36] The abandonment of the crusade allowed the French to redeploy the twelve large warships recently prepared in the Mediterranean ports and plan a major seaborne invasion of Scotland. It was the emergency thus provoked that no doubt prompted Edward III to make a personal visit to the royal dockyard at Redcliffe, below London Bridge, where on 3 April he dined aboard his ship the *Christopher* and surveyed the stock of shipping available in his personal fleet.[37] From Perth later that summer, Edward warned his subjects in England of the imminence of a French attack upon the realm.[38] In the end, Philip VI encountered significant delays in gathering both ships and men, and Edward's harrying of north-eastern Scotland foiled a French landing in the region. But the Valois fleet and army continued to grow, and it became increasingly obvious that these forces might also be used to launch raids on the south and east coasts of England. In spite of good intelligence collected by Edward's spies and general arrangements for the better defence of the south and east coasts, the French were still able to begin small-scale attacks on the shores of Suffolk and the Isle of Wight. This was the moment of no return for Edward: from the autumn of 1336, the likelihood of war was openly acknowledged by his government.[39]

At the end of July 1336, while the king was away in Scotland, the royal council met in formal session at Northampton under the presidency of Archbishop Stratford. It was decided to send a new deputation to Paris, led by the bishops of Durham and Winchester, in order to treat with the king of France and the exiled David Bruce.[40] In light of the recent humiliation suffered by English ambassadors to the Valois court, the new mission is likely to have taken an assertive stance. The inclusion of the Bruce faction, far from representing a concession to the French, probably reflected Edward III's desire to remind both parties that their withdrawal from the tripartite settlement offered in the recent draft treaty of Newcastle fully justified the more bullish position that he was now inclined to take towards them. Philip's dismissal of the envoys was therefore probably no more than the English had intended.[41] Certainly, the

[36] C 47/28/8, no. 55; *PROME*, iv, 209.

[37] E 101/387/19, m. 3.

[38] *Foedera*, II.ii, 944.

[39] J. R. Alban, 'National Defence in England, 1337–89' (University of Liverpool PhD thesis, 1976), 4–5; Sumption, i, 152–66.

[40] BL, MS Cotton Faustina B. V, fol. 77; *Foedera*, II.ii, 944–5; Haines, *Stratford*, 243; Sumption, i, 161–2.

[41] See pp. 171–2.

Northampton assembly was minded to war. A large group of merchants summoned before the council gave formal consent to an elaborate plan to mobilize the profits of the wool trade in support of impending hostilities against the French. The first stage in the plan, a temporary embargo on wool exports designed to raise the prices that could subsequently be demanded in the cloth-producing towns of the Low Countries, was duly put in place in August.[42] The second was worked out at the great council held at Nottingham at the end of September. A further group of merchants summoned to this meeting agreed to the imposition of an open-ended subsidy of £1 a sack, over and above the existing customs duties, on all wool exported out of England. Once the embargo was lifted, this would greatly increase the crown's income from the ports and help to service the large war debts that the king was already accumulating.[43] At the same time the council set a schedule of minimum prices for the domestic market in order to provide guarantees to producers against a third impending element in the new financial experiment: a compulsory purchase of wool for the king's sole use and profit.[44]

The great council of Nottingham also took extensive measures for the defence of the realm against what was now publicly acknowledged to be an imminent Scottish and French attack. An unprecedented 80,000 infantry were called out to patrol the borders and coasts, with the Home Counties being required to support the cost of wages, transport and victuals. Further large-scale purveyance of foodstuffs and military hardware followed.[45] In early January 1337 the council hammered out an agreement with representatives from the towns for the widespread requisitioning of merchant shipping.[46] All these initiatives added materially to the existing pressure to support the Scottish war and raised much anxiety over the breach of statutory limitations on the king's rights. The crown's answer was to engage in a vigorous burst of domestic propaganda that stressed universal obligation in a state of national emergency. In particular, the various arrangements for the defence of the coasts repeatedly asserted Edward III's status as 'lord of the sea of England'. This served to emphasize that the conditions already prevailing in the north of England were also now applicable in the south, and that war with the Valois was just as

---

[42] *CCR 1333–7*, 700.

[43] *RDP*, iv, 464; E. B. Fryde, 'Edward III's War Finance, 1337–41: Transactions in Wool and Credit Operations' (University of Oxford DPhil. thesis, 1947), i, 54–5; Ormrod, *Reign of Edward III*, 206.

[44] *CPR 1334–8*, 480–2; Fryde, *Studies*, chap. vi, 12.

[45] Powicke, *Military Obligation*, 193, 203; Sumption, i, 165; Maddicott, 'English Peasantry', 331. John de Watenhull was appointed receiver of wages for the troops arrayed along the south coast, but seems mostly to have been involved in raising arms and victuals for these forces: CFR *1327–37*, 497; E 358/2, m. 11d.

[46] *RDP*, iv, 469–70; Sumption, i, 178.

much about the preservation of the realm as it was about the defence or recovery of the king's titles in France.[47]

When it came, the flashpoint for Philip VI's seizure of the Plantagenet fiefs in France and the formal reopening of war was as dramatic as it was unexpected. Robert of Artois, the cousin and brother-in-law of Philip VI, had been banished from France in 1332 for his refusal to accept that the duchess of Burgundy had a better claim than he to the county of Artois.[48] In 1334 Robert had sought refuge in England and had lived there in quiet obscurity for two years. In the spring of 1336, Edward III assigned Robert a number of royal castles and a handsome pension in return for his commitment to engage in the war in Scotland. The action represented a gesture of good faith and honour to a man who Edward no doubt felt had been unjustly wronged by an overbearing and ungracious king of France. But Edward cannot have been so naïve, or ill-advised, as not to under-stand its implications. Indeed, it is difficult to avoid the conclusion that the English king's harbouring of Robert of Artois was a carefully calculated move designed to provoke Philip VI into condemning Edward as a contu-macious vassal and thus allowing the latter the excuse he so keenly sought openly to defy his suzerain of France.

In November 1336 both the king of France and the pope began to bring pressure on Edward's administration for the extradition of Robert of Artois.[49] At Christmas, Philip served an ultimatum on the seneschal of Gascony: unless Robert, 'our mortal enemy', was delivered up promptly to the agents of the French crown, great peril, travail and dissension would result.[50] Edward held firm, not least because he had a valuable counter-claim: in the early weeks of 1337 his agents in Avignon, Richard Bentworth and Paul Montefiori, were protesting about an unprovoked attack that Philip's fleet had recently attempted against the Plantagenet possessions of the Channel Islands. A parliament originally summoned to meet at York was prorogued to assemble at Westminster Palace on 3 March.[51] Back from his most recent campaign in Scotland, Edward hovered around the south-east throughout the first half of 1337. The moment had arrived in which firmly to redirect English energies towards an impending war on the continent. In 1337 and 1338 the various offices of central government that had relocated to York in 1332–3 gradually transferred back to Westminster. It was Edward III's shift of priorities in

[47] Prince, 'Army and Navy', 386, 392; *EMDP*, I.i, no. 206. Historical precedents for the claim to lordship of the Channel were reviewed in the late 1330s: C 47/28/9, nos 8, 25.

[48] Le Bel, i, 95–100; Froissart, i, 357–9. For what follows see Lucas, *Low Countries*, 176–81, 187.

[49] Déprez, *Préliminaires*, 135; Sumption, i, 172.

[50] Déprez, *Préliminaires*, 414–15.

[51] *HBC*, 558; *PROME*, iv, 229.

1337 that, more than anything else, served to make London the permanent administrative capital of the English state.[52]

Although the official record of the parliament of March 1337 is lost, it is clear that this was the moment when Edward III sought the formal consent of the political community to open hostilities with the French.[53] The continued commitment to Scotland made it imperative that the crown present a credible case to its supporters and enemies alike. Bishop Burghersh and the new earls of Huntingdon and Salisbury were dispatched to present a final statement of Edward's grievances as vassal of Philip of Valois. At the same time, authority was given for the collection of soldiers, supplies and shipping at Portsmouth in preparation for a great expedition to Aquitaine to be led in person by the king. Philip VI saw the empty blandishments of the English emissaries for what they were, and on 30 April pronounced a state of war. Three weeks later, on 24 May, he formally declared Edward III in breach of his obligations as vassal and asserted his right to confiscate the latter's fiefs in France.[54] The endless squabbles created by the treaty of Paris were once more giving way to open war.

There remained the major question as to how the warlike Edward would define his aims. In January 1337, there was a crucial discussion in closed council about the king's dynastic rights as the nearest male heir to Charles IV of France. The attempts made to lodge such a claim during the French interregnum of 1328 had been compromised by Edward's youth. It was now argued, on civil law principles, that unless Edward reasserted his claim to the throne of France before his twenty-fifth birthday (which would fall in the following November), he would lose it for ever.[55] Understanding the opportunities that this claim might offer him as leverage in his diplomacy with the Valois, Edward gave tentative support to the proposal. For the moment, however, nothing was said publicly on the matter. It therefore seems likely that the March parliament discussed the king's intentions of war solely in terms of the recovery of his territorial rights under the settlement of 1259.[56]

---

[52] Ormrod, 'Competing Capitals', 80. There was some discussion during the summer of 1338 as to whether the chancery, which also moved back to Westminster at this time, might actually follow the king to the continent: C 49/7/9, printed (though incorrectly dated) in J. F. Baldwin, *The King's Council in England during the Middle Ages* (Oxford, 1913), 478.

[53] Harriss, *King, Parliament*, 233–4, 314–20.

[54] Vale, *Angevin Legacy*, 260–3; Sumption, i, 184; Déprez, *Préliminaires*, 154 and n. 1.

[55] BL, MS Cotton Faustina B. V, fol. 79; Rogers, *War Cruel and Sharp*, 176.

[56] Fryde, 'Parliament and the French War', 244–5; Harriss, *King, Parliament*, 234; Haines, *Stratford*, 195, 246–7, 298–9. It was only the later chroniclers, Gray and Froissart, who claimed that this assembly witnessed a debate on the king's right to the French throne: *Scalacronica*, 123; Froissart, i, 359–60. Stratford's statement in 1340 was ambiguous, stating merely that the parliament of Mar. 1337 had authorized Edward to pursue his rights in France: *Anglia Sacra*, i, 29–30. For the preparation of an agenda relating to disputes with France, perhaps for one of the assemblies of 1337, see C 47/28/4, nos 28–9.

The general military strategy that emerged out of this gathering was entirely predictable. Already in 1336 the king had opened discussions with the Emperor Lewis of Bavaria and Albert of Habsburg, duke of Austria, in a deliberate attempt to rebuild Edward I's network of anti-French alliances in Germany and the Low Countries. Like his grandfather, Edward III appreciated that the recovery of his fiefs ultimately depended on his capacity to apply direct pressure on the French crown in its own heartland of the Île de France. It was to facilitate land-based invasions over the northern French border that he now actively sought out the assistance of the imperial princes. Much time was also taken up over the second half of 1337 in applying the usual reprisals against French men and women holding property in England.[57] The handful of northern French aristocratic families that still had landed interests beyond the Channel were now forced to make choices that would condition their descendants' fortunes and allegiances for centuries to come. The greatest member of this group, Raoul de Brienne, count of Eu, now lost for ever the extensive estates that his ancestors had accumulated in England and Ireland. A decade later the count's son, another Raoul, was to pay the price of war twice over, first falling prisoner to the English and then being executed for treason by the French.[58]

If the initial responses to Philip VI's declaration of war were cautious to the point of punctiliousness, Edward was soon made aware of the unwelcome limitations that traditional strategies now placed upon him. Since none of the English nobility had any significant territories on the other side of the Channel, there was no group of disinherited lords to form a natural war party in the parliaments and councils of 1337. Nor was there any real opportunity for Gascon lords to express their views; the one family that retained a regular presence at Westminster in the early fourteenth century, the Albrets, had actually fallen out with the crown over the blunt interventions of Edward II's regime and their leader in 1337, Bernard-Ezi, stood aloof from the English cause for the first few years of the new war.[59]

In constructing his case for the recovery of his fiefs in France, Edward is certainly likely to have used both constitutional and material arguments. Since Henry III had declared Aquitaine an inalienable parcel of the

[57] *Foedera*, II.ii, 982; E 101/510/18; E 199/52/8.

[58] E 159/113, rots 119, 180; GEC, v, 173–5. See also pp. 273, 327. By contrast, Isabella de la Mote, one of the queen's ladies, chose to pursue her English rather than her French interests: *Foedera*, II.ii, 987; C 143/49/3; *CPR 1338–40*, 53. The archbishop of Rouen, Pierre Roger, understanding the way that things were going in the mid-1330s, had already taken pre-emptive action by selling off English lands held by various cathedral chapters in Normandy: J. Peltzer, 'The Slow Death of the Angevin Empire', *HR*, lxxxi (2008), 557–80.

[59] SC 1/42/164, printed in *Recueil de lettres anglo-françaises (1265–1399)*, ed. F. J. Tanqueray (Paris, 1916), no. 152; Vale, *Angevin Legacy*, 95–8, 240–1, 262–3.

crown, the defence of the duchy represented – in theory at least – a direct public obligation on the people of England.[60] Potentially, too, Aquitaine offered the prospect of great riches; reconstituting the English regime there would create a self-sufficient colony and might even allow an excess that could be used, as in the past, to support the defence of other dependencies closer to home.[61] But Edward surely understood the disingenuousness of these positions. In 1294, 1322 and 1325 there had been major controversies over whether the crown could legitimately use feudal summonses and compulsory arrays to mount military expeditions to Gascony, and Mortimer's attempts to raise forces for Aquitaine in 1330 had been roundly resisted.[62] In 1337 few English nobles and knights were interested in the prospect of winning their own lands and rights in a distant land so obviously alien to their cultural and political traditions. The resulting practical constraints on his military capacity were to force Edward III to think again about the manner in which the war was presented to his subjects in England and to create much more compelling reasons for requiring their support in the recovery of his rights in France.

Edward revealed his revised strategy to the magnates and prelates meeting in two successive great councils at Westminster in late July and mid-August. He would now give up the plan to proceed in person to Gascony. The army being raised for this expedition would be downgraded and dispatched as a minor relief force under the command of John Norwich. Responsibility for the defence of Aquitaine would be devolved to the resident seneschal, Oliver Ingham, and the greatest of the loyal Gascon nobles, Jean de Grailly, captal de Buch, who would need to rely largely on local resources of men, money and supplies.[63] The king himself would take command of the current musters and cross to the Low Countries, where he would link up with his imperial allies and prepare an

---

[60] J. Le Patourel, *Feudal Empires: Norman and Plantagenet* (London, 1984), chap. viii, 301.

[61] In 1324 the English crown had estimated the annual net receipts of the duchy at £13,000: Harriss, *King, Parliament*, 523. For the earlier use of taxes from Gascony for the support of military enterprises in the British Isles, see E. A. R. Brown, 'Gascon Subsidies and the Finances of the English Dominions, 1315–1324', *Studies in Medieval and Renaissance History*, original series, viii (1971), 37–163; W. M. Ormrod, 'The English State and the Plantagenet Empire, 1259–1360: A Fiscal Perspective', *The Medieval State: Essays Presented to James Campbell*, ed. J. R. Maddicott and D. M. Palliser (London, 2000), 202–3.

[62] Powicke, *Military Obligation*, 99, 153–5; Harriss, *King, Parliament*, 53–63; Willard, *Parliamentary Taxes*, 111–14.

[63] *RDP*, iv, 475–9; Sumption, i, 205–6. A special inquiry was launched in Nov. to establish what might be the appropriate rates of pay for those serving in Gascony, and the exchequer reported the wages that had been drawn while John of Brittany was lieutenant of Aquitaine in 1294–5. These were, in fact, compatible with those that had become standard in all theatres of war by the 1330s: E 159/114, rot. 52d. John Charnels, who had been appointed receiver of victuals for Aquitaine in Mar. 1337, received no resources from the English exchequer: E 358/2, m. 5d.

invasion of northern France.[64] In a deliberate attempt to soften the blow of further taxes, Edward ordered the holding of special meetings of the county courts and local assemblies of clergy at which his commissioners would expound, 'in English', on the reasons for the war. The statements (written in bureaucratic French) that were supplied for these occasions presented the king's case merely as that of a wronged vassal who required the assistance of his loyal subjects against an oppressive and unreasonable lord. Philip was properly accorded his title as king of France, and there was no suggestion that the rights to be recovered on the continent extended beyond the lawful tenure of Aquitaine and Ponthieu. But the stress was now very clearly on the interests not of the Gascons but of the English. A war against France was as much a strike against the allies of the fickle Scots as it was an action in defence of Edward's French fiefs.[65] Both in his choices of command and in his political rhetoric, Edward worked hard in 1337 to make his war properly appealing to those who would inevitably bear the great burden of its cost.

Such sensitivity was all the more urgent given the high price that Edward was prepared to pay for the imperial alliance. A range of Netherlandish and German princes led by Edward's in-laws, the margrave of Juliers and the counts of Guelders and Hainault, rapidly fell in with Henry Burghersh's recruitment campaign and offered military assistance against Philip of Valois. But they did so only at a huge price. When the earls of Salisbury and Huntingdon met at Frankfurt with the representatives of Lewis of Bavaria in late July, they were forced to offer a subsidy of no less than £45,000. In return, Lewis accorded Edward the title of vicar-general of the Empire and thus, at least in theory, empowered him to call out all the subordinate principalities of the imperial confederation in aid of the Plantagenet cause.[66] For a short time it seemed that Edward's grand alliance would know no limits. The English philosopher William of Ockham, who was then in residence at Lewis of Bavaria's court in

[64] Sumption, i, 211–14.

[65] CCR 1337–9, 254–5; CPR 1334–8, 502–4; EHD, iv, 62–3. For the outcomes see J. F. Willard, 'Edward III's Negotiations for a Grant in 1337', EHR, xxi (1906), 727–31; W. N. Bryant, 'The Financial Dealings of Edward III with the County Communities', EHR, lxxxiii (1968), 766–8; Jurkowski, Smith and Crook, Lay Taxes, 40–2. The role of the clergy, not discussed in these studies, is demonstrated by BL, MS Cotton Faustina B. V, fols 80v–81; Register of William Melton, iii, nos 280–1; The Register of Ralph of Shrewsbury, Bishop of Bath and Wells, 1329–1363, ed. T. S. Holmes, 2 vols (Somerset Record Society, ix, x, 1895–6), i, nos 1276–8; The Register of John de Grandisson, Bishop of Exeter, ed. F. C. Hingeston-Randolph, 3 vols (London, 1894–9), i, 300–2 (which provides rare evidence of oral announcements 'in English'). For the impact of this propaganda on the chronicles see J. Barnie, War in Medieval English Society: Social Values in the Hundred Years War, 1337–99 (London, 1974), 5.

[66] Le Bel, i, 119–28, 142–53; H. S. Offler, 'England and Germany at the Beginning of the Hundred Years' War', EHR, liv (1939), 609–10; Lucas, Low Countries, 219.

Munich, began a radical treatise outlining Edward's rights to appropriate ecclesiastical property in defence of his just cause.[67] At home, too, the alliances attracted much attention: if Edward were to cross the sea with no other companion than 'Giliot of the chamber', he was surely still destined for great victory in the company of his glorious allies.[68]

Very soon, however, it was the fiscal liability of the imperial junta that would come to dominate English attitudes to the impending war. In reality, the princes required definite promises of wages, subsidies and pensions before they would sign up to the English cause. Major figures such as John III, duke of Brabant, and Rudolf II, count palatine of the Rhine, could exert considerable pressure for favourable deals. As a result, Edward was soon committed to paying out annuities of at least £124,000 by the end of 1337, over and above the enormous expenses that would accumulate as soon as the Anglo-imperial army was put into the field.[69] With the tax grant of March 1337 already heavily mortgaged against the continuing commitment in Scotland, the crown had to forge ahead with a huge campaign of fund-raising. The final element in the wool scheme was put in place in July, when a syndicate of English merchants led by William de la Pole and the Londoner Reginald Conduit agreed to act on behalf of the king and purchase 30,000 sacks of wool on credit and in accordance with the prices recently agreed at Nottingham.[70] They would be allowed special exemption from the current embargo on exports, and could thus expect to command particularly high profits when their shipments reached the wool-starved markets of the Low Countries. It was on the expectation of these riches that the new cartel agreed to loan the king £200,000. To recover their debt and, in due course, pay back the wool producers, de la Pole and his business partners would be given control of the customs service. This notably ambitious scheme offered Edward not only the prospect of an abundance of ready cash but also the opportunity to apply further diplomatic pressure to prospective allies. Unlike the other rulers of the Netherlands, the count of Flanders, Louis de Nevers, owed homage to the crown of France and was thus bound by solemn obligation to support Philip VI in the upcoming war. Edward nonetheless hoped that the current embargo on wool exports might be used to force the cloth-producing towns of Bruges, Ghent and Ypres to support his ventures and thus put pressure on Louis to take up a position of neutrality in the war of Plantagenet and Valois.[71]

[67] *Medieval Political Theory*, 207–20; C. J. Nederman, 'Royal Taxation and the English Church: The Origins of William of Ockham's *An princeps*', *Journal of Ecclesiastical History*, xxxvii (1986), 377–88.

[68] *Scalacronica*, 124–7.

[69] Fryde, *Studies*, chap. vii, 1146.

[70] *CCR 1337–9*, 148–9.

[71] Fryde, *Studies*, chap. vi, 8–24; Lucas, *Low Countries*, 186–91, 200–3, 219–23.

On 26 September a great council convened at Westminster to engage in further discussion of the war and, as the king clearly hoped, readily consent to further large-scale taxes. In structure and membership, the assembly was identical to a parliament, and many contemporaries called it such. Nevertheless, the official designation implied one important distinction. In parliaments, the king was obliged to hear both the private complaints of his subjects and the common petitions framed by the knights and burgesses. In great councils, no such obligation pertained. Edward III and his advisers had evidently determined that nothing should now be put in the way of the primary and urgent business of state. The recent attempts to excite enthusiasm in the constituencies had been met at best with indifference. Yet the commons in the great council now gave ready assent to a notably generous grant of three consecutive fifteenths and tenths, and thus committed the kingdom to a period of continuous taxation stretching forward to the early months of 1340. Where the laity went the clergy followed, and in September and November the convocations of Canterbury and York duly offered three tenths each.[72] Ironically, a great council needed no formal record, and it is therefore difficult to establish the precise nature of the royal arguments made in justification of this new and prolonged round of taxes. According to Froissart, writing two generations later, this was all to do with the eager anticipation of a polity bent on the pursuit of the king's claims. Froissart believed that the great council made ordinances encouraging the English to practise their skills in archery and to teach their children French so that they might better participate in the wars.[73] In the hard politics of the moment, it is more likely that Edward had to give a firm lead, asserting the overwhelming evidence of Philip's aggression and once more projecting the upcoming war as a defence of the integral rights of the crown and realm of England.

The most elusive element in this debate is Edward III's dynastic claim to the throne of France. The great council confirmed the king's intention to issue a formal act of defiance against Philip VI in which he divested himself of his obligations as a vassal and set out his grounds for making war against a tyrannical suzerain. Bishop Burghersh was deputed to carry this message to the court of Paris. Shortly after the conclusion of the great council Burghersh was also charged with certain confidential documents which asserted Edward III's title as 'king of France and England', empowered Edward's Netherlandish allies to take formal possession of the realm of France, and called on all the prelates and lords of France to accept Plantagenet sovereignty.[74] If Edward did indeed recognize the urgency of reasserting his claim to France before he reached his twenty-fifth birthday,

---

[72] *PROME*, iv, 231; Ormrod, *Reign of Edward III*, 205.

[73] Froissart, i, 401–3.

[74] *Treaty Rolls 1337–1339* (London, 1972), nos 87–90, 92–5; *EMDP*, I.i, no. 95; Le Patourel, *Feudal Empires*, chap. xii, 180.

then Burghersh's mission provided an obvious opportunity to do so. The envoys were rather overtaken by events; the defiance itself was not delivered but was left in abeyance for several months, and there is no evidence that the open letters of October 1337 were ever served on the people of France. Subsequent diplomacy, however, was emphatic that Burghersh did indeed protest Edward's dynastic rights on this occasion. Philip VI may have dismissed such fantasies with a knowing grin.[75] But it was from this point that Edward III also began consistently to challenge the legitimacy of Philip's position by referring to his cousin merely as de facto king of France. A diplomatic gesture at the very last possible moment had seemingly salvaged Edward's residual claim to the Capetian succession and potentially established it as an important bargaining position in any future settlement between the two realms.

It was this element in Plantagenet political rhetoric that was to persuade later historians that 1337 marked an altogether new start in Anglo-French relations and thus to justify their use of the label 'Hundred Years War' to describe the extended sequence of hostilities between 1337 and 1453. Since the mid-twentieth century, it has become fashionable to stress continuity over change and to see the war of 1337 merely as a continuation of the earlier series of disputes about the fulfilment of the 1259 treaty of Paris. In truth, the most remarkable thing about the diplomatic manoeuvres of October and November 1337 is just how little impact they had in England. The inference must be that Edward did not raise the specific point of his dynastic claim at the time that his war aims were discussed in open debate at the great council of September 1337.[76] For the following two years explicit references to the French title were confined to diplomatic correspondence. Some English minds were certainly put to work to develop elaborate legal and moral arguments in preliminary defence of the claim: at one point in 1338 Edward's canon-law machine pointed out to the pope that Christ himself had owed the title of king of the Jews to his descent in the female line, through the Virgin Mary, from King David.[77] But when Edward did eventually make public in England his decision to adopt the style of 'king of France' in January 1340, he still seems to have taken almost everyone at home by surprise.[78] For a king who set such obvious store by securing common consent for his wars, it is to say the least odd that Edward III seems never actually to have allowed the English polity the opportunity formally to approve his title to the French throne.

For twelve months after June 1337, the reality of war was delayed by successive diplomatic measures designed to allow both sides more time to

[75] Froissart, i, 404–5; Déprez, Préliminaires, 172–3.
[76] Pace the later interpolation into Froissart, i, 360.
[77] Foedera, II.ii, 1086.
[78] See pp. 212–17.

prepare for the onslaught. His forays to the north in January and March 1338 notwithstanding, Edward III now kept mainly to the south-east and East Anglia, closely observing the musters of his army and monitoring the threats posed by French shipping in the Channel. Among some of the king's potential supporters on the continent, hopes ran especially high: Jean le Bel and Froissart told the story of a group of young esquires in Hainault who swore to their ladies that they would wear eyepatches until such time as they proved their honour by feats of arms in Edward's upcoming wars.[79] Sir Walter Mauny's attack on the island of Cadzand in November 1337 caused a frisson of excitement in England, not least because it brought the king his first conspicuous prisoner of war and defector, Guy of Flanders, the bastard brother of Louis de Nevers.[80] A papal delegation arriving in December made a last-minute appeal for peace. But while receiving the envoys in the appropriate splendour of state at Westminster Palace, Edward agreed only to postpone his attack on France until the following spring.[81] As he passed Christmas at Guildford and made his lightning-speed journey to the siege of Dunbar, Edward set his mind to preparing the scenarios of war that he would present to the parliament summoned for February 1338. All seemed set for a major affray.

The king's own version of events at the 1338 parliament, recorded on the official parliament roll, kept appropriate faith with the general optimism of the previous year and the supposed eagerness of the lords and commons to support and finance the forthcoming hostilities.[82] In reality, the discussions were hard-fought. The wool scheme had recently been thrown into chaos by the decision of the king's envoys in the Low Countries to seize the first consignment of 10,000 sacks. As a consequence, the members of the merchant syndicate were left with only IOUs, which became known as Dordrecht bonds, and had no immediate prospect of being able to pay back the wool producers at home. Bishop Burghersh's speech to parliament now claimed that Edward must have the huge sum of £276,000 or 'the kingdom of England and all the other lands of the king were in danger of being lost'.[83] Reluctantly, the lords and commons agreed to convert the remaining 20,000 sacks from the original wool scheme into a prise, or legalized seizure. In return they insisted that the king suspend a number of other controversial fiscal levies put into commission in recent months. The collectors of the wool prise bore the

[79] Le Bel, i, 124; Froissart, i, 124; *EHD*, iv, 60–1.

[80] *Scalacronica*, 124–7; Prestwich, *Plantagenet England*, 345; Sumption, i, 294, 302.

[81] Murimuth, 81.

[82] *PROME*, iv, 232; Déprez, *Préliminaires*, 418–19; Fryde, 'Parliament and the French War', 245–6.

[83] C 49/67/1; S. B. Terry, *The Financing of the Hundred Years' War, 1337–1360* (London, 1914), 21; Fryde, *Studies*, chap. vi, 18.

brunt of popular resistance, and by the autumn had managed to collect fewer than 3,000 of the anticipated 20,000 sacks.[84] Public knowledge of the crown's cash crisis also significantly affected recruitment. By the summer of 1338 the king had been forced to call off both the siege of Dunbar and a prospective expedition to Gascony under the earl of Huntingdon, in order to be able to raise the 9,000 men needed for his own army of France.[85]

In mid-June Edward reached the east coast at Walton, near Ipswich, and set about the final arrangements for his embarkation. His recruiters had worked hard, but in spite of the offer of double rates of pay for men-at-arms, they had managed to raise only around 4,000 troops. Just four earls – Salisbury, Northampton, Derby and Suffolk – joined the king; the other commanders of the army were Bishop Burghersh, at the head of his own military contingent, and loyal household bannerets such as Henry Ferrers, Walter Mauny and Reginald Cobham.[86] The fragile earl of Hereford gave over the constableship of England to his energetic brother, Northampton. The king's uncle, the earl of Norfolk was seriously ill, and would die in the following September, at which point Salisbury was given the title of marshal of the army.[87] The apparently rather narrow base of aristocratic support for the campaign was, as much as anything, a function of Edward's equal concern for the home front. The earls of Arundel and Huntingdon and Lord Neville were asked to remain in England and lead a regency council under the titular presidency of the young Prince Edward. They, together with the remaining earls and a group of powerful northern barons, were also soon to take up office as keepers of the counties and lead important initiatives for the defence of the coasts and the northern border.[88] Nevertheless, it was this essential division between a relatively small group of close confidants crossing the sea with the king and a larger remnant of the nobility left in England that was later to be seen as one of the major reasons for Edward's failure to nurture and maintain a full sense of collective responsibility to the enterprise now begun.

---

[84] Fryde, *Studies*, chap. vi, 15–23; E. B. Fryde, *William de la Pole, Merchant and King's Banker* (London, 1988), 65–86; Harriss, *King, Parliament*, 236.

[85] Sumption, i, 233–8.

[86] Prince, 'Strength of English Armies', 361–2; M. Prestwich, 'Why did Englishmen Fight in the Hundred Years War?', *Medieval History*, ii[1] (1992), 60; A. Ayton, 'Edward III and the English Aristocracy and the Beginning of the Hundred Years War', *Armies, Chivalry*, ed. Strickland, 179.

[87] *CPR 1338–40*, 91, 95. Shortly after Salisbury's appointment, the king expressed a preference for the claim of Norfolk's younger daughter's husband (Salisbury's brother), Edward Montagu, to the hereditary marshalcy: E 159/115, m. 32d. However, the crown subsequently acknowledged Margaret, the older daughter, as having the right to transmit this office: GEC, ix, 599 n. (e).

[88] *CPR 1338–40*, 112, 141–2.

On 12 July, while he was still at Walton, the king sent the new chancellor, Richard Bentworth, a set of instructions devised 'by advice and counsel of our good men being about us'. Historians know these as the Walton Ordinances.[89] Their explicit aim was to prioritize the demands of the war over all other calls on the king's finances and to ensure general efficiency at a time when resources would inevitably be extremely tight. No expenditure was to be authorized by the chancery or passed by the exchequer without a specific warrant coming from the king's administration on the continent under the privy seal. The local financial officers of the crown, especially sheriffs and customs collectors, were to be elected in the localities. Far from being an attempt to promote local democracy, this was simply intended to make the relevant county and urban communities directly liable for any shortfall in the amounts due from these officials at the exchequer. The ordinances forbade any exemptions from taxation and banned the long-standing practice of allowing those owing debts at the exchequer to have respites or to pay in instalments. The whole system was to be rigorously managed by annual audits in the exchequer, the chancery and the wardrobe.

The Walton Ordinances have often been ascribed to William Kilsby, who was appointed keeper of the privy seal a few days before their issue. The influence of other household officials, such as William Norwell, keeper of the wardrobe, and Thomas Hatfield, receiver of the chamber, is also likely. In spite of Kilsby's later reputation as a bad influence on the king, however, there is little to suggest some conspiracy by senior domestic officials to take charge of the king's central administration. Rather, the high authority given to the royal household and to its main instrument, the privy seal, is readily explicable in the circumstances and the practicalities of the moment. Just as the political and military elite would be divided between home and continent, so too would the administration be split, with the household accompanying the king abroad to take overall responsibility for the administration of the war and the chancery and exchequer remaining at home to provide the necessary support structure. Far from representing an ideological division between a dominant court party led by Salisbury and Kilsby and a group of reluctant ministers and nobles left temporarily deprived of their usual discretion at home, the ordinances simply aimed to address a practical problem: how to ensure unity of purpose and action while the king was away. The stalling of repayments of royal debts in order to protect precious supplies of cash for immediate military need was a fairly regular resort, and had been applied, for example, at the beginning of Edward III's first intervention in Scotland in

[89] *Foedera*, II.ii, 1049–50; Tout, *Chapters*, iii, 68–78, 143–50. They were indeed described as 'ordinances' by contemporaries (*CCR 1337–9*, 525), but this term was used very widely for internal administrative purposes as well as more public legislative acts.

1333.[90] On several occasions during the Scottish campaigns there had also been minor misunderstandings over the home council's ability or willingness to act on Edward's personal instructions.[91] The new ordinances were therefore simply designed to pre-empt any further doubt as to the king's absolute right to drive the management of his war, and its finances, by his personal fiat.

It soon became apparent, however, that the ordinances were, in the strict letter of their application, simply impracticable. Edward himself proved reluctant to give up his right to grant respites of debts, which were often used as an inducement to lords and knights to serve in arms. In the Northampton great council of August 1338 the magnates expressed opposition, on similar grounds, to the restrictions now placed on the exchequer.[92] Local elections of officials proved unpopular because of the fiscal liabilities implied, and had quickly to be abandoned.[93] And the annual audits, which might have formed the basis of more effective budgeting, were never properly put in place.[94] Edward was to cling assiduously, and for very obvious reasons, to the principle that his military needs had absolute priority over all other forms of crown expenditure. But this core element of the ordinances was itself to be put under severe pressure by the sheer scale of Edward's subsequent demands. In this sense the Walton Ordinances were doomed from the first, for they called for ruthless economies at home but set no limits on the king's expenditure abroad.

Edward III's precise aims at the moment of departure in 1338 are something of a mystery. The transfer of the pregnant Queen Philippa, their two daughters and the entire staff and apparatus of the royal household to Antwerp certainly suggests that the king was planning a stay of some duration among his Netherlandish allies.[95] The military element would focus on a quick foray across the border between Hainault and France. In a deliberate recreation of the scorched-earth policy recently applied to such effect in north-east Scotland, Edward's forces would seek to expose

---

[90] *CCR 1333–7*, 30.

[91] SC 1/39/16 (1333); SC 1/39/33, 34 (1335); SC 1/37/170 (1336).

[92] Ormrod, *Reign of Edward III*, 108. On the very day of issue of the Walton Ordinances the king countermanded the ban on respites in favour of Sir John Segrave: E 159/115, rot. 31. For further such orders in subsequent months see E 159/115, rots 14, 27; E 159/116, *Brev. bar., passim.*

[93] B. H. Putnam, 'The Transformation of the Keepers of the Peace into the Justices of the Peace, 1327–1380', *TRHS*, 4th series, xii (1929), 35–6; Saul, *Knights and Esquires*, 119.

[94] 'An Exchequer Statement of Receipts and Issues, 1339–40', ed. H. Jenkinson and D. M. Broome, *EHR*, lviii (1943), 210–16; Ormrod, *Reign of Edward III*, 228 n. 121.

[95] Le Bel, i, 136–7; Baker, 61. SC 1/50/189, which recounts Philippa's preparations for a passage overseas with the king on 8 Mar. in an unspecified year, seems likely to date from 1338. For arrangements for the transport of the queen's ladies on this occasion see SC 1/51/4.

Philip's inadequacies as protector of his people by systematically pillaging the non-combatant population. In the event that Philip came out to meet him, Edward would then try to force some kind of open battle, at which point God and destiny would be left to decide the outcome.[96] On 16 July the English army sailed from Orwell and Yarmouth and arrived the next day at the mouth of the Scheldt, whence it made its way upriver to disembark at Antwerp on the 21st and 22nd. Philip VI's intelligence services were quickly at work, and forces were gathered at Tournai, Amiens and Saint-Quentin. Taking delivery of the Oriflamme, the great war banner of the kings of France housed at the abbey of Saint-Denis, the king of France set out promptly for the theatre of war, arriving at Amiens on 24 August.[97] Philip seemed as determined as his cousin of England to bring their differences to a quick and decisive conclusion.

Edward's arrival at Antwerp was rather less auspicious than had been hoped. On their first night in town, the king and his party had to flee for safety when fire broke out in the royal lodgings.[98] The shipments of wool from the forced loan had failed to materialize, and there was simply no cash available to pay Edward's soldiers and allies. To make matters worse, the king's allies now conveniently insisted that they could not move against the Valois army without direct authority from the emperor.[99] Edward had no choice but to seek out Lewis of Bavaria, then at Koblenz, and settle once and for all the matter of authority over the imperial forces recruited for his campaign. The resulting dash was to provide him with what proved to be his one real glimpse of the world beyond the maritime provinces of the Empire.

Travelling quickly via Herentals, Diest, Sittard and Jülich, Edward reached Cologne on 23 August. Here he made his devotions at the great shrine of the Magi and, in a rather obvious bid to please the locals, took an otherwise far-fetched vow to be buried in the cathedral church of the city.[100] Moving on to Bonn, he then travelled south to Koblenz, where the nobles of the Empire were in formal session. On 5 September, in a sumptuous ceremony in the town's marketplace, the imperial electors confirmed Edward in the title of vicar-general. Lewis of Bavaria sat in state on a high throne raised twelve feet above the ground, with Edward seated only slightly below him.[101] In a typical display of solidarity, the English king himself provided fifteen sets of tunics and robes to be worn by himself, the Emperor, the duke

[96] Rogers, *War Cruel and Sharp*, 152. In Feb. 1339 sickles and axes were provided for the king's army in obvious expectation of a campaign to destroy crops and buildings: E 358/2, m. 5; E 358/4, m. 6d.

[97] Sumption, i, 154.

[98] BL, MS Cotton Faustina B. V, fol. 82.

[99] Lucas, *Low Countries*, 289; Rogers, *War Cruel and Sharp*, 153–4.

[100] Reading, 132–3. See also the enigmatic reference to the 'church of Cologne' in *Wynnere and Wastoure*, ed. S. Trigg (EETS, ccxcvii, 1990), 16 (l. 503).

[101] Offler, 'England and Germany', 608–13.

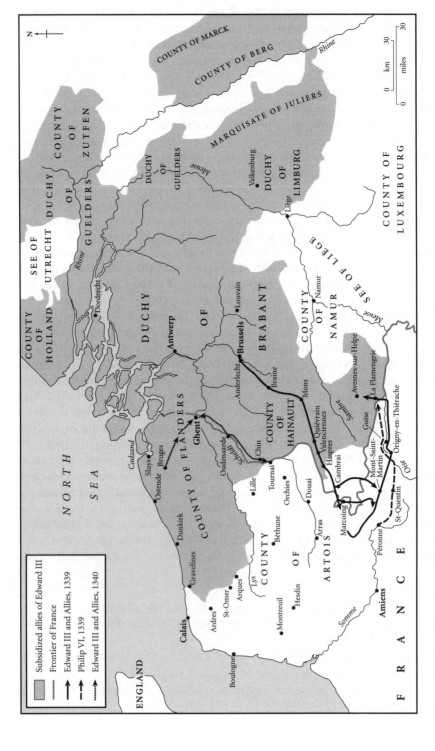

Map 4 The Low Countries, 1338–40.

of Brabant and the other chief players in this great moment of political theatre.[102] Returning quickly to Antwerp, Edward immediately began to put his new authority to use by summoning the imperial princes to appear before him in councils of war.[103] Edward's attitude to the imperial vicariate was thus every bit as pragmatic as his recent assertion of the style of king of France, with which it was obviously connected; indeed, there is some evidence that the English king threatened to take the imperial title for himself until Lewis agreed, on 15 September, to acknowledge the English monarch's status as rightful heir of the house of Capet.[104] What mattered in this moment of high urgency, however, was not the parading of notional titles but the existing commitment to a campaign against Philip VI. It was on this target that everything was now focused.

In the event, Edward would have to wait another whole year before he could make that ambition a reality. It was destined to be one of the most worrying and frustrating twelve months of his reign. Almost immediately the associated stresses become painfully evident in the correspondence between the king and the domestic administration. A week after his arrival in the Low Countries the king was writing ebulliently to the chancellor and magnates assembled at Northampton regarding the collection of the wool prise and the clerical tenths.[105] By 4 August, however, his tone had already changed. None of the money, supplies and other necessaries previously promised had materialized. Unless resources were sent to him immediately, the whole expedition would be put in jeopardy, his honour lost and the safekeeping of his realm put in jeopardy.[106] This complaint may have been written in ignorance of the decision, reached at Northampton, to retrieve the prise of wool by converting it into a straightforward tax the profits of which would all go to the king.[107] Over the following months the domestic government certainly did its best to ensure deliveries of cash and wool to the king's continental base at Antwerp.[108] Measures were set in place before and after Edward's departure to raise money by all possible means: exploiting the property recently seized from alien priories;[109]

[102] E 101/388/8, m. 1.

[103] Lucas, *Low Countries*, 291–2; Offler, 'England and Germany', 620; C 47/32/20.

[104] 'An Unknown Register of the Reign of Edward III', ed. F. Bock, *EHR*, xlv (1930), 365; Offler, 'England and Germany', 610–11.

[105] C 81/248/11261, printed in Déprez, *Préliminaires*, 418–19.

[106] Froissart, *Oeuvres*, xviii, 64–5. See also Edward's complaint of 19 Aug. that the exchequer had sent neither wool nor the fruits of the fifteenth and tenth: E 404/25, cited by Harriss, *King, Parliament*, 242 n. 2.

[107] *PROME*, iv, 233; Ormrod, 'Crown and the English Economy', 176–7.

[108] Tout, *Chapters*, 91–2; Lucas, *Low Countries*, 287.

[109] Arrangements for the leases of the alien priories seized in 1337 are found in C 270/17/4–18 and *CCR 1337–9*, 164. The 'form' for their administration in 1337 is set out in C 47/28/5, no. 50, and C 47/30/6, no. 7. Measures against alien clergy holding benefices in the English Church began in 1339: *PROME*, iv, 245.

making investigations of the king's lands;[110] encouraging advance payments on taxes;[111] and persuading the clergy of Canterbury province to
commit to yet another tenth.[112] In October the council was sufficiently
keen to have the king understand its good intent and diligent labour to put
the sentiments into a personal letter from the eight-year-old regent, Prince
Edward, to his mother.[113] But such assurances were simply not enough
either to address the king's mounting debts or to assuage his growing sense
of betrayal. The first casualty of the political tensions between the two
administrations occurred in December 1338, when Robert Woodhouse
was dismissed from the treasurership and replaced by a former household
officer and keeper of the privy seal, William Zouche.[114]

Once it became apparent to Philip VI that the English were really in no
position to move against him, he and his council wasted no time in planning a series of well-resourced counter-attacks. The fleet of ships originally intended for the crusade, reinforced by a powerful contingent of
Genoese galleys, moved out into the Channel, burning Portsmouth and
taking control of Guernsey. In October 1338 it made a major raid on
Southampton, where the French fired the town, slew those inhabitants
who attempted to put up a fight, and made off with rich plunder.[115] By the
end of the year, Plymouth, Swanage and Portsea had also been attacked,
the Isle of Wight ravaged, and all of the Channel Islands occupied. The
English coastal counties were put on high alert: beacons were to be
repaired and maintained and church bells were to be rung in the event of
enemy raids. Parliament called on the crown to require the privileged
communities of the Cinque Ports to take up their special role as 'a keeper
and wall between us and foreigners'.[116] For a while, the threat of larger-
scale invasion was very real. In 1339 the Valois government gave serious
consideration to launching a full-scale attack with an army of up to 24,000
men under the command of Philip VI's eldest son, John, duke of
Normandy.[117] Not since the invasion of Louis, son of Philip Augustus, in
1216 had England come so close to the uncomfortable reality of French
forces on its own soil.

In the face of such substantial scares, Edward III's continued absence
and inactivity could all too easily be read as an abnegation of his primary

[110] C 47/14/6, no. 36; *CFR 1327–37*, 83–4.
[111] SC 1/38/68; C 47/14/6, no. 34; *CPR 1338–40*, 122–3.
[112] *CFR 1337–47*, 98; *Foedera*, II.ii, 1069, 1092.
[113] SC 1/54/29.
[114] Fryde, *Studies*, chap. viii. In Feb. 1339 the king wrote to Zouche to urge swift delivery
of wools and money: E 159/115, rot. 99.
[115] C. Platt, *Medieval Southampton* (London, 1973), 107–18.
[116] *PROME*, iv, 243.
[117] E. Searle and R. Burghart, 'The Defense of England and the Peasants' Revolt',
Viator, iii (1972), 370–5; Alban, 'National Defence', 1–8, 190–233; Sumption, i, 245–78;
Rodger, *Safeguard of the Sea*, i, 96–7.

responsibility for the defence of England. The tournament hosted by the king at Antwerp over the Christmas season of 1338/9 to celebrate the birth of Prince Lionel created an unfortunate impression of royal feckless-ness, and the Westminster parliament of February 1339 was openly critical of the renewed pressure arising from special measures for the defence of the realm.[118] The charge that Edward was wilfully wasting both time and resources by his continued stay in the Low Countries was not altogether fair. He was careful to ingratiate himself with local political society: his visit to the shrine of the Holy Blood in Bruges and his sponsorship of other local churches and cults provided useful opportunities to parade his own Netherlandish credentials.[119] Remaining in and around Antwerp allowed him to keep a tight hold on negotiations with the emergent leader of the Flemish towns, James van Artevelde of Ghent. He also maintained close contact with John Stratford and Richard Bury who, having set up a special diplomatic commission at Arras, were now engaged in extensive covert operations designed to build up intelligence regarding French plan-ning.[120] Above all, the king was keen to manage the resources which he still confidently expected to arrive from England. This last business, however, was to prove Edward's downfall, generating a growing rift between the continental and domestic governments which in itself seriously compro-mised the crown's ability to argue a clear public case for the continuation of the war.

In May and June 1339 a series of revealing memoranda passed between the king and the home administration led by Bentworth and Zouche. Edward 'marvelled' at the lack of supplies; he complained vociferously that assignments made to his creditors were being rescinded; and he ordered that the exchequer uphold the ban on respites, even though he intended to override it in specific cases. The council protested that every-thing possible had been done to observe the king's orders. In response to Edward's threat to deprive his ministers of their fees, it commented tartly that the officers in question were quite likely to respond by resigning. It also refused the king's instruction that the treasurer attend upon him in person.[121] In expansive mode, Bentworth and Zouche reminded Edward that they had been required to take on responsibility for the whole of his

---

[118] *Scalacronica*, 126-7; *PROME*, iv, 234; C 76/14, mm. 18-14, 17d-12d; *Foedera*, II.ii, 1070-2. There is some doubt over the date of the schedule of petitions often associated with this parliament, printed in *RPHI*, 267-72. Fryde, 'Parliament and the French War', 251, dates it to Mar. 1337.

[119] Norwell, 209; Froissart, ii, 39.

[120] Le Bel, i, 131-4; E 101/311/35; Sumption, i, 240-1; Haines, *Stratford*, 255-7; Andre, *Ein Königshof auf Reisen*, 201-5.

[121] C 49/7/7, printed in Baldwin, *King's Council*, 476-8, and in Hughes, *Constitutional Tendencies*, 237-41. For discussion see Fryde, *Studies*, chap. vii, 1167; Fryde, 'Parliament and the French War', 253-4; Harriss, *King, Parliament*, 239. For the response to the request that the treasurer visit the king see also C 49/33/17.

enterprises, in Scotland and Gascony as well as in the Netherlands, and that a proportion of the profits of the realm must continue to be assigned to the proper defence of England.[122] Assuring the king that they would share in the 'shame, dishonour and great heartache' that would result from a failure of the war, the members of the home council now emphasized the insufficiency of the wool prise and wool tax and asked that the king send an envoy home to persuade parliament into yet another subsidy.[123]

It was Edward's refusal on the last of these suggestions that created the effective stand-off between the two administrations over the summer of 1339. Edward's confidence in the wool tax authorized in the Northampton great council of 1338 was, in some senses, well placed.[124] Unfortunately for him, however, the continued need to provide security for loans from Italian and English bankers meant that only just over half of the total amount of wool collected was actually sent to his agents in the Low Countries and sold there to service the debts to the allies.[125] Refusing to risk his reputation at home by making immediate demands for further taxes, the king now identified the causes of his growing deficit not as his own extravagance but as the inefficiency of the home administration. In September he declared his intention to be guided by those of his council present with him in Brussels: the margrave of Juliers, the earl of Salisbury, Bishop Burghersh, Geoffrey Scrope and William Kilsby.[126] This was simply the latest in a series of jibes and snubs launched at the regency administration by an increasingly impatient and suspicious king.

Such posturing was all very well, but in the continued absence of financial relief Edward soon found himself having to resort to desperate forms of barter in order to stave off the complete collapse of the imperial alliance. He offered his eldest son as a marriage partner for the duke of Brabant's daughter and heiress, Margaret, and dispatched the young Princess Joan to her mother's sister in Munich to be prepared for imminent betrothal to Frederick, the eldest son of Otto, duke of Austria.[127] Even the prospect of close affinity with the Plantagenets, however, was insufficient without complementary offers of fees and pensions. By September Lewis of Bavaria had clearly taken the view that Edward III

---

[122] SC 8/95/4740, printed in Harriss, *King, Parliament*, 244 n. 1.

[123] C 49/7/10, printed in Hughes, *Constitutional Tendencies*, 242–5, and Harriss, *King, Parliament*, 243 n. 2; *PROME*, iv, 246.

[124] See p. 115.

[125] Lloyd, *Wool Trade*, 154.

[126] C 47/30/8, no. 8. In June Edward had similarly asserted his right to be counselled by the 'prelates, earls, barons and others of the council in parts beyond the seas'. *CCR 1339–41*, 224.

[127] *Foedera*, II.ii, 915, 929, 940, 1083–4; Green, *Lives of Princesses*, iii, 234–9; F. Trautz, *Die Könige von England und das Reich, 1272–1377* (Heidelberg, 1961), 217, 219, 220, 279–80, 307; Lucas, *Low Countries*, 304–5.

was a diplomatic liability, and was actively seeking the opportunity to dismiss him from the position of vicar-general. The best that can be said about Edward's clinging to the wreckage of his fiscal system through the summer of 1339 was that it did at least delay the onset of yet another wave of heavy taxation of his subjects in England.

There were major questions about the crown's ability to maintain a war involving simultaneous action on so many fronts. With the king's possessions in south-western France left to fend for themselves, it was not really surprising that Philip VI's forces were now making significant headway even into the loyal heartlands of the ancient duchy of Gascony. In July 1339 the bishop of Beauvais and the count of Foix, at the head of a very large army of up to 15,000 men, seemed about to lay siege to Bordeaux. Taking fright at this emergency, Edward's government resorted to promising Gascon nobles and knights that they would be allowed to retain any lands conquered, through their own free enterprise, in the Valois-occupied territories. The only real effect of this measure, however, was to mortgage the duchy's entire fiscal resources and leave nothing available for the expenses of the beleaguered seneschal. The dreaded scenario of Valois support for the Bruce cause in Scotland also seemed set to become a reality. In the spring of 1339 the Scots broke truce and, with the assistance of a fleet of barges supplied by Philip VI, began to break England's supply routes to her remaining outposts north of the Firth of Forth. Cupar fell in May. Thomas Ughtred's garrison at Perth was finally starved out and forced to make a humiliating surrender in August. To many of his subjects in the summer of 1339, it must have seemed that the whole elaborate edifice of Edward III's strategy was about to collapse.

It was in this moment of grave crisis that the home administration was finally able to call the king's bluff. In August Edward sent his clerk, Robert Chigwell, back to Westminster with instructions that the council should provide a full summary of the current financial position.[128] By invoking the idea of a general audit of accounts envisioned in the Walton Ordinances, Edward was clearly hoping to expose what he saw as blatant deficiencies of management. Such, however, was the enormity of the fiscal deficit thus revealed that Edward was now finally persuaded to reconsider the recommendations put forward by Bentworth and Zouche in the previous months. John Stratford was to be sent home to take up presidency of the council. The home administration would be given greater discretion in such matters as the recovery of debts by instalment, the payment of fees and the appointment of officials. Most importantly, a parliament was to be summoned at which Stratford and others would finally admit the extent of the king's debts and call upon the realm, in a moment of grave

---

[128] E 159/116, rots 12, 15d. Chigwell had acted as royal envoy to the home council on at least one previous occasion: E 159/115, rot. 99.

emergency, to provide yet more subsidies.[129] In many respects the new arrangements confirmed the primacy of the war and the king's duty and right to continue his great enterprise. The increased powers of the home administration certainly did not challenge the underlying principles of the Walton Ordinances. Edward had every reason to believe that the able and loyal Stratford would work hard to achieve their agreed ends and re-establish political and fiscal stability at home. But the new accommodation would only work if there was mutual trust between king and regency. The events of the following year and a half would reveal just how damaging had been the breakdown in the relationship between the two administra-tions in 1339, and how little the return of Stratford really altered Edward III's exasperation with the domestic management of the war effort.

The king's one main purpose in agreeing to the new arrangements for the government of England was to present his allies with the prospect of financial satisfaction and thus to make it possible for them finally to embark on their long-delayed invasion of France. In early September 1339 Edward set off from Brussels in the company of the earls of Salisbury, Suffolk, Derby, Northampton, Pembroke and Warwick, Bishop Burghersh, Sir Geoffrey Scrope and a force of more than 4,600 men.[130] For some time it had been likely that the first military engagement between the Anglo-imperial and French armies would take place in the Cambrésis, a small principality ruled over by the bishop of Cambrai that was technically within the bounds of the Empire and stood at a strategic crossroads between Artois, Hainault and the kingdom of France. By the time Edward crossed into the Cambrésis on 20 September he had been joined by his brother-in-law, William, recently installed as the new count of Hainault; ten days later the duke of Brabant and his contingent also joined the growing force.

    The king now focused his hopes on an encounter with the Valois army gathering at Compiègne. But the bishop of Cambrai resisted Edward's authority as imperial vicar, and William of Hainault accordingly laid siege to the episcopal city. Edward had little interest in this interlude, and sat some miles distant from Cambrai at Marcoing. In a subsequent letter to Prince Edward recounting the course of the campaign, he provided an enthusiastic account of the devastation wreaked by his forces on the surrounding countryside and of their first foray over the French border on 25 September.[131] Eager for greater things, Edward eventually persuaded

    [129] *Foedera*, II.ii, 1091; *RDP*, iv, 503–5; Harriss, *King, Parliament*, 254.

    [130] For this and the next two paragraphs see Lucas, *Low Countries*, 328–39; Sumption, i, 278–89; Rogers, *War Cruel and Sharp*, 157–73.

    [131] Avesbury, 304–8; *The Wars of Edward III: Sources and Interpretation*, ed. C. J. Rogers (Woodbridge, 1999), 71–2.

his allies to raise the siege on 8 October, though not without repercussions. William of Hainault now decided that he had too much to lose by involving himself in a direct attack on Philip of Valois and defected to join the French army. A significant number of his troops, however, remained behind, taking advantage of the continued presence of the count's uncle, John of Hainault, in the English army. The arrival of the emperor's son, the margrave of Brandenburg, on 3 October, replenished the allied forces and gave Edward's force a semblance of strength and unity at a key moment in the campaign.

On 9 October the Anglo-imperial army made its first appearance within the territory of the crown of France. It split into three wings and spread out over a range of twenty miles, ruthlessly destroying settlements, farms and crops all along the way. The plan was to make for Péronne, where the bulk of Philip VI's army had recently moved. But this was not a suitable position or formation in which to make battle with the much larger French force, and the Anglo-German contingents moved east, crossing the Oise at Origny on 16 October and burning the town and bridges to keep the enemy at bay. Over the next few days Edward was hard pressed on all sides. The French sent several deputations demanding that he submit himself and his army to open battle. Meanwhile, the allies began to grumble that their supplies were running short. An attempt to move back across the Oise at Guise was foiled. The king reluctantly accepted the need to move north, into the Thiérarche, in order to guarantee a safe retreat into Hainault. At the same time he remained intent on as swift as possible an encounter with Philip's forces.

With the French now rapidly advancing, Edward took up a position outside La Capelle, close to the abbey of Clairfontaine and the hamlet of La Flamengrie. As at Halidon Hill, he deployed his troops at the top of an incline, with the archers divided into two wings, flanking divisions of dismounted men-at-arms and infantry. The French made camp at Buironfosse on 21 October. When Philip's advisers heard of the English dispositions, they counselled caution. They had too much to lose by risking defeat, and it would be better simply to force Edward's army to retire. The advice was sound, but it cut directly against the eagerness of the French lords to avenge the invasion. It also allowed Edward emphatically to claim the upper hand. On 23 October, the English withdrew in good order and due dignity, marching north to Avesnes and thence to Brussels where Edward held a tournament in the first week of November.[132] On both sides of the Channel, Philip was held to have behaved shamefully, failing in his first duty to protect his subjects and showing cowardice at the prospect of battle.[133] After a year of inactivity and recrimination, Edward

---

[132] Vale, *Edward III and Chivalry*, 172.
[133] Le Bel, i, 164–5; Baker, 65; Minot, *Poems*, 34–7.

had managed to turn his first foray into France to his own credit. In strategic terms, however, nothing had yet been achieved. The comparison with his spectacular campaign against the Scots in 1333 was all too obvious. If Edward were ever to make a real impression on the might of France, it was now very clear that it would take an altogether greater commitment of will and resources to accomplish it.

The events of 1339 had revealed much about the strengths and weaknesses of Edward III's character. In the phoney war of 1337–8 the king had demonstrated considerable political perspicacity, successfully arguing the compatibility between his interests and those of his people and thus committing the realm at large to the pursuit of open war against the house of Valois. After his departure from England and during his long period of inactivity in the Low Countries in 1338 and 1339, however, there is every sign that Edward gradually lost touch with reality. His wilful extravagance towards his allies left him, by the end of 1339, on the verge of bankruptcy. Apart from exposing the apparent pusillanimity of the French, his brief forays into Philip's territories had been entirely fruitless. And the complete absence of any formal engagement with the Valois left him dangerously devoid of the credibility that might yet carry him through to a new, more successful phase of fighting. Had Edward III died in the winter of 1339–40 his reign would almost certainly have been remembered by posterity as the moment when the Plantagenets lost their last vestiges of dominion on French soil.

Most ominously of all, there were already significant signs by the end of 1339 that the realm of England had reached a state of war exhaustion. There is a lively modern debate as to whether royal taxation, even of the scale and intensity experienced in the late 1330s, could have had a directly adverse impact on the economy at large.[134] For contemporaries, however, the position was all too clear. A series of poor harvests and serious live-stock epidemics in the 1330s had resulted in regular and sometimes severe food shortages. These conditions left consumers more than usually sensitive about the deleterious effects of purveyance, which reduced the amount of produce available on the open market and pushed up already inflated prices. While the crown made comparatively few large-scale trans-fers of cash to the continent in these years,[135] the general effect of high levels of taxation was to force already scarce coin out of the agrarian economy. The habitual resort to credit notes only served to intensify criti-cism and complaint of fiscal policy. A Latin and French poem known as

---

[134] Maddicott, 'English Peasantry', 329–51; A. R. Bridbury, 'Before the Black Death', *EcHR*, 2nd series, xxx (1977), 393–410.

[135] M. Prestwich, 'The Crown and the Currency: The Circulation of Money in Late Thirteenth and Early Fourteenth Century England', *Numismatic Chronicle*, cxlii (1982), 51–65.

the *Song against the King's Taxes*, written probably by a member of the English clergy in *c.*1339–40, made harsh criticisms of a ruler who ate his meals off silver plate while paying for his food with wood (a reference to the tallies given out so readily by royal purveyors and redeemed with so much difficulty by suppliers). A good king, he commented, would do precisely the reverse, eating off wooden chargers and melting down his plate to make coin for the hard-pressed people.[136] By the beginning of 1340 there were many in England who openly questioned the whole legitimacy of a war that was so obviously and directly to the jeopardy of the kingdom's own prosperity.

Ironically, Edward III shared many of the prejudices of his subjects about the operations of royal finance. When threatened with investigation, taxpayers were habitually inclined to argue that shortfalls in the system were the consequence of inefficiency and corruption among those who ran the system.[137] In particular, they believed that tax collectors and purveyors took more than they ought and made private profit from the excess: the *Song against the King's Taxes* claimed that less than half of what was taken in the name of the crown actually reached the king. This was precisely the argument to which Edward himself resorted in his exchanges with the home council during 1339 and which he attempted to address by sending Stratford home to take up the reins of government in September of that year. But the profound misgivings generated by the extraordinary burden of taxation were not to be dispelled by such tokenism, and left a permanent mark on the collective memory. Even the late fourteenth-century English *Brut* chronicle, usually so patriotic in its outlook and so fervent in its praise of Edward III, had no doubt that the opening stages of the French war marked a low point in the public credibility of the king. 'The inner love of the people was turned to hate, and their common prayers into cursing.'[138]

---

[136] *Anglo-Norman Political Songs*, ed. I. S. T. Aspin (Anglo-Norman Text Society, xi, 1953), 111, 113.

[137] E.g., *The 1341 Royal Inquest in Lincolnshire*, ed. B. W. McLane (Lincoln Record Society, lxxviii, 1988), nos 90–1, 95–6, 545, 684, 894, 991.

[138] *Brut*, ii, 293–4 (adapted).

Chapter 8

THE EDGE OF THE ABYSS, 1339–1341

On 26 January 1340, in the marketplace of the city of Ghent, Edward III was formally proclaimed king of France. For the next twenty years all his formal communications with rulers on the continent would refer to him by the double style 'king of France and England'. The new seals and heraldry adopted at this moment provided a stark comment on Edward's scale of priorities. The lilies of France were now quartered with the leopards of England in such a way as to give France perpetual precedence.[1] The chronicler Geoffrey le Baker recalled that Philip VI had earlier upbraided Edward for his temerity in putting 'little England' above 'great France'.[2] Now, quite brilliantly, Edward had beaten Philip at his own game, at once proclaiming his own dynastic aspirations in France and provoking a public debate on the legality and viability of the Valois monarchy.

There was no shortage of valid arguments that could be put forward in defence of Edward's new claim. Since the French nobility had not publicly applied the Salic law in preferring Philip VI's candidacy for the throne in 1328, Edward had every right, in theory, to continue to claim to be the true heir to Charles IV.[3] Nor, from such a perspective, was it necessarily unsustainable to put Edward's claims above those of the descendants of Charles's older brothers. Edward had been the only member of the Capetian dynasty to lodge a counter-claim in 1328. Louis X's daughter, Jeanne, had been content to take the throne of Navarre with her husband, Philip of Evreux, and their son, Charles, arguably had no right to make a retrospective bid for the throne of his uncle since he was not born until four years after the event, in 1332. Still more importantly, Edward was well aware that his and Philip of Valois's rival claims mirrored quite closely

[1] M. Michael, 'The Little Land of England is Preferred before the Great Kingdom of France: The Quartering of the Royal Arms by Edward III', *Studies in Medieval Art and Architecture Presented to Peter Lasko*, ed. D. Buckton and T. A. Heslop (Stroud, 1994), 114–26; A. Ailes, 'Heraldry in Medieval England: Symbols of Politics and Propaganda', *Heraldry, Pageantry and Social Display*, ed. Coss and Keen, 87–93.

[2] Baker, 66–7; W. M. Ormrod, 'A Problem of Precedence: Edward III, the Double Monarchy, and the Royal Style', *Age of Edward III*, ed. Bothwell, 134 n. 4. For other French reactions see W. M. Hinkle, *The Fleurs de Lis of the Kings of France, 1285–1488* (Carbondale, 1991), 27–31.

[3] *Debating the Hundred Years War*, 18–22; Taylor, 'Salic Law', 358–77; C. Taylor, 'Edward III and the Plantagenet Claim to the French Throne', *Age of Edward III*, ed. Bothwell, 155–69.

those of the two main contenders for the Scottish succession in 1290. Edward I's judgment in favour of John Balliol in 1292 had set a particularly useful precedent by putting the feudal principle of primogeniture over the Roman law principle of proximity by degree, and by acknowledging the capacity of females to transmit rights to royal title. Had these arguments been applied in France in 1328 then Edward III, as the nephew of Charles IV, would indeed have taken precedence over a mere cousin, Philip VI.[4] Finally, Edward's legal experts were careful to deny that his performance of homage to Philip VI in 1329 could be taken as committing him to the Valois succession, arguing that Edward had been a minor at the time and that the accustomed reservations expressed in his oath of simple homage had served to protect his own dynastic claim.

All of this, of course, was so much special pleading. Benedict XII, to whom Edward sent a very detailed statement of the legal arguments later in 1340, rapidly dismissed the whole thing for what it really was: a confection of ideas put together after the event in order to deflect attention from Edward's blatant act of aggression against his rightful feudal lord.[5] The English envoys to Avignon might well protest that time could not run against right, but Edward's decision to date his reign in France not from 1328 but from 1340 served only to expose the most obvious weakness in his case. For better or worse, Philip VI had now been king of France for over a decade, and any attempt to dislodge him would have to take into account the legitimacy of the acts he had undertaken in the interim. It is noticeable that, when he presented himself publicly to the people of France in February 1340, Edward skirted round the precise details of his dynastic claim. Instead, the letters announcing the double title simply played on the idea that true kings were good kings. Philip had exposed the unlawful nature of his regime through his tyrannical rule. It was Edward who would now restore the principles of sound monarchy for which their common ancestor, Louis IX, stood as exemplar.[6] He made little of it at the time, but Edward was also well acquainted with the unpopular centralizing tendencies pursued by the French monarchy since the time of Philip the Fair and would in due course seek explicitly to uphold the traditions of local autonomy favoured by the political elites of Brittany, Normandy and other powerful provinces of the kingdom of France.[7] Uneasy from the start about

[4] Prestwich, *Edward I*, 365–6. For a memorandum on the Scottish Great Cause of 1290–2 compiled in the context of Anglo-French relations in *c.*1337 see C 47/28/5, no. 9.

[5] *EMDP*, I.ii, no. 239(b).

[6] *Foedera*, II.ii, 1108–9; Avesbury, 309–10; *EHD*, iv, 66–7; *Chron. Lanercost*, 328–9. For Philip VI's response, see *Society at War: The Experience of England and France during the Hundred Years War*, ed. C. Allmand, rev. edn (Woodbridge, 1998), 149–50.

[7] Le Patourel, *Feudal Empires*, chap. xii. That such ideas were already in development by 1340 is suggested by the existence of a copy of Louis X's charter of liberties for the duchy of Normandy (1315) in a dossier of English conciliar memoranda from the 1330s: C 47/28/5, no. 44.

the credibility of his dynastic case, Edward and his apologists would always be much more inclined to rely on honour and virtue rather than simply on right as the true justification for his claim to the throne of France.

The real reason why Edward III publicly asserted the French title in January 1340, as both his allies and his enemies openly acknowledged, was his pressing need for the co-operation of the Flemish towns.[8] By the end of 1339 the king was poised to make a treaty of mutual support with James van Artevelde. Edward agreed to announce himself king of France, and thus feudal suzerain of Flanders, in order that the men of Ghent, Bruges and Ypres might argue the justice of their cause against the Valois regime and escape the penalties that might otherwise befall them for making an act of rebellion against their superior lord. In many respects, the public announcement of Edward's double title was simply an admission of the desperate diplomatic manoeuvrings to which the king had been driven by his continued shortage of financial resources. The risks of the new alliance were certainly high for the Flemings. Louis de Nevers, together with significant numbers of his nobles and knights, refused to accept the legitimacy of the treaty and sought refuge with Philip VI, while Benedict XII, furious at the contempt shown towards count and king, promptly imposed an interdict on van Artevelde and his supporters. But it was Edward III who undoubtedly bore the burden of the controversial new alliance. He was forced to offer the Flemish towns a subsidy of £140,000, the right to trade freely with England and a promise that the English wool staple would be moved to Bruges. In acknowledging the claims of Flanders to the Valois-controlled territories of Artois, Tournai, Lille and Douai, he also indicated his preparedness to subordinate his war aims to the more immediate advantage of his new allies.[9] And with his existing sources of income already completely exhausted, Edward had no hope of funding his new financial commitment to the Flemings without recourse to a further bout of heavy taxation in England. Far from representing a diplomatic tour de force, Edward's modification of his titles seemed destined to put England on the road to humiliation and ruin.

Nor was the news from home such as to suggest that the country was ready for the scale of military expenditure that might result. Much confidence had been invested in John Stratford's new role as president of the home council. At the parliament of October 1339, Stratford, together with Bishop Bury and William de la Pole, presented the king's case as a series of stark choices. Edward's recent entry into France after the siege of

---

[8] Le Bel, i, 166–8; Froissart, i, 183–8; Lucas, *Low Countries*, 339–67; Sumption, i, 296–303; D. Nicholas, *The van Arteveldes of Ghent: The Varieties of Vendetta and the Hero in History* (Ithaca, New York, 1988), 35–8.

[9] *CPR 1338–40*, 511–16.

Cambrai proved his determination to fulfil the commitments of 1337 and proceed against Philip of Valois. But Edward's debts now stood at £300,000, and without further supplies he would simply be forced to make a dishonourable peace. Anxious to demonstrate their loyalty to the regime, the lords proposed an extraordinary subsidy in kind, modelled on the ecclesiastical tithe of wool, corn and newborn lambs. The commons, by contrast, refused to give their consent to this tax until they had referred it back to their constituents in the county and borough courts. Stratford offered some crowd-pleasing measures: the confirmation of the system in place since 1338 for the maintenance of public order; new arrangements for the adequate defence of the realm; and the cancellation of all current commissions of purveyance, together with a promise of special investigation into the activities of the king's chief purveyor since 1338, William Wallingford.[10] The fact remained, however, that no new sources of war funding had been made available.

Another parliament was summoned quickly, for January 1340, to resolve the urgent and unfinished business of the previous assembly; the unprecedented order to the sheriffs to send 'belted' or fighting knights as representatives of the counties hints at a royal attempt to establish something resembling a war party in England.[11] Stratford made some headway in other assemblies meeting concurrently with parliament. He extracted offers of further tenths from both convocations of the clergy.[12] And a group of merchants summoned before the council struck a controversial deal that required those shipping wool to the continent to pay not only the customs and subsidies in English ports but also an additional 'gift' of £2 per sack to a special royal receiver at the staple of Bruges.[13] Within parliament, however, deadlock continued. The lords stuck to their offer of a ninth. The commons were equally adamant that the only viable subsidy was one to be collected in wool, and suggested a one-off levy of 30,000 sacks. Stratford and his fellow councillors felt unable to accept either offer

[10] *PROME*, iv, 235-7, 239-41, 245; Fryde, 'Parliament and the French War', 257. For Wallingford's role as receiver of victuals for the king's household and army abroad in 1338-40 see *CCR 1337-9*, 438; *CPR 1338-40*, 409; E 358/2, mm. 12, 27.

[11] *RDP*, iv, 507-9; *PROME*, iv, 247; G. O. Sayles, *The Functions of the Medieval Parliament of England* (London, 1988), 427; K. L. Wood-Legh, 'Sheriffs, Lawyers and Belted Knights in the Parliaments of Edward III', *EHR*, xlvi (1931), 385.

[12] The single tenths offered by Canterbury in Oct. 1338 and Feb. 1340 were balanced out by two tenths from the York province in Feb. 1340. These taxes are especially notable because their payment dates overlapped with those for the later years of the triennial subsidies granted in 1337. On this occasion, therefore, the clergy were persuaded away from their usual stance that concurrent taxation provided grounds for refusal of further subsidies. *Concilia Magna Britanniae et Hiberniae*, ed. D. Wilkins, 4 vols (London, 1737), ii, 622-4, 653; D. B. Weske, *Convocation of the Clergy* (London, 1937), 249, 283; Ormrod, 'Crown and the English Economy', 161-2.

[13] Fryde, *William de la Pole*, 141.

because the commons insisted on attaching a set of conditions. The details have not survived, but they are likely to have included the withdrawal of the *maltolt* and of certain prerogative taxes such as feudal aids and judicial fines. When parliament was dissolved on 19 February, the principal task with which Stratford had been charged on his return to England five months earlier – the successful negotiation of large-scale taxes – had still to be achieved.

It was the continuing refusal of parliament to bow readily to his will that finally persuaded Edward III, after a year-and-a-half's absence, to return to England and, through sheer force of personality, extract the funds for which he was so obviously impatient. Departing from the Low Countries was not a straightforward matter, for the Flemings were now pressing hard for the fulfilment of the king's financial and military obligations. Queen Philippa, heavily pregnant with her sixth child, and the earls of Salisbury and Suffolk had already been required to stand as personal surety for the debts owed to the Netherlandish princes and the Flemish towns.[14] When Edward left Bruges on 17 February with his henchman Kilsby and a few other close advisers, it was therefore at considerable risk to himself, his family and friends. Disembarking at Orwell in Suffolk on 21 February, he made straight for London and, on consultation with the council, issued writs for a parliament to assemble at the end of March.[15] As he wandered the halls of Westminster and Windsor awaiting the assembly of parliament, Edward looked about frantically for financial makeweight. On 1 March, Robert Askby was sent to the London Guildhall to ask the mayor and aldermen for an unprecedented loan of £20,000. Four days later, after much negotiation, they agreed to advance just a quarter of that sum. John Stratford, along with Kilsby and the treasurer, William Zouche, was required to put up his own estates as security. In the current state of royal finance, there was every chance that the three might indeed incur personal liability for the debt.[16]

In spite of obvious provocation, the members of the home government were not inclined to fall out publicly with the king whose enterprise they had worked so hard to sustain over the previous three years. Stratford, Arundel, Huntingdon and others now set to work on Edward to ensure that his bullying tactics would not have a negative impact on the

---

[14] Sumption, i, 305.

[15] *CCR 1339–41*, 451; *RDP*, iv, 515–18.

[16] *CLBL, F*, 45–9, 50; *CPMR 1323–64*, 120–1, 139–40, 141, 148–9, 156, 195, 203. The loan was subsequently assigned against the ninth; when this failed, attempts were made in 1343 to call in the security from Kilsby's estate, but the loan still remained substantially unsatisfied in 1347. Unwin, 'Estate of Merchants', 203; *CLBL, F*, 90–1; C 49/53/20. In 1341 the city was asked to pay an additional loan of £2,000 and offered only £1,000, of which £800 seems to have been paid: *CPMR 1323–64*, 192–201; Axworthy, 'Financial Relationship', 172–3.

negotiation of taxes. They focused first on his new and controversial style of king of France. The decision to announce this title in Flanders had been taken without any known consultation with the home administration and no public reassurances of what it might actually mean for the kingdom of England. In various documents issued during the days immediately after his arrival in England, Edward was persuaded to begin some form of explanation to a confused and disconcerted public. The order of precedence used at Ghent was reversed so that Edward became, for the purposes of domestic administration, 'king of England and France'. This exercise in damage limitation culminated in the important statute issued in the March parliament, by which the king agreed the strict separation of the two realms and guaranteed that England should never run the risk of subjection to France.[17] The council's insistence on the rebranding of the double monarchy was a significant indicator of its anxiety to impress on the king the need to pre-empt some of the serious criticism that he was about to encounter from the political community.

If Edward had thought that he could rely simply on his charisma to carry the day in the March parliament, he was therefore quickly disabused. Stratford's policy of conciliation and compromise now prevailed. The arguments put forward before the lords and commons on 1 April were essentially the same as in the previous October. Edward was about to be called back to Brussels and hand himself over as a hostage for his debts. As a consequence, 'he will be dishonoured forever and his lands both here and overseas will be in great peril'. If, however, a subsidy were forthcoming, his undertaking would be brought 'to a good end' and 'there will be peace and quiet everywhere'. Two days later, the lords' earlier proposal was revived and the commons agreed to abandon their suggestion of a wool levy and replace it with a ninth part of the wool, corn and lambs liable for ecclesiastical tithes; this subsidy, which would run for two years, would be collected in kind and then converted into cash through the sale of the proceeds on the domestic market.[18] At this point or shortly after, the lords and commons also agreed that, in return for the withdrawal of the additional subsidy negotiated with the merchants in January, they would grant a new subsidy on wool exports at the reduced rate of £1 13s 4d, to run until May 1341 or to the conclusion of the war, whichever fell first.[19]

This impressive turnaround in the king's political and financial fortunes was achieved only because of the council's insistence, against Edward's own instinct, on offering substantive reciprocal concessions. The crown

[17] *RDP*, iv, 515–17; *PROME*, iv, 261, 268; *SR*, i, 292; *EHD*, iv, 70; *Chron. Lanercost*, 333; *Scalacronica*, 128–9. See also pp. 604–5.
[18] *PROME*, iv, 267.
[19] *SR*, i, 291; *CFR 1337–47*, 196.

now agreed to consider the issues that had been raised in the conditions
set on the commons' earlier tax offer.[20] Most unusually, the points for
consideration were not put before king and council to be made up, as they
thought best, as statutes. Instead, an extraordinary committee of lords and
commons was set up to formulate remedial legislation that was eventually
approved by the king in mid-April.[21] The committee included two of
those who had recently been with the king abroad, the earl of Derby and
Sir Geoffrey Scrope. Otherwise, it was dominated by members of the
home administration: John Stratford (as effective president), his brother
Robert, the earls of Arundel and Huntingdon and Lords Wake, Percy and
Neville.

The concessions agreed by the committee with the king fell into four
broad categories. First, there were expressions of good faith that played
rather obviously to the gallery: the confirmation of Magna Carta and of
standard weights and measures; promises of stricter application of the
qualifications and terms of tenure for office-holders in the shires; the guarantee of the separation of the king's two realms; and the abolition of
'presentment of Englishry', an archaic legal practice which, in theory at
least, imposed liabilities on local communities in England for the deaths of
the king's foreign-born subjects. Secondly, there was a series of significant
promises on the abolition or restriction of some of the most contentious
forms of prerogative taxation. The crown would in future refrain from
collecting tallages (taxes on the royal domain), scutages (fines in lieu of
military service) and feudal aids (taxes imposed under certain conditions
on the king's tenants-in-chief). It would also desist from levying the
communal fines associated with visitations of the eyre and unclaimed
debts dormant in the exchequer. There was some doubt as to whether
these promises were permanently binding, but it was at least clear that the
king would have to cease such charges for the duration of the current
subsidies. In similar vein, both purveyance and the use of pardons as a
form of military recruitment would now be much more closely regulated.
To counter any suggestion about its lack of commitment to these principles, the crown also made an important statement acknowledging parliament's right to consent to all forms of extraordinary taxation.

Thirdly, there were powerful statements of the crown's accountability
to its subjects for the financial management of the war. The ninth was to

---

[20] G. L. Harriss, 'The Commons' Petition of 1340', *EHR*, lxxxviii (1963), 625–54 argues
that the extant common petitions from the parliament of Mar. 1340 repeated the substance
of the issues raised in the unknown conditions imposed on the offer of 30,000 sacks in the
Jan. assembly. For the text of these common petitions see *The Chartulary of Winchester
Cathedral*, ed. A. W. Goodman (Winchester, 1927), 131–3; Harriss, *King, Parliament*, 518–20;
PROME, iv, 275–6.
[21] *PROME*, iv, 267–8; *SR*, i, 281–94; *Calendar of the Records of the Corporation of Gloucester*,
ed. W. H. Stevenson (Gloucester, 1893), 53.

be reserved solely for the expenses of war; to ensure that this promise was upheld, the tax would be administered outside the normal processes and managed by two specially appointed receivers placed under the supervision of a group of magnates. The principle of accountability was also applied retrospectively to earlier subsidies, with the result that a string of prominent royal financiers and agents – the Bardi, William de la Pole, John Charnels, Paul Montefiori and William Melchbourn – were now subjected to close scrutiny by parliamentary commissioners.[22] Fourthly, the king's responsibility for the defence and welfare of the realm was powerfully reaffirmed. New provisions were announced for the continued defence of the north against Scottish attacks. And at the end of the assembly in May, with Edward about to return to the continent, a powerful new regency council was appointed under the presidency of Archbishop Stratford and staffed by the earls of Huntingdon, Lancaster and Surrey and Lords Percy, Wake and Neville. Many of the restrictions that had been placed on the domestic administration in 1338–9 were now eased, and the council was charged to use its comprehensive authority 'to carry out the important affairs of the realm . . . and the accomplishment of the business touching our lord the king, both here and elsewhere'.[23]

If Edward had cause to congratulate himself on the promises of supply secured during his home visit, he felt increasingly exasperated at the compromises that Stratford had effectively extracted from him. The compact worked out between September 1339 and May 1340 meant the removal or relaxation of a significant number of the detailed specifications contained in the Walton Ordinances. Edward was quick to disabuse the home administration of any notion that this allowed it to take over the management of the war. In March, he personally advised Treasurer Zouche not to meddle with the management of the alien priories, which, as he tartly reminded him, were reserved for the king's special use. On 5 May, the very day on which Stratford was installed as chancellor and Zouche was replaced at the exchequer by Robert Sadington, Edward issued the same sharp reminder to his new ministers.[24] Having already relaxed the ban of 1338 on allowing debts to the crown to be paid off by instalment, the king continued to allow such favours only as a matter of grace.[25] Most emphatically of all, on 18 May he restated the stipulation of 1338 that no assignments could be made in the exchequer without his express instruction under the privy seal.[26] So far as the king

---

[22] *PROME*, iv, 269–70; *CPR 1338–40*, 499–504; *CFR 1337–46*, 178–9.

[23] *PROME*, iv, 272–4; *Foedera*, II.ii, 1125.

[24] E 159/116, rots 92, 98d.

[25] E 101/120/20; BL, Add. Rolls 26588–26595; W. M. Ormrod, 'Edward III and the Recovery of Royal Authority in England, 1340–60', *History*, lxxii (1987), 7.

[26] E 159/116, rot. 108. The preamble to this writ contains a high-flown expression of concern for the welfare of the king's subjects in the face of such severe fiscal pressures.

was concerned, the central features of the Walton Ordinances remained emphatically in place.

Ironically, the very punctiliousness of parliament over the reservation of the ninth for the costs of war served the king's purposes in this regard. Before Edward departed the realm, he and the council agreed to assign somewhere in the region of £150,000 of the expected income from the ninth in order to cover accumulated debts to his bankers, allies and military commanders.[27] This was a high-risk strategy, for no one had any real sense of how much the new tax might actually yield. While Edward remained in England there was a reasonable expectation that the council would retain some form of realistic balance between promises and resources. But if, on his return to the Low Countries, the king were to insist on his absolute right to dictate expenditure in England, there was no telling what chaos might yet ensue. As in 1339, so now in 1340, the council could only suggest making more demands for subsidies. On 30 May writs were therefore issued for a tax-granting parliament to convene, in the king's absence, in July.[28] We catch a vivid glimpse of the likely resulting tensions within the government in a meeting between the king and Stratford at Orwell, just prior to Edward's embarkation in June, reconstructed in dramatic form by the chronicler Robert of Avesbury. The archbishop advised that a further campaign should be delayed until the king could muster more effective forces. Edward responded with a show of foot-stamping that pushed the infuriated Stratford into resigning the chancellorship. Expecting to be vindicated by the military experts, the king then called the admiral of the east coast, Robert Morley, and his lieutenant, John Crabbe, only to find that they were inclined to confirm the archbishop's concerns. Edward rounded on them all. 'I will cross the sea in spite of you,' he railed. 'You, who are afraid when there is nothing to be frightened of, can stay at home.'[29]

Avesbury's story is obviously afflicted with hindsight. Stratford did indeed resign as chancellor on 20 June, two days before the king's departure. But it was unusual for an archbishop to hold ministerial office, and the reshuffle was more likely a practical matter of providing adequate coverage for another prolonged royal absence. Certainly, Stratford had no hesitation in accepting the presidency of the regency. The new chancellor and treasurer installed shortly after the king's departure were the two bishops who had sat with Stratford on the legislative committee in the March parliament: his brother, Robert, bishop of Chichester, and the long-serving bishop of Coventry and Lichfield, Roger Northburgh.[30]

[27] Harriss, *King, Parliament*, 277–8.
[28] *RDP*, iv, 521–4.
[29] Avesbury, 311; Lucas, 'John Crabbe', 346–7.
[30] *CCR 1339–41*, 482; *PROME*, iv, 277.

There is no sense, then, of any last-minute attempt by the king wilfully to manipulate the membership and outlook of the home administration. And yet the imagined histrionics of the episode at Orwell may reveal an essential truth. Edward's begrudging attitude had sorely tried the patience of the domestic administration. His sulking had also significantly disrupted sincere efforts to settle the kingdom; even on the day of the king's departure, the council was frantically seeking his consent to a range of business still unresolved from the time of parliament.[31] Had he properly considered the implications of his visit home, Edward would surely have realized just how close he had already come to destroying both his great project and his monarchy. His failure to acknowledge the enormous debt of gratitude that he owed to Stratford would ultimately act to alienate the home administration and generate the greatest political crisis of the reign.

Edward's emphatic insistence on returning as quickly as possible to the Low Countries was in part a reaction to the news that continued to arrive from the front.[32] William of Hainault, panicked by French attacks on his territories, had decided to return to the alliance and promised to make common cause with the English and the Flemings in an attack on Tournai. But when the earls of Salisbury and Suffolk left their main force to reconnoitre the city of Lille on 11 April, they were both taken prisoner and hauled off to Paris to be locked up in the Châtelet. News of this unhappy setback reached the king as he celebrated an Easter tournament at Windsor.[33] Although the duke of Normandy and the count of Eu were repulsed from Valenciennes at the end of May by a force including the earls of Warwick and Northampton, they joined up with Philip VI to take a number of the castles recently occupied by the Hainaulters in the Cambrésis.

Most ominous of all was intelligence that the king of France had organized a large fleet to make for the estuaries of the Rivers Zwin and Scheldt and prevent Edward's planned landing in Flanders. The war at sea had gone rather better for the English over the previous six months, not least because the French had lost the support of some of the Genoese mercenaries. But the prospect of a major naval engagement exposed the weakness of Edward's position. In spite of attempts to build up his own stock of galleys in the late 1330s, Edward had only a handful of fighting ships at his direct disposal. The requisitioning of merchant shipping for a major campaign at sea was bound to jeopardize the safety of English ports and

---

[31] C 61/52, mm. 22–20; CPR 1340–3, 4.

[32] For what follows see Sumption, i, 306–29; Rogers, *War Cruel and Sharp*, 191–7.

[33] E 101/388/11, printed in 'An Armourer's Bill, temp. Edward III', ed. H. Dillon, *Antiquary*, xxii (1890), 150.

harbours. Furthermore, Edward's determination to have the earls of Derby, Northampton, Warwick, Gloucester, Arundel and Huntingdon accompany him back to the continent was at variance with the policy of maintaining a strong aristocratic presence in the commissions set up to organize the defence of the English coast. In spite of these complex and intractable issues, the state of emergency now demanded that Edward prepare for an encounter at sea. After visiting his mother at Hertford castle at the end of May, the king made his way into East Anglia to supervise the collection of shipping and manpower, and eventually set sail from Orwell on 22 June aboard his ship the *Thomas*.

The statistics did not make for comforting analysis. Edward was accompanied by a force of up to 150 vessels carrying a small army of between 2,500 and 4,000 men. The French fleet comprised in excess of 200 ships, many of them significantly larger than their English counterparts, and bore an estimated 20,000 soldiers.[34] The English dropped anchor off Blankenberg on the 23rd and sent to the Flemings for reinforcements. Anxiety mounted about the wisdom of an attack. But for all their superiority in numbers, the French were in trouble. In an age when gunpowder was in its infancy in Europe, naval engagements relied on two tactics: the loosing of arrows as the lines of ships approached each other, and the grappling together of enemy vessels in order that their forces could engage in hand-to-hand combat. The English longbowmen had a formidable range and accuracy, and many of Edward's men-at-arms were seasoned fighters with strong records of service in the Scottish wars. By contrast, neither the leadership nor the rank and file of the French forces had much experience of military or naval engagements. The two admirals, Nicholas Béhuchet and Hugh Quiéret, were at loggerheads over tactics, and in their indecision managed to offend the most experienced of their captains, the Genoese pirate Pietro Barbavera. Eventually, they decided to anchor their fleet across the opening of the River Zwin between Termuiden and the island of Cadzand, with the town of Sluys behind them. The French ships were chained together to prevent the English from breaking their line. Either they would have to risk a fight, or they would be forced to concede defeat and allow Edward's forces to sail on up the coast unchallenged.

Early on the morning of 24 June, the English king moved his ships out to sea and formed them into three battle lines. Realizing that he might have to advance directly into the glare of the sun, Edward decided to tack out further into open water, either to play for time until the sun moved south and west or to find some other means of surprise. The French understandably mistook this for a retreat, and began to break up their lines. Then disaster struck. Precisely how Edward managed so brilliantly to surprise the French remains a matter of debate. The standard account

---

[34] *Foedera*, II.ii, 1129; Rogers, *War Cruel and Sharp*, 192–3, 197.

has him waiting until the sun was behind him and then sailing suddenly forward into the French front line. Another, more intriguing, interpretation is that he ordered an abrupt diversion, sailing north and east into the estuary of the River Scheldt and then down around the eastern side of Cadzand to take the French by surprise from the rear.[35] Either way, the king's instincts proved sound. The archers let forth their flight of deadly arrows, and the knights stormed aboard the Valois ships and began systematically to eliminate the enemy. In the fierce fighting that followed, Edward III took possession of several vessels of his personal fleet that had fallen into French hands in the previous two years, including his flagship the *Christopher*. The battle was long and hard-fought, and individual engagements lasted until nightfall. The actions of the English lords and knights were soon to become the stuff of chivalric mythology. But the real winners at sea, as previously on land at Halidon Hill, were the archers, whose torrent of arrows not only wounded and killed numerous French sailors but also, crucially, prevented their captains from properly observing and responding to the manoeuvres of the English ships.

Medieval naval battles had a reputation for brutality, not least since the losers' option of flight was so obviously difficult to effect from aboard a floating castle. Even within such expectations, the battle of Sluys proved one of the bloodiest engagements of the entire Hundred Years War. Edward III gave the cautious estimate of 5,000 French dead, but the real number is likely to have been at least three times that figure. Quiéret was killed, and Béhuchet was hanged from the mast of his own ship. Those of their men who tried to swim to safety were quickly picked off on nearby beaches by the enthusiastic Flemings. There was talk of bodies washed up all along the coast of Flanders and of the sea running red with blood: every tide, reported Edward III to his son, brought up a fresh wave of dead.[36] As on land in Scotland, the English king fought in the very thick of the engagement, and emerged with his valour and honour enhanced. Had he failed, the consequences could have been devastating: with so many of the English senior command present on the occasion, a Valois victory could seriously have inhibited Edward's further prosecution of the war, not to mention depriving the king of his freedom or even his life. But Edward had chosen his moment, and his mode of operations, very well. Having failed repeatedly to engage the French on land, the king had finally achieved his aim at sea – and won a great victory in the process.

For Edward III's subjects, the great test of naval supremacy at Sluys was as emotive as it was novel: 'There,' wrote Laurence Minot, 'Englishmen

---

[35] Rodger, *Safeguard of the Sea*, i, 98–9.
[36] Le Bel, i, 178–81; *Chron. Meaux*, iii, 45; *Chron. Lanercost*, 333–4; *Scalacronica*, 130–1; Rogers, *War Cruel and Sharp*, 197 n. 133, 198 and n. 135.

learned a new dance.'[37] In the years after 1340, Edward would fully exploit the idea that this naval battle had restored and guaranteed his ancestors' claim to the title of 'sovereign of the seas'.[38] In 1343 the king had five ornamental gold ships made as permanent memorials of the victory and presented them to Walsingham Priory, St Paul's Cathedral, Gloucester Abbey and Canterbury Cathedral (the latter receiving two, one to be placed at the tomb of Becket, the other in the Lady Chapel).[39] Shortly afterwards he issued a new gold coin, the noble, bearing the image of a crowned king aboard a ship of war and the legend 'Jesus, passing through the midst of them, went his way' (Luke 4: 30).[40] This propaganda helped feed a burgeoning popular mythology that celebrated England's new-found naval prowess; such were the enemy casualties at Sluys, it was said, that the fish in the English Channel now spoke French.[41]

In the summer of 1340, however, there was scant evidence of a trans-formation in the security of the realm. In instructions sent in August to William Trussell, the admiral of the western fleet, the king reported the assembling of a further hostile navy of Normans and other French intent on destroying the fleet of England.[42] The rumours were true: the new French admiral, Robert Houdetot, had rapidly re-established a force to patrol the coasts of Picardy and Normandy, and had already begun a sequence of attempted raids on a long section of the English coastline from the Isle of Wight to Plymouth. Such was the level of public anxiety that the home council now agreed with representatives of the mercantile community the levy of a special subsidy for the provision of a standing fleet to protect commercial shipping in the Channel. This would subse-quently provide the precedent on which the crown developed the duty known as tunnage and poundage.[43]

Nor, in spite of the euphoria very obviously whipped up in England, did the political elite find much to celebrate in the summer of 1340. At the new parliament that assembled at Westminster on 12 July, the earls of

[37] Minot, Poems, 37.

[38] T. W. Fulton, The Sovereignty of the Sea (Edinburgh, 1911), 36–8; Rodger, Safeguard of the Sea, i, 77.

[39] E 36/204, fol.73. These were apparently supplied to commemorate the king's pilgrim-ages to Canterbury, Gloucester and Walsingham on his return from Brittany in Mar. 1343 (Murimuth, 135) and may in part have been thank-offerings for his safe return after an arduous sea crossing. The gift to Gloucester was offered at the high altar but later attached to the tomb of Edward II: Historia et Cartularium Monasterii Sancti Petri Gloucestriae, ed. W. H. Hart, 3 vols (RS, 1863–7), i, 47–8.

[40] Age of Chivalry, no. 664.

[41] Barnie, War in Medieval English Society, 47.

[42] C 76/15, m. 7.

[43] HBC, 559 n. 5; C 76/15, m. 3; W. M. Ormrod, 'The Origins of Tunnage and Poundage: Parliament and the Estate of Merchants in the Fourteenth Century', Parliamentary History, xxviii (2009), 210–13.

Arundel, Huntingdon and Gloucester communicated the contents of an open letter from the king. The news was double-edged. On the one hand, divine grace had brought him victory over his enemies at Sluys. On the other, he was now once more in desperate need of funds to carry through the impending land campaign. The king's letter very deliberately stressed the peril that might threaten all his English subjects if he could not continue with his great business. Parliament was therefore forced to acknowledge a state of emergency and to offer some form of financial assistance. But with the ninth only recently put into commission, the lords and commons were extremely reluctant to concede another direct tax. Instead, after a week of frantic discussion, they resorted to the idea of a forced loan. The king might have 20,000 sacks of wool from the home market, purchased on credit and repayable, during 1341–2, out of the proceeds of the second year of the ninth.[44] To many, the recent naval victory had become just another excuse for prolonging the war and the crippling level of taxation that sustained it.

Edward III had been close to the centre of action aboard ship at Sluys, and he was left with quite a significant wound in his leg. Convalescence took a fortnight, and it was not until mid-July that the king was well enough to travel on to Ghent to be reunited with Queen Philippa. In March 1340, while her husband was away in England, Philippa had given birth to another son, John. The dowager countess of Pembroke joined the queen shortly afterwards, probably with the intention of resuming her role as mistress of the royal children.[45] But with preparations now in full swing for the long-awaited allied attack on Tournai, the royal couple took the reluctant decision to send the Princesses Isabella and Joan and their two infant brothers back to England. The king could not afford the risk of losing his children to a possible Valois attack on Flanders, nor did he wish them to be caught up as hostages for the debts owed to his clamouring allies.[46] It would be another four months before Edward saw any of his children again.

The reunion of the king and queen was equally short-lived, for urgent efforts had now to be made regarding the promised march on Tournai. Edward's forces were divided in two. The first group, led by Robert of Artois, crossed into Artois but was intercepted by the duke of Burgundy on 26 July, and only a small contingent was left to join up in due course with Edward's main army. The second force, commanded by the king, proceeded through Hainault to Chin, on the banks of the Scheldt a few

---

[44] *PROME*, iv, 282–4; C 76/15, mm. 16–13. The battle of Sluys had already been announced in England on 28 June and was alluded to at the opening of parliament, so the king's letter did not actually break the news of the recent victory. Avesbury, 312–14; *CLBL*, F, 54; *PROME*, iv, 281.

[45] C 76/15, m. 9.

[46] Ormrod, 'Royal Nursery', 404–5.

miles from Tournai. Once fully assembled, and including the contingents
of the dukes of Brabant and Guelders, the margrave of Juliers, the count
of Hainault and the Flemish towns, this army would amount to as many
as 8,000 men-at-arms and 18,000 infantry.[47] At last, it seemed, Edward
had the military resources that would be a proper match for the French
and deliver the decisive outcome he had so passionately promised to his
people at home.

The siege of Tournai had no immediate strategic purpose for Edward,
and was undertaken principally for the benefit of his Flemish allies. As at
Berwick in 1333, however, Edward hoped that the siege would require
enemy forces to come to the relief of the town and thus present him with
an opportunity for open battle. Philip VI's very considerable army – some
21,000 men-at-arms, together with a much smaller group of infantry –
assembled at Arras in Artois. The moment of engagement having apparently arrived, Edward served his formal challenge to 'Philip of Valois' on
26 July. Edward was the rightful king of France and lord of Flanders, and
was now entering into his inheritance. As good Christians, the two men
should seek ways to avoid unnecessary loss of life. They might agree to
hand-to-hand combat or to an engagement between a hundred hand-
picked men on each side. If this offer was resisted, Edward would expect
Philip's entire force to make itself available for open battle before Tournai
within ten days.[48] The new emphasis on Edward's title as king of France
caused some commentators considerably to embellish the terms of this
challenge. It was said that the English king also proposed a series of tests
to prove which man had the true title to the throne of the house of Capet.
Philip and he could expose themselves to lions, which would never eat a
true king. Rather less riskily, they might have a healing contest to see which
of them was truly invested with the ability to touch for scrofula.[49] In the
latter case at least, there is a hint of authenticity: Edward had already
performed healing ceremonies in the Empire and Flanders, and was soon
to be seen imposing his miraculous powers on the French, too.[50] Such
high-flown assertions of dynastic right prompted a predictably hostile
response. On 30 July Philip VI wrote that he was the true king of France
and that both Edward and the Flemings were in unlawful revolt against
their liege lord.[51] Just as the prescriptions of just war required Edward to

[47] Rogers, *War Cruel and Sharp*, 204.

[48] SC 1/37/135, printed in *Foedera*, II.ii, 1131 and partly translated in *Wars of Edward III*,
91–2. The text of the challenge circulated widely in England: *CLBL, F*, 54; Murimuth,
110–11; Avesbury, 314–15; *Chron. Lanercost*, 334–5. For knowledge of it in France see *Grandes
Chroniques*, ix, 198–200.

[49] *Calendar of State Papers, Venice*, i (London, 1864), no. 25.

[50] Ormrod, 'Personal Religion', 862–3.

[51] *Grandes Chroniques*, ix, 200–2; Avesbury, 315–16; *Scalacronica*, 130–1; *Wars of Edward III*,
92–3.

present the quarrel as one for the recovery of dynastic title, so Philip's own case remained firmly embedded in his feudal rights as suzerain of Aquitaine and Flanders.

Edward had not even bothered to wait for Philip's reply. Crossing the Scheldt, he had advanced immediately to Tournai, where he formally commenced the siege on 1 August. The coalition army prepared for the long haul. For some weeks it contented itself with a series of *chevauchées* into the surrounding countryside. But with conditions in the camp deteriorating fast and the allies increasingly restive, Edward began to apply increased pressure on the townsmen to submit. Early in September Philip moved his army to Bouvines, only a few miles away. The French king was in no mood to talk. But his advisers advocated caution. In a powerful display of family obligation, Philip sent his sister, Jeanne, the dowager countess of Hainault, to negotiate with her English son-in-law. Under the combined pressure of the countess's blandishments and the duke of Brabant's threats of withdrawal, Edward agreed to discussions for a truce, and terms were settled at Esplechin on 25 September.[52] On 26 September Edward and his men broke camp and made their way back to Ghent, where they celebrated their safe return with the usual feasts and tournaments. Both sides tried to make the best of the recent campaign, but without a decisive engagement it continued to be uncertain as to which might be said to have carried the honour of the day.[53]

The truce of Esplechin was in many respects the saving of Edward III. It was explicitly designed not to prejudice the existing claims, alliances and conquests of any party, and permitted the Anglo-Flemish agreement to remain in force. It also applied throughout the current theatres of war. The Scots were therefore forced to give up plans to lay siege to the English garrison at Stirling, and Philip VI was required to call off a large army about to descend on Gascony. One important crumb of solace was the agreement that the earls of Salisbury and Suffolk be allowed to return to England on parole to negotiate their ransoms; in addition to relieving his conscience, this provided Edward with the prospect of a few more supportive voices in his domestic councils.[54] Above all, the nine-month truce would offer the king the opportunity to resolve some of his financial problems at home, to regroup his allies on the continent and to refocus the war that would inevitably open up again in the following June.

[52] Le Bel, i, 202–5; *Foedera*, II.ii, 1135–7; K. DeVries, 'Contemporary Views of Edward III's Failure at the Siege of Tournai, 1340', *Nottingham Medieval Studies*, xxxix (1995), 70–105. For the proclamation of the truce in England, see E 403/314, 16 Oct. 1340.

[53] Le Bel, i, 208–9.

[54] BL, MS Cotton Faustina B. V, fol. 88. Salisbury, along with Arundel, Gloucester and others, was expected to meet with the king's envoys in council at Westminster on 14 Nov. 1340: *CCR 1339–41*, 640.

None of these considerations, however, was sufficient to persuade Edward III that the cessation of hostilities had done anything other than confound his declared purpose of seeking satisfaction against Philip of Valois. Holed up at Ghent, the king began to look about him for something or someone to blame.[55] The most ready explanation lay in the dramatic failure of the ninth and the levy of wool. The assignments made on the ninth suggest that the home council expected the first year of this tax to yield between £80,000 and £100,000. By the end of 1340, however, barely £15,000 had actually been collected. Still more dramatic was the shortfall from the wool prise, which raised fewer than 1,000 of the promised 20,000 sacks.[56]

This sudden and unexpected collapse of the usually mighty English fiscal machine certainly required some explanation. The failure of the two levies must primarily be ascribed to widespread popular resistance. The assessments carried out in preparation for the ninth evoked widespread claims of poverty as a result of poor harvests, cattle murrains, and the existing pressures of purveyance and taxation. Even if the English economy was not entirely exhausted, taxpayers had clearly reached the limits of tolerance.[57] The administration of the ninth was also badly bungled. In the July parliament it was agreed that local commissioners should be required to take the highest possible price for wool, corn and animals put up for sale in markets, and that an element of compulsion might be used to force consumers to purchase such expensive commodities.[58] This created the impression of a double tax, and was quickly and openly condemned in the country. The failure of the wool prise was almost as instant. The producers were guaranteed comparatively low valuations of their wool. And since the whole of the forced loan was offset against the second year of the ninth, the failure of that tax during the summer of 1340 inevitably destroyed public confidence in the crown's ability to repay its debts the following year. The growing public discontent that had already been evident in 1339 manifested itself in 1340 in what amounted to a dramatic tax strike. This probably also explains the rumours that now began to circulate about a new wave of lawlessness in the land.[59] One chronicler claimed that the king was told by his ministers in 1340 that they dared raise no more money for fear of an uprising. And

[55] Le Bel, i, 208–9; Murimuth, 116; Baker, 71–2; Froissart, ii, 82–4.

[56] Fryde, 'Edward III's War Finance', ii, 539–63.

[57] A. R. H. Baker, 'Evidence in the "Nonarum Inquisitiones" of Contracting Arable Lands in England during the Early Fourteenth Century', *EcHR*, 2nd series, xix (1966), 518–32. Baker's work, which relied only on selected records of the ninth, is extended and revised by M. R. Livingstone, 'The Nonae: The Records of the Taxation of the Ninth in England, 1340–41' (Queen's University Belfast PhD thesis, 2003), 362–82 and Map 8.1.

[58] *PROME*, iv, 281–2.

[59] BL, MS Cotton Faustina B. V, fol. 89v; *Chron. Meaux*, ii, 387; Knighton, 7.

the *Song against the King's Taxes* was in no doubt that, should a demagogue emerge, the people would revolt.[60]

From the king's point of view, however, the temporary collapse of the tax system was all about one thing: the inefficiency of his ministers. During and after the July parliament the Stratford brothers and Roger Northburgh wrote twice to the king to assure him of a high return from the new subsidies.[61] They certainly worked hard to make the new system work. In late August, for example, the home administration tried to secure additional voluntary contributions to the war effort from the normally exempt palatinates of Chester and Durham.[62] It also, if belatedly, identified the problems raised by the attempts to force sales of the ninth; ironically, when the government eased its insistence on high prices in January 1341 it would manage to generate a further £50,000 towards the first year of the ninth.[63] On the other hand, there is a distinct air of unreality about Stratford's belief in his ability to balance the books. In an increasingly frantic attempt to shore up its credibility, the council undertook a spate of special meetings with the customs collectors and the receivers of the ninth in September and early October 1340.[64] If Stratford and his associates were really at fault, it had to do less with any obvious negligence of duty and more with their increasingly desperate efforts to delay the wrath that would fall once they finally admitted that the ninth and forced loan were indeed doomed.

Edward's attempts to force just such an admission began even before the truce of Esplechin. In early September the king sent Robert Askby and Richard Winkley home to treat with the council, calling on the earl of Arundel and others to make their way to Westminster with all speed for what no doubt proved rather fractious discussions.[65] If this initiative was meant to incite division and expose error, then it certainly seems to have been successful. A surviving anonymous letter sent from England to someone at the king's side in the same month expressed a distinctly dim

[60] *French Chronicle*, 83; *Anglo-Norman Political Songs*, 110, 113; Maddicott, 'English Peasantry', 348–9.

[61] *PROME*, iv, 290–1.

[62] C 76/15, m. 7. This appears not to have been successful in Cheshire, where there is clear evidence of tax grants in support of the earl (and thus of the king) only from 1346: Booth, *Financial Administration*, 118–19; T. Thornton, 'Taxing the King's Dominions: The Subject Territories of the English Crown in the Late Middle Ages', *Crises, Revolutions*, ed. Ormrod, Bonney and Bonney, 101–5. Attempts were made to raise the tax in Co. Durham, but seem to have been confounded by the reassertion of immunity by Bishop Hatfield in 1345: G. T. Lapsley, *The County Palatine of Durham* (Cambridge, Mass., 1924), 272–4; C. D. Liddy, 'The Politics of Privilege: Thomas Hatfield and the Palatinate of Durham, 1345–81', *Fourteenth Century England IV*, ed. Hamilton, 69.

[63] Fryde, 'Edward III's War Finance', ii, 506, 534.

[64] *CCR 1339–41*, 624, 627, 635.

[65] Ibid., 621.

view of the way in which the regency administration was running the realm and suggested that the time had come for a change of ministers.[66] The well-informed *French Chronicle of London* goes much further, claiming that an unnamed member of the home government decided to expose his fellow councillors to the king as 'false traitors'.[67] For the first few weeks of October Edward contented himself with issuing blunt reminders that he, and not the archbishop, was in control. He overrode the audit of accounts incepted in parliament in order to have Paul Montefiori return to his side and raise further loans in the Low Countries. And in a particularly high-handed personal letter to the treasurer he required that the exchequer desist immediately from attempts to inquire into the finances of his privy purse and turn its attention instead to the proper job of providing him with cash.[68]

What finally drove Edward to take action against the home ministry was the threat posed to his own and others' personal security by the continued parlous state of his finances. The king had recently been required to offer the earls of Derby, Warwick and Northampton as hostages for new loans negotiated with the merchants of Brussels and Malines. On 12 November the Bardi and Peruzzi of Florence defaulted on their own promise to repay these loans, and the king had no choice but to deliver Derby and Warwick into custody. Edward regarded the imprisonment of his cousin and his friend as particular humiliations, and was deeply angered that his repeated demands to the regency administration for the repayment of the relevant debts had been treated with such disregard for the noblemen's safety.[69] The final blow came when, by the end of November, the king himself, together with the bishop of Lincoln, the earl of Northampton, William Kilsby and Geoffrey Scrope, were required to give personal surety for the loans previously taken from the increasingly restive citizens of Ghent.[70] In a very real and hazardous way, the king was now a prisoner of his own debt.

All Edward's frustration was now focused on Stratford. In letters of credence issued in mid-November for envoys sent to Avignon, the king claimed that the archbishop of Canterbury had deliberately refused to

[66] WAM, 12195; N. M. Fryde, 'Edward III's Removal of his Ministers and Judges', *BIHR*, xlviii (1975), 154; Haines, *Stratford*, 279–80.

[67] *French Chronicle*, 83.

[68] E 159/117, rots 16, 37, 45d. Montefiori's account of receipts and sales of wool and jewels in 1338–40 (E 101/624/28) includes a statement that, since the king had been forced to pay his allies, he had had nothing left with which to pay the wages of his own men or keep his household, and that Montefiori had been authorized 'by the council' to raise further loans.

[69] *Foedera*, II.ii, 1143; 1147; Fowler, *King's Lieutenant*, 35–6; Sumption, i, 360–3. For Edward's payment of the hostages' living expenses during their custody see E 101/127/40; E 101/389/8, m. 7.

[70] *CCR 1339–41*, 649.

supply him with funds, intending thus to effect his ruin and death.[71] Writing to the citizens of Ghent while he was at sea on 28 November, he declared in similar vein that 'certain of our false councillors and ministers in England have behaved in such a manner towards us that, unless we do something about it soon, we shall be unable to fulfil the agreements made between us and you'.[72] At the considerable risk of breaking his bond with his creditors and allies, and leaving behind the newly pregnant queen,[73] Edward departed secretly in the company of a small group of trusted followers: the earl of Northampton, John Darcy, William Kilsby, Reginald Cobham, Walter Mauny, Nicholas Cantilupe and John and Giles Beauchamp. Taking ship from Sluys, this little company spent two days at sea before moving up the Thames, arriving unannounced at the watergate of the Tower of London at midnight on 30 November.[74]

The following morning, 1 December, Edward III began what was to be the most far-reaching and ruthless purge of government conducted in his long reign. Robert Stratford and Roger Northburgh were summarily dismissed as chancellor and treasurer; Sir John Stonor, chief justice of common pleas, and his four fellow justices, Richard Willoughby, John Inge, William Shareshull and John Shardlow, were placed under arrest. Sir Thomas Wake, one of the members of the regency council, together with the constable of the Tower, Sir Nicholas de la Beche, and three of the most prominent English merchant financiers, John Pulteney and William and Richard de la Pole, were all similarly imprisoned at the king's pleasure. A number of senior clerks in the chancery and exchequer were put out of office. In a striking reference to the Walton Ordinances, the exchequer was ordered to make an immediate and comprehensive inquiry into 'all manner of payments and assignments made by you since our first crossing into Brabant'.[75] All receipts from taxation currently in the hands of collectors were to be delivered not to the exchequer but to William Edington, one of the receivers of the ninth, who had evidently been appointed to organize an extraordinary treasury at the Tower of London appointed for the king's exclusive use.[76] Edward III was now intent not simply on reasserting his authority over domestic government but, very deliberately and systematically, on demonizing the Stratford ministry for its failure of will.

[71] Déprez, *Préliminaires*, 350–2, 423–6.

[72] PRO 31/8/142, fols 303–303v; Fryde, 'Edward III's Removal', 154; Haines, *Stratford*, 280.

[73] Philippa was not required to stand surety for her husband, but subsequently returned to England and was at Kings Langley by Feb. 1341.

[74] Murimuth, 116–17; *Foedera*, II.ii, 1141.

[75] E 159/117, rot. 39. Expenses were allowed for three weeks' work in drawing up the required report: E 403/314, 20 Dec. 1340. The outcome is, however, undocumented.

[76] 'The Register of Simon Montacute', *Ely Diocesan Remembrancer 1891* (Ely, 1891), 543, 555.

The search for scapegoats was not confined to Westminster. Over the following weeks Edward, allegedly egged on by the invidious influence of Kilsby,[77] carried out a selective sweep of local officials, replacing some of the customs collectors, about half the sheriffs and all of the coroners and escheators.[78] The earl of Salisbury was charged to arrest the erstwhile courtier John Molyns for his alleged betrayals of trust, and the king himself led a party to St Albans Abbey to seize Molyns's liquid wealth. The disgraced man's house at Ditton (Buckinghamshire) was immediately seized into the king's hands and for some years became one of Edward's regular haunts.[79] Edward III wrote to sheriffs and other local officials, as well as to 'the magnates and others of the community of England', announcing his intention to hold a general inquiry into the state of domestic government and ordering proclamation that all those wishing to complain against the oppressions of royal agents should send their bills to officers whom the king would appoint specifically for the task.[80] On 10 December general commissions of oyer and terminer were issued to a group of magnates, senior lawyers and substantial gentry for the purpose of hearing these complaints; the inclusion in these commissions of prominent courtiers and others soon to be marked out as champions of the king's cause – William Kilsby, Nicholas Cantilupe, Reginald Cobham, John Beauchamp, Robert Parving and Robert Bourchier – indicates Edward's very active involvement in the nominations.[81] A couple of weeks later, the king issued letters patent under the privy seal, again assuring his subjects of the firmness of his purpose in pursuing corrupt ministers. No one found guilty would be returned to office. In appropriate cases, officials would be taken around from county to county in order to ensure that everyone had an opportunity to lay charges against them.[82] A public example was made of Sir Richard Willoughby, the former chief justice of the king's bench, who was now condemned for perverting and selling the laws 'as if they were oxen or

---

[77] *French Chronicle*, 88. See also Murimuth, 117–18.

[78] Tout, *Chapters*, iii, 122 n. 3; S. T. Gibson, 'The Escheatries, 1327–41', *EHR*, xxxvi (1921), 218–25; R. L. Baker, *The English Customs Service, 1307–1343: A Study of Medieval Administration* (Philadelphia, 1961), 60–7; Fryde, 'Edward III's Removal', 156–7. On 1 Dec. Edward had ordered a list of all those who had been collectors and controllers of customs since the beginning of the reign: E 159/117, rot. 39d.

[79] *CPR 1340–3*, 83, 104; *French Chronicle*, 84; Fryde, 'Robber Baron', 201–2; *SCCKB*, vi, no. 84.

[80] CUL, MS Dd.9.38, fols 107–8; *CLBL, F*, 58; E 403/314, 6 Dec. 1340; Fryde, 'Edward III's Removal', 149; J. R. Maddicott, 'The County Community and the Making of Public Opinion in Fourteenth-Century England' *TRHS*, 5th series, xxviii (1978), 34–5.

[81] CUL, MS Dd.9.38, fols 108–9; *CPR 1340–3*, 111–12; W. R. Jones, '*Rex et ministri*: English Local Government and the Crisis of 1341', *JBS*, xiii[1] (1973), 4. See also the ensuing royal mandate for the payment of the justices' wages: *SCCKB*, v, cxxxviii.

[82] SC 1/62/85, partly translated in Maddicott, 'Parliament and the Constituencies', 85.

cows' and taken to Colchester to answer accusations brought against him by the people of Essex.[83]

It was a commonplace of medieval politics that kings returning from lengthy stays abroad made gestures of good intent by dismissing corrupt officials and taking an interest in the better maintenance of public order. Had Edward III confined himself to the disgrace of the judges and the selective investigation of some of the more notorious shire officials, there is every chance that he might have kept the co-operation of Stratford and even managed to regain some credibility among his hard-pressed subjects. In a few cases, the king was clearly prepared to admit that he had acted in haste and error. In particular, Roger Northburgh and Thomas Wake seem rapidly to have been reconciled with the king and restored to his counsels. But the extraordinary powers granted to the local commissions of inquiry excited much anxiety in the provinces. The tribunals were to investigate all alienations and infringements of royal rights and receive indictments for crimes alleged as far back as 1307. Such unusually interventionist strategies cut across the traditions of self-regulation in the shires and, rather like threatened visitations of the eyre, were actively opposed by the local landed elites.[84] The king's over-reaction to the fiscal emergency had there-fore served only to undermine the very support on which he would need to rely for relief once parliament was called into session. From this perspective it may truly be said that the political crisis brought about in the parliament of April 1341 was almost entirely of Edward III's own making.

The king began his sustained attack on John Stratford by attempting to take proceedings against the latter's brother, Robert, bishop of Chichester. On 1 December, after losing office as chancellor, Robert was immediately charged with failing to deliver funds to the king on the continent, and was given until 6 January 1341 to prepare his case.[85] The younger Stratford resisted these pressures and argued his way out of the Tower, not just because he professed innocence of the charges but also, vitally, because he was a cleric and thus had immunity from prosecution before the king's council.[86] Edward extended the deadline for the disgraced chancellor's appearance, and even tried to have him arrested by the sheriff of Sussex. But all was in vain. The king eventually had to back down completely and

[83] *French Chronicle*, 87; *Year Books 14 and 15 Edward III*, ed. L. O. Pike (RS, 1889), xxi–xxviii, 258–63; J. R. Maddicott, *Law and Lordship: Royal Justices as Retainers in Thirteenth- and Fourteenth-Century England* (Past and Present supplement, iv, 1978), 43–4; D. Crook, 'The Disgrace of Sir Richard Willoughby, Chief Justice of King's Bench', *Nottingham Medieval Studies*, xlviii (2004), 15–36. John Shardelowe, disgraced justice of the king's bench, was similarly made liable to charges in Hertfordshire: Fryde, 'Edward III's Removal', 157.

[84] See pp. 259–60.

[85] C 49/46/11.

[86] Murimuth, 117.

withdraw his charges against Robert at the end of May 1341.[87] In one particular respect, however, the bishop of Chichester's claim of clerical immunity impacted directly on subsequent royal policy. When Edward installed his new senior ministers on 14–15 December 1340, he appointed not bishops or other senior clerics, as was usual, but lay members of the judiciary: Robert Bourchier as chancellor and Robert Parving as treasurer. In the circumstances of the moment, the fact that these men would not be able to hide behind the protection of the clerical order carried very real meaning. Edward was supposed to have remarked in offhand fashion that at last he had ministers who, should they prove false, could be hanged for their crimes.[88]

John Stratford held no formal post in government in December 1340, and any attempt to make him directly answerable for his actions was therefore doubly difficult. As president of the regency administration, he had almost certainly taken a general oath of loyalty to the king.[89] For the present, however, Edward avoided the clash of jurisdictions that might ensue if he tried to use this as a basis for formal proceedings in a lay court. Instead, the first attempt to bring Stratford to heel was deliberately designed to remind him of the liabilities he had created for the king. On 3 December Edward's agent Nicholas Cantilupe sought out the archbishop at Canterbury and advised him that he should make ready immediately to cross to Louvain and stand as pledge for the king's debts there. Stratford's response was respectful, but otherwise evasive.[90] The quarrel effectively went public when William Kilsby made a speech at the London Guildhall setting out the king's case against the archbishop, and perhaps intending to provoke the kind of 'common clamour' that was used around this time to condemn the lay judge, Richard Willoughby.[91] By Christmas, with the king still so obviously intent on proceeding against clerical ministers and extending his ire to the counties, the archbishop seems to have decided that the best means of defence was attack. In light of the provocation he had sustained over the previous three months, it is only surprising that he restrained himself so long.

On 29 December, from his seat of Canterbury, John Stratford began his public campaign as self-proclaimed champion of the people against the unlawful and unreasonable behaviour of the monarch. Sentences of excommunication were to be served on those who defamed or infringed

---

[87] Fryde, 'Edward III's Removal', 159–60; Ormrod, *Reign of Edward III*, 84–5.

[88] *French Chronicle*, 86.

[89] Harriss, *King, Parliament*, 263 n. 3 argues that the councillors' oath printed in Baldwin, *King's Council*, 351–2, is probably that taken by Stratford, Huntingdon and others appointed to the council on 27 May 1340.

[90] Haines, *Stratford*, 283–4.

[91] Murimuth, 117–18; T. F. T. Plucknett, 'The Origins of Impeachment', *TRHS*, 4th series, xxiv (1950), 64–8.

the rights of the clergy, broke the clause of Magna Carta guaranteeing rights against summary arrest, disturbed the peace or challenged the rights of the church of Canterbury. While Stratford explicitly excluded the king from liability to such measures, there was no doubt that he intended them principally to be used against the unsavoury Kilsby and other cronies who were perceived to have led Edward into his current and implacable position.[92] Then, on 1 January, John wrote to the king to protest his loyal service. The whole sorry story of the collapse of the war was attributable to Edward's neglect of good advice. In behaving like the biblical King Rehoboam and relying on the counsels of fickle, selfish and scheming individuals, Edward had ended up behaving in precisely the same way as his father, and 'what happened to him for that cause, you, sire, know well'.[93] This was the closest that anyone ever came in the reign to citing a precedent for deposition. While Stratford was careful to couch his criticism in the language of loyal opposition, he must surely have understood the way in which this reference would fall on royal ears. On 4 January, the king's henchman Ralph Stafford served a formal summons on the archbishop to appear before the council at London. John now decided to refuse the order not on the basis of clerical privilege, like his brother, but in terms of his status as a peer of the realm. His argument, which drew very obviously on his long experience in the arduous politics of the 1320s, was that the secular and spiritual lords of the realm ought only to answer charges brought against them by the king when they had the opportunity to be heard before their peers in full parliament.[94] Edward himself had held firm to that principle in the condemnation of Roger Mortimer. It was now time once again for it to be asserted as a great bulwark against the arbitrary will of kings.

Such a high-handed affront served only, of course, to eliminate any remaining vestiges of sympathy that the king might have for his erstwhile first minister. Undeterred by Stratford's stinging attack, Edward kept up a powerful show of courtly spectacle by hosting tournaments over Christmas, Candlemas and Shrovetide at Reading, Kings Langley and Norwich.[95] In mid-February the king distributed to all of the bishops a formal statement of his grievances against the archbishop.[96] The document, dubbed a *libellus famosus* ('infamous libel') by the infuriated Stratford, set out a long account of the early years of the reign and the opening of the war in 1337. Throughout that time, the king argued, the archbishop had constantly

<hr/>

[92] For Edward's countermands, see *Foedera*, II.ii, 1147, 1151–2.

[93] *Foedera*, II.ii, 1143; Avesbury, 324–9; *EHD*, iv, 72–3. The biblical references are to I Kings 12: 1–19.

[94] Haines, *Stratford*, 290.

[95] The Langley event was in honour of a group of Gascons who had recently arrived at court. E 101/388/11; Baker, 73; Vale, *Edward III and Chivalry*, 173.

[96] *Foedera*, II.ii, 1147–8; Avesbury, 330–6; *Anglia Sacra*, i, 23–7.

encouraged him in his enterprises and promised him the resources with which to fight them. Yet when it had been brought to the sticking point, Stratford's will had been found wanting. Edward declared himself without personal malice and ready to guarantee the archbishop's personal safety. Nevertheless, the document concluded, the king was determined to deal decisively with an adviser whose actions had been to the general detriment of king and people. The *libellus* was attributed by some contemporaries to Adam Orleton, on the basis of his earlier rivalry with Stratford over the archbishopric of Canterbury. A more likely candidate, perhaps, is William Kilsby, not only because of his blatant animosity towards the domestic administration at large but also because he had recently set himself directly at odds with the English ecclesiastical hierarchy by challenging William Zouche for the vacant archbishopric of York.[97] Regardless of who turned the phrases, though, there can be little doubt that the substance and temper of the text were determined directly by the king.

The essence of Stratford's response was published viva voce at Canterbury and in outline letters sent to the bishops of Canterbury province in March.[98] The archbishop knew that he was on firm ground. He called into question the truth and legality of many of the king's charges and stressed the reasonableness of his request to be heard in full parliament. Edward's own position became all the more tenuous in his counterblast, which failed to respond to the points of law and merely resorted to a torrent of personal abuse.[99] It is hard, indeed, to understand why Edward could not see the trouble that he was storing up for himself through this vendetta. Presumably he felt that the inquiries now already begun into official corruption at Westminster and in the shires could not be carried forward unless he could also bring to account the man truly responsible for domestic government over most of the previous fifteen months. Objective observers may well have drawn the conclusion, however, that it was Edward, and not the archbishop, who was now behaving unreasonably and irresponsibly.

One important indication of Edward's general obstreperousness during the early weeks of 1341 was his attempt to delay the parliament for which Stratford so loudly called. It was not until 3 March that writs of summons were issued for an assembly to open at Westminster on 23 April.[100]

[97] Haines, *Stratford*, 292–3; *Fasti 1300–1541*, vi, 3, 6–7.

[98] *Anglia Sacra*, i, 27–36; Haines, *Stratford*, 309–10.

[99] *Foedera*, II.ii, 1154–5; *Anglia Sacra*, i, 36–8.

[100] The events of the following week are much contested as a result of the problem of reconciling the parliament roll (*PROME*, iv, 306–23), the Canterbury chronicle (*Anglia Sacra*, i, 38–41) and the London chronicle (*French Chronicle*, 90). This account broadly follows that provided in *PROME*, iv, 301–5, with some interventions from Haines, *Stratford*, 312–22. For other attempts to reconstruct the narrative, see G. Lapsley, 'Archbishop Stratford and the Parliamentary Crisis of 1341', *EHR*, xxx (1915), 6–18; B. Wilkinson, 'The Protest of the Earls of Arundel and Surrey in the Crisis of 1341', *EHR*, xlvi (1931), 177–93.

Edward must have intended this assembly not as an opportunity for Stratford to make his defence but for the crown to negotiate the collection of arrears on the ninth and speed up the collection dates for the second year of the tax.[101] But the arrival of the archbishop in the capital shortly after the opening of the session seriously disrupted such business. Edward's men, Ralph Stafford and John Darcy, were set at the door of Westminster Hall and instructed to inform Stratford that he could not enter parliament until he had answered a charge of non-payment of taxes outstanding against him in the exchequer. A major confrontation was now inevitable.

On 28 April matters reached a head. Stratford took up a position outside the doors of the Painted Chamber, clutching his pastoral staff and refusing to budge from the spot until he was admitted. Inside the chamber, the presence of controversial royal familiars with no right to sit as peers – Kilsby, Parving, Stafford and Darcy – provoked increasing outrage. It was left to the veteran John de Warenne, earl of Surrey, to challenge Edward III directly: 'Sir king, how goes this parliament? Parliaments were not wont to be like this. For here those who should be foremost are shut out, while there sit other men of low rank who have no business to be here.'[102] The earl of Arundel followed, requesting explicitly that the archbishop be allowed into the king's presence and given opportunity to answer the charges against him. If Stratford's fourteenth-century biography is to be believed, even the king's friends Northampton and Salisbury added their voices to the clamour.[103] Faced with such pressure, Edward could no longer resist. Stratford was given licence to enter and sit among his peers. A set of thirty-two charges was then read out before the lords and repeated two days later before the commons.

From the king's point of view the admission of the archbishop was simply another means of defaming and punishing his disgraced ministers. For almost a week, Edward therefore maintained the pressure for a summary trial. On 1 May a special committee was appointed to give expert opinion on Stratford's request for a hearing before a full parliament. But the next day, the king's men once more shouted down the archbishop when he attempted to reiterate his demand. Meanwhile, frantic attempts were being made behind the scenes to persuade Edward that it was not in his interests to pursue the matter. In a moment of rare scruple, the king had decided to honour a statute granted in March 1340 and refrain from seizing the episcopal estates of the Stratford brothers and of Roger Northburgh.[104] This made it rather easier for the prelates to

[101] *PROME*, iv, 301–2, 307–8.
[102] *French Chronicle*, 90.
[103] *Anglia Sacra*, i, 40.
[104] *SR*, i, 294.

reconcile themselves to the policy of compromise. It seems likely that some
of Edward's close friends in the lords, men such as Richard Bury and
William Montagu, now offered themselves as go-betweens and persuaded
the rival parties that it was in the public interest for them to set aside their
differences and work together for the deliverance of the realm. On 3 May,
'our lord the king came into the Painted Chamber with the archbishop of
Canterbury and the other prelates, great men and commons; and the said
archbishop humbled himself to our lord the king, requesting his good
lordship and benevolence; and our lord the king received him to his good
lordship, for which the prelates and other great men thanked him'.[105] At
the very last moment, the considerable embarrassment that might befall
from open conflict between the monarch and the archbishop of
Canterbury had been miraculously averted.

The quarrel between Edward III and John Stratford in the winter and
spring of 1340–1 was fundamentally a clash of personalities. The king was
determined to stretch to breaking point the absolute loyalty required of
those entrusted to run the realm on his behalf. The archbishop, meanwhile, was all too eager to prove his worthiness as a successor of Becket
and take up the role of martyr for the liberties of the Church. The public
ceremony performed by the two men on 3 May barely disguised the very
obvious sense of distrust that remained between them. It also failed to
resolve important issues of principle exposed by the recent row. Stratford
insisted that he have the right to clear himself of any slander contained in
the king's thirty-two articles, and a group of lords was assigned to act as
compurgators and deal with this business outside parliament.[106] Another
committee, led by Stratford's own brother and nephew and the earls of
Arundel, Salisbury, Huntingdon and Suffolk, was set up to consider the
legal issues raised by the archbishop's recent stand. It was on their recom-
mendation that, at the end of the session, the king issued a statute
declaring that 'the peers of the land', including those acting as the king's
ministers, 'should not be arrested or brought to judgment except in parliament and by their peers'.[107] In response to one of the common petitions,
the crown also offered a much more radical promise as to the liability of
its ministers to prosecution. The chancellor, treasurer and judges, as well
as the keeper of the privy seal and the senior staff of the royal household,
would in future be sworn in parliament. In every subsequent assembly, the
king would suspend their powers and make them answer publicly for their

---

[105] *PROME*, iv, 309.

[106] Ibid., iv, 303, 317; Murimuth, 120. The committee of compurgators comprised
Bishops Bury and Wyvil and the earls of Northampton, Arundel, Warwick (*in absentia*) and
Salisbury.

[107] *PROME*, iv, 308–9, 320; *SR*, i, 295. The remainder of the advisory committee
comprised Bishops Grandisson and Wyvil and Lords Wake, Percy, Neville and Basset.

actions, with any necessary punishment being meted out by judgment of their peers.[108] There can be no doubt that these two striking statements represented a public apology for the arbitrary manner in which Edward had attempted to proceed against the ministers dismissed the previous November. Stratford's striking ability to articulate his case in a manner that seemed relevant to the peers as well as to the other interest groups represented in parliament had, for a brief moment, united the polity against the king's blatant and disgraceful abuse of authority.[109] What had begun as a private quarrel between king and archbishop had turned, in effect, into a public debate on the ways in which the crown itself might be brought to account for its actions. The implications both for the future conduct of war and for the government of the realm were momentous.

In modern times the crisis of 1341 developed a reputation as one of the great set pieces of English constitutional history. The issues of high principle surrounding the rights of peers and the accountability of royal ministers seemed to mark great milestones on the long road to limited monarchy and parliamentary sovereignty.[110] Even after the Whig model of constitutional development collapsed in the mid-twentieth century, historians remained convinced that Edward III's quarrel with Stratford was a defining moment in his career. Appreciating that his own actions had damaged the interests of the crown and the viability of his wars, the king learned the lesson and changed his ways, emerging in the 1340s with a more considered military policy and a zealous commitment to the politics of consensus.[111] The parliament of 1341 therefore remains deeply embedded in the historical imagination as the moment when Edward III finally put aside childish things and became a man.

Contemporaries, who lacked the benefits of hindsight, were inevitably rather less certain about the general benefits that would accrue from the confrontation between king and archbishop. The regime that emerged in the 1340s was successful less because it represented a radically new approach and more because it held firmly to the two guiding principles of the 1330s: that the king should guarantee the good governance, quiet and prosperity of the realm; and that monarchy and people remained committed to their compact to pursue Edward's rights against his enemies abroad. In general, Edward's subjects were much more interested in re-establishing such a perceived normality than they were in championing

---

[108] *PROME*, iv, 304, 312, 320–1; *SR*, i, 296.

[109] The *gravamina* of the convocation of Canterbury were also enrolled on the parliament roll of 1341 and apparently answered in the course of the assembly: *PROME*, iv, 312–16.

[110] The classic statement is that of W. Stubbs, *The Constitutional History of England*, 4th edn, 3 vols (Oxford, 1906), ii, 409–10.

[111] Thus McKisack, *Fourteenth Century*, 270–1.

the rights of the archbishop of Canterbury. The precise legal and constitutional details on which Stratford took his stand had fleeting relevance for
the wider elite. Within a few months, indeed, the brief furore of the April
parliament seemed to have collapsed into the irrelevance of hot air.

The instinctive preference for a return to a perceived normality first
revealed itself in the new accommodation worked out between crown and
commons over the vexed issues of justice and finance. The overbearing
nature of the special inquiries launched in the counties in December 1340
had soon become apparent for, despite numerous allegations against royal
purveyors and tax collectors, very few of the senior officers of local
government were actually found to have been guilty of corrupt and
oppressive behaviour against the king's subjects.[112] In any case, the king's
thirst for vengeance was rapidly assuaged. When Edward intervened
personally in the charges of extortion brought against John Coggeshall,
sheriff of Essex, it was not with the intention of asserting his role as judge;
instead he saw it as an opportunity for a well-timed act of clemency.[113] By
the time the parliament of April 1341 opened, Edward had already indicated his willingness to accept communal fines in lieu of further proceedings in the counties, though only at rates fixed well above the amounts
charged for a standard fifteenths and tenths.[114] Faced with such blatant
attempts to force illicit taxes, the commons tried to insist that no one could
be deemed liable unless they had been present at their county courts when
the business was discussed and approved.[115] In the face of enormous pressure, the king was forced to agree at the end of parliament to suspend all
but the basic criminal functions of the special commissions.[116] For the
landed and ministerial classes in the provinces, this represented perhaps
the most immediately meaningful political gain made in the assembly. It
offered the prospect of a return to the system of locally supervised peace-
keeping that had been in place since 1338. It also amounted to a public
apology for the manner in which the king had exposed the ministerial
classes to public vilification and provided a powerful vindication of their
loyalty to the regime.

This concession also allowed Edward III to carry off what proved the
most urgent element of his political recovery in 1341: the reordering of
public finance. The lords and commons had been forcefully reminded at

---

[112] Jones, 'Rex et ministri', 1–20; W. R. Jones, 'Keeping the Peace: English Society, Local
Government, and the Commissions of 1341–44', American Journal of Legal History, xviii
(1974), 307–20; Maddicott, 'English Peasantry', 335–46.

[113] C 49/46/13. Coggeshall was made sheriff again in 1343.

[114] CFR 1337–47, 215; S. L. Waugh, England in the Reign of Edward III (Cambridge, 1991),
216.

[115] For the resulting difficulties in the collection of these fines see Bryant, 'Financial
Dealings', 762–3; Ormrod, Reign of Edward III, 244 n. 92.

[116] PROME, iv, 311–12, 323; CCR 1341–3, 143; Hughes, Constitutional Tendencies, 169–70.

the start of the assembly of the public commitment to the war made by parliament in 1337 and of the king's continued firm intention to 'conquer his rights'.[117] The time had now come to abandon the tax strike and acknowledge the need for further subsidies. With the ninth still in commission and a state of truce prevailing, there could be no question of Edward demanding additional direct taxes. Such, indeed, was public sensitivity on such matters that the crown chose also to refrain from demanding a further extension of the *maltolt* that was due to run out in May. Where the king did succeed, however, was in persuading the assembly that the ninth and the forced loan had to be replaced with some more efficient and productive source of revenue. The commons now agreed that, although the first year of the ninth would stand, the second would be commuted to a direct tax levied in wool, on the model of the successful subsidy of 1338.[118] The wool prise of 1340 would be cancelled, and anything already collected towards it would be allocated to the new tax. The new subsidy in wool was a commanding statement of the commons' sense of obligation to the war undertaken on their behalf and their commitment, for better or worse, to the fiscal policies that sustained it.

This new accommodation also marked the beginning of a remarkable transformation in Edward III's financial fortunes. The total figure on which the commons agreed for the tax in wool – 30,000 sacks – was probably selected because it mirrored the earlier forced loan of wool in 1337. On this occasion, however, there was no expectation that providers would be compensated: the new levy was to be treated as a direct tax. The county elites were reconciled to the idea because the crown agreed a formula for the fair redistribution of the total that took into account both the current county quotas for fifteenths and tenths and the relative values of wool from different regions of the country.[119] The collectors certainly faced their fair share of opposition when they began to roll out the new measure in the localities; from the perspective of the taxpayer, after all, the new scheme really amounted to another of the much-despised prises taken in the previous year.[120] In the end, however, nearly 90 per cent of this levy was raised, representing wool with a domestic market value of some £126,000. Any overall evaluation of the parliament of 1341 has to take into account not only the dramatic vocalization of opposition to the king's management of the war but also the contrary and surprising fact that the assembly consented to what proved the single heaviest tax raised in

---

[117] *PROME*, iv, 307–8.

[118] See p. 115.

[119] *PROME*, 303–4, 317–19; *SR*, i, 297–8.

[120] Maddicott, 'County Community', 39; Maddicott, 'Parliament and the Constituencies', 83; Ormrod, *Reign of Edward III*, 162. Barnes, 'Taxation of Wool', 159–60, elides the evidence of resistance to the wool prise and the wool tax.

England in the entire period between the beginning of the thirteenth and the end of the fifteenth century.[121]

This success helped, in turn, to restore some level of public confidence in the king's credit. William de la Pole and Reginald Conduit, the leaders of the 1337 wool scheme, were subjected to trial before the council on charges of embezzlement in the summer of 1341, and de la Pole remained in prison until May 1342. Already in 1340, however, a new group of English financiers, led by figures such as Walter Chiriton of London, John Goldbeter of York and John Wesenham of Lynn, had indicated its willingness to advance large loans on the basis of the wool prise. The new tax offered the opportunity to revive those credit arrangements. During the summer of 1341 the king sold large parcels of wool, often in advance of collection, to Chiriton and his associates. The temporary cessation of the *maltolt*, coupled with a brief embargo on wool exports, created expectations of high profits from sales on the continent, and the cartels were therefore prepared to pay the king at least twice the domestic market value of the goods received. In theory at least this allowed Edward to pay off the new loans raised from the merchants and to reschedule at least some of the most urgent outstanding debts owed to the Italian bankers, the Flemish merchants and the Netherlandish allies.[122] The crisis of royal finance was far from over. From the perspective of his English subjects, there were still major grievances over the king's continued refusal to honour the controversial Dordrecht bonds of 1338.[123] But with significant sources of revenue once more pouring in, Edward was soon restored to ebullient mood. By the late spring of 1341 he was insisting once again that all public expenditure had to be authorized by him in person.[124] Here was every sign of a quick and confident return to the principles of the Walton Ordinances and the royal priorities that had governed the regime since 1338.

There remained the delicate matter of winning back the confidence of the nobility. If Edward was to re-engage Philip of Valois, it was imperative that he mobilize the natural commanders of his army. Under the protection of a series of short-term extensions to the truce of Esplechin, the English elite therefore set to the task of preparing for a major onslaught against France. On 8 July the king hosted a tournament at Kings Langley to mark

---

[121] Ormrod, 'Crown and the English Economy', 176–80; Ormrod, 'England in the Middle Ages', 28, 30. There were also some cash compositions amounting to a further £5,000.

[122] *CCR 1339–41*, 614–18; *CCR 1341–3*, 255–61; *CPR 1341–3*, 257, 259, 284, 290, etc; Fryde, *William de la Pole*, 155–6, 176–9.

[123] That Chiriton and his associates may have hoped to use some of their own profits to offset the Dordrecht bonds is suggested by the king's allegations that they were withholding money due to him over the winter of 1341–2: *CCR 1341–3*, 362–3.

[124] Harriss, *King, Parliament*, 304.

the queen's rising after the birth of their new child, Edmund.[125] The royal party then made its way back to the capital for a council of war. Elaborate plans were put in place for a new army of about 13,500 men, to be funded out of the proceeds of the wool tax and sent over to Flanders to prepare for a new invasion of France. Those who signed up to serve in person or at least to provide troops for this new enterprise included stalwarts of the earlier continental regime, such as the earls of Derby and Northampton, as well as the most powerful lay members of the regency councils of 1338–40, Arundel and Huntingdon.[126] The expedition was in fact called off in September. But the series of councils held throughout that month and into early October 1341, attended by Derby, Warwick, Northampton 'and many other magnates', provided an important opportunity for king and lords to affirm their commitment to the defence of the realm.[127] It was now agreed that Edward should direct his attention once more towards Scotland and lead a campaign in the north during the coming winter. This had the effect of winning back the sympathy of the leading northern lords, Wake, Percy and Neville.[128] By the early autumn of 1341, then, Edward III seems to have managed to persuade a good proportion of the high nobility that its interests were best served by active involvement in a continuing series of wars against the Scots and, when possible, the French.

On 1 October, Edward III ordered proclamations to be made throughout England to the effect that the recent statute regarding trial of peers and accountability of ministers was contrary to the customs of the realm and had been forced from him against the tradition of free consent. With the advice and assent of the 'earls, barons and other wise men of our realm', he had therefore exercised his rightful prerogative and annulled the legislation.[129] The king evidently had good legal grounds for taking this position. The new chancellor and treasurer, Bourchier and Parving, had raised misgivings in parliament about the restrictions placed by the statute on the king's traditional prerogative right to appoint and dismiss his own ministers.[130] The nervousness of those who had led the demands for Stratford's proper treatment was also palpable: the earl of Arundel was subsequently to ask the pope to assure Edward that he had never intended to speak either for or against the archbishop.[131] Edward's recent charm offensive had evidently convinced the majority of the king's councillors that the archbishop's case was lost. On 4 October Edward and Philippa rounded off this

[125] Shenton, 'Philippa's of Hainault's Churchings', 111.

[126] RDP, iv, 532; C 76/16, mm. 20, 17, 16, 14, 12; M. Prestwich, 'English Armies in the Early Stages of the Hundred Years War: A Scheme in 1341', BIHR, lvi (1983), 102–13.

[127] Murimuth, 121; E 101/389/12.

[128] Harriss, King, Parliament, 305. For the resulting campaign see pp. 247–8.

[129] SR, i, 295, 297.

[130] PROME, iv, 304, 317.

[131] CPL, iii, 8.

sequence of political manoeuvres by hosting a triumphant tournament at Westminster for the benefit of the nobles of the realm.[132]

The one figure who still remained very obviously excluded and alienated was John Stratford. The council of the province of Canterbury that Stratford convened at St Paul's on 19 October demonstrated very clearly his comparative isolation, even within the clerical establishment. Apart from the archbishop's brother and nephew, only six other bishops bothered to attend, and any attempts to reassert Stratford's moral superiority were effectively scotched by the crown's injunction against ordinances prejudicial to the king's prerogative.[133] Had Edward been allowed his way, it is quite likely that Stratford would have been left to weep the tears of humiliation. But it was unthinkable that the king should leave the realm without readmitting the highest prelate of the land to his rightful place as royal councillor. Accordingly, on 23 October, a solemn ceremony was held in the great hall of Westminster Palace, at which the king and Archbishop Stratford marked the formal end of their disagreement by exchanging the kiss of peace.[134] In the next parliament, held in 1343, Edward agreed as an act of good faith that his earlier accusations against the archbishop were without foundation and ordered all the documents associated with the case to be destroyed.[135] All three of the Stratfords were restored to their place in court and council, and John himself was promised the considerable sum of 5,000 marks for the service he had given during his time abroad with the king in 1338–9.[136] None of this, it may be supposed, amounted to much of a personal reconciliation. The archbishop, his brother and their nephew continued to be involved in councils of regency when the king left the country, but no member of the Stratford clan ever again held government office. Posterity may have preserved a strong image of Edward III as the great conciliator, whose instinct for political peace inspired in him a great generosity of spirit and a powerful gift for friendship. In the case of John Stratford, however, it is hard to resist the conclusion that even Edward knew the exquisite pleasure of a lasting grudge.

'Crisis? What crisis?'[137] Edward III shared the instinct of many a medieval and modern political leader in preferring to deny the chaos he had

---

[132] E 101/389/12.

[133] *Records of Convocation*, ed. G. Bray, 16 vols (Woodbridge, 2005–6), iii, 172–3; xix, 36–7 (misdated); *CCR 1341–3*, 335; Haines, *Stratford*, 449.

[134] Harriss, *King, Parliament*, 306–7, 521–2; Haines, *Stratford*, 322–3.

[135] *PROME*, iv, 338.

[136] E 403/332, 17 July 1344, 23 July 1344; etc.

[137] Words ascribed to Prime Minister James Callaghan by the *Sun* newspaper in Jan. 1979 as a comment on widespread disruption arising from strike action by the trade unions. Callaghan's actual words were, 'I don't think other people in the world would share the view that there is mounting chaos.' *Oxford Dictionary of Political Quotations*, ed. A. Jay, 3rd edn (Oxford, 2006), 272, 287.

imposed on the realm in 1339/40 rather than admit the brief humiliation into which he was driven in the spring of 1341. In this sense the *affaire Stratford* exposed some of the worst features of the king's character: his unreasonableness, his bullying, and his infuriating refusal to accept realities that did not suit him. Equally, however, it revealed much about his ability, through sheer force of personality, to turn imminent disaster into survival and recovery. The issues on which Stratford had made his stand failed to capture the imagination of the wider political community and allowed the king rapidly to outwit an otherwise formidable opponent. This is not to say that the parliament of 1341 did not leave a troubled legacy. The king's obvious slipperiness in extricating himself from statutory limitations bore some comparison with Edward II's controversial abolition of the Ordinances in 1322. In the country, there was widespread dismay both at the new pressures of the wool tax and at the king's decision in 1342 to renege on the deal over the judicial inquiries and re-launch his campaign against official corruption. Such assertiveness embodied Edward's continued refusal to display contrition and his general determination to press on with business as usual.

And yet, in spite of the abundant evidence of the king's determination to press on undaunted after the crisis of 1341, there still remains an important truth in the historical tradition that the quarrel with Stratford provided Edward with an object lesson in the arts of kingship. It gave him the unintended but welcome opportunity to display the munificence of his mercy through reconciliations and pardons. Apart from Stratford, the only victim of the purge of December 1340 against whom the king bore any lasting enmity was the financier William de la Pole.[138] The crisis also made the king understand the need to choose his enemies with rather more care. In his subsequent victimization of bishops and ministers – William Thorpe in 1350–1, John Grandisson in 1350–2 and Thomas Lisle in 1355–6 – Edward managed, in spite of some criticism, to emerge generally vindicated and affirmed. It was not until the very end of the reign, in the winter of 1376–7, that the arbitrary treatment of an episcopal minister, William Wykeham, again became the rallying point for more general political opposition to the crown.[139] For three decades after 1341, Edward III held firm to the tradition that his advisers should be free to offer frank and sometimes critical views without taking the risk that their words and deeds would be construed as acts of disloyalty or treachery.

Above all, Edward came to realize after 1341 just how much his escape from complete humiliation by Stratford had relied on the goodwill of the magnates. In spite of the anxieties that some of their number were prepared to voice at the start of parliament, most of the lords temporal

---

[138] Fryde, *Studies*, chap. xii.
[139] See pp. 379, 381–3, 568.

remained loyal, moderate and neutral throughout. As a consequence, there was never any suggestion that Edward III was forced into the temporary concessions of 1341 by the threat of aristocratic insurrection. All four of his immediate predecessors had faced such acts of coercion in their moments of crisis in 1215, 1258, 1297 and 1311, and his own minority regime had experienced the spectre of armed resistance during the winter of 1328–9. Had a figure such as the earl of Arundel taken on the leadership of such a revolt in 1341, the general restiveness reported among the king's ordinary subjects during the previous few years might yet have turned into wide-spread acts of popular rebellion. The sense of loyalty that Edward had cultivated among the old and new nobility in the 1330s bore its first sweet fruits in the spring and summer of 1341. A full and abundant harvest would, in due course, follow.

Chapter 9

BRITTANY AND BACK, 1341–1346

A king less proud and determined than Edward III might well have felt in 1341 that the only way forward in relation to France was a negotiated settlement. Surely there was business enough within the British Isles to occupy even such a mighty prince as he? There are certain signs, indeed, that Edward took seriously the need to prioritize his existing territories and commitments over and above the distraction of the crown of France. In March 1341 he was busy extending to Wales and, more emphatically, to Ireland the extraordinary measures he had previously attempted to impose in England: the dismissal of high-ranking ministers, assertive interventions in the appointment of local officials and general inquiries into administrative corruption.[1] In Ireland the regime headed up by the new lieutenant John Morice had the unenviable task of implementing Edward's controversial decision to resume control of all lands granted away to the Anglo-Irish elite since the accession of his father.[2] This simply served to provoke a political crisis of its own: the parliament held at Dublin and Kilkenny over the winter of 1341–2 drew up a long series of complaints about the king's management of the lordship, and Edward was forced to withdraw the act of resumption and relax a number of the more contentious elements of his newly activist regime.[3]

It was Scotland, however, that rapidly claimed priority. In June 1341 the seventeen-year-old David Bruce returned from France to take up his claim to the northern kingdom, ousted Robert Stewart from the guardianship, and began to draw together a group of powerful nobles and prelates who would form the nucleus of a newly revived Bruce regime. Making his military debut, David led two quick raids into northern England, paying for them out of subsidies from his French allies.[4] The threat from these raids was considered sufficiently serious in England to necessitate the organization of a new campaign in the winter of 1341–2. Edward, accompanied by some of the northern lords, marched to Newcastle in November. Efforts

[1] *CPR 1340–3*, 190, 191; Hughes, *Constitutional Tendencies*, 166–7; R. A. Griffiths, *The Principality of Wales in the Later Middle Ages: The Structure and Personnel of Government. I: South Wales, 1277–1536* (Cardiff, 1972), 49; Frame, *English Lordship*, 243–4.

[2] *CFR 1337–47*, 234.

[3] *CCR 1341–3*, 508–16; R. Frame, *Ireland and Britain, 1170–1450* (London, 1998), 113–29.

[4] Bower, vii, 150–3; *Wyntoun*, vi, 159–61, M. Penman, *David II* (East Linton, 2004), 85.

were made to call up significant supplementary forces under various English earls and barons. Henry Percy went on in advance to secure the recapture of Stirling castle and make provision for the defence of the march. For a while the king lingered at Newcastle, where he and the ubiquitous William Kilsby presided over some important investigations into the civil government of the town and made a compact with Bishop Bury over the endemic problems arising when felons ran away into the privileged jurisdiction of County Durham in order to evade capture and punishment in the royal courts.[5] In early December, Edward marched into the Lowlands. But few opportunities presented for further action, and the royal party contented itself with a series of jousts and other jollifications at Melrose and Roxburgh over the Christmas season, before making a leisurely return south in January. The earl of Derby, earlier appointed royal lieutenant for the army of Scotland, now took up command and remained in the north until May to supervise the making and settlement of another truce.[6]

For all this attention to the affairs of the British Isles, Edward III was very far from giving up on his wider ambitions on the continent. Even before he marched north from Newcastle in December, Edward had announced that he would need to return swiftly to London to deal with 'the affair of France'. The commissioners of array and collectors of the wool tax were summoned en masse before the council on Edward's return to Westminster to provide information and answer for any delinquencies.[7] The results must have been somewhat dispiriting, for Edward was soon persuaded to play for more time and negotiate further extensions of the truce of Esplechin to run to June 1342. His subjects, observing the levies of wool and new efforts to raise the army of Flanders in the summer of 1341, ruefully noted the irony of a position in which Edward was simultaneously negotiating truces and preparing for war.[8]

Once the expedition to Flanders was abandoned, however, necessity and opportunity began to effect significant changes of approach towards France. In June 1341, following a rapprochement with the French, Lewis of Bavaria formally withdrew the English king's title as vicar-general of the Empire. Although he could still count on his network of in-laws in the Netherlands and western Germany, Edward now had to abandon a number of actual or potential imperial allies. The planned dynastic match with the house of Austria was finally called off. The election of Philip VI's councillor, Pierre Roger, as Pope Clement VI in the spring of 1342

---

[5] *Ancient Petitions Relating to Northumberland*, ed. C. M. Fraser (Surtees Society, clxxvi, 1966), no. 194; *CCR 1341–3*, 353–4, 364.

[6] Murimuth, 123; *Chron. Lanercost*, 335; Prince, 'Strength of English Armies', 362–3; Fowler, *King's Lieutenant*, 37.

[7] *CCR 1341–3*, 353, 369–70, 472–3, 505–8.

[8] *Foedera*, II.ii, 1160–1, 1165–6, 1168–9, 1177; Murimuth, 121.

provided a further challenge. Since 1339 Edward had been promising a marriage alliance between Prince Edward and Margaret, daughter of the duke of Brabant. But a papal dispensation was needed in order to proceed. Benedict XII had refused, and it was clear that Clement VI would never agree. Under the combined pressure of the emperor and the king of France, Edward III's north European coalition was beginning to show definite signs of strain. The time had come to identify new allies and open up new theatres of war against the Valois.[9]

The major opportunity for such diversification presented itself, unexpectedly, in the duchy of Brittany. When Duke John III of Brittany died in April 1341, he left his title in dispute between two members of his extended family, Charles of Blois and John de Montfort. One of Philip VI's sisters had been married to John III, and another was the mother of Charles of Blois. But it was strategic thinking rather than family sentiment that caused Philip to side with the Blois claim and to send his son John, duke of Normandy, to invest Brittany with French forces later in 1341. John de Montfort was persuaded to travel to Paris to discuss a resolution of his claims but, on refusing Philip's terms, was imprisoned in the Louvre. Dynastic and political relations between England and Brittany were close: after the death of his pro-English uncle, John of Brittany, in 1334, John III had been recognized as having a title to the earldom of Richmond. Edward III rapidly made contact with the Montfort party, and an agreement on military aid was reached in October 1341. Finally, at the fervent supplication of Montfort's beleaguered and determined wife, Jeanne of Flanders, Edward began to make real preparations for a campaign in the early months of 1342.[10]

The first English force dispatched to Brittany, under Sir Walter Mauny, was in fact little more than a reconnaissance party. It returned in July with depressing news: the Montfortian cause was rapidly collapsing under the pressure of further Valois reinforcements. Edward III's decision to press on with plans for an expedition had something of the chivalric adventure to it: the bravery of the bereft Countess Jeanne had struck his imagination, and he would do his very best, against all the odds, to rescue and restore her.[11] It also had its ironies: in Brittany, Philip VI and Edward III would take the opposite line to those adopted in relation to the throne of France, the former accepting the validity of female transmission of title, the latter preferring the nearest male relative. But for both sides the opening up of a new front in Brittany was a very calculated decision. Like the Flemings before them, John de Montfort and his countess were keen to represent

---

[9] *Foedera*, II.ii, 1036, 1083–4, 1140, 1164, 1166; Lucas, *Low Countries*, 305, 437, 509; D. Wood, *Clement VI: The Pontificate and Ideas of an Avignon Pope* (Cambridge, 1989), 122–41.

[10] Le Bel, i, 244–72; *Foedera*, II.ii, 1176; Le Patourel, *Feudal Empires*, chap. xii, 187.

[11] The supposed meeting between the king and the countess at York at Easter 1342, recounted by le Bel, ii, 7–8 was, however, a fiction: Froissart, iii, II–III and nn.

their cause as just. Consequently, they were eager to recognize Edward III's claim as rightful king of France and thus justify their act of resistance against Philip VI.[12] The Breton civil war of 1341–2 marked the moment at which Edward began to realize that the dynastic claim, taken up in highly pragmatic fashion as part of his diplomatic manoeuvres with the Flemings in January 1340, might also provide the basis for interventions in the other great principalities within the kingdom of France. Thus began what the historian John Le Patourel called Edward's 'provincial strategy', a diplomatic course that would, over the following twenty years, lead Edward to assert his suzerainty not just over Flanders and Brittany but also, in due course, over Normandy and Burgundy as well.[13] Viewed from this perspective, the intervention in Brittany in 1342 can indeed be seen as one of the major strategic turning points of the Hundred Years War.

This is not to say that Brittany was an easy target. At first, the English soldiers and administrators who would invest the duchy struggled to come to terms with the language, culture, politics and topography of this remote region.[14] A war to be fought in the far north-western reaches of France also created enormous logistical challenges for the English government. The preparations for the three separate expeditions planned in 1342 – those of the earl of Northampton, of Robert of Artois, and of Edward himself – were all subject to serious delays.[15] The king made some effective use of his enforced idleness. Preparations were made for the defence of the Scottish march, and the king personally supervised the sealing of charters of pardon for those promising to undertake service in Brittany.[16] New commissions of inquiry were set up in some twenty shires to deal with matters such as the illegal import of coin and export of wool and acts of desertion from the king's armies.[17] By agreeing to hand over two of his own prisoners, the earl of Moray and Herman, lord of Léon in Brittany, Edward also managed to persuade Philip VI to release the earl of Salisbury from a promise, extracted as the price of his parole, never to fight again in France. It was around this time that Edward, mindful of his responsibilities as the earl's brother in arms, may have made a substantial cash contribution to the ransom that the French had set on Montagu's

[12] 'Some Documents Relating to the Disputed Succession to the Duchy of Brittany, 1341', ed. M. Jones, *Camden Miscellany XXIV* (Camden Society, 4th series, ix, 1972), 4; M. Jones, 'Edward III's Captains in Brittany', *England in the Fourteenth Century*, ed. Ormrod, 106–7 and n. 28.

[13] Le Patourel, *Feudal Empires*, chaps xii, xv.

[14] E 36/204, the wardrobe account that covers the king's Breton campaign of 1342–3, reveals something of this cultural confusion through the notably garbled rendering of place-names.

[15] For the shipping raised for these expeditions see C 47/2/35.

[16] E 403/326, 8 July 1342; *CCR 1341–3*, 530.

[17] *CPR 1340–3*, 585–6; Verduyn, 'Attitude', 85.

head.[18] Salisbury's readying for war was part of the continuing campaign of persuasion launched in the aftermath of the Stratford crisis and designed very deliberately to re-engage the high nobility and knightly class in the pursuit of arms. The king hosted a particularly sumptuous and well-attended tournament at Dunstable in February 1342.[19] Further hastiludes followed during the spring at Northampton and Eltham. A major meeting of the great council was called at Westminster in April, attended by Warwick, Pembroke, Oxford and Suffolk, and another special council of 'earls, barons and magnates' met at Woodstock in June. This great cycle of court events culminated in a banquet at Eastry on 26 September attended by the king, queen, Prince Edward, and the earls of Derby, Warwick, Salisbury and Suffolk.[20]

On 4–5 October, already aboard the *George* at Sandwich, the king finally appointed Prince Edward keeper of the realm and made formal arrangements for the government of England during his impending absence. The written arrangements made no explicit statement about the principles that had been enshrined in the Walton Ordinances. On the other hand, with the chancery and exchequer now under the control of two of his closest supporters, Robert Parving and William Cusance, it is surely unlikely that there would be any significant difficulties over the prioritizing of Edward's own interests and business at home. The earls of Arundel, Huntingdon and Surrey joined the ministers in the young prince's council.[21] One of their first duties was to take pre-emptive action against acts of espionage and round up all Frenchmen in London.[22] Prince Edward's youth having kept him from the campaign, his subjects in Cheshire sought to declare themselves exempt from the king's attempts to array archers for the Breton expedition.[23] In other respects, though, their contribution to the contract armies put into France during this period was significant, and a number of men-at-arms from the county, such as Sir Robert Knolles and Sir Hugh Calveley, made distinguished and profitable careers in the Breton wars of the 1340s.

The king's plans for France were centred on the Channel ports of Sandwich and Winchelsea. Philip VI mistook this as a sign that the English king intended once more to cross into the Low Countries, and so

---

[18] *ODNB*, xxxviii, 774. The ransom contribution is undocumented, but is inferred here from what might be seen as a reciprocal act in which the earl left instructions to his executors to excuse a royal debt of over £6,700 owed to Montagu for war service: C 270/32, no. 33; *CPR 1345–8*, 473.

[19] See pp. 99, 143.

[20] Vale, *Edward III and Chivalry*, 173; *RDP*, iv, 537–9; Murimuth, 123; Powell and Wallis, *House of Lords*, 348–9; C 76/16, m. 39d; E 36/204, fol. 29v.

[21] *Foedera*, II.ii, 1212, 1213, 1216.

[22] *CCR 1341–3*, 660.

[23] C 47/2/34, no. 11.

diverted a significant number of his troops from the Breton front to the Pas de Calais. The crossing to Brittany was arduous and the passage around the coast of Finistère especially perilous: Edward was to send a thank-offering to the monks of Saint-Matthieu for his safe delivery around the final cape of the peninsula and into Brest.[24] By the time he landed on 27 October, the position in the duchy was beginning to look promising. Just three days later, Northampton decisively defeated Charles of Blois's Franco-Breton army at Morlaix. Although the battle had little or no strategic significance, it demonstrated the applicability in this new theatre of war of the tactics developed in Scotland during the previous decade. It also added new names to a growing catalogue of French prisoners, including Geoffrey de Charny, the commander of Blois's front line. Meanwhile, Edward's army marched west to Dinan and then south to Nantes. Eventually it was decided to head for Vannes, a strategically important position controlled by the Blois party but sited in a part of the duchy that continued to hold out for the Montfortists.[25] The fleet, under the direction of Robert of Artois, was ordered to proceed around the coast in order to cut off the port of Vannes. Robert attempted an attack in advance of the arrival of the land army, but was killed in the process; his body was taken back to England and buried at the London Blackfriars.[26]

Conditions improved little after Edward arrived outside Vannes on 29 November. Preliminary investigations had suggested that the town would fall easily, but the walls held firm against the assault, and the English were forced to dig in for the winter. Edward's forces of between 3,500 and 5,000 English and Welsh began, as always, to trickle away.[27] Writing home on 5 December, he asked his son to intercede with the chancellor and treasurer 'to send money to us, for they know well our state'.[28] But the regency administration decided that it would be unrealistic to dispatch reinforcements until the spring. It was the men already in the field with the king – Northampton, Warwick, Salisbury and the emerging young Hugh Despenser – who managed to exploit the temporary disarray of the Valois forces and launch a series of raiding parties across Brittany. Agents of Pope Clement now reopened discussions with Edward III and Philip VI for a truce, and an agreement was reached at Malestroit on 19 January.[29] The terms were extremely favourable to the English: John de Montfort

[24] E 36/204, fols 72v, 73.

[25] M. Jones, 'The Breton Civil War', *Froissart: Historian*, ed. J. J. N. Palmer (Woodbridge, 1981), 66.

[26] *Foedera*, II.ii, 1222. For the king's oblations at the time of the funeral see E 403/327, 31 Jan. 1343.

[27] Ayton, *Knights and Warhorses*, 258–64; Sumption, i, 406.

[28] Avesbury, 340–2; *Wars of Edward III*, 101–2.

[29] Murimuth, 129–35. The king entertained the papal envoys on 23 Jan.: E 36/204, fol. 37.

would be released by Philip VI and, although Vannes was to be placed under papal custody, Edward would retain control of all the positions he had occupied in the duchy. As usual, both sides vied with each other to claim that their honour had not been compromised by the settlement. The general consensus, however, was that the Plantagenet–Montfortist party had the upper hand.[30] It had been a modest start, but the campaign of 1342–3 had demonstrated that Brittany now offered by far and away the best prospects for Edward's chance of maintaining a successful war against the Valois.

Edward III arrived back in England on 2 March 1343. There had been a terrible storm in the Atlantic that had forced his fleet repeatedly back on to the west coast of Brittany and made for a highly treacherous three-day crossing. A rumour spread that the adverse conditions had been whipped up by necromancers working to the orders of the queen of France. Edward was sufficiently alarmed by the danger that he made a vow to found an abbey in return for the protection of the Virgin Mary.[31] The fleet eventually docked at Melcombe and the king proceeded via Salisbury and Winchester to London, where he was reunited with Queen Philippa.[32] After a dutiful trip to the shrine of Becket at Canterbury and other major churches, the royal couple passed Easter at Philippa's manor of Havering.[33] The countess of Montfort, exhausted by her efforts on behalf of her absent husband, arrived in England at the same time; she would live out the next thirty years of her life in the obscurity of various provincial royal castles, while her son would be brought up as an honoured member of the Plantagenet court.[34] The truce of Malestroit was designed to run until September 1346, and for the present neither Edward nor Philip VI seemed inclined to rush back to war.

Nor did the king show any eagerness for further fighting in the north. Since Edward's withdrawal from Scotland in January 1342 there had been some serious setbacks, especially the loss of control of Stirling and Roxburgh. After talks with David II's government, a three-year Anglo-Scottish truce was confirmed in June 1343 and enforced on the English side with a notable new determination.[35] Free for the moment from

[30] Sumption, i, 408.

[31] *Chron. Meaux*, iii, 51–2; *Chron. Lanercost*, 340; BL, MS Cotton Faustina B. V, fol. 90.

[32] E 36/204, fols. 37–41v.

[33] Murimuth, 135; Avesbury, 352.

[34] GEC, x, 821. For the spurious tradition that Jeanne went insane at the time of her arrival in England, see J. B. Henneman, *Olivier de Clisson and Political Society in France under Charles V and Charles VI* (Philadelphia, 1996), 27–8.

[35] *Rot. Scot.*, i, 637, 640; *Foedera*, II.ii, 1239–40; Campbell, 'England, Scotland', 191; C. J. Neville, *Violence, Custom and Law: The Anglo-Scottish Border Lands in the Later Middle Ages* (Edinburgh, 1998), 32–7.

imminent campaigning, Edward occupied himself again in sport and chivalry. The visits to Canterbury and Hereford in March were accompanied by jousts. The hastiludes at London in late June 1343, at which the king and his team dressed up as the pope and twelve cardinals, were probably held to celebrate the birth of his latest child, the brief-lived Blanche of the Tower.[36] A further major tournament followed at Windsor early in 1344.[37] Perhaps reflecting a certain thawing of their relationship, Edward began to make regular visits to his mother; in November 1344, for example, he spent his thirty-second birthday with Queen Isabella during a visit to Castle Rising.[38]

It is in this period immediately before and after the Breton expedition of 1342–3 that we also detect the first inklings of the family policy that would become Edward's very *raison d'être* later in the reign. At its core was the ambition to plant all of the king's sons (and, in due course, his sons-in-law) as royal lieutenants in the provinces of a newly enlarged Plantagenet empire. In the parliament of 1343 the king gave his eldest son the title previously held only by Edward II, and never granted to Edward III himself: that of prince of Wales. The early marriage of the four-year-old Prince Lionel to Elizabeth of Ulster in August 1342 had already hinted at the king's determination, in due course, to make his second son governor of Ireland. And the decision in September 1342 to grant the earldom of Richmond not to John de Montfort but to John of Gaunt may even suggest that Edward III had some notion of a Plantagenet succession in Brittany. Edward's decision to allow not just the prince of Wales but all of his expanding stock of sons to bear the quartered arms of France and England, differenced only by an emblem or label, was a powerful signal to the heraldic-minded elite of the day that his was indeed a collective enterprise from whose achievements all of the nuclear royal family would, in due course, benefit.[39]

Given the continued absence of any major demonstration of success in France and the tender ages of the king's younger sons, it remains unlikely that this fantasy of dynasticism as yet extended much beyond Edward's over-fertile imagination. Nevertheless, the intervention in Brittany had obviously awakened the king's interest in the great cluster of lordships in north-western and western France – Normandy, Brittany, Anjou, Maine, Touraine, Saintonge and Poitou – that had been held by his ancestors until the time of King John and Henry III. At some point between 1341 and 1343 Edward ordered a copy to be made of the twelfth-century chronicle

[36] Vale, *Edward III and Chivalry*, 173.

[37] See pp. 300–1.

[38] *The Making of King's Lynn: A Documentary Survey*, ed. D. M. Owen (London, 1984), 386; Murimuth, 231; Doherty, 'Isabella, Queen of England', 325.

[39] *RDP*, v, 43, 45; R. A. Griffiths, *King and Country: England and Wales in the Fifteenth Century* (London, 1991), 5.

of William of Newburgh, whose memorable description of an Angevin rule that extended 'from the far borders of Scotland to the Pyrenees' must surely have affirmed his own emerging sense of destiny.[40] Just as Henry II had used his sons as governors of the great provinces of his empire, so now would Edward III attempt to harness the ambitions of his children by giving them direct vested interests in a policy of imperial expansion. From 1343, England's international relations had increasingly to accommodate the personal ambitions of the king as well as his equally strong sense of responsibility to the next generation of Plantagenet princes.[41]

It was integral to the emergent provincial and dynastic strategies that Edward also commit to the long-term occupation of the principal territories that he sought to acquire. His personal withdrawal from Brittany therefore necessarily involved the planting of a permanent military establishment in the duchy. Such long-term, small-scale commitments tended to be maintained by men of knightly rather than noble rank, who could be expected to remain on the job for the duration of their service. The first non-baronial lieutenant of Brittany, John Hardreshull, was duly appointed in the spring of 1343.[42] The practical consequences of this policy soon became apparent. At the Westminster parliament of April 1343 there was a lively debate on the rights of children born to English parents abroad. The king had good reason to become personally involved, for two of his sons, Lionel and John, had arrived into the world during the court's long sojourn in the Low Countries in 1338–40. The real focus of discussion, however, was on the babies, royal or otherwise, that were now likely to be conceived in Brittany. Since French-born aliens were liable to confiscation of property in England, there was great concern over the possible jeopardizing of the family interests of Edward's loyal captains. The matter was declared both complicated and urgent, and general reassurances were provided. After the capture and occupation of Calais in 1347 the issue became pressing, and in 1351 the crown at last issued a statute guaranteeing the inheritance rights of the French-born offspring of English parents.[43]

In spite of the state of military activity that appeared to prevail for much of 1343 and 1344, the king was obviously keen to emphasize the likelihood of a speedy return to war. The parliaments of April–May 1343 and June 1344 were both summoned with the express purpose of discussing the state of the truces and the proposals now being put forward by the papacy for a final settlement to the French war.[44] In 1343 the lords and commons

---

[40] Ormrod, 'Edward III and his Family', 421–2; *EHD*, ii, 351.

[41] W. M. Ormrod, 'The Double Monarchy of Edward III', *Medieval History*, i[1] (1991), 68–80. For a caveat, see Curry, *Hundred Years War*, 54.

[42] Jones, 'Edward III's Captains', 112–13, 118.

[43] *PROME*, iv, 337–8; *SR*, i, 310; Griffiths, *King and Country*, 45–8.

[44] *RDP*, iv, 546–8, 550–1; E 403/327, 3 Mar. 1343. The great council of Apr. 1344 seems, by contrast, to have been mainly for ecclesiastical business: *RDP*, iv, 550–1; WAM, 12207.

agreed that, if the king could secure a 'good and honourable' peace with France, he ought to accept it, but if not, he could count on the support of his people to renew the efforts to bring Philip of Valois to heel. On this expectation the wool subsidy was renewed for a further three years. At the following session, Sir Bartholomew Burghersh gave a detailed account of the alleged French breaches of the truce. Philip VI's supposed ambition 'to destroy the English language and to occupy the land of England' was announced, and the commons once more obliged with a grant of further direct taxes.[45]

This heightened rhetoric of common obligation served to justify some forceful changes in domestic policy. In 1343 the commons called for the reinstatement of those elements of the cancelled 1341 statute that might be judged compatible with the royal grace. Their aim was probably to restore the principle that the senior ministers of the crown ought to be publicly accountable for their actions. The king agreed to consider the matter. But the sensitivities about the infringement of royal rights that had been provoked in 1341 remained sharp, and nothing was done.[46] Instead, the king effected some very significant changes of personnel that helped to inspire confidence in both court and country. The withdrawal of Stratford's nemesis, William Kilsby, from the keepership of the privy seal in June 1342 represented a defining moment in this respect. While Kilsby's departure from government was seemingly of his own volition, it is hard to escape the idea that he was also under some pressure to withdraw. Thwarted in his efforts to obtain the archbishopric of York, he turned his enthusiasm to a combination of exotic pilgrimage and service in war: though he never renounced his clerical status in order to be able to fight in battle, he nonetheless recruited and led his own contingents on the king's campaign in Brittany in 1342–3 and on the great Normandy expedition of 1346.[47] Kilsby's successors at the privy seal, John Offord (1342–5) and John Thoresby (1345–7), were significantly less abrasive personalities who much more readily ingratiated themselves with the established political elite. Not that this made them in any sense ambivalent about their primary responsibilities, for both Offord and Thoresby brought to the privy seal impressive records of service in the household and writing offices, and both had already proved their loyalty to Edward III in dramatic fashion by presenting the king's first complaints against John Stratford to the pope in November 1340.[48]

[45] *PROME*, iv, 325–6, 331–2, 355, 361–3. The two convocations duly followed suit: *Register of John Kirkby*, no. 756.

[46] *PROME*, iv, 339.

[47] Tout, *Chapters*, iii, 108, 116–18; v, 22.

[48] Haines, *Stratford*, 306–7.

In his selection of chancellors and treasurers, Edward revealed a similar determination to promote men unflinchingly committed to his regime. Robert Parving, one of the royal familiars denounced in the parliament of 1341, was promoted from the treasurership to the chancellorship in October of that year, but left office in 1343. The king's declared preference for lay officers of state who might be liable to justice in his courts became less relevant once he realized the abundance of well-qualified and loyal clerics about him. Parving's successors as treasurer, William Cusance (1341–4) and William Edington (1344–56), were therefore recruited in the traditional fashion from among the clerical officers of the royal household. Edington, who emerged from obscure Hampshire origins, had managed to impress the crown by his service as receiver of the otherwise ill-administered ninth of 1340; in spite of his rapid rise to seniority in the central administration, he successfully avoided the sniping of his social superiors and emerged as an administrator and politician of real stature. With John Offord's appointment to replace the last of the sequence of lay chancellors, Robert Sadington, in October 1345, the transformation was complete. Through the reshuffles of 1341–5 Edward III had managed simultaneously to throw off the dominance of the older generation of administrators inherited from his father and mother's successive regimes and to distance himself from the more controversial and outspoken of his own supporters during the crisis of 1340–1.

The consequences were first apparent in the area of royal finance. In June 1342 Edward III's government reached an initial agreement with some of the merchants yet to be compensated for loss of wools taken from them during the debacle at Dordrecht in 1338. In its eagerness to pacify this group, the crown risked the wrath of other influential parties. The new deal involved the merchants in authorizing a revival of the *maltolt*, in direct contravention of the king's promise of 1340 that he would negotiate all extraordinary taxes in parliament.[49] In April 1343 Walter Chiriton and his business partners made a further contract with the crown.[50] On the expectation that this might at last help those who had provided the wool for the royal seizure of 1337, parliament reluctantly agreed to accept the reimposition of the wool subsidy and authorized its extension, at the now standard rate of £2 a sack, until September 1346.[51] In the summer of 1343 the crown handed over the administration of the customs system to a cartel led by Thomas Melchbourn of Lynn. Its successor, formed by John Wesenham in 1345, agreed to farm the customs for an annual payment of £50,000. Between 1343 and 1351 these various merchant companies

---

[49] *RDP*, iv, 540; *CCR 1341–3*, 553; Unwin, 'Estate of Merchants', 209–10.

[50] *CCR 1343–6*, 217–18.

[51] *PROME*, iv, 327, 336–7. For the summoning of merchants at the time of parliament see *RDP*, iv, 548–50; E 403/327, 3 Apr. 1343; Fryde, *William de la Pole*, 183.

managed at once to clear debts owed on the Dordrecht bonds to the value
of over £84,000 and to pay the crown around £429,000, or about
£53,500 a year, out of their takings from the customs.[52] The initial expectations fixed upon the new farm of the customs therefore served significantly to shore up the crown's financial and political credibility in time for
the great military onslaught of 1346–7.

Another immediate and positive outcome from the parliament of 1343
was a change in monetary policy. The continuing acute shortage of silver,
coupled with the recent initiative of Philip VI in 1338–9 in launching the
first really successful gold currency in France, precipitated a decision that the
English crown should, for the first time, develop its own gold coinage alongside the existing silver sterling. The first gold coins to be issued, the florin and
half-florin, were over-valued in relation to the price of silver. But in 1344 the
crown revised the scheme and issued the successful gold noble (6s 8d), half-
noble (3s 4d) and quarter-noble (1s 8d). The new coins were intended chiefly
for use in international exchange, but were also legal currency in England:
in 1346, for example, the commons specified that payments of fifteenths and
tenths could be made in gold as well as silver.[53] So far as the silver coinage
went, the commons remained steadfast in their view that the economy was
best served by restoring the traditional fineness of sterling. In 1344, however,
the crown at once restored the fineness and reduced the weight of silver
pennies. This was an attempt to increase the number of coins in circulation
and to make it less profitable for foreigners to export English currency. Since
the reduction was not on such a scale as to cause any significant inflation of
prices, the commons seem generally to have been convinced of the feasibility of the reform, and the crown made another modest reduction in
weight in 1346.[54] The king also managed to deflect attention away from the
devaluation by pandering to the commons' marked preference for a return
to a policy of strict bullion control. In the parliament of 1343 the crown
agreed to impose a ban on papal provisions to ecclesiastical benefices in
England, with the express purpose of preventing the drain of coin into the
hands of French and Italian clerics. The resulting ordinance played on more
general public suspicion of the francophile pope, and was for a short time
enforced with some rigour.[55]

---

[52] *CCR 1343–6*, 266–7; G. Sayles, 'The "English Company" of 1343 and a Merchants'
Oath', *Speculum*, vi (1931), 177–205; Fryde, *Studies*, chap. x; Lloyd, *Wool Trade*, 193–204; Fryde,
William de la Pole, 184–5.

[53] *PROME*, iv, 334–5, 393; *Age of Chivalry*, no. 660–6.

[54] *PROME*, iv, 334–6, J. H. A. Munro, *Wool, Cloth, and Gold: The Struggle for Bullion in Anglo-
Burgundian Trade, 1340–1478* (Toronto, 1972), 34–41; T. H. Lloyd, 'Overseas Trade and the
English Money Supply in the Fourteenth Century', *Edwardian Monetary Affairs, 1279–1344*,
ed. N. J. Mayhew (British Archaeological Reports, British series, xxxvi, 1977), 110–11.

[55] *PROME*, iv, 335, 343–4, 349–50, 456; A. D. M. Barrell, 'The Ordinance of Provisors
of 1343', *HR*, lxiv (1991), 264–77.

The parliaments of 1343–4 gave important closure to the controversies raised by the crown's recent judicial policy. At the assembly of 1343, Chancellor Parving asked the commons to give their opinion on how the king's peace might best be upheld throughout the realm. The crown was eager to secure approval of its plan to launch another series of trailbaston commissions in the shires, and the commons accepted the need for a firm stance on law and order.[56] The king's personal interest in the new inquiries shows his continued inclination to apply punitive measures against anyone impeding the progress of his policies. In March 1344, during a visit to Queen Isabella at Castle Rising, Edward III made contact with the commissioners in East Anglia, gave orders for the swift payment of their expenses, and sent on to the chancellor a list of those found guilty in the local sessions so that the appropriate money penalties could be collected.[57] Given his new interest in the wide dominions of the crown, the king may also have led the initiative that imposed parallel series of judicial inquiries in Wales and Ireland.[58] But the extraordinary powers allowed to the senior members of the judiciary who presided over the tribunals in the English shires led to the belief that the crown was once more attempting to pursue the full rigours of retributive justice and reviving its attack on the ministerial classes.[59] In the parliament of 1344 the king was therefore persuaded to give up his interventionist stance and to withdraw the new inquiries. From this accommodation there emerged what proved the most enduring of all the methods of local peace-keeping attempted by the crown during the first half of Edward III's reign.

The new formula represented a working compromise between the localities' preference for self-regulation and the crown's need for continued central supervision. Since the 1344 parliament assumed that the king would soon be returning to France to continue his endeavour against the tyrant Philip, the commons' proposal amounted to a revival of the peace commissions issued before Edward's first departure for the continent, in 1338.[60] On this occasion, however, the policy of drawing larger numbers of the high nobility and baronage into direct action in the war made the crown loath to revive the supervisory role undertaken by the earlier magnate keepers of the counties. Instead, the crown hit on a comparatively new idea. The local commissioners would be empowered to undertake much of the basic work of peace-keeping by receiving indictments and bailing and imprisoning

---

[56] *PROME*, iv, 332–4, 339–49: *CPR 1343–5*, 97–8, 281–2.

[57] C 81/1331/40; C 81/1336/54–5. For these sessions see B. H. Putnam, *The Place in Legal History of Sir William Shareshull* (Cambridge, 1950), 64–5. See also Edward's personal intervention to secure a goal delivery session at Baldock in 1345: Ormrod, *Reign of Edward III*, 54.

[58] Griffiths, *Principality of Wales*, 34; R. Frame, 'The Justiciarship of Ralph Ufford: Warfare and Politics in Fourteenth-Century Ireland', *Studia Hibernica*, xiii (1973), 10–12.

[59] Verduyn, 'Attitude', 88–9. Harriss, *King, Parliament*, 405–6, supplementary inquiries that began to be issued from Jan. 1344: *CPR 1343–5*, 281–2, etc.

[60] *PROME*, iv, 364, 366, 368–9; *SR*, i, 300–1.

criminals pending trial. But they would be allowed to try cases only when they were 'afforced' by the presence of justices and sergeants-at-law from the central courts. From 1344 the crown therefore regularly assigned the professional lawyers serving on the relevant assize and goal delivery circuits to act as presidents of the local sessions of the peace.[61] The reform can probably be attributed to the group of experienced senior judges, John Stonor, Robert Parving, William Scot and William Shareshull, who had managed to survive the crisis of 1340–1 and had experienced at first hand some of the bitter hostility displayed towards the representatives of the crown during the trailbastons of 1341–4. The new system of centralized, professional supervision provided a powerful corrective to the idea that Edward III was prepared simply to allow the gentry to regulate law and order on their own terms.[62] But it also gave an effective and enduring guarantee against the perceived oppressiveness of eyres and trailbastons, and thus forged a new impression of active collaboration between crown and polity in the local operation of criminal justice.

The various measures adopted in domestic government in the early 1340s played a central part in reaffirming the king's commitment to reconciling a divided polity, promoting the peace and prosperity of his realm, and thus continuing on his great adventure in France. By effective management and a certain amount of window dressing, the king had gone a long way to recovering the support of the magnates, the knightly class and the merchants. All of this helped dispel the serious misgivings that yet remained over Edward's continuing reluctance to admit any real fault in his earlier dispute with John Stratford. Above all, the expedition to Brittany had opened up a new front in the war with Philip of Valois that offered the possibility of a sustainable military and diplomatic strategy and the prospect of material benefit for the crown and the military elite. The durability of these policies, and of the political alliance that underpinned them, would fully be put to the test during the major military commitments undertaken in 1346–7.

The confident assumptions made in England during the summer of 1344 about the imminent collapse of the Anglo-French truce were hardly propitious to the peace talks even then opening up at Avignon.[63] Edward III

---

[61] E. Powell, 'The Administration of Criminal Justice in Late-Medieval England: Peace Sessions and Assizes', *The Political Context of the Law*, ed. R. Eales and D. Sullivan (London, 1987), 48–59.

[62] A. Verduyn, 'The Commons and the Early Justices of the Peace under Edward III', *Regionalism and Revision: The Crown and its Provinces in England, 1200–1500*, ed. P. Fleming, A. Gross and J. R. Lander (London, 1998), 102.

[63] For what follows see Froissart, *Oeuvres*, xviii, 235–56; Murimuth, 136–8, 143–9; Déprez, 'La Conférence d'Avignon, 1344', 301–20; Sumption, i, 436–44; Taylor, 'Plantagenet Claim', 155–69.

had only been prepared to enter into these discussions on the basis that Clement VI would eschew the role of judge and act without prejudice as an unofficial 'friend' to both parties.[64] The earl of Derby's secret mission to the pope in the spring of 1344 yielded nothing. In August Edward dispatched the new bishop of Norwich, William Bateman, and a new rising star, John Offord, keeper of the privy seal, to treat with the curia, but they were empowered only to discuss breaches of the truce and the continuing refusal of Philip VI to free John de Montfort from detention in Paris. The French deputation was similarly restricted, with power only to discuss territorial disputes in Gascony. The pope therefore found it impossible to bring the two sides to productive discussions, and rapidly delegated the whole wretched business to two of his cardinals. These men dutifully ran through a series of old and new solutions to the impasse: that Edward III might transfer Gascony to his eldest son, or that he might give up the duchy altogether in return for financial compensation and a guarantee of his rights in Scotland. Bateman and Offord's reports revealed their increasing frustration and exhaustion. Edward claimed to be about to dispatch another embassy to the curia under Derby and Northampton, but nothing happened, and the whole peace initiative finally collapsed in March 1345.

The one point of clarity to emerge from the Avignon conference was Edward III's adamant determination to be recognized as king of France. To those in the know, the naivety of such a position was painfully obvious: in spite of the earlier success at Sluys and his recent interventions in Flanders and Brittany, there was still nothing to suggest that Edward was really capable of winning allies in the heartlands of the Valois monarchy and thus presenting himself as a serious rival to Philip VI. It is easy to dismiss Edward's insistence on the French title merely as a bargaining position and a rather cynical public relations exercise. But there are indications that, from 1344, Edward's propaganda machine began to place new emphasis on the dynastic element of the war. The new gold coinage, for example, deployed the formal style 'king of England and France' as a forceful reminder to its principal users, the international merchant community, of the reach of Edward's right. And there are at least hints that Edward was beginning to believe the force of his own arguments. A dossier of information used by Bateman and Offord in 1344 made the point that, since the king of France was sovereign in his lands, no earthly authority was empowered to arbitrate upon the title. It was for God alone to decide the outcome by divine intervention on the field of

---

[64] F. Autrand, 'The Peacemakers and the State: Pontifical Diplomacy and the Anglo-French Conflict in the Fourteenth Century', *War and Competition between States*, ed. P. Contamine (Oxford, 2000), 264–5; K. Plöger, *England and the Avignon Popes: The Practice of Diplomacy in Late Medieval Europe* (London, 2005), 33–4.

battle.[65] After six years of prevarication and frustration, it was time for Edward III, once and for all, to fulfil his prophetic destiny and assert the might of England over the tyrant of France.

Nor was Edward's back-up position scarcely less ambitious. Bateman and Offord told the cardinals that their king would consider a settlement if the Valois would acknowledge that the duchy of Aquitaine was an allod, free from French sovereignty and suzerainty.[66] It is unclear, however, whether these were the only conditions that Edward wished to impose. By 1345 the king seems to have taken the view that he would renounce the French throne only in return for a larger settlement that acknowledged his rights over Scotland and gave him suzerainty over Brittany, Flanders and other parts of the former Plantagenet dominions.[67] The well-informed Florentine chronicler Giovanni Villani believed that Edward had three orders of ambition when he went to war against Philip of Valois in 1346: to regain Gascony and Ponthieu; to redress the unlawful occupation of Normandy by the French since the time of Richard I; and to pursue his right to the throne of France.[68] By 1345 it was evident that he would refuse any terms that merely offered a restoration of the status quo ante bellum and was determined to recover as many as possible of the lands that his ancestors had ruled in France before 1259.

During the winter and spring of 1344–5 the English government put in place the diplomatic and logistical framework for the new round of hostilities. With indirect and direct taxation already more or less guaranteed until 1346, the crown could afford to be ambitious. The collapse of the imperial alliance meant the withdrawal of a number of Edward's most loyal supporters. Queen Philippa's brother, William, count of Hainault, an honoured guest at the Eltham tournament of 1342, defected to Philip VI in 1343–4 and died unexpectedly and childless in 1345. The duke of Guelders died in 1343. And in 1345 Duke John of Brabant publicly reneged on his previous deal with the English king and began negotiations for the marriage of his daughter to the son of the pro-French count of Flanders. Ultimately these setbacks proved a bonus for Edward, for they dramatically reduced his financial commitments to the princes of the Empire.[69] The search for allies now shifted to the Iberian peninsula, where English diplomats had rarely ventured during the 1330s. The impressive performances of the earls of Derby and Salisbury at the siege of Algeciras in 1343 helped frame a proposal for the marriage of the eldest son of

[65] *EMDP*, I.ii, no. 239(b); Taylor, 'Plantagenet Claim', 164.

[66] E.g., J. J. N. Palmer, 'The War Aims of the Protagonists and the Negotiations for Peace', *The Hundred Years War*, ed. K. Fowler (London, 1971), 57; *Wars of Edward III*, 145.

[67] Le Patourel, *Feudal Empires*, chap. xii, 176–7.

[68] G. Villani, 'Cronica', *Cronisti del Trecento*, ed. R. Palmarocchi (Milan, 1935), 388–9.

[69] *Grandes Chroniques*, ix, 292; Lucas, *Low Countries*, 480–546; B. D. Lyon, *From Fief to Indenture* (Cambridge, Mass., 1957), 214–17.

Alfonso XI of Castile with the English Princess Joan, and in 1344 Derby and Arundel were empowered, as lieutenants of Aquitaine, to broker alliances with the rulers of Castile, Aragon and Portugal.[70] Over the next few years Edward III spent a good deal of time in courting the Castilians, simultaneously corresponding with Alfonso's wife and mistress in pursuit of a final agreement on the dynastic alliance.[71]

Meanwhile, a certain amount of effort was concentrated in and around Brittany. The increasingly threatening behaviour of Philip VI towards those lords of western France who sought to use the Breton succession dispute as a means to their own ends was beginning to create defectors to Edward's cause. Philip's attempt to set an example for such men by executing the powerful Oliver III Clisson in 1343 rebounded badly on him.[72] In March 1345 John de Montfort escaped from Valois custody and fled to England. On 20 May, in a ceremony at Lambeth Palace witnessed by Archbishop Stratford and the earl of Northampton, John duly performed liege homage to Edward III as king of France.[73] Another of those who took up the offer of alternative sovereignty was Godfrey Harcourt, lord of Saint-Sauveur-le-Vicomte in the Cotentin peninsula of Normandy. He had rebelled against Philip's heir, John, duke of Normandy in 1343 and had been forced into exile in Brabant, whence he now transferred to England to perform homage to Edward III as king of France in June 1345.[74]

The preparations for the new offensive were the first to incorporate the idea of a simultaneous and co-ordinated attack on Philip VI from a number of different fronts. Edward was not satisfied simply with sending armies of occupation into Aquitaine and Brittany while he led an offensive into north-western France. This time, he was determined to ensure that all his resources could, if necessary, be directed towards a decisive engagement with the elusive Valois. By the spring of 1345 this grand strategy was firmly in place. Three armies were to be assembled. The first, whose numerical force was not specified, would muster at Portsmouth and proceed to Brittany under the command of the earl of Northampton.[75] The second, of 2,000 men, would embark from

[70] Fowler, *King's Lieutenant*, 45–7.

[71] P. E. Russell, *The English Intervention in Spain and Portugal in the Time of Edward III and Richard II* (Oxford, 1955), 8–9.

[72] S. H. Cuttler, *The Law of Treason and Treason Trials in Later Medieval France* (Cambridge, 1981), 146–51; Henneman, *Olivier de Clisson*, 26–7; *Foedera*, III.i, 35, 45.

[73] Murimuth, 243; *Foedera*, III.i, 39.

[74] *Foedera*, III.i, 44; Baker, 78–9; R. Cazelles, *La Société politique et la crise de la royauté sous Philippe de Valois* (Paris, 1958), 136–40. For payments of fees to various other Norman knights coming into Edward's homage in this period see E 403/336, 20 Dec. 1345, 28 Jan., 6 Apr. 1346.

[75] *Foedera*, III.i, 37.

Southampton under the earl of Derby and would make for Gascony.[76] Both of these forces would, it was expected, be considerably swollen in size once they joined up with local allies and subjects of the king in Brittany and Aquitaine. Edward himself would command the third force, which was to gather at Sandwich, and which would be the centrepiece of operations against Philip. This was intended to be the largest army yet raised in England for service overseas, amounting to as many as 20,000 men.[77]

To realize such enormous forces required a huge push on the part of the English logistical machine. Commissions of array were issued in the counties south of the Trent in 1345–6 to levy around 4,000 foot archers. The towns were required to supply a further 2,000 men, mainly mounted archers and hobelars. Some 7,000 archers and spearsmen were to be levied in Wales. Of these targets, the king's commissioners were eventually able to raise a total of around 9,000 men. Large numbers of criminals were also recruited as archers by the time-honoured inducement of royal pardons. To assuage public concern on this matter, the crown insisted that such men provide a full term's service, without pay, and find appropriate sureties before their pardons would be validated.[78] Between 2,500 and 3,000 men-at-arms and around the same number of mounted archers were raised as volunteers by members of the king's household.

Much more controversially, the crown attempted to assess all lay landholders to perform military service as men-at-arms or light cavalry on a sliding scale according to relative wealth. This breached the conventions on conscription for overseas service and created a predictable outcry among the gentry in the shires. The crown therefore agreed to a compromise that would reduce the level of service required and would allow those assessed to send others in their place.[79] The king gave the vital reassurance that all those who served, either by traditional or by experimental methods of recruitment, would be paid for the duration of the campaign.[80] Nevertheless, the new attempts to extend the basis of compulsory service were roundly condemned in the parliament of 1346.[81] In the later stages of the 1346–7 campaign, the towns in particular were to be put under enormous pressure to generate additional forces. When complaints were voiced about these unreasonable demands, the crown again had to reduce

[76] Fowler, *King's Lieutenant*, 230–2.

[77] For the figures that follow, see A. Ayton, 'The English Army and the Normandy Campaign of 1346', *England and Normandy in the Middle Ages*, ed. D. Bates and A. Curry (London, 1994), 261–8; Rogers, *War Cruel and Sharp*, 423–6; *Battle of Crécy*, 159–251.

[78] Ayton, *Knights and Warhorses*, 144–5; SC 1/39/144. For the use of conditional pardons for service in Scotland in 1343 see SC 1/39/154.

[79] C 47/2/31, 34, 36–41, 52, 58; *CPR 1343–5*, 414, 427–8; *Crecy and Calais from the Public Records*, ed. G. Wrottesley (London, 1898), 66.

[80] *Crecy and Calais*, 191–204; Prestwich, *Armies and Warfare*, 84–5.

[81] *PROME*, iv, 392–3; Powicke, *Military Obligation*, 195–8.

the quotas, convert them to cash payments, and promise that such levies would not set a precedent.[82] If the long arm of the English war state reached out further in 1344–7 than at almost any other time in the reign, it was to have its fingers repeatedly nipped by a polity more than usually sensitive to the preservation of its own rights.

Behind this great drive to put England into a state of war lay the power of Edward III's personality. The king put in considerable time to negotiate fresh loans for the war, and was instrumental in a new initiative to charge taxes on foreign monks resident in his kingdom.[83] In February 1346 he supervised a gathering of the prelates and lords of southern England which gave consent to a two-year extension of the *maltolt* and thus ensured the continued viability of the farm of the customs.[84] He was also actively involved in the enormous operation to raise shipping for the transport of troops and supplies.[85] His personal attention to the recruitment campaign was especially evident. When he was at Portchester in May 1346, for example, Edward ordered that a list be drawn up of all those who had refused the discipline of the array and returned to their homes. He then sent the names of the deserters by personal correspondence to the chancellor in order that action should be taken against such 'rebels'.[86] The force of between 14,000 and 15,000 that Edward eventually led across the Channel may have been rather smaller than he had originally hoped, but it was still the largest army that had yet been raised in England for service overseas, and represented to a significant degree the mixture of persuasion and compulsion that the king had brought to bear upon his realm.

It is at the very highest levels of strategy, however, that we can best see Edward's personality at work. Throughout the planning for the new campaign, the king kept himself fully informed of the state of diplomacy.[87] He cleverly avoided the personal conferences that successive papal envoys demanded of him, making it known to them that he considered it his moral duty aggressively to pursue his rights in France and rather disingenuously informing them, at the eleventh hour, that it was now simply too late to start discussions for peace.[88] In particular, Edward put a high premium on secrecy, refusing to declare anywhere outside the closest of circles precisely what he intended to do, and achieve, in the forthcoming expedition. In fact, it was never actually specified during the long

---

[82] *Foedera*, III.i, 107; *CFR 1337–47*, 497, 500–4; Ormrod, *Reign of Edward III*, 180, 249 n. 67.

[83] *CCR 1343–6*, 636–7, 651. For loans raised in 1345–6 see Harriss, *King, Parliament*, 324–6; Axworthy, 'Financial Relationship', 30, 150–1.

[84] Harriss, *King, Parliament*, 445.

[85] SC 1/40/91; C 81/908/6; C 81/1331/13. This was part of a long-term interest of Edward's: Ormrod, *Reign of Edward III*, 52.

[86] C 81/1332/1.

[87] C 49/7/15; E 403/327, 2 Apr. 1343.

[88] Murimuth, 190–1; *Foedera*, III.i, 80, 84.

preparations of 1344–6 where the king's own army would land in France.[89] After this force disembarked in Normandy in 1346, Sir Bartholomew Burghersh claimed that it had originally been destined for Gascony. It remains a moot point whether this was a truth, an error or a deliberate red herring intended to deceive Philip VI's information service.[90] Whatever the case, Burghersh's testimony suggests that Edward achieved his principal aim of depriving the enemy of effective intelligence and arming himself with the weapon of surprise.

In spite of his calculated vagueness over strategy, Edward was emphatic about the need to keep the non-combatant population of England properly informed of his war aims and his progress towards their fulfilment. The preparations for the 1346 campaign brought new heights of sophistication to the government's domestic propaganda. Not content with the regular system that disseminated news through prayers ordered in parish churches, Edward now enlisted the assistance of the great public preachers of the day, the Dominican friars. In the spring of 1346 the chancery supplied the head of the Dominican order in England with a detailed account of the causes of the French war so that the members of his order might 'inform the intellects and enliven the hearts of the faithful'.[91] As in the information circulated to the localities in 1337, the emphasis was on Philip of Valois's systematic abuses of his former status as Edward's feudal lord. Little was said specifically about the claim to the French throne, and most commentators were complicit with the king's general preference to keep the war agenda as generalized and flexible as possible.[92] Some, however, were in no doubt that Edward was intent on making himself ruler of France.[93] By a slow and subtle process, the king had begun to reconcile some of the more belligerent sections of English society to the potential attractions of the dual monarchy. What was now needed was the great victory that would allow peace to be established firmly on Edward's terms.

By June 1345 everything seemed in a state of readiness. Northampton departed for Brittany, where one of his commanders, Sir Thomas Dagworth, immediately cut a dash by defeating a small force led by Charles of Blois near Josselin. The fleet destined for Gascony was delayed

[89] Murimuth, 199; Baker, 79.

[90] *The Life and Campaigns of the Black Prince*, ed. and trans. R. Barber (Woodbridge, 1979), 14. A. H. Burne, *The Crecy War* (London, 1954), 137, suggests that the king asked the clergy to disseminate news of a departure for Gascony in order to mislead French intelligence. But the relevant instructions to the prelates state only that Edward intended to go to 'parts overseas': *Foedera*, III.i, 81.

[91] *Foedera*, III.i, 72–3.

[92] E.g., *AC*, 19.

[93] *Chron. Lanercost*, 341–2.

by adverse winds. In early June the king went down to survey Derby's troops gathering at Southampton, before heading off to make the necessary oblations at Canterbury. Henry of Grosmont eventually left in late July and landed at Bordeaux on 9 August. Ralph Stafford, recently installed as seneschal of Gascony, had already begun to rally Plantagenet support in the duchy and, with the help of Bernard and Bérard Ezi, Arnaud de Durfort and the new captal de Buch, Jean de Grailly, set about plans for a major offensive in the Dordogne.

Edward III joined his own army at Sandwich in mid-June. The king had decided that the fifteen-year-old Edward of Woodstock should now make his military debut and join him in the campaign. On 1 July the infant Prince Lionel was accordingly appointed keeper of the realm and provided with a council of executive officers and advisers, including the three Stratfords and the elderly earls of Lancaster and Surrey. The queen also came down to join the king at Sandwich and finally waved her husband off on 3 July.[94] But at the very last moment the main expedition had to be postponed in order to allow Edward to make a dash to Flanders. The king had been warned that Jacob van Artevelde was about to be toppled from power and that the support of the towns of Ghent, Ypres and Bruges would thus be imperilled or lost. On 17 July, the king's worst fears seemed to be fulfilled when van Artevelde was ambushed and murdered in Ghent. In fact, Edward and his advisers had exaggerated van Artevelde's importance. Remaining aboard ship in the waters of Sluys, the king conducted a frantic bout of negotiations which, on 19 July, secured a successful agreement. The men of the three towns guaranteed that they would not accept Louis de Nevers as count of Flanders unless Louis in turn recognized Edward as king of France.[95] The emergency averted, Edward set sail on 22 July to link up with the main force departing from Sandwich. Their destination remained undisclosed. But a violent storm dispersed the fleet, driving some of the king's ships back into the North Sea and forcing most of them to take refuge in the Channel ports. Landing at Sandwich on the 26th, Edward proceeded to Canterbury to give more than usually heartfelt thanks for his safekeeping. He then moved rapidly on to Westminster to consult about a way forward. To the king's bitter regret, the council decided that the expedition would have to be cancelled and a new army called together as soon as events allowed.[96]

Edward's frustration was all the greater given the spectacular news trickling back from Aquitaine. On 24 August, the earls of Derby and Pembroke, Sir Walter Mauny and Ralph Stafford took the stronghold of Bergerac, securing a quiverful of valuable hostages and plundering the

[94] *CCR 1343–6*, 634; *Foedera.*, III.i, 50.
[95] Lucas, *Low Countries*, 516–27.
[96] *Foedera*, III.i, 55–6; *Crecy and Calais*, 58–61.

'vast riches' to be had from the town.[97] Moving on into the Périgord, Henry of Grosmont defeated the count of l'Isle at Auberoche in October and recaptured La Réole on the Garonne in January. Again, there were huge profits to be made: contemporary estimates put the ransoms negotiated for French captives taken at Auberoche at around £50,000.[98] Stafford then led the attack on the Agenais, where he took Aiguillon and negotiated numerous defections to the English cause. The profits of war went straight to the commander, Derby, to be shared as appropriate with his captains. The news from Brittany, however, was bleak. John de Montfort made an abortive attempt to lay siege to Quimper in August and fell ill after withdrawing to Hennebont, where he died on 26 September. His heir, the titular Duke John V, was only about five years old and lived in the security of the English court. Northampton and his commanders were left to rally Montfortist support as best they could. A difficult winter campaign in the north of the duchy yielded few results other than the capture of La Roche-Derrien. Caution had to prevail. Plans to send relief forces to Brittany and Gascony were set aside, and the date of embarkation for Edward III's main army, now reconvening at Portsmouth, was put off until 15 May 1346.

To the anxious and eager Edward, these long weeks of waiting must have seemed all too reminiscent of the successive delays experienced at the start of the French war in 1337–8. But there was a major difference. Since the king now remained within his realm, he was able not only to provide direct supervision of the logistical machine of the state but also to take a good deal of the credit for the well-timed measures being put in place to provide for the general security of the realm. The position in Scotland demanded urgent attention. News of further incursions over the border, and a serious raid on Carlisle in October 1345, forced Edward to attempt another of his habitual rushes to the north. He was thwarted by the onset of a brief and unspecified illness, and seems to have got no further than Nottingham before turning south again for London and moving off to Woodstock for the Christmas season.[99] But during the winter councils of war were also held in London with various prelates and lords of the north. In mid-January 1346, when Edward made another progress into the Midlands, accompanied by his wife and mother, to attend the funeral of the earl of Lancaster at the hospital of the Newarke in Leicester, he probably took the opportunity for further discussion of the great affairs of France and Scotland with the assembled prelates and magnates. On the king's personal instruction, the sheriffs of Northumberland and Cumberland were now absolved of their normal

---

[97] Knighton, 53.
[98] Fowler, *King's Lieutenant*, 60–1.
[99] Mortimer, *Perfect King*, 220.

responsibilities to appear at the exchequer so that they could remain on the alert in the defence of the border. Powerful new commissions to keep the Scottish marches were also issued in the spring of 1346.[100] In April there came an equally affirmative response to public concern about the possible corruption of government and justice in the event of another prolonged royal absence from England. The Ordinance of Justices, duly proclaimed in the shires, required the staff of the central courts and those serving on oyer and terminer, gaol delivery and assize commissions to swear that they would be impartial in all their judgments and eschew the fees and robes habitually offered as sweeteners by private parties. It also created a new framework for the regulation of those county officials, especially the sheriffs and escheators, who serviced the courts in the provinces.[101] If all of this was, from Edward's point of view, a rather inadequate substitute for military action, it at least made very clear that the peace and security of the realm now stood appropriately high on the list of the king's concerns.

At the end of May 1346, Edward III finally took up a position at Portchester outside Portsmouth in preparation for his departure to France. He nevertheless had to sit tight for over a month before army, fleet and wind were all ready. When the moment came, the king was still keeping his counsel on where his forces might land; the order that no one leave the realm for a week after the departure of the royal fleet was a dramatic sign of Edward's resolve to deprive his enemies of information for as long as possible.[102] The French may well have suspected that the English king would do as before and make for Flanders. In reality, though, Edward was intent on a different theatre. For a while, he seems to have given serious consideration to a landing in Brittany.[103] There also remained the real possibility of a royal appearance in Gascony, for the French had laid siege to Henry of Grosmont's forces in La Réole and Aiguillon, and Edward was well aware of his contractual obligation to go, if necessary, to the assistance of this army.

In the end the decision was reached to make for the Cotentin peninsula in Normandy. There were good practical reasons for such a choice. The prevailing winds were likely to allow a well-organized landing in Normandy, and Godfrey Harcourt's defection to the English cause created the assurance of a safe haven in the Cotentin. Moving forward from such

[100] *RDP*, iv, 556–8; Knighton, 54–5; *Hist. Angl.*, i 266; E 159/122, rot. 56; Neville, *Violence, Custom and Law*, 37–8.

[101] *SR*, i, 303–6; P. Nightingale, 'The Intervention of the Crown and the Effectiveness of the Sheriff in the Execution of Judicial Writs, *c*.1355–1530', *EHR*, cxxiii (2008), 32.

[102] C 76/23, m. 23d; Alban, 'National Defence', 319. In instructions to the exchequer in May and June, the king referred obliquely to his impending 'passage' and his eventual return 'from over there': E 159/122, rots 64, 80.

[103] *Crecy and Calais*, 11.

a position, the king would be able to link up with other local defectors and
with the English forces installed in Brittany. From the start, however, the
invasion of Normandy was seen not as a means of relieving the
Montfortists but as an end in itself. Froissart dramatized his account of
the 1346 campaign with a conversation aboard ship between Edward III
and Godfrey Harcourt:

'Normandy,' said Sir Godfrey, 'is one of the richest countries in the
world. I promise you, on my life, that once you reach it, it will be easy
to land there. There will be no serious resistance, for the inhabitants
have no experience of arms and the whole cream of the Norman
knights are at the siege of Aiguillon with the duke [of Normandy].You
will find large towns and fortresses completely undefended, in which
your men will win enough wealth to make them rich for twenty years to
come. Your fleet will be able to follow you almost as far as Caen. If you
see fit to take my advice, you and all of us will profit by it. We shall have
gold, silver, food supplies and everything in abundance.'[104]

This episode may be the product of Froissart's overactive imagination,
but the practical benefits that it highlighted were very real considerations
in the summer of 1346. English men-at-arms were attracted to the
pleasing notion that, just as a duke of Normandy had conquered the
kingdom of England in 1066, so now would a king of England occupy
the duchy of Normandy. Just as the English armies operating in Brittany
and Aquitaine had begun to realize the enormous private profits to be
made from plunder and ransoms, so now did the fabled wealth of
Normandy offer the real prospect of material gain. The campaign that
ensued has long taken its historical label from the great conflict at Crécy
in which it reached its triumphant conclusion. It was the *viage de Normandie*
or 'way of Normandy', however, that the veterans of 1346 were always to
name their great moment in the sun.[105]

[104] Froissart, trans. Brereton, 69. This elaborates on le Bel, ii, 70, 76.
[105] SC 1/39/180, 187, 192; SC 1/40/111, 128, 143, 211; SC 1/42/2, 39; W. M. Ormrod,
'England, Normandy and the Beginnings of the Hundred Years War, 1259–1360', *England
and Normandy*, ed. Bates and Curry, 202.

Chapter 10

THE WAY OF VICTORY, 1346–1347

Edward III landed at Saint-Vaast-la-Hougue on the north-eastern coast of the Cotentin on 12 July 1346. One of the king's first actions on disembarking was to knight his eldest son, along with the new earl of Salisbury and the young Roger Mortimer. In Edward's party were the earls of Arundel, Huntingdon, Northampton (recently recalled from Brittany), Oxford, Suffolk and Warwick and the vigorous former royal clerk Thomas Hatfield, who had recently been elevated to the bishopric of Durham. Over the next few days they worked to devise a definitive strategy. The army would split into three divisions, with the king commanding the centre, the prince of Wales the vanguard and Bishop Hatfield the rear. From the start, the campaign was to be tightly focused on the king's strategic needs. The absence of a preliminary statement as to the nature and details of such planning simply confirms the success of Edward's continuing policy of secrecy and surprise.

It used to be thought that Edward III designed the *chevauchée* through Normandy in the summer of 1346 as a conscious alternative to a set-piece engagement.[1] According to this view, the English king wished only to expose the inability of Philip VI to defend his realm and people and thus to demonstrate the moral validity of the Plantagenet cause. The intention was to force Philip into a truce and allow Edward to take the dominant role in discussions aimed at securing a final peace. Open battle was both unnecessary and purposefully to be avoided, and the great victory at Crécy in which the campaign culminated happened only because the

---

[1] The main sources for the campaign of 1346–7 comprise a group of chronicles and newsletters with an extremely complex textual and editorial history. See, in particular, *Battle of Crécy*, 287–350; K. Fowler, 'News from the Front: Letters and Despatches of the Fourteenth Century', *Guerre et société*, ed. Contamine, Giry-Deloison and Keen, 63–92. Some of the chronicles and newsletters are translated in *Life and Campaigns*, 13–48. This chapter relies chiefly on the accounts of the campaign provided by Sumption, i, 489–586; K. DeVries, *Infantry Warfare in the Early Fourteenth Century: Discipline, Tactics, and Technology* (Woodbridge, 1996), 155–75; Rogers, *War Cruel and Sharp*, 238–85; and *Battle of Crécy*, 35–107. These, like the medieval sources on which they are based, sometimes take significantly different positions. Other full-length accounts of the campaign are to be found in Burne, *Crecy War*; H. de Wailly, *Crécy 1346: Anatomy of a Battle* (Poole, 1987); and M. Livingstone and M. Witzel, *The Road to Crécy: The English Invasion of France, 1346* (Harlow, 2005).

French themselves were determined to see the whole thing to a final conclusion.[2]

In recent years, interpretations of the expedition of 1346 have changed considerably. Jonathan Sumption has suggested, controversially, that it was an attempt to mirror recent strategy in Brittany and to undertake a war of conquest and occupation that would realize Edward III's claims over his ancestors' duchy of Normandy.[3] It is the arguments of Clifford Rogers and Andrew Ayton, however, which have largely informed the new orthodoxy. These suggest that Edward aimed, consistently and explicitly, to provoke an open confrontation in battle, and that the *chevauchée* was the essential means by which he sought to draw Philip VI into such an affray. The damage to the economic infrastructure of Normandy and the merciless treatment of the non-combatant population were intended to impose an overwhelming political and moral obligation on the Valois to defend the realm in arms.[4] It might be added that Philip VI also actively sought just such a confrontation. After the criticisms he had suffered for withdrawing without a fight in 1339 and 1340, he had come to realize that a major battle was the only means by which he could fully vindicate his rule in France, confront the rebels in Aquitaine, Brittany, Normandy and Flanders, and reassert his feudal suzerainty over the king of England. In July 1346 both sides were intent on a decisive confrontation. It only remained to decide when, where and how such a battle would be fought.

The clear-sightedness of English royal strategy is evident in the high level of discipline instilled into the great army from the time of muster at Saint-Vaast-la-Hougue. It is possible that Edward III in 1346 issued something akin to the ordinances of war later promulgated on the eve of major campaigns by Richard II in 1385 and Henry V in 1419. Certainly, a semi-official account of the ensuing campaign known as the *Acta bellicosa* or *Acts of War of Edward III* suggests a particular effort to ensure that English soldiers behaved in a way befitting to their commander-in-chief's status as rightful ruler of France:

> The English king, feeling for the suffering of the poor people of the country, issued an edict throughout the army that no town or manor was to be burnt, no church or holy place sacked, and no old people, children or women in his kingdom of France were to be harmed or molested; nor were they to threaten people, or do any kind of wrong, on pain of life or limb.[5]

---

[2] See p. 594.

[3] Sumption, i, 532–3.

[4] *Wars of Edward III*, 265–83; Rogers, *War Cruel and Sharp*, 230–7; *Battle of Crécy*, 35–107, 139–57.

[5] CCCC, MS 170, printed in J. Moisant, *Le Prince Noir en Aquitaine* (Paris, 1894), 157–74 and translated in *Life and Campaigns*, 26–40 (quotation at 28–9); *Battle of Crécy*, 296–9.

This hopeful expression of high discipline accords ill with some of the other descriptions of the campaign, with their keen emphasis on the orgy of destruction and plunder that ensued. Yet there are signs that Edward's commanders were usually able to keep in check the random acts of violence and theft in which the English infantry so obviously and readily wallowed. Importantly, it was the king, and not his soldiers, who determined the relative speed at which the army would move.[6] It was to Edward's great benefit that he encountered such little resistance over the first few days of the campaign and that he was able to develop and test collective responsibility to a shared strategic goal. Godfrey Harcourt's considerable influence in the Contentin peninsula ensured a relatively easy march south. In spite of local efforts to impede the English advance through the marshes of the Douve, the first major town along the way, Carentan, immediately surrendered and was promptly sacked. Moving on eastwards across the Vire to Saint-Lô, the English army spread out into a fan shape, covering an area fifteen to twenty miles wide, in order to wreak maximum damage on the fields and villages that stood in its path.[7]

By 25 July the king was within a few miles of Caen, the second city of Normandy and the first significant source of resistance to the English invasion. The castle of Caen was held by the counts of Eu and Tancarville, respectively constable of France and chamberlain of Normandy, together with a force somewhere in excess of 1,000 soldiers. On the 26th, Edward's men descended on the town. It was not an orderly engagement: English archers launched an unsupported attack on the enemy, and the earls of Warwick and Northampton, sent by the king to order retreat, were themselves caught up in a potentially ruinous mêlée.[8] But the outcome was a triumph. The bridge over the River Orne was taken, and Edward's soldiers ran amok through the town. French knights, frightened for their safety, frantically searched out English captains who might agree to spare their lives in return for ransoms. The count of Eu himself surrendered to Sir Thomas Holland, who later sold this prized prisoner to Edward III for the magnificent sum of £12,000. Holland, with an eye to the main chance, was subsequently to use some of his new-found wealth to prosecute a controversial case in the papal court at Avignon in order to secure the hand of the nineteen-year-old Joan of Kent, wife of the second earl of Salisbury, with whom he claimed to have undertaken a clandestine but binding promise of marriage in 1340. Holland's success in achieving this prestigious marriage with the king's cousin provides a striking example of the genuinely transformative impact of luck in war.

---

[6] *Battle of Crécy*, 62–5.

[7] Murimuth, 215; Avesbury, 358; C. J. Rogers, 'By Fire and Sword: *Bellum hostile* and the "Civilians" in the Hundred Years War', *Civilians in the Path of War*, ed. M. Grimsley and C. J. Rogers (Lincoln, Nebr., 2002), 36–7.

[8] *Life and Campaigns*, 17–18.

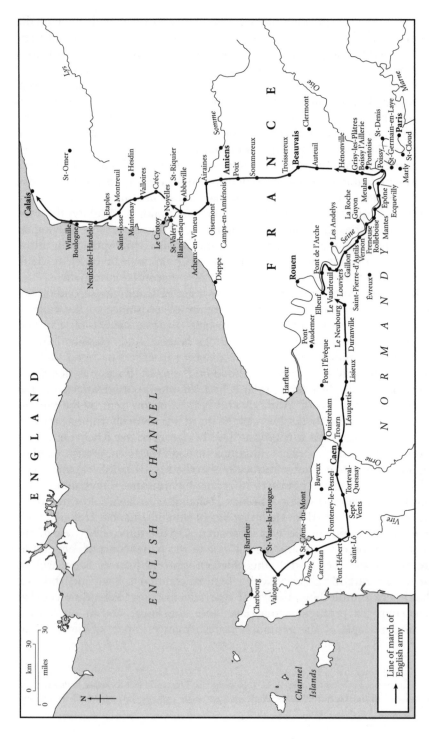

Map 5 The Normandy Campaign, 1346.

For most of his fellows, though, the sense of gratification was rather more in the instant. As at Carentan, so now at Caen, English soldiers gorged on food and drink, raped women and made off with vast amounts of moveable wealth.[9]

The prisoners and spoils taken at Caen became a matter of legend in England, and two generations later Thomas Walsingham was to write about the fine linens and plate of Normandy with which the matrons of England had proudly adorned their tables in the aftermath of the great campaign.[10] Behind this breathtaking display of unrestrained greed, however, lay some important strategic achievements. The sack of the town marked an ultimatum to Philip VI: if he did not appear and fight, then Edward would continue to march eastwards towards the Île-de-France and wreak yet further destruction on the heartlands of the French crown. The English king was especially careful to order that the French lords and knights taken at Caen be shipped home and not put to ransom until his aims, defined in notably general terms, were properly advanced towards conclusion.[11] Although a number of the lesser prisoners of war rapidly organized their release on parole, the counts of Eu and Tancarville remained in prison in England for some time. Edward later used them to apply leverage on Philip VI for the better treatment of some of the English prisoners of war taken in Normandy, Brittany and Aquitaine, including his old friend Sir Walter Mauny.[12]

As Edward had predicted, the sack of Caen did much to galvanize French opinion and policy. On 29 July the Valois king ordered major reinforcements for the sizeable army already mustered at Rouen, and began a westward march. It was his evident intention to meet Edward's forces before they could cross the Seine, enter the Île de France, and threaten the city of Paris. Within a few days, however, he turned back, apparently in alarm at news that Edward III's Flemish allies, led by the English knight Hugh Hastings, had crossed the Lys and entered northern France. After hosting a banquet on the evening of 30 July, Edward and his army set off the following day over the floodplain of the River Dives, arriving at Lisieux on 2 August. Philip's only remaining hope was to cut off the further advance of the English army by destroying all the bridges along the Seine. Edward's scouts advised that the king's obvious target, the city of Rouen, was too powerfully invested to risk attack. The English therefore reached the Seine at Elbeuf on 7 August and marched along its western side to seek possible alternative crossing points. On 13 August they entered Poissy, a mere fifteen miles from Paris. The conventual church of

[9] CPR 1345–8, 337, 538–9; le Bel, ii, 80, 83; Froissart, iii, 146–7; ODNB, xxx, 138.

[10] Knighton, 58–9; T. Walsingham, Chronicon Angliae, ed. E. M. Thompson (RS, 1874), 26; Barnie, War in Medieval English Society, 36–7.

[11] Life and Campaigns, 18.

[12] Sumption, i, 511, 556.

Poissy had been founded by Edward's maternal grandfather, Philip the Fair, whose heart was buried in the choir there.[13] The king reportedly ordered the priory spared as a mark of honour to the memory of his illustrious French forebear. Faced with widespread panic, Philip VI evacuated the town and ordered out the remains of his dwindling military forces to Saint-Cloud. This simply gave Edward the opportunity he needed to take the crossing at Poissy, and by 14 August his engineers had managed to erect a temporary wooden bridge that would give the English baggage train access to the right bank. The episode keenly demonstrated the superiority of the English logistical and tactical machine and threw the French court into something approaching real panic.[14]

Philip VI's attempt to rely on a natural rather than a human barrier had proved a failure. With Edward's advance upon Paris now apparently unstoppable, his only recourse was to immediate battle. On 14 August Philip wrote to Edward to demand that he present himself south of Paris or north of Poissy and fight out their dispute to an honourable and definitive conclusion. If this was precisely what the English king had wanted all along, it was also a risky ultimatum. Edward appreciated the severe perils involved in allowing his enemy to determine the place and time of battle. On 15 August he marked the Feast of the Assumption by attending mass at Philip the Fair's priory church. Thus replenished with Capetian zeal, he promptly wrote to the Valois that he had come to recover the throne of France and to punish those who resisted his rule. If Philip the tyrant wished to challenge Edward's rightful authority, he would have to come and find him.[15]

Behind this act of bravado there were clear signs of strain. After a month in the field, Edward's army was seriously fatigued. Despite the orgy of consumption that had gone on in Normandy, the supplies brought over from England had begun to run low. Deciding to avoid battle in the Seine basin, Edward now moved due north via Beauvais and headed for the Somme. It is easy to interpret this move as a retreat and to see the ensuing week as one in which the Valois had the English on the run. But Edward's forces remained in good order. The plan was to link up with the relief forces and provisions due to be sent over from England to the port of Le Crotoy, and thence to move to a position where effective battle might at last be engaged.[16] With uncharacteristic decisiveness and speed, however, Philip now moved to foil the English advance. On 23 August the Valois marched west from Amiens, pushing Edward towards Oisemont and

[13] P. Lee, *Nunneries, Learning and Spirituality in Late Medieval English Society: The Dominican Priory of Dartford* (York, 2001), 15–17.

[14] Le Bel, ii, 85–8; *Life and Campaigns*, 19, 21–3, 37–8.

[15] *CPR 1345–8*, 516–17; *Life and Campaigns*, 38–9; Froissart, iii, 148–50, 382–3.

[16] C 81/314/17803, printed in Fowler, 'News from the Front', 83–4 and translated in *Wars of Edward III*, 125–6.

Acheux. The English king suddenly found himself in a highly dangerous position, caught between the coast and the marshlands of the Somme. His only immediate recourse was to cross the river, buy some time and make proper preparation for the battle to which he remained so keenly committed. It was in this moment of high drama that Edward demonstrated, once more, the personal conviction that helped sustain his credibility among his captains and men.

During the night of 23–24 August, Edward's commanders accomplished the skilful manoeuvre that successfully delivered the king's forces from imminent ambush and transferred the entire English army across the Somme at the ford of Blanchetaque, to the west of Abbeville.[17] At daybreak and low tide, the earl of Northampton and Reginald Cobham waded through the river and held the beach against Philip's commander, Godemar du Fay. The whole episode represented in dramatic fashion Edward III's ability to combine major logistical and tactical manoeuvres with supreme feats of individual bravery. In subsequent accounts of this episode circulated in England, a whole variety of explanations was offered for the success at Blanchetaque. Some asserted a miracle and implied a parting of the waters akin to Moses's crossing of the Red Sea.[18] The later Meaux chronicler offered the more prosaic but perhaps more authentic explanation that Edward's army was assisted by the insider knowledge of a Yorkshireman who had been living in the area for the previous sixteen years.[19] The story is a reminder that, on successfully crossing the river, Edward III had arrived in his own ancestral county of Ponthieu. There was no shortage of loyalists in the region, or indeed captains in the army, who had reasonably good knowledge of viable crossing places in the Somme basin. Contemporaries were equally well aware that the ensuing engagement at Crécy was fought on ground that formed part of the Plantagenet inheritance unjustly seized by the Valois in 1337.[20] Even if the manoeuvre was a matter of exigency, it was a powerful reminder of Edward's publicly declared commitment to recover his rights in France.

The English took promptly to the forest of Crécy, which spread out for some ten miles to the north of the Somme. Using the natural cover to their advantage, they managed to elude the dispirited French during the night of 24 August. The next day, Edward marched his army to the northern edge of the forest near the village of Crécy. Edward had been here before, as a young man, en route to and from his fraught meeting with Philip VI at Amiens in 1329, and he may well have felt that the site offered an appropriate position in which finally to challenge the authority that the Valois

---

[17] Le Bel, ii, 96–8; *Life and Campaigns*, 22, 24. For what follows see *Battle of Crécy*, 85–98.
[18] Murimuth, 216; Avesbury, 368.
[19] *Chron. Meaux*, iii, 57.
[20] Le Bel, ii, 99, 105; Froissart, iii, 165, 402.

had earlier and so aggressively asserted over him. The king was also aware that Philip's son John was now marching northwards with relief forces, and judged it best to make battle without further delay. On Saturday 26 August, Philip VI moved to prevent Edward III's advance further north, apparently believing that the English intended to join up with the Flemings at Hesdin. In fact, Edward was already drawing up his lines. His scouts had identified a suitable defensible site between Crécy and Wadicourt, comprising a ridge about 2,000 yards long facing south-east and fronted by a valley, known as the Vallée des Clercs, that opened at its southern point on to the little River Maye. Edward deployed his army such that the left flank would have level ground in front of it, the right flank would be protected by the sloping terrain, and the rearguard would be defended by the thick woodland of the Bois de Crécy-Grange. The conventional interpretation has it that Philip VI deployed his own forces on the rising ground to the east of the Vallée des Clercs. Running down the valley was a steep-sided bank that would have been readily seen by both sides as a serious impediment both to a cavalry charge and to an organized retreat. Unless Philip believed that he would be able to manoeuvre around this bank, he must have been aware from the outset that the topography was almost entirely to the benefit of the English. Some of the French chroniclers, desperate to seek consolation from the ensuing defeat, were later to suggest that Edward had behaved dishonourably by not giving Philip VI due notice of the intention to fight.[21] But whatever the relative states of preparedness of the two armies, it was now clear that battle would have to be joined.

The confrontation at Crécy is one of the most intensely studied military engagements of the Hundred Years War. Yet the sources are oddly confused as to detail. Consequently, no one knows precisely how the two armies were arranged on the field.[22] The dismounted English men-at-arms and infantry were lined up in three 'battles' led by the king, the prince of Wales and the earl of Northampton. But it remains uncertain whether these divisions were stretched out in a single line or arranged in consecutive groupings, one behind the other. There is also a major issue as to the deployment of the English archers. These are conventionally supposed to have been organized in wedge formations or circles between the battles. But it is also possible that they were ordered to spread out in long lines in front of them. The best guess is that Edward III's division kept to the rear, where the baggage carts were used as additional impromptu defence works; that the other two battles formed up alongside each other, with the prince's forming the vanguard; and that the archers were placed partly in triangular wings on the flanks and partly as a screen

[21] *Battle of Crécy*, 273–7.
[22] Ibid., 139–57.

in front of the men-at-arms.[23] The French, meanwhile, seem to have placed their mercenary forces, the Genoese crossbowmen, in the front battalion, and then formed a number of divisions of mounted cavalry behind them. They deployed the infantry on the flanks. Reliable numbers are much more difficult for Philip's than for Edward's army, but the French may have had between 20,000 and 25,000 men on the field – anything up to 10,000 in excess of the English.[24] That Edward III intended to take what was now his accustomed defensive position is clear from the fact that the English soldiers dug pits to act as foot traps for the oncoming French forces.

There was a novel piece of technology in use on the English side. Guns and gunpowder had been employed for a few years before 1346 by both English and French armies, but only during sieges. The reference to a number of cannon being used by Edward III's forces on the field of Crécy therefore represents the first recorded employment of firearms by the English in pitched battle. These guns were small and crude, and fired bolts and grapeshot rather than the large projectiles associated with later warfare. Although they inflicted some damage on the Genoese, the guns at Crécy were mostly intended to scare the enemies' horses and add to the general mayhem of the mêlée.[25]

Unlike his son in his later military career in Aquitaine and Spain, Edward III does not seem to have gone in for making formal orations to the massed ranks of his army during the immediate preparations for battle. Considering the elaborate mythology that was to build so quickly around the victory of Crécy, it is striking indeed that the likes of Jean le Bel and Jean Froissart resisted the temptation to reconstruct an imagined battlefield speech replete with the predictable evocations of divine pleasure and chivalric adventure. Rather, Jean le Bel claimed that Edward made an informal tour of the ranks while they were still in their tents or digging the pits. Froissart, embroidering this story, had the king mounted on a white palfrey and carrying a white baton as he rode among his troops, rousing the frightened to acts of heroism.[26] Edward's style, as the Rochester chronicler noted, was thus to provide informal and intimate encouragement to his soldiers 'by words, gifts and deeds'.[27] A Roman chronicle that provides an interesting independent account of the ensuing battle similarly reports that Edward comforted his men and commended

---

[23] R. Hardy, 'The Longbow', *Arms, Armies and Fortifications in the Hundred Years War*, ed. A. Curry and M. Hughes (Woodbridge, 1994), 178.

[24] Sumption, i, 526. Other estimates tend to suggest smaller numbers for the French: *Battle of Crécy*, 18.

[25] Tout, *Collected Papers*, ii, 238–40; Prestwich, *Armies and Warfare*, 320–1.

[26] Le Bel, ii, 106; Froissart, iii, 408; Ainsworth, *Jean Froissart*, 289–90.

[27] *Wars of Edward III*, 44.

himself to God.[28] Giovanni Villani put it more prosaically: having disposed his cavalry and foot, Edward left the men to the consolations of food and drink.[29]

The battle lines were ready by late afternoon on 26 August. Philip's advisers counselled that he should hold his ground and wait until the following morning to decide how best to proceed. But many of the nobles and knights gathered in this great array of chivalry regarded such caution as a slur on their honour, and pressed for an immediate attack. As rain began to fall and the light deteriorated, the French began their onslaught. Very few of those in the Valois command had seen English longbowmen in action before. Consequently, when the Genoese failed to make headway against the hail of arrows from the other side, Philip and his supporters began to believe that some kind of treachery was being committed. In their panic, they immediately ordered the cavalry to charge. Philip's brother the count of Alençon tore forward, managing to reach the lines of the prince of Wales. The French divisions behind him, eager to join in, re-formed in a line roughly parallel to the English. But the costs of this reckless charge were high indeed. A hail of English arrows now brought French horses and riders low. The Welsh infantry moved forward to dispose of the grounded elite, slipping their deadly daggers in between the plates of their enemies' armour. In this frantic state, many of the Genoese were left trampled under the hooves of their own allies' horses. Those French knights who made it into the thick of the mêlée were quickly aware that they had disastrously forfeited their initial advantage of numbers and fallen victim, like the Scots before them, to the success of English defensive tactics.

Throughout the battle Edward III kept to the rear, taking up a position near a windmill that provided a commanding view of the field. Given his previous and subsequent eagerness to be involved in the thick of the action during lesser battles and affrays, this move to the comparative safety of operational headquarters seems surprising. No doubt the king, recognizing the very high risks, was keen to demonstrate a sense of responsibility in his role of commander-in-chief. Philip VI, by contrast, by placing himself in the vanguard of his army, created a liability for his men by incurring serious injury and risking capture by the English.[30] In the end, though, Edward's decision was probably motivated less by dispassionate calculations over his personal security than by personal concerns about status and honour. If he was indeed the rightful king of France and Philip VI a mere impostor, then strictly speaking it was unnecessary – and even demeaning – for Edward to fight in person. Above all, there were the

---

[28] Anonimo Romano, *Cronica*, ed. G. Porta (Milan, 1979), 134–5.
[29] Villani, 'Cronica', 395.
[30] *Life and Campaigns*, 19–20; *Eulogium*, iii, 210–11.

rights and reputation of a new generation to consider. Just as the English king had had his day at Halidon Hill and Sluys, so now should the young Edward of Woodstock be given the opportunity to take the palm of glory at Crécy. Froissart later claimed that Edward III refused to send aid to the prince on the field in order not to compromise the latter's claim to valour and honour: the chronicler's rendering of Edward's bold retort, 'Let the boy win his spurs', was to become one of the great set pieces of the later national mythology of Crécy. If the details of the story are apocryphal, then its essence seems to be accurate, for the Black Prince did indeed find himself at the very centre of action and seems only to have been saved from capture or worse by the loyalty and bravery of his personal standard-bearer, Sir Richard Fitzsimon.[31] Froissart's account captures an essential truth about Edward III's uncompromising adherence, even in a moment when the stakes were set so terrifyingly high, to the imperatives of chivalric kingship.

Nightfall brought an end to the battle. John of Hainault, that recent defector from the English cause, led Philip VI from the field. At the start of the battle, the French king had ordered the unfurling of the Oriflamme to signal that this would be *guerre mortelle*, a battle to be fought to the death. Edward had responded by sporting his own banner of the Dragon. But Philip's attempt to ensure that his forces were not distracted from the fight by the search for prisoners, ransoms and booty had rebounded badly. Edward III now responded with equal severity, insisting that no quarter be given to enemy troops found alive in the surrounding countryside. The Oriflamme itself lay, abandoned and tattered, on the field. The heraldic surcoats of the fallen chivalry of France were gathered up for display in Edward's pavilions, where relief and exhilaration soon gave way to story-telling and general inebriation. The English men-at-arms and archers left in the field at the king's instruction lit bonfires and settled down to a rest-less night, broken by the moans of the wounded and dying.[32]

It was not until the mist rose on the following morning that the full extent of the victory was understood. Among the bodies found on the field was that of Philip's courageous ally, the blind King John of Bohemia, who had made a suicide pact with his supporters and ridden to certain death against the English. A veritable pantheon of French nobles lay with him, including the duke of Lorraine and the counts of Alençon, Auxerre, Blois, Flanders, Harcourt and Sancerre. Jean le Bel commented that no one could remember so many great princes dying in a single encounter.[33] All

---

[31] R. Barber, *Edward, Prince of Wales and Aquitaine* (London, 1978), 67.

[32] Murimuth, 247; Baker, 81–2; *Récits d'un Bourgeois de Valenciennes*, 235; C. Given-Wilson and F. Bériac, 'Edward III's Prisoners of War: The Battle of Poitiers and its Context', *EHR*, cxvi (2001), 804–5.

[33] Le Bel, ii, 109.

told, the French had lost between 1,500 and 2,000 men-at-arms. No one
even bothered to count the number of archers and infantry who had died.
But in one of his campaign reports, Edward III recorded that a further
4,000 French men-at-arms and Genoese archers had lost their lives when
pursued in flight from the field of Crécy. If the battle had been bloody,
then its aftermath was evidently still more so.[34]

The English losses, in dramatic contrast, were minimal. The official
tally of knights and esquires was around 300. But even this comparatively
modest figure may be an exaggeration, since it seems to include men-at-
arms who died during the subsequent siege of Calais.[35] Such miraculous
deliverance could only be ascribed to divine intervention. In a sermon
preached before the king and his commanders later in the year, Thomas
Bradwardine, one of the clerks who had been present with the king's party
at Crécy, mobilized predictable but potent arguments to prove that the
recent victories had been won by God's will.[36] After nearly ten years of
arduous, expensive and often unfruitful war, the moment of transformation had at last arrived. Crécy was indeed a defining moment in the king's
life. Some years later, when the English regime was properly re-established
in the county of Ponthieu, Edward would have the particular satisfaction
of furnishing his English feasts with wild boar hunted in the forest of
Crécy.[37] But the victory of 1346 was far more than an act of personal
revenge. It was the single greatest military accomplishment of Edward's
reign, the benchmark against which all his subsequent achievements of
war, and those of his successors, would be judged. For the king's subjects
at home and his allies abroad, it provided spectacular affirmation of the
justice of Edward's cause and of the apparent feasibility of his increasingly ambitious war aims.

News of the astonishing victory spread quickly throughout England, not
least because of the careful propaganda campaign that Edward III's home
administration quickly mounted.[38] After the sack of Caen, the king had
sent orders home for the summoning of parliament. Financial considerations made this inevitable: the subsidy granted in 1344 had run out, and
the crown was already taking out loans on the apparent expectation of a
renewal of taxation.[39] At Caen, Edward's soldiers had discovered a text of
the detailed plan drawn up in 1339 between Philip VI and the nobility of

[34] *Wars of Edward III*, 131.

[35] Rogers, *War Cruel and Sharp*, 270; *Battle of Crécy*, 191.

[36] J. Coleman, *English Literature in History, 1350–1400: Medieval Readers and Writers* (London,
1981), 266; Carey, *Courting Disaster*, 82–5; H. S. Offler, *Church and Crown in the Fourteenth
Century* (Aldershot, 2000), 1–40.

[37] E 159/144, *Brev. bar.*, Mich., rots 13d, 15.

[38] *Foedera*, III.i, 89.

[39] *PROME*, iv, 383–4.

Normandy to invade England.[40] The compact had promised that the assets of the English crown would be given to Philip's son in his capacity as duke of Normandy and that the nobles would be able to take possession of all other lay property beyond the Channel. This fanciful proposal had long since collapsed, and there was no real threat to the security of England in the summer of 1346. But the text was perfectly suited to the domestic political needs of the crown. Archbishop Stratford had the French invasion plan read aloud to the Londoners in St Paul's churchyard in a deliberate attempt to drum up suspicion of the enemy and provoke appropriate patriotic responses.[41] Bartholomew Burghersh, sent home specially to make report to parliament on the latest developments at the front, formally announced the victory of Crécy to the lords and commons and invoked the 1339 ordinance as direct proof that the people of France and Normandy remained intent 'to destroy and ruin the whole English language and nation'. Only constant vigilance could ensure that the realm would in due course properly benefit from the new Plantagenet supremacy in France.[42]

Hardly had parliament dissolved on 20 September than further news broke of divine pleasure in English arms. Under the terms of their alliance with the French, the Scots were more or less bound to come to Philip VI's assistance by making diversionary moves against northern England. Already in late October 1345 David II had ordered a raid into Cumberland.[43] During the summer of 1346 he began to consider how a more ambitious invasion would improve his own international standing and force a peace with Edward III. The English crown had been well aware of these dangers when planning the French campaign; the taxes and infantry raised north of the Trent were reserved for the defence of the northern border, and the magnates of the marches were encouraged to remain at home and prepare for their own war.[44] A truce had been extended to the end of September 1346, but such was the likelihood of an imminent invasion that sixteen of the northern English lords and prelates had been given exemption from attending the Westminster parliament.[45] Leadership of the military operations in the north passed to the

---

[40] Froissart, *Oeuvres*, xviii, 67–75; P. Contamine, 'The Norman "Nation" and the French "Nation" in the Fourteenth and Fifteenth Centuries', *England and Normandy*, ed. Bates and Curry, 227–8.

[41] Murimuth, 211–12; Avesbury, 363–4.

[42] *PROME*, iv, 388–93; D. Green, 'National Identities and the Hundred Years War', *Fourteenth Century England VI*, ed. C. Given-Wilson (Woodbridge, 2010), 119. For other uses of this discourse in the build-up to the 1346 campaign see *Foedera*, III.i, 67; C 76/22, mm. 27, 25.

[43] *Chron. Lanercost*, 341; *Wyntoun*, vi, 175–7.

[44] *Rot. Scot.*, i, 668–71; Harriss, *King, Parliament*, 348–54.

[45] *Rot. Scot.*, i, 667, 674; *RDP*, iv, 558–61.

archbishop of York, Lords Percy, Neville, Umfraville, Lucy and Mowbray and others including the prominent sheriff of Yorkshire, Thomas Rokeby.[46]

By early October a Scottish force comprising 2,000 well-armed troops and as many as 10,000 basic infantry had gathered on the western march. Many of the Highlanders actually returned home before the army crossed into England, but this army still had sufficient resources to launch a major offensive into Cumberland, raiding monasteries and villages and forcing Carlisle to pay ransom for release from the threat of pillage.[47] As the enemy forces made their way east into Northumberland and crossed the Tyne and Derwent, heading for Durham, the English prepared for major action. About 6,000 men, mostly arrayed infantry, were mustered at Richmond in Yorkshire and marched thence to Bishop Auckland.[48] On 17 October the opposing forces met at Neville's Cross outside Durham.

Even more than for Crécy, the chroniclers' accounts of the battle of Neville's Cross are confused and contradictory.[49] Whether it was the hail of arrows from the English archers or the constraints of the topography that drove the Scottish schiltrons to destruction remains a matter of keen debate. After three hours of struggle, however, it was evident that the English had inflicted a decisive defeat, and Robert Stewart and the earl of March left the field with their supporters, beating a hasty retreat northwards. The effect was disastrous for the remaining Scots, who were now driven from the field. The earls of Moray and Strathearn and the marshal, constable, chancellor and chamberlain of Scotland were all dead; the earls of Wigtown, Menteith and Fife, David's great commander, William Douglas of Liddesdale, and a host of Scottish nobles and knights were captive. David II himself, wounded in the face by two English arrows, was taken prisoner by the Northumberland esquire John Coupland.[50] The precise sites both of the battle and of David's capture remain a matter of keen dispute. But the city of Durham was quick to claim the victory as its own, and the banners of the king of Scots and his English victors hung in the cathedral church for at least two hundred years in commemoration of that vivid moment when the city was so miraculously delivered from the thrall of the Bruce.

[46] *CDS*, iii, no. 1463; *Rot. Scot.*, i, 675.

[47] *CDS*, v, no. 803; *Chron. Lanercost*, 344–6; *AC*, 24; A. Grant, 'Disaster at Neville's Cross: The Scottish Point of View', *The Battle of Neville's Cross, 1346*, ed. D. Rollason and M. Prestwich (Stamford, 1998), 22; Penman, *David II*, 125–6; Campbell, 'England, Scotland', 194.

[48] M. Prestwich, 'The English at the Battle of Neville's Cross', *Battle of Neville's Cross*, ed. Rollason and Prestwich, 6–7.

[49] *Chron. Lanercost*, 347–52; Bower, vii, 252–61; *Wyntoun*, vi, 177–87; Murimuth, 218–19; Avesbury, 376–7; Baker, 87–9; *AC*, 26–8.

[50] *Wyntoun*, vi, 185.

Messengers sped south immediately after the battle to bring the happy news to the regency administration in London, and the king was soon informed of the dramatic change of fortunes in the north.[51] Edward was delighted. From his new base at Calais, he issued personal orders for the deployment of the clutch of prominent Scottish prisoners.[52] He could now be assured – in a way that had not been the case since he left Scotland in the late 1330s – of the security of the northern border and of the remaining English strongholds in the Scottish Lowlands. In May–June 1347, Edward Balliol led an army of 1,000 men into Scotland and took effective control of significant parts of Berwickshire and Roxburghshire.[53] For a brief and precious moment, it seemed that Edward III was about to fulfil his ambitions in Scotland, to assert his suzerainty over a subordinate Balliol regime and to restore his sovereignty in the Lowlands.

It was the triumph at Neville's Cross and the apparent revival of English fortunes of the Scottish march that also made possible Edward III's continued stay on the continent. For one of the most unusual things about the French campaign of 1346 is that the king did not call a halt after the battle of Crécy. On 26 August he raised his tents and made northwards to Calais, arriving before the gates of the town on 3 September. When parliament met at Westminster a week later, it was told that Edward had laid siege to Calais. He intended to remain there until the town had fallen and he had gone again in pursuit of Philip of Valois.[54] To choose Calais as the site of such a final confrontation was both emotive and pragmatic. After the battle of Sluys, Edward III had listed Calais as one of the northern French ports that continued to pose a threat to English supremacy in the Channel.[55] The English polity was also well aware that the capture of the town and its temporary or permanent occupation could prove highly beneficial both for military operations and for the pursuit of trade. With some grumbling about the impact of recent taxes and military burdens, and on the understanding that the war would continue, the commons therefore acceded to the crown's request and granted two further fifteenths and tenths.[56] The lords, informed of the prince of Wales's recent knighting, also assented unilaterally to the collection of a customary aid to

---

[51] E 403/339, 1 Dec. 1346.

[52] *CDS*, iii, no. 1482.

[53] E 101/25/10; *CDS*, iii, nos 1479, 1492; *Foedera*, III.i, 113; Knighton, 74–7; *Wyntoun*, vi, 187–9.

[54] *PROME*, iv, 389–90; Rogers, *War Cruel and Sharp*, 273–85; S. Rose, *Calais: An English Town in France, 1347–1558* (Woodbridge, 2008), 7–22. Precisely the same point was made by the king in his letter to Sir Thomas Lucy: *Life and Campaigns*, 23.

[55] C 76/15, m. 7d.

[56] *PROME*, iv, 388–93. The same discourse had also been used in the build-up to the 1346 campaign: *Foedera*, III.i, 67; C 76/22, mm. 27, 25.

be levied on the tenants-in-chief of the crown.[57] A major new round of purveyance was ordered, and fresh supplies of troops were summoned to muster at Sandwich on 15 October and cross to Calais to support the forces gathered there.[58] Faced with this resounding affirmation of royal policy, the clergy had little choice but to follow and, in the meetings of convocation held in October 1346 and January 1347, duly granted the crown two further tenths.[59] Crown and polity had powerfully affirmed its compact and provided the fiscal and logistical basis for a further, major extension of the war.

If the siege of Calais was the means by which Edward hoped to draw Philip VI into a final, devastating encounter, then it soon became evident that this aim could not be quickly realized. Philip, having sent his forces home, was directionless until the arrival of John of Normandy in early September. A new force was called to muster at Compiègne on 1 October and march against Calais. In the interim, Edward III's allies and commanders in other arenas seized the opportunity of the temporary crisis of Valois authority to advance their causes. The Flemings plunged into Artois, took the town of Thérouanne and laid temporary siege to Saint-Omer. The withdrawal of the duke of Normandy's army from south-west France also allowed the English to make significant advances in Aquitaine.[60] In September–October 1346 Henry of Grosmont, who had succeeded to the earldom of Lancaster on the death of his father the previous year, led a small army north from La Réole and reached as far as Poitiers, whose inhabitants were murdered and plundered without discrimination. Along the way, small garrisons were planted in Saintonge and Poitou. Lancaster's Gascon supporters, the Albret brothers and Alexandre de Caumont, led raids into the Agenais and Bazardais that won back many positions lost since the 1320s. All of this caused much confusion and concern in Paris, forcing Philip VI to abandon the army of Compiègne and order a new army to muster at Orléans and march south against Lancaster. When he arrived at Arras in May 1347, at last intent on a confrontation with Edward III, Philip called a two-month postponement to his operations. His attempts to cut off Edward's supply and communication routes into Flanders had failed miserably. Faced with a major crisis of confidence among his own commanders, Philip limped his way to Hesdin, some fifty miles south of Calais, to watch and wait for Edward's next move.

---

[57] *PROME*, iv, 401–2, 403; E 175/2/22; *Antient Kalendars*, i, 162–3. For the parallel aid levied by the prince in his lands see *BPR*, i, 34.

[58] *Foedera*, III.i, 135–6; E 358/2, mm. 24d, 26d, 29d, 31, 31d, 32, 35; C 47/2/41/11; C 47/2/61/11, 13, 15.

[59] Ormrod, *Reign of Edward III*, 205. The northern clergy, like parliament, made the second year of the grant conditional upon the continuation of the war: SC 1/42/140; C 270/14/3.

[60] Avesbury, 372–4; Fowler, *King's Lieutenant*, 67–70.

Edward III remained at Calais more or less permanently from September 1346 to October 1347. His army had a difficult and dispiriting winter. Many of those who had thrived on the adrenalin of the Normandy campaign and survived the risks of battle at Crécy were now laid low by food poisoning, dysentery and malaria. Among the senior members of the army thus afflicted were the former royal official and confidant William Kilsby, who died at Calais in the first month of the siege, and the prominent East Anglian knight Hugh Hastings, whose death in England in July 1347 is probably attributable either to a severe blow to the mouth or to chronic sickness contracted in the besieging English army.[61] For some, such ordeals and risks were simply too much: notwithstanding the transformation in the relative moral authority of Plantagenet and Valois, Godfrey Harcourt now thought better of his defection to Edward's side and sought pardon and restoration from Philip VI.[62] At home, too, there were some distinctly unwelcome consequences arising from the extended siege of Calais. At a great council held at Westminster in March 1347, the regency administration sought consent for no fewer than four new taxes: a prospective grant of the *maltolt* for three years from 1348; a forced loan of 20,000 sacks of wool; a permanent customs duty on the export of cloth; and a six-month levy of tunnage and poundage.[63] Over the spring and summer of 1347 considerable pressure was applied to raise loans from a wide range of religious houses and towns for 'the defence and safety of England'.[64] Privy seal writs sent to the bishops to try to speed up the payment of the current clerical tenth stressed the obligation of all right-thinking people to support an enterprise undertaken for the common good.[65] Edward retained a high view of his fiscal prerogatives and of his continued right to exploit the realm for the full pursuit of his enterprise abroad. At least some taxpayers were drawn to the reluctant but inevitable conclusion that that the liberation of France was only to be achieved by the oppression of England.[66]

In some respects Edward's long period of residence at Calais in 1346–7 bore public comparison with the extended stay in Antwerp and Bruges in 1338–40. Considerable resources were allocated for the comfort of the

[61] B. Hooper, S. Rickett, A. Rogerson and S. Yaxley, 'The Grave of Sir Hugh de Hastings, Elsing', *Norfolk Archaeology*, xxxix (1984–7), 88–99.

[62] E. Déprez, 'La Double Trahison de Godefroi de Harcourt (1346–1347)', *Revue historique*, xcix (1908), 32–4.

[63] Harriss, *King, Parliament*, 445, 450–1, 457, 460. There is evidence that selected merchants and masters of ships were involved in the councils of Feb. 1346 and Mar. 1347: *PROME*, iv, 395–6; Ormrod, *Reign of Edward III*, 251.

[64] *CCR 1346–9*, 360; G. L. Harriss, 'Aids, Loans and Benevolences', *Historical Journal*, vi (1963), 15; Jurkowski, Smith and Crook, *Lay Taxes*, 50; C. D. Liddy, *War, Politics and Finance in Late Medieval English Towns: Bristol, York and the Crown, 1350–1400* (Woodbridge, 2005), 24–6.

[65] *Registrum Johannis de Trillek, episcopi Herefordensis*, ed. J. H. Parry (CYS, viii, 1912), 267–8.

[66] *PROME*, iv, 407–8, 447, 448.

royal household and other great commanders. A complete new town, known as Villeneuve-la-Hardie, was thrown up on the outskirts of Calais, with mansions for the commanders and viewing galleries from which the royal party could observe the siege. The queen, who bore her tenth child, Margaret, at Windsor in July 1346, subsequently moved across to Calais, and arrangements were put in place for the two older princesses, Isabella and Joan, to join their parents there for the duration.[67] The gathering of so many family, friends and hangers-on in the camp at Calais led one or two commentators in England to conclude that the prolonged siege was nothing more than an excuse for laziness and luxury.[68] This attitude may not have been typical, but it is a reminder that the apparent inactivity of the king during the long siege of Calais could, under different circumstances, have provoked precisely the same kinds of public criticism that had worked so negatively against Edward's reputation during his sojourn in the Low Countries in 1338–40.

These hints of misgiving must have been compounded by the serious crises of diplomacy now facing the English crown. From his base at Calais Edward kept in close contact with events in Aquitaine and Brittany and maintained direct diplomatic contact with the emperor and the rulers of Castile and Navarre.[69] He also personally received the homage of the French and Netherlandish knights and lords who continued steadily to be drawn to his cause.[70] Edward showed particular interest in developments in Burgundy, where the defection of a group of disillusioned nobles allowed him to make his first faltering interventions against Philip VI's brother-in-law, Duke Odo.[71] None of this, however, could disguise the fact that the diplomatic strategy purchased at such vast expense in 1337–40 was now in a state of almost complete collapse. Since the death of the childless William of Hainault in 1345, Edward and the emperor had formed an increasingly bitter rivalry concerning the succession rights of the deceased count's sisters, their respective wives Philippa and Margaret. In October 1346 Queen Philippa met the empress at Ypres to agree a moratorium on their quarrel.[72] But the resulting impasse further compromised English

---

[67] Trautz, *Könige von England*, 336; *Foedera*, III.i, 118: E 358/2, m. 35d. The tradition that Queen Philippa was present at the battle of Neville's Cross is false: le Bel, ii, 126–9; Froissart, iv, 20–6, 231–7; Prestwich, 'English at Neville's Cross', 8–9.

[68] *Political Poems*, i, 158–9.

[69] E 101/391/4, mm. 1–2.

[70] BL, Add. Ch. 11307, printed in Déprez, *Etudes de diplomatique anglaise*, 50; E 101/391/4, m. 3.

[71] Sumption, i, 562.

[72] *Récits d'un Bourgeois de Valenciennes*, 242–3; Lucas, *Low Countries*, 558–9. For Margaret's subsequent sojourn in England in 1351 in connection with the pursuit of the sisters' claims, see E 403/359, 12. Dec. 1351, 29 Feb. 1352; E 403/362, 18 May 1352; Fowler, *King's Lieutenant*, 119.

diplomacy, and a special conference at Calais failed to mobilize the towns of Hainault in joint action with the Flemings. Edward's young nephew, Reginald of Guelders, also deserted the English cause in May 1347.

Still more ominous was the failure of continuing efforts to win over the rulers of Flanders and Brabant. In March 1347 Edward III's household moved to Bergues outside Dunkirk where, amidst much feasting, the king sealed an agreement with Louis de Mâle, who after the death of his father at Crécy had succeeded as count of Flanders. Louis undertook a preliminary ceremony of betrothal to Edward's eldest daughter, the fourteen-year-old Isabella of Woodstock. In return, he was offered the attractive prospect of controlling the Plantagenet counties of Ponthieu and Montreuil, with cash compensation while they remained in hostile Valois hands.[73] But the count only went through these formalities to appease his pro-English subjects. Within a matter of weeks he had wriggled free of the arrangement and rejoined Philip VI in France. The fiasco caused considerable personal humiliation to the English princess and her father. Then, in June, Duke John of Brabant, the most powerful of the Netherlandish princes, finally made his peace with Philip VI. In a joint ceremony in July, Louis de Mâle and Reginald of Guelders signalled their own public adherence to the Valois cause by their double marriage with Duke John's two daughters, Margaret and Marie.[74] By the later summer of 1347 only the Flemish towns and William of Juliers remained steadfast in support of the English alliance. The family networks that had sustained English interests in the Low Countries since the beginning of the reign had truly entered the terminal stage of their long decline.

The news from Brittany was a good deal more encouraging. In June 1347 the king's lieutenant in the duchy, Sir Thomas Dagworth, enjoyed a spectacular victory against Charles of Blois at La Roche-Derrien. Charles lost half his army in the struggle, including several of his principal supporters, and was himself taken prisoner.[75] The battle had comparatively little effect in terms of the number of positions that the English could claim as their own within the duchy; La Roche-Derrien itself, stoutly defended by Dagworth in the battle, was again lost to the French within a matter of weeks. But possession of the Valois-backed contender for the ducal title greatly improved the prospect of a Montfort succession and gave the English a strong negotiating position as and when Philip might again be drawn into talks. Dagworth, who was rewarded with £3,500 for his endeavours, transferred his prisoners to England. Arriving at the

[73] Paris, Bibliothèque Nationale, MS Fr. 693, fols 222v–223; G. le Muisit, *Chronique et annals de Gilles le Muisit, abbé de Saint-Martin de Tournai (1272–1352)*, ed. H. Lemaître (Paris, 1906), 169; *Foedera*, III.i, 111–12; *CPR 1345–8*, 569; 'A Letter to Louis de Mâle, Count of Flanders', ed. B. Wilkinson, *BJRL*, ix (1925), 177–87.

[74] *Récits d'un Bourgeois de Valenciennes*, 250, 256.

[75] Le Bel, ii, 144–9; *Grandes Chroniques*, ix, 28–306.

Tower of London, Charles of Blois found himself in exalted company. David II, who had been taken after Neville's Cross to Wark, Bamburgh and York, had been transferred to the Tower in December 1346, his earlier gaolers, Coupland and Rokeby, having been richly rewarded for their enterprise and loyalty to the crown of England.[76] The principal captives of Caen, the counts of Eu and Tancarville, were also there. England was indeed becoming a great repository of royal and noble hostages whose release might prove the essential stock needed to broker future definitive settlements with the Scots and the French.

The siege of Calais brought into being the largest army ever mobilized by the English crown in France during the Hundred Years War. As a result of the crown's energetic efforts to recruit supplementary forces, the army that had fought at Crécy was doubled in size over the winter of 1346–7, to somewhere in the region of 26,000 men.[77] There was a strong element of compulsion in some of the recruitment strategies, and desertion from the ranks of the infantry was a constant problem. But members of the English chivalric class were keenly aware of the importance that might in due course be attached to the roll call of the decisive engagement now promised against Philip of Valois. Among the earls, only the elderly and infirm – Surrey, Gloucester, Hereford and Devon – were denied the chance to join in the anticipated celebration of English arms.[78] Lancaster and Pembroke, who had missed Crécy because of their campaign in the south-west, returned to England late in 1346 and subsequently joined the king at Calais the following spring. After Neville's Cross a number of the northerners, including Thomas Lucy and William Greystoke, also crossed over to join the army of Calais. Other English barons were called over in May 1347, and the earl of Kildare arrived in July.[79] With hundreds of English knights and esquires gathering in the retinues of these great lords, the siege of Calais turned into one of the greatest gatherings of English chivalry known in the later Middle Ages.

In this general atmosphere of excited anticipation, it took all the king's leadership skills to maintain order and morale. The leaders of the army were not immune to the ravages of disease, and a number of prominent captains, such as Sir Maurice Berkeley of Uley, died in the course of the siege.[80] Nor was the enforced inactivity conducive to the expressions of

[76] *Foedera*, III.i, 99; *CDS*, iii, nos 1474–5, 1478; M. C. Dixon, 'John de Coupland – Hero to Villain', *Battle of Neville's Cross*, ed. Rollason and Prestwich, 36–49; R. Frame, 'Thomas Rokeby, Sheriff of Yorkshire, Justiciar of Ireland', *Peritia*, x (1996), 374–96. In the 1350s there was a lance kept at the Tower of London that Rokeby had given to Edward III, perhaps as a memorial of the battle: E 101/392/14, m. 6.

[77] *Battle of Crécy*, 267.

[78] *Foedera*, III.i, 120.

[79] *Crecy and Calais*, 6, 7, 183; *Foedera*, III.i, 120.

[80] Ayton, 'English Army', 266–7.

valour and honour that English knights and esquires so eagerly craved. The veteran lord Robert Morley used the lull in fighting to claim the right to bear the coat of arms of the defunct baronial family of Burnell. Edward III, appreciating the importance that the elite attached to such things, took up personal presidency of a court of chivalry convened to determine the matter. It was later reported that Morley had a robust exchange with the king, swearing 'by God's flesh' that, were his claims confounded, he would never again fight for Edward's cause in France. There is a ring of truth about this, for Morley had also been named as one of those who had dared question the king's military policies in the summer of 1340. But whereas Edward had earlier bitten back, he now took Morley's challenge in good part and duly confirmed him in possession of the Burnell heraldry.[81] The episode reflected well on Edward III's new found ability, since the time of his quarrel with Archbishop Stratford, properly to distinguish between open rebelliousness and mere plain speaking.

In the end, it was less the size or distinction of the English army and more the close attention to logistics that eventually allowed Edward III to prevail at Calais. Despite the repeated failure of his men to breach and scale the walls of the town, the king remained secure in the knowledge of an effective supply line from England and could well afford to sit and wait. In the spring of 1347, English land forces managed to capture the Rysbank, the narrow spit of land that controlled the harbour of Calais. Edward promptly invested it with troops and cannon. Although the English army never quite succeeded in enforcing a complete blockade of the town's port, their new position helped guarantee the ready flow of equipment and provisions across the Channel and accentuated the intense problems now experienced by the beleaguered forces within Calais. Edward had good cause to consider the benefits that had accrued from the achievement of naval supremacy since the battle of Sluys. By June the situation inside the town was indeed critical. According to a letter intercepted by Edward's spies sent by the French captain of Calais, Jean de Vienne, to Philip VI, the populace was reduced to eating horses, dogs and rats, and contemplating the need for cannibalism. Unless Philip finally came to his aid, Vienne would have no other option but to surrender.[82]

Stirred by such alarming information, Philip could no longer prevaricate. In late July he reached Sangatte, six miles south of Calais, with a force of between 15,000 and 20,000 men. Edward, anxious about their approach, wrote at least one personal letter to a member of the English clergy requesting prayers for his 'just cause' (*droite querele*) in this moment

---

[81] A. Ayton, 'Knights, Esquires and Military Service: The Evidence of the Armorial Cases before the Court of Chivalry', *The Medieval Military Revolution*, ed. A. Ayton and J. L. Price (London, 1998), 98 n. 22.

[82] Avesbury, 386; Knighton, 78–9.

of peril.[83] But Philip had no intention of risking a military engagement. Arrangements were put in place for discussions between representatives of the two sides. The French offered terms by which the whole of Aquitaine would be delivered back to Edward III as a fief of the Valois crown. When the English deputation, led by Lancaster and Northampton, scoffed at such a conservative offer, the French came back with an offer of battle, but only if the English would come out beyond the marshes that surrounded Calais and fight Philip's army on open ground. It was an appeal to the same traditions of honour that Philip had employed when Edward was at Poissy. But hard-nosed sense won the day. The English categorically refused to give up their strong position, and left it to Philip to decide a further course of action.

On the night of 1–2 August Philip delivered his answer. The French army raised its tents and skulked away in a southerly retreat. The sense of humiliation was palpable, and nowhere more so than within Calais itself, which had now been effectively abandoned by its sovereign lord. On 3 August the inhabitants of the town formally surrendered. Under the conventions of war, their year-long resistance entitled Edward III to take everything: their homes, their possessions, even their lives. The king had already demonstrated his ruthlessness in refusing refuge to the elderly and infirm ejected from the town when supplies had run short. Now, though, some degree of clemency was deemed appropriate. While they would forfeit all their property, the citizens would at least be spared their lives. The keys of the town were to be handed over to the king by six of the most prominent townsmen, who should present themselves with nooses round their necks as a sign of their utter submission to his will and pleasure. Jean Froissart claimed that Queen Philippa acted as champion of the wretched burghers and successfully pleaded with her husband for their release from otherwise certain death. It is likely, though, that Philippa's intervention was simply the public acting out of a policy already determined by the king and confirmed by his advisers.[84] In the sweetness of success, it behoved Edward III to show due clemency to a conquered and abject people.

* * *

[83] SC 1/37/174.

[84] Le Bel, ii, 165–7; Froissart, iv, 61–2; L. Chalon, 'La Scène des bourgeois de Calais chez Froissart et Jean le Bel', *Cahiers d'analyse textuelle*, x (1968), 68–84; Ainsworth, *Jean Froissart*, 297–9; P. Strohm, *Hochon's Arrow: The Social Imagination of Fourteenth-Century Texts* (Princeton, 1992), 99–105; J. C. Parsons, 'The Pregnant Queen as Counsellor and the Medieval Construction of Motherhood', *Medieval Mothering*, ed. J. C. Parsons and B. Wheeler (New York, 1996), 39–61. *Récits d'un Bourgeois de Valenciennes*, 253–4, 260–1, claims that Edward pretended to send Queen Philippa home to England in the summer of 1347 to avoid her being caught up in the efforts of her mother to make a peace, but also affirms her presence at the subsequent surrender of Calais. Anonimo Romano, *Cronica*, 134–5, ascribes the act of mercy to the interventions of the queen and 'a certain master of theology'.

The victories of 1345–7 transformed Edward III's reputation at home and abroad. In England, the great rush of successes represented by Auberoche, Crécy, Neville's Cross, La Roche-Derrien and Calais had the effect of persuading even some of the king's sternest critics that his war aims were legitimate and feasible. After their years in the wilderness, the English could once more proclaim their status as the new Israel, God's true chosen people on earth.[85] The acerbic Rochester chronicler had earlier commented on the apparent ludicrousness of Edward's claim to the French throne: for all the good it did him, he might just as well have called himself sultan of Babylon or king of heaven.[86] In the aftermath of Neville's Cross, Crécy and Calais, however, English writers became wildly enthusiastic about the prospect of subordinating the entire kingdom of France to the will of their monarch. One typical piece of vicious bigotry composed in the mid-fourteenth century, the Latin *Dispute between an Englishman and a Frenchman*, turned the traditional image of the French as lechers on its head, claiming that over-indulgence in sex had softened England's enemies and turned valiant men into sissies.[87] Certainly, the collapse of the massed ranks of the French elite made instant heroes of the English and Welsh veterans of Crécy, giving rise to late medieval popular mythology of the stout yeoman archer.[88] Among both his apologists and more neutral commentators on the continent, Edward III was now hailed as the leader of one of the mightiest regimes on earth. Jean le Bel remarked that when Edward became king no one in Europe talked of the prowess or bravery of the English, whereas after Crécy people held them to be the noblest combatants in the western world.[89] And Giovanni Villani played on the David and Goliath story to represent Edward's army as a little band of heroes united against the arrogant and vainglorious giant of France.[90]

Beyond the inevitable contemporary preoccupation with chivalric prowess and divine grace, a broader analysis of the entire campaign of 1346–7 reveals just how much the great victories of Crécy and Calais owed to effective leadership, sound strategy and good discipline. The secrecy that surrounded the planning of the campaign was successfully maintained only because of the powerful *esprit de corps* established in the ranks of high command. In the constable and marshal of the army, the earls of Northampton and Warwick, Edward found loyal and capable

---

[85] *Chron. Lanercost*, 344; A. Hastings, *The Construction of Nationhood: Ethnicity, Religion and Nationalism* (Cambridge, 1998), 35–65.

[86] BL, Cotton MS Faustina B. V, fol. 88; Rogers, *War Cruel and Sharp*, 215.

[87] See p. 323.

[88] Minot, *Poems*, 43–8; J. Bradbury, *The Medieval Archer* (Woodbridge, 1985), 171–9.

[89] Le Bel, i, 155–6.

[90] Villani, 'Cronica', 400–1. David and Goliath were also, interestingly, the subjects of a hanging kept for many years in Edward's court: E 101/396/18; E 101/397/2.

commanders prepared to act together in pursuit of a defined set of strategic aims. The sheer size of the royal army maintained in France in 1346–7 was testimony to the careful planning put into the *chevauchée*, battle and siege. Major logistical feats such as the bridging of the Seine at Poissy and the fording of the Somme at Blanchetaque also revealed the highly developed skills of engineers, scouts and logisticians. Above all, Edward's ability to dispose and order his troops on the field of Crécy exposed the very high level of discipline required to carry off the defensive tactics of the mixed formation successfully. Soon all – even the French – were attempting to do what the English had done, and abandon the traditional cavalry charge in preference for hand-to-hand combat between dismounted men-at-arms. It was to take some time before war leaders realized that this tactic was only successful when supported by archers; lacking the skill and experience of the English and Welsh longbowmen, Edward's contemporaries continued to find it very difficult to emulate the Plantagenet mode of fighting with any degree of success. It says much for the extraordinary international impact of Crécy, however, that within a generation English knights and bowmen, fighting in a recognizably 'English' style, were being employed as mercenary forces as far away as Portugal, Italy and Hungary.[91]

No military campaign succeeds without an effective support system behind it, and one of the principal reasons for the success of the 1346 expedition was the high degree of co-operation and co-ordination maintained between the king's army in France and the regency administration in England. It is easy to suppose that this was only achieved because Edward III was persuaded to abandon the principles of the Walton Ordinances and to allow his ministers at home to manage his war finances and domestic policy.[92] To assume that Edward was any less determined to ensure the priority of the war effort during his absence in 1346–7 is, however, palpably false. As in 1338, so in 1346, domestic government was closely managed through a stream of official correspondence maintained from the king's continental administration and communicated by the new keeper of the king's privy seal, John Thoresby.[93] Shortly after arriving at

[91] Ayton, *Knights and Warhorses*, 21.

[92] Thus Tout, *Chapters*, iii, 165–6; McKisack, *Fourteenth Century*, 212; Harriss, *King, Parliament*, 324.

[93] W. M. Ormrod, 'Edward III's Government of England, *c.*1346–*c.*1356' (University of Oxford DPhil. thesis, 1984), 75–8; Ormrod, 'Accountability and Collegiality', 69; C. Carpenter, 'War, Government and Governance in England in the Later Middle Ages', *Conflicts, Consequence and the Crown in the Late Middle Ages*, ed. L. Clark (Woodbridge, 2007), 6–7. The originals of warrants for exchequer issues do not survive for the period 1346–7, but the notes made against individual entries in the issue rolls demonstrate the flow of such instructions under the king's privy seal: E 403/338, 339, *passim*. In 1346–7, as in 1338–40, the regent was permitted to authorize issues of a routine nature: E 404/4/24, 25, *passim*.

Calais, Edward sent private instructions to Chancellor Offord to have his military plight advertised and thus hasten the dispatch of relief forces.[94] Members of the king's inner circle – Bartholomew Burghersh in September 1346 and Ralph Stafford in February 1347 – were sent home from time to time to impart the king's views to parliament and council.[95] During his sojourn at Calais, Edward adjudicated on the affairs of Ireland and intervened personally to protect the interests of his eldest son in Cornwall and Wales.[96] And within a few days of the taking of the town, Edward dispatched another personal representative, John Montgomery, to report to the council his plans for the disposition of his new conquest.[97] Here were all the signs of a ruler intent on the full assertion of his prerogatives and the uncompromising submission of his ministers to his own priorities.

The real explanation for the sustainability of government during the campaign of 1346-7 lies not, then, in any marked change of attitude on the part of Edward III. Rather, it is to be found in the improved efficiency of an administration now better able to sustain the demands that Edward continued to place on his realm of England. The council appointed to support the young Prince Lionel's keepership of the realm in 1346 had a significantly different composition from those of 1338-40. With almost the whole of the nobility actively occupied in war on several fronts, no earls and barons were formally associated with the home government; instead, John Stratford and his relatives were once more included. But neither the king nor his officers of state would brook any insubordination from that quarter. They stamped down on some of the bishops' attempts to override a recent parliamentary injunction and permit the raising of subsidies in their dioceses for the expenses of the papal peace talks. And in the summer of 1347 Edward sent home personal instructions, carried by Bradwardine, ordering the chancellor to convene the council and take pre-emptive measures against any prejudicial ordinances that might emanate from an upcoming ecclesiastical council summoned by Archbishop Stratford.[98] It was the new generation of loyal senior ministers, headed by the obedient Chancellor Offord and Treasurer Edington, that dominated the domestic administration in 1346-7 and ensured that the king's will remained the primary driver of all policy.

It was Edington's particular talent and diligence that also allowed Edward III to achieve the previously impossible and mount a major

---

[94] C 81/1332/10.

[95] *RDP*, iv, 561-2.

[96] C 81/1332/24; *RP*, ii, 180; Frame, *English Lordship*, 282 and n. 79.

[97] C 81/1332/31.

[98] SC 1/39/198, printed in B. Wilkinson, *The Chancery under Edward III* (Manchester, 1929), 198; *Records of Convocation*, iii, 249-512; xix, 42; Haines, *Stratford*, 358-9.

campaign without seriously jeopardizing the solvency of the crown. Edington's earlier experience as receiver of the ill-fated ninth and administrator of the emergency treasury set up at the Tower in the winter of 1340–1 had made him acutely aware of the embarrassments and dangers that arose when crown resources became over-committed. A schedule of royal debts drawn up at the start of his treasurership reveals his special concern to quantify and manage the deficit left over from the first stage of the French war.[99] In the era of Crécy, his strategy depended to a great degree on minimizing such outstanding obligations. Military contractors were called sharply to account: the exchequer took the position, for example, that Sir James Audley of Heighley, by failing to serve in person on the Gascon expedition of 1345, had broken the terms of his contract and would therefore incur personal liability for the wages of the men-at-arms and archers whom he had sent over under a substitute captain, John Tromwyn.[100] In similar vein, the successive bankruptcies of the Bardi and Peruzzi companies in 1343 and 1346 became convenient excuses for delaying – though not, in the end, reneging on – the repayment of the loans brokered through the Lombard companies before 1340.[101] There was also some distinctly sharp practice with regard to the repayment of the Dordrecht bonds. Creditors were required to sell these to the farmers of the customs at large discounts of 1 shilling or 2 shillings in the pound; the farmers were then allowed to redeem them at their full face value out of the profits of the ports. This had the unpredicted effect of encouraging unscrupulous individuals to take illicit advantage from counterfeit bonds; it also served to convince the polity that the farm of the customs was simply becoming a source of private profit for a small and unpopular cartel of merchants.[102] In a curious way, however, growing public suspicion of the rescheduling of public debt played increasingly to Edington's advantage. In 1346, as again in 1348, the commons made it a condition of their grants of direct taxation that the revenues should be used not for the settling of old debts, but solely for current military expenditure.[103] It was this principle that Edward III himself rather piously asserted when, at the end of the siege of Calais, he declared his opposition to a proposal that his debts to the city of London might be offset against taxes; the subsidies in

[99] BL, Harl. Roll CC. 30.

[100] N. Gribit, 'Accounting for Service in War: The Case of Sir James Audley of Heighley', *Journal of Medieval Military History*, vii (2009), 147–67.

[101] For details of the repayments made to these companies between 1343 and 1391 see E. Russell, 'The Societies of the Bardi and the Peruzzi and their Dealings with Edward III, 1327–45', *Finance and Trade*, ed. Unwin, 125–9; A. Beardwood, *Alien Merchants in England, 1350 to 1377* (Cambridge, Mass., 1931), 6–9, 122–33.

[102] SC 1/42/177; *PROME*, iv, 426–7; Fryde, *Studies*, chap. x, 14 and n. 4.

[103] *PROME*, iv, 392–3, 453.

question had been ordained solely for the costs of war, and 'the king will not depart from this faith'.[104]

The direct consequences of these and other efforts at systematic retrenchment in royal finance are best and most obviously judged by analysis of the expenditure undertaken by the principal war office, the wardrobe of the king's household. Over a period of twenty-two months in 1338-40, the wardrobe had run up expenses of just under £400,000 on war wages and other related expenditure, of which £135,000 represented overspend and IOUs. By contrast, the wardrobe account covering the Crécy-Calais campaign reveals expenditure of some £200,000, with over-spend and outstanding obligations running at only £16,000.[105] Such figures are far from representing a complete military budget for the relevant periods. It is quite possible, for example, that the costs of war handled by sheriffs, purveyors and other local officials were significantly higher in 1346-7 than they had been in 1338-40 as a consequence of the many logistical challenges involved in supporting the army of Calais.[106] Nor did the greater efficiency represented by Edington's regime prevent a barrage of short-tempered complaints about the simultaneous pressures of taxation and further government borrowing in 1347-8.[107] Nonetheless, the new and robust management of the credit system and the proper targeting of resources upon immediate needs meant that Edward III was never in any risk in 1346-7, as he had so obviously been in 1339-40, of having to withdraw from France before achieving victory. And for those inclined to make the point, the spectacularly successful *viage* and siege of 1346-7 could surely be said to represent astonishingly good value for money.

For most contemporaries, what ultimately explained that great duet of victories of Crécy and Calais was not the government's management of finance, effective or otherwise, but the charisma of the king. After his bruising experiences in 1338-40, Edward III was more than usually appreciative of the resulting good press and all the more eager to capitalize on it. From the moment of his first major success at the sack of Caen, the king actively demonstrated his belief in the power of good news. Through the long months that followed, he personally led the programme of systematic

[104] C 49/53/20. This document seems to have been presented to Edward immediately on his return to England in 1347: the response to its suggestion for a ban on the export of corn links with a proclamation issued on 16 Oct., warranted by the secret seal: *Foedera*, III.i, 139; *CLBL, F*, 170.

[105] Tout, *Chapters*, iv, 104-6, 115-18.

[106] S. Rose, *Medieval Naval Warfare, 1000-1500* (London, 2002), 60; M. Kowaleski, *Local Markets and Regional Trade in Medieval Exeter* (Cambridge, 1995); S. J. Burley, 'The Victualling of Calais, 1347-65', *BIHR*, xxxi (1958), 49-57.

[107] SC 1/38/52, 147; *Calendar of Ancient Correspondence Concerning Wales*, ed. J. G. Edwards (Cardiff, 1935), 185; *Historical Papers and Letters from the Northern Registers*, ed. J. Raine (RS, 1873), 390-2; 'The Register of Thomas de Insula', *Ely Diocesan Register 1894* (Ely, 1894), 227; Harriss, *King, Parliament*, 450-7. See also pp. 323-4.

dissemination that brought unusually detailed reports of the campaign both to the citizens of London and to the towns, marketplaces and parish churches of provincial England.[108] And in the period after his triumphant return, he helped create one of the most enduring series of memorials to the achievements of chivalry known in medieval England. Through the foundation of the Order of the Garter in the summer of 1348, Edward celebrated his personal feats of arms and honoured the great leaders of the recent victories in France. Thus inspired, Thomas Bradeston raised the great east window of Gloucester Abbey as a permanent record in glass of the local lords and knights who had served at Crécy.[109] Other great worthies of 1346–7, such as Bartholomew Burghersh, Reginald Cobham and Hugh Hastings, were to use their family mausolea as opportunities to commemorate their own and their companions' contributions to the great endeavours of Crécy and Calais.[110] It was this sense of collective achievement among the military elite which, more than anything else, was to sustain Edward's political regime for the rest of his long life. Like his descendant Mary Tudor, but for very different reasons, Edward III could indeed be said to have had Calais inscribed upon his heart.

[108] C 81/314/17803, printed in Fowler, 'News from the Front', 83–4; *Foedera*, III.i, 89–90; *Records of the Borough of Leicester, 1103–1509*, ed. M. Bateson, 2 vols (London, 1899–1901), ii, 68; *Registrum Johannis de Trillek*, 279–81.

[109] Saul, *Knights and Esquires*, 77; J. Kerr, 'The East Window of Gloucester Cathedral', *Medieval Art and Architecture at Gloucester and Tewkesbury*, ed. T. A. Heslop and V. A. Sekules (Norwich, 1985), 116–29.

[110] A. M. Morganstern, *Gothic Tombs of Kinship in France, the Low Countries and England* (University Park, Penn., 2000), 103–16; N. Saul, *Death, Art and Memory in Medieval England: The Cobham Family and their Monuments, 1300–1500* (Oxford, 2001), 149–68; *Age of Chivalry*, no. 678; L. Dennison and N. J. Rogers, 'The Elsing Brass and its East Anglian Connections', *Fourteenth Century England I*, ed. Saul, 167–93; F. Lachaud, 'La Répresentation des liens personnels sur les tombeaux anglais du XIVe siècle', *Liens personnels, réseaux, solidarities en France et dans les îsles Britanniques (XIe–XXe siècle)*, ed. D. Bates and V. Gazeau (Paris, 2006), 137–44, 150.

Chapter 11

FOR ARTHUR AND ST GEORGE, 1344–1355

Edward III returned in triumph from Calais on 12 October 1347.[1] A serious storm had blown up in the Channel during the king's crossing, and Edward made his habitual appeal to the Virgin Mary for deliverance from peril.[2] The royal party landed at Sandwich on 12 October and proceeded straight to a thanksgiving service at Canterbury. From there they moved on to the capital and the great pile of accumulated business that awaited the king's attention. In due course plans were made for not one but two successive parliaments, called for January and March 1348, to give the seal of approval to the king's recent successes and to discuss diplomatic and military strategy in light of the capture of David II and the defeat of Philip VI.[3] For the present, however, the king was much more inclined to devote himself to celebration. After spending Christmas at Guildford and the New Year at Windsor, Edward embarked on a great round of tournaments: at Reading and Bury St Edmunds in February, at Lichfield and Eltham in May, at Windsor in late June and, finally, at Canterbury in July.[4] Most of these were comparatively small-scale events attended mainly by members of the household along with David of Scotland and some of the honoured French captives.[5] Even so, spectacle and excess abounded. The great release of ecstatic energy manifested itself particularly in the fantastic costumes commissioned for these parties. At Christmas, various members of the royal party dressed up as swans, peacocks and dragons, and during the Bury tournament the king himself made a

---

[1] *CCR 1346–9*, 396–7; E 101/390/11. The tradition that Edward visited Portsmouth, Southampton and Winchester after his return home is erroneous: M. Biddle et al., *King Arthur's Round Table: An Archaeological Investigation* (Woodbridge, 2000), 513 and n. 2.

[2] 'Annales Monasterii de Oseneia', *Annales Monastici*, iv, 352; Reading, 105; *Polychronicon*, viii, 344; *Eulogium*, iii, 213; *Hist. Angl.*, i, 271–2; *CCR 1346–9*, 396–7; E 101/390/11. The Saint-Omer chronicle mentions the bad weather but not the divine deliverance: Paris, Bibliothèque Nationale, MS français 693, fol. 233.

[3] *RDP*, iv, 572–7; E 403/340, 22 Nov. and 24 Dec. 1347, 1 Mar. 1348.

[4] Vale, *Edward III and Chivalry*, 173–4; W. M. Ormrod, 'For Arthur and St George: Edward III, Windsor Castle and the Order of the Garter', *St George's Chapel Windsor*, ed. Saul, 19 and n. 30; J. Munby, R. Barber and R. Brown, *Edward III's Round Table at Windsor: The House of the Round Table and the Windsor Festival of 1344* (Woodbridge, 2007), 35.

[5] E 101/391/5; 'Observations', 92.

surprise appearance as a pheasant in an elaborate outfit complete with flapping wings made up from copper piping covered with real feathers.[6] It was during this great round of celebrations that Edward also conceived the idea of founding the chivalric fellowship that, within a year, was to develop into the Order of the Garter.

To understand the context and meanings of the Order of the Garter, it is necessary to go back some four years to another great tournament held at Windsor early in 1344. On 19 January that year, before the assembled court and nobility and a great multitude of the chivalric elite, Edward declared his intention to found a 'Round Table' of 300 knights 'in the same manner and condition as Arthur, formerly king of England, established it'. The scale and splendour of this event surpassed all previous feasts hosted by Edward III. The king wore a specially commissioned set of red robes lined with ermine and was supported by over 200 retainers dressed in fresh livery.[7] Expenditure on entertainment reached unparalleled heights, with the costs of the king's hall over the week from Saturday 17 January running to almost £2,000.[8] Beyond the excuses for jollification, the commitment to the new order was a very real one. Edward III promptly issued detailed personal instructions for the erection of a circular arena in the upper ward at Windsor to provide a defined space for the feats of arms in which the members of the new order would engage and delight.[9] The open area inscribed by the building was 200 feet in diameter, and a roofed building some twelve feet deep ran around the circumference to provide seating and dining space for spectators. The works, led by two of the leading masters of the day, William Ramsey and William Hurley, proceeded through the spring and summer. Although there is no record of the commissioning of an actual table at which the king and his fellow knights might re-enact the Arthurian feasts, it is more than probable that Edward's planning included at least an ornamental round table like the one produced for Edward I that still hangs in Winchester castle.[10] Everything about the Windsor festivities of January 1344 suggests that Edward III was intent, on a scale previously never imagined, to present himself as the European chivalric patron par excellence.

In November 1344, however, and without apparent warning, the whole elaborate project was called off. The unfinished building in the upper ward of the castle would eventually be pulled down in the late 1350s, and there is no evidence that Edward ever formally announced the proposed

---

[6] Vale, *Edward III and Chivalry*, 69–71.

[7] Murimuth, 155–6, 231–2; le Bel, ii, 34–5; E 101/390/5.

[8] E 36/205, fols 65v–66.

[9] SC 1/40/92; SC 1/41/163; *CPR 1343–5*, 279.

[10] Biddle et al., *King Arthur's Round Table*, 337–92; M. Morris, 'Edward I and the Knights of the Round Table', *Foundations of Medieval Scholarship*, ed. Brand and Cunningham, 57–76.

membership of his abortive order of the Round Table.[11] The reasons for the collapse of the plan were never made explicit and remain a matter of some keen speculation. Secular orders of chivalry of this kind were still quite a new phenomenon in the Europe of the 1340s, and many were the fruits of initial failure and prolonged experiment. The most obvious immediate reason for the collapse of the scheme, however, was the untimely death of William Montagu, earl of Salisbury on 30 January 1344, just a fortnight after taking part in the lists at the great foundation tournament.[12] A period of court mourning set in. The king attended a special memorial mass held at St Paul's Cathedral on 4 February before the earl's remains were removed for final interment at Bisham Priory. Perhaps as a mark of respect, and with the plans for the forthcoming campaign now in full train, the first meeting of the Round Table at Windsor over the Feast of Pentecost on 23 May was also cancelled.[13] Although the work on the tournament arena continued for some months, the original impetus for the order had clearly been lost. With the king now distracted by the preparations for his major onslaught on France, the Round Table slipped so far down his order of priorities as to make further financial investment in the project both unnecessary and unwise. Edward III's first serious engagement with the social and political institutions of chivalry, proclaimed with such obvious energy and excitement, had simply withered into extinction.

The likely link between the death of the earl of Salisbury and the failure of the Round Table seems also to have been responsible for an enduring but spurious legend about the subsequent foundation of the Order of the Garter. Writing in the late fourteenth century, Froissart merged these events and supposed that the Garter itself was founded in 1344. By the early sixteenth century, English antiquarians had in turn elided this story with Froissart's separate account of Edward III's liaison with the countess of Salisbury. Consequently, in Tudor times, it was widely held that the Order of the Garter had its origins in a ball held to celebrate the victories of Crécy and Calais, at which Edward sought to confound critics of his extramarital liaison by elevating an intimate item of female underwear, the garter, into a symbol of chivalric honour.[14] The story may

[11] Munby, Barber and Brown, *Edward III's Round Table*, 155–77, 191–239.

[12] Much has been made of the passage in Murimuth, 232, describing Salisbury as *frustratus*. GEC, xi, 388, n. (a) and many others interpret this as indicating that the earl was wounded in the lists and died from the resulting infection and complications. Richard Barber, on advice from Michael Lapidge, assures me that the passage cannot have this meaning, and simply indicates that Salisbury had been defeated at the tournament.

[13] E 36/204, fol. 73v; *Age of Chivalry*, no. 679; Vale, *Edward III and Chivalry*, 173.

[14] Froissart, ii, 304; Munby, Barber and Brown, *Edward III's Round Table*, 188–9; H. E. L. Collins, *The Order of the Garter, 1348–1461: Chivalry and Politics in Late Medieval England* (Oxford, 2000), 12, 270–2; S. Trigg, 'The Vulgar History of the Order of the Garter', *Reading the Medieval in Early Modern England*, ed. G. McMullan and D. Matthews (Cambridge, 2007), 91–105.

well contain a residual truth about the notorious immorality of the Plantagenet court. At almost exactly the time that he announced his intention to found a Round Table in 1344, Edward III was actively supporting the unscrupulous efforts of the earls of Surrey and Arundel to wriggle out of their respective marriage vows and marry ladies of the court, respectively Isabella Holland and Eleanor Beaumont, with whom they had been conducting openly adulterous liaisons. And although the king was subsequently persuaded to drop his support for Surrey's remarriage on the basis that it would damage the inheritance rights of Arundel, Edward was especially indulgent of the latter's affair and personally presided over the earl's nuptials with Lady Beaumont in February 1345.[15] In such an excess of sexual libertinism, it is possible that Edward, too, might have been led into an illicit relationship with William Montagu's wife. In that case, the cancellation of the Round Table late in 1344 could also be plausibly read as a belated act of atonement for Edward's offence in cuckolding his deceased best friend. It is not surprising, then, that the popular foundation legend of the Garter continues to this day to have at least some degree of credibility.[16]

In the end, however, we have also to admit that this whole elaborate edifice is built entirely on speculation. There is absolutely nothing in the contemporary sources to indicate that the countess of Salisbury was understood to have played the role of femme fatale in the inception either of the Round Table or subsequently of the Garter. The only possible English evidence that Edward was engaged in extramarital affairs during this period comes in the so-called *Prophecies of John of Bridlington*, completed in *c*.1350. This claims that an elusive figure identified as 'Diana' had presided over a scandalous regime of depravity in the royal camp at Calais in 1346–7.[17] Even so, the *Prophecies* fall distinctly short of accusing Edward of an act of adultery. Above all, Froissart's unfortunate eliding of events in 1344 and 1348, and the resulting confusion of English historiography, failed to acknowledge the veritable transformation, over the intervening period, in Edward's reputation. In 1344, Edward was still a king in search of a cause, a ruler whose ambitions tended to outstretch his reach and one

---

[15] For Surrey, see GEC, xii (pt i), 511, n. (k); F. R. Fairbank, 'The Last Earl of Warenne and Surrey, and the Distribution of his Possessions', *Yorkshire Archaeological Journal*, xix (1907), 244–5; Prestwich, *Edward I*, 128. Surrey's estranged wife, Joan of Bar, a granddaughter of Edward I, remained closely associated with the household of Queen Isabella and was present at Hertford castle at the time of Isabella's death in 1358: *CPR 1327–30*, 21; BL, MS Cotton Galba E. XIV, fols 11, 16–17, 24. For Arundel see *CPP*, 99; GEC, i, 243 and n. (d); Ormrod, 'For Arthur and St George', 31.

[16] Ingledew, *Gawain*, 57–80, 93–157. For other recent discussions see C. S. Jaeger, *Ennobling Love: In Search of a Lost Sensibility* (Philadelphia, 1999), 140–3; Crane, *Performance of Self*, 137–8.

[17] *Political Poems*, i, 158–9. For the date of this text see A. G. Rigg, 'John of Bridlington's Prophecy: A New Look', *Speculum*, lxiii (1988), 596–613; Coote, *Prophecy*, 118–19.

who was readily satirized by hostile commentators at home and abroad. By 1348, in contrast, he had become a giant among men, truly the greatest monarch of his age. If the Round Table had been but a natural extension of the court's general commitment to Arthuriana, the Garter was to be the king's special contribution to the wider programme of commemoration that aimed very consciously to promote the martial values displayed by his great men on the fields of Crécy and Calais.

Since the seventeenth century, when historians first began to give serious attention to the circumstances in which the Order of the Garter was founded, it has been understood that the enigmatic imagery that Edward chose for his chivalric fraternity related most obviously and directly to his acts of war with France. The garter was a fashionable, decorative element worn by high-status men both in civilian and in military dress; the new short tunics and tights adopted by the young men of the court provided opportunities for conspicuous decorative features of this kind, and both Edward III and Henry of Grosmont had sported garters in their youth.[18] More pointedly, the choice of the distinctive blue as the colour of the order's robes marked a departure from the English royal colour of red favoured at the inception of the Round Table in 1344, and seems to have been a very deliberate reference to the blue field on the French royal arms. In like vein the motto, *Honi soit qui mal y pense* ('Shame on him who thinks ill of it'), was most likely a public challenge to anyone who might defy Edward's dynastic right to the throne of France.[19] The garter motif was adopted by Edward some time shortly before the summer of 1348. Two large streamers 'with images of St Laurence . . . on a white background powdered with blue garters' may have been in use on the royal ship either for the king's outward journey to Normandy in 1346 or (as might seem more credible) for his victorious return in 1347.[20] The same emblem was adopted as the king's personal badge at the Eltham tournament of May 1348, when Edward wore a robe decorated with twelve embroidered garters.[21] The round of celebrations culminated in a large-scale tournament and feast at Windsor on 24 June 1348 to mark the queen's churching following the delivery of another son, the brief-lived William of Windsor. It was only at, or perhaps even shortly after, this event that Edward seems

[18] Mortimer, *Perfect King*, 266.

[19] E. Ashmole, *The Institution, Laws and Ceremonies of the Most Noble Order of the Garter* (London, 1672), 76, 184; G. F. Beltz, *Memorials of the Order of the Garter* (London, 1841), xlvii; Barber, *Edward, Prince of Wales*, 87–9; Collins, *Order of the Garter*, 12.

[20] 'Observations', 33–4, as interpreted by Vale, *Edward III and Chivalry*, 79–81; *Battle of Crécy*, 4. It remains possible, however, that the streamers were only commissioned in 1348, in preparation for Edward's crossing to meet the count of Flanders at Calais and Dunkirk later that year or as part of the advanced preparations for an aborted campaign to Gascony in 1349. See pp. 289, 325.

[21] Vale, *Edward III and Chivalry*, 76–82; Collins, *Order of the Garter*, 237.

eventually to have hit on the idea of institutionalizing his commitments to
the chivalric ideal and his rights in France by forming a knightly fraternity
whose members would wear his recently adopted personal badge. In this
sense, the founding of the Order of the Garter was less an event than a
process.

The relatively relaxed and informal mode in which the order was first
conceived is particularly evident in the diverse, not to say rather random,
profile of its founder knights. These were, in all probability, the members
of the two jousting teams, each of twelve men, put together under the
captaincies of the king and the prince of Wales for the tourneys at
Windsor. The roll of honour was dominated, predictably enough, by great
lords such as the earls of Lancaster, Warwick and Salisbury and the captal
de Buch. But it also included a significant number of bannerets and
knights of the king's and prince's households, such as Lords Stafford,
Burghersh, Courtenay and Grey, Miles Stapelton, John Chandos, James
Audley, Walter Pavely and Richard Fitzsimon, whose claim to their new
distinction rested less on status and much more on the personal contributions they had recently made to the campaigns in Gascony and northern
France.[22] It remains striking, too, that so many other prominent
commanders and captains of 1346–7 were omitted from the founding
fellowship. The inclusion of the two Hainaulters, Eustace d'Aubrichecourt
and Henry Eam, and of the otherwise obscure younger brother of
Sir Thomas Holland, Sir Otes, can only really be explained by their being
in the right place at the right time. Indeed, these lesser men may not have
lasted very long in such auspicious company, for within a short while they
seem to have been required to give up their places to more prominent
members of the high command, including the earls of Suffolk and
Northampton.[23] That said, the list of original knights of the Garter also
serves to emphasize a special feature that was to endure from that day to
this: membership was the peculiar gift of the monarch, used just as much
to acknowledge personal bonds and private friendships as to reward
conspicuous public service.

Given the dimensions of the proposed Round Table of 1344, it comes
as something of a surprise that Edward III did not simply take the tournament teams of 1348 as the basis of a larger fraternity that might be seen
as more representative and inclusive of the high military command of his
earls and barons. The rationale for restricting the membership to twenty-
four knights, along with the monarch and the heir apparent, lay in
the parallel religious foundation that Edward established at Windsor on

[22] Vale, *Edward III and Chivalry*, 82, 86–7.

[23] I owe to a forthcoming publication by Richard Barber the identification of the myste-
rious 'Sanchet' d'Aubrichecourt as Eustace, and my inference that some of the more
obscure founder members were set aside in favour of others rather than, as usually argued,
vacating their positions through early death.

6 August 1348 to provide a permanent headquarters for the order. The existing royal chapel of Edward the Confessor was to be refounded with a triple dedication to the Confessor, the Virgin and St George. It would be staffed by a permanent college of twenty-four secular canons and twenty-six veteran or 'poor' knights who would stand as permanent representatives of the members of the order in the regular round of religious observance performed on their behalf.[24] In 1344 Philip VI's eldest son, the duke of Normandy, had conceived his earliest proposals for the Company of the Star as a fraternity of knights served by a special collegiate church dedicated to the Virgin and St George, and it is quite likely that in 1348 Edward III set out consciously to emulate that precedent.[25] St George's Chapel and its resident clergy thus provided the institutional infrastructure that at once determined the size of the knightly confraternity and guaranteed its longer-term survival.

The king's strong and continuous commitment to the Order of the Garter is all the more remarkable given the extreme conditions in which he and his subjects found themselves in the summer of 1348. In the previous winter, reports had begun to trickle in of a terrible pestilence spreading through Italy and southern France. The epidemic later acquired the fearsome nickname of the Black Death. The exact nature of the disease was a matter of speculation at the time and remains so today; the conventional modern diagnosis, bubonic plague, has many times been challenged, though the alternatives proposed – anything from influenza to anthrax – have usually failed to convince.[26] What was certainly not in dispute at the time was the virulence of the outbreak: commentators were generally agreed that, across the urban centres of southern Europe, the death rate was running well in excess of 50 per cent. As his kingdom braced itself for the onset of this great natural disaster, Edward III received the baleful news that the fourteen-year-old Princess Joan, who was on her way to Spain to be married to the heir to the throne of Castile, had died suddenly from the plague at Bordeaux on 1 July.[27] Over the course of July and August, the plague entered England via one of the southern ports, reputedly Melcombe, Bristol or Southampton, and during the early autumn it tightened its grip on the West Country and the West

---

[24] *CPR 1348–51*, 144; E 403/341, 13 Aug. 1348. For the seals provided for the new collegiate establishment see E 101/391/20, m. 1.

[25] D'A. J. D. Boulton, *The Knights of the Crown: The Monarchical Orders of Chivalry in Later Medieval Europe, 1325–1520* (Woodbridge, 1987), 167–210. In contrast to the Garter, the Star had a large fellowship of up to 500 knights, and was wound up within a generation.

[26] For the most recent challenge to the orthodoxy of bubonic plague (though offering no precise alternative diagnosis), see S. K. Cohn, *The Black Death Transformed: Disease and Culture in Early Renaissance Europe* (London, 2002).

[27] E 101/391/17; Ormrod, 'Royal Nursery', 413, n. 83. For Edward's letter of 15 Sept. announcing the death to the king of Castile see *Foedera*, III.i, 171.

Midlands. As if to intensify the king's grief and anxiety, the latest addition to the royal nursery, Prince William, now fell sick and died at Windsor. The unusually flamboyant funeral subsequently held for the infant at Westminster Abbey suggests an intense feeling of loss in this time of general sorrow.[28] Certainly, the activities of the court were immediately and severely curtailed. The king spent August and September at his rural retreats of Hampstead Marshall, Clarendon, Hurstbourne Priors and Woodstock. And following the Christmas and New Year revels at Otford and Merton, the royal household went into a kind of quarantine at the royal manors of Kings Langley and Woodstock for most of the first six months of 1349. The king's relic collection was sent down to Langley, the better to preserve the safety of the imperilled monarch.[29]

With so many other aspects of court life and government activity shut down during the emergency, it says much for Edward's personal commitment to the Garter that he determinedly moved ahead with his plans for the first formal meeting of the order at Windsor on St George's Day, 23 April 1349.[30] The event itself brought news of further tragedy: in a curious coincidence, the reputed dedicatee of the Garter, Catherine Montagu, dowager countess of Salisbury, breathed her last on the very day that the knights of the fraternity gathered for their first patronal feast.[31] But in spite of such inauspicious auguries, the king kept faith with this new and pivotal moment in the social calendar of the court. Unlike the earlier Round Table, the new chivalric fraternity did not falter or fail. It was from 1349 that the Order of the Garter was subsequently able to trace, through its annual meetings at Windsor, a continuous tradition that both commemorated its founder and celebrated the ongoing cult of arms and honour.[32]

The foundation of the Garter and the associated college of St George at Windsor castle involved Edward III in his first major, sustained architectural project. Between 1350 and 1353, William Hurley took charge of extensive refurbishments to the existing chapel and outbuildings in the lower ward of Windsor castle. Over the following few years other master masons completed the new vestry, treasury, chapter house, lodgings and domestic services provided for the canons and poor knights of St George's. The king showed a particular personal interest in the adornment of the

---

[28] The funeral took place on 5 Sept.: 'Observations', 50. E 403/344, 11 Dec. 1348, gives the period from the death of the prince to the funeral as 58 days, suggesting that William died on 9 July. Invitations to the funeral were issued by 11 Aug.: E 403/341. See also *Issues*, 153.

[29] W. M. Ormrod, 'The English Government and the Black Death of 1348–49', *England in the Fourteenth Century*, ed. Ormrod, 175–7.

[30] E 403/347, 4 July 1349.

[31] E 101/391/8, m. 6; *CIPM*, ix, nos 64, 310; GEC, xi, 388.

[32] L. Jefferson, 'MS Arundel 48 and the Earliest Statutes of the Order of the Garter', *EHR*, cix (1994), 356–85.

new chapel. Splendid sets of vestments and plate were commissioned. The most precious item in the royal relic collection, the Croes Nawdd, was provided with a splendid new reliquary and donated to the chapel of St George. In 1354 Edward claimed in a petition to the pope that he intended to be buried in his new chapel at Windsor.[33] This resolution was not fulfilled, but it suggests that the king briefly entertained some high-flown notions of making St George's a new sacral headquarters of English monarchy, superseding both Westminster and Saint-Denis as the chief necropolis of a new line of joint rulers of England and France.

It was in the abortive knightly fraternity and the successful enterprise of the Garter that Edward III first began to present himself not merely as one of the knights of the Round Table but specifically and consistently as their patron, Arthur. In writing up the failed scheme of 1344, Jean le Bel (and, after him, Froissart) made the comment that Edward's birthplace of Windsor had itself been founded by King Arthur.[34] Edward was quick to exploit this newly imagined association. In 1348–9, just as the detailed arrangements for the Order of the Garter were being made at Windsor, the round table of Edward I was hung on the wall of the great hall in Winchester castle. The associated remodelling of the hall included the use of Edward III's badge of the sunbeam, whose pun on 'winds' and '*or*' served as a reminder of Windsor's newly prominent Arthurian connections.[35] The visual imagery of the Order of the Garter included no direct allusions to Arthur. Nevertheless, Edward's presidency of an order of chivalry set up specifically to celebrate the great feats of a close group of companions-in-arms served as a powerful statement of his Arthurian credentials. The Round Table motif itself remained firmly fixed in court culture. Bishop Edington of Winchester, for instance, owned a spectacular set of plate decorated with images of animals, birds, roses, ladies and 'knights of the Round Table'.[36] After 1349, such generalized references were complemented by a new and much more specific imagery that represented Windsor as the true Camelot and cast Edward of Windsor as a true and worthy successor to Arthur. It is hardly surprising that polite culture in the second half of the fourteenth century so readily assumed a special association between England's two greatest rulers: the Middle English Alliterative *Morte Arthure*, for example, resonates with implied parallels between the glorious careers of Arthur and Edward III.[37]

[33] E 101/392/4, m. 2; *CPP*, 265–6.
[34] Le Bel, ii, 26; Froissart, iii, 37.
[35] Biddle et al., *King Arthur's Round Table*, 393–424.
[36] *Antient Kalendars*, i, 263–5.
[37] G. R. Keiser, 'Edward III and the Alliterative *Morte Arthure*', *Speculum*, xlviii (1973), 37–51; P. DeMarco, 'An Arthur for the Ricardian Age: Crown, Nobility, and the Alliterative *Morte Arthure*', *Speculum*, lxxx (2005), 464–93.

The foundation of the Garter marked a further step forward in the development of Plantagenet iconography. The garter itself was quickly established as a recognizable element in the visual repertoire of war: Edward III's ship, the *Thomas*, was decked out in 1351 with pennons bearing garters on a white pale, and in 1353–4 the royal armoury at the Tower of London included a stockpile of *pavises* (large rectangular shields propped up on the ground during battle) decorated with the royal arms and blue garters.[38] On the other hand, public understanding of the arcane symbols and rituals of the new order of chivalry remained quite restricted for some time, and at least until the great St George's Day feast of 1358 there was little sense in which Edward sought to deploy the garter as a means of expressing the triumphal spirit of the realm at large.[39] Rather, the new chivalric order served simply to confirm and accelerate the process, already well under way in the 1330s, whereby the arms of St George were themselves coming to be regarded as the closest thing England had to a national banner. In 1350, for example, a thousand pennants of St George were ordered for the arraying of the king's ships in preparation for his naval confrontation with the Castilians.[40] This affirmation of George's patronage of English arms also meant that figurative representations of the saint, previously confined to manuscript illumination and the decorative schemes of private royal chapels, were now also employed in the public imagery of monarchy. In 1360 George was depicted, along with the Virgin, as the principal supporter of the king on the great seal of England.[41] It was the special association established between the Garter and St George that ultimately provided fourteenth-century England with the heavenly champion who was seen to compete worthily – and apparently triumphantly – with his counterpart of France, St Denis.[42]

The Order of the Garter and St George's Chapel, Windsor are the best known, because the most enduring, of Edward III's foundations. But they were part of a larger group of religious institutions developed by the king during the late 1340s, all of which were designed quite obviously to secure the salvation of his soul through purgatory and to glorify his memory on earth. The mature Edward was clearly committed to the image of the pious ruler. Although records are lacking after 1344, it is highly likely that he continued the practice of touching for scrofula during the middle and later years of his reign; significantly, it is from the late 1340s that he also began to show keener interest in the Good Friday liturgy that proclaimed his (and

---

[38] 'Observations', 136; pers. comm., T. Richardson.

[39] For the feast of 1358, see pp. 388–9.

[40] E 101/392/4, m. 2. For further examples see pp. 325, 329.

[41] *Age of Chivalry*, no. 672.

[42] S. J. E. Riches, *St George: Hero, Martyr and Myth* (Stroud, 2002); J. Good, *The Cult of St George in Medieval England* (Woodbridge, 2009), 68–73, 95–121.

now also the queen's) miraculous powers to heal epilepsy.[43] But the king's endowment of churches, monasteries and colleges served much more emphatically to publicize and perpetuate his Christian credentials. Edward's foundations fell into three groups. First, there was the chartering of an existing society of scholars at Cambridge to create the King's Hall in 1337.[44] Then there were the two new colleges of secular canons established simultaneously at Windsor and at St Stephen's Chapel, Westminster in 1348.[45] Finally there were the religious houses: the priory of Dominican nuns at Dartford granted papal licence in 1349, and the Cistercian monastery of St Mary Graces set up adjacent to the Tower of London in 1350.[46]

The personal preferences and choices that went to make up this programme reveal much about the spiritual and practical concerns of the king. The foundation of the King's Hall was part of a notable phase in the development of the universities, and may in turn have prompted Philippa of Hainault's chaplain, Robert Eglesfield, to establish the Oxford hall that was later formally named the Queen's College. Halls and colleges of scholars were intended as much for the daily observation of prayers for their founders as they were for the pursuit of knowledge. Nevertheless, Edward III had at least some appreciation of the practical utility of scholarship. Oxford and Cambridge provided the training in civil and canon law that was becoming an essential qualification for employment in international diplomacy and promotion to the episcopal bench.[47] Later in his reign Edward would employ radical Oxford theologians to give justification to his opposition to the power of the papacy.[48] The king was

[43] Bloch, *Royal Touch*, 102–3; Ormrod, 'Personal Religion, 863–5.

[44] *CPR 1334–8*, 541; A. B. Cobban, *The King's Hall within the University of Cambridge in the Later Middle Ages* (Cambridge, 1969), 9–28.

[45] *CPR 1348–50*, 144, 147. For Edward's endowment of these chapels see A. K. B. Roberts, *St George's Chapel, Windsor Castle, 1348–1416: A Study in Early Collegiate Administration* (Windsor, 1948); *VCH London*, i, 566–7; C. Given-Wilson, 'Richard II and his Grandfather's Will', *EHR*, xciii (1978), 320–37. The fact that the letters patent of foundation of both colleges were dated 6 Aug. 1348 suggests a deliberate attempt to establish their equality: Ormrod, 'For Arthur and St George', 21 n. 38. In 1356 the canons of St Stephen's managed to get an important new royal charter of privilege backdated to 1353: SC 8/247/12304; C 81/366/23044; *CChR 1341–1417*, 133–7. In 1360 the king acknowledged that there was still a shortfall of £51 on the total agreed endowment of £656 for St George's, and allowed that this should be collected from the farm of the alien priory of Takeley (Essex): *CPR 1358–61*, 364. With the restoration of the estates of the alien priories during the peace of 1360–9, the commitment had to be maintained by cash payments from the exchequer: E 403/408, 14 June 1361; etc.

[46] *CPP*, 187; *CPR 1348–50*, 484; M. B. Honeybourne, 'The Abbey of St Mary Graces, Tower Hill', *Transactions of the London and Middlesex Archaeological Society*, new series, xi (1952–4), 16–26.

[47] J. Dunbabin, 'Careers and Vocations', *The History of the University of Oxford, I: The Early Oxford Schools*, ed. J. I. Catto (Oxford, 1984), 580, 581–96.

[48] See p. 520.

also prepared to provide suitable support to those who sought serious academic training. Edward and Philippa both financed the Oxford careers of their respective godsons, Edward Paumart and Philip Beauchamp.[49] And in 1368 Edward donated a copy of Justinian's *Corpus iuris civilis* to the King's Hall.[50] Such an understanding of the role of the universities, while admittedly basic and utilitarian, does at least hint that the early guidance of Richard Bury had created in Edward a residual respect for the authority and value of higher learning.

The particular religious orders selected as the beneficiaries of the king's foundations also indicate the conservative nature of Edward's instincts in matters spiritual. The nunnery at Dartford was something of an anomaly, being the only female Dominican house successfully established in medieval England. Its real purpose, in fact, was to provide financial support for the house of Dominican friars founded by Edward II at Kings Langley. Because female houses were allowed to hold real estate, the nunnery was intended to act as custodian of a property portfolio the income of which would go to Kings Langley. The links are nicely captured in the person of John Woodrove, who was simultaneously prior of Kings Langley and Dartford, royal confessor and supervisor of the king's new building works at the nunnery during the 1350s.[51] Dartford was also very obviously intended as a royal residence: in 1346 the king announced his intention to build not only a church, cloister and dormitory but also 'halls, chambers and other houses necessary for our visits'.[52] Far from representing a bold and novel response to the aspirations of female piety, then, the house at Dartford emerged simply as a pragmatic response to Edward's existing family commitments. It is a nice irony that a king whose regime invested so much time in ousting French clergy from English monasteries and church offices should have colonized his new house of nuns from the great French Dominican convent of Poissy.[53]

New Cistercian houses were rare in fourteenth-century England and it is not immediately clear why Edward III should have chosen this order for the monastic foundation established hard by the Tower of London in 1350. Had the king been more in tune with contemporary trends, he might have followed the lead set by his son and some of his courtiers and patronized regular canons of the order of St Augustine or its offshoot, the *Boni homines*.[54] One plausible explanation for the choice of the order of Cîteaux is the

[49] For Paumart see E 403/433, 3 Jan. 1368; E 403/434, 9 Aug. 1368. For Beauchamp see *BRUO*, i, 136–7.

[50] *CCR 1364–8*, 408–9.

[51] A. B. Emden, *A Survey of Dominicans in England* (Rome, 1967), 486; Lee, *Nunneries*, 15–17.

[52] E 159/122, rot. 83.

[53] Lee, *Nunneries*, 15.

[54] H. F. Chettle, 'The *Boni Homines* of Ashridge and Edington', *Downside Review*, lxii (1944), 40–55; G. St. John, 'The Religiosity of English Men-at-Arms in the Fourteenth Century', *Monastic Research Bulletin*, xiv (2008), 44–6.

king's particular desire to honour the Virgin, patron of all Cistercian monasteries: the foundation of the house represented the fulfilment of the vow earlier made by Edward on his stormy crossing from Brittany in 1343. Another reason was royal tradition. Edward III was a regular patron and (later in the reign) visitor to King John's Cistercian foundation of Beaulieu, which he chose as the mother house of St Mary Graces.[55] He must also have been aware of Edward I's ambitious plans to create England's largest and grandest Cistercian foundation at Vale Royal in Cheshire; in 1353 the Black Prince took up this unfinished project and invested considerable (though ultimately inadequate) resources towards its completion.[56] Respect for his dynastic past echoes through so much of Edward III's religious observation as to suggest that it was the dominant organizing framework of his acts of piety.

Very few of the buildings erected at Edward III's ecclesiastical foundations in the fourteenth century now survive. The King's Hall at Cambridge was knocked down to make way for Henry VIII's foundation of Trinity College. Similarly at Windsor, much of Edward's work in the lower ward was swept away to accommodate Edward IV's great rebuilding of St George's Chapel. Some of the domestic elements of this complex, especially the canons' cloister, preserve some of their fourteenth-century fabric and appearance. A particularly important survival is the Aerary Porch, which formed the principal entrance to the reconfigured chapel and collegiate buildings. It may have been built to plans made by the talented master mason William Ramsey before his death in 1349. The porch incorporates a range of architectural features that would become part of the mainstream of the Perpendicular style, and its influence has been detected in later fourteenth-century work at Winchester Cathedral and Westminster Abbey.[57] Edward III's chapel was very largely a remodelling of the existing building, and the records suggest that the changes were not so much structural as functional and decorative: the new stalls provided for the Garter knights and their vicars, painted glass, a statue of St George, a series of panel paintings and eventually, in 1367, a new alabaster reredos for the high altar.[58] Nevertheless, Edward was clearly keen to turn St George's into something of a tourist attraction, and campaigned with the papacy for special indulgences to be granted to those who made pilgrimage to the great relic of the True Cross housed in the royal chapel at Windsor.[59]

[55] *VCH London*, i, 461; Ormrod, 'Personal Religion', 874 and n. 141; E. Jamroziak, 'St Mary Graces: A Cistercian House in Late Medieval London', *The Uses and Abuses of Sacred Places in Late Medieval Towns*, ed. P. Trio and M. de Smet (Leuven, 2006), 154.

[56] *VCH Cheshire*, iii, 156, 160.

[57] J. A. A. Goodall, 'The Aerary Porch and its Influence on Late Medieval English Vaulting', *St George's Chapel Windsor*, ed. Saul, 165–202.

[58] *King's Works*, ii, 872–3; *Issues*, 160, 185, 187, 188, 193.

[59] *CPP*, 188, 265–6.

In terms of high artistic patronage, however, the real focus of Edward's projects in the 1350s was not so much Windsor as Westminster. St Stephen's Chapel, which stood within the precinct of Westminster Palace, had been conceived by Edward I in conscious emulation of Louis IX's Sainte-Chapelle at Paris. The building programme had been subject to long delays, but Edward III took it up again early in his reign and the structure was finally completed by 1348.[60] Although the upper chapel was destroyed in the great fire that swept through Westminster Palace in 1834, enough information survives to reconstruct the decorative scheme installed between 1351 and 1360. Under the direction of Hugh of St Albans, an army of painters covered every available surface of wall and ceiling with biblical scenes, images of military saints, leopards and *fleurs-de-lys*, angels, doves, elephants and castles, and the coats of arms of the royal family and the English baronage, all executed in the highest-quality materials of silver, gold, ultramarine and vermilion.[61] The high point of the scheme was a major sequence of paintings on the east wall depicting St George with Edward III, Queen Philippa and their children kneeling in devotion before a cycle of paintings of the Birth of Christ. The sumptuous altar frontals and clerical vestments that had been commissioned for the trousseau of the ill-fated Princess Joan were given by the king to St Stephen's in 1349.[62] And in 1358, as the work was drawing to a close, Edward spent the large sum of £80 on the provision of a holy water stoop, two silver candelabra and a silver cross for the chapel.[63] The whole ensemble was of superb quality, representing the very best that the contemporary International Gothic style had to offer. In particular, the dynastic scheme on the east wall, with its representation of Edward III, Philippa of Hainault and their children, epitomized the king's strong commitment to his family and its collective enterprise and salvation.[64]

The two royal chapels at Westminster and Windsor were the major architectural commissions of the middle period of Edward III's reign. But there were other building projects that also commanded Edward's attention at this time. In the early 1340s a memorandum on the dilapidations of Westminster Palace was compiled for the attention of the king and

[60] C. Wilson, 'The Origins of the Perpendicular Style and its Development to *circa* 1360' (University of London PhD thesis, 1979), 34–80; *Age of Chivalry*, nos 324–5.

[61] J. Cherry and N. Stratford, *Westminster Kings and the Medieval Palace of Westminster* (London, 1995), 28–49; Binski, *Westminster Abbey*, 182–5; *King's Works*, i, 518–19.

[62] E 403/344 (inventory and memorandum at end of roll).

[63] E 403/388, 12 Oct. 1357; E 403/392, 18 May 1358; *The Issue Roll of Thomas of Brantingham*, ed. F. Devon (London, 1835), xxxviii.

[64] V. Sekules, 'Dynasty and Patrimony in the Self-Construction of an English Queen: Philippa of Hainault and her Images', *England and the Continent in the Middle Ages: Studies in Memory of Andrew Martindale*, ed. J. Mitchell and M. Moran (Stamford, 2000), 165–7; E. Howe, 'Divine Kingship and Dynastic Display: The Altar Murals of St Stephen's Chapel, Westminster', *Antiquaries Journal*, lxxxi (2001), 259–303.

council.[65] This may have been the catalyst for some new activity in the public and private spaces of the complex. Carpenters and others working on the privy palace in 1344 were paid special Sunday rates in order to speed completion.[66] In 1351–2 the king's bathroom was upgraded to incorporate that ultimate medieval luxury, hot and cold running water. At the royal manor of Eltham, Edward carried out considerable improvements and built a complete new range of royal apartments in the 1350s. There were significant works at various smaller manor houses and hunting lodges, such as Clarendon, Henley on the Heath, Easthampstead and Hampstead Marshall. In 1353 Edward began in earnest a major building programme on a brand new royal residence at Rotherhithe. At Windsor, too, the sweeping away of the existing royal apartments to make space for the new collegiate buildings of St George's Chapel prompted some refurbishments in the High Tower (now known as the Round Tower). These provided temporary accommodation for the court pending the major new building campaign in the upper bailey that was to follow later in the reign. It was in the 1350s that Edward III thus began to devote himself to the monumental schemes that were to be one of his most tangible and enduring legacies.[67]

Considering the twin perils of war and plague that beset him so obviously in the middle years of his life, Edward III seems to have remained in very good health until well into his forties and early fifties. Some of this is no doubt explicable in terms of genetic predisposition. Henry III and Edward I had lived well into their sixties; Edward II had been famed for his physical fitness, and Queen Isabella remained spry until shortly before her death, at the age of sixty-two, in 1358. It also had to do with the quality of care. The king retained both a physician and a surgeon in his household, and had ready access to the very best that contemporary medicine could offer. In the summer of 1353, eight months after his fortieth birthday, occur the first explicit references to the provision of medicines for Edward III's personal use.[68] It would seem likely that the king was beginning to suffer the perennial complaints of middle age: old war wounds, stiffening joints, dental, digestive and urinary complaints. Nevertheless, the omission of any further references to the provision of drugs suggests that Edward showed remarkable resilience to the effects of ageing. His active lifestyle must surely have helped in this respect. Although fate determined that he would see little action for nearly a decade after the fall of Calais, Edward remained constantly committed to

[65] E 101/683/56.
[66] E 403/335, 16 Oct. 1344. Carpenters were impressed in Kent for the works at Westminster in 1350: E 403/353, 19 July.
[67] *King's Works*, i, 545–6, 550–1; ii, 875–6, 917, 926, 931–3, 955–6, 961, 990–3.
[68] E 101/392/12, fol. 17.

the prospect of resuming his personal leadership of the war in France. This was publicly affirmed by the king's resolute adherence to physical sports. Whenever circumstance permitted, the mature Edward III spent his summers in the pleasures of the chase. On either side of the naval affray of 1350, for example, the king went forth to hunt, first in Rockingham Forest and then in Sherwood Forest. And in July–September 1354 he made an extensive tour of the royal hunting grounds both in the Isle of Wight and Hampshire and, later, in the forest of Rockingham. Queen Philippa may have suffered gynaecological problems during and after her last pregnancy in 1354–5, and was forced to give up hunting after a serious fall in 1358.[69] Edward himself, by contrast, continued to be a fearless and strenuous horseman until well into his sixties.

The energy, charisma and personal style of the mature king are vividly captured in two rare contemporary vignettes. The first occurs in the Middle English poem *Winner and Waster* (*Wynnere and Wastoure*), which is usually dated to around 1352. At the beginning of the poem, the anonymous narrator has a vision of a 'comely king' with a 'berry-brown' beard, seated in majesty in an elaborate pavilion decorated with blue garters and surmounted by what appears to be a vernacular rendering of the motto of the new Order of the Garter: 'Hethyng [shame] have the hathell [knight] that any harme [slander] thynkes.' The king is dressed in tunic and mantle of the finest quality, embroidered with golden falcons and bearing an intricately worked 'garter of inde [blue]'.[70] There must inevitably be some question as to the accuracy of some of the physical details. But if the author of *Winner and Waster* had never actually set eyes on the visage of Edward III, his rendering of the Garter imagery is all the more powerful, denoting the degree to which the iconography of the new order had so quickly come to imprint itself upon the public image of monarchy.

The second pen portrait of Edward III was written by Jean Froissart. Froissart came to England only in the early 1360s and began to write his *Chronicles* a decade or so later. There is every reason, however, to trust the essence of his celebrated description of Edward III aboard his ship of war, the *Thomas*, on the eve of the battle of Winchelsea in 1350:

> He stood in the bow of his own ship, wearing a black velvet jerkin and a black beaverskin cap, which greatly suited him. On that day, I was told by some who were with him, he was in a gayer mood than he had ever been before. He told his minstrels to strike up a dance tune which Sir John Chandos, who was there beside him, had recently brought back from Germany. And out of sheer high spirits he made Sir John sing with the minstrels, to his own vast amusement.[71]

[69] *Eulogium*, iii, 227.
[70] *Wynnere and Wastoure*, 4–5 (ll. 59–98); Vale, *Edward III and Chivalry*, 73–5.
[71] Froissart, trans. Brereton, 115.

The royal household accounts amply confirm these texts' emphasis on the importance of clothing to the royal self-image. For some years, as Froissart attests, Edward III wore the new figure-hugging ensemble of jerkin and hose that became all the rage in court fashion after 1340. Clerics had a distinct aversion to these styles, dubbing those who wore the revealing hose 'harlots'. Later, the king became too stout to carry off such a youthful look: as he approached fifty, Edward had to have one of his fancy belts, made of velvet and gold, let out to accommodate an expanding royal waistline. For ceremonial occasions, the king and queen continued to wear the traditional garb of multi-layered, floor-length robes imagined with such loving detail by the poet of *Winner and Waster*. If anything, the state robes were still more sumptuous than those worn in the couple's youth. Satin, much used for collars and cuffs as well as to provide sumptuous linings for fine clothes, made its first appearance in court costume during the 1340s. Edward's robes for the Garter feast in 1350 were made from luxurious cloth of gold imported, via Venice, from the Far East. Jewels, plate and embroidery added to the shimmering effect; a few years later, Edward took delivery of a suit of robes adorned with pelicans and golden tabernacles.[72] One item of clothing in which Edward particularly indulged his taste for finery was, as Froissart intimated, the hat. For the Christmas festivities of 1337 Edward had commissioned a veritable menagerie of a headpiece, decorated with tigers, trees, a castle, and a man riding a horse and all decorated with pearls, imitation jewels, and gold and silver plate.[73] The crests worn over helmets in tournaments offered particular opportunities for extravagant display: in 1352 the king had a crest of red velvet embroidered with wild men and branches and topped off with a gold leopard and a crown of gold and silver decorated with sapphires.[74]

The depiction of the king in *Winner and Waster* provides a good reminder of the way in which Edward III used the heraldic and the textual to reinforce the message of majesty. In 1340 Edward had worn his newly quartered arms of England and France on a sumptuous tunic and horse-trapper in red and blue velvet, with the leopards and *fleurs-de-lys* worked in gold.[75] The use of the English and French royal colours was potent: later, in 1373, the citizens of Bristol were to have a royal charter illuminated with a representation of Edward III wearing a scarlet robe (for

[72] Newton, *Fashion*, 34, 53–4, 56; Monnas, 'Silk Cloths', 285, 288; *Issues*, 189.

[73] E 101/388/8.

[74] K. Staniland, 'Medieval Courtly Splendour', *Costume*, xiv (1980), 20. See also the hood of black cloth lined in scarlet with a border embroidered with pearls and a buckle decorated with pearls and emeralds provided for the king in the early 1350s: E 159/133, *Brev. bar.*, Mich., rot. 24d. In Nov. 1363 Edward took delivery in his chamber of a hood made from red woollen cloth and embroidered with eagles and the letter E in gold, pearls and silk thread: E 101/394/16, m. 12.

[75] E 101/389/4.

England) under a blue cloak (for France) and a crown of *fleurs-de-lys*.[76] Mottos were also frequently worn on, and borne around, the royal person. At the Dunstable tournament of 1342, the king's state bed and the hoods provided for the jousters had been embroidered with the enigmatic motto, 'It is as it is'. The exuberant couplet 'Hay hay the wythe swan/By Godes soule I am thy man', mentioned in *c*.1348, was also probably used as the theme for a tournament. A little later the king would also use the tag 'Syker as ye wodebynd' ('As strong as the woodbine'), with its striking connotations of tenacity and perseverance.[77] And in 1364 Edward gave the queen two robes embroidered with Philippa's own sayings, 'Ich wyndemuth' ('I twine myself [around you]') and 'Myn biddeneye' ('My bidding').[78] In these ways the king's and queen's bodies became fields upon which the values and ideologies of court life were, quite literally, inscribed.

Froissart's depiction of Edward III aboard his ship of war reminds us that music was another integral element both of military activity and of court life in this period. A significant amount of the music performed at court was provided by itinerant minstrels, some of them sent as messengers by foreign princes. Queen Philippa's fellow Hainaulter, Jean de la Mote, who had a successful double career as minstrel and poet, visited the English court on several occasions.[79] At rare times, local amateurs might be brought in: in 1331, for example, while she was at Clipstone, the young queen had heard an impromptu concert of singing by a group of women from nearby Bilsthorpe.[80] In the first half of his reign, Edward III had a troop of around twenty designated musicians in his service, including not only trumpeters and drummers but also men skilled on harp, lute, viol, psaltery and guitar.[81] Merlin the fiddler was a regular performer in the king's and the queen's households, and Henry the fiddler was with Edward at Calais in 1346.[82] The king continued to have his own lutenist in the 1350s, and Queen Philippa had an organist in her service.[83] For the rest of the reign Edward's court was regularly entertained by a corps of twelve to

[76] See p. 523.
[77] 'Observations', 43; Vale, *Edward III and Chivalry*, 64–5. For robes embroidered with unspecified 'texts' and 'sayings' of the king in the late 1340s, see also 'Observations', 25, 44, 49.
[78] E 101/394/16, m. 12.
[79] N. Wilkins, 'Music and Poetry at Court: England and France in the Late Middle Ages', *English Court Culture*, ed. Scattergood and Sherborne, 191–2; M. A. Rouse and R. H. Rouse, 'The Goldsmith and the Peacocks: Jean de la Mote in the Household of Simon de Lille', *Viator*, xxviii (1997), 293–4.
[80] JRUL, MS Latin 235, fol. 19r. See also the two female dancers/acrobats who performed before the queen in the same year: ibid., fol. 18v
[81] E 101/385/4.
[82] Bullock-Davies, *Register*, 115; JRUL, MS Latin 234, fol. 27r; E 101/391/9, fols 10–10v.
[83] E 403/355, 25 Nov. 1350; E 101/392/12, fol. 37; *CPR 1364–7*, 29.

fifteen pipers, trumpeters and drummers retained as permanent members of the royal household.[84]

We misunderstand and underrate the musical capacity and sophistication of the court, however, if we consider only secular performers. At least as significant were the clerks who organized the liturgical music provided in the royal chapel. After 1348 this group was very significantly enlarged as a result of the setting up of permanent staffs of singers – men and boys – to service the new collegiate establishments at Windsor and Westminster.[85] John II's imprisonment in England after 1357 facilitated interactions between French and English church musicians, and the celebrated French composer Matheus de Sancte Johanne spent some years in Queen Philippa's chapel. A surviving motet, *Sub Arturo plebs*, composed some time between the 1360s and the 1380s, celebrated England as a land where knights and clergy flourished together, free of the tyranny that pervaded foreign lands. Two other motets of *c.*1370, *Singularis laudis digna* and *Regem regum collaudemus*, similarly contemplated Edward III's victory on earth and future apotheosis in heaven.[86] It is clear that the king expected liturgical music, like all the performing and figurative arts, to enhance the image of his court and articulate the supreme political confidence of his mature monarchy.

Throughout the 1350s Edward III continued to rely heavily on his family and household to provide the daily comfort of human society. With the passage of time, however, the composition of these more intimate networks altered quite significantly. By 1347 Edward had made arrangements for the endowment of the three younger princes, John, Lionel and Edmund, respectively from the earldoms of Ulster and Richmond and the Yorkshire estates of the deceased earl of Surrey.[87] A decade later they were allocated £2,000 from the public purse to maintain their own bachelor establishment, and by 1358 both Lionel and John had fully developed households of their own.[88] The oldest princess, Isabella, who was still unmarried at the time of her twenty-first birthday in 1353, was also given

[84] *Issue Roll of Brantingham*, 54–7, 296–8, 301, 380, 423, 453, 489; E 101/397/20, mm. 27, 32. The lists of Edward III's minstrels provided in R. Rastall, 'The Minstrels of the English Royal Households, 25 Edward I–1 Henry VIII: An Inventory', *Royal Musical Association Research Chronicle*, iv (1964), 15–20, are far from complete.

[85] R. Bowers, 'The Music and Musical Establishment of St George's Chapel in the Fifteenth Century', *St George's Chapel, Windsor, in the Late Middle Ages*, ed. C. Richmond and E. Scarffe (Windsor, 2001), 172–5.

[86] A. Wathey, 'The Peace of 1360–1369 and Anglo-French Musical Relations', *Early Music History*, ix (1989), 129–74; R. Bowers, 'Fixed Points in the Chronology of English Fourteenth-Century Polyphony', *Music and Letters*, lxxi (1990), 313–35.

[87] Wolffe, *Royal Demesne*, 242–3.

[88] E 403/384, 13 Feb. 1357; E 403/387, 6 May 1357; E 403/388, 4 Oct. 1357, 16 Feb. 1358; E 403/392, 11 May 1358; E 101/393/2; Ormrod, 'Royal Nursery', 411.

an independent landed estate, complete with her own town house in London.[89]

The landed endowments of his children heralded Edward III's new determination to have the next generation paraded before his subjects as proof of his own, and the country's, good fortune. Lionel, John and Edmund made public appearances at the Windsor tournament of 1348. Over the following five years they also made a number of independent visits to some of the great churches and shrines of England at Canterbury, York, Hailes, Walsingham and Bury St Edmunds. In 1353 the three younger princes were sent down to Gloucester to attend the requiem mass that marked the anniversary of their grandfather Edward II.[90] The generations were indeed moving on. In August 1355, eight months after the birth of his last child, Thomas of Woodstock, Edward III became a grandparent for the first time, when Lionel of Antwerp's wife gave birth to a daughter named Philippa.[91] All of this necessarily meant that, in spite of his own more leisured existence, Edward's contacts with his older offspring became more spasmodic and formal. It was no doubt something of a delight to the royal couple that so many of their adult children at least continued to trek to court for the celebrations and great halls that marked the cycle of major religious festivals.[92]

The partial withdrawal of the princes coincided with a decline in the number of high-ranking bannerets and knights retained in the household as the king's daily companions and confidants. This was the practical consequence of the fact that the king's household did not go to war at any point between 1347 and 1355. There was certainly no hint that the elite found the court an unfriendly place: Thomas Beauchamp and Thomas de Vere, heirs to the earldoms of Warwick and Oxford, were both members of the household in the 1350s, and the heads of a number of baronial and gentry families, such as the Warrs, Lisles, Says and Swynnertons, had younger brothers and sons serving as knights and esquires to Edward III

---

[89] Wolffe, *Royal Demesne*, 243–4; E 403/375, 22 Nov. 1354. In 1355 the king spent nearly £350 on plate for Isabella's use: E 403/377, 20 June.

[90] 'Observations', 37; *AC*, 30; E 36/205, fol. 11; E 101/392/12, fols 34–34v, 35; SAL, MS 208, fols 3–3v.

[91] *GEC*, viii, 447–8. The queen's midwife, Margaret Gaunt, attended the Countess Elizabeth, and the king's physician subsequently visited her: E 403/378, 30 Nov. 1355; *Issues*, 164. Prince Lionel is supposed to have consummated his marriage in 1352, when he was fourteen, and a payment to the king's physicians for the care of Lionel's wife in 1353 may perhaps refer to a miscarriage: E 403/368, 7 June. Lionel and Elizabeth's second daughter died shortly after birth in 1357: 'Chaucer as Page in the Household of the Countess of Ulster', *The Chaucer Society Publications: Life-Records of Chaucer*, ed. W. D. Selby, F. J. Furnivall, E. A. Bond and R. E. Kirk, 4 vols (London, 1875–1900), iii, 99; *BPR*, iv, 251. Elizabeth was reported ill again in 1361: E 403/408, 6 July.

[92] E 101/393/15, mm. 3–4; E 101/394/16, m. 13; etc.

in this period.[93] Even within the comparatively small corps of twenty or so household knights, however, there now emerged a close, elite group coming more and more regularly to be designated as the knights of the chamber. In *c*.1348 these were named as John Grey, John Lisle, Walter Mauny, Robert Ferrers, Roger Beauchamp, Guy Brian and Richard la Vache.[94] Grey took over as steward of the household from the veteran Richard Talbot in 1350 and served until 1359, while the chamberlainship was held successively by Bartholomew Burghersh (1347–55) and John Charlton (1356–60). It was in the period between Calais and Poitiers, then, that Edward III's more settled and domesticated existence began to have the accidental consequence of a diminishing aristocratic presence within the royal household.

It is a measure of Edward's instinctive sociability that, faced with this situation, he sought out the quotidian fellowship of other, lesser members of his domestic service. The sergeants-at-arms, who provided for the king's personal security and fulfilled a wide range of ceremonial and administrative responsibilities, yielded a number of close associates in this period. Walter Hanley was one especially valued sergeant; another was John atte Wode, a well-connected Worcestershire man who used loyal service and royal favour very much to his own advantage, emerging in his own right as a knight of the chamber by 1370.[95] The king also particularly enjoyed the company of a newly designated group of 'henchmen', the precursors of the later grooms of the body. They usually worked in pairs, and were almost always referred to in the household records by nicknames. Verjuice and Vinegar (Richard Vergeous and Richard Vynegre), who appear in 1353, went on to successful military careers in France and Ireland.[96] Their replacements, Mustard and Garlic, are more elusive; it is possible that these men came from the retinue of John II, and their names could well reflect Edward III's personal sense of humour about national gastronomic stereotypes.[97] A third pair, Solaz and Hans, presumably of Netherlandish or German extraction, moved from the household of the Black Prince to serve the king in the 1360s.[98] The punning

[93] E 101/392/12, fols 40, 41; E 101/393/11, fols 76, 76v; G. T. O. Bridgeman, 'An Account of the Family of Swynnerton of Swynnerton', *Collections for a History of Staffordshire*, vii[1] (1886), 35–41.

[94] 'Observations', 24.

[95] For Hanley, see R. Partington, 'Edward III's Enforcers: The King's Sergeants-at-Arms in the Localities', *Age of Edward III*, ed. Bothwell, 94, 97. For atte Wode see E 101/392/12, fol. 41; E 101/393/11, fol. 76; E 101/395/2, no. 236; E 101/395/10; E 159/146, *Brev. bar.*, Pasch, rot. 5; *John of Gaunt's Register, 1371–1375*, ed. S. Armitage-Smith, 2 vols (Camden Society, 3rd series, xx–xxi, 1911), i, nos 57, 261; J. S. Roskell, L. Clark and C. Rawcliffe, *The House of Commons, 1386–1421* (4 vols, Stroud, 1993), iv, 892.

[96] E 101/392/12, fol. 42v; SC 8/247/12310. Verjuice is the acid juice of unripe apples.

[97] E 403/401, 17 July 1360; Wathey, 'Peace of 1360–1369', 143.

[98] *BPR*, iv, 71; E 101/393/15, m. 11. Hans was in Prince Lionel's entourage at Pavia in 1368: E 159/145, *Brev. bar.*, Trin., rot. 10d.

joviality expressed in the naming of the henchmen strongly suggests that, like Richard II, Edward III enjoyed a notable informality in his relationships with at least some of his bodyguards and personal servants.[99]

If Edward's private persona was sufficiently assured to admit of such intimacies, however, it is also very clear that the 1350s witnessed an increasing emphasis on the formalities of royal ceremonial. Here again, the Order of the Garter can be said to have had a major impact on the rhythm and style of court life. From 1349 until the very end of his reign, Edward III was almost always at Windsor castle for the annual Feast of the Garter on 23 April. From the early 1350s the household accounts and chronicles begin to reveal the manner of the annual celebrations and the public attention they drew. These involved three key elements: a solemn mass performed in memory of deceased members, a tournament, and a great banquet. The preparations for the event were on an ambitions scale: in 1353, for example, the Feast of St George accounted for the largest expenditure in the king's hall during the entire year, amounting to nearly £250.[100] It was to service the Garter and its ceremonies that Edward III now reorganized and expanded his existing staff of heralds.[101] William, known variously as Volaunt ('the flying one', perhaps an allusion to the 'golden wings' of Windsor) or Vaillant (courageous, spirited, valiant), seems to have managed many of the Garter feasts in the first decade of the order's existence. He was joined during the later 1350s and 1360s by heralds bearing titles such as Falcon, Havering and Windsor.[102] St George's Day had now effectively joined Easter, Pentecost, All Saints and Christmas as one of the major feasts on which the king, his family and household gathered together for the celebration of great halls.[103]

It had also thereby become one of the principal regular assembly points, not just for the knights of the Garter but for larger meetings of the social and political elite. A reference to the provision of robes for Princess Isabella for the feast in 1350 suggests that Edward III was already forming the support group of royal and aristocratic women who later became known as the Ladies of the Fraternity of St George.[104] The Black Prince

---

[99] N. Saul, *Richard II* (London, 1997), 394.

[100] E 101/392/12, fols. 10. 34; Collins, *Order of the Garter*, 211–12. For works carried out in preparation for this event see E 101/391/1, fol. 15.

[101] Andrew 'Claroncell' (Clarenceux) appears in 1334: BL, Add. MS 46350, rot. 7. For the first appearance of the later Norroy King of Arms in 1338, see A. R. Wagner, *Heralds and Heraldry in the Middle Ages* (Oxford, 1939), 35.

[102] E 403/378, 21 Dec. 1355; E 403/388, 24 Jan. 1358; *Issues*, 169, 171; E 403/391, 4 May, 7 Sept. 1358; E 403/396, 7 June 1359; E 403/408, 4 May 1361; E 101/393/11, fol. 76v; E 101/395/10; Wagner, *Heralds*, 35–6, 37; Vale, *Edward III and Chivalry*, 152 n. 112. Volaunt was in royal service from at least 1349: *CFR 1347–56*, 187–8; E 159/133, *Brev. bar.*, Mich., rot. 2d. For (Colinet) Falcon see also E 101/398/9, fol. 82; Froissart, vi, 110–12.

[103] E 101/392/14, m. 2.

[104] E 101/392/4, m. 2; J. L. Gillespie, 'Ladies of the Fraternity of St George and of the Society of the Garter', *Albion*, xvii (1985), 259–78.

took an extensive entourage of knights, heralds and minstrels to the Garter feast at Windsor in 1352.[105] The bishop of Winchester attended regularly as prelate of the order, and other high-ranking clergy such as the abbot of Westminster also received formal invitations to attend.[106] In 1357 St George's Day fell while parliament was in session at Westminster. A recess was called over the weekend of 21–23 April in order to allow the king and at least a proportion of the assembled lords temporal and spiritual to move to Windsor for the feast that would celebrate the prince's recent victory against the French at Poitiers.[107] For all the apparent exclusiveness of the little band of twenty-six royals, nobles and knights who made up the immediate membership of the order, then, Edward III worked consistently in the first decade of the Garter's existence to promote the annual feast at Windsor as a great meeting-point for the wider political elite. England's new Arthur was not just a military hero: he was also emerging as an astute political manager.

In the dozen or so years that followed the great victories of 1346–7, Edward III's enhanced esteem among his own followers and his growing reputation on the international stage encouraged the development of a more consistent and confident court style. The king, now confirmed as the great hero of chivalry, gave significant attention to the refoundation of Arthur's imagined seat of Windsor to provide a fitting context for the celebration of Plantagenet monarchy and English arms. The feasting and jousting that had been crucial in Edward III's bid to revive the glamour of the court in the 1330s now became part of a more elaborate and increasingly ritualized ceremonial played out in an emerging annual cycle of courtly activity built around the annual Garter feast on 23 April. The English court showed itself capable of commissioning the work of some of the finest craftsmen, artists and performers in Europe. All this spoke to an increasingly expansive world vision of a monarchy fully engaged in public celebration of its military and political achievements.

---

[105] *BPR*, iv, 72–3.
[106] Biddle et al., *King Arthur's Round Table*, 513–18; WAM, 12211.
[107] *CPR 1354–8*, 527; *PROME*, iv, 130.

Chapter 12

THE ROAD TO POITIERS, 1347–1356

When he returned to England after the triumphant conclusion to the siege of Calais in the autumn of 1347, Edward III found himself gaoler to an altogether exceptional group of prisoners of war: David Bruce, Charles of Blois, the counts of Eu and Tancarville and a host of other Scottish and French nobles and knights. For the following decade, Plantagenet strategy aimed to deploy these high-status captives as bargaining counters for territorial settlements in Scotland and France and as hostages for final peace. At times, it seemed that the only gains to be made were financial ones: in difficult circumstances, Edward III was just as inclined to be tempted by the offer of a fat ransom as to hold out for a more ambitious settlement. Equally, the king would reveal his willingness to sacrifice less realistic goals in return for firm territorial gains and/or monetary compensation. Above all, it became apparent that Edward regarded the claims to suzerainty over Scotland and to sovereignty over France as expendable assets to be renounced as and when other terms proved sufficiently favourable. Beyond these immediate diplomatic considerations, however, the king also began to give serious consideration to the interests of his family and to the possibility that his descendants might one day recover the former Angevin empire and establish their rule over the whole of the British Isles and the great lordships of northern and western France. The opportunism that sometimes led Edward into quick compromises should not blind us to the skilful manoeuvres by which he aimed to preserve residual rights and, in due course, exploit them to his own and his sons' collective benefit.

On 28 September 1347 the representatives of Edward III and Philip VI agreed a nine-month truce in all theatres of war.[1] The most urgent issue now facing the English crown was to capitalize on its de facto control of Calais and establish some form of effective regime that would guarantee the new bridgehead into France.[2] Although Edward reserved the right to expel all the native French from Calais, he was also keen to accept the allegiance of as many of the inhabitants as would succumb. His confirmation of the Calaisians' 1317 charter from Mahaut, countess of Artois, was thus

---

[1] *Foedera*, III.i, 136–8; Avesbury, 396–406; Baker, 92–5; *Anon. Cant.*, 14–15; Paris, Bibliothèque Nationale, MS Fr. 693, fols 232v–233.
[2] *Foedera*, III.i, 138–45, 158.

a well-timed advertisement of good faith in his new subjects.[3] The need to attract loyal settlers – to fill up the town with 'pure' Englishmen, as Froissart put it – also encouraged the development of a faltering economic policy. Financial inducements, including significant tax breaks, were offered to new settlers, and for a short while in 1348 the crown established a staple at Calais for English exports of lead and cloth.[4] Nevertheless, it was the sheer cost of the maintenance of Calais that inevitably attracted most public interest in England. Until 1355, it took some £8–£10,000 a year to maintain the permanent garrison needed to defend the town. In 1351 there was vociferous complaint in parliament about the scale of recent purveyance for Calais. The crown was forced significantly to reduce such compulsory purchases and to rely instead on the purchase of food-stuffs on the open market.[5] By capturing Calais, Edward III had shown that he was capable of winning a major strategic position in enemy terri-tory. Determined to hold on to it, he had to remain resolute against both the scheming of his enemies and the occasional ambivalence of his own subjects.

In spite of the pause in hostilities over the winter and spring of 1347–8, doubt soon emerged as to whether the French might be forced into accepting a final settlement. At the parliament of January 1348, the earls of Lancaster and Northampton promised the commons the prospect of peace.[6] Their reception may have been rather mixed, for the more rampantly xenophobic of the king's subjects were clearly convinced that he should resist the blandishments of his enemies of Scotland and France and press on to the final conquests that now seemed within his grasp. In the wake of the fall of Calais some educated men in England gave vent, in sophisticated Latin poetry, to some of the worst excesses of populist anti-French prejudice.[7] One such composition from around this time cari-catured the French as emasculated 'capons', implying that they were at best softies and at worst sodomites.[8] There is every indication that this new wave of viciousness towards the enemy served to harden the hearts of the political community. In a further parliament convened in March, it was reported that discussions towards a treaty had indeed foundered and that

[3] Le Patourel, *Feudal Empires*, chap. xiv, 232–3.

[4] Froissart, iv, 296; *Foedera*, III.i, 158, 178; C 76/26, mm. 8, 16d.

[5] Harriss, *King, Parliament*, 328–9; Sumption, ii, 20–2; *CFR 1347–56*, 273–7, 288–91; *PROME*, v, 5–6, 13–14; Burley, 'Victualling of Calais', 49–57.

[6] *PROME*, iv, 412–13, 452.

[7] *Political Poems*, i, xix, xxi–xxii, 26–51, 53–8; A. G. Rigg, 'Propaganda of the Hundred Years War. Poems on the Battles of Crecy and Durham (1346), A Critical Edition', *Traditio*, liv (1999), 169–211.

[8] *Political Poems*, i, 91–3; James, 'John of Eltham', 64; R. F. Green, 'Further Evidence for Chaucer's Representation of the Pardoner as a Womanizer', *Medium Ævum*, lxxi (2002), 308.

the treacherous French were again gathering an army (so it was claimed) for the invasion of England. Albeit begrudgingly, the commons acknowledged their obligation to support such a return to arms, conceded that the current *maltolt* should run its course and granted three successive fifteenths and tenths.[9] During the summer, concern mounted over events in Flanders, where the new count, Louis de Mâle, was beginning to assert control over the rebellious towns and force them to withdraw from their rebellious alliance with Edward. When the truce of Calais expired in June, Philip VI immediately sent a force led by Charles of Spain and Geoffrey de Charny to cut off the communications routes between Calais and Flanders. Plans were made to extend the truce, but in October Edward announced that he would lead an army across the Channel. At the end of that month he moved to Sandwich to await news from his representatives at the court of France, Henry of Lancaster and William Bateman.[10] Those English patriots who assumed that the fall of Calais would lead on to the general conquest of France braced themselves for the last and greatest encounter.

In reality, the natural disaster and human tragedy of the plague of 1347–9 left all sides with no choice but to stall hostilities.[11] On 13 November 1348 the Anglo-French truce was extended until the following September. A few days later Edward crossed to Calais, accompanied by Bishop Edington, to complete a new and unexpected accord with the count of Flanders. The treaty, formally ratified by deputations from the king and count at Dunkirk on 4 December, required that Edward give up his separate alliance with the towns of Ghent and Ypres. Louis agreed that, in the event of French refusal to render to him the lands that he claimed by hereditary right in Artois, Lille and Douai, he would renounce his homage to the Valois and support Edward's claim to the French throne.[12] The offer of military assistance was kept secret and ultimately proved worthless: once the count secured the submission of Ghent and Ypres, he simply ignored his obligations to the English alliance. Equally, a brief rapprochement with Alfonso XI of Castile proved a failure. By the summer of 1349, Castilian ships were beginning to make common cause with Norman squadrons along the French coast. As England and France

---

[9] *PROME*, iv, 451–3, 459; Jurkowski, Smith and Crook, *Lay Taxes*, 47, 50. Knighton, 88, thought that the second parliament was an adjourned session of the first, and it is noticeable that a high number of those who had sat in the commons in Jan. were re-elected in Mar.: K. L. Wood-Legh, 'The Knights' Attendance in the Parliaments of Edward III', *EHR*, xlvii (1932), 406, 408.

[10] *Foedera*, III.i, 166, 172–4, 175–6; *CLBL*, F, 185.

[11] *Foedera*, III.i, 182–3, 184–5, 188.

[12] Ibid., III.i, 177–9; *EMDP*, I.ii, no. 256; E 403/344, 14 Nov., 21 Nov., 1 Dec., 17 Dec. 1348; Chaplais, *Essays*, chap. xiii, 193; Fowler, *King's Lieutenant*, 75–83. Parliament was summoned to discuss this diplomatic initiative, but this assembly was later abandoned on account of the plague: *CCR 1346–9*, 607–8.

limped back to some kind of normality after the devastation of the Black Death, Edward III must have been keenly aware just how little his great victories of 1346–7 had really altered the diplomatic landscape.

The one glimmer of hope in these dark days lay in a possible revival of the Anglo-imperial alliance. After the death of Lewis of Bavaria in October 1347, a group of electors approached Edward III with the proposition that he become a candidate for the title of emperor. When he declined in May 1348, people in England greeted the news as a welcome sign that he was no longer susceptible to flattery and would not be deflected from his existing commitments in France.[13] In fact, Edward knew that his purposes were rather better served by giving his backing to the main contender for the vacant title: Charles IV of Bohemia. Although Charles had fought with his blind father on the Valois side at Crécy, he was eager to reach an accommodation with Edward and now offered both to support Queen Philippa's claims to a portion of her deceased brother's lands and to withdraw any further imperial support for Philip VI. By 1349 Edward faced the real prospect of rebuilding his alliances with the estranged princes of the Empire and of once more recruiting significant German and Netherlandish forces to his cause in France.[14]

In the summer of 1349 Philip VI finally resolved to reopen hostilities with the English. Guy de Nesle was appointed to lead a large army to the south-west. The gains made by Henry of Grosmont in the mid-1340s had left English soldiers and sympathizers in control of numerous positions in Saintonge, Poitou, the dioceses of Limoges, Cahors and Périgueux, and the Agenais. Edward III seems to have expected to raise an appreciable force in retaliation. Large numbers of painted sails and flags, including 300 bearing the arms of St George, were procured for the 'voyage of Gascony' in 1349.[15] In the end, however, the earl of Lancaster took a mere 350 men to Aquitaine and his ensuing winter campaign was manned almost entirely by contingents of loyal Gascons. Lancaster led a *chevauchée* down the Garonne and beyond the Agenais, marching all the way to the walls of Toulouse. But it was impossible to make any really lasting impression with such small forces. Retreating to La Réole and thence to Bordeaux, Grosmont asserted the powers granted him under the form of his lieutenancy and negotiated a short truce to last until April 1350.[16]

Edward III, meanwhile, had been buoyed up by a great adventure in Calais. On 24 December 1349, as the court was busy preparing the Christmas Day celebrations at the queen's manor of Havering in Essex, the king was made aware of a plot launched by Geoffrey de Charny to recapture Calais. Aimeric of Pavia, an Italian mercenary serving in the English

[13] *Foedera*, III.i, 161; Baker, 97; Knighton, 90–3.
[14] Offler, 'England and Germany', 629–31, Trautz, *Könige von England*, 344–52.
[15] E 101/391/1, fol. 4.
[16] Sumption, ii, 58; Fowler, *King's Lieutenant*, 84–8.

garrison of the town, had turned traitor and promised to open the gates to the French in a secret midnight operation. Edward, accompanied by the prince of Wales, immediately mounted a small force of household retainers and sailed secretly for Calais. While Charny was at Saint-Omer convening with his co-conspirators, Edward managed surreptitiously to gain access to the town and hid himself and his men amidst its great jumble of alleys and buildings. Among the stalwarts of this clandestine force was the twenty-two-year-old Roger Mortimer, grandson and namesake of Edward's former nemesis the first earl of March. Ironically, it was not since the dramatic events of the older Mortimer's downfall at Nottingham in 1330 that the king had undertaken a covert military operation so crucial in strategic importance and so perilous in possible consequence.

Before dawn on 2 January 1350 Aimeric of Pavia raised the standard of France over the citadel of Calais. When the first contingents of French entered the gates under direction from Aimeric's followers, however, the English soldiers secreted above the gatehouse broke the drawbridge, preventing further reinforcements from outside. They fell upon the invaders with cries of 'To the death, to the death!' Sensing betrayal, Charny retreated, but the king and the Black Prince rushed out of the town and routed the enemy in strenuous hand-to-hand combat amidst general cries of 'Edward and St George!' The event was widely celebrated as proof of Edward III's ability to react decisively in the face of emergency, and as general testimony to his superior military intelligence. Above all, it provided fresh and abundant proof of his personal bravery. Froissart particularly relished the chivalric values of the skirmishes on the streets of Calais and its environs. Just as Edward had earlier fought incognito in tournaments and travelled in disguise on confidential missions abroad, so now he reputedly took on the arms of a simple knight and fought under the banner of Sir Walter Mauny. Observing the convention of honouring the defeated, the king accorded the honour of the day to the captive French governor in the march of Flanders, Eustace de Ribemount.[17]

The hazard posed by the betrayal of Calais and the strategic importance of its recapture in 1350 may well have been somewhat exaggerated in the countless retellings of this colourful episode over subsequent generations. It is possible that Aimeric of Pavia was acting under instruction from Edward III and that his supposed betrayal was part of a plan to double-cross Charny and put a decisive end to his hostile designs on the town. If Edward did act spontaneously, then the whole escapade might easily be condemned as beyond the bounds of acceptable risk: had it turned out another way, it might have spelled complete disaster for England. On the other hand, the king's presence was probably vital to restoring order and loyalty among the

---

[17] Le Bel, ii, 176–82; Froissart, iv, 70–81; Baker, 103–8; *AC*, 30–1; *Anon. Cant.*, 16–17; *Hist. Angl.*, i, 273–4; le Muisit, *Chronique*, 262–3; BL, MS Cotton Faustina B. V, fol. 100; *Society at War*, 23–4; Crane, *Performance of Self*, 130–1; Rose, *Calais*, 31–2.

1 The royal parents: Edward II and Queen Isabella, represented together in a treatise by Walter de Milemete dedicated to the young Edward III.

2 Edward II in state: the tomb at Gloucester Abbey, perhaps commissioned by Edward III in the 1330s and visited by him on a number of occasions in his reign.

3 The coronation: an illumination in the order of service as used in 1327 provides a striking artist's impression of an early fourteenth-century crowning ceremony.

4 The second great seal of Edward III: the seal used for all major acts of government between 1327 and 1338, showing the king enthroned in majesty.

5 York Minster: the west front, under construction at the time that Edward III and Queen Philippa were married inside the cathedral church in 1328.

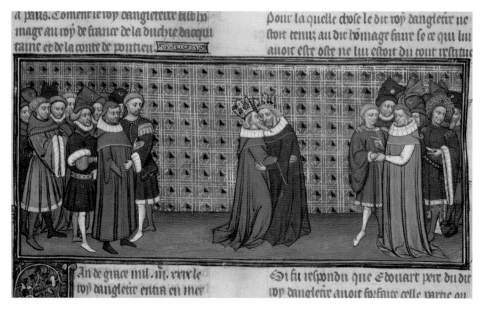

a paus. Comenr le roy dangleterre sillt lo
mage au roy de france de la duchie dacqui
taine et de la conte de ponticu

Pour la quelle chose le dit roy dangleterre ne
stoit tenuz au dit hômage faur se ce qui lui
auoit este oste ne lui estoit du tout restitue

An de grace mil. iij. xxix le
roy dangleterre entra en mer

Si fu respondu que Edouart pere du dit
roy dangleterre auoit forfaire celle varne ou

6 Edward III and Philip VI: the meeting between the royal cousins at Amiens in 1329, as depicted in a late fourteenth-century illuminated manuscript of the *Chroniques de France*.

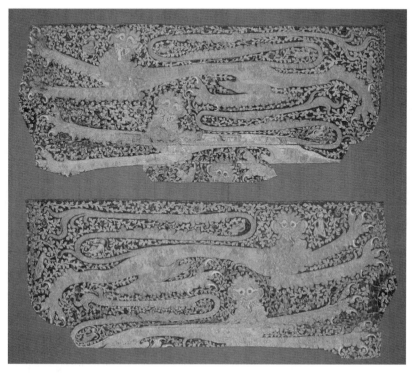

7 A rare piece of English fourteenth-century embroidery depicting the heraldic leopards of England, possibly used for Edward III's meeting with the emperor at Koblenz in 1338.

8 The gold noble of Edward III: first introduced in 1344, the coin depicts the king aboard a ship of war in commemoration of the battle of Sluys of 1340.

9 The silver groat of Edward III: this coin, an innovation in the silver currency of England, was introduced in the coinage reform of 1351 and had a face-value equivalent to four pennies.

10 Castle Rising, Norfolk: the castle, held by Queen Isabella, witnessed reunions of Edward III and his mother on several occasions and later passed into the hands of the Black Prince.

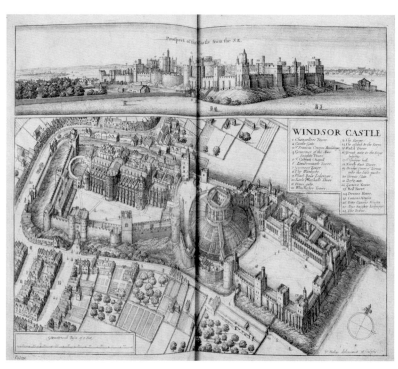

11 Windsor castle: this seventeenth-century engraving shows the upper ward of the castle much as it was left after Edward III's great rebuilding project in the 1350s and 1360s.

12 For England and St George: drawings undertaken in the eighteenth century of the wall paintings made for Edward at St Stephen's Chapel, Westminster in the 1350s.

13 The seventh great seal of Edward III: used between 1360 and 1369, the so-called Brétigny seal is notable for the use of the figures of the Virgin Mary and St George flanking the enthroned king.

14 Three kings in search of titles: a depiction of John II's submission to Edward III after the battle of Poitiers, from a psalter commissioned by the Bohun family; the crowned figure at the foot may be Charles II of Navarre or the future Charles V of France.

15 Brothers in peace: Edward III and David II of Scotland at the time of the treaty of Berwick of 1357, from an illuminated collection of diplomatic documents compiled in the reign of Richard II.

16 The Jewel Tower, Westminster: one of the few remaining structures from the medieval palace of Westminster, this was originally built by Edward III in the 1360s.

17 Trinity College, Cambridge: the college was built by Henry VIII on a site previously occupied by the King's Hall, and Henry commemorated Edward III and six of his sons on the façade of the great gate.

18 Prince of Aquitaine: the letters patent declaring Edward of Woodstock's new title to Aquitaine in 1362, decorated with the prince's badge of ostrich feathers and other motifs.

19 Edward III as king of France: in spite of the declining fortunes of the second war, the citizens of Bristol illuminated their 1373 charter with a vivid representation of Edward in French coronation robes.

20 The mother of England: Philippa of Hainault as stately matron in the strikingly life-like tomb effigy commissioned in the queen's own lifetime from the craftsman Jean de Liège.

21 Remember me: the tomb of Edward of Woodstock, the Black Prince, erected at Canterbury Cathedral in the reign of Richard II.

22 The funerary achievements of the Black Prince, originally hung about his tomb (and since replaced by replicas); a similar set of shield, sword and gauntlets once adorned the tomb of Edward III at Westminster.

23 The funeral of Edward III: a possible depiction of the lying-in state of Edward III, with temporary tomb and wooden effigy, during the solemn rites at Westminster Abbey in 1377.

24 The original wooden funeral effigy of Edward III, modelled from a death mask complete with vestiges of paint and hair; the lifelike qualities extend to the twisted mouth, which suggests the effects of a series of strokes on the elderly king.

25 The apotheosis of Edward III: the gilt-bronze effigy of the deceased monarch lies atop a tomb-chest designed with six niches on each long side to hold miniature figures of the king's twelve children.

26 Two gothic heroes: Edward III and the Black Prince at the battle of Crécy in 1346, as imagined by the American artist Benjamin West in a 1788 commission by George III for Windsor castle.

27 The happy couple: Queen Victoria and Prince Albert as Philippa of Hainault and Edward III
at the great costume ball held at Buckingham Palace in 1842, subsequently captured for posterity
in this portrait by Sir Edward Landseer.

garrison and non-combatants of the town itself. And it is hard to deny that Edward's very swiftness in springing to arms in that Christmas season of 1349–50 made a significant contribution both to preserving the English hold on Calais and to the deeply felt English conviction of the righteousness of the king's cause against France.

The expedition also served to revive Edward's general appetite for war. Although Lancaster's truce was honoured and new talks with the French were opened up at Guînes outside Calais, Edward was now set upon another major intervention in France. Councils of war were summoned in late March 1350 and archers and ships were ordered to be made ready for a departure in June. It may well have been against the king's own instincts that the council induced him, at the last moment, to accept a further twelve-month truce.[18] Philip VI died on 22 August, and the coronation of his son, John II, stirred up renewed comment in England about the Valois usurpation of Plantagenet rights.[19] John committed a very serious error at the beginning of his reign by ordering the execution of Raoul de Brienne, count of Eu, who had recently evaded captivity in England and returned to France to negotiate his ransom. The French polity was united in its hostility to this arbitrary judgment, and Edward III evidently had hopes that the scandal would result in further defections to his cause.[20] The visit to the English court in October 1350 of Thomas de la Marche, John's highly visible illegitimate son, may also have been designed as a deliberate snub to the new king of France; in seeking out Edward to act as patron of the duel he planned with a fellow French knight, Thomas was very obviously making a statement about the deficiencies of his father's own chivalric credentials.[21] Without the continuing caution of his advisers, then, it seems that Edward III would have much preferred to capitalize on John II's early difficulties and make a swift return to arms.

With his plans for a land campaign temporarily thwarted, the king directed his attention instead to the threat posed by the Castilian fleet. This hostile force was threatening the superiority that England had enjoyed in the Channel over the previous decade. Edward turned his domestic publicity machine on the Spanish, ordering prayers against an imagined Castilian invasion of the realm.[22] In early August the new king

---

[18] *RDP*, iv, 587; *Foedera*, III.i, 192–5, 196, 197–8, 200. The knights of the king's retinue received summonses that are likely to have been in connection with these plans: E 403/353, 28 May 1350.

[19] Baker, 111; C. Given-Wilson, *Chronicles: The Writing of History in Medieval England* (London, 2004), 186–7.

[20] Le Bel, ii, 198–200; Froissart, iv, 123–5; *Chron. J&C*, i, 28–30; *Chron. QPV*, 19–20; Cazelles, *Philippe VI*, 247–52; Cuttler, *Law of Treason*, 154; Given-Wilson and Bériac, 'Edward III's Prisoners', 821–2. That the count's return to France was against Edward III's instructions for his custody is made clear by *SCCKB*, vi, no. 45.

[21] *CPR 1350–4*, 8; SC 8/246/12280.

[22] *Foedera*, III.i, 201–2; London, Lambeth Palace Library, Register of Simon Islip, fol. 22.

of Castile, Peter I 'the Cruel', agreed to become a party to the recent French truce with England.[23] It was apparently in response to news of this rapprochement that Edward III cut short his summer hunting expedition to Northamptonshire and returned for a council of war in London. Ships were requisitioned and men-at-arms were recruited for a reasonably substantial force of around fifty cogs to be commanded by the king, Prince Edward and the earls of Lancaster, Northampton and Warwick. Edward took ship from Rotherhithe and sailed off down the Thames estuary. After lying in wait for nearly two weeks at Sandwich in Kent, he moved west beyond Dungeness Point hoping to pounce upon a convoy of two dozen Castilian ships now known to be making its way through the Channel laden with goods from Flanders.

On the evening of 29 August Edward's impromptu navy successfully intercepted this potentially hostile force off the shores of Winchelsea. The battle was hard fought, for the Spanish galleys were much larger in size than the English. Missiles from catapults hailed down on the decks of Edward's vessels, and both the king's and the prince's ships were badly damaged as they attempted to ram the enemy. Once they managed to grapple and board the Castilian ships, however, Edward's men-at-arms rapidly proved their superiority in hand-to-hand fighting. A bloody but glorious victory, often named thereafter as *les Espagnols sur mer*, was proclaimed.[24] The Black Prince presented his father with his trophy vessel, the *Bilbao*. The English fleet remained in service for some weeks, achieving modest success in picking off stragglers.[25] Edward himself disembarked at Rye and made his way over to Canterbury to provide thank-offerings at the shrine of Becket before returning north to resume his equal passion for the chase.

In comparison with the battle of Sluys a decade earlier, the engagement at Winchelsea was of an admittedly much lesser scale and strategic significance. Continental chroniclers, such as the abbot of Saint-Martin at Tournai, regarded the episode merely as a minor and inconclusive skirmish. Indeed, *les Espagnols sur mer* may have been as much a triumph of propaganda as of deeds, for the effective control of the narrow seas remained a matter of some dispute throughout the early 1350s.[26] For a sympathetic domestic audience, however, there was no doubt as to the sense of deliverance, and the battle of Winchelsea duly took its place in the great and growing catalogue of Edward III's miraculous victories over foreign powers. To the list of crude

[23] *Foedera*, III.i, 228–9; *CLBL, F*, 234.

[24] Froissart, iv, 88–98; Baker, 109–11; *Anon Chron., 1333–81*, 31; *Hist. Angl.*, i, 274–5; Rodger, *Safeguard of the Sea*, i, 104.

[25] E 101/24/14, no. 1.

[26] Le Muisit, *Chronique*, 276. For le Muisit's world-view, see B. Guenée, *Between Church and State: The Lives of Four French Prelates in the Late Middle Ages*, trans. A. Goldhammer (Chicago, 1991), 71–101.

racial stereotypes that represented their most hated enemies, the English now gleefully added the figure of the 'blackbeard' of Spain.[27]

The battle seems to have created a significant and lasting legacy for the stock of royal ships that formed the core of the king's naval forces. In the mid-1350s Edward III had twenty-eight vessels at his personal disposal, including purpose-built ships of war such as the *Jerusalem*, the *Edward* and the *Falcon* and requisitioned commercial craft such as the *St Mary* of Winchelsea and the *Thomas* of Hull.[28] After 1350 the government also became involved in setting up a convoy system to protect the wine fleet plying its trade between Bordeaux and the ports of southern England, and made periodic levies of tunnage and poundage to support armed patrols in the busy seaways of the Channel.[29] It was in the context of these more gradual advances that the victory of 1350 came to represent and reinforce Edward III's claim to suzerainty of the seas. Some time shortly after the naval battle of Winchelsea, the king's clerk of ships, William Clewer, took possession of a new stock of 367 streamers bearing painted shields with the arms of St George on a blue background.[30] Like the knights of the Garter, the fleet itself was becoming a kind of perpetual memorial both to Edward's continued aspirations in France and to the divine protection accorded to his followers by the intercessions of England's adopted saint.

The success of Winchelsea was not emulated by all of Edward's commanders scattered across western and southern France. Throughout 1351 the story of the English positions in these areas was one of continued struggle and frequent loss. Henry of Grosmont managed a successful *chevauchée* through Artois and Picardy. Anglo-Gascon forces achieved a victory at Saintes, where Guy de Nesle was captured and many French nobles slain. But Lancaster's secret mission to negotiate a marriage between John of Gaunt and the baby heiress to the county of Flanders proved a failure, and Louis de Mâle's open defection to the French represented a particularly serious blow to English diplomacy. The loss of the position of Saint-Jean-d'Angély in Aquitaine was another major humiliation, and Edward III had no choice but to accept proposals for a further extension of the Anglo-French truce to September 1352.[31]

The continued suspension of hostilities did not prevent significant levels of military activity under the guise of local defence, and early in January 1352 a small group of English soldiers captured the town of Guînes, five

[27] Minot, *Poems*, 54–5.

[28] E 101/24/14, no. 8.

[29] C. Richmond, 'The War at Sea', *Hundred Years War*, ed. Fowler, 100–1; M. K. James, 'The Fluctuations of the Anglo-Gascon Wine Trade during the Fourteenth Century', *EcHR*, 2nd series, iv (1951), 181–8; Ormrod, 'Origins of Tunnage and Poundage', 210–14. For Edward's personal interest in the wine convoy see C 81/1333/61.

[30] E 159/133, *Brev. bar.*, Mich., rot. 24d.

[31] *Foedera*, III.i, 224, 230–2; Rogers, *War Cruel and Sharp*, 287–8; Fowler, *King's Lieutenant*, 100–1.

miles south of Calais. The attack, led by a fortune hunter named John Doncaster, had not apparently been authorized, and the French immediately complained about what they regarded as a clear breach of the truce. Edward found a convenient way to reconcile the conundrum by declaring Guînes forfeited to himself, as Doncaster's superior lord.[32] The fortress and its hinterland were thus incorporated into the emergent pale of Calais and remained in English hands until 1558. The controversy raised by the capture of Guînes seems to have been the spark to a series of statements made by William Shareshull and Bartholomew Burghersh in the parliament that opened at Westminster on 13 January. They reminded the lords and commons that parliament had supported the war in the past, announced that John II himself had now wilfully broken the truces in Gascony, Brittany and Scotland, and pointed out the obligation now placed upon the king's subjects to counter the 'malice and deceit' of his enemies. In a mood of cautious excitement, the commons agreed that the king should have three continuous years of direct taxes to support the defence of the realm.[33]

Over the following six months, a new set of strategic plans slowly emerged. Since 1351 Sir Walter Bentley had been busy avenging the ambush and murder of Thomas Dagworth, his predecessor as lieutenant of Brittany. This was a war of attrition rather than of set-piece encounters, though it had its more memorable moments. An otherwise trivial episode in 1351, based on the model of the tournament mêlée, involved hand-to-hand combat between thirty selected men-at-arms from the rival garrisons of Josselin and Ploërmel; the chivalric enthusiasm of those present, which tended to take precedence over the technical victory of the French side, was much commemorated in verse and prose, and the 'battle of the Thirty' became a great set piece of subsequent romanticized accounts of the Hundred Years War.[34] In 1352, however, it was announced that Bentley would recruit further reinforcements for his army and redouble serious operations in the duchy. The earl of Stafford would also be sent to Gascony with a new expeditionary force. And a special army of 6,000 men, led by the king, would invade northern France via Calais. The royal expedition was soon abandoned in preference for a smaller force sent over to help the garrison of Calais defend its local positions. But the more impressive victories for which Edward so keenly hoped were eventually reported over the course of the summer. In Aquitaine, Stafford successfully captured Blaye and took command of almost all the positions around the Garonne estuary. And in Brittany there were still more spectacular gains. On 14 August, at Mauron, Bentley mounted a miniature

[32] Baker, 116–18; Avesbury, 414–15.

[33] *PROME*, v, 33–4, 41–2.

[34] Le Bel, ii, 194–7; 'La Bataille de trente Anglois et de trente Bretons', ed. H. R. Brush, *Modern Philology*, ix (1911–12), 511–44; x (1912–13), 82–136.

version of the English battle plan used at Halidon Hill and Crécy and inflicted a tremendous defeat on a Franco-Breton army significantly superior in numbers and equipment. The French commander, Guy de Nesle, was slain, along with some 800 men-at-arms.[35] By the autumn of 1352, Edward II's commanders in France had gone a long way to establishing effective control in Aquitaine, Brittany and the Pas de Calais. The key question for Edward III was how to persuade the Valois that any peace settlement would need to accommodate not just the territories that had been in dispute at the start of war in 1337 but also England's more recent gains in northern and western France.

David II's capture at the battle of Neville's Cross in 1346 had a profound impact both on the internal politics of Scotland and on Anglo-Scottish relations. Robert Stewart took over the regency for the captive king, but any semblance of political unity in the northern kingdom rapidly withered. By early 1348, English sovereignty was once again established in Roxburgh, Jedburgh, Peebles, Selkirk, Dumfries and Galloway. Far from reverting to the idea of a puppet monarchy under Edward Balliol, however, Edward III's diplomatic strategy now underwent a radical realignment.[36] In essence, Edward sought to play a double game. On the one hand, he wanted the Scots to believe that he would accept the kingship of David Bruce as a necessary preliminary to the ransoming of the imprisoned monarch. On the other, he intended to do nothing to infringe his own rights in Scotland until such time as that ransom was negotiated and paid. It was typical of Edward III that he should want to have his diplomatic cake and eat it, and at least some of the obfuscation and delay to Anglo-Scottish negotiations after 1347 is attributable to the English king's confident belief in the strategic and moral superiority of his position. Out of the resulting conundrum, however, would emerge a new proposal: for the future succession of a Plantagenet prince to the Scottish throne. The prolonged debate over the ransoming of David Bruce thus marked the first indications of Edward III's ambition to accommodate the kingdom of the Scots within his emerging vision of empire.

Very little progress was made between David's imprisonment in the Tower of London in 1346 and Edward III's return from Calais in the autumn of 1347. The key event in this period was the execution of another prisoner, the earl of Menteith, who was declared guilty of treason against the English crown for his earlier defection from the Balliol cause.[37]

[35] Sumption, ii, 92–8; Rogers, *War Cruel and Sharp*, 288.
[36] A. A. M. Duncan, '*Honi soit qui mal y pense*: David II and Edward III, 1346–52', *Scottish Historical Review*, lxvii (1988), 113–41.
[37] *Foedera*, III.i, 108; *CDS*, iii, nos 1486–7; Bellamy, *Law of Treason*, 53–4. The earl of Fife was also condemned to death but was subsequently pardoned because of his wife's kinship to Edward III: GEC, v, 374.

Discussion of Anglo-Scottish affairs was on the agenda for the Westminster parliament of March 1348, but for most of that year Edward's government did little more than discuss the fates of various Scottish nobles imprisoned at Bristol, Windsor and other English royal castles.[38] When an embassy visited London late in 1348, however, the English shifted on to the diplomatic offensive. In return for his release, David would be required to pay liege homage to the king of England. All the English lords disinherited from their rightful claims in Scotland had to be reinstated. If David were to die without a direct heir, then the Scottish throne would devolve to the crown of England. The English were to remain in control of all castles and lands currently in their possession until the other terms of the settlement were fulfilled.[39]

Such uncompromising terms were not so much a serious basis for effective peace as an opening salvo. The Scottish response is not recorded, though it is hardly surprising that the envoys felt unable to give definitive answers and returned home with only an extension to the truce.[40] Stalemate ensued until 1350, when David II himself expressed a willingness to accept terms and to press for their adoption in Scotland. It was at this point that Edward III finally admitted his effective abandonment of Edward Balliol. The man adopted as vassal king of Scots in 1333–4 was now in his sixties, still unmarried and childless, and it is easy to see why the English regarded him as readily expendable. This is not to say that he was easily silenced: accusing Edward III of duplicity and dishonour, Balliol put up a significant show of opposition by refusing to be a party to any agreement between Plantagenet and Bruce.[41] The negotiations were sufficiently sensitive to necessitate a strict code of secrecy, and nothing was said publicly on the matter at the English parliament of February 1351.[42] Edward III was working with speed and determination to find an advantageous solution; showing his hand to the political community at this moment was deemed likely only to compromise his chances.[43]

In Scotland, by contrast, the peace proposals were openly debated in a general council and parliament held in the first half of 1351. The resulting

[38] *Foedera*, III.i, 153; Wyntoun, vi, 225; *CDS*, iii, nos 1488–9, 1491, 1496, 1504, 1517, 1519–20; Given-Wilson and Bériac, 'Edward III's Prisoners', 813 n. 59. One of the captives of Neville's Cross, the earl of Wigtown, escaped back to Scotland in 1347: *CPR 1345–8*, 314; *CCR 1346–9*, 311.

[39] *Foedera*, III.i, 163, 167, 169, 175; *CPP*, i, 203; E. W. M. Balfour-Melville, 'David II's Appeal to the Pope', *Scottish Historical Review*, xli (1962), 86; Duncan, '*Honi soit qui mal y pense*', 116–18, 138–9.

[40] *Rot. Scot.*, i, 722–4; *Foedera*, III.i, 175.

[41] 'Negotiations for the Release of David Bruce in 1349', ed. C. Johnson, *EHR*, xxxvi (1921), 57–8, re-dated and reinterpreted by Duncan, '*Honi soit qui mal y pense*', 121–3, and (with differences of detail) by Penman, *David II*, 163–4.

[42] *PROME*, v, 1–32.

[43] This explains the notable confusion of the chroniclers over these negotiations: Baker, 96–7; Knighton, 112–13; le Bel, ii, 241–2.

documentation makes it clear that Edward III had already significantly modified his position. Now, there was no talk of homage, liege or otherwise. The rights of the disinherited were still very much to the fore. For the first time, a price – of £40,000 – was set for the release of King David. But to the prospect of Scottish independence the English king was determined to add an important rider. It was now proposed that, should David fail to produce a direct heir, he would be succeeded in due course by a younger son of Edward III.[44] This surprising suggestion may have made it on to the agenda as a result of David's own intervention; subsequent events were to reveal that he clung yet more consistently than Edward to the idea of a dynastic reconciliation between the houses of Plantagenet and Bruce. But the response of the Stewart administration was uncompromising. The proposals were rejected out of hand, and the Scots began to look once more to France for support in the event that hostilities might reopen with England.[45]

In the face of this obduracy, Edward had little choice but to reduce his terms for peace. David II was transferred to Newcastle for a new round of talks in August–September 1351, and a statement was drawn up summarizing each side's demands. In many ways, this was the most reasonable compromise proposed since 1333. The Scots held out for David's release without ransom and for the restoration of the boundaries of their kingdom as in the time of Robert I. But they were also prepared to accept Edward III's difficulty in acknowledging David II's title and suggested that the issue could be resolved if the two sides agreed to a long-term truce rather than a final treaty. On the English side, the rights of the disinherited were again reserved, and military assistance was required of the Scots; otherwise, the only substantive condition was that David should be succeeded by one of Edward III's younger sons.[46] David was in an optimistic mood when he returned temporarily to his kingdom to present his case to a parliament at Scone in February–March 1352.[47] But once more his cause was roundly rejected by his subjects, who were simply not prepared to see Edward III dictate terms for the release of their king.

Edward was not present at the Newcastle talks of 1351, and it is not altogether easy to determine how seriously he took the settlement there proposed. In the Westminster parliament of January 1352 he blatantly

[44] 'Papers Relating to the Captivity and Release of David II', ed. E. W. M. Balfour-Melville, *Scottish History Society Miscellany IX* (Scottish History Society, 3rd series, i, 1958), 37, 44–5. Duncan, '*Honi soit qui mal y pense*', 122–3, argues that John of Gaunt may already have been identified as Edward's nominee to succeed David, but the evidence is inconclusive, and concurrent plans to marry John to the heiress of Flanders may suggest that Edward was deliberately keeping his options open with regard to Scotland.

[45] Froissart, *Oeuvres*, xviii, 336–7; Campbell, 'England, Scotland', 197; *PROME*, v, 40.

[46] *Acts of the Parliaments of Scotland*, 12 vols (Edinburgh, 1814–75), i, 494–5, re-dated by Duncan, '*Honi soit qui mal y pense*', 127–32, 139–41.

[47] *Foedera*, III.i, 230–1, 234, 237; *CDS*, iii, no. 1569.

overrode the territorial dispositions then under discussion by confirming
the rights of his subjects in the Lowland shires attached to the English
crown since 1334.[48] The king had good reason for such a bullish stance. In
1348 the commons had demanded that neither David Bruce nor William
Douglas of Liddesdale be ransomed except as part of a lasting agreement
with the Scots.[49] Edward may well have felt that his subjects would regard
the new draft treaty as a distinctly inadequate return for the release of
these prisoners. In July 1352 he also undermined the current proposals by
making a separate agreement with Douglas on condition that the latter
paid him liege homage in return for his freedom.[50] But if Edward was
temporizing, it was only because his new interest in the Scottish succession
had created an impasse in diplomacy. His resolve to have one of his sons
succeed David Bruce represented a direct challenge to the interests of the
guardian, Robert Stewart, who as a grandson of Robert Bruce had an
obvious claim to be David's heir presumptive.[51] It was these dynastic
imperatives that caused the breakdown of diplomacy after the parliament
of Scone and provoked the descent into further, if brief, armed conflict
between England and Scotland in 1355–6.

There are important personal dimensions to the series of negotiations
around the release of David II. The English and Scottish kings had never
met before Edward III's return to London from Calais in 1347, but they
soon developed a fairly strong bond of friendship based in their kinship
and their common delight in courtliness and chivalry. Edward was keen to
ensure that David had all the comforts that custody could afford, and
made his brother-in-law an honoured guest in his household.[52] In June
1348 David was present, with other prisoners of war, at the spectacular
Windsor tournament, where he wore a surcoat of red velvet worked with
a silver-white rose.[53] Queen Philippa, too, developed a close attachment to
the exiled monarch.[54] It is clear that David found his enforced leisure
rather agreeable. But it is unfair to assume that he was less than resolute
in his desire to return to Scotland.[55] The offer to adopt one of Edward's
sons as his heir may itself have been a deliberate gamble: David was still
a young man – only twenty-two at the time of his imprisonment – and
there was no particular reason to think that he would not in due course

[48] *PROME*, v, 38–61; SC 8/143/7112; *Foedera*, III.i, 237; *Rot. Scot.*, i, 747.

[49] *PROME*, iv, 453.

[50] *Rot. Scot.*, i, 752–3. Douglas was subsequently murdered by his kinsman, William, Lord
Douglas.

[51] This in turn explains the rumours in 1352–3 that the Scots might depose David and
set up Stewart as king: Knighton, 120–3; Wyntoun, vi, 224; Penman, *David II*, 171.

[52] Duncan, *'Honi soit qui mal y pense'*, 119.

[53] 'Observations', 42; Penman, *David II*, 150 (misdating the event).

[54] Froissart, iv, 235–6.

[55] B. Webster, 'David II and the Government of Fourteenth-Century Scotland', *TRHS*,
5th series, xvi (1966), 115–30.

produce a son of his own. The opportunities were certainly there. Queen Joan, who had initially remained in Scotland, visited her husband in London on several occasions. Edward III, who had not seen her since 1328, treated his long-lost sister with genuine affection.[56] David had already developed a reputation as a philanderer by the time he was taken prisoner,[57] and this seems to have put some strain on his relationships not only with Joan but also with her brother. For the first few years, however, Edward and David seem to have maintained both a genuine amity and a mutual confidence in their ability to achieve a lasting settlement between their realms.

Edward III's decision to abandon the Balliol cause and negotiate directly with the Bruce regime in Scotland was the first in a series of remarkable diplomatic about-turns of the mid-1350s. As with Scotland, so now with Brittany: Edward was prepared to consider recognizing the legitimacy of his erstwhile enemies in return either for large ransoms or for the expectation of territorial gain. On 1 March 1353 he reached an agreement with the envoys of Joan of Penthièvre, the wife of his enemy and captive, Charles of Blois, in the draft treaty of Westminster. Charles would be released on the expectation of a ransom of £50,000 sterling payable over six or eight years, depending on whether peace or war prevailed. The agreement included the specification that both sides should support each other against their enemies. But it made no mention of a requirement that Charles perform homage to Edward and was in theory a settlement between equal parties, to be confirmed in due course by a marriage between Charles's heir, John, and the English Princess Margaret.[58]

Edward was well aware of the possible liabilities of this scheme. It represented a blatant act of betrayal of the Montfortist party in Brittany to which he had previously given such eager and emphatic support, and a gross abuse of his role as protector to Jeanne de Montfort and her infant son, John. It suggested the same kind of unscrupulous opportunism to which another abandoned ally, Edward Balliol, had recently taken such grave exception. But it also prefigured a position that was to be adopted repeatedly in the later 1350s, whereby Edward III sought at once to levy heavy ransoms for the release of prestigious captives and to hold back from recognizing their titles. Consequently, the new compact attempted

---

[56] *Foedera*, III.i, 174, 262; E 101/393/10; E 101/393/15, m. 3; Green, *Lives of Princesses*, iii, 139–40, 144. SC 1/56/82 records Joan's need for a waiting woman at the 'great revels' at Windsor, probably the Garter feast of 1358.

[57] Rigg, 'Propaganda of the Hundred Years War', 193.

[58] 'Some New Documents Illustrating the Early History of the Hundred Years War (1353–1356)', ed. F. Bock, *BJRL*, xv (1931), 63–6, 84–91. For the expenses of the king's council and the Breton deputation in the making of this treaty, see E 403/365, 21 Feb., 1 Mar., 18 Mar. 1353.

with Joan of Penthièvre did not in itself preclude the possibility that Edward might gain the ransom and, in due course, revert to the Montfortist cause.[59] Such calculated duplicity helps to explain why the king kept the ransom deal strictly confidential. News only leaked out slowly after his confessor, John Woodrove, was dispatched to Avignon and secured the necessary papal dispensation for the impending marriage on 6 May.[60] Thereafter the negotiations faltered. But a new channel of diplomacy had been opened up, and the secret treaty of 1353 would later allow Edward to manipulate both the Blois and the Montfortist factions to his own distinct advantage.

A major reason for the secrecy surrounding the treaty of Westminster was Edward's desire to play along with the initiatives currently being put in place by the curia for a lasting settlement between England and France. Pope Clement VI died late in 1352, and his successor, the elderly Innocent VI, deputed the role of peacemaker to Guy of Boulogne, cardinal of Porto, a powerful prince of the Church who had close family and political ties with the court of France. Extensive preparations were made during the early months of 1353 for a peace conference to be held, under Guy's presidency, at Guînes. The English envoys to the talks, Archbishop Simon Islip of Canterbury, Henry of Grosmont and the earl of Arundel, were clearly under instruction to delay proceedings until Edward had reached an accommodation in Brittany. In late April the ambassadors claimed, surely rather disingenuously, that they could not make an offer because a council called by Edward III to discuss the matter had been poorly attended and that no parliament was scheduled to meet.[61]

While the filibustering continued at Guînes, Edward was nonetheless prepared to show his hand to the pope. During his visit to Avignon in 1353, John Woodrove told Innocent VI that Edward III was prepared, if necessary, to give up his claim to the throne of France. In return, however, he expected not only full sovereign control over Aquitaine, Ponthieu and Calais but also suzerainty of Flanders and possession of the duchy of Normandy and all the lands in Brittany and other parts of France that he and his men had taken by conquest during the war. It is difficult to know how seriously Edward intended this agenda. It certainly represented a shift away from the position taken at the Avignon peace talks of 1344–5, when the king had been so notably insistent on preserving his title to France. The willingness to withdraw that right therefore provides strong evidence of a new sense of realism on the part of the English crown. Equally, though, the insistence on an exceptionally generous territorial settlement

---

[59] For the subsequent agreement of 1356, which specifically reserved Edward's alliance with the house of Montfort, see p. 354.

[60] *CPL*, iii, 614, 615; 'Some New Documents', 64 n. 2.

[61] 'Quatre lettres du cardinal Guy de Boulogne (1352–1354)', ed. E. Perroy, *Revue du Nord*, xxxvi (1954), 162.

reflects the very important gains of war that had been made since 1345 and the king's increasing preoccupation with the idea of recovering as many as possible of the lands formally held in France by his Norman and Angevin ancestors. Admittedly those claims flew in the face of reality: the treaty with Charles of Blois had recently stated that all positions in Brittany controlled by the English would be handed over to the duke, and the claim to the suzerainty of the county of Flanders took no account of the recent rapprochement between Louis de Mâle and John the Good. It seems probable, then, that the ambitious scope of Edward's demands in 1353 was more by way of an ultimatum to John II. In an important great council of lords and commons held at Westminster Palace in October 1353, Sir Bartholomew Burghersh laid out the details of Woodrove's mission. The assembly concurred that war was both likely and appropriate, and on that expectation granted an extension of the wool subsidy for three years.[62]

Edward's newly articulated policy of using his residual claims to the northern French principalities as leverage for a final settlement focused on Aquitaine, Ponthieu and Calais came under enormous strain over the winter of 1353–4. In particular, the idea that Edward could realistically argue for control of Normandy was challenged by the dramatic intervention of the young Charles II 'the Bad', king of Navarre. As the grandson of Louis X, Charles was a potential rival to Edward III for the Capetian succession. As the son-in-law of John II, he enjoyed especially privileged rights and status at the French court. And as count of Evreux and Mortain, he was also a major landholder in Normandy. In January 1354, Charles organized the ambush and murder of the constable of France, Charles of Spain. The English took this as a definite sign of his defection from the Valois cause and immediately began to make plans for a joint Anglo-Navarrese offensive in northern France.[63] In February, however, John II managed to win Charles the Bad back by pardoning the murder and greatly enlarging his already considerable interests in Normandy. Their formal agreement, the treaty of Mantes, represented a serious setback to English diplomacy, and helps to explain the significant differences of detail between the proposals presented to Innocent VI in 1353 and the outline of an Anglo-French peace drawn up under the guidance of Guy of Boulogne at Guînes on 6 April 1354.[64] The emergence into the military and diplomatic arena of the cunning and unpredictable Charles of Navarre added new complexity to the relations of England and France.

[62] *PROME*, v, 81–3.

[63] Sumption, ii, 128–9.

[64] Fowler, *King's Lieutenant*, 122–9; R. Cazelles, *Société politique, noblesse et couronne sous Jean le Bon et Charles V* (Geneva, 1982), 85–90; 'Some New Documents', 70–3, 91–3. After his return from Avignon, John Woodrove had been sent to take part in the discussions at Guînes: E 403/371, 25 Jan. 1354. He then went back to the curia: L. Mirot and E. Déprez, *Les Ambassades anglaises pendant la Guerre de Cent Ans* (Paris, 1900), nos 166–7.

Under the terms of the treaty of Guînes, it was proposed that Edward III would renounce the French throne in return for full sovereignty over Aquitaine, Poitou, Anjou, Maine, Touraine, Limoges and Ponthieu, and the town and region of Calais. Nothing was said of Edward's claims in Brittany, Normandy or Flanders. This omission must have reflected an understanding that Charles of Blois, Charles of Navarre and Louis de Mâle were all likely to resist the assimilation of the three great principalities into a reconfigured Plantagenet empire. In recognition of recent setbacks, then, the English negotiators retreated to a position of less resistance. It is easy to assume that these new, more modest demands represented Edward's genuine aims by reasserting the true causes for which he had originally gone to war in 1337.[65] But there is a danger in too readily assuming that Edward had given up the fantasy of a larger regime stretching right along the northern and western coasts of France from Calais to Bayonne. Even at such a difficult moment, the English commission insisted on the inclusion of Poitou, Anjou, Maine and Touraine, lordships that stood outside the bounds of Aquitaine and which had been explicitly renounced by Henry III under the terms of the treaty of Paris. Guînes set only a preliminary agenda, which would have to be worked out in much more detail at a future peace conference planned at Avignon. The necessary inclusion of Brittany, Normandy and Flanders in those talks might still allow Edward opportunities either to work towards a more advantageous settlement or, just as likely, to call John II's bluff and provoke a return to war.

It was this pragmatic but steadfast approach that was duly reported to the English parliament of May 1354. Once again Sir Bartholomew Burghersh addressed the lords and commons, advising them that there was a good chance of establishing a lasting settlement. When asked whether they felt prepared to commit to a 'treaty of perpetual peace', the commons replied with a unanimous 'Yes, yes!'[66] The official report is very brief, and it is unclear whether Burghersh relayed any of the detail of the draft treaty of Guînes. Events over the following months were certainly to reveal the advantage of continued flexibility. In November 1354 John the Good abandoned the treaty of Mantes and announced the confiscation of Charles the Bad's possessions throughout the kingdom of France.[67] Edward immediately sought out the slippery Charles with seductive offers of alliance. If he would recognize Edward as king of France and make common cause in a war of conquest, Charles could have Normandy, Brie and Champagne for himself.[68]

[65] Curry, *Hundred Years War*, 56; C. J. Rogers, 'The Anglo-French Peace Negotiations of 1354–60 Reconsidered', *Age of Edward III*, ed. Bothwell, 193–213.

[66] *PROME*, v, 114.

[67] Sumption, ii, 139.

[68] BL, MS Cotton Caligula D. III, no. 61, printed in 'Premières négociations de Charles le Mauvais avec les Anglais (1354–1355)', ed. R. Delachenal, *Bibliothèque de l'Ecole des Chartes*, lxi (1900), 280–2. For the dating of this document see Ormrod, 'England, Normandy', 204 n. 42.

As in the earlier discussions with Joan of Penthièvre, Edward was taking the calculated risk of supporting rival claimants to the northern principalities in the expectation that, once a peace was made with the Valois, they would remain loyal to the Plantagenet cause and even, perhaps, pay homage to the crown of England.

The Avignon peace conference of 1354–5 was one of the great diplomatic spectacles of the Hundred Years War. Edward III's principal ambassador, the duke of Lancaster, managed to run up an expense account of over £5,600 as a result of the extravagant entertaining expected by the various distinguished parties that gathered at the papal court.[69] Prior to their departure for the continent, Lancaster and Arundel were instructed that they must demand English possession of Aquitaine and Ponthieu, Anjou, Maine, Touraine, Poitou and Angoulême, Quercy and the Limousin, and all other lands acquired by conquest during the war. Significantly, Normandy was also now included in the list, though with the specification that it, like Angoulême, Cahors and Quercy, could be bargained away if necessary.[70] In the end, however, the conference accomplished nothing. In the recriminations that followed, each side inevitably blamed the other, and it remains difficult to establish precisely what the real sticking points might have been. Most English and pro-English chroniclers assumed that the French showed bad faith by attempting to shift the agenda and demanding new conditions not mentioned at Guînes.[71] Henry Knighton provided a rather different account of events, claiming that Henry of Lancaster refused at the last minute to accept the demand that Edward III give up the title and arms of France.[72] This story may be true, but it does not necessarily mean that Edward had suddenly shifted away from the policy, openly proclaimed in the great council of 1353, of renouncing his dynastic title in return for a more solid territorial settlement.[73] Rather, it suggests that the conference of 1354–5 marked the first occasion on which Edward's agents stated that the king intended to use the French royal style as warranty for peace, and that he would be prepared to renounce it only *after* John II had agreed and carried out the transfers of sovereignty in the lands passing to Plantagenet control. Whilst this introduced a complicating factor into the discussions, its integration into the subsequent settlement of 1360 suggests that it cannot have been the sole or principal reason for the collapse of the Avignon conference.

To some extent it would be fair to say that both the English and the French envoys to the papal summit of 1354–5 were rapidly overwhelmed

[69] 'Some New Documents', 96–7; Fowler, *King's Lieutenant*, 136–7.

[70] 'Some New Documents', 74–6, 94–6; *EMDP*, I.i, no. 124.

[71] Froissart, *Oeuvres*, xviii, 364–5; *AC*, 31–2; Avesbury, 421; Baker, 123–5; Reading, 116.

[72] Knighton, 126–7; Le Patourel, *Feudal Empires*, chap. xii, 177; M. Prestwich, *The Three Edwards: War and State in England, 1272–1377* (London, 1980), 179.

[73] Rogers, 'Anglo-French Peace Negotiations', 197–8.

by the sheer complexity and intractability of the issues raised and that the
momentum for peace all too rapidly dissipated. The presence of troublesome third parties certainly tested the commitment of the principals.
Charles the Bad, who attended in person, made contact with Lancaster in
January 1355 and began a series of top-secret negotiations around Edward
III's recent proposals for an anti-Valois alliance.[74] In the end, however, it
was John II who most obviously revealed his lack of commitment to the
cause of peace. The French ambassadors to Avignon argued that the
cession of sovereignty in Aquitaine and Ponthieu conflicted directly with
the law and constitution of the realm of France and would amount to a
direct breach of John's coronation oath. This was much more than mere
positioning. John was deeply and very personally committed to redeeming
the honour lost by his father on the field of Crécy. By the end of 1354 he
had evidently decided on a rematch that would be revenge for the humiliations of 1346–7 and, equally importantly, give him strategic advantage in
any subsequent round of peace talks.[75] Plans were being made for a new
Valois offensive in the south-west, the systematic occupation of Charles of
Navarre's castles in Normandy, and the renewal of joint actions with the
Scots.[76] The two sides had become completely entrenched. Ultimately, the
only achievement of these vastly expensive talks was to provide both sides
with time to prepare for war.

The decision of John II and his council to force a further military
encounter with the English in 1354 helps to explain the collapse of the
Anglo-Scottish ransom agreement reached at Newcastle on 13 July of that
year.[77] By this draft treaty, the Scots were required to pay an increased
ransom of £60,000 over nine years for the release of David Bruce. A final
settlement would come only after the last instalment of the ransom; in the
meantime, a state of truce would prevail between the two realms. In that
it made no mention of English suzerainty over the northern kingdom or
required any territorial concessions either to Edward III or to the disinherited, the Newcastle settlement has often been seen as a triumph of Scottish
diplomacy. But it also offered advantages to the English. The formal text
did not actually admit David's title as king of Scots and thus reserved for
future discussion the possibility both of a Balliol and of a Plantagenet
succession. Just as Edward was indicating his determination to cling to
the French royal title as leverage for a territorial settlement on the continent, so too was he attempting artfully to make the ransom of David II a
condition for any final peace with the Scots.

---

[74] *EMDP*, I.i, no. 156; *AC*, 32; Ormrod, 'England, Normandy', 204.
[75] Perroy, *Hundred Years War*, 129; Rogers, 'Anglo-French Peace Negotiations', 198;
Rogers, *War Cruel and Sharp*, 290–2.
[76] Sumption, ii, 138–9.
[77] *Foedera*, III.i, 279, 281–2.

Such manoeuvrings reckoned without the astuteness of David's regency administration. The royal party in Scotland deliberately dragged out the negotiations in the hope that the likely collapse of the Anglo-French talks would render ratification impossible. When David Bruce was transferred to Newcastle in November 1354 in preparation for his delivery to Scotland, there were obvious signs of tension. The Scots demanded that the English accord David his title, and Edward felt bound to impose a further delay on his brother-in-law's release.[78] In March 1355 the sire de Garencières was dispatched from the French court to organize Scottish attacks on northern England. Edward took swift precautions, ordering David's safe return south and his lodging in close confinement at Odiham castle in Hampshire.[79] This was a security issue rather than a personal punishment, and David returned to the Tower during April and May to participate in the ongoing talks.[80] But it is likely that Edward III's patience with his long-standing guest was beginning to wear thin. Once more, the Scots had shown that they were content to bide their time. Nine years after the battle of Neville's Cross, Edward's ambitious plans for the disposition of Scotland remained embarrassingly far from fruition.

The repeated cancellation of royal military expeditions after the victory of *les Espagnols sur mer* and the continuation of truces with the French and the Scots meant that Edward III entered into a rather more settled phase of life. Despite outward appearances, Edward indubitably regarded the substitute activities of tournaments and hunting as only partial compensation for the thrill of war. But if active military engagement remained beyond his sights, he could at least take full command of diplomacy. In early June 1353 the king presided over a banquet at which he, Henry of Lancaster and Charles of Blois entertained a deputation of French knights.[81] His attentiveness to the high-level discussion at Avignon in 1354–5 was especially assiduous. Messengers were regularly dispatched to and fro to relay confidential correspondence between the king and the duke of Lancaster.[82] It was Edward's own agenda, duly approved in council, which continued emphatically to determine English foreign policy throughout this period.

Following the dissolution of the Avignon summit, the pope's envoy, the abbot of Cluny, was sent to England to try to prevent the now imminent collapse into war. In their meeting at Westminster in April 1355, however, Edward told the abbot frankly that, while he was prepared to take counsel on the proposed extension of the Anglo-French truce, he was personally

---

[78] *Foedera*, III.i, 291, 293; Bower, vii, 304–5; Wyntoun, vi, 231–3.
[79] Bower, vii, 278–9; 'Papers Relating to the Captivity and Release of David II', 9–35; *CDS*, iii, nos 1610, 1615, 1627; Penman, *David II*, 181.
[80] E 403/387, 22 June 1357.
[81] E 101/392/12, fol. 13.
[82] E 403/375, 5 Dec. 1354; E 403/377, 23 May 1355.

disinclined to accept it.[83] For the first time since 1347, plans were now firmly established for a major campaign, on multiple fronts, in France. A small force of 800 men-at-arms and 1,400 archers, led by the prince of Wales and including the earls of Warwick, Suffolk, Oxford and Salisbury, would proceed to Gascony, link up with contingents in the duchy and confront the Valois army now being gathered in the south-west. A second and much larger expedition, led by the king, with the duke of Lancaster and the earls of Northampton, Stafford and March and numbering 9,000 men in all, would cross to northern France and make common cause with Charles the Bad and his supporters.[84]

The two armies of 1355 reflected recent changes in recruitment practice. The combined operations were treated as the common cause of the realm, and their costs – amounting to over £100,000 – were met out of public funds, most especially the six-year extension of the wool subsidy granted by the commons in November 1355.[85] But there was also an important element of private enterprise. In a landmark statute in 1352, the crown had agreed to give up its earlier and controversial experiments in conscripting soldiers on the basis of landed wealth.[86] Almost all of the men-at-arms and archers recruited for the campaigns of 1355 were therefore volunteers raised by aristocratic captains and senior military figures of the royal household and funded by large cash advances from the exchequer.[87] The extant indenture made between the king and the prince of Wales reveals the extent to which the contract system now allowed generous terms to the leaders of armies operating outside the control of the royal household. In addition to wages of war, the captains of the army of Gascony would receive a bonus known as *regard*. And while Edward III would retain exclusive control over the 'head of the war' in the event of his capture, his son would have all other prisoners, ransoms and plunder, and could do as he saw fit in sharing out the spoils of war with his own captains.[88] Many of the nobles and men-at-arms who joined both the king and Edward of Woodstock in 1355 came out of a sense of loyalty to the crown and a duty to their martial estate. Far more than ever before, however, they were able to weigh the risks against the potential gains and to introduce into their calculations the prospect of immense material profit.

A great deal of mystery and confusion surrounded the precise nature and aims of Edward III's proposed expedition to northern France in 1355. As in 1346, the king relied heavily on the tactics of surprise. An extant letter from Sir Bartholomew Burghersh emphasizes the top-secret nature

---

[83] Avesbury, 424.

[84] Sumption, ii, 153–5.

[85] *PROME*, v, 122; Harriss, *King, Parliament*, 344–5.

[86] See p. 364.

[87] Prince, 'Payment of Army Wages', 155–6.

[88] *BPR*, iv, 143–5.

of the associated planning.[89] The chroniclers believed that Edward deliberately sought to confuse the French by giving command to Lancaster and therefore suggesting that he would not cross in person.[90] This may suggest that Edward's original scheme included the idea of splitting his force in two, one part to be sent into Normandy under Lancaster and the other being reserved for a surprise landing in Calais and a new *chevauchée* through Picardy and the Île-de-France.[91] By 1 July preparations were well in hand, and the king appointed the six-month-old Prince Thomas as keeper of the realm pending his imminent departure. But adverse weather made progress unexpectedly slow. It took over two weeks to muster the fleet in the Thames estuary at Northfleet near Gravesend. Strong winds in the Channel then dispersed the ships, driving them to seek refuge in the harbours of Deal, Winchelsea and Portsmouth. For much of August and September the king remained on the south coast, busily reordering his forces and awaiting the conditions that might yet allow for the proposed crossings to Normandy and Calais.[92]

Edward III had good reason to regret the overtures that he had made towards Charles the Bad in preparation for the offensive of 1355. On 10 September John II managed to pre-empt the imminent war in Normandy by once more reaching an accommodation with Charles at Valognes.[93] The prince of Wales's fleet had set off for Gascony on the very day before the Franco-Navarrese treaty was sealed. Any failure on Edward III's part to mount an operation in northern France would breach the spirit of the prince's contract and compromise his ability to make headway in the south. Edward was therefore forced significantly to revise his plans. Lancaster would do what he could in Normandy and Brittany, but most of the forces raised for his expedition would now be reassigned to support the king's proposed expedition to Calais. On 22 October the parliament due to meet on 12 November was postponed until the 23rd.[94] In public terms this suggested that Edward intended simply to launch a quick *chevauchée* beyond the Pas de Calais that might provide brief but sufficient distraction from the prince's invasion of Aquitaine.[95] Fleetingly at least, he may also have had a grander strategy in mind. John II had already abandoned his plans to send his eldest son, Charles, against Edward of Woodstock, and at this particular moment it seemed that any major encounter between royal forces was much more likely to take place in the north-east than the

[89] SC 1/41/19.

[90] Avesbury, 425–6; Baker, 125.

[91] Prestwich, *Three Edwards*, 179. Compare the discussion in Rogers, *War Cruel and Sharp*, 293 n. 38.

[92] *CPR 1354–8*, 269; C 81/908/10; *AC*, 32–3; Avesbury, 425–6; Rogers, *War Cruel and Sharp*, 295.

[93] Delachenal, i, 107.

[94] *RDP*, iv, 603–6; *PROME*, v, 116.

[95] C 76/33, m. 6; *Foedera*, III.i, 312; Fowler, *King's Lieutenant*, 148; Avesbury, 427.

south-west of France. Jean le Bel certainly believed that Edward intended
to do battle against King John in 1355, and the report subsequently made
to the English parliament said much the same thing.[96]

Edward disembarked at Calais at the end of October. Including the
thousand or so Netherlandish and German men-at-arms who flocked to
his standard, he had around 10,000 men at his disposal.[97] Although a
good deal smaller than the army of 1346–7, this was still a substantial
fighting force, larger than those with which Edward had earlier faced
down Philip VI in 1339 and 1340. As soon as they reached the limits of the
English conquests and arrived at Ardres, the king's forces began to burn
and destroy everything that stood in their way. Moving south via Alquines
and Thérouanne, Edward was visited by the French knight Jean le
Maingre, better known as the Marshal Boucicaut, to whom he delivered a
direct challenge on 5 November: King John should come out and fight
within the next three days, or Edward would return home. The aim was
to force battle as quickly as possible, and before the English ran out of
supplies. Edward's bravura performance was also intended to send the
clear message that he, rather than John, ought to dictate when the king of
France might prove himself in arms.[98] While Edward prepared himself at
Blagny between 6 and 8 November, John deliberately stalled. The prevarication was proof enough for the English, who now headed north again,
reaching Calais on the 11th. The French, realizing that there were still
points to be scored, sent a deputation to the English camp to propose duels
between members of the rival royal families and alternative dates for a
military engagement.[99] But Edward refused to be taken in, reminding the
envoys that he had already challenged John and that it was certainly not
his intention to be dictated to by a cowardly enemy. Leaving as quickly as
he had come, Edward arrived back in England on 12 November.[100] At the
very least, the fortnight's outing had been a piece of military theatre on a
par with the English invasion of the Cambrésis in 1339. On its own,
however, the Picardy campaign could make no real impression on the
current state of diplomacy. Edward was acutely aware that everything
now rested on the fortunes of his son's army in the south-west.

Had he been able to conjure up further resources, Edward III might
have lingered longer at Calais in 1355 or returned in the following spring to
resume the challenge to John II. But circumstances in Scotland dictated
otherwise. Early in 1355, as part of the preparations for his departure to
the continent, Edward had put the north of England in a state of defence.
A nine-month Anglo-Scottish truce agreed in September allowed him,

[96] Le Bel, ii, 211, 212–13; *PROME*, v, 121; Rogers, *War Cruel and Sharp*, 296.
[97] Le Bel, ii, 212; E 43/69.
[98] Le Bel, ii, 214.
[99] *Chron. J&C*, i, 53–4; *Chron. QPV*, 31.
[100] Rogers, *War Cruel and Sharp*, 301–4; Sumption, ii, 173.

unexpectedly, to redeploy some of his northern forces in support of the French campaign: both Henry Percy and Ralph Neville planned to serve with Edward abroad in 1355.[101] But de Garencières had sealed his negotiations with the Scottish lords by delivering a substantial subsidy – the equivalent of £10,000 sterling – to those prepared to make common cause against the English. Early in October a small Scottish army led by the earl of March and William, lord of Douglas, regained control of the remaining English positions in the Lowlands, crossed the Tweed and descended on Northumberland. It was the first really significant incursion since 1346 and, like that earlier emergency, demanded a decisive campaign of retaliation.

Edward III was aware of these developments before he left for Calais. At first it was deemed sufficient to send Neville north to resume his accustomed responsibilities for the defence of the border. But on 6 November, while the king was in France, the Scottish earls of March and Angus launched a surprise attack on Berwick, captured the town and laid siege to the castle.[102] The campaign now had the full support of the regency government of Scotland, and Robert Stewart took charge of operations. It was this emergency, more than anything else, that determined Edward III's notably swift withdrawal of his *chevauchée* in France.[103] In a plenary session of parliament on 25 November, Sir Walter Mauny recounted in some detail the bad faith shown by the French over the previous eighteen months and the king's recent campaign against John II. Then Sir William Shareshull announced the 'hot news' of the loss of Berwick. It was essential both for the security of the north and for the king's personal honour that the town be retaken. A muster of Welsh and northern English archers and infantry was ordered at Newcastle, and Edward moved north in early December to prepare for the relief of Berwick.[104] It was the first time since 1345 that Edward had visited the northern extremities of his kingdom, and his arrival was almost as much of a surprise to his subjects as it was to the enemy beyond the border. The king later complained that the shortage of victuals in Newcastle had forced him to supply wine from his own stocks to support the Christmas revels in the entourages of the princes Lionel and John, the duke of Lancaster, and the earls of Northampton and March.[105]

The significant show of English arms rapidly had its effect. On 13 January 1356 the remainder of the Scottish army at Berwick submitted. Since they had shown no resistance, the enemy forces were allowed to

[101] *Rot. Scot.*, i, 775–6; Sumption, ii, 169–70.

[102] *AC*, 33; Bower, vii, 280–3; Froissart, iv, 141–3.

[103] Froissart, iv, 149–50.

[104] *PROME*, v, 120–1; *Foedera*, III.i, 314–15. For prises ordered to be brought northwards see C 81/908/13. For the campaign see Avesbury, 431–2; Baker, 126–7; Reading, 122; le Bel, ii, 216–19; *AC*, 33–4; Bower, vii, 286–95; Wyntoun, vi, 203–7; *Liber Pluscardensis*, ed. F. J. H. Skene, 2 vols (Edinburgh, 1877–80), i, 297–9; ii, 227–9.

[105] E 159/140, *Brev. bar.*, Mich., rot. 32.

retreat northwards without further punishment.[106] But the raising of the siege marked the beginning of a brutal campaign of retribution. Edward marched on Roxburgh. The lord of Douglas managed to secure a short truce in order to evacuate his lands, but the earl of March was not a party to the agreement. On 26 January Edward's army moved eastward to the coast and thence up through March's estates, indulging in a frenzy of destruction and pillage along the way. Froissart painted a dramatic picture of the king's arrival at Edinburgh – the Paris of Scotland, as he called it – where the widow of William Douglas of Liddesdale supposedly interceded for the inhabitants. The lower town, however, was set to the torch.[107] Edward then moved on to Haddington, which was systematically destroyed. Supply lines proved insecure, and in the harshness of winter Edward could not risk moving across the Forth. The march south proved hazardous, and the king narrowly escaped ambush by Douglas in the forests around Melrose. It was the sheer devastation that accompanied this punitive raid that was most keenly remembered in England and Scotland alike. Posterity would dub the campaign the 'Burned Candlemas'.[108]

The decision to extend the techniques of the *chevauchée* even into those parts of the Lowlands that had been annexed by Edward III under the terms of the original settlement of Scotland in 1333 was an unusually dramatic statement of the king's decision to move away from earlier power-sharing schemes and resolve once and for all the matter of the Bruce succession. On 20 January 1356, at Roxburgh, Edward Balliol formally renounced his title and homage as king of Scots.[109] Edward III remained at Bamburgh during the proceedings, probably aware that the personal dynamics would be somewhat tense: Balliol apparently made it plain to those attending that this was final proof of the English monarch's perfidy.[110] But the former titular king of Scots was at least partly placated by the offer of compensation: the English crown absolved him of all his debts, gave him 5,000 marks to pay off his other creditors, and agreed to a very generous annuity of £2,000 for the remainder of his life. The old pretender was therefore more than content to retire to self-imposed obscurity in the north of England.[111] By the time he arrived back in the south-east in mid-March, Edward III had good reason to believe that his display of force, coupled with the final abandonment of Balliol, would remove any further impediments to a resolution with the Stewart regency

---

[106] *Wars of Edward III*, 157.

[107] Froissart, iv, 155–6. The veracity of this scene and the possible identity of the intercessor remain uncertain.

[108] Sumption, ii, 187–90; Penman, *David II*, 183–5.

[109] *Foedera*, III.i, 317, 318–19; *CDS*, iii, nos 1591–2.

[110] Fordun, *Chronica*, i, 373–4; Bower, vii, 286–9; *Scalacronica*, 141.

[111] *CDS*, iii, no. 1598; E 159/132, *Brev. bar.*, Hil., rot. 6d; *Foedera*, III.i, 319–20, 327, 345. In 1363 Edward purchased Balliol's rights in the county of Ponthieu for 1,000 marks: *Issues*, 178.

and allow him finally to capitalize on his continued possession of the captive David Bruce.

The prince of Wales's expedition to Gascony had been delayed by the problems created by the strong south-westerly winds of the summer of 1355. But it had set off from Plymouth in early September and, after ten days' good sailing, arrived at Bordeaux on 20 September. The following day, a large assembly of the local nobility gathered in the cathedral to do the prince homage and offer their support; in return, Edward of Woodstock swore, in the Gascon tongue, to be a good and loyal lord.[112] Preparations were immediately made for a major *chevauchée*.[113] Like the Normandy campaign of 1346 on which it was modelled, this was intended as much more than a mere raid. The aim was threefold: to make an example of those lords beyond the frontiers of Aquitaine who continued to resist Edward III's rightful title to the crown of France; to subject their lands to the systematic destruction that served to undermine the moral and political force of Valois rule; and to draw into open battle John II's principal lieutenant in the region, Jean, count of Armagnac.[114]

The Anglo-Gascon army was divided into three, with the prince, Warwick and Salisbury respectively leading the centre, the van and the rear. Marching south-eastwards and entering enemy territory, the divisions fanned out in the usual manner, destroying and plundering as they went, ransoming lesser castles and towns and firing more important strategic positions. At first, Armagnac showed no inclination to fight. Since Prince Edward did not have the resources to lay siege to the count's citadel of Toulouse, it was decided to press on further east into the heart of Languedoc. By mid-November the Anglo-Gascon forces had penetrated as far as Carcassonne, where the prince refused the offer of a tempting pay-off from the cowed inhabitants and instead ordered the burning of the fortified upper town. At Narbonne, news reached the English command that Armagnac now intended to meet Edward of Woodstock in battle. The prince regrouped and about-faced, but when the French army did not materialize it was decided to recommence the *chevauchée* in an organized retreat. Along the way, at Boulbonne on 17 November, Prince Edward formally recruited to his cause the powerful Gaston Phoebus, count of Foix, the sworn enemy of the count of Armagnac. The weather and the search for supplies were now becoming serious problems; slowed down by flooded rivers, the army began to be harassed by Armagnac's raiding parties. By the beginning of December Edward had managed to

[112] Barber, *Edward, Prince of Wales*, 116–17.

[113] *Life and Campaigns*, 61–70.

[114] Rogers, *War Cruel and Sharp*, 304–24; P. Hoskins, 'The Itineraries of the Black Prince's *Chevauchées* of 1355 and 1356: Observations and Interpretations', *Journal of Medieval Military History*, vii (2009), 13–25, 37.

bring his forces back in reasonable order into the English territories. After disbanding much of the army, he invited the captains to take up positions along the border from which they could mount forays against the enemy.[115] The prince himself returned to Bordeaux to take stock, receive news from England, and plan his next move. In spite of the absence of a confrontation, the expedition was deemed a success. Jean le Bel condemned Armagnac's inactivity as deeply cowardly, and the prince's man Sir John Wingfield, who had something of an accountant's eye for such matters, wrote eagerly to the king's treasurer that the general campaign of destruction and plundering had deprived John II of over half the revenue of his kingdom.[116]

The winter and spring of 1355–6 witnessed yet another change in the position of that notorious exponent of the art of self-preservation, Charles of Navarre. As early as November 1355, Navarre was plotting to overthrow John II and put the dauphin on the throne. Charles's leadership of the resistance to royal taxation in Normandy forced John finally to take decisive action, and Navarre and his co-conspirators were arrested even as they sat at dinner with Prince Charles at Rouen on 5 April 1356.[117] The hostile local political reaction to such strong-armed tactics provided Edward III with the opportunity he had sought in the previous year to send a military expedition into Normandy. Such swift repositioning involved some duplicity: at the very moment that Charles's supporters were engaging in negotiation with him, Edward was also bluffing his way through a correspondence with the pope in which he claimed never to have consorted with such perfidious adventurers and always to have treated Charles as his enemy.[118] By May, however, any such pretence was removed. It was now decided that Henry of Lancaster's long-delayed expedition would make for Normandy, there to join up with Charles the Bad's brother, Philip of Navarre, and make common cause against the Valois. On 28 May Philip of Navarre, Godfrey Harcourt and their principal allies issued formal letters of defiance against John the Good.[119] Edward III's provincial strategy was about to admit yet another dimension.

John II had been preparing for some time to march against the Black Prince's army of Gascony, and his forces were due to muster at Chartres in the spring. The arrival of Henry of Grosmont at Saint-Vaast-la-Hougue on 18 June created a much more immediate threat to the security of the kingdom. Appointing his teenage son, John, count of Poitiers, as commander of the army of the south-west, the French king set out with a large force to counter Lancaster's rapid advance through Normandy. With

[115] Rogers, *War Cruel and Sharp*, 325–9.
[116] Le Bel, ii, 222; *Life and Campaigns*, 52.
[117] Delachenal, i, 135–57; Cuttler, *Law of Treason*, 160–2.
[118] *Foedera*, II.i, 329, 330, 331; *Antient Kalendars*, i, 180, 181; Sumption, ii, 209–10.
[119] Froissart, iv, 180–6.

the reinforcements provided by the Navarrese, Lancaster had about 1,000 men-at-arms and 1,400 mounted archers at his disposal.[120] He advanced eastwards to relieve Pont-Audemer and Breteuil, and reached Verneuil by early July. Having seen off the enemy on several occasions and relieved important Navarrese strongholds, Lancaster could perfectly reasonably claim the upper hand, and now organized a dignified retreat to the Cotentin peninsula. King John was left looking discredited and foolish.[121]

At the end of Lancaster's notable campaign, Godfrey Harcourt formally acknowledged Edward III as both king of France and duke of Normandy.[122] This newfangled style neatly expressed Edward's support for the strong tradition of provincial independence in Normandy.[123] It was never asserted in England, since the title to France was held to incorporate any rights that the king had in the duchy. But it hinted at a new preoccupation on the part of Edward III. On 4 August Philip of Navarre, who had crossed to England for personal talks with the king at Clarendon, also performed liege homage to the king of England as 'king of France and duke of Normandy'.[124] The cousins of England and Navarre no doubt greeted each other with the studied courtesy of seasoned strategists. But they also found a way out of their rivalry and mutual suspicion by establishing a form of words that might at once admit of Edward's sovereignty in France and yet hint at his willingness to use his title to Normandy as a means of advancing Charles's interest in northern France. Lancaster's campaign had already aroused memories of the *viage de Normandie* of 1346–7 and proved once again that England had effective military control of the duchy. In that respect, it too may well have reawakened Edward's own interest in pursuing the rights of his ancestors and reassembling not just the attenuated continental empire of Henry III but also the great clutch of titles once enjoyed by Henry II.[125] With the prospect of more glories to come, the English clergy confidently roused the king's subjects to a further bout of fervent prayer.[126]

On 4 August 1356 the Black Prince set off northwards from Bergerac on a second great march, accompanied by an Anglo-Gascon force of up to 7,000 men. He had three interlinked objectives: to pursue the count of Poitiers's army at Bourges; to join Lancaster in the Loire valley; and, in the

[120] Fowler, *King's Lieutenant*, 151; Rogers, *War Cruel and Sharp*, 341.

[121] Avesbury, 462–5; Knighton, 138–43; Froissart, iv, 188–91.

[122] *Foedera*, III.i, 332–3.

[123] J. Le Patourel, 'Edouard III, "roi de France et duc de Normandie" ', *Révue historique du droit français et étranger*, 4th series, xxxi (1953), 317–18. The king's separate title to Normandy was still being asserted at the time of the Reims campaign in 1359–60: C 76/38, m. 7.

[124] E 30/72, printed in *Foedera*, III.i, 338, 339, 340; Froissart, iv, 184–6.

[125] BL, MS Cotton Caligula D. III, nos 43–53; Ormrod, 'England, Normandy', 205–6.

[126] BIA, Register 11, fol. 37v.

event that his father decided to cross to France, to combine with the latter on further activities that might, under the right circumstances, lead to a decisive battle.[127] Edward III did not make any known preparations for an expedition of his own in 1356, but he remained under obligation to support the prince if the latter were in grave danger. Had things turned out differently, then, it is quite likely that he would once more have taken up arms in the autumn of 1356. In fact, the original plan had to be significantly modified when John II decided to abandon efforts to lay siege to Breteuil and marched south at the head of his own army. By the time the prince reached Romorantin at the end of August, the French were beginning to take up bases at Orléans and Tours. John, meanwhile, had ordered the destruction of the bridges along the Loire. The duke of Lancaster, who advanced as far as Angers, was therefore unable to cross the river and was forced to retreat to Brittany. If there was to be a major encounter between Plantagenet and Valois, fate had now determined that the prince of Wales would command it alone.

The French king moved south and re-mustered at Loches on 13 September. By this time Edward of Woodstock had also turned south from Tours, and for the next few days the two armies jostled for position, each side uncertain whether the other intended to give battle or retreat. Cardinal Talleyrand of Périgord attempted to arbitrate a peaceful withdrawal, and the English and French went through the usual motions of setting out terms for a truce. In reality, both were now busy reconnoitring suitable locations for battle. On 18 September lines were drawn up outside the city of Poitiers, in the fields between Savigny-l'Évescault and the woods of Nouaillé.[128] Prince Edward divided his army into three, the van being led by Warwick and Oxford with the captal de Buch and other Gascon lords, the rearguard by Suffolk and Salisbury, and the centre by the prince himself, with his close associates Bartholomew Burghersh the younger, James Audley, John Chandos and Reginald Cobham. All told, the English force was probably between 6,000 and 8,000 men. It is very difficult to establish the size of John II's army, but it was certainly larger – perhaps twice as large as that of Prince Edward. It was deployed in a complex formation with the two marshals, Audrehem and Clermont, leading small forces of mounted men-at-arms as phalanxes to a front division led by the dauphin and two further divisions, led by the duke of Orléans and the king, to the rear. In the French army was William,

[127] Delachenal, i, 192–7; D. Green, *The Black Prince* (Stroud, 2001), 61; Fowler, *King's Lieutenant*, 154–5.

[128] For detailed accounts of Poitiers (which differ, often quite significantly, in their various interpretations of the evidence) see Burne, *Crecy War*, 297–321; H. J. Hewitt, *The Black Prince's Expedition of 1355–1357* (Manchester, 1958), 110–39; Barber, *Edward, Prince of Wales*, 137–48; Sumption, ii, 233–9; Rogers, *War Cruel and Sharp*, 372–84; D. Green, *The Battle of Poitiers, 1356* (Stroud, 2002); F. Bériac-Lainé and C. Given-Wilson, *Les Prisonniers de la bataille de Poitiers* (Paris, 2002), 39–52; Hoskins, 'Itineraries', 25–36.

lord of Douglas, whose experience against the English in Scotland was brought to bear significantly on tactical planning. In response to the nature of the local terrain and the now well understood dangers of unsupported cavalry attacks, the Valois council of war ruled that the great part of its men-at-arms should prepare to fight on foot. The lessons of Crécy were, it seemed, finally being understood by the French high command.[129]

The implications for the English were ominous indeed. Both in size and in deployment, the French army represented an enormous threat to the prince of Wales's hopes of victory in pitched battle. Not surprisingly, some of John II's generals, and many later historians, believed that Edward of Woodstock decided at the last moment simply to withdraw from the field. The earl of Warwick seemingly moved off with the vanguard to conduct the English baggage train south across the boggy land around the River Miosson. But this manoeuvre is also susceptible to other interpretations. On the model of his father's great victories at Halidon Hill and Crécy, Edward had planned to take a defensive position and placed his troops behind the thick hedges that skirted the forest of Nouaillé. Lacking water and supplies, and realizing that the French were perfectly happy to starve them out, the English saw that they had no option but to break the dead-lock. In a later letter to the citizens of London, the prince explained that 'it was agreed that we should take a path traversing their front, in such a way that, if they wanted the battle, or would come towards us in a place that was not too greatly to our disadvantage, we would fight them'.[130] Such a manoeuvre was difficult and dangerous, and speaks volumes for the iron discipline on which the prince could count within his ranks, as well as the overwhelming confidence that those men vested, at this dark moment, in the son of the redoubtable Edward III.

Against the strong sense of English unity in adversity sat the squabbling battalions of France. When Audrehem observed the earl of Warwick's movements he immediately assumed the English to be in retreat and, abandoning the plan to remain in defensive formation, ordered his forces forward in a traditional cavalry charge. Not to be outdone, Clermont responded by attacking the earl of Salisbury's division. Such impetuous advances, reminiscent of the English earl of Hereford's reckless charge at Bannockburn, demonstrated the continuing lack of firm co-ordination within the French army. Audrehem was quickly isolated and taken prisoner. Clermont fell, along with so many of the flower of French chivalry, as they attempted to push their way through the thickets that protected the English archers and knights. Seemingly unaware of the disaster occurring further down the field, King John ordered the massed rank of dismounted

---

[129] The figures are inevitably conjectural. See Green, *Black Prince*, 64.

[130] *Memorials of London*, 206, translated and analysed by Rogers, *War Cruel and Sharp*, 373 and n. 140.

men-at-arms to advance. But the carnage was soon evident, and many of the men in Orléans's division simply fled the field.

With no contingency plan in place, John II himself now moved forward. At the sight of this advance, Prince Edward's men-at-arms, led by Audley, mounted their horses and charged, forcing the French off the hill. Meanwhile the captal de Buch led a flanking movement to cut off John's forces in the rear. In a field by the Miosson known as the Champ Alexandre, during a desperate hand-to-hand encounter in the afternoon, John the Good was finally forced to surrender up his body. Immediately, a dispute arose as to who might claim this exalted prize, but the Gascon soldiers who had set upon the king were ordered off, and the earl of Warwick and Reginald Cobham led John away to safety.

By this time the battle's outcome was all too clear. Many of King John's forces attempted to escape, keenly pursued by English and Gascon bounty-hunters. The French losses were indeed terrible: the dukes of Athènes and Bourbon were dead, along with the gallant standard-bearer Geoffrey de Charny and a host of other nobles, knights and esquires. What principally marked out the English victory of Poitiers, however, and gave it such a lasting legacy in the minds of the elite, was the spectacular array of prisoners taken. It seems likely that somewhere in the region of 2,000 French men-at-arms were captured on the field or in flight. In addition to John II himself, these included the king's son Philip, count of Touraine, the archbishop of Sens, Marshal Audrehem, and the counts of Vendôme, Tancarville, Eu, Ponthieu, Ventadour, Longueville, Dammartin and Auxerre. In one and the same blow, the French elite had been stripped of a significant part of its political and military high command. And by the same action, numerous English nobles and knights had at last been delivered the much-promised means of profit from the enterprises of war. It was with the spoils of Poitiers, for example, that Thomas Beauchamp, earl of Warwick, concluded the major rebuilding programme that he had earlier undertaken at Warwick castle; the self-consciously French 'look' of the extant round tower there, known as Caesar's Tower, probably built in the 1360s, is vivid testimony to the natural superiority felt by those English lords who had accompanied the prince of Wales on the campaign of 1356.[131]

Sweet indeed was the alcohol-fuelled euphoria that swept through Edward of Woodstock's victorious army. Especially for the young nobles and knights of the prince's generation who had gained positions of leadership since the heady days of Crécy and Calais, the success at Poitiers represented a truly life-defining moment. The young earl of Salisbury and his companions were remembered as fighting 'more fiercely than lions'.[132]

---

[131] K. B. McFarlane, *The Nobility of Later Medieval England* (Oxford, 1973), 30; R. K. Morris, 'The Architecture of the Earls of Warwick in the Fourteenth Century', *England in the Fourteenth Century*, ed. Ormrod, 161–74.

[132] *Life and Campaigns*, 100.

Nor, in their triumph, did the English forget the obligations of the victorious. At a banquet held in his pavilions on the evening following the battle, Edward of Woodstock made honoured guests of his captives and, in a piece of highly charged chivalric theatre, insisted graciously on deferring to John II as the hero of the hour. The Valois leader may have lost the day, but his bravery on the field and his dignity and fortitude in adversity had won him the laurel of honour.[133]

Edward III was well informed about the activities of his son and other commanders in France during 1355–6. Thomas the Messenger and John Dagenet carried information from Prince Edward to his father and vice versa. The king sent the herald John Mushon to seek out his son in Gascony, and other envoys arrived in England with letters from the prince to Queen Philippa.[134] The Black Prince and his steward, John Wingfield, both wrote accounts of the 1355 *chevauchée* through Languedoc, which they sent to Edward III's right-hand man, William Edington, bishop of Winchester.[135] The news of the great victory was communicated to Edward III by at least three different men: John le Cok of Cherbourg, Geoffrey Hamelyn and Thomas the Messenger.[136] It must have reached him by no later than 10 October 1356, when the bishops were asked to order prayers of thanksgiving for the capture of 'John de Valois, usurper of the kingdom of France'.[137] Around the same time letters from the prince to various churchmen and to the citizens of London began to arrive in England.[138]

It was out of this general information network that there emerged one of the most sustained mythologies of victory in the whole history of the Hundred Years War. The prince was predictably hailed as England's latest and greatest hero. Just as Edward III had been linked with the Arthurian prophetic tradition in the 1330s and proclaimed the 'boar of Windsor', so now was Prince Edward celebrated as the 'boar of Cornwall'.[139] In the sixteenth century Edward of Woodstock acquired the nickname with which he was always later associated, the 'Black Prince', a reference to his

---

[133] Froissart, v, 63–4; *EHD*, iv, no. 35.

[134] E 403/378, 12 Oct., 23 Oct. 1355, 11 Apr. 1356; E 403/380, 1 June, 10 June 1356; E 403/382, 7 Oct. 1356.

[135] Avesbury, 434–9; *Life and Campaigns*, 50–5; Hewitt, *Black Prince's Expedition*, 78–81.

[136] Hewitt, *Black Prince's Expedition*, 194; Bériac-Lainé and Given-Wilson, *Prisonniers*, 61.

[137] *CCR 1354–60*, 334.

[138] Froissart, *Oeuvres*, xviii, 389–92; *Memorials of London*, 285–8; *Life and Campaigns*, 57–9; *Chartulary of Winchester Cathedral*, 162–4; Fowler, 'News from the Front', 77–8. See also the account by Bartholomew Burghersh: Froissart, *Oeuvres*, xviii, 385–7, translated in *Wars of Edward III*, 163–4. The king's council was recorded as sitting in special session at the time the news of Poitiers reached London: E 403/382, 14 Oct. 1356; *Issues*, 166; Hewitt, *Black Prince's Expedition*, 194.

[139] Baker, 152; *Life and Campaigns*, 80.

alleged use of ceremonial black armour.[140] But in the aftermath of Poitiers and the prince's subsequent career in the 1360s, his contemporaries seem to have given him a different accolade, celebrating their king-in-waiting under the informal style of Edward IV. In the general euphoria of the moment, unofficial and often scurrilous stories also began to circulate among an eager public about the abject humiliation of England's enemies. In particular, the new victory seemed to vindicate the increasing wave of popular hostility to a pro-French papacy. The chronicler of St Mary's Abbey, York, reported gleefully a rumour that the pope had been wrongly informed of the outcome of the battle and ordered general jubilation at Avignon, only to have to call the whole thing off on hearing the devastating news of John II's captivity.[141] Writing later in the century, Henry Knighton reported with satisfaction the scandalous verses that had supposedly circulated on the continent in the aftermath of Poitiers: 'The pope has become a Frenchman and Jesus an Englishman. Now we shall see who will do better, the pope or Jesus!'[142]

As the Black Prince withdrew to Bordeaux for the winter, Edward III busied himself in deciding how best to exploit his new gains of war. A number of special councils were held over the winter and, after a gap of some sixteen months, parliament was summoned to meet at Westminster on 17 April 1357.[143] Under the terms of Prince Edward's appointment as lieutenant of Aquitaine, the right to hold and ransom John II belonged to the king alone. All other prisoners were legally under the control of the captains who had claimed them on the field, and the negotiations of their ransoms would therefore be private business transactions. But Edward III quickly realized the advantages to be had from taking control of all the principal captives held by the prince's men. The discussions held with the parties of Charles of Blois and David II in 1356–7 indicated that Edward had been right to insist that prisoners not be released until he was able to dictate advantageous terms. In August 1356, just a few weeks before the battle of Poitiers, it had finally been agreed that Charles of Blois be ransomed for the astonishingly high figure of 700,000 écus (£116,667). Furthermore, Edward now made explicit the point that had seemed to be lost in 1353, insisting that he reserve the right to continue supporting the Montfort cause in Brittany.[144] By the spring of 1357 it seemed that a similar deal was about to be made for the release of David Bruce, in which Edward would secure the Scots' commitment to payment of a hefty

[140] Barber, *Edward, Prince of Wales*, 242.

[141] *AC*, xxxiii, 22, 39, 160.

[142] Knighton, 150–1 (translation adapted).

[143] E 403/382, 18 Nov. 1356; E 403/384, 19 Dec. 1356, 10 Feb., 11 Mar. 1357; *RDP*, iv, 611–13.

[144] M. Jones, 'The Ransom of Jean de Bretagne, Count of Pethièvre: An Aspect of English Foreign Policy, 1386–1388', *BIHR*, xlv (1972), 9–10; Harriss, *King, Parliament*, 490; Given-Wilson and Bériac, 'Edward III's Prisoners', 822–4.

ransom while keeping open his right to intervene in the future succession to the northern kingdom.[145] How much more might Edward gain if not only John II but the entire clutch of great French lords taken at Poitiers were brought under his control and used actively to influence the peace settlement that might ensue.

In spite of his very public adherence to the conventions of war, Edward III's treatment of the prisoners of Poitiers revealed an even deeper commitment to the rights and interests of the crown. Over the winter of 1356–7 the Black Prince brokered a series of agreements by which the king promised to pay in the region of £44,000 in order to secure exclusive rights to the ransoming of the major French nobles taken at Poitiers. Edward III was certainly not blind to the profit motive and must have been aware that, in the event that they were ransomed off separately, the Valois lords might yield handsome profits on his initial investment. But although the counts of Auxerre and Dammartin did indeed attempt to strike private deals with the king for their ransom and release, the majority (and probably all) of the sixteen major captives of Poitiers purchased by Edward were held as additional leverage for the Anglo-French peace settlement that Edward now hoped to secure.[146] If John himself was to be released – and this was the inference right from the start of the ensuing round of diplomacy – Edward might usefully deploy the other prisoners as continuing hostages both for the payment of John's ransom and for the implementation of the other elements of the peace. In the systematic buying up of aristocratic prisoners after the battle of Poitiers, Edward III revealed himself as much more than a mere profiteer. Above all, the scheme demonstrated his resolve not to be drawn into a binding peace without full guarantees that the Valois would fulfil their side of any lasting settlement. It was these fundamental principles to which Edward was to cling over the following years, as he set about forcing the French into a great final settlement for the ransoming of John II and the re-establishment of effective English rule in western and northern France.

[145] See pp. 388–91.
[146] Given-Wilson and Bériac, 'Edward III's Prisoners', 814, 817, 818–20, 830–2.

Chapter 13

PESTILENCE AND POLITICS, 1348–1358

In the decade between the victories of Crécy and Poitiers Edward III emerged as a statesman of true stature. The impressive achievements of the king and the prince of Wales dispelled many of the public anxieties over domestic policy that had been so keenly expressed in the early years of the French wars, and helped to convince the polity that the continuing military effort genuinely served the common interests of king and kingdom. But the recovery of royal authority was very far from reliant on military success alone. The public confidence that had been slowly re-established since the debacle of 1341 required Edward to provide regular, bold and imaginative leadership to the internal government of England. In the third decade of his reign, most of Edward's subjects were inevitably a good deal more preoccupied with the huge challenge created by the plague of 1348–9 than they ever were with the prospects of further victories against England's enemies abroad. It was in his government's decisive and creative responses to the onset and aftermath of the Black Death that Edward III fully revealed the expansiveness and vision of his regime, and his own equally remarkable capacity for political leadership.

To understand the extent of that achievement is to acknowledge that many middling members of the polity, especially among the gentry and the mercantile classes that provided the core constituencies of the parliamentary commons, were decidedly unconvinced in the late 1340s about the supposed benefits accruing from a perpetual state of war. If Edward thought that the great clutch of victories in 1346–7 would buy him the ready acquiescence of the political community, he was to be quickly disabused of the idea. In the parliaments of January and March 1348 the commons submitted long lists of complaints about the operation of the law, the abuse of pardons, the regulation of the coinage, the wool staple, the crown's recent attempts to levy troops on the basis of landed wealth, the continuing burden of purveyance, the injurious effects of the monopoly over the customs, and the dubious legality of the feudal aid and forced loan of 1346. The king, who must have been expecting rather more gratitude for his recent military achievements, took a distinctly high-handed approach and, apart from promising that there would be statutory concessions in the future, insisted that the public commitment to war took precedence over the private interests of the subject. Had events not taken an altogether unexpected course, there is every sign that this state of tension might have continued, not least because Edward's new-found success in war, the strong devotion of the nobility, and the relative financial stability of the regime now rendered him a good deal less vulnerable to political attack than in 1339–41.[1] Ironically, it would take the unimaginable disaster of the plague to prove to the political community that the king did indeed recognize his obligation to the principle of the general good and would work actively with his greater subjects to guarantee effective and beneficent rule.

The surviving evidence relating to the Black Death of 1348–9 offers few certainties to modern historians. The most likely explanation is that the pandemic arose as a result of the introduction into Europe from the Far East of a particularly virulent strain of bubonic plague transmitted by fleas borne on the backs of rats. The impact was certainly swift, devastating and terrifying: those who criticize the hyperbole of the chroniclers would do well to remember the very real panic aroused by the widespread belief that the disease marked the beginning of the end of the world. England offers the richest demographic data in the whole of Europe, though even here the figures are a matter of dispute. The population, which had been rising steadily since the time of Domesday Book (1086) seems to have reached a peak around 1300, when England probably had between 4.5 and 6 million inhabitants. In 1377, by contrast, when the first national poll tax was collected, there were no more than 2.75 million people left in the realm. Even assuming that the level had already fallen as a consequence of the earlier period of famine in the 1310s and 1320s, the plague of 1348–9 and subsequent outbreaks in the 1360s and 1370s brought about a cumulative drop in the population of between 30 and 50 per cent in the course of single generation. There is every reason to believe what Edward III's contemporaries said: that England underwent a human disaster of unimaginable scale in the eighteen months following the first arrival of the Black Death in the summer of 1348.[2]

The eruption of the plague in London after September forced the crown to take emergency preventive measures for the safety of its servants and subjects. A parliament that had been due to open at Westminster in January 1349 was postponed until Easter.[3] Treasurer Edington quitted the capital

[1] *PROME*, iv, 413–32, 453–61; Harriss, *King, Parliament*, 366–75, 513–17; Verduyn, 'Attitude', 98–106.

[2] J. L. Bolton, ' "The World Upside Down": Plague as an Agent of Economic and Social Change', *The Black Death in England*, ed. W. M. Ormrod and P. G. Lindley (Stamford, 1996), 17–78; P. J. P. Goldberg, *Medieval England: A Social History, 1250–1550* (London, 2004), 71–87, 163–7; S. H. Rigby, 'Introduction', *A Social History of England, 1250–1500*, ed. R. Horrox and W. M. Ormrod (Cambridge, 2006), 1–30. B. M. S. Campbell, *English Seigniorial Agriculture, 1250–1450* (Cambridge, 2000), 399–406, suggests a more conservative figure for the pre-plague population.

[3] *CCR 1346–9*, 613–14, 615; *CCR 1349–54*, 1.

after Christmas and spent most of the rest of the winter at his manor houses in Surrey and Hampshire.[4] For those who remained, the prospects were indeed grim. At the end of January 1349 it was reported that the barons of the exchequer and the sheriffs called to account there did not dare to do their business for fear of their lives. By the spring, it was decided that the courts would have to close for the rest of the legal year and that the impending session of parliament must be cancelled.[5] Archbishop Stratford had died, of old age, on the eve of the plague's arrival in August 1348. His designated successor at Canterbury, the already frail Chancellor Offord, died from the pestilence in the London suburbs on 20 May 1349, and the otherwise robust scholar and royal clerk Thomas Bradwardine, elected archbishop in his stead, also fell victim just three months later.[6] Edward III, who had so magnificently kept the French and Scots at bay, now stood by, seemingly helplessly, as the plague wreaked its terrible vengeance on his kingdom.

Governments across Europe were severely hampered by their general ignorance of the causes and nature of the plague. The English crown not unreasonably assumed a general link with poor public sanitation, and the king expressed his personal anxiety about such matters by initially opposing the new plague cemetery set up at the initiative of the bishop of London at East Smithfield, in the close vicinity of the Tower.[7] If any kind of coherent public policy did evolve in the autumn and winter of 1348-9, it was based principally on the belief that the new disease was a manifestation of divine wrath. Early in the emergency, Edward III requested the clergy to perform rites that would 'protect [his] realm of England from these plagues and mortality'.[8] Later, in August 1349, his chancery wrote to the bishops with dire warnings:

We are amazed and appalled that the few people who still survive have been so ill-fated, so ungrateful towards God and so stiff-necked that they are not humbled by the terrible judgments and lessons of God. For, if their works are any guide, sinfulness and pride are constantly increasingly in the people, and charity has grown more than usually cold in them. This seems to presage a much mightier calamity that might happen unless God, who has been offended by their guilt, is pacified by the performance of penance for sin and by the prayers of the faithful.[9]

---

[4] *The Register of William Edington, Bishop of Winchester, 1346–1366*, ed. S. F. Hockley, 2 vols (Hampshire Record series, vii–viii, 1986–7), i, nos 314–468.

[5] E 368/121, rot. 144d; *CCR 1349–54*, 28, 66; Baker, 99.

[6] *CCR 1349–54*, 84; *Fasti 1300–1541*, iv, 3.

[7] C 81/1332/56. For the excavations conducted on this site in the 1980s see I. Grainger, D. Hawkins, L. Cowal and R. Mikulski, *The Black Death Cemetery, East Smithfield, London* (London, 2008).

[8] *The Black Death*, ed. R. Horrox (Manchester, 1994), 113–14.

[9] *Registrum Hamonis de Hethe, diocesis Roffensis*, ed. C. Johnson, 2 vols (CYS, xlviii, xlix, 1948), ii, 894–5, translated in *Black Death*, 117–18.

This stern assessment of the state of public morality seems to have captured at least the essence of the monarch's own views. As the plague dissipated, Edward III indicated his commitment to acts of atonement by making his way to Hereford in October 1349 to attend the translation of the remains of St Thomas Cantilupe. Soon after, he also sent special alms to the shrine of Thomas Becket at Canterbury Cathedral.[10] Some commentators were convinced that the moral defects identified in the king's letter to the bishops were common in all levels of society. Henry Knighton, for example, later described the shocking antics of a group of women who had allegedly moved around the tournament circuit in the months immediately before the arrival of the plague, tempting the flower of English knighthood to neglect its responsibilities to the divine order.[11] Almost inevitably, however, the prevailing attitude – and the one quickly espoused as official policy – was that the lower orders were really to blame.

After his long period of semi-quarantine at Woodstock, Edward III left in July and early August 1349 to make a tour of his hunting grounds in Gloucestershire, Wiltshire, Dorset and Hampshire. Some of these areas had taken the full force of the plague during the previous year, and Edward observed for himself the dramatic effects upon the rural economy: home-steads abandoned, tenancies unfilled, fields left unploughed and unsown.[12] The most pressing issue was finding the labour that would bring in the harvest and allow the survivors to eat over the coming winter. In some parts of the realm, lords were being forced to pay up to 50 per cent more than in the previous decade to persuade the meagre surviving workforce out into the fields.[13] The king had already been to Westminster for urgent discus-sions with the council in mid-June, and from his seat in the capital on 18 August he promulgated the emergency legislation that would become known as the Ordinance of Labourers. All able-bodied adults and 'sturdy beggars' were forcibly to be put to work. They were to see out the full dura-tion of their contracts, and were to accept pre-plague rates of pay. These regulations would also apply to those artisans – smiths, leatherworkers, builders, and so on – whose work was essential to the rural and urban economies alike. The ordinance reiterated the contemporary notion that there should be a just price for foodstuffs and manufactures to prevent unscrupulous retailers from exploiting current shortages. Finally, the bishops were supplied with a parallel ordinance for the regulation of the wages of unbeneficed mass-priests and church workers. The idea that everyone should stand by their responsibility to assist in restoring economic

[10] R. C. Finucane, *Miracles and Pilgrims: Popular Belief in Medieval England* (Basingstoke, 1995), 179; *Litterae Cantuariensis*, ii, 296.

[11] Knighton, 92–5. See also Baker, 97; *Melsa*, iii, 69.

[12] The route and chronology of the plague through England are analysed by O. J. Benedictow, *The Black Death, 1346–1353: The Complete History* (Woodbridge, 2004), 123–45.

[13] D. L. Farmer, 'Prices and Wages [i]', *The Agrarian History of England and Wales, II: 1042–1350*, ed. H. E. Hallam (Cambridge, 1988), 816–17.

stability was to be powerfully articulated again a few months later when, on the grounds of the exhaustion of the realm, the crown temporarily forbade all its subjects from travelling abroad either for war or for pilgrimage.[14]

In spite of the apparent radicalism of these measures, there was nothing essentially new about the Ordinance of Labourers. Many of the principles of wage regulation had been deeply embedded in village by-laws since the end of the thirteenth century.[15] The Irish parliament had adopted the paradigm of reasonable wages fifty years before the plague, and there had already been some faltering steps towards national price regulation in England since Edward II's time.[16] A number of Edward III's contemporaries in continental Europe issued proclamations about wage levels in the aftermath of the plague, and the English legislation may originally have been intended, like these, as a simple statement of solidarity with hard-pressed employers.[17] This explains why no particular measures were at first taken to enforce the ordinance of 1349 in the royal courts.[18] Instead, lesser courts were simply encouraged to take the initiative as local conditions required. By the end of 1349 the authorities in London were already adapting the Ordinance of Labourers to fit the needs of the industrial and commercial economies of the city.[19] Rather than seeing the plague as an opportunity to extend the reach of criminal justice, the crown simply hoped that a cautious statement of general encouragement would be enough to ride out the emergency.

The king also used the administration of the royal estates as an example of the self-help practices that he commended to his subjects. With so many tenants-in-chief falling victim to the plague, and a significant proportion of them lacking adult heirs, the exchequer successfully channelled the resulting profits of wardship to create a new income stream for the royal household.[20] It took a stern line with the administrators of these and other

---

[14] *SR*, i, 307–8; *Foedera*, III.i, 191, 198–9; *CCR 1349–54*, 206–7; *CLBL, F*, 192, 199, 201; *CIM*, iii, no. 50; B. H. Putnam, 'Maximum Wage-Laws for Priests after the Black Death', *American Historical Review*, xxi (1915–16), 12–32.

[15] A. Musson, 'New Labour Laws, New Remedies? Legal Reaction to the Black Death "Crisis" ', *Fourteenth Century England I*, ed. Saul, 76.

[16] *Statutes and Ordinances . . . of Ireland*, 214–17; R. H. Britnell, *The Commercialisation of English Society, 1000–1500* (Cambridge, 1993), 31–7; R. Braid, 'Economic Behavior, Markets and Crises: The English Economy in the Wake of Plague and Famine in the 14th Century', *Economic and Biological Interactions in Pre-Industrial Europe from the 13th to the 18th Centuries*, ed. S. Cavaciocchi (Florence, 2010), 345–51. For the enforcement of the English legislation of 1349–51 in Ireland, see *Statutes and Ordinances . . . of Ireland*, 366 n. 1.

[17] R. S. Gottfried, *The Black Death* (London, 1983), 95; J. N. Hillgarth, *The Spanish Kingdoms, 1250–1516*, 2 vols (Oxford, 1976–8), ii, 4–5.

[18] Putnam, 'Transformation', 43.

[19] *CLBL, F*, 212–13; S. Rees Jones, 'Household, Work and the Problem of Labour: The Regulation of Labour in Medieval English Towns', *The Problem of Labour in Fourteenth-Century England*, ed. J. Bothwell, P. J. P. Goldberg and W. M. Ormrod (York, 2000), 139.

[20] *SCCKB*, v, cliii; *CIPM*, ix, vii; E 368/123, mm. 20d–21; SC 1/40/100, printed in Tout, *Chapters*, iv, 123 n. 1.

royal lands and insisted on careful inquiries into local conditions before it would relax its demands for rents and other dues.[21] Queen Philippa and the Black Prince quickly followed the king's lead. Under the former courtier, now queen's steward, Sir John Molyns, and the chief justice of king's bench, Sir William Shareshull, the queen and prince launched ruthless investigations on their estates in Essex and Cheshire with the intention of increasing their income from judicial penalties.[22] These initiatives encouraged landholders across the realm to compensate for short-term reductions in profit margins by maximizing their yield from entry fines and other accidents of lordship. Far from admitting that things could never really be the same again, Edward III's view was that the landed elite must draw together in a vigorous recreation of the economic conditions that had prevailed before the plague.

It was the very enthusiasm engendered by this stance that, in due course, required the crown to give more systematic attention to the enforcement of the labour legislation. When parliament eventually met in February 1351, the commons complained that financial penalties were not enough to control wage demands and called for a new regime of corporal punishment. The resulting Statute of Labourers specified day rates for a wide variety of workers, prevented free labourers from leaving their normal places of residence, and required that stocks be made available in every town and village for the public humiliation of those who breached this rule. It was the first time that national legislation had mentioned this basic but effective form of punishment, and there is ample evidence of resulting activity: at Norwich, for example, the woodwork, ironwork and lock of the city stocks were repaired in 1351.[23] Most importantly of all, the statute required that the labour laws be enforced by specially appointed judicial commissions sitting at least four times a year in each county. In March 1351 the Ordinance and Statute of Labourers were formally included in the powers granted to newly appointed commissioners of the peace for each shire in England. Then, from December 1352, the legislation was gradually hived off and made the responsibility of a seperate series of commissioners known as the justices of labourers. These new specialists were mainly members of the local gentry, the very people who were most likely to gain from vigorous enforcement of the

[21] E. Fryde, 'The Tenants of the Bishops of Coventry and Lichfield and of Worcester after the Plague of 1348–9', *Medieval Legal Records*, ed. Hunnisett and Post, 224–5, 261–2; Ormrod, 'English Government and the Black Death', 180–2.

[22] M. K. McIntosh, *Autonomy and Community: The Royal Manor of Havering, 1200–1500* (Cambridge, 1986), 58–63; P. H. W. Booth, 'Taxation and Public Order: Cheshire in 1353', *Northern History*, xii (1976), 16–31. Note also the co-operation between crown and prince in implementing the profitable trailbastons of Devon and Cornwall in 1354: Putnam, *Shareshull*, 73–4.

[23] *PROME*, v, 14; *SR*, i, 311–13; *The Records of the City of Norwich*, ed. W. Hudson and J. C. Tingey, 2 vols (Norwich, 1906–10), ii, 40.

new laws.[24] With wage regulation firmly established in the repertoire of royal justice, the other element of the 1349 ordinance, relating to prices, could now be elaborated. Between 1351 and 1363 a number of attempts were made at the national level to fix reasonable prices for raw materials, manufactured goods, wine, and foodstuffs such as fish and poultry.[25] Out of the crisis of 1348–9 the crown had been encouraged not merely to set the tone but also to establish an elaborate new infrastructure for the regulation of the economy.

All of these initiatives were, of course, driven by a class prejudice that assumed the God-given right of lords and employers to deprive workers of the benefits that might otherwise have accrued from declining rents and rising wages. The notorious and often vicious feudal reaction of the elite in the years after the plague also included stern measures against unfree peasants. In 1352, at the instigation of the commons, the crown agreed to make it easier for lords to repossess runaway serfs and force them to take up customary tenancies on their manors.[26] It was, however, the labour laws, which imposed a kind of 'second serfdom' on previously free wage-earners, that created the keenest sense of injustice. A few brave souls were prepared to take a stand. In Hertfordshire, the hermit and radical preacher Richard of Fulham openly denounced the labour laws and threatened those responsible for their enforcement with excommunication.[27] Urban and rural communities soon found a host of more subtle ways by which to strike a balance between royal prescription and the local reality of market forces.[28] Nevertheless, the sense of alienation created by the labour laws was very widespread. In assessing the remarkable success of Edward III's regime during the 1350s, we should never forget that social and political stability was achieved partly because the state demonstrated its readiness to subordinate the interests of the many to preserving the advantages of the few.[29]

* * *

[24] *CPR 1350–4*, 85–92; B. H. Putnam, *The Enforcement of the Statute of Labourers* (New York, 1908), App., 21–4, 35–42.

[25] Seabourne, *Royal Regulation*, 77.

[26] *PROME*, v, 52–3; *SR*, i, 323; P. R. Hyams, 'The Action of Naifty in the Early Common Law', *Law Quarterly Review*, xc (1974), 331.

[27] *SCCKB*, vi, no. 72.

[28] S. A. C. Penn and C. Dyer, 'Wages and Earnings in Late Medieval England: Evidence from the Enforcement of the Labour Laws', *EcHR*, 2nd series, xliii (1990), 356–76; L. R. Poos, *A Rural Society after the Black Death: Essex, 1350–1525* (Cambridge, 1991), 241–2; E. Clark, 'Medieval Labor Law and English Local Courts', *American Journal of Legal History*, xxvii (1983), 330–53.

[29] C. Dyer, 'Villeins, Bondmen, Neifs, and Serfs: New Serfdom in England, c.1200–1600', *Forms of Servitude in Northern and Central Europe: Decline, Resistance, and Expansion*, ed. P. Freedman and M. Bourin (Turnhout, 2005), 430–1.

The crown's inclination to pander to the prejudices of the elite manifested itself more generally during the 1350s in a series of important realignments with two key groups within the political community: the lay nobility, and the gentry and merchants whose representatives made up the commons in parliament. It is easy to assume that, in achieving this new accommodation, the government of Edward III traded power for popularity, acknowledging the limitations of its reach and accepting that the elite ought to have rights of self-determination within and beyond the bounds of the state. In its most expansive sense, the point has much merit. For better or worse, the style of governance that emerged out of the social and economic crisis of the plague, and remained in place for three hundred years and more, was based emphatically on the principle of consensus, in which power and responsibility were shared out between the crown and the landed and commercial elites. Viewed in close-up, however, the 1350s emerge not as a starting point in the inexorable decline of late medieval royal authority but as the period in which Edward III came closest to establishing his vision of a truly sustainable war state. In particular, the king's continued dynamism during his forties provided the sense of mission and purpose that properly justified the continued assertion of strong monarchy.

It was in the middle decades of the reign that the high nobility came most perfectly to represent the values and ethos of the Edwardian regime. The deaths of the veteran earls of Lancaster and Surrey in 1345 and 1347 marked the end of the generation of lords that had dominated the fractious politics of the 1320s. But the demise of Salisbury, Gloucester and Huntingdon between 1344 and 1354 also served to remind Edward III that his own earlier creations of 1337 were not immune to the ravages of time. The restocking of the titled nobility in the 1350s was, for the most part, a matter of promotion from within the existing peerage. In the parliament of 1351, Ralph, Lord Stafford, a stalwart courtier and soldier, was made earl of Stafford and endowed out of the estate of the deceased earl of Gloucester, whose daughter he had abducted and married. At the same time the king marked out his cousin, Henry of Grosmont, for particular honour by raising him from earl to duke of Lancaster and giving him palatine authority over the county of Lancashire. Finally, in 1354, the grandson of Edward's old enemy Roger Mortimer, also named Roger, was restored to the earldom of March. This last action signalled in particularly dramatic form Edward III's resolve to transcend the factionalism of the 1320s and honour the new generation of young lords who had become some of his principal commanders and councillors since the campaigns of 1346–7.[30]

---

[30] *CChR 1341–1417*, 124; *CPR 1350–4*, 60; *PROME*, v, 98; R. Somerville, *History of the Duchy of Lancaster* (London, 1953), 40–5; C. Rawcliffe, *The Staffords, Earls of Stafford and Dukes of Buckingham, 1394–1521* (Cambridge, 1978), 8–10; Fowler, *King's Lieutenant*, 172–5; Given-Wilson, *English Nobility*, 40–2.

It was very much in the same spirit that Edward agreed in the parliament of 1352 to issue the great Statute of Treasons. This set strict limits on the crimes that could rightly be categorized as high treason: plotting the death of the king, queen or heir to the throne; abducting the queen, the eldest princess or the wife of the heir apparent; making open war against the king or giving assistance to his enemies; forgery of the king's seals and coinage; smuggling counterfeit money into the realm; and killing the chancellor, treasurer or senior judges.[31] The statute reflected general anxiety about recent controversial attempts in the courts to apply the penalties of treason to a wide range of criminal actions vaguely classified as 'accroachments' (usurpations) of royal power.[32] But it also appealed greatly to the the nobility, who remained keenly aware that a less benevolent king than Edward III might use the ambiguity of the charge of treason unscrupulously to pursue his political enemies. Sir John Maltravers, who had been in exile since 1330 for his part in the demise of Edmund of Kent, had begun a concerted campaign for rehabilitation in the 1340s. Possibly because of the impending majority of Edward III's cousin John, the new earl of Kent, Maltravers was allowed to appeal *in absentia* at the parliament of 1351, where he secured pardon for his involvement in the plot against the king's uncle in 1330.[33] After his return to England and his summons to sit among the peers in the parliament of 1352, Maltravers submitted a further petition to have his pardon confirmed and put on the official parliamentary record.[34] It is likely that the Maltravers case was an uncomfortable reminder of the vengeance meted out by successive regimes to members of the nobility between 1322 and 1330 and drove the earls and barons to request clarification of the offence of treason.[35] From a personal point of view, the king may have been just as much motivated by the desire to contrast himself with John II, whose recent treatment of the count of Eu had generated such a storm of protest among the elite in France.[36] Either way, the Statute of Treasons of 1352 quickly established itself as the most compelling possible statement of Edward III's public commitment to the preservation of the rights of the nobility.

The reason why treason was such an emotive issue for the aristocracy lay not merely in the threat of the death penalty but in the fact that the crown had the right permanently to confiscate the offender's titles and lands and thus, in theory at least, to drive his surviving family and future descendants to ruin. The implications were particularly evident to Richard Fitzalan, earl of Arundel, whose father had been put to death for

---

[31] *SR*, i, 319–20.

[32] *PROME*, v, 44–5; Bellamy, *Law of Treason*, 59–101.

[33] *CPR 1343–5*, 535; *PROME*, iv, 432–3; v, 6; *CPR 1350–4*, 110; *CCR 1349–54*, 312.

[34] *PROME*, v, 54–6; *CPR 1350–4*, 224; Powell and Wallis, *House of Lords*, 358.

[35] M. V. Clarke, *Fourteenth Century Studies* (Oxford, 1937), 125–32.

[36] See p. 327.

treason during the revolution of 1326. On two successive occasions, in 1351 and 1354, Arundel sought formal confirmation of the annulment of the judgment against his father on the basis of which he had been allowed to succeed to the family title in 1330. This was no mere tokenism. In 1351 Arundel was extremely concerned about hostile claims from the up and coming earl of Kent, whose father and brother had held part of the Fitzalan estate between 1326 and 1330.[37] Having seen off this threat, Arundel set out to repeat the process when it became apparent that the king intended to restore Roger Mortimer to the earldom of March. In the spring of 1354 Fitzalan and Mortimer agreed that they would work together to deprive a third party, the second earl of Salisbury, of his interest in the estates confiscated in 1330 from the first Roger Mortimer. The joint applications for annulment of the penalties against their fore-bears in the parliament of 1354 were thus a vital element in ensuring the greater security of the newly reconfigured Arundel and Mortimer inheri-tances, and the necessary prelude to the formal investiture of the new earl of March.[38]

It is easy to see the Statute of Treasons and the cancellation of earlier judgments of treason as representing an inclination on the part of a compliant Edward III to bow to the nobles' demands for enhanced secu-rity of tenure and greater autonomy in the disposition of their estates. In the 1350s Edward III also showed himself willing to support the creation of so-called enfeoffments to use, or trusts, on the estates of his tenants-in-chief. These legal devices ensured that, in the event of sudden death on campaign, the nobleman's land would not fall to the mercies of the king's escheators but remain, during the minority of the heir, in the hands of family and friends. By the beginning of Richard II's reign it had become accepted as a point of law that lands enfeoffed to use were normally immune from confiscation for felony and treason.[39] In 1361, moreover, the king allowed that, when persons were declared guilty of treason after their own deaths, the family estate would only be subject to forfeiture in cases of open rebellion.[40] Clearly, the strong sense of co-operation between crown and nobility that was helping to win such great victories abroad was

---

[37] *PROME*, v, 6, 11–12.

[38] Ibid., v, 95–101; Holmes, *Estates*, 15–17. In 1354 Arundel specifically retained the right to the Mortimer lordship of Chirk. He agreed in 1355 that this might pass back to Mortimer, but only in return for important guarantees and handsome compensation: Bothwell, *Falling from Grace*, 198.

[39] J. M. W. Bean, *The Decline of English Feudalism, 1215–1540* (Manchester, 1968), 105–26, 312–14; McFarlane, *Nobility*, 218–19; R. C. Palmer, *English Law in the Age of the Black Death, 1348–81: A Transformation of Governance and Law* (London, 1993), 110–30. See, in similar vein, the king's concession in Aug. 1359 that, should his eldest son die on campaign, the fruits of the prince's estates would be made available to his executors for four years for the clearing of his debts: *CPR 1358–61*, 268.

[40] *SR*, i, 367–8.

also being reflected in a significant increase in the legal rights of the peerage.

It would be quite wrong, however, to suggest that any of these developments were seen seriously to compromise the authority of the crown. In some respects, indeed, the 1350s witnessed forceful efforts to limit the privileges of the nobility. Between 1344 and 1351 Edward III had made free with life grants of sheriffdoms as forms of patronage to various earls and barons of the realm. The county communities were suspicious of this practice, since it seemed to place the relevant shires at the whim of private lords. Although the existing grants were honoured, no more were now made. Conditions and limits were also attached. Lancashire, which became a virtually separate entity under the personal control of Henry of Grosmont after its elevation to a palatinate in 1351, nevertheless failed to secure the fiscal immunity enjoyed by the inhabitants of Cheshire and County Durham, and continued to pay taxes to Westminster.[41] The absence, before 1359, of any great campaign involving a levy en masse of the aristocracy also meant that the crown was able to restrict those fiscal or judicial incentives of war, such as the postponement of debts at the exchequer, for which the nobility had fought so keenly in 1338. Indeed, from 1352 to 1359 the crown actually challenged those lords who held the right to collect the fines imposed by royal judges on their tenants in order, once again, to maximize the profits accumulated by the exchequer from the exercise of justice.[42]

Above all, through the 1350s Edward III retained a very personal control over grants of patronage that served constantly to remind the nobility of the conditional nature of royal largesse. In 1353–4 the king repeatedly intervened in the courts, often in quite arbitrary ways, to effect a dramatic redistribution of the great lordships of north and south Wales. The earl of Warwick won Gower, the earl of Arundel, Chirk, and the new earl of March, Denbigh. What is perhaps most notable in such cases is the response of the losers. William Montagu, second earl of Salisbury, son of the king's deceased great favourite, had already been defeated in the papal court by the parvenu Thomas Holland in their celebrated quarrel over the right to marry Joan of Kent. Now, in the 1350s and 1360s, Montagu's interests were repeatedly to be set aside by the king in preference for the earl's brother-in-law, Roger Mortimer, for Robert Wyvil, bishop of Salisbury, and finally for John of Gaunt.[43] Wyvil's tomb brass, with its forceful representation of the bishop's recovery of Sherborne castle from the hands of the earl, stands today as testimony to the repeated snubs

---

[41] Ormrod, *Reign of Edward III*, 110; J. W. Alexander, 'The English Palatines and Edward I', *JBS*, xxii[2] (1983), 11–12.

[42] Ormrod, 'Edward III and the Recovery of Royal Authority', 7–8.

[43] Holmes, *Estates*, 15–16, 39; M. W. Warner, 'The Montagu Earls of Salisbury *circa* 1300–1428' (University of London PhD thesis, 1991), 22–4, 60–9; Bothwell, *Peerage*, 123.

suffered by the luckless Montagu.[44] Yet there is every sign that the long-suffering Salisbury was convinced of the virtues of loyalty as well as the necessity of stoicism, and he emerged in the later years of Edward III's reign as a consistently active courtier, counsellor and military commander. The same point may apply even to Richard Fitzalan, earl of Arundel, whose particularly conspicuous service in war, politics and finance can to a degree be read as a sustained act of contrition for the public support he had dared to give Archbishop Stratford during the crisis of 1341.[45] The real secret of Edward III's success with the nobility in the 1350s lay not, then, in unrestricted and indiscriminate liberality, but in the king's unusual ability to persuade even those less favoured by his regime that they remained valued members of it. If Edward was more subtle and deft in his treatment of the nobles during the 1350s, it does not follow that either he or they regarded his management of them as anything other than active, direct and rigorous.

The accommodation with the county and urban communities was predictably rather harder won than that with the nobility. But it, too, revealed the mature Edward III's adeptness in the arts of political management. In contrast to the rather tense and often unfruitful negotiations of the 1340s, the parliaments of the early 1350s generated a large programme of reformist legislation designed to appease provincial political society. In particular, the assembly of 1352 saw the crown in magnanimous and expansive mood. In return for a new triennial fifteenth and tenth to subsidize the war effort, Edward III made three important concessions. Feudal aids would in future only be levied with parliamentary consent. Royal purveyors would be bound to observe the existing laws on the provisioning of the king's household and army. And, with the exception of those owing feudal service to the crown, no one would ever again be compelled to serve, or provide troops, for the king's wars without the consent of parliament. The polity recognized these as serious points of principle, and in the years that followed was to be notably resistant to any royal attempts to use a national emergency as a means of overriding the limitations imposed on the war state in 1352.[46]

The king's deliberate efforts to play to the gallery were also apparent in a new bout of anti-papal legislation. Since the Ordinance of Provisors of 1343, the commons had continued to argue that the English Church was being packed with foreigners who were acting as French spies and

---

[44] *Age of Chivalry*, no. 98.

[45] Vale, *Edward III and Chivalry*, 89–91, argues that Edward III deliberately excluded both Arundel and the earl of Huntingdon from the Order of the Garter as punishment for their part in the 1341 crisis. Huntingdon's case is different from Arundel's: he was not at Crécy and may have been suffering ill health by that time: *ODNB*, xii, 152.

[46] *SR*, i, 319, 321, 322; Harriss, *King, Parliament*, 395–400.

draining the country of money. In 1351 the knights and burgesses returned to the theme, going so far as to claim that the pope was now making more from the realm than the king. The royal response, the Statute of Provisors, prohibited the execution of all papal provisions to benefices in England. In 1353, furthermore, the crown issued the Statute of Praemunire, which sought to prevent challenges to its own and other patrons' rights over church offices by explicitly banning appeals to the curia.[47] The king certainly benefited directly from this round of legislation. But given the general complicity of the papacy around this time in accepting Edward's own nominees for senior appointments in the English Church, it is doubtful that the crown would have bothered to make such hostile statements for its own purposes.[48] The 1353 statute in particular offered valuable opportunities for private patrons of English benefices and their appointees to bring successful actions against papal provisors in the royal courts.[49] From the royal point of view, then, the immediate significance of the new legislation lay in its symbolic statement of the crown's claims to sovereignty over the English Church and its equally obvious appeal to popular prejudices against the Avignon papacy.

The desire to provide a new framework of legislation that responded explicitly to the priorities of a broader political constituency is most obvious in the economic policies worked out by the crown in the early 1350s. The Statute of York of 1335, which upheld the principle of freedom to trade in English markets, was confirmed and reinforced in 1351. Important legislation was also passed in 1351 guaranteeing the ready passage of traffic on English waterways and confirming the existing laws against forestalling (the practice of buying up goods before they reached the open market in order to push up demand and thus inflate retail prices). And in 1352 the crown not only reiterated its habitual commitment to standard weights and measures but also, more unusually, began an ambitious programme of enforcement in the shires, the towns and the ports.[50]

Above all, a solution was now found to the regulation of the wool trade that seemed, at last, to suit both the commercial interests of the wool producers and the fiscal interests of the crown. The cartel led by Walter Chiriton that had farmed the customs since 1346 collapsed in 1348–9, unable to sustain its commitments in light of the temporary collapse of

[47] *PROME*, iv, 399, 427, 432; v, 14, 25–7, 83; *SR*, i, 323–4, 329.

[48] F. Cheyette, 'Kings, Courts, Cures, and Sinecures: The Statute of Provisors and the Common Law', *Traditio*, xix (1963), 295–349; W. R. Jones, 'Relations of the Two Jurisdictions: Conflict and Cooperation in England during the Thirteenth and Fourteenth Centuries', *Studies in Medieval and Renaissance History*, original series, vii (1970), 102–32.

[49] E. B. Graves, 'The Legal Significance of the Statute of Praemunire', *Anniversary Essays Presented to C. H. Haskins*, ed. C. H. Taylor (New York, 1929), 57–80; D. Martin, 'Prosecution of the Statutes of Provisors and Premunire in the King's Bench, 1377–1394', *Fourteenth Century England IV*, ed. Hamilton, 109–23.

[50] *SR*, i, 270–1, 314–16, 321; Ormrod, *Reign of Edward III*, 79.

overseas trade during the plague. A new group led by John Malwayn took over the farm and limped on until early 1352. But the failure of these schemes to deliver adequate credit to the crown or to deal fairly with the holders of Dordrecht bonds meant that the monopoly schemes that had dominated since 1343 were now largely discredited.[51] The lack of public confidence was reflected in the distinctly muted response to the king's call for another general round of borrowing in 1351. Although some merchants made private deals that would ensure them repayment out of the wool subsidy, many balked at Edward's demands. In London, an attempt to impose a forced loan of 20,000 marks collapsed when complaints arose that the deal had been struck by the king and the mayor without the proper consent of the civic community.[52] In 1351–2 the crown decided to abandon monopolistic practices and resume direct management of the customs system. Out of this decision emerged the fourteenth century's most successful scheme for the promotion and exploitation of overseas trade.

In the summer of 1353 the crown established a new series of domestic wool staples at Newcastle upon Tyne, York, Lincoln, Norwich, Westminster, Winchester, Exeter and Bristol.[53] The Ordinance of the Staple, issued at the great council held at Westminster in September, defined the principles and mechanisms that would govern the new system.[54] A key element of the new strategy was an open-ended ban on the export of wool by denizen merchants. This was a drastic measure, but it sent the powerful message that the king no longer intended to pursue private commercial deals with English mercantile monopolies. Within a month Edward's government instituted a series of show trials against the former financier William de la Pole.[55] These conveniently relieved the crown of most of its remaining obligation to the debts left over from the late 1330s. More publicly, it served once more to advertise the king's new determination to rely on a free and open credit market. The result was a great boom in trade that lasted throughout the following decade and took the volume of wool exports to around 35,000 sacks a year, a level unknown since the very beginning of the fourteenth century and one not to be surpassed again for the rest of the Middle Ages.[56]

[51] Fryde, *Studies*, chap. x, 16–17.

[52] *CLBL, G*, 235, 236–7; *Calendar of Letters from the Mayor and Corporation of the City of London*, ed. R. R. Sharpe (London, 1885), no. I; Ormrod, *Reign of Edward III*, 185; Liddy, *War, Politics*, 24, 26.

[53] Hull, Canterbury and Chichester were subsequently added. C 67/22, m. 25d; *PROME*, v, 64–5; *Records of the Borough of Leicester*, ii, 79–80; Lloyd, *Wool Trade*, 205–8.

[54] C 67/22, mm. 22–21; *PROME*, v, 70–81; *SR*, i, 332–43; H. G. Richardson and G. O. Sayles, *The English Parliament in the Middle Ages* (London, 1981), chap. xxi (pt 2), 13 n. 4; Cam, *Law-Finders and Law-Makers*, 139–40.

[55] Fryde, *Studies*, chap. xii.

[56] E. M. Carus-Wilson and O. Coleman, *England's Export Trade, 1275–1547* (Oxford, 1963), 122.

In order to ensure that the new ban on denizen merchants carrying wool abroad did not adversely affect the English economy, the crown introduced a series of measures designed to encourage alien merchants to trade in English wool, and to protect the nascent domestic cloth industry. In 1351, the crown had reinstated the aulnage, a system whereby all cloth sold in domestic markets was required to conform to standard measures. This had created serious disruptions in the market: no less figures than Queens Isabella and Philippa had been quick to report to the king their dismay that cloth purchased by their agents from the London merchant John Pecche had been subject to confiscation under the new regulations.[57] At the great council of 1353 the government was persuaded to abandon this practice and allow cloth producers and merchants to buy and sell freely. This, along with the confirmation of the liberties of foreign cloth-iers working in England, provided a notable boost to domestic manufac-tures, and the 1350s witnessed a significant increase in exports both of broadcloths and of the cheaper ranges known as kerseys and worsteds.[58] Such was the general satisfaction with the new rules for the wool and cloth trades that, in the parliament of 1354, the commons successfully petitioned to have the Ordinance of the Staple reissued as a statute 'to last forever'.[59]

The commercial principles established in 1351–4 were to survive for nearly twenty years, and fundamentally conditioned English political atti-tudes to the regulation of overseas trade throughout the second half of Edward III's reign. Not surprisingly, the ban on denizen exports of wool proved rather less sustainable. From 1357 the king began to sell licences to English merchants, allowing them once more to export wool in return for loans. Some of the merchants involved in these transactions, such as Henry Picard, Thomas Dolesley, John Pyel and Thomas Perle, had been close associates of the earlier monopolists.[60] Rather than condoning a return to restrictive practices, however, the crown was generally content to allow all denizen merchants to export wool on the simple but effective condition that they pay the alien rates of duty at the ports. For the first time since 1336, there had emerged a series of principles for the manage-ment of overseas trade that were at once popular with the polity, viable for the English merchant community, and highly profitable to the king.

In tracing the accommodation between crown and polity through the legislative programme of the early 1350s, historians have long since given up the notion that Edward III simply capitulated to political pressure and

[57] *SR*, i, 314; Ormrod, *Reign of Edward III*, 192; E 159/132, *Brev. bar.*, Pasch, rot. 2.

[58] *PROME*, v, 83–4; *SR*, i, 330–1; *CFR 1347–56*, 385; *CPR 1350–4*, 232; *Records of the City of Norwich*, ii, 330–2; Carus-Wilson and Coleman, *England's Export Trade*, 47–8, 75–7; H. L. Gray, 'The Production and Exportation of English Woollens in the Fourteenth Century', *EHR*, xxxix (1924), 13–35; A. R. Bridbury, *Medieval English Clothmaking* (London, 1982), 88–9.

[59] *PROME*, v, 89–90, 101; *SR*, i, 348–9; C 67/22, m. 20.

[60] Lloyd, *Wool Trade*, 208–9; Ormrod, *Reign of Edward III*, 185.

wilfully alienated his authority as a means of buying continued financial support for the war.[61] The campaign of law enforcement adopted in the 1350s provides an instructive case in point. In 1351 the crown affirmed the policy, in place since 1344, of having the peace commissions supervised by lawyers from the central courts.[62] As if to reinforce the point, the king's bench moved from Westminster in 1351–3 and made an extensive tour of the south-east, East Anglia and the West Midlands, where it assumed control over all criminal and civil actions pending in the relevant counties. By the time the court reached Kingston upon Thames in the autumn of 1353, Chief Justice Shareshull had set special terms of reference that included inquiries into corrupt local officials and the vigorous enforcement of recent economic legislation.[63] In 1352 parliament reacted unfavourably to this apparent resumption of the policy of trailbaston. But the king replied abruptly that he would send his court wherever he saw fit. Throughout the 1350s the commons' own preferred mechanism for local law enforcement, the commissions of the peace, continued to function principally in a support capacity, binding suspected criminals over to appear before the professional judges who came down into the counties on the assize and gaol delivery circuits.[64] Only in the new courts set up to administer the labour laws were local gentry and men of law allowed to act as royal justices and deliver judgments of their own. The delegation to these special tribunals in 1357 of powers to hear offences under the weights and measures legislation signalled an awareness of their potential as clearing houses for a wider range of minor criminal offences.[65] Otherwise, however, the story of judicial administration in the decade after the Black Death was of continued emphasis on an integrated system closely supervised by the central courts and senior judiciary.

That Edward III and his ministers knew their own mind on matters of policy in the 1350s is perhaps most obviously demonstrated by the management of the currency. In June 1351 the crown finally hit on a successful formula that would balance the silver and gold currencies and control the

---

[61] B. H. Putnam, 'Chief Justice Shareshull and the Economic and Legal Codes of 1351–1352', *University of Toronto Law Journal*, v (1943–4), 251–81; G. L. Harriss, 'The Formation of Parliament, 1272–1377', *English Parliament*, ed. Davies and Denton, 45–9; Ormrod, *Reign of Edward III*, 46–50, 63–8, 78–80.

[62] *CPR 1350–4*, 85–91.

[63] *SCCKB*, vi, xlvii; *Le liver des assises & plees del corone . . . en temps du Roy Edward le Tiers* (London, 1679), 27 Edw III, Mich. pl. 44; Putnam, 'Chief Justice Shareshull', 275–80.

[64] *PROME*, v, 36, 42–3; Putnam, *Shareshull*, 110–11; Musson and Ormrod, *Evolution*, 51, 61.

[65] *PROME*, iv, 434, 454; v, 36, 42–3, 84, 91, 101; Putnam, *Enforcement*, App., 25–7; Verduyn, 'Attitude', 116–22. Local justices sometimes exceeded their official powers and heard cases relating to the actions of sheriffs and bailiffs and to forestalling: *Proceedings before the Justices of the Peace in the Fourteenth and Fifteenth Centuries*, ed. B. H. Putnam (Ames Foundation, 1938), cxxi–cxxii, 64, 67, 68, 81, 82, 349, 368, 370; Putnam, *Enforcement*, App., 166–9.

efflux of bullion from the realm. This involved a further reduction in the weight of sterling and the introduction of two new silver coins, the groat and half-groat (4d and 2d). The resulting general re-coinage publicly confirmed the king's apparent resolve to press on with his dynastic destinies, for the new high-denomination silver coins bore (for the first time in the history of sterling) the title 'king of England and France'.[66] In economic terms, however, the reform did not meet with universal approval, for many believed that the new, lighter pennies contributed to a general inflation of prices and suspected that the re-coinage was merely a ruse by which Treasurer Edington sought to maximize the profits of the mints.[67] The commons had become committed to the restoration of sterling standard and to forms of protectionism that would supposedly drive out the counterfeit coins, known as Lushbournes, that had been imported in large quantities during the 1340s. In 1352, they actually managed to extract a promise from the king that the ancient standard would be restored 'as soon as a good way is found'.[68] Nothing, however, was done. After the mid-1350s, when the stability of the new coinage began to become apparent, the polity was forced to admit that the government's instincts had been sound. As in these, so in many other matters, the king would routinely request the opinions of parliament on what might be most beneficial for the realm, but remained entirely free to make up his own mind about the direction of policy. Ultimately, it has to be said that the politics of the 1350s was consensual only because Edward III allowed it to be so.

The measures adopted in response to the dislocation of the plague and the various economic challenges of the early 1350s reflected the vision and ability of the new generation of royal ministers led by William Edington, John Thoresby and William Shareshull. Key to the strong sense of corporate responsibility and endeavour established by this group was the greater institutional identity and effectiveness of the administrative council. In 1343 the council was given its first designated place of assembly in the famous Star Chamber in Westminster Palace. Within two decades, the exchequer was routinely covering the costs of heating the Star Chamber, providing cooking facilities for its staff and meeting the travel and subsistence of council members.[69] Royal sergeants-at-arms were increasingly

[66] *CCR 1349–54*, 379–81; A. Feaveryear, *The Pound Sterling*, 2nd edn (Oxford, 1963), 17–20; Ormrod, 'Problem of Precedence', 150 and n. 68. The silver penny continued to bear only the title 'king of England'.

[67] Reading, 113; Walsingham, *Chronicon Angliae*, 29; *Hist. Angl.*, i, 275–6. The total profits of the mints in 1351–5 amounted to some £11,000, but most of this was eaten up in production costs: Ormrod, 'Edward III's Government', 272–9.

[68] *PROME*, iv, 394–5, 417; v, 15, 20, 48, 84, 107. For an attempt to instigate a campaign against Lushbournes in Wales in 1349 see C 81/341/20507.

[69] C 49/47/7; *Issues*, 16; E 403/392, 19 May 1358; E 403/398, 16 Nov. 1359; E 403/412, 17 Feb. 1363; Baldwin, *King's Council*, 355–6.

employed to follow up the council's instructions to sheriffs, to undertake inquiries on its behalf in the localities, and to bring suspected persons back to London pending investigation.[70] After 1350, the staff of the privy seal office also settled more or less permanently at Westminster Palace and began to assist the chancery in the implementation of council policy. The status of the keeper of the privy seal was thereby enhanced, and by the time John Buckingham held the office in 1360–3, the keeper had emerged alongside the chancellor and treasurer as a third great minister of state.[71]

The successive chancellors John Offord (1345–9) and John Thoresby (1349–56), also helped strengthen the council's judicial arm. Thoresby invented the famous *sub pena* writ, which summoned persons to appear for unspecified causes before the chancellor or council and imposed a penalty of fine or forfeiture for default.[72] By the end of the reign, the chancery was beginning to take on some of the functions that would turn it, in due course, into a specialized court of equity. In the later 1350s it also developed a number of new common law writs that provided remedies in the courts against parties who were negligent in performing agreed services and contractual promises. Like the labour laws, these novelties were strongly indicative of the crown's policy, after the shock of the plague, of reinforcing traditional social values of trust and obligation.[73]

The decade after the Black Death witnessed equally significant reforms in government finance. William Edington's long tenure as treasurer of the exchequer (1344–56) spanned both the Crécy and the Poitiers campaigns. Between the two, the industrious and capable Edington implemented far-reaching changes that created much closer co-ordination between the exchequer and the royal household. The aim was to give the exchequer the overall view of royal finance that had been envisioned in the Walton Ordinances, and thus to allow for much more effective budgeting. For at least a short while in the mid-1350s, the sense of co-ordination that had proved so difficult in the late 1330s came close to reality.[74]

In effecting these changes, it was emphatically not Edington's intention to force unwelcome regulation or economy on the king's domestic offices. Indeed, Edward III was convinced of the wisdom of the new policy only because of its comparative generosity. The royal household was relieved of most of its responsibilities for the costs of war outside those periods when the king himself led campaigns. The chamber, the office of the privy purse, was given a block grant of 10,000 marks (£6,667) a year from the

---

[70] Partington, 'Edward III's Enforcers', 99–105.

[71] Tout, *Chapters*, v, 30–4, 68–74; Ormrod, 'Edward III's Government', 66–72; Ormrod, 'Accountability and Collegiality', 73–5; A. L. Brown, *The Early History of the Clerkship of the Council* (Glasgow, 1969).

[72] W. M. Ormrod, 'The Origins of the *sub pena* Writ', *HR*, lxi (1988), 11–20.

[73] Palmer, *English Law*, 104–32, 169–306; Musson, 'New Labour Laws', 73–88.

[74] W. M. Ormrod, 'The Protocolla Rolls and English Government Finance, 1353–1364', *EHR*, cii (1987), 622–32.

exchequer to cover spending on the jewels, plate, personal gifts, falcons and (very occasionally) books purchased for the king's personal use.[75] Thus comfortable in his own luxury, Edward felt able to relax his previous insistence on reserving prerogative revenues and other windfalls for the support of his personal treasury. When, in 1352, Robert Gyene of Bristol was accused of concealing £20,000 in money and goods confiscated a quarter of a century earlier from the younger Despenser and Robert Baldock, the sum was directly assigned to the energetic earl of Stafford in 1353 to be used towards the costs of a new campaign in Gascony.[76] Normally, the king would have treated such spoils as a private asset and sent them to the chamber. The disposition of the Despenser hoard therefore had considerable implications, and set an important precedent for the channelling into public enterprises of the profits that also began to fall to the English crown during the later 1350s from foreign ransoms.[77]

General expressions of good intent would have been to little avail, of course, had the exchequer not found adequate resources to finance the on-going burden of war. In many ways Edington could be counted lucky, for the cancellation of the larger expeditions that Edward III intended repeatedly to lead to the continent helped appreciably to reduce the military budget. In the late 1340s the exchequer already had sufficient resources to contemplate a quite ambitious scheme for paying off £150,000 worth of old debts.[78] On the other hand, the treasurer faced what was surely the greatest fiscal emergency ever encountered in medieval England. In France, the existing structure of royal taxation virtually collapsed for some years after the Black Death and was only properly rebuilt, to a very different design, after John II's capture at Poitiers.[79] In 1350 Edington was poised to consider the impact of a similar crisis of public finance in England. It was lucky indeed that England had in the treasurer of the exchequer one of the most scrupulous, as well as the most ambitious and persistent, financial managers of the later Middle Ages.

Initially at least, the English fiscal system proved resilient to the impact of plague. The triennial lay and clerical subsidies granted in 1348 ran up a slightly higher level of arrears than was normal, but in general the king's tax collectors continued, against all the odds, to render their dues. The crown was assisted by the block quotas charged on communities for fifteenths and tenths, which in theory protected it from the sudden reduction in the number of households. Edward III and his ministers were also vigilant and unyielding in their attitude to the requests for tax relief

---

[75] Tout, *Chapters*, iv, 290–1, 315–18; Given-Wilson, *Royal Household*, 85–6.

[76] *CPR 1350–4*, 522; E 403/359, 10 Mar. 1352; *CCR 1349–54*, 618; E 368/126, *Recorda*, Mich., rot. 13; E 101/333/23, no. 2; E 101/508/18.

[77] See pp. 416, 479.

[78] Harriss, *King, Parliament*, 338.

[79] J. B. Henneman, 'The Black Death and Royal Taxation in France, 1347–1351', *Speculum*, xliii (1968), 405–28.

that began to flood in during 1348–9.[80] Equally, though, the spirit of co-operation that prevailed in the parliaments of the early 1350s required some well-judged concessions to hard-pressed taxpayers. In 1352, when a new triennial subsidy was granted in parliament, the adept Edington devised a scheme to reserve the profits from the labour sessions for the support of poverty-stricken communities. In some areas this meant that a heavy burden of current taxation was borne, indirectly, by wage-labourers previously considered too poor to pay taxes to the crown. The experiment was not repeated in this form after 1355, probably because of the obvious social tensions that it created. In 1357 the crown did agree, for the dura-tion of the current subsidy only, that the communal fines associated with the eyre could be used to provide some temporary tax relief. In this case, however, the results were much more modest.[81] The real lesson to be learned from the fiscal experiment of the 1350s was that England could no longer afford the levels of direct taxation that had prevailed in the previous two decades. It was out of this uncomfortable reality that Edington brought to triumphant conclusion the process that, since the later 1330s, had gradually been shifting the burden of war finance away from direct and towards indirect taxation.

The abandonment of the farm of the customs in 1351 and the efforts in 1353 to revive wool exports provided the crown with a strong inducement to maximize its revenues from the ports. The collectors of customs were now subjected to close scrutiny; authorized weighing machines were sent to the staples and ports in order to prevent deception; and measures were taken to deal with the endemic problem of smuggling. The boom in exports, coupled with the insistence that all wool sent out of the realm be liable to the alien rates of duty, meant a vast increase in royal revenue. In the financial year 1353–4 the customs and subsidies raised the astonishing sum of £113,000. Although revenue fell away slightly after this, the annual average income from the ports in the decade 1353–62 was still some £87,500. By the mid-1350s, then, Edward III was raising five times the amount that his government had been realizing from the ports twenty years earlier.[82] It was this success that allowed the canny Edington to effect a major reduction in the burden of direct taxation.

Between 1344 and 1354 the laity and the clergy had paid a virtually uninterrupted series of direct subsidies. Both groups showed signs of strain during this difficult decade: in particular, their attempts to ensure that the king did not collect taxes in times of truce and that he spent the profits solely on the enterprise of war reflected continued suspicion about the tense relationship between public need and royal greed. In 1352 the

[80] Ormrod, 'English Government and the Black Death', 183–4.

[81] SR, i, 327–8, 352; Putnam, *Enforcement*, 98–149; Harriss, *King, Parliament*, 345–6.

[82] W. M. Ormrod, 'The English Crown and the Customs, 1349–63', *EcHR*, 2nd series, xl (1987), 27–37.

clergy even conducted a six-month tax strike to force the crown into accepting their demand for the confirmation of ecclesiastical liberties.[83] In preparation for the campaign of 1355, by contrast, no direct subsidies were initially sought. For the first time since the start of the Hundred Years War, the crown seemed about to finance a major expedition solely out of the profits of indirect taxation. Early in 1356 it apparently withdrew from this position and issued the clergy with a request for an unprecedented double-weighted tax of six tenths to be collected over three consecutive years. The convocation of Canterbury expressed general outrage and, resisting the arguments of a royal deputation led by Sir Walter Mauny, eventually conceded only a single tenth. It took the victory at Poitiers, and a frank exchange of views between the king and the archbishops of Canterbury and York in 1357, for the convocations to relax the restrictions imposed on this grant and pay the second half of the subsidy.[84] For most of the king's clerical subjects, the prospects of a lasting remission from the burden of taxation looked distinctly far off.

Beyond the public posturing, however, the royal altercation with the clergy in 1356–7 generated some major new agreements about the overall distribution of the tax burden. The ubiquitous Edington – who was promoted to the chancellorship at the end of 1356 – and his successor as treasurer, John Sheppey, bishop of Rochester, persuaded Edward that the convocations would be mollified if he agreed to ask the 1357 parliament for a parallel fifteenth and tenth.[85] Still more importantly, they were able to demonstrate, through their newly integrated budgeting machine, that the revenue from indirect and direct taxation would be more than sufficient to cover the immediate costs of the Black Prince's campaign and the ongoing defence of English positions in France. Throughout the 1350s Edington had been able to build up cash surpluses from the profits of direct taxation; to such an extent that he was able (against all the precepts of parliament) to divert significant sums to the domestic expenditure of the king, the queen and their children.[86] Above all, the very real prospect of realizing the ransoms of Charles of Blois, David Bruce and John of Valois seemed set to transform Edward III into the richest monarch in Europe. The time had therefore come to acknowledge the principle of proportionality and hold back, wherever possible, from imposing further direct taxes. Edward III expressed enthusiastic thanks to Edington and Sheppey for this new dispensation by promptly discharging them of their

[83] C 270/13, no. 1; C 270/14, no. 5; *Foedera*, III.i, 230; *CCR 1349–54*, 322; *PROME*, v, 56–61; *Concilia*, iii, 23–5, 28–9; *SR*, i, 324–6; P. Heath, *Church and Realm, 1272–1461* (London, 1988), 137; Harriss, *King, Parliament*, 320–7.

[84] *Records of Convocation*, iii, 267; *The Register of Gilbert Welton, Bishop of Carlisle, 1353–1362*, ed. R. L. Storey (CYS, lxxxviii, 1999), nos 125, 167, 200; SC 1/38/80, 82; SC 1/40/181; SC 1/56/4.

[85] Jurkowski, Smith and Crook, *Lay Taxes*, 52–3. See also p. 387.

[86] Harriss, *King, Parliament*, 335–40; Ormrod, 'English Crown and the Customs', 35–6.

personal contributions to the recent clerical tax.[87] This was not perhaps the best way to win public confidence in the probity of senior ministers. But the structural transformation worked. The chronicler John of Reading made the revealing comment that William Edington had sought, in all his public policies, to preserve a balance between the interests of the crown and those of the realm.[88] It was in the 1350s that Edward III came closest to persuading his subjects that the war state was not only a necessary but also a genuinely sustainable reality.

Fourteenth-century notions of good governance did not assume that rulers had to be deeply involved in the routine business of state, and Edward III was not the kind of king to take very close control of the minutiae of public business. Although he had lifted his pen early in the reign to autograph the *pater sancte* letter to Pope John XXII, the only other known example of Edward's handwriting comes in the sign manual *E Rex* applied on a letter to the king of Castile in 1362.[89] This is not to suggest that Edward only ever exerted himself to deal with administration when it involved diplomacy and war. With the separation of the privy seal from the king's household, letters under the king's so-called secret seal (replaced in the mid-1350s by the signet) became an essential channel of communication between monarch and ministers and may act as an index of royal activism. They reveal Edward III regularly exercising his rights to appoint to ecclesiastical benefices and to a wide range of secular offices, to dispose of lands and other assets at pleasure, and to expedite petitions.[90] In 1348 when the poor people of Finstock and Topples Wood in Oxfordshire requested relief, on account of their poverty, from earlier levies in wool, a special note was made that their petition was heard in person by the king.[91] And in 1354, when he reluctantly consented to the temporary incarceration of his cousin, Margaret Marshal, for contempt in going abroad without licence, Edward III was quick to issue personal instructions to ensure that the lady was well looked after by her gaolers at Somerton castle in Lincolnshire.[92] Very occasionally such interventions hint at a sense of royal impatience. In 1353, for example, when there was another flare-up in Queen Isabella's long-standing feud with the prior of Coventry, the clerk of the secret seal wrote an instruction to Chancellor Thoresby to call the council together and discuss the case. A postscript to the order seems to have been added at the king's personal dictation: 'We charge you

---

[87] E 159/134, *Brev. bar.*, Mich., rot. 6d; Hil., rot. 3; E 159/135, *Brev. bar.*, Mich., rot. 1.

[88] Reading, 113.

[89] *Foedera*, III.ii, 657; Chaplais, *Essays*, chap. xxii, 181. For a reference to a letter written in the hand of the Black Prince see *BPR*, iv, 131.

[90] C 81/1333, 1334. Many of the petitions that originally accompanied these letters of secret seal are found in SC 8/246, 247.

[91] SC 8/244/12167; C 81/330/19418; *CIM*, ii, no. 2075; *CCR 1349-54*, 2-3.

[92] C 49/7/27; *CIM*, iii, no. 50; C 81/1334/10; *CCR 1354-60*, 27.

go to no final judgment without consulting us.'[93] And in June 1356 when the council took it upon itself to dismiss the sheriff of Herefordshire, Thomas atte Barre, the king wrote sharply to the chancellor to insist that Thomas be restored and not removed without express royal orders.[94] It was by this kind of attention to the fine grain of administration that Edward was able constantly to reaffirm the principle that the apparatus of government existed primarily to reflect and serve his own will.

Much of Edward III's understanding of his regime in the 1350s derived from interactions with his subjects, great and small, either in personal meetings or through the process of petitioning. The king, for example, regularly received new tenants-in-chief in order to take their homage and admit them to their inheritances.[95] It is tempting to suggest that such encounters, reinforced by regular engagement with the baronage and gentry on campaigns and in parliament, gave Edward at least passing acquaintance with many of those who made up the post-plague polity. Wherever he went, the monarch was pursued by groups of petitioners eager to have their grievances and requests addressed in person by the king. In 1350, when two of the canons of Merton Priory requested permission to go on pilgrimage to Rome, the king dictated a personal response: 'We have heard this petition and will that our chancellor have writs of passage made for them.'[96] The vivid image of Edward III receiving and answering petitions while out hunting in Wychwood Forest in 1362 is consonant with one of the major medieval tropes of good kingship: King Alfred was said to have given judgments while washing his hands, and Henry IV and Henry V were later said to have received bills while lying down each day after dinner.[97]

It was in the general disposition of justice that Edward III undoubtedly involved himself most actively during the middle years of his reign. The conventions of the day gave the king two distinct and not always easily compatible roles. On the one hand, he was required to uphold the due process and impartiality of the law. On the other, he was expected to soften the harshness of justice in deserving cases. Much of the king's

---

[93] C 81/1333/58.

[94] C 81/1334/37. For possible context of Barre's temporary dismissal see *CPR 1354–8*, 435. For similar intervention in the appointment of the sheriff of Somerset in 1360 see C 81/1334/49.

[95] SC 1/40/127, 162; SC 1/41/40, 74.

[96] SC 8/246/12268, printed in H. C. Maxwell-Lyte, *Historical Notes on the Use of the Great Seal of England* (London, 1926), 147–8. Galbraith, *Kings and Chroniclers*, chap. i, 103 n. 47 argues that the royal response was in fact in Edward III's own hand.

[97] W. M. Ormrod, *Political Life in Medieval England, 1300–1450* (Basingstoke, 1995), 33; C. Wilson, 'The Royal Lodgings of Edward III at Windsor Castle: Form, Function, Representation', *Windsor*, ed. Keen and Scarff, 43. Edward's model for French kingship, Louis IX, was similarly believed to have given judgments while resting under an oak tree: Jean de Joinville and Geoffrey de Villehardouin, *Chronicles of the Crusades*, trans. M. R. B. Shaw (Harmondsworth, 1963), 176–7.

reputation as just arbiter rested on his role as overseer of the council and on the special judicial commissions often set up to deal with high-profile cases. Sometimes Edward overreached himself. In 1352, for example, he permitted the authorities of the University of Cambridge special powers to deal with offences committed against its members by men of the town. But this was stoutly resisted by the agents of Queen Isabella, who held the farm of the town of Cambridge, and Edward was forced to withdraw his grant to the university.[98] In Oxford, by contrast, unexpectedly dramatic circumstances allowed for a more decisive affirmation of privileges. In February 1355 the habitual tensions between town and gown erupted into a major affray known as the St Scholastica's Day Riot. A special royal commission was appointed to investigate the causes. The resounding judgment that it delivered in favour of the scholars at once advertised the king's support for the university and affirmed his strong commitment to public order.[99]

Tensions between royal will and due process were evident in a minor scandal surrounding the dismissal of Sir William Thorpe from the office of chief justice of king's bench in 1350. The Ordinance of Justices of 1346 had proved successful as a general statement of the crown's policy to root out corruption in the judicial system.[100] Until the arrest of Thorpe in October 1350, however, there had been no discernible efforts to expose venality in high places.[101] Thorpe was accused of having taken bribes during the sessions of the king's bench held at Lincoln in 1349. In demonstrating his displeasure at this breach of faith, however, Edward raised some awkward points of legal principle. Thorpe was subjected to investigation before an ad hoc tribunal of the council under the earls of Warwick, Arundel and Northampton and the steward and chamberlain of the king's household, who duly found him guilty and sentenced him to be hanged. The prospect of a senior minister being executed without due process before the lords of the realm raised uncomfortable memories of the treatment of the Stratfords some ten years before. When parliament met in February 1351, the king was therefore persuaded into a compromise. In plenary session, the peers agreed to confirm the judgment against Thorpe and to declare the king's right to try his ministers in courts other than parliament. In return, Edward conceded that his campaign against Thorpe was unnecessarily vindictive and promptly issued the disgraced chief justice with a full and unconditional pardon.[102] A year later, Thorpe

[98] CPR 1350–4, 374, 392.

[99] VCH Oxon, iv, 53–7.

[100] A. Musson, 'Second "English Justinian" or Pragmatic Opportunist? A Re-examination of the Legal Legislation of Edward III's Reign', Age of Edward III, ed. Bothwell, 81–2.

[101] For what follows see Foedera, III.i, 208–10; SCCKB, vi, xxv–xxvi; Maddicott, Law and Lordship, 40–51; R. C. Kinsey, 'Legal Service, Careerism and Social Advancement in Late Medieval England: The Thorpes of Northamptonshire, c.1200–1391' (University of York PhD thesis, 2009), 137–51.

[102] PROME, v, 13; CPR 1350–4, 61–2.

was back in royal service as a judge in the court of the exchequer. If the case served its general purpose of acting as an example to others, it had also demonstrated very clearly that the king could not afford to proceed against the will of the peerage on matters concerning the trial and punishment of ministers of state.

The restoration of Sir William Thorpe, like the pardon of John Maltravers and the annulments of the judgments against the former earls of Arundel and March, provided strong proof of the importance attached to the royal prerogative of mercy. Inevitably, royal pardons were not always universally praised. Throughout the 1340s Edward had persisted with his practice of granting pardons to convicted felons in return for military service, sometimes holding formal ceremonies at which pre-prepared charters of pardon were solemnly sealed in the presence of his councillors and military commanders.[103] As part of the package of concessions to the political community after the plague, it was agreed in 1353 that pardons for military service should not give recipients carte blanche, but had to include both the names of the military captains who had sought them and the specific crimes that were condoned. In spite of anxiety over the disruptive influence of demobilized soldiers in 1361, the king's subjects seem to have been satisfied with the new compromise and reverted to the view that pardons were a necessary and usually beneficial ingredient of the judicial system.[104] The symbolic nature of the process was captured in a story about a bungled hanging at Leicester in 1363. Edward III, who knew a good miracle when he saw one, set the offender free: 'As God gave you life, so shall we give you a charter.'[105] The figure of 'King Edward' in the fifteenth-century *Gest of Robin Hood* articulated precisely the same principles in the act of pardon by which Robin was restored to royal grace and readmitted to the wholeness of the king's peace.[106]

If the mature Edward III displayed an appropriate commitment to the arts of conciliation, there nonetheless remained a strong streak of obstreperousness about the royal personality. In the middle year of the reign this manifested itself most consistently in relations with the prelates. After John Stratford's death in 1348 the other members of his family, Ralph (d. 1354) and Robert (d. 1362) played little active role in politics. As the older generation of bishops died off, the English hierarchy was gradually filled with men who had a strong and continuing record of personal service to Edward III. Simon Islip of Canterbury (1349–66), John

---

[103] *CCR 1341–3*, 530; *CCR 1343–6*, 347.

[104] *PROME*, v, 85; *SR*, i, 330, 364; Lacey, *Royal Pardon*, 105.

[105] Knighton, 188–91; *CPR 1361–4*, 422.

[106] *Robin Hood and Other Outlaw Tales*, ed. S. Knight and T. Ohlgren, 2nd edn (Kalamazoo, 2000), 142; W. M. Ormrod, 'Robin Hood and Public Record: The Authority of Writing in the Medieval Outlaw Tradition', *Medieval Cultural Studies: Essays in Honour of Stephen Knight*, ed. R. Evans, H. Fulton and D. Matthews (Cardiff, 2006), 67–9.

Thoresby of York (1352–73), Thomas Hatfield of Durham (1345–81) and Michael Northburgh of London (1354–61) had all, for example, served as keepers of the privy seal.[107] The prominence of current and former civil servants generated some sneering: Pope Clement VI was supposed to have declared at the time of Hatfield's promotion that Edward III might just as well recommend an ass as bishop.[108] In most cases, however, the imputation that such men lacked formal academic training was actually unfounded. A number of the new bishops of this period – William Bateman of Norwich (1344–55), Gilbert Welton of Carlisle (1353–62) and Thoresby himself – had been recruited into royal service in the first place because they had higher degrees in canon and civil law that equipped them to deal with the complex processes of international diplomacy.

Nor was Clement VI entirely fair to imply that royal nominees were mere placemen. In the later 1340s there were some notable conflicts of jurisdiction between crown and episcopate. William Bateman elicited little support from his fellow bishops when, as a consequence of his disputes with the townsmen of Lynn and the abbot of Bury St Edmunds, his temporalities were seized by the crown in 1346–7.[109] But the crown's general campaign to assert rights of patronage over the canonries of English cathedrals, which resulted in the brief confiscation of the estates of Bishop John Grandisson of Exeter in 1350, pushed the prelates into outspoken opposition, and the king was forced to relax his policy and confirm the privileges of the Church in 1352.[110] In neither of these disputes were there obvious or lasting clashes of personality: Bateman, for example, was quickly reconciled with the king, who acted as a benign arbiter in the bishop's continuing disputes with Lynn and Bury St Edmunds, and even recommended his appointment as a cardinal. A few years later, however, Edward's blatantly retributive pursuit of Thomas Lisle, bishop of Ely, was once more to provoke major issues relating to the legal rights of churchmen and prove a major test of loyalty for the ministers and bishops.

Thomas Lisle was an English-born Dominican friar who had been unexpectedly elevated to the bishopric of Ely by Clement VI in 1345. With no significant connections in the universities, the civil service or the episcopate, he was something of an outsider and perhaps easy prey for a monarch in search of a cause. Lisle had a long-standing feud with the

---

[107] Islip and Thoresby achieved a notable compromise in the long-standing dispute over the rights of the archbishop of York to bear his cross within the province of Canterbury: *Concilia*, iii, 31–2.

[108] Walsingham, *Chronicon Angliae*, 20; J. R. L. Highfield, 'The English Hierarchy in the Reign of Edward III', *TRHS*, 5th series, vi (1956), 131–2.

[109] A. H. Thompson, 'William Bateman, Bishop of Norwich, 1344–1355', *Norfolk Archaeology*, xxv (1935), 118–24; *Making of King's Lynn*, 34–7; Ormrod, *Reign of Edward III*, 56, 129, 221 n. 95, 237 n. 49; Palmer, *English Law*, 40–1, 45–52.

[110] *PROME*, v, 59–60.

king's cousin, Blanche of Lancaster, dowager Lady Wake. In 1354–5 this
erupted into serious violence between the servants of the two parties that
led to the murder of one of Blanche's tenants, William Holm.[111] In the
parliament of November 1355 Lady Wake submitted an appropriately
colourful appeal for direct royal assistance and Edward, breaking the ceremonial silence that normally surrounded the monarch on such occasions,
announced his decision with his own lips: 'I take the dispute into my
hands.'[112] From the bishop's point of view, this merely served to confirm
the king's obvious partiality. According to the Ely chronicler, Edward was
infuriated by Lisle's attempts to claim the moral high ground and lost his
temper: 'You will have the law without the favour of the law!'[113] Edward
III's obvious sense of chivalric obligation to his kinswoman, and his
equally blatant distaste for the uppity bishop, had seriously compromised
the authority that he now claimed as arbiter in the case.

The 1355 parliament was called to a hasty conclusion as a result of the
king's need to head off for his winter campaign against the Scots. In his
impatience to have the Lisle–Wake feud resolved, Edward ordered
Chancellor Thoresby to issue instructions for the seizure of the bishop of
Ely's estates. This action was in clear contravention of one of Edward's
own statutes of 1340, and Thoresby was faced with a major conflict of
interests. From Newcastle on 30 December, Edward wrote to the chancellor and treasurer complaining of their prevarication and reminding
them of their obligation to obey his instructions. But Thoresby was on
firm ground. He convened a special meeting of the judicial experts of the
council and confirmed the illegality of the process being required by the
king.[114] Not only for the higher clergy but for the judges too, the whole
affair had distinct parallels with the king's attack on the Stratford brothers
in the winter of 1340–1. For the moment, reason prevailed. Edward was
forced to withdraw the threat of confiscation and to allow the case to be
heard in the king's bench. It was not until October 1356 that the judges
delivered a judgment of felony against Lisle for receiving the murderers of
William Holm. Instructions were then finally issued for the confiscation of
the bishop's temporalities. Even with the proprieties properly observed,
however, this was too much for John Thoresby. Within a month of the
confiscation of the Ely estates, in November 1356, he resigned the chan-

[111] For what follows see J. Aberth, *Criminal Churchmen in the Reign of Edward III: The Case
of Bishop Thomas de Lisle* (University Park, Penn., 1996), 117–85, 240–50.

[112] *PROME*, v, 128.

[113] *Anglia Sacra*, i, 657; Aberth, *Criminal Churchmen*, 134–5.

[114] SC 1/56/27, printed in B. Wilkinson, 'A Letter of Edward III to his Chancellor and
Treasurer', *EHR*, xlii (1927), 249; C 49/67/5, printed in Richardson and Sayles, *English
Parliament*, chap. xxv, 32 n. 73. The abolition of the practice of applying forfeited lands to
the upkeep of the royal chamber on 20 Jan. 1356 looks suspiciously like a pre-emptive
strike by the ministers against Edward's plans for the Ely temporalities: Tout, *Chapters*,
iv, 305 n. 2; Ormrod, 'Edward III's Government', 257–8.

cellorship.[115] On account of his obvious partiality and his determination to drive Lisle to humiliation and ruin, the king had lost the services of one of the most able and loyal ministers of his entire reign.

Had Lisle and Thoresby elicited sympathy for their respective plights in the winter of 1356–7, it is possible that the affair might have escalated into a very significant confrontation between Church and crown. As things turned out, however, Lisle's unreasonableness tended to alienate the majority of the episcopate. The astute William Edington, less convinced than Thoresby that real damage had been done by the king's actions, immediately stepped in as chancellor. Archbishop Islip, with the instincts of a peacemaker, advised Lisle to seek purgation in the ecclesiastical courts and a personal reconciliation with the king. But in November 1356 Lisle left the realm for Avignon, intent on lodging an appeal. Innocent VI was just as offended as Edward had been by the bishop's self-righteousness, but nevertheless felt obliged to issue formal excommunications against William Shareshull and Robert Thorpe, the royal justices who had delivered the judgment against Lisle in the king's court. Edward immediately deployed the recent Statute of Praemunire to argue that anyone abetting Lisle's appeal would be subject to prosecution in England. The threat was enough to persuade most of the bishops into tactful neutrality and only one prelate, John Gynewell of Lincoln, risked royal wrath by promulgating the excommunications of the judges. In 1358 the parliamentary commons did their best to confound papal initiatives towards a settlement for the release of John II on the grounds that the Lisle case had exposed Innocent VI's prejudice against the English crown.[116] When Lisle died unexpectedly during the second outbreak of the plague at Avignon in 1361, almost all of Edward III's leading subjects considered the king not only fully vindicated in his attack on the bishop but also more generally affirmed in his claims to moral and jurisdictional authority over the English Church.[117] If Edward was lucky in this outcome, the case had also amply demonstrated his new-found ability to turn high-profile causes distinctly to his own advantage and thus greatly to reinforce public confidence in his claims to sovereign jurisdiction within his realm.

The decade after the Black Death marked a period of remarkable reconstruction for the English crown. The firm leadership provided by Edward III persuaded the landed and commercial elites that it was plausible to consider restoration of the social and economic conditions that had prevailed before the plague. Although the labour laws sat within a much longer tradition of regulation by the crown, they also marked a great leap

---

[115] E 403/382, 21 Oct. 1356; *CCR 1354–60*, 332; Ormrod, 'Edward III's Government', 258–9.

[116] *Scalacronica*, 150–3.

[117] *Hist. Angl.*, i, 285–6.

forward in the scope of royal interventionism, creating the forms of coercion on which the proprietary classes were to become increasingly dependent for the preservation of their own private interests. Strikingly, the crown's active involvement in the campaign to resist any improvement in the material conditions of the lower orders suggests a concerted effort to marginalize the third estate from the benefits of the state.[118] Whether these wider implications were fully understood at the time is less certain. The government of the 1350s can scarcely have predicted the outbreak of the Peasants' Revolt in 1381. Nor, in spite of his more obvious social prejudices, can Edward III be suspected of deliberately exploiting the crisis of 1348–9 to abnegate his responsibilities to the less affluent and influential of his free subjects. At least in the immediate aftermath of the pestilence, his instinct was altogether more pragmatic, a simple matter of muddling through until such time as a reasonable sense of normality returned. It remains all the more impressive, then, that the 1350s also produced so many new and successful developments in royal government. Edward III's well-timed rapprochements with the nobility, the parliamentary commons and, at least belatedly, the clergy provided him with the firm base of support on which the likes of Thoresby, Shareshull and Edington were able to build significant improvements in administration, justice and finance. Around the time that the Black Prince won his great victory over John II in 1356, Edward III could indeed be said to be presiding over the most sophisticated governmental machine yet known in the long and illustrious history of the English medieval state.

---

[118] Harriss, *King, Parliament*, 509–17; Palmer, *English Law*, 11–13. For a different perspective see Walker, *Political Culture*, 75–6.

Chapter 14

THE RANSOMING OF RULERS, 1356–1360

If any confirmation was needed of the invincibility of English arms after the time of Crécy and Neville's Cross, then the battle of Poitiers provided it in truly miraculous form. Edward III and the Black Prince had never stood higher in the estimation of their subjects at home or their allies and enemies abroad. Edward's possession of both his principal enemies, David of Scotland and John of France, seemed set to transform the crown of England into the most powerful political force in western Europe. Speculation was rife as to the likely reach of the settlement that might follow. In March 1357 the Oxford scholar John Ashenden completed an astrological treatise in which he predicted that, after another great spate of pestilence, tempest and war, the kingdom of France would be utterly ruined and the king of England would finally have full dominion there.[1]

The great challenge that faced Edward III between 1356 and 1360 was to balance his allies' and subjects' inflated expectations of such a settlement against the many practical impediments that still stood in its way. Considering the great flurry of diplomatic activity that resulted from the battle of Poitiers, the negotiations with the Scots and French are surprisingly poorly documented. Both Edward and his captives recognized the perilous path they had to tread, and at times the three kings seem to have entered into a pact of secrecy to which neither their advisers nor posterity had any real access. English chroniclers of the period were often misinformed and confused. Furthermore, the official records of parliament are missing for the period 1357–61.[2] In broad terms, however, it is evident that Edward III tried to formulate a diplomatic strategy based on three firm principles. The first was to secure as large a ransom as possible for the release of David Bruce and John of Valois. The second was to effect, as quickly as possible, a territorial settlement in France that would allow England to take control, in full sovereignty, of its ancient rights and new conquests in Aquitaine, Ponthieu and Calais. The third, which proved the trickiest position to sustain, was to reserve Edward's own claims to the thrones of Scotland and France as a means both of guaranteeing the ransoms and of securing promises of further titles and territories to follow. By charting the ways in which the king sought to balance these three

---

[1] Carey, *Courting Disaster*, 85–90.
[2] Given-Wilson, *Chronicles*, 190–1; *PROME*, v, 130–4.

objectives, we can reach a reasonable understanding of the aims of Edwardian diplomacy and of the problematic reactions it sometimes provoked not only in Scotland and France but also among the political elite within England.

Edward III spent the winter and spring of 1356–7 in careful consideration of his new position in France.[3] John II, now languishing in the archiepiscopal palace in Bordeaux, frantically sought means by which to secure his release and restore order to his imperilled realm. But neither the king of England nor the French government showed any enthusiasm for John's proposal to draw in the emperor, Charles IV, as an arbiter for peace. Sir Nigel Loring, dispatched by the Black Prince to inquire as to the king's intentions, returned to Bordeaux at the end of December. The prince was empowered to represent the king in discussions with the French but was to make no offers or promises until the Valois stated their own terms. Once he had made a truce, he and his exalted prisoner should transfer immediately to England.

Edward evidently intended to use the continued presence of his forces in the northern and western provinces of France to bring further pressure to bear on the temporarily paralyzed Valois regime. Lancaster and Philip of Navarre undertook extensive operations in Normandy and Brittany, investing a string of positions in central Normandy, laying siege (though ultimately unsuccessfully) to Rennes, and sending a small army of 1,000 men deep into the Île de France as far as Chartres and the environs of Paris. The control exercised over English-held positions in the north and west had been much enhanced since Sir Thomas Holland's reforms in Brittany in 1354–5, and by 1357 Lancaster was extending to Lower Normandy, Anjou and Maine the forms of military contract that were gradually turning the war into a longer-term process of occupation and conquest.[4] Neither Edward III nor his supporters in these areas were prepared to jeopardize their achievements in the north of France to gain a territorial settlement based on the treaty of Paris of 1259. The written form of the king's instructions to the prince of Wales stated simply, but boldly, that he was seeking 'perpetual liberty' (unconditional sovereignty) over every one of the lands that the French might be forced to concede.[5]

On 18 March 1357 parties representing John the Good and the prince of Wales, negotiating under the presidency of the cardinal of Périgord at Bordeaux, produced a set of terms for a treaty of peace. On the expectation of a successful outcome, a two-year truce was instituted five days later.[6] The draft peace has not survived, and there is no knowing its

[3] *EMDP*, I.i, no. 52.
[4] Sumption, ii, 263–4, 272–7.
[5] 'Some New Documents', 77–9, 97–9.
[6] *Foedera*, III.i, 340, 348–51; *Chron. J&C*, i, 107.

detailed specification. If it was generous to the English, as might well be expected, then it would simply have exposed the major difference of opinion that now existed between King John, eager to establish terms for his release, and the royal council in Paris, which was focusing on the unenviable task of rebuilding the royal war treasury. The duke of Lancaster was quick to see off the suggestion in the truce that he should raise the siege of Rennes, arguing that the war in Brittany was a separate issue and that he was within his rights to continue the siege until such time as Rennes capitulated.[7] Edward III himself was intent on making a further campaign into France in the summer 'to bring an end to his war, with the help of God', and summoned parliament at Easter to grant the necessary tax.[8] Prince Edward and John II took ship from Bordeaux on 11 April 1357 and arrived on English shores at Plymouth, as planned, on 5 May.[9] Public expectation in England therefore seems to have rested not on any template for peace conditionally approved by the prince of Wales but on the terms that Edward III himself might now be able to set for the release of King John. It was such discussions that presumably kept the lords and knights of the shires in session at Westminster Palace until 16 May.[10]

The royal progress from Plymouth was a leisurely event, and it was not until 24 May that Edward of Woodstock and his exalted prisoner entered London. The event had been carefully planned for full theatrical effect. A thousand citizens dressed in their guild liveries marched through the streets of the capital to meet the new arrivals, large quantities of free wine were distributed to the crowd, and young maidens scattered gold and silver leaf over the procession.[11] Froissart claimed that John of Valois rode on a white horse, with the prince following him on a black hackney.[12] At a great banquet held in Westminster Palace, Edward III sat between his two royal prisoners, John II at his right and David II on his left.[13] Thus began one of the most sustained and purposeful demonstrations of royal magnificence witnessed in medieval England. For four years after Poitiers, said the herald of Sir John Chandos in his verse *Life* of the Black Prince, the English court and its guests 'danced, hunted, hawked, jousted and feasted, just as in King Arthur's time'.[14]

[7] *AC*, 40.

[8] *EMDP*, I.i, no. 53; *PROME*, v, 130. When this campaign was called off, large parts of the subsidy were used to settle the debts owing for that of 1355–6: Harriss, *King, Parliament*, 345.

[9] *Foedera*, III.i, 348; Knighton, 148–51.

[10] *CCR 1354–60*, 401; E 403/387, 11 May 1357.

[11] Knighton, 150–1; *AC*, 41; *Anon. Cant.*, 34–7.

[12] Froissart, v, 83.

[13] *The Kirkstall Abbey Chronicles*, ed. J. Taylor (Thoresby Society, xlii, 1952), 62; M. Bennett, 'Isabelle of France, Anglo-French Diplomacy and Cultural Exchange in the Late 1350s', *Age of Edward III*, ed. Bothwell, 218.

[14] *Vie du Prince Noir*, 89 (ll. 1513–1516), translated in *Life and Campaigns*, 104.

It was central to the conventions of war and chivalry that the captor should honour the status of his prisoners and show due concern for their physical and spiritual welfare. Some of the French nobles taken at Poitiers, now installed in various English royal castles, were indeed allowed a relatively relaxed regime: the marshal Audrehem, the count of Tancarville and others were regularly given parole to visit that venerable doyenne of the Anglo-French connection, the dowager Queen Isabella, at Hertford castle.[15] For obvious reasons, the security around the person of John II was rather tighter. Initially he was placed under house arrest in the duke of Lancaster's palace of the Savoy in London.[16] A group of bargemen were paid to stay 'day and night' on the Thames to minimize the risk of a surreptitious royal escape by water.[17] John's entourage was also quickly disabused of any expectation of unconditional hospitality, and many of the household expenses of the exiled king had to be borne by subventions sent over from Paris.[18] Clearly, however, Edward III was very much aware of the political capital to be made out of proper displays of graciousness. In September or early October 1357 the king hosted a great tournament at Smithfield at which John of Valois and David Bruce were again the principal guests.[19] Through such events Edward sought very deliberately to remind his subjects and enemies alike of the new strength of his strategic position.

This campaign of calculated magnificence reached its climax at the Garter feast of April 1358.[20] John II had already spent much of the winter at Windsor being introduced to the wonders of the newly rebuilt St George's Chapel and the fast-growing association between the castle and the cult of King Arthur.[21] The forthcoming Garter ceremonies were planned not only to impress the great assemblage of foreign dignitaries now held hostage in England but also to proclaim Edward's status as international patron of chivalry. Heralds were sent to France, Germany and the Low Countries to announce the forthcoming jousts, and the duke of Luxembourg and a large contingent of Gascon knights were among those

[15] BL, MS Cotton Galba E. XIV, fols 5r–17r; 'Notices of the Last Days of Isabella, Queen of Edward the Second', ed. E. A. Bond, *Archaeologia*, xxxv (1853), 456–62; Bennett, 'Isabelle of France', 219–21.

[16] Froissart, v, 83–4; *Chron. J&C*, i, 110; Fowler, *King's Lieutenant*, 290 n. 2.

[17] *Foedera*, III.i, 413; E 403/387, 16 June, 23 June, 1 July 1357; E 403/388, 6 Oct. 1357; Delachenal, ii, 57 n. 2.

[18] 'Notes et documents relatifs à Jean, roi de France, et à sa captivité en Angleterre', ed. H. E. P. L. d'Orléans, duc d'Aumale, *Miscellanies of the Philobiblon Society*, ii (1855); J. B. Henneman, *Royal Taxation in Fourteenth-Century France: The Captivity and Ransom of John II, 1356–1360* (Philadelphia, 1976), 88–9. Henry of Grosmont was subsequently awarded £30 compensation for the damages that John's entourage had inflicted at the Savoy: E 403/401, 11 July 1360.

[19] Reading, 129, 272.

[20] Knighton, 158–9; *Eulogium*, iii, 227.

[21] E 403/388, 16 Feb. 1358.

who answered the call. The elderly Queen Isabella made what was to be her last trek to Windsor for the Feast of St George, and 'diverse lords and ladies of England' were invited to witness the impressive spectacle. Twenty-four minstrels, two waits and the jester Little Robert provided the entertainment.[22] John the Good was reported in one English chronicle to have remarked adversely on the disproportionate extravagance of the occasion, using the same trope employed nearly twenty years earlier in the *Song against the King's Taxes* and criticizing the English king for living off credit while dining from gold and silver plate. On the whole, however, sympathetic observers were eager to see such extravagance as a true expression of Edward's authority over a vanquished and humiliated rival for the throne of France.[23]

The arrival of John II in England sharpened Edward III's resolve over the ransoming of David II of Scotland. Edward's government understood that, unless it could reach its own agreement with David's regency administration, the French were quite likely to insist that their alliance with the Scots be taken into account in the Anglo-French negotiations. David Bruce himself attempted to facilitate the process by holding discussions with Chancellor Edington and seeking Edward's permission for a well-timed pilgrimage to Canterbury.[24] Preliminary terms were agreed at Westminster in early May 1357 and may have been discussed in the parliament then sitting at the palace.[25] They were eventually settled at Berwick on 3 October in a treaty confirmed on the English side by the archbishop of York, the bishops of Durham and Carlisle and Lords Percy and Neville.[26] David II was to be released on the promise of a ransom of £66,667, payable in instalments over ten years and guaranteed by hostages selected from the noble families of Scotland. In case of default, David would be obliged to surrender his own body, or those of his most senior earls, to the English king. For the duration of the ransom payments, a truce would hold between the two realms.

The treaty of Berwick was, in essence, a rerun of the terms first proposed at Newcastle in 1354. For both sides, it represented a realistic

---

[22] E 403/388, 9 Mar., 12 Mar. 1358; E 403/392, 13 Apr., 4 May 1358; Knighton, 158–9; *Eulogium*, iii, 227; Reading, 130; *Scalacronica*, 150–1; *Anon. Cant.*, 42–5; 'Notices', 459. For heralds of the Black Prince at the 1358 jousts see *BPR*, iv, 252.

[23] *A Chronicle of London from 1089 to 1483*, ed. N. H. Nicolas (London, 1827), 63–4; A. Steele, *The Receipt of the Exchequer, 1377–1485* (Cambridge, 1954), xxxiv–xxxv; Collins, *Order of the Garter*, 238–9. The trope is also found in *Chartularies of St Mary's Abbey, Dublin*, ed. J. T. Gilbert, 2 vols (RS, 1884–6), ii, 392–3.

[24] *CDS*, iii, no. 1610 (incorrectly dated); 'Papers Relating to the Captivity and Release of David II', 21–9; Penman, *David II*, 188–9.

[25] *CDS*, iii, no. 1629; *RDP*, iv, 611–13; *PROME*, v, 130.

[26] *Foedera*, III.i, 372–4; *Rot. Scot.*, i, 811–14; *Acts of the Parliaments of Scotland*, i, 518–21; *EHD*, iv, no. 37; *BPR*, iii, 291. For David's journey to Berwick at this time see 'Papers Relating to the Captivity and Release of David II', 18–28; Wyntoun, vi, 233.

approach to the problem of a final settlement by offering agreement on the question of the ransom and buying time in which to consider future diplomatic strategy.[27] There is certainly an element of desperation about the way in which the English crown decided, after a decade of inconclusive talks, to sell back the tiresome David II to his subjects without securing any other definitive concessions. The treaty required no territories to be ceded to the English and said nothing about the Plantagenets' historical claims to suzerainty over the northern kingdom. On the other hand, it did effectively reserve Edward's rights in these and other matters by insisting that the guarantee of the Scots' claims to self-determination was entirely dependent on the payment of the ransom. The rights of certain third parties supportive of the English cause were also protected. These included the semi-autonomous lord of the Western Isles, John Og of Islay, the group of English lords disinherited by the treaty of 1328, and the earl of Salisbury, whose claim to the Isle of Man was vigorously defended by Edward III.[28] In Scotland, as shortly in France, Edward's tactic was evidently to hold on as long as possible to his claims to sovereignty and suzerainty, and to use this position as the most powerful possible leverage for a more enduring peace.

In adopting this holding position, Edward III gave fresh consideration to the prospect of a dynastic settlement in Scotland. The official form of the treaty of Berwick had conceded the point for which the Scots had argued so fiercely at Newcastle, and accorded David his royal title. Immediately after the settlement, however, the English crown reverted to its earlier position and refused to recognize the legitimacy of the Bruce monarchy.[29] In theory at least, the conditional nature of the treaty allowed Edward III continued discretion to grant the title to the Scottish throne and, by extension, to decide the succession upon David II's death. While many members of the political community in Scotland informally accepted Robert Stewart as their king-in-waiting, the treaty of Berwick offered no guarantee of such a prospect, and actually required that Stewart deploy one of his own sons, John, as hostage for David's ransom. Edward III's vivid memory of his head-on confrontation with Robert Stewart at Halidon Hill in 1333 must surely have coloured his attitude to the continuing question of the Scottish succession. And since Edward Balliol had renounced his own royal title in 1356, it had become possible for Edward III to respond more freely to David II's long-held notion of adopting a Plantagenet prince as his heir. David raised this idea again at the time of his release and return to Scotland late in 1357, suggesting that

[27] 'A Question about the Succession, 1364', ed. A. A. M. Duncan, *Miscellany of the Scottish History Society XII* (Scottish History Society, 5th series, vii, 1994), 7.

[28] *Munimenta de Insula Manniae*, ii, 199–202.

[29] *The Acts of David II, King of Scots, 1329–1371*, ed. B. Webster (Regesta Regum Scottorum, vi, 1982), nos 148, 150; Campbell, 'England, Scotland', 200.

he might be able to persuade his council to accept a Plantagenet succession in return for a reduction in the ransom payments.[30]

In the summer of 1358 Edward III accordingly went to work to devise a new and ambitious plan for the assimilation into his family of a number of royal and noble titles whose interests spanned England, Wales, Ireland and Scotland. In a triple betrothal ceremony performed in the queen's chapel, the twelve-year-old Princess Margaret was promised to the eleven-year-old John Hastings, earl of Pembroke; Prince Lionel's daughter, Philippa, then just three, was affianced to the six-year-old Edmund Mortimer, son of the earl of March; and John of Gaunt, at the relatively advanced age of eighteen, vowed to marry the twelve-year-old Blanche, co-heiress of Henry of Grosmont, duke of Lancaster.[31] The latter engagement was designed to provide Gaunt with a power base in northern England from which he might more easily control interests marked out for him in due course within the realm of Scotland. As if to denote his complicity with this policy, in February 1359 David II granted the duke of Lancaster a title of Scottish nobility as earl of Moray.[32] In an emerging plan for the deployment of the extended royal family to run the English crown's existing dependencies within the British Isles, Edward III was beginning to consider the serious possibility of having his third son succeed to the kingdom of the Scots.

Prince John's wedding to Blanche of Lancaster was celebrated at Reading Abbey in May 1359 in a flamboyant ceremony attended by the king and queen and the massed ranks of the English court. A splendid tournament followed at Smithfield in London, where the king, his sons and various nobles dressed up as the mayor and aldermen of the city. Edward III was provided with armour for this event, and may well have demonstrated his continued martial vigour by fighting in the lists.[33] Not least of the honoured guests was Edward's sister, Joan of the Tower. Joan had informally separated from the adulterous David II and retreated to England to take the veil alongside her elderly mother. But she had also continued to work as an agent of Anglo-Scottish peace. It was Joan, for example, who negotiated the delay that David sought in the payment of his ransom around the time of his grant of the earldom of Moray to Lancaster.[34] Joan's presence in England was also a ready reminder that David might at any time divorce, remarry and sire a direct heir. If

[30] Penman, *David II*, 189–90.

[31] *Issues*, 170, 172; E 403/394, 11 Dec. 1358, 15 Feb. 1359; 'Chaucer as Page', 100.

[32] *Acts of David II*, no. 211; *CDS*, iv, no. 9; Fowler, *King's Lieutenant*, 175; Ormrod, 'Edward III and his Family', 411 n. 50; Penman, *David II*, 222–4, 320–1.

[33] *CPL*, iii, 605; E 101/393/10; *Issues*, 170; E 159/139, *Brev. bar.*, Hil., rot. 25; *Anon. Cant.*, 48–9; *Brut*, ii, 309; Reading, 131–3; *BPR*, iv, 324; A. Goodman, *John of Gaunt: The Exercise of Princely Power in Fourteenth-Century Europe* (Harlow, 1992), 34–5. The king met John of Brittany's expenses for the tournament: E 403/394, 29 Jan., 2 Mar. 1359; *Issues*, 172.

[34] *Scalacronica*, 150–1, 246; *Foedera*, III.i, 419; *CDS*, iv, nos 27, 37, 65; 'Question about the Succession', 7–8; E 101/393/10.

Edward III was concerned about the feasibility of his son's adoption as heir presumptive to Scotland, it was all the more important that he act as soon as possible. The idea that Edward might extend his colonial model to Scotland, and thus create a new kind of dynastic unity within the British Isles, would provide a key dimension to the English crown's continuing negotiations with the Scots until the the mid-1360s.[35]

By 1357 the idea of separating off a ransom settlement and leaving territorial and dynastic issues for later discussion had been employed, with some considerable success, in relation both to Charles of Blois and to David Bruce. It seems likely that Edward III sought at first to apply the same formula in the discussion that opened with the representatives of John II's government after the battle of Poitiers. He surely had every expectation of success. The fact that the papal delegates to the discussions, Cardinals Talleyrand and Capocci, took up residence in London rather than hosting sessions at the usual venues of Avignon and Guînes is testimony to the great authority enjoyed by the king of England at this stage of the war. According to Henry Knighton, Edward received the envoys 'arrayed in his imperial state, and with the face of a lion', and informed them that he was confident of recovering the lands lost by his ancestors; what now remained at issue was the crown of France.[36]

Such tales may be make-believe, but there is no denying that the king took a highly interventionist approach to the ensuing talks. William Tirrington, a prominent member of the English diplomatic service, was provided with a horse in order that he could make haste to bring Edward any significant news.[37] In December 1357, when he agreed that four of John's fellow prisoners, the archbishop of Sens, the counts of Tancarville and Vendôme and the lord of Derval, should be released to assist in the making of a peace, Edward wrote in some displeasure to Chancellor Edington to insist that no letters of safe passage be allowed to any of the other French captives. And the king made it a requirement of their parole that these envoys should send an account of their discussions in Paris within a week of the opening of the parliament planned for February 1358.[38] As usual, Edward's input came to a halt over the festive season. The royal family moved off to Queen Philippa's castle of Marlborough for the Christmas revels of 1357 and then on to her seat at Bristol castle for Epiphany and Circumcision. The unusual torchlit tournament held at Bristol was yet another opportunity to celebrate the Black Prince's spectacular victory over the French and to raise public expectations for the fulfilment of a glorious peace.[39]

[35] See pp. 427–30.
[36] Knighton, 152–3.
[37] E 403/387, 5 July 1357. For Tirrington see Chaplais, *Essays*, chap. xxii, 174.
[38] SC 1/56/32, printed in Delachenal, ii, 396–7.
[39] Bennett, 'Isabelle of France', 220.

By January 1358, those charged to continue the talks with the French had managed to produce a draft Anglo-French agreement, known to modern historians as the first treaty of London.[40] A huge ransom of 4 million *écus* (£666,667) was to be set for the release of King John, and Edward III was to be guaranteed sovereign possession of Aquitaine, Saintonge, Poitou and Limousin, together with Ponthieu, Montreuil and the town and region of Calais. There was no mention of Edward's claims in Anjou, Maine, Touraine and Normandy, and the confirmation of his suzerainty over Brittany was intended as no more than an interim arrangement. The only extant text of this treaty, written from the English point of view, makes no direct reference to the obvious concession that would be expected in return: Edward's renunciation of the title to the crown of France. It is just possible that this reflected the king's determination to press on with that claim. In the aftermath of John's capture at Poitiers, France had become paralyzed by the increasingly radical demands for reform put forward by the Estates-General. If he wished, the king of England might easily use these conditions to restate his earlier challenge to the legitimacy of the Valois regime. It is far more likely, however, that the omission of the renunciation from the draft treaty simply reflected Edward's decision to reserve that position until such time as the French gave proper assurances of their inclination to accept the other terms.[41] This explains the way in which Edward's prisoner was referred to in the text of the treaty. If John of Valois was currently still only 'the adversary of France', then the fulfilment of the agreement would make him and his successors 'kings of France'. The major issue over the winter of 1357–8, then, was not *whether* Edward III would renounce the French throne but *when*, and under what circumstances.

Edward III presented at least the essence of the terms set out in the first treaty of London to the parliament of 1358. If the chroniclers Sir Thomas Gray and Thomas Walsingham are to be believed, the commons expressed themselves as surprisingly discontented with the settlement. Their opposition was couched principally in terms of the partiality of the cardinals: keen to demonstrate that England was not in thrall to the papacy, the knights and burgesses demanded that Innocent VI abandon his recent attempts to collect arrears of the tribute payable in recognition of King John's acceptance of the suzerainty of Innocent III in 1213. But they were also suspicious of the threat to English dignity arising out of the compromises that Edward now proposed over the French royal title.[42] In Paris the precise terms of the draft treaty seem to have been kept

[40] BL, MS Cotton Caligula D. III, nos 84–8; *Chron. J&C*, 143–4; Knighton, 163; Delachenal, ii, 62–3, 402–11; Sumption, ii, 309–10.

[41] Rogers, 'Anglo-French Peace Negotiations', 199–203.

[42] *RDP*, iv, 614–16; *PROME*, v, 131; *Scalacronica*, 150–3; *Hist. Angl.*, i, 285; Delachenal, ii, 73–6.

secret.[43] It was only John II's strong sense of personal commitment to the English king that probably kept the talks going at this point. On 24 March, while he was still in London, John purchased 'a great skin of parchment' and ink 'to write the treaty of the king [of France] and the king of England'.[44] During the Garter feast in April, Edward and John seem to have reached some form of private agreement on the pressing issue of the latter's ransom and release, agreeing that other matters might await further talks to be held under the presidency of the cardinals over the summer.[45] The date of 1 November 1358, fixed for the first instalment of the ransom, set an implied deadline for the conclusion and ratification of the expected treaty.[46] English commentators were later to argue that the French deliberately delayed their responses to this initiative, thus maliciously forcing its collapse.[47] In spite of his public show of commitment to the terms agreed at London and Windsor, however, there were strong signs that Edward himself had begun to have second thoughts about the advantages of an immediate and binding peace.

In March 1358 the dauphin Charles had had to flee from Paris under threats from Etienne Marcel and the radicals who demanded far-reaching political reforms. At the end of May the peasantry of the regions around Beauvais and Soissons rose in the rebellion known to posterity as the Jacquerie. Charles of Navarre, who had escaped from imprisonment at the end of 1357, led the bloody suppression of the revolt and was hailed by many of the French nobility as the hero of a dark hour. But he then moved on to take control of Paris and made common cause with Marcel, resisting the efforts of the dauphin to return to his capital. Laying siege to Paris, the dauphin offered terms: Navarre would be given a substantial landed settlement and cash sum, while the citizens would be pardoned in return for paying the first instalment of John II's ransom. There was widespread distrust among the various factions making up the revolutionary government of the city, and after Marcel was murdered on 31 July the dauphin's cause was assured. On 1 August, in a desperate bid to recover his position, Charles of Navarre drew up proposals at Saint-Denis for an alliance with England. This would deliver a veritable partition of France: Charles would have Normandy, Chartres, Picardy, Champagne and Brie, while Edward III would take the throne and have sovereign control of all other territories in the kingdom.[48] Such a far-fetched plot could do little to deflect Edward from his main purpose of forcing peace with the Valois,

---

[43] *Chron. J&C*, i, 176–7.

[44] 'Notes et documents', 113.

[45] *EMDP*, I.i, no. 201; *Anon. Cant.*, 44–7; *Foedera*, III.i, 425; BL, MS Cotton Caligula D. III, no. 129; Delachenal, ii, 66 and n. 1.

[46] *Scalacronica*, 152–3; Delachenal, ii, 69.

[47] *Anon. Cant.*, 44–7.

[48] *Foedera*, III.i, 228; Delachenal, ii, 421–3.

not least because Charles was now fully exposed as a notorious and unscrupulous turncoat.[49] The English response to the Navarrese plan was therefore cautious, and specifically refused to countenance Charles's claim to the sovereignty of Normandy.[50] But the whole episode threw into sharp relief the parlous state of the dauphin's position and the considerable potential for the English to exploit the disunity of the French nobility.

With the assistance of the mixed Navarrese, English, Picard and Norman forces that had gathered in his service, Charles of Navarre now invested a series of strongholds along the Seine basin from Poissy to Honfleur. Across western and southern France, English and pro-English troops were taking advantage of the pause in hostilities to invest in strategic positions and extract ransoms, known as *pâtis*, from the non-combatant population. The Navarrese occupation of fortresses in the Île de France brought this system within a short distance of Paris itself. Suddenly the enticing prospect of control over the northern and western provinces seemed in Edward III's sights. Faced with the increasing likelihood of a final military showdown with the Valois, Edward deliberately stalled the peace negotiations. The cardinals were unable to break the impasse, and eventually left England in September.[51] In November, with no sign either of the promised first instalment of the ransom or of the hostages that he had demanded for future payments, Edward informed the dauphin that he intended to resume the war.[52] In November and December plans were made for a great English army of invasion timed to coincide with the expiration of the truce of Bordeaux in April 1359.[53] And while Edward opposed the use of English troops in the current operations in the Île de France, he was careful to keep open the threat of an alliance with Charles of Navarre, promising his slippery cousin that no final agreement would be reached between Plantagenet and Valois without Charles himself being included as a party to peace.[54] Everything in English royal policy over the winter of 1358-9 therefore indicated an imminent return to full-scale hostilities.

It was only the personal intervention of John II that allowed his benighted realm temporarily to fend off such a terrible prospect. At the eleventh hour, John persuaded Edward III to postpone his military expedition and agree to an extension of the truce on 18 March.[55] A week later,

[49] Delachenal, ii, 79-80.

[50] *Foedera*, III.i, 228; E. Déprez, 'Une Conference Anglo-Navarraise en 1358', *Révue historique*, xcix (1908), 34-9; S. Luce, 'Négociations des Anglais avec le roi de Navarre pendant la révolution parisienne de 1358', *Mémoires de la société de l'histoire de Paris et de l'Ile de France*, i (1875), 113-31; Ormrod, 'England, Normandy', 207.

[51] Foedera, III.i, 405; E 101/508/27; *Anon. Cant.*, 46-7.

[52] Le Patourel, *Feudal Empires*, chap. xiii, 28-9; Sumption, ii, 374-5.

[53] Froissart, v, LV n. 3; *Foedera*, III.i, 415-16, 426, 427-8, 440-1.

[54] E. Perroy, 'France, England, and Navarre from 1359 to 1364', *BIHR*, xiii (1935-6), 151-2.

[55] C 76/37, m. 17d.

on the 24th, the two kings set their seals to the so-called second treaty of London.[56] The documentary evidence for this settlement is rather firmer than that for the draft treaty of 1358, and provides explicit proof of Edward's willingness to renounce the French throne on condition that the Valois first carry out the transfers of territory enumerated in the other clauses.[57] The ransom of John II remained at 4 million écus, but the first instalment of 600,000 écus (£100,000) was to be paid by 1 August. The real difference came in the list of territories over which Edward now demanded control. These included not only greater Aquitaine, Saintonge and Poitou, together with Ponthieu, Montreuil and Calais, but also Anjou, Maine, Touraine, Normandy and the county of Boulogne, all in full sovereignty, together with the suzerainty of Brittany. The effect would have been to re-establish virtually the entirety of the ancient Angevin empire and to give England uninterrupted control of the coastline of France from Calais to Bayonne.

So apparently outrageous were these demands that the second treaty of London has often been seen simply as a piece of blatant war-mongering by Edward III.[58] In some ways, in fact, the treaty represented a deliberate calling of bluff by both Edward and John, the means by which they hoped to force the troublesome Charles of Navarre to become a third party to a final peace. The new proposals suggested an extension of the Anglo-French truce to 24 June, specifically to allow Charles time to settle his own claims; if he failed to respond, Edward and John would then take common action against him.[59] But the treaty also had a serious purpose of its own. The audacious claim to English control of Normandy, Anjou, Maine, Touraine and Brittany reflected not only Edward's fantasy of reclaiming the entire sequence of ancestral titles lost since 1259 but also the significant reality of English occupation in the northern and western provinces. It thus recognized an increasingly powerful pressure group: the English soldiers who had invested in long-term careers of service in Brittany and Normandy and expected their gains there to be incorporated and guaranteed in any final settlement with the French. The idea that the English deliberately overstated their case in order to force the dauphin to choose between a more realistic settlement or another, potentially disastrous, war does not necessarily preclude the possibility that Edward III saw the impending final encounter as capable of delivering him just such an ambitious agenda. In this, the centenary year of the treaty of Paris, Edward intended finally and triumphantly to avenge the humiliation of his ancestors and secure possession of the largest

---

[56] Froissart, *Oeuvres*, xviii, 413–33; Delachenal, ii, 81 n. 1; 'Unknown Register', 370; 'Notes et documents', 113.

[57] Le Patourel, *Feudal Empires*, chap. xiii, 29.

[58] Ibid., chap. xiii, 30; Curry, *Hundred Years War*, 57.

[59] Sumption, ii, 400–1.

possible swathe of territories within the boundaries of the kingdom of France.

The ruinous terms that John II was prepared to countenance in order to secure his much-desired peace with Edward served to reveal the enormous gulf that had now opened up between the exiled Valois ruler and the regency administration of his son. Charles demonstrated his utter contempt for the proposals by refusing to have any part in his father's treaty.[60] Edward III responded by making some subtle but indicative changes in John's conditions of custody. In January 1359 there had already been a plan to remove John far from the circles of influence by sending him to stay at Somerton castle in Lincolnshire.[61] In the spring the French king was forced to leave the Savoy and take up residence at Hertford castle, a royal seat vacant since the death, the previous August, of Queen Isabella. John was clearly displeased. He sulked over the inadequacy of a little boat provided for him to take his pleasure on the river. More ominously, he fell quite seriously ill during April and May 1359.[62] If Edward's captive were to die before even a ransom settlement was worked out, then almost all the diplomatic capital built up by the English since Poitiers would collapse and the peace talks would once more founder and fail. It was imperative, then, that no further impediments should be put in the way of that great invasion of France which Edward had been planning, on and off, for the previous six months.

Edward III's decision to launch the campaign of 1359 revealed just as much about his supremacy in domestic politics as it did about the strength of his strategic position in France. No parliament was held in England between February 1358 and May 1360. The second treaty of London was therefore not put to public debate, and Edward sought no formal affirmation for his return to hostilities in the summer of 1359. Such unilateral decisions could, as Edward's grandfather and father had both found out, be very controversial.[63] But the parliament of 1358 had already made clear the suspicions of the political community about too ready a recourse to peace, and it may be that Edward regarded this as sufficient affirmation of the policy of war newly pursued in 1359. The whole manner in which the campaign was planned also served to stress the reasonableness of the king's actions. By funding the expedition entirely out of existing grants of the wool subsidy and from the profits of the ransom of David II, the king showed that he was still fully committed to the recent policy of

[60] Henneman, *Ransom of John II*, 93–4.

[61] *CPR 1338–61*, 142, 221; 'Notes et documents', 101–2, 132.

[62] 'Notes et documents', 117, 118, 127–8, 129–30, 132, 133.

[63] M. Prestwich, 'The Ordinances of 1311 and the Politics of the Early Fourteenth Century', *Politics and Crisis in Fourteenth-Century England*, ed. J. Taylor and W. Childs (Gloucester, 1990), 5.

avoiding direct taxation and minimizing the burden on his subjects at home.[64]

Just as significantly, Edward represented the new campaign as intended unquestionably for the defence of England. The king requested the usual round of prayers and processions invoking divine favour for his enterprise. Archbishop Islip embraced the opportunity to remind his flock of the evils of Sunday trading and the desirability of going to church to pray for the king.[65] Plans were made to prevent breaches of security by the various French captives held in England. The practice of allowing prisoners of war release on parole, used extensively in 1357–8, was now stopped. Many members of John II's household were sent back to France, and John and his son were transferred, in much-reduced circumstances, to the remoteness of Somerton.[66] On the eve of his departure in October, Edward made the usual preparations for the defence of the coasts while he and so many members of the military elite would be out of the realm.[67] When the regency council subsequently suggested that the wealthier gentry might contribute arms and provisions for the troops raised for this purpose, the county elites were quick to remind it that this contravened the legislation of 1352, and alternative measures had to be put in place to raise a special subsidy in the localities intended solely for the support of the defence forces.[68] In 1359–60, the crown went out of its way to prove that the new campaign represented a natural continuation of a war already many times affirmed by the polity, conducted in line with its own strict new principles of fiscal sustainability and prosecuted with England's interests very much to the fore.

Most importantly of all, Edward III was entirely confident of an enthusiastic response to his new call to arms. The army put together during the summer of 1359 came to around 10,000 men. This was only half the size of that planned for the Crécy campaign of 1346. But it had a much higher proportion of men-at-arms and mounted archers and was therefore much more socially exclusive than its predecessors. The four older princes all

---

[64] The wage bill for the campaign of 1359–60 amounted to just under £134,000: *Anon. Cant.*, 51 n. 131. The customs alone supported some £75,000 of expenditure in connection with this campaign: Ormrod 'English Crown and the Customs', 37. The wardrobe account covering the expedition, kept by William Farley, indicated a deficit of around £30,000: Tout, *Chapters*, vi, 90–1.

[65] *Foedera*, III.i, 442; *Register of John de Grandisson*, ii, 1201–2; H. J. Hewitt, *The Organization of War under Edward III* (Manchester, 1966), 162–3.

[66] *Foedera*, III.i, 436, 438–9; *CPR 1358–61*, 251; *Comptes de l'argenterie des rois de France au XIVe siècle*, ed. L. Douët-d'Arcq (Société de l'Histoire de France, 1851), 210–11, 213, 215; E 403/396, 29 July 1359; Delachenal, ii, 142–3; Bériac-Lainé and Given-Wilson, *Prisonniers*, 138, 143, 153–4, 149, 154–5.

[67] *Foedera*, III.i, 449–50.

[68] *RDP*, iv, 619–21; C 47/2/45, no. 1; C 47/2/56, nos 1–9; Harriss, *King, Parliament*, 395–400. The parallel single tenth requested from the clergy was also granted for the specific purpose of local defence: Ormrod, *Reign of Edward III*, 204, 205, 240 n. 111.

served, as did the duke of Lancaster, the earls of Stafford, Northampton, Warwick, Suffolk, March and Salisbury, Lords Basset, Percy, Zouche, Mauny, Burghersh, Cobham and Ughtred, and a host of other lords and knights.[69] In fact, the participation rate of the English nobility and gentry was probably higher on this expedition than on any other continental campaign of the fourteenth century.[70] Such eagerness had much to do with excitement at the king's resumption of the role of commander-in-chief. Edward showed appropriate concern for the welfare of his knights. John, the young grandson of the king's former staunch supporter Henry Beaumont, was made a personal gift of £100 to help defray the costs of equipment.[71] On the eve of their departure Edward promised Sir John Cobham, son of the dowager countess of Norfolk, that he would act in good faith towards Cobham's estates and tenants in the event that John were to die abroad.[72] And for the more optimistic, the king was quick to offer the guarantee of material profit. Indentures of war were not issued for this campaign, for the practical reason that the royal household now resumed its traditional role as a paymaster's office in the field. But noble and gentry captains seem to have been offered the terms that had become the norm in recent contract armies: wages, *regard*, costs of passage, compensation for horses lost on campaign, and the right to half of the spoils of war taken by their men.[73]

What did the military elite think Edward III intended to gain from another invasion of France? The king reputedly informed the participants before their departure that he intended to remain in France until he had achieved his aims, and was prepared to die in the attempt.[74] As usual, however, he kept the specific details highly confidential. Observation alone would have made it clear that this was intended as a sustained campaign intended to provoke a full-scale encounter with the dauphin. Unlike the army that Edward had led into Picardy in 1355, the force of 1359 was extremely well equipped and supplied. Indeed, the commissioning of leather boats, milling machines and portable ovens to help to provide fresh fish and bread to the troops must partly account for the delay of over two months in Edward's embarkation.[75] Exceptional arrangements were also made for the king's safety, with a group of forty archers from the forest of

---

[69] *Anon. Cant.*, 50–3; Ayton, *Knights and Warhorses*, 265–7. The earl of Arundel also originally intended to serve: A. Ayton, 'English Armies in the Fourteenth Century', *Arms, Armies and Fortifications*, ed. Curry and Hughes, 28 n. 17. John of Gaunt received a personal gift of £500 from the king to cover his expenditure in preparing to go overseas: E 403/396, 11 Aug. 1359.

[70] Ayton, 'English Armies', 28–9.

[71] E 159/137, *Brev. bar.*, Mich., rot. 28.

[72] *PROME*, vi, 17–19.

[73] Ayton, *Knights and Warhorses*, 118–19, 127–32.

[74] Le Bel, ii, 298–90; Froissart, v, 198–9; Reading, 133.

[75] *Society at War*, 63; Fowler, *King's Lieutenant*, 200.

Knaresborough assigned to be continually about Edward's person.[76] This was to be no mere dash through the northern French countryside. Edward's silence on the specifics served to heighten the army's expectation of some imminent moment of supreme destiny.

The king passed September and October of 1359 either with Queen Philippa at Leeds castle or among his gathering troops at Thorne in Thanet. The barge *Blanche* of Winchelsea, which had been used on earlier occasions for royal transports, was once more requisitioned to carry him as he went about surveying his gathering fleet. Edward eventually took ship from Sandwich and crossed, without event, to Calais aboard the *Philip* of Dartmouth on 28 October.[77] Moving south-east, the army divided into the usual three formations, under the king, Lancaster and the prince of Wales, and progressed through territory now familiar to Edward and many of his followers. The king's own division proceeded via Arras into the Cambrésis and on via Saint-Quentin and Craonne. After making slow progress in difficult weather, the three divisions mustered in the environs of Reims on 4 December. The king set up headquarters in the abbey of Saint-Basle near the village of Verzy, high up on the hill outside the city.

Edward's decision to make for Reims was based at least in part on the symbolic significance of the city as the traditional coronation place of the kings of France. The twentieth anniversary of his formal claim to the throne of his Capetian forebears was looming in January 1360. If he were to manage to take the city, then the archbishop, Jean de Craon, might be cajoled into performing some kind of crowning ceremony that would prove once and for all Edward's entitlement to the throne of John II.[78] In preparation for such a stunt, the king gave careful orders that there should be no violence and looting in the city.[79] It is noticeable, however, that the English chroniclers saw nothing special about Reims, and simply interpreted the campaign in general terms as one designed to protect and pursue the king's rights.[80] Rather, it was in France that the particular reverberations of an

---

[76] E 403/401, 5 June 1360.

[77] *Anon. Cant.*, 50–1; *Foedera*, III.i, 452; C 76/28, m. 5; E 101/24/14, no. 8; E 159/136, *Brev. bar.*, Trin., rot. 5. Edward had earlier hoped to leave on 10 or 11 October: SC 1/60/80; *CCR 1354–60*, 656–7.

[78] Rogers, *War Cruel and Sharp*, 407.

[79] Delachenal, ii, 157.

[80] Knighton, 170–1, 176–7; *Life and Campaigns*, 104; *AC*, 44–5; *Scalacronica*, 170–5, 187–8; *Hist. Angl.*, i, 287. It seems particularly significant that John Ergholme's commentary on the *Prophecies* of John of Bridlington, which set some store by Edward's claim to France, made no mention of Reims and represented the campaign of 1359–60 simply as a destructive raid: *Political Poems*, i, 179. Nor do le Bel, ii, 300, 302, or Froissart, v, 211–12, have anything to say about the significance of Reims as a target. The appointment of commissioners to receive the fealty of the people of France in preparation for the campaign was regular practice when Edward planned to cross to France, and seems to have carried no special significance in 1359: *Foedera*, III.i, 45, 417.

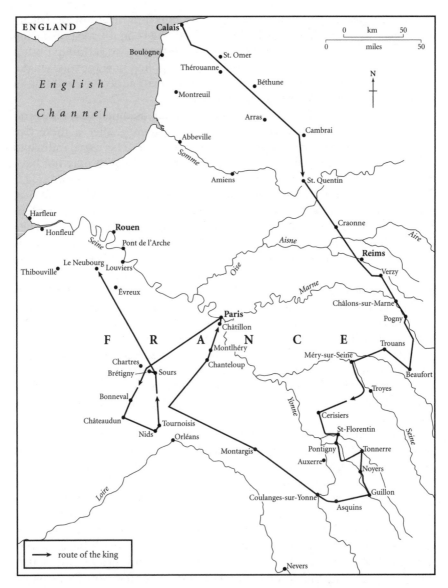

Map 6 The Reims campaign, 1359–60.

attack on this city were understood, and it is from these sources that modern historians have developed the idea that Edward conceived the operation as a 'coronation campaign'.[81] The French were also well aware

[81] *Chronique de Richard Lescot, religieux de Saint-Denis*, ed. J. Lemoine (Société de l'Histoire de France, 1896), 142–3; *The Chronicle of Jean de Venette*, trans. J. Birdsall and ed. R. A. Newhall (New York, 1953), 96; Delachenal, ii, 145–6; Burne, *Crecy War*, 328.

that the English hoped to use the siege of Reims as a means of provoking the regent to battle. If Edward III did indeed entertain the idea of having himself crowned at Reims in the winter of 1359–60, we certainly do not need to suppose that this was a reversal of the policy, now pursued single-mindedly for some years, to promise the renunciation of the royal title in return for a favourable territorial settlement.

By the same token, it need not be too readily assumed that Edward's decision to raise the siege of Reims in mid-January, after a mere five weeks, represented the collapse of such a strategy. The city's walls had only recently been repaired and extended, and the English may not have realized the stout defence that its inhabitants were capable of mounting.[82] With the dauphin refusing to be drawn out, Edward decided that his best course was to withdraw in good order. Many assumed that he was planning to head west and attempt to lay siege to the altogether bigger prize of Paris.[83] But at Reims Edward had been approached by some of the disaffected nobles of Burgundy with a plan for an alliance. They despised the undue influence that John II was exerting in the duchy as a result of his marriage to Jeanne of Auvergne, the widowed mother of the infant duke, Philip de Rouvres, and were ready to throw in their lot with the English. Here was an opportunity for Edward to extend his successful provincial strategy into Burgundy and even, through the marriage then being considered between Duke Philip and the heiress of Louis de Mâle, to draw Flanders back into the Plantagenet alliance. Edward also hoped to overwinter in a region free of the ravages inflicted by his own armies and by the freebooters or *routiers* who were now regularly rampaging through the Île de France.

Leaving Reims around 11 January, the English army proceeded south, again splitting into three divisions in order to ease the daily challenge of supply. The king's contingents moved through southern Champagne via Châlons to Trouans, and then marched west and south to avoid the hazards of Troyes and thus on into Burgundy. This was new territory for Edward III, and he took time to appreciate its charms. The army gathered together at Pontigny, where the king visited the great Cistercian monastery and its shrine to Edmund Rich, the English saint on whose feast day Edward had been christened.[84] The *Anonimalle* chronicler insisted that Edward spared the monks of Pontigny, but most contemporaries assumed that, like all else in the army's wake, the abbey was viciously plundered.[85] In spite of such incentives, not all was well in the ranks. Disease was

[82] M. Jones, 'War and Fourteenth-Century France', *Arms, Armies and Fortifications*, ed. Curry and Hughes, 117–19.

[83] Rogers, *War Cruel and Sharp*, 408.

[84] E 101/393/11, fol. 61.

[85] *AC*, 45–6, 167.

proving a significant problem: the earl of March, marshal of the army, and another prominent commander, Robert Morley, both died during the descent into Burgundy.[86]

The king at least remained in buoyant mood. On 19 February Edward reached Guillon, where he received Jean de Neufchâtel and the other ducal ambassadors. A treaty was agreed on 10 March. In return for Edward's protection, the duke of Burgundy would pay an indemnity of 200,000 *moutons* (£40,000) and provide military support. An interesting stipulation was added that in the event that Edward chose to be crowned as king of France and the duke refused to support him as a peer of the realm, their truce would be nullified.[87] A number of similar agreements were made around the same time with lesser French nobles.[88] The references to an imminent coronation again suggest that French provincial elites sympathetic to the English cause considered their own interests best served by Edward's swift return to Reims and the fulfilment of his dynastic destiny.

First, though, it would be necessary to confront the regent. If the dauphin refused to come out and fight, then Edward would have to proceed to Paris. In late March, with hopes that the weather was now improving, the English army set off from Guillon, rampaging across the Gâtinais as far as Chanteloup, south of Paris, where Edward arrived at the end of the month and mustered his forces in preparation for a final engagement.[89] As papal envoys arrived to attempt a truce, Edward moved to establish a base of operations at Châtillon and to encircle the French capital. On Good Friday, the king again advertised his royal status in France by performing his usual ritual of donating money for the provision of cramp rings.[90] There was high tension when Edward's forces appeared before Paris the following Tuesday, 7 April. But the dauphin, wisely resisting the impetuosity that had driven both his father and his grand-father to seek honourable outcomes through battle, resisted all offers of engagement. The position was now critical for Edward. There was no prospect that he could lay effective siege to the city and, with Charles having called his bluff, he had no reserve position. Supplies were running low. Since Charles of Navarre was at least temporarily reconciled with the dauphin, there was also no chance of any significant relief forces joining Edward at the gates of Paris.[91]

Froissart believed that, in leaving the environs of Paris and moving west on 13 April, Edward III intended to make for Brittany and regroup there

[86] *Scalacronica*, 174–5; Knighton, 178–9; *Anon. Cant.*, 56–7.
[87] *Foedera*, III.i, 473–4.
[88] Fowler, *King's Lieutenant*, 206.
[89] *Scalacronica*, 182–3.
[90] E 101/393/11, fol. 61.
[91] Delachenal, ii, 437.

before launching a new onslaught on the French capital.[92] Whatever his
original purpose, the king's own willpower, and the morale of his men,
seem finally to have faltered. On the first day of their march, as they
passed the city of Chartres, Edward's forces were overcome by a freak
storm.[93] The majority of the army managed some kind of shelter from the
torrent of rain and hail, but many horses and much equipment in the
baggage train were lost. 'Black Monday' or 'Bad Monday' seemed, at least
in hindsight, to mark the beginning of the end for this campaign. The
disease that had already carried off the earl of March was now rife, and it
was later reputed that a thousand English soldiers died on this campaign.[94]
A number of others, including the young squire Geoffrey Chaucer, were
taken prisoner in the minor skirmishes to which the English forces were
subjected all along the way.[95] The army continued as best it could from
Chartres to Châteaudun, and then turned east towards Orléans. But
while Edward's forces regrouped at Tournoisis and Nids, the abbot of
Cluny approached with the offer of talks. Bedraggled and dispirited, the
king of England had little choice but to resort, once more, to the power
of words.

The decision to call a halt to his army's progress and make terms with the
dauphin was not one that came easily to Edward III. Papal envoys had
been in contact since the beginning of March, and both Lancaster and
Prince Edward had advocated the way of peace for some time.[96] Given the
right circumstances, however, it seems that the king would have much
preferred to bring the campaign to a resounding climax in battle. At home,
there had been considerable panic over the serious attack launched by a
French fleet on the port of Winchelsea in March. The Canterbury chronicler, genuinely shocked by the ferocity of the invaders, listed the victims
and chastised the perpetrators for their acts of pillage and rape and (in his
view) their equally outrageous offence of eating meat in Lent.[97] Such was
the general panic that some of the bishops considered offering spiritual
indulgences to those prepared to defend the coasts. In the end, however, the
scare proved short-liked. Successful reprisals in the Channel restored confidence at home and offset any notion that Edward might have to withdraw
from France in order to come to the salvation of his own realm.[98]

---

[92] Froissart, vi, 1.
[93] Fowler, King's Lieutenant, 208–9.
[94] Hist. Angl., i, 288.
[95] EHD, iv, no. 693.
[96] Rogers, War Cruel and Sharp, 415.
[97] Anon. Cant., 58–63; T. Walsingham, Ypodigma Neustriae, ed. H. T. Riley (RS, 1876), 303.
[98] Alban, 'National Defence', 27–8; N. Housley, 'France, England, and the "National
Crusade", 1302–1386', France and the British Isles in the Middle Ages and Renaissance, ed. G.
Jondorf and D. N. Dumville (Woodbridge, 1991), 190; Sumption, ii, 435–8, 444–8.

Accepting the overtures of the abbot of Cluny was therefore an act of some humiliation for the English king. Froissart rationalized the whole episode in terms of religious obligation. During the storm outside Chartres, Edward had supposedly taken an oath to the Virgin Mary to accept peace if he and his men were saved in their moment of peril.[99] There is a certain ring of authenticity to this story. It remains unlikely, however, that Edward would have been persuaded to call an immediate halt to his military operations had he not some sense of expectation about the offered talks. If Black Monday had been read so emphatically as divine displeasure with his defeat, it is much more likely that Edward would have made immediately for the northern coast of France and returned his dispirited army to the safety of England. By keeping his forces in the field during the preliminary stages of the peace talks, he was able at once to denounce the dauphin for his dishonourable avoidance of battle and to cling at least notionally to his own continued invincibility in arms. Ever the pragmatist, Edward quickly worked out how to make the best of a bad situation, to recover a proper sense of his own dignity, and to enter into the new talks still confident in his expectation of a highly advantageous settlement.

At the end of April Edward moved back towards Chartres and took up residence at Sours. Formal discussions opened on 1 May at the tiny hamlet of Brétigny. The speed with which the arbitrators worked out a draft formula of peace reflects the two sides' readiness to pick up where they had left off with the first treaty of London. Under the terms of the preliminary settlement sealed on 8 May, Edward III would have sovereign control over the duchy of Aquitaine as defined in 1259, together with Poitou, Saintonge and Angoumois. In the north, he would have his inheritances of Ponthieu and Montreuil and his new acquisition of Calais with its hinterland, as well as the county of Guînes. In return, he would give up his title to the French throne. The other former Plantagenet lands in Normandy, Anjou, Maine and Touraine were to remain part of the kingdom of France. John II's ransom was set at 3 million écus (£500,000). In a pact of mutual and perpetual peace, John would promise not to support the Scots against the English, and Edward would give up assisting the Flemings against the French.[100] Both sides expressed themselves prepared to make proper concessions in order to secure the settlement. The French offered some additional territories: Thouars and Belleville were to be added to the county of Poitou, and Rodez and Rouergue to the duchy of Aquitaine. And in addition to accepting the reduction in the value of John's ransom, the English agreed that the 3 million écus should now be taken to cover the separate ransoms that might otherwise have been set for the sixteen nobles bought by Edward III as prisoners of war after the battle of Poitiers.[101]

[99] Froissart, vi, 4–5.
[100] *Foedera*, III.i, 487–94; *Chron. J&C*, i, 267–300.
[101] Given-Wilson and Bériac, 'Edward III's Prisoners', 814–20, 830–3.

In many respects, Edward must have felt highly satisfied with this agenda of peace. It gave him everything – and a good deal more – that he had vowed to fight for at the outbreak of hostilities in 1337. To have added substantially to the territorial settlement of the treaty of Paris through such a notable extension to the boundaries of the duchy of Aquitaine, to have secured French agreement to the cession of Calais, and to have all of this in the expectation of full sovereignty was, by any estimation, a truly impressive achievement. There is no evidence that Edward felt embarrassed by the treaty at the time it was drafted. News of the settlement was quickly dispatched home to England. John II, who had earlier been moved back to London, received the tidings of peace from Philippa of Hainault's messengers, and dined with the queen at Westminster Palace a few days later.[102] When the officers of the city of Winchester recorded a payment to a royal herald sent home to announce the accompanying truce, their clerk wrote a heartfelt note in the margin of his accounts: 'Thanks be to God.'[103]

And yet grave doubts remained as to the wisdom and viability of this settlement. Hindsight reveals that it was not John II and the dauphin Charles but Edward himself who was chiefly responsible for the eventual collapse of the treaty of Brétigny. It is therefore quite probable that the settlement of 1360 represented a momentary wobble when Edward, faced with his recent failure to replicate the achievement of 1346 and bring the enemy to battle, felt constrained to accept compromises that he had regarded as unconscionable just a year before.[104] This is not, however, to argue (as the historian John Le Patourel controversially did) that Edward simply could not bring himself to accept the humiliation of resigning his title to the throne of France.[105] After all, the king's representatives had repeatedly offered just such a concession, in 1344, 1354 and 1358, in return for sovereign control of old and new territories in France. For Edward, the fundamental problem arose from two much more substantive and practical issues: the geographical extent of the territorial concessions, and the willingness of the French to fulfil the necessary transfers of sovereignty in the ceded provinces. In seeking guarantees of good faith on the agenda of

[102] *Foedera*, III.i, 470, 475–6; E 403/401, 25 Aug. 1360; *Comptes de l'argenterie*, 237, 241–2, 245, 247, 249, 251; Bériac-Lainé and Given-Wilson, *Prisonniers*, 140.

[103] *City Government of Winchester from the Records of the XIV and XV Centuries*, ed. J. S. Furley (Oxford, 1923), 144.

[104] 'Some Documents Regarding the Fulfilment and Interpretation of the Treaty of Brétigny, 1361–1369', ed. P. Chaplais, *Camden Miscellany XIX* (Camden Society, 3rd series, lxxx, 1952), 5–8; M. Jones, 'Relations with France, 1337–1399', *England and her Neighbours*, ed. Jones and Vale, 252–3; K. Fowler, *The Age of Plantagenet and Valois* (New York, 1967), 62–6; Palmer, 'War Aims', 53–4, 60–2; C. Allmand, *The Hundred Years War* (Cambridge, 1988), 18–19; Curry, *Hundred Years War*, 58–9; Rogers, 'Anglo-French Peace Negotiations', 208–11; G. L. Harriss, *Shaping the Nation: England, 1360–1461* (Oxford, 2005), 405–7.

[105] Le Patourel, *Feudal Empires*, chap. xii, 189; chap. xiii, 31–3.

Brétigny, the king would soon be driven back to precisely the position implied in the first treaty of London, insisting that he would resign his claim to the crown of France only *after* the Valois had begun to pay the ransom and handed over the agreed territories. In 1360 Edward III tried hard to convince all parties that he had the right to claim the victor's prerogative and determine the order in which the various elements of the settlement were fulfilled. Ironically, the resulting manoeuvrings served only to compound the already unrealistic expectations of his subjects in England as to what might be achievable in peace with the French.

The agreements made at Brétigny included a four-month truce, which, it was judged, would be sufficient time to allow for the discussion of unresolved issues and prepare for final confirmation.[106] It had been agreed that John the Good would be transferred to Calais by 15 July, and dates had already been proposed for the payment of his ransom and the transfer of territories into English possession. As yet, though, there was no agreement on the mechanism and timescale for the renunciations that would have to be made by both sides. It was these issues, together with the detailed arrangements to be made for the provision of hostages for John II's ransom, that were deferred to the talks scheduled to open at Calais in July.[107] For the moment, then, there was nothing to keep Edward in France, and the king marched quickly through Normandy to the port of Honfleur; taking ship for England, he landed at Rye on 18 May.[108]

On 3 April the regency government of Prince Thomas had put out summonses to a parliament to meet on 15 May. Edward III must have presented at least an outline of the Anglo-French accord to this assembly, and one chronicle goes so far as to say that each article of the proposed peace was declared and approved.[109] Under a certain amount of pressure from the crown, any backsliders apparently felt it politic, for the present, to keep silent. For the next few weeks there was a good deal of ceremony around the preparations for John II's departure. Edward's household took up residence at Westminster against 'the concord made with the adversary of France'. And on 14 June, at a banquet in the Tower of London, King John gave his consent to the treaty and agreed with Edward that they and their sons should be true brothers, properly committed to a state of perpetual amity.[110] The Feast of St John the Baptist was celebrated with a grand service at St Paul's Cathedral and a performance of minstrelsy before the two kings, the prince of Wales and the duke of Lancaster. On 28 June Edward entertained John to dinner at Westminster Palace and

---

[106] *Foedera*, III.i, 485; *Chronicle of Jean de Venette*, 104-5.

[107] Le Patourel, *Feudal Empires*, chap. xiii, 33.

[108] *CCR 1360-4*, 112-13; E 101/393/11, fol. 49.

[109] *RDP*, iv, 622-4; *PROME*, v, 132; CCCC, MS 78, fol. 182. *AC*, 47-8, is notably more cautious in its account of Edward's transactions with this parliament.

[110] E 403/401, 5 June 1360; *Chron. J&C*, i, 319; *Brut*, ii, 312; *EMDP*, I.i, no. 202.

presented him with a sword-belt and an eagle (apparently a live bird rather than a crest). At the end of the month John left London, escorted by Prince Edward. After making lavish oblations at Canterbury Cathedral he moved on to Dover. Before crossing to Calais on 8 July he received a parting gift of Edward III's personal drinking vessel, and sent back to London his equivalent receptacle, the cup of St Louis.[111]

In late August the English lords commissioned to represent the king at the Calais summit – the prince of Wales, the duke of Lancaster, Prince Lionel, the earls of Arundel, Stafford and Salisbury and Chancellor Edington – made their way across the Channel.[112] It was understood that Edward would follow for the final ratifications. The only clue to the king's attitudes during this period comes from a private letter that he sent to one member of the delegation on 6 September.[113] Edward reported that he had removed to the Isle of Sheppey where, with his ships close at hand, he was well placed to cross to Calais at short notice. While he conveyed his usual impatience with technical details, he made it very clear that there were certain unspecified matters that he alone should decide. The letter suggests that the English representatives were under direct instruction to filibuster. The terms established in May had required that the 600,000 écus (£100,000) comprising the first instalment of John's ransom should be paid within four months of the latter's arrival in Calais, and the French government was finding it predictably difficult to raise such a mighty sum.[114] The closer the English could force the talks to the deadline for the ransom, the more pressure Edward's ambassadors might be able to apply for modifications to the draft settlement. Already by early September, there were signs that Edward had begun to reconsider the implications of the Brétigny agreement and to seek ways in which he might delay or avoid some of its more restrictive elements.

This strategy became explicit in the new terms worked out after the king's transfer to Calais on 9 October.[115] Edward's arrival was the occasion for much extravagant feasting. His agents had purchased considerable quantities of jewels for the celebrations that would accompany the summit, and the king received rich cloth and a sword from John the Good at the moment of their reunion. Heralds organized elaborate ceremonies of

[111] *Chron. J&C*, i, 319; *Anon. Cant.*, 62–5; *Comptes de l'argenterie*, 269–74. The 'goblet of the king of England' was among the items of plate that John II brought back to England in 1363–4: 'Notes et documents', 155.

[112] E 403/401, 6 Aug. 1360; E 101/314/2–5, 9–10, 12; Le Patourel, *Feudal Empires*, chap. xiii, 35–6.

[113] SC 1/55/87, printed in 'Some Documents Regarding the Fulfilment of the Treaty of Brétigny', 7 n. 1.

[114] 'The Ransom of John II, King of France, 1360–1370', ed. D. M. Broome, *Camden Miscellany XIV* (Camden Society, 3rd series, xxxvii, 1926), vii–viii; Henneman, *Ransom of John II*, 110–16.

[115] *HBC*, 39.

hospitality, and minstrels passed back and forth between the households of the kings and other great lords assembled in the town.[116] Behind the scenes, a great deal of hard work was done. Edward made proper show of his graciousness in the cause of peace. He agreed to release John after he had received payment of only a portion, 400,000 écus, of the first instalment of the ransom; he relaxed the deadline for the French cession of La Rochelle; he freed fourteen of the major prisoners of war taken at Poitiers; and he agreed that the continuing succession dispute in Brittany should be separated off and made the subject of a different arbitration so as not to jeopardize the main settlement.[117] In return for Edward's promise to withdraw his troops from Normandy, the Île de France and the Loire provinces, the Valois also guaranteed that Ponthieu, Saintonge and Angoumois would be delivered into English control by March 1361, and brought forward the date for the final transfer of the other territories from September to June of the same year. Such ostentatious displays of liberality allowed the two sides to reach a binding confirmation on the bulk of the Brétigny agenda, and on 24 October Edward III, John II and their heirs finally set their seals to a new and binding treaty of Calais.[118]

All of this goodwill, however, was really only by way of distraction from the major sticking point that remained: the manner and timing of the renunciations to be made by the two kings. Someone on Edward's side – most likely one of the professional diplomat-clerks, John Carlton, Adam Houghton, John Barnet, William Loughborough or John Branketre – came up with the clever solution of removing from the main text of the treaty the clauses that required the Valois to resign sovereignty over the ceded territories and Edward to renounce the throne of France. These were now placed in a subsidiary agreement, subsequently referred to by the rather oblique title of the littere cum clausula c'est assavoir ('the letters with the clause "that is to say ..." '), which was ratified alongside the main treaty of Calais.[119] The littere stated that John II should complete the transfer of all lands and rights in the ceded territories by midsummer 1361. After this, both sides would send written confirmation of their respective renunciations to a diplomatic conference at Bruges on 15 August, at which the two monarchs would simultaneously undertake their acts of renunciation. Should those dates prove impossible, then a postponement would be allowed until November 1361.

[116] *Issues*, 176; *EMDP*, I.ii, no. 412; E 101/624/40; E 403/401, 25 Aug. 1360; E 403/405, 8 Mar. 1361.

[117] *Foedera*, III.i, 533; 'Ransom of John II', viii; *EMDP*, I.ii, no. 302; Given-Wilson and Bériac, 'Edward III's Prisoners', 819 and n. 84; M. Jones, *Ducal Brittany, 1364–1399* (Oxford, 1970), 15.

[118] Le Patourel, *Feudal Empires*, chap. xiii, 38.

[119] E 403/401, 6 Aug. 1360; *Foedera*, III.i, 514–18, 520, 522–5; Chaplais, *Essays*, chap. xxii, 181, 184.

The *littere cum clausula c'est assavoir* represented a diplomatic masterstroke for the English, who were immediately delivered three powerful advantages. First, the English king would not be required to give up his own claim to the French throne until the Valois government had made good its promise of a ransom for John II. In this respect, the treaty represented a more complex form of the strategy already applied in the cases of Charles of Blois and David II, where matters of right were delayed until the appropriate financial compensation was seen to flow into English coffers. Second, Edward would be able to use his French title as a means of pressuring the Valois into speedy withdrawal from the Plantagenet territories in greater Aquitaine, Ponthieu and the marches of Calais. This would avoid the spectacle, witnessed repeatedly between 1259 and 1337, of English kings being promised their lands in France only then to be denied full access to them. Finally, the linking of Edward's renunciation of the French crown with John's resignation of sovereignty over the ceded territories had the ironic effect of requiring the Valois to acknowledge implicitly that the English king did indeed possess a valid dynastic claim. As and when the moment of renunciation arrived, Edward would thus be able to make the point that he had a perfectly sustainable right to the throne of France but had simply decided, of his own free will and for the sake of peace, to give it up.

All of this may have helped convince Edward III that he could emerge from the treaty of Calais with his integrity and dignity intact. As an important marker of his personal commitment to the peace, Edward chose to alter his royal style from the very day that the treaty of Calais was confirmed and announce himself 'king of England, lord of Aquitaine and Ireland'. Equally, and in order to emphasize that this was an act of pure discretion that would not be binding until such time as the renunciation clauses were fulfilled, he insisted on retaining the quartered heraldry adopted in 1340 with its striking representation of the Capetian and Plantagenet inheritances.[120] In similar vein, the novel title of lord of Aquitaine articulated Edward's strong desire to behave as though the French had already performed their side of the renunciation deal and given him full sovereign control of his newly configured territories in south-west France. Presented in such terms, Edward hoped, the treaty of Calais would be seen as a spectacular piece of diplomatic manoeuvring that locked the French into their side of the bargain and ensured that the settlement would be fulfilled in a manner that was entirely to the advantage of England.

Edward III returned to England on 1 December 1360 and made straight for Westminster, where he called his council about him and

---

[120] *EMDP*, I.i, no. 95; Ormrod, 'Problem of Precedence', 149. For numerous references to gold and silver plate quartered with the arms of England and France in use in the royal household during the 1360s see E 101/396/10.

promptly issued proclamations announcing the new peace.[121] Summonses were issued for a parliament to meet in January 1361 and give its formal consent to the diplomatic fait accompli.[122] At this assembly the king continued scrupulously to avoid any requests for taxes. He also offered some well-timed legislation that guaranteed the rights of denizen merchants to export wool, addressed the threat posed to public order by returning soldiers, and set some limits on peacetime purveyance.[123] A cycle of celebration was rounded off at Windsor on St George's Day, when the princes Lionel, John and Edmund were formally installed as knights of the Garter. Such advertising techniques seem by and large to have worked, and Edward was given every reason to believe that his subjects had greeted the announcement of peace with unalloyed enthusiasm.[124]

There remained, however, one group that was decidedly unconvinced by the general excitement surrounding the treaty of Calais: the English men-at-arms who had occupied substantial parts of the north-western provinces of France in the course of the previous decade. At the great council of 1353 the crown had given assurances that it would press for possession of the lands conquered in Normandy, Anjou, Maine and Touraine, and the control of some or all of these areas had again been high on the political agenda at Guînes and Avignon in 1354–5. By the terms of the treaty of Calais, however, Edward had apparently reneged on that commitment and instead bound himself to the systematic evacuation of English-held positions in most of northern France.[125] The fact that his forces were allowed to remain in Brittany pending separate settlement offered at least some compensation to the hard-nosed professional soldiers holed up in the Loire provinces; many of them now simply moved inside the boundaries of Brittany and continued their fortune-hunting there. By transferring the lordship of Saint-Sauveur-le-Vicomte to Sir John Chandos in 1359, Edward had also created a mechanism by which displaced captains might retreat into the Cotentin and join in the systematic occupation and ransoming of local castles and villages without technically breaking the spirit of the new peace.[126] Nevertheless, the many captains ordered to quit their positions elsewhere in the north of France in 1360–1 had ample reason for resentment, and even more opportunity to

---

[121] *HBC*, 39; E 403/402, 5 Nov., 10 Nov. 1360.

[122] *RDP*, iv, 624–7; E 403/405, 12 Dec. 1360; *PROME*, v, 133. At the end of this assembly 'divers magnates of England . . . sat at table for the expediting of the king's business': E 403/405, 26 Feb. 1361.

[123] *SR*, i, 364–70.

[124] Reading, 147–8; *Hist. Angl.*, i, 294; *Brut*, ii, 313.

[125] *Foedera*, III.i, 535–6; K. Fowler, *Medieval Mercenaries, I: The Great Companies* (Oxford, 2001), 25.

[126] K. Fowler, 'Les Finances et la discipline dans les armées anglaises en France au XIVe siècle', *Les cahiers vernonnais*, iv (1964), 72; Ormrod, 'England, Normandy', 206–7; Sumption, ii, 458–9.

create trouble. Prominent among the aggrieved were members of the duke of Lancaster's military retinue, Sir Thomas Uvedale, Sir Thomas Fogg, Richard Sholl and William Tutbury.[127] Many others had similar strong connections of service and blood with the English baronage and gentry. The resulting sense of betrayal felt by certain members of the domestic polity was articulated powerfully by the York chronicler, who fantasized that, had Edward III only persevered with the war in 1360, 'the captains [of the occupied castles and towns] and their men could easily have conquered the kingdom of France, to the advantage of the king of England and his heirs'.[128]

These anxieties in turn gave expression to the wider view, emerging in the months and years after the treaty of Calais, that Edward III had sold out his rights and dignity for the sake of a quick peace. This debate focused, inevitably, on the double monarchy. In France, Edward's gracious gesture in dropping his claim to the throne was taken as an unmistakable admission of defeat: one chronicler gleefully noted that this was a moment of no return, when the English finally and incontrovertibly acknowledged the Valois as legitimate kings of France.[129] The Scots, too, were quick to see the renunciation of the French throne as a stain on the English king's honour.[130] Edward's advisers must have been keenly aware that there were also parties in England that were bound to regard his change of policy as having compromised his good name and the reputation of his realm. The chronicler Sir Thomas Gray, whose sympathies lay very much with the displaced garrisons in Normandy, went so far as to argue that the abandonment of the claim to the French throne was an act of culpable negligence on the part of the king.[131] And William Langland, the minor cleric who wrote the first version of his great poem *Piers Plowman* in the early 1360s, railed against a monarch who had sold his birthright for silver.[132] If Edward had assumed the French royal title in a moment of haste in 1340, then the intervening twenty years of public commitment to that cause left many in England feeling that its renunciation in 1360 required a fulsome apology and a good deal more justification than Edward had yet provided.

* * *

[127] Fowler, *King's Lieutenant*, 280 n. 50; G. Bois, *The Crisis of Feudalism: Economy and Society in Eastern Normandy, c.1300–1550* (Cambridge, 1984), 294–7.

[128] *AC*, 49, translated in Barnie, *War in Medieval English Society*, 13.

[129] *Chron. QPV*, 119.

[130] Bower, vii, 314–17.

[131] *Scalacronica*, 187–8; A. King, 'War and Peace: A Knight's Tale. The Ethics of War in Sir Thomas Gray's *Scalacronica*', *War, Government*, ed. Given-Wilson, Kettle and Scales, 153–4, 155–8. Knighton, 190–1, in a somewhat frantic attempt to vindicate Edward's actions, claimed that John II actually apologized on his deathbed for taking the crown of France away from the king of England.

[132] D. N. Baker, 'Meed and the Economics of Chivalry in *Piers Plowman*', *Inscribing the Hundred Years' War in French and English Cultures*, ed. D. N. Baker (Albany, NY, 2000), 55–72.

The treaty of Calais was seen by the public in 1360–1 as at once Edward III's greatest personal triumph and his kingdom's greatest humiliation. The treaty left the crown with the prospect of very substantial territorial gains in a newly enlarged Aquitaine, possession of the strategic bridge-head of Calais, and unprecedented riches in the form of the ransom of John II. It marked a historic breakthrough in the long sequence of disputes over England's continued presence in France since the treaty of Paris of 1259, and represented the fulfilment of long-held ambitions to establish the Plantagenets in full sovereign control of their continental possessions. As a response to contemporary circumstances, however, it was seriously flawed. Edward III was too ready to suppose that the bond of honour existing between himself and John II would commit the French government to pay the ransom and implement the transfers of territory. The withdrawal of the renunciation clauses into the *littere cum clausula c'est assavoir* may have avoided an impasse in 1360, but it also reduced the force of the main treaty and in the end simply allowed the dauphin to mimic Edward's own strategy of deferral. No one in England could, of course, predict quite how the implementation of the treaty would proceed, and some of the larger questions over the wisdom of the peace arose only after the return to open war in 1369. Yet even in the moment of optimistic cele-bration during the winter of 1360–1, the seeds of doubt were yielding young shoots of protest. Edward III had raised domestic expectations to a level higher than could ever possibly have been fulfilled by a binding treaty of peace. It was to be his tragic legacy that a settlement intended to draw to a close one century of Anglo-French hostility would end up merely provoking another hundred years of war.

Chapter 15

INTIMATIONS OF EMPIRE, 1360–1368

Between the treaties of Berwick and Calais of 1357 and 1360 and the re-opening of the French war in 1369, Edward III devoted enormous personal energy to the disposition of his titles in the British Isles and France and to new opportunities for diplomatic and military intervention in other parts of continental Europe. Much of this enterprise was driven by a dynastic imperative. Edward wanted to establish his sons and sons-in-law in semi-autonomous lordships in the outposts of his dominions and other satellite states, and thus perpetuate a Plantagenet confederation of western European powers bound together by dynastic and feudal ties. Of the various historical models available to him, it was Henry II's 'family firm' that most readily appealed to Edward's imagination.[1] But there was also the more recent example, on the maternal side of the family, of Philip IV of France, who had tried through the marriage of Edward II and Queen Isabella to present the descendants of the couple as part of a general Capetian diaspora.[2] The precedents were there; it was now time for Edward to exploit them in rolling out a new Plantagenet empire.

There was some real urgency about the long-term security of the royal family. By 1360, Edward's surviving brood numbered five sons and three daughters. Of these, only the second and third sons, Lionel and John, were married, and each had but a single daughter, named in both instances after their grandmother, Philippa. The king's youngest daughter, Margaret of Windsor, was engaged to the earl of Pembroke but would die in 1361 before the marriage could be solemnized. Most remarkably, the king's eldest son and daughter, Edward and Isabella, who were both now approaching their thirties, remained unmarried. This was not for want of trying. As a child and teenager, the Black Prince had been put up for marriage successively with the Capetian house of France and the ruling dynasties of Brabant, Castile and Portugal. And Isabella of Woodstock, having been jilted in so outrageous a manner by the count of Flanders in 1347, had come similarly close to marrying Bérard, the son of the major

---

[1] The phrase is that of J. Gillingham, *The Angevin Empire* (London, 1984), 29–33. It does not appear in the 2nd (2001) edition of this work.

[2] Brown, 'Political Repercussions of Family Ties', 573–95.

Gascon lord Bernard-Ezi d'Albret, in 1351.[3] In the 1350s, however, the pace of negotiation around the futures of Edward III's eldest children had slackened noticeably. If this denoted a deliberate attempt to reserve them as the major prizes in a grand scheme of empire, its only immediate result was to leave the future of the dynasty notably and unexpectedly fragile.

Edward's more active deployment of his family as a diplomatic resource after 1360 was also prompted by the potentially hostile initiatives of the Valois dauphin, Charles. It is quite likely that, in their private discussions between 1357 and 1360, John II suggested to Edward III that they might revive the plan built into the earlier draft treaty of Guînes and agree one or more marriages between their younger children. At just that moment, however, John's sons were busying themselves with alternative marriage plans. In 1359 the dauphin organized the wedding of his brother, John, to the daughter of one of the greatest lords of the south-west, the count of Armagnac. And in 1360 another brother, Louis of Anjou, married the daughter of Edward's sometime prisoner and claimant to the duchy of Brittany, Charles of Blois.[4] In October 1360, John II set his seal of approval on these formidable challenges to Edward III's authority in the French provinces by raising Louis, John and the youngest of the Valois brood, Philip, to the rank of duke and giving them the titles respectively of Anjou, Berry and Touraine.[5] When Edward III in turn created his second and third sons, Lionel of Antwerp and John of Gaunt, dukes of Clarence and Lancaster in November 1362, he was acting very consciously in emulation of recent French practice.[6] Edward's diplomacy in the 1360s can thus be seen to have been driven by a constant and keen sense of direct dynastic competition with John II and his successor, Charles V.

The Anglo-French negotiations that proceeded from the treaty of Calais of October 1360 revolved around three main issues: the payment of John II's ransom; the withdrawal of French armies from greater Aquitaine and of English forces from northern and western France; and the simultaneous transfers of territory and acts of renunciation to be undertaken by Edward III and John the Good. At first, the English had little to complain about with regard to the ransom. Having allowed John to delay one-third of the total of 600,000 écus of the first instalment, Edward received full and prompt satisfaction of the entire sum by March 1361. But the super-human effort that this required of the French fiscal machine simply could

[3] Barber, *Edward, Prince of Wales*, 26, 33, 46; J. Lutkin, 'Isabella de Coucy, Daughter of Edward III: The Exception Who Proves the Rule', *Fourteenth Century England VI*, ed. Given-Wilson, 135–6.

[4] *Chronicle of Jean de Venette*, 127; F. Autrand, ' "Hôtel de seigneur ne vaut rien sans dame": Le mariage de Jean, comte de Poitiers, et de Jeanne d'Armagnac, 24 juin 1360', *Guerre, pouvoir et noblesse*, ed. Paviot and Vergier, 51–61.

[5] Delachenal, ii, 255–6.

[6] *PROME*, v, 152; *CChR 1341–1417*, 174; *RDP*, v, 53–4.

not be replicated year after year. The Valois regime was temporarily saved from bankruptcy by the co-ruler of Milan, Galeazzo Visconti, who was prepared to pay a very high price for the prestigious marriage of his heir to Isabella, the younger daughter of John II. By early 1364 John II seems to have paid the English crown some 999,200 écus, or £166,667, towards his ransom. When compared with the sums that Edward managed to extract from Charles of Blois and David II, this represented a major triumph. But the figure was still only 45 per cent of the total debt of 2.2 million écus that was due to be paid on the ransom by the end of 1364. The sums involved were simply too large to be passed over. Edward was intent on using his income from the ransoms to support the defence of his existing and new possessions in Calais, Ponthieu, Aquitaine and Ireland. It was not just greed or pride that was at stake: the very sustainability of Edward's new peacetime regime depended, to a significant degree, on continued pressure being applied for the delivery of the French royal ransom.[7]

The fault lines in the 1360 settlement also soon began to reveal themselves in relation to the difficult issue of clearing the troops from the French territories occupied during the war. The earl of Warwick, who had been given overall charge of the English evacuation force, found constant tension between the public imperatives of the treaty and the personal rights of conquest claimed by Edward III's captains in the northern and western territories. Henry of Grosmont, under pressure from the captains he had deployed in the occupation of Normandy a few years earlier, insisted that the withdrawals should be seen as voluntary. A handful of English fortune hunters reluctantly transferred allegiance to the Valois in the hope of retaining their possessions. Those who had made their way into Brittany were also causing trouble by raiding across the border into Normandy and Maine: Sir Hugh Calveley captured Bertrand du Guesclin in such an encounter in late 1360. Finally, significant contingents of men from England and Wales, Brittany, Gascony, Navarre, the Low Countries and Germany refused to demobilize and began to re-form themselves into larger forces – the free companies, as they became known – and to run amok across France. By the end of 1360 the self-styled Great Company, which included the famous English captain John Hawkwood, was posing a major threat to Valois positions in the Languedoc and casting greedy eyes on the papal capital of Avignon.[8]

The emergence of the free companies was a sensitive issue for Edward III, who found himself caught between the necessary public condemnation of their actions and a private appreciation of their possible usefulness to his cause. The brigands Matthew Gournay and John St Loo were

[7] 'Ransom of John II'; *EMDP*, I.ii, nos 303, 305; Delachenal, ii, 231–7; Henneman, *Ransom of John II*, 102–22, 161–70; Harriss, *King, Parliament*, 466–508.

[8] Sumption, ii, 455–503; Fowler, *Medieval Mercenaries*, 24–43.

arrested and temporarily imprisoned in the Tower of London in 1361 for their 'contempt and rebellion' against the king, and in 1363 Edward formally denounced Hugh Calveley and James Pipe as being among the most notorious of those who continued illegally to pillage and rob in the kingdom of France.[9] But in new crucibles of conflict the king was quite prepared to condone the actions of the companies. In November 1361 the young duke of Burgundy, Philip de Rouvres, died unexpectedly as a result of a riding accident, leaving no direct heir. Although John II promptly announced that the duchy had fallen, by default, to the French crown, Edward III confirmed the treaty of Guillon and thus restated his commitment to the independence of the duchy.[10] The commanders of the Great Company, quick to spot an opportunity, immediately marched on the area. The prospect of a new war of succession in Burgundy thus raised major issues over the inclination of the English to assist in eradicating the disruptive presence of the *routiers* within the boundaries of France.

It was in relation to the third element of the 1360 settlement, the transfer of sovereignty and the mutual acts of renunciation by Edward III and John the Good, that there emerged the first open conflicts between the courts of Westminster and Paris. In the autumn of 1361 a French delegation arrived in London to request that the English king undertake his renunciation of the rights to the crown of France and to his ancestral lands in Normandy, Maine, Anjou and Touraine. Given John's failure to pay the second instalment of his ransom, such a unilateral demand seemed more than a little impertinent. But since the initial deadline set for the mutual renunciations had now passed, both sides agreed to explore the possibility of revised terms. A number of diplomatic conferences over the winter of 1361–2 facilitated the work of Sir John Chandos in establishing English control over Poitou, Saintonge, Angoumois, Rouergue and the threes dioceses of Périgueux, Cahors and Limoges. But Edward's representatives now also began to insist that the English should have control over the lordship of Belleville in Poitou, which had been reserved under the 1360 agreement, and that the count of Armagnac should be required to do homage to the English king and surrender to him the county of Gaure. Crucially, no revised deadline was agreed for the exchange of renunciations.[11]

From late 1361 Edward III thus began to advertise what had probably been his intention all along: to separate out the agendas of the 1360 settlement and to press on with the fulfilment of the territorial and financial

---

[9] *CPR 1361–4*, 144, 186; *CCR 1360–4*, 299–300; C 76/45, m. 1.

[10] Froissart, vi, 77, 271; *Chronicle of Jean de Venette*, 109. At the time that Philip de Rouvres died, Otto de Grandisson and Jacques de Vienne were in London negotiating a delay in the ransom payment from the duchy, agreed with members of the king's council at Westminster on 19 Nov. 1361: BL, Add. Ch. 1257. Instalments of the ransom continued to be paid until May 1363: Harriss, *King, Parliament*, 492.

[11] 'Some Documents Regarding the Fulfilment of the Treaty of Brétigny', 5–50.

clauses while deliberately prevaricating over the final ratification of the *littere cum clausula c'est assavoir*. The aim, quite blatantly, was to secure those elements of the treaty most advantageous to his side while holding open the claim to the French throne in the hope of making still further territorial gains. This devious strategy became apparent in two initiatives taken during 1361–2: the king's decision to establish, by unilateral diktat, a sovereign regime in greater Aquitaine; and his efforts to undermine the integrity of the 1360 treaty through independent negotiations with the French princes held in England as hostages for John II's ransom.

Ever since the Black Prince's spectacular campaign in south-west France in 1355–6, Edward III's aspirations for the recovery of Plantagenet authority in Aquitaine had probably included the notion that his eldest son might one day act as resident lieutenant of the newly constituted duchy. As such a phenomenon loomed into view in the aftermath of the treaty of Calais, the prince's status as the greatest bachelor of Europe became more and more a focus of ambition for prospective English allies. It was directly in response to the expectation of a Plantagenet presence in the shadow of the Pyrenees that the rival rulers Peter I of Castile and Pere IV of Aragon both avidly sought dynastic matches with the English royal house in 1360–1.[12] To widespread consternation, however, Edward III announced late in 1361 that his son had taken to wife not one of the great princesses of Europe but his own cousin, Joan, the daughter of Edward II's half-brother, Edmund of Kent and, since the death of her brother in 1352, titular countess of Kent in her own right.

By the standards either of the fourteenth or of the twenty-first century, Joan of Kent made an unlikely candidate for princess of Wales. Within the limits of memory, no direct heir to the throne had married an English noblewoman, even one of such esteemed lineage. Furthermore, Joan was no virgin bride but a widow and mother with a colourful marital career already behind her. The court cases in the late 1340s that had seen Joan released by the pope from her marriage to the second earl of Salisbury and handed back to her original fiancé, Thomas Holland, had probably already given her the reputation for sensuality later captured in the partly sardonic nickname of 'Fair Maid of Kent'. Between the confirmation of her marriage to Holland in 1349 and the latter's death in 1360, Joan had borne at least five children, including two sons, Thomas and John, who in the continuing absence of grandsons for Edward III might easily be seen by a wider public as potential cuckoos in the royal nest. Also, the precise circumstances of Joan's engagement with Edward of Woodstock were highly controversial. The couple were forbidden by the laws of consanguinity from marrying without papal licence. But in the spring of 1361

---

[12] Russell, *English Intervention*, 25.

they simply forced the issue by undertaking a preliminary, clandestine wedding in advance of the necessary dispensations – and thus, in the process, potentially managed to offend the principles of all loyal members of the Church.[13]

Contemporary chroniclers, looking askance at these various breaches of convention, assumed not unreasonably that Edward III was embarrassed and angered by his son's irresponsible behaviour in 1361 and remained implacably opposed to such an eccentric match. One French commentator even suggested that Edward of Woodstock's subsequent dispatch to Aquitaine was by way of punishment for this act of disobedience.[14] All of this was grist to the mill of a later, spurious legend that Edward III wished to confound the marriage because he himself had earlier taken Joan as his mistress.[15] That the king was initially frustrated at his son's behaviour is, indeed, scarcely to be doubted. Equally, however, he quickly rationalized the fait accompli and realized its potential as a statement of English independence from both Paris and Avignon. What better way to signal the English crown's equality with that of France than to allow its heir to marry in the same manner as so many recent Capetian and Valois rulers, by taking to wife one of his father's own relatives and subjects? Accordingly, Edward III worked actively with the couple to secure the papal licences needed to legitimize their match, and organized a triumphant wedding ceremony at Windsor castle on 10 October attended by a great array of English royals, lords and prelates.[16] In the process of his negotiations with Avignon, moreover, he managed to persuade Innocent VI that a papal subsidy of £15,000 about to be demanded from the English clergy should actually be diverted into a contribution towards the ransom of John II.[17] At the Cheapside tournament subsequently held by the prince to proclaim

[13] K. P. Wentersdorf, 'The Clandestine Marriages of the Fair Maid of Kent', *JMH*, v (1979), 203–32. For the sexualized nature of Joan's later reputation, see Barber, *Edward, Prince of Wales*, 173–4; Strohm, *Hochon's Arrow*, 48, 175; W. M. Ormrod, 'In Bed with Joan of Kent: The King's Mother and the Peasants' Revolt', *Medieval Women: Texts and Contexts in Late Medieval Britain*, ed. J. Wogan-Browne, R. Voaden, A. Diamond, A. Hutchinson, C. M. Meale and L. Johnson (Turnhout, 2000), 277–92.

[14] *Anon. Cant.*, 116–17; *Polychronicon*, viii, 360; *Chron. QPV*, 123–5.

[15] M. Galway, 'Joan of Kent and the Order of the Garter', *Birmingham Historical Journal*, i (1947), 13–50, attempts to argue the case for the authenticity of this legend.

[16] Nicholas Lovayne was employed twice by the crown to go to the curia, once carrying the prince's petition for this dispensation and once the king's: E 101/314/17; *Foedera*, III.ii, 626; *CPP*, 376; Wentersdorf, 'Clandestine Marriages', 222–3. See also *BPR*, iv, 476. The business of the trips was described in a privy seal writ as 'touching both us and our beloved son the prince of Wales': E 159/138, *Brev. bar.*, Mich., rot. 11d. At the end of his second trip, Lovayne travelled directly to the king at Windsor to bring him news of the grant of the dispensation: Mirot and Déprez, *Ambassades anglaises*, no. 214.

[17] 'Ransom of John II', 13–22; Lunt, *Financial Relations*, ii, 95–103; Wentersdorf, 'Clandestine Marriages', 218, 219. The crown's active engagement in the collection of the subsidy is demonstrated by correspondence with the bishops recorded in E 403/417, 24 Feb. 1364.

the nuptials to the citizens of London, the royal family cocked a snook at continuing clerical sensibilities about the marriage by adopting the notably provocative theme of the Seven Deadly Sins.[18]

It was entirely in line with these statements of self-determination that the king now revealed his plans to settle the prince of Wales as his resident viceroy in Aquitaine. The great tournament hosted by Edward of Woodstock at Smithfield in May 1362 was probably organized in anticipation of just such a statement.[19] When it eventually came, at Westminster Palace on 19 July, there was a surprising dimension to the ceremony. The Black Prince performed homage to his father not as lieutenant or duke, but as prince of Aquitaine: that is, as ruler of an independent territory held under the direct lordship of the crown of England.[20] Here, at last, was the crucial act of defiance which Edward III had been building up to since the sealing of the treaty of Calais, by which he pre-empted the enactment of the renunciation clauses and simply asserted the right to sovereign authority over Aquitaine. The whole manner in which the prince's new title was put in place suggests a deliberate effort to reaffirm, for both domestic and foreign audiences, Edward III's supreme commitment to the positive achievements of the 1360 settlement.

Equally importantly, the dispatch of the new prince of Aquitaine indicated the king's desire to drive the territorial settlement to a speedy conclusion. The prince and his commanders, the earl of Warwick and Sir John Chandos, contracted to take a total of 300 men-at-arms and 400 archers with them; these, together with further forces raised in Gascony, would complete the task of evacuating the territories still occupied by the French and the free companies and thus realize England's long-held dream of control in greater Aquitaine.[21] The victory of Poitiers had given Edward of Woodstock huge political capital among the nobility of Gascony, and the first year of his regime in Aquitaine was organized very deliberately as a means of advertising the positive benefits of Plantagenet rule. Gaston Phoebus, count of Foix, may have refused to give homage for the lordship of Béarn, but the prince achieved some notable success in winning over Jean, count of Armagnac, from his recent dynastic alliance with the Valois.[22]

---

[18] *Foedera*, III.ii, 626–7; *Anon. Cant.*, 118–19; Reading, 151; 'Wigmore Chronicle', 292.

[19] Reading, 152–3; *Anon. Cant.*, 120–1.

[20] *Foedera*, III.ii, 667–70. The original, illuminated deed survives as E 30/1105, reproduced in facsimile in *Foedera*, III.ii, plate opp. 667. For the argument that Edward III may briefly have entertained the notion of establishing Aquitaine as an independent kingdom, see G. Pépin, 'Towards a New Assessment of the Black Prince's Principality of Aquitaine: A Study of the Last Years (1369–1372)', *Nottingham Medieval Studies*, l (2006), 60.

[21] The troop numbers are derived from E 403/411, 26 July 1362. The king paid for a further 200 archers in 1363: E 403/415, 9 May.

[22] P. Capra, 'Les Bases sociales du pouvoir anglo-gascon au milieu du xive siècle', *Le Moyen Age*, lxxxi (1975), 293–9; M. Vale, 'The War in Aquitaine', *Arms, Armies and Fortifications*, ed. Curry and Hughes, 81; Barber, *Edward, Prince of Wales*, 180–1; Green, *Black Prince*, 106–7; Sumption, ii, 494.

Early in 1365, at Angoulême, Princess Joan bore the couple's first child, a boy named, predictably enough, Edward. The celebrations that followed were reported in England as a huge extravaganza, involving a great ten-day sequence of tournaments and feasts attended by a thousand lords and knights.[23] The Chandos Herald later described the prince's honeymoon period in Aquitaine in telling terms: 'All his subjects and his men loved him well, because he did so much good for them.'[24]

If this ambitious programme of reconstruction in Aquitaine had any innate weakness, it was fiscal. Edward III was quite prepared to invest English resources, including the profits of the French royal ransom, in the initial efforts to establish order in the new principality. Thereafter, however, the assumption was that the regime in Aquitaine should be self-supporting.[25] Had Edward of Woodstock chosen to confine his interventions within the borders of his principality, all might have been well. But by 1364 the prince was persuaded to involve himself, as an autonomous power, in disputes in northern France. His first intervention, in sending reinforcements led by the captal de Buch to assist Charles of Navarre's attempts to recover lands in Normandy, ended in disaster; the Anglo-Navarrese army was decisively defeated at the battle of Cocherel on 16 May, the captal was taken prisoner, and Charles II was forced into a humiliating peace with the French crown. Thereafter, English fortunes improved; in September 1364, Sir John Chandos led the combined Breton, English and Gascon forces that won John de Montfort's momentous victory at Auray in Brittany.[26] Either way, however, such adventures had to be subsidized by the available resources of Aquitaine. In 1364 Prince Edward secured consent for the imposition of a *fouage* (hearth tax) throughout his principality. The high rate at which the tax was set, coupled with the problem of enforcing payment in areas claiming privileged status, created considerable frictions. Although Jean of Armagnac realized that the time was not yet right for outright defection, he determinedly resisted the levy of the subsidy in his territories.[27] Edward III's plan to override the delays in Anglo-French diplomacy and create a self-regulating regime in Aquitaine had served only to reveal the continuing difficulties of establishing a stable Plantagenet presence in south-west France.

The second major scheme employed by Edward III in 1361–2 to force the pace in the fulfilment of the treaty of Calais involved the members of the French royal family held as hostages for the settlement in England.

[23] *AC*, 51; *Eulogium*, iii, 236; 'A Fourteenth-Century Chronicle of the Grey Friars of Lynn', ed. A. Gransden, *EHR*, lxxii (1957), 271.

[24] *Vie du Prince Noir*, 92 (ll. 1620–3), translated in *Life and Campaigns*, 105.

[25] *EMDP*, I.ii, no. 305; Harriss, *King, Parliament*, 474–8.

[26] *Vie du Prince Noir*, 93–4 (ll. 1649–68); Green, *Black Prince*, 87, 142 n. 23.

[27] Henneman, *Ransom of John II*, 247–8.

Under the terms of the 1360 settlement, forty nobles and forty leading townsmen of France were to stand surety for John's release and the continuing payment of his ransom. The contingent of French lords dispatched to England during the winter of 1360/1 included four high-ranking princes: John II's second and third sons, Louis of Anjou and John of Berry; his brother Philip, duke of Orléans; and the dauphin's brother-in-law, Louis II, duke of Bourbon.[28] Although these prisoners lived at their own expense, Edward III and Queen Philippa were keen to expose them to the famed generosity of the English court, and laid on lavish feasts and entertainments in their honour.[29] The affections thus forged were, indeed, of lasting consequence: some years later, after his return to France, the duke of Berry was to write personally to Edward and Philippa with the happy news of the birth of a son.[30] It is equally clear, however, that Edward was quite ruthless in his determination to derive full diplomatic benefit from possession of these valuable house guests.

The principal hostages were due to be released by the end of 1361. However, the delays in the delivery of the second instalment of John II's ransom allowed Edward III to insist on redefining the conditions for their release. Full of confident bravado, the king demanded immediate delivery of all of greater Aquitaine, a delay in the evacuation of English-occupied areas, and the remarkable stipulation that John should undertake his own renunciation of sovereignty in advance of Edward's abandonment of the French royal title. When John II's government refused such outrageous demands, the conventions of diplomacy allowed Edward to make his own private settlement with the stranded hostages. On 21 November 1362, Anjou, Berry, Orléans and Bourbon were constrained to seal the so-called treaty of the *fleurs-de-lys*.[31] They and six other nobles would be released on bail. In return, they would negotiate with John to have Edward confirmed in possession of all remaining disputed territories, including Belleville and Gaure, and to be absolved of further responsibility for the expulsion of the English and Gascon garrisons from French lands. The transfers, and the payment of 200,000 *écus* towards the ransom, were to be carried out by 1 November 1363. It was only with regard to the renunciations that Edward would accept a compromise: returning to the spirit of 1360, he stated his agreement to undertake them simultaneously with John II. The Paris administration had no real alternative but to accept this deal and eventually ratified the treaty on 13 March 1363. Two months later, the four

[28] *Foedera*, III.ii, 604; Cazelles, *Jean le Bon et Charles V*, 380–2.

[29] Henneman, *Ransom of John II*, 152–3, 165; Wathey, 'Peace of 1360–1369', 142–3. BL, Add. Ch. 3332 records payment of £300 by the duke of Anjou to Adam Bury of London for the provision of (unspecified) goods for his maintenance.

[30] *Issues*, 190. The duke of Orléans made a gift of a lion and two lionesses to the king's menagerie in the Tower: E 403/422, 10 July 1365.

[31] *Foedera*, III.ii, 681; Froissart, vi, 86–7, 280–1; *Antient Kalendars*, i, 199; Delachenal, iii, 340–1.

French royal dukes were accordingly transferred from Dover to Calais.[32] By a notably dextrous manoeuvre, Edward III had at once brought new pressure to bear for the confirmation of the financial and territorial clauses and successfully modified the terms of the Calais settlement to his own great advantage.

For the French, the treaty of the *fleurs-de-lys* proved no less serious in the breach. In September 1363 the duke of Anjou broke his parole and fled from Calais into France, where he was received by his brother, the dauphin. With a keen understanding of the workings of John II's mind, Edward III declared that such behaviour besmirched the reputation of French chivalry.[33] The dukes of Berry and Orléans stood by their honour and agreed to return to England. But Anjou absconded. At the end of November, John II therefore announced that he must go to England and stand as hostage for his son's bad faith.[34] The French king arrived in London in early January 1364 with a great entourage of 200 people and a gift for Edward of thirty wild boars.[35] John clearly hoped that his presence would be enough to resolve the diplomatic impasse: he wrote 'in his own hand' to Edward III on the subject of the duke of Anjou, and probably made a personal request for the renegotiation of his ransom. But neither Edward nor his subjects were in any mood for compromise.[36] John's health, moreover, was far from robust. On 8 April the worst fears of the French councillors were fulfilled, when their forty-four-year-old king died in London.[37] John the Good's desperate efforts to undo the damage of the treaty of the *fleurs-de-lys* had resulted only in political humiliation and personal tragedy.

The death of John II marked a watershed in Anglo-French relations. Until 1364 Edward III's efforts to establish an enduring peace had been built firmly on the agenda of the treaty of Calais. Even when he extended himself beyond its limits, as in the creation of the principality of Aquitaine and the negotiations with the French hostages, he did so in the main only to apply further pressure for the fulfilment of the agenda of 1360. With John's demise, however, much of the impetus for peace was lost. The new French king, Charles V, did not share his father's sense of personal loyalty to the terms established at Brétigny and Calais. Charles is

---

[32] *Foedera*, III.ii, 685, 694; SC 1/63/220.

[33] *Foedera*, III.ii, 755–7; *Chronicle of Jean de Venette*, 115–16; *Anon. Cant.*, 128–31 and n. 286.

[34] Froissart, vi, 93–4; *Chronicle of Jean de Venette*, 116; *Chron. QPV*, 129–30, 134–5; *Chronique de Richard Lescot*, 159–60; E. Perroy, 'Charles V et le traité de Brétigny', *Le Moyen Age*, xxxviii (1928), 257; Cazelles, *Jean le Bon et Charles V*, 447–8.

[35] *EMDP*, I.ii, no. 326; *Foedera*, III.ii, 718, 719; Froissart, vi, 94; Reading, 162–3; E 403/417, 17 Feb. 1364. An identical gift of wild boars is recorded from Charles V in 1366: *Issues*, 189.

[36] *Antient Kalendars*, i, 201; *Eulogium*, iii, 232; Knighton, 190–1.

[37] *Chronique de Richard Lescot*, 162; *Chron. QPV*, 143; *Chronicle of Jean de Venette*, 120; *Anon. Cant.*, 132–5; 'Wigmore Chronicle', 293. For the obsequies in England see pp. 468–9.

supposed to have declared to his secretary in 1364 that, after bringing home the hostages, he would ally with the Scots and wreak a terrible vengeance on the English in France.[38] In the moment of succession, diplomatic niceties required appropriate expressions of amity. Edward III sent his cousin a set of ceremonial robes, and Charles responded a little later with a gift of the finest wine of Beaune.[39] None of this, however, could disguise the damage inflicted upon Anglo-French relations by John's untimely death. After 1364 Edward III had to accept that the treaty of Calais was unlikely to provide a template for lasting peace, and was increasingly forced to seek out alternative diplomatic strategies designed to minimize the resulting damage and prepare for an eventual renewal of war.

First, however, the king had to turn his attention to the disposition of the British Isles. During the 1360s Edward III made a series of significant statements of intent with regard to his existing lordship of Ireland and his ambitions for the future of Scotland. His aim, as in Aquitaine, was to develop vigorous, self-supporting regimes presided over by resident members of the royal family. There was already an obvious model for such devolved rule in the British Isles, in Edward of Woodstock's principality of Wales and earldom of Chester. Throughout the 1340s and 1350s, the prince's officials had been asserting his rights and authority with the express intention of increasing revenues and thus helping to support the war effort in France.[40] The victims of this bracing regime were rather less inured than their counterparts in England to royal oppression, and Wales and Cheshire witnessed a number of rumoured and attempted revolts in the middle decades of the century. Far from prompting a relaxation of pressure, however, the rumblings simply provided the prince's agents with the excuse to launch further heavy-handed judicial inquiries and levy punitive fines to ensure future good behaviour.[41] Edward of Woodstock's controversial rule in Wales was hardly a prototype for consensual colonial government. But it did appear to suggest that the wider dominions of the English crown might indeed be run in such a way as to make each of them a fully sustainable entity within a larger confederation of Plantagenet states. It was to this beguiling notion that Edward III firmly directed his family policy during the 1360s.

The immediate reason for the dispatch of Prince Lionel to Ireland in 1361–2 was an alarming escalation in the armed resistance put up by the

[38] Delachenal, iii, 551–3. See also *Anon. Cant.*, 136–7.

[39] E 101/394/16, m. 14; *EMDP*, I.ii, no. 413.

[40] R. R. Davies, *Conquest, Coexistence and Change: Wales, 1063–1415* (Oxford, 1987), 401–3; Booth, *Financial Administration*, 133–41; D. Green, *Edward the Black Prince: Power in Medieval Europe* (Harlow, 2007), 190.

[41] *Calendar of Ancient Correspondence Concerning Wales*, 231–5; Booth, 'Taxation and Public Order', 16–31.

Gaelic clans to English rule in the lordship. A great council held at Kilkenny in 1360 had sent Edward III a dire report of the threat thus posed, especially from the mighty MacMurrough alliance in the ancient kingdom of Leinster, and had explicitly demanded the presence of a senior English lord to relieve the desperate situation.[42] Lionel of Antwerp had long been identified as the member of the English royal family most suited to take up command of Ireland. His infant betrothal to Elizabeth de Burgh, heiress to the earldom of Ulster, in 1342, had been proclaimed at the time as a new initiative towards peace in the lordship, and the appointment of Elizabeth's stepfather, Ralph Ufford, as justiciar had seemed at the time as though it were a preparation for the prince's eventual assumption of rule.[43] Lionel's appointment, on 1 July 1361, as lieutenant of Ireland therefore raised considerable excitement on both sides of the seas, heralding it seemed a new stage in the history of Plantagenet rule in the island.[44]

The twenty-two-year-old prince travelled from Liverpool to Dublin in late August 1361 with a force of some 900 men, a plentiful supply of arms and armour for war and the jousts, banners bearing the arms of St George, England and Ulster, a 'little gun' and 16 pounds of gunpowder. The veteran earl of Stafford was sent over to provide much-needed military and political counsel.[45] Lionel's wife transferred to Dublin in the summer of 1362 with a generous dress allowance of £400 from the king; she was to die in Ireland during the winter of 1363–4.[46] Few of those English lords with landed interests in the lordship responded to the royal demand that they serve with Lionel in 1361 or make other arrangements for the defence of their interests in Ireland.[47] But in June 1362, absentees were forced to agree to pay the next two years' issues from their Irish estates for the defence of the lordship. The regular resort to such measures in the mid-1360s revealed a notable new determination on the part of the Westminster government to restore effective authority in Ireland.[48]

[42] SC 8/258/12900, printed in *Parliaments and Councils of Mediaeval Ireland*, ed. H. G. Richardson and G. O. Sayles (Dublin, 1947), 19–22; Frame, *English Lordship*, 318–25. See also the follow-up petition sent to the English parliament in February 1361: SC 8/171/8545; P. M. Connolly, 'Lionel of Clarence and Ireland, 1361–1366' (University of Dublin PhD thesis, 1977), 288.

[43] *Foedera*, II.ii, 1159; Frame, *English Lordship*, 51; Frame, 'Justiciarship of Ralph Ufford', 7–47.

[44] *Foedera*, III.ii, 621–2.

[45] E 101/28/21; E 101/394/2; E 101/396/6; *Handbook and Select Calendar of Sources for Medieval Ireland in the National Archives of the United Kingdom*, ed. P. Dryburgh and B. Smith (Dublin, 2005), 321, 323.

[46] E 403/411, 7 July 1362; E 403/412, 9 Dec. 1362; *Foedera*, III.ii, 704; Reading, 159; Knighton, 190–1; 'Wigmore Chronicle', 293. For her funeral see p. 467.

[47] *CCR 1360–4*, 254, 278, 384.

[48] *RDP*, iv, 627–9; *HBC*, 563 n. 1; *CFR 1356–68*, 244, 303; *CCR 1360–4*, 451; *CCR 1364–8*, 15, 42, 213; *CPR 1364–7*, 35; *Handbook . . . of Sources for Medieval Ireland*, 326–7.

The most obvious sign of this commitment was, of course, the presence of the prince himself. Lionel remained in Ireland until April 1364, and returned to the lordship again from December 1364 to November 1366. Edward III never devolved sovereignty on his second son: Lionel remained lieutenant, rather than prince, of Ireland. But the English and Anglo-Irish elites were well aware that the prince and his young son-in-law, the earl of March, offered the closest thing possible to a lasting vice-regal presence in Dublin. The new status of duke of Clarence bestowed on Lionel, *in absentia*, in the English parliament of 1362 carried an important message about his formal primacy among the resident and absent nobles of Ireland. The major question on all sides was the degree to which his regime might now be brought to emulate the well advertised successes of the Black Prince's rule in Wales and Aquitaine.

In many respects, Edward III could consider Lionel's lieutenancy of Ireland a significant achievement. The MacMurroughs' leader, Art Kavanagh, and his heir, Domhnall Riabhach, were both captured in 1362 and died shortly afterwards in Trim castle.[49] During the prince's absence in 1364, the earl of Ormond also managed temporarily to regain control of the Gaelic-occupied Athlone castle. And in his second residency, Lionel succeeded in re-establishing effective English control throughout much of central and eastern Ireland. The result was an instant and major increase in the revenues of the Dublin treasury.[50] At the English parliament of May 1366 the chancellor, Simon Langham, announced the king's confident expectation that Ireland might once more be profitable to the crown.[51] In point of fact, the aspiration was quite unrealistic: less than a fifth of the cost of English rule was being borne by the ordinary revenues of Ireland, and after 1362 the Irish parliament simply refused to countenance any further requests for extraordinary taxes within the lordship.[52] The pattern already observed in Aquitaine was now being repeated in Ireland, to still more serious effect: initial strong investment followed by over-reliance on fragile local resources served only to compromise efforts towards the effective establishment of colonial rule.[53]

Lionel of Clarence's personal rule was also undermined by the suspicious attitude of the Anglo-Irish establishment. Since the lieutenancy of Ralph Ufford in the 1340s, Edward III had encouraged the earls of Ormond and Kildare to provide loyal and effective leadership in Ireland.

---

[49] *CPR 1361–4*, 368.

[50] P. Connolly, 'The Financing of English Expeditions to Ireland, 1361–1376', *England and Ireland in the Later Middle Ages: Essays in Honour of Jocelyn Otway-Ruthven*, ed. J. Lydon (Blackrock, 1981), 104–11.

[51] *PROME*, v, 192.

[52] Connolly, 'Lionel', 266 calculates that only 17 per cent of recorded expenditure on Lionel's regime in Ireland came from Irish revenues.

[53] J. F. Lydon, *Ireland in the Late Middle Ages* (Dublin, 1973), 97–8; Ormrod, 'The English State and the Plantagenet Empire', 211–12.

In particular, Ormond's appointment as justiciar in 1359 had been taken as an important statement of the crown's new willingness to engage the resident nobility in the running of the lordship.[54] Prince Lionel's arrival seemed to present a direct challenge to this new spirit of autonomy. Fears of an overly intrusive style of government reached a head in 1364, when the prince's paymaster, Walter Dalby, was appointed treasurer of Ireland and many of the existing members of the Dublin administration were replaced by Englishmen. The Anglo-Irish political community appealed over the prince's head, via the earl of Kildare and others, to Edward III, and during the course of the following winter most of the new personnel, including Dalby, had to be dismissed in order to placate public opinion in the lordship.

The most controversial of Lionel's interventions to establish metropolitan authority in the lordship came in 1366, with the notorious Statutes of Kilkenny. This legislative code was an ambitious attempt to address the problem of relations between the 'old English' (residents) and the 'new English' (incomers). Residents loyal to the crown were confirmed as having full legal rights and political status. In return, however, they were required to eschew the Gaelic culture that many of them had openly embraced and to hold faith with the customs of their counterparts in England, practising the gentle arts of archery and tilting, using English names and speaking in the English tongue.[55] Such deeply intrusive regulations carried rather less force at the time than in later cultural clashes between England and Ireland, for neither the duke of Clarence nor his immediate successors showed much commitment to the comprehensive enforcement of the new code. But in hindsight at least, Edward III's decision to recall Prince Lionel late in 1366 seemed like something of a statement of political defeat. Edward's attempt to respond to the concerns of the Anglo-Irish by imposing a programme of vigorous direct rule had simply exacerbated the chronic suspicion that now existed between the polities of Westminster and Dublin, and thus to sour all subsequent efforts towards the settlement of the lordship.

As in Ireland, so in Scotland; the story of Edward III's attempts to further his family's interests within the British Isles during the 1360s followed a pattern of initial high expectation followed by cautious but undeniable retreat. David II's government proved unable or unwilling to meet the ransom terms set by the treaty of Berwick, and after managing to deliver the whole of the first two annual instalments, amounting to a total of £13,333, allowed payments to fall into abeyance

---

[54] Frame, *English Lordship*, 279–80, 282–3, 288–91.
[55] *Statutes and Ordinances . . . of Ireland*, 431–69; S. Duffy, 'The Problem of Degeneracy', *Law and Disorder in Thirteenth-Century Ireland: The Dublin Parliament of 1297*, ed. J. F. Lydon (Dublin, 1997), 86–106; R. R. Davies, 'The Peoples of Britain and Ireland, 1100–1400, III: Laws and Customs', *TRHS*, 6th series, vi (1996), 12–16.

after 1360.[56] Edward III clearly saw this as an opportunity to force the Scots back into negotiation over the final settlement that had eluded him in 1357. This was brought into fresh focus by a sequence of changes in the English and Scottish ruling families. With the death in quick succession of Henry of Grosmont and of his eldest daughter, Maud, countess of Holland and Zeeland, the entirety of the Lancastrian estate devolved upon John of Gaunt who, in November 1362, was duly granted the title of duke of Lancaster. The prodigious wealth of the ducal estate, calculated at around £12,000 a year, might now realistically be made available to support the prince's dynastic ambitions north of the border.[57] Equally, the death in September 1362 of Edward III's sister and David II's wife, Queen Joan, raised the possibility that David might remarry and produce a direct heir. If Edward was ever to gain Scotland for his son, now was the time to act.

In November 1363 the king of Scots and his new queen, Margaret Drummond, travelled to Westminster. At the conference table, Edward III put on a bravura performance. Abandoning the position taken up since 1333, he now demanded the right of direct succession to the Scottish throne, asserting it not for one of the cadet branches of his family but for himself and his heirs in the senior Plantagenet line. In return, he offered to restore the territorial bounds of Scotland as they had existed before his interventions and to compensate from his own resources the English lords dispossessed in Scotland after the 1328 settlement. In arguing that the two realms should be at once under a single ruler and maintain their individual constitutional integrities, the English king was consciously harking back to Edward I's initial attempts to resolve the Scottish succession crisis through the treaty of Birgham of 1290. He was also – though he did not know it – paving the way for the eventual unions of Scotland and England in 1603 and 1707.[58]

It is difficult to take the startling new agenda of 1363 at anything like its face value. Virtually nothing in English military or diplomatic strategy since the battle of Neville's Cross had suggested or warranted such ambition. Like the second treaty of London, the proposals of 1363 acted merely as a timely reminder of Edward's residual rights over the northern kingdom and as a means of applying leverage for an alternative peace.[59] The resort to dynastic formulas did, however, have one notable outcome. David II now repeated the suggestion he had made on a number of

[56] Harriss, *King, Parliament*, 490–1.

[57] S. Walker, *The Lancastrian Affinity, 1361–1399* (Oxford, 1990), 19–20; *ODNB*, xxx, 175. There were rumours among the vulgar sort that Maud had been poisoned in order to free the way for an undivided inheritance: Knighton, 184–5.

[58] *Acts of the Parliaments of Scotland*, i, 492–4; *Foedera*, III.ii, 715–16; A Grant, *Independence and Nationhood: Scotland 1306–1469* (London, 1984), 37–8.

[59] Knighton, 188–9; Penman, *David II*, 308.

occasions in the 1350s, and offered to adopt one of Edward's younger sons – either John of Gaunt or, as some contemporaries now believed, Lionel of Clarence – as his heir.[60] This, however, was to be the last occasion on which Anglo-Scottish diplomacy explicitly addressed this suggestion. Edward's blunt refusal of David's compromise proposal stood as an open admission that the scheme was simply untenable.[61] The Scots certainly thought likewise: the political assembly at Scone in March 1364 roundly condemned David's proposals and stated its strong preference for the recognition of Robert Stewart as heir to the royal title.[62] In 1363–4 Edward III came to the reluctant but realistic conclusion that the personal circumstances of the English and Scottish ruling houses no longer allowed the former to claim direct control over the latter.

The consequences were swift. In the new round of negotiations that opened up in 1365, it was taken for granted that England and Scotland would remain distinct realms under the control of separate ruling houses. The issue was now simply over the degree to which the interim settlement of 1357 remained binding. The English insisted that the ransom payments must be resumed and that the Scots should pay additional compensation for lands still formally claimed by the English crown and the disinherited lords in the Lowlands. At first, David II attempted to wriggle free of continued obligation to his ransom. But the offers that his envoys made in return – aid to Lionel of Clarence in Ireland, and the succession of one of Edward's sons to the Galloway estates of the recently deceased Edward Balliol – were not sufficient to compensate for the loss of potential revenue to the English crown.[63] What emerged was therefore very much a compromise. On 10 May 1365 it was agreed to extend the Anglo-Scottish truce to 1370. David II's ransom would be reinstated and raised from £66,667 to £100,000, but would be paid in much smaller instalments of just £4,000 a year.[64]

This position was not one that either Edward III or David II regarded as satisfactory. But it was the Scots who undoubtedly emerged from the latest encounter with the greater claim to moral victory. They had successfully reduced the burden of the ransom on the kingdom's public finances. With the payment period extending so far beyond the current

[60] 'Question about the Succession', 10, 11–12.

[61] Penman, *David II*, 311, 321.

[62] Fordun, *Chronica*, i, 381–2; Wyntoun, vi, 251–3; Bower, vii, 321–3; 'Question about the Succession', 13, 49; M. Penman, '*Diffinicione successionis ad regnum Scottorum*: Royal Succession in Scotland in the Later Middle Ages', *Making and Breaking the Rules: Succession in Medieval Europe, c.1000–c.1600*, ed. F. Lachaud and M. Penman (Turnhout, 2008), 55–6.

[63] 'Question about the Succession', 13–14; *Acts of the Parliaments of Scotland*, i, 495–6. An older argument that Edward also tried to secure the homage of David II in 1366 is refuted in 'Question about the Succession', 17–18; Penman, *David II*, 345–6.

[64] *CDS*, iv, no. 108; *Foedera*, III.ii, 766, 770; 'Question about the Succession', 15–17; *Issues*, 186; E 403/422, 15 July 1365.

truce, moreover, they were more than likely to be able to find some future pretext for reneging on the whole deal. Edward III's only compensation was that he had not been forced to make a final surrender of sovereignty. He thus resorted to face-saving gestures. In 1367 the English king dismissed the Scottish ambassadors sent to his court since, as he put it, there was no apparent prospect of a final peace. Although David himself planned a further visit south in 1368, the collapse of his marriage to Margaret Drummond and his plans to marry his new mistress, Agnes Dunbar, created too many pressing political issues to allow him to leave the kingdom.[65] Edward held the line on the truce and urged his subjects in the north to show restraint in the face of cross-border raids.[66] But the deterioration of Anglo-French relations in 1368 raised inevitable fears about a revival of the Auld Alliance and added new impediments to ongoing discussions between Plantagenet and Bruce.

Expectations of a final peace with the Scots were probably lower in 1368 than at any point since the treaty of Berwick. Most seriously for Edward III, David II's increasingly open acknowledgement of the likelihood of a Stewart succession had brought an end, once and for all, to the notion that John of Gaunt might one day become king of Scots. Edward's ambition of sharing out the parcels of Britain between his sons and their descendants had always contained an element of fantasy, driven more by the model of King Arthur's alleged achievement of uniting the British Isles than by the real possibility of direct Plantagenet rule. But if the collapse of such hopes in the mid-1360s was a reluctant nod to reality, it hardly lessened Edward's resolve to have the members of his family assume their rightful place as political leaders of Western Christendom. In the short term, in fact, the collapse of his British dream in the mid-1360s merely refocused Edward III's dynastic aspirations on the principalities of continental Europe.

The attempts made by Edward III in the years after the treaty of Calais to draw the great lordships of Brittany, Flanders and Burgundy into the Plantagenet network were a natural continuation of the so-called provincial strategy pursued since the opening stages of the Hundred Years War. In contrast with his increasingly lukewarm attitude to a Plantagenet succession in Scotland, Edward showed great obstinacy in the plans he made after 1361 to plant members of his family in the great principalities that owed allegiance to the crown of France. These manoeuvres were not always easily compatible with the Anglo-French peace, and after 1364 Edward acted disingenuously in insisting that he was still committed to the treaty of Calais. As in his own territory of greater Aquitaine, Edward was

---

[65] Penman, *David II*, 368–9; Penman, '*Diffinicione successionis*', 56.
[66] *The Register of Thomas Appleby, Bishop of Carlisle, 1363–1395*, ed. R. L. Storey (CYS, xcvi, 2006), nos 70, 176.

driven by growing awareness of the unlikelihood of a full confirmation of the 1360 settlement, and thus by the need to establish a pro-English network of allies within an increasingly hostile kingdom of France.

Since their flight from Brittany in 1343, the Countess Jeanne de Montfort and her two children, John and Jeanne, had been residents in England. The two infants were of an age with Edward III's middle children, and were brought up largely in the household of Queen Philippa.[67] John de Montfort made his military debut with Henry of Grosmont in Brittany in 1356–7.[68] He seems to have been unwell at the time of the Reims campaign in 1359–60, but was present at the negotiations at Calais in October 1360 and returned to the continent for discussions on the future of Brittany at a conference at Saint-Omer in the spring of 1361.[69] John was thus set, with full English backing, to resume his father's claim to the duchy of Brittany. A key element in this settlement was John's marriage to Edward's second surviving daughter, Mary of Waltham. The wedding was already planned in 1359–60, when the necessary papal dispensations were being sought, and it took place at Woodstock in June 1361.[70] The sixteen-year-old princess died in England early in the following year, perhaps from the complications of a first pregnancy.[71] But John was persuaded not to remarry without Edward's explicit consent, and remained closely bound to the English court after his return to Brittany in the summer of 1362.[72]

It was against the terms of the Anglo-French peace for Edward III to reassert the feudal suzerainty that he had claimed over Duke John's father in 1342. But Edward's particular determination to keep Brittany within his orbit resulted in an independent bilateral treaty of alliance between king and duke in 1362.[73] It was with the assistance of Lord Latimer, the former royal lieutenant in the duchy, that John accordingly set about defeating his rivals, Joan of Penthièvre and her husband Charles of Blois for the ducal title. At Auray on 29 September 1364 John achieved the definitive victory that his supporters had so long sought. Blois was defeated and killed on the field. His two sons, John and Guy de Bretagne, had already been

[67] Jones, *Ducal Brittany*, 16; SAL, MS 208, fols 3–3v; JRUL, MS Latin 326, fols 2, 2v, 5, 5v, 6v.

[68] *AC*, 48; E 403/396, 11 July 1359.

[69] E 101/393/11, fol. 63r (a litter and other 'instruments' provided for the duke, described as infirm); E 403/401, 4 July 1360; E 403/405, 20 Feb. 1361; E 101/393/11, fol. 64r; E 101/393/15, mm. 4–5; *Foedera*, III.i, 607, 608, 612; E 101/314/16; E 372/206, rot. 43; Jones, *Ducal Brittany*, 15, 40.

[70] E 101/393/11, fol. 64; E 101/393/15, m. 4; GEC, x, 823; Green, *Lives of the Princesses*, iii, 286–7. Assuming the king's presence, the date of the wedding can probably be identified as 13 June: C 81/1334/16; *CPR 1361–4*, 29, 32.

[71] Walsingham, *Chronicon Angliae*, 19; Reading, 150.

[72] *Foedera*, III.i, 662–4. A prest of 2,000 marks was paid to the duke in preparation for his departure to Brittany on 26 July 1362: E 403/411.

[73] *Foedera*, III.ii, 662.

surrendered up to the king of England as hostages for their father's ransom in 1356, and Edward was certainly not about to compromise Montfort's interests by releasing them. Indeed, they remained in custody in England for the rest of the reign and long beyond.[74] The new French king Charles V had no choice but to renounce Valois support for the cause of Joan of Penthièvre and, by the treaty of Guérande of April 1365, to recognize Montfort as duke of Brittany.

This recognition came, as ever, at a price, for Charles expected John to perform homage. But Montfort proved worthy of his kinship with Edward III. Having first prevaricated over the ceremony, he then insisted that his homage ought to be considered simple rather than liege.[75] Edward therefore had every expectation that Brittany would remain loyal to his cause. In January 1366 he invited his former son-in-law to spend the coming hunting season with him, rather presumptuously suggesting that 'two or three good and loyal Englishmen' could be deputed to look after the duchy in the interim.[76] Within a short while of the treaty of Guérande, the new duke asserted his independence of Valois suzerainty by making an alliance of mutual support with Edward of Woodstock as prince of Aquitaine. And in the spring of 1366 John actually married the Black Prince's step-daughter, Joan Holland. Edward III's scheme for a dynastic alliance with Brittany thus seemed to have reached an advanced stage of development, fixing itself firmly in the hearts both of the king and, equally significantly, of his heir.

It was this successful application of the dynastic formula that led Edward III to believe that he might achieve similar independent alliances with Burgundy and Flanders.[77] The death of Philip of Rouvres in 1361 had created an undignified scramble both for the vacant duchy of Burgundy and for possession of Philip's widow, the ten-year-old Margaret of Flanders. Margaret was the sole heiress to three great agglomerations of titles: through her father, Louis de Mâle, to Flanders, Nevers and Rethel; through her mother, Margaret of Brabant, to Brabant and Limburg; and through her grandmother, Margaret of France, to Artois and the county of Burgundy (a separate palatinate within the empire, distinct from the duchy of Burgundy itself). Not surprisingly, John II moved with alacrity to claim Margaret's hand for his youngest son, Philip, duke of Touraine, later known as Philip the Bold.[78] The threat thus posed to English interests – especially, in immediate terms, to the security of

---

[74] E 364/7, rot. 1d; Jones, *Ducal Brittany*, 20, 64, 85.

[75] Jones, *Ducal Brittany*, 19.

[76] *EMDP*, I.i, no. 72.

[77] For what follows, see J. J. N. Palmer, 'England, France, the Papacy and the Flemish Succession, 1361–9', *JMH*, ii (1976), 339–64. My interpretations, however, sometimes differ significantly from Palmer's.

[78] *Chronique de Richard Lescot*, 151.

Calais – required Edward III to take action, and in the winter of 1361–2 the English king launched a counter-bid for Margaret's marriage to his fourth surviving son, Edmund of Langley.[79] Realizing the advantages to be had from some calculated fence-sitting, Louis de Mâle sought to make the rivals for his daughter's hand work exceptionally hard to win his favour. The decision by Edward III's government to move the English wool staple to Calais in 1363 represented one of many Plantagenet manoeuvres towards this tantalizing end.[80] In June 1363, however, John II asserted the obvious advantages of a Valois match by declaring the duchy of Burgundy an apanage of the French crown and devolving it directly on Philip.[81] If Philip were indeed to marry Margaret, Edward III and his successors would face the unsettling prospect of a newly powerful and hostile Valois presence both in Burgundy and in Flanders.

Edward retaliated with some quick-footed diplomacy. Nicholas Lovayne was sent to the curia in September 1363 to open negotiations for the papal dispensation that would allow a marriage between Edmund and Margaret. Shortly after John II's death in the spring of 1364, the English king also dispatched two successive embassies to Calais, the first led by the bishop of London and the second by John of Gaunt, to discuss and agree a dynastic alliance with Flanders.[82] In October the court moved down to Kent to prepare for the ceremonies of confirmation, and Louis de Mâle crossed the narrow seas to meet Edward at Dover. After travelling up to Canterbury to make common oblations at the tomb of Becket, the two men returned to Dover where, on 19 October, in the presence of the princes John and Edmund and the earl of Arundel, they set their seals to the new treaty.[83] The terms made for dramatic reading. Edmund of Langley would be assigned all of the Plantagenet possessions left in northern France after the settlement of 1360 – Calais, Marck, Guînes and Ponthieu – along with Queen Philippa's claims to a third of the territories of her deceased brother, the count of Hainault.[84] Even more astonishingly, the whole of the newly constituted principality forged by the marriage of Margaret and Edmund would in future be held as a fief of the English crown. In one brilliant stroke, Edward had outflanked the Valois and subverted the peace of 1360 by asserting that it was England, not France, that would act as suzerain of the great power bloc set to emerge around the county of Flanders. It was certainly no surprise to hear that Edward,

[79] Foedera, III.ii, 636.

[80] See pp. 482–3.

[81] R. Vaughan, Philip the Bold: The Formation of the Burgundian State, new edn (Woodbridge, 2002), 3; P. Contamine, Des Pouvoirs en France, 1300–1500 (Paris, 1992), 63–4.

[82] E 101/314/27, 31–4; Foedera, III.ii, 709, 744; E 403/418, 17 July, 22 July, 26 Aug. 1364; E 403/421, 12 Nov., 27 Nov. 1364; Issues, 187.

[83] Foedera, III.ii, 750–1; Anon. Cant., 140–3. For exchanges of gifts on this occasion see E 403/421, 31 Oct., 10 Dec. 1364; Issues, 185–6.

[84] Trautz, Könige von England, 390–3.

Count Louis and their supporters ended the talks in an all-night drinking session.[85]

In almost every respect, however, the treaty of Dover represented a serious liability to the English cause. It was all very well arguing that the creation of a new Anglo-Flemish state on the other side of the North Sea might justify the handsome subsidies that Edward now promised the count. But it was quite another thing to persuade the English polity that the town of Calais should be handed over to such an unreliable ally as Louis de Mâle. Even Edward's counsellors and family members seem to have expressed misgivings.[86] In the course of the summer of 1364, the Black Prince had already been apprised that Charles V was trying to force his own alliance with Louis.[87] Following the ratification of the treaty, in December, Charles went public on such plans by marrying his sister Marie to Robert, duke of Bar, the man who, if succession in the male line were to be enforced, would be next in line to the county of Flanders. A letter sent by Edward III to Pope Urban V expresses the deep frustration that the king felt over such manoeuvres: if the pope had granted a dispensation to allow this marriage, how could he possibly withhold his consent in the case of Edmund and Margaret?[88] Far from revealing the strength of Edward's position in the autumn of 1364, then, the treaty of Dover reflected the increasingly desperate attempts that the English crown was being forced to make in order to confound the Valois takeover of Burgundy and Flanders.

Not surprisingly, Edward III proved notably coy about revealing too much to his own subjects about the recent Anglo-Flemish rapprochement. In spite of intense pressure from Westminster, the pope eventually announced himself implacably opposed to the marriage of Edmund and Margaret in December 1364.[89] Edward tried, with increasing desperation, to assure Count Louis that all might yet be well.[90] Meanwhile he sought to take revenge on the obstructive Urban V. Severe reprisals were ordered against Avignon, including a prohibition on the bringing of injurious papal bulls into England and a ban on the export of English money to the

---

[85] Reading, 220.

[86] Special meetings of the council, attended by the duke of Lancaster and Bishop Edington, were held at Westminster on 8 and 12 Nov. to discuss 'secret business': E 403/421, 16 Nov. 1364.

[87] Delachenal, iii, 551–4, analysed by Palmer, 'England, France', 351–2.

[88] BL, Add. MS 24062, fols 186v–187r.

[89] Mirot and Déprez, *Ambassades anglaises*, nos 238, 240, 242–3; E 372/209, rot. 51; *Foedera*, III.ii, 941.

[90] *EMDP*, I.ii, no. 260; Mirot and Déprez, *Ambassades anglaises*, nos 244–5, 248–9, 251, 254, 256; *Foedera*, III.ii, 758, 761; E 403/422, 13 June, 28 Aug. 1365; E 403/425, 30 Oct., 19 Nov. 1365. For a short time in the spring of 1365 it seemed possible that Charles V might concur with the Emperor Charles IV's plan to marry Elizabeth of Slavonia, niece of the king of Hungary, to Philip of Burgundy: Delachenal, iii, 220.

curia.[91] The publication of recent papal legislation against the holding of church offices in plurality was also prohibited, much to the relief of many of the king's own civil servants.[92] The parliament that met at Westminster in January 1365 enthusiastically endorsed such policies by confirming the Statutes of Provisors and Praemunire. Even so, the king did not apparently dare to share with the rank and file of the parliamentary estates the controversial details of his attempted alliance with the Flemish.[93] After 1365 the treaty of Dover gradually became the dominant feature of Edward's policy, as he strove to confound the machinations of Charles V and to realize at least an element of his own dynastic imperialism. Ironically, most people in England did not appreciate the liabilities involved in such an enterprise until it had already collapsed and the realm was once more embarked on full-scale war with France.[94]

Throughout the mid-1360s the pressing issue of John II's ransom remained central to the course of Anglo-French diplomacy. Charles V later claimed that he had paid a total of just under 600,000 écus between his accession in 1364 and the reopening of war in 1369.[95] There is a strong suspicion, however, that the French double-counted some of the payments. The English records (which may, of course, be similarly biased) suggest that the Valois delivered no more than 292,000 écus to Edward III between 1364 and 1369. This lower figure would bring the grand total of the ransom payments between 1360 and 1369 to just 1,291,200 écus, or some £215,200. Whichever side we believe, it is obvious that Charles allowed the arrears to accumulate at a significantly faster rate than his father.[96] Neither Edward nor Charles necessarily saw the falling away of the ransom as reason in itself for a return to open hostilities. Rather, the drying up of supplies was simply taken by Edward's government as yet more evidence of Charles's wilful determination to undermine the settlement of 1360 and challenge Edward's remaining authority and influence within the kingdom of France.

[91] J. J. N. Palmer and A. P. Wells, 'Ecclesiastical Reform and the Politics of the Hundred Years War during the Pontificate of Urban V (1362–70)', *War, Literature and Politics in the Late Middle Ages*, ed. C. T. Allmand (Liverpool, 1976), 169–89.

[92] Heath, *Church and Realm*, 133–4.

[93] *PROME*, v, 172–3, 176, 177–81; *SR*, i, 385–7. E 403/421, 22 Feb. 1365, records a three-day meeting of the council at the end of parliament (which was dismissed on 17 Feb.), attended by the chancellor and treasurer, the duke of Lancaster, the bishop of Winchester, the earls of Arundel and Hereford and 'other lords'; it may have been at this meeting, rather than in plenary session of parliament, that the details of diplomacy were discussed.

[94] Among the chronicles, *Eulogium*, iii, 235, 237, provides some references to the Anglo-Flemish treaty, but only *Anon. Cant.*, 140–3, grasps the detail. Froissart, vi, 80–1, 274, clearly understood the significance of the marriage plan.

[95] Delachenal, ii, 325–31.

[96] 'Ransom of John II', ix–xiv, 37–8.

For some while, Edward III was content to play out the issue of the ransom chiefly in relation to the ongoing question of the princely hostages. After 1364 the dukes of Berry, Orléans and Bourbon were allowed periodic passes to travel to France, but otherwise remained firmly bound by their bond.[97] The collapse of the treaty of the *fleurs-de-lys* allowed Edward III to take control of Orléans's lordships of Chizé, Melle, Civray and Villeneuve-la-Comtesse in Saintonge, and in late 1364 he had the duke make these over to the youngest of the Plantagenet princes, Thomas of Woodstock.[98] In January 1366, when the English and French kings agreed to an adjudication of their continuing dispute over Belleville, Edward finally allowed for the conditional release of the hostages. But he was adamant that none of these arrangements excused the French from continued commitment to the ransom, and pointedly asked what Charles was going to do to address the arrears.[99]

The summit conference on the future of Belleville was an important admission by both sides of the many unresolved issues that remained over the settlement of 1360. Later in 1366, a similar tribunal was established at Montreuil-sur-Mer to determine whether certain lands held by tenants of John of Artois, count of Eu, ought to be included within Edward's county of Ponthieu or remain in subjection to the king of France.[100] It is hard to escape the conclusion, however, that both Charles and Edward saw such processes simply as another means of avoiding the more intractable elements in the treaty of Calais. In 1366–8, while agreeing repeatedly to extend the deadline for the resolution of the dispute over Belleville, Edward was already making advanced preparations for war by rebuilding and garrisoning his castles in Ponthieu and the pale of Calais.[101] In this stand-off, substantive diplomacy was almost completely halted.[102] Edward's regular envoy to Paris, Nicholas Louth, receiver of Ponthieu, was confined to ceremonial and shopping duties, delivering a gift of salt

---

[97] Delachenal, iii, 19; iv, 224–5; *Chron. J&C*, i, 343; *Foedera*, III.ii, 768, 772, 782–3, 814; *Antient Kalendars*, i, 210, 211; *Issues*, 184. In 1367 the English chancery made a number of exemplifications of the oaths undertaken by John II and the dauphin in 1360 to uphold the terms agreed at Brétigny: *Foedera*, III.ii, 819, 829.

[98] Delachenal, ii, 340–1; *Foedera*, III.ii, 758–9; *Antient Kalendars*, i, 205, 209. Sir John Chandos took control of these lands in 1365, and William Seriz 'laboured' there for the prince's interests in the mid-1360s: E 30/1509; E 36/81; *Foedera*, III.ii, 796; E 159/143, *Brev. bar.*, Trin., rot. 2. The Black Prince commissioned John of Gaunt and Edmund of Langley to take Thomas of Woodstock's homage for the lordships in 1368: DL 41/412. The possessions were lost after the fall of La Rochelle in 1372: SC 8/227/11327.

[99] *EMDP*, I.ii, nos 307, 359; *Foedera*, III.ii, 781–3, 785, 826–7; C 76/49, mm. 17, 13; Perroy, 'Charles V', 259.

[100] C 76/49, mm. 10, 8.

[101] *Foedera*, III.ii, 826–7, 832, 841; C 76/49, mm. 7, 6, 4, 3; C 76/50, m. 11.

[102] Mirot and Déprez, *Ambassades anglaises*, 35–7. In 1368 there was a minor quickening of activity, including the dispatch of personal letters from Edward III to Charles V: E 101/315/27–9; E 364/17, m. D.

venison to the French king and making purchases of the expensive walnut oil so much prized at Edward's table.[103] Until such time as a new provocation might arise, the courts of England and France seemed content to sit out the impasse in an interminable round of meaningless niceties.

In 1365 an opportunity arose to redirect the conflict towards a new arena and play out the Anglo-French dispute within the civil war that had begun in the kingdom of Castile. Peter I of Castile, known to posterity as the Cruel, was engaged in a major dispute with his bastard brother, Henry of Trastamara, over their rival claims to the throne. Since Peter was firmly allied to the English cause under the terms of a treaty established in June 1362,[104] Henry was almost bound to seek alliance with the French. It was with support provided by Charles V, along with Pere IV of Aragon and Charles II of Navarre, that Henry duly set about a military operation in Castile. The Valois regime wanted to use the new conflict as a means of clearing the free companies from French soil, and as a consequence a number of English freelance captains, including Matthew Gournay and Hugh Calveley, now combined forces with their erstwhile enemy, Bertrand du Guesclin. By the spring of 1366 Trastamara had taken control of his brother's throne and established a pro-Valois presence south of the Pyrenees. The implications for Anglo-French relations were profound. Up to 1364 it was Edward III who had set the diplomatic pace, pushing the French to confirm their half of the 1360 settlement before he was required to fulfil his own. By 1366 the position in Castile seemed set to reverse that state and to give Charles V the powerful negotiating position he needed to force a new settlement upon the English.

It says something for Edward III's understanding of the dangers involved that he considered for so long a direct involvement in the war in Castile. The presence of some of his own subjects in du Guesclin's invasion force was no doubt an embarrassment to the English king and called for deft repositioning. For some while, there were serious attempts to develop alternative diplomatic strategies that might better suit the overall English cause. In July 1365, at an ostentatious ceremony held at Windsor castle, the thirty-three-year-old English Princess Isabella was married to one of the former French hostages, the young Enguerrand, lord of Coucy, who was subsequently created earl of Bedford.[105] Long tradition has it that this, like the marriage of the Black Prince and Joan of Kent, was a love match condoned by an over-indulgent royal father. But it also had very serious diplomatic intent. Coucy had defected from the Valois allegiance after the collapse of the treaty of the *fleurs-de-lys* and, by performing

[103] E 159/144, *Brev. bar.*, Mich., rots 12d, 13d, 15; E 159/146, *Brev. bar.*, Mich., rot. 8.

[104] *Foedera*, III.ii, 656–8; *EMDP*, II.ii, no. 259; *Antient Kalendars*, i, 197. For what follows see Russell, *English Intervention*, 1–81.

[105] *PROME*, v, 196; *CChR 1341–1417*, 193; Reading, 170; *Eulogium*, iii, 236; *Polychronicon*, viii, 365.

homage to Edward, had successfully re-established his family's ancient rights to important estates in the north of England.[106] Edward also now managed to secure Charles V's permission to have the county of Soissons transferred to Coucy and held under the suzerainty of the English, rather than the French, crown.[107] Like John of Brittany's successive marriages to members of the Plantagenet clan, then, Enguerrand de Coucy's match with Princess Isabella stood as a striking statement of Edward III's continuing ability to draw members of the French nobility into his own allegiance and thus to challenge the moral and constitutional authority of the Valois monarchy.

It was to provide a similar test of French authority that Edward now pressed ahead, with renewed determination, in the matter of the Flemish marriage. In October–November 1365, John of Gaunt was dispatched to Calais with Prince Edmund. Edward III was evidently gambling on being able to persuade Louis de Mâle into a preliminary betrothal ceremony that would exert the necessary moral pressure upon the papacy to grant the much-delayed dispensation.[108] Louis had urgent considerations of his own: those of the free companies that had not signed up to the new hostilities in Castile were posing a severe threat to his daughter's claimed territories in and around the imperial county of Burgundy. Although he balked at the idea of a pre-emptive betrothal, Louis was therefore prepared to render himself indebted to Edward for assistance in forcing the companies out of Rethel, Nevers and Burgundy.[109] The consequence of this pragmatic alliance was a series of joint Anglo-Flemish communiqués to Paris and Avignon stating that continued refusal to license the wedding of Edmund and Margaret would be taken as direct justification for open war.

As if to prepare for that eventuality, Edward now began to reconstruct at least part of his former network of alliances with the princes of the empire.[110] Queen Philippa's nephew, Albert, duke of Bavaria, who was lieutenant for his brother William, count of Holland, was encouraged away from a French alliance and invited to England on several occasions

---

[106] *CPR 1361–4*, 427; *CPR 1364–7*, 190; *Foedera*, III.ii, 773. At the same time Coucy also asserted his right to lands in Roxburghshire and Berwickshire: SC 8/192/9591. The relevant English estates were in the hands of Sir John Coupland (d. 1363) and his wife Joan (d. 1375). In 1367, Coucy granted the reversion back to the king, but this may only have been intended to protect the integrity of the estates, since Edward honoured the original arrangements and delivered them to Coucy on Joan Coupland's death: *CCR 1364–8*, 403–4; *CFR 1368–77*, 323; *CPR 1374–7*, 144–5.

[107] Sumption, iii, 244–6.

[108] E 159/142, *Brev. bar.*, Mich., rot. 29; E 403/425, 6 Dec. 1365. *Eulogium*, iii, 237, places this episode 'after Christmas'. The Black Prince gave his consent to the expected marriage in May: *Antient Kalendars*, i, 208.

[109] *Foedera*, III.ii, 777; A. D. Carr, *Owen of Wales: The End of the House of Gwynedd* (Cardiff, 1991), 22. For the draft of a personal letter from the king to Ieuan Wyn, then serving as one of the commissioners for the evacuation, see C 81/908/27.

[110] Trautz, *Könige von England*, 388–402; *EMDP*, I.i, no. 24.

to discuss a lasting solution to Philippa's own claims on the Hainault inheritance.[111] In June 1366 another of the queen's nephews, William II, duke of Juliers, visited England and, in return for a handsome subsidy, did homage to Edward III in a grand ceremony at Westminster Palace.[112] Urban V's threat to excommunicate Edward III late in 1365 was taken as a pretext for further hostile gestures towards Avignon.[113] The pope's recent ill-judged demand for the payment of the annual census known as Peter's Pence prompted the crown to return to demands made by the commons back in 1358 and formally to repudiate the feudal suzerainty asserted by Innocent III over King John.[114] At the same time, major preparations were put in place for the defence of England in the event of imminent hostilities.[115] Edward III was continuing, with some success, to mobilize the prejudices of his own subjects in the service of his still semi-secret plan to outmanoeuvre Charles V and take over the county of Flanders.

Ultimately, however, this continued focus on the politics of north-western Europe could not wholly prevent the English from becoming embroiled in the war in Castile. Some time before December 1365 Peter I sent one of his prominent advisers, Martin Lopez of Cordoba, to Edward's court, charged to offer any or all of Peter's three young daughters as brides for available English princes.[116] Although this proposal was rebuffed, it heralded a sequence of dynastic alliances that would have far-reaching political repercussions in Iberia during the 1370s and 1380s. In the summer of 1366 preparations were being made in England to raise a small army under John of Gaunt that might proceed to Aquitaine and make common cause with the Black Prince against the French and Aragonese supporters of Henry of Trastamara. In August, Peter the Cruel and his entourage arrived in Gascony requesting refuge and aid. Among the many temptations that the deposed monarch laid out before the Black Prince was an offer to install the young Edward of Angoulême as titular king of Galicia.[117] The council at Bordeaux, like its counterpart at

[111] *CPR 1361–4*, 26, 96, 125, 191, 247, 416; *CPR 1367–70*, 55; Reading, 170–1.

[112] C 47/28/6, no. 13; C 47/30/8, nos 5–9; *Foedera*, III.ii, 791–4; E 403/427, 9 June 1366; *Antient Kalendars*, i, 208–9. William's father had died in 1361; his title of earl of Cambridge had been granted to Edmund of Langley in 1362, and William II formally renounced his claims to the title during the visit of 1366: GEC, ii, 493.

[113] These are likely to have been the subject of discussion at the great council called for Jan. 1366: E 403/425, 6 Dec. 1365.

[114] *PROME*, v, 190, 193–4; *Eulogium*, iii, 239; Reading, 171; *Brut*, ii, 316; Palmer, 'England, France', 355. While the tribute of 1,000 marks associated with the papal suzerainty was thus also repudiated, Peter's Pence itself continued to be collected in England after 1366 and was only finally abolished under Henry VIII: Lunt, *Financial Relations*, ii, 6–25; McKisack, *Fourteenth Century*, 283–4.

[115] *CPR 1364–7*, 364–6, 430–2; *CCR 1364–8*, 370–1; Palmer, 'England, France', 355.

[116] Russell, *English Intervention*, 37–9.

[117] Reading, 174–5; Green, *Black Prince*, 93.

Westminster, remained ambivalent. But the prince was fully persuaded that Peter deserved his support against an illegitimate rival and unjust usurper.[118] There followed some delicate communications between the two Edwards in which the prince's envoy, Aquitaine Herald, played a crucial role.[119] The king was prepared to license his son's invasion of Castile, but would provide no direct financial support from England. When Edward of Woodstock met with Charles the Bad and Peter I at Libourne in September 1366, he was therefore careful to set stringent financial conditions. Peter would have to pay all the costs of the impending campaign of reconquest and, in due course, cede to his allies some small but significant territories in the far north-east of Spain.[120]

Shortly after the birth of his second son, Richard of Bordeaux, in January 1367, the Black Prince set out for Castile. John of Gaunt, who had left England in November, had taken the land route through Normandy and Poitou and met up with his brother at Dax. The assembled force was dominated by the Gascon retinues led by the count of Armagnac, the lord of Albret and the captal de Buch, together with a cluster of free companies recently recruited by Sir John Chandos. All told, there may have been as many as 8,500 men.[121] Since Henry of Trastamara had already dismissed most of the English captains and troops recruited for his recent coup, the prince of Wales was relieved of the prospect of making war against his father's own subjects, and quickly recruited the nimble Hugh Calveley to make a march on Pamplona and cajole Charles of Navarre into some form of co-operation. As yet, Charles was reluctant to offer any material support, but the show of force was enough to persuade him to allow the Anglo-Gascon army to pass undisturbed through his kingdom en route for Castile.

After avoiding battle for some time, Trastamara eventually met his enemies on the field at Nájera on 3 April. Henry had the support of prominent French commanders in the persons of the Marshal Audrehem and Bertrand du Guesclin. Seasoned in the Anglo-French encounters of the previous decade, these men sought to emulate the tactics of Edward III by taking up a defensive position and trying to force the English to attack. But the Black Prince's unexpected decision to move his army to face the left flank of the Franco-Castilian forces required du Guesclin to undertake an emergency regrouping, and in the panic that followed it was decided to launch a cavalry charge against the English vanguard. This advance force was quickly cut off and sustained terrible casualties. The rest of Trastamara's army showed itself either unable or unwilling to move forward, and simply fled the field. The formal fight thus quickly over, the English gave themselves enthusiastically to the task of collecting

---

[118] Froissart, vi, 204–9, 366–7; *Vie du Prince Noir*, 99–102 (ll. 1867–64).
[119] E 403/429, 23 Nov. 1366.
[120] *Foedera*, III.ii, 800–6.
[121] Barber, *Edward, Prince of Wales*, 194; Green, *Black Prince*, 95.

and redistributing their prisoners. Prince Edward claimed du Guesclin for himself. The count of Denia, captured by the English esquire Robert Hawley and his follower Richard Henry, offered a particularly attractive proposition for ransoming, and was bought up first by the Black Prince and subsequently by Edward III.[122] Henry of Trastamara himself managed to escape and fled temporarily to France. A few days after the battle of Nájera Peter I was symbolically reinstated at Burgos as king of Castile. Edward of Woodstock wrote to Princess Joan with an account of his safe delivery, and immediately dispatched messengers to his father to announce the victory.[123] Queen Philippa's harper, Massyet, who was with the prince, later returned to England with news of his progress, and one of the prince's valets brought back the dramatic trophy of a horse seized from Henry the Bastard.[124]

The battle of Nájera was soon to be appropriated by English chroniclers and poets as another great military achievement for the English and a third proof, after Crécy and Poitiers, of the Black Prince's miraculous invincibility in war. 'The greatest battle to be fought in our days' is how Knighton summarized the event; Froissart hailed the victorious prince as 'the flower of all the chivalry of the world'.[125] The immediate outcomes, however, were rather less glorious. When the Anglo-Gascon forces eventually left Castile in September 1367 they were out of pocket, hungry and, in a number of cases, incapacitated by malaria and dysentery. The prince himself seems never fully to have recovered from the illnesses he contracted during this campaign.[126] Meanwhile, Henry of Trastamara had already made his way back to his brother's kingdom. In August 1367 he entered into a new alliance with the duke of Anjou at Aigues-Mortes in order to make common cause against those 'sons of Satan', the Black Prince and Charles the Bad.[127] And in the following summer he renewed his alliance with Charles V.[128] Edward of Woodstock had now to face the cheerless prospect of involvement in an altogether more protracted and expensive civil war for the crown of Castile.

The particular challenge of paying for his recent intervention south of the Pyrenees also served to expose the existing fiscal and political

[122] E. Perroy, 'Gras profits et rançons pendant la Guerre de Cent Ans: L'affaire du comte de Denia', *Mélanges d'histoire du moyen âge dédiés à la mémoire de Louis Halphen* (Paris, 1951), 573–80; A. Rogers, 'Hoton versus Shakell: A Ransom Case in the Court of Chivalry, 1390–5', *Nottingham Mediaeval Studies*, vi (1962), 74–108; vii (1963), 53–78.

[123] SC 1/42/33, printed in 'A Letter of Edward the Black Prince Describing the Battle of Nájera in 1367', ed. A. E. Prince, *EHR*, lxi (1926), 415–18; *AC*, 171; *Foedera*, III.ii, 825.

[124] E 403/433, 2 Dec. 1367; *Issues*, 191.

[125] Knighton, 194–5; Froissart, vii, 52–4. See also *AC*, 53–5; *Anon. Cant.*, 150–1; Reading, 182–5; *Political Poems*, i, 94–6; *Polychronicon*, viii, 367; *Brut*, ii, 318.

[126] *Vie du Prince Noir*, 153–4 (ll. 3815–38); *AC*, 56.

[127] Delachenal, iii, 557–62.

[128] *Foedera*, III.ii, 850–2.

fragilities of the prince's regime in Aquitaine. Caught between his father's continued refusal to subsidize the Castilian venture and the demands of his own lords for payment of war wages, Edward of Woodstock was forced to summon a meeting of the Estates of Aquitaine at Angoulême in January 1368 and to request an unprecedented five-year *fouage*. The assembly conceded, but only in return for a charter which promised that the tax would not be taken as a precedent and guaranteed the privileges of the lords and towns of the principality.[129] This crisis of resources would force the English crown to admit that the Black Prince's regime could no longer be entirely self-supporting and to send over a series of subsidies to the hard-pressed administration at Bordeaux.[130] But the political tensions created by the new *fouage* proved still more intractable. There was now an acknowledged incompatibility between the sovereign rule of the prince and the immunities and exemptions so dear to the lords of eastern Aquitaine. It was the decision of Charles V once more to intervene in the resulting jurisdictional disputes within the principality that was destined to prompt the return to full-scale war between England and France in 1369.

Yet in the immediate aftermath of the battle of Nájera it was the matter of the Flemish succession that seemed most likely to provoke renewed hostilities. On 17 April 1367, Urban V made what was perhaps the key diplomatic decision of the entire decade, by granting the dispensation that would allow Margaret of Flanders to be married not to Edmund of Langley but to the French prince Philip of Burgundy.[131] Louis de Mâle had already been showing signs of reluctance to pursue the English alliance, and the pope's provocative siding with Charles V ought to have been sufficient to persuade Edward III that he should simply cut his losses and abandon the enterprise. Over the previous year, however, Edward had begun to invest the futures of several of his sons in the continuing campaign for an Anglo-Flemish alliance. The decision to press the ancient claims of the house of Lancaster to territorial rights in Provence was a deliberate attempt to threaten the stability of the curia at Avignon.[132] More startlingly still, Edward's decision to withdraw Lionel of Clarence from Ireland and embroil him in a war with the papacy in far-off Italy revealed the extent to which the king was now prepared to compromise the security of his existing dominions for the increasingly desperate pursuit of the Flemish marriage.

[129] Barber, *Edward, Prince of Wales*, 210–11.

[130] It is possible that some of the payments that Charles V claimed to have made towards his father's ransom and which were denied by the English exchequer had in fact been diverted by Edward III into funding for the prince's campaign in Castile: Harriss, *King, Parliament*, 499.

[131] Delachenal, iii, 505.

[132] *Foedera*, III.ii, 830; Palmer, 'England, France', 356.

In July 1366 envoys led by the earl of Hereford had been dispatched to Milan to discuss a marriage between Prince Lionel and Violante, the daughter of Galeazzo Visconti, lord of Pavia and co-ruler of Lombardy. Terms were finally settled in May 1367. Violante brought with her the promise of a dowry payment of around £15,000 and a string of towns and castles in Piedmont to the value of £12,000 a year.[133] In the spring of 1368 the couple were married at Milan Cathedral; the banquet that followed was said to have offered enough food for 10,000 people.[134] Later English writers liked to fantasize that Lionel could, in different circumstances, have gone on to be lord of Milan, king of the Romans and even emperor.[135] But it is difficult to believe that Edward III took seriously the idea of a lasting English presence beyond the Alps. Rather, the intention was almost entirely pragmatic. The involvement of Sir John Hawkwood in the Anglo-Milanese marriage negotiations had been a clear sign of things to come. Lionel was now instructed to draw together the Milanese forces and the free companies and prepare a full-scale onslaught upon the papal states in central Italy.[136] Out of this dramatic initiative, Edward III hoped at last to wrest the elusive dispensations required to effect the Flemish match.

The opening up of a new front in northern Italy, and the perceived threat to papal interests, were certainly taken very seriously in 1368. Urban V moved to Viterbo and Montefiascone the better to supervise the defence of Rome, and was vocal in his criticism of the unwelcome English presence in Milan.[137] Edward III put up a notably tart defence, arguing that he had 'many sons to marry' and that the only other available bride in Europe to match Violante – that, is, Margaret de Mâle – was currently denied them.[138] In the end, however, the Milanese alliance simply imploded. Lionel died unexpectedly at Alba on 17 October 1368.[139] His second-in-command, Edward Despenser, felt compelled to avenge the inevitable rumour that Lionel had been murdered, and turned his forces and the free companies in hostile attack on Galeazzo Visconti. The Italian interlude had not only failed to change Urban V's mind about the Flemish

[133] *Foedera*, III.ii, 797. For gift-giving accompanying the 1367 settlement, see E 101/396/3. Cash payments towards the dowry amounting to £11,667 were delivered to London in May 1368: *Foedera*, III.ii, 843; *CFR 1356–68*, 379; E 101/315/30; E 43/233.

[134] *Foedera*, III.ii, 817, 827–8, 842, 845; *Issues*, 192; E 403/436, 6 Mar. 1369; *Chron. QPV*, 195–6; *Chron. J&C*, ii, 40–1; *ODNB*, xxxiii, 951; W. Caferro, *John Hawkwood* (Baltimore, 2006), 134.

[135] J. Hardyng, *The Chronicle of John Hardyng*, ed. H. Ellis (London, 1812), 332–3.

[136] F. S. Saunders, *Hawkwood: Diabolical Englishman* (London, 2004), 123–5.

[137] *CPL*, iv, 27.

[138] *AC*, 172; J. R. L. Highfield, 'The Promotion of William of Wickham to the See of Winchester', *Journal of Ecclesiastical History*, iv (1953), 41, 51–3.

[139] For prayers ordered for the prince's soul see *Wykeham's Register*, ed. T. F. Kirby, 2 vols (London, 1896–9), 564–5; *Register of Thomas Appleby*, no. 214. Edmund Rose escorted eight of the prince's best horses back from Pavia, via Paris, to Windsor, at a cost of £91: E 404/9/59, privy seal writ, 13 July 1369.

marriage; it had also deprived Edward III of one of the five sons in whose
favour he had so obviously attempted to develop his imperial policy over
the previous decade.

If there was any strategic justification for Edward's continued pursuit of
the Flemish marriage after 1366, it lay in the need to stall an alliance
between Louis de Mâle and Charles V. The count of Flanders was not
disposed to lose the advantage of independence from the crown of France,
and Edward remained convinced that he could exploit the stand-off now
existing between Louis and Charles over possession of the border territories of Lille, Douai and Orchies. Just a few weeks after the issue of the
dispensation for the Flemish–Burgundian marriage, Edward actually
managed to re-establish an alliance of mutual aid with Louis de Mâle.[140]
When Urban V chose to appoint the recently elevated archbishop of
Canterbury, Simon Langham, to the post of cardinal in 1368, the king
quickly made it known who was in charge in England: Langham was
forced to resign the archbishopric and thus formally to forfeit his place on
the royal council. Following the deaths of Lionel of Clarence and the
young duchess of Lancaster, Edward wrote to Louis de Mâle in December
1368 to suggest that his second surviving son, John of Gaunt, now be
substituted as the long-awaited English bridegroom for Margaret of
Flanders.[141] But the consequence was further humiliation. Over the
autumn of 1368, Louis effectively eliminated any remaining commitment
to the Anglo-Flemish alliance by coming to terms with the rulers of
Brabant and Holland and promising to abandon Edward's proposal to
assimilate Hainault into the county of Flanders.[142] In May 1369 Louis and
Charles V finally resolved the remaining impediments to the Franco-
Flemish alliance. The following month, at Ghent, Margaret de Mâle was
duly given in marriage to Philip of Burgundy.[143] If the scheme to create a
Plantagenet satellite in Flanders was not, in the end, the actual sparking
point of the return to armed conflict, there is no doubt that its collapse
represented a severe setback to Edward's ambitions and security at the
very moment when England and France once more contemplated the full
tumult of war.

Between 1361 and 1368 Edward III attempted a radical reconfiguration of
the Plantagenet dominions. By giving his first and second sons command
of Aquitaine and Ireland, he consciously confirmed the special sovereign

---

[140] *EMDP*, I.ii, no. 349; *Foedera*, III.ii, 826. Edward also probably encouraged the Anglo-
Gascon free companies to move out of Castile in the autumn of 1367 and inflict themselves
on the Burgundian territories of Philip the Bold: Delachenal, iii, 441–4; Palmer, 'England,
France', 348–9.

[141] J. J. N. Palmer, 'The Historical Context of the Book of the Duchess: A Revision',
Chaucer Review, viii (1974), 253–5.

[142] Palmer, 'England, France', 360–1.

[143] *Chron. J&C*, ii, 16–31; Froissart, viii, 129–31; Vaughan, *Philip the Bold*, 5–6.

status that he now asserted over all his dependencies, in France as well as in the British Isles. His willingness to abandon the prospect of an English succession to Scotland after 1365 revealed his reluctance to pursue dynastic dreams when offered the prospect of a substantive peace. But the failure of his efforts to drive John II and Charles V towards the full implementation of the treaty of Calais also led him to fixate on the idea of setting up his younger sons and sons-in-law in new Plantagenet fiefdoms in Brittany, Soissons, Poitou, Flanders and Burgundy, and to redeploy his two oldest sons in increasingly high-risk ventures in Castile and northern Italy. After 1365 the dynastic imperative became all too obviously a liability, at once creating unrealistic expectations of Edward's true reach and seriously distracting English diplomacy from the main purpose of effecting a long-term settlement with France. For twenty years the king had successfully avoided the spectre of conflict within the royal family by persuading his children of their entitlement to a share in the spoils of his foreign wars. It remained to be seen whether the strong sense of unity that still prevailed within the royal ranks would survive once the new war put a decisive end to so many of those Plantagenet dreams.

Chapter 16

THE HOUSE OF MAGNIFICENCE, 1358–1369

In spite of the serious diplomatic problems that Edward III encountered during the 1360s, his international reputation as warrior and statesman stood never so high as in the era of Poitiers and Nájera. In 1360, the great Italian poet Francesco Petrarch commented that a generation earlier the English had been the 'meekest of the barbarians', humbled even by the 'wretched Scots'. Yet now, 'they are a fiercely bellicose nation. They have overturned the ancient military glory of the French by victories so numerous that they have reduced the entire kingdom of France by fire and the sword.'[1] Eight years later, Petrarch was among the guests at the wedding of Lionel of Clarence and Violante Visconti in Milan. In the English party at this same event was the Hainaulter Jean Froissart, who had arrived in England in 1361–2 and, in the interim, had visited some of the spheres of Edward's influence in Scotland, the Welsh marches, Brittany, Aquitaine and Provence. Geoffrey Chaucer may also have been there; he had been in Edward III's service since the Reims campaign, and had already travelled extensively on royal business to Scotland, Gascony and Navarre.[2] The possibility of this meeting between three great literary figures – one old and esteemed, the other two young and budding – provides a vivid reminder of the cosmopolitanism to which the court of Edward III so obviously subscribed. In the 1360s Edward made ready use of his international cultural credentials to promote his status as leader of Europe. Increasingly, however, this involved a confident espousal of characteristically insular English forms. For those of his subjects conditioned by several generations of royal propaganda to believe that the French were nothing but treacherous, evil and degenerate, Edward III was now more than willing to parade his personal and cultural credentials as a true son of England.

In the period 1358–65 Edward III perfected the arts of spectacle that had been such an important element of his self-image since the beginning of his personal rule. Magnificence was regarded as a positive virtue in later

---

[1] R. Boutruche, 'The Devastation of Rural Areas during the Hundred Years War and the Agricultural Recovery of France', *The Recovery of France in the Fifteenth Century*, ed. P. S. Lewis (London, 1971), 26.

[2] Pearsall, *Life of Geoffrey Chaucer*, 53–4, 102–5, 106–9.

medieval rulers, the means by which the potency of monarchy was expressed for the benefit both of the elite and of a wider public. The natural environment for such performances was, of course, the court. A century later, under Edward IV, a treatise defined the above-stairs elements of the royal household as the 'house of magnificence'.[3] The text in question was informed in part by ordinances, now lost, from the time of Edward III. Had such documents survived, we might have a rather firmer sense of the detailed protocols that accompanied royal display in the 1360s. Enough still exists in the financial accounts of the royal household, however, to provide at least a glimpse of the scale and style of courtly extravaganzas at this high point of Edwardian self-confidence.

The most tangible index of magnificence is provided by the levels of staffing and expenditure of the royal household. At the end of the French war it had seemed for one brief moment that the domestic establishments of the royal family might enter a period of retrenchment. By the late 1350s, Queen Philippa's domestic finances were close to collapsing under the strain of high expenditure.[4] In 1360 it was accordingly decided to merge the administration of the queen's domestic establishment with that of the king. Thereafter, Philippa had only to contribute £10 a day to cover the basic costs of housing her retainers; all excesses and other special expenditures would be underwritten by the crown.[5] But since the royal couple continued to maintain two complete entourages, the expected economies of scale were not altogether forthcoming. Whereas Edward III's household had numbered 368 heads in the mid-1350s and Philippa's perhaps up to 100, the combined staffs of the two domestic establishments was still running at nearly 450 in the mid-1360s.[6] A number of other royals and nobles such as the king's sister, Joan, his youngest son, Thomas of Woodstock, and the duke of Brittany's sister, Jeanne, also received regular subsidies for the maintenance of their domestic staffs.[7] When Edward III

[3] *The Household of Edward IV*, ed. A. R. Myers (Manchester, 1959), 76–197.

[4] *CPR 1358–61*, 237–9; E 159/136, *Brev. bar.*, Mich., rot. 1d; Wolffe, *Royal Demesne*, 56, 238–9. A long list of those awaiting payment for foodstuffs purveyed by the queen's officials, compiled in *c*.1357, provides striking evidence of the dire state of her finances: JRUL, MS Latin 237.

[5] C. Given-Wilson, 'The Merger of Edward III's and Queen Philippa's Households, 1360–9', *BIHR*, li (1978), 183–7.

[6] Given-Wilson, *Royal Household*, 278.

[7] Joan of Scotland drew a subsidy of £200 a year after her return to England in 1358: E 403/392, 5 July 1358; E 403/394, 9 Oct. 1358. When Joan died in 1362, Edward paid the fees due to a number of her ladies and household servants: *CPR 1361–4*, 10; E 403/415, 8 May 1363. After John de Montfort's return to Brittany, his sister drew an allowance of £100 a year from the exchequer, but Queen Philippa also continued to claim the £200 a year that she had earlier been granted for the upkeep of John and Jeanne: *Foedera*, III.ii, 607; E 403/422, 6 May 1365; E 403/425, 4 Dec. 1365. Subsidies for the king's three middle sons largely ceased after 1362 and were then restricted to the maintenance of Thomas of Woodstock; in 1366 Thomas's tutor or 'keeper', Roger la Warde, and other of the prince's staff were being supported within the king's entourage: E 101/396/2, fol. 56.

dispensed liveries to the members of his family, their personal attendants and the massed ranks of the king's and queen's household for the funeral of Philippa of Hainault in January 1370, the list ran to some 635 men and women.[8] If we were to include the associated followings of the lords and ladies still being supported directly by the crown at this date, that total would easily rise to well over a thousand people.

The pattern of household expenditure tells a similar story. In 1362, as an act of political goodwill, Edward III elaborated on preliminary promises made the previous year and, representing the concession as an act of unforced generosity, promulgated the great Statute of Purveyors. This effectively abolished the controversial compulsory seizures of foodstuffs previously made by the king's household officials and required that provisions be purchased for ready cash on the open market.[9] Ironically, the most immediate effect of the statute was to add significantly to the already escalating costs of maintaining the court. The expenditure of the king's wardrobe rose from about £16,000 a year at the start of the 1360s to £25,000 a year in the middle of the decade.[10] In 1367, Edward gave permission for some of the debts that had accumulated in the household to be met from loans out of the private treasury created to hold the profits of John II's ransom.[11] Thereafter, an element of stringency set in, and domestic expenditure fell back to around £15,000 a year by 1368–9. It was only following the break-up of Queen Philippa's entourage and with the new challenges of war finance after 1369, however, that the king's household made real efforts to cut back on its costs. If scale alone was a measure of magnificence, the early 1360s marked the apogee of Edward III's regal splendour.

The same period witnessed important developments in the architectural settings employed for displays of courtly magnificence. After he had completed St Stephen's Chapel, Westminster and St George's Chapel, Windsor in the 1350s, Edward III gave most of his attention to monumental schemes of secular architecture. There was a strong sense of competition in all of this: across Europe, the design and decoration of palaces underwent major changes in the fourteenth century as popes, emperors, kings and princes sought to express the relationship between architecture and power. In particular, the sequence of major building

---

[8] E 101/395/2, no. 236, printed in 'Enrolments and Documents from the Public Record Office', *Chaucer Society Publications*, ed. Selby, Furnivall, Bond and Kirk, iv, 172–5; Wathey, 'Peace of 1360–1369', 144. The total excludes an additional 266 ancillary staff hired especially for the event.

[9] *PROME*, v, 137, 142–5; *SR*, i, 371–3. The 1362 statute restricted purveyance to the households of the king and queen. The heir to the throne had been included in 1361; in 1362 the omission of the Black Prince was presumably made possible, rather conveniently, by the latter's creation as prince of Aquitaine and impending departure from the realm.

[10] Given-Wilson, *Royal Household*, 77; C. Given-Wilson, 'Purveyance for the Royal Household, 1362–1413', *BIHR*, lvi (1983), 163.

[11] E 159/144, *Brev. bar.*, Mich., rot. 17.

programmes conduced from *c.*1360 by the dauphin and later king of France, Charles V, probably influenced the prodigious outlay that Edward III undertook during the same period, principally at Windsor castle but also at several other major and lesser royal residences in the south of England.[12] Architecture, as the English chroniclers readily understood, had become a crucial element in the performance of good kingship.[13]

The rebuilding of the royal apartments in the upper ward at Windsor between the late 1350s and the mid-1360s was the greatest single royal investment in castle-building in England known in the entire Middle Ages; together with some lesser additional bills run up between 1365 and 1377, expenditure on these works reached a total of around £44,000.[14] Although much of Edward III's work was swept away in another great spate of architectural activity in the seventeenth century, the archaeological work undertaken after the major fire at the castle in 1992 has done much to allow a better understanding of the original scheme.[15] The principal rooms were situated in the long south range of the new work, with the great chamber, chapel and great hall arranged in a line looking into the ward. In the Rose Tower, which stood at the west end of the south range, was a grand second-floor chamber which enjoyed commanding views of the surrounding countryside. Behind the great chamber and chapel were the private apartments of the king and queen, linked by a connecting door between their bedrooms. The sheer size of the buildings created its own challenges: in the 1370s significant efforts had to be put into ensuring that enough firewood was collected in Windsor Great Park 'to warm the chimneys of the chambers and the bathhouse' of the castle.[16] At great feasts and other ceremonies, the normally bare public rooms would be dressed with furniture, plate and wall hangings and staffed by a veritable army of liveried servants. A rare glimpse of the kinds of pictorial themes that might have been used at Windsor comes in a set of hangings subsequently given by Edward III to St Mary Graces Abbey, which included a set of representations of kings and earls, another depicting the legend of Solomon and Marcolf, and a length of worsted embroidered with crests and peacock feathers.[17]

Edward III's personal identification with the work in the upper ward at Windsor is best demonstrated by the new frequency with which he chose

---

[12] P. Crossley, 'Architecture', *The New Cambridge Medieval History, VI: c.1300–c.1415*, ed. M. Jones (Cambridge, 2000), 235–9; M. Whiteley, 'The Courts of Edward III of England and Charles V of France: A Comparison of their Architectural Setting and Ceremonial Functions', *Fourteenth Century England I*, ed. Saul, 153–66.

[13] CCCC, MS 78, fol. 181v; *Hist. Angl.*, i, 328; *Brut*, ii, 333. For more critical comment see *Polychronicon*, viii, 359.

[14] *King's Works*, i, 163; ii, 881; R. A. Brown, *English Castles*, 2nd edn (London, 1976), 208.

[15] For what follows see Wilson, 'Royal Lodgings', 15–94.

[16] E 159/153, *Brev. bar.*, Trin., rot. 6d.

[17] E 159/144, *Brev. bar.*, Hil., rot. 1d.

to reside there. Now that the king's birthplace more adequately accommodated the enormous ceremonial and logistical machine of the royal household, it was at last suitable as a major venue for court festivities. Having
never previously passed Christmas or New Year at Windsor, Edward held
one or other (and usually both) of these midwinter feasts there every year
from 1361–2 to 1368–9. In addition, the annual removal of the court for
the Garter ceremonies on St George's Day was now often extended to
include one or more of the great springtide festivals. The king spent Easter
at Windsor on seven out of a possible eleven occasions between 1359 and
1369.[18] And in 1365 Edward was in residence at Windsor, with interim
visits away, for the entire sequence of feasts from Easter (13 April) through
St George's Day (23 April), Ascension (22 May) and Pentecost (1 June) to
the Nativity of John the Baptist (24 June).

It is not easy to establish either the numbers of attendees or the scale of
celebration that accompanied these moments in an emergent Windsor
'season'. Edward III certainly expected the members of his extended
family to attend whenever possible. On the guest list for the midwinter
revels of 1366–7, for example, were the princes Lionel, John, Edmund and
Thomas, Princess Isabella, and the young earls of Pembroke and March;
the considerable expenditure of £255 for the feast on Christmas Day
suggests that other members of the political elite may also have been
present.[19] The general absence of notices of the Garter feasts in the
chronicles of the 1360s tends to suggest that Edward III did not pursue the
precedent of 1358 and attempt to turn the St George's Day meetings into
general gatherings of European chivalry.[20] On the other hand, as founder
members of the Garter died off, the fraternity was itself coming to include
many of the most important members of the English elite. Those enrolled
in the later 1350s and 1360s included the king's three middle sons, Lionel,
John and Edmund, the earls of Hereford, Bedford and Pembroke, and
senior figures in the royal household such as Edward Despenser, William
Latimer and John Neville. That the Order of the Garter was taking on a
more general function as a privileged social circle around the king is
suggested by occasional summonses issued to the knights to convene for
ceremonial and social occasions beyond their regular commitment on
St George's Day.[21]

It is in the celebrations of the weddings of the king's two eldest children
at Windsor in 1361 and 1365 that we can best glimpse the opulent environment created in the newly modelled castle. Edward of Woodstock and

[18] The exceptions were 1360 (when Edward was in France), 1363 (Kings Langley), 1364
and 1367 (both Eltham).

[19] E 101/395/10; E 101/396/2, fols 26, 30, 31v.

[20] Collins, *Order of the Garter*, 212.

[21] E 403/465, 16 Nov. 1352; E 403/409, 19 Jan. 1362; E 403/412, 14 Mar. 1363;
E 404/6/40, great seal writ, 8 Feb. 1361.

Joan of Kent's public nuptials in October 1361 were attended by the king and queen, the princes and princesses, Edward III's sister Joan of Scotland and a great array of the English prelacy and nobility.[22] The king spent at least £1,500, and probably much more, on jewels as gifts for the couple.[23] At Princess Isabella's marriage to Enguerrand de Coucy there seems to have been a similar general gathering of the elite: among those who received personal invitations to this event were the earl of Stafford, the bishops of Salisbury, London, Winchester and Durham, the abbot of Chertsey, Abbot Litlington of Westminster, the dowager countess of Pembroke, and Ladies Say, Wake and Mohun.[24] The records, such as they are, suggest an even greater emphasis on display: the jewels and plate procured by the crown for this occasion ran up a staggering expenditure of £4,500.[25] By 1365 Windsor had become the definitive venue at which, through carefully articulated displays of extravagance, Edward III affirmed his commitment to the cults of monarchy and chivalry and the spectacular achievements of his military and political regime.

At the king's lesser residences too, there was a good deal of new building that signalled a greater emphasis on luxury and display. Leeds castle (Kent) and Sheen (Surrey) reverted to the crown after the death of Queen Isabella in 1358 and were significantly refurbished. The royal lodge at Gravesend (Kent) was almost completely rebuilt. Further afield, in 1363 Edward purchased the castle of Moor End (Northamptonshire) as a new base for hunting expeditions in Whittlewood Forest, and remodelled the lodgings in appropriately sumptuous style. The existing castle at Hadleigh (Essex) underwent extensive rebuilding in order to turn it into both a bastion against possible enemy attacks and a suitable venue for royal visits. In September 1366 the works at Hadleigh were sufficiently advanced to allow the king to entertain the earls of Warwick, Suffolk and Salisbury there.[26] Concern for the comfort of the king and his visitors was evident throughout; fireplaces feature prominently in the works carried out at these and other lesser residences during the 1360s, and the stews (bathhouses) at Easthampstead and Kings Langley were overhauled or rebuilt to bring them into line with similar facilities earlier installed for the king at Westminster.[27]

Edward III's personal interest in such schemes is most especially attested in the case of Queenborough castle at Rushenden in the Isle of Sheppey (Kent). After Windsor, this was the king's greatest architectural project, accounting for expenditure in the region of £25,000 between 1361

[22] *Anon. Cant.*, 118–19; Reading, 151; 'Wigmore Chronicle', 292.

[23] E 403/409, 15 Oct. 1361.

[24] WAM, 12213; E 403/411, 8 July, 12 July 1365.

[25] J. A. Lutkin, 'Goldsmiths and the English Royal Court, 1360–1413' (University of London PhD Thesis, 2008), 44, 47–8, 305; Harriss, *King, Parliament*, 526.

[26] E 101/396/2, fol. 44v.

[27] *King's Works*, ii, 926, 974.

and 1369. The new works were formally begun on 9 May 1361.[28] Edward went down to survey progress on a regular basis from 1363, at first staying in makeshift accommodation and later taking advantage of the suite of apartments completed in 1365–6 inside the central tower of the complex. In 1366–7 a new town was planted in the shadow of the emergent castle, and in June 1367 Edward held a feast on the site at which he announced his intention to name both town and castle in honour of his queen.[29] Queenborough differed from most of Edward's other residences in its very obvious military function. The castle was built to a novel ground plan, with a central rotunda surrounded by a concentric circle of high and thick walls. Situated across the Thames estuary from Hadleigh, it was probably conceived as part of a larger plan for the protection of the waterborne approaches to London. As such, however, it also projected a powerful public symbolism, declaring to the multitude of shipping moving up and down the Thames the king's resolute command of the seas and his stout defence of the security and sovereignty of his realm.

If Windsor and Queenborough were closest to Edward's heart, then the royal residences within the capital might equally be said to have ruled his head. It was at the Tower of London and Westminster Palace that the king tended most frequently to hold audiences of state during the second half of his reign.[30] After the plague, Edward became increasingly concerned that the appalling open sewers running down many of the streets of the capital might compromise his safety and dignity, and from the mid-1350s he retained his own 'boonraker', at a fee of £2 a year, to clear away the filth whenever the royal party rode through London.[31] Such preventive measures helped create a suitable environment for the lavish royal tournaments that continued to be held in the great open-air spaces around the city at Smithfield and Cheapside. Over the winter of 1363–4 Edward III acted as host in the capital to royal visits, in rapid succession, from David II of Scotland and John II of France. Peter I of Cyprus was also in London, busily recruiting volunteers for a crusade to reconquer

---

[28] The commission to levy stonemasons for the site required them to appear before the king on 5 May: *CPR 1361–4*, 68; *King's Works*, i, 163. Edward's presence there on 9 May is attested by E 101/394/8 and C 81/1334/55. For a great iron anvil sent over from Calais to be used in the construction work see E 101/178/21.

[29] The date can be deduced from the fact that the earliest privy seal writ in C 81/409 naming the site as Queenborough is dated 20 June 1367. E 403/431, 15 July 1367 records a payment of £100 to the (unnamed) damsels of the queen at the time when the king 'gave' the castle to his wife. The town was formally incorporated in 1368: *CChR, 1341–1417*, 211; *CLBL, G*, 228.

[30] C. J. Given-Wilson, 'The Court and Household of Edward III, 1360–1377' (University of St Andrews PhD thesis, 1975), 115–16. From *c.*1360 Edward also adopted the convention of making Christmastide distributions to male and female recluses in and around the city of London: E 403/405, 16 Dec. 1360; E 403/409, 16 Dec. 1361; E 403/412, 12 Dec. 1363.

[31] E. L. Sabine, 'City Cleaning in Mediaeval London', *Speculum*, xii (1937), 27–9; E 403/375, 28 Nov. 1354; E 403/377, 2 May 1355; E 403/378, 12 Dec. 1355; etc.

Alexandria, and he and David duly accepted Edward's invitation to a great tournament at Smithfield, possibly held on David's arrival (but before John's) in late November 1363. Here Edward probably appeared in a new and no doubt resplendent suit of armour recently made for him by the craftsman John of London.[32] Within a generation it was believed that Waldemar IV of Denmark had also come to England at this time, and a myth developed of a 'feast of five kings' hosted by the prominent London vintner and recent mayor of London, Henry Picard.[33] Even if it could only ever be a fiction, this story provides a strong indicator of the close links between the court and the commercial elite of the city, and provides at least a hint of Edward III's ease and graciousness in accommodating the social aspirations of the London merchants and their wives.

The real locus of royal magnificence within the capital was the great complex of buildings that made up the palace and abbey of Westminster. Here Edward III made early use of Henry Yevele and Hugh Herland, the two great craftsmen who would go on to mastermind Richard II's superb remodelling of the great hall.[34] While most of the works carried out at Westminster in the 1360s were small-scale and cosmetic, they did include some notable changes to the external appearance of the palace. Two new structures were erected. The Jewel Tower, designed as a repository for royal valuables, stands to this day as one of a very few buildings of the medieval palace to survive the disastrous Westminster fire of 1834. Much more conspicuous in its own time was the campanile erected close to the great hall to house a clock and a four-ton bell known as 'Edward of Westminster'. Edward III turns out to have had something of a penchant for timepieces: his innovations at Westminster and elsewhere provide some of the earliest documented references to the presence of mechanical clocks in medieval England.[35] The bells for the clocks at Westminster,

---

[32] *Chronicle of Jean de Venette*, 114; E 101/394/16, m. 17; E 403/417, 9 Oct. 1363; *Eulogium*, iii, 233; P. W. Edbury, *The Kingdom of Cyprus and the Crusades, 1191–1374* (Cambridge, 1991), 11–12, 164–5. Peter made Edward the gift of a leopard on this occasion, and the English king responded with various items of plate: E 403/417, 6 Nov., 20 Nov. 1363; *Antient Kalendars*, i, 254.

[33] Reading, 158, 311–12; Knighton, 188–9; C. L. Kingsford, 'The Feast of the Five Kings', *Archaeologia*, lxvii (1915–16), 119–26. In 1359 Waldemar IV had threatened to launch an attack on eastern England in support of the Valois cause. He was therefore encouraged to come to the talks occasioned by John II's return to London in 1364, but does not seem to have attended in person: Cazelles, *Jean le Bon et Charles V*, 350–1; *Foedera*, III.ii, 719; Reading, 337–8; *Issues*, 186; E 159/141, *Brev. bar.*, Mich., rot. 11d. Reading, 179–81 (and hence *Brut*, ii, 317), suggests that there were Danish attacks on England in 1366–7. But there also seems to have been a temporary rapprochement with Waldemar after 1367: Palmer, 'England, France', 363 n. 6; E 403/438, 7 May 1369.

[34] *CPR 1358–61*, 449, 452.

[35] R. A. Brown, 'King Edward's Clocks', *Antiquaries Journal*, xxxix (1959), 283–6; A. G. Rigg, 'Clocks, Dials, and other Terms', *Middle English Studies Presented to Norman Davies*, ed. D. Gray and E. G. Stanley (Oxford, 1983), 256–7.

Queenborough and Kings Langley were commissioned, as a job lot, from the founder John Gloucester in 1367.[36] 'Edward of Westminster' itself survived for some three hundred years, and there is every reason to suppose that it carried at least something of the iconic significance that attaches today to the striking of Big Ben.

The public nature of much of the royal ritual conducted in the Palace of Westminster is demonstrated most obviously in sessions of parliament. Edward III hosted opening plenary meetings of parliament in Henry III's Painted Chamber, where he presided from a bed of state decorated with his quartered arms of France and England.[37] The opening speech to parliament, usually delivered by a member of the king's household or a senior minister, was increasingly accompanied by a sermon that played on Edward III's beneficence. In 1365, for example, the bishop of Ely preached on the text 'Justice and judgement are the habitation of Thy throne' (Psalms 89: 14).[38] After 1358 we find references to royal sergeants-at-arms charged to attend upon the will of the king and council, appar-ently as masters of ceremonies, during the time of parliament.[39] There is also a hint of better provision for the dignity and comfort of the king and lords: in 1358 three valets of the royal household were appointed to 'array' the king's chamber for parliament, and in 1363 bolsters were purchased for 'the house of parliament'.[40] Westminster was indeed emerging under Edward III as a true theatre of politics.

The greatest set pieces in the ceremony of parliament tended to come on the last day of business in a plenary assembly again convoked, in the king's presence, in the Painted Chamber. In 1362 parliament was artifi-cially prolonged so that its final meeting could coincide with the king's fiftieth birthday on Sunday, 13 November. The chancellor expounded the many blessings bestowed by the Almighty on the fortunate king. Edward then installed his three middle sons as dukes of Clarence and Lancaster and earl of Cambridge. There followed a quite brilliant articulation of the benefits of Edward's rule when, appropriating the Judaeo-Christian notion of jubilee, the crown announced the issue of a general pardon.[41] No previous monarch had made his life events into occasions of public celebration, and Edward III's jubilee of 1362 marked a valuable first step

[36] E 208/7, file 42 Edward III, privy seal writ, 24 Sept. 1367.

[37] *A Collection of the Wills of the Kings and Queens of England*, 61. For the disposition of this room, see P. Binski, *The Painted Chamber at Westminster* (London, 1986).

[38] *PROME*, v, 176.

[39] E 403/388, 16 Feb., 17 Feb., 22 Feb. 1358; E 403/427, 13 May 1366; E 403/434, 27 May 1368; E 403/438, 16 July 1369; *Issue Roll of Brantingham*, 290.

[40] E 403/388, 22 Feb. 1358; E 101/394/16, m. 17.

[41] *PROME*, v, 139, 151–2; W. M. Ormrod, 'Fifty Glorious Years: Edward III and the First English Royal Jubilee', *Medieval History*, new series, i[1] (2002), 13–14. For chronicle notices of the jubilee, see CCCC, MS 78, fol. 183; *Anon. Cant.*, 126–9; *Hist. Angl.*, i, 297–8; Walsingham, *Ypodigma*, 307.

towards the systematic integration of royal anniversaries within the English cult of monarchy. The proceedings of 1362 were presumably rounded off with a great parliamentary feast like that held in 1368, when the king invited the lords and 'many of the commons' to a banquet in the great hall of the palace.[42] The inclusion of the knights of the shires and the urban representatives in such formalities marked a departure in the protocols of the court. As in the open-air spectacles conducted in London, so now also in the business of politics, Edward III had deliberately set out to draw a wide cross-section of the political community into the ceremonial apparatus of the English state.

The lavish expressions of royal magnificence between 1358 and 1365 were very definitely intended to proclaim England as an inviolable, independent state and to indulge Edward III's Arthurian fantasies of general world domination. Part of this campaign played on the strident chauvinism of English political culture. In 1362, as part of the jubilee celebrations, the crown responded to a request for a change in the spoken language of the law courts and declared that in future proceedings should be undertaken not, as in the previous hundred years and more, in French, but in the native tongue of Englishmen. After 1362, moreover, the opening speech to parliament was no longer delivered as a matter of course in the Anglo-Norman French of the ruling elite, but in English.[43] These symbolic measures pandered to innate prejudice against all things foreign and helped represent the recent treaty of Calais as England's final liberation from the political and cultural hegemony of France.[44] The dramatic challenges issued to Urban V's authority similarly played to the isolationist preferences of the gallery. Even the royal jubilee was something of a snub to the pope, for it emphatically appropriated to secular use the practice, revived at Rome in 1300 and 1350, of celebrating every fiftieth anniversary of the birth of Christ. Throughout the 1360s, Edward III quite unashamedly manipulated the rampant xenophobia and anti-papalism of parliament to suggest that he fully shared the cultural isolationism of the middling and lower orders of his realm.

Equally, of course, the growing sense of England's destiny as a global power necessarily required a royal commitment to internationalism. During the 1360s Edward received envoys and gifts from a veritable

[42] *PROME*, v, 213–14. E 101/397/5 fol. 60v records the considerable expenditure of £98 for the costs of the king's hall on 25 Nov. 1372, suggesting a feast after the dismissal of parliament the day before. For references to the parliamentary feasts of July 1376 and Feb. 1377 see E 101/397/12; E 101/398/9, fol. 12.

[43] *PROME*, v, 140, 152–3, 158, 176; *SR*, i, 375–6.

[44] W. M. Ormrod, 'The Use of English: Language, Law, and Political Culture in Fourteenth-Century England', *Speculum*, lxxxviii (2003), 750–87. For the broader context, see J. Catto, 'Written English: The Making of the Language, 1370–1400', *Past and Present*, clxxix (2003), 24–59.

pantheon of European rulers, including the Emperor Charles IV of Bohemia and the kings of Norway, Sweden, Hungary and Sicily.[45] In Peter of Cyprus's entourage on his visit to London in 1363 were several pagan and Muslim princes; one, calling himself 'lord of Jerusalem' was converted to Christianity, with the king of England himself acting as godfather, and was duly christened Edward.[46] Interactions with the world beyond Christendom fitted naturally with the contemporary courtly fashion for the exotic. A copy of Marco Polo's *Divisament dou monde* may have been in circulation at the English court,[47] and the Anglo-Norman *Travels* of John Mandeville, written shortly after Poitiers and supposedly dedicated to Edward III, provided a celebrated account of the distant reaches of a world inhabited variously by great civilizations, wild men and monsters. In 1366, when Edward III was in the middle of a hunting expedition in the New Forest, he was informed of the arrival of one John Balbat, who claimed to be the son of the high king of India. Suspicions were raised about the visitor's true identity, and he was eventually deported.[48] Even when they were spurious, however, such engagements with the Orient were taken as proof of Edward's increasingly expansive moral dominion. Mandeville's dedication addressed his king as 'the most excellent prince, to be chiefly reverenced above all mortals . . ., credit and ornament of Christendom, patron of all men at arms and pattern of probity and strength'.[49] And a petitioner to the crown in 1360 used the high-flown salutation, 'To our most honoured and most redoubted, gracious and most powerful king of the whole world.'[50]

This heady mix no doubt helps to explain why, in spite of his pandering to the linguistic nationalism of parliament, Edward III remained deeply committed to the French-speaking culture prevalent throughout the courts of Europe. We should not take too seriously Henry of Grosmont's claim in his devotional treatise, the *Livre de seyntz medicines*, written in the mid-1350s, that 'Je sui anglais, et n'ai pas moelt hauntee le franceis' ('I am English, and have had but little acquaintance with French').[51] Henry was one of the great European princes of his age, and the facility and origi-nality of his writing very obviously belie this conventional expression of

[45] *EMDP*, I.ii, no. 414 n. 36; E 403/396, 24 Aug. 1359; E 403/411, 1 June 1362; E 403/429, 6 Feb. 1367; E 403/438, 7 May 1369. For a later visit from a herald of Louis I of Hungary see E 403/451, 21 Mar. 1373.

[46] *Eulogium*, iii, 233.

[47] M. J. Bennett, '*Mandeville's Travels* and the Anglo-French Moment', *Medium Ævum*, lxxv (2006), 281.

[48] E 101/396/2, fol. 38v; E 403/427, 11 July, 28 July, 1366; E 403/429, 16 Oct., 19 Oct. 1366.

[49] *Mandeville's Travels*, ed. P. Hamelius, 2 vols (EETS, cliii–cliv, 1919–23), ii, 14. For arguments in favour of the authenticity of the dedication, see Bennett, '*Mandeville's Travels*', 276–8.

[50] SC 8/247/12318; Ormrod, 'Problem of Precedence', 152.

[51] *Le livre de seyntz medicines*, ed. E. J. Arnould (Anglo-Norman Texts, ii, 1940), 239.

authorial humility. It is no surprise to find, then, that the contents of Edward III's own library continued to be dominated by French romance literature. All of the works that can be identified in an admittedly highly selective list of eighteen books inherited by Richard II from Edward III were romances in French, such as the *Romance du Roy Arthure* and the *Quest de Saint Grael*.[52]

The francophone tradition of the court was inevitably reconfirmed after 1356 as a result of the presence in England of John II and the other high-status French captives and hostages. The celebrated musician-poet Guillaume de Machaut wrote the *Dit de la fonteinne amoureuse* for the duke of Berry while the latter was a house guest of Edward III in the 1360s.[53] Much the same can be said of the Hainault connection. Jean de la Mote, a distinguished poet and musician who had earlier been retained by Edward III and had written an elegy on the death of Queen Philippa's father, seems to have returned to England in the late 1350s.[54] Then, in 1361–2, de la Mote's fellow Hainaulter Jean Froissart arrived at Edward's court bearing a verse chronicle in French which he dedicated and presented to his countrywoman, the queen. The flattery had the desired effect, and Froissart remained in Philippa's service until her death, composing 'pretty ditties and treatises of love' for her delectation.[55]

None, of this, however, precludes the possibility that English also had a distinct place in court culture in the later years of Edward III's reign. Much of the French influence on the king relied on the continuing presence of the two queens, Isabella and Philippa, and a circle of powerful French-born ladies led by the dowager countesses of Surrey (d. 1361) and Pembroke (d. 1377). It was in Philippa's household, rather than the king's, that the Brabançon knight Franc van Halle took up service after his arrival in England and his admission to the Order of the Garter in the late 1350s.[56] Yet in spite of the influence of John II's household, the little colonies of francophony gathered around the queens were already becoming somewhat beleaguered. In 1359, a tense moment in Anglo-French relations,

[52] R. F. Green, 'King Richard II's Books Revisited', *Library*, xxxi (1976), 235–9; N. Saul, 'The Kingship of Richard II', *Richard II: The Art of Kingship*, ed. A. Goodman and J. Gillespie (Oxford, 1999), 43. See also, more generally, M. J. Bennett, 'France in England: Anglo-French Culture in the Reign of Edward III', *Language and Culture in Medieval Britain: The French of England, c.1100–c.1500*, ed. J. Wogan-Browne (York, 2009), 320–33.

[53] E. Salter, *English and International: Studies in the Literature, Art and Patronage of Medieval England* (Cambridge, 1988), 241–2; W. Calin, *The French Tradition and the Literature of Medieval England* (Toronto, 1994), 8.

[54] N. Wilkins, '*En regardant vers le païs de France*: The Ballade and the Rondeau, a Cross-Channel History', *England in the Fourteenth Century*, ed. Ormrod, 298–302.

[55] Froissart, *Oeuvres*, xiv, 1; A. Butterfield, 'French Culture and the Ricardian Court', *Essays on Ricardian Literature in Honour of J. A. Burrow*, ed. A. J. Minnis, C. C. Morse and T. Turville-Petre (Oxford, 1997), 89–93.

[56] Van Halle's status as a knight of the queen's household is construed from E 101/395/2, n. 236. For other aspects of his career see Collins, *Order of the Garter*, 55 and n. 94.

several of the retainers of Queen Philippa and Marie de Saint-Pol had to take out special licences exempting them from the general expulsion of alien enemies.[57] With the death of Isabella in 1358 and Philippa in 1369, the most obvious courtly patrons of continental French literature may be said to have been removed from the English cultural scene. It is for good reason that the departure of Froissart from England after Queen Philippa's funeral is often taken as a symbolic moment in the Plantagenet court's abandonment of French and adoption of English as a valid medium of cultural expression.[58]

Nor was the international dimension in Edward III's own household any longer sufficient to require the exclusive use of French. Very few of the Netherlandish and German knights and esquires recruited to Edward's service in the late 1320s and 1330s remained there a generation later. Sir Walter Mauny, still a prominent presence at court, had been elevated to the peerage in 1348 and had made a prestigious marriage to the king's cousin Margaret Marshal, countess of Norfolk.[59] Froissart, for whom Mauny was a great hero, imagined that his conversations with the king took place very self-consciously 'in the English tongue'.[60] Others may have followed suit. The d'Aubrichecourts, for example, were well on their way to becoming members of an English-speaking provincial gentry society in Nottinghamshire by the time that the latest generation of the family, Colard and Nicholas, joined the ranks of the king's household in the 1360s and 1370s. And Thierry (or 'Canon') Robersart, lord of Escaillon, who renewed his family's long-standing connections with the English court in 1365, was part of a family soon to be revealingly dubbed 'English at heart'.[61] Even Edward III's minstrels and heralds seem, by the later years of the reign, to have been mostly natives of the realm: to judge from names, the only continental presence among the court performers was now maintained by Peter of Burgundy and Nicholas of Prague.[62] All of this provides strong *prima facie* evidence to suggest that, at least in their everyday exchanges, the king and his inner household tended to use English as their language of default. Just as Edward III's enigmatic mottoes had been routinely expressed in English, so too were other forms

---

[57] C 76/37, m. 9.

[58] Fowler, *Age of Plantagenet and Valois*, 192; M. Zink, *Froissart et le temps* (Paris, 1998), 16–17.

[59] *ODNB*, xxxvii, 445–8; R. E. Archer, 'The Estates and Finances of Margaret of Brotherton, 1320–1377', *BIHR*, lx (1987), 264–80. C 76/37, m. 9, lists two 'Picards' in the household of the countess marshal in 1359.

[60] A. Butterfield, *The Familiar Enemy: Chaucer, Language, and Nation in the Hundred Years War* (Oxford, 2009), 163–4.

[61] E 101/395/10; E 101/396/2, fol. 56; E 101/397/5, fols 43, 82; Froissart, viii, 1 n. 3; J. W. Sherborne, *War, Politics and Culture in Fourteenth-Century England* (London, 1994), 11; Collins, *Order of the Garter*, 54–5.

[62] E 403/417, 24 Oct. 1363; E 403/417, 17 Feb. 1364; E 403/429, 15 Oct. 1366; E 403/438, 15 Sept. 1369.

of the elaborate wordplay in which the court so obviously delighted. The wry inscription 'Who may hald [hold] that will away', found engraved on a silver-gilt goblet in the royal collection in 1371, suggests a natural preference for riddles and puns expressed in the mother tongue of the majority.[63]

It is fruitful to ask, then, whether the court of Edward III should have sought to confirm its anglophone credentials by hosting performances of the new body of Middle English literature becoming available to polite audiences in the second half of the fourteenth century.[64] One obvious candidate is the romance *Guy of Warwick*, an early fourteenth-century adaptation of an Anglo-Norman work celebrating the deeds of a heroic fictional ancestor of the Beauchamp family. In the 1350s and 1360s Thomas Beauchamp, earl of Warwick, had numerous relatives at Edward's court, including his son and heir, Thomas, his younger brother, John, and their distant cousins John and Roger, sons of Giles Beauchamp of Powick.[65] The English *Guy of Warwick* appears in an important miscellany of Middle English works known as the Auchinleck Manuscript, compiled in the 1330s. Although its patron is often assumed to have been a London merchant, Auchinleck contains precisely the kinds of text that would have appealed directly to the tastes of the Beauchamps and, indeed, of the Plantagenets: a verse chronicle of the history of England; action-adventure romances of Arthur and Richard the Lionheart; and a liberal splash of oriental fantasy.[66] Rather than seeing the circle of Edward III as hermetically sealed against infection from vulgar vernacularism, it is surely much more reasonable to assume that the mid-fourteenth-century court responded readily to a new Middle English literature that so often complemented its own evolving sense of cultural identity.

The still more intriguing possibility arises as to whether Edward's court might have been receptive to that greatest text of the fourteenth-century Middle English Alliterative Revival, *Sir Gawain and the Green Knight*. Although the sole surviving manuscript is usually dated around the end of the fourteenth century, this poem may have been written as early as *c*.1350. William Montagu, second earl of Salisbury, and Henry of Grosmont, duke of Lancaster, have both been suggested as plausible

---

[63] *Antient Kalendars*, iii, 273.

[64] What follows pursues preliminary suggestions by A. I. Doyle, 'English Books in and out of Court from Edward III to Henry VII', *English Court Culture*, ed. Scattergood and Sherborne, 164–6.

[65] E 101/392/12, fols 40, 41; E 101/393/11, fol. 76; E 101/396/2, fol. 56; E 101/396/11, fol. 17; GEC, ii, 44–5.

[66] For arguments in favour of the Auchinleck Manuscript as a Beauchamp commission, see Turville-Petre, *England the Nation*, 108–41; R. Field, 'From *Gui* to *Guy*: The Fashioning of a Popular Romance', *Guy of Warwick: Icon and Ancestor*, ed. A. Wiggins and R. Field (Woodbridge, 2007), 44–60.

patrons.[67] In such cases, it is easy to see how *Gawain* might have found its way to the royal court. The scribe of the manuscript added, after the end of the poem, the motto of the Order of the Garter, as if to draw additional meaning from the green girdle worn by the hero. Since the poem involves the sexual temptation of Gawain by the wife of his host, Sir Bertilak, it is just possible that it was intended as a deliberate counter to the French-inspired rumour of Edward III's rape of the countess of Salisbury. A loyal audience would surely, however, have been much more inclined to identify Edward with the figure of King Arthur, the president of the Christmas feast with which the poem opens and the judge of Gawain's honour at its end. If *Sir Gawain and the Green Knight* was not written with a royal patron directly in mind, it is nonetheless hard to escape the conclusion that its author replicated very precisely the moral values and social mores that prevailed at the Edwardian court.

The most powerful suggestion of Edward III's greater inclination to engage with anglophone culture during the 1360s is provided by the work of Geoffrey Chaucer. Chaucer was not, in any true sense, a court poet: there is no evidence that any of his literary output was the result of direct royal commission.[68] Yet it is almost impossible to believe that Geoffrey's decision to begin writing in English was not influenced by his experience as a member successively of the households of the countess of Ulster, Edward III and John of Gaunt.[69] Chaucer's first major English poem, *The Book of the Duchess*, was written in response to the tragic death of Gaunt's first wife, Blanche of Lancaster, in 1368. The *Book* was a spectacular demonstration of the capacity of Middle English to express those heightened sensibilities so long thought a preserve of French courtly verse. Soon, indeed, the process of emulation was working in the opposite direction. Froissart used *The Book of the Duchess* as direct inspiration for his *Dit dou Bleu Chevalier*. And the esteemed French poet Eustace Deschamps later complimented Chaucer (if perhaps in a slightly back-handed manner) on his attempt at a working English translation of the *Roman de la Rose*.[70] By the end of Edward III's reign, English was thus well on its way to establishing a respected position, alongside French and Italian, as one of the major European literary vernaculars.

[67] W. G. Cooke, '*Sir Gawain and the Green Knight*: A Restored Dating', *Medium Ævum*, lviii (1989), 34–48; Ingledew, *Gawain*, 133–57; W. G. Cooke and D'A. J. D. Boulton, '*Sir Gawain and the Green Knight*: A Poem for Henry of Grosmont?', *Medium Ævum*, lxviii (1999), 42–54.

[68] D. Pearsall, 'The *Troilus* Frontispiece and Chaucer's Audience', *Yearbook of English Studies*, vii (1977), 68–74; G. Olson, 'Geoffrey Chaucer', *The Cambridge History of Medieval English Literature*, ed. D. Wallace (Cambridge, 1999), 566–70.

[69] Pearsall, *Life of Geoffrey Chaucer*, 47–8, 95–102.

[70] J. I. Wimsatt, 'The *Dit dou Bleu Chevalier*: Froissart's Imitation of Chaucer', *Mediaeval Studies*, xxxiv (1972), 388–400; Butterfield, *Familiar Enemy*, 143–51.

It was entirely of a piece with Edward III's increasing sense of his own status among the princes of Christendom, then, that his court should have sought in some way to associate itself with English vernacular literature. It is important not to exaggerate the point. Edward neither initiated the Middle English revival nor commissioned any known writing in the English tongue. Nor did he show any interest, in the way that Henry IV and Henry V were to do, in the use of English as a language of written communication between the crown and its subjects. Edward's flirtations with vernacular culture in the 1360s were credible only so long as the king and his subjects continued to believe in their comfortable fiction of England's dominance over France. After the reversals of diplomacy in 1366 and the return to war in 1369, the fragility of that idea was thoroughly exposed. For all the caveats, however, there is reason to believe that Edward III very deliberately complemented the extravagant assertions of national sovereignty made in the parliaments of the 1360s by representing himself and his court as recognizably English in composition, customs and culture. In this respect, Edward's reign may be said to have marked a key stage in the long and complex process whereby the descendants of the dukes of Normandy transformed themselves into true-born Englishmen.[71]

If the early 1360s marked the high point of Edward III's achievement in the performance of magnificence, the later years of the decade witnessed a definite diminution in such activity. Outside the annual meetings of the Garter at Windsor, there is no evidence that Edward hosted any major tournaments between 1364 and 1376.[72] Royal tours of the provinces were also notably scaled down. Edward's last public visit to the Midlands came in 1363, when he and the queen, together with some of the French princely hostages and the full panoply of the royal household, made a progress through the royal hunting grounds of Northamptonshire, Leicestershire and Nottinghamshire, calling at the Augustinian priories of Launde and Newstead and making formal state appearances in the towns of Leicester and Nottingham.[73] The tour culminated in a formal hall and feast at Nottingham castle on 8 September, at which Edward granted the townsmen the right to collect the profits from the royal ferry on the River Trent to finance the reconstruction of the public bridge.[74] In 1366, by contrast, the king's summer tour was on a much more modest scale. The queen now remained, with most of the royal household, at Windsor and Havering, and Edward set off with a small entourage for sport in the New

---

[71] J. S. Hamilton, *The Plantagenets: History of a Dynasty* (London, 2010), 225–6.

[72] See p. 532.

[73] For the act of pardon performed at Leicester, see p. 380.

[74] *CPR 1361–4*, 419; *Records of the Borough of Nottingham, 1155–1399*, ed. W. H. Stevenson (London, 1882), 182–3; A. Cooper, *Bridges, Law and Power in Medieval England, 700–1400* (Woodbridge, 2006), i, 55, 125. See also *CPR 1361–4*, 396.

Forest. The earl of Salisbury set in provision at Canford Magna in the hope of hosting the royal party for a night or two,[75] and the king made several solemn visits to the royal foundation of Beaulieu Abbey. But the move down to Corfe, and then back in a leisurely loop via Clarendon to be reunited with the queen at Havering, seems to have been treated purely as a private excursion devoid of the ceremonial set pieces that had accompanied royal itineraries until 1363.

This change in the character and function of royal visitations was reflected in the more restricted geographical range of the royal travels. After 1363, Edward never again visited his hunting lodges of Clipstone and Bestwood in Sherwood Forest, and usually confined his pursuit of game to the royal reserves in Surrey, Hampshire, Berkshire and Northamptonshire. Outside the hunting season, and when the ritual performances of the spring season were not upon him, the king would tend to quit Westminster and Windsor and seek the comparative intimacy of a string of lesser castles, manors and lodges in the south-east, at Sheen, Kings Langley, Gravesend, Rotherhithe, Eltham, Queenborough, Hadleigh and Havering. Increasingly too, as on the expedition of 1366, Edward chose to be accompanied on his movements through the Home Counties not by the full staff of the royal household but by a *privata familia*, or select entourage, numbering no more than about fifty personal attendants and domestic servants.[76] This in turn made some modest contribution to domestic economy. On several occasions in the later 1360s, cooks and bakers attached to the household were laid off and billeted out from Windsor upon the nearby nunnery at Burnham (Buckinghamshire).[77]

Edward III's resort to a more informal and settled lifestyle reflected his advancing age. Froissart later claimed that the king responded to the request of his guest, Peter of Cyprus, for assistance in crusade in 1363–4 by saying (conveniently enough) that he was too old for such adventures and would rather leave them to his sons.[78] Edward was certainly less disposed to the rigours of itineration. One of the last occasions on which he slept in a tent within his own realm was on an impromptu visit to the queen's manor of East Tytherley (Hampshire) in 1366.[79] The king also now required more regular medical attention. In the 1360s the apothecaries William Stanes and William Nerve were frequently commissioned to supply medicines for Edward's use, and the physicians John Glaston and John Paladyn were in more frequent attendance at court. The costs of

[75] *Calendar of Ancient Correspondence Concerning Wales*, 222–3.

[76] Tout, *Chapters*, iv, 177–81; Given-Wilson, *Royal Household*, 33; McIntosh, *Autonomy and Community*, 22.

[77] E 403/427, 18 July 1366; E 404/9/59, privy seal writ, 26 Jan. 1369.

[78] Froissart, vi, 90–2, 280–4. Cf. *Chron. QPV*, 128, which claims (probably satirically) that Edward told Peter that he should render Cyprus to the English crown as recognition of Richard I's earlier conquest of the island.

[79] E 101/396/2, fol. 42v.

such treatments could be very high: one bill for drugs alone in 1367 ran to £54, the annual income of a wealthy knight.[80] Since there is no indication that the king ever suffered prolonged periods of illness in the 1360s, it may well be suspected that at least some of this expenditure was actually on potions and palliatives for the ailing Philippa of Hainault. In the spring of 1366 Edward made a payment to the queen's ladies for their attentiveness during Philippa's recent recuperation from a serious, though undefined, malady.[81] Given the manner in which Edward III's court ceremonial had so consistently presented his monarchy as a royal partnership, the increasing frailty of the queen may be accounted one of the principal reasons for the diminution of public ceremonial in the later 1360s.

The main consequence of the notable scaling down of royal magnificence was the dramatic decline in the number of senior, above-stairs staff in the royal household. By the middle of the 1360s there were no more than a dozen or so knights retained at any one time in the king's personal service. Furthermore, there was now a much firmer distinction between the rank and file and the elite group, known as the knights of the chamber, who attended upon the king in his private apartments.[82] The decline in the number of household knights may have been a simple response to the new logistics, but it had a strong impact on wider perceptions of the representativeness of the royal household and the openness of the court. By the later 1360s the only members of noble families still in formal employ in the household were the earl of Oxford (as hereditary chamberlain), Lords Percy and Latimer, Thomas Beauchamp and Gilbert Despenser, uncle of Edward, Lord Despenser.[83] Most of the other senior figures came from a relatively small and self-perpetuating nexus of courtly families. Philip la Vache, a household knight of the 1370s and friend of Chaucer, owed his promotion directly to his father, Richard, who was the deputy chamberlain of the household in the mid-1360s.[84] Similarly, Sir John atte Wode, a knight of the chamber by 1370, owed much of his prominence to a very advantageous marriage with one of the queen's ladies-in-waiting, Lucy, daughter of the established courtier Sir John Beauchamp of

[80] E 101/393/15, m. 2; E 101/394/16, m. 16; E 101/396/2, fol. 40v; E 101/396/11, fol. 15; E 159/144, *Brev. bar.*, Mich., rots 12, 14d; Tout, *Chapters*, iv, 182; Talbot and Hammond, *Medical Practitioners*, 151, 174.

[81] E 404/7/47, privy seal writ 13 May 1366; E 403/427, 19 May 1366.

[82] Given-Wilson, *Royal Household*, 280–1.

[83] E 101/395/2, no. 236; E 101/395/10; Given-Wilson, *Royal Household*, 281; M. J. Lawrence, 'Power, Ambition and Political Rehabilitation: The Despensers, *c*.1281–1400' (University of York PhD thesis, 2005), 37. For Oxford's assertion of the right to act as chamberlain and his resulting presence at court during the 1360s see Tout, *Chapters*, iv, 338–9; Given-Wilson, 'Royal Charter Witness Lists', 69, 71.

[84] Tout, *Chapters*, vi, 43, 47; G. Chaucer, *The Riverside Chaucer*, ed. L. D. Benson, 3rd edn (Oxford, 1987), 653 (ll. 1084–5).

Holt.[85] There was nothing particularly unusual about such strong social networks. But as recruitment from outside those circles dwindled, the impression of cliquishness was bound to take hold. It is in the changes made to the functioning and personnel of the household during the later 1360s that we can see the seeds of a problem that would ultimately lead the polity in 1376 to identify the king's household as a cradle of faction, rivalry and corruption.

If the changes in the performance and personnel of the court were all readily explicable in a manner acceptable to the wider political elite, there remains the fact that Edward III did now have something very serious to hide. In 1364 one of the queen's waiting women, Alice Perrers, bore the king a son named John Southray. Two daughters, Joan and Jane, followed in quick succession.[86] Whatever the possibility of earlier peccadilloes, there had never been any rumour or suggestion that Edward had previously sired illegitimate children. In a court society that often took a frank approach to such matters, the liaison may not have been considered morally abhorrent. But wider knowledge of a mistress was bound to call into question Edward's much advertised commitment to family life and expose him as a philandering hypocrite. David II's highly public liaisons had recently fomented much political dissent in Scotland; the murder of his mistress, Katherine Mortimer, in 1360 and his marriage to Margaret Drummond in 1363 were both matters of keen gossip at the very time that Alice Perrers first set her head on Edward III's pillow.[87] The English political establishment was quick to close ranks in a deliberate effort to counter rumours about the royal affair. Edward was only too keen to comply with such damage limitation. He had removed Alice from the queen's entourage by 1366, and although he allowed his mistress to draw a livery of wine in his own household, his only other direct patronage came in the form of a solitary wardship in distant Cumberland.[88] So long as Queen Philippa lived, there remained some hope that the liaison would quietly run its course and that Perrers and her bastards could soon be pensioned off into convenient obscurity.

This, however, was to reckon without the royal mistress's formidable resourcefulness. Alice was a self-made woman who had left a family of modest freeholders in East Hanney (Berkshire) for an early marriage to a

---

[85] Wode's status as knight of the chamber is attested in E 159/146, *Brev. bar.*, Pasch, rot. 5. For his career and full references, see p. 319.

[86] C. Given-Wilson and A. Curteis, *The Royal Bastards of Medieval England* (London, 1984), 136–42.

[87] Penman, *David II*, 245–6, 269, 293.

[88] *CPR 1364–7*, 321, 396, 397, 418. For deliveries of the grant of wine in the king's household, see E 101/396/2, fol. 34; E 101/397/5, fols 45v, 84v; E 101/397/20. Alice's name does not appear on the extant livery lists for the queen's ladies in 1366 and 1369: 'Enrolments and Documents', 162–70.

London-based trader, Janyn Perrers. As a young widow in the early 1360s she had already begun to build up connections of her own in the commercial world.[89] Faced with the prospect that the king might not publicly acknowledge their son, she set about alternative means of building a future for John Southray. From 1364 to 1369 Alice secretly drew cash from the royal coffers which she invested in properties in London and an expanding portfolio of rural estates in the Home Counties, the South Midlands and beyond. Those with whom she came into contact would later have much to say about the imperious and unscrupulous manner in which Alice conducted her private business affairs during the 1360s.[90]

Despite the court's best efforts to disguise the truth, then, there is every possibility that Alice Perrers was already becoming the subject of salacious speculation by 1368. It is often assumed that Alice was the model for the figure of Lady Meed, the infamous embodiment of moral and legal corruption in William Langland's *Piers Plowman*. In fact, the first version of this poem was written in the early 1360s, before Alice was in the public eye; it was only later, in his successive revisions of the poem in *c*.1377 and *c*.1381, that Langland adapted Meed to reflect some of the details of Perrers's career.[91] The earliest credible hints of public debate about the king's mistress come instead in a commentary written by the distinguished friar John Erghome on the *Prophecies of John of Bridlington*. This was probably completed in Queen Philippa's own lifetime, and certainly by 1372. Erghome was appropriately cautious about making too direct an allusion to Alice. But in referring to the biblical stories of Samson and Delilah and David and Bathsheba, he seemed to tap into a current discourse about the way in which lascivious behaviour was depriving the ageing Edward III of his physical vigour and political judgement.[92] As Philippa of Hainault moved from sickbed to deathbed, the court faced the deeply worrying prospect that Alice Perrers might replace the queen not only in Edward's arms but also in the public formalities of the state.

If there was one area of activity in which Edward III consistently demonstrated his allegiance to the principles of magnificence throughout the 1360s, it was in the cult of the dead. During this phase of his life,

[89] W. M. Ormrod, 'Who was Alice Perrers?', *Chaucer Review*, xl (2006), 219–29.

[90] J. Bothwell, 'The Management of Position: Alice Perrers, Edward III, and the Creation of a Landed Estate, 1362–1377', *JMH*, xxiv (1998), 31–51; W. M. Ormrod, 'The Trials of Alice Perrers', *Speculum*, lxxxiii (2008), 381–6.

[91] M. Giancarlo, '*Piers Plowman*, Parliament, and the Public Voice', *Yearbook of Langland Studies*, xvii (2003), 135–74.

[92] *Political Poems*, i, 141, 142, 159, 161; Barnie, *War in Medieval English Society*, 145–7; C. D. Fletcher, 'Corruption at Court: Crisis and the Theme of *luxuria* in England and France, *c*.1340–1422', *The Court as Stage: England and the Low Countries in the Late Middle Ages*, ed. S. Gunn and A. Janse (Woodbridge, 2006), 28–38.

Edward lost his mother, Queen Isabella (d. 1358), his sister, Joan of
Scotland (d. 1362), his wife, Queen Philippa (d. 1369), two of his daughters, Margaret (d. 1361) and Mary (d. 1362), his second son, Lionel (d. 1368)
and two of his daughters-in-law, Elizabeth of Clarence (d. 1363) and
Blanche of Lancaster (d. 1368). In the face of such tragedies, the king
naturally began to give serious consideration to the provision for the souls
of family members. In 1361 he secured for St Stephen's Chapel,
Westminster the privilege of baptizing and burying the children of the
kings of England.[93] Later in the decade he paid out at least £100 for a
tomb commissioned by Queen Philippa for their daughters Margaret and
Mary at Abingdon Abbey, and erected windows in memory of the
princesses at the royal foundation of Kings Langley. Towards the end of
his reign he also commissioned a new tomb at Westminster for two of his
children who had died in the 1340s, Blanche of the Tower and William of
Windsor.[94] And when the baleful news of Lionel of Clarence's death
reached England in 1368, the magnates of realm were summoned en
masse to attend elaborate exequies for the prince's soul at Westminster
Abbey in January 1369.[95]

Not surprisingly, it was in this period that Edward III became more
keenly preoccupied with his own mortality. On the eve of his expedition
to France in 1359, and properly mindful of the need to prepare for the
eventuality of death on campaign, he handed all the jewels currently in his
possession to Queen Philippa with instructions that, should he fail to
return, they might be considered a permanent gift and not reclaimed by
his executors.[96] Around the same time, the king gave renewed attention to
the endowment of his religious foundations. In 1362 he spent £2,000 on
the purchase of the personal estate of Juliana Leybourne, dowager
countess of Huntingdon, to provide landed income for St Mary Graces, St
Stephen's Westminster and the friary of Kings Langley.[97] He also made
definitive plans for his own burial. After toying with the fanciful idea of a

---

[93] *CPP*, 363.

[94] E 403/429, 26 Oct 1366; E 403/429, 17 Feb 1367; E 403/434, 27 May 1368; *King's Works*, i, 262, 486.

[95] Lionel's body was not brought back to England until the very end of the reign.
E 403/436, 16 Dec. 1368; *Collection of the Wills*, 88; *AC*, 56–7; E 101/397/20, m. 9.

[96] *CPR 1358–61*, 269.

[97] *CCR 1360–4*, 362–4; Wolffe, *Royal Demesne*, 62; Harriss, *King, Parliament*, 485; Given-
Wilson, 'Richard II and his Grandfather's Will', 320–37. The estates in Sussex earlier
acquired from Roger Bavent were also now assigned to the endowment of Kings Langley:
CIPM, x, no. 387; *CFR 1347–56*, 294; *CFR 1356–68*, 22–3; N. Saul, *Scenes from Provincial Life:
Knightly Families in Sussex, 1280–1400* (Oxford, 1986), 181. It is likely that Edward originally
intended to do similarly with the estates demised to him by Sir John Cobham in 1359, for
which the king rewarded the latter with a payment of 2,000 marks, an annuity of 100
marks and a life interest in the relevant properties. As it happened, however, Cobham
outlived Edward III. See *PROME*, vi, 17–19; *CCR 1360–4*, 529; *CPR 1361–4*, 479; E 403/417,
20 Oct. 1363.

mausoleum at Cologne in 1338 and the more plausible suggestion of interment at Windsor in 1354, the king reverted to a decision, first recorded as
long ago as 1339, to be buried in the south arcade of Edward the
Confessor's Chapel at Westminster Abbey.[98] On a visit to the monks of
Westminster in 1359, Edward declared his intention to be interred in the
abbey church near 'that most illustrious and courageous soldier, and the
most prudent statesman', Edward I.[99] The king's abiding sense of dynastic
identity and obligation had at last prevailed in a powerful statement of
Westminster's emerging status as the premier royal mausoleum of
England.

Court life was habituated to honouring the deaths and memories of the
political elite, and for practical reasons it was quite impossible for Edward
III to attend all major funerals in person. When members of the high
nobility were interred outside the capital, the convention was for the king
to send down lengths of cloth of gold that would be draped, as a sign of
special distinction, over the hearse and coffin.[100] Occasionally, however,
Edward went further. In 1360, when the earl of March died on the royal
campaign in France, the king sent special instructions home for a
commemoration service to be held, at his expense, at Windsor castle.[101]
The funeral of Edward's cousin, Henry of Grosmont, at Leicester in April
1361 clashed with a pre-existing royal commitment to an important
meeting of the council, but three of the princes, Edward, John and
Edmund, were sent to represent their father at this major event.[102] In the
spring of 1364 the king was again detained by his negotiations with John
II from attending the memorial services for Elizabeth of Clarence at her
family's religious foundations of Bruisyard and Clare in Suffolk, but took
time to dictate a personal letter to the bishop of Norwich authorizing the
latter to preside at the duchess's interment at Clare.[103] Such interventions
suggest Edward's keen awareness of the sense of dignity that derived even
from his indirect presence at the solemnities of death.

[98] WAM 6300*, printed in Ormrod, 'Personal Religion', 868 n. 109; Binski, *Westminster
Abbey*, 195; D. M. Palliser, 'Royal Mausolea in the Long Fourteenth Century (1272–1422)',
Fourteenth Century England III, ed. Ormrod, 9–10.

[99] Reading, 132–3; A. Gransden, *Historical Writing in England*, 2 vols (London, 1974–82), ii,
108. See also *Brut*, ii, 309; *The Great Chronicle of London*, ed. A. H. Thomas and I. D.
Thornley (London, 1938), 40.

[100] In 1360–1 liveries of cloth were recorded for the funerals of the king's cousin,
Elizabeth, Lady Clare, at the Convent of the Minoresses in London, of Sir John
Beauchamp at St Paul's Cathedral, and of the earl of Northampton at Walden Abbey
(Essex): E 101/393/15, m. 10.

[101] E 101/393/11, fol. 61v.

[102] *RDP*, iv, 627–9; *Collection of the Wills*, 84; *BPR*, iv, 73; E 403/408, 8 Apr. 1361;
Goodman, *John of Gaunt*, 36. Cloth of gold was again provided by the king: E 101/393/15
m. 14.

[103] E 101/394/16, m. 3; E 101/394/19; E 361/4, rot. 12.

It was in the funeral arrangements of Queen Isabella, John II of France and Queen Philippa that Edward III most obviously demonstrated his mastery of the ceremonies of burial and commemoration. Queen Isabella had long decided that she would be buried at the great Franciscan friary in London, which already housed Eleanor of Provence's heart and Margaret of France's tomb, and Joan of Scotland would also elect to be interred there a few years after her mother.[104] Nevertheless, it took some three months from the queen's death in late August 1358 to put in place the elaborate arrangements for a major public funeral. Large numbers of the royal family and the lay and clerical elite were said to have attended the solemnities in London in late November.[105] In keeping with Edward's insistence on the symbolic healing of wounds left over from the revolution of 1326–7, the queen was buried in her wedding robes and with an urn containing the heart of her long-dead husband.[106] The crown spent the significant sum of £550 on alms distributed to the poor of the city of London and assorted gifts to the friary church.[107] Nor did the spectacle end there. A month after the funeral, in December, Chancellor Edington, Treasurer Sheppey and the mayor and aldermen of London attended a special requiem mass in honour of the queen's soul and took refreshments of wine and confectionery.[108] The subsequent services held to mark the anniversary of the queen's death involved the dressing of the tomb in cloth of gold, torchlit processions and distributions of alms to the residents of Newgate prison and various religious houses in the city.[109] Nothing, it seemed, quite became Queen Isabella's performance of queenship like the leaving of it.

The death of John II in England in the spring of 1364 gave Edward III a notable opportunity to display his munificence for the benefit of both national and international audiences. Edward readily concurred with the view that John's body should be carried back to France for burial at

---

[104] J. C. Parsons, ' "Never was a body buried in England with such solemnity and honour": The Burials and Posthumous Commemorations of English Queens to 1500', *Queens and Queenship in Medieval Europe*, ed. A. J. Duggan (Woodbridge, 1997), 330–1. For Joan's funeral see E 403/412, 20 Oct. 1362; *Issues*, 184.

[105] *Eulogium*, iii, 311.

[106] F. D. Blackley, 'Isabella of France, Queen of England (1308–1358), and the Late Medieval Cult of the Dead', *Canadian Journal of History*, xv (1980), 26, 27, 30; F. D. Blackley, 'The Tomb of Isabella of France, Wife of Edward II of England', *International Society for the Study of Church Monuments Bulletin*, viii (1983), 161–4; Ormrod, 'Sexualities of Edward II', 45–6.

[107] E 403/394, 29 Nov. 1358; E 361/4, m. 1d.

[108] E 403/394, 8 Feb 1359.

[109] E 101/393/7; E 101/394/10, 18; E 101/395/5; E 101/397/1, 13, 18, analysed by Blackley, 'Isabella of France', 34–7, and J. Catto, 'Religion and the English Nobility in the Later Fourteenth Century', *History and Imagination: Essays in Honour of H. R. Trevor-Roper*, ed. H. Lloyd-Jones, V. Pearl and B. Worden (London, 1981), 47. For the anniversary of 1360, see E 101/393/11, fol. 6iv.

Saint-Denis. But this did not prevent significant preliminary ceremonies from being conducted in England. The royal corpse was borne in state, accompanied by a hundred torch-bearers, to St Paul's Cathedral, where a requiem mass was sung in the presence of the English royal family, the bishops and abbots and a great array of nobles. A screened platform was erected in the cathedral church for Edward's use during the service.[110] The king then accompanied the procession two leagues from the city before entrusting Sir Nicholas Damory with the task of conducting the cortège, via Canterbury, to Dover.[111] English chroniclers believed that John's entrails and heart, removed in the course of embalming, were interred respectively at St Paul's and Canterbury. The facts were confused, but the moral was obvious: it was on Edward III's good grace that the lives and deaths of his rivals of France continued to hang.[112]

Like her mother-in-law, Philippa of Hainault had definite ideas about the manner of her funeral and ample time in which to elaborate plans for her own commemoration. Some time before February 1365, the queen asked the dowager countess of Pembroke to commission her a tomb in Paris, and by January 1366 at the latest the contract had gone to Jean de Liège, a celebrated craftsman much patronized by the Valois court.[113] Just as the king had already declared his intention to be buried opposite his grandfather at Westminster, so now Philippa's tomb was erected, in advance of her death, in the easternmost bay of the south side of St Edward's Chapel, directly opposite that of Edward I's queen, Eleanor of Castile. The effigy, carved in white marble, was a very personal state- ment of artistic preference with its depiction of the queen not in angelic perfection but as an aged matron complete with thick waist and double chin. Equally, the elaborate iconography of the tomb proclaimed a forceful political message about Philippa's royal dignity, her distinguished birth and her major diplomatic contribution to her husband's emergence as a leader of the Western world.

---

[110] E 101/394/16, mm. 11, 1; E 361/4, rot. 12; E 403/418, 11 Apr. 1364. Cloth of gold was purchased to hang over the heads of king and queen at the ceremonies, and Edward III had a new set of robes for the occasion: E 101/394/16, m. 15. For the king's special alms at St Paul's see *Issues*, 183.

[111] 'Wigmore Chronicle', 293; E 364/7, rot. 1d; *Chronique de Richard Lescot*, 245; *Issues*, 183; *Chronicle of Jean de Venette*, 120. For the inventory of John's plate returned to France after his death see 'Notes et documents', 153-6.

[112] Reading, 216; *AC*, 51; Hardyng, *Chronicle of John Hardyng*, 330; Delachenal, iii, 17-18.

[113] E 101/508/30; *Issues*, 189. For the dating and significance of these references see W. M. Ormrod, 'Queenship, Death and Agency: The Commemorations of Isabella of France and Philippa of Hainault', *Memory and Commemoration in Medieval England*, ed. C. M. Barron and C. Burgess (Donington, 2010), 96-103. For analyses of the tomb see Morganstern, *Gothic Tombs*, 73-80; L. L. Gee, *Women, Art and Patronage from Henry III to Edward III, 1216-1377* (Woodbridge, 2002), 115-18; Sekules, 'Dynasty and Patrimony', 169-73.

Philippa died, at Windsor castle, on 15 August 1369.[114] War with France was now once more within the king's sight, but Edward was forced to postpone his command of the army while the funeral and the period of official mourning were completed. It took nearly five months to organize the appropriate exequies. By December a date had been fixed, and a large number of prelates and lords and ladies were told to make the winter trek to the capital.[115] The queen's body was moved from Windsor on 3 January, accompanied by a large group of household officials and a phalanx of male and female paupers dressed in the black of deep mourning. Taken first by water to the bishop of London's residence at Fulham, it was then borne along the Thames to the church of St Mary Overy, Southwark, before being transported through the streets of London to St Paul's Cathedral on 8 January for the liturgy that accompanied the vigil of burial. The next day, Philippa's remains were interred in Westminster Abbey. At each stage of the journey, elaborate wooden hearses or catafalques were erected to hold the coffin and support the torches and candles that burned constantly around it; the hearse at the abbey was left *in situ* until at least the first month's special mass for the queen's soul.[116] Since Edward III's wife had died just before the anniversary of Queen Isabella, the annual services performed in their memory were arranged, after 1370, as one continuous sequence, attended by bishops and abbots and at least some members of the royal family and court. Not surprisingly, however, the king was careful to distinguish the relative importance of the two queens, and expenditure on alms and hospitality at Philippa of Hainault's memorial masses significantly outstripped those dispensed for Isabella of France.[117]

There is no particular reason to doubt the sincerity of Edward III's devotion to the memory of Philippa of Hainault. Froissart later conjured up an imaginary scene in which the dying Philippa exhorted her grieving spouse to affirm his commitment to lie with her in death.[118] If this contained a barbed hint at the king's lack of faith within marriage, there was never any real danger that Edward would wilfully compromise Philippa's public memory. In a later parliament the chancellor would remark that '[no] Christian king or other lord in the world ever had so noble and gracious a lady for his wife or such children – princes, dukes and others – as our lord the king has had'.[119] Philippa's role as a fecund mother

---

[114] Sherborne, *War, Politics*, 3, 88–9. *ODNB*, xliv, 37, gives the date as before 14 Aug.

[115] *Issue Roll of Brantingham*, 408–9; WAM, 12214, partially printed in Ormrod, 'Personal Religion', 868 n. 115.

[116] *AC*, 58; *Issue Roll of Brantingham*, 98, 282, 383, 389, 492; 'Enrolments and Documents', 172; E 101/395/2, no. 236; E 404/10/65, privy seal writ, 23 Mar. 1370.

[117] Blackley, 'Isabella of France', 34–7; Catto, 'Religion and the English Nobility', 47.

[118] Froissart, vii, 181–3.

[119] *PROME*, v, 395.

of great men lent itself readily to comparison with the Virgin Mary, on the Feast of whose Assumption the queen had died. Some time shortly after her death a monk of Westminster wrote a skilful poem in praise of the deceased Philippa, perhaps intended as the basis of an epitaph to be inscribed or painted on her tomb:

Let the whole of England have time for prayers
Because Queen Philippa lies dead, closed up in death.
While she flourished she was full of grace to the English.
The people were not in want; neither was her country in need of grain.
It is clear to everyone now that she was successful.
She would call upon Christ while she lived so that the kingdom should not lack for its harvest.
Hence, that piety of Christ could not die
But her own goodness would have to come to the supreme joys [of heaven].[120]

Here, as in a wider tradition that established itself in the chronicles during the fifteenth century, Philippa's readiness to take on the cultural and political identity of her husband's court bred the enduring idea of a bond of reciprocal love between her and the English people.[121] The sentiment may have been fanciful, but its strength was palpable, not least because of the convenient refuge it came to provide from the seamier realities of court politics in the 1370s.

---

[120] WAM, 15169:

Anglia tota vacet precibus quia sub libitina
Mortua regina clausa Philippa iacet
Hec quia dum viguit fuit Anglis gracia plena
Plebs non indiguit nec patria farris egena
Omnibus apparet iam profuit illa vocaret
Christum dum degeret ne regnum messe careret
Hinc Christi pietas illa non possit perire
Sic sua set bonitas ad gaudia summa veniret.

[121] Barnie, *War in Medieval English Society*, 118; Ormrod, 'Personal Religion', 850.

Chapter 17

THE THRONE OF PEACE, 1360–1369

For a quarter of a century before the treaties of Berwick and Calais, England had been in a more or less permanent state of war. If the polity was concerned from the start about the precise terms of the settlements of 1358–60, it must also have hailed the prospective dividends of peace: a significant reduction in levels of taxation and other burdens of war, and an opportunity once more to address perennial domestic issues such as the state of the economy and the preservation of public order. In keeping his focus of attention very firmly on the international stage, Edward III may have imagined that the mere absence of war was enough to convince his subjects of the continuing benefits of his rule. But the dynamics of peacetime politics proved rather more challenging than the king had expected. With the withdrawal of the powerful rhetoric of national emergency that had previously been deployed to justify so much domestic policy, there was a good deal of uncertainty over the nature of the reciprocal bond of obligation between crown and people. The traditions of negotiation and consent on which Edward had placed such emphasis during the war were now taken up with confidence by parliament, which expected the energies of the state to be directed into an ambitious programme of social, economic and legal reform. Edward III's instinct for laissez-faire did not always sit comfortably with such goals and sometimes significantly compromised the capacity of his government to implement clear and coherent strategies. The politics of peace thus set challenges for both the style and the substance of royal policy throughout the 1360s.

Edward III's confident expectation of a rapid return to stability and plenty was rudely confounded by the return of the Black Death in the spring of 1361. The second pestilence raged through England over the summer and autumn and lingered on in some outlying parts of the country throughout the following winter. While the proportion of the population that succumbed was lower than in the first pandemic, contemporaries commented that the plague of 1361 struck down more men than women and killed an especially large number of children.[1] Either by coincidence

---

[1] Knighton, 184–5; *Anon. Cant.*, 114–15; Bolton, ' "World Upside Down" ', 27–8; Cohn, *Black Death Transformed*, 130.

or as a direct effect of the pestilence, many of the lay and clerical elite also died in 1361–2, including the king's two younger daughters, his cousin Henry of Grosmont and Bishops Northburgh of London and Stratford of Chichester.[2] Preventive measures had promptly to be put in place. The Church ordered public penance to assuage divine wrath. The central courts were closed down in the spring of 1361, and business was temporarily suspended in the upper exchequer in order that local officials did not have to travel up to Westminster during the emergency. Edward III himself retreated to the country for almost the whole of the period from May to September 1361, moving first to Hadleigh and then on, via Woodstock and Easthampstead, to the safety of isolation in the New Forest.[3]

Just as it seemed that some degree of normality might be restored, the vagaries of nature imposed a second cruel blow on the realm. On 15 January 1362 the British Isles suffered one of the most severe hurricanes in their history, known to posterity as St Maurus's Wind. As well as causing the collapse of numerous churches and other public and domestic buildings, the tempest destroyed woodlands and orchards, mills, barns and fences. Some major lords carried out extensive repairs, complaining bitterly of the high prices that building contractors were charging at this time of national misfortune. Many lesser folk were left in a much worse predicament, unable to restore their properties because the recent plague had intensified the existing shortage of skilled and unskilled workers.[4]

For the crown, the storm provided some unexpected bonuses. Forest officials adroitly recognized a business opportunity and started selling off fallen wood.[5] And Edward III took a keen interest in his rights to treasure trove from ships wrecked during the tempest in the port of Plymouth.[6] On the other hand, the hurricane added significantly to the problems of the king's own estate officials, and the exchequer had little choice but to accept pleas for temporary reductions in farms and rents 'on account of the time of the wind'.[7] In the face of the twin misfortunes of plague and storm, Edward III's council understood that the first great test of the peacetime regime would lie in its commitment to the re-establishment of economic and social stability.

[2] *CCR 1360–4*, 197–8; *Anon. Cant.*, 114–17; McFarlane, *Nobility*, 168–71.

[3] BIA, Register 11, fol. 48; *CCR 1360–4*, 181–2; E 159/137, *Brev. bar.*, Trin., rot. 1; E 159/137, *Recorda*, Pasch., rot. 14; W. M. Ormrod, 'The Politics of Pestilence: Government in England after the Black Death', *Black Death*, ed. Ormrod and Lindley, 150.

[4] Reading, 151; *Anon. Cant.*, 118–19; Knighton, 185; *AC*, 50; *Anon. Cant.*, 118–19; 'Wigmore Chronicle', 292; *Chronicle of London*, 65; C. E. Britton, *A Meteorological Chronology to A.D. 1450* (London, 1937), 144–5.

[5] E 159/140, *Brev. bar.*, Mich., rot. 28. For similar practice on the queen's estates see *CFR 1356–68*, 159.

[6] SC 8/247/12320; C 81/1335/39; *CPR 1361–4*, 209.

[7] *CIM*, iii, no. 605; *CFR 1356–68*, 341; E 368/135, *Precepta*, Pasch.

The 1360s represented a challenging moment for such policy-making. In the aftermath of the second pestilence, employers grew obsessed with the notion that the labouring classes were taking advantage of the newly competitive market to press for easy terms and unreasonably high wages. The author of *Winner and Waster* had criticized those peasants with too much money and time on their hands who, careless of the future, made off to the tavern with gleeful cries of 'Wee hee!' Even such a relatively sympathetic commentator as William Langland, the author of *Piers Plowman*, complained in the 1360s that labourers previously content to eat old vegetables now expected 'fresh flesh, or fish fried'.[8] The establishment reacted with a predictable appeal to traditional values. In 1364 Archbishop Thoresby issued constitutions for the province of York banning lewd entertainments on the eve of feasts and funerals. The crown followed up with an unusual proclamation prohibiting football, cock-fighting and other sports 'of no value' on high days, and exhorted all able-bodied men to devote their leisure time to practising the productive art of archery.[9]

If such rhetoric proved popular with the proprietary elite, it also belied the bleak realities of many peasants' everyday existence. The great storm was merely one manifestation of a larger, and very alarming, environmental crisis. With the aid of modern scientific techniques, it is now possible to demonstrate that England, in common with much of Europe and the wider world, suffered a serious and sustained climatic deterioration during the second and third quarters of the fourteenth century. The winter of 1350–1 had been the severest for a century, and in the 1360s conditions deteriorated still further. Although there were now many fewer mouths to be fed, there was also much less land being put to the plough, and the onset of bad weather was therefore just as likely to produce shortages as it had before the plague: indeed, the famine of 1369 was one of the worst suffered in England during the entire Middle Ages. The resulting high price charged for basic foodstuffs seriously compromised the real purchasing power of wages, and until the mid-1370s the income of most agricultural contract-workers at best only kept pace with inflation.[10] The golden age of the English labourer was still a long way off.

In its effort to provide a reasoned response to the economic problems of the 1360s, Edward III's government pursued a pragmatic course that attempted at once to respond to the concerns of the landed and commercial elites and to keep their more vindictive characteristics in check. This

---

[8] *Wynnere and Wastoure*, 10 (ll. 274–82); W. Langland, *Piers Plowman: The A Version*, ed. G. Kane (London, 1960), 344–5 (Passus VII, ll. 286–95).

[9] *Records of Convocation*, xiii, 153–4; *Foedera*, III.ii, 704.

[10] B. M. S. Campbell, 'Physical Shocks, Biological Hazards, and Human Impacts: The Crisis of the Fourteenth Century Revisited', *Economic and Biological Interactions*, ed. Cavaciocchi, 15–20; D. L. Farmer 'Prices and Wages [ii]', *The Agrarian History of England and Wales, III: 1348–1500*, ed. E. Miller (Cambridge, 1991), 434, 502, 516, 520–1; C. Dyer, *Standards of Living in the Later Middle Ages* (Cambridge, 1989), 262.

was first revealed in relation to the labour laws. In November 1359, in order to release members of the knightly class for service in the Reims campaign, the crown had withdrawn the specialist commissions set up in 1352 to deal with breaches of this legislation.[11] At the parliament of January 1361 the commons pressed for further extension of the labour regulations, and the crown responded by authorizing imprisonment and even branding as punishments against serious offenders.[12] As yet, however, no efforts were made to revive the specialist commissions of labourers and thus create the capacity for a vigorous campaign of enforcement of wage policy in the localities.

It was only with the coming of the plague and the hurricane in 1361–2 that the government once more considered a more proactive approach to economic regulation. Proclamations were issued announcing that the king would punish those who quitted their jobs on his building projects in pursuit of better terms, and local investigations were ordered into the reported escalating costs of roofing materials and builders' wages.[13] After further agitation by the commons in the parliament of October 1362, the council agreed to empower the commissioners of the peace as justices of labourers and have them enforce the legislation of 1349–51 in their newly regularized quarter sessions.[14] Even then, however, the crown continued to show some concern about the possibility of over-zealous and vindictive prosecutions. It refused to revive the practice of paying the expenses of the local justices out of the financial penalties taken under the labour laws.[15] And in 1364 it again dropped reference to the labour laws in the peace commissions, instead encouraging the provincial judiciary to focus on the economic offence of forestalling.[16]

A similar cautious approach was adopted in response to the parliamentary demand in 1363 for measures to address the problem of rising prices. The government proposed three solutions. First, artisans and merchants should restrict themselves to working in one commodity ('vintners to wine, wool merchants to wool, drapers to cloth, shoemakers to shoes, tailors to tailoring'). Secondly, the old idea of a reasonable or 'just' price for foodstuffs would be revived. Thirdly, and more unusually, each rank of society should dress according to its estate, with strict rules applied as to relative qualities of cloth and gradations of fur, headgear and jewellery. The

[11] Powell, 'Administration', 52; Musson, 'New Labour Laws', 84. Continuing efforts were made to levy outstanding fines and amercements imposed by the former justices of labourers: E 159/136, *Brev. bar.*, Mich., rot. 20d; Hil., rot. 7d; Pasch., rot. 9.

[12] *SR*, i, 366–7.

[13] *CCR 1360–4*, 238–9, 262–3, 391; *CIM*, iii, no. 473.

[14] *SR*, i, 374; *CPR 1361–4*, 291–3.

[15] *PROME*, v, 148.

[16] *CPR 1361–4*, 528–31; R. H. Britnell, '*Forstall*, Forestalling and the Statute of Forestallers', *EHR*, cii (1987), 89–102.

meticulous, not to say obsessive, quality of this new sumptuary law may perhaps suggest a regime with rather too much time on its hands and a distinctly inflated view of the reach of its authority. In fact, though, the crown seems to have decided to call the commons' bluff. The proposed legislation on clothing struck out less at uppity peasants than at those merchants and gentry who attempted to ape the fashions of their aristocratic betters. The chancellor therefore offered a get-out clause: if the legislation proved inoperable, it could be withdrawn at the next parliament. When the commons unsurprisingly reported in January 1365 that the trading and sumptuary ordinances had indeed failed, the crown promptly struck them from the record.[17] It is hard to avoid the conclusion that the king and council, who remained wedded to the general principles of the free market, had intended just such an outcome. Although Edward III's immediate successors sometimes concurred with parliament's desire to limit the market in luxury goods, the precedent of 1363 was a continuing and salutary reminder that attempts to impose comprehensive sumptuary legislation were almost always destined to fail.[18]

In comparison with the moderation displayed in 1361–4, the crown's reaction to the third outbreak of the plague in 1368 indicated a much greater willingness to align public policy with the divisive social agenda of the commons. The latter were also much more astute in the manner in which they now articulated their demands. At the parliament of May 1368, which met even as the third pestilence was rising in London,[19] the knights and burgesses asked for the revival of the labour laws. Significantly, they claimed to be acting not for themselves but for the peasant freeholders and modest craftsmen who lived 'by the fruits of their lands and trade, and do not have lordships and villeins to serve them'. This expressed a beguiling notion, much developed over the following decade, that the labour laws promoted the common good by protecting the interests of the majority against the acquisitiveness of the few.[20] Faced with such a powerful discourse, the government had little choice but to abandon its former scruples and issue a statute declaring that the labour laws would henceforth be permanently enforceable in the peace sessions.[21]

The commons' other perennial concern – the preservation of public order – was rather less stridently expressed during the 1360s. Initial

[17] *PROME*, v, 161–2, 164–8 166, 169–70, 182; *SR*, i, 378–82; 'Wigmore Chronicle', 292; K. M. Phillips, 'Masculinities and the Medieval English Sumptuary Laws', *Gender and History*, xix (2007), 22–42.

[18] *PROME*, xiii, 108–11; xiv, 392–5, 459–60; F. E. Baldwin, *Sumptuary Legislation and Personal Regulation in England* (Baltimore, 1926), 34–119; Woolgar, *Great Household*, 174–5.

[19] *CCR 1364–8*, 426; E 159/144, *Brev. bar.*, Pasch, rot. 13d.

[20] *PROME*, v, 211, 337–40; C. Given-Wilson, 'The Problem of Labour in the Context of English Government, c.1350–1450', *Problem of Labour*, ed. Bothwell, Goldberg and Ormrod, 87.

[21] *SR*, i, 388.

worries that demobilized soldiers might turn to a life of crime proved unfounded, not least because so many undesirables chose to remain abroad as freebooters and mercenaries. In December 1363 John Coupland, the hero of Neville's Cross, was murdered by a gang of Northumberland worthies led by John Clifford. The affair caused a sensation: Clifford's dramatic escape from the realm and his eventual securing of a royal pardon dramatically illustrated the practical limits to the due processes of justice.[22] This case apart, however, the kinds of organized criminality that had created such an outcry at the beginning of the reign were notably absent in the 1360s.[23] The crown also offered timely reminders of its commitment to eradicating corruption in high places. In 1365 the chief justice of king's bench, Henry Green, and the chief baron of the exchequer, William Skipwith, were charged with 'enormous dereliction' of their duties. The king managed to avoid the political errors made in the earlier trial of Chief Justice Thorpe, and simply allowed the judges to pay hefty fines in lieu of formal prosecution.[24] In 1366 Edward also took a very active interest in the trial before the council of the disgraced sheriff of Yorkshire, Thomas Musgrave, and issued personal instructions for the appointment of a successor, Marmaduke Constable.[25] For the most part, such well-judged activism helped to maintain general confidence in the king's acknowledged role as protector of his subjects from the depredations of his own officers.

The remaining major political issue concerned less the quality and more the overall capacity of the criminal justice system. The parliamentary commons expected that the restoration of peacetime conditions would allow further devolution of judicial powers to the commissions of the peace. At first, Sir William Shareshull's successors in the senior ranks of the judiciary and council held firm to their previous policy of close central supervision. The king's bench was dispatched to York in 1362, the West Country in 1363 and East Anglia in 1364.[26] And when the commons in the parliament of 1365 complained about the intrusive nature of such visitations, they were rebuffed just as sharply as they had been in 1352: 'the king neither will nor can desist from sending his bench wherever he pleases'.[27] Yet despite this, the government inadvertently played to the

[22] M. Prestwich, 'Gilbert de Middleton and the Attack on the Cardinals, 1317', *Warriors and Churchmen in the High Middle Ages: Essays Presented to Karl Leyser*, ed. T. Reuter (London, 1992), 179–94; Dixon, 'John de Coupland', 36–49.

[23] Harriss, 'Formation of Parliament', 51 and n. 53.

[24] Knighton, 192–3; *ODNB*, xxiii, 507–8; l, 881; *SCCKB*, vi, xxvi; Maddicott, *Law and Lordship*, 60. In 1366 the king personally remitted the fine imposed on Skipwith: SC 1/40/165.

[25] *Select Cases before the King's Council, 1243–1482*, ed. I. S. Leadam and J. F. Baldwin (Selden Society, xxxv, 1918), 54–60; SC 1/56/91.

[26] *SCCKB*, vi, xlviii–xlix; Knighton, 184–7; KB 9/29, 141, 143.

[27] *PROME*, v, 182–3.

commons' belief in the merits of a devolved system of justice by making
some badly judged changes in the peace commissions. In 1361–4 it abandoned the system, in place since 1344, of reserving cases of felony for trial
before special quorums and instead reverted to the earlier practice of
sending such business before the members of the central courts acting in
the shires as justices of assize.[28] If this aimed consciously to restore the
conditions prevailing before 1338, its only obvious result was to throw a
now well-established system into some confusion. By 1368 the crown was
forced to admit that the recent division of powers had left the justices of
the peace significantly compromised in their ability to deliver judgments
on serious offences as well as on the increasingly wide range of petty tres-
passes that made up the bulk of business in their sessions.[29]

Faced with such difficulties, Edward III's council had no real option but
to acknowledge its mistakes and resurrect the system that had prevailed
between 1344 and 1361. The new peace commissions issued in 1368
restored the unity of local criminal justice. They were staffed by a mixture
of magnates, gentry and local lawyers, with a quorum of experts from the
central courts who would make themselves available, as necessary, for the
trial of serious crimes.[30] The return to a strong reliance on the justices of
the peace at this time could be amply justified as a result of the onset of
the third plague and the growing likelihood of a return to war with
France.[31] But it also proved to be a lasting change. The authority and
composition of the local benches endured, with no further significant
alteration, for the rest of the reign. And after some further experiments in
the 1380s and a relaxation of the quorum in 1390, the peace commissions
of 1368 formed the essential model for local criminal justice throughout
the fifteenth century.[32] If Edward III did not actually invent the justices of
the peace, it was to his reign and his vision that posterity would inevitably
ascribe their emergence as the very bedrock of the English judicial
system.[33]

Of all the issues confronting the peacetime administration of the 1360s,
the most intractable was that of finance. In the immediate context of the
treaty of Calais, king and parliament shared a confident belief that the
ending of war would bring on a regime of plenty in which the country

---

[28] Verduyn, 'Attitude', 153–4; Musson and Ormrod, *Evolution*, 61.

[29] *CPR 1367–70*, 191–6; *Sessions of the Peace for Bedfordshire, 1355–1359 and 1363–1364*, ed.
E. G. Kimball (Bedfordshire Historical Record Society, xlviii, 1969), 4–5.

[30] *CPR 1367–70*, 191–4.

[31] In Mar. 1369, with hostilities inevitable, the formula of 1338 was consciously restored
and the justices of the peace and sheriffs were charged, *ex officio*, to organize the array and
defence of the shires: *CPR 1367–70*, 264–5.

[32] Powell, 'Administration', 52–4.

[33] *Early Treatises on the Practice of the Justices of the Peace in the Fifteenth and Sixteenth Centuries*,
ed. B. H. Putnam (Oxford Studies in Social and Legal History, vii, 1924), 191–4.

would be relieved of its wartime taxes and the cost of maintaining the king's newly configured empire would be met from the vast riches now expected to flow in from the French royal ransom. The sheer scale of the ransom created false expectations about its capacity to cover all the king's various expenses, and the manner of its administration was to cause serious tension between Edward, his ministers and parliament that rumbled on throughout the early 1360s.

It was entirely consonant with Edward III's close adherence to the laws of war that he should have upheld for himself, as for his commanders, the principle that ransoms were a form of private income.[34] This is not to say that the king regarded such perquisites merely as pocket money to be squandered on personal luxuries. As need and opportunity arose, Edward was quite prepared to reinvest the profits of his French and Scottish wars in the major enterprises of the state. By the end of 1360, for example, the king had accumulated around £40,000 from the ransoms of Charles of Blois and David II of Scotland and the indemnity offered for his withdrawal from the duchy of Burgundy. The entirety of this sum was in due course allocated to help cover the costs associated with the English withdrawal from northern France and other similar expenses.[35]

Where the king did remain resolute was in his insistence that such well-directed distributions of his wealth remained entirely at his own discretion. When the first instalment of John II's ransom was transferred from Calais to London in October 1360, Edward III gave orders that it be placed in a separate strongroom in the Tower of London and forbade any record of the transaction to be made in the exchequer. The hoard was to be kept intact and only re-coined into English gold nobles as and when the king gave personal authority for its disbursement.[36] By the time of the death of John II in 1364, the equivalent of about £163,700 had been received under this scheme in cash deposits at the Tower.[37] Eventually, at least £110,000 of this sum was in fact to be channelled via the exchequer into the clearing of debts left over from the campaign of 1359–60, the evacuation of the northern French provinces, the ongoing costs of the

---

[34] D. Hay, 'The Division of the Spoils of War in Fourteenth-Century England', *TRHS*, 5th series, iv (1954), 91–109; K. B. McFarlane, *England in the Fifteenth Century* (London, 1981), 151–74; M. K. Jones, 'Ransom Brokerage in the Fifteenth Century', *Guerre et société*, ed. Contamine, Giry-Deloison and Keen, 221–35. For the reservation of the profits from the farms of English-held positions in Normandy and Brittany to the king's chamber, see Tout, *Chapters*, iv, 317–18.

[35] Harriss, *King, Parliament*, 490–1.

[36] 'Ransom of John II', xv, 4. Seignorage taken at the mint on the re-coinage of the ransom hoard was also to be paid directly to the king's chamber: E 159/145, *Brev. bar.*, Mich., rot. 13d.

[37] This represents the figure of £166,667 for which John had received quittances by the time of his death, minus the sum of £3,000 still to be paid at this point out of the £15,000 assessed on the English clergy: 'Ransom of John II', 18–22.

garrisons at Roxburgh, Berwick and Calais, and the initial investment in the new princely establishments in Aquitaine and Ireland.[38] The problem raised by the French ransom lay not in the appropriateness of Edward's choices about its expenditure but in the growing speculation as to the size and possible uses of the unspent surplus.

The king and the small number of chamber officials privy to the true value of the Tower hoard understood rather better than anyone else how exaggerated were public expectations of the scale of his new-found wealth. They comprehended, in a way that often seemed lost even on experienced members of political society, that the profits of war were non-renewable and that it therefore made sense to try to store up some of these windfalls against hard times to come. Even so, Edward III's attitudes laid him open to charges of disingenuousness. His earlier purchases of the sixteen French nobles taken at Poitiers had been funded by the exchequer. Once the release of these prisoners was made conditional on the payment of John II's ransom, the treasurer, Simon Langham bishop of Ely, hoped that the king might choose to pay back that commitment. It quickly became apparent that this would not happen. Parliament, too, seems to have become aware that Edward was trying to have his cake and eat it. In his initial refusal to acknowledge the surplus from the ransoms and his decision to press ahead with a controversial plan for the extension of wartime taxation, Edward III set an unexpected test both for the solidarity of his government and for his own skills as a political manager.

In 1355 parliament had granted, without further restriction, a six-year extension of the wool subsidy to run from September 1356 to September 1362.[39] If there were some merchants and wool-growers who hoped that the king might reduce or drop the associated charges at the outbreak of peace in 1360, they were soon disabused. By 1362, moreover, it was clear that the crown simply could not afford to give up the precious income stream it had now enjoyed for twenty years and more from the profits of the wool trade. Ordinary revenues from the shires, the permanent customs duties and feudal prerogatives were running at between £30,000 and £40,000 a year. This was barely sufficient to cover the basic costs of government and of royal annuities. The wool subsidy, by contrast, had recently grossed around £60,000 a year.[40] Over the course of the final year of the 1355 subsidy, Edward III accordingly began regular consultations at which he and his advisers inched towards the arguments that would allow them, for the first time in the history of this tax, to request a new grant of the *maltolt* during peacetime.[41]

[38] Harriss, *King, Parliament*, 493–5.

[39] *PROME*, v, 122.

[40] Harriss, *King, Parliament*, 526; Ormrod, *Reign of Edward III*, 207.

[41] *RDP*, iv, 631–3; E 403/409, 30 Oct., 13 Nov. 1361, 29 Jan., 19 Feb. 1362; E 403/411, 30 June, 26 July, 8 Aug., 3 Sept. 1362.

The resulting strategy was first played out in the parliament of October–November 1362. The crown claimed that the evacuation of Normandy and the ongoing defence of Calais represented a state of 'great necessity' that justified a three-year extension of the wool subsidy. In granting the Statute of Purveyors and the jubilee pardon, the king plainly acknowledged the need to make substantive concessions on the royal prerogative as the price of continued public support. Edward even broke his usual silence in plenary parliamentary session to announce the principal legislation of the assembly 'from his own mouth' (presumably, as in the opening speech to the same assembly, in English) and to thank the lords and commons in notably emollient terms for their great service to him. Under the weight of such blandishments, the commons readily conceded to the king's requests. But they required a formal guarantee that native merchants be free to export wool, forced a statute guaranteeing parliament's exclusive right to authorize future grants of the wool subsidy, and insisted that the rate of the tax be reduced from £2 to £1 per sack.[42] Not since 1339–41 had Edward III had to give so much ground in order to rescue the finances of the state.

The commons and their constituents thus had every reason to consider the accommodation of 1362 a major triumph. Although the Statute of Purveyors reflected a shift away from compulsory purchase and towards open contracts for the raising of foodstuffs, it set very definite limits on the crown's ability to supply its household and its armies from the controversial fruits of a prerogative tax.[43] The wider relevance of the legislation became dramatically apparent in 1363, when Edward III was twice obliged to promise that the new statute also applied to compulsory levies of manpower and thus agreed that English craftsmen and labourers press-ganged for the royal works at Calais would have to be guaranteed a proper market wage.[44] Not surprisingly, the parliament of 1365 ranked the Statute of Purveyors alongside Magna Carta and the Charter of the Forests as one of the great buttresses of the country's political freedom.[45] And after the return to war in 1369, various aggrieved parties were quick to cite the 1362 legislation in their protests about illegal seizures of foodstuffs within the realm.[46]

In similar manner, the general pardon of 1362 came to be regarded as a touchstone of civil liberties and a precedent to be vigorously followed. In 1363, the townsmen of Oxford tried to argue, on rather tendentious

---

[42] *PROME*, v, 136–7, 148, 151–3, 160; *SR*, i, 371–8; *CFR 1356–68*, 250, 251–2; Harriss, *King, Parliament*, 420–49, 467–8.

[43] Burley, 'Victualling of Calais', 53; M. M. Postan, *Essays on Medieval Agriculture and General Problems of the Medieval Economy* (Cambridge, 1973), 57.

[44] C 76/46, m. 20.

[45] *PROME*, v, 181.

[46] Ibid., v, 312, 370–1; Ormrod, *Reign of Edward III*, 47–8; McIntosh, *Autonomy and Community*, 80.

grounds, that the jubilee pardon ought to release them from the penalties imposed after the St Scholastica's Day riots in 1355.[47] In 1372 the parliamentary commons also attempted to instigate supplementary legislation that might define and amplify the scope of the earlier amnesty.[48] Taken all in all, the political settlement of 1362 seems to have fired the imagination of a large and diverse audience among the king's subjects and offered the enticing prospect of new political capital to be had from the condition of peace.

Subsequent parliaments accordingly pressed ahead with further demands for reform. Since 1360 the crown had been considering the idea of relocating the staple to Calais, and in May 1361 it had held an important meeting of representatives from the English ports and the French community of Calais to consider the matter.[49] The knights and burgesses proved uncharacteristically relaxed on this subject in 1362, suggesting merely that that the king should consult with the merchants and decide what was best.[50] As a consequence, the council took the initiative, transferring the staple to Calais in February 1363 and appointing a group of twenty-six prominent English merchants, led by John Wroth and John Wesenham, to run the wool market there.[51] In the parliament of October 1363, however, the commons returned to the issue with a much greater sense of purpose. The prominent place accorded to Wesenham in the new scheme had prompted memories of the cartels of the 1340s, and parliament now sought to restrict the charging of extra fees for the processing of wool at Calais and other forms of 'trickery' allegedly performed for private gain by the merchants of the staple.[52] The crown agreed to an inquiry, and in 1364 it withdrew the charter to the twenty-six and imprisoned Wesenham in the Tower. This put paid, for the present, to the anxiety that commercial operations at Calais might be usurped by a private Company of the Staple, and instead put the staple in the hands of a series of merchant governors who could be assumed to be properly accountable to the government and parliament at Westminster.[53] Native

---

[47] SC 8/257/12809, printed in *Parliamentary Petitions Relating to Oxford*, ed. L. Toulmin Smith (Oxford Historical Society, xxxii, 1896), 139; *CPR 1361–4*, 380, 392, 400, 408, 494, 517. In Feb. 1368 the king exercised his grace in pardoning the people of Doncaster a communal fine of £5 for the goods and chattels of an offender from the town: E 159/144, *Brev. bar.*, Pasch, rot. 2.

[48] *PROME*, v, 260–1.

[49] *CCR 1360–4*, 267–8; C 49/47, no. 5; Reading, 297.

[50] *PROME*, v, 140, 142.

[51] Lloyd, *Wool Trade*, 208–10.

[52] *PROME*, v, 160–1; Fryde, *Studies*, chap. x, 3–5.

[53] The idea that the charter of 1363 marked the foundation of the later incorporated and powerful Company of the Staple of Calais, perpetuated inter alia by E. Power, *The Wool Trade in English Medieval History* (Oxford, 1941), 98–103, is therefore a modern rather than a medieval fiction: see R. L. Baker, 'The Government of Calais in 1363', *Order and*

wool producers were further placated by the council's agreement to keep in place the courts that had been operating in the English provincial staples since 1353 and which had proved popular venues for a range of commercial litigation.[54] The new compromise, which survived without further disruption until the reopening of the war, seems rapidly to have convinced most of the domestic political community of the virtues of the Calais staple and established the abiding fiction, much discussed in 1376, that this institution was itself the creation of parliament.[55]

It was against this background that the king's advisers began to plan a political strategy for the further extension of the wool subsidy. Between the spring of 1363 and February 1364, Simon Langham, now promoted as chancellor, and his successor as treasurer, John Barnet, ordered a series of statements of income and expenditure stretching back to 1359.[56] The returns seemed to indicate a continuing and very significant deficit of between £55,000 and £65,000 a year. In fact, as the councillors knew perfectly well, this was a fiction of bookkeeping arising from the fact that the profits of the ransoms had been left out of the income side of the budget. Langham and Barnet seem indeed to have made these calculations with the express intention of impressing upon the king the urgent need to open up the undisclosed contents of his private treasury at the Tower.[57] They were especially anxious about the fact that Edward was siphoning off significant sums from the profits of the wool subsidy to cover his mounting domestic expenditure and the bills for his building projects at Windsor.[58] Well aware of parliament's sensitivity about the misuse of public funds, Langham and Barnet felt that the only way to make a credible case for a further extension of the *maltolt* was to go public on the true value of the liquid wealth accumulating in the king's private treasury.

Such scruples reckoned without Edward III's stubbornness on this matter. Just before John II's death, on 2 April 1364, the king and his keeper of the privy seal, William Wykeham, called a special meeting of the council at Westminster where, in Langham's presence, Edward ordered that the unspent contents of the Tower hoard be handed over to the

---

Innovation in the Middle Ages: Essays in Honor of Joseph R. Strayer, ed. W. C. Jordan, B. McNab and T. F. Ruiz (Princeton, 1976), 205–14. In the late fifteenth century, the Company of the Staple asserted the right to trace its history back as far as the foundation of the staple of Bruges in 1341, but the formal incorporation of the company does not seem to have taken place until the time of Henry IV: BIA, Staple 2, fols 4–5; Rose, *Calais*, 41, 44–6.

[54] Ormrod, 'Origins of the *sub pena* Writ', 14 and n. 23.

[55] See pp. 553 and n. 8.

[56] For what follows see T. F. Tout and D. M. Broome, 'A National Balance Sheet for 1362–3', *EHR*, xxxix (1924), 404–19; Harriss, *King, Parliament*, 470–502, 527–30.

[57] Ormrod, 'Protecolla Rolls', 630–1; G. L. Harriss, 'Budgeting at the Medieval Exchequer', *War, Government and Aristocracy*, ed. Given-Wilson, Kettle and Scales, 182.

[58] Harriss, *King, Parliament*, 487, 494–5; Given-Wilson, *Royal Household*, 94; Ormrod, 'English Crown and the Customs', 25–6.

receiver of the chamber, Helming Leget. An undisclosed sum, later reported to be the equivalent of £47,171 sterling, was thus moved into the office of the king's privy purse, the most independent of the financial agencies of the household and the one that was most obviously free of any sense of accountability either to exchequer or to parliament.[59] The whole dramatic encounter was designed to impress upon the ministers of state Edward's determination, against all the odds, to treat the accidents of war as a private perquisite of the monarch.

Faced with such intransigence, Langham and his associates had no option but to press ahead with political negotiations on the basis that the recently calculated deficit could only be covered through renewed taxation. In this they were clearly directed by Edward's strong preference for a new charm offensive in parliament. At the assembly which opened in January 1365, the chancellor announced the business in the most expansive and consensual manner: 'Now sitting and presiding in his own land on his throne of peace, [the king] desires above all the peace and tranquillity of the nobles, great men and commonalty of his land.' A week later, at a meeting with a select group of the lords, Langham announced that the costs of defending Aquitaine, Ponthieu, Calais and Ireland could not be sustained by ordinary revenues and that a renewal of the wool subsidy was necessary. If there was any demur, the parliament roll certainly does not record it. Instead, the lords and commons accepted the arguments with due resignation and quickly offered to authorize the *maltolt* for three further years. They even agreed that the tax should be restored immediately to its wartime rate of £2 per sack of wool.[60] Edward III's high-risk strategy had paid off. Disagreements within the council had been overcome and the wool subsidy had moved one step closer to becoming a permanent peacetime imposition. It was one of those rare but revealing moments in which Edward III was able to dismiss the natural caution of his counsellors and, by sheer force of will, pull off a major political triumph.

The only real reverberations of this episode were felt in the exchequer. Over the winter of 1364–5, Ralph Brantingham and Richard Piriton, two officials of the exchequer of receipt, brought a series of charges of corruption and malpractice against their colleague Ralph Chesterfield. At the top of the list was the accusation that Chesterfield had embezzled some of the money received by the exchequer in disbursements from the Tower treasury. After two formal hearings, Chesterfield was exonerated.[61] But this otherwise routine case had raised some quite significant issues of

[59] 'Ransom of John II', xvi, 4.

[60] *PROME*, v, 176, 181; G. Dodd, *Justice and Grace: Private Petitioning and the English Parliament in the Late Middle Ages* (Oxford, 2007), 112–13.

[61] *CCR 1364–8*, 114–25; E 159/141, *Recorda*, Pasch, rots 11–14; *CPR 1364–7*, 93, 251–2, 258; Tout, *Chapters*, iii, 249–51.

principle relating to the exchequer's liability in the administration of the ransom revenues. Extensive inquiries were launched to establish whether the office had indeed properly observed the king's close instructions on those parts of the Tower treasure handed over for reinvestment in the regimes in Aquitaine and Ireland.[62] To prevent any further misunderstandings, Edward III now reluctantly agreed that Barnet's staff should make a post-dated entry on the receipt and issue rolls to cover the sum of £47,171 sent from the Tower to the chamber in April 1364. By making this small bureaucratic concession, the king managed at once to extricate himself from suspicion of unscrupulous behaviour and to re-establish the functionality and honour of the exchequer. Not everything was restored to normality: some of the more intricate elements of William Edington's earlier system of financial co-ordination had to be abandoned in the process of this new accommodation.[63] In all political respects, however, the outcome was positive, finally resolving the remaining tensions between the king and Langham and thus restoring the ministerial unity on which the wider credibility of the crown depended.

Over the course of 1364–5 Edward III had managed not only to bluff his way through the negotiations for the wool tax but also very emphatically to stamp his authority on the senior ranks of government. Thereafter, so long as the peace continued, his financial position seemed assured. In the parliament of May 1368, the king and Langham repeated the persuasion tactics of 1365 almost to the letter, and the lords and commons granted the wool subsidy for a further two years.[64] As a result of the restoration of the wartime rate in 1365 and 1368, the income from the customs and subsidies rose from about £40,000 a year in 1362–4 to an annual average of just under £70,000 for the five fiscal years 1364–9.[65] Even given the fact that Edward had to make rather larger injections of cash into the Black Prince's faltering government at Bordeaux, this revenue continued to be more than ample to cover the general costs of defence in the dominions. Consequently – and to his very obvious satisfaction – Edward was able to hoard all new accidents of war, including the further instalments of the French and Scottish ransoms as well as a substantial repayment of personal loans earlier advanced to the duke of Brittany. By early 1369 the king's private treasury contained at least £135,000, and in all likelihood much more.[66] Edward III amassed what was probably the greatest personal fortune held by any late medieval king while simultaneously persuading parliament that his peacetime regime had to be subsidized from the

[62] 'Ransom of John II', xvi–xvii; Tout, *Chapters*, iii, 246–8.
[63] Ormrod, 'Protecolla Rolls', 632.
[64] *PROME*, v, 209, 214.
[65] Ormrod, *Reign of Edward III*, 207.
[66] Harriss, *King, Parliament*, 499–502, adding the payment for the Milanese marriage of Lionel of Clarence as discussed by Given-Wilson, *Royal Household*, 88.

proceeds of indirect taxation. That he did so without discernible public challenge or criticism is one of the most astonishing achievements not just of the decade but of the entire reign.

In the 1360s Edward III reached a pinnacle of accomplishment in his plan to have his family take up their rightful places as leaders of English aristocratic society. For much of the decade the king focused mainly on his third son, John of Gaunt, duke of Lancaster. Gaunt was able to use some of the huge resources derived from the Lancastrian estates to create a new and more extensive political affinity. Employing the still relatively novel device of the contract of life service, the prince extended his reach beyond the traditional confines of the noble household to include a growing number of baronial and gentry families in midland and northern England.[67] As a consequence, royal government in these areas was often placed very largely in the hands of Lancastrian retainers.[68] Gaunt's influence is particularly evidenced by the introduction of a number of his senior staff into the central administration; one of his most distinguished advisers, Sir John Ipres, for example, became controller of the king's household in 1368.[69] With Edward of Woodstock occupied in Gascony and Castile and Lionel of Antwerp heavily involved first in Ireland and then in Lombardy, Gaunt was now rapidly emerging as the principal buttress of his father's political regime in England.

The king also spent a good deal of time working through plans for the junior league of Plantagenets. The spate of royal weddings between 1358 and 1365 served its purposes well in creating a new generation of royals, and by 1369 Edward III had eight surviving grandchildren: by the Black Prince, Edward of Angoulême (b. 1365) and Richard of Bordeaux (b. 1367); by Princess Isabella, Marie (b. 1366) and Philippa de Coucy (b. 1367); by Prince Lionel, Philippa of Clarence (b. 1355); and by John of Gaunt, Philippa (b. 1360), Elizabeth (b. 1364) and Henry of Bolingbroke (b. 1367).[70] On the unexpected death of the earl of March in France in 1360, Edward took particular steps to reassure the Mortimers of his commitment to the existing betrothal of their heir, Edmund, to Philippa

---

[67] Walker, *Lancastrian Affinity*, 11, 14, 18–20; H. Castor, *The King, the Crown, and the Duchy of Lancaster: Public Authority and Private Power, 1399–1461* (Oxford, 2000), 22.

[68] A. Goodman, 'John of Gaunt: Paradigm of the Late Fourteenth-Century Crisis', *TRHS*, 5th series, xxxvii (1987), 140–3.

[69] Tout, *Chapters*, vi, 29, 44; Given-Wilson, *Royal Household*, 31, 62, 161–2, 219, 232; Walker, *Lancastrian Affinity*, 12, 28–9, 38, 47 n. 35.

[70] Gaunt had a number of other children who died at birth: S. Armitage-Smith, *John of Gaunt* (London, 1904), 21, 94; J. Coleman, 'Philippa of Lancaster, Queen of Portugal – and Patron of the Gower Translations?', *England and Iberia*, ed. Bullón-Fernández, 136–9; I. Mortimer, 'Henry IV's Date of Birth and the Royal Maundy', *HR*, lxxx (2007), 567–76. For the king's gift to Princess Isabella's physician after the birth of her second child, see E 403/433, 18 Nov. 1367.

of Clarence. He kept the young teenagers close about him after Philippa's return from Ireland in 1364, and made careful preparations for Edmund's admission to his titles at the end of the decade.[71] In 1368 the young earl of Pembroke, John Hastings, who had formerly been affianced to Princess Margaret, was reaffirmed as a member of the royal circle through the new marriage organized for him, on the eve of his coming of age, with Anne Mauny, daughter of the king's cousin, Margaret of Brotherton. In similar vein, Edward hatched an early plan to betroth Princess Isabella's second daughter to Robert de Vere, the youthful heir of the earl of Oxford.[72]

These various schemes served to highlight Edward III's continuing and unflagging determination to have his family members assume the major dukedoms and earldoms of England, and thus to establish a solid phalanx of support for the crown in future generations. Ironically, though, the emphasis on forward planning left the king somewhat short of friends and allies within the current generation of senior peers. Outside the immediate royal family, only four titled noblemen appeared regularly at meetings of the council in the 1360s: Richard Fitzalan, earl of Arundel; Thomas Beauchamp, earl of Warwick; Robert Ufford, earl of Suffolk; and Thomas de Vere, earl of Oxford.[73] Suffolk, who died in 1369, was the last survivor of the six earls created in 1337; his bequest to his successor, William, of the sword with which he had been invested with his title by Edward III neatly typifies the sense in which a personal commitment to the monarch could be converted into a more lasting sense of dynastic loyalty.[74] Other than Suffolk, however, only one other of the earls of 1337, Salisbury, had an heir who continued to be actively involved in public life during the later years of the reign. All of this meant that the responsibilities of status now rested on the shoulders of a very small number of premier lords. No fewer than eighteen of the peace commissions appointed in 1368 were headed by just five men: the duke of Lancaster (nine jurisdictions spread over five counties), the earl of Hereford (three counties) and the earls of Warwick, Arundel and Suffolk (two counties each).[75] Such positions were, of course, largely honorific; the effectiveness of royal justice relied less on the active involvement of such token

---

[71] Holmes, *Estates*, 45–6; *Foedera*, III.ii, 725; *Handbook . . . of Sources for Medieval Ireland*, 327. The king gave Edmund and Philippa expense accounts of £100 each to maintain their estate at court before Edmund came into possession of his earldom: E 403/427, 6 Nov. 1365; E 403/429, 26 Nov. 1366, 4 Feb. 1367; etc.

[72] GEC, x, 226, 391–3. Pembroke performed homage to the king on 12 Sept. 1369: E 159/145, *Brev. bar.*, Pasch. rot. 2.

[73] Given-Wilson, 'Royal Charter Witness Lists', 55, 68–71; Given-Wilson, *Royal Household*, 155. See also *CCR 1360–4*, 393–4, 514, 529; *CCR 1364–8*, 403, 404, 465, 494; *CCR 1369–74*, 93, 108–9.

[74] *Testamenta Vetusta*, ed. N. H. Nicolas (London, 1826), 73–4.

[75] *CPR 1367–70*, 191–5. The earls of Salisbury, Devon, Suffolk and Stafford headed one commission each.

presidents than on the lesser barons, county gentry and men of law who comprised the working element of the commissions of the peace. Nevertheless, in a system that expected the titled nobility and the more powerful of the barons to set standards of service and behaviour for the lower reaches of political society, it was now questionable whether royal government in the localities could ever really be effectively managed by such heavy dependence on a handful of king's friends.

Edward III was not unaware or neglectful of this challenge. Indeed, he worked hard to build effective political leadership by restocking the lower levels of the peerage.[76] By 1362 the number of barons receiving personal summonses to parliament had dropped to just twenty-nine, the lowest figure for the entire reign. During the following six years, in contrast, a series of prominent knights, some of them descendants and relatives of noble families, were newly recruited into the lords. The earl of Stafford's brother, Richard Stafford, was summoned as a baron in his own right from 1370,[77] and the veteran earl of Suffolk's second son, William Ufford, was elevated to the peerage before the death of his older brother made him heir, in turn, to the family earldom. After 1369, the crown put still further effort into the process of upward recruitment: at the parliament of 1371 there were sixteen new barons, bringing the total capacity of the non-titled peerage to fifty-one. The value of this group was demonstrated in the last set of peace commissions issued by Edward III, in 1375, when established barons such as Gilbert Umfraville and Henry Percy were brought in to replace the over-committed John of Gaunt as presidents of a number of the county benches in the East Midlands and Yorkshire.[78]

In the end, however, the comparative liveliness of recruitment into the baronage simply accentuated the effective block that Edward III had now set on the creation of new earls. Among the more obvious candidates for promotion from the baronage to the titled nobility were Edward, Lord Despenser (d. 1375), holder of the great lordship of Tewkesbury; Lord Percy, head of a great northern family with seats in Yorkshire and Northumberland; and John Mowbray (d. 1368) and his son, also John, successive lords of the Isle of Axholme. In Richard II's reign these three families went on to hold the earldoms of Gloucester, Northumberland and Nottingham. Since these and other men were already amply supplied with the landed resources to support titles of nobility, Edward III's hesitation about allowing such advancement cannot simply have been a matter of resource. Instead, it was a direct consequence of the much more practical difficulty he faced in providing for his two youngest sons. Edmund of Langley's title of earl of Cambridge was funded by a portion of the

---

[76] For what follows see Powell and Wallis, *House of Lords*, 362–70.

[77] For his career see K. B. McFarlane, *Lancastrian Kings and Lollard Knights* (Oxford, 1972), 174–5.

[78] *CPR 1374–7*, 135–9.

defunct earldom of Surrey. But there was as yet no sign of the additional estates that might allow the prince to take his place alongside his older brothers as a duke.[79] Throughout the 1360s Edward was also searching for the means to provide Thomas of Woodstock with a landed estate. He eventually found it in 1373, after the sudden death of his cousin, Humphrey Bohun, earl of Hereford and Northampton. In the following year, Thomas was married to Humphrey's daughter and co-heiress, the eight-year-old Eleanor.[80] The king arranged for Eleanor's younger sister, Mary, to be placed in a nunnery so that the inheritance might pass undivided to his precious son.[81] Even so, Thomas remained without a title at the time of his father's death, and it was left to his nephew Richard II to make him earl of Buckingham in 1377.[82] Ultimately, then, Edward III's reluctance to elevate members of the baronage to earldoms in the 1360s was the direct consequence of his unfulfilled obligation to the proper promotion of the princes of the blood.

For some of the small group of senior lords in the inner sanctum of royal favour, the new sense of social exclusiveness was, by all accounts, somewhat intoxicating. Richard Fitzalan, earl of Arundel, although one of the king's most conspicuously loyal supporters, was increasingly inclined during the 1360s to push at the limits of his entitlement. He entered into a long-standing conflict with William Lenn, bishop of Chichester, over rents and rights of patronage. As in the earlier dispute between Lady Wake and Bishop Lisle, the king was rather too quickly persuaded to apply the full rigours of the law against a recalcitrant bishop, and a major political confrontation with the Church was only narrowly averted when Lenn was cajoled into an out-of-court settlement in 1366.[83] In the same year, Arundel attempted, unsuccessfully, to pull rank in the council by insisting that a special hearing to resolve a disputed marriage settlement between the children of Lord Audley and Alice, Lady Beaumont should not go ahead without his being present.[84] In his local spheres of influence the earl was still more assertive. At the time of his death in 1376, the county community

---

[79] When Richard II made Langley duke of York in 1385, he had to provide a cash annuity of £1,000 to help sustain his uncle's estate: Wolffe, *Royal Demesne*, 242–3; Given-Wilson, *English Nobility*, 43–4.

[80] *CPR 1370–4*, 472. In addition to this grant, Thomas was given £300 a year to support Eleanor during the king's custody of the Bohun estates: E 403/456, 11 Dec. 1374, 28 Feb. 1375; E 403/457, 1 May, 14 May 1375; etc.

[81] Mary was placed in the custody of her mother, Joan: E 403/461, 7 Nov. 1376. For subsequent changes to the Bohun inheritance as a result of Mary's marriage to Henry of Bolingbroke, see GEC, v, 720–2; vi, 474–5; Holmes, *Estates*, 24 and n. 6; A. Goodman, *The Loyal Conspiracy: The Lords Appellant under Richard II* (London, 1971), 5, 88–90.

[82] McFarlane, *Nobility*, 259–66; Ormrod, 'Edward III and his Family', 416–20.

[83] C. Given-Wilson, 'The Bishop of Chichester and the Second Statute of Praemunire, 1365', *HR*, lxiii (1990), 128–42.

[84] *CCR 1364–8*, 237–9; Palmer, *English Law*, 128–9.

of Sussex was to complain vociferously about the manner in which Fitzalan had abused his prerogative jurisdiction to appropriate the shire court for his own use and profit.[85] Such aristocratic high-handedness convinced at least some that the king was reverting to the behaviour of his youth and failing to instil in the aristocracy a proper sense of personal discipline and public obligation. Just as the narrowing of the upper ranks of the household in the later 1360s was almost bound to create the impression of faction, so too was it increasingly easy for outsiders to believe that court and council were becoming closed to the wider participation of the elite and overly indulgent of the ambitions of the few.

The sense of exclusion was greatly reinforced by the emergence on to the political scene of a new chief minister, William Wykeham. Wykeham was a clerk of relatively humble Hampshire stock who had been brought into royal service by William Edington and had risen to prominence as keeper of the works at Windsor from 1357.[86] Such was the king's confidence in this junior official that Edward had actually included William in the group of senior civil servants taken to the peace talks at Calais in October 1360.[87] On their return, the king and his clerk dined together on the building site at Windsor, where Edward charged Wykeham to assist in the preparations of the upcoming meeting of the Garter at Windsor.[88] Firm friendship brought quick preferment. Wykeham became receiver of the chamber and keeper of the secret seal in 1361, then keeper of the privy seal in 1363. By 1366 extensive grants of church offices had given him an income of at least £850 a year, putting him on an equal footing with some of the greatest barons in the land.[89] In 1367 Edward engineered Wykeham's appointment to the most valuable see in England, the bishopric of Winchester, and elevated him to the presidency of his council as chancellor of England.[90] The influence that Wykeham had already achieved in the inner circles of power was thus dramatically proclaimed to the wider polity.

Much of the distrust generated by Wykeham's rise to greatness was the product of straightforward prejudice; rather like William Kilsby before him, the newly favoured royal clerk's supposed pride and prickliness were

[85] C 49/46/5; *PROME*, v, 356–7.

[86] *CPR 1354–8*, 463; C 81/910, no. 29; Maxwell-Lyte, *Great Seal*, 55; Tout, *Chapters*, iii, 236 and n. 8; V. Davis, *William Wykeham* (London, 2007), 17–30.

[87] E 159/137, *Brev. bar.*, Mich., rot. 1.

[88] E 101/394/8: E 403/401, 2 May 1360.

[89] *Registrum Simonis de Sudburia diocesis Londoniensis, A.D. 1362–1375*, ed. R. C. Fowler, 2 vols (CYS, xxxiv, xxxviii, 1927–38), ii, 164–5; Davis, *William Wykeham*, 41.

[90] *EMDP*, I.i, no. 77; Reading, 177–8; Highfield, 'Promotion of William of Wickham', 37–54. The appointment to the chancellorship is dated by *HBC*, 86, as between 10 and 17 Sept. E 403/431, 16 Sept. 1367, suggests that Wykeham had still to assume office on 15 Sept., so the appointment can be narrowed to either 16 or 17 Sept.

as much the spiteful invention of his social superiors as an accurate judgement of his character. The English ecclesiastical hierarchy had a strong aversion to the admission to its ranks of a man of such low birth and no university education. William's predecessor at the privy seal, John Buckingham, had also been the butt of much sarcastic comment following his elevation, at Edward III's behest, to the bishopric of Lincoln in 1363.[91]

All that said, Wykeham seems to have cared little for the customary political arts of deference and subtlety, and his abrupt and ambitious manner created widespread suspicion and offence. Edward had insisted that, as keeper of the privy seal, William should be constantly at his side to attend briskly to all his personal commands.[92] The high-handed manner in which Wykeham interpreted this role is glimpsed in a letter he wrote in 1366 instructing that no arrangements be made for the recently vacated archbishopric of Canterbury until he brought verbal instructions from the king. The fact that one of the recipients of this correspondence, Chancellor Langham, had already been promised the relevant see simply underscores the impertinence of the intervention.[93] After his own promotion to replace Langham as chancellor in 1367, William continued to regard himself very much as keeper of the king's conscience and chief watchman of royal rights. The resulting tendency to involve himself in minutiae caused real concern, and occasional disruption, in the lower ranks of the chancery.[94] As Froissart snidely put it, 'everything was done by him, and nothing was done without him'.[95]

Under such circumstances it is not surprising that ministers, magnates and, ultimately, the commons came to regard Wykeham as something of a liability to the administration of Edward III. Much of this, it must be said, was the wisdom of hindsight. In 1376–7, when Wykeham fell from grace, it proved very convenient to attach to his name some of the major policy errors of the 1360s. He was accused of levying heavy fines on Matthew Gournay, Thomas Fogg, John St Loo and other captains operating in Normandy during the early 1360s, and thus of intensifying the bad feeling between the crown and the English military forces left in France after the settlement of 1360. Most particularly, Wykeham was thought to have been the primary architect of fiscal policy during the years of peace. In 1376 it was claimed that he had jealously guarded the unspent residues of the ransoms of John II, David II and the duchy of

---

[91] *Polychronicon*, viii, 365; Reading, 155; *EMDP*, I.i, no. 23; A. K. McHardy, 'The Promotion of John Buckingham to the See of Lincoln', *Journal of Ecclesiastical History*, xxvi (1975), 127–35.

[92] *CPR 1361–4*, 444; *CPR 1364–7*, 97. For Wykeham's drawing down of the special allowance of £1 a day provided for this purpose, see, e.g., E 403/427, 28 July 1366; E 403/429, 24 Oct. 1366.

[93] SC 1/56/125.

[94] Ormrod, *Reign of Edward III*, 91–2.

[95] Froissart, vii, 101; Tout, *Chapters*, iii, 239.

Burgundy, along with other prerogative revenues of the crown, and refused to allow them to be used to the common profit.[96] It is certainly hard to deny that the wily Wykeham played a key part in the decision to build up an independent private treasury administered through the chamber, or that his strong identification with that policy at the fateful meeting with Langham in April 1364 did not exacerbate the king's conflict with his ministers at the time of the 1365 parliament. Until the reopening of the French war, however, the general determination of the royal council to present a united front meant that parliament had no real opportunity to imagine and exploit divisions within the top ranks of the government. For the time being, Wykeham's reputation was simply that of a slightly sinister 'fixer', the proverbial *éminence grise* of the Edwardian peacetime regime.

It was not Wykeham but the royal steward, Sir John atte Lee, who first fell victim to growing public disquiet with the record of royal government in the later 1360s. Since the combining of the king's and queen's households into one administrative unit from 1360, the crown had showed renewed interest in the practice of funding royal domestic expenditure out of the profits of feudalism.[97] A number of the most valuable wardships that became available following the deaths of tenants-in-chief in the early 1360s were reserved to provide additional support for Philippa of Hainault and her entourage.[98] To maximize the potential of such feudal prerogatives, the crown now developed a general campaign for the investigation and recovery of feudal rights, at first specifically on the queen's estates but increasingly from 1365 on the king's as well.[99] The area subject to most frequent visitation stretched from Norfolk, Suffolk and Essex through Cambridgeshire and Hertfordshire to Oxfordshire, Berkshire, Wiltshire, Somerset and Dorset. Given the kingdom's expectations of quiet rule after 1360, such inquiries seemed ill judged, serving to raise the hostility of the tenants-in-chief, the gentry and other substantial freeholders in the shires.

The man who sued out most of these commissions to investigate royal rights in the 1360s, and the formal president of many of them, was Sir John atte Lee, the joint steward of the combined royal households. Lee's

---

[96] *AC*, 96–100, 184.

[97] The wardrobe estate created in the aftermath of the first plague had been wound up in 1359 in order to free the king's wardrobe from the complicated business of estate management and allow it to resume its role as a paymaster's office for the Reims campaign: E 159/136, *Recorda, Mich.*, rot. 8; Ormrod, 'Edward III's Government', 260–1.

[98] *CPR 1358–61*, 451, 501; *CPR 1361–4*, 75, 86, 135, 142, 218, 236, 260, 272, 399; *CFR 1356–68*, 208, 389.

[99] *CPR 1358–61*, 217, 278, 279, 404, 409, 518; *CPR 1361–4*, 135, 148, 207, 288, 361, 369, 371, 452, 546; *CPR 1364–7*, 66, 150, 152, 200–1, 206, 210, 287–8, 289, 356, 370; *CPR 1367–70*, 138, 189–90; J. G. Bellamy, *Robin Hood: An Historical Inquiry* (London, 1985), 88–9, 95. Only two returns to commissions of inquiry issued before 1368 survive: *CIM*, iii, no. 614; JUST 1/748.

tours of East Anglia and the South Midlands were often interpreted as visitations of the unpopular court of the verge.[100] The high priority given to Philippa of Hainault's rights in many of his sessions had the effect of reviving long-standing prejudices against senior officials of the queen. Lee's predecessor as Philippa's steward, the former courtier Sir John Molyns, had clawed his way back into royal favour after the crisis of 1341 only to be exposed once more as a notorious and unscrupulous bully in 1357.[101] Hardly less controversial was John Bampton of Essex, former steward of the queen's manor of Havering, who served on many of Lee's commissions in East Anglia. Bampton was later to be murdered by the rebels of 1381, who gleefully celebrated the demise of this despicable character in popular verse.[102] For some while in the 1360s, it seemed that Lee and his associates were unassailable. In 1367, Sir John added to his portfolio the keepership of the forests south and north of the Trent, thus assuming comprehensive powers to investigate the crown's rights under the special laws and customs of the forest.[103] Soon after, however, it became apparent that Lee's campaigns in the shires were motivated as much by personal greed as by official policy. The scale and consequences of this scandal are indicative both of public sensitivity to official corruption and of the crown's increasing vulnerability to such criticism.

In the parliament of May 1366 it was revealed that a group of Kent-based gentlemen and lawyers had colluded to have one of the king's wards, William Septvans, declared of age ahead of time and thus to force the young man to give them possession of his family's estates. Because the associated investigation, led by Lord Cobham, was confined to Kent, the personal involvement of Sir John atte Lee was not yet publicly revealed.[104] Within the year, however, it became known that Lee had himself illicitly purchased Septvans's Essex manor of Little Wigborough.[105] The lawyer-poet John Gower, one of the lessees in Kent caught up in the scandal, was later to comment ruefully in his *Mirour de l'Omme* on the king's duty to separate the good sheep from the bad and dismiss 'villains' from his

---

[100] *PROME*, v, 215.

[101] Tout, *Chapters*, iii, 123 n. 3; Ormrod, *Reign of Edward III*, 111.

[102] McIntosh, *Autonomy and Community*, 270; *The Peasants' Revolt of 1381*, ed. R. B. Dobson, 2nd edn (London, 1983), 124; N. Brooks, 'The Organization and Achievements of the Peasants of Kent and Essex in 1381', *Studies in Medieval History Presented to R. H. C. Davis*, ed. H. Mayr-Harting and R. I. Moore (London, 1985), 250–1; S. Justice, *Writing and Rebellion, England in 1381* (Berkeley, Calif., 1994), 133 and n. 66.

[103] *CFR 1356–68*, 353.

[104] SC 8/247/12329; C 81/1335/50; *PROME*, v, 196–201; ' "Probatio Aetatis" of William de Septvans', ed. L. B. Larking, *Archaeologia Cantiana*, i (1858), 124–36.

[105] Bellamy, *Robin Hood*, 85. The matter was in process in chancery in 1366: C 44/5/9.

household.[106] By February 1368 Edward III was apparently persuaded that Lee did indeed pose a direct liability to the reputation of his crown. The steward was discreetly removed from office and exiled from the court, to be replaced by Sir William Latimer of Corby.[107]

The council clearly hoped that such a pre-emptive move would be sufficient to assuage anger at Lee's recent inquests in the shires. But when parliament opened in May, it became apparent that public opinion would only be fully placated if Lee were put up for public trial. From the outset, the commons seem to have insisted that the essential price of their consent to the further extension of the wool subsidy would be the withdrawal of Lee's inquiries and the hearing of formal charges against the dismissed steward.[108] On the last day of the assembly, Edward III invited the lords and some of the commons to join him in the White Chamber at Westminster and hear the announcement by Chief Justice Robert Thorpe of formal charges against the defamed and disgraced steward. Predictably enough, these focused on the recent controversial inquiries into the crown's feudal rights and confirmed existing suspicion that the villainous Lee had oppressed innocent parties and sought to make private profit from the market in royal wardships. But they also addressed a matter of high principle by claiming that Lee had seriously exceeded his authority as steward and exercised forms of prerogative justice that were for king and council alone to dispense. Lee was allowed to plead his defence. But the lords quickly deemed it insufficient, and the former steward was placed in custody at the Tower to await the king's pleasure.[109]

The matter did not end there. Such was the scale of the public outcry that the king was persuaded to send the two chief justices down to the eastern counties to inquire into the oppressions allegedly committed by Lee and his unsavoury associates. In Hertfordshire, complainants flocked to tell tales of John atte Lee's embezzlement of fines and of his merciless hounding of two local worthies, Edward and Thomas Kendal.[110] When the tribunal moved to Cambridgeshire, attention fell on another of the queen's officials, Roger Harlestone, who was referred to the council for

[106] J. Gower, *Complete Works*, ed. G. C. Macaulay, 4 vols (Oxford, 1899–1902), I, 252 (ll. 22885–96). This possible topical reference adds some weight to the argument that Gower began work on the *Mirour* as early as the late 1350s and resumed it *c.*1368 before eventually completing it around 1376: R. F. Yeager, 'Politics and the French Language in England during the Hundred Years' War: The Case of John Gower', *Inscribing the Hundred Years' War*, ed. Baker, 127–57. Gower's acquisition of a moiety of the manor of Aldington had been properly subjected to inquiry and approved by the crown in 1365: C 143/356/11; *CPR 1364–7*, 99.

[107] Tout, *Chapters*, vi, 43.

[108] *PROME*, v, 210–11.

[109] Ibid., v, 214–16. Apart from those mentioned on the parliament roll, at least two other petitions against Lee were received on this occasion: SC 8/47/2326; SC 8/65/3227.

[110] JUST 1/339/1; KB 9/37, no. 9.

further investigation.[111] In 1369, the king's council took Lee's refusal to attend proceedings over the Little Wigborough dispute to be an admission of guilt and ordered the manor to be returned to William Septvans.[112] The hounded Sir John was not quite a ruined man: he seems to have secured his release from the Tower on payment of a hefty fine in lieu of further proceedings, and actually managed to retain most of his landed interests. But he was never purged of the allegations against him and died, still in official disgrace, in 1370.

Both the circumstances and the reverberations of Lee's case were quite different from those that had obtained in the downfalls of Sir William Thorpe in 1350–1 and of Sir Henry Green and Sir William Skipwith in 1365. In 1351, particularly, the king had successfully deployed the parliamentary trial of Thorpe as a means of advertising his commitment to the integrity and impartiality of justice. In 1368, by contrast, it was the commons who took much of the initiative, sharply rebuking the crown for its failure to regulate a senior official and using their right of assent to taxation to force through a humiliating exposure of corruption in high places. Above all, the implied attack on the court and on the king's absolute right to appoint and discipline his domestic staff looked ahead to the trials in the Good Parliament of 1376 and the fierce public debates over the political influence of Richard II's household in the mid-1380s. Far from being a minor exercise in royal face-saving, the trial of John atte Lee represented a defining moment in parliament's understanding of its right to challenge royal prerogative and its duty to monitor and regulate the whole panoply of royal government.

The final irony in this momentous sequence of events lies in the appointment of Lee's successor as steward, Sir William Latimer. In many ways Latimer was an obvious and admirable choice for this post. He came from a well-established baronial family. His father had been one of Edward III's co-conspirators at Nottingham in 1330, and William himself had long been retained as a knight, and then banneret, of the royal household.[113] He was also an experienced career soldier who had become heavily involved in the English support for Breton independence and had fought with distinction at the battle of Auray in 1364. His up-to-date knowledge of affairs in France may particularly have commended him to the king, who employed him on a number of occasions in 1368 to communicate messages to the court of Charles V.[114] Such service had its proper rewards, and Latimer remained in office for nearly eight years, first as steward (to 1370) and then as chamberlain of the household (1371–6).

[111] *CPR 1367–70*, 189–90; JUST 1/102, rots 5–6, 7, 8; JUST 1/339/1; KB 9/37, no. 9.

[112] C 44/5/9; *CCR 1369–74*, 9–10. For the subsequent dispute between Septvans and Lee's son, Walter, over this manor see SC 8/142/7091; *CCR 1374–7*, 463–4.

[113] E 101/392/12, fol. 40; E 101/393/11, fol. 76.

[114] E 159/145, *Brev. bar.*, Mich., rot. 10.

Ultimately, however, William Latimer's promotion was to prove an enormous liability to the unity of Edward's government and the reputation of his crown. The fact that Latimer was soon found to be investing heavily in the purchase of royal wardships for his own use prompted inevitable speculation that he was just as inclined as his predecessor to trade the king's rights for personal profit.[115] Like William Wykeham, Latimer was also quickly implicated in the other great political controversy rumbling on during the late 1360s, the reservation of the ransoms as a store of private wealth for the king.[116] Three years after Lee's fall from grace, Wykeham himself was to be forced out of office by public anxiety over his management of the first, disastrous phase of the new war with France. Latimer would survive rather longer. But he too would in due course become a victim by association of the faltering military and financial regime of the 1370s. In the Good Parliament of 1376 the detested triumvirate of William Latimer, Alice Perrers and the London merchant Richard Lyons would be denounced as an unscrupulous faction intent on their own private gain at the direct cost of crown and country. For late fourteenth-century political society, it was clear enough that the general collapse of unity and integrity at Edward III's court had first become evident during the disastrous stewardship of Sir John atte Lee.[117]

Edward III's domestic regime during the years of peace must be judged a significant success. The notable adroitness with which the king manoeuvred parliament into accepting the extension of the wool subsidy marked a major leap forward in the fiscal stability of the English state. It was in the 1360s, too, that crown and polity reached a successful accommodation over the management of the post-plague economy and finally agreed a lasting formula for the maintenance of law and order in the shires. In other respects, royal government lacked some of the dynamic qualities it had shown in the previous decade, too readily resorting to self-congratulation and shying away from a programme of peacetime reconstruction. In the warm afterglow of the treaty of Calais and the general pardon of 1362, the polity was sometimes inclined to conspire in this complacency: in 1363, for example, the commons expressed effusive thanks to the Almighty for giving them 'such a lord and ruler who has prevented them from being subject to other lands, and has freed them from many charges which they have sustained in times past'.[118] As the decade wound on, however, the

---

[115] G. Holmes, *The Good Parliament* (Oxford, 1975), 66.

[116] *CPR 1367–70*, 189.

[117] See in this regard the proposals of 1404 for the recovery of royal rights and estates lost since the fortieth year of Edward III's reign (1366): *PROME*, viii, 291–4; B. P. Wolffe, 'Acts of Resumption in the Lancastrian Parliaments, 1399–1456', *Historical Studies*, ed. Fryde and Miller, ii, 65–6.

[118] *PROME*, v, 160; McKisack, *Fourteenth Century*, 221.

inconsistencies and shortcomings of the regime became a source of some unease. Edward III's stubbornness, to the point of perversity, over the reservation of the profits from the ransoms very nearly forced a rift in the ranks of the council in 1364 and was to be a continuing source of aggravation to the king's subjects for the rest of the decade and beyond. It was in the disgrace of Sir John atte Lee that the commons first expressed their concern that government policy was being abused by unscrupulous individuals intent on their own advancement and neglectful of the common good. By the late 1360s there were already real signs that Edward III's increasing withdrawal into a semi-private existence was jeopardizing the representative nature and the unity of his court and council. As the polity braced itself for a return to war in 1368–9, the major question everywhere was whether the king had it in him to resume the leadership so desperately required at this supreme moment of national emergency.

Chapter 18

RETREAT AND DEFEAT, 1368–1375

Ever since the label of the 'Hundred Years War' was first used in the nineteenth century, there has been debate as to whether it is really valid to represent the sequence of Anglo-French hostilities between 1337 and 1453 as a single, coherent dispute. Edward III and his advisers considered the re-opening of the French war in 1369 as a new phase in Anglo-French relations, one whose agenda was fixed not by the treaty of Paris of 1259 but by the imperative of defending the terms of the 1360 treaty of Calais. Nonetheless, it has to be said that few of the king's subjects shared this perspective. The 'second war', as they called it,[1] was very obviously seen as a natural continuation of the conflict begun in 1337, and more specifically by Edward's announcement of his entitlement to the French crown in 1340. At the reopening of hostilities in 1369, Edward III resumed the double title of 'king of England and France' dropped, as a matter of discretion, since the peace of 1360. For those who had expressed misgivings over the wisdom of the Calais settlement, this seemed for one precious moment to represent a renewed statement of commitment to the conquest of France. Such high hopes were rapidly and rudely dashed. The challenge facing Edward III's regime after 1369 was therefore two-pronged: to maintain the increasingly beleaguered Plantagenet possessions on the continent, and to placate a domestic political community confused and disillusioned by such a devastating decline in English military fortunes.

The crucible of the new conflict was the principality of Aquitaine. There were a number of prominent defectors from the meeting of the Estates at Angoulême in January 1368 at which the Black Prince extracted the heavy *fouage* needed to cover the costs of the Nájera campaign. Chief among these was Jean, count of Armagnac. Jean's refusal to allow the collection of the *fouage* in his territories was not necessarily a declaration of outright war against the Plantagenets. But it was exactly the kind of self-interested stand that might appeal to Gascon lords otherwise strongly supportive of the English regime.[2] The real threat to the Black Prince's security came as a result of the long-standing alliance between the Armagnacs and the Albrets, the pre-eminent noble family in 'ancient' Gascony.

[1] *AC*, 96.
[2] Sumption, ii, 569–70.

The Albrets had been loyal to Edward III since 1340, their allegiance shored up by a generous annuity of £1,000 from English revenues. Bernard-Ezi d'Albret had contributed significant forces to the Black Prince's army at Poitiers in 1356, and the head of the family from 1358, Arnaud-Amanieu, did similar conspicuous service as one of Edward III's commissioners for the evacuation of northern France in the early 1360s.[3] But Arnaud-Amanieu was also bound to support the count of Armagnac against their common enemy, Gaston Phoebus, count of Foix. The debts that Albret owed as a result of his capture by Foix at Launac in 1362 remain the most likely explanation for his fateful decision to defy the Black Prince's authority and make common cause with Armagnac in 1368.[4] In early May of that year, Albret married Margaret of Bourbon, sister of Charles V's queen, Jeanne. A few weeks later he performed homage to Charles and received promise of a handsome pension.[5] Spurred on by these events, Armagnac lodged a formal appeal at the court of Charles V against the prince's *fouage*. He and Albret were joined by a third powerful defector, Archambaud, count of Périgord. On 30 June, the king of France made a secret alliance with the three lords, offering them generous guarantees of rights, lands and pensions in return for their support in the war that his own provocations had now made more or less inevitable.[6]

The Black Prince and his father were both well informed of events in Paris and understood all too clearly the implications of the Valois' public posturing.[7] Charles's claim to hear Armagnac's appeal conflicted directly with the sovereign status accorded by Edward III to Aquitaine in 1362, and effectively demoted the English crown, represented by the prince, to the status of a vassal of France. If Charles chose to interpret Edward of Woodstock's resistance as an act of contumacy, then Edward III would be forced to intervene to preserve his rights and protect his territorial interests as defined in the treaty of Calais. For some months it remained uncertain whether the squabble would result in open war. The return of plague in the spring and summer of 1368 inclined the English government to further temporizing. Edward summoned a great council to meet at Guildford at the end of July to discuss arrangements for the government of Ireland consequent upon Lionel of Clarence's recent departure for Italy.[8] The king used

---

[3] G. Loirette, 'Arnaud Amanieu, sire d'Albret, et l'appel des seigneurs gascons en 1368', *Mélanges offerts à M. Charles Bémont* (Paris, 1913), 318–19; K. Fowler, 'Truces', *The Hundred Years War*, ed. Fowler, 191–3.

[4] Vale, *Angevin Legacy*, 96; Henneman, *Ransom of John II*, 178–9.

[5] Loirette, 'Arnaud Amanieu', 324; Henneman, *Ransom of John II*, 250–1.

[6] Froissart, *Oeuvres*, xviii, 485–8; Delachenal, iv, 85–91.

[7] Correspondence between the king and his son is noted in E 403/434, 6 May 1368.

[8] *Foedera*, III.ii, 845, 848. 'Earls and knights of the north who have lands in Ireland' were among those summoned to the council: E 403/434, 21 July 1368. A good deal of domestic business was also settled at this assembly, including an important ordinance relating to freedom of trade in the city of London: *CCR 1364–8*, 483.

the occasion to secure consent for the raising of new military contingents in
England and Wales, at the cost of the English exchequer, to be sent over to
Aquitaine under John of Gaunt and assist in any actions necessary to defend
the principality.[9] But the death of Gaunt's wife Blanche in September meant
that the expedition was delayed, and it was only dispatched under Edmund
of Langley and the earl of Pembroke in the following spring.[10]

Meanwhile, the diplomatic stand-off continued. In September 1368,
Lords Neville and Latimer were sent to Paris. They returned merely with
a vague promise that the count of Tancarville would soon be coming to
England to propose a solution.[11] The lord of Albret played the situation
significantly to his own advantage, on the one hand encouraging the
English to believe that he preferred to recognize Edward III as his superior lord of Gascony and on the other asserting his right, in the face of
unreasonable behaviour by Edward of Woodstock, to appeal to Charles V.
Such unscrupulous manoeuvring for a moment threatened to create a
breach between Edward III, who was still intent on preserving the peace,
and the prince, who was much more readily reconciled to the inevitability
of war.[12] With Louis of Anjou now actively inviting the nobles and
townsmen living on the fringes of the Plantagenet dominions to defect to
the Valois cause, it is indeed surprising that the truce held as long as it did.
The most likely explanation lies in the personal circumstances of Prince
Edward, who in the autumn fell seriously ill with the disease, probably
chronic dysentery, that he had contracted while fighting in Castile. In
November Charles V summoned the prince to appear in person at the
parlement of Paris on 2 May 1369.[13] The Chandos Herald dramatized
Edward of Woodstock's response to the news: 'Lords, I think, from what I
hear, that the French believe I am dead; but if God gives me comfort, and
I can get up from this bed, I will cause them harm enough yet, because
God knows that they complain of me now without good cause.'[14] If the
prince was in belligerent mode, he was also in no position to take
command of the war that he now so eagerly sought.

It was in this uneasy state of limbo that Edward III launched his final
effort to avert conflict and reclaim the settlement of 1360. In a memorandum sent to the French court in March 1369, the English king set out
three ways towards a peaceful resolution of differences: the fulfilment of
the renunciations required by the treaty of Calais; the completion of the

[9] E 403/434, 9 Aug. 1368; Sherborne, *War, Politics*, 3 n. 7.
[10] Goodman, *John of Gaunt*, 46, 66 n. 22; E 403/436, 14 Nov. 1368, 6 Mar. 1369;
Sherborne, *War, Politics*, 77–8.
[11] E 101/315/28; *Foedera*, III.ii, 850.
[12] E. Perroy, 'Edouard III d'Angleterre et les seigneurs gascons en 1368', *Annales du Midi*,
lxi (1948–9), 93, 95–6.
[13] Loirette, 'Arnaud Amanieu', 330, 334–5.
[14] *Vie du Prince Noir*, 155 (ll. 3881–8), translated in *Life and Campaigns*, 135. Cf. Froissart, vii,
96–7.

conference set up in 1366 to adjudicate the bounds of the lordship of Belleville; and the confirmation of the extent of English possessions in Ponthieu, Montreuil, Calais and Marck.[15] Privately, Edward may also have been considering the advantages of wiping off the outstanding debt owed by the French government on John II's ransom. But the sheer scale of such proposed or implied concessions served to expose the fragility of the English position. For a moment at least, the marriage of Margaret of Flanders and Philip of Burgundy in June 1369 threatened severely to disrupt Edward's network of alliances in the Low Countries and the empire and thus to imperil his strategic position in northern France. Some of the king's numerous in-laws could still be counted as allies. Philippa of Hainault's nephews Edward, duke of Guelders, and William, duke of Juliers, together with her sister's husband, Robert of Namur, remained publicly committed to the English cause in 1369; Robert's induction to the Order of the Garter at the St George's Day feast of 1370 was a potent reminder of the enduring obligations of family ties. But with the rulers of Flanders, Brabant and Hainault adopting calculated neutrality, the prospects of significant support in the Low Countries remained bleak, and were to deteriorate further as the 1370s progressed.[16]

Hardly less serious to English security was the news from Spain. Late in 1368 the French once more entered into alliance with the pretender to the Castilian throne, Henry of Trastamara.[17] When Peter I appealed for assistance, Edward III insisted on holding the position he had earlier taken up with regard to the Nájera campaign: military aid was entirely a matter for the prince of Aquitaine. But if Edward thought that a recent defensive alliance with Pere IV of Aragon would be sufficient to offset the dangers arising from a possible regime change in Castile, he was quickly disabused of the idea.[18] In March 1369 Bertrand du Guesclin led a small French force in support of Trastamara at the battle of Montiel. Peter I was roundly defeated, and a few days later was ambushed and murdered.[19] The belated commitments that Edward was persuaded to undertake in Castile were simply, and ironically, to provide further distraction from the main task of defending the territorial settlement in France.

In mid-January 1369 Edward held a great council at Westminster attended by a full array of the lords spiritual and temporal of the realm.[20]

---

[15] *EMDP*, I.ii, no. 308; *Chron. J&C*, ii, 76–116.

[16] Trautz, *Könige von England*, pp. 400–3.

[17] *Foedera*, III.ii, 850–2.

[18] E 30/1553, printed in Russell, *English Intervention*, 555–6 and *EMDP*, I.i, no. 73; *Foedera*, III.ii, 855–6; Curry, *Hundred Years War*, 65.

[19] Russell, *English Intervention*, 147–8.

[20] This is likely to have been the occasion of the writs sent out to a long list of named recipients in Dec. 1368: E 101/315/25. See also *AC*, 59. SC 8/227/11346 that refers to actions taken in Feb. 1369, which recalls that this great council had included the chancellor, treasurer and chief justice of king's bench, the duke of Lancaster, the earls of Arundel and Salisbury, William Latimer and 'other lords and justices'.

The news of Charles V's challenge to the sovereignty of Aquitaine was discussed, and further commitments of cash and soldiers were made for the defence of the principality.[21] Plans already put in place the previous autumn to dispatch the household knight William Windsor to Ireland as the new lieutenant of the lordship were brought forward in order to fend off possible French attempts to foment crisis in the colony.[22] It was agreed that men-at-arms and archers be invited to come forward and assist in the defence of Ponthieu and Calais, and that money be sent over to the treasurers of the king's dominions in northern France to support such initiatives.[23] Despite these measures, the English seem to have been caught unawares by Charles V's decision to pre-empt the formal declaration of war and begin the occupation of Edward's French possessions. English control of Ponthieu crumbled during the spring, and the surrender of Abbeville in late April created grave concern over the general state of defence in the Plantagenets' northern French provinces.

What really galvanized public opinion in England in 1369 was the risk of losing Calais. The great European entrepôt had become both a symbol and a mechanism of England's strategic strength in the Channel. Calais was now the obvious point of disembarkation for the great majority of English soldiers travelling to France: a vivid sense of the resulting conditions in the town is provided by a slightly later complaint from its burgesses about the endless mountains of manure left on their streets by incoming English warhorses.[24] Now that English wool-growers and exporters had been converted to the benefits of the compulsory wool staple established there since 1363, Calais was also seen as offering unique economic benefits.[25] At the outbreak of war in 1369 the crown temporarily closed the staple and resurrected the scheme of 1353 by which only aliens were permitted to export wool to the continent. By August 1370, however, when the initial scare had passed, the ban was lifted and the Calais staple was duly re-established.[26] After the outbreak of war, considerable efforts were put into ensuring the safekeeping of the town. From 1369 Edward III maintained a permanent garrison of around 500 men in Calais and a further 1,000 at various fortresses in the Pale. The associated costs rose

---

[21] E 403/436, 16 Dec. 1368, 26 Jan., 31 Jan., 3 Feb. 1369; *Foedera*, III.ii, 857.

[22] *Foedera*, III.ii, 850, 853–5; E 403/436, 31 Jan. 1369; Connolly, 'Financing', 111, 112, 117.

[23] *Foedera*, III.ii, 861–4; E 403/436, 5 Mar., 29 Mar. 1369; E 403/438, 14 Apr. 1369.

[24] SC 8/262/13081.

[25] *PROME*, v, 174–5; Lloyd, *Wool Trade*, 212–13.

[26] *PROME*, v, 226; *SR*, i, 390–1; *CLBL, G*, 248. There remained significant hostility to the crown's attempts to make a range of other commodities, including worsted cloth, subject to the staple: see D. Greaves, 'Calais under Edward III', *Finance and Trade*, ed. Unwin, 340–7. After the 1376 ordinance re-establishing the liability of worsteds to the Calais staple, the clothiers of Norfolk successfully sought exemption through parliament on the basis of a quaint argument that the market for cheap cloths was mainly among the 'Saracens': SC 8/85/4243.

accordingly, from around £12,000 a year in the 1350s to more than £20,000 a year in the 1370s.[27] Far from being the dung-heap of Europe, Calais had emerged by general consensus as the greatest jewel in the Plantagenets' imperial crown.

The defence of such rights was prominent in the new master plan worked out by the English council during the first half of May 1369. The king, accompanied by John of Gaunt and the earl of Hereford, would lead an expedition for the defence of Calais and the recovery of Ponthieu.[28] Edward prepared for his impending campaign by forestalling Charles V's efforts to revive the Franco-Scottish alliance. In May–June, David II made what was to be his last visit to his former brother-in-law.[29] On 18 June the two kings agreed an important modification to the treaty of Berwick that at once extended the Anglo-Scottish truce from 1370 to 1384 and spread still further the period allowable for payment of the outstanding portion of David's ransom. Nothing was said about the succession to the northern kingdom, and both monarchs now clearly agreed that the Scottish throne was almost bound to pass, in due course, to Robert Stewart. But Edward had the great satisfaction of knowing that he had succeeded in the strategy recently attempted with Charles V, using his right to relax the terms of an existing treaty as leverage for the peace that he sought so steadfastly to maintain. He also found much consolation in the subtext, for David seems to have given a confidential promise of military aid against the French.[30]

By the time this agreement was made, the English political community had already declared itself enthusiastically committed to full-scale war. In a manner typical of his *politique*, Edward III invited the secular peers to arrive at Westminster a week ahead of the parliament due to convene on 3 June 'for hard and secret business touching the king and the kingdom, to ordain and array for the king to go against his adversary of France'.[31] But if Edward's preferred strategy was to take a holding position and attempt merely to resist the Valois encroachments upon his territories, it soon became evident that the martial elite favoured a much more aggressive stance. When parliament opened, the lords and commons declared their unanimous support for war and made a generous new grant of the wool subsidy in recognition of the impending state of emergency.

---

[27] E. Perroy, 'L'Administration de Calais en 1371–2', *Revue du Nord*, xxxiii (1951), 218–27; *Compte de William Gunthorpe, trésorier de Calais, 1371–2*, ed. E. Perroy (Mémoires de la commission départementale des monuments historique du Pas de Calais, x, 1959); Harriss, *King, Parliament*, 329, 475; Rose, *Calais*, 34–5.

[28] E 403/438, 5 May, 12 May, 16 May, 17 May, 18 May, 29 May 1369. In 1372, two of the hostages then held at Stamford were transferred back to London: E 403/444, 17 Mar. 1372.

[29] *Rot. Scot.*, i, 928–33; Penman, *David II*, 383–4, 385. For gifts of jewels and plate to the bishop of Glasgow and other Scottish envoys see E 403/438, 14 June, 27 June 1369.

[30] *Foedera*, III.ii, 873, 877, 878–9; *CDS*, iv, no.154; E 403/438, 16 June 1369; *CLBL, G*, 246; Penman, *David II*, 385.

[31] E 403/438, 18 May 1369.

A week later, as a result of further debate among the high command, existing military plans were significantly revised. The army would now proceed in two stages, the first to be led by John of Gaunt and the second and larger force, departing in August, by the king.[32] The original idea of re-establishing control in Calais and Ponthieu was now giving way to a full-scale *chevauchée* on the models of 1346 and 1359. At the end of the parliamentary session, Chancellor Wykeham confirmed that everyone involved in the new invasion of France should be entitled to whatever lands and rights they might take by conquest.[33] This was an obvious sop to those who had lost out earlier in the decade by the forced evacuation of the English positions in Normandy, Anjou, Maine and Touraine. Similar incentives were subsequently communicated to the lords of Aquitaine, who were also promised remission of undue taxes and a general amnesty for any acts that might be construed as sympathetic to the Valois cause.[34] Before parliament closed, the commons were properly reassured that arrangements would be made for the internment of enemies, the confiscation of the alien priories and the defence of the coasts; in the latter case, the crown took the opportunity to establish a new principle that included the clergy in the general liability to local arrays. On the last day of the session, 11 June, Edward III formally resumed the style 'king of England and France', and thus once more laid down a direct challenge of war to the usurping Valois.[35]

It was with mixed feelings that Edward III girded himself for his forth-coming campaign. At fifty-six, he was of an age when at least the majority of nobles and knights had retired from the rigours of campaigning. The only leading nobleman of Edward's own generation to serve on the resulting expedition, the earl of Warwick, was actually to die, reputedly of plague, at Calais later in 1369.[36] Over the summer the king busied himself with the special defensive measures ordered, rather belatedly, against the menacing fleet gathered by Charles V in the Seine.[37] Gaunt's arrival at Calais with the vanguard of his army at the end of July saw off this threat,

[32] *Foedera*, III.ii, 870–1.

[33] *PROME*, v, 221, 223, 226–7.

[34] *Foedera*, III.ii, 874; Froissart, vii, lxxix–xc. There was a plan in 1370 to repeat the first of these communications throughout France, but it is unclear that it was implemented: *Foedera*, III.ii, 908.

[35] *PROME*, v, 221–2, 223, 224, 227; *Foedera*, III.ii, 864–6, 874, 876; *CLBL, G*, 242, 246; B. McNab, 'Obligations of the Church in English Society: Military Arrays of the Clergy, 1369–1418', *Order and Innovation*, ed. Jordan, McNab and Ruiz, 296–7. Detailed arrangements had been made in May for the transfer of the French townsmen held as hostages for John II's ransom to various provincial castles: E 403/438, 18 May 1369. For the hostages' subsequent efforts to secure release see P.-C. Timbal *et al.*, *La Guerre de Cent Ans vue à travers les registres du parlement (1337–1369)* (Paris, 1961), 401, 407–32.

[36] *Hist. Angl.*, i, 308; *AC*, 62.

[37] Froissart, vii, 157–8; *Issue Roll of Brantingham*, 396; *Foedera*, III.ii, 874–5.

forcing Charles to abandon the naval muster at Rouen and Harfleur and to send his brother, the duke of Burgundy, to head off the English prince as he rode into Picardy and towards the Île de France.

Until the very last moment, Edward III declared himself fully committed to joining the second army now gathering at Sandwich and departing for Calais on 18 August. On the 14th, with John of Gaunt already across the Channel and rumours of French preparations for imminent battle, Edward issued urgent orders from Eltham for a further force, at enhanced rates of pay, to muster in short order at Dover. But the death of Queen Philippa on the 15th left the king and his family unexpectedly marooned by the protocols of court mourning. The muster itself was ordered to go ahead as planned, but the enforced royal absence had significant impact on its scale and viability.[38] Edward had earlier ordered armour of war to be delivered to the earl of Arundel, as well as to his son-in-law, Enguerrand de Coucy, and his youngest son, the fourteen-year-old Thomas of Woodstock, in preparation for this expedition.[39] None of these, however, sailed with the force that crossed belatedly to Calais on 12 September, and just four earls – the veteran Thomas Beauchamp of Warwick, together with Thomas de Vere of Oxford, William Montagu the younger of Salisbury and Edmund Mortimer of March – eventually linked up with the advance party led by Lancaster and Hereford. The combined strength of the two armies amounted to around 6,000 men, including at least 1,000 recruited on the continent by William of Juliers and his captains.[40]

It was hardly surprising that the confident anticipation of glory rapidly gave way to an altogether more prosaic and inconclusive campaign. There was a significant stand-off between the dukes of Lancaster and Burgundy at Tournehem in mid-September when, in spite of adverse numbers, the English allegedly determined to fight. The French decision to withdraw was inevitably proclaimed an admission of cowardice, though it was also well understood to be part of Charles V's strategic planning. Gaunt now made for the coast, linking up with an English fleet sent across from Sandwich and working his way through the Pays de Caux in an orgy of destruction reminiscent of his father's earlier *viage de Normandie*. On his way back to Calais, Lancaster also made some attempts to breach the defences of Harfleur. None of these modest achievements was sufficient, however, to justify the enormous cost of the campaign, which came to at least £85,000.[41] At home, the risk of seaborne invasion continued to provoke panic, especially when the remnant of Charles V's fleet was employed by the adventurer Owain of Wales to attack the Black Prince's lordships in

[38] E 403/438, 14 Aug., 1 Sept. 1369; E 101/29/40.
[39] E 101/396/15.
[40] E 403/438, 25 July 1369; Sherborne, *War, Politics*, 2–6, 79–80.
[41] Froissart, viii, 164–7, 185–8, 191–5, 387–9; Sherborne, *War, Politics*, 93–6.

North Wales.[42] The English crown could only respond with its now accustomed resort to the rhetoric of necessity, instructing lords to return to their castles on the coasts and prepare for a war that threatened otherwise to destroy the principality of Wales and wipe the English language from the face of the earth.[43]

Charles V belatedly formalized his right to confiscate the English possessions in Aquitaine in November 1369, on the grounds that the Black Prince had continued to resist all attempts to draw him into the jurisdiction of the *parlement* of Paris. By this stage, many of the outer reaches of the English lands in south-west France had already fallen. Nobles and townsmen otherwise inclined to remain loyal to the English cause were either bullied into submission by the strong-armed tactics of the duke of Anjou or seduced into accepting Charles V's promise to confirm their customary privileges.[44] As if Edward of Woodstock's own health was not sufficient cause for concern, his regime suffered the additional misfortune of losing two of its greatest commanders, James Audley and John Chandos, within the first six months of hostilities.[45] In spite of initiatives taken by the earls of Cambridge and Pembroke and their lieutenants at Bourdeilles, La Roche-sur-Yon and Montauban,[46] the English had already lost effective control of Quercy and Périgord by the end of 1369. Edward III responded to Charles's announcement of confiscation by resuming authority to act on appeals from Aquitaine and distributing to his loyal Gascon subjects carefully worded statements of the wrongs suffered at the hands of the unreasonable and malicious Valois.[47] For those veterans who could remember as far back as the dark days of 1337–9, the reversals of 1369 were probably not sufficient to create an immediate sense of panic. The major question that remained was precisely how the crown would build a diplomatic and military strategy that could adequately challenge French aggression and drive Charles V back into negotiations for a revised peace.

In February 1370, in an interesting attempt to re-enact the first campaign of the Hundred Years War, Edward III proclaimed his intention of mustering an army at Orwell, proceeding to the Low Countries, and thence invading the kingdom of France. This rather fanciful plan was first rescheduled as a crossing from the Channel ports to Calais, and then abandoned altogether.[48] The reason for this notable wavering of royal

---

[42] Carr, *Owen of Wales*, 23–4; Sumption, iii, 44–5.

[43] *Foedera*, III.ii, 883, 900–2.

[44] Pépin, 'New Assessment', 59–114.

[45] *Vie du Prince Noir*, 157 (ll. 3941–54); Froissart, viii, 163, 206–7; *Hist. Angl.*, i, 312.

[46] Froissart, viii, 118–19, 150–3, 159–63, 337–8, 362–4, 368–9; *Vie du Prince Noir*, 156 (ll. 3915–34).

[47] *Foedera*, III.ii, 883–5.

[48] *Issue Roll of Brantingham*, 458; *Foedera*, III.ii, 889, 890.

policy was the re-entry into Anglo-French affairs of Charles of Navarre. Eager to exploit the differences between his Plantagenet and Valois cousins, Charles had moved to Brittany and Normandy and now offered to assist with a landing in the Cotentin. His condition was both straight-forward and potentially very costly: namely, that the English should with-draw from the stronghold at Saint-Sauveur-le-Vicomte, now the centre of operations for an extensive system of *pâtis* and plunder extracted by the freelance English warlords still installed in western Normandy.[49]

On the advice of a great council in February, Edward III agreed to send over a force of 4,000 men to join Charles's supporters and help stir up provincial opposition to Valois rule.[50] It was the unusual nature of this expedition, designed as a relief force rather than an independent invasion, that caused the crown to give command not to some high-ranking lord but to a self-made soldier Sir Robert Knolles. Nevertheless, the implied mark of distinction offended many conservatively minded soldiers, including some of Knolles's fellow contractors, and leadership of the army had subsequently to be renegotiated with Alan Buxhull, Thomas Grandisson and Thomas Bourchier.[51] The summer campaign began auspiciously enough, and the English swept through Picardy, Champagne, Normandy and Maine. But French strategy soon prevailed, and Knolles was eventu-ally surprised and defeated at Pontvallain, north of Tours, in December. Rather vindictively, the English council chose to punish the commander of Normandy by temporarily depriving him of the lands earlier given him as an up-front incentive of service.[52]

The only other significant military expedition of 1370 was that sent under John of Gaunt, Edmund of Langley and the earl of Pembroke in July to assist the enfeebled Edward of Woodstock in his beleaguered outpost of Gascony. Although the king was prepared to allocate significant amounts of his personal treasure in subsidies to support this initiative, he remained loath to encourage large numbers of English knights to take service in Aquitaine. A French fleet attacked merchant vessels in the Channel and burned the town of Gosport, and it was necessary for the moment to prioritize the defence of the English coasts. The entire army of Gascony, including the contingents from the prince's lands in Wales and Cheshire, was planned to be only around 1,500 men.[53] The prince and his brothers made a summer foray as far as Limoges, whose bishop had recently surrendered his part of the city to the duke of Berry. Froissart

---

[49] Holmes, *Good Parliament*, 38; N. Wright, *Knights and Peasants: The Hundred Years War in the French Countryside* (Woodbridge, 1998), 58.

[50] Sumption, iii, 64–7. For the contracts made in preparation for this expedition see *Issue Roll of Brantingham*, 128–30; E 101/68/4, no. 90; E 101/30/25; Prince, 'Strength of English Armies', 369–70; Sherborne, *War, Politics*, 6–7; Fowler, *Medieval Mercenaries*, 289.

[51] *Froissart*, v, 366; *ODNB*, xxxi, 954–5.

[52] Froissart, viii, 1–5; Sumption, iii, 84–94; Fowler, *Medieval Mercenaries*, 292–7.

[53] *Foedera*, III.ii, 894, 895, 896; E 101/29/40; Sumption, iii, 69–70.

grossly exaggerated in his famous account of the ruthless punishments
meted out to the non-combatant population of Limoges, but his reflections on the prince's bad health and resulting short temper remain enlight-
ening.[54] The raid had little lasting value, and by the end of the year almost
all of the Limousin and the Agenais had fallen to the advancing Valois
forces. The prince returned to Angoulême to find his wife deep in
mourning for the recent death of their first son. In the face of such overwhelming loss, Edward of Woodstock gave up all pretence of ability to
command the principality. After handing the lieutenancy of Aquitaine to
the more robust Gaunt, he made swift preparations to retire to England,
where he eventually arrived with Princess Joan and Richard of Bordeaux
in January.[55] With them went any residual hope that the territorial and
constitutional settlement forged by Edward III in 1360–2 might yet be
sustained.

At home, attention had again moved back to the possibility of intervention in the great principalities of France. In July–August 1370 Charles the
Bad crossed from Cherbourg to meet with his English cousin at the royal
hunting lodge of Clarendon. The wily king of Navarre set stringent terms
for the encounter: Edward would pay the entirety of Charles's expenses,
and would hand over the bishop of Durham and the new earls of
Warwick and Suffolk to stand surety for his own good faith.[56] An outline
proposal emerged in December, by which Charles agreed to recognize and
support Edward III in return for generous offers of cash and lands both in
northern France and in greater Aquitaine. Edward accordingly began to
apply pressure on Sir Alan Buxhull, who had taken possession of Saint-
Sauveur, to hand over the castle to Charles's agents. But the Black Prince,
who was a necessary party to any agreement, judged the whole process too
risky, and after Knolles's defeat at Pontvallain the king rapidly gave up any
further efforts to promote this unlikely alliance.[57]

No sooner had the Anglo-Navarrese talks collapsed than Edward's
attention was drawn back into that other great theatre of his earlier
provincial strategy, the duchy of Brittany. Like his counterparts in
Flanders and elsewhere, Duke John V of Brittany was disposed to take a

---

[54] Froissart, vii, 243–5, 248–53, 422–7; *Vie du Prince Noir*, 159–60 (ll. 4026–56); Barber,
Edward, Prince of Wales, 224–6; Pépin, 'New Assessment', 86–8.

[55] *John of Gaunt's Register, 1371–5*, i, no. 9; Froissart, viii, 9–10; *AC*, 67. Edward of
Angoulême's remains were subsequently translated by Richard II to the secondary royal
mausoleum at Kings Langley: 'The Accounts of John de Stratton and John Gedeney,
Constables of Bordeaux, 1381–90', ed. J. R. Wright, *Mediaeval Studies*, xlii (1980), 304
and n. 76.

[56] E 159/147, *Brev. bar.*, Hil., rot. 3; E 159/147, *Brev. bar.*, Mich., rot. 6d; *Foedera*, III.ii,
899–900.

[57] *EMDP*, I.i, no. 26; *Foedera*, III.ii, 907–8; *AC*, 66; *Hist. Angl.*, i, 312; Delachenal, iv,
365–7; Jones, *Ducal Brittany*, 63; Barber, *Edward, Prince of Wales*, 226–7; Sumption, iii,
72–4, 93.

neutral stance in the new Anglo-French hostilities. He was keen to oust the English from the castle of Bécherel, and found some ready potential support for such an enterprise in the person of Charles V. But he was also determined not to lose the advantage of good relations with his former father-in-law and protector, Edward III. Edward, in turn, was eager to offer handsome terms for a renewal of the Anglo-Breton alliance. He provided solid assurances that the two sons of John's former rival, Charles of Blois, would remain in custody in England.[58] He promised Montfort the Poitevin lordships previously marked out for Thomas of Woodstock and Charles the Bad, and allowed him to reassert his ancestral rights to the honour of Richmond in Yorkshire currently held by John of Gaunt. Most unexpectedly, Edward released the duke of Brittany from performing the act of homage due to him as king of France. Unfortunately for both men, the agreement finally ratified in November 1372 simply had the effect of unleashing serious Valois recriminations. A small English force led by Lord Neville was quickly overwhelmed by du Guesclin's army. Duke John was forced, like his father before him, to seek refuge at the English court and was reunited with his former patron at Windsor in May 1373.[59] Far from helping to deflect Charles V's energies from the main arenas of war, the attempted alliances with Charles of Navarre and John de Montfort had served only to compromise Edward III's diplomatic strength and dissipate his already overstretched military resources.

Ironically enough, it was in his dealings with Flanders that Edward actually had most military and diplomatic success in the early 1370s. In spite of permitting his daughter's marriage to Philip of Burgundy, Louis de Mâle had no intention of giving active assistance to Charles V in the new war and was keen to preserve his county's important commercial links with England. By 1370 an Anglo-Flemish trade agreement had already been drafted. There were delays in its ratification, and during 1371 there were small-scale skirmishes at sea that once more gave rise to nervous predictions of co-ordinated French and Flemish actions in the Channel.[60] In May Edward's council redoubled its efforts for coastal defence. A naval force assembled at Southampton to transport the earl of Hereford to Brittany was redeployed in the Bay of Bourgneuf against the Flemish salt fleet returning from La Rochelle, and won what turned out to be the last

[58] Jones, *Ducal Brittany*, 64 n. 3; *Anglo-Norman Letters and Petitions from All Souls MS 162*, ed. M. D. Legge (Anglo-Norman Text Society, iii, 1941), no. 265; *Foedera*, III.ii, 988; E 403/461, 21 Jan., 13 Feb., 10 Mar. 1377.

[59] *EMDP*, I.i, no. 96; *Foedera*, III.ii, 964–5; *AC*, 71–2; Jones, *Ducal Brittany*, 64–74; M. Arvanigian, 'A Lancastrian Polity? John of Gaunt, John Neville and the War with France, 1368–88', *Fourteenth Century England III*, ed. Ormrod, 131–2; Holmes, *Good Parliament*, 25.

[60] Before the end of Feb. 1371 John Tipet, valet of the king's chamber, was sent to Rye to view seven Flemish vessels recently taken 'by our lieges' in the Channel and reported back to the king and council at London on the matter: E 101/620/17; E 159/147, *Brev. bar.*, Hil., rot. 12.

naval victory of Edward III's reign.[61] The action served as a timely warning against further prevarication, and Louis de Mâle finally asserted his neutrality in the war by confirming the trade agreement with England in 1372.[62]

The least disruptive of all the cluster of events on the international stage in 1371 was the death, on 22 February, of David II of Scotland. In making his contributions to the funeral expenses and tomb of his deceased brother-in-law, Edward III necessarily deployed the conditional forms used since the treaty of Berwick and denied David the title of king.[63] Equally, though, he put up no objection to the speedy succession of Robert Stewart to the vacant monarchy. Edward's advisers understood that their best way forward was to enter into negotiations with Stewart as de facto ruler and affirm the recently extended Anglo-Scottish truce. At a meeting to hand over the latest ransom payment at Berwick in June 1372, Robert II's representatives created a minor fracas by objecting to the English habit of omitting the Scottish royal style from written confirmations of receipt.[64] But this hardly detracted from the Stewart king's own keenness to preserve good relations. Robert's first parliament sent a deputation to the court of Charles V to renew the customary alliance of mutual support between their realms. At the same time, however, it refused to accept Charles's offer that he would pay off David II's ransom in return for being allowed to invade England through Scotland.[65] Nor were recent initiatives to regulate cross-border quarrels seriously undermined by the change of dynasty in Scotland. Even a potentially vicious vendetta between Henry Percy and William, earl of Douglas, over rights in Jedburgh was for the most part contained until 1377.[66] If English policy towards Scotland had necessarily to remain a holding operation, then Edward III also had good reason to believe that it now more effectively served his interests in France than at almost any time since 1357.

If there is a single explanation for the failure of Edward III's strategy regarding France in the 1370s, it lies in his continued willingness to be distracted by the succession crisis in Castile. Peter I's two surviving teenage daughters, Constanza and Isabella, had been placed in the custody of the Black Prince as hostages for their father's debts after the battle of Nájera, and continued to find refuge in Gascony after Peter's murder in 1369.[67]

[61] E 403/442, 4 June 1371; *AC*, 68–9, 177. *Hist. Angl.*, i, 313–14, misdates the engagement to 1372, as does the later *Chronicle of London*, 69.

[62] *Foedera*, III.ii, 938–9; *EMDP*, I.i, no. 112; Lloyd, *Wool Trade*, 218–19.

[63] *Foedera*, III.ii, 920, 942, 980.

[64] *CDS*, v, no. 846; S. I. Boardman, *The Early Stewart Kings: Robert II and Robert III, 1371–1406* (East Linton, 1996), 110. For subsequent English insistence on the denial of the title see *Foedera*, III.ii, 967–8.

[65] *Foedera*, III.ii, 925–6; Bower, vii, 382–9; Campbell, 'England, Scotland', 203 and n. 1.

[66] Neville, *Violence, Custom and Law*, 52–6.

[67] *AC*, 55, 69.

Under the terms of her father's will, Constanza was the rightful heiress to the kingdom, though it would be for her future husband to make good that title by force of arms. Peter himself had twice proposed a marriage with one of the Plantagenet princes as part of his rapprochement with the English court in the 1360s.[68] In September 1371, with his father's blessing, John of Gaunt married the seventeen-year-old Constanza at Roquefort near Mont-de-Marsan. Given the earlier attempts to set up his third son as heir to the Scottish throne, it is perfectly possible that the English king was persuaded to view Gaunt's new interest in Castile as a serious ambition. In January 1372 the Westminster council gave consent to Prince John's new style of king of Castile and Léon and began discussing plans for direct military intervention against Henry of Trastamara. Returning to England, John and Constanza set about creating a full-scale court-in-exile, complete with Castilian staff, language and fashions.[69]

Such a shift of dynastic alignment was really only justifiable because of the significant threat that a hostile Castile might pose to the security of Aquitaine and to English supremacy at sea.[70] By the spring of 1372 the English government was aware of plans for major Franco-Castilian naval manoeuvres in the Bay of Biscay and the English Channel. Charles V's go-between, Owain of Wales, made a serious, though unsuccessful, attempt to invade Guernsey; the picturesque local tradition that the maidens of the island stirred their young men to feats of arms by giving them hats decorated with violets and other spring flowers rather belies the major emergency thus prompted.[71] Meanwhile, a minor expedition led by the earl of Pembroke and intended for Aquitaine arrived outside La Rochelle on 22 June to find a massed Castilian fleet blockading the harbour. Urgently in need of reinforcements, Pembroke called for assistance from the seneschal of Saintonge, Sir John Harpeden. But the result of the encounter was never in doubt. By the afternoon of 23 June the entirety of Pembroke's small fleet had been destroyed or captured, his war treasury of £12,000 had been seized, and he and most of the Anglo-Gascon notables who had come to his rescue had been captured. Pembroke was confined by Henry of Trastamara in infamously gruesome conditions at the castle of Curiel.[72] It is difficult to escape the conclusion that the wedding of Edmund of Langley and Isabella of Castile, celebrated at Wallingford castle in July 1372, marked a desperate attempt to signal England's determination for vengeance upon Trastamara for the devastating defeat at La Rochelle.[73]

[68] Russell, *English Intervention*, 38–9, 145.

[69] *AC*, 69; *Hist. Angl.*, i, 313; Knighton, 194–7; Froissart, viii, 32–3; Russell, *English Intervention*, 175 and n. 1; Sumption, iii, 122–3.

[70] Froissart, viii, 29–30; Russell, *English Intervention*, 190–203; Goodman, *John of Gaunt*, 112–13.

[71] *Chron. QPV*, 230–1; Carr, *Owen of Wales*, 27–30.

[72] Froissart, viii, 36–49; *AC*, 70–1; Sherborne, *War, Politics*, 41–5; Sumption, iii, 138–42.

[73] Goodman, *John of Gaunt*, 50–1.

To such symbolic reactions had to be added the full force of English military and naval might. Since February 1372 most of the government's efforts had been put into planning a land-based campaign ostensibly for the relief of the siege of Thouars in Poitou.[74] On 10 July, however, Edward III dramatically announced his intention 'to go upon the sea . . . to resist the malice of his enemies'.[75] Over the summer a large force of 3,000 men-at-arms and 3,000 archers was assembled at Sandwich.[76] As in 1359, a contingent of archers from the Forest of Knaresborough was assigned as the king's personal guard for the campaign.[77] Edward was joined at Sandwich at the end of August by the principal captains of his new army: the three older princes, Edward, John and Edmund, together with his ailing cousin the earl of Hereford, the vigorous and valiant earls of March and Salisbury, and two recent newcomers to the comital ranks, William Ufford of Suffolk and Thomas Beauchamp the younger of Warwick. The ardent seventeen-year-old Thomas of Woodstock seems also to have made ready to take ship with his father, for it was not he but the infant Richard of Bordeaux who, on 31 August, was appointed titular keeper of the realm for the duration of the king's absence.[78]

By the time Edward set sail, the situation at La Rochelle had become still more serious. On 7 September, under intense pressure from the French and Castilians by land and sea, the remaining English forces in the area had been required to surrender the town. If Edward intended to go directly to the relief of La Rochelle, he may have planned to land in Brittany and take the land route south.[79] Alternatively, his sights may have been set on lingering in the Channel until such time as the Castilian fleet could be drawn into a conscious re-enactment of the great English victory of *les Espagnols sur mer*. In the end, the weather took control. For over a month the English tried to make headway through the Channel against strong south-westerly winds. Putting in at Winchelsea, the king was forced to disband most of his men in the first week of October, though he only finally abandoned the expedition and took to dry land again on the 14th. Public frustration vented itself in wild speculation about the amounts of money squandered in the aborted campaign.[80] A month before his sixtieth birthday, the exasperated Edward III had to confront the fact that time, the elements and divine will were all running against him. It was one of the most deeply frustrating moments of his entire military career.

---

[74] Froissart, viii, 93–4.

[75] *John of Gaunt's Register, 1371–5*, i, no. 63; Sherborne, *War, Politics*, 47–8.

[76] C 76/55, m. 28. Public prayers for the expedition were ordered on 11 Aug.: *Foedera*, III.ii, 960.

[77] E 403/447, 21 Oct. 1372.

[78] *CPR 1370–4*, 195; *HBC*, 39. For a memorandum setting out Richard's powers as *custos regni* see C 49/47/9.

[79] Sumption, iii, 153.

[80] *Hist. Angl.*, i, 315; *PROME*, v, 258.

The one positive outcome from the shock of La Rochelle was a significant change in English naval policy. During the years of peace Edward III
seems to have used some of his jealously guarded private income from
ransoms to build new ships such as *Dieu la garde* and the *Grace Dieu*. A
possibly incomplete list of the king's personal fleet in 1370 names twenty-
five seagoing vessels, including the *Merlin*, the *George*, the *Christopher*, the
Edward and the *Philippa*. This force formed the core of the ill-fated armada
of 1372.[81] However, on its own it was insufficient to provide either for the
defence of the coasts or for military transportation, both of which activities continued to depend heavily on the requisitioning of commercial
vessels.[82] Already in 1370 the council had begun the process of extending
to inland towns the general obligation to contribute ships and mariners for
coastal defence.[83] In the parliaments of the early 1370s the commons also
took up what they identified as the serious deterioration in the naval
capacity of the realm, nostalgically recalling the period in the middle
decades of the century when 'the fleet of the realm was so noble and so
plentiful . . . that all countries called our lord the "king of the sea"'.[84] The
most significant of the resulting initiatives was that rolled out after the
defeat of La Rochelle in 1372, when a series of prominent towns were
ordered to construct and maintain some seventy purpose-built vessels of
war. If England was still far from having anything akin to a dedicated
navy, the new provincial flotillas instituted in 1372 went a long way to
relieving the pressure on merchant shipping, and for the rest of Edward
III's reign they contributed significantly to the twin burdens of military
transport and coastal defence.[85]

If such measures helped reassure the domestic political community of
a resolute commitment to maintain the security of England, they could do
nothing to alter the dismal catalogue of defeats still being reported from
France. The one remaining significant Plantagenet force left in Gascony,
under the redoubtable Jean de Grailly, captal de Buch, was forced to stand
by as the mighty city of Poitiers fell to the French invaders. At Soubise in
late August, Grailly attempted to ambush a small detachment of French
led by Owain of Wales. But both he and the seneschal of Poitou, Sir
Thomas Percy, were captured in the ensuing skirmish. Soubise thus
marked the end of any effective resistance to the Valois in Poitou,

---

[81] E 159/152, *Brev. bar.*, Mich., rot. 13; E 403/446, 23 July 1372; Sherborne, *War,
Politics*, 32.

[82] Rodger, *Safeguard of the Sea*, i, 118–25.

[83] C 81/416/28092–C 81/417/28131.

[84] *PROME*, v, 245, 261–2, 284–5.

[85] E 403/447, 22 Nov. 1372; Sherborne, *War, Politics*, 34, 72; Liddy, *War, Politics*, 44, 46–8,
53–5; M. Kowaleski, 'Warfare, Shipping, and Crown Patronage: The Impact of the
Hundred Years War on the Port Towns of Medieval England', *Money, Markets and Trade in
Later Medieval Europe: Essays in Honor of John H. A. Munro*, ed. M. Elbl, I. Elbl and L.
Armstrong (Leiden, 2007), 237–8.

Saintonge and Angoumois. By the end of September virtually the whole of the Agenais was also overrun by Charles V's forces. In the same month the dukes of Berry, Bourbon and Burgundy marched into Brittany to protest against the recently revealed alliance between Duke John and Edward III. In December they successfully forced the Anglo-Gascon army remaining at Thouars to surrender, and returned in triumph to Paris.[86]

In the midst of such a torrent of bad news, the English elite had to stand witness to the public humiliation of its royal heroes. On 5 November 1372 in a plenary session of parliament Sir Guy Brian announced that, since Edward of Woodstock's independent principality of Aquitaine was no longer viable, the prince had decided to renounce his title and surrender all his claims to his father as superior lord.[87] There were obvious practical reasons for this formal transfer of powers; not least, it would give the king authority to appoint a new sequence of military lieutenants to the high command at Bordeaux. But it was also a dangerous admission of the effective collapse of sovereign control over the Plantagenets' ancestral lands in France. Just five weeks later, at the Louvre Palace in Paris, the duke of Berry did homage to Charles V for Poitou. The systematic dismemberment of the principality of Aquitaine had begun. Edward III and his sons stood by in helpless horror as their Valois cousins gleefully paraded the titles and spoils of victory.

The withdrawal of the 1372 expedition marked the end of the military careers of both Edward III and the Black Prince; never again would either mighty commander don the armour of war in defence of honour and right. Like his eldest son, the king was becoming prone to infirmity; he had already suffered a first bout of serious illness in the late summer of 1371, and from 1373 he was to give himself up increasingly to the feebleness of old age.[88] At the November parliament of 1372 Sir Guy Brian gave the assurances of continued military commitment that were necessary to generate further grants of taxation, but was careful to avoid creating a false impression that the king or the prince might join any future campaign.[89] The aspirations of the royal family and political community were now becoming fixed on the king's third son, John of Gaunt, duke of Lancaster. From 1373 to the end of the reign it was to be Gaunt's unenviable task to steer a course between the English polity's increasingly strident demand for victory against the Valois, the crown's grave concern to retrieve at least something from the Anglo-French settlement of 1360, and his own ambitions for conquest and rule in Castile. It was the real or

[86] Froissart, viii, 67–71; Sumption, iii, 145–55, 159.

[87] *PROME*, v, 258; *Foedera*, III.ii, 974.

[88] See pp. 529–31.

[89] *PROME*, v, 258–60.

perceived tension between these various commitments that would in turn create the growing suspicion that Gaunt had ambitions for the crown of England itself.

Plans for a new campaign emerged slowly over the early months of 1373. John of Gaunt would be joined in high command by three new earls of his generation, Stafford, Suffolk and Warwick. John de Montfort signed up, offering to raise a thousand men of his own in England. A group of minor Gascon nobles who had recently found refuge with the Black Prince also agreed to serve, and a handful of Hainaulters planned to join the army on its arrival in France. But none of Edward III's remaining princely allies in the Netherlands and the empire was to turn out in support of this army.[90] The comparatively large force pieced together by Gaunt, which numbered close on 6,000 men, was made up overwhelmingly of contract forces raised in England, especially from the duke of Lancaster's own mighty network of military retainers.[91]

The prominence of John de Montfort and the fixing of the original muster at Plymouth made it reasonably evident that the campaign of 1373 was first intended to land in Brittany and undertake an extended march southwards to relieve what little remained of English Gascony.[92] There may initially have been some idea of opening up a second front, presumably in northern France, under the leadership of Edmund of Langley.[93] In the end, though, the muster was moved to Dover and Sandwich, and Gaunt's army transferred to Calais in late July.[94] The revised aim was to make the accustomed show of strength in the Île de France and provoke Charles V to take up arms for the defence of Paris. But Gaunt faced even stouter resistance than his father had in 1359, and Charles V refused to be dislodged from his position at Troyes. Faced with such an impasse, Prince John decided to head off for his original destination of Aquitaine. There followed what later became known as the 'great *chevauchée*' through the Limousin and down the Dordogne to Bordeaux, where the English army arrived at Christmas.[95] Valois supporters kept their distance in the hope that Lancaster's forces would simply wither away; logistical problems, combined with incessant local skirmishes through La Marche and the

---

[90] *AC*, 73, 178–9; Froissart, viii, 126–8, 137–8; *Chron. QPV*, 215–20; *Chron. J&C*, ii, 158–9. When Edward III subsequently apologized to Henry, count of Holstein, for the fact that the financial pressures of Gaunt's expedition had delayed payment of the count's fee, he made no suggestion that Henry might need to excuse his recent absence from Lancaster's campaign: *EMDP*, I.i, no. 25.

[91] *John of Gaunt's Register, 1371–5*, i, no. 52; Walker, *Lancastrian Affinity*, 40, 48–9; Sherborne, *War, Politics*, 10–12.

[92] *John of Gaunt's Register, 1371–5*, no. 310; Sumption, iii, 175.

[93] *AC*, 73, claims that Edmund accompanied Gaunt, but there is no documentary evidence to support this.

[94] *John of Gaunt's Register, 1371–5*, i, no. 310.

[95] Delachenal, iv, 480–503.

lower Limousin, certainly resulted in heavy losses of English men and horses. The constable of Gaunt's army, Edward Despenser, was one of several prominent English soldiers who contracted chronic illnesses during this harsh and heroic trek.[96]

Modern historians have been much more inclined than their medieval counterparts to give John of Gaunt credit for the leadership, adaptability and organizational skills that he showed in the campaign of 1373.[97] For some, there is a lingering doubt as to whether the duke saw the descent into Aquitaine as an end in itself or merely as a prelude to the prosecution of his claims in Castile. Gaunt and his captains had contracted with the crown for a full year's service, of which only six months had been performed by the time they arrived at Bordeaux. During the winter and spring of 1372–3 the English crown had already attempted, and failed, to secure the support of Fernando I of Portugal against Henry of Trastamara.[98] By early 1374 Gaunt himself was in active discussion with the count of Foix and the kings of Navarre and Aragon for a joint expedition across the Pyrenees. All such plans foundered, however, on the rock of finance. There is absolutely no suggestion that Edward III now deviated from his previous position and attempted to divert the profits of English taxation to pay for Gaunt's ambitions in Spain.[99] It was not until 1385, under Richard II, that the crown was to take this fateful step and open up a rift between Gaunt's private interests and his public responsibilities.[100] The duke of Lancaster's sudden decision in April 1374 to abandon his prospective allies in the Midi and return to England stands as the firmest possible evidence that his father's government had simply refused to extend its commitments to Castile.[101] And in spite of the sense of frustration likely to have been forged, the prince's action reveals what still undoubtedly remained his strongest motivation: an unswerving loyalty to his father's cause.

Gaunt's withdrawal from Aquitaine marked the end of recent attempts to revive the English set piece of the *chevauchée* and to draw out the French into open battle. It also heralded further retreat from the remaining pockets of Plantagenet control. With the French capture of La Réole, English Aquitaine was reduced to a narrow coastal strip between Bayonne and Bordeaux and a fragile string of strategic castles stretching through the lower Dordogne as far as Bergerac.[102] Not surprisingly, the ordinary

---

[96] Froissart, viii, 171.

[97] *Hist. Angl.*, i, 315–16; *Chron. J&C*, ii, 174; J. J. N. Palmer, *England, France and Christendom, 1377–99* (London, 1972), 6; Goodman, *John of Gaunt*, 233–4.

[98] *Foedera*, III.ii, 966, 981, 983–5; *EMDP*, I.i, nos 261, 360, 415; Russell, *English Intervention*, 196–203.

[99] *PROME*, v, 278, 279–80; Holmes, *Good Parliament*, 25–9.

[100] *PROME*, vii, 6; J. S. Roskell, *The Impeachment of Michael de la Pole, Earl of Suffolk, in the Context of the Reign of Richard II* (Manchester, 1984), 43, 71.

[101] Holmes, *Good Parliament*, 29; Sumption, iii, 200–2.

[102] *Hist. Angl.*, i, 317; Delachenal, iv, 507–15; Fowler, *Age of Plantagenet and Valois*, 69.

revenues of the duchy were now in steep decline, and the constable of Bordeaux, Robert Wykford, was forced to draw down increasingly large amounts of cash from Westminster.[103] A rare victory in a skirmish between the young count of Saint-Pol and the garrisons of Calais and Guînes in early August 1374, at which the count and numerous French captains were taken prisoner, gave a welcome indication that the defences of Calais remained secure.[104] But the English surrender of Bécherel in November and the major French siege of Saint-Sauveur-le-Vicomte now seriously jeopardized the English presence in the north of France.[105] Plans for a relief expedition under the joint command of Montfort and Edmund of Langley were repeatedly postponed.[106] The king's sense of frustration comes across vividly in a personal letter to the captain of the muster, Guy Brian, who was briskly berated for the general laxity of arrangements for the departure of the fleet from the ports of Devon.[107] The army eventually sailed in April 1375, but was soon sacrificed to the opening of peace talks and recalled from the field after barely three months' action.[108] Its withdrawal seriously called into question the crown's commitment to the continuing English presence in Brittany and Normandy and appeared to render redundant that promise, expressed so confidently in 1369, that the second war might yet become a source of private enterprise and profit.

Ever since his election in 1370, Pope Gregory XI had been attempting to encourage the English and French back into negotiation. These initiatives had an important personal dimension: Gregory's brother, Roger Beaufort, had been taken prisoner by the English at the sack of Limoges, and it was incumbent on the pope to do everything possible to facilitate Roger's ransom and release. In 1371 Gregory had dispatched as his envoy to Edward's court Simon Langham, the former archbishop of Canterbury and chancellor of England and, since 1368, a cardinal of the Church. But such obvious efforts to exploit Edward's goodwill were ironically confounded by Langham's over-anxiety to please: the cardinal's rash decision to doff his cap before the king of England was said to have aroused much condemnation among the hierarchically minded authorities of Avignon.[109] Some further desultory discussions had taken place under the

---

[103] T. Runyan, 'The Constabulary of Bordeaux: The Accounts of John Ludham (1372–73) and Robert de Wykford (1373–75)', *Mediaeval Studies*, xxvi (1974), 228–9.

[104] Froissart, viii, 182–7; *AC*, 76–7, 180; *Chron. QPV*, 249–50.

[105] For what follows see C. C. Bayley, 'The Campaign of 1375 and the Good Parliament', *EHR*, lv (1940), 370–83.

[106] *Foedera*, III.ii, 1018–19, 1021; Froissart, viii, 194–5; Sherborne, *War, Politics*, 12–13.

[107] Holmes, *Good Parliament*, 40–1; Sumption, iii, 898 n. 16. For complaints from the people of Devon about the activities of Montfort's troops see SC 8/14/655; *PROME*, v, 370–1, 386.

[108] *Foedera*, III.ii, 1034–5; Froissart, viii, 210–12; Jones, *Ducal Brittany*, 80; Henneman, *Olivier de Clisson*, 87.

[109] *Eulogium*, iii, 337.

presidency of Gregory's delegates at Calais in 1372 and Bruges in 1373.[110]
Now, in the early summer of 1374, the special papal envoy Pileo de Prata,
archbishop of Ravenna, visited the English court. The French remained
convinced that Edward would refuse all offers of talks. However, the
increasingly dire military position left the English government with no real
choice, and measures were finally put in place in January 1375 for a peace
summit to be held after Easter at Bruges. It was an important marker of
England's seriousness of purpose that Gaunt himself was named as
Edward III's principal delegate to the talks.[111]

The conference of Bruges opened in late March 1375 in a flourish of
ceremony and spectacle. The English were naturally quick to reserve their
negotiating position by asserting Edward III's right to the throne of
France and insisting that he would only renounce this when duly compensated for loss of sovereignty and invested with all the ancestral lands held
by the English crown in the time of King John. If this had represented a
substantive agenda in the 1350s, it was now resurrected only as a means of
forcing the French to concede the terms of the treaty of Calais. The duke
of Burgundy predictably retorted that, since the English themselves had
breached the 1360 settlement, the talks ought to revert to the position that
had applied in 1337 and thus allow the reopening of the whole question of
the former feudal status of Aquitaine. Rarely since the 1340s had the two
sides adopted agendas that were so obviously unrealistic, and so diametri-
cally opposed.

Faced with this posturing, the papal deputies, the archbishop of Ravenna
and the bishop of Carpentras, tried hard to find a third way. Their most
radical solution was that Edward III should dissolve the constitutional unity
of England and Gascony and give up all claims to the duchy. In return,
John of Gaunt would be recognized as duke of Aquitaine and would
hold the title in feudal homage to the French crown. To provide guarantees
against future conflicts of interest, Gaunt should give up his own lands and
rights in England – though not, significantly, in Castile. Lancaster, for
whom the scheme might be thought to have had some appeal, nevertheless
rejected it out of hand.[112] Despite this, there followed an amended
plan for a three-way division of Aquitaine, with the provinces south of
the Dordogne being retained in full sovereignty by Edward III and the

[110] *Foedera*, III.ii, 934, 969–70; *AC*, 70; *Hist. Angl.*, i, 313; Mirot and Déprez, *Ambassades anglaises*, nos 314–15.

[111] *Chron. QPV*, 214; *Foedera*, III.ii, 1021, 1022–3, 1024–5. For what follows, see 'The Anglo-French Negotiations at Bruges, 1374–1377', ed. E. Perroy, *Camden Miscellany XIX* (Camden Society, 3rd series, lxxx, 1952).

[112] Palmer, *England, France*, 34–5. For the attempts after 1390 to revive this scheme, see J. J. N. Palmer, 'The Anglo-French Peace Negotiations, 1390–1396', *TRHS*, 5th series, xvi (1966), 94; M. G. A. Vale, *English Gascony, 1399–1453* (Oxford, 1970), 28–9; A. Tuck, 'Richard II and the Hundred Years War', *Politics and Crisis*, ed. Taylor and Childs, 118–19.

remaining areas split between Charles V and a cadet branch of the Plantagenets. It was agreed that this scheme should be referred back to Edward III and Charles V and that the negotiators would reconvene in May to pursue the new basis for peace. The ever active William Latimer was entrusted with the delicate task of communicating the proposals to his master in England.

On 16 May a great council convened at Westminster to consider the reports from Bruges and Edward III's initial responses to them. There was little enthusiasm for the specifics. But in the hope of saving Saint-Sauveur and preventing further incursions into Gascony, the crown authorized Gaunt to play for time.[113] On 27 June the duke of Lancaster accordingly gave royal consent to a year-long cessation of hostilities intended to become fully operative by early August.[114] A month later the king gave personal instructions to the earl of March and other commanders operating in the northern French provinces to return home immediately. Acknowledging that there was a very slim chance of quick payment of wages, a number of English men-at-arms men decided to dig in and await further developments.[115] In theory, their confidence was well placed, for the truce of Bruges provided important guarantees against further English losses. On 3 July, however, the English captain Thomas Catterton was induced to surrender the fortress of Saint-Sauveur into French hands. Charles V's agents paid the garrison the enormous sum of 40,000 francs (£6,667) and promised Catterton an additional reward of 12,000 francs (£2,000).[116] The loss of Saint-Sauveur became quickly fixed in the minds of many members of the English polity as a moment of terrible betrayal and humiliation. By the spring of 1376, it was openly claimed in England that Catterton's actions had been treasonable and that he had been incited to commit such outrages by his alleged patron, the former captain of Saint-Sauveur and now royal chamberlain, William Latimer.[117] It was the loss of Saint-Sauveur, above all, that established Latimer's reputation as unscrupulous operator and evil counsellor. Completing the *Mirour de l'Omme* around this time, John Gower railed against those Englishmen who

[113] E 403/457, 7 May 1375; Sumption, iii, 227–8, 230.

[114] 'Anglo-French Negotiations', nos XIX–XXIII; *Foedera*, III.ii, 1029, 1031–4; *Hist. Angl.*, i, 318.

[115] Holmes, *Good Parliament*, 45 and n. 2; S. Walker, 'Profit and Loss in the Hundred Years War: The Sub-contracts of Sir John Strother, 1374', *HR*, lxviii (1985), 100–6.

[116] 'Anglo-French Negotiations', nos XXIV–XXVI; L. Delisle, *Histoire du château et des sires de Saint-Sauveur-le-Vicomte* (Valognes, 1867), 242–5, 261; Sumption, iii, 230–1, 236–7. 40,000 francs was, in fact, the precise figure set by the truce of Bruges for the compensation to be paid to Edward III in the event that Saint-Sauveur was subsequently handed over to French control.

[117] *Foedera*, III.ii, 903, 917; J. G. Bellamy, 'Sir John Annesley and the Chandos Inheritance', *Nottingham Mediaeval Studies*, x (1966), 94–105; J. G. Bellamy, 'Appeal and Impeachment in the Good Parliament', *BIHR*, xxxix (1966), 35–46.

had put covetousness before honour and sullied the good reputation of chivalry in their blatant scramble for profit.[118]

The loss of Saint-Sauveur was not the only reason for the distinctly negative reception given to the truce of Bruges in England. Gregory XI also took advantage of the peace talks of 1375 to elicit a controversial concordat with the English crown. For several years, the pope had been seeking the opportunity to tax the English clergy in order to fund his wars in Italy. Such ambitions tested the limits the crown had imposed on papal authority in 1365–6, so were a matter of considerable political sensitivity: at a debate in council in June 1373, the tetchy prince of Wales was reported to have called out 'You ass' when Archbishop Whittlesey of Canterbury dared to prevaricate on the king's rights to ring-fence clerical wealth for his own purposes.[119] In its determination to mount a vigorous defence of its rights, the crown quickly sought out the top minds of the day: the great Oxford scholar Uthred Boldon and his equally eminent sparring partner, John Wyclif, were both employed to argue Edward's case in delegations sent to Avignon in 1373 and 1374.[120] Following Whittlesey's death in 1374, however, Edward III made a notable concession. In order to avoid the appointment to Canterbury of another proponent of papal sovereignty, William Courtenay, and to secure the elevation of his own preferred candidate, Simon Sudbury, Edward now allowed Gregory to raise a papal subsidy of 60,000 florins (£9,000) from the English Church.[121] For the domestic political community, these unwelcome developments not only compromised the anti-papal policy to which Edward had so publicly committed himself; it smacked of just the same kind of grubby opportunism even now being played out in the surrender of Saint-Sauveur.

For some months the court worked hard to hold the line of confidence in its new diplomatic strategy. From his hunting grounds in Rockingham Forest over the summer, Edward advised Lancaster, Sudbury, the earls of Cambridge and Salisbury and Lords Latimer and Cobham to join him in London 'or wherever we might be' in September to discuss a new delegation to Bruges. The terms of reference for the resulting embassy were agreed at Westminster on 23 September, and the Hereford Herald, who had moved into royal service after the death of Humphrey Bohun in 1373, was put in charge of the communications network that would keep the king in close contact with his envoys.[122] Even if it was no more than a

[118] Gower, *Complete Works*, i, 260–7 (ll. 23593–24180).

[119] *Eulogium*, iii, 337–9; J. I. Catto, 'An Alleged Great Council of 1374', *EHR*, lxxxii (1967), 764–71.

[120] E. Perroy, *L'Angleterre et le grand schisme d'occident* (Paris, 1933), 32–7; A. Larson, 'English Embassies during the Hundred Years War', *EHR*, lv (1940), 431; Holmes, *Good Parliament*, 14–15, 19–20.

[121] Perroy, *L'Angleterre et le grand schisme*, 45; Holmes, *Good Parliament*, 46–9.

[122] 'Anglo-French Negotiations', App., no. VI; *Foedera*, III.ii, 1040, 1041; *EMDP*, I.ii, no. 327; E 159/152, *Brev. bar.*, Pasch, rot. 9.

temporizing measure, this high-powered commission represented a powerful statement of Edward III's desperate need to find a diplomatic solution that would prevent the spectacle of his final and abject defeat in France.

After nearly three months of wearied debate, all parties to the Bruges conference were forced to admit that the initiative had failed. For a brief moment there seemed a real possibility that the English and French would accept the lesser solution of a forty-year truce, during which the political map of France would be frozen and the Valois would pay an annual subsidy to the crown of England by way of compensation for lost rights and profits. The English had only recently made a very similar deal with the Scots, and were later to apply the idea with some success in relation to France in 1396.[123] But in 1375–6 there was endless quibbling over rival claims to key positions, the value of the subsidy and the involvement of third parties. Above all, the English delegates at Bruges were infuriated by the Valois demand that Edward III desist from using the title of king of France during the truce.[124] On 12 March 1376, both sides agreed to salvage what little consensus remained and content themselves with an extension of the current truce until 1 April 1377.[125]

In accounting for the dramatic reversal in English military fortunes during the short period between 1369 and 1376, contemporaries were quick to denounce Charles V as an unscrupulous opponent who refused to be bound by the conventions of chivalry and put political advantage before personal honour. 'A false man, a liar and a perjurer' is how the anonymous York chronicler memorably summed up the French king.[126] The main focus of such criticism was Charles's well-known Fabian strategy, which constantly frustrated the English preference for open battle and relied on the gradual grinding effect of small-scale sieges and skirmishes. Yet battle avoidance was not by any means the only reason for the spectacular recovery of Valois power. Whereas Philip VI's financial resources at the beginning of the first war had compared unfavourably with those of Edward III, the transformation of French taxation resulting from the emergency of John II's captivity meant that French royal receipts under Charles V were running at up to twice the level of those of England.[127] Charles also learned much from Edward's earlier practice of reserving senior prisoners as leverage for diplomatic gain. He kept the captal de

---

[123] 'Anglo-French Negotiations', no. XXXI; Palmer, *England, France*, 166–79.

[124] Froissart, viii, 216–19, 321; 'Anglo-French Negotiations', nos XXXII–XXXIII, XXXVIII–XXXIX.

[125] *Foedera*, III.ii, 1048, 1049, 1054.

[126] *AC*, 58–9. See also *Hist. Angl.*, i, 317–18.

[127] Ormrod, 'West European Monarchies', 138–49; J. Watts, *The Making of Polities: Europe, 1300–1500* (Cambridge, 2009), 227.

Buch as his special prize from the battle of Soubise and refused to allow him to be paroled under the terms of the truce of Bruges, retaining him under strong security in Paris as a stark warning to the remaining pro-English community in Gascony.[128] Similarly, Charles is likely to have been instrumental in Bertrand du Guesclin's purchase of the earl of Pembroke from Henry of Trastamara and in imposing successive delays in the release of this senior prisoner of war. The English chivalric elite greeted with genuine shock the news that du Guesclin – and, by implication, Charles – had so worn down the pitiful Pembroke that the twenty-seven-year-old earl collapsed and died within a few weeks of his release in 1375, while still en route from Paris to Calais.[129]

Faced with such complex and bewildering changes in the strategy of war, the financing of campaigns and the conventions of ransoming, many members of the English elite took refuge in a more straightforward expla-nation of military failure: the crisis of leadership. The Chandos Herald completed his *Life of the Black Prince* with a roll call of the captains who had lost their lives in defending English Aquitaine in the 1370s.[130] The demise of the earl of Warwick in 1369, of Sir Walter Mauny, that great chivalric adventurer, and of the steadfast earls of Oxford and Stafford in 1371–2, marked the effective end of an older generation of high command. And the trust placed in a new generation of aspiring commanders was brutally dashed by the premature death of the earl of Hereford in 1373 and of the two young heroes, the earl of Pembroke and Sir Edward Despenser in 1375.[131] Within the immediate royal family, only John of Gaunt, Edmund of Langley and their honorary brother-in-law John de Montfort remained actively involved in the war after 1372. The king's one remaining son-in-law, Enguerrand de Coucy, preferred simply to avoid a conflict of interests arising from his status as subject of both Edward III and Charles V by taking himself off into a private dispute with the duke of Austria over rival claims in Alsace and Switzerland. While Coucy managed to retain a degree of credibility and dignity in England, his evasiveness was a signifi-cant embarrassment for the otherwise united royal family. His residual personal loyalty to the English crown was to be eradicated on Edward III's death, when he finally renounced his allegiance and declared himself publicly for Charles V.[132]

---

[128] Froissart, viii, xxxix and n. 2; *AC*, 70; 'Anglo-French Negotiations', nos XVI, XVII, XIX, XXI; Delachenal, iv, 288–9, 295–6, 428; Holmes, *Good Parliament*, 43.

[129] *AC*, 70–1; *Polychronicon*, viii, 383; *Hist. Angl.*, i, 319–20; Carr, *Owen of Wales*, 32–3; *ODNB*, xxv, 768.

[130] *Vie du Prince Noir*, 164–5 (ll. 4189–252).

[131] *AC*, 56–7, 62, 70–1, *Hist. Angl.*, i, 308, 314, 319–20; Beltz, *Memorials*, 142; Lawrence, 'Power, Ambition', 88–9. The king provided cloth of gold for the funeral of Despenser at Tewkesbury Abbey in 1375: E 101/397/20, m. 24.

[132] Froissart, *Oeuvres*, xxi, 41–2.

Above all, of course, it was the personal circumstances of the English king and his eldest son that were believed to have dashed hopes of recovery during the war of 1369–75. Whether the outcomes of the various *chevauchées* planned and dispatched between 1369 and 1373 would have been different under the direct command of the king or prince remains necessarily a matter of conjecture. Their presence would undoubtedly have helped recruitment. It would also have allowed the English to make much more of the argument that the Valois' refusal to engage in open battle amounted to an admission of dishonour and failure. As it was, the English political community simply retreated into the fiction that, because it was sanctioned by God and right, the Plantagenet cause was somehow bound to prevail. It was indeed difficult to argue otherwise in Edward III's lifetime: even such sharp intellectuals as John Wyclif and John Gower, who would later openly challenge the legal and moral justifications for the Anglo-French war, were fully committed to the necessity of conflict so long as its instigator remained alive.[133] In 1373, just as the English government was reluctantly accepting the pope's continuing overtures for truce and peace, the city authorities of Bristol had their new royal charter illuminated with the quartered royal arms and a full-length image of Edward III dressed in coronation robes as king of France.[134] The more unrealistic the French claim became, the more tenaciously Englishmen now seemed to cling to it as a point of royal, and national, honour.

[133] R. F. Yeager, '*Pax Poetica*: On the Pacifism of Chaucer and Gower', *Studies in the Age of Chaucer*, ix (1987), 103–8; M. Wilks, *Wyclif: Political Ideas and Practice* (Oxford, 2000), 117–77; N. Saul, 'A Farewell to Arms? Criticism of Warfare in Late Fourteenth-Century England', *Fourteenth Century England II*, ed. Given-Wilson, 134.

[134] Liddy, *War, Politics*, 56–7. See also E. Danbury, 'English and French Artistic Propaganda during the Period of the Hundred Years War: Some Evidence of Royal Charters', *Power, Culture and Religion in France, c.1350–c.1550*, ed. C. T. Allmand (Woodbridge, 1989), 75–97; W. M. Ormrod, 'The Domestic Response to the Hundred Years War', *Arms, Armies and Fortifications*, ed. Curry and Hughes, 99–100.

Chapter 19

A FRAGILE TENURE, 1369–1376

The crisis of leadership that gradually emerged between the opening of the second war and the truce of Bruges was manifest in the domestic politics of England as well as in the campaigns sent over to France. As Edward III's subjects sought explanations for the reversal of English fortunes abroad, it was almost inevitable that they should diagnose the problem as a loss of unity and will within the royal family, the court and the government. In particular, it was a matter of public scandal that royal policy was being manipulated by a group of royal favourites led by William Latimer and Alice Perrers. These and other members of the king's inner circle became the principal scapegoats both for the humiliating defeats in France and for the rampant corruption that was thought to have infected the war machine at home. The court covine (a word that had powerful connotations of cliquishness and conspiracy) certainly had a baleful influence on royal patronage and on some aspects of fiscal policy.[1] However, the great political debacle in the parliament of 1376 reflected a much wider and more general crisis. Faced with ever higher demands for taxes to fight an increasingly hopeless war, the various elements of political society – the landed interest, the clergy and the merchants – were set at odds with each other. When they did come together to make common cause, it was too often in support of vindictive measures against vulnerable groups, such as the labouring classes and foreigners, who were least able to defend their own interests. In trying to understand this descent into social conflict, contemporaries were drawn back repeatedly to the corporal imagery of the state and the notion that the dysfunction of the body was a direct consequence of illness in the head. The great public dilemma of Edward III's last years was between a strong and continuing sense of personal devotion to the king and the prince of Wales and a pragmatic admission that their twin infirmities were becoming a serious threat to the stability of the Plantagenet crown.

In spite of the apparent relish with which great councils and parliament greeted the prospect of the renewal of hostilities with France in 1368–9, the resulting financial dispositions revealed a stubborn determination on the part of the polity to secure proper safeguards against the undue

---

[1] Given-Wilson, *Royal Household*, 147.

oppressions of the war state. The scheme worked out at the Guildford great council in the summer of 1368 was consciously modelled on that of the Reims campaign of 1359–60. Borrowing was to be kept to a minimum, no direct taxes were to be levied on the laity, and as much expenditure as possible would be assigned to revenue from the customs system. It was on the effective promise of continued immunity from direct taxation that Chancellor Wykeham and Treasurer Barnet were able successfully to argue the case for a new grant of the wool subsidy for three years, at the unprecedentedly high rate of £2 3s 4d a sack.[2] But it seems more than likely that the Guildford council had set a precondition for this new tax by requiring that the king release for the war effort the reserves of cash accumulated from the French and other ransoms. Of the £135,000 or so held in the special treasury at the Tower of London, at least £133,400 had been transferred to the exchequer between November 1368 and June 1369. Around £40,000 of this was used up immediately in advances for William Windsor's expedition to Ireland and the Black Prince's preparations for the defence of Aquitaine. Most of the rest was rapidly swallowed up by the high costs of John of Gaunt's *chevauchée* of 1370.

Edward III seems to have been persuaded to hand over his jealously guarded personal wealth in the mistaken belief that the investment would reap instant dividends in France. Ironically, however, the failure of such a conscious gamble left a difficult legacy for the fiscal politics of the 1370s. With the outstanding remainder of the ransom of John II now effectively written off and the annual instalments of David II's ransom much reduced, the Tower treasury was incapable of funding further large-scale expeditions to France. For the rest of the reign only a paltry £26,600 was transferred from the king's private hoard to the exchequer, and by the time of his death Edward III had effectively stripped himself of the entirety of his once fabled war treasure.[3] Had the king not been required to make this statement of personal commitment to the war fought in his name, it seems likely that he would have continued to use the Tower hoard to realize the ambitions of his younger sons, possibly including the war of private enterprise that Gaunt sought in pursuit of his wife's claims in Castile. As it was, Edward's initial heavy outlay in 1369 simply perpetuated the public illusion of a renewable and inexhaustible resource that would allow England to wage war on the cheap.

In responding to the squeeze, the government had to resort to a wider range of extraordinary fiscal measures. John Barnet retired from the treasurership of the exchequer in June 1369 and was replaced by the energetic Thomas Brantingham, who had extensive experience in the royal household and the financial administration of Calais, and was shortly after

[2] *PROME*, v, 223.
[3] Given-Wilson, *Royal Household*, 88; Harriss, *King, Parliament*, 499–501; Sherborne, *War, Politics*, 56, 62.

raised to the bishopric of Exeter. In December 1369 the escheators were ordered to impose anew the communal fines that had accumulated since the general pardon of 1362. In January and February 1370 the convocations of Canterbury and York were also cajoled into offering their counterpart to the wool subsidy, a triennial tenth on clerical incomes. And at meetings with representatives of the ports and inland towns in November 1369 and January 1370, the council warned of the king's upcoming need to raise significant loans. Over the following spring and summer Edward wrote to many lords, clerics and urban authorities requesting loans of £66,667 to fund Knolles's expeditions and a further £16,667 for Charles of Navarre's vastly extravagant visit to the English court.[4]

The strident tone of these letters suggests a degree of pressure unknown since the 1340s. Some quite significant corporate loans were duly forthcoming. The city of London contributed £5,000, Bristol £900, York £833 and Norwich £800, and a further £1,500 was raised from individual London merchants. There were a few spontaneous acts of personal generosity: the earl of Devon sent in £200 as a free gift. But beyond the civic groups, there were only three significant investors in the crown's new enterprise: William Wykeham, who contributed £3,000; the steward of the royal household, William Latimer, who put in some £1,133; and the earl of Arundel, who drew on his own exceptional liquid capital to lend an extraordinary £20,000 to the exchequer and a further £6,667 to the chamber. All told, the borrowing campaign of 1370 yielded something over £40,000, just half the sum intended.[5] The first major test of public commitment had generated a distinctly tepid response and revealed the king's heavy reliance on a few large-scale investors from his own inner circle of advisers.

Even the reduced borrowing commitment proved too much for the crown's overstretched resources. As a result of the temporary closure of the Calais staple and reintroduction of the ban on English merchants exporting wool to the continent, the customs system raised just £49,000 in the financial year 1369–70, by far the lowest figure since the return to wartime rates in 1365.[6] The high priority that the council set on the repayment of Arundel's loan left other lenders dangerously exposed. In May 1370 the sheriffs, escheators and collectors of clerical taxes were told to ignore existing commitments and instead deliver all their proceeds to the

---

[4] *Issue Roll of Brantingham*, 126, 129–30, 138, 202, 379, 400, 408–9; *CCR 1369–74*, 111; *CFR 1369–77*, 72; *CLBL, G*, 255, 256, 263; *Records of Convocation*, iii, 47–8; xiii, 163–5; xix, 47–8; *Register of Thomas Appleby*, nos 232, 249–53, 255; *Hist. Angl.*, i, 309; Liddy, *War, Politics*, 26–7.

[5] E 401/500, 26 Mar. 1370; E 401/501, 1 July, 18 July, 27 July, 15 Sept. 1370; E 401/503, 7 Dec. 1370; *CLBL, G*, 263, 275–6; C. Given-Wilson, 'Wealth and Credit, Public and Private: The Earls of Arundel, 1306–1397', *EHR*, cvii (1991), 6, 25–6; Liddy, *War, Politics*, 24, 26; Sherborne, *War, Politics*, 63–4.

[6] Ormrod, *Reign of Edward III*, 92, 206, 207.

exchequer in cash.[7] This desperate resort to the principles of the Walton Ordinances effectively turned the current round of credit deals into forced loans. Arrangements for repayment of the corporate loan from London and many others were cancelled, and the creditors were left with no immediate prospect of satisfaction.[8] Indeed, many of the provincial towns received belated satisfaction only in the winter of 1376–7 or during the early years of Richard II's reign; the well-meaning canons of Lichfield Cathedral, who had lent £100, were especially shabbily treated and did not manage to get Edward III's debt reassigned in the exchequer until as late as 1393.[9]

The financial scandal of 1370 left the crown no option but to appeal to parliament for a grant of direct taxation, and an assembly was convoked at Westminster on 24 February 1371, with Edward III presiding in person. Wykeham made a carefully crafted opening speech in which he set out the obligation of the king's subjects to assist in the state of emergency and to provide new taxes amounting to the prodigious figure of £100,000. To cushion the blow, the crown organized a rare academic debate in which two Austin friars argued the case that the clergy must contribute their fair share of this exceptional sum. The convocation of Canterbury was subsequently summoned to a meeting at the Savoy Palace and forced to commit itself, and by extension its counterparts in York, to accepting the prince of Wales's arguments for a special clerical subsidy of £50,000. Back in parliament, the lords and commons declared that the lay contribution of £50,000 should be raised by assigning a standard quota of £1 2s 3d to each parish in England and requiring that richer districts subsidize poorer ones. The calculations were badly bungled, and a supplementary session of the parliament had to be called at Winchester in June. Armed with new statistical information, the crown pointed out that the number of parishes in the country was much smaller than had been thought. The lords and commons were therefore obliged to acknowledge that the standard quota of parishes would have to be raised fivefold, to £5 16s.[10]

The administration had shown how cleverly and determinedly it could still turn a financial crisis to its advantage and secure the prospect of a significant increase in tax revenues. But it was painfully clear that parliament required very significant concessions in return. The commons

[7] *Issue Roll of Brantingham*, 126, 138–9, 186.

[8] E 401/501; E 401/503.

[9] E 401/501, 29 Apr. 1370.

[10] E 403/441, 17 Jan. 1371; E 403/442, 16 Apr., 29 Apr., 14 May, 8 July 1371; *PROME*, 229–30, 231–2, 235, 236–7; V. H. Galbraith, 'Articles Laid before the Parliament of 1371', *EHR*, xxxiv (1919), 579–82; *Records of Convocation*, iii, 305–16; M. Aston, ' "Caim's Castles": Poverty, Politics and Disendowment', *The Church, Politics and Patronage in the Fifteenth Century*, ed. R. B. Dobson (Gloucester, 1984), 51; W. M. Ormrod, 'An Experiment in Taxation: The English Parish Subsidy of 1371', *Speculum*, lxiii (1988), 59–64; Davis, *William Wykeham*, 54–5.

insisted that the crown confirm, by proclamation, that no further levies would be imposed at the ports for the duration of the wool subsidy of 1369–72.[11] Reflecting their abiding suspicion that the king was still holding on to significant personal reserves, the knights and burgesses made two other radical demands. The next time Edward needed to raise an army, they suggested, it should be at his own expense. Still more outspoken was their unprecedented request that the proceeds of the new tax be placed under the direct control of a group of lords who would see to it that the money was spent solely on the needs of war. Such was the shock felt in official quarters at these incursions upon the king's rights that the text of the two petitions was struck through on the official record of parliament.[12]

On one other front, however, the commons managed to achieve striking success. They asked that all the chief ministers of the crown should in future be laymen who would be fully accountable to the king for their actions. Before the end of the Westminster session of the parliament on 29 March, the king was therefore persuaded to give up the services of his three principal clerical ministers, Chancellor Wykeham, the treasurer, Thomas Brantingham, and the keeper of the privy seal, Peter Lacy. The crown salvaged some dignity from the fact that its right to choose and dismiss its ministers was not formally compromised, and the king emerged from the encounter with the assurance that his own man, Wykeham, would continue as a prominent member of the council. The fact remained, however, that Edward III had once more been forced, in a manner painfully reminiscent of the debates of 1340–1, to sacrifice his most trusted and conspicuous servants on the altar of public finance.[13]

The dismissals of 1371 were seen by some contemporaries and many later historians as proof of the emergence of an aristocratic opposition led by the earl of Pembroke and intent on giving more decisive direction to the military high command.[14] In reality, the commons seem to have been driven mainly by their preoccupation with greater accountability which would help prevent a repeat of the credit scandal of 1370. The men appointed to the vacant offices of state were certainly not chosen for their connections with Pembroke, but for their conspicuous loyalty to the crown and their general fitness for the task of financial and political recovery. Following the precedent of the lay chancellors of 1340–5, Edward promoted a senior member of the judiciary, Sir Robert Thorpe, brother of the former chief justice William, to the chancellorship. Similarly, the new keeper of the privy seal, Sir Nicholas Carew, had well-known

[11] *Foedera*, III.ii, 918.

[12] *PROME*, v, 240–1. For later successful efforts to have taxes reserved under the control of special treasurers of war see Given-Wilson, *Royal Household*, 123–30.

[13] *PROME*, v, 230, 238.

[14] Stubbs, *Constitutional History*, ii, 441 and n. 1; Tout, *Chapters*, vi, 271–2; McKisack, *Fourteenth Century*, 384–5; A. Tuck, *Richard II and the English Nobility* (London, 1973), 5.

connections with the royal household, where his grandmother, Joan, had presided for many years as a prominent lady-in-waiting to Queen Philippa.[15] If there was an expectation of reform in 1371, it was still very much acknowledged as working to the king's own agenda and benefit.

The most interesting choice in the new ministerial triumvirate was the new treasurer, Sir Richard Scrope. He was a younger son of the former royal judge, Henry, and nephew of Geoffrey Scrope, the prominent chief justice of king's bench at the beginning of Edward III's reign. Unlike Thorpe and Carew, Richard owed his rise less to family tradition than to the patronage of two very powerful noblemen: his cousin (and Geoffrey's eldest son) Henry Scrope, who was now steward of the king's household; and his principal lord, John of Gaunt, who had retained him as a member of the Lancastrian retinue since 1367. Robert Thorpe's successor as chief justice of common pleas, William Finchdean, had also previously served Gaunt as steward of Pontefract and Tickhill. In November 1371, yet another of Gaunt's life retainers, John Neville, succeeded Henry Scrope as steward of the royal household; at the same time, Neville's close associate and future father-in-law, William Latimer, took over as chamberlain.[16] When Gaunt returned to England at the end of 1371, he therefore had every reason to suppose that, either by accident or by design, his influence was now well established in high places. Ironically and rather perversely, the net effect of the reshuffle of 1371 was greatly to reinforce the authority within government of a relatively small and closed group of royal courtiers and Lancastrian retainers.

John of Gaunt's rapid emergence as the de facto leader of domestic government during the winter of 1371–2 is most obviously explained by a recent major crisis in the king's health. While the royal household was in residence at Marlborough castle in August 1371,[17] Edward III was suddenly taken ill at the nearby village of Everleigh. The king's regular physician, John Glaston, being absent, messengers were dispatched to Oxford and London to summon no fewer than five medical experts – the physican William Wymondham, the surgeons William Holm, Adam Leche and William Stodeley, and an unnamed friar – to deal with the emergency. Glaston himself arrived a little later with various newly acquired potions for the relief of his royal patient. No one recorded the experts' diagnosis, and there is no detail in the medicaments to give clues to the nature of Edward's indisposition. If we read back from the end of

---

[15] *ODNB*, x, 49, 52–3; Roskell, Clark and Rawcliffe, *House of Commons, 1386–1421*, i, 483.

[16] *ODNB*, xlix, 560; Walker, *Lancastrian Affinity*, 281; Kinsey, 'Legal Service', 156–7; Arvanigian, 'Lancastrian Polity?', 122–4, 126–7.

[17] Some repairs were carried out in preparation for this visit, and the court arrived in time for Thomas of Woodstock to be present in the castle chapel for the commemoration of Queen Philippa's anniversary: E 101/397/5, fols 11, 34.

his life, it is tempting to suggest that he had suffered a minor stroke. But it is just as likely that he had taken a bad fall while out hunting. After three weeks of enforced rest, the king was judged well enough to move, though it took a whole ten days for Edward, travelling by litter, to reach the security of Windsor.[18] In October, the members of the medical team were thanked for 'labouring and dwelling upon a good cure for the king when he was ill' and presented with generous *ex gratia* payments of between 10 and 25 marks each.[19]

The king's recovery from his recent indisposition was presumably reported and celebrated at the great council held at Westminster at the end of September, which Edward himself seems to have attended.[20] It was sufficient to make credible the king's renewed promise of personal involvement in the coming round of campaigns planned in France and his intended departure on the ill-fated naval expedition to avenge the defeat of La Rochelle. But ailments continued. Further medicines were provided by Glaston and by the London apothecary William Wandsworth in the summer of 1372.[21] After that time, the court seems quickly to have accepted that neither the king nor, indeed, his eldest son would ever again be in a position to command an English army or navy. A month after Edward's sixtieth birthday, in December 1372, it was decided that it was no longer appropriate for the royal household to continue in its role as a paymaster's office for an impending royal campaign and that a separate war treasury should instead be established under the direction of Adam Hertington, one of the chamberlains of the lower exchequer.[22] The public announcements made by the clergy in June 1373 of Gaunt's leadership of the war removed any further ambiguity in the public mind as to Edward III's ability to rally his ailing body in personal defence of his own just cause in France.[23]

In the absence of detailed accounts of the royal household between 1372 and 1376 it is difficult to establish the extent or speed of the deterioration of the king's health in his last years. The tradition that Edward III became senile is not supported by contemporary sources and seems to be the product of a later assumption that his old age was necessarily associated with dementia. The crown was certainly careful to avoid any public admission of royal frailty. Instructions to the bishops for prayers for the

---

[18] E 101/397/5, fols 13, 36, 46; Tout, *Chapters*, iv, 182; Talbot and Hammond, *Medical Practitioners*, 402–3, 420.

[19] E 403/444, 4 Oct. 1371. Wymondham was also given profitable ecclesiastical preferment, and Holm was marked out for special thanks with an annuity of £10 and the particular right to hunt in the king's forests (the latter perhaps itself a rueful reference to a hunting accident?): *CPR 1370–4*, 134, 135, 140.

[20] E 403/442, 19 July 1371.

[21] E 101/397/5, fol. 79.

[22] This agency functioned until early 1374: Given-Wilson, *Royal Household*, 122–3.

[23] *Foedera*, III.ii, 983.

realm made no reference to the king's health before the spring of 1376.[24] Edward continued his ceremonial appearances, presiding at the opening and closing of the parliaments of 1372 and 1373 and probably putting in at least a token appearance at the great councils that sat in October 1374 and May 1375.[25] Petitions requiring dispensations of grace were still sent on for the king's personal approval, and at least a trickle of letters under Edward's personal seal, the signet, informed the direction of patronage until 1375.[26] The few surviving items of the king's private correspondence suggest that he also retained something of the self-importance, not to say wilfulness, of his younger self. Edward was roused to order the arrest of John Isleham for the serious offence of murdering one of the staff of the royal household, John Kingston, while the latter was in residence with the king.[27] And in December 1374, against the better judgement of the chancellor, the king insisted on giving a comprehensive pardon to a notorious brigand recently turned king's evidence, William Daniel.[28] Otherwise, however, the administrative records after 1373 are more or less bereft of any sign that royal policy continued to be driven in any meaningful way by Edward III's own personal prejudices and preferences.

What can still be traced with a degree of precision for these years are the king's whereabouts. The main apparatus of the royal household restricted its movements to the circuit of castles and manor houses in the south-east. An expense account for the transport of the king's gold and silver plate, for example, lists the household's places of residence for the period September 1372 to August 1376 as Westminster, Gravesend, Eltham, Queenborough, Leeds, Hadleigh, Sheen, Kings Langley, Henley on the Heath and Woodstock.[29] Edward certainly travelled further than this with his private entourage. In June 1373, he spent a significant time at his deceased wife's former residence of Havering-atte-Bower in Essex. We also catch sight of him bestowing a new charter on Selborne Priory during a visit to Hampshire in June 1374.[30] Even if he could no longer ride to hunt, Edward may still have been able to shoot, and he clearly continued to enjoy being a spectator to the general carnage that resulted from his visits to the royal forests. Throughout the 1370s notable efforts were put into the maintenance and stocking of the parks at the royal residences of Eltham, Gravesend, Leeds castle and Banstead, and in the forest of Windsor at Wychemere in Old Windsor, Foliejohn in Winkfield, Eton and

---

[24] *CCR 1369–74*, 563; *CCR 1374–7*, 96, 224; E 403/449, 22 June 1373; E 403/456, 7 May 1375.

[25] *PROME*, v, 251, 256, 272, 277; *RDP*, iv, 653–9; E 403/446, 16 Sept. 1372; E 403/454, 22 Sept. 1374; E 403/457, 7 May 1375.

[26] C 81/422–445; C 81/1336/28–41.

[27] SC 1/43/53, printed in Maxwell-Lyte, *great seal*, 58.

[28] SC 1/41/54; *CPR 1374–7*, 37–9.

[29] E 101/397/12.

[30] *CPR 1370–4*, 277, 296, 301, 317, 319, 450, 455; *CChR 1341–1417*, 229.

Easthampstead.[31] In 1374 and 1375 the king was still fit enough to travel as far as Northamptonshire in pursuit of his accustomed summer sports.

Nor was the cycle of courtly celebration much affected by Edward's descent into old age. After 1369 the traditional Christmas festivities were normally held at Kings Langley or Eltham; at the latter venue, in the winter of 1372–3, the costs of the king's hall for Christmas Day and New Year's Day came to a mighty £370.[32] John of Gaunt and Constanza of Castile arrived in the kingdom too late in 1371 to join Edward for Christmas, but were careful to send him a pair of fancy buckles as a seasonal gift.[33] Considerable preparations were made for a special royal Christmas party at Woodstock in 1373, when the sheriff of Oxfordshire was ordered to have all bridges of the county well maintained to ease the passage of the king's falconers through the county.[34] Gaunt presented the king with a pair of cups previously given him by the prince and princess of Wales, and it was on this occasion that Edward may have given Constanza a golden crown encrusted with emeralds, rubies and pearls.[35] The king's withdrawal from active engagement in the lists no doubt explains the general absence of references to royal tournaments in the early 1370s; the one large-scale event at which knightly feats of arms are likely to have been celebrated, the reception of Gaunt and Constanza as king and queen of Castile at Cheapside in January 1372, was hosted not by the king but by Edward of Woodstock.[36] Late in June 1374, however, instructions were given for the delivery to the king's chamber, 'for his will', of two basinets, three helmets, two crests, four coats of mail, a detachable visor and several sets of body armour.[37] Even in advanced age, Edward III still apparently clung to the martial image that had so long proved the basis of his good fortune and fame.

Apart from Christmas, the other occasion in the court season that was marked consistently during the 1370s was, not surprisingly, the annual Garter feast on 23 April.[38] Ironically, the renewal of the war compromised attendance at this symbolically important event. Whereas the Black Prince was usually present at Windsor on St George's Day after his return to

---

[31] E 101/540/28; E 159/153, *Brev. bar.*, Trin., rot. 6d.

[32] E 101/397/5, fols 18, 20, 20v, 34, 62, 62v, 63, 77; E 101/397/11. John Cavendish, John Meres and Edmund Chelrey received knighthood from the king at the Christmas court of 1371: E 101/397/3.

[33] *AC*, 69; Goodman, *John of Gaunt*, 49.

[34] *Foedera*, III.ii, 990.

[35] Gaunt also probably attended the king's Christmas court at Eltham in 1374: *John of Gaunt's Register, 1371–5*, ii, nos 915, 1133, 1343, 1661.

[36] *AC*, 69.

[37] E 101/396/15.

[38] The associated costs of the king's hall for this occasion were £127 (1371), £185 (1372), £162 (1373): E 101/396/11, fol. 8; E 101/397/5, fols 28v, 71v. See also Collins, *Order of the Garter*, 208.

England in 1371, John of Gaunt, Edmund of Langley and the earls of Pembroke, Warwick and Salisbury were often absent. The heavy military responsibilities undertaken by some of the international members recently admitted into the order, such as Robert of Namur and the Poitevin lord Guichard d'Angle, meant that attendance was further reduced. In 1374 just thirteen of the twenty-four knights of the Garter joined the king and the prince of Wales at the patronal feast.[39] The following year, even Edward III seems to have stayed away, possibly because of indisposition or perhaps as a result of formal mourning for the earl of Pembroke.[40] It was only at the very end of the reign, in 1376 and 1377, that serious efforts were again made to revive the Windsor feast as a major event in the political calendar.[41]

A similar pattern emerges in the attendance of the magnates at meetings of the council.[42] The earl of Arundel, banker extraordinaire to the military expeditions of these years, was still heavily involved in government business: Edward III's gift to the earl of a litter formerly in the possession of Queen Philippa hints at his anxiety to keep the elderly Fitzalan mobile and active.[43] Others of the older generation, however, tended to drift away. Walter Mauny ceased to involve himself in public affairs from 1368 and died in 1372,[44] while Sir Guy Brian largely gave up attending meetings of the council after 1373. John of Gaunt and Edmund of Langley were present whenever their commitments allowed. But the new generation who succeeded as earls of March, Suffolk, Warwick, Oxford and Stafford in 1369-72 were too busy with service abroad to make more than erratic appearances. Otherwise, the business of the king's council appears to have been largely controlled by the chancellor, treasurer and keeper of the privy seal, along with John Neville and William Latimer and that continuing presence without portfolio, William Wykeham. As wider aristocratic involvement fell away, public perception inevitably shifted, and the court and council of Edward III, once famed for their openness and accessibility, came to be seen as closed shops dominated by the influence and ambition of the few.

[39] The comparable figures are seventeen in 1371, eighteen in 1372, fourteen in 1373 and seventeen in 1375: E 101/396/18; E 101/396/20; E 101/397/3; E 101/397/4; E 101/397/9; E 101/397/16; E 101/397/20, m. 23.

[40] The evidence of place-dates points entirely to residence at Eltham through the relevant period: C 81/440/30478–C 81/441/30504.

[41] See pp. 548, 573-4.

[42] For what follows see Given-Wilson, 'Royal Charter Witness Lists', 71-3, 87-8. See also evidence of council attendance in E 403/444, 13 Mar. 31 Mar. 1371; E 404/447, 11 Dec. 1372, 10 Jan. 1373; E 403/459, 8 Nov. 1375; CCR 1368-74, 93, 108-9, 109-10, 287-8, 321-2, 424, 445, 461; CCR 1374-7, 248-9.

[43] E 159/152, Brev. bar., Mich., rot. 4.

[44] The king provided cloth of gold for Mauny's obsequies: E 101/397/4. According to Froissart, viii, 33, Edward also attended the funeral in person. For Mauny's tomb see D. Knowles and W. F. Grimes, Charterhouse (London, 1954), 87-92.

The resulting problems first became apparent in the actions of the chamberlain, Lord Latimer. In 1371 when Edward lay ill at Marlborough, the earl of Pembroke had visited him in an attempt to secure personal royal intervention in a complex inheritance dispute that had broken out with Lord Grey of Ruthin. But on arriving at the castle the earl was given the brush-off, told that the king was indisposed and that he would have to present his case through Latimer.[45] The chamberlain had the undeniable authority to determine who could pass from the public space of the hall to the king's private apartments. To refuse so distinguished a supplicant as John Hastings was, however, an outrageous abuse of power and a major affront to the nobility's trust in the politics of access.

The situation did not ease after the king recovered his health. In 1372 Edward III marked out Latimer and the steward, Lord Neville, by ordering that their robes as knights of the Garter, like those worn by the princes of the blood and other titled nobles, should be trimmed with pure ermine.[46] Such personal indulgence helps to explain how Latimer was able so quickly to assume effective control of the systems of royal patronage that operated within the chamber. The privy seal and chancery were now required to accept notes made by the chamberlain's clerks on petitions heard before the king as direct authority for the issue of royal grants.[47] Other members of Edward's inner circle, such as Nicholas Carew, were quick to exploit this new process, and sought out Latimer's co-operation in their bids for favour.[48] The image of a clique of royal courtiers conspiring to receive a disproportionate amount of the stock of royal patronage proved all too vivid for a polity eager to find easy scape-goats for its general frustration with the conduct of the war.

Gradually throughout the mid-1370s, then, the court came to be seen by outsiders as a veritable matrix of corruption. The inner core was readily identified as comprising William Latimer, John Neville and Alice Perrers. Around them clustered some of the principal officers: Helming Leget, receiver of the chamber; Sir John Ipres, controller of the house-hold; Nicholas Carew, who remained at the privy seal until Edward III's death; and Sir Robert Ashton, who succeeded Richard Scrope as treasurer

[45] R. I. Jack, 'Entail and Descent: The Hastings Inheritance, 1370–1436', *BIHR*, xxxviii (1965), 6. The dating of this encounter to somewhere before mid-Sept. 1371 means that Latimer's assumption of the chamberlainship needs to be placed earlier than 10 Oct., the date proposed by Tout, *Chapters*, vi, 47.

[46] E 101/397/4.

[47] Ormrod, *Reign of Edward III*, 118 and 235 n. 142. This new process did, in fact, become fairly regular practice after 1376. For petitions processed by Latimer's successor as cham-berlain, Roger Beauchamp, see SC 8/179/8946; SC 8/189/9419; SC 8/191/9517; SC 6/227/11346; SC 8/305/15277. For developments after 1377 see Ormrod, *Political Life*, 20; G. Dodd, 'Parliamentary Petitions? The Origins and Provenance of the "Ancient Petitions" (SC 8) in the National Archives', *Medieval Petitions*, ed. Ormrod, Dodd and Musson, 43–4.

[48] SC 6/227/11349; *CPR 1374–7*, 72–3.

in 1375. Among the rank and file of the household, those who emerged as the most conspicuous manipulators of royal patronage included the chamber knight, constable of the Tower of London and keeper of Saint-Sauveur, Sir Alan Buxhull, and up-and-coming royal knights and esquires such as Philip la Vache, John Salisbury and John Beverley.[49] One man early marked out as a public enemy was the chamber knight and emerging royal familiar, Richard Sturry, whose conscience Thomas Walsingham memorably compared to a tepid ice-drop.[50]

These and other alleged parasites upon the crown were all the more visible for their high level of involvement in the provinces. After Queen Philippa's death, Alice Perrers set aside all remaining modesty and extended her property empire to include sixty manors stretching from Devon to Northumberland, from Shropshire to Norfolk. Alice's famously acrimonious dispute with Abbot Thomas de la Mare of St Albans over control of the manor of Oxney Walround became, in the mind of the abbey chronicler Thomas Walsingham, a microcosm of the general crisis.[51] Hardly less notorious were the royal household retainers George Felbrigg and John Herlyng, who managed to gain a dominant position in the political life of East Anglia. They accumulated life interests in royal hundreds, secured leases on alien priories, gained the constableships of the royal castles of Castle Rising, Hadleigh and Colchester, and even took over part of the customs administration at Yarmouth.[52]

What particularly angered those left out of this orgy of patronage were the highly preferential terms that the courtiers often secured for crown leases, and their infuriating habit of trading such titles on their own internal market. Philip la Vache openly bartered with Alice Perrers the right to control the marriage of John, Lord Mowbray.[53] And Lord Percy was deeply offended by the fact that the wardship of his half-sister's independent inheritance, the Orby estate, was granted to Alan Buxhull and then sold on, without Percy's consent, to Perrers.[54] Such blatant commercialization quickly created an impression that the courtiers were engaged in nothing less than a systematic stripping of some of the principal financial assets of the crown.[55]

[49] Given-Wilson, *Royal Household*, 149–50; W. M. Ormrod, 'Alice Perrers and John Salisbury', *EHR*, cxxiii (2008), 383–5.

[50] *St Albans*, i, 30–1, 56–9.

[51] Bothwell, 'Management of Position', 49–51; Ormrod, 'Trials of Alice Perrers', 382–4; Given-Wilson, *Royal Household*, 145–6.

[52] *CPR 1370–4*, 419–20; *CPR 1374–7*, 76, 186–7, 193, 213, 284, 311, 368, 397; *CFR 1368–77*, 108, 133, 220, 223, 361, 357, 365. Herlyng was also steward of the liberty of Bury St Edmunds.

[53] *CCR 1374–7*, 280.

[54] *ODNB*, xliii, 695.

[55] Ormrod, *Reign of Edward III*, 118–19.

The growing public criticism of the king's close circle inevitably tended to imagine the court covine as a tight-knit, cohesive group. In reality, the notorious abrasiveness of Latimer and Perrers and their general nervousness over the impending mortality of the king meant that even those apparently on the inside were often at odds with each other. There was little love lost, for example, between Latimer and Wykeham.[56] John Beverley was later to claim that Alice Perrers had always been suspicious of him and had been careful never to speak to the king in his presence for fear that Beverley might use her careless talk against her.[57] Even Princess Isabella fell out with Alice over the latter's efforts to lay her hands on one of Enguerrand de Coucy's northern manors.[58]

The chronic instability within the group of parasitical royal cronies was particularly revealed in 1371–2 in a major row over the lieutenancy of Ireland. William Windsor had proved a highly controversial choice for command in the lordship, allegedly using threats and arbitrary imprisonments to coerce the Anglo-Irish political community into a new round of heavy taxation.[59] But the decision of the Westminster administration to respond to complaints from Ireland and recall Windsor in the spring of 1372 precipitated a bout of faction-fighting within the court. Alice Perrers, who was already probably involved in private business deals with Windsor, chose to champion his cause. Robert Ashton also had designs on the lieutenancy. The council's preferred nominee, Sir Richard Pembridge, one of the senior and most respected knights of the royal household, came under such pressure from both Perrers and Ashton that he felt obliged to turn down the offer.[60] And when Ashton, rather than Windsor, was appointed as the new lieutenant, Alice took out her frustration by persuading the beleaguered king to make an example of the hapless Pembridge. Reluctantly, the enfeebled Edward III exiled Sir Richard from court, deprived him of his other public offices and refused him admission to the Garter feasts of 1372 and 1373.[61] The king's wrath was assuaged only when Perrers belatedly triumphed over Ashton and had Windsor appointed lieutenant later in 1373.[62] The whole affair had served to confirm the contemporary belief that closed political systems had a tendency to implode, and that the ultimate effect of faction was simply to produce a paralysis of the state.

[56] *AC*, 93.

[57] *PROME*, vi, 29.

[58] SC 8/41/2011, printed in 'Petition by the Lady Isabella, Countess of Bedford', ed. J. Bain, *Archaeological Journal*, xxxvi (1879), 174–6.

[59] P. Crooks, 'Representation and Dissent: "Parliamentarianism" and the Structure of Politics in Colonial Ireland, *c*.1370–1420', *EHR*, cxxv (2010), 8–9.

[60] S. Harbison, 'William of Windsor, the Court Party and the Administration of Ireland', *England and Ireland*, ed. Lydon, 159.

[61] *CCR 1369–74*, 420; E 101/397/3; E 101/397/9.

[62] *CPR 1374–7*, 340. Pembridge was partially restored to royal favour in 1374, but died in 1375.

The moral scandal of Edward III's open affair with Alice Perrers generated broader interest in the perceived offences of the courtiers and sent a frisson of prurient horror through the polity at large. The illicit relationship, so long kept under wraps, was sufficiently well understood by 1371 for even the pope to begin to seek out Alice's help in making supplications to her lover.[63] In 1373 Edward gave Alice possession of the dead queen's jewels. Cash gifts allowed her to build up her treasure still further, and in 1377 an inventory of her goods included a stock of over 20,000 pearls.[64] From her London base off Thames Street and her great Middlesex manors of Gunnersbury and Pallenswick, Perrers presided over her business empire with an arrogance founded in the secure knowledge of immunity from the normal strictures of the law. The victims of her oppression who came forward after Edward III's death complained over and over again of her wilful neglect of her debts, her blatant reneging on property deals and her flagrant abuse of the due processes of justice. Gold and silver, said one petitioner, had indeed been worthless when confronted with Alice's unassailable influence in the courts.[65]

Most scandalous of all was the public parading of Perrers's bastard son. Edward III never went quite so far as publicly to name John Southray as his own, but in February 1374 he made his first formal provision for the ten-year-old boy by granting him a considerable annuity of £100.[66] By October 1375 at the latest, Southray had joined Lord Beaumont and other young aristocrats of the court as an esquire of the king's chamber.[67] If the pearl-encrusted brooch that the king commissioned in 1374 with the inscriptions *Pensez de moi* ('Think of me') and *Sanz departir* ('Never apart') was intended as a gift for Alice Perrers, which seems highly likely, then it gives a vivid glimpse of the aged Edward's pitiful eagerness to play the role of ardent lover to the mother of his bastard.[68] Knowing well the stock figure of the elderly man driven to foolishness by a young woman, commentators became understandably obsessed with the notion that Edward's surrender to Alice's bewitching wiles was stripping him of his remaining vigour and rendering him a laughing stock among his subjects and enemies alike. John Gower expressed the problem with frankness around 1376: 'No king will ever be feared who prefers to give up his shield and wage battle in bed.'[69]

* * *

[63] *CPL*, iv, 96.

[64] *Foedera*, III.ii, 989; E 101/334/17.

[65] SC 8/103/5132; Ormrod, 'Trials of Alice Perrers', 382–4.

[66] *CPR 1370–4*, 338; M. Galway, 'Alice Perrers's Son John', *EHR*, lxvi (1951), 242.

[67] E 101/397/20, mm. 3, 9.

[68] E 101/509/20.

[69] Gower, *Complete Works*, i, 251 (ll. 22816–18). For the literary theme of the *senex amans*, or elderly male lover, see J. H. Burrow, *The Ages of Man: A Study in Medieval Writing and Thought* (Oxford, 1986), 156–62.

Alongside the mismanagement of the war and the manipulation of patronage, it was for their dealings in government finance that the courtiers of Edward III were to be most sharply reprimanded when the full wrath of the polity eventually descended in 1376. There had been some initial optimism over the revival of royal finance following the parliament of February 1371. Richard Scrope instituted a period of financial stringency, continued to insist on a strict limit to the number of assignments on existing forms of revenue, made a careful review of the likely value of the customs, and even attempted some kind of overall statement of the king's outstanding commitments.[70] The special subsidies of £50,000 granted by the laity and clergy contributed a net £92,000 to the royal coffers, all of it raised in cash and most of it already paid in by the spring of 1372. Scrope's administration had, however, reckoned without the strongly negative reactions of powerful vested interests. A controversial decision to apply the clerical subsidy to specially privileged ecclesiastical institutions met with undisguised contempt: the canons of the king's free chapels at Bridgnorth and Shrewsbury, normally completely exempt from such charges, were said to have dismissed the tax collectors by threatening to throw them into the River Severn.[71] Similarly, the attempt to extend the lay portion of the tax into the independent palatinates was much resented, and the people of County Durham and Cheshire only belatedly offered free-will offerings as recompense.[72] The commons' declared intention in 1371 that the parish subsidy should be treated as a one-off also effectively prevented the crown from making any further reform of direct taxation before 1377.

Nor did parliaments and convocations bend easily to the rod of fiscal conservatism. In the parliament of November 1372 the king secured a two-year extension of the *maltolt*; only after it was shown (perhaps in budget form) that this was inadequate to cover planned expenditure were the commons reluctantly persuaded to make a grant of tunnage and poundage and to authorize the imposition of one fifteenth and tenth.[73] In November 1373, the crown's usual persuasion tactics gave way to more strong-armed techniques. John Knyvet, who had replaced Robert Thorpe as chancellor, announced that no petitions, common or private, would be

---

[70] Ormrod, *Reign of Edward III*, 92–3. For the investigation of the customs, see E 159/148, *Brev. retorn.*, Hil.; E 159/149, *Brev. retorn.*, Hil. In 1371, and again in 1373, the government reactivated its right to levy collective fines for the goods and chattels of outlaws: E 403/444, 12 Dec. 1371; E 403/451, 1 Mar. 1373.

[71] SC 1/56/3.

[72] Ormrod, 'Experiment in Taxation', 64–81; Ormrod, *Reign of Edward III*, 204; Liddy, 'Politics of Privilege', 71–3; Booth, *Financial Administration*, 123.

[73] *PROME*, v, 258–60; *CFR 1368–77*, 191–3, 197; Jurkowski, Smith and Crook, *Lay Taxes*, 55. For subsequent alterations to the terms of the grant of tunnage and poundage, see Ormrod, 'Origins of Tunnage and Poundage', 215. For plans to levy loans on the expectation of its revenues, see SC 1/55/88.

heard until the commons had satisfied the king's need for taxes. Under obvious pressure, the knights and burgesses agreed to a further two-year extension of the wool subsidy, which would take it to September 1376; two further years of tunnage and poundage, to Christmas 1375; and two fifteenths and tenths, to be collected in four equal instalments until June 1375. They insisted that collection of the second year of each of these grants should be dependent on the continuation of the war. But any hope that the crown might honour such conditions was seriously undermined when the council reneged on its own assurance about petitions. The commons were kept in a state of limbo for nearly two weeks until their grievances were addressed, and none of their suggestions was ultimately taken up as the basis for new statutory legislation. The closing of the 1373 parliament may thus be said to have marked the effective end of the long tradition of political reciprocity that had so successfully underpinned Edward III's military regime in the 1340s and 1350s.[74]

If anything, the clergy were still more restive. At the convocation of Canterbury in December 1373 a royal deputation led by the earls of Salisbury and March, together with lords Latimer and Brian and Richard Sturry, argued the case for further taxes on the Church. Even with the amenable bishop of London, Simon Sudbury, deputizing for Archbishop Whittlesey, however, the debate proved particularly hard-fought. A single tenth was conceded, but only at the cost of open rupture in the ranks of the hierarchy. The vocal bishop of Hereford, William Courtenay, now declared himself implacably opposed to the levy, and the crown faced the very real prospect of a concerted clerical tax strike in some parts of the kingdom.[75]

The growing public exasperation with the pressure of taxation was all the keener, given the very real hardships that had now befallen the realm. Further outbreaks of the Black Death in 1368 and 1375 reversed any demographic recovery that might have occurred since the second pestilence and further reduced the number of adult heads of population available to service the fragile economy. It seems clear that the per capita burden of the direct taxes collected between 1370 and 1375 was at least as great, and probably considerably heavier, than that experienced during the great spate of fiscal exaction in 1336–42. As in the 1330s, the principal victims were the small tenant farmers who continued to pay most of the contributions to fifteenths and tenths. The only effective resort for this group was to insist that a larger proportion of the fixed tax quotas on their villages should be met by smallholders and landless labourers. But these

[74] *PROME*, v, 275–8, 279–80; G. Dodd, 'The Lords, Taxation and the Community of Parliament in the 1370s and Early 1380s', *Parliamentary History*, xx (2001), 290.

[75] *Foedera*, III.ii, 993; *Records of Convocation*, iii, 317–32; J. H. Dahmus, *William Courtenay, Archbishop of Canterbury 1381–1396* (University Park., Penn., 1966), 12; Holmes, *Good Parliament*, 18–19.

latter groups were also suffering hardships of their own in the early 1370s, when a new run of bad weather once more drove up the price of food and put a tight squeeze on many peasant budgets.[76]

Meanwhile, the landed elite was redoubling its efforts to restore its advantage by reimposing old labour services on villein tenants and calling for resolute enforcement of the labour laws. In the 1370s those who exercised lordship over a dependent peasantry came closer to full-scale class war than at any time since the first arrival of the plague.[77] In 1376–7 parliament began a vicious attack on the lower orders, who were said to be taking to a life of vagrancy, mendicancy and robbery rather than sticking to their social and legal obligations of work. The inevitable hostile reaction was felt particularly in some parts of the south of England, where by 1376 communities of unfree tenants were beginning to mount concerted resistance against the tyrannies of their lords.[78] Under such circumstances, the elite became convinced that its economic interests were being directly jeopardized by the crown's unreasonably large share of the total national wealth, and that the overall burden of public taxation would simply have to be reduced to more realistic and manageable levels.

To these urgent concerns were added serious worries about the state of the commercial economy. Severe disruptions in the chief markets for English wool, Flanders and northern Italy, meant that exports of wool were some 25 per cent lower in the 1370s than they had been in the 1350s. Thanks principally to the hike in the value of the *maltolt* after 1369, the crown's finances did relatively well, with the customs and subsidies raised at the ports still generating a gross income of around £70,000 a year up to 1375. But while the balance of trade remained broadly in profit, the decline in wool exports had a serious effect on the amounts of bullion being drawn back into England. In the 1370s the mint at the Tower of London was producing only about 30 per cent of the amount of sterling that it had generated in the previous decade, and just 20 per cent of the amount of gold coin. The output of the Calais mint also declined dramatically after 1373. England was moving slowly but inexorably into a serious monetary crisis.[79]

As they desperately looked around for explanations of the trade recession, the parliamentary commons resorted to some distinctly distasteful rhetoric. Foreigners – especially the pope, alien clergy holding benefices in England, and the much-despised Italian merchants – were quickly blamed

[76] Ormrod, 'Poverty and Privilege', 642.

[77] Farmer, 'Prices and Wages [ii]', 502–3, 521; E. B. Fryde, *Peasants and Landlords in Later Medieval England, c.1380–c. 1525* (Stroud, 1996), 38–42.

[78] *PROME*, v, 336–40; vi, 47–8; R. Faith, 'The "Great Rumour" of 1377 and Peasant Ideology', *The English Rising of 1381*, ed. R. H. Hilton and T. H. Aston (Cambridge, 1984), pp. 43–73.

[79] Lloyd, 'Overseas Trade', 96–124; Ormrod, *Reign of Edward III*, 207; J. H. A. Munro, 'Mint Policies, Ratios and Outputs in the Low Countries and England, 1335–1420', *Numismatic Chronicle*, cxli (1981), 106.

for removing large stocks of bullion from the English currency. In 1376 the commons claimed that the Lombards (meaning, specifically, the members of the merchant society of Lucca) were 'Jews and Saracens and secret spies', and that they had introduced into the land the 'most horrible vice that cannot be named', the sin of sodomy.[80] It is significant that Thomas Walsingham, for one, believed that Alice Perrers's first husband had been part of the Lombard community of London.[81] The crown played to such deep-seated bigotry by stepping up its wartime measures against foreigners resident in the realm.[82] In 1373 the prior of the Dominican convent at Oxford was ordered to expel friars who, masquerading as scholars of the university, were allegedly acting as agents provocateurs for Charles V.[83] Even some of the French men and women present in the households of the royal family once more began to feel the pressure of xenophobia. Princess Isabella was particularly frustrated at the way in which the war was used as a front to refuse one of her clerks, Jean Jehan of Paris, entry to a west country benefice.[84]

Behind this headline-seeking hyperbole, there actually lay some serious thinking about the parlous state of the economy. As on previous occasions, the commons showed a good understanding of how the weight and value of the currency could affect England's ability to draw in new supplies of bullion. In 1371 and 1373 they expressed concern about the exchange rate with the Scottish currency and persuaded the crown to take measures to prevent the flow of sterling across the northern border.[85] In their attacks on the Italians they were also much influenced by the efforts of the city of London, finally achieved in 1376, to claw back its right to regulate trade and thus challenge the privileged position allowed to alien merchants.[86] The Londoners' campaign was part of a wider challenge to the principles of free exchange set down in the Statute of York of 1335. In the face of a deteriorating balance of trade, parliament now sought refuge in the forms

---

[80] *PROME*, v, 263–4, 285–6, 318, 331–7.

[81] *St Albans*, i, 42–3; Ormrod, 'Who was Alice Perrers?', 223–4.

[82] For surveys of alien clergy during this period see SC 1/38/28; SC 1/55/90; SC 1/55/122; *Register of Thomas Appleby*, no. 228; E 403/451, 16 Mar. 1374; *Register of Thomas de Brantyngham, Bishop of Exeter*, ed. F. C. Hingeston-Randolph, 2 vols (London, 1901–6), i, nos 51, 53; *Royal Writs Addressed to John Buckingham, Bishop of Lincoln, 1363–1398*, ed. A. K. McHardy (Lincoln Record Society, lxxxvi, 1997), no. 116, App. A, no. 27; *Wykeham's Register*, ii, 567; Durham University Library, Durham Cathedral Muniments, Register of Thomas Hatfield, fol. 91v.

[83] *Foedera*, III.ii, 991. See also the withdrawal in 1373 of the right of alien priories to lease back their estates from the crown: A. K. McHardy, 'The Alien Priories and the Expulsion of Aliens from England in 1378', *Studies in Church History*, xii (1975), 135.

[84] SC 1/40/187.

[85] *PROME*, v, 248–9, 281; *SR*, i, 395; *Foedera*, III.ii, 919, 994.

[86] See p. 560. For disputes between Lombards and London traders see *Select Cases before the King's Council*, 42–7; A. Beardwood, *Alien Merchants in England, 1350 to 1377* (Manchester, 1968), 11–14.

of protectionism that were thought, according to nascent mercantilist principles, to be the best means of promoting a healthy economy.[87]

Most seriously from the vantage point of the crown, the economic crisis of the early 1370s caused a severe disruption to the credit markets and made it increasingly difficult to raise loans.[88] Edward III would have found it more or less impossible to make the up-front payments to his military captains in these difficult years without the continued commitment of his chief banker, the earl of Arundel.[89] In spite of some pressure, neither London nor any of the provincial towns were persuaded to make corporate loans to Edward III after 1370.[90] And among individual London capitalists, only a handful of major operators were now prepared to risk further undertakings.[91] Three of the most prominent members of this select group were John Pyel, Adam Bury and William Walworth.[92] The ringleader, however, was Richard Lyons, a London vintner of obscure (possibly Flemish) origins. Lyons already had good contacts with the court in his capacity as a supplier to the royal household, and had previously done business with Alice Perrers. It was he who accordingly acted as the facilitator for most of the commercial loans raised in Edward III's name between 1372 and 1375.[93]

Suspicion of this cartel focused predictably on the highly advantageous terms offered to its members by the crown. The interest rates on the new loans were later alleged to have been set at 50 per cent or more. Further benefits followed. Lyons and his associates were offered the opportunity to purchase and trade both Edward III's remaining debts to the Bardi bank and the cancelled tallies of assignment held by those who had loaned money to the crown in 1370. They were later accused of buying up these debts at large discounts and making a 100 per cent profit on the redemptions at the exchequer.[94] The most outrageous case concerned the crown's debts to Thomas Hatfield, bishop of Durham. In 1374–5 Hatfield made a series of generous grants of wardships in his palatinate to Alice Perrers in order to gain her assistance in the satisfaction of his earlier loans. But

---

[87] *PROME*, v, 281, 318–19; W. M. Ormrod, 'Parliament, Political Economy and State Formation in Later Medieval England', *Power and Persuasion: Essays on the Art of State Building in Honour of W. P. Blockmans*, ed. P. Hoppenbrouwers, A. Janse and R. Stein (Turnhout, 2010), 134–8.

[88] P. Nightingale, 'Monetary Contraction and Mercantile Credit in Later Medieval England', *EcHR*, 2nd series, xliii (1990), 565.

[89] Given-Wilson, 'Wealth and Credit', 6–7, 26.

[90] *CLBL, G*, 330–1; SC 1/55/84; Ormrod, *Reign of Edward III*, 185–6.

[91] For the remainder of this section see Holmes, *Good Parliament*, 69–79.

[92] *A Calendar of the Cartularies of John Pyel and Adam Fraunceys*, ed. S. J. O'Connor (Camden Society, 5th series, ii, 1993), 22–36; Barron, *London*, 333–4. For Pyel and Bury's involvement as royal envoys in the negotiations that led to the trade agreement with Flanders in 1372 see E 101/315/37; E 101/316/1; E 364/5, rot. H.

[93] *ODNB*, xxxiv, 935–6.

[94] *AC*, 86, 87.

Alice simply used Hatfield's credit instruments for her own purpose, and traded them in at a massive discount to wipe off £1,000 of her own debts to the crown.[95] All of this smacked of the sharp practices associated with the monopolist companies of the 1340s and generated widespread suspicion and anger among the many members of the polity still awaiting repayment of loans made to the exchequer in 1370.

Nor were these the only dubious business deals in which Latimer, Perrers and Lyons became involved. In the early 1370s the crown began to sell permissions for merchants to export wool not to Calais but to Middelburg, Dordrecht and various ports in Flanders.[96] Wool producers and small-scale exporters represented in the parliamentary commons understandably looked askance at a development that so fundamentally destabilized Calais's important contribution to the recycling of bullion. By 1372 the commons were therefore arguing strongly that the best guarantee of general prosperity resided in the requirement that every merchant, without exception, take his wool through the Calais staple.[97] By this time, however, the licensing scheme was simply too much part of the fabric of royal revenue-raising to be dropped. Crucially, the market in permissions was run not from the exchequer and chancery but by the king's personal financial office, the chamber. Those discommoded by the scheme quickly reached the reasonable conclusion that Lord Latimer and his associates had invented the whole thing as a means of simultaneously raising fees for the king and backhanders for themselves.

Eventually, the London-based capitalists came under suspicion for their involvement in the customs system. In 1372–3 the so-called petty customs (the duties on exports and imports of cloth and of general merchandise) and the subsidy of tunnage and poundage in all English ports were farmed out to Richard Lyons and another of his merchant contacts, John Hedingham. From 1373 to 1375, Lyons operated the farm alone, acting through his own locally appointed receivers. Ironically, this was to bring Lyons into direct conflict with another member of the court circle, George Felbrigg, who with William Ellis had a prior claim to the farm of the relevant duties at the port of Yarmouth.[98] Public perception, however, had it that this was all so much gain for the grasping Lyons. In 1373 another of the court's connections in London, the fishmonger and alderman John Pecche, was granted exclusive control of the sale of sweet wines in the capital on condition that he shared the resulting enhanced profits with the king.[99] The

[95] *Northern Petitions*, ed. C. M. Fraser (Surtees Society, cxciv, 1982), pp. 220–1; Liddy, 'Politics of Privilege', 76–7.

[96] Lloyd, *Wool Trade*, 216–19.

[97] *PROME*, v, 254, 270, 271.

[98] *CFR 1368–77*, 197–8, 227, 231, 273; *CPR 1370–4*, 382–4; Holmes, *Good Parliament*, 116.

[99] *CFR 1368–77*, 225; P. Nightingale, *A Medieval Mercantile Community: The Grocers' Company and the Politics and Trade of London, 1000–1485* (London, 1995), 228, 232, 242.

selling of licences to evade the Calais staple and the re-establishment of
monopoly rights in the customs system smacked strongly of the discredited
activities of William de la Pole in the late 1330s and 1340s and seemed set
to dismantle the whole of the trade policy erected around the staple system
since the 1350s.

It also served to confirm the growing public suspicion about corruption
in high places. By 1376 it was widely believed that the Londoners were a
mere front, and that the capital being put up for royal loans was actually
being drawn by William Latimer and Richard Lyons out of the king's own
private funds held in the chamber. Far from making a contribution to
public finance, the recent system of loans had therefore been nothing
more than an elaborate exercise in money-laundering from which the
courtiers and their cronies had sought to make huge illicit profits.[100]
Behind this complicated tissue of rumour lay the abiding suspicion that
the king continued to sit upon enormous reserves of personal wealth accumulated from the ransoms of the 1360s. To the more awkward truth that
there was in fact nothing left of Edward III's once brimming treasure at
the Tower of London, the response was all too obvious: it was the parasitical courtiers and their friends among the London merchants who were to
blame.

If the administration of Edward III emerged from the truce of Bruges of
June 1375 with any positive expectation, it was presumably that the lull in
fighting would at least allow some opportunity for financial retrenchment
and political realignment at home. In fact, the making of the truce coincided with the latest outbreak of plague, and for some months the members
of the government were preoccupied with the dangers to their own and to
the king's health. Among the likely victims of this latest epidemic were
Queen Isabella's old servant Robert Wyvil, bishop of Salisbury, and the
distinguished soldier Edward, Lord Despenser. The plague of 1375 also
carried off several senior civil servants, including the trusted notary, John
Branketre, and the senior exchequer clerk and encyclopaedist, James le
Palmer.[101] It was imperative that the frail king be kept away from possible
sources of infection. Edward spent most of June and July at Windsor,
Sheen and Guildford. Then in early August he moved northwards into
Northamptonshire, Leicestershire and Rutland, proceeding via Yardley
Hastings, Drayton, Nassington and Blatherwycke and then on to the royal
castles of Oakham, Moor End and Rockingham.[102] His entourage passed

[100] Holmes, *Good Parliament*, 66–7.

[101] *AC*, 77; *Hist. Angl.*, i, 319; Ormrod, 'Politics of Pestilence', 178; L. F. Sandler, *Omne
bonum: A Fourteenth-Century Encyclopaedia of Universal Knowledge*, 2 vols (London, 1996).

[102] Oakham castle had recently been refurbished, conceivably in preparation for this
visit: *King's Works*, ii, 766. For the expenses undertaken by the forester of Rockingham,
Amaury St Amand, against the king's visit there, see E 159/152, *Brev. bar.*, Mich., rot. 13.

the time in field sports: in preparation for the visit, the king had ordered forty-eight painted bows for 'the ladies in our company upon the chase in this coming hunting season'.[103] Whether Edward was fit enough to be able to shoot is not recorded. But this was the most energetic itinerary that he had managed since the mid-1360s, and it surely says something for the state of his health at this moment that the king was judged able to cope with the discomforts of a provincial progress.

The summer expedition to the Midlands was all the more significant for its social and political dimensions. For the first time in some years, the king took the privy seal and its keeper, Nicholas Carew, with him on his itinerary.[104] Other senior ministers caught up with the royal party at various locations. On 10 August there was an impromptu meeting of the council at Yardley Hastings attended by Chancellor Knyvet and Treasurer Scrope, at which the king undertook a commitment to pay £2,000 for the purchase of a French prisoner of war earlier taken by Lord Basset of Drayton.[105] Gaunt, who had recently returned from Bruges and taken up residence at his own great midland strongholds of Leicester and Kenilworth, may well have been present at this and other business meetings held in the king's travelling court over the summer.[106] But if the fresh air of Rockingham Forest helped keep the plague at bay, it could do little to dispel the odour of corruption. As Latimer and Carew worked their way through the new stock of patronage arising from from the deaths of tenants-in-chief and office-holders, it was members of the court covine – Philip la Vache, Alice Perrers and Latimer himself – who once more gained conspicuous advantage.[107] If anything, the emergency evacuation of the king in the summer of 1375 simply confirmed the view that his government had succumbed to the full infection of faction.

This impression was greatly reinforced by the crown's continuing refusal to summon parliament and give public account of its recent disastrous record. In referring the truce of Bruges to a great council of lords rather than a full session of parliament, the king had undoubtedly acted within his rights. The return of the military leadership to England during the truce also had the fortunate effect of increasing the aristocratic presence at meetings of the administrative council and restoring some measure of confidence among the elite. In the autumn and winter of 1375–6 council sessions were regularly attended by the earls of March, Suffolk, Warwick and Stafford along with members of the lesser nobility such as lords Montagu, Lovell and Lisle.[108] None of this, however, had much impact on the attitude

---

[103] E 101/396/15.

[104] C 81/441/30590–C 81/442/30658.

[105] *CPR 1374–7*, 134.

[106] Goodman, *John of Gaunt*, 54.

[107] *CPR 1370–4*, 131, 134; *CFR 1368–77*, 293–4.

[108] *PROME*, v, 385; E 403/459, 5 Feb. 1376; Ormrod, *Reign of Edward III*, 117.

of the wider polity. Those who held firm to the view that English soldiers should be entitled to continue their war of private enterprise in Normandy and Brittany received the truce of Bruges with undisguised consternation.[109] More generally, the delay in the summoning of parliament exposed the crown's bad faith on matters of public finance. Under the conditions set by the commons in 1373, the wartime rate of the wool subsidy should have ceased from September 1375, but instead of summoning parliament and making a rational case for the extension of the *maltolt* in time of truce, the government now took matters into its own hands and insisted that the wartime rates continue.[110] With the exception of the long intermission between the assemblies of 1348 and 1351, the gap in parliaments between 1373 and 1376 marked the longest delay to the normal conventions of politics in the collective political memory. It is hardly surprising that the commons of 1376 were to return to an old concern and ask the crown to renew its commitment to holding parliament at least once a year 'to correct errors and deceits in the realm'.[111]

The refusal to call together the estates of the realm was all the more anomalous given the imminence of war. Right from the start, there were real concerns about the stability of the truce of Bruges. News of the surrender of Saint-Sauveur in July 1375 raised expectations that the crown would be obliged to launch a new expedition to Normandy. A still more pressing matter was Henry of Trastamara's refusal to be bound by the new agreement. In August, just a week after the truce became effective, an English fleet returning home from Bordeaux was attacked by a Castilian force off La Rochelle and sustained what the York chronicler called 'the greatest loss ever suffered at sea'. The defeat raised once more the spectre of a hostile Castilian presence in the Channel and the unwelcome prospect of joint ventures with the French. Such alarm was well founded: Charles V's admiral, Jean de Vienne, was taking full advantage of the temporary withdrawal of hostilities to build up an impressive new naval force in the Clos des Galées at Rouen.[112] In the winter of 1375–6 England was put on high alert. The new justices of the peace approved in December were appointed en masse to commissions of array issued for the coastal counties in January. The crown ordered new levies of shipping for defence, the maintenance of beacons to provide a system of advanced warning, and the return of lords to their coastal residences for the impending struggle against enemy invaders.[113] Such measures merely

---

[109] *AC*, 79.

[110] *CFR 1368–77*, 302, 307–8, 310.

[111] *PROME*, v, 373; J. G. Edwards, ' "Justice" in Early English Parliaments', *Historical Studies*, ed. Fryde and Miller, i, 292–3.

[112] *AC*, 77, 79; 'Anglo-French Negotiations', no. XXXIX; Russell, *English Intervention*, 224–5; Perroy, *Hundred Years War*, 168; Holmes, *Good Parliament*, 56–8.

[113] *CPR 1374–7*, 135–9; *Foedera*, III.ii, 1045–6, 1049; *CCR 1374–7*, 290, 302; E 403/459, 22 Dec. 1375, 12 Jan. 1376; Verduyn, 'Attitude', 169.

reinforced existing and widespread public rumours that the realm once more stood in imminent danger of external attack.

It was in the context of this new emergency that the crown was finally persuaded, in December 1375, to summon a parliament to meet at Westminster the following February. In the event, a further delay was announced in late January and the assembly was eventually convoked only at the end of April 1376.[114] In the interim, frantic efforts were made to buy further time, and in March Gaunt was able to secure the consent of the French deputation to Bruges for an extension of the truce to 1 April 1377.[115] It was in order to approve this, to give further assurances of good faith to the lords and to discuss the agenda of the upcoming parliament that a further meeting of the great council was called at Westminster in late March 1376.[116] Much as it might defend its position, however, the crown's continued prevarication over the holding of parliament served merely to confirm public suspicion of the uselessness of the truce. In the spring of 1376 it was widely believed that, as the York chronicler put it, 'the kingdom of England was in peril and on the point of being destroyed by sea and land by the enemies of France, Spain, Gascony, Flanders, Scotland and other nations'.[117]

Faced with such a crisis of public confidence, the government sought to make easy political capital out of what still remained its greatest asset, the person of the king. The royal household celebrated the midwinter feasts of 1375–6 in some style: Princess Isabella and Thomas of Woodstock went down to Eltham to join their father for Christmas, and the aptly named Hugh Joye was appointed lord of misrule for the season.[118] The death of Richard Fitzalan, earl of Arundel in January was a doleful moment marked by the dispatch of cloth of gold from the king's household for the funeral at Lewes.[119] But this was no time for mourning. The very day after Arundel's death, 25 January, was the start of Edward III's fiftieth year as king of England. As at the time of his fiftieth birthday in 1362, the court sought actively to exploit this symbolic marker of good fortune, planning a series of public spectacles to provide a convenient distraction from current discord and create something of a rallying point for the political elite.

The first event in this new round of royal festivities was a week-long tournament held at Smithfield before the beginning of Lent in February 1376. In excited anticipation of its first major celebration of martial culture for over ten years, the royal household prepared painted shields

[114] *PROME*, v, 289, 385.
[115] *Foedera*, III.ii, 1048.
[116] E 403/459, 27 Mar. 1376.
[117] *AC*, 80.
[118] E 101/397/20, m. 5.
[119] GEC, i, 244; E 101/397/20, m. 24.

and trumpeters' pennants for the hastiludes. Even in his feeble state, the king seems to have been well enough to move up from Sheen to sit as president in the lists.[120] But Edward's impresarios reckoned without Alice Perrers's tendency to hijack the event for self-advertisement. In later generations the Smithfield festivities were to be remembered as the time when the royal mistress had ridden through the streets of London dressed as the 'lady of the sun'.[121] Alice's obvious attempt to steal the show was all the more brazen given that her costume was probably taken as a reference to Edward's personal badge of the sunburst. The jubilee year had got off to a distinctly false start.

Rather more political goodwill seems to have been achieved through the meeting of the Order of the Garter at Windsor castle on 23 April.[122] The king, as usual, was there, dressed in a specially commissioned red robe decorated with the order's motif. The resident poor knights who acted as vicars to the members of the fraternity were decked out in new caps and in mantles bearing the arms of St George. In comparison with recent years, the turnout of members of the fraternity was high. Prince Edward was there, as were John of Gaunt and Edmund of Langley. Their brother-in-law, Enguerrand de Coucy, took advantage of the truce to make a now rare appearance at the English court, and the princess of Wales's son-in-law, the duke of Brittany, arrived on a diplomatic visit in time to take up the stall to which he had been elected the previous year.[123] The earls of Warwick and Salisbury attended, together with Lords Latimer and Neville, and William Wykeham presided over the liturgy in his capacity as prelate of the order. With several stalls having recently fallen vacant, Edward III admitted no fewer than five new members: the earls of Stafford and Suffolk, Sir Thomas Percy, Sir Thomas Banastre and the princess of Wales's eldest son, Sir Thomas Holland.[124] The St George's Day celebrations of 1376 was the largest social gathering at Windsor castle since Princess Isabella's wedding in 1365, and represented a conscious effort to revitalize the social and political role of the Garter at a moment when the future of crown and realm stood in peril. It was in the place of his birth and the castle of his dreams that Edward III acted out the elaborate tableaux that hailed his achievement of fifty glorious years as king.

---

[120] E 101/397/20, mm. 18, 19, 21.

[121] *Chronicle of London*, 70. The chronicle dates the event within the mayoral year Oct. 1374–Oct. 1375, perhaps supposing that it was connected with the truce of Bruges or reflecting an understanding that it was in this year that Walworth and Lyons served respectively as mayor and sheriff of the city. But the episode also sits within a section of the chronicle that takes significant liberties with the chronology of the last years of Edward III's reign and manages, in the process, to misplace even the deaths of the Black Prince and the king.

[122] For what follows see E 101/397/20, mm. 6, 15, 18, 25.

[123] Froissart, viii, 224; Jones, *Ducal Brittany*, 79.

[124] GEC, ii, 536; Beltz, *Memorials*, 10.

Thus emboldened, the crown decided to launch a further public tournament to be held at Smithfield on the Feast of Pentecost, 4 June. Preparations were made over the spring, when Princess Isabella and Alice Perrers were provided with cloth of gold and taffeta for their new costumes. But the financial records are emphatic: closer to the time, the spectacle was cancelled.[125] It is not difficult to understand why. While acknowledging that the jubilee ought to be a time of 'grace and joy', the parliament that had opened at Westminster at the end of April had made it all too clear that such distractions must be set aside and the business of the realm properly focused on the punishment of traitors.[126] The death of the Black Prince on 8 June also plunged the court and the wider elite into a period of deep mourning. The king, who had retired to Havering after the opening of parliament, had been able to visit his son at Kennington at the beginning of June. But within a short while he, too, took seriously ill with an affliction that incapacitated him for much of the latter part of 1376.[127] Against these great waves of political crisis and human tragedy the jubilee proved, for the moment at least, all too fragile a defence, and the crown's energies had perforce to be directed to the much more urgent task of settling the kingdom and securing the succession.

It is hard to deny that the slow collapse of Edward III's military and political regime over the period from 1369 to 1376 was owed in large measure to the king's failing health and the crisis of leadership that resulted. If the image of the empty throne remains technically inaccurate before 1376, it is nonetheless clear that Edward gradually turned into a mere passive cipher for the ambitions of the unscrupulous Latimer and Perrers. Had the king suffered repeated bouts of serious illness like that experienced in the late summer of 1371, it is indeed possible that the polity might have come more quickly to the view that the royal office had to be put into commission. Equally, however, the events of the last year of Edward's life were to demonstrate that the medieval constitution, which adapted relatively easily to the problem of minority, had no real solution to that ultimate anomaly: the adult king who, through infirmity of body or mind, could not exercise the personal will from which all grace and good governance was believed to flow.[128]

---

[125] E 101/397/20, m. 6.
[126] *PROME*, v, 333.
[127] *AC*, 92, 94; Froissart, viii, 224.
[128] J. Watts, *Henry VI and the Politics of Kingship* (Cambridge, 1996), 21–31.

Chapter 20

THE YEAR OF SORROWS, 1376–1377

The last fourteen months of Edward III's life were the bleakest phase in his long and tumultuous reign. The death of the Black Prince and the king's slow decline into his final infirmity forced their subjects to acknowledge the unthinkable: that the great heroes of Crécy, Calais and Poitiers were mere mortals, and that the very longevity of the Edwardian regime had become its own biggest liability. The great outpouring of frustration by the political community in the parliament of April–July 1376 and the equally dramatic reassertion of royal authority in the assembly of January–March 1377 were both direct reactions to the king's chronic incapacity and the chilling prospect of his succession by the young Richard of Bordeaux. In this state of intense vulnerability, all sides found themselves driven to actions which, under normal political circumstances, would have been regarded as inappropriate and even unlawful. To the polity's strident claim that it was acting for the common good, the crown, in the person of John of Gaunt, responded by resorting to the justifications of necessity. Although many of the initiatives taken by parliament and council in 1376–7 were aborted in the short term, there survived a vivid memory of the political set pieces of 1376–7 that would significantly inform public life in succeeding generations. Not the least interesting element of that legacy was the new fashion for labelling political assemblies according to their perceived sympathies and outcome. The contemporary or near-contemporary epithets of 'Good' and 'Bad' applied to the successive parliaments of 1376 and 1377 seem to have lodged in the collective political memory, and were very consciously deployed during the revival of historical and constitutional interest in the Middle Ages between the seventeenth and the nineteenth century.[1]

The government must surely have known that the passage of business through the parliament eventually called into session at Westminster in

---

[1] *St Albans*, i, lxxi; T. F. Tout, 'Parliament and Public Opinion, 1376–88', *Historical Studies*, ed. Fryde and Miller, i, 298–315; Harriss, *Shaping the Nation*, 441–4; C. Fletcher, 'Virtue and the Common Good: Sermons and Political Practice in the Good Parliament, 1376', *Charisma and Religious Authority: Jewish, Christian, and Muslim Preaching, 1200–1500*, ed. K. L. Jansen and M. Rubin (Turnhout, 2009), 199–216; C. Oliver, *Parliament and the Origins of Political Pamphleteering* (York, 2010).

1376 would be both circuitous and hazardous. No one on either side, however, could possibly have predicted the intensity and bitterness of the debate that followed, or the series of dramatic challenges to the crown's constitutional authority. The genuine sense of astonishment is palpable in the official record of the assembly; the anonymous compiler of the parliament role was simply unable to keep up with the scale and complexity of the business, and generated an imperfect and confused account of proceedings. Much of the detail is, in fact, recoverable only because two writers, Thomas Walsingham and the anonymous monk who wrote the chronicle of St Mary's Abbey, York, preserved others' eyewitness accounts of the dramatic events of 1376. Both these narratives are broadly sympathetic to the perspective of the commons. But it is the latter that captures the mood of high excitement and expectation among the knights and burgesses, and hints at the consciously radical elements of their agenda.[2]

This momentous parliament opened at Westminster Palace, in the presence of the ailing king, on 28 April 1376. The following day, with Edward again in attendance, the lords and commons were informed by Chancellor Knyvet of the urgent business for which they had been summoned: to provide for the good government of the kingdom, to make better provision for the defence of the realm, and to consider the possibility of further wars in France and elsewhere. A specific request was then added for new grants of direct and indirect taxation. The lords and commons were asked to treat separately on the matter, and the knights and burgesses were allotted the chapter house of Westminster Abbey in which to conduct their discussions. The king then withdrew, either to his private quarters in the palace or to one of his suburban manors within easy reach of the capital.[3]

Such a royal withdrawal was not thought untoward, and certainly did not betoken incapacity. But Edward's ministers were aware of the restive mood infecting the members of the assembly of 1376 and may have felt it better that their master put some distance between himself and his critics. Such preventive measures were apparently vindicated when, on 29 April, the commons agreed to take an oath 'loyally to treat and ordain for the profit of the kingdom'. This was not standard procedure, and may well have been construed as having revolutionary overtones: the last time that a sworn confederacy of this kind had been employed in the political sphere was, after all, during the deposition crisis of 1326–7.[4] During May

---

[2] *PROME*, v, 289–387; *St Albans*, i, 3–53; *AC*, 79–94, translated in Taylor, *English Historical Literature*, 301–13; A. Goodman, 'Sir Thomas Hoo and the Parliament of 1376', *BIHR*, xli (1968), 139–49; C. Oliver, 'The First Political Pamphlet? The Unsolved Case of the Anonymous Account of the Good Parliament', *Viator*, xxxviii (2007), 251–68.

[3] *PROME*, v, 295; *AC*, 79–80.

[4] *AC*, 80–1; W. M. Ormrod, 'The Good Parliament of 1376: Commons, *Communes* and "Common Profit" in Fourteenth-Century English Politics', *Comparative Perspectives on History and Historians: Essays in Memory of Bryce Lyon*, ed. D. Nicholas, B. S. Bachrach and J. M. Murray (Kalamazoo, 2010).

and June 1376, some of the more important decisions forced upon the council were to be referred to the king for ratification. But Edward III's active role in the proceedings of parliament ceased almost entirely after the end of April and, with the Black Prince's swift decline into his final illness, the role of president passed by default to the king's third son, John of Gaunt.

The crown's request for taxation dominated the early discussions of the commons and helped to frame the unusual proposals that emerged. The knights and burgesses were entirely opposed to further direct taxes, partly because of the intolerable economic burden that such impositions represented and partly because of their resistance, on principle, to the levying of such subsidies during time of truce. They were more inclined to accept the inevitability of the request for the wool subsidy, agreeing to continue the *maltolt* of 1373 at wartime rates and conceding the tax for a further three years from September 1376. But they were adamant in their determination to wring definite concessions in return. In discussions over the first week of May, they reached the conclusion that the salvation of the realm depended on three imperatives: the restoration of the crown estate, in order to provide a more adequate resource from which to finance future wars; the cancellation of licences to evade the wool staple at Calais, which would guarantee equality of opportunity to all exporters and restore the stability of the English bridgehead in France; and a general inquiry into the private profits made from the king's credit transactions by Lord Latimer and Richard Lyons.

The commons were greatly assisted in reaching these conclusions by the oral summaries of their transactions provided by one of their number, Sir Peter de la Mare, the steward of the earl of March and representative for Herefordshire. When Sir Alan Buxhull arrived at the chapter house on 9 May to request a conclusion and outcome to their debates, the knights and burgesses agreed unanimously that de la Mare ought to act as their spokesman before the duke of Lancaster.[5] Thus began, by accident rather than design, a discernibly continuous history to the present-day office of Speaker of the House of Commons.

On his first appearance before John of Gaunt on 9 or 10 May, de la Mare chose not to reveal the commons' findings but rather to insist on two procedural points: that all his fellow members be admitted to the discussions; and that a deputation of lords be assigned to liaise with the knights and burgesses. Such requests, duly honoured, reflected the commons' understanding of the importance both of their own collective and of the support to be had in high places. The first of de la Mare's nominees for the consulting committee was the most outspoken of the prelates, William Courtenay, bishop of London. The majority of the others, however, comprised loyal servants of the king such as the earls of Warwick, Stafford

---

[5] *PROME*, v, 290, 297–8; *AC*, 81–3.

and Suffolk. There were also at least two men, Henry Percy and Henry Scrope, who had known connections with Gaunt. The most powerful figure on the list was the charismatic Edmund Mortimer, earl of March, the king's grandson-in-law. The commons clearly identified the advantage to be had from Peter de la Mare's existing connections with the earl, and seem to have been aware that March was at odds with the duke of Lancaster over the Anglo-French truce.[6] The meeting between the commons and the selected lords on Monday 12 May served chiefly as an opportunity to reassure the knights and burgesses that they would be allowed to speak openly, without recriminations, before the king's council. Walsingham – who admittedly bore a venomous hatred of John of Gaunt – believed that the duke wanted to intimidate the presumptuous commons, mere 'degenerate knights of the hedgerows', by a forceful show of majesty.[7] The guarantee of free speech was therefore a necessary and important preliminary to the impending encounter.

Thus emboldened, de la Mare and all his colleagues made their way into the palace complex to meet with the duke of Lancaster. The Speaker reiterated and elaborated the three points of the commons' agenda. Lord Latimer, the only person explicitly named in the accusations who was actually present, immediately went on the defensive, pointing out (correctly) that the management of the Calais staple was entirely a matter for the king and his council. Sir Peter, ever resourceful, retorted by pulling out a handbook of statutes and claiming authority, probably from the Statute of York of 1322, that what was originally ordained in parliament ought only to be changed there.[8] When he turned to the question of the squandering of resources, de la Mare added further to the court's discomfort by referring directly to the king's mistress. The sycophantic Alice Perrers, he said, had two or three thousand pounds a year from the public purse, for which she did nothing; for the good of the kingdom, she should now be forcibly removed from the king's presence. But the attempts to force judicial proceedings were, for the moment, thwarted. Apart from agreeing that the commons might have the co-operation of the former treasurers, Thomas Brantingham and Richard Scrope, Gaunt did nothing, and for another two weeks there ensued something akin to stalemate.

On 19 May de la Mare's party achieved a minor breakthrough in demonstrating before Gaunt that the injurious rates of interest charged on loans raised by William Latimer and Richard Lyons had been unnecessary.

[6] *PROME*, v, 297; *AC*, 83–5; McKisack, *Fourteenth Century*, 392; J. S. Roskell, *The Commons and their Speakers in English Parliaments* (Manchester, 1965), 119–20.

[7] *St Albans*, i, 10–11.

[8] *AC*, 85–6. De la Mare's possible point of reference has been a cause of considerable debate: ibid., 183; Lloyd, *Wool Trade*, 221–2. Note also a common petition in the next parliament, which (in the context of the existing Statute of Purveyors) argued that 'the statutes made and to be made in parliament ought not to be annulled except in parliament and with the assent of parliament': *PROME*, v, 391, 410.

William Walworth, one of the representatives of the city of London in the commons, when called before the duke, assured the council that he and others would have been quite ready to lend large sums of money, on reasonable terms, had Latimer, Lyons and John Pyel not sought to manipulate the system for their own profit. Pyel, who was also present as a member for London, then wriggled out of liability by insisting that a loan of 20,000 marks levied in 1374, with which the commons were especially preoccupied, had been entirely the work of Latimer and Lyons. According to the York chronicle, Pyel also hinted that the money thus invested had been smuggled out of the king's own treasury, and thus played to the commons' suspicion that the whole thing had been engineered to create pure profit for the chamberlain and his cronies. When the commons demanded that Latimer and Lyons be punished, however, the former quickly claimed his rights as a lord of the realm and announced his intention of answering the charges made against him.[9] The fate of the financiers now depended entirely on Gaunt's ability to resist the commons' demand for blood and to bring the assembly to a speedy close.

It was at this pivotal moment that the political views of the bishops and nobles became particularly relevant. On 24 May the lords invited the commons to come, en masse, to their chamber. There is no indication that Gaunt and Latimer were present, and de la Mare clearly took the opportunity to cultivate those elements he identified as sympathetic to the commons' cause. Playing on the accustomed aristocratic formula for resolving crises of royal authority, he now called for the appointment of a continual council of three bishops, three earls and three barons whose advice and consent would be necessary for every major act of government issued by the crown. These proposals were duly repackaged and submitted along with the formal grant of the wool subsidy.

On 26 May the duke of Lancaster secured the king's consent to the new measures. The council, named by the lords, was to comprise the recently elevated archbishop of Canterbury, Simon Sudbury, together with Bishops Courtenay of London and Wykeham of Winchester, the earls of March and Stafford and the new earl of Arundel, and Lords Percy, Brian and Beauchamp. These were specifically charged to work closely with the king's sons, John and Edmund.[10] With the exception of Courtenay, the new councillors formed a solid phalanx of royal supporters. But they were also instinctively suspicious of faction and division, and may well have been identified for their reputations as peacemakers. Hugh Stafford, for example, who had succeeded his father as earl of Stafford in 1372, had been a close supporter of Edward of Woodstock and basked in the reflected glory of the frail prince's popular reputation. Several of their number, especially Edmund Mortimer, had also earlier been identified as

[9] AC, 88–90.
[10] AC, 90–2; St Albans, i, 50–3; PROME, v, 297–9.

possible commons' sympathizers. But the continual council was, in the main, a triumph for those moderately minded loyalists among the peers who were eager to find some way out of the current undignified stand-off between de la Mare and Gaunt. Far from perpetuating faction, the new experiment in collective rule was an attempt to set aside rancour and difference and reunite the realm in a sense of common purpose.

It says an enormous amount for the commons' powerful sense of responsibility for the common good that they did not content themselves with this optimistic compromise but pressed ahead with their demand for the disgrace of the courtiers and financiers. It was Alice Perrers who proved most easily disposable. On 18 May Bishop Brinton of Rochester had delivered a general exhortation to expose and punish offenders, in which he specifically denounced the king for allowing Alice to hold the keys of the kingdom.[11] Under pressure from Gaunt, Edward III was now persuaded to exile his mistress from court. Perrers was not subjected to any formal trial and was allowed continued enjoyment of her lands and titles. But she was made subject to an extraordinary parliamentary ordinance which stated that, should she ever again dare to meddle in the operations of finance and justice, she would be liable both to forfeiture and to banishment from the realm.[12]

It was to make this particular compromise stick that Gaunt seems around this time to have made a private deal with Alice's fellow courtier, William Windsor. Windsor's second lieutenancy of Ireland had been still more controversial than his first, and the refusal of the 1375 parliament of Kilkenny to cede any further taxes had forced the English government to take the unusual step of summoning Irish parliamentary representatives to Westminster in February 1376. The long deposition that this group made against Windsor and his senior officers was initially taken up by the crown, and when Windsor returned to England towards the end of the session of the Good Parliament he was arrested and held at the Tower of London in preparation for trial. Before the proceedings could properly get under way, however, the whole investigation was quietly suppressed.[13] The most likely explanation of this about-face is that the duke of Lancaster offered Windsor immunity from prosecution in return for his accepting responsibility for Alice Perrers. Just as Perrers had sprung to Windsor's defence in 1372, so now should William stand as guarantor for Alice's good behaviour. This putative deal was what lay behind the clandestine contract of marriage between Windsor and Perrers probably undertaken in the late summer of 1376 and subsequently made public after the death of Edward III.

[11] *The Sermons of Thomas Brinton, Bishop of Rochester (1373–1389)*, ed. M. A. Devlin, 2 vols (Camden Society, 3rd series, lxxxv–lxxxvi, 1953–4), ii, 316–21.

[12] *PROME*, v, 313; *AC*, 92; *St Albans*, i, 44–7; T. Walsingham, *Gesta abbatum monasterii Sancti Albani*, ed. H. T. Riley, 3 vols (RS, 1867–9), iii, 320–32.

[13] Clarke, *Fourteenth Century Studies*, 154–9.

Far from being an expression of Alice's independent spirit, the secret contract with Windsor served only to take away her legal independence and subject her to the custody of a controlling husband. Walsingham, wise after the event, was quick to criticize Gaunt for a scheme that had the unintended effect, on Alice's subsequent return to court, of leading the aged king into the mortal sin of adultery. The duke himself had recently taken a mistress, Katherine Swynford, another of Queen Philippa's former waiting-women and sister-in-law to Geoffrey Chaucer. In banishing Alice Perrers, Walsingham therefore felt that Gaunt had simply revealed the blatant moral hypocrisy of his own domestic situation.[14]

The obvious relief at the departure of the irksome Perrers did little to abate the commons' determination to institute formal proceedings against the male courtiers and financiers. Between 26 and 28 May de la Mare again appeared before the lords, asking that Latimer be arrested and Lyons be brought to judgment. William Latimer once more pleaded time. But Bishop Wykeham, who seems to have taken very seriously his new role as a member of the continual council, spoke out and declared that a trial should follow promptly.[15] Faced with such alarming fissures within the establishment, Lancaster finally conceded that judicial proceedings should begin. But because the duke refused to have the crown act as prosecutor, it was left to the commons to provide the detailed charges on which the trial could proceed. In this way, de la Mare and his fellows stumbled, unintentionally, upon a new parliamentary process. Impeachment was already a well-established procedure in the common law courts, involving a joint charge brought by a group of accusers acting in the name of the king.[16] Now, in 1376, it was employed in parliament, with the charges being heard and tried by the lords under the presidency of Gaunt. The invention of parliamentary impeachment meant, for the first time, that state trials could technically be initiated by the commons. If this precedent was to be very rarely employed in the decades and centuries after 1376, its implications were nevertheless momentous.

The trials of Richard Lyons and William Latimer progressed simultaneously over a period of some two weeks from 26 May to 12 June.[17] The charges against Lyons focused on his abuses of office as mayor of Calais, his trading in licences to evade the staple, his unlawful imposition of arbitrary charges on bullion exports from the realm and his involvement in the loan of 20,000 marks raised for the crown in 1374, from which the commons believed that he and his fellow conspirators had made a profit of 10,000 marks. The

---

[14] St Albans, i, 46–51; Ormrod, 'Trials of Alice Perrers', 371–4, 379.
[15] AC, 93–4.
[16] G. Lambrick, 'The Impeachment of the Abbot of Abingdon in 1368', EHR, lxxxii (1967), 250–76; Strohm, Hochon's Arrow, 171–2.
[17] CFR 1368–77, 348; CLBL: H, 30; PROME, v, 291–2.

commons may also have included allegations about the embezzlement of funds from the ransom of John II. Lyons, arrested and brought into the parliament chamber, protested that everything he had done had been on the direct orders of the king and his council. It was this chancy statement that sealed his fate. When asked to produce the appropriate written authorization, he said that he had only ever received verbal instructions. It was then reported that the absent king, when consulted on the matter, had denied ever giving Lyons power to undertake such responsibilities. On Edward III's personal testimony, Richard was put in prison to await a financial penalty. It was only at the further insistence of the commons that Gaunt and the lords were finally persuaded to order the penalties of treason, to have all Lyons's property confiscated to the crown, and thus to put the disgraced financier entirely at the mercy of the king's grace.[18]

All of this high drama was only really a sideshow to the main event: the trial of Lord Latimer. To the accusations of private profit made from the loan of 1374, the licences for evasion of the Calais staple and other irregular impositions on wool exports were added, in his case, serious allegations about the conduct of the French war. It was said that Latimer had made a huge fortune from various protection rackets organized during his time as captain of Saint-Sauveur-le-Vicomte, and that he had been directly responsible for the surrender of Bécherel and Saint-Sauveur in 1374–5. This last charge reflected the commons' keenness to have the discredited chamberlain subjected to the full rigours of the law of treason. In the end, it was difficult to establish definite proof of Latimer's responsibility for the withdrawal from Brittany and Normandy. The judgment, when it came, was instead the result of the testimony provided by Richard Scrope and William Walworth, both of whom asserted that Latimer had forced through the loan of 20,000 marks in 1374 for private gain. Like Lyons, Latimer was originally sent to prison to await a fine but was then subjected, on the insistence of the commons, to the greater penalty of the loss of all crown offices.[19] All of this, of course, merely confirmed long and powerfully held suspicions about the outrages committed by the court covine: their blatant manipulation of public finance and their gross perversion of foreign policy. The dismissal of Alice Perrers and the impeachment of Richard Lyons and William Latimer had turned public scandal into bitter political humiliation.

* * *

[18] *PROME*, v, 300–2; A. R. Myers, 'The Wealth of Richard Lyons', *Essays in Medieval History*, ed. Sandquist and Powicke, 301–29; Holmes, *Good Parliament*, 111–14. The crown immediately redistributed some of Lyons's real estate to Princes Edmund and Thomas and to John Ipres. This would cause difficulties after Lyons was restored in 1377: *CPR 1374–7*, 298; *PROME*, vi, 26.

[19] *PROME*, v, 291–2, 302–7; Holmes, *Good Parliament*, 126–34; Given-Wilson, 'Court and Household', 215–16.

If the commons felt buoyed up by these spectacular successes, then the urgent state of the realm did not as yet allow for a sense of triumph. The Black Prince, who had been present at the beginning of the parliamentary session, was struck down by serious illness in May and retired to his suburban manor of Kennington, where the king reputedly made him a visit around 1 June. After this, the prince was taken back to Westminster Palace, where he died a week later, on 8 June. The associated religious obligations caused disruptions and delays to the proceedings of the parliament. Little business was done during the fortnight after the prince's demise. Most unusually during parliament time, the king actually left the capital and departed for the royal manor of Havering, where he remained in the quiet seclusion of mourning until early July.[20]

Between his return from Aquitaine and his death, Edward of Woodstock had been an intermittent and not always a very constructive influence upon domestic politics. The ability to tolerate and control the niceties of politics had never been his particular métier, and the notion that his succession might mark the dawn of a new age of glory had already begun to wear thin, at least for those who observed directly his descent into ill health and short temper. On the other hand, his death had a serious and profound impact on the progress of reform. Although they may have had the ear of figures such as the earl of March and Bishop Wykeham, de la Mare and his fellows had put their principal trust in the prince of Wales. His accession to the throne, they argued, would have provided a lasting guarantee and vindication of their own political stance. A story subsequently circulated as to how, in the early stages of the Good Parliament, the prince had firmly rejected the bribes sent him by Richard Lyons in a last-ditch attempt to win protection and evade prosecution.[21] With their supposed champion gone and the duke of Lancaster now firmly in charge, the commons were for the moment bereft of a symbolic royal patron, and thus of much of the moral authority that they claimed for their cause.

The tragedy in the royal family created intense public anxiety over the succession. If Edward III were to die while Prince Richard was still a child, then reason of state might dictate that the ambitious and able John of Gaunt could step in and take the throne. This was precisely what had happened in 1199 when another John, the son of Henry II, had usurped the rights of his nephew, Arthur of Brittany. In court circles it was well understood that both Edward III and John of Gaunt had provided the Black Prince on his deathbed with verbal assurances of the boy Richard's right to succeed.[22] The king was as good as his word. He immediately

---

[20] *AC*, 92, 94.

[21] *St Albans*, i, 18–21, 32–7; *AC*, 92.

[22] *Vie du Prince Noir*, 162–3 (ll. 4139–64); M. J. Bennett, 'Edward III's Entail and the Succession to the Crown, 1376–1471', *EHR*, cxiii (1998), 584–5.

acknowledged his young grandson as earl of Chester and took him under the special protection of the royal household, where a suit of black clothes was ordered for the grieving boy.[23] But such private expressions of familial loyalty did little to calm public concerns. On 25 June the king's grandson was brought into parliament 'so that the lords and commons of the realm could see and honour [him] as the true heir apparent'. The commons further asked that Richard might be styled prince of Wales, but were reminded that such a decision lay exclusively with the king; since Edward III was still absent, the title had to remain in abeyance.[24] In the tense political relations prevailing between court and parliament, even such an innocuous exchange was open to malicious misinterpretation. The conniving chamber knight Richard Sturry allegedly tried to stir up mischief by reporting back to the king that the commons wanted nothing less than to depose him, 'as they had previously done with his father', and have Richard as their new lord.[25] The sacred question of the succession was seemingly being subordinated, like everything else, to the politics of faction.

If Gaunt hoped that the plenary session held on 25 June might allow him to draw the vexatious parliament to a close, he had clearly reckoned without the commons' ability to regroup and press on after the temporary setback of the Black Prince's death. They now demanded a second wave of dismissals and impeachments. John Neville was removed from the office of steward of the household and charged with corruption and negligence in war. William Ellis of Yarmouth and the Londoners John Pecche and Adam Bury were condemned for malpractice in the administration of the customs, the retail trade in wine, the raising of loans and the brokerage of royal debts. The identification of yet a third group of lesser conspirators – Hugh Fastolf, John Leicester, Walter Sporier and Henry Medbourne – indicated just how far the commons were prepared to reach in their campaign to eradicate corruption.[26] On 24 July the council at once affirmed the Calais staple and forbade further licences for its evasion in a new ordinance requiring that all wool, together with lead, tin, worsted cloth and other lesser commodities exported to the continent should, without exception, pass through the entrepôt of Calais. The resulting proclamations represented the clearest public statement to date of the crown's defeat at the hands of the commons' sworn league.[27]

---

[23] E 101/397/20, m. 6. On 31 July the exchequer issued £20 for the prince's use: E 403/460.

[24] *PROME*, v, 315.

[25] *St Albans*, i, 30–1. It is this episode, and Sturry's resulting temporary disgrace, that are probably alluded to in the otherwise erroneous statement of *AC*, 92, about Sir Richard Stafford's removal from the continual council.

[26] *PROME*, v, 292, 307–14, 385, 424–6; Given-Wilson, *Royal Household*, 151. For Medbourne, see also SC 8/227/11346; and for Sporier, see Holmes, *Good Parliament*, 112 n. 5.

[27] *CCR 1374–7*, 441–2. These arrangements were confirmed in Dec.: C 76/59, m. 3.

The knights and burgesses had also used the intermissions between the trials and other discussions with the lords and council to notable effect for the drawing up of the longest set of common petitions yet known in the entire history of parliament. [28] Much of this agenda represented spin-offs from the recent round of trials. Thus the impeachments of William Ellis and Hugh Fastolf led the knights and burgesses to take up a whole series of disputes over coastal fishing rights between the towns of Yarmouth and Lowestoft. [29] Of significantly more general import was the commons' decision to support the authorities of London in a new, and this time successful, bid to challenge the crown's free-trade policies and reassert the city's right to regulate its own trade. [30]

The most noticeable feature of the common petitions, however, was the way in which they so emphatically reiterated the programme of reform declared at the beginning of the assembly. Regrouping and recovering from the temporary setback of the death of the prince of Wales, de la Mare and his followers had once more found their moral purpose and political voice. The request that the king should reserve the profits arising from his feudal rights 'for the maintenance of his honour and of his wars' echoed directly one of the recommendations made by de la Mare in his meeting with John of Gaunt on 12 May. In like manner, the commons now demanded promises that those already impeached would not be granted pardons, and that proceedings still under way should continue to judgment and sentence. [31] Both the ambition and the consistency of the commons' programme in 1376 were of a scale rarely observed before. Nevertheless, such assertiveness had its own neuroses. Behind de la Mare's long and resolute campaign lurked an acute understanding of the vulnerability of his achievements and a growing concern that business done in this parliament might all too easily be undone thereafter.

After nearly eleven weeks in session, the Good Parliament was brought to a close on 10 July 1376. The manner of dismissal was unusual, and reflected the continuing state of political emergency. By 8 July the enfeebled and exhausted king had moved from Havering to Eltham to be close at hand for the closing ceremony. At the last moment, however, it was reported that Edward was too fragile to undertake the short journey up

---

[28] *PROME*, v, 316–79; W. M. Ormrod, 'On – and off – the Record: The Rolls of Parliament, 1337–77', *Parliamentary History*, xxiii (2004), 52–3; Dodd, *Justice and Grace*, 148–52.

[29] A. Saul, 'Local Politics and the Good Parliament', *Property and Politics: Essays in Later Medieval English History*, ed. A. Pollard (Gloucester, 1984), 156–71.

[30] *CLBL: H*, 38–41; *PROME*, v, 354–5; Ormrod, *Reign of Edward III*, 174; Barron, *London*, 137, 143. The crown confirmed its decision on the regulation of trade later in the year and upheld it again, albeit tacitly, in the parliament of Jan. 1377: *CPR 1374–7*, 389; *CLBL: H*, 53; *PROME*, v, 406–7.

[31] *PROME*, v, 374–5; *AC*, 87–8.

the Thames to Westminster. Instead, the lords and commons were asked to attend upon him at Eltham, where the impeachments were confirmed, the continual council ratified, and the available replies to the common petitions announced.

The official compiler of the parliament roll insisted that the royal pronouncements at Eltham elicited high and unanimous praise. But the commons' increasing nervousness about Gaunt's inconstancy was also ominously substantiated. One of the reasons why Lancaster had kept parliament open for so long was the hope that the knights and burgesses might be forced into making the grant of direct taxation they had so vigorously resisted at the start of the assembly. Once it became plain that such a concession would never be forthcoming, the crown decided to exercise its own prerogative and refuse to issue any of its responses to the common petitions in the form of public statutes. In a final expression of exasperated pique, Gaunt even declined to preside at the customary end-of-session feast. Accordingly it was left to Peter de la Mare and his fellow knights of the shire to organize an impromptu celebration in the capital, to which they invited Prince Edmund, the earl of March, and several of the lords recently nominated to the continual council.[32]

It is easy to exaggerate the importance of the Good Parliament. The chroniclers claimed that the commons had wanted to impeach the chancellor and treasurer, and even perhaps Gaunt himself.[33] But there seems to be no direct evidence that de la Mare and his supporters wished to go beyond the disgracing of a hard core of discredited courtiers. In particular, they made no bid, either for themselves or for others, to take charge of the executive. The continual council that they helped to create was only ever intended to provide advice and consent; the actual direction of government was freely acknowledged as remaining with the king and thus, in reality, with the duke of Lancaster. Peter de la Mare was a man of genuine substance and bravery, who has a rightfully enduring place in the longer history of the English parliament. But the backwoodsmen who kept faith with their Speaker were unlikely revolutionaries, and there is little sense that they appreciated the fuller implications of his outspokenness. In fact, it was John of Gaunt who probably best comprehended the seriousness of the constitutional issues raised in 1376, and thereby set himself the unenviable task of dismantling what he saw as unconscionable and illegal challenges to the royal prerogative. The main significance of the Good Parliament lies rather in its new and open admission of three great political taboos of the 1370s: that the war with France was unsustainable; that

[32] *PROME*, v, 315; *AC*, 94.

[33] *AC*, 90–1. The *Brut* continuation found in CCCC, MS 78, fol. 188, claimed that in 1376 'the duke of Lancaster, Lord Latimer and other officers of the king were accused [*encoupes*] of evil governance'.

the realm had been betrayed by persons of influence around the king; and
that Edward III could not long resist the moment of mortality. Once
public debate was opened up to these alarming realities, the politics that
had prevailed for the previous thirty years could never be quite the same
again.

The summer recess of 1376 offered little immediate prospect of cheer for
the beleaguered court. Much of the government's attention in the first
weeks after the Good Parliament was given over to the disposition of the
Black Prince's estate and preparations for his funeral. In August the king
personally instructed his son's executors that they must fulfil the prince's
dying wish and distribute almost all the game available at Castle Rising as
alms to local people.[34] Eventually it was decided to call a great council at
Westminster at Michaelmas, an event timed to coincide with the official
ceremonies for the prince of Wales's soul at Westminster and London
and the transfer of his remains for burial at Canterbury Cathedral on
5 October. A select group comprising Archbishop Sudbury and other
unspecified bishops, earls and barons was also asked to meet a week before
the great council and prepare the way for its business.[35] Clearly, every
effort was being made to ensure a carefully controlled agenda and a properly respectful political mood at the forthcoming meeting of the political
elite.

In the midst of these manoeuvres came the difficult news of another
serious deterioration in the king's health. The shock of the Black Prince's
death had taken its toll on Edward III, who had quickly set about the
much delayed completion of the tombs of Queen Philippa and of two of
their other children, William of Windsor and Blanche of the Tower, at
Westminster Abbey.[36] In July and August the king was still well enough to
undertake a modest progress round Kent and Essex, including a unique
visit to Pleshey castle, the former seat of the Bohuns and now the prized
possession of Thomas of Woodstock. It may have been at this time that
the royal family gathered for the nuptials of the king's granddaughter, the
nine-year-old Philippa of Bedford, and the teenage Robert de Vere, earl
of Oxford.[37] For at least two months from the end of August 1376,
however, Edward seems to have been seriously indisposed. His acts of
grace continued to be communicated to Westminster by written and oral
warrants, but public appearances were obviously out of the question.
Confined to his sickbed at Havering, Edward was forced to give up all
hopes of attending either the Michaelmas great council or the exequies of

[34] E 101/398/5.
[35] E 403/460, 31 July, 29 Aug., 18 Sept. 1376; Barber, *Edward, Prince of Wales*, 236;
Holmes, *Good Parliament*, 159–60.
[36] *Issues*, 199–200; *King's Works*, i, 486.
[37] The marriage had taken place by Oct.: *CPR 1374–7*, 368.

the prince. The royal household had to content itself with arranging for cloth of gold to be offered on the king's behalf by Thomas of Woodstock and Richard of Bordeaux as Edward of Woodstock's funeral procession made its long passage from London, via Dartford, Rochester and Faversham, to Canterbury.[38]

The precise nature of the king's affliction during this period remains a mystery. Walsingham, who saw himself as something of an expert on psychosomatic illnesses, thought that Edward was smitten by a combination of grief and frustrated lust at the temporary loss of Alice Perrers.[39] The York chronicler's explanation was much more medically precise. He believed that the problem was an aposteme, a generic word used to describe an ulcer, abscess or cancerous growth. In the very same year that Edward fell ill, the renowned English physician John Arderne, who had seen service in the wars with Henry of Grosmont, wrote a treatise on rectal cancer describing in detail the foods and enemas used to facilitate the extraction of tumours and restore the health of the patient. In quite similar vein, the chronicle account of Edward's condition says that the king eventually managed to pass a 'large aposteme' and slowly recovered on a soft diet of stewed meats, soups and milksops.[40] This cluster of circumstantial evidence apart, there remains the further possibility that Edward had suffered the first of the sequence of strokes that were to carry him off in 1377. Whatever its exact nature, the king's illness was regarded as extremely serious. At least six physicians and surgeons were brought to attend upon the royal person during this testing time, and special provision was made for two members of the royal household to get up in the middle of the night to stand vigil by Edward's bed.[41]

For a while in early October, it seemed that the end had indeed arrived. Archbishop Neville of York wrote from the capital on 2 October to order urgent prayers in his diocese for the king's recovery.[42] Over three days from 5 to 7 October, while most of the royal family were down at Canterbury, there was intense activity at Havering. Edward's private estates were put in order, the endowments of his sons and grandchildren were confirmed and enhanced, arrangements were made to fulfil his commitments to his religious foundations, and his final will was drawn up

[38] E 101/397/20, m. 29.

[39] *St Albans*, i, 56–7; D. Green, 'Masculinity and Medicine: Thomas Walsingham and the Death of the Black Prince', *JMH*, xxxv (2009), 34–51.

[40] *AC*, 95; C. P. Swain, 'A Fourteenth-Century Description of Rectal Cancer', *World Journal of Surgery*, vii (1983), 304–7.

[41] E 101/397/20, m. 8.

[42] *Historical Papers and Letters*, 410–11. It may be that Neville also commissioned the tomb of Edward's son, William of Hatfield, at York Minster around this time: S. Oosterwijk, ' "A swathe feire graue": The Appearance of Children on Medieval Tomb Monuments', *Family and Dynasty*, ed. Eales and Tyas, 183–4.

and agreed.[43] Rumours of an impending crisis were rife. Those unnerved by the idea that the duke of Lancaster might seize power sought refuge in a scurrilous story that Gaunt was no true son of Edward III but the offspring of a Flemish woman smuggled into Queen Philippa's birthing chamber in 1340 to replace a dead baby girl. A still more subversive tale, circulating in France, told of how Edward III, who had once killed his own father, was now afflicted with premonitions that he, in turn, would be poisoned or drowned by his son.[44]

Had the gossipmongers but known it, there was in fact some official basis for their suspicion. Shortly after the Black Prince's funeral the senior members of the king's family convened at Havering to consider how to deal with the fact that the little Richard of Bordeaux, once king, was unlikely to produce a direct heir for some years. One proposal at least reached draft stage. This declared that, in the event that Richard were to die childless, the crown should devolve not upon the descendants of Lionel of Clarence through his daughter Philippa, countess of March, but upon John of Gaunt and his heirs male. Failing that line, the throne would then pass, in order, to the descendants in the male line of Edmund of Langley and Thomas of Woodstock. If Gaunt was unflinching in his support for the impending kingship of the Black Prince's son, then the secret debates in the royal circle during the autumn of 1376 revealed that he was equally determined to have himself declared heir presumptive to the future Richard II.[45]

In the end, this scheme was never promulgated. Against all expectations, Edward III rallied after 7 October and gradually regained some control of his mental and physical faculties. There is no evidence that crown or polity felt bound thereafter by the discussions that had taken place at Havering. And it remained an open question as to whether the king was even entitled to make such proleptic arrangements for the succession. Lancaster's pre-emptive strike stood in real danger of being interpreted as a malicious attack on the earl of March for the latter's defection to the commons in the Good Parliament. And although the earl's two-year-old son, Roger Mortimer, did represent something of a problematic candidate for the title of heir general to Richard of Bordeaux, there is no reason to suppose that Edward III himself was inclined permanently to override the rights of his favourite granddaughter, Philippa of Clarence. Two of Edward's greatest historical heroes, Henry II and Edward I, had both asserted the legitimacy of the

---

[43] *CPR 1374–7*, 327, 337, 347–8, 354, 355, 359, 368; *Collection of the Wills*, 59–64; Given-Wilson, 'Richard II and his Grandfather's Will', 320–1; Bennett, 'Edward III's Entail', 588–9.

[44] *St Albans*, i, 56–7, 60–1; *AC*, 95, 104–5; *Chron. QPV*, 261–2.

[45] Bennett, 'Edward III's Entail', 586–94, 607–9. Walsingham believed that Gaunt had (unsuccessfully) presented just such a scheme to the Good Parliament: *St Albans*, i, 38–41.

female line, the first by claiming the throne through his mother and the second by devolving the succession, in the absence of surviving sons, upon the descendants of his eldest daughter.[46] Such precedents strongly suggest that the attempted designation of Lancaster as Richard's heir had happened only because Gaunt himself had been temporarily making free with the exercise of the royal grace.

Above all, of course, both Edward III and his sons perfectly well understood the severe compromises that the entailing of the English crown would impose on their international status and reputation. In 1328, 1337, 1340 and 1369 the king had repeatedly asserted that descent in the female line from the house of Capet gave him a legitimate and sustainable claim to the throne of France. Charles V's attempts in 1374 to lay down a scheme for a regency in the event of the premature succession of his own young son, the Dauphin Charles, had prompted commentators on the continent to consider once more the recent conventions of succession in the kingdoms of France, England and Navarre.[47] To have denied Plantagenet women the very right that Edward had so fervently argued for his mother in France would simply have been to expose him as a perjurer and a fraud.[48] As a consequence, the detailed proposals raised in the family conference of October 1376 were quickly hushed up, and the only public statement to arise from the recent emergency of the king's health was the one that the English polity most obviously sought: that Richard of Bordeaux was indeed the rightful and designated heir to the throne. On 20 November the investiture ceremony requested in the Good Parliament finally took place, and Richard was created prince of Wales and duke of Cornwall with an income of 4,000 marks to maintain his estate as heir apparent of Edward III.[49]

Much less happily, the Havering council of October 1376 also marked the moment at which the crown formally asserted its right to rescind the actions of the Good Parliament and rehabilitate the group of courtiers condemned there. Although the continual council of prelates, earls and barons appointed in May had barely survived in an organized manner beyond the end of the Good Parliament, Gaunt seems to have kept up some kind of informal consultation with various groups of magnates and

[46] *Foedera*, I.ii, 742.

[47] *Chron. J&C*, ii, 177–8, 224–6; Delachenal, iv, 530–48; Sherborne, *War, Politics*, 161.

[48] It was precisely such anxieties to preserve intact English dynastic claims in France that seem later to have caused parliament to oppose Henry IV's plan of 1406 to entail the crown of England on his male heirs: Bennett, 'Edward III's Entail', 600.

[49] *CChR 1341–1417*, 231; *Foedera*, III.ii, 1075; Tout, *Chapters*, iii, 312. For the independent household established for the prince, at the king's expense, from 1 Jan. 1377, see E 101/398/9; Tout, *Chapters*, iv, 190–1; Saul, *Richard II*, 18. Froissart, viii, 226–7, claims that a great feast was held at Westminster at Christmas 1376, to which the king invited the prelates, lords and knights of England and raised Richard as his heir. Since Christmas was spent at Havering, it seems likely that the reference is really to the parliament of Jan. 1377.

prelates over the summer and autumn of 1376.[50] In early November, for example, a great council that was convened to discuss the regulation of office-holding in the city of London included the chancellor, treasurer and keeper of the privy seal, the archbishops of Canterbury and York, the bishop of London and six other prelates, the earls of Salisbury, Stafford, Suffolk and Warwick, together with Lord Percy and other barons. Even Gaunt's recent sparring partner the earl of March was there.[51] Six months after their appointment to the failed commission, a minimum of five of the original nine continual councillors were thus still firmly implicated at least in the normal processes of royal government.

This sense of corporate obligation allowed the duke of Lancaster to claim counsel and consent for altogether more controversial measures. On 8 October, in the presence of Prince John, the bishops of Lincoln and Worcester and the senior officers of state, the fragile Edward III was lifted from his sickbed to give his authority for the formal pardon of William Latimer.[52] While Richard Lyons remained for the moment in custody, the other London and Yarmouth financiers impeached in parliament were bailed and released pending similar acts of mercy.[53] Over the summer those of the covine who had managed to escape the commons' wrath, such as Nicholas Carew, Richard Sturry, John Beverley and John Salisbury, had continued to help themselves to the handsome pickings of royal patronage.[54] The return to court of the senior members of that clique therefore represented a clear statement that the king's friends were fully intent on resuming their political ascendancy. Latimer, along with the newly restored John Neville, promptly took up his place in the council, where the two men were soon joined by three powerful members of Gaunt's circle, Henry Percy, Ralph Basset and Walter Fitzwalter.[55] Under the combined influence of the restored courtiers and the Lancastrian affinity, the king's authority had been released from the unwarranted limitations imposed by his enemies and his prerogative had once more been triumphantly vindicated.

For the wider political public, the element of this process that created the most obvious impression was the return to court of the universally despised figure of Alice Perrers. On 22 October, in a perverse act of will, the king released Alice from liability to any actions brought against her

[50] AC, 95–6.

[51] SC 8/59/2909. For the outcomes see CPR 1374–7, 387; Barron, London, 137.

[52] SC 8/180/8960; CPR 1374–7, 353–4; St Albans, i, 54–5; Holmes, Good Parliament, 160; Dodd, 'Parliamentary Petitions?', 42–3 and n. 88.

[53] Tout, Chapters, iii, 308 and n. 3.

[54] CPR 1374–7, 342–3 347–8.

[55] SC 8/59/2909; SC 8/227/11346. Percy, Fitzwalter and Basset were also nominated by Gaunt to the committee of lords to intercommune with the commons in the Bad Parliament, and seem to have been recognized there as his cronies: Tout, Chapters, iii, 313; Arvanigian, 'Lancastrian Polity?', 137.

since her banishment from his presence. On the same day he ordered new gowns in preparation for her return to his company. Drawing extensively on biblical references, Walsingham graphically compared Perrers to the dog that returns to its own vomit (Proverbs 16: 11).[56] If Edward III remained ignorant of his mistress's recent marriage contract, no one else at court was under much illusion as to what was going on. In early December Alice persuaded Edward to countermand an important decision of the council to send Nicholas Dagworth to Ireland and reopen the inquiries against William Windsor. Gaunt himself was later to complain about Alice's blatant interference in this matter, ascribing her untoward influence to a night spent in the king's bed.[57] There is good reason to believe that it was Alice's outrageous behaviour in this and other matters that drove Lancaster to the point of desperation and caused him seriously to overreach himself in his efforts to recover the reputation of his father's tottering regime.

At the end of November 1376, orders went out from Westminster for the arrest of Peter de la Mare and his detainment at Nottingham castle. Since no formal charges were brought, de la Mare's supporters were forced to assume that the former Speaker was being punished for the exercise of free speech, and Peter was predictably hailed as an innocent victim and popular hero.[58] Then, on 1 December, de la Mare's employer, the earl of March, was deprived of the office of marshal in favour of Lancaster's man, Lord Percy.[59] Around the same time, Gaunt and Percy launched a singularly ill-judged attack on the judicial privileges of the Londoners.[60] On the pretext of a spate of violence that had broken out in the capital, the crown threatened, for the first time in nearly fifty years, to confiscate the liberties of the city and subject it to the direct jurisdiction of the steward and marshal of the royal household. If this was a misguided attempt to force the mercantile elite of London back into proper co-operation in the crown's credit schemes, it merely caused further damage to Gaunt's political credibility. Mobs whipped up by the London demagogue John Northampton threatened the Savoy, causing Lancaster to flee for his life and take refuge with Prince Richard at Kennington. The reconciliation that was eventually patched together proved a bitter personal humiliation for the duke, whose attempt to have a monumental pillar erected

[56] CPR 1374–7, 364–5; E 101/397/20, m. 8; St Albans, i, 56–9; Holmes, Good Parliament, 160–1.

[57] PROME, vi, 27–8. Clarke, Fourteenth Century Studies, 160, dated this episode to early Nov. 1376, but it seems more likely to relate to the commission issued to Dagworth on 20 Nov. and rescinded on 4 Dec.: CPR 1374–7, 416; CCR 1374–7, 469.

[58] CCR 1374–7, 397; St Albans, i, 56–9.

[59] St Albans, i, 62–3; Holmes, Good Parliament, 183.

[60] P. Nightingale, 'Capitalists, Crafts and Constitutional Change in Late Fourteenth-Century London', Past and Present, cxxiv (1989), 3–35.

to his honour in Cheapside was determinedly resisted by the embittered citizens of London.[61]

The most daring and foolish of Gaunt's acts of revenge was his attack on the Church. In September, John Wyclif was called down from Oxford to advise the council. Since his temporary engagement as a royal diplomat in 1373–4, Wyclif had been busy writing his *De civilo dominio*, a disquisition on the nature of lordship which concluded that the priesthood had no role to play in the exercise of temporal authority. This radical position provided Gaunt with a crude but effective opportunity to punish the bishops who had recently dared to speak out against the court. Over the winter of 1376–7 Wyclif preached a series of radical sermons in various London churches that helped foment popular hatred against the prelates.[62] In early November the duke of Lancaster also forced the council to make an example of William Wykeham for his betrayal in supporting the commons at the Good Parliament. The bishop was accused of a series of irregularities committed during his time as chancellor before 1371. The only one that really stuck was the quite minor charge that he had remitted fines due from certain recipients of royal favour. But this was taken as sufficient pretext for vengeance, and on 17 November orders went out from the government for the seizure of the temporalities of the see of Winchester. The heated reaction of the other bishops to this gross abuse of ecclesiastical liberties could no doubt have been predicted. What Gaunt had failed to realize, however, was the capacity of the case to provide a rallying point for wider discontent. Unlikely as it seemed, Gaunt's actions seemed set to turn Wykeham into a political martyr.[63] The duke of Lancaster's increasingly frantic and indiscriminate campaign against the perceived allies of the commons in the Good Parliament appeared fundamentally to jeopardize the strong tradition of royal magnanimity and simply accentuated the dangerous political isolation of the court.

Edward III's slow recovery from his recent collapse was sufficiently advanced by the beginning of December to allow the council to issue writs summoning a new parliament for 27 January 1377.[64] In the intervening period, various factions within the court competed for the king's attention and favour. Alice Perrers persuaded Edward that the Christmas and New Year festivities at Havering should be given over to celebrating the marriage of John Southray to Alice's ward, the infant Mary Percy. The new steward, Lord Percy, was furious at what he saw as the disparagement of his half-sister. The ceremony therefore served to entrench the hostile

[61] *AC*, 104–6; Goodman, *John of Gaunt*, 60–2.

[62] *Issues*, 200; *St Albans*, i, 74–81; *AC*, 103; A. Kenny, *Wyclif* (Oxford, 1985), 45–53.

[63] *AC*, 96–100, 184–5; *CCR 1377–81*, 36; Tout, *Chapters*, iii, 310–12; Ormrod, *Reign of Edward III*, 93, 230 n. 157; Davis, *William Wykeham*, 65–7.

[64] *RDP*, iv, 669–71; E 403/461, 12 Dec. 1376.

positions now taken up by Perrers and Percy's patron, Gaunt.[65] Shortly afterwards, on 11 January, John Knyvet and Robert Ashton were replaced as chancellor and treasurer by Adam Houghton, bishop of St David's, and Henry Wakefield, bishop of Worcester. Houghton and Wakefield were loyal moderates, and their selection suggests an attempt by Gaunt to offer a token of reconciliation on the eve of a new parliament.[66] But the move also breached the convention, honoured since the parliament of 1371, of having the principal offices of state occupied by laymen who might be made publicly accountable for their actions. The crown's good intentions were further undermined when Robert Ashton was redeployed to the office of chamberlain. Ashton had already been strongly implicated in the financial scandals exposed in the Good Parliament. His promotion to high office in the household suggested, rightly or wrongly, that the court regarded itself as entirely exempt from the norms and values of public life.

To these issues were added anxieties over relations with France. In July 1376 a new round of negotiations had opened at Bruges to find a way forward to lasting peace. The papal representatives returned briefly to the idea of a division of Aquitaine, first proposed the previous year, but offered a revised version of the scheme. Dropping the idea that one portion of the territory should be given to a cadet branch of the Plantagenet crown, they proposed a three-way split between Edward III (whose share would be held in sovereignty for the remainder of his life), Richard of Bordeaux (who would hold his share as a fief of France), and Charles V. Neither side was happy with such a compromise. But in spite of the nuncios' attempts to redraw the partition to his obvious advantage, Charles himself made it very clear that he intended to extend his rights to every part of his kingdom. In a blistering attack delivered by his new envoy, the abbot of Saint-Vaast at Arras, Charles maliciously accused Gaunt of wishing to take an army into France so that he might be able to re-enter England by force and usurp his father and nephew.[67] As active preparations continued for a major Valois onslaught across the Channel, French commanders used their status as conservators of the truce to whittle away at what remained of the Plantagenet regime in the Périgord and other parts of greater Aquitaine.[68] Such shows of force only made more urgent the summons of the English parliament and the reiteration of Edward III's continuing need for supplies towards an imminent reopening of war.

* * *

[65] E 101/397/20, mm. 9–10; Given-Wilson and Curteis, *Royal Bastards*, 138; Ormrod, 'Trials of Alice Perrers', 375. For a set of bed hangings given to Mary Percy by the king on her wedding see E 101/397/20, m. 20.

[66] Tout, *Chapters*, iii, 312–13; vi, 15–15, 23.

[67] Anglo-French Negotiations', nos XLVII-LVII.

[68] M. Jones, 'Bertrand du Guesclin, the Truce of Bruges and Campaigns in the Périgord (1376)', *Soldiers, Nobles and Gentlemen*, ed. Coss and Tyerman, 183–97.

The lords and commons who assembled at Westminster at the end of January 1377 came, in many cases, with a distinct sense of foreboding. John of Gaunt, acting on the conviction that it was his duty above all to protect the crown from its detractors, had clearly attempted to fix the parliament before it met. A select group of lords and prelates was summoned to meet with the council a week before the official opening in order to pick off potential critics and set up the business of the assembly. It was also rumoured that Gaunt had manipulated the elections of the knights of the shires. Whether this latter interference had much impact is difficult to tell. Only a dozen or so of the returned MPs were actually fee'd retainers of the duke of Lancaster. But few of those who had sat in the Good Parliament were re-elected, and the new parliament seems to have contained a significant number of conservatively minded men prepared to lend at least passive support to Gaunt's programme. In an obvious demonstration of what was to come, the commons agreed that Lancaster's own steward, Sir Thomas Hungerford, knight of the shire for Wiltshire, should on this occasion act as their Speaker.[69]

The parliament opened with a rather obvious but symbolically powerful call for co-operation. With the king reported still too weak to attend in person, the role of president was taken not by the controversial Gaunt but by the instantly appealing figure of the ten-year-old heir apparent. In this Epiphany season, the chancellor called on all present to show the prince of Wales the same reverence that the Magi had once shown to the Christ-child. A little later, the Londoners hosted a great parade in the prince's honour, featuring a group of mummers dressed as the emperor, pope and twenty-four cardinals, and delivered gifts to the prince, his mother and his uncles at Kennington. Such powerful evocations of unity were greatly reinforced by the fact that the parliament coincided with the completion of Edward III's jubilee year as monarch. On 28 January, Adam Houghton made a finely wrought speech, part sermon, part political manifesto, in which he reported the king's recovery to health, his purging from sin, and the start of a new and glorious phase of his reign. If his subjects were to have the benefits of royal grace in this special moment of achievement, however, they too must be free of all vice and reconciled as members of a whole and healthy body politic. If the crown's earlier efforts to exploit the jubilee had proved largely futile, Edward III's ministers and family remained nonetheless determined to make all possible political capital out of its completion.[70]

The preliminaries thus dispensed with, the lords and commons were requested to assemble separately and discuss the failure of the Anglo-French truce. The commons, repairing to the chapter house of

[69] *PROME*, v, 423; *St Albans*, i, 68–71; J. S. Roskell, *Parliament and Politics in Late Medieval England*, 3 vols (London, 1981), ii, 15–44; Walker, *Lancastrian Affinity*, 239.
[70] *PROME*, v, 394–7; *AC*, 102; Wilks, *Wyclif*, 130–2.

Westminster Abbey, spent over three weeks locked in debate. Gaunt was clearly anxious to influence them into a speedy resolution. A committee of peers including the earls of Arundel, Warwick, Salisbury and Stafford and the lords Percy, Ros, Fitzwalter and Basset was sent across to the abbey to impart the spirit of the discussions in the upper house. On Shrove Tuesday, 10 February, Edward III made his first public appearance in many months when he was rowed down the Thames en route from Havering to Sheen. The lords were again induced to put on a show of unity for the benefit of the commons, and came out in their own boats as the royal barge passed Westminster Palace to provide a fleet of honour in celebration of the royal jubilee.[71]

Faced with these and other less subtle forms of political pressure, the commons reached the reluctant conclusion that they could not sustain the opposition mounted by their counterparts in the summer of 1376. William Langland satirized the arguments in the B-text of *Piers Plowman*, written shortly after the Bad Parliament. A 'rat of renown' (Peter de la Mare) had previously argued for putting a bell on the cat (John of Gaunt) so that the people might better know his actions and avoid his threats. But now a mouse 'that had good sense' (Hungerford) argued that it would be better for the rats and mice to remove the bell and let the cat concentrate his reprisals upon another group, the rabbits (who, in the immediate context, might be assumed to represent the French).[72] The new urgency attached to the state of imminent invasion, coupled with a widespread sense of the inevitability of a royalist recovery, made the 1377 parliament altogether different in outlook and action from that of 1376 and much more readily disposed to accept the essential wisdom of a proper restoration of royal authority.

On 22 February a deputation of lords and ministers was sent to Sheen to secure formal royal assent to the package agreed in parliament. The commons would concede the urgent need for supplies towards a now imminent renewal of war. But they refused to grant a single or multiple fifteenth and tenth and resorted, as they had done in 1371, to experimentation. They proposed a subsidy of one groat, or 4d, on every head of population over the age of fourteen. The rationale behind this fateful formulation was not given. The knights and burgesses were probably concerned to avoid any new assessment of real wealth that might increase

[71] *AC*, 103.
[72] W. Langland, *The Vision of Piers Plowman: A Complete Edition of the B-text*, ed. A. V. C. Schmidt (London, 1978), 6–8 (Prologue, ll. 146–208). Interpretations of this fable are many and various. See, among other recent studies, A. Gross, 'Langland's Rats: A Moralist's View of Parliament', *Parliamentary History*, ix (1990), 286–301; G. Dodd, 'A Parliament Full of Rats? *Piers Plowman* and the Good Parliament of 1376', *HR*, lxxix (2006), 21–49; M. Giancarlo, *Parliament and Literature in Late Medieval England* (Cambridge, 2007), 181–3; N. Lassahn, 'Langland's Rats Revisited: Conservatism, *Commune*, and Political Unanimity', *Viator*, xxxix (2008), 127–55.

their own liability to taxation. But it is hard to escape the conclusion that they also saw the new poll tax as another means by which to express their growing frustration at the supposed affluence of the lower orders. Either way, they wanted due accountability, and called for the appointment of special treasurers of war, along the lines demanded in 1371 and adopted in 1372, to ensure that the new tax revenues were spent solely on the purposes for which they had been granted. In return for supplies, the knights and burgesses expected favourable answers, if possible made up as statutes, to their common petitions. The council's responses to the petitions, duly authorized by the king, were communicated in a joint session of lords and commons held the next day, 23 February.[73]

Under normal circumstances the parliament would have closed at this point. But a number of outstanding issues served to prolong the session. Chancellor Houghton's earlier allusions to the realm's enjoyment of Edward III's special state of grace had raised the prospect of a new general pardon following the precedent of that of 1362. The commons' long request for the updating and extension of the earlier pardon suggests that they hoped to use the new amnesty to secure the release of Peter de la Mare and to indemnify their predecessors of 1376 from any possible further reprisals. In the event, the crown proved rather less than accommodating. The council, consulting with the king, agreed to extend the range of offences covered by the pardon to include some lesser felonies, abuses of the crown's feudal rights and unresolved debts owed by sheriffs and tax collectors. This was a very significant concession to the interests of the office-holding classes and their constituents, over 2,500 of whom went on to purchase copies of the general pardon in the following six months. But far from simply representing an act of reconciliation, the amnesty also served to advertise and perpetuate current divisions within the political elite. The commons were forced to request that the benefits of the pardon be duly extended to William Latimer, Richard Lyons, Alice Perrers and the lesser offenders impeached in 1376. At the same time, the crown explicitly barred William Wykeham from the benefits of grace.[74] With de la Mare still languishing in prison and Wykeham under penalty of forfeiture, those who hoped for some recognition of the reform programme of 1376 had good reason to feel tricked and betrayed.

That sense of grievance was compounded by the obvious triumphalism of the court. On 28 February the clergy of the southern province meeting in session at St Paul's Cathedral were forced to concede a poll tax of their own. They had the satisfaction of receiving royal guarantees on their own petitions submitted in parliament. But their request for the restoration of the bishop of Winchester went unanswered, and the convocation was left

[73] *PROME*, v, 399–401; Given-Wilson, *Royal Household*, 122–3.
[74] *PROME*, v, 401–3, 420, 423–6; *SR*, i, 396–7; Lacey, *Royal Pardon*, 113–26.

with no further effective means to resolve this continuing outrage.[75] The same day witnessed the equally dramatic announcement in parliament that the palatine powers previously enjoyed by Henry of Grosmont in the county of Lancaster were to be bestowed, for life, on John of Gaunt.[76] Within the royal family only Richard of Bordeaux, as earl of Chester, enjoyed equivalent rights. On 1 March the heir to the throne probably presided at the feast held, as the royal household accounts rather forebodingly had it, to celebrate the 'grant of groats'. The following day the knights and burgesses were finally given licence to depart.[77] They did so in the full knowledge not merely that the crown was once more restored to the uninhibited enjoyment of its prerogative but also that John of Gaunt was now established in virtually unassailable control of his father's regime. Shortly after parliament went down, the grateful king made proper token of gratitude by supplying his loyal third son with a spectacular gown of red silk trimmed with ermine.[78]

The confident public reports of Edward III's recovery to good health did not long outlive the Bad Parliament. From mid-February to mid-April 1377, Edward III remained locked away from the public gaze at Sheen. According to Walsingham, he now sat like a statue, unable either to move or to speak.[79] Medicines were sent down for the king's use in early March, and at the end of that month the household carefully scaled down the Easter celebrations out of respect for Edward's continued indisposition.

Such concerns notwithstanding, plans were now put in place for a major gathering of the court and the political elite at the forthcoming Garter ceremonies. A suit of robes was commissioned for the king to wear on this occasion. A sumptuous new throne, upholstered in stencilled cloth of gold fixed with a thousand gilded pins, was also commissioned, seemingly in preparation for the event.[80] On the vigil of the Garter feast, three princes of the blood, Richard of Bordeaux, Thomas of Woodstock and Henry of Bolingbroke, received knighthood at the king's hand. They were followed by a group of young lords, including the earl of Oxford and Lord Beaumont, the heirs of the earls of Stafford and Salisbury, and no fewer than three sons of Lord Percy. The last and most controversial dubbing was that of the bastard Southray. Then, on St George's Day itself, Richard of Bordeaux and his cousin Bolingbroke were installed as new knights of the Garter. A tournament ensued, for which the young prince of Wales

[75] The convocation of York granted its own poll tax in April: *PROME*, v, 422–3; *Records of Convocation*, iii, 337–50; xiii, 185–8; xix, 50–1.

[76] *The Charters of the Duchy of Lancaster*, ed. W. Hardy (London, 1845), no. 11.

[77] E 101/398/9, fol. 12; *CCR 1374–7*, 535–7.

[78] E 101/397/20, m. 10.

[79] *St Albans*, i, 102–3.

[80] E 101/397/20, m. 10; E 101/398/9, fol. 23.

was provided with ornamental armour.[81] In many ways Edward III's last Garter feast represented the epitome of his *politique*, a coming together of the royal family and its most trusted associates in a powerful public display of unity and loyalty. It was Edward's particular tragedy that he was now too frail either to enjoy or to comprehend such vivid reminders of the miracle he had wrought.

The general need for a rallying of the elite was all the more pressing given the imminent threat of war. Even before the formal end of the truce on 1 April, there was great concern about England's ability to withstand the rumoured Valois onslaught. Conspiring again with Owain of Wales and drawing into the confederacy a turncoat English knight, John Minsterworth, Charles V began to plan a combined Franco-Castilian armada that would harry the south coast of England and land a major army in Wales. Envoys were also dispatched to Scotland to try to persuade Robert II to repudiate his truce with the English. In optimistic mood, Charles's principal commanders planned to strike simultaneously at the key English positions in Calais, Brittany, Gascony and the Auvergne.[82] Minsterworth was intercepted and taken back to England, where he was subjected to a show trial and put to death for treason, his quartered body distributed to the four corners of the realm as a ghoulish reminder of the penalties of defection. In the mood of uncertainty that now prevailed, however, the polity was rather less convinced of the government's case. Far from becoming a convenient butt of public wrath, Minsterworth was rumoured to have been put to death for threatening to expose some unstated trickery on the part of Lord Percy and John of Gaunt.[83]

In the midst of such confusion, the crown found its efforts to launch a military counter-offensive severely compromised by a general lack of resources and will. The south coast was put on a state of high alert, and special efforts were made to concentrate naval forces in the mouth of the Thames against an attempted attack on the capital.[84] Royal castles throughout the south of England were made ready for war: the great palace of Windsor was itself invested with a garrison in May.[85] Bishops, earls and other lords were regularly called to sit with Gaunt, Archbishop Sudbury and the chancellor and treasurer at Westminster and develop some kind of coherent strategy. In such troubled times the earl of March agreed temporarily to give up his feud with the duke of Lancaster and

---

[81] E 101/397/20, mm. 10, 11, 28; E 101/398/8; *AC*, 106; Beltz, *Memorials*, 11; *Issues*, 202–3; Galway, 'Alice Perrers' Son', 244; Holmes, *Good Parliament*, 194; Ormrod, 'Edward III and his Family', 419–20.

[82] Sumption, iii, 268–70.

[83] *St Albans*, i, 106–9; *Issues*, 202.

[84] Sumption, iii, 276–8.

[85] E 101/396/15.

resume his seat in council.[86] In the end, however, it was agreed that the only possible solution was to beg for time and seek some further brief intermission of truce.

The French were well aware of the strength of their position. They would concede only a slight reprieve, allowing the truce to be extended in short measure to 1 May and then to 24 June. Recognizing that this was a mere postponement of the inevitable, the standing peace conference at Bruges declared its business over in early April.[87] In June, indentures were sealed for an impending continental expedition of 4,000 men to be led by Gaunt, the duke of Brittany, the earl of Warwick, Lord Latimer, Sir Richard Sturry and Sir Philip la Vache, together with two new royal commanders, Thomas of Woodstock and Richard of Bordeaux. But even these well-advanced plans subsequently foundered and collapsed as the lifeblood drained from Edward III.[88]

Early in May 1377 the king was once more moved from Windsor. Apart from a short visit back to his birthplace at the beginning of June, Edward would spend the last remaining weeks of his life in the seclusion of his manor of Sheen. For his household clerks it was, perforce, business as usual. The great wardrobe confidently ordered new gowns and hoods for Edward and the 'earls, barons, ladies, knights, esquires and valets' who would supposedly accompany him on his sports in the new hunting season. Repairs were also carried out at Clarendon Palace in anticipation of a royal progress into the New Forest. Such fantasies of immortality were quickly belied by the further round of medicines ordered up by John Glaston. But rather than taking him quickly, death seemed to taunt the paralyzed monarch. In April and May news reached the court of the demise of two of the oldest and most respected members of the aristocracy, Marie, dowager countess of Pembroke, and Hugh Courtenay, earl of Devon. In early June the king's chapel performed solemn rites on the first anniversary of the death of the Black Prince.[89] The country held its breath for news of the next, and now surely imminent, fatality.

In this atmosphere of high tension the restored members of the court covine rushed to exploit their last moments in the company of the dying king. In May, Alice Perrers made a daring attempt to improve the terms of the pardon that had been allowed to Richard Lyons after the Bad Parliament. Lyons was to be released from an outstanding debt owed to the crown and to be given a gift of 1,000 marks as compensation for his

[86] Issues, 204; E 403/462, 6 Apr., 9 Apr., 16 Apr., 27 Apr., 16 May, 25 May 1377; Given-Wilson, 'Royal Charter Witness Lists', 73.

[87] Sumption, iii, 278.

[88] Goodman, John of Gaunt, 64.

[89] St Albans, i, 110–11; E 101/397/20, mm. 10, 29; E 101/398/9, fols 23, 25; A Richardson, The Forest, Park and Palace of Clarendon, c.1200–c.1650 (British Archaeological Reports, British series, cccvii, 2005), 62.

recent bout of bad fortune. When Alice's lobbying for Lyons was later exposed, two of her erstwhile allies, Nicholas Carew and Alan Buxhull, would claim that she had directed the whole process from her position at the head of the old king's bed as he lay incapacitated at Sheen.[90] Thomas Walsingham suggested that the pardon belatedly offered to William Wykeham on 18 June was likewise won only when the contrite bishop abased himself before the king's mistress.[91] If these were the convenient musings of misogynists, they are confirmed by the official record. In the very last month of Edward III's life Alice Perrers took delivery in the royal household of new ermine-trimmed gowns and hoods and a gold cup valued at nearly £40.[92] And on 4 June she secured a new and enlarged version of her own pardon, which confirmed her in full enjoyment of the recent general amnesty and exempted her from any financial liability for the lavish gifts of money, jewels, plate and fine cloth accumulated over the whole time of her service to Queen Philippa and Edward III.[93] There could surely be no more dramatic a representation of the full cycle through which Fortune's wheel had turned in the previous year.

[90] *CPR 1374–7*, 439–40, 444; *PROME*, vi, 26–30.

[91] *CPR 1374–7*, 483; *St Albans*, i, 108–11. In fact, the decisive intervention is likely to have been that of the princess of Wales: *St Albans*, i, 88–95.

[92] E 101/397/20, m. 11; E 403/462, 15 June 1377; E 101/509/20.

[93] *CPR 1374–7*, 478.

Chapter 21

EDWARD THE GREAT

Edward III died at his manor of Sheen alongside the Thames in Richmond on the evening of 21 June 1377. Quite who was in attendance at this terrible moment remains unclear. Thomas Walsingham, writing in the 1380s, imagined Edward as bereft and betrayed. In this colourful rendering of the episode, even the parasitical Alice Perrers chose to strip the rings from Edward's fingers before fleeing, and only a single unnamed priest remained to seek out the signs of contrition appropriate to the making of a good death. In Jean Froissart's depiction of the scene, by contrast, the administration of the last rites was attended, as might be thought properly fitting, by a great clutch of the king's adoring and grieving family. If Froissart's intention was principally to emphasize the sense of common purpose within the dynasty at this defining moment, it is his account that also ultimately has the great claim to veracity. While the prince of Wales and his mother kept vigil at their palace of Kennington, the princes John, Edmund and Thomas, the duke of Brittany and the earl of March were all almost certainly with Edward III at the time of his death. It was at Sheen on the following day, 22 June, that these and other members of the royal family also gathered to mark the first day of the official reign of the new Richard II.[1]

With the Anglo-French truce about to expire and the urgent need to secure the succession, the regime gave rapid attention to the ceremonies of transition.[2] The French sack of Rye on 29 June was a stark reminder of the hazards of an overlong interregnum, and invitations were soon issued for the funeral that would take place on 5 July and the coronation that would follow hard upon it. Roger Chaundler of London was employed to eviscerate and embalm the corpse of Edward III, and sumptuous fabrics were rapidly procured to be made up into a pillow and drapes for the coffin. For nearly two weeks the deceased king's remains lay in a chamber hung with black cloth within his house at Sheen. Then on Sunday 28 June the full staff of his household, kept in place to deal with the logistics of the exequies, moved down from Windsor to set in train the slow and solemn

---

[1] *St Albans*, i, 118–31; Froissart, viii, 230.
[2] For what follows see C. Given-Wilson, 'The Exequies of Edward III and the Royal Funeral Ceremony in Late Medieval England', *EHR*, cxxiv (2009), 257–82.

progress that would take Edward's body to its final resting place at Westminster Abbey.

Some time before the interment Stephen Hadley, the craftsman who had recently built the king's new throne, was commissioned to provide a lifesized mannequin in the likeness of the dead monarch, together with replicas of the coronation regalia. The wooden figure that he created still survives as the oldest extant funeral effigy in the ghoulish collection of royal memorabilia at Westminster. The dummy was made from wood and straw, but the face was made of plaster moulded in a death mask taken from the corpse. The dramatic effect was heightened by painted eyes, lips and cheeks and the application of a wig and beard; the hair of a little brown dog was used to create lifelike eyebrows.[3] The idea was not new: fifty years earlier, a temporary likeness of the deceased monarch had been used during Edward II's interment at Gloucester Abbey. In contrast to 1327, however, there is obviously no suggestion that the dummy was employed to disguise the true identity of the deceased or to cover up some act of foul play. Edward III's embalmed body was displayed in an open casket, with the face exposed, at both Sheen and Westminster.[4] The mannequin seems to have been created simply to provide a powerful symbolic representation of the royal presence during the open-air procession up to the capital and on the double-decker wooden platform erected to hold the coffin inside Westminster Abbey. It may also have been employed on the temporary box-tomb thrown up in the abbey church to receive the body in advance of the creation of a permanent memorial.[5] Whatever its precise liturgical function, the figure provides the closest thing we have to a contemporary likeness of Edward III. If its height, 5 feet 10½ inches, is at all indicative, then the king may be attributed with at least something of the tall physique for which his grandfather and father were rather better known.[6] The most arresting feature, however, is the distortion of the mouth, a virtually unmistakable sign of a series of serious, and ultimately fatal, strokes.[7]

---

[3] E 101/389/9, fol. 23v, transcribed in W. St J. Hope, 'On the Funeral Effigies of the Kings and Queens of England', *Archaeologia*, lx (1907), 532; A. Harvey and R. Mortimer, *The Funeral Effigies of Westminster Abbey* (Woodbridge, 1994), 30–5; J. Steane, *The Archaeology of the Medieval English Monarchy* (London, 1999), 56–7.

[4] E 101/397/20, m. 12; Froissart, viii, 231.

[5] An illuminated image in a text of the royal funeral service preserved in the *Liber regalis* at Westminster Abbey, compiled some time shortly after 1382, seems to depict just such a usage of the funeral effigy atop a makeshift tomb: London, Westminster Abbey, MS 38, fol. 33v.

[6] Walsingham described him as 'not excessively tall': *St Albans*, i, 988–9.

[7] It has been argued that the famous lifelike profile portrait of John II now in the Louvre was once part of a quadriptych including portraits of Charles V of France (either as dauphin or as king), the Emperor Charles IV and Edward III. Since John's portrait is usually dated *c.*1360, it remains a matter of speculation as to whether the artist charged with the likeness of Edward III attempted anything more than a conventional representation of

The funeral cortège of Edward III left Sheen on Friday 3 July and progressed via Wandsworth to Southwark, where the coffin was transferred to a larger hearse for its public reception into London.[8] Crossing London Bridge, the procession moved on to St Paul's Cathedral, where the body would lie overnight. Given the speed with which all this was arranged, the sheer scale of the event is all the more impressive. Four hundred torch-bearers walked in doleful attendance on either side of the coffin, which was followed by the entire cast of the royal household; all told, the procession included at least a thousand people, and perhaps even as many as two thousand. At St Paul's the coffin was placed on a bier set up between the choir and the high altar, at which prayers and masses were said through the night. The whole of Saturday was given over to a stately progress through the city to the abbey of Westminster. For this leg of the journey, the members of the household were joined again by John of Gaunt, Edmund of Langley and Thomas of Woodstock, along with John of Brittany and the earl of March. To allow precedence to the deceased, the new King Richard did not take part in these public ceremonies. But he may well have attended the service in Westminster Abbey, sitting with his mother and other royal ladies in the privacy of the royal pew high above the monastic choir.[9] There was much lamentation on the streets, and generous alms were bestowed on the poor who thronged the way.[10] At Westminster the coffin was placed on an elaborate, multi-level catafalque complete with black curtains, canopy, and painted shields of the royal arms. Here it lay in state before interment on the following day. Edward III had said little in his will about arrangements for his funeral other than the general injunctions that it should be conducted 'in a regal manner' and without undue ostentation.[11] It was the former rather than the latter sentiment that prevailed in the rites carried out in July 1377.

The funeral ceremony performed by Archbishop Sudbury on Sunday 5 July followed the broad outlines of a liturgical tradition preserved in the memory of the Westminster monks since the time of Henry III. The deceased king's body was wrapped in red samite decorated with a white cross and the sealed coffin, placed inside the temporary tomb, was draped

---

kingship. A. Martindale, 'Painting for Pleasure: Some Lost Fifteenth-Century Secular Decorations of Northern Italy', *The Vanishing Past: Studies of Medieval Art, Liturgy and Metrology Presented to Christopher Hohler*, ed. A. Borg and A. Martindale (British Archaeological Reports, international series, cxi, 1981), 112–13; F. Hepburn, *Portraits of the Later Plantagenets* (Woodbridge, 1986), 5.

[8] Hope, 'Funeral Effigies', 532; Given-Wilson, 'Exequies', 268–9.

[9] Richard's only known involvement in the funeral comes in a reference to mourning clothes provided for the event: E 101/397/20, m. 13. It seems significant that Froissart excluded him from the list of those who were involved in the public elements of the funeral.

[10] Froissart, viii, 230–1; E 101/398/9, fol. 24.

[11] *Collection of the Wills*, 60.

with a rich brocade of double silk. It is likely that at least some of the robes and insignia that Edward had borne at his coronation fifty years earlier were also buried with him. Despite the opposition of the ecclesiastical authorities, medieval royal convention generally allowed for the separate burial, at different sites, of the heart and viscera removed from the corpse during the embalming process.[12] It is perhaps surprising that Edward III did not leave instructions for the interment of his organs at St George's, Windsor or St Stephen's, Westminster. Had his tomb been opened during the craze for antiquarian investigation of mortal remains in the eighteenth and nineteenth centuries, we might know whether an urn containing the entrails was interred with the corpse. But in the absence of any other evidence it seems reasonable to conclude that the body and viscera were buried together in the appointed position next to Queen Philippa's tomb on the south side of the Confessor's Chapel at Westminster.

If the interment of Edward III followed well-established liturgical practice, there was nevertheless one significant innovation in 1377. A knight bearing the heraldry of the deceased monarch entered the abbey church during the ceremonies and made an offering of a shield and, probably, a sword.[13] In the 1370s it was becoming fashionable for aristocratic families to present the military accoutrements of the deceased to their mausolea, and the Black Prince's helm, crest, gauntlets, coat armour and shield had been presented to Canterbury Cathedral at the time of his funeral in 1376.[14] The adoption of the practice as a recognized element in Edward III's funeral in 1377 seems to be a very deliberate attempt to recall the great deeds of the warrior-king.

There is every reason to believe that the sword and shield presented at the funeral were the same as those that continued to be reported on display around the tomb of Edward III until at least the eighteenth century.[15] The original sword, while a surprisingly crude piece of craftsmanship, still survives in the abbey's collections; the shield that accompanies it, once thought to be genuine, is more likely to be a sixteenth- or seventeenth-century replica.[16] A similar ceremonial sword was placed soon after Edward's death above the royal stall in St George's, Windsor as a permanent memorial to the founder of the Garter, and remains on

[12] For this practice in relation to Edward I and II see Westerhof, *Death and the Noble Body*, 90.

[13] Given-Wilson, 'Exequies', 271–9.

[14] *Age of Chivalry*, nos 626–33; C. Wilson, 'The Medieval Monuments', *A History of Canterbury Cathedral*, ed. P. Collinson, N. Ramsay and M. Sparks (Oxford, 1995), 497–8.

[15] D. A. L. Morgan, 'The Political After-life of Edward III: The Apotheosis of a Warmonger', *EHR*, cxii (1997), 874; W. Thornbury, *Old and New London*, 6 vols (London, 1878), iii, 431–50.

[16] G. F. Laking, *A Record of European Arms and Armour through Seven Centuries*, 5 vols (London, 1920–2), ii, 223–7, 329–30; WAM, 62481–62485; Given-Wilson, 'Exequies', 274 n. 75.

display to this day in the south choir aisle of the chapel.[17] The icono-
graphical importance attached by contemporary and later political culture
to such precious relics was considerable, and explains why the next martial
monarch to be buried at Westminster, Henry V, chose in this, as in so much
else, to copy Edward III and have his own funeral achievements displayed
for posterity around his tomb.[18]

Edward III and his courtiers had made no attempt in the last few
months of his life to update the royal will made in October 1376, and the
personal bequests ordered by this document therefore tended to reflect not
the fickle whim of a malleable old man but the robust conservatism of his
children. To his successor he gave the state beds at Westminster and the sets
of hangings stored in the great wardrobe for the adornment of royal halls.
Princess Joan had gracious release from liability to a recent advance of
cash; and Princess Isabella, 'our most beloved daughter', was accorded a
supplementary pension out of the estates of her son-in-law, Robert de Vere.
Significantly, Alice Perrers and her toadies got nothing by way either of
memento or pension from the estate of the old king. Rather, the whole of
Edward's personal possessions – plate, jewels, cash and land acquired in a
private capacity – were to be placed in the hands of a group of executors
and trustees, led by Gaunt and Archbishop Sudbury, and used to fulfil his
endowments of St Stephen's Chapel, St Mary Graces and Kings Langley.[19]

At the time that the will was made, these pious commitments had seemed
to Edward's courtiers and advisers entirely uncontroversial and straightforward. But the royal family had reckoned without the force of the new idea
articulated in the Good Parliament that the king's personal resources –
including, of course, that mythical hoard of ransom moneys piled up in his
private treasury – should not be squandered at will but reserved for the
public business of the realm.[20] The situation was exacerbated by the fact

[17] Laking, *Record of European Arms*, ii, 330–2. A number of other swords and daggers now
held in collections abroad have been argued to have connections with Edward III, but the
arguments for such provenance are tendentious and have not been well received:
E. Oakshott, *Records of the Medieval Sword* (Woodbridge, 1991), 268–83.

[18] *Gothic: Art for England, 1400–1547*, ed. R. Marks and P. Williamson (London, 2003),
no. 54.

[19] *Collection of the Wills*, 61–4; *CPR 1374–7*, 347–8. At the same time Edward had made
provision for the future of the estates held in life interest by Marie de Saint-Pol, countess
of Pembroke (who was still alive at the time). Most of these lands were reserved for
Edmund of Langley, but three Hertfordshire manors were assigned to St Mary Graces:
CPR 1374–7, 354, 374; Wolffe, *Royal Demesne*, 243.

[20] It is significant that the special council appointed to inquire into the state of royal
finances and government in the Wonderful Parliament of 1386 was empowered to inquire
into 'the jewels and goods which were of our grandfather [Edward III] at the time of his
death, what these were and of what price or value and what has become of them': *SR*, ii,
44–6; *The Westminster Chronicle, 1381–1394*, ed. L. C. Hector and B. F. Harvey (Oxford, 1982),
171. Part of Richard II's prevarication over the fulfilment of Edward's will had therefore to
do with a stubborn and continuing belief among the political community that the old king
had left a significant treasure that ought to be put to public use.

that the group of trustees of the old king's will included a number of the leading members of the newly resurrected court covine: Robert Ashton, Nicholas Carew, John Ipres and even, most outrageously, William Latimer. Over the following five years there was to be a running battle between the executors and the exchequer over whether the former were entitled to have control of all of Edward's landed acquisitions or merely – as was finally agreed in 1382 – the former estates of the great heiress Juliana Leybourne, countess of Huntingdon. Even then, it would be another sixteen years and more before Edward III's will was finally declared fully performed.[21]

Nor was Richard II's government initially much more punctilious about the need to provide a suitable permanent memorial to his grandfather. As the site of Edward III's tomb had been so long identified, it might be suspected that Edward had given at least some thought to the manner of his representation in tomb and permanent effigy. He and his counsellors perhaps discussed such ideas with John Orchard, the craftsman commissioned in 1376 to provide copper angels for Queen Philippa's adjacent sepulchre.[22] The eventual decision to place in the niches of Edward's tomb-chest twelve miniature bronze images of his children surely reflects the stated preference of a king so renowned for his commitment to dynasty.[23] Even so, the task of commissioning the tombs both of Edward III and of the Black Prince fell almost entirely to the regime of Richard II, and was only taken up with a degree of purpose at some point in the 1380s.[24] Our final impression of the old king thus says at least as much about Richard II's interest in the history and destiny of his monarchy as it does about Edward III's own personal style.

This conscious incorporation of Edward's memory into Richard's vision of kingship also helps to account for the very obvious contrast between Queen Philippa's extremely personalized effigy and the flawless, timeless and universalized figure preferred for Edward III's tomb. The gilt-bronze figure, variously associated with John Orchard, John de Liège (the artist of Queen Philippa's effigy) and Henry Yevele (the master put in charge of Richard II's tomb), may have been based loosely on the temporary funeral effigy of Edward III, but was entirely devoid of its lifelike

---

[21] Given-Wilson, 'Richard II and his Grandfather's Will', 320–37.

[22] *King's Works*, i, 487.

[23] All twelve were still *in situ* in the sixteenth century, but those on the north side were lost thereafter and only six now survive, on the south side, representing Edward of Woodstock, Joan of the Tower, Lionel of Clarence, Edmund of Langley, Mary of Waltham and William (more likely, from his position in the scheme, William of Windsor rather than, as often stated, William of Hatfield). See A. P. Stanley, *Historical Memorials of Westminster Abbey*, 3rd edn (London, 1869), 147.

[24] Binski, *Westminster Abbey*, 95–9. In 1386 a cargo of Purbeck marble purchased for Edward III's tomb was reported to be lying aboard ship at Poole awaiting departure for Westminster: *CPR 1385–9*, 127.

blemishes. Instead, the king was portrayed as a venerable and eternal figure unmarked by the ravages of age and infirmity. The effigy kept faith with a traditional iconography that represented kings in long, flowing robes of state rather than (as in the case of the Black Prince) in the armour of war. The head of the figure was designed to bear a crown, though any such circlet has long since disappeared. The effigy was thus entirely of a piece with the six stone sculptures of past kings commissioned by Richard II in the mid-1380s to adorn the walls of Westminster Hall.[25] That scheme, and the supposed likeness of Edward III in the Westminster tomb, became in turn the prototypes for the representations of Edward and his fellow rulers found on the fifteenth-century choir screens at York and Canterbury and in the mass-produced portraits of monarchs that adorned the long galleries of sixteenth-century country houses.[26]

The strongest indicator of Richard II's involvement in the design of his grandfather's tomb is the Latin inscription that runs around the edge:

Here is the glory of the English, the paragon of past kings,
The model of future kings, a merciful king, the peace of the peoples,
Edward the Third, fulfilling the jubilee of his reign.
The unconquered leopard, he was a powerful Maccabeus in his wars.
While he lived prosperously, he restored to life his kingdom in probity.
He ruled mightily in arms; now in heaven may he be a heavenly king.[27]

This was quite unlike the laconic epitaphs on earlier royal tombs at Westminster, which consisted of simple identifiers in Anglo-Norman ('Here lies . . .') and brief invocations of prayers. Its interest to posterity is amply attested to by the existence, even before the Reformation, of a transcription and translation of the text found hanging upon the tomb as an aid to visitors.[28] In its original conception, the new-style epitaph seems to have been something of a foil to that found on the nearby tomb of Richard II, with which it shared both a language and a recognizable form, the Leonine hexameter. Indeed, there is more than a hint that Richard

[25] *King's Works*, i, 486–7; 192; L. Stone, *Sculpture in Britain: The Middle Ages* (Harmondsworth, 1955), 192; Cherry and Stratford, *Westminster Kings*, 68–72.

[26] J. H. Harvey, 'Architectural History from 1291 to 1558', *A History of York Minster*, ed. G. E. Aylmer and R. Cant (Oxford, 1977), 181–6; R. Strong, *Tudor and Jacobean Portraits*, 2 vols (London, 1969), i, 85.

[27] *An Inventory of the Historical Monuments in London I: Westminster Abbey* (London, 1924), 30:

Hic decus anglorum, flos regum pretitorum,
Forma futurorum, rex clemens, pax populorum,
Tertius Edwardus, regni complens jubileum.
Invictus pardus, bellis pollens Machabeum.
Prospere dum vixit, regnum probitate revixit.
Armipotens rexit; jam cello celice rex sit.

[28] R. Fabyan, *The New Chronicles of England and France*, ed. H. Ellis (London, 1811), 487–8.

commissioned the two epitaphs as a complementary pair. Against Edward's record as the new Maccabeus, Richard presented himself as the new Homer; to Edward's instinctive generosity and mercy he countered with the qualities of prudence or wisdom; and for Edward's liberality Richard substituted the proper rigours of the law.[29] If Edward III's monarchy was indeed acknowledged as a model for the future, then Richard II's instinct was much more obviously to cast his grandfather as the epitome of an older tradition of rule now superseded by his own supposedly more sophisticated *politique*. Time would tell which vision of kingship might yet prevail.

Far from releasing the crown from the captivity of ill governance, the death of Edward III was widely held to be the precipitant of a still more ominous threat to the integrity of the realm of England. For fifty years, Edward had provided a focus of unity and a sense of permanence in a fickle and fast-changing world. Now, that certainty was lost. The continued threat of attack from France and the problem of establishing a viable regime for the minority of Richard II caused many to believe that no remedy would be forthcoming. After attending the rapidly organized coronation of Richard II on 16 July, the lords and prelates of the realm sat down to address the formidable challenge of minority.[30] The idea of a regency on the model of 1216 was rapidly abandoned, just as it had been in 1327. Instead, the decision was taken to set up another continual council representative of the principal estates of the realm – bishops, earls, barons, bannerets and knights – which would ensure that all actions undertaken in the name of the youthful monarch were properly directed and vetted according to the principles of counsel and consent.

In essence, this device was no more than an elaborate form of the councils set up in the parliaments of 1327 and 1376 to guarantee the custody of Edward III's regime during his nonage and dotage. But there was one very important difference. In 1327 and 1376 Edward III's council had either included, or been explicitly instructed, to work with the senior members of the royal family. In 1377, by contrast, Richard II's continual council omitted Gaunt and his brothers, admitted Lancaster's supposed adversary the earl of March as its leading member, and accommodated in its lower ranks a strong representation from the household of the Black Prince. If none of this was intended to deprive Gaunt of de facto presidency of the

---

[29] *Inventory of Historical Monuments: Westminster Abbey*, 29, 31; Saul, *Richard II*, 357. The epitaph of the Black Prince at Canterbury was quite different, for it did not mention the deceased and merely commented on the transitory nature of life. In fact, it was taken verbatim from a text in wide circulation in fourteenth-century England. D. B. Tyson, 'The Epitaph of Edward the Black Prince', *Medium Ævum*, xlvi (1977), 98–104.

[30] N. B. Lewis, 'The "Continual Council" in the Early Years of Richard II, 1377–80', *EHR*, xli (1926), 246–51.

informal regency, it did give the impression that the lords were intent on squeezing the duke out of politics and bred further rumours that the king's uncle might seek, in his pique, to confound the regime and take the throne for himself.

Nor did the new council's well-intended measures to distance itself from the factions of Edward III's court go very far to placate the polity. William Wykeham received a belated pardon for his recent offences against the crown and Peter de la Mare was quickly released from prison, returning to London to be proclaimed a kind of Becket of the people.[31] But at the first parliament of the new reign, the provincial elites quickly made known their dissatisfaction with the recent record of government. A large number of those who had sat in the Good Parliament were returned to the Westminster assembly of October 1377. In an excitement of anticipation, the commons once more selected de la Mare as their Speaker. They pressed for the take-up of the programme of reformist measures proposed during the crisis of 1376. They forced the removal from the continual council of the remaining members of Edward III's court, Sir Roger Beauchamp, Sir John Knyvet and the notorious Lord Latimer. And they required Gaunt to subject the now-vulnerable Alice Perrers to a show trial that finally deprived her of all the lands and goods that she had managed miraculously to retain throughout and beyond the last year of her lover's reign.[32]

This last action, in particular, provided much-needed proof of the new regime's commitment to the eradication of the evil forces that had surrounded the dying Edward III. In spite of the subsequent success of William Windsor in recovering possession of a large portion of the Perrers estate, Alice's public career was effectively over after 1377. With it, very obviously, went any hope that her son might be able to transcend the disabilities of illegitimacy and establish himself as an independent political force. In 1380 Mary Percy was to file for divorce from John Southray on the grounds that Alice had cajoled her unwillingly into marriage and that her husband, as she so strikingly put it, was a man of ignoble birth.[33] Edward III's bastard took refuge in military service to John of Gaunt and Edmund of Langley but disappears from records after 1383 and is presumed to have died while still only in his early twenties. Alice herself, widowed in 1384, continued a vigorous campaign for the recovery of her property, which was taken up in due course by her surviving daughter, Joan Skerne. But any hope that the discredited Perrers clan might regain

[31] St Albans, i, 130–1.

[32] Ibid., i, 168–71; N. B. Lewis, 'Re-election to Parliament in the Reign of Richard II', EHR, xlviii (1933), 380–5; Ormrod, 'Trials of Alice Perrers', 375–9.

[33] M. Aston, Thomas Arundel: A Study of Church Life in the Reign of Richard II (Oxford, 1967), 44.

admittance to the charmed circle of royal and aristocratic society had long
since evaporated when Alice eventually died, still ranting against her
enemies, in the winter of 1400–1.[34]

Despite the well-timed victimization of Alice Perrers, the reputation of
Richard II's early regime rapidly foundered on that other great impediment to political stability, the war. The decision of the royal uncles and
other nobles to re-commit to the military and diplomatic agenda of 1369
meant that much of the energy of the crown was diverted into a faltering
sequence of campaigns and truces. The duke of Lancaster tried to impress
upon a disillusioned elite the benefits of a so-called 'barbican policy',
which aimed to create a string of bastions around the north and west coast
of France and thus restore England's much-prized primacy at sea. But the
acquisition of the castles of Cherbourg and Brest, and the series of military expeditions that sought unsuccessfully to take further coastal positions
at Saint-Malo, Harfleur and Nantes, served only to escalate the costs of
the war and thus in turn to alienate significant portions of the English
population from its further prosecution.[35]

The culmination of this ruinous strategy came in the fateful decision of
the Northampton parliament of November 1380 to reinstate a flat-rate
poll tax on the model of 1377. The raising of the standard contribution to
a rate of 1 shilling a head meant that the more affluent members of village
communities were no longer able to subsidize their poorer neighbours
without greatly prejudicing their own livelihoods. In June 1381 various
leaders of peasant communities and associated hotheads in Essex and
Kent took matters into their own hands, mustered large numbers of disaffected leaseholders and labourers, and marched on London. Beginning as
a tax strike, the Peasants' Revolt rapidly exploded into a full-scale condemnation of the economic, social and legal disabilities to which the lower
orders had become prey during the difficult decade of the 1370s.

In the face of this unprecedented crisis of authority, the fourteen-year-
old Richard II somehow managed to navigate a route that won at least the
initial admiration both of the rebels and of the establishment. But in the
great public soul-searching that followed the revolt, the crown revealed
itself unable to find any real solutions to corruption in high places, to fiscal
reform, or to the restoration of a harmonious social order. The landed
classes were now deeply divided between those who argued for renewed
efforts to punish the laziness and presumption of the peasantry and those
who felt that the only answer was a radical programme of social and
economic reconstruction. But in the absence of strong leadership from
on high, the polity gradually retreated into a resigned and resentful

[34] Given-Wilson and Curteis, *Royal Bastards*, 136–42; Ormrod, 'Trials of Alice Perrers',
366, 388–92.
[35] *PROME*, vi, 78–9; Jones, *Ducal Brittany*, 84–5; Sherborne, *War, Politics*, 66–9.

conservatism.[36] Langland altered his depiction of the political system of England in his C-text of *Piers Plowman*, written shortly after 1381, to suppress any notion that the king exercised sovereignty as the gift of the common people of the realm.[37] And Chaucer represented the legacy of 1381 as a cacophonous *Parliament of Fowls* in which rational argument had been drowned out by the anarchic screeches of the lower orders: 'Kek, kek! Kokkow! quek quek!'[38]

It was in this febrile atmosphere that contemporaries began, predictably enough, to seek imaginative refuge in the notion of a lost golden age during the ascendancy of Edward III. In the century after 1377 there developed a lively tradition that imbued Edward with all the attributes of greatness and represented his regime as the epitome of beneficent monarchy. Not surprisingly, this posthumous cult rested firmly on the military achievements of the reign. The representation of Edward in his tomb inscription as *invictus pardus*, the 'unconquered leopard', played on the convenient fact that none of the campaigns led in person by this great monarch had suffered open defeat. Walsingham proclaimed the deceased king's record in similar terms: 'In all his battle encounters, by land or sea, he always triumphantly and gloriously gained the victory.'[39] This statement, and the full-length encomium of which it was part, found their way into a number of other histories, including two of the most widely circulated English-language chronicles of the late fourteenth century, the translation and continuation of Ranulph Higden's *Polychronicon* and the English prose *Brut*.[40] The posthumous cult of Edward III had indeed got off to a swift and resounding start.

The emphasis on martial values was, of course, to have very obvious and fresh relevance when, in 1415, Henry V set about reviving his ancestor's claims on the continent and once more engaged in full-scale war with France.[41] In the euphoria that surrounded the early victories at Harfleur and Agincourt, the deeds of Edward III and the Black Prince were inevitably much in mind. In the parliament of 1416, for example, Chancellor Beaufort represented the battle of Agincourt as the latest in the great sequence of victories, begun at Sluys in 1340 and continued at Poitiers in 1356, whereby God had shown His favour to the chosen people of England.[42] Such vivid

---

[36] A. Tuck, 'Nobles, Commons and the Great Revolt of 1381', *English Rising of 1381*, ed. Hilton and Aston, 194–212; W. M. Ormrod, 'The Peasants' Revolt and the Government of England', *JBS*, xxix (1990), 1–30.

[37] A. P. Baldwin, *The Theme of Government in Piers Plowman* (Cambridge, 1981), 12–13.

[38] Chaucer, *Riverside Chaucer*, 392 (ll. 498–9); D. Aers, '*Vox populi* and the Literature of 1381', *Cambridge History of Medieval English Literature*, ed. Wallace, 439–51.

[39] *St Albans*, i, 988–9.

[40] *Westminster Chronicle*, xviii–xix; *Brut*, ii, 333–4.

[41] V. J. Scattergood, *Politics and Poetry in the Fifteenth Century* (London, 1971), 49–50.

[42] *Gesta Henrici Quinti: The Deeds of Henry the Fifth*, ed. F. Taylor and J. S. Roskell (Oxford, 1975), 122–5; *PROME*, ix, 132, 135–6.

memories of Edward's great victories were scarcely dimmed by the subsequent collapse of Henry V's dream of conquest and colonization in France. On the final withdrawal from Normandy and Gascony in the 1450s, English chivalry found at least some salve for its wounded pride in the idea that the descendants of Edward III, while losing the war, had always won its major battles. Noting with relief the coincidence of the birthplaces of Edward III and Henry VI, aficionados of the art of prophecy evoked the image of the boar of Windsor in a flight of wishful thinking that cast Henry VI and his son, the prophetically named Edward, as truly worthy successors to their strenuous forebears.[43]

Much the same was expected, and with rather better reason, of Henry's usurper, Edward IV. Tracing his claim to the throne by descent through both Lionel of Antwerp and Edmund of Langley, Edward very consciously set out to emulate the achievements and exploit the memory of his fourteenth-century ancestor and namesake.[44] His rebuilding of the Garter chapel at St George's, Windsor, was but one in a series of public acts affirming commitment to the personal and political style of Edward III. It was in Edward IV's reign that intellectuals began to construct astrological charts of former kings to exemplify the personal qualities they had brought to their office. Conveniently deciding that Edward III had been born at the propitious moment of dawn on 13 November 1312, the astrologers were able to demonstrate the overwhelming dominance of Mars and the benign influence of Fortune on the former king's life and deeds.[45] When Edward IV and, later, Henry VIII attempted symbolically to reopen the Hundred Years War and launch attacks on France, they therefore did so explicitly on the model of Edward III's *chevauchées* of 1346–7 and 1359–60 and on the basis of the dynastic rights that those expeditions had purported to prove.[46] A surviving Latin lament on the death of Edward IV, which confidently announces his achievement in subduing the Scots and making the French bend to his will, demonstrates

---

[43] Coote, *Prophecy*, 205–7.

[44] A. Allan, 'Yorkist Propaganda: Pedigree, Prophecy and the "British History" in the Reign of Edward IV', *Patronage, Pedigree and Power in Later Medieval England*, ed. C. Ross (Gloucester, 1979), 171–92; Morgan, 'Political After-life', 856–81.

[45] BL, MS Royal 12 F. XVII, fols 153–153v, discussed by Carey, *Courting Disaster*, 119–25; H. Wayment, 'The Medieval Stained Glass', *A History of the Stained Glass of St George's Chapel, Windsor Castle*, ed. S. Brown (Windsor, 2005), 57 and fig. 51.

[46] J. R. Lander, *Crown and Nobility, 1450–1509* (London, 1976), 220–41; C. S. L. Davies, 'Henry VIII and Henry V: The Wars in France', *The End of the Middle Ages? England in the Fifteenth and Sixteenth Centuries*, ed. J. L. Watts (Stroud, 1998), 235–62. In 1515 Sir Robert Wingfield, Henry VIII's ambassador to the imperial court, informed Thomas Wolsey that he was pressing the king's claims to France, 'which and it had not been perfect and good it is not to be esteemed that so wise a prince [as Edward III] would have wilfully put [the duchy of Aquitaine] in peril . . ., and beside that make war with so mighty a realm as France': *Letters and Papers, Foreign and Domestic, of the Reign of Henry VIII*, 21 vols (London, 1864–1932), II.i, no. 1265.

just how far the identities of Edward III and the Black Prince had now become bound up in that of England's first Yorkist king.[47] It was only with the final withdrawal of the English regime from Calais in 1558 that the Tudor history machine began, very tentatively, to admit that Edward III's wars in France might in fact have been damaging to the interests of the English state and thus to find some justification for the otherwise abject humiliation brought about at the end of two hundred years of conflict with the Valois.[48]

The mythology of Edward III that was emerging in the fifteenth century thus rested solidly and enduringly on his martial prowess. But it was far from restricted by it. By 1400 there was already a parallel tradition that Edward's wars had sustained a benign policy in which production and trade had flourished and the realm had achieved untold prosperity. In 1429 the parliamentary commons looked back with nostalgia to a time in Edward's reign when the wool farmers and cloth-workers of England could command top prices for their products on the international market and when exotic spices and fine wines imported from the continent, Africa and the Orient could be had in England at bargain-basement prices.[49] The *Libelle of Englyshe Polycye*, a polemic composed in *c*.1435–6 to promote the principle of English trade in English hands, cast Edward III as a veritable hero of commerce who had promoted shipping, won Calais, kept open the seas, taken guarantees for the good behaviour of foreign traders and 'loved [his English merchants] heartily'.[50] So enduring were such traditions that when, from the sixteenth century, commentators began to attempt to develop a statistical approach to the issue of the balance of trade, they chose as their crucial historical benchmark the *annus mirabilis* immediately following the issue of the Ordinance of the Staple in 1353. By 1700 Edward III was thus ironically but firmly established in the minds of many of its proponents as the true originator, *avant la lettre*, of the doctrine of mercantilism.[51]

To this facet of the Edwardian achievement were added still others. Edward's reputation as a monarch just and merciful in his dealings with

[47] A. F. Sutton, L. Visser-Fuchs and R. A. Griffiths, *The Royal Funerals of the House of York at Windsor* (London, 2005), 90–2.

[48] M. Aston, 'Richard II and the Wars of the Roses', *The Reign of Richard II: Essays in Honour of May McKisack*, ed. F. R. H. Du Boulay and C. M. Barron (London, 1971), 314–15.

[49] *PROME*, x, 430.

[50] *The Libelle of Englyshe Polycye: A Poem on the Use of Sea Power, 1436*, ed. G. Warner (Oxford, 1926), 10 (ll. 186–9), 13 (ll. 240–5), 50–1 (ll. 980–1009).

[51] E. Misselden, *The Circle of Commerce: or, The Balance of Trade* (London, 1623), 116, 119–22, 127–30; D. C. Coleman, 'Mercantilism Revisited', *Historical Journal*, xxiii (1980), 781–2; P. Slack, 'Government and Information in Seventeenth-Century England', *Past and Present*, clxxxiv (2004), 40–1, 51–2. Because of a misunderstanding over the dating of the financial year under Edward III, these calculations in fact drew down the figures for 1354–5: Ormrod, 'English Crown and the Customs', 39–40.

all his subjects, great and small, was sentimentalized in the century
following his death in such ballads as *King Edward and the Shepherd*, *King
Edward and the Hermit*, and the *Gest of Robin Hood*, where Edward 'our
comely king' takes on the role of peacemaker by recognizing the essential
goodness of criminal outlaws and restoring them to his grace and
service.[52] The idea that Edward perfected the balance between the rigours
of the law and the need to reconcile recidivist elements to the king's peace
was also kept alive by the regular resort of fifteenth-century monarchs to
his important precedent of granting general pardons.[53] Edward IV's
accession prompted many calls for the emulation of this and other
domestic policies of the king's esteemed namesake. A remarkable petition
dating from the long parliament of 1472–5 captures a vivid and rounded
memory of Edward of Windsor, 'this noble prince, this princely knight,
this knightly conqueror so loved', in whose days 'God [was] obeyed, the
course and recourse of merchandise [was] justly kept, and the order of the
law [was] duly observed'.[54]

This same sense of perfection also rendered Edward III immune from
the obvious criticism that, by having too many sons, he had in some way
been responsible for the Wars of the Roses. Henry VIII, that most dynas-
tically minded of rulers, saw Edward's great quiverful of boy children as
an unmitigated blessing, and decorated the gatehouse of his new foundation of Trinity College, Cambridge, built on the site of the King's Hall,
with the arms of all six of Edward's then known male offspring.[55] Nor did
the generation of the Virgin Queen easily admit that the rivalry between
the houses of Lancaster and York might be traced back to Edward's family
policy.[56] Shakespeare emphatically saw the Wars of the Roses as arising
directly from the deposition of Richard II. The recent discovery that the
anonymous history play *The Reign of King Edward III*, first published in
1596, flowed in full or in part from Shakespeare's pen does not mean that
the bard intended to incorporate Edward into the cycle that began with
Richard II and ended with *Richard III*. Instead, the play seems to stand
alone, offering its original audience a rendition of the newly established

---

[52] A. J. Pollard, *Imagining Robin Hood* (London, 2004), 200–4.

[53] R. L. Storey, *The End of the House of Lancaster*, new edn (Gloucester, 1986), 210–16; E.
Powell, *Kingship, Law, and Society: Criminal Justice in the Reign of Henry V* (Oxford, 1989), 125,
134–6, 187–9, 190–1, 229–32.

[54] WAM, 12235, printed in Morgan, 'Political After-life', 873 (spelling modernized).

[55] C. Carpenter, *The Wars of the Roses: Politics and the Constitution, c.1437–1509* (Cambridge,
1997), 9 and n. 8.

[56] Aston, 'Richard II', 288 and n. 16; K. Dockray, 'The Origins of the Wars of the
Roses', *The Wars of the Roses*, ed. A. J. Pollard (Basingstoke, 1995), 72–3. At the time of Mary
I's marriage to Philip II of Spain the crown had sought to emphasize the latter's descent
from Edward III as a means of placating public nervousness: S. Anglo, *Spectacle, Pageantry
and Early Tudor Policy* (Oxford, 1969), 92; J. Loach, 'The Marian Establishment and the
Printing Press', *EHR*, ci (1986), 144.

mythology surrounding the creation of the Order of the Garter and – to the obvious satisfaction of the groundlings – a great sequence of heroic battle scenes comparable to those found in the better-known action adventure, *Henry V*.[57]

Above all, it was the qualities of statesmanship attributed to Edward III by his posthumous encomiasts that ensured him a lasting place in the pantheon of English monarchy. By the end of his life, Edward was already firmly cast as the classical model of a king who governed not for his own ambitions but for the common good. 'To live under him was to reign', was Walsingham's fulsome judgement.[58] Later medieval assessments certainly admitted that the faction-fighting of the court during Edward's old age had seriously imperilled that happy state. In general, however, the growing nostalgia for the era of Crécy and Poitiers meant that Edward III was accorded, without further qualification, an unassailable position as the guarantor of harmonious, inclusive and participatory politics.[59] Confronted with the harsh realities of Tudor and Stuart masterfulness, political dissidents increasingly took the view that the reign had witnessed a veritable high point of constitutionalism.[60] In the 1628 controversies that generated the Petition of Right, Charles I's opponents put their trust in Magna Carta and the series of important confirmations, glosses and extensions issued by Edward III in the so-called 'six statutes' of 1331, 1352, 1354, 1362, 1363 and 1368. Edward Coke may have singled out Edward I as England's Justinian, but for those who sought to resist Charles I's tyranny it was Edward III and parliament who, by rescuing Magna Carta from oblivion, had most obviously perfected the liberties of freeborn Englishmen.[61]

Almost uniquely among medieval rulers, then, Edward III seemed readily adaptable to almost every political condition that arose in the three centuries that followed his death. Underpinning much of the establishment's trust in his example was the enduring importance attached to his great campaign of anti-papal legislation and his resulting position as the

[57] R. Proudfoot, '*The Reign of King Edward the Third* (1596) and Shakespeare', *Proceedings of the British Academy*, lxxi (1985), 159–85; *King Edward III*, ed. G. Melchiori (Cambridge, 1988); E. Slater, *The Problem of the Reign of King Edward III: A Statistical Approach* (Cambridge, 1988); *Shakespeare's Edward III: An Early Play Restored to the Canon*, ed. E. Sams (New Haven, 1996); T. Merriam, '*Edward III*', *Literary and Linguistic Computing*, xv (2000), 157–86. The play was revived as part of the Shakespearean apocrypha in 1986–7; with the development of arguments in favour of authenticity in the 1990s, the Royal Shakespeare Company put on its first production of the play in London in 2002.

[58] *St Albans*, i, 988–9.

[59] E.g., *Political Poems*, i, 215–18.

[60] G. L. Harriss, 'Medieval Doctrines in the Debates on Supply, 1610–1629', *Faction and Parliament: Essays on Early Stuart History*, ed. K. Sharpe (London, 1978), 73–103.

[61] F. Thomson, *Magna Carta: Its Role in the Making of the English Constitution, 1300–1629* (Minneapolis, 1948), 86–97, 326–35.

instigator of the sovereignty later asserted over the English Church by Henry VIII.[62] The slender evidence of his employment of John Wyclif was taken as ready proof by the Anglican ascendancy of the sixteenth to eighteenth century that Edward III must indeed have been a proto-Protestant.[63] In a monolithic culture that allowed so little space for devotional or intellectual diversity, it was comparatively easy to maintain such ill-informed notions. Towards the end of the seventeenth century a much more rigorous form of historical scholarship began to apply itself to the reign: Elias Ashmole's *Institution, Laws and Ceremonies of the Most Noble Order of the Garter* (1672) and Joshua Barnes's *History of that Most Victorious Monarch Edward III* (1688) were impressive feats of research and came to stand, for two centuries and more, as essential points of reference for those engaged in wider narratives of the island story. Yet not even Barnes could resist the hyperbolic mode, proclaiming Edward in his final sentences as 'the best king, the best captain, the best lawgiver, the best friend, the best father and the best husband in his days'.[64]

For all the interest shown by elite cultures of the fifteenth to the seventeenth century in the achievements of an ascendant Edward the Great, it was in the time of George III and the young Victoria that the cult may be said to have reached its true apotheosis. The new Gothic craze in art, architecture and literature focused attention on the royal heroes of England's medieval past. It also caused a re-evaluation and reapplication of the principles of chivalry. At Windsor castle George III remodelled the royal apartments, commissioned Benjamin West to create a cycle of historical paintings based on the exploits of Edward III and the Black Prince, and developed a set of consciously archaic ceremonies around Edward's prestigious foundation, the Order of the Garter. More significantly still, George encouraged polite and bourgeois society to associate with the values of personal honour and national pride that he saw as attributes of the fourteenth century and to absorb these into the newly emerging culture of Britishness.[65] The elevation of the Black Prince to near-equal status with his father provided two princes of Wales, George II's son Frederick and the later George IV, with valuable precedents in support of their own demands for a greater say in politics and government. Increasingly, too, Edward of Woodstock's imagined role as champion of the commons in 1376 turned

---

[62] J. W. McKenna, 'How God became an Englishman', *Tudor Rule and Revolution: Essays for G. R. Elton from his American Friends*, ed. D. J. Guth and J. W. McKenna (Cambridge 1982), 25–43.

[63] Aston, 'Richard II', 292–300; A. Hudson, *Lollards and their Books* (London, 1985), 247–8.

[64] Barnes, *Edward III*, 911.

[65] M. Girouard, *The Return to Camelot: Chivalry and the English Gentleman* (London, 1981), 21–6; L. Colley, 'The Apotheosis of George III: Loyalty, Royalty and the British Nation, 1760–1820', *Past and Present*, cii (1984), 94–129; W. Greenhouse, 'Benjamin West and Edward III: A Neoclassical Painter and Medieval History', *Art History*, viii (1985), 178–91; L. Colley, *Britons: Forging the Nation, 1707–1837* (London, 1994), 212–17.

him into a political hero of almost equivalent stature to the supposed founder of parliament, Simon de Montfort.[66]

After Queen Victoria's marriage to Albert of Saxe-Coburg, the potent mythology of Edward III's domesticity and dynasticism proved an equally inescapable lure both for the court and for the emergent middle classes. In 1842, the young royal couple dressed as Philippa of Hainault and Edward III for the great fancy-dress ball that they hosted at Buckingham Palace, their picture of marital bliss preserved in a portrait subsequently painted by Sir Edwin Landseer. A year later, in the open competition to design the decorative scheme for the House of Lords in the recently rebuilt Palace of Westminster, the trio of Edward III, Philippa of Hainault and the Black Prince featured prominently among the submitted cartoons, and Charles Cope won a commission to produce a large fresco of *Edward the Black Prince Receiving the Order of the Garter from Edward III*. The distinguished antiquary Sir Nicholas Harris Nicolas complained bitterly, on the basis of his recent researches in the Public Records, that the Garter and its fellowship had not been instituted in the manner being depicted by Cope. The controversy was deemed of sufficient importance to be referred all the way up to the Prime Minister, Robert Peel. After careful thought, however, Peel seems to have judged it too much bother to change the subject at such a late stage. Not for the first or last time in the posthumous history of Edward III, strict historical veracity was conveniently subordinated to a combination of the political, the pragmatic and the picturesque.[67]

It was inevitable that such time-honoured orthodoxies should be challenged by the onward march of history. Even before the new breed of professional historians turned their scientific method to the fourteenth century, gentlemen-scholars of the mid-Victorian era began to question Edward's claims to greatness. William Longman's *Life and Times of Edward the Third* of 1869, the first full-scale biography to be published in two hundred years, concluded in a manner reflecting its author's progressive views that the gallantry of Edward III and the Black Prince was simply not sufficient to compensate either for the sheer brutality of their military methods or for their selfish disregard of the interests of their subjects.[68] In similar vein, William Stubbs's *Constitutional History of England*, first published in the 1870s and the essential text for all university-trained

[66] B. L. Gribling, 'Nationalizing the Hero: The Image of Edward the Black Prince in English Politics and Culture, 1776–1903' (University of York PhD thesis, 2009), 66–84, 193–224, 251–9.

[67] Ibid., 290–328.

[68] W. Longman, *The History of the Life and Times of Edward the Third*, 2 vols (London, 1869), ii, 297–8. See also W. Warburton, *Edward III* (London, 1875); J. Mackinnon, *The History of Edward III (1327–1377)* (London, 1900).

historians over the following seventy years, denounced Edward as 'ambitious, unscrupulous, selfish, extravagant, and ostentatious'. For Stubbs, the only compensation of the 'long and tedious reign' was that it served the purposes of democracy by establishing parliament, once and for all, as an essential element of the constitutional structure of the realm.[69] It was left to Stubbs's younger Oxford colleague, Charles Plummer, to deliver the final blow. Edward's reign, Plummer claimed, had marked the beginning of 'bastard feudalism', the term he so fatefully coined to describe the contractual relationship between great lords and their affinities and which he believed to have fundamentally hobbled the authority of the late medieval crown. At one stroke, Edward was exposed as the inventor of the 'over-mighty subject', the nobleman with the resources and pretensions to be king. It was Edward's famed liberality that had thus set England hurtling down the path to civil war in the fifteenth century.[70]

The legacy of these attacks was enormous. While English and North American scholarship went on in the 1920s and 1930s to invest great energy in the constitutional and administrative history of the fourteenth century, the personal reputation of Edward III remained in the deepest doldrums. In 1937 the influential constitutional historian Bertie Wilkinson could bring himself only so far as to dub Edward's *politique* 'clever opportunism'.[71] The real low point came, however, when the king was openly denounced by those whose views he might be thought most to have respected: the military strategists. Assuming that Edward's *chevauchées*, if they had any real purpose at all, were intended as an alternative to battle, Sir Charles Oman and others argued that even the great set piece of Crécy was no more than a magnificent accident in which the king defied all the principles of high command to pluck a lucky victory from the near-inevitability of defeat.[72] Such scathing attacks no doubt explain why no biography of the king was published in the entire first half of the twentieth century. The fact that this was the time of some of the greatest popular and academic interest in the hero of Agincourt, Henry V, simply accentuates the reversal of fortunes that Edward III's reputation suffered in the era of the two world wars.[73]

---

[69] Stubbs, *Constitutional History*, ii, 393–4.

[70] J. Fortescue, *The Governance of England*, ed. C. Plummer (Oxford, 1885), 15–16; McFarlane, *England in the Fifteenth Century*, 23–43; J. Fortescue, *On the Laws and Governance of England*, ed. S. Lockwood (Cambridge, 1997), xvi–xviii; Carpenter, *Wars of the Roses*, 8–10.

[71] B. Wilkinson, *Studies in the Constitutional History of the Thirteenth and Fourteenth Centuries*, 2nd edn (Manchester, 1952), 167.

[72] See the critical discussion of these views by C. J. Rogers, 'Edward III and the Dialectics of Strategy, 1327–1360', *TRHS*, 6th series, iv (1994), 83–4.

[73] J. H. Wylie and W. T. Waugh, *The Reign of Henry the Fifth*, 3 vols (Cambridge, 1914–29); E. F. Jacob, *Henry V and the Invasion of France* (London, 1947); A. Curry, *The Battle of Agincourt: Sources and Interpretations* (Woodbridge, 2000), 1–8, 370–405.

In the second half of the twentieth century, the charismatic historian K. B. McFarlane and his disciples gradually but inexorably tore down the Stubbsian paradigm. They produced a new model of medieval monarchy that was less inclined to judge the past in relation to modern bourgeois values and much more readily admitted the logistical and conceptual limitations acting upon the exercise of authority in the Middle Ages. On the scale of the possible, Edward was acknowledged to have done rather well. Historians particularly acknowledged his success in restoring the power and prestige of the monarchy after the ruinous civil strife of the 1320s. May McKisack, who did more than any other twentieth-century historian to rehabilitate Edward, represented him as a king with a keen awareness of the responsibilities of his office and one who, within the perhaps rather limited reach of his intellect, did his best to promote and perpetuate political harmony in the realm. McKisack and her contemporaries set particular store by this last achievement and noted with satisfaction the absence of any act of armed rebellion against the crown, either aristocratic or popular, for two whole generations between 1330 and 1380. Such a dispensation, unparalleled in duration since the Norman Conquest or again until the eighteenth century, set Edward's example apart even from the other great models of successful kingship of the later Middle Ages: Henry II, Edward I and Henry V. For the generation of the 1960s, Edward III's legacy was, above all, that of peace.[74]

This assessment contained a hollow irony, for there remained the undeniable fact that Edward's domestic policy had been so obviously subordinated to the pursuit of military glory. In the face of a great explosion of new scholarship on the history of the Hundred Years War, it was – and, in many respects, still is – difficult to avoid the uncomfortable conclusion that Edward III set England on course for disaster by engaging her not just in one but in three unwinnable wars: in France, in Scotland and in Castile. This great conundrum – the 'tragic dilemma', as A. R. Myers called it in 1952 – accounts in significant ways for the continuing reluctance of academic historians in the 1960s and 1970s to engage in personal studies of Edward III.[75] Whereas the sixth hundredth anniversary of the Black Prince's death in 1976 prompted the publication of two well-informed biographies of Edward of Woodstock,[76] no one thought to mark the

---

[74] McKisack, *Fourteenth Century*, 270–1; M. McKisack, 'Edward III and the Historians', *History*, xlv (1960), 1–15. For the influence of McKisack's work on later generations see the various summaries of the Edwardian achievement by Prestwich, *Three Edwards*, 238–44; Ormrod, 'Edward III and the Recovery of Royal Authority', 4–19; Ormrod, *Reign of Edward III*, 200–3; Waugh, *England in the Reign of Edward III*, 230–6; Mortimer, *Perfect King*, 392–402.

[75] A. R. Myers, *England in the Later Middle Ages*, 8th edn (Harmondsworth, 1971), 15–36. For Myers's attempt to write a biography of Edward III in the 1970s see p. x.

[76] Barber, *Edward, Prince of Wales*; B. Emmerson, *The Black Prince* (London, 1976); J. H. Harvey, *The Black Prince and his Age* (London, 1976).

equivalent anniversary of Edward III in the following year. The three popular books on Edward published between 1973 and 1992 were entirely devoid of originality, and it was only as recently as 2006 that Ian Mortimer finally produced a fitting successor to Joshua Barnes's study in his ambitious, stimulating and sometimes over-dramatized biography, tellingly titled *The Perfect King*.[77]

In spite of such ambivalence, new directions in medieval history since the 1980s have reinforced the significance of Edward III's reign as a pivotal point in the history of the English crown and state. Three great historical processes are now seen to have reached their culmination in this period. The first – and the one in which Edward might most readily have had a guiding hand – was the phenomenon now sometimes labelled the 'medieval military revolution'. The change of battle tactics to a defensive mode of fighting, originating under Edward I and reaching its perfection at Halidon Hill and Crécy, had implications far beyond the battlefield. In order to provide and equip the small, mobile and increasingly professionalized forces favoured for campaigns in France, the crown abandoned systems of direct recruitment and supply and instead relied on private contracts with military captains and merchant capitalists. The accompanying fiscal revolution, with its great shift away from direct and towards indirect taxation, came close to making the English war state a genuinely sustainable enterprise. Most notably, the practices and values of chivalry were revived to create a strong sense of shared identity among the nobility and gentry, the classes from which most men-at-arms, and an increasing number of mounted archers, sprang. Edward III's enthusiasm for the knightly ideal thus appears in revisionist thinking not as some refuge of fantasy but as a truly dynamic force in the military success and political stability of mid-fourteenth-century England.[78]

The second historical process understood to have reached its culmination under Edward III is the growth of a broad-based consensual politics. Until the reign of Edward II the crown had treated the emerging institution of parliament mainly as a talking-shop for barons and bishops, and it was only in the mid-1320s that the commons began consistently to assert an independent political voice. The efforts of Edward III to engage the commons, demonstrated in striking manner in the parliament of 1327, quickly established both the tone and the substance of a new

[77] P. Johnson, *The Life and Times of Edward III* (London, 1973); M. Packe, *King Edward III* (London, 1983); B. Bevan, *Edward III: Monarch of Chivalry* (London, 1992).
[78] C. J. Rogers, 'The Military Revolutions of the Hundred Years' War', *Journal of Military History*, lvii (1993), 241–78; M. Prestwich, 'Was there a Military Revolution in Medieval England?', *Recognitions: Essays Presented to Edmund Fryde*, ed. C. Richmond and I. Harvey (Aberystwyth, 1996), 19–38; A. Ayton and J. L. Price, 'Introduction: The Military Revolution from a Medieval Perspective', *Medieval Military Revolution*, ed. Ayton and Price, 1–22; A. Ayton, 'Armies and Military Communities in Fourteenth-Century England', *Soldiers, Nobles*, ed. Coss and Tyerman, 215–39.

politics.[79] In the 1340s the Oxford clerk Walter Burley argued that England was a perfect example of Aristotle's notion of mixed monarchy, the sharing of rule between king and people, and for the first time in scholastic writing specified that the institution of parliament was the essential guarantee of the principles of good governance.[80] Burley was the apologist of a system, not of a king: had he an eye to recent events, he might well have shared the outrage at Edward's recent record of bad faith and bullying in the parliaments of 1340–1. In the end, however, the tradition of mixed government prevailed. Unlike other fourteenth-century rulers in France and Iberia, Edward III showed no inclination to use the emergency of war as an excuse for overriding the conventions of consent. Instead, he and his ministers actively sought to engage the commons in the process of reform, in a manner that at once pandered to their prejudices and ameliorated some of the more divisive aspects of their social and economic programme. Even those historians who regard Edward as rather too ready to give up the initiative in return for a quiet life now freely acknowledge the considerable creative power of this partnership.[81] It was under Edward III that parliament first began to refer to its business as being undertaken for 'the common profit of the king and the kingdom'. In so doing, it adopted those principles that, over the following two centuries, would come to form the better-known discourse of the commonweal.[82]

The third of the long-term processes understood to have reached fulfilment in Edward III's reign is the development of a new accommodation between crown and aristocracy. Recent close work on Edward III's relations with the peerage has confirmed McFarlane's general sense that the king's fabled indulgence of the nobility was in fact highly conditional in nature, imposing a heavy moral obligation on the elite to give unstinting

[79] M. Prestwich, 'Parliament and the Community of the Realm', *Parliament and Community*, ed. A. Cosgrove and J. I. McGuire (Belfast, 1983), 5–24; A. Harding, *England in the Thirteenth Century* (Cambridge, 1993), 217–19; J. R. Maddicott, *The Origins of the English Parliament, 924–1327* (Oxford, 2010), 359–66.

[80] S. H. Thomson, 'Walter Burley's Commentary on the *Politics* of Aristotle', *Mélanges Auguste Pelzer* (Louvain, 1947), 557–78; C. J. Nederman, 'Kings, Peers, and Parliament: Virtue and Corulership in Walter Burley's *Commentarius in VIII Libros Politicorum Aristotelis*', *Albion*, xxiv (1992), 391–407.

[81] E.g., M. H. Keen, *England in the Later Middle Ages: A Political History*, 2nd edn (London, 2003), 132–3.

[82] A. Harding, *Medieval Law and the Foundations of the State* (Oxford, 2002), 257–63; J. Watts, 'Public or Plebs: The Changing Meaning of "The Commons", 1381–1549', *Power and Identity in the Middle Ages: Essays in Memory of Rees Davies*, ed. H. Pryce and J. Watts (Oxford, 2007), 242–60; Ormrod, 'Good Parliament'; C. Fletcher, 'De La Communauté du royaume au *common weal*: Les requêtes anglaises et leurs stratégies au XIVᵉ siècle', *Revue française de l'histoire des idées politiques*, xxxi (2010), 359–72.

respect, loyalty and service to the crown.[83] A very similar point might be made about the gentry. The decision of Edward III's regime to delegate significant authority to the resident landholders in the shires, above all in their new role as justices of the peace, is still regarded by some as placing serious constraints on the crown's ability to regulate the ministerial classes and thus prevent an explosion of corruption and lawlessness in the provinces.[84] There are certainly reasons to suppose that the lower orders regarded the new-found authority of their employers as a direct challenge to their own economic well-being and sense of self-determination in the generation between the Black Death and the Peasants' Revolt.[85] But many historians are now inclined to see the longer-term process of judicial devolution as the essential mechanism by which the English monarchy harnessed the energies and aspirations of a wider polity in the service of an expanding state.[86] In this sense the effect of Edward III's judicial reforms was not to make justice either better or worse, but to increase the range of human activity over which it claimed jurisdiction and thus more fully to weave it into the social and economic fabric of the realm. This process was one of the most enduring legacies of the reign, establishing the tradition of the squire-magistracy that continued to dominate English rural society and local government in the seventeenth, eighteenth and even the nineteenth century.[87]

In light of such emphasis on the formative influences of Edward's reign, we may justifiably ask to what degree the achievements of the regime reflected the king's personal priorities. Medieval commentators would hardly, of course, have made the distinction: for them, the success or failure of a regime was itself very largely determined by the strength or weakness of a ruler's personality. For a modern audience, however, there is the key question of whether Edward entirely deserved the universal adulation accorded him within the realm and the almost equally over-

[83] McFarlane, *Nobility*, 156–63; J. S. Bothwell, 'Edward III and the "New Nobility": Largesse and Limitation in Fourteenth-Century England', *EHR*, cxii (1997), 1111–40; J. S. Bothwell, ' "Until he receive the equivalent in land and rent": The Use of Annuities as Endowment Patronage in the Reign of Edward III', *HR*, lxx (1997), 146–69; Bothwell, *Peerage*, 154–60.

[84] Kaeuper, *War, Justice, and Public Order*, 181–2.

[85] A. Harding, 'The Revolt against the Justices', *English Rising of 1381*, ed. Hilton and Aston, 165–93; A. Musson, *Medieval Law in Context: The Growth of Legal Consciousness from Magna Carta to the Peasants' Revolt* (Manchester, 2001), 241–55.

[86] Powell, *Kingship, Law*, 19–20; G. L. Harriss, 'Political Society and the Growth of Government in Late Medieval England', *Past and Present*, cxxxviii (1993), 28–57; Carpenter, *Wars of the Roses*, 47–66; Musson and Ormrod, *Evolution*, 42–74.

[87] G. L. Harriss, 'The Dimensions of Politics', *The McFarlane Legacy: Studies in Late Medieval Politics and Society*, ed. R. H. Britnell and A. J. Pollard (Stroud, 1995), 1–20; Palmer, *English Law*, 1–12; P. Coss, *The Origins of the English Gentry* (Cambridge, 2003), 239–54.

whelming respect paid him by his friends and enemies throughout the known medieval world.

To address this question is immediately to acknowledge that Edward was a relatively uncomplicated man of honest instincts and straightforward manner. This had both benefits and liabilities. Edward's greatest attribute was his sense of honour, which expressed itself in his commitment to the code of chivalry, his unflinching support of those loyal to his cause, his high moral sense of even-handedness and fairness, and his adherence to the abiding political principles of counsel and consent. Among his negative traits, we might particularly consider his rather limited intellect, his stubborness in accepting realities that did not accord with his own ambitions, and an exasperating belief that his mere fiat somehow made all things possible. If he had the great assets of natural charm and easy congeniality, he could also at times be petulant, wilful, vulgar and boorish. His attitude to religion, education and the arts was chiefly driven by the opportunities they offered for the adornment of his monarchy. While he had an innate belief in his own destiny, there is little indication that he was inclined to reflect on the deeper implications or repercussions of his ambitions. And although he proved to be one of England's most vigorous warrior-kings, he was ultimately too easily persuaded that the trappings of power could compensate for the mundane practicalities and hard grind of rule.

Such a frank acknowledgement of Edward's limitations does comparatively little, however, to detract from the fact that his character and ambitions remained absolutely at the heart of English royal policy for at least forty years. In assessing Edward's creative and dynamic contribution to the regime that bore his name, we are bound to begin with the relationships he forged within his family, his entourage and the wider courtly elite of the high nobility. As the product of a deeply dysfunctional marriage, Edward clearly set exceptional store by his emotional bonds with his wife and children. His marriage to Philippa of Hainault developed into a genuine partnership of trust and love that made a deep impression on their great brood of sons and daughters. Edward may have fallen short of creating adequate English titles and endowments for all his sons, but he refused to fall into the trap that befell so many other long-lived monarchs and leave his children with nothing to do. All five surviving boys, Edward, Lionel, John, Edmund and Thomas, were fully engaged as young teenagers in the military destiny that their father had designed for them. While younger members of the wider family circle, like the earls of Pembroke and March, took a more critical stance towards royal policy in the 1370s, the princes of the blood were far too heavily invested in the regime to do anything other than remain resolutely loyal to the cause through the successive crises of Edward's last illness and death. Nor, indeed, did that important unity break down easily once their father was no longer there. It was Richard II's gross mishandling of family relationships that caused Thomas of Woodstock and Gaunt's son,

Henry of Bolingbroke, to take on the mantle of loyal opposition in 1386. And it was only Richard's belated and quite unwarranted act of vengeance against his uncle and cousin after 1397 that caused the last surviving son of Edward III, Edmund of Langley, finally to defect from the faith of 1377 and to support the usurpation that in 1399 brought Henry IV to the throne of England.[88]

Edward III's ability to inspire the trust and loyalty of his sons extended, in a very obvious way, to his circle of friends in court and council. His early devotion to his mentor Richard Bury and his companion-in-arms William Montagu seems to have represented a very real need for a surrogate father and brother. The nature of the king's personal relationships inevitably changed as the friends of his youth began to die off and he retreated into a quieter and more private mode of living. But the constancy and tenacity of Edward's affections were rarely in doubt. Occasionally, of course, that could cause troubles of its own. Edward's perverse insistence on pursuing his extramarital relationship with Alice Perrers in the face of mounting political and financial scandal not only made a fool of the king but was a serious blot on his reputation for moderation and control in matters both personal and political. For the most part, however, Edward was blessed with the good fortune of being surrounded by men and women of real integrity, ability and substance. The long and loyal service he enjoyed from high aristocrats such as Henry of Grosmont, duke of Lancaster, Robert Ufford, earl of Suffolk, William Bohun, earl of Northampton, Thomas Beauchamp, earl of Warwick, Richard Fitzalan, earl of Arundel, Marie de Saint-Pol, dowager countess of Pembroke, and a host of other aristocratic supporters and friends over the long years of his reign provide abundant proof of the king's great gift of friendship and his ability to inspire not only respect but often deep-felt affection among the social elite of his day. The good judgement that he demonstrated in the selection and promotion of ministers of the stature of John Thoresby, William Edington and William Shareshull suggests that, at the height of his powers, Edward was capable of sustaining the loyalty of some of the most capable strategic minds of his day. If successful government and politics in the Middle Ages was all about making the very most of others' talents, then in the full maturity of his regime Edward III surely and abundantly exhibited many of the traits that his fellow Englishmen regarded as essential to true statesmanship.

Another quality that Edward's contemporaries are likely to have commended in their king was his natural glamour and his talent as a

---

[88] Goodman, *Loyal Conspiracy*, 74–104, 153–6; C. Given-Wilson, 'Richard II, Edward II, and the Lancastrian Inheritance', *EHR*, cix (1994), 553–74; D. L. Biggs, ' "A wrong whom conscience and kindred bid me to right": A Reassessment of Edmund of Langley, Duke of York, and the Usurpation of Henry IV', *Albion*, xxvi (1994), 253–72; D. L. Biggs, *Three Armies in Britain: The Irish Campaign of Richard II and the Usurpation of Henry IV, 1397–1399* (Leiden, 2006), 111–47, 237–60.

showman. That the young and middle-aged Edward had a winning personal style is hardly to be gainsaid; that he knew how to use it and adapt it to different audiences is, perhaps, still too little appreciated. For the friends and servants entertained at his great halls and Christmas courts, Edward was quick to identify as one of the boys, and even to set himself up as the butt of the occasional well-choreographed joke. In his more public parading through the streets of London to the great tournaments of Cheapside and Smithfield, he might use the conceit of costume and disguise to proclaim his devotion to team spirit and to heighten the excitement of the moment when he raised his visor and revealed himself in majesty. Equally, though, Edward knew the power of proper solemnity. In his engagements with foreign rulers and their envoys, his presidency of councils and parliaments, his performance of healing miracles and his observation of the public rituals surrounding the births, marriages and deaths of his fellow royals, the king showed his natural ability to command the dramaturgy of state. It was to extend the courtly cult of magnificence to a wider audience that he also concentrated so many of his resources on that monumental memorial to his kingship, Windsor castle. And in the jubilees of 1362 and 1377 Edward and his family, more explicitly than ever before, made a systematic effort to project the monarchy as a kind of alternative English religion. Finally, the persistent commitment to the itinerant lifestyle that continued to some degree until the mid-1360s allowed a surprisingly large number of his subjects at least a fleeting glimpse of the man remembered so fondly in folk memory as the good King Edward. For Edward III, style was not some arcane retreat from reality but an essential proof of his constant dedication to good kingship.

It was for much the same purpose, of course, that Edward emphatically and fatefully committed himself and his realm to the pursuit of war. It is hard to exaggerate the degree to which public attitudes to the great succession of campaigns in Scotland and France from the 1330s to the 1370s was informed, and transformed, by the personal example of the king. While the chroniclers no doubt sometimes exaggerated the point, Edward could surely have never kept his armies so long in the field and in such good order without a real talent for leadership that rested in a deep understanding of the capabilities of his men, a close and persistent attention to detail, the ability to respond to the unexpected, and an exceptional aptitude for inspiring loyalty and sustaining morale. If at Crécy in 1346 Edward kept a careful distance from the fighting, then the stories that circulated of his valour at Halidon Hill in 1333, his wounds at Sluys in 1340 and his personal bravery at the attempted betrayal of Calais in 1350 demonstrated vividly his firmness of purpose. And while he showed quite ruthless determination to make strategic capital from the conventions of ransom-taking, his gracious treatment of his great prisoners, above all of David II and John II, revealed him as the model of chivalric generosity and led the whole of Europe, friend and enemy alike, to hail him as a truly noble prince.

To say that Edward fulfilled magnificently the role of the valiant hero and martial monarch is not the same, of course, as saying that he always had a clear sense of the purpose and responsibilities of his actions in war. Throughout the campaigns of the 1330s and 1340s Edward maintained a coherent strategy based on the debilitating impact of the *chevauchée*, the forcing out of the enemy into pitched battle, and the famous defensive mode of fighting with the tactics of the mixed formation. Until the mid-1340s, too, the aims of such strategy were reasonably consistent: to establish a puppet monarchy in Scotland and to force Philip VI to cede back as much as possible of the Plantagenets' ancestral lands in France. After the great victories of 1346–7, however, there are signs that Edward's conviction in his invincibility compromised his ability to bring the war to a good end. By the 1360s Edward was left with the unenviable task of balancing four competing agendas: his genuine desire to find a lasting agreement with the Scots and the French; his tendency to fulfil only those parts of peace settlements that suited him; his increasing sense of obligation to his sons' ambitions for lands and titles in the British Isles and the principalities of France; and the strident demand of a proportion of the military elite that he should uphold his French title and thus deliver them their former conquests in his ancestors' ancient lordships of Normandy and greater Anjou. Edward must take major responsibility for failing sufficiently to control these competing forces and to manage public expectations of the possible. So also must he take the blame, at least until his withdrawal from active leadership after 1372, for the failure to find a true focus for the second French war. If Edward III went a very long way to achieving his aims in the 1340s and 1350s, then his most serious deficiency as man and monarch was his inability to hold the peace of the 1360s.

Beyond this uncomfortable conclusion remains Edward's undeniable and compelling ability to engage the hearts and minds of so many of his subjects, combatant and non-combatant alike, in the major military enterprises of the English crown. To suggest that Edward III was some kind of English chauvinist is obviously to ignore his strong attachment to the transnational cult of chivalry and to his Norman, Angevin and Capetian heritage. It is easy to suppose that his domestic propaganda, with its consistent emphasis on the interests of England, was but a disguise for the cynical decision to submit his subjects to the peril of war with foreign powers. Yet there is also good reason to argue that, just as he occasionally allowed himself from the mid-1340s to indulge in the fantasy of a conquest of France, so too did Edward genuinely believe that his war aims were compatible with the strategic, commercial and political interests of England. In the 1350s and 1360s Edward III strongly identified himself with the more jingoistic elements among his subjects by promoting the cults of King Arthur and St George, celebrating his release from the tyrannical suzerainty of Valois kings and pro-French popes, and enhancing the political and cultural authority of the English language. It is entirely plausible that, with his resolute determination to upstage his foreign rivals, Edward felt quite at home in these newly assumed trappings of Englishness. And if nationalism was never the dominant force in his psychological make-up, it may yet prove the one feature of Edward's performance of monarchy that allows us seriously to consider him for readmission to the ranks of the royal greats. Not since the Norman Conquest had the subjects of the English crown been able, so readily, to consider the king genuinely one of their own.

Edward III lived and reigned too long to allow any easy generalizations about his personality, career and reign. The Edward who came to power as a young teenager amidst the trauma of his father's deposition in 1326–7 and the death of his mother's lover in 1330 was very different from the glorious monarch who caroused in triumph after the great victories of 1346–7, and still more from the fragile old man who sat slumped upon a golden throne at his last Garter feast in April 1377. It is probably this sheer longevity and stark variety that accounts, as much as anything, for the persistent belief among historians that Edward III was less of a man, and less of a king, than that other late medieval contender for greatness, Henry V. But it is also the most emphatic proof of his supreme statesmanship that Edward endured for as long as he did. To say that this king transcended the initial problems of his minority, survived the grave threat to his authority in the crisis of 1340–1, rode out public concerns about the feasibility of the peace in the 1360s, outlasted the serious controversies of his last year and died peacefully in his own bed may not be to give the most exciting and glamorous synopsis of such a long and action-packed reign. But Edward's successful avoidance of any hint of armed revolt among his subjects for over four decades – an achievement unparalleled in historical memory, and not surpassed again for at least two centuries – is a vivid reminder of the enviable state of stability for which he stood, both in his own age and in posterity. In a century whose political history saw the deposition of not one but two kings, and in a decade that witnessed widespread political discontent and growing social unrest, the dignified end accorded to the deceased king in 1377 says something very important about the powerful aura that persisted around this monarch. Edward III had demonstrated, in a manner all too often lost on other medieval kings, that the security and prosperity of the realm ultimately lay in the affective relationship established between ruler and people. Not until the time of Gloriana would England again so powerfully imagine, and so enthusiastically celebrate, such a happy state of mutual regard.

THE TITLES AND SEALS OF EDWARD III

From 25 January 1327 to 25 January 1340 Edward III's style, as expressed on all formal documents issued in his name, was that used by his predecessors since the time of the treaty of Paris of 1259: 'King of England, lord of Ireland and duke of Aquitaine'. Wales, conquered by Edward I, was treated as a parcel of the English crown to be delegated, at pleasure, as a dependent principality held by the heir to the throne; it was not considered a separate entity within the royal title itself. Nor did Edward III's intervention in Scotland require changes: until the time of the treaty of Berwick, Edward assumed the position of feudal lord of Scotland and treated the throne either as vacant and in his gift (in 1333–4 and 1356–7) or as in the hands of his vassal, Edward Balliol (in 1334–56). Scotland was therefore deemed, as it had been under Edward I and Edward II, to be under the direct jurisdiction of the crown of England and did not warrant its own mention in the Plantagenet royal style.

Before 1340, some consideration was given to adapting the royal style to reflect Edward III's claims in France. A memorandum probably drawn up in the early 1330s articulated his full range of titles as 'king of England, lord of Ireland and Gascony and the Channel Isles, duke of Aquitaine, count of Ponthieu and Montreuil'.[1] The only recorded deviation from the standard form of the royal title before 1340 came in a handful of documents issued on 7 October 1337 and intended for Edward's allies in France and the Low Countries, which asserted his dynastic right to the French throne by declaring him 'king of France and England, lord of Ireland and duke of Aquitaine' (in some of the documents the order was reversed, with England appearing before France).[2] The unique assertion of the title of count of Toulouse in 1339 was merely a *pièce d'occasion*, designed to win over dissidents in southern France against Philip VI.[3] Otherwise Edward's royal style remained entirely settled and unchanged.

The formal declaration of the assumption of the title to France in 1340 occurred, conveniently enough, on 26 January, which was the day following the anniversary of Edward III's accession to the English throne.

---

[1] See p. 184.

[2] See p. 195.

[3] C. Johnson, 'An Act of Edward III as Count of Toulouse', *Essays in History Presented to R. L. Poole*, ed. H. W. C. Davis (Oxford, 1927), 399–404.

The day of 25 January 1340 was therefore taken to mark the beginning both of his fourteenth regnal year as king of England and of his first as king of France. While he remained on the continent in early 1340, Edward styled himself 'king of France and England and lord of Ireland'.[4] After his return to England on 21 February 1340, and for the rest of the period down to the sealing of the treaty of Calais on 24 October 1360, however, he used two parallel styles. For the business of England, Wales, Ireland, Scotland and Gascony, he reflected public anxieties about the precedence recently accorded to France by calling himself 'king of England and France'. For business relating to the kingdom of France and for his relations with other foreign rulers and the papacy, by contrast, he favoured the original form, 'king of France and England'.[5] Occasionally during this period the king also asserted titles relevant to particular arenas of war: the pragmatic use of the title of 'duke of Normandy' in the mid-1350s reflected his keenness to appeal to the separatist tendencies of his supporters in this great principality of France.[6]

From 24 October 1360 to 30 December 1369, during which period he agreed as a matter of discretion to drop the French royal title, Edward III used the style 'king of England, lord of Ireland and Aquitaine'. The title cannot have been fully countenanced by the French, for it asserted, in advance of the fulfilment of the treaty of Calais, Edward's right to hold Aquitaine, as he did Ireland, in full sovereignty.[7] The style was not affected by his grant of the title of prince of Aquitaine to Edward of Woodstock in 1362, since the latter held in dependent tenure of the king. In 1369, however, Edward was forced by the reopening of war with the Valois to return to the simultaneous double-styles 'king of England and France'/'king of France and England' as observed between 1340 and 1360.[8] There were also some further implications for the status of some of the territories claimed by the English crown in France. Between 1360 and 1369 Edward III had attempted to incorporate the town of Calais (formally part of the county of Artois) along with its dependencies into the county of Ponthieu, one of his ancestral territories claimed in full sovereignty under the terms of the treaty of Brétigny. But after 1369 it was necessary to revert to the official position adopted in 1347–60 and treat Calais simply as a parcel of Edward's crown of France and/or a conquest of the crown of England.[9]

---

[4] Ormrod, 'Problem of Precedence', 137–9.

[5] P. Chaplais, 'English Diplomatic Documents to the End of Edward III's Reign', *The Study of Medieval Records: Essays in Honour of Kathleen Major*, ed. D. A. Bullough and R. L. Storey (Oxford, 1971), 50–4; Ormrod, 'Problem of Precedence', 146–9.

[6] See p. 349.

[7] See p. 411.

[8] *EMDP*, I.i, no. 95.

[9] Le Patourel, *Feudal Empires*, chap. XIV. For the existence of a seal for 'the sovereignty of Ponthieu, Guînes, Marck and Calais' in the 1360s see S. B. Storey-Challenger, *L'Administration anglaise du Ponthieu, 1361–1369* (Abbeville, 1975), 102.

The great seal of England was changed on several occasions under Edward III, mainly in order to reflect alterations in the royal style.[10] The first great seal, employed until 4 October 1327, was simply that of Edward II, on to which two *fleurs-de-lys* were carved in order to provide simple differentiation between the two rulers. The second great seal (the first to be specifically designed for Edward III) remained in use until 1338 when the king's departure abroad required two seals to be put into commission: the second great seal was taken to the Low Countries and used there until the time that Edward asserted his claim to the French throne in 1340, and a new (third) great seal was created for the domestic administration under the titular presidency of Edward of Woodstock.

On 8 February 1340, at Ghent, Edward took delivery of a new (fourth) great seal, bearing the legend 'king of France and England, lord of Ireland and duke of Aquitaine'. On 20 June 1340, however, just before the king's return to the continent, two new seals were put into use, one (the fifth great seal) being for the home administration and the other (the sixth great seal) for the king's use abroad. There were two other significant innovations on these twinned great seals: they employed the style 'king of France and England and lord of Ireland'; and the legends were preceded by a hand of divine blessing issuing from clouds, perhaps in vindication of Edward's otherwise outrageous act of presumption in claiming the French throne. No attempt was made to ensure that there would be full compatibility between the legends on the seals and the order of precedence in the written documents to which impressions of the seals were attached; all business, whether relating to England or to France, was therefore sealed with seals bearing the legend 'king of France and England'.

Following Edward III's return to England late in 1340, the fifth great seal became the principal seal of state for the next twenty years; the sixth great seal was only again put into commission during the king's formal absences overseas in 1342–3, 1345, 1346–7, 1348 and 1359–60. Following the treaties of Brétigny and Calais, Edward commissioned a new (seventh) great seal with the legend 'king of England, lord of Ireland and Aquitaine', which he used throughout the peace of the 1360s. This seal is notable for its elaborate iconography: on the 'majesty' side it depicts the king flanked by the figures of the Virgin Mary and St George, the principal patrons of the Order of the Garter. Following the reopening of the war and the reassertion of the French royal title in 1369, Edward reverted to the seals put into use in 1340, seemingly adopting the sixth because it had been used rather less than the fifth and was thus inclined to provide sharper impressions. The king's attempt to lead his own forces into France

---

[10] The numbering system that follows is that employed by W. de G. Birch, *Catalogue of Seals in the Department of Manuscripts in the British Museum*, 6 vols (London, 1887–1900), i, 21–8. Cf. A. B. Wyon and A. Wyon, *The Great Seals of England* (London, 1887), 28–41.

again in 1372 once more seemed about to require the simultaneous operation of two seals, and the splendid seventh seal was re-engraved (as the
eighth great seal) to have the legend comply with the newly asserted style
'king of France and England, lord of Ireland'. When Edward's expedition
was called off, the sixth great seal was put out of commission and the
eighth became the seal for all business conducted for the rest of the reign.

The history of Edward III's privy seal follows a pattern broadly similar
to that of the great seal, with the legend giving primacy to France during
those periods, 1340–60 and 1369–77, when the king asserted the double
royal style.[11] The king's most personal seal, the secret seal, of which there
were at least three different matrices, bore a badge (rather than a coat of
arms) and did not have a legend. After 1354, however, it was replaced by
a signet on a ring, which bore the figure of a knight surrounded by *fleurs-
de-lys* and the legend 'king of England and France'. The reversal of the
order found on the great and privy seals denotes the fact that the signet
was used mainly to authorize private letters to the king's advisers and
subjects within England, though it was also occasionally used on correspondence with the Valois. Interestingly, it appears that this seal was not
altered when Edward dropped the claim to the French throne between
1360 and 1369.[12]

The deputed great seal employed in the exchequer under Edward III
dated from Edward II's time and was not replaced either in 1327 or in
1340; it therefore continued to use the post-1259 royal style, though the
documents to which it was attached certainly used the form 'king of
England and France'.[13] In 1369 when all the extant great seals were called
in, in order to make a review pending the reassertion of the French title,
it was said that some of these might bear the legend 'king of England and
France'.[14] So far as can be established, however, it seems that the only seals
(apart from the signet) that used this order of precedence were the two
deputed great seals created in 1344 to validate judicial writs issued by the
courts of common pleas and king's bench.[15] The decision to drop a separate claim to Aquitaine in the legends of June 1340 may have created some
anxiety in Gascony, where loyalists were adamant that they held Edward
in his capacity not as king of France but as ruler of England. This explains
why the English chancery preferred to use the style 'king of England and
France' on documents relating to Gascony and why the deputed seal
employed by the seneschal of Gascony for royal acts issued within the

[11] Tout, *Chapters*, v, 136–42.

[12] Ibid., v, 171–8.

[13] E 43/645; C. L. Kingsford, 'On Some Ancient Deeds and Seals Belonging to Lord De
L'Isle and Dudley', *Archaeologia*, lv (1913), 257–8.

[14] *Foedera*, III.ii, 868.

[15] B. Wilkinson, 'The Seals of the Two Benches under Edward III', *EHR*, xlii (1927),
397–401.

duchy remained unchanged and continued to display the pre-1340 unquartered arms of the leopards of England.[16]

It was only under Henry IV that the royal style inscribed on successive great seals since 1369 was reversed in accordance with the written text of so much of the output of the English royal chancery and expressed as 'king of England and France'.[17] Nonetheless, Henry's successors still understood the importance of Edward III's preferred order of precedence. In 1420, Henry V actually exhumed Edward's eighth great seal in order to reassert his great-grandfather's preferred style on the occasion of the confirmation of the treaty of Troyes.[18] The claim to the throne of France, first formally incorporated into the English royal style in 1340, thus remained at least a residual element of the English and British royal family's titles far beyond the Hundred Years War, and was not finally dropped until as late as 1801.[19]

[16] Ormrod, 'Problem of Precedence', 144 and n. 47.

[17] Wyon and Wyon, *Great Seals*, 43–6.

[18] H. Jenkinson, 'The Great Seal of England: Deputed or Departmental Seals', *Archaeologia*, lxxxv (1935), 310.

[19] *HBC*, 47.

THE ITINERARY OF EDWARD III,
1325–1377

This itinerary draws on Edward III's household accounts, instruments under the privy seal, secret seal and signet (including those transcribed into other government documents and occasionally preserved in private archives), chronicles, the rolls of parliament, and records of council meetings at which the king's presence was noted. The quantity and quality of this evidence varies greatly over the reign. From the end of 1326 until the mid-1340s, it is possible to track Edward's whereabouts on a virtually daily basis. An unpublished handlist in the search rooms at the National Archives, 'The Itinerary of Edward III and his Household: Regnal Years 1–7', provides a particularly valuable source for the period 1327–33. A detailed itinerary has also been published by Dr Caroline Shenton for the years 1327–45.[1] The summaries below draw partly on these two lists, but the data have been rechecked, revised and supplemented, especially in relation to the king's movements in Scotland and on the continent. Dr Shenton's itinerary, compiled according to well-established principles, properly distinguishes between the travels of the household and those of the privy seal; when these are at variance, I rely on contextual evidence to suggest which one more accurately reflects the king's own movements. I also correct a number of identifications of English, Scottish and continental place-names. The cumulative result is that, especially after 1337, I tend to deviate in some details from Dr Shenton's conclusions. Dr Shenton also omitted to use the relevant household account for Edward's period in the Low Countries and Germany in 1338–40, and for this period I generally follow the useful independent itinerary published by Dr Elsbeth Andre.[2]

The comparative brevity and incompleteness of the lists during the last thirty years of the reign is, in part, indicative of Edward III's more sedentary lifestyle during this period. The main reason, however, is that instruments under the privy seal, which supply the most consistent data for the early years, cease to provide a regular and sure guide to the king's travels after his return from the siege of Calais in 1347. The seal and its staff no

---

[1] Shenton, *Itinerary of Edward III*.
[2] Andre, *Ein Königshof auf Reisen*, 230–51.

longer moved around as a matter of course with the king's entourage, but usually remained fixed, like the chancery, at Westminster.[3] The privy seal clerks, like their counterparts at the chancery, still sometimes recorded the place where the king had been (or rather the place where they thought him to have been) on the day that he gave his personal consent to the relevant matter of grace. But the vast majority of privy seal instruments were now place-dated at Westminster. Letters under the secret seal and signet continued to reflect the king's movements, but the number of originals and transcriptions of instruments under these personal seals remains very small during the second half of the reign. This, when combined with a notable decline in the survival rate and level of detail of the household accounts, means that there are inevitably many gaps in our knowledge about Edward III's whereabouts during his later years.

In a few cases the predictable rhythms of the political and ceremonial year mean that the king's presence can be surmised. Unless there is definite evidence otherwise, for example, I have assumed that Edward III was in attendance during the known date-spans of sessions of parliament and (after 1349) at Windsor for the Garter feast on St George's Day, 23 April. Generally, however, the king is only given a location when his presence in a place is firmly attested. Question marks replace dates when Edward can be positively identified in the relevant place during the period (usually from chronicle accounts), even though no specific date is available. A forward slash denotes that there are good grounds for assuming that the king visited both (or all) the places named on the relevant day, in the order given; where one place-name simply allows for several identifications within a given area, these are marked as either/or options. Question marks attached to place-names indicate cases where identifications of fourteenth-century spellings remain conjectural. Italics denote those instances where I have been unable to provide even a speculative identification of a place-name, which is then left in the original spelling. More obscure English locations, and those with common names, are identified by their historic counties; where such place-names recur within a given year, only the first occurrence is thus denoted. In cases of royal residences such as Windsor and Clarendon, no distinction is made between the main house and the smaller lodges, though particularly in the case of visits to Windsor it should be noted that the king quite often stayed not at the castle but in one of the dependent hunting parks.

1325   AUGUST 12–13 Stratford (Essex). 14 Bromley. 15 Sevenoaks. 16–17 Tonbridge. 18–19 Leeds (Kent). 21–2 Canterbury. 23–7 Dover. 28–31 Elham. SEPTEMBER 1–3 Elham. 4–11 Dover. 12 At sea. 22 Paris. 24 Bois de Vincennes. OCTOBER 14 Poissy. 15–17 Paris. 22 Le Bourget. 23

---

[3] Tout, *Chapters*, v, 72–4; Ormrod, 'Accountability and Collegiality', 68–76.

Louvres/Senlis. 24 Rully/Béthisy-Saint-Pierre. 25 Béthisy-Saint-Pierre. 26 Verberie. 27 Pierrefonds. 28 Ambleny/Soissons. 29 Braine/Fismes. 30 Jonchery-sur-Vesle/Reims. NOVEMBER 1 Reims. 2 Fismes. 3 Braine/Soissons. 4 Jaulzy. 5–6 Compiègne. 7 Verberie/Pont-Sainte-Maxence. 8–10 Pont-Sainte-Maxence. 11 Senlis/Louvres. 12 Paris.

1326 AUGUST 27 Mons. SEPTEMBER 23 Dordrecht. 24 Walton (Suff.). SEPTEMBER/OCTOBER ? Bury St Edmunds. ? Cambridge. ? Dunstable. ? Wallingford. ? Oxford. ? Gloucester. ? Berkeley. ? Bristol. OCTOBER 26–8 Bristol. NOVEMBER 4–22 Hereford. 26 Much Marcle. 27 Newent. 28 Gloucester. 29 Coberley. 30 Cirencester. DECEMBER 1 Lechdale. 2 Witney. 3–21 Woodstock. 22 Osney. 23–9 Wallingford. 30 Reading. 31 Windsor.

1327 JANUARY 1 Windsor. 2 Chertsey. 3 Merton. 4–31 Westminster. FEBRUARY 1–28 Westminster. MARCH 1–12 Westminster. 13 Dartford. 14 Rochester. 15 Faversham. 16 Canterbury. 17 Ospringe. 18 Leeds (Kent). 19 Malling. 20 Eltham. 21–9 Westminster. 30–1 Waltham Abbey. APRIL 1 Hertford. 2 Bassingbourn. 3 Huntingdon. 4–7 Ramsey. 8–17 Peterborough. 18–25 Stamford. 26 Whissendine. 27 Stamford/Old Dalby. 28–30 Nottingham. MAY 1–16 Nottingham. 17 Clipstone. 18 Blyth. 19 Doncaster. 20–1 Pontefract. 22 Sherburn in Elmet. 23–31 York. JUNE 1–30 York. JULY 1–2 Overton. 3 Beningborough. 4 Newton-on-Ouse/Aldwark. 5 Myton-on-Swale. 6–12 Topcliffe. 13 Northallerton. 14 Darlington. 15–16 Durham. 17–18 Tudhoe. 19 Bishop Auckland. 20 Bagraw. 21–6 Haydon Bridge. 27 Ratton Row *or* Rattenraw. 28 Haltwhistle. 29 Blanchland. 30–1 Stanhope. AUGUST 1–6 Stanhope. 7–9 Durham. 10 Darlington. 11 Northallerton. 12 Myton-on-Swale. 13–23 York. 24 Sherburn in Elmet. 25 Pontefract. 26 Doncaster. 27 Blyth. 28 Clipstone. 29–31 Nottingham. SEPTEMBER 1–13 Nottingham. 14 Newark. 15–27 Lincoln. 28 Newark. 29–30 Nottingham. OCTOBER 1–31 Nottingham. NOVEMBER 1–10 Nottingham. 11 Newstead. 12–15 Clipstone. 16 Blyth. 17 Doncaster. 18–24 Pontefract. 25 Doncaster. 26 Blyth. 27–9 Clipstone. 30 Newstead. DECEMBER 1–2 Nottingham. 3 Loughborough. 4–6 Leicester. 7 Warwick/Earl Shilton. 8 Nuneaton. 9–11 Coventry. 12 Kenilworth. 13 Warwick. 14 Stratford-upon-Avon. 15 Chipping Campden. 16–17 Winchcombe. 18 Cheltenham. 19–20 Gloucester. 21 Tewkesbury. 22 Pershore. 23–7 Worcester. 28 Droitwich. 29 Bromsgrove. 30 Birmingham. 31 Lichfield.

1328 JANUARY 1 Lichfield. 2 Burton upon Trent. 3 Tutbury. 4 Darley Abbey. 5–7 Nottingham. 8 Newark. 9–14 Clipstone. 15 Blyth. 16 Doncaster. 17–18 Rothwell. 19 Sherburn in Elmet. 20–8 York. 29–31 Knaresborough. FEBRUARY 1–2 Knaresborough. 3–29 York. MARCH 1–8 York. 9 Sherburn in Elmet. 10 Pontefract. 11 Doncaster. 12 Blyth. 13

Clipstone. 14–15 Southwell. 16–17 Newark. 18 Eagle. 19–22 Lincoln. 23–7 Barlings. 28 Lincoln. 29 Navenby. 30 Sleaford. 31 Sempringham. APRIL 1–5 Sempringham. 6 Bourne. 7–15 Stamford. 15 Wansford. 16–21 Oundle. 22 Thorpe Waterville. 23 Wellingborough. 24–30 Northampton. MAY 1–23 Northampton. 24 Warwick. 25–26 Alcester. 27 Worcester. 28 Credenhill. 29–30 Worcester. 31 Hereford. JUNE 1 Leominster. 2–3 Ludlow. 4 Bromyard. 5 Evesham. 6 Chipping Norton. 7–8 Woodstock. 9 Chipping Norton. 10–19 Worcester. 20–1 Pershore. 22–6 Evesham. 27 Rous Lench. 28–9 Holloway (Hanbury). 30 Bordesley. JULY 1 Bordesley. 2–3 Hailes. 4 Dudley. 5 Bridgnorth. 6–8 Much Wenlock. 9–10 Shrewsbury. 11 High Ercall. 12 Penkridge. 13 Lichfield. 14 *Newport.* 15 Elford. 16–17 Burton upon Trent. 18 Derby. 19–21 Nottingham. 22–6 Clipstone. 27 Blyth. 28 Doncaster. 29 Pontefract. 30 Sherburn in Elmet. 31 York. AUGUST 1–17 York. 18 Sherburn in Elmet. 19–21 Pontefract. 22–3 Doncaster. 24 Blyth. 25 Clipstone. 26–7 Nottingham. 28–31 Clipstone. SEPTEMBER 1–3 Nottingham. 6 Lincoln. 7–9 Barlings. 11 Revesby. 12 Boston. 13 Swineshead. 14 Spalding. 15 Long Sutton. 16 Wisbech. 17–18 King's Lynn. 19 Castle Rising. 20 Little Walsingham. 21 North Elmham. 23 Norwich. 24 Wymondham. 25 Thetford. 26 Bury St Edmunds. 27 Cambridge. OCTOBER 1 Salisbury. 4–7 Gloucester. 8 Malmesbury. 10 Salisbury/Vastern. 12–13 Marlborough. 16–31 Salisbury. NOVEMBER 1–3 Salisbury. 4–6 Winchester. 7 Hurstbourne Priors/Newbury. 8–13 Wallingford. 14 Reading. 15–20 Windsor. 21–30 Westminster. DECEMBER 1–4 Westminster. 7 Abingdon. 9 Faringdon. 10 Cirencester. 11–22 Gloucester. 24–7 Worcester. 30–1 Warwick.

1329 JANUARY 1 Warwick. 2 Coventry. 5 Hinckley. 6–12 Leicester. 14–15 Northampton. 17–18 Odell. 19 Newnham. 20–1 Bedford. 23 Dunstable/St Albans. 24–5 St Albans. 26 Kings Langley. 27 Amersham. 28–31 Windsor. FEBRUARY 1–6 Windsor. 7–12 Tower of London/ Isleworth. 13–21 Westminster. 22–8 Eltham. MARCH 1 Eltham. 2 Kingston upon Thames. 3–5 Newark Priory (Surrey). 6–9 Guildford. 10–13 Chertsey. 14 Uxbridge. 15 West *or* High Wycombe. 16 Thame. 17 Islip. 18–26 Woodstock. 27 Eynsham. 28 Abingdon. 29–31 Wallingford. APRIL 1–26 Wallingford. 27 Reading. 28 Windsor/Sheen. 29–30 Eltham. MAY 1–16 Eltham. 17 Dartford. 18 Rochester. 19 Orpington *or* Ospringe. 20–3 Canterbury. 24–5 Dover. 26–7 Wissant. 28 Boulogne. 29 Montreuil. 30 Crécy. 31 Saint-Riquier. JUNE 1 Saint-Riquier. 2 Longueau *or* Long. 3–8 Amiens. 9 Crécy. 10 Wissant/Dover. 11–12 Dover. 13–19 Canterbury. 20 Faversham. 21–4 Rochester. 25 Dartford. 26–30 Eltham. JULY 1 Eltham. 2–3 Reigate. 4–6 Guildford. 7 Witley. 8 Midhurst. 9–14 Chichester. 15 Durford. 16 Upper *or* Lower Farringdon. 17 Odiham. 18 Easthampstead. 19–27 Windsor. 28 Reading. 29–31 Wallingford. AUGUST 1 Wallingford. 2 Osney. 3–8 Woodstock. 9–10 Burford. 11 Withington. 12–31 Gloucester. SEPTEMBER 1–4 Gloucester. 8–13 Hereford. 14–26 Gloucester. 27

Hanley Castle. 28–30 Worcester. OCTOBER 1–7 Worcester. 8–9 Evesham.
10 Chipping Campden. 11 Banbury. 12 Brackley. 13–14 Stony Stratford.
15–19 Water Eaton *or* Eaton Bray. 20 Dunstable. 21–2 Toddington. 23 Stony
Stratford. 24 Towcester. 25–8 Daventry. 29–31 Kenilworth. NOVEMBER
1–30 Kenilworth. DECEMBER 1–31 Kenilworth.

1330 JANUARY 1–2 Kenilworth. 3 Alcester. 4–11 Worcester. 12
Pershore. 13 Evesham. 14 Chipping Campden. 15 Chipping Norton. 16
Woodstock. 17 Osney. 18 Wallingford. 19 Reading. 20 Easthampstead. 21
Merton. 22–31 Eltham. FEBRUARY 1–6 Eltham. 7–17 Tower of London.
18 Westminster. 20–2 Windsor. 23 Chobham/Guildford. 24–8 Guildford.
MARCH 3–23 Winchester. 24–5 Reading. 26–7 Wallingford. 28 Osney.
29–31 Woodstock. APRIL 1–30 Woodstock. MAY 1–31 Woodstock. JUNE
1–20 Woodstock. 21 Burford. 22 Cirencester. 23–6 Gloucester. 27
Tewkesbury. 29 Hanley Castle. 30 Worcester. JULY 1 Worcester. 5–7
Woodstock. 9–11 Osney. 12–15 Woodstock. 16–17 Westminster. 18
Woodstock. 19 Westminster. 20 Woodstock. 21 Windsor. 22–7 Woodstock.
28 Brackley. 29–31 Northampton. AUGUST 1–3 Northampton. 5
Rockingham. 6–8 King's Cliffe. 9–15 Bourne. 16–17 Folkingham. 18–21
Heckington. 22 Cawthorpe. 23–6 Lincoln. 28 Newark. 29–31 Clipstone.
SEPTEMBER 1–4 Clipstone. 5–20 Nottingham. 22–3 Clipstone. 25
Worksop. 29–30 Pontefract. OCTOBER 6 Doncaster. 13–20 Nottingham.
21 Castle Donington. 22–6 Leicester. 27 Lutterworth. 28–9 Daventry. 30
Brackley/Woodstock. 31 Woodstock. NOVEMBER 1–4 Woodstock. 7
Wantage. 9 Bedwyn. 11–16 Clarendon. 18 Salisbury. 20 Romsey. 21
Alton. 22 Waverley. 25 Kingston upon Thames. 26–30 Westminster.
DECEMBER 1–21 Westminster. 25–31 Guildford.

1331 JANUARY 1–6 Guildford. 8–25 Westminster. 26 Waltham Abbey.
27–8 Hertford. 29 Hatfield. 30 St Albans. 31 Kings Langley. FEBRUARY
1–7 Kings Langley. 8–18 Windsor. 21–8 Croydon. MARCH 1 Westminster.
2 Eltham. 3 Croydon. 4 Orpington. 5–14 Otford. 15–19 Eltham. 20–4
Westminster. 25–31 Eltham. APRIL 1–2 Eltham. 3 Dover. 4 Wissant. 7
Saint-Just-en-Chaussée. 12–17 Pont-Sainte-Maxence. 20 Dover/
Wingham. 21–2 Wingham. 23 Canterbury. 24 Ospringe. 25 Rochester. 26
Dartford. 27–8 Stratford. 29–30 Havering-atte-Bower. MAY 1–21
Havering-atte-Bower. 22 Chelmsford. 23 Braintree. 24 Sudbury. 25–30
Bury St Edmunds. JUNE 1–4 Bury St Edmunds. 5 Thetford. 7
Wymondham/Norwich. 8–10 Norwich. 11–13 Barnwell. 16–19 Stepney.
20–4 Norwich. 25 North Elmham. 26 Little Walsingham. 27 Coxford. 28
King's Lynn/Gaywood. 29 Gaywood/Little Walsingham. 30 Wisbech.
JULY 1 Spalding. 2 Swaton. 3 Navenby. 4–22 Lincoln. 23–4 Southwell.
25–7 Clipstone. 28–31 Sheffield. AUGUST 1 Sheffield. 2–5 Clipstone. 5–6
Newstead. 7–11 Nottingham. 12 Rockingham. 13 Melton Mowbray. 14
Preston (Rutland). 15 Melton Mowbray. 16 Preston. 20 Bedford. 23

Rockingham. 24–7 King's Cliffe. 28 Melton Mowbray. 29 Nottingham. 30 Derby. 31 Ashbourne. SEPTEMBER 1–4 Tideswell. 5–8 Castleton. 9 Bakewell. 10 Derby. 11 Loughborough. 12 Melton Mowbray. 13 Market Harborough. 14 Northampton. 15 Stony Stratford. 16–17 Kings Langley. 20 Sheen. 21–31 Westminster/London. OCTOBER 1–17 Westminster 20–4 Windsor. 25–6 Odiham. 27–8 Newbury. 29–30 Hungerford. 31 Marlborough. NOVEMBER 1–3 Marlborough. 4–5 Ludgershall. 6 Andover. 7 Wherwell. 9–10 Odiham. 11 Wokingham. 12–15 Windsor. 16–17 Guildford. 18 Waverley. 19–20 Chawton. 21 Bishop's Sutton. 22–3 Winchester. 24–30 Clarendon. DECEMBER 1–2 Clarendon. 4 Christchurch. 5–6 Wimborne Minster. 7 Wareham. 8 Bindon Abbey. 9 Wareham. 10–11 Broadmayne. 12–13 Frampton. 14–15 Cerne Abbas. 16–17 Sherborne. 18 Marston Magna. 19 North or South Cadbury. 20 Ditcheat. 21–2 Glastonbury. 23–31 Wells.

1332 JANUARY 1–6 Wells. 7 Paulton. 8 Bath. 9 Chippenham. 10 Avebury. 11–12 Hungerford. 13 Newbury. 14 Aldermaston. 15 Reading. 16 Maidenhead. 17 Stanwell. 18 Brentford. 19–31 Westminster. FEBRUARY 1–4 Waltham Abbey. 5–7 Hertford. 8 Waltham Abbey. 9 Epping Forest. 10–15 Hertford. 16–20 Waltham Abbey. 22–6 Kings Langley. 27 Havering-atte-Bower. MARCH 6–10 Havering-atte-Bower. 12–14 Stratford. 16–27 Tower of London/Westminster. 28–9 Tower of London. 30 Waltham Abbey. 31 Hertford. APRIL 1 Hertford. 2 Buntingford. 3 Ickleton. 4 Barnwell. 5 Cambridge. 6–7 Huntingdon. 8 Sawtry. 9 Wansford. 10–21 Stamford. 22–3 Oakham. 24–9 Nottingham. 30 Daventry/Woodstock. MAY 1–31 Woodstock. JUNE 1–30 Woodstock. JULY 1 Vastern. 2–6 Devizes. 7–12 Clarendon. 15–17 Abingdon. 18–26 Woodstock. 26–7 Evesham. 28–9 Pershore. 30–1 Hanley Castle. AUGUST 1–2 Hanley Castle. 3 Ledbury. 4 Bromyard. 5 Leominster. 6–11 Wigmore. 12 Ludlow. 13–16 Cleobury. 17 Earnwood. 18–21 Kidderminster. 22–4 Halesowen. 25 Alvechurch. 26–7 Feckenham. 28 Henley in Arden. 29 Long Itchington. 30 Daventry. 31 Northampton. SEPTEMBER 1–5 Northampton. 6 Kings Langley. 7–14 Westminster.[4] 15–17 Waltham Abbey. 18 Hitchin. 19 Newport Pagnell. 20–4 Northampton. 25 Cottesbrooke. 26–7 Sulby. 28–30 Leicester. OCTOBER 1 Leicester. 2 Loughborough. 3–8 Nottingham. 9–10 Clipstone. 11 Worksop. 12 Tickhill. 13 Doncaster. 14–15 Pontefract. 16 Sherburn in Elmet. 17–31 York. NOVEMBER 1–4 York. 8–30 Knaresborough. DECEMBER 1 Knaresborough. 3–19 York. 21 Driffield. 23–31 Beverley.

---

[4] A letter of 21 Sept. 1332 states that the king and queen had recently been at Canterbury: *Litterae Cantuariensis*, i, 496–8. Unless this is a reference back to the visit of Apr. 1331, it is perhaps most likely that the royal couple went down to Canterbury after the conclusion of parliament on 12 Sept.

1333 JANUARY 1–2 Beverley. 4–11 Burstwick. 12 Meaux. 18–31 York. FEBRUARY 1–6 York. 7–28 Pontefract. MARCH 1–8 Pontefract. 9–13 Cowick. 14–22 Pontefract. 23–4 Cowick. 26–31 Pontefract. APRIL 1 Pontefract. 2–5 Knaresborough. 6 Helperby/Northallerton. 7 Crayke/ Darlington. 8–16 Durham. 19–27 Newcastle upon Tyne. 28 Newminster. 29 Alnwick. 30 Belford. MAY 1–8 Belford/Fenwick. 9–16 Tweedmouth. 17–31 Berwick-upon-Tweed. JUNE 1–30 Berwick-upon-Tweed. JULY 1–30 Berwick-upon-Tweed. 31 Newbiggin-by-the-Sea. AUGUST 1–3 Newcastle upon Tyne. 4 Durham. 5 Darlington. 6 Northallerton. 7 Topcliffe. 8–15 Knaresborough. 16 Criddling Stubbs. 17 Scrooby. 18 Navenby. 19 Moulton. 20 Wisbech/Castle Rising. 21 Little Walsingham. 22–3 Wymondham. 24–5 Great Yarmouth. 26 Botesdale. 27 Redgrave/Bury St Edmunds/Long Melford. 28 Chelmsford. 29–30 Westminster. 31 Eltham. SEPTEMBER 1 Eltham. 2 Ospringe. 3–8 Eltham. 9–12 Windsor.[5] 13–14 Odiham. 15–16 Stansted Park (Hants). 17 Guildford. 18 Westminster. 19 Chelmsford. 20 Bury St Edmunds. 21–2 Newton (Suff.) *or* Newton (Norf.). 23 Wymondham. 24 Newmarket. 25 Bishop's Stortford. 26–30 Waltham Abbey. OCTOBER 1–2 Waltham Abbey. 3–9 Havering-atte-Bower. 10–12 Lambeth. 13–18 Sheen. 19–22 Windsor. 23–4 Odiham. 26–9 Hurstbourne Priors. 30 Ludgershall. 31 Marlborough. NOVEMBER 1–2 Marlborough. 3 Denford. 4 Hampstead Marshall. 5 Chilton Foliat. 6 Marlborough. 7–8 Ludgershall. 9 Enford Down. 10–21 Clarendon. 22 Sherborne. 25 Wincanton/Yarlington. 26 Stoke Trister/Warminster. 28–30 Marlborough. DECEMBER 1–9 Marlborough. 10 Aldermaston. 11 West *or* High Wycombe. 12 Dunstable. 13 Royston. 14 Newmarket.[6] 15 Swaffham. 16 West Acre. 17 Mildenhall. 18 Babraham. 19 Hitchin. 20 Berkhamsted. 21–31 Wallingford.

1334 JANUARY 1–9 Wallingford. 10 Abingdon. 11–13 Woodstock. 14–15 Ivinghoe. 16–26 Dunstable. 30 Woodstock. FEBRUARY 1–6 Woodstock. 9 Newmarket. 10–14 Woodstock. 15 Leicester. 16 Nottingham. 17 Blyth. 18–19 Pontefract. 20–8 York. MARCH 1–9 York. 10–12 Woodstock. 13–14 Bicester. 16–17 Towcester. 18–22 Northampton. 23–31 Rockingham. APRIL 1–4 Rockingham. 5 Thrapston. 6 Kimbolton. 7 St Neots. 8–10 Huntingdon. 11 Somersham. 12–13 St Ives. 16–17 Ramsey. 18 Sawtry. 21 Peterborough. 22–3 Market Deeping. 24 Bourne. 27–9 Folkingham. 30 Sleaford. MAY 1 Sleaford. 2 Navenby. 4–6 Lincoln. 7 Fillingham/Scotton. 8 Scotton. 12 Thornton (Lincs). 16–18 Burstwick. 20–4 Beverley. 25 Malton. 26 Pickering. 31 Helmsley. JUNE 1 Helmsley. 2 Thirsk. 3 Yarm. 4 Aycliffe. 5 Durham. 6–21 Newcastle upon Tyne. 22–3 Raby castle. 24–30

---

[5] It was probably during this or the Oct. visit to Windsor, or his residence at Wycombe in Dec., that Edward laid the foundation stone of Bisham Priory: *Age of Chivalry*, no. 498.

[6] The letter of secret seal found in SC 8/243/12150, dated on its guard as 1347, is more likely to relate to this visit.

Barnard Castle. JULY 1–2 Newburgh. 3–4 York. 5 Sherburn in Elmet. 6 Doncaster. 7–11 Clipstone. 12–17 Nottingham. 22 Northampton. 23 Stony Stratford. 24 Reading. 31 Woodstock/Windsor. AUGUST 1–5 Windsor. 7–8 Odiham. 11 Highclere/Kingsclere. 12 Kingsclere. 14–22 Clarendon. 24 London/Westminster. 26–8 Waltham Abbey. SEPTEMBER 1 Waltham Abbey. 2 Bitterne. 3 Clarendon. 5 Guildford. 7 Selborne. 11–12 Guildford. 13–30 Westminster. OCTOBER 1 Westminster. 3–4 St Albans. 8 Walsingham. 11 Somerton. 12 Pontefract. 13 York. 17–18 York/Bishopthorpe. 19–20 Knaresborough. 21–3 York. 26 Topcliffe. 28 Northallerton. 29 Durham. 31 Newcastle upon Tyne. NOVEMBER 1–14 Newcastle upon Tyne. 15 Newminster. 18 Alnwick. 20 Doddington (Northumb.). 22–30 Roxburgh. DECEMBER 1–31 Roxburgh.

1335 JANUARY 1–31 Roxburgh. FEBRUARY 1–3 Roxburgh. 6–7 Alnwick. 11–25 Newcastle upon Tyne. 26–8 Darlington. MARCH 1–3 Pontefract. 4 York. 6 Hatfield (Yorks). 9–10 Coventry. 13 Walsingham. 15 Cattawade. 18 Tower of London. 19 Westminster. 24 London. 26–31 Nottingham. APRIL 1–5 Nottingham. 11–30 Clipstone. MAY 1–2 Clipstone. 3–4 Tickhill. 5–6 Hatfield. 7–9 Cowick. 12 Pontefract. 13–14 Cowick. 15 Pontefract. 17–20 Knaresborough. 23–31 York. JUNE 1–9 York. 10–12 Pickering. 13–16 Newburgh. 17 Northallerton. 20 Durham. 22–30 Newcastle upon Tyne. JULY 1–6 Newcastle upon Tyne. 7–9 Carlisle. 10 Arthuret. 11 Dalswinton. ? Glasgow. 25–30 Airth. AUGUST 9–30 Perth. SEPTEMBER 5 Perth. 6 Linlithgow. 7 Kirkliston. 10–16 Edinburgh. 15 Haddington. 17–24 Cockburnspath. 28–30 Wooler. OCTOBER 1 Bamburgh. 3–17 Berwick-upon-Tweed. 18–30 Roxburgh. 31 Doddington (Northumb.). NOVEMBER 1 Doddington. 2–10 Alnwick. 11 Berwick-upon-Tweed. 15–30 Newcastle upon Tyne. DECEMBER 1–18 Bishop Auckland. 20–9 Newcastle upon Tyne. 31 Alnwick.

1336 JANUARY 1 Alnwick. 6–30 Berwick-upon-Tweed. 31 Belford. FEBRUARY 2–9 Knaresborough. 10–16 Walsingham. MARCH 1 Hertford. 6 Sheen. 9–21 Westminster. 22 Eltham. 23 Westminster. 24–7 Tower of London. 29–31 Eltham. APRIL 1–2 Eltham. 3–4 Tower of London. 5–6 Havering-atte-Bower. 7–11 Waltham Abbey. 12–17 Tower of London. 18–28 Guildford. 29 Isleworth. 30 Westminster. MAY 1–5 Westminster. 6–15 Windsor. 16 Reading. 17–21 Wallingford. 22 Abingdon. 23–31 Woodstock. JUNE 1–3 Woodstock. 4 Towcester. 5 Northampton. 6 Leicester. 7 Topcliffe. 8 Northallerton. 9 Pontefract. 10 Durham. 11–12 Newcastle upon Tyne. 13 Morpeth. 14 Wooler. 15 Kelso. 16 Newbattle. 17 Linlithgow. 18 Gask. 19 Perth. 24 Alyth. 25 ?Kirkton of Lethendy. 26 Birnam. 27–30 Perth. JULY 1–11 Perth. 12 *Aughtreganen*. 13 Blair Atholl. 14 Kingussie. 15 Lochindorb. 16 *Aberskarf.* 17 Forres/Kinloss. 18 Elgin. 19 Cullen. 20 Fyvie. 21–3 Aberdeen. 24 Muchalls/Dunnottar. 25 Brechin. 26 Forfar. 27 Coupar Angus. 28–31 Perth. AUGUST 1–31 Perth.

SEPTEMBER 1–3 Perth. 4 Kinkell Bridge. 5 Cambuskenneth. 6 Stirling. 10–15 Berwick-upon-Tweed. 16 Belford. 17 Newcastle upon Tyne. 18 Bishop Auckland. 19 Darlington. 20 Knaresborough. 21–2 Blyth. 23–9 Nottingham. 30 Leicester. OCTOBER 1 Leicester. 2 Blyth. 3 York. 4 Northallerton. 5 Bishop Auckland. 6–13 Newcastle upon Tyne. 14 Hexham. 15 Thirlwall. 16 Castleton. 17 Hawick. 18 Peebles. 19 Carnwath. 20 Stonehouse. 21–31 Bothwell. NOVEMBER 1–30 Bothwell. DECEMBER 1–4 Bothwell. 5 *Brounleghs*. 6 *Simondeston*. 7–8 ?Stobo. 9 Cornhill-on-Tweed. 10–14 Berwick-upon-Tweed. 15 Alnwick. 16 Newcastle upon Tyne. 17 Darlington. 18 Boroughbridge. 19 Pontefract. 21–3 Doncaster. 24–7 Hatfield (Yorks).

1337 JANUARY 5–16 Tower of London. 17 Cliffe (Kent). 18 Canterbury. 19 Cliffe. 20–2 Tower of London. 28–30 Hatfield (Yorks). FEBRUARY 1–2 Hatfield. 4 Kings Langley. 5–6 Westminster. 8–12 Tower of London. 14–18 Hatfield. 28 Tower of London. MARCH 1 Tower of London. 2–25 Westminster. 26–8 Windsor. 30 Tower of London. APRIL 1–5 Tower of London. 6–7 Windsor. 8 Chertsey. 10–20 Windsor. 21 Mortlake. 22–3 Westminster. 24–30 Windsor. MAY 1 Windsor. 2 Tower of London. 3–4 Dunstable. 5–7 Nottingham. 8–16 York. 17 Kingston-upon-Hull. 18 York. 19–25 Clipstone. 26–31 Stamford. JUNE 1 Grantham/King's Cliffe. 2 Stamford. 3 Boroughbridge/Northallerton. 5 Newcastle upon Tyne. 6–12 Berwick-upon-Tweed. 13 Ettrick. 14–15 Stirling. 17 Newcastle upon Tyne. 20–9 Stamford. 30 Huntingdon. JULY 3–15 Tower of London. 17–28 Westminster. 30 Clarendon. AUGUST 1–4 Clarendon. 5–9 Westminster. 10–16 Tower of London. 17–31 Westminster. SEPTEMBER 1–7 Westminster. 8–13 Woodstock. 14–16 Gloucester. 17–18 Woodstock. 20–5 Tower of London. 26–30 Westminster. OCTOBER 1–5 Westminster. 6–12 Tower of London. 13–19 Westminster. 20–1 Stanwell. 23–31 Thame. NOVEMBER 1–3 Thame. 4 Quarrendon. 5–7 Leighton Buzzard. 9–11 Thame. 12–15 Quarrendon. 16 Newmarket. 20 Quarrendon. 22 Thame. 23–30 Reading. DECEMBER 2 Reading. 3–4 Newbury. 5–7 Reading. 8 Odiham/Windsor. 9–10 Windsor. 11 Aldermaston. 12–23 Westminster. 24–30 Guildford.

1338 JANUARY 1–5 Tower of London. 6–8 Hertford. 11 Blyth. 12 Aberford. 13–14 Newcastle upon Tyne. 16–17 Berwick-upon-Tweed. 20 Newcastle upon Tyne. 24 Whitekirk. 26–7 Berwick-upon-Tweed. 28 Newcastle upon Tyne. 29 Aberford. FEBRUARY 2 Hatfield (?Herts). 3–29 Westminster. MARCH 1–4 Westminster. 5–16 Tower of London. ? Darlington. 19–24 Newcastle upon Tyne. 26–8 Alnwick. 29 Newcastle upon Tyne. 30 Durham/Darlington. APRIL 1 Nottingham. 5 Kings Langley. 7–18 Havering-atte-Bower. 20–30 Westminster. MAY 1–2 Westminster. 3–17 Tower of London. 18 Windsor. 19–25 Tower of London. 26 Babraham. 27–31 Bury St Edmunds. JUNE 1–4 Bury St

Edmunds. 6–12 Lopham. 13–18 Ipswich. 19–30 Walton (Suff.). JULY 1–11 Walton. 12–16 Orwell. 17–18 At anchor in the Scheldt off Sluys. 19–20 Arnemuiden. 21–31 Antwerp. AUGUST 1–11 Antwerp. 13–15 Malines. 16–18 Antwerp. 19 Herentals. 20 Diest. 21 Sittard. 22 Jülich. 23–4 Cologne. 25 Bonn. 26–8 Sinzig. 29 Andernach. 30–1 Neuwied. SEPTEMBER 1–6 Koblenz. 8 Bonn. 9 Düren. 10 Sittard. 11 Diest. 12 Herentals. 13 Antwerp. 16–20 Malines. 21–30 Antwerp. OCTOBER 1–7 Antwerp. 10 Liège. 12–14 Diest. 15 Liège. 17–25 Antwerp. 26–9 Malines. NOVEMBER 1–30 Antwerp. DECEMBER 1 Antwerp. 2–7 Liège. 10–18 Antwerp. 25–30 Antwerp.

1339 JANUARY 1–31 Antwerp. FEBRUARY 1–28 Antwerp. MARCH 1–5 Antwerp. 6–30 Vilvoorde. APRIL 1–24 Vilvoorde. 25–6 Malines. 27–30 Antwerp. MAY 1 Malines. 3–9 Antwerp. 10–14 Malines. 16–24 Antwerp. 28–9 Diest. 30–1 Antwerp. JUNE 1–3 Antwerp. 5–10 Diest. 11 Antwerp. 14 Diest. 16–20 Antwerp. 25–30 Vilvoorde. JULY 3–6 Vilvoorde. 7–9 Brussels. 10 Bruges. 11–12 Brussels. 24–31 Vilvoorde. AUGUST 1–5 Brussels. 6–11 Vilvoorde. 12–14 Brussels. 16 Malines. 17–22 Brussels. 23–4 Oudenaarde/Anderlecht/Brussels. 25–7 Brussels. 28 Anderlecht. 31 Brussels. SEPTEMBER 1 Brussels. 4–5 Anderlecht. 6 Braine-l'Alleud. 12–15 Mons. 16 Quiévrain. 18–20 Valenciennes. 21–5 Haspres. 26–31 Marcoing. OCTOBER 1–11 Marcoing. 12–14 Mont-Saint-Martin. 15–16 Origny-en-Thiérache. 18 Guise. 21–2 La Flamengrie (Picardie). 23–4 Avesnes-sur-Helpe. 28–30 Brussels. NOVEMBER 1–6 Brussels. 8–30 Antwerp. DECEMBER 1–31 Antwerp.

1340 JANUARY 1–4 Antwerp. 5 Ghent. 6–8 Antwerp. 11 Lier. 15–26 Ghent. FEBRUARY 1–16 Ghent. 17 Bruges. 18–20 Sluys. 21 Orwell. 28–9 Westminster. MARCH 1–16 Westminster. 18–23 Windsor. 24 Kings Langley. 26–31 Westminster. APRIL 1–11 Westminster. 12–18 Windsor. 19–30 Westminster. MAY 1–15 Westminster. 16–24 Tower of London. 25–7 Westminster. 28–30 Hertford. JUNE 1 Hertford. 4–12 Shotley/Ipswich. 14–15 Newton (Suff.). 17–19 Shotley. 20–2 Orwell. 23 Blankenberg. 24 At sea off Sluys. 27–30 Sluys. JULY 1–7 Sluys. 8–9 Bruges. 10–16 Ghent. 19–20 Oudenaarde. 26 Chin. 27–31 Tournai. AUGUST 1–31 Tournai. SEPTEMBER 1–26 Tournai. 27 Oudenaarde. 28–30 Ghent. OCTOBER 1–31 Ghent. NOVEMBER 1–27 Ghent. 28 Sluys. 29 At sea. 30 Tower of London. DECEMBER 1–20 Tower of London. 21 Ditton (Bucks). ? St Albans. 25 Reading. 29 Guildford. 31 Ditton.

1341 JANUARY 2–11 Westminster. 12 Fulham. 13–18 Tower of London. 20–7 Westminster. 28–9 Tower of London. 30 Westminster. 31 Kings Langley. FEBRUARY 1–7 Kings Langley. 8 Hemel Hempstead. 10–11 Kings Langley. 12 Royston. 17 Norwich. 21–8 Woodstock. MARCH 1–3 Woodstock. 5–19 Kings Langley. 20–3 Ditton. 24–8 Sheen. 29–31 Tower of

London. APRIL 1 Westminster. 2–20 Kings Langley. 22–30 Westminster. MAY 1–27 Westminster. 28 Eltham. 29 Windsor. JUNE 1–10 Kings Langley. 11–19 Tower of London. 20–4 Kings Langley. 25 Ditton. 26–30 Kings Langley. JULY 1–10 Kings Langley. 11 London. 14 Waltham Abbey. 16–17 Tower of London. 18 Waltham Abbey. 20 Tower of London. 21–31 Havering-atte-Bower. AUGUST 1–6 Havering-atte-Bower. 8–15 Tower of London. 16 Sheen. 17–22 Tower of London. 23 Odiham. 24–7 Tower of London. 28 Windsor. 31 Sheen. SEPTEMBER 1–13 Westminster/Tower of London. 14 Chertsey. 15–30 Westminster. OCTOBER 1–7 Westminster. 8–14 Chertsey. 20 Kings Langley. 23–8 Westminster. NOVEMBER 1–19 Stamford. 20–1 Lyddington. 22 Newark/Retford. 26–30 Newcastle upon Tyne. DECEMBER 1–7 Newcastle upon Tyne. 10 Cornhill-on-Tweed. 11–14 Ancrum. 15 Forest of Selkirk. 16–31 Melrose/Roxburgh.

1342 JANUARY 1 Melrose/Roxburgh. 3–7 Newminster. 8–17 Melrose. ? Berwick-upon-Tweed. 20 Newcastle upon Tyne/Morpeth. 21 Durham. 22 Darlington. 23 Northallerton. 24 Boroughbridge. 25 Wetherby. 26 Nottingham. 27–31 Castle Rising. FEBRUARY 1–3 Castle Rising. 4–8 Kings Langley. 9–13 Dunstable. 14–15 Kings Langley. 16–28 Westminster. MARCH 1–15 Westminster/Tower of London. 16–31 Eltham. APRIL 1–4 Eltham. 5–7 Ditton (Bucks). 8–9 West *or* High Wycombe/ Thame/Brackley. 10–14 Northampton. 16 Windsor. 25–6 Woodstock. 27–30 Westminster/Tower of London. MAY 3–7 Westminster. 9 Eltham. 16 Westminster/Mortlake. 22 Woodstock. 26–31 Windsor. JUNE 1 Windsor. 6–8 Hadleigh. 9–12 Woodham Ferrers. 13 Castle Rising. 16 Dunstable. 17–26 Woodstock. 28–9 Mortlake. 30 Tower of London. JULY 1–13 Westminster/Tower of London. 14–16 Windsor. 17 Henley on the Heath. 18–20 Windsor. 21–3 Tower of London. 24–8 Guildford. 29–31 Tower of London. AUGUST 1–26 Tower of London. 27 Leeds (Kent). 28 Sandwich. 29–31 Eastry/Sandwich. SEPTEMBER 1–30 Eastry/Sandwich. OCTOBER 1–3 Eastry/Sandwich. 4 Aboard ship at Sandwich. 5–11 Eastry/Sandwich. 12 Aboard ship at Sandwich. 13–23 At sea off the Goodwin Sands. 24–5 At sea. 26 At sea off Pointe-Saint-Mathieu. 27–8 At anchor in port of Brest. 29–31 Le Rosier (Plougastel-Daoulas). NOVEMBER 1–5 Le Rosier. 6–7 Sizun. 8–9 ?Saint-Herbot. 10–11 Carhaix-Plouguer. 12 ?Langonnet. 13–19 ?Pont-Calleck. 20 ?Pont-Scorff. 21 ?Pluvigner. 22–8 Grand-Champ. 29–30 Vannes. DECEMBER 1–31 Vannes.

1343 JANUARY 1–25 Vannes. 26–31 Port of Vannes. FEBRUARY 1–10 Port of Vannes. 11–12 Belle-Île. 13 La Rade de Brest. 14–15 Plage des Blancs Sablons. 16–18 Le Conquet. 19–22 Port of Crozon. 23–7 Plage des Blancs Sablons. 28 At sea. MARCH 1 Melcombe/Weymouth. 2–3 Salisbury/Winchester. 4 Tower of London/Westminster. 5 Westminster. 6–7 Lamberhurst. 10–? Sittingbourne/Canterbury. 14 Tower of London. 20–? Castle Rising/Walsingham. ? Gloucester/Hereford. 31 Havering-atte-Bower. APRIL 1–19 Havering-atte-Bower. 20–4 Mortlake. 25–30 Westminster. MAY 1–24 Westminster. 25 Stratford (Essex). 26–8 Hertford. 29 Woodford (Essex). 31 Havering-atte-Bower. JUNE 1–4 Havering-atte-Bower. 9 Rochford. 14–23 Windsor. 24–7 London/Westminster. 28–30 Windsor. JULY 1–2 Windsor. 3 Farnham. 4–6 Midhurst. 8 Arundel. 9–10 East Dean. 12–14 Bishop's Waltham. 15 Arundel. 16 Carisbrooke. 20 Chichester. 22–9 Clarendon. AUGUST 1–6 Clarendon. 10–26 Westminster. 28–31 King's Cliffe. SEPTEMBER 1–3 King's Cliffe. 10–11 Clipstone/Rockingham/Nottingham. 14 Mortlake. 22 Tower of London. 26 Woodford. 29 Westminster. OCTOBER 4–5 Leeds. 11–16 Mortlake. 20–6 Castle Rising. 28 Newmarket. 29 Lakenheath/Hitchin. 31 Kings Langley. NOVEMBER 1–7 Kings Langley. 8 Wheathampstead. 10–11 Holywell (Cambs.)/Long Melford. 12–15 Kings Langley. 21–5 Ditton (Bucks). 26–7 Mortlake. 28 Acton. 29–30 Ditton. DECEMBER 1–2 Ditton. 3 Westminster. 4 Duxford. 7 Thetford. 8–9 Castle Rising. 12–14 Ditton. 22 Brill. 23–8 Woodstock.

1344 JANUARY 2 Ditton (Bucks). 3 Woodstock. 6 Reading. 8 Windsor. 9–13 Ditton. 14 Woodstock. 15–24 Windsor. 25–31 Westminster. FEBRUARY 1–3 Westminster. 4 London. 8 Waltham Abbey. 10 Mortlake. 13 Westminster. 19 Henley on the Heath. 25–8 Westminster. MARCH 5 Tower of London. 6 Westminster. 8 Swaffham. 11–15 Castle Rising. 18 Ware. 21–7 Westminster/Tower of London. APRIL 1–9 Marlborough. 14 Tower of London. 16–17 Canterbury. 18 Westminster/Havering-atte-Bower. 24 Marlborough. 26 Reading. MAY 4–8 Castle Rising. 10–14 Berkhamsted. 15 Marlborough. 16 Corsham/Ludgershall. 17–26 Marlborough. 28 Hertford. JUNE 1 Lambeth. 2–30 Westminster. JULY 1–12 Westminster. 13–14 Clarendon. 18–28 Mere (Wilts). AUGUST 3–4 Castle Rising. 8 Kenninghall (Norf.). 11 London. 13–15 Ditton. 16–22 Westminster. 25–7 Bishop's Waltham. 31 Hurstbourne Priors. SEPTEMBER 2–7 Bishop's Waltham. 10 Mere. 11–20 Corfe Castle. 26 Bishop's Waltham. 29–30 Tower of London. OCTOBER 4–11 Bishop's Waltham. 17–31 Long Melford. NOVEMBER 1–14 Long Melford/Castle Rising. 15–18 Orsett. 20–30 Hoxne. DECEMBER 1–15 Hoxne. 17 Rickinghall. 18–20 Ashwellthorpe. 21–7 Norwich. 28–9 Taverham.

1345 JANUARY 1–2 Wymondham. 3–5 Norwich. 10–23 Westminster. 23–31 Mortlake. FEBRUARY 1–4 Mortlake. 5 Ditton (Bucks). 16 Westminster. 21–4 Teynham (Kent). 28 Westminster. MARCH 1–17 Westminster/Tower of London. 18 Sheen. 19–23 Windsor. 27–9 Guildford. 30 Tower of London. APRIL 1–3 Tower of London. 4–5 Eltham. 6–26 Westminster. 28 Tower of London. 30 Ware. MAY 1 Pickenham (Norf.). 5–7 Reading. 9–12 Westminster. 15–16 Eltham. 17–19 Westminster. 20 Lambeth. 26–8 Westminster. JUNE 6 Reading. 8 Southampton. ? Canterbury. 12 Sturry (Kent). 13–17 Tower of London.

18–19 Aboard ship at Sandwich. 20–30 Sandwich. JULY 1–2 Sandwich. 3
At sea. 4 At sea off Sluys. 5–21 At anchor off Sluys. 22–5 At sea. 26–7
Sandwich. 28 Canterbury. 29 Rochester. AUGUST 1–5 Westminster. 6–9
Hertford. 12 Kings Langley. 13 Woodstock. 14 Princes Risborough. 17
Woodstock. 21–31 Westminster. SEPTEMBER 1 Westminster. 6 Havering-
atte-Bower. 8–10 Tower of London. 11 Hertford. 14–16 Windsor. 18–30
Woolmer Green (Herts). OCTOBER 1 Kings Langley. 3–30 Westminster.
NOVEMBER 1–5 Kings Langley. 7 Mortlake. 9–12 Westminster. 16
Baldock/Rockingham. 17–26 Rockingham. 27 Melton Mowbray. 28
Oakham. 26 Rockingham. 29 Nottingham. 30 Rockingham.
DECEMBER 1–3 Rockingham. 4–5 Clipstone. 6 Lyddington. 7–15
Clipstone. 16 Ware. 18–21 Westminster. 25–31 Woodstock.

1346 JANUARY 1–3 Woodstock. 14 Aylestone. 15 Leicester. 16–21
Aylestone. FEBRUARY 1–4 Kings Langley. 6–28 Westminster. MARCH
1–31 Westminster. APRIL 1–7 Westminster. 9–12 Tower of London. 16–18
Guildford. MAY 3–18 Westminster. 21–4 Guildford. 25–7 Portchester. 28
Portsmouth. 29–31 Portchester. JUNE 1–28 Portchester. 29 Portsmouth. 30
Portchester. JULY 1 Portchester. 2–3 Isle of Wight. 4–5 Freshwater. 6–8
Yarmouth (Isle of Wight). 9 Freshwater. 12–17 Saint-Vaast-la-Hougue. 18
Valognes. 19 Saint-Côme-du-Mont. 20 Carentan. 21 Pont Hébert. 22
Saint-Lô. 23 Sept-Vents. 24 Torteval-Quesnay. 25 Fonteney-le-Pesnel.
26–30 Caen. 31 Troarn. AUGUST 1 Léaupartie. 2–3 Lisieux. 4
Duranville. 5–6 Le Neubourg. 7 Elbeuf. 8 Pont de l'Arche/Le Vaudreuil.
9 Gaillon/Saint-Pierre-d'Autils. 10 Vernon/Freneuse. 11 Rolleboise/
Mantes/Epône. 12 Ecquevilly. 13–15 Poissy. 16 Boissy l'Aillerie/Grisy-les-
Plâtres. 17 Hénonville/Auteuil. 18 Beauvais/Troissereux. 19 Sommereux.
20 Poix-de-Picardie/Camps-en-Amiénois. 21–2 Airaines. 23 Acheux-en-
Vimeu/Blanchetaque. 24–5 Forest of Crécy. 26–7 Field of Crécy. 28
Valloires (Argoules). 29 Maintenay. 30 Saint-Josse. 31 Neufchâtel-
Hardelot. SEPTEMBER 1 Neufchâtel-Hardelot. 2–3 Wimille. 4–30
Calais. OCTOBER 1–31 Calais. NOVEMBER 1–30 Calais.
DECEMBER 1–31 Calais.

1347 JANUARY 1–31 Calais. FEBRUARY 1–28 Calais. MARCH 1–12
Calais. 13 Bergues. 14–31 Calais. APRIL 1–30 Calais. MAY 1–31 Calais.
JUNE 1–30 Calais. JULY 1–31 Calais. AUGUST 1–31 Calais.
SEPTEMBER 1–30 Calais. OCTOBER 1–11 Calais. 12 Sandwich. 13
Canterbury. 14 Dartford/Westminster. 15–20 Westminster. 28 Newmarket.
NOVEMBER 11–13 Westminster. 14–18 Kings Langley. 23–30
Westminster. DECEMBER 1–9 Westminster. 10–15 Iver. 20 Westminster.
21 Chertsey. 22 Guildford. 23 Chertsey. 24–8 Guildford.

1348 JANUARY 1–3 Windsor. 6 Reading. 8–9 Windsor. 14–31
Westminster. FEBRUARY 1–12 Westminster. ? Reading. ? Bury St

Edmunds. MARCH 1–7 Windsor. 8 Westminster. 12 Hertford. 26–31 Westminster. APRIL 1–17 Westminster. 18–23 Mortlake. 24–6 Windsor. 27–9 Woodstock. 30 Banbury. MAY 1–2 Kenilworth. 4–12 Lichfield. 14–19 Windsor. 20 Eltham. 27–30 Windsor. JUNE 5 Westminster. 7 Hertford. 8 Woodstock. 14–21 Windsor. 23 Iver. 24–30 Windsor. JULY 9 Mortlake. 12 Hadleigh. 14–15 Canterbury. 21 Windsor. 30 Eltham. AUGUST 8–14 Odiham. 15–20 Woodstock. 21 Hampstead Marshall. 22–31 Woodstock. SEPTEMBER 5 Westminster. 11–12 Clarendon. 14 Hurstbourne Priors. 15–18 Woodstock. OCTOBER 15 Sandwich. 21–6 Tower of London/Westminster. 28–31 Sandwich. NOVEMBER 1–29 Sandwich. 30 Calais. DECEMBER 1–2 Calais. 3 Sandwich. 10–14 Westminster/Tower of London. 17–22 Otford. 23 Sandwich. 24–7 Otford. 29 Westminster.

1349 JANUARY 1–6 Merton. 9 Otford. 10 Rotherhithe. 18 Hatfield (Hert). 20–8 Kings Langley. 30 Westminster. FEBRUARY 1–2 Westminster. 4–9 Kings Langley. 10–22 Castle Rising. 23–8 Kings Langley. MARCH 1–6 Kings Langley. 7–16 Westminster. 17–28 Kings Langley. APRIL 1–5 Kings Langley. 10–11 Woodstock. 12–19 Kings Langley. 20–8 Windsor. 30 Woodstock. MAY 1–31 Woodstock. JUNE 1–12 Woodstock. 13–23 Westminster. 24–5 Windsor. 28 Henley on the Heath. 29–30 Selborne. JULY 1 Selborne. 3 Highclere. 6 Goodworth Clatford. 7–14 Clarendon. 15–19 Lyndhurst. 20 Stanley (Dorset)/Corfe Castle. 21–2 Corfe Castle. 23 Cranborne. 24–30 Clarendon. 31 Marlborough. AUGUST 5–6 Marlborough. 7 Devizes. 8–10 Stanley (Wilts). 11 Corsham. 14–16 Mortlake. 17–27 Westminster. 28 Rotherhithe. 29 Sonning. 31 Gloucester. SEPTEMBER 1 Forest of Dean. 2 Sonning. 3–4 Flaxley. 7 Weston-under-Penyard. 10–14 Bicknor (Glos.). 16–18 Marlborough. 21–8 Westminster. 30 Mortlake. OCTOBER 3–6 Sheen. 9 Mortlake. 12–16 Westminster. 19 Mortlake. 24–8 Hereford. 29–30 Rotherhithe. NOVEMBER 1–7 Orsett. 12 Canterbury. 14–17 Faversham. 29 Rotherhithe. DECEMBER 5–7 Orsett. 25–8 Havering-atte-Bower.

1350 JANUARY 2 Calais. 10–20 Havering-atte-Bower. 23 Kings Langley. 26 Westminster. FEBRUARY 10 Bobbing. 11–23 Westminster. 24–8 Croydon. MARCH 1–3 Croydon. 5 Rotherhithe. 15–31 Croydon. APRIL 1 Croydon. 5 Windsor. 7 Henley on the Heath. 8–14 Selborne. 15 Westminster. 17–26 Windsor. 30 Westminster. MAY 2–4 Rotherhithe. 5–6 Windsor. 7–8 Westminster. 13 St Albans. 16–26 Windsor. 28 Hertford. JUNE 1 Henley on the Heath. 4 Windsor. 6 Henley on the Heath. 7 Wherwell. 8–15 Selborne. 16 Henley on the Heath. 18 Westminster. 20 Mortlake. 30 Westminster. JULY 2 Boxworth. 4 Rotherhithe. 12–13 Westminster. 16 Havering-atte-Bower. 20–4 Westminster. 25–6 King's Cliffe. 27–31 Blatherwycke. AUGUST 1 Blatherwycke. 2 Rockingham. 6 Westminster. 7 London/Rotherhithe. 8–10 Rotherhithe. 14–27 Sandwich. 28 Winchelsea. 29 At sea off Winchelsea. 30–1 Rye. SEPTEMBER 1–3

Rye. 4 Winchelsea. 6 Canterbury. 7–8 Rotherhithe. 9–11 Hertford. 14–19 Bestwood. 20–4 Clipstone. 30 Westminster. OCTOBER 4–12 Westminster. 20 Mortlake. 26 Westminster. NOVEMBER 1 Mortlake. 2–3 Westminster. 6 Mortlake. 9 Reading. 10–14 Hampstead Marshall. 18–24 Westminster. 25–30 Reading. DECEMBER 1–8 Reading. 17 Castle Rising. 20–8 Ludgershall.

1351 JANUARY 3 Rotherhithe. 5–20 Tower of London. FEBRUARY 9–28 Westminster. MARCH 1–16 Westminster. 17–20 Eltham. 23–7 Queenborough.[7] 28–9 Croydon. APRIL 15–18 Eltham. 23–5 Windsor. 28 Mortlake. MAY 1–12 Westminster. 13–14 Rotherhithe. 15–20 Westminster. 26 Eltham. JUNE 4–5 Eltham. JULY 1 Hertford. 21 Eltham. 31 Windsor. AUGUST 1 London. 5–7 Henley on the Heath. 23–4 Odiham. SEPTEMBER 4–6 Tower of London. 15 Woodstock. 28 Chertsey. OCTOBER 15 Chertsey. 16 Mortlake. NOVEMBER 1 Mortlake. 25 Reading. DECEMBER 1 Salden. 12 St Albans. 26–7 Woodstock.

1352 JANUARY 13–31 Westminster. FEBRUARY 1–14 Westminster. MARCH 3 Thurrock. 6 Westminster. 15 Mortlake. 27 Queenborough. 28 Windsor. APRIL 1–3 Thurrock. 6–10 Havering-atte-Bower. 16–30 Windsor. MAY 9–14 Windsor. 20 ?Epping. 23–4 Rotherhithe. 27–30 Eltham. JUNE 1 Westminster. 2 Windsor. 6 Eltham. 16 Rotherhithe. 26–30 Windsor. JULY 1–5 Windsor. 6 Stratfield Mortimer. 8–12 Windsor. 15 Thurrock. 17 Henley on the Heath. 19 Guildford. AUGUST 1 Hadleigh. 7–10 Henley on the Heath. 16–25 Westminster. SEPTEMBER 9–12 Hertford. 16 Windsor. 24–5 Thurrock. OCTOBER 13 Windsor. 24 Westminster. 27 Great *or* Little Coxwell. NOVEMBER 1 Mortlake/ Windsor. 2–4 Windsor. 7 Rotherhithe. 18–28 Windsor. DECEMBER 5 Windsor. 15 Biggleswade. 25–9 St Albans. 30 Windsor.

1353 JANUARY 3–7 Windsor. 14 Tower of London. 20 Hertford. 30 Duxford. FEBRUARY 16 Mortlake. 20 Windsor. 22 Rotherhithe. 24 Thurrock. MARCH 1 Westminster. 8 Mortlake. 19–27 Eltham. APRIL 5–12 Mortlake. 18 Westminster. 20 Chertsey. 21–6 Windsor. 29 Mortlake. MAY 1 Windsor. 12 Thurrock. 17 Mortlake. JUNE 5–6 Westminster. 7 Kingston upon Thames/Henley on the Heath. 8 Guildford. 9 Alton. 10 Winchester. 11 Salisbury.[8] JULY 1 Westminster. 2–16 Windsor. 18

---

[7] Until 1367, when the king's castle and new town were styled Queenborough, the site was referred to as Rushenden; the name Queenborough is used throughout this itinerary in order to avoid confusion.

[8] The household remained at Salisbury until the beginning of Aug. and then moved off via Warminster, Malmesbury and Cirencester to Gloucester, where it remained between 19 Aug. and 16 Sept. It then moved by stages to Northampton, where it remained for the period 19 Sept.–7 Dec. before making its way back, via Dunstable and St Albans, to Eltham

Havering-atte-Bower. 20 Windsor. 28 Odiham. 31 Clarendon. AUGUST 6 East Tytherley. 18–26 Woodstock. SEPTEMBER 2 Flaxley. 4 Woodstock. 23–30 Westminster. OCTOBER 1–15 Westminster. 21 Mortlake. 24 Westminster. NOVEMBER 1–13 Woodstock. DECEMBER 7–9 Windsor. 25–31 Eltham.

1354 JANUARY 1–6 Eltham. 16 Windsor. 22 Westminster. 30–1 Colchester. FEBRUARY 1–4 Colchester. 5 Bury St Edmunds. 6–12 Colchester. 20 Rotherhithe. MARCH 4 Mortlake. 20 Westminster. APRIL 9–13 Eltham. 28–30 Westminster. MAY 1–20 Westminster. 23 Windsor. 27 Swallowfield. 28 Chertsey. JUNE 1 Chertsey. 5 Windsor. 10 Chertsey. JULY 2 Havering-atte-Bower. 15 Arundel. 20–2 Carisbrooke. 23 Lyndhurst. 25–7 Clarendon. AUGUST 2–6 Woodstock. 10–13 Blatherwycke. 14–25 Rockingham. 26–31 Clipstone. SEPTEMBER 1 Clipstone. 3 Daventry. 9 Woodstock. 26 Hampstead Marshall. 28 Woodstock. OCTOBER 4 Mortlake. 5–8 Westminster. 12 Hampstead Marshall. 14–15 Woodstock. 29 Hampstead Marshall. 31 Westminster. NOVEMBER 6 Woodstock. 7 Tower of London. 20 Westminster. 30 Hampstead Marshall. DECEMBER 5–16 Clarendon. 24–30 Hampstead Marshall.

1355 JANUARY 1–4 Hampstead Marshall. 24 Woodstock. FEBRUARY 10–26 Woodstock. MARCH 12 Hampstead Marshall. APRIL 1 Woodstock. 9 Shabbington. ? Westminster. 23–4 Windsor. MAY 5 Chertsey. 7 Basingstoke. 16 Windsor. 20 Rotherhithe. 23 Windsor. 24 Eltham. JUNE 17 Odiham. JULY 1–6 Northfleet. 8 Erith. 10 Westminster. 11–22 Northfleet. 26 Winchelsea. 28–31 Deal. AUGUST 4 Deal. 5–12 Winchelsea. SEPTEMBER 9 Portsmouth. 10–13 Southwick (Hants). 14 Portsmouth. 23–9 Sandwich. 30 Eltham. OCTOBER 2–6 Eltham. 16–28 Sandwich. ?29–31 Calais. NOVEMBER 1–11 Calais. 12 Sandwich. 13–14 Eltham. 23–30 Westminster. DECEMBER 3 Huntingdon. 13 Markham Moor. 20 Northallerton. 23 Durham. 25–31 Newcastle upon Tyne.

1356 JANUARY 1–11 Newcastle upon Tyne. 13 Berwick-upon-Tweed. 16–23 Bamburgh. 25 Roxburgh. FEBRUARY ? Edinburgh. ? Haddington. 12–15 Bamburgh. 16–24 Newcastle upon Tyne. MARCH 12 Mortlake. 17 Eltham. 20 Windsor. 22 Henley on the Heath. 26–8 Eltham. APRIL 7–9

on 21 Dec. Tout, *Chapters*, iv, 179, supposed that the king followed this itinerary. But the relevant account, E 101/392/12, provides no direct evidence that Edward III was present at any of these locations in person, and states (fol. 34) that he was at Woodstock on 1 Nov. The progress into the West Midlands seems rather to have been laid on as a tour of religious sites by the king's children (see p. 318). Apart from a reference to a royal visit to Flaxley on 2 Sept., the privy seal evidence suggests that the king moved no further west than Woodstock during this period.

Clarendon. 13–28 Windsor. MAY 3–15 Windsor. 18 Basingstoke/
Clarendon. 19–28 Clarendon. 30 Reading. JUNE 11–12 Hertford. 14–15
Woodstock. 18 Kings Langley. 23 Windsor. 26 Westminster. JULY 8
Easthampstead. 13 Henley on the Heath. 18 Westminster. 25 Henley on
the Heath. AUGUST 1–10 Westminster. 14 Bramshaw. SEPTEMBER 4
Clarendon. 14 Canford Magna. 19 Lyndhurst. OCTOBER 4 Reading. 26
Mortlake. NOVEMBER 1–2 Reading. 4–10 Mortlake. 22 Dartford. 27
Westminster. DECEMBER 25–7 Eltham.

1357 JANUARY 6 Reading. FEBRUARY 4 Mortlake. 23 Ludgershall.
25–7 Reading. MARCH 6 Buckden. 10–30 Reading. APRIL 2–12 Kings
Langley. 17–20 Westminster. 21–3 Windsor. 24–30 Westminster. MAY 1–?8
Westminster. 14 Mortlake. 24 London/Westminster. 27 Woodstock. 30
Reading. JUNE 3–17 Woodstock. 23–4 Mortlake. 26–8 Henley on the
Heath. JULY 13 Westminster. AUGUST 3 Woodstock. 15 Beckley (Oxon).
16 Westminster. SEPTEMBER 9 Woodstock. 17 Clarendon. 18 Marwell
(Hants). 23 Hurstbourne Priors. ? London. OCTOBER ? London. 6
Woodstock. NOVEMBER (no evidence). DECEMBER 24–7
Marlborough. 28 Hampstead Marshall. 30 Marlborough.

1358 JANUARY 6–14 Bristol. 16 Marlborough. 28 Hampstead
Marshall. 30–1 Easthampstead. FEBRUARY 5–27 Westminster. MARCH
2 Kings Langley. 15 Mortlake. 20 Hertford. 24–31 Kings Langley. APRIL
1–13 Kings Langley. 20–5 Windsor. MAY 1 London. 17–20 Havering-atte-
Bower. 22–24 London. JUNE 5 Clarendon. 6 Henley on the Heath. 12–24
Westminster. 25–6 Henley on the Heath. JULY 4 Hadleigh. 8–10
Havering-atte-Bower. 12 Hertford. 22 Westminster. AUGUST 1–4
Windsor. 10 Corsham. SEPTEMBER 7–18 Marlborough. 24–30
Ramsbury. OCTOBER 1 Ramsbury. 3 Windsor. 4–5 Mortlake. 21
Reading. NOVEMBER 3 Reading. 27 London. DECEMBER 4
Westminster. 25–8 Havering-atte-Bower.

1359 JANUARY (no evidence). FEBRUARY 23 Sheen. MARCH 24
Westminster. APRIL 6 Hadleigh. 11–12 Rotherhithe. 19–30 Windsor. MAY
3 Windsor. 11 Eltham. 20 Reading. 27–9 London. JUNE (no evidence).
JULY 20 Westminster. 23 Duxford. AUGUST 5 Easthampstead. 9
Havering-atte-Bower. 15 Westminster. 27–31 Leeds (Kent). SEPTEMBER
1–4 Leeds. 5–15 Sandwich/Thorne. 16 Leeds. 18 Sandwich/Thorne.
20–6 Leeds/Sandwich. 28 Sandwich. OCTOBER 1–7 Sandwich/
Thorne. 8–27 Great Stonar/Sandwich. 28–31 Calais. NOVEMBER
1–3 Calais. ? Arras. ? Saint-Quentin. ? Craonne. DECEMBER 4–31
Verzy.

1360 JANUARY 1–11 Verzy. ? Châlons-sur-Marne. 18–26 Pogny. ?
Trouans. ? Méry-sur-Seine. FEBRUARY ? Troyes. ? Cerisiers. ? Saint-

Florentin. ? Pontigny. ? Tonnerre. ? Noyers. 19–28 Guillon. MARCH 1–10 Guillon. ? Asquins. ? Coulanges-sur-Yonne. ? Montargis ? Chanteloup (Saint-Germaine-lès-Arpajon). APRIL 1–10 Chanteloup. ? Montlhéry. ? Châtillon. 13 Chartres. ? Bonneval. ? Châteaudun. ? Nids. 18–28 Tournoisis. MAY 5–6 Sours. 8 Brétigny/Sours. 9 Sours. ? Le Neubourg. 12–16 Thibouville. 17 Honfleur. 18 Rye. 19–31 Westminster. JUNE 1–30 Westminster. JULY 1–7 Westminster. 8–13 Eltham. 20–31 Havering-atte-Bower. AUGUST 5–12 Havering-atte-Bower. SEPTEMBER 5–15 Queenborough. 17 Hadleigh. 18 Thorne (Kent). 19 Great Stonar/ Hadleigh. 20–1 Hadleigh. 24 Thorne. 25–6 Great Stonar. 27–30 Thorne. OCTOBER 2–3 Thorne. 4–5 Great Stonar. 6 Queenborough. 8 Great Stonar. 9–31 Calais. NOVEMBER 1 Calais. 2–3 Westminster. 5–13 Havering-atte-Bower. 15–16 Sheen. 18 Chertsey. DECEMBER 5 Windsor. 6 West or High Wycombe. 9–31 Woodstock.

1361   JANUARY 1–6 Woodstock. 7 Thame. 8 West or High Wycombe. 9 Windsor. 10–11 Henley on the Heath. 12–23 Sheen. 24–31 Westminster. FEBRUARY 1–18 Westminster. 19–27 Sheen. 28 Rotherhithe. MARCH 1 Thurrock. 3 Hadleigh. 8 Graveney. 9 Hadleigh. 11 Rotherhithe. 12–15 Sheen. 18–28 Windsor. 31 Sheen. APRIL 1–2 Sheen. 3 Windsor. 5 Rotherhithe. 6 Hadleigh. 8 Queenborough. 11 Westminster. 13 Sheen. 18–19 Westminster. 23–5 Windsor. 29 Sheen. 30 Westminster. MAY 3 Woodford (Essex). 6 Rotherhithe. 7 Hadleigh. 9 Queenborough. 10–21 Hadleigh. JUNE 8 Kings Langley. 11 Windsor. 13 Woodstock. 20–4 Windsor. 25 Clarendon. 29–30 Tower of London. JULY 1 Hertford. 12 Windsor. 19–20 Henley on the Heath. 21–4 Easthampstead. 25–6 Henley on the Heath. 27–8 Swallowfield. AUGUST 1 Ludgershall. 5 Clarendon. 6–12 Brockenhurst. 13–24 Beaulieu. 25 Carisbrooke. 28–31 Beaulieu. SEPTEMBER 1 Hathebergh Lodge (Hants). 3–7 Beaulieu. 13 Beaulieu/Hathebergh Lodge. 14–15 Clarendon. 18 Ludgershall. 20 Windsor. 22 Rotherhithe. 23–5 Windsor. 26 Hadleigh. 30 Windsor. OCTOBER 4–13 Windsor. 18 Sheen. 23 Windsor. 25 Westminster. 30 Thurrock. NOVEMBER 1 Hadleigh. 19–20 Windsor. 25 Reading. 26 Windsor. DECEMBER 24–31 Windsor.

1362   JANUARY 1–6 Windsor. 12–14 Thurrock. 17 London. 23 Beaulieu. 31 Windsor. FEBRUARY 6–8 Windsor. 13–22 Windsor. MARCH 6 Windsor. 18–21 Westminster. APRIL 6–7 Windsor. 10 Westminster. 12–24 Windsor. 26 Westminster. 27–8 Windsor. MAY 1–5 Westminster/Tower of London. 14 Westminster. JUNE 12 Sheen. 22–5 Westminster. JULY 7–19 Westminster. 24 Easthampstead. 25–30 Havering-atte-Bower. AUGUST 6–9 Havering-atte-Bower. 14 Windsor. 20–8 Woodstock. 29 Shipton-under-Wychwood. SEPTEMBER 3–5 Beckley. 6–11 Woodstock. 13 Easthampstead. 15 Beckley. 17–18 Farnham. 23–5 Queenborough. OCTOBER 1 Thurrock. 13–31 Westminster/Sheen.

NOVEMBER 1–17 Westminster/Sheen/Chertsey. DECEMBER 2 Windsor. 28 Windsor.

1363 JANUARY 2–8 Windsor. 18 Sheen. 24 Windsor. 27–30 Kings Langley. FEBRUARY 1 Westminster/Windsor. 2–5 Windsor. 6 Eltham. 7 Sheen. 19 Westminster. MARCH 1 Westminster. 25 Kings Langley. 30 Eltham. APRIL 2–6 Kings Langley. 22–3 Windsor. MAY 26–7 Westminster. 29 Windsor. JUNE 5 Kings Langley. 10–16 Salden. 23–5 Northampton. 27–9 Drayton (Northants). JULY 3–11 Nassington. 12–16 Rockingham. 20–1 Launde. ? Leicester. 25–31 Clipstone. AUGUST 1–10 Clipstone. 18–19 Newstead. 21–31 Bestwood. SEPTEMBER 1–7 Bestwood. 8 Nottingham. 9 Moor End. 12–14 Kings Langley. 23 Queenborough. 26 Hadleigh. OCTOBER 6–30 Westminster/Sheen. NOVEMBER 1 Windsor. 10–13 Sheen. ? London. 27 Westminster. DECEMBER 6–30 Windsor.

1364 JANUARY 7–9 Sheen. 10 Windsor. 11–24 Eltham. FEBRUARY 2 Sheen. 4 Eltham. 12 Sheen. 13–16 Westminster. 17–20 Eltham. 21 Sheen. 22 Eltham. 25 Sheen. MARCH 1–7 Eltham. 18 Windsor. 21–5 Eltham. APRIL 2 Westminster. 6 Windsor. 11–14 Eltham. ? London. 23 Windsor. MAY 1–4 Eltham. 9–10 Gravesend. 13–15 Queenborough. JUNE 8–13 Chertsey. 15 Salden. 16 Moor End. 20 Chertsey. 22–3 Sheen. JULY 20–1 Westminster. 24–5 Havering-atte-Bower. 26–7 Hadleigh. 28–30 Havering-atte-Bower/Gravesend. AUGUST 2–3 Eltham. 7 Lewes. 8 Rotherhithe/Havering-atte-Bower. 10–15 Havering-atte-Bower. 20 Windsor. 21–5 Henley on the Heath. 26 Easthampstead. 28 Windsor. SEPTEMBER 3 Windsor. 12–13 Woodstock. 15 Beckley. 18 Kings Langley. 20 Windsor. 25 Gravesend. 27 Queenborough. OCTOBER 1 Dover. 2–3 Canterbury. 4–20 Dover. NOVEMBER 1 Kings Langley. 13 Windsor. 20 Westminster. DECEMBER 3 Sheen. 18–30 Windsor.

1365 JANUARY 1 Windsor. 7–11 Woodstock. 12–13 Beckley. 14 Thame. 15–18 Windsor. 20–31 Westminster/Eltham. FEBRUARY 1–?17 Westminster/Windsor/Sheen. 22 Westminster. 25 Windsor. 27–8 Kings Langley. MARCH 1 Moor End. 6 Kings Langley. 7–9 Windsor. 12–14 Hadleigh. 18 Gravesend. 19–20 Eltham. 23–31 Windsor. APRIL 1–27 Windsor. MAY 20–31 Windsor. JUNE 1–7 Windsor. 14 Gravesend. 20 Westminster. 23–4 Windsor. 25–8 Henley on the Heath. JULY 2 Easthampstead. 3 Selborne. 13–15 Easthampstead. 16–17 Stratfield Mortimer. 18–31 Windsor. AUGUST 1–8 Windsor. 9 Hurstbourne Priors. 15–31 Marlborough. SEPTEMBER 5 Vastern. 6 Windsor. 8–9 Stanley (Wilts). 12 Marlborough. 16–30 Windsor. OCTOBER 1–2 Windsor. 3–8 Thame. 11 Windsor. 12 Kings Langley. 30 Windsor. NOVEMBER 2 Windsor. 5 Gravesend. 8–11 Queenborough. 20–1 Windsor. 23 Kings

Langley. 29–30 Windsor. DECEMBER 6 Westminster. 7–9 Windsor. 10–20 Kings Langley. 21–28 Windsor.

1366 JANUARY 2–7 Kings Langley. 13 Westminster. 24–6 Windsor. 27–8 Kings Langley. 29–31 Moor End. FEBRUARY 1–9 Moor End.[9] 10–13 Kings Langley. 15–21 Windsor. ? Westminster. 27 Queenborough. MARCH 1 Hadleigh. ? Westminster. 8–9 Queenborough. 10 Gravesend. 14–19 Windsor. 20 Sheen. 25 Leeds (Kent). 27–30 Windsor. APRIL 1–8 Windsor. 13 Queenborough. 23–8 Windsor. MAY 1 Eltham. 4–12 Westminster. 18 Windsor. 24 Queenborough. 25–7 Leeds. 28–31 Queenborough. JUNE 2 Milton (Kent). 4–6 Windsor. 8 Eltham. 13 Westminster/Sheen. 15 London. 17–18 Windsor. 19 Chertsey. 20–3 East Tytherley. 25–9 Clarendon. JULY 1 Downton. 3 Breamore. 4–11 Hathebergh Lodge (Hants). 13–16 Brockenhurst. 17–19 Beaulieu. AUGUST 3 Henley on the Heath. 4 Beaulieu. 6 Brockenhurst. 8 East Tytherley. 9 ?Canford Magna. 10 Corfe Castle. 12 Kingswood. 14–18 Corfe Castle. 19–20 Cranborne. 23–6 Dinton. SEPTEMBER 1–5 Clarendon. 9–17 Havering-atte-Bower. 18 Burstead (Essex). 19 Hadleigh. 21–6 Queenborough. 29 Gravesend. 30 Sheen. OCTOBER 13–14 Sheen. 15–16 Westminster. 19 Windsor. 23 Sheen. 24–5 Westminster. 26 Sheen. 28 Westminster. 30 Windsor. 31 Chertsey. NOVEMBER 1 Chertsey. 2 Westminster. 3 Sheen/Westminster. 5 Sheen. 6 Chertsey. 8–11 Windsor. 13 Beckley. 14 Woodstock. 15–20 Shipton-under-Wychwood. 22–5 Woodstock. 26–30 Windsor. DECEMBER 1–2 Windsor. 3–4 Westminster. 5 Gravesend. 6 Westminster. 9 Eltham. 12–15 Queenborough. 18 Windsor. 21 Kings Langley. 25–31 Windsor.

1367 JANUARY 1–2 Windsor. 5–7 Sheen. 9–14 Windsor. 15–18 Sheen. 20–2 Windsor. 23 Sheen/Windsor. 24–6 Windsor. 27 Sheen. 28–31 Kings Langley. FEBRUARY 1–2 Moor End. 10 Westminster. 13 Sheen. 26 Eltham. MARCH 2–14 Queenborough. 18 Gravesend. 22–31 Queenborough. APRIL 1–7 Queenborough. 8 Gravesend. 10–19 Eltham. 22–7 Windsor. 29 Sheen/Eltham. MAY 1–7 Sheen. 13–15 Westminster. 19–29 Queenborough. JUNE 5–6 Sheen. 8–9 Eltham. 10–14 Canterbury. 16 Leeds (Kent). 20–6 Queenborough. 28 Eltham. JULY 1–2 Eltham. 10 Henley on the Heath. 12–14 Eltham/Rotherhithe. 16–17 Henley on the Heath. 18–19 Easthampstead. 22 Windsor. 30 Hadleigh. AUGUST 3–11 Havering-atte-Bower. 14–15 Eltham. 17–20 Havering-atte-Bower. 22 Gravesend. 28 Hadleigh. 30–1 Havering-atte-Bower. SEPTEMBER 1 Havering-atte-Bower. 7 Windsor. 9–10 Easthampstead. 20 Rotherhithe. OCTOBER 23 Windsor. NOVEMBER 3–4 Westminster. 5 Sheen. 8

---

[9] From 1 Feb. 1366 to 31 Jan. 1367 the royal household remained permanently fixed either at Windsor or at Havering-atte-Bower: E 101/396/2; Tout, *Chapters*, iv, 179.

Windsor. 10–14 Westminster. 16 Windsor. 17–22 Westminster. 26–30 Windsor. DECEMBER 3–6 Westminster. 7–9 Eltham. 12 Leeds. 14–16 Queenborough. 18 Eltham. 27–9 Windsor.

1368 JANUARY 4–5 Windsor. 16 Kings Langley. FEBRUARY 25 Westminster. MARCH 8 Queenborough. 14 Sheen. 16 Windsor. APRIL 7–22 Windsor. MAY 1–21 Westminster. 23–6 Windsor. JUNE 1 Gravesend. 9–10 Rotherhithe. 29 Preston (Kent). JULY 1 Windsor. 7 Leeds (Kent). 13–20 Windsor. 27–9 Guildford. 30 Henley on the Heath. AUGUST 1 Windsor. 6 Kings Langley. 22 Moor End. 30–1 Woodstock. SEPTEMBER 1–2 Woodstock. 10 Freemantle Forest (Hants). 11–22 Windsor. OCTOBER 2 Rotherhithe. 4 Gravesend. NOVEMBER 9 Sheen. 20 Windsor. 25 Gravesend. 28 Westminster. DECEMBER 7 Kings Langley. 8–11 Sheen. 25 Windsor.

1369 JANUARY 1 Windsor. 12 Sheen. 16 Westminster. FEBRUARY 10 Westminster. 12 Sheen. MARCH 19 Rotherhithe. 20 Windsor. APRIL 1–3 Windsor. 5 Sheen. 10–11 Gravesend. 12–15 Queenborough. 16–17 Gravesend. 23–5 Windsor. MAY 14 Canterbury. 20 Windsor. 28–30 Westminster. JUNE 1–18 Westminster. 26 Rotherhithe. JULY 1 Gravesend. 7 Rotherhithe. AUGUST 12 Sheen. 18–25 Eltham. 26–9 Rotherhithe. SEPTEMBER 1 Eltham. 6–7 Preston (Kent). 15 Rotherhithe. OCTOBER 1 Eltham. 3 Rotherhithe. 8 Tower of London. 10 Eltham. NOVEMBER 9–10 Eltham. 18 Westminster. DECEMBER 21 Kings Langley.

1370 JANUARY. 8 Westminster. 21 Westminster. FEBRUARY. ? Westminster. MARCH 26–8 Eltham. APRIL 23 Windsor. MAY 2 Gravesend. 20 Sheen. JUNE 4 Westminster. 20 Rotherhithe. JULY 27–31 Clarendon. AUGUST 1–14 Clarendon. 28 Eltham/Havering-atte-Bower. SEPTEMBER 5 Havering-atte-Bower. OCTOBER 4 Eltham. 7–16 Sheen. NOVEMBER 26 Westminster. DECEMBER 22 Sheen. 28 Kings Langley.

1371 JANUARY 8 Sheen. FEBRUARY 24–8 Westminster. MARCH 1–29 Westminster. APRIL 4–11 Kings Langley. 23 Windsor. MAY 5 Henley on the Heath. 6–13 Guildford. 14 Canterbury. 19–26 Windsor. JUNE 8–22 Winchester. JULY 8–15 Windsor. 27 Westminster. AUGUST 10 Clarendon. 12 Hurstbourne Priors. ? Everleigh. 22–31 Marlborough. SEPTEMBER 1–14 Marlborough. 20 Stratfield Mortimer. 24 Windsor. 29 Westminster. OCTOBER (no evidence). NOVEMBER 12–20 Gravesend. DECEMBER 25–31 Eltham.

1372 JANUARY 1 Eltham. 6 Sheen. 26 Westminster. FEBRUARY 2 Eltham. 6 Sheen. 13 Westminster. 14 Kings Langley. MARCH 26–31 Eltham. APRIL 1 Canterbury. 4–5 Westminster. 23–5 Windsor. MAY 6

Sheen. 16 Windsor. 22 Sheen. JUNE 25 London. JULY 5–10 Henley on the Heath. ? Wallingford. AUGUST 1 Eltham. 8 Westminster. 12 Gravesend. 14 Leeds (Kent). 17 Godmersham. 18 Canterbury/Preston (Kent). 19–26 Preston. 27–31 Aboard ship at Sandwich. SEPTEMBER 1–6 Aboard ship at Sandwich. 15–30 Aboard ship at Winchelsea. OCTOBER 1–14 Aboard ship at Winchelsea. 20 Banstead. 21 Sheen. NOVEMBER 1–2 Sheen. 3–24 Westminster. DECEMBER 12 Eltham. 15–16 Sheen. 25–31 Eltham.

1373 JANUARY 1–3 Eltham. 5–6 Sheen. 30 Sheen. FEBRUARY 2 Sheen. 4 Kings Langley. 19 Sheen. MARCH 9 Kings Langley. APRIL 15–18 Kings Langley. 23–7 Windsor. MAY. ? Windsor. JUNE 11–15 Havering-atte-Bower. JULY 1 Havering-atte-Bower. 5 Sheen. 10 Kings Langley. 11–13 Windsor. 15 Easthampstead. 17–30 Windsor. AUGUST 3 Westminster. 5–8 Woodstock. 12 Beckley. 17 Nutley (Bucks). 22 Preston (Kent). SEPTEMBER 22 Sheen. 23 Windsor. 29 Queenborough. OCTOBER 24–31 Sheen. NOVEMBER 1–3 Sheen. 21–30 Westminster. DECEMBER 1–10 Westminster. 14–31 Woodstock.

1374 JANUARY 1–8 Woodstock. 14 Kings Langley. 23 Sheen. FEBRUARY 2 Sheen. MARCH 10 Sheen. APRIL 1–3 Kings Langley. 7–12 Sheen. 23–4 Windsor. 30 Kings Langley. MAY 1 Sheen. 10 Wychemere (Berks). 12 Windsor. JUNE 3 Kings Langley. 4 Sheen. 19–20 Selborne. JULY 24 Moor End. AUGUST 4 Moor End. SEPTEMBER (no evidence). OCTOBER 6 Westminster. NOVEMBER 8 Queenborough. DECEMBER 10–15 Kings Langley. 19 Sheen. 26–31 Eltham.

1375 JANUARY 1–4 Eltham. FEBRUARY 2 Sheen. MARCH 30 Queenborough. APRIL 18 Gravesend. 19–26 Eltham. 28–9 Gravesend. MAY 1 Windsor. 4–9 Eltham. 16 Westminster. 24 Sheen. JUNE 12 Windsor. 15 Sheen. 16–23 Windsor. JULY 19–20 Guildford. 27–8 Windsor. 29 Denham. AUGUST 1 Kings Langley. 6–10 Yardley Hastings. 11–16 Drayton (Northants). 17–19 Nassington. 21–5 Blatherwycke. 27–9 Oakham. 30–1 Rockingham. SEPTEMBER 1–9 Rockingham. 10 Kettering. 11 Yardley Hastings. 19 Sheen. 23 Westminster. OCTOBER 11 Eltham. 14–15 Sheen. NOVEMBER 8 Sheen. 18 Kings Langley. DECEMBER 23–31 Kings Langley.

1376 JANUARY 1–2 Kings Langley. 6 Sheen. 17 Kings Langley. 20 Sheen. FEBRUARY 3 Sheen. 5 Hatton (Middx). 13 Sheen. ? London. 24 Hatton. 25 Sheen. MARCH 10 Sheen. 26 Westminster. APRIL 11–16 Eltham. 23 Windsor. 26–9 Westminster. MAY ? Westminster. JUNE ?1 Kennington. ? Havering-atte-Bower. JULY 8–10 Eltham. 23 Leeds (Kent). 29 Hadleigh. AUGUST 1–4 Rayleigh. 8–17 Havering-atte-Bower. 19–28

Pleshey. 29–31 Havering-atte-Bower. SEPTEMBER 1–30 Havering-atte-Bower. OCTOBER 1–31 Havering-atte-Bower. NOVEMBER 1–30 Havering-atte-Bower. DECEMBER 1–31 Havering-atte-Bower.

1377 JANUARY 1–31 Havering-atte-Bower. FEBRUARY 1–9 Havering-atte-Bower. 10 Aboard barge from Havering-atte-Bower via London and Westminster to Sheen. 11–28 Sheen. MARCH 1–31 Sheen. APRIL 1–18 Sheen. 22–30 Windsor. MAY 1–2 Windsor. 7–31 Sheen. JUNE 1 Windsor. 2–21 Sheen.

BIBLIOGRAPHY

MANUSCRIPT SOURCES

Cambridge, Corpus Christi College

MS 20: coronation *ordo*
MS 78: *Brut* chronicle and continuation
MS 170: *Acta bellicosa* of Edward III

Cambridge University Library

MS Dd.9.38: formulary book
MS Mm.3.21: coronation *ordo*

Durham University Library

Durham Cathedral Muniments, Register of Richard Bury
Durham Cathedral Muniments, Register of Thomas Hatfield

Kew, The National Archives

C 44: Court of Chancery: Common Law Pleadings, Tower Series
C 47: Chancery Miscellanea
C 49: Chancery and Exchequer, King's Remembrancer: Parliament and Council Proceedings
C 61: Chancery: Gascon Rolls
C 67: Chancery: Supplementary Patent Rolls
C 76: Chancery: Treaty Rolls
C 81: Chancery: Warrants for the Great Seal (Series I)
C 143: Chancery: Inquisitions *Ad Quod Dampnum*
C 219: Chancery and Lord Chancellor's Office: Parliament Election Writs and Returns
C 270: Chancery: Ecclesiastical Miscellanea
DL 10: Duchy of Lancaster: Royal Charters
DL 41: Duchy of Lancaster: Miscellanea
E 30: Exchequer, Treasury of Receipt: Diplomatic Documents
E 36: Exchequer, Treasury of Receipt: Miscellaneous Books
E 43: Exchequer, Treasury of Receipt: Ancient Deeds, Series WS
E 101: Exchequer, King's Remembrancer: Various Accounts
E 142: Exchequer, King's Remembrancer: Extents, Inquisitions and Valors of Forfeited Lands
E 159: Exchequer, King's Remembrancer: Memoranda Rolls
E 179: Exchequer, King's Remembrancer: Particulars of Account, Lay and Clerical Taxation
E 199: Exchequer, King's Remembrancer: Sheriffs' Accounts

632

E 208: Exchequer, King's Remembrancer: *Brevia Baronibus* files
E 356: Exchequer, Pipe Office: Customs Accounts Rolls
E 358: Exchequer, Pipe Office: Miscellaneous Enrolled Accounts
E 361: Exchequer, Pipe Office: Enrolled Wardrobe and Household Accounts
E 364: Exchequer, Pipe Office: Foreign Accounts Rolls
E 368: Exchequer, Lord Treasurer's Remembrancer: Memoranda Rolls
E 372: Exchequer, Pipe Office: Pipe Rolls
E 401: Exchequer of Receipt: Receipt Rolls
E 403: Exchequer of Receipt: Issue Rolls
E 404: Exchequer of Receipt: Warrants for Issues
JUST 1: Justices in Eyre, of Assize, of Oyer and Terminer, of the Peace, etc: Rolls and Files
KB 9: King's Bench, Crown Side: Indictments Files
KB 27: King's Bench, Plea and Crown Sides: *Coram rege* Rolls
PRO 1: Public Record Office: General Correspondence
SC 1: Special Collections: Ancient Correspondence of the Chancery and Exchequer
SC 7: Special Collections: Papal Bulls
SC 8: Special Collections: Ancient Petitions

London, British Library

Additional Charters
Additional MS 9951: Wardrobe account book
Additional MS 17362: Wardrobe account book
Additional MS 24062: Formulary of Thomas Hoccleve
Additional MS 35181: Wardrobe receipt book
Additional MS 46350: Wardrobe account roll
Additional MS 47680: *Secreta secretorum*
Additional Rolls 26588–26595: Estalment Rolls
Cotton Charters
Harley Rolls
MS Cotton Caligula D. III: Diplomatic documents
MS Cotton Faustina B.V: Rochester chronicle
MS Cotton Galba E. III: Account book of Queen Philippa
MS Cotton Galba E. XIV: Account book of Queen Isabella
MS Cotton Nero C. VIII: Wardrobe account books
MS Cotton Vitellus C. XII: Coronation *ordo*
MS Lansdowne 451: Coronation *ordo*
MS Royal 12 F. XVII: Astrological charts of kings and princes

London, Lambeth Palace Library

Register of Simon Islip

London, Society of Antiquaries

MSS 120–122: Chamber account books
MS 208: Household account of Queen Philippa
MS 543: Household account of Queen Isabella

London, Westminster Abbey

MS 38: *Liber regalis*
Muniments 6300*, 12195, 12207, 12213, 12214, 15169, 51112, 62481–62485

Manchester, John Rylands University Library

MS Latin 234–237: Household accounts of Queen Philippa

Oxford, Christ Church

MS 92: Walter Milemete, *De nobilitatibus, sapientiis et prudentiis regum*

Paris, Bibliothèque Nationale

MS français 693, fols 248–279v: Saint-Omer chronicle

York, Borthwick Institute for Archives

Register 11: Register of John Thoresby
Staple 2: Charters of the English Company of the Staple

PRINTED PRIMARY SOURCES

The 1341 Royal Inquest in Lincolnshire, ed. B. W. McLane (Lincoln Record Society, lxxviii, 1988).
'An Account of the Expenses of Eleanor, Sister of Edward III, on the Occasion of her Marriage to Reynald, Count of Guelders', ed. E. W. Safford, *Archaeologia*, lxxvii (1927).
'The Accounts of John de Stratton and John Gedeney, Constables of Bordeaux, 1381–90', ed. J. R. Wright, *Mediaeval Studies*, xlii (1980).
The Acts of David II, King of Scots, 1329–1371, ed. B. Webster (Regesta Regum Scottorum, vi, 1982).
Acts of the Parliaments of Scotland, 12 vols (Edinburgh, 1814–75).
Ancient Petitions Relating to Northumberland, ed. C. M. Fraser (Surtees Society, clxxvi, 1966).
Anglia Sacra, ed. H. Wharton, 2 vols (London, 1691).
'The Anglo-French Negotiations at Bruges, 1374–1377', ed. E. Perroy, *Camden Miscellany XIX* (Camden Society, 3rd series, lxx, 1952).
Anglo-Norman Letters and Petitions from All Souls MS 162, ed. M. D. Legge (Anglo-Norman Text Society, iii, 1941).
Anglo-Norman Political Songs, ed. I. S. T. Aspin (Anglo-Norman Text Society, xi, 1953).
Anglo-Scottish Relations, 1174–1328, ed. E. L. G. Stones, revised edn (Oxford, 1970).
'Annales de Bermundeseia', *Annales Monastici*, ed. H. R. Luard, 5 vols (RS, 1863–8), iii.
'Annales Londoniensis', *Chronicles of the Reigns of Edward I and Edward II*, ed. W. Stubbs, 2 vols (RS, 1882–3), i.
'Annales Monasterii de Oseneia', *Annales Monastici*, ed. H. R. Luard, 5 vols (RS, 1863–8), iv.
'Annales Paulini', *Chronicles of the Reigns of Edward I and Edward II*, ed. W. Stubbs, 2 vols (RS, 1882–3), i.
The Anonimalle Chronicle, 1307–1334, ed. W. R. Childs and J. Taylor (Yorkshire Archaeological Society record series, cxlvii, 1987).
The Anonimalle Chronicle, 1333–1381, ed. V. H. Galbraith (Manchester, 1927).
ANONIMO ROMANO, *Cronica*, ed. G. Porta (Milan, 1979).
The Antient Kalendars and Inventories of the Treasury of His Majesty's Exchequer, ed. F. Palgrave, 3 vols (London, 1836).
'An Armourer's Bill, temp. Edward III', ed. H. Dillon, *Antiquary*, xxii (1890).
Autobiography of Emperor Charles IV and his Legend of St Wenceslas, ed. B. Nagy and F. Schaer (Budapest, 2001).
AVESBURY, R., *De gestis mirabilibus regis Edwardi Tertii*, ed. E. M. Thompson (RS, 1889).
BAKER, G., *Chronicon Galfridi le Baker de Swynebroke*, ed. E. M. Thompson (Oxford, 1889).

'La Bataille de trente Anglois et de trente Bretons', ed. H. R. Brush, *Modern Philology*, ix (1911–12); x (1912–13).

The Black Death, ed. R. Horrox (Manchester, 1994).

BOWER, W., *Scotichronicon*, ed. D. E. R. Watt, 9 vols (Aberdeen, 1993–8).

The Brut, or, The Chronicles of England, ed. F. W. D. Brie, 2 vols (EETS, original series, cxxxi, cxxxvi, 1906–8).

Calendar of Ancient Correspondence Concerning Wales, ed. J. G. Edwards (Cardiff, 1935).

A Calendar of the Cartularies of John Pyel and Adam Fraunceys, ed. S. J. O'Connor (Camden Society, 5th series, ii, 1993).

Calendar of Chancery Warrants 1244–1326 (London, 1927).

Calendar of Charter Rolls, Henry III–Henry VIII, 6 vols (London, 1903–27).

Calendar of Close Rolls, Edward II–Richard II, 24 vols (London, 1892–1927).

Calendar of Documents Relating to Scotland, ed. J. Bain, G. G. Simpson and J. D. Galbraith, 5 vols (Edinburgh, 1881–1987).

Calendar of Entries in the Papal Registers Relating to Great Britain and Ireland: Papal Letters, ii–iv (London, 1895–1902).

Calendar of Entries in the Papal Registers Relating to Great Britain and Ireland: Petitions to the Pope, 1342–1419 (London, 1896).

Calendar of Fine Rolls, Edward II–Richard II, 10 vols (London, 1912–29).

Calendar of Inquisitions Miscellaneous, Henry III–Henry V, 7 vols (London, 1916–69).

Calendar of Inquisitions Post Mortem, Edward I–Richard II, 17 vols (London, 1904–88).

Calendar of Letter Books of the City of London, ed. R. R. Sharpe, 11 vols (London, 1899–1912).

Calendar of Letters from the Mayor and Corporation of the City of London, ed. R. R. Sharpe (London, 1885).

Calendar of Memoranda Rolls (Exchequer), Michaelmas 1326–Michaelmas 1327 (London, 1968).

Calendar of Patent Rolls, Edward II–Richard II, 27 vols (London, 1894–1916).

Calendar of Plea and Memoranda Rolls of the City of London, ed. A. H. Thomas and P. E. Jones, 6 vols (Cambridge, 1926–61).

Calendar of the Records of the Corporation of Gloucester, ed. W. H. Stevenson (Gloucester, 1893).

Calendar of State Papers, Venice, i (London, 1864).

CAPGRAVE, J., *John Capgrave's Abbreuiacion of Cronicles*, ed. P. J. Lucas (EETS, cclxxxv, 1983).

CHANDOS HERALD, *La vie du Prince Noir*, ed. D. B. Tyson (Tübingen, 1975).

The Charters of the Duchy of Lancaster, ed. W. Hardy (London, 1845).

Chartularies of St Mary's Abbey, Dublin, ed. J. T. Gilbert, 2 vols (RS, 1884–6).

The Chartulary of Winchester Cathedral, ed. A. W. Goodman (Winchester, 1927).

CHAUCER, G., *The Riverside Chaucer*, ed. L. D. Benson, 3rd edn (Oxford, 1987).

'Chaucer as Page in the Household of the Countess of Ulster', *Chaucer Society Publications: Life-Records of Chaucer*, ed. W. D. Selby, F. J. Furnivall, E. A. Bond and R. E. Kirk, 4 vols (London, 1875–1900), iii.

Chronica Monasterii de Melsa, ed. E. A. Bond, 3 vols (RS, 1866–8).

The Chronicle of Jean de Venette, trans. J. Birdsall and ed. R. A. Newhall (New York, 1953).

A Chronicle of London from 1089 to 1483, ed. N. H. Nicolas (London, 1827).

Chronicon Anonymi Cantuariensis: The Chronicle of Anonymous of Canterbury, 1346–1365, ed. C. Scott-Stokes and C. Given-Wilson (Oxford, 2008).

Chronicon de Lanercost, ed. J. Stevenson (Edinburgh, 1839).

Chronique des quatre premiers Valois (1327–1393), ed. S. Luce (Société de l'Histoire de France, 1862).

Chronique de Richard Lescot, religieux de Saint-Denis, ed. J. Lemoine (Société de l'Histoire de France, 1896).

Chroniques des règnes de Jean II et Charles V, ed. R. Delachenal, 4 vols (Société de l'Histoire de France, 1910–20).

City Government of Winchester from the Records of the XIV and XV Centuries, ed. J. S. Furley (Oxford, 1923).

A Collection of the Wills of the Kings and Queens of England, ed. J. Nichols (London, 1780).

Compte de William Gunthorpe, trésorier de Calais, 1371–2, ed. E. Perroy (Mémoires de la commission départementale des monuments historique du Pas de Calais, x, 1959).

Comptes de l'argenterie des rois de France au XIVe siècle, ed. L. Douët-d'Arcq (Société de l'Histoire de France, 1851).

Concilia Magna Britanniae et Hiberniae, ed. D. Wilkins, 4 vols (London, 1737).

Crecy and Calais from the Public Records, ed. G. Wrottesley (London, 1898).

Croniques de London, ed. J. G. Aungier (Camden Society, original series, xxviii, 1844).

De speculo regis Edwardi Tertii, ed. J. Moisant (Paris, 1891).

Debating the Hundred Years War: Pour ce que plusieurs (La Loy Salique) and A Declaracion of the Trew and Dewe Title of Henry VIII, ed. C. Taylor (Camden Society, 5th series, xxix, 2006).

'Documents Relating to the Death and Burial of King Edward II', ed. S. A. Moore, *Archaeologia*, l (1887).

Early Treatises on the Practice of the Justices of the Peace in the Fifteenth and Sixteenth Centuries, ed. B. H. Putnam (Oxford Studies in Social and Legal History, vii, 1924).

English Coronation Records, ed. L. G. Wickham Legge (London, 1901).

English Historical Documents, II: 1042–1189, ed. D. C. Douglas and G. W. Greenaway, 2nd edn (London, 1981)

English Historical Documents, III: 1189–1327, ed. H. Rothwell (London, 1975).

English Historical Documents, IV: 1327–1485, ed. A. R. Myers (London, 1969).

English Medieval Diplomatic Practice, ed. P. Chaplais, 2 vols in 3 parts (London, 1975–82).

The Enrolled Customs Accounts, ed. S. Jenks, 5 vols (List and Index Society, ccciii, cccvi, cccvii, cccxiii, cccxiv, 2004–6).

'Enrolments and Documents from the Public Record Office', *Chaucer Society Publications: Life-Records of Chaucer*, ed. W. D. Selby, F. J. Furnivall, E. A. Bond and R. E. Kirk, 4 vols (London, 1875–1900), iv.

Eulogium Historiarum, ed. F. S. Haydon, 3 vols (RS, 1858–63).

The Exchequer Rolls of Scotland, 1264–1359, ed. J. Stuart (Edinburgh, 1878).

'An Exchequer Statement of Receipts and Issues, 1339–40', ed. H. Jenkinson and D. M. Broome, *EHR*, lviii (1943).

'Extracts from the *Historia Aurea* and a French "Brut" (1317–1377)', ed. V. H. Galbraith, *EHR*, xliii (1928).

The Eyre of Northamptonshire 3–4 Edward III, A.D. 1329–1330, ed. D. W. Sutherland, 2 vols (Selden Society, xcvii, cxviii, 1983–4).

FABYAN, R., *The New Chronicles of England and France*, ed. H. Ellis (London, 1811).

'The First Journal of Edward II's Chamber', ed. J. C. Davies, *EHR*, xxx (1915).

Foedera, Conventions, Literae et Cujuscunque Generic Acta Publica, ed. T. Rymer, 3 vols in 6 parts (London, 1816–30).

FORDUN, J., *Chronica gestis Scotorum*, ed. W. F. Skene (Edinburgh, 1871).

FORTESCUE, J., *The Governance of England*, ed. C. Plummer (Oxford, 1885).

—— *On the Laws and Governance of England*, ed. S. Lockwood (Cambridge, 1997).

'A Fourteenth-Century Chronicle of the Grey Friars of Lynn', ed. A. Gransden, *EHR*, lxxii (1957).

FROISSART, J., *Chronicles*, trans. G. Brereton (Harmondsworth, 1978).

—— *Chroniques*, ed. S. Luce et al., 15 vols (Société de l'Histoire de France, 1869–1975).

—— *Oeuvres complètes: Chroniques*, ed. J. M. B. C. Kervyn de Lettenhove, 25 vols (Brussels, 1867–77).

'Gesta Edwardi de Carnarvan auctore canonico Bridlingtoniensi, cum continuatione', *Chronicles of the Reigns of Edward I and Edward II*, ed. W. Stubbs, 2 vols (RS, 1882–3), ii.

Gesta Henrici Quinti: The Deeds of Henry the Fifth, ed. F. Taylor and J. S. Roskell (Oxford, 1975).

GOWER, J., *Complete Works*, ed. G. C. Macaulay, 4 vols (Oxford, 1899–1902).

Les Grandes Chroniques de France, ed. J. Viard, 10 vols (Société de l'Histoire de France, 1920–53).

GRAY, T., *Scalacronica*, ed. and trans. A. King (Surtees Society, ccix, 2005).

The Great Chronicle of London, ed. A. H. Thomas and I. D. Thornley (London, 1938).

Handbook and Select Calendar of Sources for Medieval Ireland in the National Archives of the United Kingdom, ed. P. Dryburgh and B. Smith (Dublin, 2005).

HARDYNG, J., *The Chronicle of John Hardyng*, ed. H. Ellis (London, 1812).

HIGDEN, R., *Polychronicon*, ed. C. Babington and J. R. Lumby, 9 vols (RS, 1865–82).

Historia et Cartularium Monasterii Sancti Petri Gloucestriae, ed. W. H. Hart, 3 vols (RS, 1863–7).

Historia Dunelmensis Scriptores Tres, ed. J. Raine (Surtees Society, ix, 1839).

Historical Papers and Letters from the Northern Registers, ed. J. Raine (RS, 1873).

The Household Book of Queen Isabella of England, 8th July 1311 to 7 July 1312, ed. F. D. Blackley and G. Hermansen (Edmonton, 1971).

The Household of Edward IV, ed. A. R. Myers (Manchester, 1959).

'Inquisition on the Effects of Edward II', ed. C. H. Hartshorne, *Archaeologia Cambrensis*, 3rd series, ix (1863).

An Inventory of the Historical Monuments in London I: Westminster Abbey (London, 1924).

The Issue Roll of Thomas of Brantingham, ed. F. Devon (London, 1835).

Issues of the Exchequer, Henry III–Henry VI, ed. F. Devon (London, 1847).

Johannis de Trokelowe et Henrici de Blandeforde Chronica et Annales, ed. H. T. Riley (RS, 1866).

John of Gaunt's Register, 1371–1375, ed. S. Armitage-Smith, 2 vols (Camden Society, 3rd series, xx–xxi, 1911).

JOINVILLE, J. de and VILLEHARDOUIN, G. de, *Chronicles of the Crusades*, trans. M. R. B. Shaw (Harmondsworth, 1963).

King Edward III, ed. G. Melchiori (Cambridge, 1988).

The Kirkstall Abbey Chronicles, ed. J. Taylor (Thoresby Society, xlii, 1952).

KNIGHTON, H., *Chronicon Henrici Knighton*, ed. J. R. Lumby, 2 vols (RS, 1889–95).

—— *Knighton's Chronicle, 1337–1396*, ed. G. H. Martin (Oxford, 1995).

LANGLAND, W., *Piers Plowman: The A Version*, ed. G. Kane (London, 1960).

—— *The Vision of Piers Plowman: A Complete Edition of the B-text*, ed. A. V. C. Schmidt (London, 1978).

Le BEL, J., *Chronique de Jean le Bel*, ed. J. Viard and E. Déprez, 2 vols (Société de l'Histoire de France, 1904–5).

Le MUISIT, G., *Chronique et annals de Gilles le Muisit, abbé de Saint-Martin de Tournai (1272–1352)*, ed. H. Lemaître (Paris, 1906).

'A Letter of Edward the Black Prince Describing the Battle of Nájera in 1367', ed. A. E. Prince, *EHR*, lxi (1926).

'A Letter to Louis de Mâle, Count of Flanders', ed. B. Wilkinson, *BJRL*, ix (1925).

Letters and Papers, Foreign and Domestic, of the Reign of Henry VIII, 21 vols (London, 1864–1932).

Letters of the Queens of England, 1100–1547, ed. A. Crawford (Stroud, 1994).

The Libelle of Englyshe Polycye: A Poem on the Use of Sea Power, 1436, ed. G. Warner (Oxford, 1926).

Liber Pluscardensis, ed. F. J. H. Skene, 2 vols (Edinburgh, 1877–80).

The Life and Campaigns of the Black Prince, ed. and trans. R. Barber (Woodbridge, 1979).

List of Welsh Entries in the Memoranda Rolls, 1282–43, ed. N. Fryde (Cardiff, 1974).

Litterae Cantuarienses, ed. J. B. Sheppard, 3 vols (RS, 1887–9).

Le liver des assises & plees del corone . . . en temps du Roy Edward le Tiers (London, 1679).

Le livre de seyntz medicines, ed. E. J. Arnould (Anglo-Norman Texts, ii, 1940).

The Making of King's Lynn: A Documentary Survey, ed. D. M. Owen (London, 1984).

Mandeville's Travels, ed. P. Hamelius, 2 vols (EETS, cliii–cliv, 1919–23).

Medieval Political Theory – A Reader: The Quest for the Body Politic, 1100–1400, ed. C. J. Nederman and K. L. Forhan (London, 1993).

Memorials of London and London Life in the XIIIth, XIVth, and XVth Centuries, ed. H. T. Riley (RS, 1868).

MILEMETE, W., *De nobilitatibus, sapientiis et prudentiis regum*, ed. M. R. James (Oxford, 1913).

MINOT, L., *Poems*, ed. T. B. James and J. Simons (Exeter, 1989).

MISSELDEN, E., *The Circle of Commerce: or, The Balance of Trade* (London, 1623).

Monumenta Ritualia Ecclesiae Anglicanane, ed. W. Maskell (London, 1847).

Munimenta de Insula Manniae, ed. J. R. Oliver, 3 vols (Manx Society Publications, iv, vii, ix, 1860–2).

MURIMUTH, A., *Continuatio chronicarum*, ed. E. M. Thompson (RS, 1889).

'Negotiations for the Release of David Bruce in 1349', ed. C. Johnson, *EHR*, xxxvi (1921).

Northern Petitions, ed. C. M. Fraser (Surtees Society, cxciv, 1982).

'Notes et documents relatifs à Jean, roi de France, et à sa captivité en Angleterre', ed. H. E. P. L. d'Orléans, duc d'Aumale, *Miscellanies of the Philobiblon Society*, ii (1855).

'Notices of the Last Days of Isabella, Queen of Edward the Second', ed. E. A. Bond, *Archaeologia*, xxxv (1853).

'Observations on the Institution of the Most Noble Order of the Garter', ed. N. H. Nicolas, *Archaeologia*, xxxi (1846).

The Original Chronicle of Andrew of Wyntoun, vi, ed. F. J. Amours (Edinburgh, 1908).

Original Letters Illustrative of English History, ed. H. Ellis, 3rd series, 3 vols (London, 1866).

'Papers Relating to the Captivity and Release of David II', ed. E. W. M. Balfour-Melville, *Scottish History Society Miscellany IX* (Scottish History Society, 3rd series, i, 1958).

The Parliament Rolls of Medieval England, ed. and trans. P. Brand, A. Curry, C. Given-Wilson, R. E. Horrox, G. Martin, W. M. Ormrod and J. R. S. Phillips, 16 vols (Woodbridge, 2005).

Parliamentary Petitions Relating to Oxford, ed. L. Toulmin Smith (Oxford Historical Society, xxxii, 1896).

Parliamentary Writs and Writs of Personal Summons, ed. F. Palgrave, 2 vols in 4 parts (London, 1827–34).

Parliaments and Councils of Mediaeval Ireland, ed. H. G. Richardson and G. O. Sayles (Dublin, 1947).

The Peasants' Revolt of 1381, ed. R. B. Dobson, 2nd edn (London, 1983).

Peter Langtoft's Chronicle, ed. T. Hearne, 2 vols (Oxford, 1725).

'Petition by the Lady Isabella, Countess of Bedford', ed. J. Bain, *Archaeological Journal*, xxxvi (1879).

The Piers Plowman Tradition, ed. H. Barr (London, 1993).

The Poems of the Pearl Manuscript: Pearl, Cleanness, Patience, Sir Gawain and the Green Knight, ed. M. Andrew and R. Waldron, rev. edn (Exeter, 1987).

Political Poems and Songs Relating to English History, ed. T. Wright, 2 vols (RS, 1859–61).

'Premières négociations de Charles le Mauvais avec les Anglais (1354–1355)', ed. R. Delachenal, *Bibliothèque de l'Ecole des Chartes*, lxi (1900).

' "Probatio Aetatis" of William de Septvans', ed. L. B. Larking, *Archaeologia Cantiana*, i (1858).

Proceedings before the Justices of the Peace in the Fourteenth and Fifteenth Centuries, ed. B. H. Putnam (Ames Foundation, 1938).

'Quatre lettres du cardinal Guy de Boulogne (1352–1354)', ed. E. Perroy, *Revue du Nord*, xxxvi (1954).

'A Question about the Succession, 1364', ed. A. A. M. Duncan, *Miscellany of the Scottish History Society XII* (Scottish History Society, 5th series, vii, 1994).

'The Ransom of John II, King of France, 1360–1370', ed. D. M. Broome, *Camden Miscellany XIV* (Camden Society, 3rd series, xxxvii, 1926).

READING, J., 'Chronicon', *Chronica Johannis de Reading et Anonymi Cantuariensis*, ed. J. Tait (Manchester, 1914).

Récits d'un Bourgeois de Valenciennes, ed. Kervyn de Lettenhove (Louvain, 1877).

Records of the Borough of Leicester, 1103–1509, ed. M. Bateson, 2 vols (London, 1899–1901).

Records of the Borough of Nottingham, 1155–1399, ed. W. H. Stevenson (London, 1882).

The Records of the City of Norwich, ed. W. Hudson and J. C. Tingey, 2 vols (Norwich, 1906–10).

Records of Convocation, ed. G. Bray, 16 vols (Woodbridge, 2005–6).

Recueil de lettres anglo-françaises (1265–1399), ed. F. J. Tanqueray (Paris, 1916).

Register of Edward the Black Prince, 4 vols (London, 1930–3).

The Register of Gilbert Welton, Bishop of Carlisle, 1353–1362, ed. R. L. Storey (CYS, lxxxviii, 1999).

The Register of John de Grandisson, Bishop of Exeter, ed. F. C. Hingeston-Randolph, 3 vols (London, 1894–9).

The Register of John Kirkby, Bishop of Carlisle, 1332–1352, and the Register of John Ross, Bishop of Carlisle, 1325–1332, ed. R. L. Storey, 2 vols (CYS, lxxix, lxxxi, 1993–5).

The Register of Ralph of Shrewsbury, Bishop of Bath and Wells, 1329–1363, ed. T. S. Holmes, 2 vols (Somerset Record Society, ix, x, 1895–6).

'The Register of Simon Montacute', *Ely Diocesan Remembrancer 1891* (Ely, 1891).

The Register of Thomas Appleby, Bishop of Carlisle, 1363–1395, ed. R. L. Storey (CYS, xcvi, 2006).

Register of Thomas de Brantyngham, Bishop of Exeter, ed. F. C. Hingeston-Randolph, 2 vols (London, 1901–6).

'The Register of Thomas de Insula', *Ely Diocesan Register 1894* (Ely, 1894).

The Register of Walter de Stapeldon, Bishop of Exeter (A.D. 1307–1326), ed. F. C. Hingeston-Randolph (London, 1892).

The Register of William Edington, Bishop of Winchester, 1346–1366, ed. S. F. Hockley, 2 vols (Hampshire Record series, vii–viii, 1986–7).

The Register of William Melton, Archbishop of York, 1317–1340, ed. R. M. Hill, D. Robinson, R. Brocklesby and T. C. B. Timmins, 5 vols (CYS, lxx, lxxi, lxxvi, lxxxv, xciii, 1977–2002).

The Registers of Roger Martival, Bishop of Salisbury, 1315–1330, III, ed. S. Reynolds (CYS, lix, 1965).

Registrum Hamonis de Hethe, diocesis Roffensis, ed. C. Johnson, 2 vols (CYS, xlviii–xlix, 1948).

Registrum Johannis de Trillek, episcopi Herefordensis, ed. J. H. Parry (CYS, viii, 1912).

Registrum Simonis de Sudburia diocesis Londoniensis, A.D. 1362–1375, ed. R. C. Fowler, 2 vols (CYS, xxxiv, xxxviii, 1927–38).

Registrum Thome de Charlton, episcopi Herefordensis, ed. W. C. Capes (CYS, ix, 1913).

Report from the Lords Committee for All Matters Touching the Dignity of a Peer, 5 vols (London, 1820–9).

Robin Hood and Other Outlaw Tales, ed. S. Knight and T. Ohlgren, 2nd edn (Kalamazoo, 2000).

Rotuli Parliamentorum, 6 vols (London, 1787).

Rotuli Parliamentorum Angliae hactenus inediti, ed. H. G. Richardson and G. O. Sayles (Camden Society, 3rd series, li, 1935).

Rotuli Scotiae, 2 vols (London, 1814–19).

The Royal Charter Witness Lists of Edward II (1307–1326), ed. J. S. Hamilton (List and Index Soc., cclxxxviii, 2010).

Royal Writs Addressed to John Buckingham, Bishop of Lincoln, 1363–1398, ed. A. K. McHardy (Lincoln Record Society, lxxxvi, 1997).

Select Cases before the King's Council, 1243–1482, ed. I. S. Leadam and J. F. Baldwin (Selden Society, xxxv, 1918).

Select Cases in the Court of King's Bench, ed. G. O. Sayles, 7 vols (Selden Society, lv, lvii, lviii, lxxiv, lxxvi, lxxxii, lxxxviii, 1936–71).

The Sermons of Thomas Brinton, Bishop of Rochester (1373–1389), ed. M. A. Devlin, 2 vols (Camden Society, 3rd series, lxxxv–lxxxvi, 1953–4).

Sessions of the Peace for Bedfordshire, 1355–1359 and 1363–1364, ed. E. G. Kimball (Bedfordshire Historical Record Society, xlviii, 1969).

Shakespeare's Edward III: An Early Play Restored to the Canon, ed. E. Sams (New Haven, 1996).

Society at War: The Experience of England and France during the Hundred Years War, ed. C. Allmand, rev. edn (Woodbridge, 1998).

'Some Documents Regarding the Fulfilment and Interpretation of the Treaty of Brétigny, 1361–1369', ed. P. Chaplais, *Camden Miscellany XIX* (Camden Society, 3rd series, lxxx, 1952).

'Some Documents Relating to the Disputed Succession to the Duchy of Brittany, 1341', ed. M. Jones, *Camden Miscellany XXIV* (Camden Society, 4th series, ix, 1972).

'Some New Documents Illustrating the Early History of the Hundred Years War (1353–1356)', ed. F. Bock, *BJRL*, xv (1931).

Statutes and Ordinances, and Acts of the Parliament of Ireland, King John to Henry V, ed. H. F. Berry (Dublin, 1907).

Statutes of the Realm, 11 vols (London, 1810–28).

Testamenta Vetusta, ed. N. H. Nicolas (London, 1826).

Three Coronation Orders, ed. J. Wickham Legge (London, 1900).

Treaty Rolls 1234–1325 (London, 1955).

Treaty Rolls, 1337–1339 (London, 1972).

'An Unknown Register of the Reign of Edward III', ed. F. Bock, *EHR*, xlv (1930).

VILLANI, G., 'Cronica', *Cronisti del Trecento*, ed. R. Palmarocchi (Milan, 1935).

Vita Edwardi Secundi, ed. and trans. W. R. Childs (Oxford, 2005).

The Vows of the Heron (Les Voeux du heron): A Middle French Vowing Poem, ed. J. L. Grigsby and N. J. Lacy (New York, 1992).

WALSINGHAM, T., *Chronicon Angliae*, ed. E. M. Thompson (RS, 1874).

—— *Gesta abbatum monasterii Sancti Albani*, ed. H. T. Riley, 3 vols (RS, 1867–9).

—— *Historia Anglicana*, ed. H. T. Riley, 2 vols (RS, 1863–4).

—— *The St Albans Chronicle: The 'Chronica Maiora' of Thomas Walsingham*, ed. J. Taylor, W. R. Childs and L. Watkiss, in progress (Oxford, 2003—)

—— *Ypodigma Neustriae*, ed. H. T. Riley (RS, 1876).

The War of Saint-Sardos (1323–1325): Gascon Correspondence and Diplomatic Documents, ed. P. Chaplais (Camden Society, 3rd series, lxxxvii, 1954).

The Wardrobe Book of William de Norwell, ed. M. Lyon, B. Lyon, H. S. Lucas and J. de Sturler (Brussels, 1983).

The Wars of Edward III: Sources and Interpretation, ed. C. J. Rogers (Woodbridge, 1999).

The Westminster Chronicle, 1381–1394, ed. L. C. Hector and B. F. Harvey (Oxford, 1982).

Wykeham's Register, ed. T. F. Kirby, 2 vols (London, 1896–9).

Wynnere and Wastoure, ed. S. Trigg (EETS, ccxcvii, 1990).

Year Books 14 and 15 Edward III, ed. L. O. Pike (RS, 1889).

PRINTED SECONDARY SOURCES

ABERTH, J., *Criminal Churchmen in the Reign of Edward III: The Case of Bishop Thomas de Lisle* (University Park, Penn., 1996).

AERS, D., '*Vox populi* and the Literature of 1381', *The Cambridge History of Medieval English Literature*, ed. D. Wallace (Cambridge, 1999).

Age of Chivalry: Art in Plantagenet England, 1200–1400, ed. J. Alexander and P. Binski (London, 1987).

AILES, A., 'Heraldry in Medieval England: Symbols of Politics and Propaganda', *Heraldry, Pageantry and Social Display*, ed. P. R. Coss and M. H. Keen (Woodbridge, 2002).

AINSWORTH, P. F., *Jean Froissart and the Fabric of History* (Oxford, 1990).

ALEXANDER, J. J. G., 'Painting and Manuscript Illumination for Royal Patrons in the Later Middle Ages', *English Court Culture in the Later Middle Ages*, ed. V. J. Scattergood and J. W. Sherborne (London, 1983).

ALEXANDER, J. W., 'The English Palatines and Edward I', *JBS*, xxii[2] (1983).

ALLAN, A., 'Yorkist Propaganda: Pedigree, Prophecy and the "British History" in the Reign of Edward IV', *Patronage, Pedigree and Power in Later Medieval England*, ed. C. Ross (Gloucester, 1979).

ALLEN, M., 'The Volume of the English Currency, 1158–1470', *EcHR*, 2nd series, liv (2001).

ALLMAND, C., *The Hundred Years War* (Cambridge, 1988).

ANDRE, E., *Ein Königshof auf Reisen: Der Kontinentaufenthalt Eduards III von England, 1338–40* (Cologne, 1996).

ANGLO, S., *Spectacle, Pageantry and Early Tudor Policy* (Oxford, 1969).

ARCHER, R. E., 'The Estates and Finances of Margaret of Brotherton, 1320–1377', *BIHR*, lx (1987).

ARMITAGE-SMITH, S., *John of Gaunt* (London, 1904).

ARVANIGIAN, M., 'A Lancastrian Polity? John of Gaunt, John Neville and the War with France, 1368–88', *Fourteenth Century England III*, ed. W. M. Ormrod (Woodbridge, 2004).

ASHMOLE, E., *The Institution, Laws and Ceremonies of the Most Noble Order of the Garter* (London, 1672).

ASTON, M., ' "Caim's Castles": Poverty, Politics and Disendowment', *The Church, Politics and Patronage in the Fifteenth Century*, ed. R. B. Dobson (Gloucester, 1984).

—— 'Richard II and the Wars of the Roses', *The Reign of Richard II: Essays in Honour of May McKisack*, ed. F. R. H. Du Boulay and C. M. Barron (London, 1971).

—— *Thomas Arundel: A Study of Church Life in the Reign of Richard II* (Oxford, 1967).

ATKINSON, T. D., 'Queen Philippa's Pews in Ely Cathedral', *Proceedings of the Cambridge Antiquarian Society*, xli (1948).

AUTRAND, F., ' "Hôtel de seigneur ne vaut rien sans dame": Le mariage de Jean, comte de Poitiers, et de Jeanne d'Armagnac, 24 juin 1360', *Guerre, pouvoir et noblesse au Moyen Age: Mélanges en l'honneur de Philippe Contamine*, ed. J. Paviot and J. Vergier (Paris, 2000).

—— 'The Peacemakers and the State: Pontifical Diplomacy and the Anglo-French Conflict in the Fourteenth Century', *War and Competition between States*, ed. P. Contamine (Oxford, 2000).

AYTON, A., 'Armies and Military Communities in Fourteenth-Century England', *Soldiers, Nobles and Gentlemen: Essays in Honour of Maurice Keen*, ed. P. Coss and C. Tyerman (Woodbridge, 2009).

—— 'Edward III and the English Aristocracy and the Beginning of the Hundred Years War', *Armies, Chivalry and Warfare in Medieval Britain and France*, ed. M. Strickland (Stamford, 1998).

—— 'English Armies in the Fourteenth Century', *Arms, Armies and Fortifications in the Hundred Years War*, ed. A. Curry and M. Hughes (Woodbridge, 1994).

—— 'The English Army and the Normandy Campaign of 1346', *England and Normandy in the Middle Ages*, ed. D. Bates and A. Curry (London, 1994).

—— 'Knights, Esquires and Military Service: The Evidence of the Armorial Cases before the Court of Chivalry', *The Medieval Military Revolution*, ed. A. Ayton and J. L. Price (London, 1998).

—— *Knights and Warhorses: Military Service and the English Aristocracy under Edward III* (Woodbridge, 1994).

—— 'Sir Thomas Ughtred and the Edwardian Military Revolution', *The Age of Edward III*, ed. J. S. Bothwell (York, 2001).

—— and PRESTON, P., with AUTRAND, F., PIEL, C., PRESTWICH, M. and SCHNERB, B., *The Battle of Crécy, 1346* (Woodbridge, 2005).

—— and PRICE, J. L., 'Introduction: The Military Revolution from a Medieval Perspective', *The Medieval Military Revolution*, ed. A. Ayton and J. L. Price (London, 1998).

BAKER, A. R. H., 'Evidence in the "Nonarum Inquisitiones" of Contracting Arable Lands in England during the Early Fourteenth Century', *EcHR*, 2nd series, xix (1966).

BAKER, D. N., 'Meed and the Economics of Chivalry in *Piers Plowman*', *Inscribing the Hundred Years' War in French and English Cultures*, ed. D. N. Baker (Albany, New York, 2000).

BAKER, J. H., *The Common Law Tradition: Lawyers, Books and the Law* (London, 2000).

BAKER, R. L., *The English Customs Service, 1307–1343: A Study of Medieval Administration* (Philadelphia, 1961).

—— 'The Government of Calais in 1363', *Order and Innovation in the Middle Ages: Essays in Honor of Joseph R. Strayer*, ed. W. C. Jordan, B. McNab and T. F. Ruiz (Princeton, 1976).

BALDWIN, A. P., *The Theme of Government in Piers Plowman* (Cambridge, 1981).

BALDWIN, F. E., *Sumptuary Legislation and Personal Regulation in England* (Baltimore, 1926).
BALDWIN, J. F., 'The King's Council', *The English Government at Work, 1327–1336*, ed. J. F. Willard, W. A. Morris and W. H. Dunham, 3 vols (Cambridge, Mass., 1940–50), i.
—— *The King's Council in England during the Middle Ages* (Oxford, 1913).
BALFOUR-MELVILLE, E. W. M., 'David II's Appeal to the Pope', *Scottish Historical Review*, xli (1962).
BARBER, R., *Edward, Prince of Wales and Aquitaine* (London, 1978).
BARKER, J. R. V., *The Tournament in England 1100–1400* (Woodbridge, 1986).
BARNES, F. R., 'The Taxation of Wool, 1327–1348', *Finance and Trade under Edward III*, ed. G. Unwin (Manchester, 1918).
BARNES, J, *The History of that Most Victorious Monarch Edward III* (Cambridge, 1688).
BARNIE, J., *War in Medieval English Society: Social Values in the Hundred Years War, 1337–99* (London, 1974).
BARRATT, N., 'English Royal Revenue in the Early Thirteenth Century and its Wider Context, 1130–1330', *Crises, Revolutions and Self-Sustained Growth: Essays in European Fiscal History, 1130–1830*, ed. W. M. Ormrod, M. Bonney and R. Bonney (Stamford, 1999).
BARRELL, A. D. M., 'The Ordinance of Provisors of 1343', *HR*, lxiv (1991).
BARRON, C. M., *London in the Later Middle Ages: Government and People, 1200–1500* (Oxford, 2004).
BARROW, G. W. S., 'The Aftermath of War', *TRHS*, 5th series, xxviiii (1978).
—— *Robert Bruce and the Community of the Realm of Scotland*, 3rd edn (Edinburgh, 1988).
BAYLEY, C. C., 'The Campaign of 1375 and the Good Parliament', *EHR*, lv (1940).
BEAN, J. M. W., *The Decline of English Feudalism, 1215–1540* (Manchester, 1968).
BEARDWOOD, A., *Alien Merchants in England, 1350 to 1377* (Cambridge, Mass., 1931).
BEAUNE, C., *The Birth of an Ideology: Myths and Symbols of Nation in Late-Medieval France*, trans. S. R. Huston (Berkeley, Calif., 1991).
BELL, A., BROOKS, C. and MOORE, T. K., 'Interest in Medieval Accounts: Examples from England, 1272–1340', *History*, xciv (2009).
BELLAMY, J. G., 'Appeal and Impeachment in the Good Parliament', *BIHR*, xxxix (1966).
—— 'The Coterel Gang: An Anatomy of a Band of Fourteenth-Century Criminals', *EHR*, lxxix (1964).
—— *The Law of Treason in England in the Later Middle Ages* (Cambridge, 1970).
—— *Robin Hood: An Historical Inquiry* (London, 1985).
—— 'Sir John Annesley and the Chandos Inheritance', *Nottingham Mediaeval Studies*, x (1966).
BELTZ, G. F., *Memorials of the Order of the Garter* (London, 1841).
BENEDICTOW, O. J., *The Black Death, 1346–1353: The Complete History* (Woodbridge, 2004).
BENNETT, M. J., 'Edward III's Entail and the Succession to the Crown, 1376–1471', *EHR*, cxiii (1998).
—— 'France in England: Anglo-French Culture in the Reign of Edward III', *Language and Culture in Medieval Britain: The French of England, c.1100–c.1500*, ed. J. Wogan-Browne (York, 2009).
—— 'Isabelle of France, Anglo-French Diplomacy and Cultural Exchange in the Late 1350s', *The Age of Edward III*, ed. J. S. Bothwell (York, 2001).
—— '*Mandeville's Travels* and the Anglo-French Moment', *Medium Ævum*, lxxv (2006).
BÉRIAC-LAINÉ, F. and GIVEN-WILSON, C., *Les Prisonniers de la bataille de Poitiers* (Paris, 2002).
BEVAN, B., *Edward III: Monarch of Chivalry* (London, 1992).
BIDDLE, M., 'Seasonal Festivals and Residence: Winchester, Westminster and Gloucester in the Tenth to Twelfth Centuries', *Anglo-Norman Studies*, viii (1985).
—— et al., *King Arthur's Round Table: An Archaeological Investigation* (Woodbridge, 2000).
BIGGS, D. L., *Three Armies in Britain: The Irish Campaign of Richard II and the Usurpation of Henry IV, 1397–1399* (Leiden, 2006).

—— ' "A wrong whom conscience and kindred bid me to right": A Reassessment of Edmund of Langley, Duke of York, and the Usurpation of Henry IV', *Albion*, xxvi (1994).

BINSKI, P., *The Painted Chamber at Westminster* (London, 1986).

—— *Westminster Abbey and the Plantagenets* (London, 1995).

BIRCH, W. de G., *Catalogue of Seals in the Department of Manuscripts in the British Museum*, 6 vols (London, 1887–1900).

BLACKLEY, F. D., 'Adam, the Bastard Son of Edward II', *BIHR*, xxxvii (1964).

—— 'Isabella and the Bishop of Exeter', *Essays in Medieval History Presented to Bertie Wilkinson*, ed. T. A. Sandquist and M. R. Powicke (Toronto, 1969).

—— 'Isabella of France, Queen of England (1308–1358), and the Late Medieval Cult of the Dead', *Canadian Journal of History*, xv (1980).

—— 'The Tomb of Isabella of France, Wife of Edward II of England', *International Society for the Study of Church Monuments Bulletin*, viii (1983).

BLOCH, M., *The Royal Touch: Sacred Monarchy and Scrofula in England and France*, trans. J. E. Anderson (London, 1973).

BOARDMAN, S. I., *The Early Stewart Kings: Robert II and Robert III, 1371–1406* (East Linton, 1996).

BOIS, G., *The Crisis of Feudalism: Economy and Society in Eastern Normandy, c.1300–1550* (Cambridge, 1984).

BOLTON, J. L., ' "The World Upside Down": Plague as an Agent of Economic and Social Change', *The Black Death in England*, ed. W. M. Ormrod and P. G. Lindley (Stamford, 1996).

BOOTH, P. H. W., *The Financial Administration of the Lordship and County of Chester, 1272–1377* (Chetham Society, 3rd series, xxviii, 1981).

—— 'Taxation and Public Order: Cheshire in 1353', *Northern History*, xii (1976).

BOTHWELL, J. S., 'Agnes Maltravers (d. 1375) and her Husband, John (d. 1364)', *Fourteenth Century England IV*, ed. J. S. Hamilton (Woodbridge, 2006).

—— *Edward III and the English Peerage* (Woodbridge, 2004).

—— 'Edward III and the "New Nobility": Largesse and Limitation in Fourteenth-Century England', *EHR*, cxii (1997).

—— *Falling from Grace: Reversal of Fortune and the English Nobility, 1075–1455* (Manchester, 2008).

—— 'The Management of Position: Alice Perrers, Edward III, and the Creation of a Landed Estate, 1362–1377', *JMH*, xxiv (1998).

—— 'The More Things Change: Isabella and Mortimer, Edward III, and the Painful Delay of a Royal Majority (1327–1330)', *The Royal Minorities of Medieval and Early Modern England*, ed. C. Beem (New York, 2008).

—— ' "Until he receive the equivalent in land and rent": The Use of Annuities as Endowment Patronage in the Reign of Edward III', *HR*, lxx (1997).

BOULTON, D'A. J. D., *The Knights of the Crown: The Monarchical Orders of Chivalry in Later Medieval Europe, 1325–1520* (Woodbridge, 1987).

BOUTEL, C., *Boutell's Heraldry* (London, 1973).

BOUTRUCHE, R., 'The Devastation of Rural Areas during the Hundred Years War and the Agricultural Recovery of France', *The Recovery of France in the Fifteenth Century*, ed. P. S. Lewis (London, 1971).

BOWERS, R, 'Fixed Points in the Chronology of English Fourteenth-Century Polyphony', *Music and Letters*, lxxi (1990).

—— 'The Music and Musical Establishment of St George's Chapel in the Fifteenth Century', *St George's Chapel, Windsor, in the Late Middle Ages*, ed. C. Richmond and E. Scarffe (Windsor, 2001).

BOYLE, L. E., 'William of Pagula and the *Speculum Regis Edwardi III*', *Mediaeval Studies*, xxxii (1970).

BRADBURY, J., *The Medieval Archer* (Woodbridge, 1985).

BRAID, R., 'Economic Behavior, Markets and Crises: The English Economy in the Wake of Plague and Famine in the 14th Century', *Economic and Biological Interactions in Pre-Industrial Europe from the 13th to the 18th Centuries*, ed. S. Cavaciocchi (Florence, 2010).

BRAND, P., 'The Languages of the Law in Later Medieval England', *Multilingualism in Later Medieval Britain*, ed. D. A. Trotter (Cambridge, 2000).

BRIDBURY, A. R., 'Before the Black Death', *EcHR*, 2nd series, xxx (1977).

―― *Medieval English Clothmaking* (London, 1982).

BRIDGEMAN, G. T. O., 'An Account of the Family of Swynnerton of Swynnerton', *Collections for a History of Staffordshire*, vii¹ (1886), 35–41.

BRIGGS, C. F., *Giles of Rome's De regimine principum: Reading and Writing Politics at Court and University, c.1275–c.1525* (Cambridge, 1999).

BRITNELL, R. H., *The Commercialisation of English Society, 1000–1500* (Cambridge, 1993).

―― '*Forstall*, Forestalling and the Statute of Forestallers', *EHR*, cii (1987).

BRITTON, C. E., *A Meteorological Chronology to A.D. 1450* (London, 1937).

BROOKS, N., 'The Organization and Achievements of the Peasants of Kent and Essex in 1381', *Studies in Medieval History Presented to R. H. C. Davis*, ed. H. Mayr-Harting and R. I. Moore (London, 1985).

BROOME, D. M., 'Exchequer Migrations to York in the Thirteenth and Fourteenth Centuries', *Essays in Medieval History Presented to T. F. Tout*, ed. A. G. Little and F. M. Powicke (Manchester, 1925).

BROWN, A. L., *The Early History of the Clerkship of the Council* (Glasgow, 1969).

―― *The Governance of Late Medieval England, 1272–1461* (London, 1989).

BROWN, E. A. R., 'Diplomacy, Adultery and Domestic Politics at the Court of Philip the Fair: Queen Isabelle's Mission to France in 1314', *Documenting the Past: Essays in Medieval History Presented to G. P. Cuttino*, ed. J. S. Hamilton and P. J. Bradley (Woodbridge, 1989).

―― 'Gascon Subsidies and the Finances of the English Dominions, 1315–1324', *Studies in Medieval and Renaissance History*, original series, viii (1971).

―― 'The Marriage of Edward II of England and Isabelle of France: A Postscript', *Speculum*, lxiv (1989).

―― 'The Political Repercussions of Family Ties in the Early Fourteenth Century: The Marriage of Edward II of England and Isabelle of France', *Speculum*, lxiii (1988).

―― 'The Prince is Father of the King: The Character and Childhood of Philip the Fair of France', *Mediaeval Studies*, xlix (1987).

BROWN, M., *The Wars of Scotland, 1214–1371* (Edinburgh, 2004).

BROWN, R. A., *English Castles*, 2nd edn (London, 1976).

―― 'King Edward's Clocks', *Antiquaries Journal*, xxxix (1959).

――, COLVIN, H. M. and TAYLOR, A. J., *The History of The King's Works: The Middle Ages*, 2 vols (London, 1963).

BRYANT, W. N., 'The Financial Dealings of Edward III with the County Communities', *EHR*, lxxxiii (1968).

BUCK, M., *Politics, Finance and the Church in the Reign of Edward II: Walter Stapeldon, Treasurer of England* (Cambridge, 1983).

BULLOCK-DAVIES, C., *A Register of Royal and Baronial Domestic Minstrels, 1272–1327* (Woodbridge, 1986).

BURDEN, J., 'How do You Bury a Deposed King? The Funeral of Richard II and the Establishment of Lancastrian Royal Authority in 1400', *Henry IV: The Establishment of the Regime, 1399–1406*, ed. G. Dodd and D. Biggs (York, 2003).

―― 'Re-writing a Rite of Passage: The Peculiar Funeral of Edward II', *Rites of Passage: Cultures of Transition in the Fourteenth Century*, ed. N. F. McDonald and W. M. Ormrod (York, 2004).

BURLEY, S. J., 'The Victualling of Calais, 1347–65', *BIHR*, xxxi (1958).

BURNE, A. H., *The Crecy War* (London, 1954).

BURROW, J. H., *The Ages of Man: A Study in Medieval Writing and Thought* (Oxford, 1986).

BUTTERFIELD, A., *The Familiar Enemy: Chaucer, Language, and Nation in the Hundred Years War* (Oxford, 2009).

—— 'French Culture and the Ricardian Court', *Essays on Ricardian Literature in Honour of J. A. Burrow*, ed. A. J. Minnis, C. C. Morse and T. Turville-Petre (Oxford, 1997).

CAFERRO, W., *John Hawkwood* (Baltimore, 2006).

CALIN, W., *The French Tradition and the Literature of Medieval England* (Toronto, 1994).

CAM, H. M., *Law-Finders and Law-Makers in Medieval England* (London, 1962).

—— *Liberties and Communities in Medieval England* (London, 1963).

CAMERON, S. and ROSS, A., 'The Treaty of Edinburgh and the Disinherited (1328–1332)', *History*, lxxxiv (1999).

CAMPBELL, B. M. S., *English Seigniorial Agriculture, 1250–1450* (Cambridge, 2000).

—— 'Physical Shocks, Biological Hazards, and Human Impacts: The Crisis of the Fourteenth Century Revisited', *Economic and Biological Interactions in Pre-Industrial Europe from the 13th to the 18th Centuries*, ed. S. Cavaciocchi (Florence, 2010).

CAMPBELL, J., 'England, Scotland and the Hundred Years War in the Fourteenth Century', *Europe in the Late Middle Ages*, ed. J. R. Hale, J. R. L. Highfield and B. Smalley (London, 1965).

CAPRA, P., 'Les Bases sociales du pouvoir anglo-gascon au milieu du xiv⁰ siècle', *Le Moyen Age*, lxxxi (1975).

CAREY, H. M., *Courting Disaster: Astrology at the English Court and University in the later Middle Ages* (Basingstoke, 1990).

CARPENTER, C., 'War, Government and Governance in England in the Later Middle Ages', *Conflicts, Consequence and the Crown in the Late Middle Ages*, ed. L. Clark (Woodbridge, 2007).

—— *The Wars of the Roses: Politics and the Constitution, c.1437–1509* (Cambridge, 1997).

CARPENTER, D., *The Minority of Henry III* (London, 1990).

—— *The Reign of Henry III* (London, 1996).

CARR, A. D., *Owen of Wales: The End of the House of Gwynedd* (Cardiff, 1991).

CARUS-WILSON, E. M. and COLEMAN, O., *England's Export Trade, 1275–1547* (Oxford, 1963).

CASTOR, H., *The King, the Crown, and the Duchy of Lancaster: Public Authority and Private Power, 1399–1461* (Oxford, 2000).

CATTO, J. I., 'An Alleged Great Council of 1374', *EHR*, lxxxii (1967).

—— 'Religion and the English Nobility in the Later Fourteenth Century', *History and Imagination: Essays in Honour of H. R. Trevor-Roper*, ed. H. Lloyd-Jones, V. Pearl and B. Worden (London, 1981).

—— 'Written English: The Making of the Language, 1370–1400', *Past and Present*, clxxix (2003).

CAZELLES, R., *La Société politique et la crise de la royauté sous Philippe de Valois* (Paris, 1958).

—— *Société politique, noblesse et couronne sous Jean le Bon et Charles V* (Geneva, 1982).

CHALON, L., 'La Scène des bourgeois de Calais chez Froissart et Jean le Bel', *Cahiers d'analyse textuelle*, x (1968).

CHAMBERLIN, C. L., 'A Castilian in King Edward's Court: The Career of Giles Despaigne, 1313–27', *England and Iberia in the Middle Ages, 12th–15th Century: Cultural, Literary and Political Exchanges*, ed. M. Bullón-Fernández (Basingstoke, 2007).

CHAPLAIS, P., 'English Arguments Concerning the Feudal Status of Aquitaine in the Fourteenth Century', *BIHR*, xxi (1948).

—— 'English Diplomatic Documents to the End of Edward III's Reign', *The Study of Medieval Records: Essays in Honour of Kathleen Major*, ed. D. A. Bullough and R. L. Storey (Oxford, 1971).

—— *Essays in Medieval Diplomacy and Administration* (London, 1981).

—— *Piers Gaveston: Edward II's Adoptive Brother* (Oxford, 1994).

CHERRY, J. and STRATFORD, N., *Westminster Kings and the Medieval Palace of Westminster* (London, 1995).

CHETTLE, H. F., 'The *Boni Homines* of Ashridge and Edington', *Downside Review*, lxii (1944).

CHEYETTE, F., 'Kings, Courts, Cures, and Sinecures: The Statute of Provisors and the Common Law', *Traditio*, xix (1963).

CHILDS, W. R., 'Edward II, John of Powderham and the Chronicles, 1318', *Church and Chronicle in the Middle Ages: Essays Presented to John Taylor*, ed. I. Wood and G. A. Loud (London, 1991).

CLANCHY, M. T., *England and its Rulers, 1066–1272*, 2nd edn (Oxford, 1998).

CLARK, E., 'Medieval Labor Law and English Local Courts', *American Journal of Legal History*, xxvii (1983).

CLARKE, M. V., *Fourteenth Century Studies* (Oxford, 1937).

—— *Medieval Representation and Consent* (London, 1936).

COBBAN, A. B., *The King's Hall within the University of Cambridge in the Later Middle Ages* (Cambridge, 1969).

COHN, S. K., *The Black Death Transformed: Disease and Culture in Early Renaissance Europe* (London, 2002).

COKAYNE, G. E., *The Complete Peerage of England, Scotland, Ireland, Great Britain and the United Kingdom*, rev. V. Gibbs et al., 13 vols (London, 1910–59).

COLEMAN, D. C., 'Mercantilism Revisited', *Historical Journal*, xxiii (1980).

COLEMAN, J., *English Literature in History, 1350–1400: Medieval Readers and Writers* (London, 1981).

—— 'Philippa of Lancaster, Queen of Portugal – and Patron of the Gower Translations?', *England and Iberia in the Middle Ages, 12th–15th Century: Cultural, Literary and Political Exchanges*, ed. M. Bullón-Fernández (Basingstoke, 2007).

COLLEY, L., 'The Apotheosis of George III: Loyalty, Royalty and the British Nation, 1760–1820', *Past and Present*, cii (1984).

—— *Britons: Forging the Nation, 1707–1837* (London, 1994).

COLLINS, H. E. L., *The Order of the Garter, 1348–1461: Chivalry and Politics in Late Medieval England* (Oxford, 2000).

CONNOLLY, P., 'The Financing of English Expeditions to Ireland, 1361–1376', *England and Ireland in the Later Middle Ages: Essays in Honour of Jocelyn Otway-Ruthven*, ed. J. Lydon (Blackrock, 1981).

CONTAMINE, P., 'The Norman "Nation" and the French "Nation" in the Fourteenth and Fifteenth Centuries', *England and Normandy in the Middle Ages*, ed. D. Bates and A. Curry (London, 1994).

—— *Des Pouvoirs en France, 1300–1500* (Paris, 1992).

COOKE, W. G., '*Sir Gawain and the Green Knight*: A Restored Dating', *Medium Ævum*, lviii (1989).

—— and BOULTON, D'A. J. D., '*Sir Gawain and the Green Knight*: A Poem for Henry of Grosmont?', *Medium Ævum*, lxviii (1999).

COOPER, A., *Bridges, Law and Power in Medieval England, 700–1400* (Woodbridge, 2006).

COOTE, L. A., *Prophecy and Public Affairs in Later Medieval England* (York, 2000).

COSS, P., *The Knight in Medieval England, 1000–1400* (Stroud, 1993).

—— *The Origins of the English Gentry* (Cambridge, 2003).

CRANE, S., *The Performance of Self: Ritual, Clothing, and Identity during the Hundred Years War* (Philadelphia, 2002).

CROOK, D., 'The Disgrace of Sir Richard Willoughby, Chief Justice of King's Bench', *Nottingham Medieval Studies*, xlviii (2004).

—— 'The Later Eyres', *EHR*, xcvii (1982).

—— *Records of the General Eyre* (London, 1982).

CROOKS, P., 'Representation and Dissent: "Parliamentarianism" and the Structure of Politics in Colonial Ireland, c.1370–1420', *EHR*, cxxv (2010).

CROSSLEY, P., 'Architecture', *The New Cambridge Medieval History, VI: c.1300–c.1415*, ed. M. Jones (Cambridge, 2000).

CRUMP, C. G., 'The Arrest of Roger Mortimer and Queen Isabel', *EHR*, xxvi (1911).

CURRY, A., *The Battle of Agincourt: Sources and Interpretations* (Woodbridge, 2000).

—— *The Hundred Years War*, 2nd edn (Basingstoke, 2003).

CUTTINO, G. P., *English Diplomatic Administration, 1259–1339*, 2nd edn (Oxford, 1971).

—— *English Medieval Diplomacy* (Bloomington, 1985).

—— and LYMAN, T. W., 'Where is Edward II?', *Speculum*, liii (1978).

CUTTLER, S. H., *The Law of Treason and Treason Trials in Later Medieval France* (Cambridge, 1981).

DAHMUS, J. H., *William Courtenay, Archbishop of Canterbury 1381–1396* (University Park., Penn., 1966).

DANBURY, E., 'English and French Artistic Propaganda during the Period of the Hundred Years War: Some Evidence of Royal Charters', *Power, Culture and Religion in France, c.1350–c.1550*, ed. C. T. Allmand (Woodbridge, 1989).

DAVIES, C. S. L., 'Henry VIII and Henry V: The Wars in France', *The End of the Middle Ages? England in the Fifteenth and Sixteenth Centuries*, ed. J. L. Watts (Stroud, 1998).

DAVIES, J. C., *The Baronial Opposition to Edward II* (Cambridge, 1918).

DAVIES, R. R., *Conquest, Coexistence and Change: Wales, 1063–1415* (Oxford, 1987).

—— *The First English Empire: Power and Identities in the British Isles, 1093–1343* (Oxford, 2000).

—— *Lordship and Society in the March of Wales, 1282–1400* (Oxford, 1978).

—— 'The Peoples of Britain and Ireland, 1100–1400, III: Laws and Customs', *TRHS*, 6th series, vi (1996).

DAVIS, R. H. C., *The Medieval Warhorse* (London, 1979).

DAVIS, V., *William Wykeham* (London, 2007).

De VILLE, O., 'The Deyvilles and the Genesis of the Robin Hood Legend', *Nottingham Medieval Studies*, xliii (1999).

De WAILLY, H., *Crécy 1346: Anatomy of a Battle* (Poole, 1987).

DELACHENAL, R., *Histoire de Charles V*, 5 vols (Paris, 1909–31).

DELISLE, L., *Histoire du château et des sires de Saint-Sauveur–le–Vicomte* (Valognes, 1867).

DeMARCO, P., 'An Arthur for the Ricardian Age: Crown, Nobility, and the Alliterative *Morte Arthure*', *Speculum*, lxxx (2005).

DENHOLM-YOUNG, N., *Collected Papers* (Cardiff, 1969).

DENNISON, L. and ROGERS, N. J., 'The Elsing Brass and its East Anglian Connections', *Fourteenth Century England I*, ed. N. Saul (Woodbridge, 2000).

DÉPREZ, E. 'Une Conference Anglo-Navarraise en 1358', *Révue historique*, xcix (1908).

—— 'La Conférence d'Avignon, 1344', *Essays in Medieval History Presented to Thomas Frederick Tout*, ed. A. G. Little and F. M. Powicke (Manchester, 1925).

—— 'La Double Trahison de Godefroi de Harcourt (1346–1347)', *Revue historique*, xcix (1908).

—— *Etudes de diplomatique anglaise* (Paris, 1908).

—— 'La Mort de Robert d'Artois', *Revue historique*, xciv (1907).

—— *Les Préliminaires de la Guerre de Cent Ans* (Paris, 1902).

DeVRIES, K., 'Contemporary Views of Edward III's Failure at the Siege of Tournai, 1340', *Nottingham Medieval Studies*, xxxix (1995).

—— *Infantry Warfare in the Early Fourteenth Century: Discipline, Tactics, and Technology* (Woodbridge, 1996).

DIXON, M. C., 'John de Coupland – Hero to Villain', *The Battle of Neville's Cross, 1346*, ed. D. Rollason and M. Prestwich (Stamford, 1998).

DOCK, G., 'Printed Editions of the *Rosa Anglica* of John of Gaddesden', *Janus*, viii (1907).

DOCKRAY, K., 'The Origins of the Wars of the Roses', *The Wars of the Roses*, ed. A. J. Pollard (Basingstoke, 1995).

DODD, G., *Justice and Grace: Private Petitioning and the English Parliament in the Late Middle Ages* (Oxford, 2007).

—— 'The Lords, Taxation and the Community of Parliament in the 1370s and Early 1380s', *Parliamentary History*, xx (2001).

—— 'A Parliament Full of Rats? *Piers Plowman* and the Good Parliament of 1376', *HR*, lxxix (2006).

—— 'Parliamentary Petitions? The Origins and Provenance of the "Ancient Petitions" (SC 8) in the National Archives', *Medieval Petitions: Grace and Grievance*, ed. W. M. Ormrod, G. Dodd and A. Musson (York, 2009).

DOHERTY, P. C., 'The Date of the Birth of Isabella, Queen of England (1308–58)', *BIHR*, xlviii (1975).

—— *Isabella and the Strange Death of Edward II* (London, 2003).

DOYLE, A. I., 'English Books in and out of Court from Edward III to Henry VII', *English Court Culture in the Later Middle Ages*, ed. V. J. Scattergood and J. W. Sherborne (London, 1983).

DRAGE, C., 'Nottingham Castle', *Transactions of the Thoroton Society*, xciii (1989).

DUFFY, S., 'The Problem of Degeneracy', *Law and Disorder in Thirteenth-Century Ireland: The Dublin Parliament of 1297*, ed. J. F. Lydon (Dublin, 1997).

DUNBABIN, J., 'Careers and Vocations', *The History of the University of Oxford, I: The Early Oxford Schools*, ed. J. I. Catto (Oxford, 1984).

—— 'Government', *The Cambridge History of Medieval Political Thought, c.350–c.1450*, ed. J. H. Burns (Cambridge, 1988).

DUNCAN, A. A. M., '*Honi soit qui mal y pense*: David II and Edward III, 1346–52', *Scottish Historical Review*, lxvii (1988).

DYER, C., *Standards of Living in the Later Middle Ages* (Cambridge, 1989).

—— 'Taxation and Communities in Late Medieval England', *Progress and Problems in Medieval England: Essays in Honour of Edward Miller*, ed. R. Britnell and J. Hatcher (Cambridge, 1996).

—— 'Villeins, Bondmen, Neifs, and Serfs: New Serfdom in England, c.1200–1600', *Forms of Servitude in Northern and Central Europe: Decline, Resistance, and Expansion*, ed. P. Freedman and M. Bourin (Turnhout, 2005).

EDBURY, P. W., *The Kingdom of Cyprus and the Crusades, 1191–1374* (Cambridge, 1991).

EDWARDS, J. G., ' "Justice" in Early English Parliaments', *Historical Studies of the English Parliament*, ed. E. B. Fryde and E. Miller, 2 vols (Cambridge, 1970), i.

—— 'Ranulph, Monk of Chester', *EHR*, xlvii (1932).

EMDEN, A. B., *Biographical Register of the University of Oxford to 1500*, 3 vols (Oxford, 1957–9).

—— *A Survey of Dominicans in England* (Rome, 1967).

EMMERSON, B., *The Black Prince* (London, 1976).

EVANS, M., *The Death of Kings: Royal Deaths in Medieval England* (London, 2003).

FAIRBANK, F. R., 'The Last Earl of Warenne and Surrey, and the Distribution of his Possessions', *Yorkshire Archaeological Journal*, xix (1907).

FAITH, R., 'The "Great Rumour" of 1377 and Peasant Ideology', *The English Rising of 1381*, ed. R. H. Hilton and T. H. Aston (Cambridge, 1984).

FARMER, D. L., 'Prices and Wages [i]', *The Agrarian History of England and Wales, II: 1042–1350*, ed. H. E. Hallam (Cambridge, 1988).

—— 'Prices and Wages [ii]', *The Agrarian History of England and Wales, III: 1348–1500*, ed. E. Miller (Cambridge, 1991).

FAWTIER, R., *Hand-List of Additions to the Collection of Latin Manuscripts in the John Rylands Library, 1908–1920* (Manchester, 1921).

FEAVEARYEAR, A., *The Pound Sterling*, 2nd edn (Oxford, 1963).

FERNSTER, J., *Fictions of Advice: The Literature of Counsel in Late Medieval England* (Philadelphia, 1996).

FIELD, R., 'From *Gui* to *Guy*: The Fashioning of a Popular Romance', *Guy of Warwick: Icon and Ancestor*, ed. A. Wiggins and R. Field (Woodbridge, 2007).

FINUCANE, R., *Miracles and Pilgrims: Popular Belief in Medieval England* (Basingstoke, 1995).

FLETCHER, C. D., 'De la Communauté du royaume au *common weal*: Les requêtes anglaises et leurs stratégies au XIVe siècle', *Revue française de l'histoire des idées politiques*, xxxi (2010).

—— 'Corruption at Court: Crisis and the Theme of *luxuria* in England and France, *c*.1340–1422', *The Court as Stage: England and the Low Countries in the Late Middle Ages*, ed. S. Gunn and A. Janse (Woodbridge, 2006).

—— *Richard II: Manhood, Youth and Politics, 1377–99* (Oxford, 2008).

—— 'Virtue and the Common Good: Sermons and Political Practice in the Good Parliament, 1376', *Charisma and Religious Authority: Jewish, Christian, and Muslim Preaching, 1200–1500*, ed. K. L. Jansen and M. Rubin (Turnhout, 2009).

FOWLER, K., *The Age of Plantagenet and Valois* (New York, 1967).

—— 'Les Finances et la discipline dans les armées anglaises en France au XIVe siècle', *Les cahiers vernonnais*, iv (1964).

—— *The King's Lieutenant: Henry of Grosmont, First Duke of Lancaster, 1310–1361* (London, 1969).

—— *Medieval Mercenaries, I: The Great Companies* (Oxford, 2001).

—— 'News from the Front: Letters and Despatches of the Fourteenth Century', *Guerre et société en France, en Angleterre et en Bourgogne, XIVᵉ–XVᵉ siècle*, ed. P. Contamine, C. Giry-Deloison and M. H. Keen (Lille, 1991).

—— 'Truces', *The Hundred Years War*, ed. K. Fowler (London, 1971).

FRAME, R., *English Lordship in Ireland, 1318–1361* (Oxford, 1982).

—— *Ireland and Britain, 1170–1450* (London, 1998).

—— 'The Justiciarship of Ralph Ufford: Warfare and Politics in Fourteenth-Century Ireland', *Studia Hibernica*, xiii (1973).

—— 'Overlordship and Reaction, *c*.1200–*c*.1450', *Uniting the Kingdom? The Making of British History*, ed. A. Grant and K. J. Stringer (London, 1995).

—— 'Thomas Rokeby, Sheriff of Yorkshire, Justiciar of Ireland', *Peritia*, x (1996).

FRYDE, E. B., 'Parliament and the French War, 1336–40', *Historical Studies of the English Parliament*, ed. E. B. Fryde and E. Miller, 2 vols (Cambridge, 1970), i.

—— *Peasants and Landlords in Later Medieval England, c.1380–c.1525* (Stroud, 1996).

—— *Studies in Medieval Trade and Finance* (London, 1983).

—— 'The Tenants of the Bishops of Coventry and Lichfield and of Worcester after the Plague of 1348–9', *Medieval Legal Records*, ed. R. F. Hunnisett and J. B. Post (London, 1978).

—— *William de la Pole, Merchant and King's Banker* (London, 1988).

FRYDE, N. M., 'Edward III's Removal of his Ministers and Judges', *BIHR*, xlviii (1975).

—— 'A Medieval Robber Baron: Sir John Molyns of Stoke Poges, Buckinghamshire', *Medieval Legal Records*, ed. R. F. Hunnisett and J. B. Post (London, 1978).

—— *The Tyranny and Fall of Edward II, 1321–1326* (Cambridge, 1977).

FULTON, T. W., *The Sovereignty of the Sea* (Edinburgh, 1911).

GALBRAITH, V. H., 'Articles Laid before the Parliament of 1371', *EHR*, xxxiv (1919).

—— *Kings and Chroniclers: Essays in English Medieval History* (London, 1982).

GALWAY, M., 'Alice Perrers's Son John', *EHR*, lxvi (1951).

—— 'Joan of Kent and the Order of the Garter', *Birmingham Historical Journal*, i (1947).

GEE, L. L., *Women, Art and Patronage from Henry III to Edward III, 1216–1377* (Woodbridge, 2002).

GIANCARLO, M., *Parliament and Literature in Late Medieval England* (Cambridge, 2007).

—— '*Piers Plowman*, Parliament, and the Public Voice', *Yearbook of Langland Studies*, xvii (2003).

GIBSON, S. T., 'The Escheatries, 1327–41', *EHR*, xxxvi (1921).

GILLESPIE, J. L., 'Ladies of the Fraternity of St George and of the Society of the Garter', *Albion*, xvii (1985).

GILLINGHAM, J., *The Angevin Empire* (London, 1984).

GIROUARD, M., *The Return to Camelot: Chivalry and the English Gentleman* (London, 1981).

GIVEN-WILSON, C., 'The Bishop of Chichester and the Second Statute of Praemunire, 1365', *HR*, lxiii (1990).

—— 'Chronicles of the Mortimer Family, *c.* 1250–1450', *Family and Dynasty in Late Medieval England*, ed. R. Eales and S. Tyas (Donington, 2003).

—— *Chronicles: The Writing of History in Medieval England* (London, 2004).

—— *The English Nobility in the Late Middle Ages* (London, 1987).

—— 'The Exequies of Edward III and the Royal Funeral Ceremony in Late Medieval England', *EHR*, cxxiv (2009).

—— 'The Merger of Edward III's and Queen Philippa's Households, 1360–9', *BIHR*, li (1978).

—— 'The Problem of Labour in the Context of English Government, *c.*1350–1450', *The Problem of Labour in Fourteenth-Century England*, ed. J. Bothwell, P. J. P. Goldberg and W. M. Ormrod (York, 2000).

—— 'Purveyance for the Royal Household, 1362–1413', *BIHR*, lvi (1983).

—— 'Richard II and his Grandfather's Will', *EHR*, xciii (1978).

—— 'Richard II, Edward II, and the Lancastrian Inheritance', *EHR*, cix (1994).

—— 'Royal Charter Witness Lists, 1327–1399', *Medieval Prosopography*, xii² (1991).

—— *The Royal Household and the King's Affinity: Service, Politics and Finance in England, 1360–1413* (London, 1986).

—— 'Wealth and Credit, Public and Private: The Earls of Arundel, 1306–1397', *EHR*, cvii (1991)

—— and BÉRIAC, F., 'Edward III's Prisoners of War: The Battle of Poitiers and its Context', *EHR*, cxvi (2001).

—— and CURTEIS, A., *The Royal Bastards of Medieval England* (London, 1984).

GODDARD, R., *Lordship and Medieval Urbanisation: Coventry, 1043–1355* (Woodbridge, 2004).

GOLDBERG, P. J. P., *Medieval England: A Social History, 1250–1550* (London, 2004).

GOOD, J., *The Cult of St George in Medieval England* (Woodbridge, 2009).

GOODALL, J. A. A., 'The Aerary Porch and its Influence on Late Medieval English Vaulting', *St George's Chapel Windsor in the Fourteenth Century*, ed. N. Saul (Woodbridge, 2005).

GOODER, A. and E., 'Coventry before 1355: Unity or Division?', *Midland History*, vi (1981).

GOODMAN, A., *John of Gaunt: The Exercise of Princely Power in Fourteenth-Century Europe* (Harlow, 1992).

—— 'John of Gaunt: Paradigm of the Late Fourteenth-Century Crisis', *TRHS*, 5th series, xxxvii (1987).

—— *The Loyal Conspiracy: The Lords Appellant under Richard II* (London, 1971).

—— 'Sir Thomas Hoo and the Parliament of 1376', *BIHR*, xli (1968).

Gothic: Art for England, 1400–1547, ed. R. Marks and P. Williamson (London, 2003).

GOTTFRIED, R. S., *The Black Death* (London, 1983).

GRAINGER, I., HAWKINS, D., COWAL, L. and MIKULSKI, R., *The Black Death Cemetery, East Smithfield, London* (London, 2008).

GRANSDEN, A., 'The Alleged Rape by Edward III of the Countess of Salisbury', *EHR*, lxxxvii (1972).

—— *Historical Writing in England*, 2 vols (London, 1974–82).

—— 'Propaganda in English Medieval Historiography', *JMH*, i (1975).

GRANT, A., 'Disaster at Neville's Cross: The Scottish Point of View', *The Battle of Neville's Cross, 1346*, ed. D. Rollason and M. Prestwich (Stamford, 1998).

—— *Independence and Nationhood: Scotland 1306–1469* (London, 1984).

—— 'Scottish Foundations: Late Medieval Contributions', *Uniting the Kingdom? The Making of British History*, ed. A. Grant and K. J. Stringer (London, 1995).

GRAVES, E. B., 'The Legal Significance of the Statute of Praemunire', *Anniversary Essays Presented to C. H. Haskins*, ed. C. H. Taylor (New York, 1929).

GRAY, H. L. 'The Production and Exportation of English Woollens in the Fourteenth Century', *EHR*, xxxix (1924).

GREAVES, D., 'Calais under Edward III', *Finance and Trade under Edward III*, ed. G. Unwin (Manchester, 1918).

GREEN, D., *The Battle of Poitiers, 1356* (Stroud, 2002).

—— *The Black Prince* (Stroud, 2001).

—— *Edward the Black Prince: Power in Medieval Europe* (Harlow, 2007).

—— 'Masculinity and Medicine: Thomas Walsingham and the Death of the Black Prince', *JMH*, xxxv (2009).

—— 'National Identities and the Hundred Years War', *Fourteenth Century England VI*, ed. C. Given-Wilson (Woodbridge, 2010).

GREEN, M. A. E., *Lives of the Princesses of England*, 6 vols (London, 1849–55).

GREEN, R. F., *A Crisis of Truth: Literature and Law in Ricardian England* (Philadelphia, 2002).

—— 'Further Evidence for Chaucer's Representation of the Pardoner as a Womanizer', *Medium Ævum*, lxxi (2002).

—— 'King Richard II's Books Revisited', *Library*, xxxi (1976).

—— *Poets and Princepleasers: Literature and the English Court in the Later Middle Ages* (Toronto, 1980).

GREENHOUSE, W., 'Benjamin West and Edward III: A Neoclassical Painter and Medieval History', *Art History*, viii (1985).

GRIBIT, N., 'Accounting for Service in War: The Case of Sir James Audley of Heighley', *Journal of Medieval Military History*, vii (2009).

GRIFFITHS, R. A., *King and Country: England and Wales in the Fifteenth Century* (London, 1991).

—— *The Principality of Wales in the Later Middle Ages: The Structure and Personnel of Government. I: South Wales, 1277–1536* (Cardiff, 1972).

—— *The Reign of King Henry VI* (London, 1981).

GROSS, A., 'Langland's Rats: A Moralist's View of Parliament', *Parliamentary History*, ix (1990).

GUENÉE, B., *Between Church and State: The Lives of Four French Prelates in the Late Middle Ages*, trans. A. Goldhammer (Chicago, 1991).

—— *States and Rulers in Later Medieval Europe*, trans. J. Vale (Oxford, 1985).

HADWIN, J. F., 'The Medieval Lay Subsidies and Economic History', *EcHR*, 2nd series, xxxvi (1983).

HAINES, R, M., *Archbishop John Stratford: Political Revolutionary and Champion of the Liberties of the Church, ca. 1275/80–1348* (Toronto, 1986).

—— *The Church and Politics in Fourteenth-Century England: The Career of Adam Orleton* (Cambridge, 1978).

—— *Ecclesia Anglicana: Studies in the English Church of the Later Middle Ages* (Toronto, 1989).

—— '*Edwardus redivivus*: The "Afterlife" of Edward of Caernarvon', *Transactions of the Bristol and Gloucestershire Archaeological Society*, cxiv (1996).

—— *King Edward II: Edward of Caernarfon, his Life, his Reign, and its Aftermath, 1284–1330* (Montreal, 2003).

—— 'Simon de Montacute, Brother of William, Earl of Salisbury, Bishop of Worcester (1333–7) and of Ely (1337–45)', *Fourteenth Century England I*, ed. N. Saul (Woodbridge, 2000).

—— 'The Stamford Council of April 1327', *EHR*, cxxii (2007).

—— 'Sumptuous Apparel for a Royal Prisoner: Archbishop Melton's Letter, 14 January 1330', *EHR*, cxxiv (2009).

HALLAM, E. M., *The Itinerary of Edward II and his Household* (List & Index Society, ccxi, 1984).

HAMILTON, J. S., *Piers Gaveston, Earl of Cornwall 1307–1312* (London, 1988).

—— *The Plantagenets: History of a Dynasty* (London, 2010).

—— 'Some Notes on "Royal" Medicine in the Reign of Edward II', *Fourteenth Century England II*, ed. C. Given-Wilson (Woodbridge, 2002).

HANAWALT, B. A., *Crime and Conflict in English Communities, 1300–1348* (Cambridge, Mass., 1979).

Handbook of British Chronology, ed. E. B. Fryde, D. E. Greenway, S. Porter and I Roy, 3rd edn (Cambridge, 1986).

HARBISON, S., 'William of Windsor, the Court Party and the Administration of Ireland', *England and Ireland in the Later Middle Ages: Essays in Honour of Jocelyn Otway-Ruthven*, ed. J. Lydon (Blackrock, 1981).

HARDING, A., *England in the Thirteenth Century* (Cambridge, 1993).

—— *Medieval Law and the Foundations of the State* (Oxford, 2002).

—— 'The Revolt against the Justices', *The English Rising of 1381*, ed. R. H. Hilton and T. H. Aston (Cambridge, 1984).

HARDY, B. C., *Philippa of Hainault and her Times* (London, 1910).

HARDY, R., 'The Longbow', *Arms, Armies and Fortifications in the Hundred Years War*, ed. A. Curry and M. Hughes (Woodbridge, 1994).

HARRIS, S. J., 'Taking your Chances: Petitioning in the Last Years of Edward II and the First Years of Edward III', *Medieval Petitions: Grace and Grievance*, ed. W. M. Ormrod, G. Dodd and A. Musson (York, 2009).

HARRISS, G. L., 'Aids, Loans and Benevolences', *Historical Journal*, vi (1963).

—— 'Budgeting at the Medieval Exchequer', *War, Government and Aristocracy in the British Isles, c.1150–1500: Essays in Honour of Michael Prestwich*, ed. C. Given-Wilson, A. Kettle and L. Scales (Woodbridge, 2008).

—— 'The Commons' Petition of 1340', *EHR*, lxxxviii (1963).

—— 'The Dimensions of Politics', *The McFarlane Legacy: Studies in Late Medieval Politics and Society*, ed. R. H. Britnell and A. J. Pollard (Stroud, 1995).

—— 'The Formation of Parliament, 1272–1377', *The English Parliament in the Middle Ages*, ed. R. G. Davies and J. H. Denton (Manchester, 1984).

—— *King, Parliament and Public Finance in Medieval England to 1369* (Oxford, 1975).

—— 'Medieval Doctrines in the Debates on Supply, 1610–1629', *Faction and Parliament: Essays on Early Stuart History*, ed. K. Sharpe (London, 1978).

—— 'Political Society and the Growth of Government in Late Medieval England', *Past and Present*, cxxxviii (1993).

—— *Shaping the Nation: England, 1360–1461* (Oxford, 2005).

HARVEY, A. and MORTIMER, R., *The Funeral Effigies of Westminster Abbey* (Woodbridge, 1994).

HARVEY, J. H., 'Architectural History from 1291 to 1558', *A History of York Minster*, ed. G. E. Aylmer and R. Cant (Oxford, 1977).

—— *The Black Prince and his Age* (London, 1976).

HASTINGS, A., *The Construction of Nationhood: Ethnicity, Religion and Nationalism* (Cambridge, 1998).

HAY, D., 'The Division of the Spoils of War in Fourteenth-Century England', *TRHS*, 5th series, iv (1954).

HEATH, P., *Church and Realm, 1272–1461* (London, 1988).

HENNEMAN, J. B., 'The Black Death and Royal Taxation in France, 1347–1351', *Speculum*, xliii (1968).

—— 'France in the Middle Ages', *The Rise of the Fiscal State in Europe, c.1200–1815*, ed. R. Bonney (Oxford, 1999).

—— *Olivier de Clisson and Political Society in France under Charles V and Charles VI* (Philadelphia, 1996).

—— *Royal Taxation in Fourteenth-Century France: The Captivity and Ransom of John II, 1356–1360* (Philadelphia, 1976).

—— *Royal Taxation in Fourteenth-Century France: The Development of War Financing, 1320–1356* (Princeton, 1971).

HEPBURN, F., *Portraits of the Later Plantagenets* (Woodbridge, 1986).

HEWITT, H. J., *The Black Prince's Expedition of 1355–1357* (Manchester, 1958).

—— *The Organization of War under Edward III* (Manchester, 1966).

HIGHFIELD, J. R. L., 'The English Hierarchy in the Reign of Edward III', *TRHS*, 5th series, vi (1956).

—— 'The Promotion of William of Wickham to the See of Winchester', *Journal of Ecclesiastical History*, iv (1953).

HILL, M. C., *The King's Messengers, 1199–1377* (London, 1961).

HILL, R. M. T., 'An English Archbishop and the Scottish War of Independence', *Innes Review*, xxii (1971).

HILLGARTH, J. N., *The Spanish Kingdoms, 1250–1516*, 2 vols (Oxford, 1976–8).

HINKLE, W. M., *The Fleurs de Lis of the Kings of France, 1285–1488* (Carbondale, 1991).

HOLMES, G. A., *The Estates of the Higher Nobility in Fourteenth-Century England* (Cambridge, 1957).

—— *The Good Parliament* (Oxford, 1975).

—— 'Judgement on the Younger Despenser, 1326', *EHR*, lxx (1955).

—— 'The Rebellion of the Earl of Lancaster, 1328–9', *BIHR*, xxviii (1955).

HONEYBOURNE, M. B., 'The Abbey of St Mary Graces, Tower Hill', *Transactions of the London and Middlesex Archaeological Society*, new series, xi (1952–4).

HOOPER, B., RICKETT, S., ROGERSON, A. and YAXLEY, S., 'The Grave of Sir Hugh de Hastings, Elsing', *Norfolk Archaeology*, xxxix (1984–7), 88–99.

HOPE, W. H. St J., 'On the Funeral Effigies of the Kings and Queens of England', *Archaeologia*, lx (1907).

—— *Windsor Castle: An Architectural History*, 3 vols (London, 1913).

HORROX, R., 'Caterpillars of the Commonwealth? Courtiers in Late Medieval England', *Rulers and Ruled in Late Medieval England: Essays Presented to Gerald Harriss*, ed. R. E. Archer and S. Walker (London, 1995).

HOSKINS, P., 'The Itineraries of the Black Prince's *Chevauchées* of 1355 and 1356: Observations and Interpretations', *Journal of Medieval Military History*, vii (2009).

HOUSLEY, N., 'France, England and the "National Crusade", 1302–1386', *France and the British Isles in the Middle Ages and Renaissance*, ed. G. Jondorf and D. M. Dumville (Woodbridge, 1991).

—— *The Later Crusades, 1274–1580* (Oxford, 1992).

HOWE, E., 'Divine Kingship and Dynastic Display: The Altar Murals of St Stephen's Chapel, Westminster', *Antiquaries Journal*, lxxxi (2001).

HOYT, R. S., 'The Coronation Oath of 1308', *EHR*, lxxi (1956).

HUDSON, A., *Lollards and their Books* (London, 1985).

HUGHES, D., *A Study of Social and Constitutional Tendencies in the Early Years of Edward III* (London, 1915).

HUNT, E. S., *The Medieval Super-Companies: A Study of the Peruzzi Company of Florence* (Cambridge, 1994).

—— 'A New Look at the Dealings of the Bardi and Peruzzi with Edward III', *Journal of Economic History*, l (1990).

HUNTER, J., 'On the Measures taken for the Apprehension of Sir Thomas de Gournay', *Archaeologia*, xxvii (1838).

HYAMS, P. R., 'The Action of Naifty in the Early Common Law', *Law Quarterly Review*, xc (1974).

INGLEDEW, F., *Sir Gawain and the Green Knight and the Order of the Garter* (Notre Dame, 2006).

JACK, R. I., 'Entail and Descent: The Hastings Inheritance, 1370–1436', *BIHR*, xxxviii (1965).

JACOB, E. F., *Henry V and the Invasion of France* (London, 1947).

JAEGER, C. S., *Ennobling Love: In Search of a Lost Sensibility* (Philadelphia, 1999).

JAMES, M. K., 'The Fluctuations of the Anglo-Gascon Wine Trade during the Fourteenth Century', *EcHR*, 2nd series, iv (1951).

JAMES, T. B., 'John of Eltham, History and Story: Abusive International Discourse in Late Medieval England, France and Scotland', *Fourteenth Century England II*, ed. C. Given-Wilson (Woodbridge, 2002).

JAMROZIAK, E., 'St Mary Graces: A Cistercian House in Late Medieval London', *The Uses and Abuses of Sacred Places in Late Medieval Towns*, ed. P. Trio and M. de Smet (Leuven, 2006).

JEFFERSON, L., 'MS Arundel 48 and the Earliest Statutes of the Order of the Garter', *EHR*, cix (1994).

JENKINSON, C. H., 'The Great Seal of England: Deputed or Departmental Seals', *Archaeologia*, lxxxv (1935).

—— 'Mary de Sancto Paulo, Foundress of Pembroke College, Cambridge', *Archaeologia*, lxvi (1915).

JOHNSON, C., 'An Act of Edward III as Count of Toulouse', *Essays in History Presented to R. L. Poole*, ed. H. W. C. Davis (Oxford, 1927).

JOHNSON, P., *The Life and Times of Edward III* (London, 1973).

JOHNSTONE, H., 'The Eccentricities of Edward II', *EHR*, xlviii (1933).

—— 'Isabella, the She-Wolf of France', *History*, xxi (1936–7).

—— 'The Queen's Household', *The English Government at Work, 1327–1336*, ed. J. F. Willard, W. A. Morris and W. H. Dunham, 3 vols (Cambridge, Mass., 1940–50), i.

JONES, M., 'Bertrand du Guesclin, the Truce of Bruges and Campaigns in the Périgord (1376)', *Soldiers, Nobles and Gentlemen: Essays in Honour of Maurice Keen*, ed. P. Coss and C. Tyerman (Woodbridge, 2009).

—— 'The Breton Civil War', *Froissart: Historian*, ed. J. J. N. Palmer (Woodbridge, 1981).

—— *Ducal Brittany, 1364–1399* (Oxford, 1970).

—— 'Edward III's Captains in Brittany', *England in the Fourteenth Century: Proceedings of the 1985 Harlaxton Symposium*, ed. W. M. Ormrod (Woodbridge, 1986).

—— 'The Ransom of Jean de Bretagne, Count of Pethièvre: An Aspect of English Foreign Policy, 1386–1388', *BIHR*, xlv (1972).

—— 'Relations with France, 1337–1399', *England and her Neighbours, 1066–1453: Essays in Honour of Pierre Chaplais*, ed. M. Jones and M. Vale (London, 1989).

—— 'War and Fourteenth-Century France', *Arms, Armies and Fortifications in the Hundred Years War*, ed. A. Curry and M. Hughes (Woodbridge, 1994).

JONES, M. K., 'Ransom Brokerage in the Fifteenth Century', *Guerre et société en France, en Angleterre et en Bourgogne XIVᵉ-XVᵉ siècle*, ed. P. Contamine, C. Giry-Deloison and M. H. Keen (Lille, 1991).

JONES, T., *Chaucer's Knight: The Portrait of a Medieval Mercenary*, rev. edn (London, 1985).

JONES, W. R., 'The Court of the Verge: The Jurisdiction of the Steward and Marshal of the Household in Later Medieval England', *Journal of British Studies*, xˡ (1970).

—— 'The English Church and Royal Propaganda during the Hundred Years War', *JBS*, xixˡ (1979).

—— 'Keeping the Peace: English Society, Local Government, and the Commissions of 1341–44', *American Journal of Legal History*, xviii (1974).

—— 'Purveyance for War and the Community of the Realm in Late Medieval England', *Albion*, vii (1975).

—— 'Relations of the Two Jurisdictions: Conflict and Cooperation in England during the Thirteenth and Fourteenth Centuries', *Studies in Medieval and Renaissance History*, original series, vii (1970).

—— '*Rex et ministri*: English Local Government and the Crisis of 1341', *JBS*, xiiiˡ (1973).

JORDAN, W. C., *The Great Famine: Northern Europe in the Early Fourteenth Century* (Princeton, 1996).

JURKOWSKI, M., SMITH, C. L. and CROOK, D., *Lay Taxes in England and Wales, 1188–1688* (London, 1998).

JUSTICE, S., *Writing and Rebellion, England in 1381* (Berkeley, Calif., 1994).

KAEUPER, R. W., 'Law and Order in Fourteenth-Century England: The Evidence of Special Commissions of Oyer and Terminer', *Speculum*, liv (1979).

—— *War, Justice, and Public Order: England and France in the Later Middle Ages* (Oxford, 1988).

KANTOROWICZ, E. H., *The King's Two Bodies* (Princeton, 1957).

KAYE, J., *Economy and Nature in the Fourteenth Century* (Cambridge, 1998).

KEEN, M. H., *England in the Later Middle Ages: A Political History*, 2nd edn (London, 2003).

—— *Nobles, Knights and Men-at-Arms in the Middle Ages* (London, 1996).

—— *The Outlaws of Medieval Legend*, rev. edn (London, 1977).

KEISER, G. R., 'Edward III and the Alliterative *Morte Arthure*', *Speculum*, xlviii (1973).

KENNY, A., *Wyclif* (Oxford, 1985).

KERR, J., 'The East Window of Gloucester Cathedral', *Medieval Art and Architecture at Gloucester and Tewkesbury*, ed. T. A. Heslop and V. A. Sekules (Norwich, 1985).

KING, A., 'War and Peace: A Knight's Tale. The Ethics of War in Sir Thomas Gray's *Scalacronica*', *War, Government and Aristocracy in the British Isles, c.1150–1500: Essays in Honour of Michael Prestwich*, ed. C. Given-Wilson, A. Kettle and L. Scales (Woodbridge, 2008).

KINGSFORD, C. L., 'The Feast of the Five Kings', *Archaeologia*, lxvii (1915–16).

—— 'On Some Ancient Deeds and Seals Belonging to Lord De L'Isle and Dudley', *Archaeologia*, lv (1913).

—— 'Sir Otho de Grandison, 1238?–1328', *TRHS*, 3rd series, iii (1909).

KNOWLES, D. and GRIMES, W. F., *Charterhouse* (London, 1954).

KOWALESKI, M., *Local Markets and Regional Trade in Medieval Exeter* (Cambridge, 1995).

—— 'Warfare, Shipping, and Crown Patronage: The Impact of the Hundred Years War on the Port Towns of Medieval England', *Money, Markets and Trade in Later Medieval Europe: Essays in Honor of John H. A. Munro*, ed. M. Elbl, I. Elbl and L. Armstrong (Leiden, 2007).

LACEY, H., *The Royal Pardon: Access to Mercy in Fourteenth-Century England* (York, 2009).

LACHAUD, F., 'Un "Miroir au prince" méconnu: Le *De nobilitatibus, sapienciis et prudenciis regum* de Walter de Milemete (vers 1326–1327)', *Guerre, pouvoir et noblesse au Moyen Âge: Mélanges en l'honneur de Philippe Contamine*, ed. J. Paviot and J. Verger (Paris, 2000).

—— 'La Réprésentation des liens personnels sur les tombeaux anglais du XIVᵉ siècle', *Liens personnels, réseaux, solidarities en France et dans les îsles Britanniques (XIᵉ-XXᵉ siècle)*, ed. D. Bates and V. Gazeau (Paris, 2006).

LAKING, G. F., *A Record of European Arms and Armour through Seven Centuries*, 5 vols (London, 1920–2).

LAMBRICK, G., 'The Impeachment of the Abbot of Abingdon in 1368', *EHR*, lxxxii (1967).

LANDER, J. R., *Crown and Nobility, 1450–1509* (London, 1976).

LAPSLEY, G., 'Archbishop Stratford and the Parliamentary Crisis of 1341', *EHR*, xxx (1915).

—— *The County Palatine of Durham* (Cambridge, Mass., 1924).

LARSON, A., 'English Embassies during the Hundred Years War', *EHR*, lv (1940).

LASSAHN, N., 'Langland's Rats Revisited: Conservatism, *Commune*, and Political Unanimity', *Viator*, xxxix (2008).

LEE, P., *Nunneries, Learning and Spirituality in Late Medieval English Society: The Dominican Priory of Dartford* (York, 2001).

LE NEVE, J., *Fasti Ecclesiae Anglicanae, 1300–1541*, comp. H. P. F. King, J. M. Horn and B Jones, 12 vols (London, 1962–7).

LE PATOUREL, J., 'Edouard III, "roi de France et duc de Normandie" ', *Révue historique du droit français et étranger*, 4th series, xxxi (1953).

—— *Feudal Empires: Norman and Plantagenet* (London, 1984).

LEWIS, N. B., 'The "Continual Council" in the Early Years of Richard II, 1377–80', *EHR*, xliv (1926).

—— 'The Organisation of Indentures of Retinue in Fourteenth-Century England', *TRHS*, 4th series, xxvii (1945).

—— 'The Recruitment and Organization of a Contract Army, May to November 1337', *BIHR*, xxxvii (1964).

—— 'Re-election to Parliament in the Reign of Richard II', *EHR*, xlviii (1933).

—— 'The Summons of the English Feudal Levy, 5 April 1327', *Essays in Medieval History Presented to Bertie Wilkinson*, ed. T. A. Sandquist and M. R. Powicke (Toronto, 1969).

LEWIS, P. S., 'War, Propaganda and Historiography in Fifteenth-Century France and England', *TRHS*, 5th series, xv (1965).

LIDDY, C. D., *The Bishopric of Durham in the Late Middle Ages: Lordship, Community and the Cult of St Cuthbert* (Woodbridge, 2008).

—— 'Bristol and the Crown, 1326–31: Local and National Politics in the Early Years of Edward III's Reign', *Fourteenth Century England III*, ed. W. M. Ormrod (Woodbridge, 2004).

—— 'The Politics of Privilege: Thomas Hatfield and the Palatinate of Durham, 1345–81', *Fourteenth Century England IV*, ed. J. S. Hamilton (Woodbridge, 2006).

—— *War, Politics and Finance in Late Medieval English Towns: Bristol, York and the Crown, 1350–1400* (Woodbridge, 2005).

LINDLEY, P., *Gothic to Renaissance: Essays on Sculpture in England* (Stamford, 1995).

LIPSON, E., *The Economic History of England, I: The Middle Ages*, 10th edn (London, 1949).

LIVINGSTONE, M. and WITZEL, M., *The Road to Crécy: The English Invasion of France, 1346* (Harlow, 2005).

LLOYD, T. H., *England the German Hanse, 1157–1611* (Cambridge, 1991).

—— *The English Wool Trade in the Middle Ages* (Cambridge, 1977).

—— 'Overseas Trade and the English Money Supply in the Fourteenth Century', *Edwardian Monetary Affairs, 1279–1344*, ed. N. J. Mayhew (British Archaeological Reports, British series, xxxvi, 1977).

LOACH, J., 'The Marian Establishment and the Printing Press', *EHR*, ci (1986).

LOBEL, M. D., 'A Detailed Account of the 1327 Rising at Bury St Edmunds and the Subsequent Trial', *Proceedings of the Suffolk Institute of Archaeology*, xxi (1933).

LOIRETTE, G., 'Arnaud Amanieu, sire d'Albret, et l'appel des seigneurs gascons en 1368', *Mélanges offerts à M. Charles Bémont* (Paris, 1913).

LONGMAN, W., *The History of the Life and Times of Edward the Third*, 2 vols (London, 1869).

LORD, C., 'Queen Isabella at the Court of France', *Fourteenth Century England II*, ed. C. Given-Wilson (Woodbridge, 2002).

LUCAS, H. S., 'John Crabbe: Flemish Pirate, Merchant, and Adventurer', *Speculum*, xx (1945).

—— *The Low Countries and the Hundred Years' War, 1326–1347* (Ann Arbor, 1929).

LUCE, S., 'Négociations des Anglais avec le roi de Navarre pendant la révolution parisienne de 1358', *Mémoires de la société de l'histoire de Paris et de l'Ile de France*, i (1875).

LUNT, W. E., 'The Collectors of Clerical Subsidies Granted to the King by the English Clergy', *The English Government at Work, 1327–1336*, ed. J. F. Willard, W. A. Morris and W. H. Dunham, 3 vols (Cambridge, Mass., 1940–50), ii.

—— *Financial Relations of the Papacy with England*, 2 vols (Cambridge, Mass., 1939–62).

LUTKIN, J., 'Isabella de Coucy, Daughter of Edward III: The Exception Who Proves the Rule', *Fourteenth Century England VI*, ed. C. Given-Wilson (Woodbridge, 2010).

LYDON, J. F., *Ireland in the Late Middle Ages* (Dublin, 1973).

LYON, B. D., *From Fief to Indenture* (Cambridge, Mass., 1957), 214–17.

—— 'What Were Edward III's Priorities: The Pleasures of Sports or Charity?', *Revue d'histoire ecclesiastique*, xcii (1997).

MADDICOTT, J. R., 'The Birth and Setting of the Ballads of Robin Hood', *EHR*, xciii (1978).

—— 'The County Community and the Making of Public Opinion in Fourteenth-Century England' *TRHS*, 5th series, xxviii (1978).

—— 'The English Peasantry and the Demands of the Crown, 1294–1341', *Landlords, Peasants and Politics in Medieval England*, ed. T. H. Aston (Cambridge, 1987).

—— *Law and Lordship: Royal Justices as Retainers in Thirteenth- and Fourteenth-Century England* (Past and Present supplement, iv, 1978).

—— *The Origins of the English Parliament, 924–1327* (Oxford, 2010).

—— 'Parliament and the Constituencies, 1272–1377', *The English Parliament in the Middle Ages*, ed. R. G. Davies and J. H. Denton (Manchester, 1984).

—— *Thomas of Lancaster, 1307–1322: A Study in the Reign of Edward II* (Oxford, 1970).

MARTIN, D., 'Prosecution of the Statutes of Provisors and Premunire in the King's Bench, 1377–1394', *Fourteenth Century England IV*, ed. J. S. Hamilton (Woodbridge, 2006).

MARTINDALE, A., 'Painting for Pleasure: Some Lost Fifteenth-Century Secular Decorations of Northern Italy', *The Vanishing Past: Studies of Medieval Art, Liturgy and Metrology Presented to Christopher Hohler*, ed. A. Borg and A. Martindale (British Archaeological Reports, international series, cxi, 1981).

MATHESON, L. M., *The Prose* Brut: *The Development of a Middle English Chronicle* (Tempe, 1998).

MATTHEWS, D., *Writing to the King: Nation, Kingship and Literature in England, 1250–1350* (Cambridge, 2010).

MAXWELL-LYTE, H. C., *Historical Notes on the Use of the Great Seal of England* (London, 1926).

MAYHEW, N. J., 'From Regional to Central Minting, 1158–1464', *A New History of the Royal Mint*, ed. C. E. Challis (Cambridge, 1992).

McFARLANE, K. B., *England in the Fifteenth Century* (London, 1981).

—— *Lancastrian Kings and Lollard Knights* (Oxford, 1972).

—— *The Nobility of Later Medieval England* (Oxford, 1973).

McHARDY, A. K., 'The Alien Priories and the Expulsion of Aliens from England in 1378', *Studies in Church History*, xii (1975).

—— 'The English Clergy and the Hundred Years War', *Studies in Church History*, xx (1983).

—— 'Paying for the Wedding: Edward III as Fundraiser, 1332–3', *Fourteenth Century England IV*, ed. J. S. Hamilton (Woodbridge, 2006).

—— 'The Promotion of John Buckingham to the See of Lincoln', *Journal of Ecclesiastical History*, xxvi (1975).

—— 'Some Reflections of Edward III's Use of Propaganda', *The Age of Edward III*, ed. J. S. Bothwell (York, 2001).

—— 'Religious Ritual and Political Persuasion: The Case of England in the Hundred Years War', *Journal of Moral and Social Studies*, iii (1988).

McINTOSH, M. K., *Autonomy and Community: The Royal Manor of Havering, 1200–1500* (Cambridge, 1986).

McKENNA, J. W., 'How God Became an Englishman', *Tudor Rule and Revolution: Essays for G. R. Elton from his American Friends*, ed. D. J. Guth and J. W. McKenna (Cambridge 1982).

MacKINNON, J., *The History of Edward III (1327–1377)* (London, 1900).

McKISACK, M., 'Edward III and the Historians', *History*, xlv (1960).

—— *The Fourteenth Century* (Oxford, 1959).

—— 'London and the Succession to the Crown during the Middle Ages', *Studies in Medieval History Presented to Frederick Maurice Powicke*, ed. R. W. Hunt, W. A. Pantin and R. W. Southern (Oxford, 1948).

McNAB, B., 'Obligations of the Church in English Society: Military Arrays of the Clergy, 1369–1418', *Order and Innovation in the Middle Ages: Essays in Honor of Joseph R. Strayer*, ed. W. C. Jordan, B. McNab and T. F. Ruiz (Princeton, 1976).

McNAMEE, C., *The Wars of the Bruces: Scotland, England and Ireland, 1306–1328* (East Linton, 1997).

MENACHE, S., 'Isabella of France, Queen of England: A Reconsideration', *JMH*, x (1984).

MERRIAM, T., '*Edward III*', *Literary and Linguistic Computing*, xv (2000).

MEYER, E., *Charles II, roi de Navarre, comte d'Evreux, et la Normandie au XIVe siècle* (Paris, 1898).

MICHAEL, M. A., 'The Iconography of Kingship in the Walter of Milemete Treatise', *Journal of the Warburg and Courtauld Institutes*, lvii (1994).

—— 'The Little Land of England is Preferred before the Great Kingdom of France: The Quartering of the Royal Arms by Edward III', *Studies in Medieval Art and Architecture Presented to Peter Lasko*, ed. D. Buckton and T. A. Heslop (Stroud, 1994).

—— 'A Manuscript Wedding Gift from Philippa of Hainault to Edward III', *Burlington Magazine*, cxxvii (1985).

MILESON, S. A., *Parks in Medieval England* (Oxford, 2009).

MIROT, L. and DÉPREZ, E., *Les Ambassades anglaises pendant la Guerre de Cent Ans* (Paris, 1900).

MITCHELL, L. E., *Portraits of Medieval Women: Family, Marriage, and Politics in England, 1225–1350* (Basingstoke, 2003).

MOISANT, J., *Le Prince Noir en Aquitaine* (Paris, 1894).

MONNAS, L., 'Silk Cloths Purchased for the Great Wardrobe of the Kings of England, 1325–1462', *Textile History*, xx (1989).

—— 'Textiles for the Coronation of Edward III', *Textile History*, xxxii (2001).

MORGAN, D. A. L., 'The Banner-Bearer of Christ and Our Lady's Knight: How God Became an Englishman Revisited', *St George's Chapel Windsor in the Fourteenth Century*, ed. N. Saul (Woodbridge, 2005).

—— 'The Political After-life of Edward III: The Apotheosis of a Warmonger', *EHR*, cxii (1997).

MORGAN, P., *War and Society in Medieval Cheshire, 1277–1403* (Chetham Society, 3rd series, xxxiv, 1987).

MORGANSTERN, A. M., *Gothic Tombs of Kinship in France, the Low Countries and England* (University Park, Penn., 2000).

MORRIS, M., 'Edward I and the Knights of the Round Table', *Foundations of Medieval Scholarship: Records Edited in Honour of David Crook*, ed. P. Brand and S. Cunningham (York, 2008).

MORRIS, R. K., 'The Architecture of the Earls of Warwick in the Fourteenth Century', *England in the Fourteenth Century: Proceedings of the 1985 Harlaxton Symposium*, ed. W. M. Ormrod (Woodbridge, 1986).

MORTIMER, I., 'The Death of Edward II in Berkeley Castle', *EHR*, cxx (2005).

—— *The Greatest Traitor: The Life of Sir Roger Mortimer* (London, 2003).

—— 'Henry IV's Date of Birth and the Royal Maundy', *HR*, lxxx (2007).

—— *The Perfect King: The Life of Edward III* (London, 2006).

—— 'Sermons of Sodomy: A Reconsideration of Edward II's Sodomitical Reputation', *The Reign of Edward II*, ed. G. Dodd and A. Musson (York, 2006).

MUNBY, J., BARBER, R. and BROWN, R., *Edward III's Round Table at Windsor: The House of the Round Table and the Windsor Festival of 1344* (Woodbridge, 2007).

MUNRO, J. H. A., 'Mint Policies, Ratios and Outputs in the Low Countries and England, 1335–1420', *Numismatic Chronicle*, cxli (1981).

—— *Wool, Cloth, and Gold: The Struggle for Bullion in Anglo-Burgundian Trade, 1340–1478* (Toronto, 1972).

MUSSON, A., *Medieval Law in Context: The Growth of Legal Consciousness from Magna Carta to the Peasants' Revolt* (Manchester, 2001).

—— 'New Labour Laws, New Remedies? Legal Reaction to the Black Death "Crisis" ', *Fourteenth Century England I*, ed. N. Saul (Woodbridge, 2000).

—— 'The Prior of Coventry v. Queen Isabella of England: Re-assessing the Archival Evidence', *Archives*, xxxii (2007).

—— *Public Order and Law Enforcement: The Local Administration of Criminal Justice, 1294–1350* (Woodbridge, 1996).

—— 'Second "English Justinian" or Pragmatic Opportunist? A Re-examination of the Legal Legislation of Edward III's Reign', *The Age of Edward III*, ed. J. S. Bothwell (York, 2001).

—— and ORMROD, W. M., *The Evolution of English Justice: Law, Politics and Society in the Fourteenth Century* (Basingstoke, 1999).

MYERS, A. R., *England in the Later Middle Ages* (Harmondsworth, 1971).
—— 'The Wealth of Richard Lyons', *Essays in Medieval History Presented to Bertie Wilkinson*, ed. T. A. Sandquist and M. R. Powicke (Toronto, 1969).
NEDERMAN, C. J., 'Kings, Peers, and Parliament: Virtue and Corulership in Walter Burley's *Commentarius in VIII Libros Politicorum Aristotelis*', *Albion*, xxiv (1992).
—— 'Royal Taxation and the English Church: The Origins of William of Ockham's *An princeps*', *Journal of Ecclesiastical History*, xxxvii (1986).
NEVILLE, C. J., *Violence, Custom and Law: The Anglo-Scottish Border Lands in the Later Middle Ages* (Edinburgh, 1998).
NEWTON, S. M., *Fashion in the Age of the Black Prince* (Woodbridge, 1980).
—— 'Queen Philippa's Squirrel Suit', *Documenta Textila*, ed. M. Flury-Lemberg and K. Stolleis (Munich, 1981).
NICHOLAS, D., *The van Arteveldes of Ghent: The Varieties of Vendetta and the Hero in History* (Ithaca, New York, 1988).
NICHOLSON, R., *Edward III and the Scots: The Formative Years of a Military Career* (Oxford, 1965).
—— *Scotland: The Later Middle Ages* (Edinburgh, 1974).
NIGHTINGALE, P., 'Capitalists, Crafts and Constitutional Change in Late Fourteenth-Century London', *Past and Present*, cxxiv (1989).
—— 'The Intervention of the Crown and the Effectiveness of the Sheriff in the Execution of Judicial Writs, c.1355–1530', *EHR*, cxxiii (2008).
—— *A Medieval Mercantile Community: The Grocers' Company and the Politics and Trade of London, 1000–1485* (London, 1995).
—— 'Monetary Contraction and Mercantile Credit in Later Medieval England', *EcHR*, 2nd series, xliii (1990).
OAKSHOTT, E., *Records of the Medieval Sword* (Woodbridge, 1991).
OFFLER, H. S., *Church and Crown in the Fourteenth Century* (Aldershot, 2000).
—— 'England and Germany at the Beginning of the Hundred Years' War', *EHR*, liv (1939).
OGGINS, R. S., *The Kings and their Hawks: Falconry in Medieval England* (London, 2004).
OHLGREN, T., '*Edwardus redivivus* in *A Gest of Robyn Hode*', *Journal of English and Germanic Philology*, xcix (2000).
OLIVER, C., 'The First Political Pamphlet? The Unsolved Case of the Anonymous Account of the Good Parliament', *Viator*, xxxviii (2007).
—— *Parliament and the Origins of Political Pamphleteering* (York, 2010).
OLSON, G., 'Geoffrey Chaucer', *The Cambridge History of Medieval English Literature*, ed. D. Wallace (Cambridge, 1999).
OOSTERWIJK, S., ' "A swathe feire graue": The Appearance of Children on Medieval Tomb Monuments', *Family and Dynasty in Late Medieval England*, ed. R. Eales and S. Tyas (Donington, 2003).
ORME, N., *From Childhood to Chivalry: The Education of the English Kings and Aristocracy, 1066–1530* (London, 1984).
ORMROD, W. M., 'Accountability and Collegiality: The English Royal Secretariat in the Mid-Fourteenth Century', *Ecrit et pouvoir dans les chancelleries médiévales: Espace français, espace anglais*, ed. K. Fianu and D. J. Guth (Louvain la Neuve, 1997).
—— 'Agenda for Legislation, 1322–c.1340', *EHR*, cv (1990).
—— 'Alice Perrers and John Salisbury', *EHR*, cxxiii (2008).
—— 'Coming to Kingship: Boy Kings and the Passage to Power in Fourteenth-Century England', *Rites of Passage: Cultures of Transition in the Fourteenth Century*, ed. N. F. McDonald and W. M. Ormrod (York, 2004).
—— 'Competing Capitals? York and London in the Fourteenth Century', *Courts and Regions in Medieval Europe*, ed. S. Rees Jones, R. Marks and A. J. Minnis (York, 2000).
—— 'The Crown and the English Economy, 1290–1348', *Before the Black Death: Studies in the 'Crisis' of the Early Fourteenth Century*, ed. B. M. S. Campbell (Manchester, 1991).

—— 'The Domestic Response to the Hundred Years War', *Arms, Armies and Fortifications in the Hundred Years War*, ed. A. Curry and M. Hughes (Woodbridge, 1994).

—— 'The Double Monarchy of Edward III', *Medieval History*, i[1] (1991).

—— 'Edward III and his Family', *JBS*, xxvi (1987).

—— 'Edward III and the Recovery of Royal Authority in England, 1340–60', *History*, lxxii (1987).

—— 'England in the Middle Ages', *The Rise of the Fiscal State in Europe, c.1200–1815*, ed. R. Bonney (Oxford, 1999).

—— 'England, Normandy and the Beginnings of the Hundred Years War, 1259–1360', *England and Normandy in the Middle Ages*, ed. D. Bates and A. Curry (London, 1994).

—— 'The English Crown and the Customs, 1349–63', *EcHR*, 2nd series, xl (1987).

—— 'The English Government and the Black Death of 1348–49', *England in the Fourteenth Century: Proceedings of the 1985 Harlaxton Symposium*, ed. W. M. Ormrod (Woodbridge, 1986).

—— 'The English State and the Plantagenet Empire, 1259–1360: A Fiscal Perspective', *The Medieval State: Essays Presented to James Campbell*, ed. J. R. Maddicott and D. M. Palliser (London, 2000).

—— 'An Experiment in Taxation: The English Parish Subsidy of 1371', *Speculum*, lxiii (1988).

—— 'Fifty Glorious Years: Edward III and the First English Royal Jubilee', *Medieval History*, new series, i[1] (2002).

—— 'For Arthur and St George: Edward III, Windsor Castle and the Order of the Garter', *St George's Chapel Windsor in the Fourteenth Century*, ed. N. Saul (Woodbridge, 2005).

—— 'The Good Parliament of 1376: Commons, *Communes* and "Common Profit" in Fourteenth-Century English Politics', *Comparative Perspectives on History and Historians: Essays in Memory of Bryce Lyon*, ed. D. Nicholas, B. S. Bachrach and J. M. Murray (Kalamazoo, 2011).

—— 'In Bed with Joan of Kent: The King's Mother and the Peasants' Revolt', *Medieval Women: Texts and Contexts in Late Medieval Britain*, ed. J. Wogan-Browne, R. Voaden, A. Diamond, A. Hutchinson, C. M. Meale and L. Johnson (Turnhout, 2000).

—— 'The King's Secrets: Richard de Bury and the Monarchy of Edward III', *War, Government and Aristocracy in the British Isles, c.1150–1500: Essays in Honour of Michael Prestwich*, ed. C. Given-Wilson, A. Kettle and L. Scales (Woodbridge, 2008).

—— 'On – and off – the Record: The Rolls of Parliament, 1337–77', *Parliamentary History*, xxiii (2004).

—— 'The Origins of the *sub pena* Writ', *HR*, lxi (1988).

—— 'The Origins of Tunnage and Poundage: Parliament and the Estate of Merchants in the Fourteenth Century', *Parliamentary History*, xxviii (2009).

—— 'Parliament, Political Economy and State Formation in Later Medieval England', *Power and Persuasion: Essays on the Art of State Building in Honour of W. P. Blockmans*, ed. P. Hoppenbrouwers, A. Janse and R. Stein (Turnhout, 2010).

—— 'The Peasants' Revolt and the Government of England', *JBS*, xxix (1990).

—— 'The Personal Religion of Edward III', *Speculum*, lxiv (1989).

—— *Political Life in Medieval England, 1300–1450* (Basingstoke, 1995).

—— 'The Politics of Pestilence: Government in England after the Black Death', *The Black Death in England*, ed. W. M. Ormrod and P. G. Lindley (Stamford, 1996).

—— 'Poverty and Privilege: The Fiscal Burden in England (XIIIth–XVth Centuries)', *La fiscalità nell'economia europea secc. XIII–XVIII*, ed. S. Cavaciocchi, 2 vols (Prato, 2008), ii.

—— 'A Problem of Precedence: Edward III, the Double Monarchy, and the Royal Style', *The Age of Edward III*, ed. J. S. Bothwell (York, 2001).

—— 'The Protecolla Rolls and English Government Finance, 1353–1364', *EHR*, cii (1987).

—— 'Queenship, Death and Agency: The Commemorations of Isabella of France and Philippa of Hainault', *Memory and Commemoration in Medieval England*, ed. C. M. Barron and C. Burgess (Donington, 2010).

—— *The Reign of Edward III: Crown and Political Society in England, 1327–1377* (London, 1990).

—— 'Richard II's Sense of English History', *The Reign of Richard II*, ed. G. Dodd (Stroud, 2000).

—— 'The Road to Boroughbridge: The Civil War of 1321–2 in the Ancient Petitions', *Foundations of Medieval Scholarship: Records Edited in Honour of David Crook*, ed. P. Brand and S. Cunningham (York, 2008).

—— 'Robin Hood and Public Record: The Authority of Writing in the Medieval Outlaw Tradition', *Medieval Cultural Studies: Essays in Honour of Stephen Knight*, ed. R. Evans, H. Fulton and D. Matthews (Cardiff, 2006).

—— 'The Royal Nursery: A Household for the Younger Children of Edward III', *EHR*, cxx (2005).

—— 'The Sexualities of Edward II', *The Reign of Edward II: New Perspectives*, ed. G. Dodd and A. Musson (York, 2006).

—— 'The Trials of Alice Perrers', *Speculum*, lxxxiii (2008).

—— 'The Use of English: Language, Law, and Political Culture in Fourteenth-Century England', *Speculum*, lxxxviii (2003).

—— 'The West European Monarchies in the Later Middle Ages', *Economic Systems and State Finance*, ed. R. Bonney (Oxford, 1995).

—— 'Who was Alice Perrers?', *Chaucer Review*, xl (2006).

Oxford Dictionary of National Biography, ed. H. C. G. Matthew and B. H. Harrison, 60 vols (Oxford, 2004).

Oxford Dictionary of Political Quotations, ed. A. Jay, 3rd edn (Oxford, 2006).

PACKE, M., *King Edward III* (London, 1983).

PALLISER, D. M., 'Royal Mausolea in the Long Fourteenth Century (1272–1422)', *Fourteenth Century England III*, ed. W. M. Ormrod (Woodbridge, 2004).

PALMER, J. J. N., 'The Anglo-French Peace Negotiations, 1390–1396', *TRHS*, 5th series, xvi (1966).

—— *England, France and Christendom, 1377–99* (London, 1972).

—— 'England, France, the Papacy and the Flemish Succession, 1361–9', *JMH*, ii (1976).

—— 'The Historical Context of the Book of the Duchess: A Revision', *Chaucer Review*, viii (1974).

—— 'The War Aims of the Protagonists and the Negotiations for Peace', *The Hundred Years War*, ed. K. Fowler (London, 1971).

—— and WELLS, A. P., 'Ecclesiastical Reform and the Politics of the Hundred Years War during the Pontificate of Urban V (1362–70)', *War, Literature and Politics in the Late Middle Ages*, ed. C. T. Allmand (Liverpool, 1976).

PALMER, R. C., *English Law in the Age of the Black Death, 1348–81: A Transformation of Governance and Law* (London, 1993).

PARSONS, J. C., *Eleanor of Castile: Queenship and Society in Thirteenth-Century England* (Basingstoke, 1995).

—— 'Mothers, Daughters, Marriage, Power: Some Plantagenet Evidence, 1150–1500', *Medieval Queenship*, ed. J. C. Parsons (Stroud, 1994).

—— ' "Never was a body buried in England with such solemnity and honour": The Burials and Posthumous Commemorations of English Queens to 1500', *Queens and Queenship in Medieval Europe*, ed. A. J. Duggan (Woodbridge, 1997).

—— 'The Pregnant Queen as Counsellor and the Medieval Construction of Motherhood', *Medieval Mothering*, ed. J. C. Parsons and B. Wheeler (New York, 1996).

—— 'The Year of Eleanor of Castile's Birth and her Children by Edward I', *Mediaeval Studies*, xlvi (1984).

PARTINGTON, R., 'Edward III's Enforcers: The King's Sergeants-at-Arms in the Localities', *The Age of Edward III*, ed. J. S. Bothwell (York, 2001).

PEARSALL, D. A., *The Life of Geoffrey Chaucer* (Oxford, 1992).

—— 'The *Troilus* Frontispiece and Chaucer's Audience', *Yearbook of English Studies*, vii (1977).

PELZER, J., 'The Slow Death of the Angevin Empire', *HR*, lxxxi (2008).

PENMAN, M., *David II* (East Linton, 2004).

—— '*Diffinicione successionis ad regnum Scottorum*: Royal Succession in Scotland in the Later Middle Ages', *Making and Breaking the Rules: Succession in Medieval Europe, c.1000–c.1600*, ed. F. Lachaud and M. Penman (Turnhout, 2008).

PENN, S. A. C. and DYER, C., 'Wages and Earnings in Late Medieval England: Evidence from the Enforcement of the Labour Laws', *EcHR*, 2nd series, xliii (1990).

PÉPIN, G., 'Towards a New Assessment of the Black Prince's Principality of Aquitaine: A Study of the Last Years (1369–1372)', *Nottingham Medieval Studies*, l (2006).

PERROY, E., 'L'Administration de Calais en 1371–2', *Revue du Nord*, xxxiii (1951).

—— *L'Angleterre et le grand schisme d'occident* (Paris, 1933).

—— 'Charles V et le traité de Brétigny', *Le Moyen Age*, xxxviii (1928).

—— 'Edouard III d'Angleterre et les seigneurs gascons en 1368', *Annales du Midi*, lxi (1948–9).

—— 'France, England, and Navarre from 1359 to 1364', *BIHR*, xiii (1935–6).

—— 'Gras profits et rançons pendant la Guerre de Cent Ans: L'Affaire du comte de Denia', *Mélanges d'histoire du moyen âge dédiés à la mémoire de Louis Halphen* (Paris, 1951).

—— *The Hundred Years War*, trans. W. B. Wells (London, 1951).

PETERS, E., *The Shadow King: Rex Inutilis in Medieval Law and Literature, 751–1327* (New Haven, 1970).

PETIT, K., 'Le Mariage de Philippa de Hainault, reine d'Angleterre', *Le Moyen Age*, lxxxvii (1981).

PHILLIPS, J. R. S., *Aymer de Valence, Earl of Pembroke 1307–1324* (Oxford, 1972).

—— *Edward II* (London, 2010).

—— 'Edward II and the Prophets', *England in the Fourteenth Century: Proceedings of the 1985 Harlaxton Symposium*, ed. W. M. Ormrod (Woodbridge, 1986).

—— ' "Edward II" in Italy: English and Welsh Political Exiles and Fugitives in Continental Europe, 1322–1364', *Thirteenth Century England X*, ed. M. Prestwich, R. H. Britnell and R. Frame (Woodbridge, 2005).

—— 'An Englishman in Rome, 1330–1334', *Dublin in the Medieval World: Studies in Honour of Howard B. Clarke*, ed. J. Bradley, A. J. Fletcher and A. Simms (Dublin, 2009).

—— *The Medieval Expansion of Europe* (Oxford, 1988).

PHILLIPS, K. M., 'Masculinities and the Medieval English Sumptuary Laws', *Gender and History*, xix (2007).

PIRENNE, H., 'La Première Tentative Faite pour reconnoitre Edouard III d'Angleterre comme roi de France (1328)', *Annales de la Société de'Histoire et d'Archéologie de Gand*, v (1902).

PLATT, C., *Medieval Southampton* (London, 1973).

PLÖGER, K., *England and the Avignon Popes: The Practice of Diplomacy in Late Medieval Europe* (London, 2005).

PLUCKNETT, T. F. T., 'The Origins of Impeachment', *TRHS*, 4th series, xxiv (1950).

—— 'Parliament', *The English Government at Work, 1327–1336*, ed. J. F. Willard, W. A. Morris and W. H. Dunham, 3 vols (Cambridge, Mass., 1940–50), i.

POLLARD, A. J., *Imagining Robin Hood* (London, 2004).

POOS, L. R., *A Rural Society after the Black Death: Essex, 1350–1525* (Cambridge, 1991).

POSTAN, M. M., *Essays on Medieval Agriculture and General Problems of the Medieval Economy* (Cambridge, 1973).

POULET, A., 'Capetian Women and the Regency: The Genesis of a Vocation', *Medieval Queenship*, ed. J. C. Parsons (Stroud, 1994).

POWELL, E., 'The Administration of Criminal Justice in Late-Medieval England: Peace Sessions and Assizes', *The Political Context of the Law*, ed. R. Eales and D. Sullivan (London, 1987).

—— *Kingship, Law, and Society: Criminal Justice in the Reign of Henry V* (Oxford, 1989).

POWELL, J. E. and WALLIS, K., *The House of Lords in the Middle Ages* (London, 1967).

POWER, E., *The Wool Trade in English Medieval History* (Oxford, 1941).

POWICKE, M., *Military Obligation in Medieval England* (Oxford, 1962).

PRESTWICH, M., *Armies and Warfare in the Middle Ages: The English Experience* (London, 1996).

—— 'Cavalry Service in Early Fourteenth Century England', *War and Government in the Middle Ages: Essays in Honour of J. O. Prestwich* (Woodbridge, 1984).

—— 'The Crown and the Currency: The Circulation of Money in Late Thirteenth and Early Fourteenth Century England', *Numismatic Chronicle*, cxlii (1982).

—— *Edward I* (London, 1988).

—— 'England and Scotland during the Wars of Independence', *England and her Neighbours, 1066–1453: Essays in Honour of Pierre Chaplais*, ed. M. Jones and M. Vale (London, 1989).

—— 'The English at the Battle of Neville's Cross', *The Battle of Neville's Cross, 1346*, ed. D. Rollason and M. Prestwich (Stamford, 1998).

—— 'English Armies in the Early Stages of the Hundred Years War: A Scheme in 1341', *BIHR*, lvi (1983).

—— 'Gilbert de Middleton and the Attack on the Cardinals, 1317', *Warriors and Churchmen in the High Middle Ages: Essays Presented to Karl Leyser*, ed. T. Reuter (London, 1992).

—— 'Military Logistics: The Case of 1322', *Armies, Chivalry and Warfare in Medieval Britain and France*, ed. M. Strickland (Stamford, 1998).

—— 'The Ordinances of 1311 and the Politics of the Early Fourteenth Century', *Politics and Crisis in Fourteenth-Century England*, ed. J. Taylor and W. Childs (Gloucester, 1990).

—— 'Parliament and the Community of the Realm', *Parliament and Community*, ed. A. Cosgrove and J. I. McGuire (Belfast, 1983).

—— *Plantagenet England, 1225–1360* (Oxford, 2005).

—— *The Three Edwards: War and State in England, 1272–1377* (London, 1980).

—— 'The Victualling of Castles', *Soldiers, Nobles and Gentlemen: Essays in Honour of Maurice Keen*, ed. P. Coss and C. Tyerman (Woodbridge, 2009).

—— 'War and Taxation in England in the XIIIth and XIVth Centuries', *Genèse de l'état moderne: Prélèvement et redistribution*, ed. J.-P. Genet and M. le Mené (Paris, 1987).

—— 'Was there a Military Revolution in Medieval England?', *Recognitions: Essays Presented to Edmund Fryde*, ed. C. Richmond and I. Harvey (Aberystwyth, 1996).

—— 'Why did Englishmen Fight in the Hundred Years War?', *Medieval History*, ii[1] (1992).

PRINCE, A. E., 'The Army and Navy', *The English Government at Work, 1327–1336*, ed. J. F. Willard, W. A. Morris and W. H. Dunham, 3 vols (Cambridge, Mass., 1940–50), i.

—— 'The Indenture System under Edward III', *Historical Essays in Honour of James Tait*, ed. J. G. Edwards, V. H. Galbraith and E. F. Jacob (Manchester, 1933).

—— 'The Payment of Army Wages in Edward III's Reign', *Speculum*, xix (1944).

—— 'The Strength of English Armies in the Reign of Edward III', *EHR*, xlvi (1931).

PROUDFOOT, R., '*The Reign of King Edward the Third* (1596) and Shakespeare', *Proceedings of the British Academy*, lxxi (1985).

PUTNAM, B. H., 'Chief Justice Shareshull and the Economic and Legal Codes of 1351–1352', *University of Toronto Law Journal*, v (1943–4).

—— *The Enforcement of the Statute of Labourers* (New York, 1908).

—— 'Maximum Wage-Laws for Priests after the Black Death', *American Historical Review*, xxi (1915–16).

—— *The Place in Legal History of Sir William Shareshull* (Cambridge, 1950).

—— 'Shire Officials: Keepers of the Peace and Justices of the Peace', *The English Government at Work, 1327–1336*, ed. J. F. Willard, W. A. Morris and W. H. Dunham, 3 vols (Cambridge, Mass., 1940–50), iii.

—— 'The Transformation of the Keepers of the Peace into the Justices of the Peace, 1327–1380', *TRHS*, 4th series, xii (1929).

RAMSAY, J. H., *A History of the Revenues of the Kings of England, 1066–1399*, 2 vols (Oxford, 1925).

RASTALL, R., 'The Minstrels of the English Royal Households, 25 Edward I–1, Henry VIII: An Inventory', *Royal Musical Association Research Chronicle*, iv (1964).

RAWCLIFFE, C., *The Staffords, Earls of Stafford and Dukes of Buckingham, 1394–1521* (Cambridge, 1978).

REDSTONE, V. B., 'Some Mercenaries of Henry of Lancaster, 1327–1330', *TRHS*, 3rd series, vii (1913).

REES JONES, S., 'Household, Work and the Problem of Labour: The Regulation of Labour in Medieval English Towns', *The Problem of Labour in Fourteenth-Century England*, ed. J. Bothwell, P. J. P. Goldberg and W. M. Ormrod (York, 2000).

RICHARDSON, A., *The Forest, Park and Palace of Clarendon, c.1200–c.1650* (British Archaeological Reports, British series, cccvii, 2005).

RICHARDSON, H. G., 'The *Annales Paulini*', *Speculum*, xxiii (1948).

—— 'The Coronation in Medieval England: The Evolution of the Office and the Oath', *Traditio*, xvi (1960).

—— 'The English Coronation Oath', *Speculum*, xxiv (1949).

—— and SAYLES, G. O., 'Early Coronation Records', *BIHR*, xiv (1936–7).

—— *The English Parliament in the Middle Ages* (London, 1981).

RICHES, S. J. E., *St George: Hero, Martyr and Myth* (Stroud, 2002).

RICHMOND, C., 'The War at Sea', *The Hundred Years War*, ed. K. Fowler (London, 1971).

RIGBY, S. H., 'Introduction', *A Social History of England, 1250–1500*, ed. R. Horrox and W. M. Ormrod (Cambridge, 2006).

RIGG, A. G., 'Clocks, Dials, and other Terms', *Middle English Studies Presented to Norman Davies*, ed. D. Gray and E. G. Stanley (Oxford, 1983).

—— *A History of Anglo-Latin Literature, 1066–1422* (Cambridge, 1992).

—— 'John of Bridlington's Prophecy: A New Look', *Speculum*, lxiii (1988).

—— 'Propaganda of the Hundred Years War. Poems on the Battles of Crecy and Durham (1346), A Critical Edition', *Traditio*, liv (1999).

ROBERTS, A. K. B., *St George's Chapel, Windsor Castle, 1348–1416: A Study in Early Collegiate Administration* (Windsor, 1948).

RODGER, N. A. M., *The Safeguard of the Sea: A Naval History of Britain*, 2 vols (London, 1997–2004).

ROGERS, A., 'Hoton versus Shakell: A Ransom Case in the Court of Chivalry, 1390–5', *Nottingham Mediaeval Studies*, vi (1962); vii (1963).

ROGERS, C. J., 'The Anglo-French Peace Negotiations of 1354–60 Reconsidered', *The Age of Edward III*, ed. J. S. Bothwell (York, 2001).

—— 'By Fire and Sword: *Bellum hostile* and the "Civilians" in the Hundred Years War', *Civilians in the Path of War*, ed. M. Grimsley and C. J. Rogers (Lincoln, Nebr., 2002).

—— 'Edward III and the Dialectics of Strategy, 1327–1360', *TRHS*, 6th series, iv (1994).

—— 'The Military Revolutions of the Hundred Years' War', *Journal of Military History*, lvii (1993).

—— *War Cruel and Sharp: English Strategy under Edward III, 1327–1360* (Woodbridge, 2000).

ROSE, S., *Calais: An English Town in France, 1347–1558* (Woodbridge, 2008).

—— *Medieval Naval Warfare, 1000–1500* (London, 2002).

ROSKELL, J. S., *The Commons and their Speakers in English Parliaments* (Manchester, 1965).

—— *The Impeachment of Michael de la Pole, Earl of Suffolk, in the Context of the Reign of Richard II* (Manchester, 1984).

—— *Parliament and Politics in Late Medieval England*, 3 vols (London, 1981).

—— 'The Problem of the Attendance of the Lords in Medieval Parliaments', *BIHR*, xxix (1956).

——, CLARK, L. and RAWCLIFFE, C., *The House of Commons, 1386–1421*, 4 vols (Stroud, 1993).

ROUND, J. H., 'The Landing of Queen Isabella in 1326', *EHR*, xiv (1899).

ROUSE, M. A. and ROUSE, R. H., 'The Goldsmith and the Peacocks: Jean de la Mote in the Household of Simon de Lille', *Viator*, xxviii (1997).

RUDDICK, A., 'Ethnic Identities and Political Language in the King of England's Dominions: A Fourteenth-Century Perspective', *Identity and Insurgency in the Late Middle Ages*, ed. L. Clark (Woodbridge, 2006).

RUNYAN, T., 'The Constabulary of Bordeaux: The Accounts of John Ludham (1372–73) and Robert de Wykford (1373–75)', *Mediaeval Studies*, xxvi (1974).

RUSSELL, E., 'The Societies of the Bardi and the Peruzzi and their Dealings with Edward III', *Finance and Trade under Edward III*, ed. G. Unwin (Manchester, 1918).

RUSSELL, P. E., *The English Intervention in Spain and Portugal in the Time of Edward III and Richard II* (Oxford, 1955).

SABINE, E. L., 'City Cleaning in Mediaeval London', *Speculum*, xii (1937).

SALTER, E., *English and International: Studies in the Literature, Art and Patronage of Medieval England* (Cambridge, 1988).

SANDLER, L. F., *Gothic Manuscripts, 1285–1385*, 2 vols (London, 1985).

—— *Omne bonum: A Fourteenth-Century Encyclopaedia of Universal Knowledge*, 2 vols (London, 1996).

SAUL, A., 'Local Politics and the Good Parliament', *Property and Politics: Essays in Later Medieval English History*, ed. A. Pollard (Gloucester, 1984).

SAUL, N., *Death, Art and Memory in Medieval England: The Cobham Family and their Monuments, 1300–1500* (Oxford, 2001).

—— 'The Despensers and the Downfall of Edward II', *EHR*, xcix (1984).

—— 'A Farewell to Arms? Criticism of Warfare in Late Fourteenth-Century England', *Fourteenth Century England II*, ed. C. Given-Wilson (Woodbridge, 2002).

—— 'The Kingship of Richard II', *Richard II: The Art of Kingship*, ed. A. Goodman and J. Gillespie (Oxford, 1999).

—— *Knights and Esquires: The Gloucestershire Gentry in the Fourteenth Century* (Oxford, 1981).

—— *Richard II* (London, 1997).

—— *Scenes from Provincial Life: Knightly Families in Sussex, 1280–1400* (Oxford, 1986).

SAUNDERS, F. S., *Hawkwood: Diabolical Englishman* (London, 2004).

SAYLES, G. O., 'The "English Company" of 1343 and a Merchants' Oath', *Speculum*, vi (1931).

—— *The Functions of the Medieval Parliament of England* (London, 1988).

SCAMMELL, J., 'Robert I and the North of England', *EHR*, lxxiv (1958).

SCATTERGOOD, V. J., *Politics and Poetry in the Fifteenth Century* (London, 1971).

SEABOURNE, G., *Royal Regulation of Loans and Sales in Medieval England* (Woodbridge, 2003).

SEARLE, E. and BURGHART, R., 'The Defense of England and the Peasants' Revolt', *Viator*, iii (1972).

SEKULES, V., 'Dynasty and Patrimony in the Self-Construction of an English Queen: Philippa of Hainault and her Images', *England and the Continent in the Middle Ages: Studies in Memory of Andrew Martindale*, ed. J. Mitchell and M. Moran (Stamford, 2000).

SHENTON, C., 'Edward III and the Coup of 1330', *The Age of Edward III*, ed. J. S. Bothwell (York, 2001).

—— 'Edward III and the Symbol of the Leopard', *Heraldry, Pageantry and Social Display*, ed. P. R. Coss and M. H. Keen (Woodbridge, 2002).

—— *The Itinerary of Edward III and his Household, 1327–1345* (List & Index Society, cccxviii, 2007).

—— 'Philippa of Hainault's Churchings: The Politics of Motherhood at the Court of Edward III', *Family and Dynasty in Late Medieval England*, ed. R. Eales and S. Tyas (Donington, 2003).

—— 'Royal Interest in Glastonbury and Cadbury: Two Arthurian Itineraries, 1278–1331', *EHR*, cxiv (1999).

SHERBORNE, J. W., *War, Politics and Culture in Fourteenth-Century England* (London, 1994).

SHERMAN, C. R., *Imagining Aristotle: Verbal and Visual Representation in Fourteenth-Century France* (Berkeley, Calif., 1995).

SLACK, P., 'Government and Information in Seventeenth-Century England', *Past and Present*, clxxxiv (2004).

SLATER, E., *The Problem of the Reign of King Edward III: A Statistical Approach* (Cambridge, 1988).

SMITH, J. B., *Llywelyn ap Gruffudd, Prince of Wales* (Cardiff, 1998).

SMYTH, J., *The Lives of the Berkeleys*, 2 vols (Gloucester, 1883).

SNEDDON, S. A. , 'Words and Realities: The Language and Dating of Petitions, 1326–7', *Medieval Petitions: Grace and Grievance*, ed. W. M. Ormrod, G. Dodd and A. Musson (York, 2009).

SOMERVILLE, R., *History of the Duchy of Lancaster* (London, 1953).

SPENCER, A. M., 'Royal Patronage and the Earls in the Reign of Edward I', *History*, xciii (2008).

SPONSLER, C., 'The King's Boyfriend: Froissart's Political Theater of 1326', *Queering the Middle Ages*, ed. G. Burger and S. F. Kruger (Minneapolis, 2001).

ST JOHN, G., 'The Religiosity of English Men-at-Arms in the Fourteenth Century', *Monastic Research Bulletin*, xiv (2008), 44–6.

STACEY, R. C., 'Parliamentary Negotiation and the Expulsion of the Jews from England', *Thirteenth Century England VI*, ed. M. Prestwich, R. H. Britnell and R. Frame (Woodbridge, 1997).

STANILAND, K., 'Clothing and Textiles at the Court of Edward III, 1342–52', *Collectanea Londiniensia*, ed. J. Bird et al. (London and Middlesex Archaeological Society Special Paper, ii, 1978).

—— 'Medieval Courtly Splendour', *Costume*, xiv (1980).

STANLEY, A. P., *Historical Memorials of Westminster Abbey*, 3rd edn (London, 1869).

STANTON, A. R., 'Isabelle of France and her Manuscripts, 1308–1358', *Capetian Women*, ed. K. Nolan (New York, 2003).

—— *The Queen Mary Psalter: A Study of Affect and Audience* (Philadelphia, 2001).

STEANE, J., *The Archaeology of the Medieval English Monarchy* (London, 1999).

STEELE, A., *The Receipt of the Exchequer, 1377–1485* (Cambridge, 1954).

STONE, L., *Sculpture in Britain: The Middle Ages* (Harmondsworth, 1955).

STONES, E. L. G., 'An Addition to the "Rotuli Scotiae" ', *Scottish Historical Review*, xxix (1950).

—— 'The Folvilles of Ashby Folville, Leicestershire, and their Associates in Crime, 1326–1347', *TRHS*, 5th series, vii (1957).

—— 'Sir Geoffrey le Scrope (*c*.1280 to 1340), Chief Justice of the King's Bench', *EHR*, lxix (1954).

—— 'The Treaty of Northampton, 1328', *History*, xxxviii (1953).

STOREY, R. L., *The End of the House of Lancaster*, new edn (Gloucester, 1986).

STOREY-CHALLENGER, S. B., *L'Administration anglaise du Ponthieu, 1361–1369* (Abbeville, 1975).

STRAYER, J. R., 'Introduction', *The English Government at Work, 1327–1336*, ed. J. F. Willard, W. A. Morris and W. H. Dunham, 3 vols (Cambridge, Mass., 1940–50), ii.

—— *On the Medieval Origins of the Modern State* (Princeton, 1970).

STRICKLAND, A., *Lives of the Queens of England*, 6 vols (London, 1842).

STROHM, P., *England's Empty Throne: Usurpation and the Language of Legitimation, 1399–1422* (London, 1998).

—— *Hochon's Arrow: The Social Imagination of Fourteenth-Century Texts* (Princeton, 1992).

STRONG, R., *Tudor and Jacobean Portraits*, 2 vols (London, 1969).

STUART, E. P., 'The Interview between Philip V and Edward II at Amiens in 1320', *EHR*, xli (1926).

STUBBS, W., *The Constitutional History of England*, 4th edn, 3 vols (Oxford, 1906).

SUGGETT, H., 'The Use of French in England in the Later Middle Ages', *TRHS*, 4th series, xxviii (1946).

SUMPTION, J., *The Hundred Years War*, in progress (London, 1990—).

SUTTON, A. F., VISSER-FUCHS, L. and GRIFFITHS, R. A., *The Royal Funerals of the House of York at Windsor* (London, 2005).

SWAIN, C. P., 'A Fourteenth-Century Description of Rectal Cancer', *World Journal of Surgery*, vii (1983).

TALBOT, C. H. and HAMMOND, E. A., *The Medical Practitioners in Medieval England: A Biographical Register* (London, 1965).

TANQUEREY, F. J., 'The Conspiracy of Thomas Dunheved, 1327', *EHR*, xxi (1916).

TAYLOR, A. J., 'Edward I and the Shrine of St Thomas of Canterbury', *Journal of the British Archaeological Association*, cxxxii (1979).

TAYLOR, C. D., 'Edward III and the Plantagenet Claim to the French Throne', *The Age of Edward III*, ed. J. S. Bothwell (York, 2001).

—— 'English Writings on Warfare and Chivalry during the Hundred Years War', *Soldiers, Nobles and Gentlemen: Essays in Honour of Maurice Keen*, ed. P. Coss and C. Tyerman (Woodbridge, 2009).

—— 'The Salic Law, French Queenship, and the Defense of Women in the Late Middle Ages', *French Historical Studies*, xxix (2006).

—— 'The Salic Law and the Valois Succession to the French Crown', *French History*, xv (2001).

TAYLOR, J., *English Historical Literature in the Fourteenth Century* (Oxford, 1987).

—— 'The Judgement on Hugh Despenser the Younger', *Medievalia et Humanistica*, xii (1958).

TERRY, S. B., *The Financing of the Hundred Years' War, 1337–1360* (London, 1914).

THOMPSON, A. H., 'William Bateman, Bishop of Norwich, 1344–1355', *Norfolk Archaeology*, xxv (1935).

THOMSON, F., *Magna Carta: Its Role in the Making of the English Constitution, 1300–1629* (Minneapolis, 1948).

THOMSON, S. H., 'Walter Burley's Commentary on the *Politics* of Aristotle', *Mélanges Auguste Peltzer* (Louvain, 1947).

THORNBURY, W., *Old and New London*, 6 vols (London, 1878).

THORNTON, T., 'Taxing the King's Dominions: The Subject Territories of the English Crown in the Late Middle Ages', *Crises, Revolutions and Self-Sustained Growth: Essays in European Fiscal History, 1130–1830*, ed. W. M. Ormrod, M. Bonney and R. Bonney (Stamford, 1999).

TIMBAL, P.-C. et al., *La Guerre de Cent Ans vue à travers les registres du parlement (1337–1369)* (Paris, 1961).

TOLLEY, T., 'Eleanor of Castile and the "Spanish" Style in England', *England in the Thirteenth Century: Proceedings of the 1989 Harlaxton Symposium*, ed. W. M. Ormrod (Stamford, 1991).

TOUT, T. F., *Chapters in the Administrative History of Medieval England*, 6 vols (Manchester, 1920–33).

—— *Collected Papers*, 3 vols (Manchester, 1932–4).

—— *The History of England from the Accession of Henry III to the Death of Edward III* (London, 1905).

—— 'Parliament and Public Opinion, 1376–88', *Historical Studies of the English Parliament*, ed. E. B. Fryde and E. Miller, 2 vols (Cambridge, 1970), i.

—— *The Place of the Reign of Edward II in English History*, 2nd edn (Manchester, 1936).

—— and BROOME, D. M., 'A National Balance Sheet for 1362–3', *EHR*, xxxix (1924).

TRAUTZ, F., *Die Könige von England und das Reich, 1272–1377* (Heidelberg, 1961).

TRIGG, S., 'The Vulgar History of the Order of the Garter', *Reading the Medieval in Early Modern England*, ed. G. McMullan and D. Matthews (Cambridge, 2007).

TROTTER, D., 'Walter of Stapeldon and the Pre-marital Inspection of Philippa of Hainault', *French Studies Bulletin*, xlix (1993).

TUCK, A., 'A Medieval Tax Haven: Berwick-upon-Tweed and the English Crown, 1333–1461', *Progress and Problems in Medieval England: Essays in Honour of Edward Miller*, ed. R. Britnell and J. Hatcher (Cambridge, 1996).

—— 'Nobles, Commons and the Great Revolt of 1381', *The English Rising of 1381*, ed. R. H. Hilton and T. H. Aston (Cambridge, 1984).

—— *Richard II and the English Nobility* (London, 1973).

—— 'Richard II and the Hundred Years War', *Politics and Crisis in Fourteenth-Century England*, ed. J. Taylor and W. Childs (Gloucester, 1990).

TUDOR-CRAIG, P., 'The Fonts of St George's Chapel', *St George's Chapel Windsor in the Fourteenth Century*, ed. N. Saul (Woodbridge, 2005).

TURVILLE-PETRE, T., *England the Nation: Language, Literature, and National Identity, 1290–1340* (Oxford, 1996).

TYERMAN, C., *England and the Crusades, 1095–1588* (Chicago, 1988).

—— 'Philip VI and the Recovery of the Holy Land', *EHR*, c (1985).

TYSON, D. B., 'The Epitaph of Edward the Black Prince', *Medium Ævum*, xlvi (1977).

UNDERHILL, F. A., *For Her Good Estate: The Life of Elizabeth de Burgh* (Basingstoke, 1999).

UNWIN, G., 'The Estate of Merchants, 1336–1365', *Finance and Trade under Edward III*, ed. G. Unwin (Manchester, 1918).

VALE, J., *Edward III and Chivalry: Chivalric Society and its Contexts, 1270–1350* (Woodbridge, 1982).

—— 'Image and Identity in the Prehistory of the Order of the Garter', *St George's Chapel Windsor in the Fourteenth Century*, ed. N. Saul (Woodbridge, 2005).

VALE, M. G. A., *The Angevin Legacy and the Hundred Years War, 1250–1340* (Oxford, 1990).

—— 'The Anglo-French Wars, 1294–1340: Allies and Alliances', *Guerre et société en France, en Angleterre et en Bourgogne XIVᵉ–XVᵉ siècle*, ed. P. Contamine, C. Giry-Deloison and M. H. Keen (Lille, 1991).

—— *English Gascony, 1399–1453* (Oxford, 1970).

—— *The Princely Court: Medieval Courts and Culture in North-West Europe* (Oxford, 2001).

—— 'The Return of the Event', *Times Literary Supplement*, 16 Aug. 1996.

—— 'The War in Aquitaine', *Arms, Armies and Fortifications in the Hundred Years War*, ed. A. Curry and M. Hughes (Woodbridge, 1994).

VALENTE, C., 'The Deposition and Abdication of Edward II', *EHR*, cxiii (1998).

—— 'The "Lament of Edward II": Religious Lyric, Political Propaganda', *Speculum*, lxxvii (2002).

—— *The Theory and Practice of Revolt in Medieval England* (Aldershot, 2003).

VAUGHAN, R., *Philip the Bold: The Formation of the Burgundian State*, new edn (Woodbridge, 2002).

VERDUYN, A., 'The Commons and the Early Justices of the Peace under Edward III', *Regionalism and Revision: The Crown and its Provinces in England, 1200–1500*, ed. P. Fleming, A. Gross and J. R. Lander (London, 1998).

—— 'The Politics of Law and Order during the Early Years of Edward III', *EHR*, cviii (1993).

—— 'The Selection and Appointment of Justices of the Peace in 1338', *HR*, lxviii (1995).

Victoria County History of Berkshire, iii, ed. P. H. Ditchfield and W. Page (London, 1923).

Victoria County History of Cheshire, iii, ed. C. R. Elrington and B. E. Harris (London, 1980).

Victoria County History of London, i, ed. W. Page (London, 1909).

Victoria County History of Oxfordshire, iv, ed. A. Crossley and C. R. Elrington (London, 1979).

Victoria County History of Warwickshire, viiii, ed. W. B. Stephens (London, 1969).

Victoria County History of Yorkshire: The City of York, ed. P. M. Tillott (London, 1961).

VIOLLET, P., 'Comment les Femmes ont été exclues, en France, de la succession à la couronne', *Mémoires de l'Académie des Inscriptions et Belles-lettres*, xxxiv (1895), 125–78.

WAGNER, A. R., *Heralds and Heraldry in the Middle Ages* (Oxford, 1939).

WALKER, S., *The Lancastrian Affinity, 1361–1399* (Oxford, 1990).

—— *Political Culture in Later Medieval England*, ed. M. J. Braddick (Manchester, 2006).

—— 'Profit and Loss in the Hundred Years War: The Sub-contracts of Sir John Strother, 1374', *HR*, lxviii (1985).

WALLACE, D., *Chaucerian Polity: Absolutist Lineages and Associational Forms in England and Italy* (Stanford, 1997).

WARBURTON, W., *Edward III* (London, 1875).

WARD, J., *Women of the English Nobility and Gentry, 1066–1500* (Manchester, 1995).

WATHEY, A., 'The Marriage of Edward III and the Transmission of French Motets to England', *Journal of the American Musicological Society*, xlv (1992).

—— 'The Peace of 1360–1369 and Anglo-French Musical Relations', *Early Music History*, ix (1989).

WATTS, J., *Henry VI and the Politics of Kingship* (Cambridge, 1996).

—— *The Making of Polities: Europe, 1300–1500* (Cambridge, 2009).

—— 'Public or Plebs: The Changing Meaning of "The Commons", 1381–1549', *Power and Identity in the Middle Ages: Essays in Memory of Rees Davies*, ed. H. Pryce and J. Watts (Oxford, 2007).

WAUGH, S. L., *England in the Reign of Edward III* (Cambridge, 1991).

WAYMENT, H. W, 'The Medieval Stained Glass', *A History of the Stained Glass of St George's Chapel, Windsor Castle*, ed. S. Brown (Windsor, 2005).

WEBSTER, B., 'David II and the Government of Fourteenth-Century Scotland', *TRHS*, 5th series, xvi (1966).

WENTERSDORF, K. P., 'The Clandestine Marriages of the Fair Maid of Kent', *JMH*, v (1979).

WESKE, D. B., *Convocation of the Clergy* (London, 1937).

WESTERHOF, D., *Death and the Noble Body in Medieval England* (Woodbridge, 2008).

—— 'Deconstructing Identities on the Scaffold: The Execution of Hugh Despenser the Younger, 1326', *JMH*, xxxiii (2007).

WHITELEY, M., 'The Courts of Edward III of England and Charles V of France: A Comparison of their Architectural Setting and Ceremonial Functions', *Fourteenth Century England I*, ed. N. Saul (Woodbridge, 2000).

WILKINS, N., '*En regardant vers le païs de France*: The Ballade and the Rondeau, a Cross-Channel History', *England in the Fourteenth Century: Proceedings of the 1985 Harlaxton Symposium*, ed. W. M. Ormrod (Woodbridge, 1986).

—— 'Music and Poetry at Court: England and France in the Late Middle Ages', *English Court Culture in the Later Middle Ages*, ed. V. J. Scattergood and J. W. Sherborne (London, 1983).

WILKINSON, B., 'The Authorisation of Chancery Writs under Edward III', *BJRL*, viii (1924).

—— 'The Chancery', *The English Government at Work, 1327–1336*, ed. J. F. Willard, W. A. Morris and W. H. Dunham, 3 vols (Cambridge, Mass., 1940–50), i.

—— *The Chancery under Edward III* (Manchester, 1929).

—— 'The Deposition of Richard II and the Accession of Henry IV', *Historical Studies of the English Parliament*, ed. E. B. Fryde and E. Miller, 2 vols (Cambridge, 1970), i.

—— 'A Letter of Edward III to his Chancellor and Treasurer', *EHR*, xlii (1927).

—— 'Notes on the Coronation Records of the Fourteenth Century', *EHR*, lxx (1955).

—— 'The Protest of the Earls of Arundel and Surrey in the Crisis of 1341', *EHR*, xlvi (1931).

—— 'The Seals of the Two Benches under Edward III', *EHR*, xlii (1927).

—— *Studies in the Constitutional History of the Thirteenth and Fourteenth Centuries*, 2nd edn (Manchester, 1952).

WILKS, M., *Wyclif: Political Ideas and Practice* (Oxford, 2000).

WILLARD, J. F., 'The Crown and its Creditors, 1327–33', *EHR*, xlii (1927).

—— 'Edward III's Negotiations for a Grant in 1337', *EHR*, xxi (1906).

—— *Parliamentary Taxes on Personal Property, 1290 to 1334* (Cambridge, Mass., 1934).

—— 'The Scotch Raids and the Fourteenth-Century Taxation of Northern England', *University of Colorado Studies*, v (1907–8).

—— 'The Taxes upon Moveables of the Reign of Edward III', *EHR*, xxx (1915).

WILLIAMS, G. A., *Medieval London: From Commune to Capital* (London, 1963).

WILSON, C., 'The Medieval Monuments', *A History of Canterbury Cathedral*, ed. P. Collinson, N. Ramsay and M. Sparks (Oxford, 1995).

—— 'The Royal Lodgings of Edward III at Windsor Castle: Form, Function, Representation', *Windsor: Medieval Archaeology, Art and Architecture in the Thames Valley*, ed. L. Keen and E. Scarff (Leeds, 2002).

WIMSATT, J. I., 'The *Dit dou Bleu Chevalier*: Froissart's Imitation of Chaucer', *Mediaeval Studies*, xxxiv (1972).

WISWALL, F. L., III, 'Politics, Procedure and the "Non-Minority" of Edward III: Some Comparisons', *The Age of Richard II*, ed. J. L. Gillespie (Stroud, 1997).

WOLFFE, B. P., 'Acts of Resumption in the Lancastrian Parliaments, 1399–1456', *Historical Studies of the English Parliament*, ed. E. B. Fryde and E. Miller, 2 vols (Cambridge, 1970), ii.

—— *The Royal Demesne in English History* (London, 1971).

WOOD, C. T., *Joan of Arc and Richard III: Sex, Saints, and Government in the Middle Ages* (Oxford, 1988).

WOOD, D., *Clement VI: The Pontificate and Ideas of an Avignon Pope* (Cambridge, 1989).

WOOD-LEGH, K. L., 'The Knights' Attendance in the Parliaments of Edward III', *EHR*, xlvii (1932).

—— 'Sheriffs, Lawyers and Belted Knights in the Parliaments of Edward III', *EHR*, xlvi (1931).

WOOLGAR, C. M., *The Great Household in Late Medieval England* (London, 1999).

WRIGHT, J. R., *The Church and the English Crown, 1305–1334* (Toronto, 1980).

WRIGHT, N., *Knights and Peasants: The Hundred Years War in the French Countryside* (Woodbridge, 1998).

WYLIE, J. H. and WAUGH, W. T., *The Reign of Henry the Fifth*, 3 vols (Cambridge, 1914–29).

WYON, A. B. and WYON, A., *The Great Seals of England* (London, 1887).

YEAGER, R. F., '*Pax Poetica*: On the Pacifism of Chaucer and Gower', *Studies in the Age of Chaucer*, ix (1987).

—— 'Politics and the French Language in England during the Hundred Years' War: The Case of John Gower', *Inscribing the Hundred Years' War in French and English Cultures*, ed. D. N. Baker (Albany, New York, 2000).

ZEIKOWITZ, R. E., *Homoeroticism and Chivalry: Discourses of Male Same-Sex Desire in the Fourteenth Century* (New York, 2003).

ZINK, M., *Froissart et le temps* (Paris, 1998).

UNPUBLISHED THESES

ALBAN, J. R., 'National Defence in England, 1337–89' (University of Liverpool PhD thesis, 1976).

AXWORTHY, R. L., 'The Financial Relationship of the London Merchant Community with Edward III, 1327 to 1377' (University of London PhD thesis, 2001).

BENZ, L., 'Queen Consort, Queen Mother: The Power and Authority of Fourteenth-Century Plantagenet Queens' (University of York PhD thesis, 2009).

BURDEN, J., 'Rituals of Royalty: Prescription, Politics and Practice in English Coronation and Royal Funeral Rituals, *c.*1327–*c.*1485' (University of York DPhil. thesis, 1999).

CONNOLLY, P. M., 'Lionel of Clarence and Ireland, 1361–1366' (University of Dublin PhD thesis, 1977).

DOHERTY, P. C., 'Isabella, Queen of England, 1296–1330' (University of Oxford DPhil. thesis, 1977).

DRYBURGH, P. R., 'The Career of Roger Mortimer, First Earl of March (*c.*1287–1330)' (University of Bristol PhD thesis, 2002).

FRYDE, E. B., 'Edward III's War Finance, 1337–41: Transactions in Wool and Credit Operations' (University of Oxford DPhil. thesis, 1947).

GIVEN-WILSON, C. J., 'The Court and Household of Edward III, 1360–1377' (University of St Andrews PhD thesis, 1975).

GRIBLING, B. L., 'Nationalizing the Hero: The Image of Edward the Black Prince in English Politics and Culture, 1776–1903' (University of York PhD thesis, 2009).

KINSEY, R. C., 'Legal Service, Careerism and Social Advancement in Late Medieval England: The Thorpes of Northamptonshire, c.1200–1391' (University of York PhD thesis, 2009).

LAWRENCE, M. J., 'Power, Ambition and Political Rehabilitation: The Despensers, c.1281–1400' (University of York PhD thesis, 2005).

LIVINGSTONE, M. R., 'The Nonae: The Records of the Taxation of the Ninth in England, 1340–41' (Queen's University Belfast PhD thesis, 2003).

LUTKIN, J. A., 'Goldsmiths and the English Royal Court, 1360–1413' (University of London PhD thesis, 2008).

MARSHALL, A. F., 'Thomas of Brotherton, Earl of Norfolk and Marshal of England: A Study in Early Fourteenth-Century Aristocracy' (University of Bristol PhD thesis, 2006).

ORMROD, W. M., 'Edward III's Government of England, c.1346–1356' (University of Oxford DPhil. thesis, 1984).

SHENTON, C., 'The English Court and the Restoration of Royal Prestige, 1327–1345' (University of Oxford DPhil. thesis, 1995).

VERDUYN, A., 'The Attitude of the Parliamentary Commons to Law and Order under Edward III' (University of Oxford DPhil. thesis, 1991).

WARNER, M. W., 'The Montagu Earls of Salisbury circa 1300–1428' (University of London PhD thesis, 1991).

WILSON, C., 'The Origins of the Perpendicular Style and its Development to circa 1360' (University of London PhD thesis, 1979).

INDEX

Garter, Order of the
  foundation of 298, 303–8
  meetings of 320–1, 388–9, 394, 411,
    450, 461, 490, 501, 532–3, 536,
    548, 573–4
  members of 304–5, 367 n.45, 411,
    450, 457, 501, 532–3, 536, 548, 573
  motto of 303, 460
  origins of 299–303
Gascony, duchy of 64, 90, 574
  and Edward III 64, 184–6, 261, 262
  French occupation of 31
  military expeditions to 192, 263–4,
    266–7, 325, 330, 342, 347, 507
  military expeditions to (planned) 22,
    86, 192, 198, 268
  negotiations concerning 31, 64, 261
  nobility of 184–5, 191, 192, 207, 420,
    440, 498–9
  seneschals of 607–8 see also Ingham;
    Stafford
  sovereignty over 27, 184–6
  war in 207
  see also Aquitaine, duchy of
Gask (Perthshire) 616
Gaunt, Margaret 318 n.91
Gaure, county of 417, 422
Gaveston, Piers (d. 1312), earl of Cornwall
  5–6, 17
Gawain, Arthurian knight, 15, 459–60
Gaywood (Norf.) 613
Genoa (Italy), ships from 204, 221
  mercenaries from 221, 222,
    279–80, 282
George III, king of the United Kingdom
  and Hanover 1, 592
George IV, king of the United Kingdom
  and Hanover 592
Gest of Robin Hood 380, 590
Ghent (Belgium) 194, 202, 212, 214, 225,
  227, 228, 267, 324, 444, 618 passim
  loans from 230–1
Glamorgan, lordship of 84
Glasbury, lordship of 108
Glasgow 167, 168, 616
Glasgow, bishop of see Wardlaw
Glaston, John
Glastonbury (Somerset) 98, 614
  abbey 98
Gloucester 18, 43, 74 n.105, 611 (ter), 612
  passim, 613, 617, 619, 622, 623 n.8
  abbey 68, 224 & n.39, 298; tomb of
    Edward II at 68–9, 76, 88, 121–2,
    123, 224 n.39, 318, Pl. 2

Gloucester, earls and countesses of
  see Audley; Clare
Gloucester, John, bell founder 454
Gloucester, John, groom 24
Gloucester, Richard 33
Godmersham (Kent) 630
Goldbeter, John 242
Goodwin Sands (English Channel) 619
Goodworth Clatford (Hants) 622
Gosport (Hants) 507
Gournay, Matthew 416–17, 437, 491
Gower, John 493, 494 n.106, 523, 537
  Mirour de l'Omme 493–4 & n.106,
    519–20
Gower, lordship of 366
Graham, John (d. 1347), earl of Menteith
  284, 331
Grailly, Jean II de (d. 1343), captal de
  Buch 192
Grailly, Jean III de (d. 1377), captal de
  Buch 267, 304, 350, 352, 421, 440,
  513–14, 521–2
Grand-Champ (dép. Morbihan) 619
Grandisson, Catherine, countess of
  Salisbury, wife of William Montagu 135,
  145, 302–3, 306
Grandisson, John, bishop of Exeter 238
  n.107, 245, 381
Grandisson, Otto de (d. 1328) 8
Grandisson, Otto de 417 n.10
Grandisson, Thomas 507
Grantham (Lincs) 617
Graveney (Kent) 626
Gravesend (Kent) 451, 462, 531, 627–9
  passim, 630 (ter)
Gravesend, Stephen, bishop of London
  56, 75, 88, 95, 166
Gray, Sir Thomas, of Heton 2, 96, 412
Great Company 416–17
great seal 45, 47, 48, 49, 78, 99, 308,
  606–8, Pl. 4, Pl. 13
  of absence 45, 49
Great Yarmouth see Yarmouth, Great
Green, Henry, chief justice of king's
  bench 477, 495
Greet, Peter 132
Gregory XI, pope 517–18, 520, 537
Greneville, Joan, Lady Mortimer, wife of
  Roger Mortimer 92–3
Grey, John (d. 1359), Lord Grey of
  Rotherfield, steward of the king's
  household 139–40, 304, 319, 379
Grey, Reynold (d. 1388), Lord Grey of
  Ruthin 534